UNDERSTANDING HUMAN SEXUALITY

UNDERSTANDING HUMAN SEXUALITY

THIRD EDITION

JANET SHIBLEY HYDE
Denison University

McGRAW-HILL BOOK COMPANY

New York St. Louis San Francisco Auckland Bogotá Hamburg Johannesburg London Madrid Mexico Montreal New Delhi Panama Paris São Paulo Singapore Sydney Tokyo Toronto

UNDERSTANDING HUMAN SEXUALITY

1 2 3 4 5 6 7 8 9 0 VNHVNH 8 9 8 7 6 5

ISBN 0-07-031581-7

See Acknowledgments on pages 680–683. Copyrights included on this page by reference.

This book was set in Garamond by University Graphics, Inc. (ECU).
The editors were James D. Anker, Stephanie K. Happer, and David Dunham;
the designer was Robin Hessel;
the cover was designed bt Rafael Hernandez;
the cover photograph was taken by John Pinderhughes;
the production supervisor was Joe Campanella.
The photo editor was Caroline Anderson.
New drawings were done by Bruce Lemevise.
Von Hoffmann Press, Inc., was printer and binder.

Library of Congress Cataloging in Publication Data

Hyde, Janet Shibley.
Understanding human sexuality.

Bibliography: p.
Includes index.
1. Sex. 2. Sex customs. 3. Sexual hygiene.
4. Sex—Psychology. I. Title.
HQ12.H82 1986 612.6 85-7875
ISBN 0-07-031581-7
ISBN 0-07-031582-5 (instructor's manual)
ISBN 0-07-031587-6 [text bank (microexaminer)]

ABOUT THE AUTHOR

Janet Hyde is Professor of Psychology at Denison University, having received her education at Oberlin College and the University of California at Berkeley. She has taught a course in human sexuality since 1974, first at Bowling Green State University and then at Denison. Her research interest is in gender-role development in children. In addition, she is investigating the effects of human sexuality courses on the students who take them. Author of the textbook *Half the Human Experience: The Psychology of Women,* she is a Fellow of the American Psychological Association and has received other honors, including an award for excellence in teaching at Bowling Green State University. She is married and has two children.

To my husband, Clark,
and my mother and father,
Dorothy and Grant,
without whom this would not have been possible.

CONTENTS IN BRIEF

CONTENTS

CHAPTER 21. SEXUALITY TRANSMITTED DISEASES 561

CHAPTER 22. ETHICS, RELIGION, AND SEXUALITY 593

CHAPTER 23. SEX AND THE LAW 625

PREFACE

I suspect that my motivation for writing this text was quite similar to that of many people who write textbooks. When I began teaching an undergraduate course in human sexuality, in the fall of 1974, I was unable to find a text that suited my needs or tastes. One text treated the biological aspects of sexuality with so many forbidding Latin terms that students seemed too intimidated to study it effectively. Another had a preaching tone and a bias in favor of very traditional gender roles, neither of which seemed to be in touch with today's students. Others were far too brief and omitted important topics. As a result, I set out to write a text that would meet the needs that the other texts neglected.

Today, approximately 10 years later, there are many sexuality texts available, and many of them are quite good. Nonetheless, I feel that this text has a unique combination of three features that are of utmost importance in a textbook: a writing style that is readable and appealing to the student; coverage that is interdisciplinary and comprehensive; and excellent scholarship. Of the other texts available, some are quite readable, but they tend to be weak in scholarship. Some are very scholarly, but they are not readable. And others lack comprehensiveness, omitting such important topics as the legal aspects of sexuality, or focusing on biology to the exclusion of psychology. My goal in this text is to provide the best in all three of these features—readability, scholarship, and comprehensiveness. This approach has been well-received in the previous editions, and I have worked to maintain and improve these features in the third edition.

PLAN OF THE BOOK

First and foremost, I tried to keep in mind at all times that students *want* to learn about sexuality and that my job as writer was to help them learn. I covered topics completely, in as clear a presentation as possible, and made a special effort to use language that would enlighten rather than intimidate; because students so often know only slang terminology regarding sex, I have included slang terms in parentheses following definitions of scientific sexual terms, to connect the two terminologies. Similarly, in the selection and preparation of illustrations for the book, the goal was always to convey as much information as possible, simply and clearly.

The book assumes no prior college courses in biology, psychology, or sociology.

It is designed as an introduction following the three major objectives of my own course in human sexuality:

1. To provide practical information needed for everyday living (information about sexual anatomy, contraception, and venereal disease, for example) and to deal with problems in a more psychological area (such as impotence or inability to have an orgasm)
2. To help students feel more comfortable with thinking and talking about sex, both to minimize their own personal anguish about a tension-causing topic and to help them become rational decision makers in an important aspect of their lives
3. To familiarize students with methods used in research on sexual behavior, and particularly with problems inherent in some of these methods, so that they can read research reports critically and intelligently.

My own course is a survey course, designed to provide students with a broad range of information about sexuality. Reflecting that approach, this book is intended to be complete and balanced in its coverage, so that students will want to save it after the course for use as a reference in future years. My own training was quite compatible with this interdisciplinary, survey approach. My original graduate training was in psychology, with specialties in behavior genetics and statistics; later my interests expanded to include psychology of women and gender roles. As a result, I feel comfortable in discussing sexuality from biological, psychological, and sociological viewpoints. I did not want to write a book just about the biology of sex, nor just about the psychology of sex, nor just about the sociology of sex. I wanted to cover all those areas with integrity.

Nonetheless, for instructors who feel they lack the time to deal with all the material or who are not prepared to cover certain topics, the chapters have been written to be fairly independent. For example, any of the following chapters could be omitted without loss of continuity: Chapter 13, "Love and Attraction"; Chapter 18, "Sexual Coercion"; Chapter 22, "Ethics, Religion, and Sexuality"; Chapter 23, "Sex and the Law."

It is my belief that, in modern American culture, we are in danger of taking sex far too seriously. We may not be serious about it in the same way as were our Victorian ancestors, but we are serious nonetheless—serious about whether we are using the best and most up-to-date sexual techniques, serious about whether our partners are having as many orgasms as possible, and so on. To counteract this tendency, I have tried to use a light touch, with occasional bits of humor, in this book. I am not advocating that we treat sex in a flippant or frivolous manner, but rather that we keep it in perspective and remember that there are some very funny things about it.

THE THIRD EDITION

This third edition represents a major revision. What is new about the third edition? There are some new chapters and coverage of many new topics, designed to provide the most up-to-date information in the field. There is a comprehensive set of new learning aids for the student. And there are some special new features.

NEW CHAPTERS AND TOPICS

Several chapters are new or received major revisions. Chapter 21, "Sexually Transmitted Diseases," received major attention, with a new section on AIDS and updates on statistics and medical advances related to many other diseases such as chlamydia and herpes. Chapter 2, "Theoretical Perspectives," is a new chapter. It includes the section on theories that was in Chapter 1 of the previous edition, and a major new section on sociological theories has been added. Depending on the focus of a specific course, instructors may want to emphasize or omit this chapter; those teaching an applied course in a health education department might want to omit it, whereas those teaching in psychology or sociology departments who want to focus on the theoretical basis of sex research may want to emphasize it.

Chapter 18, "Sexual Coercion," is a new chapter in this edition. To the coverage of rape from the previous edition, I have added new material on incest, child molestation, and sexual harassment. Chapter 19, "Sex for Sale," is also a new chapter. It includes the material on prostitution from previous editions and a new section on pornography, with a careful review of research on this controversial topic.

Chapter 16, "Sexual Orientation: Gay, Straight, or Bi?," is a major revision of the chapter on homosexuality and bisexuality in the second edition. Reflecting new concepts and research in the field, I have shifted the focus away from explaining homosexuality to explaining sexual orientation—why people become homosexual or heterosexual. New research on long-term gay relationships has been included. In order to avoid ghettoizing the topic of homosexuality, I also did some mainstreaming of that material; for example, the section on techniques in gay lovemaking is now found in Chapter 9, "Techniques of Arousal and Communication." In making all these revisions, I was mindful of the fact that approximately 10 percent of the students (and faculty) who read this book are gays or lesbians. They have a right to see their techniques discussed alongside heterosexuals' techniques, their patterns of communication alongside heterosexuals', and so on.

Chapter 23, "Sex and the Law," received a major overhaul to reflect trends in sex laws in the 1980s. And Chapter 25, "Sexuality in the Future," has a new section—The Sexual Revolution: Is It Over?—which considers the data on a return to fewer partners, less experimentation, and more emphasis on long-term relationships.

To give you some idea of the extent of the revision, there were more than 700 references included in the second edition of the book; some 350 new references were added in the third edition. But don't worry about the readability having been affected by the inclusion of more references. I positioned the references carefully and the writing style remains the same as in the second edition.

LEARNING AIDS

In the third edition I also emphasize learning aids for the student. By expanding to a larger size book, I was able to include a running glossary of terms, with pronunciations, with plenty of space for students to take notes. Chapter outlines appear at the opening of each chapter. Since research in cognitive psychology indicates that learning and memory are improved considerably if the learner knows the organization of the material in advance, the chapter outlines should facilitiate this learning. I have added Review Questions and Questions for Thought, Discussion, and Debate at the end of each chapter. These questions should help students review for exams as well as stimulate them to think beyond the material presented in the text.

SPECIAL FEATURES

Finally, there is a new Appendix—"A Directory of Resources in Human Sexuality." It lists the names, addresses, and functions of many major organizations in the field of human sexuality, on topics ranging from birth control to toll-free hotlines for sexually transmitted diseases, to scholarly journals. I hope this listing will serve as a useful reference for both instructors and students.

ACKNOWLEDGMENTS

Special thanks go to reviewers who went over major portions of the revised text: James F. Calhoun, University of Georgia; Frank Carl, Western Illinois University; Sarah Cirese, College of Marin; John DeLamater, University of Wisconsin-Madison; Randy D. Fisher, University of Central Florida; William A. Fisher, The University of Western Ontario; Gere Fulton, The University of Toledo; Harold Gaines, Maryville College—St. Louis; Ronald Murdoff, San Joaquin Delta College; Lauralee Rockwell, The University of Iowa; and Michael D. Storms, California School of Professional Psychology, Los Angeles. Special authorities who reviewed individual chapters have also been most helpful: Rhonda R. Rivera, College of Law Criminal Programs, The Ohio State University; and Dr. Frederick Sparling, School of Medicine, The University of North Carolina, Chapel Hill. Any errors, or course, remain my responsibility.

Of course, important contributions remain from reviewers of the second edition: James H. Price, University of Toledo; William R. Stayton, Thomas Jefferson University Medical College; Bernie Zilbergeld, Oakland, California; Howard Markman, University of Denver; Alan Bell, Indiana University; Lynn Miller, Lucas and Miller, P. C.; Rober Moss, California State University, Northridge; Robert Sabalis, University of South Carolina, School of Medicine; Leslie McBride, Portland State University; and Helen H. Lambert, Northeastern University.

Important contributions were also made by reviewers of the first edition, and these contributions remain in the third edition. Reviewers of the first edition included: Betsy Allgeier, State University of New York at Fredonia; Gere Fulton, University of Toledo; Valerie Pinhas, Nassau Community College; B. W. Wickersham, Pennsylvania State University; Gordon Bermant, Washington D.C.; James A. Briley, Jefferson State Junior College; Stanley Brodsky, University of Alabama; Benjamin H. Glover, University Hospitals, Madison, Wisconsin; Jeanne Gullahorn, Michigan State University; Cecil M. Hampton, Jefferson College; Margaret Hayes, Borough of Manhattan Community College; the Reverend Richard Hettlinger, Kenyon College; Rosemary Huerter, School of Nursing, University of Minnesota; the Reverend Leo Kelty, Family Life Bureau, Diocese of Trenton; Neil Kirschner, Bowling Green State University; Susan Matusak, Institute for Sex Research, Indiana University; Margaret L. May, Virginia Commonwealth University; Helen McAllister, Monmouth College; Charles McCaghy, Bowling Green State University; Martha Mednick, University of Connecticut; Dee Pridgen, Law School of Catholic Universities, Washington, D.C.; Ira Reiss, University of Minnesota; Charity Runden, Montclair State University; Bruce Salender; Gunter Schmidt, University of Hamburg; Robert Staples, University of California at San Francisco; Rhoda K. Unger, Montclair State University; Russell Veitch, Bowling Green State University; Ruth Westheimer, Cornell University Medical Center, New York; and Bettie Wysor, author and free-lance writer. To the people with whom I have team-taught the course—Neil Kirschner, Howard Markman, and Don Ragusa—thanks are extended for the insights they have provided me about sexuality. The Interlibrary Loan staff at Denison, particularly Roger Blaine, also deserve my heartiest thanks. They have tracked down some pretty obscure references and have contributed to the scholarship of this book.

Finally, I owe many thanks to the editors and staff at McGraw-Hill: Stephanie Happer, developmental editor, whose ideas have improved the book enormously; David Serbun, psychology editor, who has offered consistent support and encouragement for the book; and David Dunham, editing supervisor, who patiently carried things to completion.

I've enjoyed writing and rewriting this text and using it to teach my own course. I hope that you will enjoy reading it, learning from it, and teaching with it.

JANET SHIBLEY HYDE

[redacted]

CHAPTER • 1

SEXUALITY IN PERSPECTIVE

Her voice was the merest whisper as he slowly undressed her, until at last she stood before him, tiny, perfectly formed, her flesh shining in the moonlight, her blond hair almost silver. He picked her up then and slid her into the bed, and carefully took off his own clothes, dropped them to the floor, and slid in beside her. The feel of her satin skin was almost more than he could bear, and he had a hunger for her that was impossible to control as he lay beside her. But it was she who took his face in her hands, who held him close as she arched her body toward him, as slowly, like a forgotten memory come to life with a delicious vengeance, she felt him slip inside her, and she soared to heights that, even with Jeffrey, she had never known.*

* *Source:* Danielle Steel. (1982). *Once in a lifetime.* New York: Dell Publishing, p. 130.

The biologist considers sexual behavior to be of fundamental significance because it leads to perpetuation of the species and thus to the continuity of life itself. The psychologist finds in the sexual impulse wellsprings of human conduct, deep reservoirs of motivation that impel men and women to action and furnish the driving force for many of their day-to-day activities. Sociologists recognize the integrating, cohesive functioning of sex as contributing to the stability of the family unit and thus to the entire structure of the social group. For the moralist, man's perpetual attempt to reconcile his basic sexual tendencies with the ethical standards and ideal demands of his social group presents a primary problem.†

†*Source:* Clellan S. Ford and Frank A. Beach. (1951). *Patterns of sexual behavior.* New York: Harper & Row, p. 1.

CHAPTER HIGHLIGHTS

Odd though it may seem, both of the quotations on page 1 are talking about the same thing—sex. The first quotation is from a romance novel. It stimulates the reader's fantasies and arousal response. The second is from a scholarly book about sex. It stimulates the brain but not the genitals. From these two brief excerpts we can quickly see that the topic of sexuality is diverse, complex, and fascinating.

Introductory textbooks on most subjects generally begin with a section designed to motivate students to study whatever topic it is that the text is about. No such section appears in this book; the reason why people want to study sex is obvious, and your motivation for studying it is probably already quite high. Sex is an important force in many people's lives, and so there are practical reasons for wanting to learn about it. Most people are curious about sex, particularly because exchanging sexual information is somewhat taboo in our culture, and so curiosity also motivates us to study sex. Finally, most of us at various times experience problems with our sexual functioning or wish that we could function better, and we hope that learning more about sex will help us. This book is designed to meet all those needs. And so, without further ado, let us consider various perspectives on sexuality. This will give you a glimpse of the forest before you study the trees: sexual anatomy and physiology (the "plumbing" part), and sexual behavior, which is discussed in the later chapters (the "people" part).

SEX AND GENDER

We sometimes use the word "sex" ambiguously. Sometimes it refers to being male or female, and sometimes it refers to sexual behavior or reproduction. In most cases, of course, the meaning is clear from the context. If you are filling out a job application form and one item says, "Sex: ———," you do not write, "I like it" or "As often as possible." It is clear that your prospective employer wants to know whether you are a male or female. In other cases, though, the meaning is ambiguous. For example, when a book has the title *Sex and Temperament in Three Primitive Societies,* what is it about? Is it about the sexual practices of primitive people and whether having sex frequently gives them pleasant temperaments? Or is it about the kinds of personalities that males and females are expected to have in those societies? Not only does this use of "sex" create ambiguities, but it also clouds our thinking about some important issues.

Gender:
The state of being male or female.

To remove—or at least reduce—this ambiguity, the term "sex" will be used in this book to refer specifically to sexual anatomy and sexual behavior, and the term gender will be used to refer to the state of being male or female. This convention will be maintained throughout the book, in the hope that it will help clarify some issues as we proceed.

This is a book about sex, not gender; it is about sexual behavior and the biological, psychological, and social forces that influence it. Of course, although I am arguing that sex and gender are conceptually different, I would not try to argue that they are totally independent of each other. Certainly gender roles—the ways in which males and females are expected to behave—exert a powerful influence on the way people behave sexually, and so one chapter will be devoted to gender roles and their effects on sexuality.

Sexual behavior:
Behavior that produces arousal and increases the chance of orgasm.

How should we define "sex," aside from saying that it is different from "gender"? A biologist might define sexual behavior as "any behavior that increases the likelihood of gametic union [union of sperm and egg]" (Bermant and Davidson, 1974). This definition emphasizes the reproductive function of sex. However, particularly in the last few decades, technologies have been developed that allow us to separate reproduction from sex. Most Americans now use sex not only for procreation but also for recreation.[1]

[1]Actually, even in former times sex was not always associated with reproduction. For example, a man in 1850 might have fathered 10 children; using a very conservative estimate that he engaged in sexual intercourse 1500 times during his adult life (once a week for the 30 years from age 20 to age 50), one concludes that only 10 in 1500 of those acts, or less than 1 percent, resulted in reproduction.

Kinsey defined "sex" as behavior that leads to orgasm. While this definition has some merits (it does not imply that sex must be associated with reproduction), it also presents some problems. If a wife has intercourse with her husband but does not have an orgasm, was that not sexual behavior for her?

To try to avoid some of these problems, "sexual behavior" will be defined in this book as *behavior that produces arousal and increases the chance of orgasm.*[2]. The term "sexual anatomy," then, refers to the parts of our bodies that are involved in sexual behavior (particularly intercourse) and reproduction.

UNDERSTANDING SEXUALITY

Religion

Throughout most of recorded history, at least until about 100 years ago, religion (and rumor) provided most of the information that people had about sexuality. Thus the ancient Greeks openly acknowledged both heterosexuality and homosexuality in their society and explained the existence of the two in a myth in which the original humans were double creatures with twice the normal number of limbs and organs; some were double males, some were double females, and some were half male and half female. The gods, fearing the power of these creatures, split them in half, and forever after each one continued to search for its missing half. Thus heterosexuals were thought to have resulted from the splitting of the half male, half female; male homosexuals, from the splitting of the double male; and female homosexuals, from the splitting of the double female. It was through this mythology that the ancient Greek understood sexuality.

The fifteenth-century Christian believed that "wet dreams" (nocturnal emissions) resulted from intercourse with tiny spiritual creatures called *incubi* and *succubi,* a notion put forth in a papal bull of 1484 and a companion book, the *Malleus Maleficarum* ("witch's hammer"); the person who had wet dreams was thus guilty of sodomy (see Chapter 21) as well as witchcraft.

The Muslim believed that sexual intercourse was one of the finest pleasures of life, reflecting the teachings of the great prophet Muhammad.

Science

It was against this background of religious understandings of sexuality that the scientific study of sex began in the late nineteenth century, although, of course, religious notions continue to influence our ideas about sexuality to the present day. In addition, the groundwork for an understanding of the biological aspects of sexuality had already been laid by the research of physicians and biologists. The Dutch microscopist Anton van Leeuwenhoek (1632–1723) and his student John Ham had discovered sperm swimming in human semen. In 1875 Oscar Hertwig first observed the actual fertilization of the egg by the sperm in sea urchins, although the ovum in humans was not directly observed until the twentieth century.

---

[2]This definition, though an improvement over some, still has its problems. For example, consider a woman who feels no arousal at all during intercourse. According to the definition, intercourse would not be sexual behavior for her. However, intercourse would generally be something we would want to classify as sexual behavior. It should be clear that defining "sexual behavior" is very difficult. The definition given is good, though not perfect.

(a)

(b)

FIGURE 1.1

Two important early sex researchers. (*a*) Sigmund Freud. (*b*) Henry Havelock Ellis.

A major advance in the scientific understanding of the psychological aspects of human sexuality came with the work of the Viennese physician Sigmund Freud (1856–1939), founder of psychiatry and psychoanalysis. His ideas will be discussed in detail in Chapter 2.

It is important to recognize the cultural context in which Freud and the other early sex researchers began their research and writing. They began their work in the Victorian era, the late 1800s, both in the United States and Europe. Norms about sexuality were extraordinarily rigid and oppressive. Historian Peter Gay characterized this repressive aspect of Victorian cultural norms as

> . . . a devious and insincere world in which middle-class husbands slaked their lust by keeping mistresses, frequenting prostitutes, or molesting children, while their wives, timid, dutiful, obedient, were sexually anesthetic and poured all their capacity for love into their housekeeping and their child-rearing. (Gay, 1984, p. 6)

Certainly traces of these Victorian attitudes remain with us today. Yet at the same time the actual sexual behavior of Victorians was sometimes active and in violation of societal norms (see Focus 1.1: A Victorian Sex Survey). In his history of sexuality in the Victorian era, Peter Gay documents the story of Mabel Loomis Todd who, though married, carried on a sensual and lengthy affair with Austin Dickinson, a community leader in Amherst, Massachusetts. Many people actually knew about the "secret" affair, yet Mrs. Loomis did not become an outcast (Gay, 1984). Doubtless, this wide discrepancy between Victorian sexual norms and actual behavior created a great deal of personal tension. That tension probably propelled a good many people into Dr. Freud's office, providing data for his theory that emphasizes sexual tensions and conflict.

F • O • C • U • S
1.1

A VICTORIAN SEX SURVEY

In the late 1800s Queen Victoria reigned in England, and both there and in the United States the ideal seemed to be to repress sexuality as much as possible. Women, particularly, were to have no sexual desires. And standards of modesty were so great that pianos had "limbs" rather than vulgar "legs."

Out of the Victorian environment emerged a remarkable woman, Dr. Clelia Mosher. Born in Albany, New York, in 1863, she began college at Wellesley and finished at Stanford. For her Masters degree from Stanford, she collected data to debunk a popular myth of the time: that women could breathe only high in the chest, whereas men breathed deeply using the diaphragm. Mosher concluded, quite reasonably, that any differences resulted purely from women being laced into tight-fitting corsets. Mosher began medical school at Johns Hopkins when she was 32 and earned her M.D. degree four years later. Interestingly, Gertrude Stein, the famous author, entered the same medical school one year after Mosher, but never finished her degree.

Over a period of 30 years, beginning when she was an undergraduate, Mosher conducted a sex survey of Victorian women, most of whom were born around the time of the Civil War. In all, she administered her nine-page questionnaire to 47 women. The sample is, admittedly, small and nonrandom. Many of the women were faculty wives at universities, or women from Mosher's medical practice, and surely they were a select sample to agree to answer the questions; 81 percent had attended college, a high level of education for women in those days. Nonetheless, the survey is remarkable because—despite well-known ideas about Victorian women—this is the only actual survey of those women known to exist. Here are some interesting findings from the study:

- Despite the stereotype that Victorian women felt no sexual desire, 35 of the 44 women answering the question said that they felt a desire for sexual intercourse.
- Thirty-four of the women indicated that they experienced orgasm. Interestingly, Mosher worded the question "Do you always have a venereal orgasm?" thus assuming that orgasm was to be expected.
- Mosher suspected that women's longer time to reach orgasm might be a cause of marital conflicts. Many of her respondents supported this idea. One said that sex had been unpleasant to her for years because of her "slow reaction," but "orgasm [occurs] if time is taken." Another complained that "Men have not been properly trained." And for some, not reaching orgasm was psychologically devastating (one can't help thinking that things haven't changed so much from the 1880s to the 1980s).
- At least 30 of the women used some form of birth control. Douching was the most popular method, followed by withdrawal and "timing." Several women's husbands used a "male sheath," and two women used a "rubber cap over the uterus." One woman used cocoa butter. She did not explain how or why.

Clelia Mosher's survey is fascinating because it demonstrates that, despite the Victorian era's repressive teachings, some women still managed to enjoy sex. True, some were affected by Victorian mores; three of the women said their ideal would be to abstain from intercourse entirely. But the majority of the women still expressed sexual desires and experienced orgasms and seemed to enjoy sex with their husbands.

Source: Kathryn A. Jacob. (1981). The Mosher report. *American Heritage,* pp. 57–64.

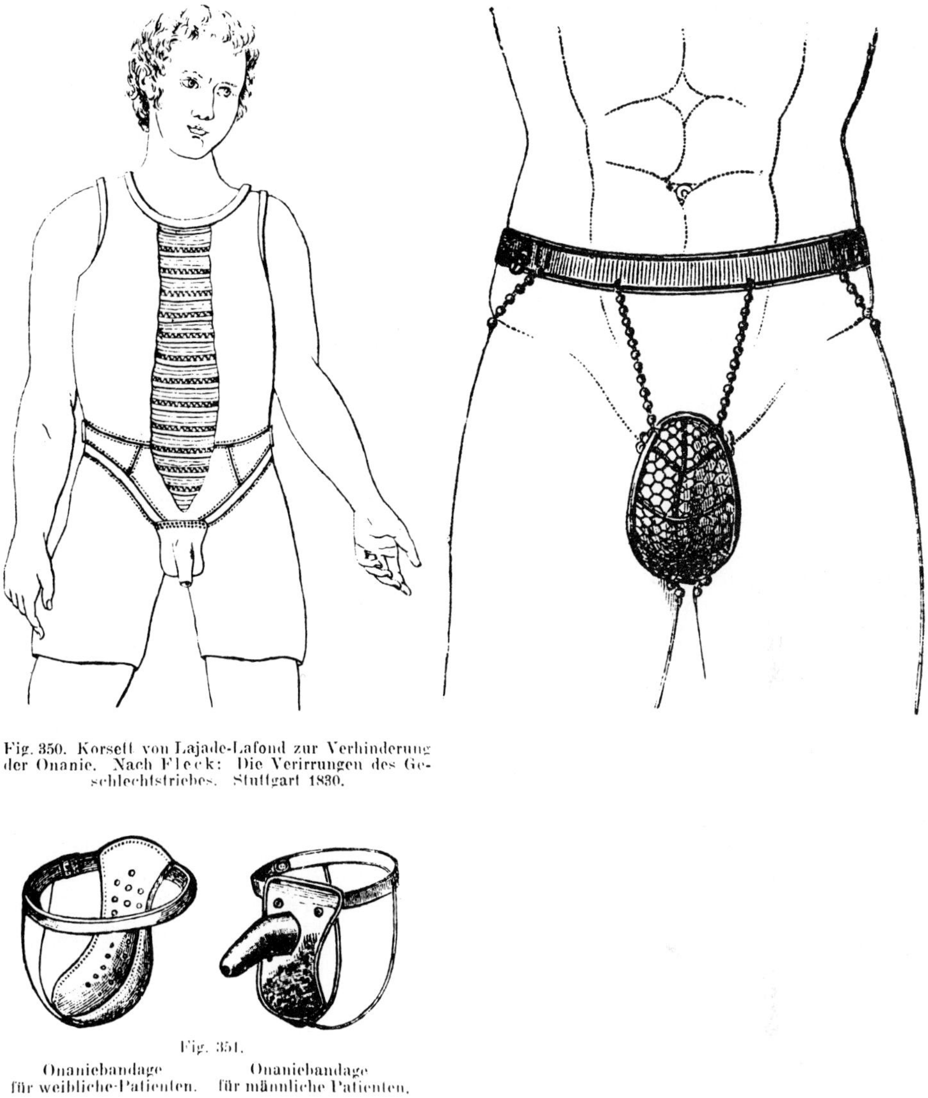
Fig. 350. Korsett von Lajade-Lafond zur Verhinderung der Onanie. Nach Fleck: Die Verirrungen des Geschlechtstriebes. Stuttgart 1830.
Fig. 351.
Onaniebandage für weibliche Patienten.
Onaniebandage für männliche Patienten.

FIGURE 1.2

The Victorian era, from which Freud and Ellis emerged, was characterized by extreme sexual repression. Here are apparatuses that were sold to prevent onanism or masturbation.

An equally great—though not so well known—early contributor to the scientific study of sex was Henry Havelock Ellis (1859–1939). A physician in Victorian England, he compiled a vast collection of information on sexuality—including medical and anthropological findings, as well as case histories—which was published in a series of volumes entitled *Studies in the Psychology of Sex* beginning in 1896. Havelock Ellis was a remarkably objective and tolerant scholar, particularly for his era. A sexual reformer, he believed that sexual deviations from the norm were often harmless, and he urged society to accept them. In his desire to collect information about human sexuality rather than to make judgments about it, he can be considered the forerunner of modern sex research (for an autobiography, see Ellis, 1939; numerous biographies also exist).

Another important figure in nineteenth-century sex research was Richard von Krafft-Ebing (1840–1902). His special interest was "pathological" sexuality, and he managed to collect over 200 case histories of pathological individuals, which appeared in his book entitled *Psychopathia Sexualis.* His work tended to be neither objective nor tolerant. One of his case histories is presented in Chapter 17.

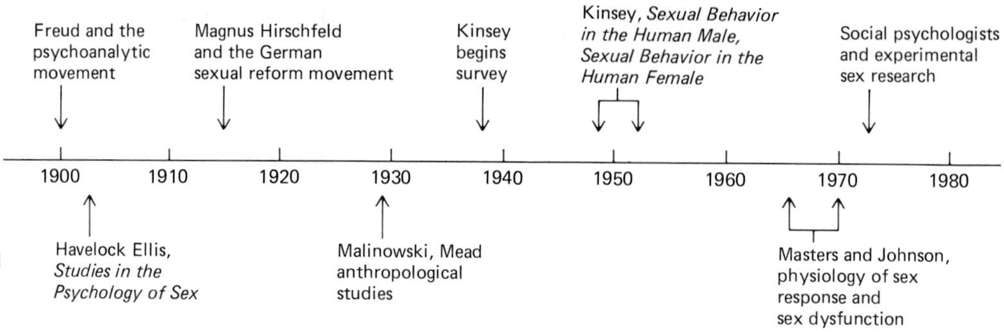

FIGURE 1.3
The history of scientific research on sex.

One other early contributor to the scientific understanding of sexuality deserves mention, the German Magnus Hirschfeld (1868–1935). He founded the first sex research institute and administered the first large-scale sex survey, obtaining data from 10,000 people on a 130-item questionnaire. Unfortunately, most of the information he amassed was destroyed by Nazi hoodlums. Hirschfeld also established the first journal devoted to the study of sex, established a marriage counseling service, worked for legal reforms, and gave advice on contraception and sex problems. His special interest, however, was homosexuality. Doubtless some of his avant-garde approaches resulted from the fact that he was himself both a homosexual and a transvestite, but his contributions as a pioneer sex researcher cannot be denied (Bullough, 1976).

Homosexual:
A person who is sexually attracted to, or engages in sexual activity primarily with, members of his or her own gender.

Transvestite:
A person (usually a man) who dresses in the clothing of the opposite gender.

In the twentieth century, major breakthroughs in the scientific understanding of sex came with the massive surveys of human sexual behavior in the United States conducted by Alfred Kinsey and his colleagues in the 1940s and with Masters and Johnson's investigations of sexual dysfunctions and the physiology of sexual response. At about the same time that the Kinsey research was being conducted, some anthropologists—most notably Margaret Mead and Bronislaw Malinowski—were beginning to collect data on sexual behavior in other cultures. Other, smaller investigations also provided important information.

The scientific study of sex has still not emerged as a separate, unified academic discipline like biology or psychology or sociology. Rather, it tends to be interdisciplinary—a joint effort by biologists, psychologists, sociologists, anthropologists, and physicians. In a sense, this is a major virtue in our current approach to understanding sexuality, since it gives us a better view of humans in all their sexual complexity.

Let us now consider the perspectives on sexuality provided by cross-cultural observations of humans in a wide variety of societies.

CROSS-CULTURAL PERSPECTIVES

We tend to be ethnocentric in our understanding of human sexual behavior. That is, most of us have had experience with sexuality in only one culture—the United States—and we tend to view it as the only pattern of sexual behavior in existence, and certainly as the only "natural" pattern. But anthropologists have discovered that there are wide variations in sexual behavior and attitudes from one culture to the next. Considering these variations should help us to put our own sexual behavior in perspective.

The data on the enormous variations in sexual behavior from one culture to the next will be reviewed below. First, however, some generalizations that emerge in cross-cultural studies will be considered. A major source of data for the conclusions that will be drawn is the classic study of anthropologist Clellan Ford and psychologist Frank Beach (1951), who surveyed sexual behavior in 190 societies around the world and also sexual behavior across various animal species. Another major source is a recent, massive cross-cultural survey of sexual practices, done by anthropologist Edgar Gregersen (1983).

Before proceeding it is worth noting that Ford and Beach concluded, in 1951, that the United States culture was a relatively sexually restrictive one; the majority of the others studied were far more permissive. This may help us put our own standards in better perspective. On the other hand, most people would agree—and scientific research supports the notion (see Chapters 10 to 12)—that sexual behavior

FIGURE 1.4

Sexual behaviors and customs vary widely in human cultures different from our own. (*a*) Asmat boys from New Guinea jokingly imitate parents copulating. (*b*) Trobriand Island girls from New Guinea sing bawdy songs and dance to attract boys. (*c*) Bride and groom, from the Asmat tribe in New Guinea, during their wedding ceremony.

(a)

(b)

(c)

F · O · C · U · S 1.2

SEXUALITY IN TWO SOCIETIES

INIS BEAG

Inis Beag is a small island off the coast of Ireland. It is probably one of the most naive and sexually repressive societies in the world.

The people of Inis Beag seem to have no knowledge of a number of sexual activities such as French kissing, mouth stimulation of the breast, or hand stimulation of the partner's penis, much less cunnilingus, fellatio, or homosexuality. Sex education is virtually nonexistent; parents do not seem to be able to bring themselves to discuss such embarrassing matters with their children, and they simply trust that, after marriage, nature will take its course.

Menstruation and menopause are sources of fear for the island women because they have no idea of their physiological significance. It is commonly believed that menopause can produce insanity; in order to ward off this condition, some women have retired from life in their mid-forties, and a few have confined themselves to bed until death years later.

The men believe that intercourse is hard on one's health. They will desist from sex the night before they are to do a job that takes great energy. They do not approach women sexually during menstruation or for months after childbirth; a woman is considered dangerous to the male at these times.

The islanders abhor nudity. Only babies are allowed to bathe while nude. Adults wash only the parts of their bodies that extend beyond their clothing—face, neck, lower arms, hands, lower legs, and feet. The fear of nudity has even cost lives. Seamen

and attitudes among Americans have undergone substantial changes in the 35 years since Ford and Beach wrote their book. It would be interesting to know whether they would now classify us as a permissive or a restrictive society.

Generalizations

The major generalization that emerges from cross-cultural studies is that all societies regulate sexual behavior in some way, though the exact regulations vary greatly from one culture to the next (Gebhard, 1971; Jensen, 1976b). Apparently no society has seen fit to leave sexuality totally unregulated, perhaps because social disruption would result. As an example, incest taboos are nearly universal: sex is regulated in that intercourse between relatives is prohibited. Most societies also condemn forced sexual relations, such as rape.

Incest taboo: A regulation prohibiting sexual interaction between blood relatives, such as brother and sister or father and daughter.

Beyond this generalization, though, regulations vary greatly from one society to the next, and sexual behavior and attitudes vary correspondingly. The ways in which who never learned to swim because it involved wearing scanty clothing have drowned when their ships have sunk.

Premarital sex is essentially unknown. In marital sex, foreplay is generally limited to kissing and rough fondling of the buttocks. The husband invariably initiates the activity. The male-on-top is the only position used, and both partners keep their underwear on during the activity. The man has orgasm quickly and falls asleep almost immediately. Female orgasm is unknown, or at least it is doubted to exist or is considered deviant.

MANGAIA

In distinct contrast to Inis Beag is Mangaia, an island in the South Pacific. For the Mangaians, sex—for pleasure and for procreation—is a principal interest.

The Mangaian boy hears of masturbation when he is about 7, and he may begin to masturbate at age 8 or 9. At around age 13 he undergoes the superincision ritual (in which a slit is made on the top of the penis, along its entire length). This ritual initiates him into manhood; more important, however, the expert who performs the superincision gives him sexual instruction. He shows the boy how to perform cunnilingus, how to kiss and suck breasts, and how to bring his partner to orgasm several times before he has his own orgasm. About two weeks after the operation, the boy has intercourse with an experienced woman, which removes the scab. She provides him with practice in various acts and positions and trains him to hold back until he can have simultaneous orgasms with his partner.

After this, the Mangaian boy aggressively seeks out girls, or they seek him out; soon he has coitus every night. The girl, who has received sexual instruction from an older woman, expects demonstration of his virility as proof of his desire for her. What is valued is the ability of the male to continue vigorously the in-and-out action of coitus over long periods of time while the female moves her hips "like a washing machine." Nothing is despised more than a "dead" partner who does not move. A good man is expected to continue his actions for 15 to 30 minutes or more.

The average "nice" girl will have three or four successive boyfriends between the ages of 13 and 20; the average boy may have 10 or more girlfriends. Mangaian parents encourage their daughters to have sexual experiences with several men. They want her to find a marriage partner who is congenial.

At around age 18, the Mangaians typically have sex most nights of the week, with about three orgasms per night. By about age 48, they have sex two or three times per week, with one orgasm each time.

All women in Mangaia apparently learn to have orgasms. Bringing his partner to orgasm is one of the man's chief sources of sexual pleasure.

Sources: John C. Messenger. Sex and repression in an Irish folk community. Donald S. Marshall. Sexual behavior on Mangaia. Both in D. S. Marshall and R. C. Suggs (Eds.), (1971). *Human sexual behavior.* New York: Basic Books.

various societies treat some key areas of human sexual behavior will be considered below.

Sexual Techniques

Kissing is one of the most common sexual techniques in our culture. It is also very common in most other societies (Gregersen, 1983). There are a few societies, though, in which kissing is unknown. For example, when the Thonga of Africa first saw Europeans kissing, they laughed and said, "Look at them; they eat each other's saliva and dirt." There is also some variation in techniques of kissing. For example, among the Kwakiutl of Canada and the Trobriand Islanders, kissing consists of sucking the lips and tongue of the partner, permitting saliva to flow from one mouth to the other. Many Americans might find such a practice somewhat repulsive, but other peoples find it sexually arousing.

Grooming and delousing are widespread forms of behavior that act as a prelude to sexual relations. Describing the Siriono of South America, one observer wrote:

> Lovers also spend hours in grooming one another—extracting lice from their hair or wood ticks from their bodies, and eating them; removing worms and spines from their skin; gluing feathers into their hair; and covering their faces with utuku . . . paint. This behavior often leads up to a sexual bout, especially when conditions for intercourse are favorable. (Holmberg, 1946, p. 182)

Cunnilingus (mouth stimulation of the female genitals) is fairly common in our society, and it occurs in a few other societies as well, especially in the South Pacific. A particularly exotic variation is reported on the island of Ponape; the man places a fish in the woman's vulva and then gradually licks it out prior to coitus.

Inflicting pain on the partner is also a part of the sexual technique in some societies. The Apinaye woman of South America may bite off bits of her partner's eye-

FIGURE 1.5

The sexual behavior of gorillas. (*a*) The female "presents" to the male, soliciting copulation. (*b*) Copulation in the rear-mount position. (*c*) Copulation in the face-to-face position, which is rare among nonhumans.

brows, noisily spitting them aside. Ponapean men usually tug at the woman's eyebrows, occasionally yanking out tufts of hair. The Trukese women of the South Pacific poke a finger into the man's ear when they are highly aroused. People of various societies bite their partners to the point of drawing blood and leaving scars; most commonly it is the woman who inflicts the pain on the man (Ford and Beach, 1951).

The frequency of intercourse for married couples varies considerably from one culture to the next. The lowest frequency seems to be among the Keraki of the South Pacific, who copulate only about once a week. The Irish natives of Inis Beag, discussed in the Focus, may hold a record by having an even lower frequency than this, perhaps only once or twice a month; however, the anthropologists who studied them were unable to determine how often couples did have sex because so much secrecy surrounds the act. At the opposite extreme, the Aranda of Australia have intercourse as often as three to five times a night, sleeping between episodes; the Mangaians, described in the Focus, seem to have an equally high frequency, at least among the young. The Santals of southern Asia copulate as often as five times per day every day early in marriage (Gregersen, 1983). Our own culture, then, at the time of the Kinsey report, had a low frequency of intercourse compared with other societies. Surveys of United States sexuality in the 1970s and 1980s would indicate our frequency of intercourse is now about average compared with other societies (e.g., Hunt, 1974).

Masturbation

Masturbation:
Self-stimulation of the genitals to produce sexual arousal.

Attitudes toward masturbation vary widely across cultures. Some societies tolerate or even encourage masturbation during childhood and adolescence, while others condemn the practice at any age. Almost all human societies express some disapproval of adult masturbation, ranging from mild ridicule to severe punishment (Gregersen, 1983). On the other hand, at least some adults in all societies appear to practice it.

Female masturbation certainly occurs in other societies. The African Azande woman does it with a phallus made of a wooden root; however, if her husband catches her masturbating, he may beat her severely. The following is a description of the Lesu of the South Pacific, who are one of the few societies that express no disapproval of adult female masturbation:

> A woman will masturbate if she is sexually excited and there is no man to satisfy her. A couple may be having intercourse in the same house, or near enough for her to see them, and she may thus become aroused. She then sits down and bends her right leg so that her heel presses against her genitalia. Even young girls of about six years may do this quite casually as they sit on the ground. The women and men talk about it freely, and there is no shame attached to it. It is a customary position for women to take, and they learn it in childhood. They never use their hands for manipulation. (Powdermaker, 1933, pp. 276–277)

Homosexuality

There is a wide range of attitudes toward homosexuality in various cultures. At one extreme are societies that strongly disapprove of homosexual behavior for people of any age. In contrast, some societies tolerate homosexual behavior for children but disapprove of it in adults. Yet other societies actively force all their male members to engage in some homosexual behavior, usually in conjunction with puberty rites. In Africa, prominent Siwan men lend their sons to one another, and they discuss their homosexual love affairs as openly as they discuss the love of women. A few societies have a formalized role for the adult male homosexual which gives him status and dignity.

While there is wide variation in attitudes toward homosexuality and in homosexual behavior, four general rules do seem to emerge (Ford and Beach, 1951; Whitam, 1983): (1) no matter how a particular society treats homosexuality, the behavior always occurs in at least some individuals—that is, homosexuality is found universally in all societies; (2) males are more likely to engage in homosexual behavior than females; (3) homosexual behavior is never the predominant form of sexual behavior for adults in any of the societies studied; and (4) the incidence of homosexuality is stable across cultures and across time and does not exceed 5 percent of the total population.

Standards of Attractiveness

In all human societies physical characteristics are important in determining whom one chooses as a sex partner. What is considered attractive varies considerably, though. In the United States, the ideal is a slim woman with large eyes and a lovely complexion and long, shapely legs. For us, physical characteristics are probably less important in determining a man's attractiveness. More important is what he *does;* he is attractive if he is a star athlete or a wealthy businessman. But his physical characteristics are also considered important; the ideal is a tall, trim man with broad shoulders, narrow hips, and a firm jaw.

The region of the body that is judged for attractiveness varies considerably from one culture to the next. For some peoples, the shape and color of the eyes are especially significant. For others, the shape of the ears is most important. Some societies go directly to the heart of the matter and judge attractiveness by the appearance of the external genitals. In a few societies, elongated labia majora (the pads of fat on either side of the vaginal opening in women) are considered sexually attractive, and it is common practice for a woman to pull on hers in order to make them longer. Elongated labia majora among the Nawa women of Africa are considered a mark of beauty and are quite prominent.

Our society's standards are in the minority in one way: in most cultures, a plump woman is considered more attractive than a thin one.

One standard does seem to be a general rule: a poor complexion is considered unattractive in the majority of human societies.

Gender Roles

Margaret Mead did some of the most important studies on gender roles in cultures other than our own, and her books, among them *Sex and Temperament in Three Primitive Societies,* are classics. Those studies will not be discussed in detail here because they are well known; the interested reader may consult them directly.

The point that emerges from the cross-cultural studies is that gender roles vary tremendously from one society to the next. In particular, the roles that males and females play in sexual relations may be quite different from the ones that are played in our own society. For example, there are a few societies in which the girl generally begins all love affairs (for example, the Maori and the Kwoma of the South Pacific and the Mataco of South America). Although the gender roles in our society lead us to believe that rape is always committed by men against women, Malinowski described a regular process of women raping men among the Trobriand Islanders of the South Pacific:

> If they perceive a stranger, a man from any village but their own, passing within sight, they have a customary right to attack him, a right which by all accounts they exercise with zeal and energy.
>
> The man is the fair game of the women for all that sexual violence, obscene cruelty, filthy pollution, and rough handling can do to him. Thus first they pull off and tear up his pubic leaf, the protection of his modesty and, to a native, the symbol of his manly dignity. Then by masturbatory practices and exhibitionism, they try to produce an erection in their victim and, when their manoeuvres have brought about the desired result, one of them squats over him and inserts his penis into her vagina. After the first ejaculation he may be treated in the same manner by another woman. Worse things are to follow. Some of the women will defecate and micturate all over his body. . . . Local informants from the south confirmed this account in all essentials. They were by no means ashamed of their custom, regarding it rather as a sign of the general virility of the district, and passing on any possible opprobrium to the stranger-victims.(1929)

Suffice it to say that some cultures have gender roles very different from our own.

Social-Class and Ethnic-Group Variations in the United States

The discussion so far may have seemed to imply that there is one uniform standard of sexual behavior in the United States and that all Americans behave alike sexually. In fact, though, there are large variations in sexual behavior within our culture. Some of these subcultural variations can be classified as social-class differences and some as ethnic differences.

TABLE 1.1

SOCIAL CLASS VARIATIONS IN THE SEXUAL BEHAVIOR OF AMERICANS AT THE TIME OF THE KINSEY STUDIES

	Educational Level		
	0–8 Years of Education, %	9–12 Years of Education, %	13 or More Years of Education, %
Males having premarital sex by age 20	83	75	44
Males having sex with a prostitute before marriage	80	61	35
Males having performed cunnilingus on their wives	4	15	45
Females who had never had an orgasm by the fifth year of marriage	28	17	15

Sources: Alfred C. Kinsey, Wardell B. Pomeroy, and Clyde E. Martin. (1948). *Sexual behavior in the human male.* Philadelphia: Saunders, pp. 352, 368, 550. Alfred C. Kinsey, Wardell B. Pomeroy, Clyde E. Martin, and Paul H. Gebhard. (1953). *Sexual behavior in the human female.* Philadelphia: Saunders, p. 401.

F · O · C · U · S 1.3

SOVIET SEX

Little is known about sex in the Soviet Union because the Soviets officially have no sex research. They view studies such as the Kinsey Report as indicative of the moral decadence of the West. (Ironically, during the McCarthy era Kinsey was accused of being a communist!) The publication, in 1980, of Mikhail Stern's *Sex in the USSR* provided a new and fascinating glimpse of the taboo topic. Stern was a physician in the Soviet Union for 30 years and spent his last three years in Russia in a labor camp, then left for France. There is no sex therapy in the U.S.S.R., so people with sex problems consult physicians with specialties such as endocrinology, which was Stern's work. His experiences as a physician and in the labor camp provided the data for his book.

According to Stern, marital sex is a rather grim business. Intercourse is typically accomplished in the doggy position (called "crayfish" by the Soviets). There is little sophistication in technique; the woman is relatively inexperienced and passive, while the man uses little foreplay and may even be brutal. Most men are unaware that the clitoris exists or has a sexual function. For men, sex is seen mainly as being a performance for them, an indication of strength and masculinity. Further, it is believed that the man should not delay his orgasm—indeed, "holding back" is regarded as a perversion. It is medical dogma that delaying orgasm is injurious and can lead to serious consequences such as impotence, neurosis, and psychosis. A medical journal gave its opinion that the ideal duration of the sexual act was two minutes.

The state has taken on the role of moral overseer. Its attitude can be described only as puritanical; the attempt has been officially to banish sex. For example, "immoral" young people—unmarried lovers

Social Class and Sex

Kinsey found large social-class differences in sexual behavior (he generally used amount of education as a measure of social class). For example, Table 1.1 shows that males in his study who did not go beyond grade school were nearly twice as likely as males who attended college to have had premarital sex by the age of 20 (83 percent, as compared with 44 percent). Almost none of the grade school males had ever performed cunnilingus on their wives, whereas nearly half of the college-educated men had. Considerably more of the uneducated wives had never had an orgasm after five years of marriage, compared with wives who had had a high school or a college education.

Gender roles tend to be more rigid in the lower class, and this tends to extend to the realm of sexuality. As sociologist Lee Rainwater (1971) has noted, among the who are seen kissing in public—may have their pictures posted prominently in a village square.

Given all the above, it is not surprising that Stern reports an early loss of sexual appetite among Soviets, with the frequency of intercourse declining from once a day in the 20 to 25 age range to once a month in the 35 to 40 age range.

Impotence, according to Stern, is at epidemic proportions. He attributes this in part to the stresses of everyday life in the Soviet Union, with the constant threat of harassment by the government; to the high rate of alcoholism; and to the high incidence of malnutrition. Stern also believes that "frigidity" is common, although his estimate is that the percentage has declined from 70 during the Stalin years (about the time of the Kinsey report in the United States) to about 45 percent of women who currently have orgasms never or infrequently.

Despite all this, there seems to be a sexual revolution in the U.S.S.R. parallel to the one in the United States, with substantial increases in the incidence of premarital intercourse. One sociological study estimated that 64 percent of Soviet women engaged in it by age 21. The attitude of Soviet young people, though, is cynical. They view sex in practical terms—a physical need that must be satisfied. Love seems to have been banished even more than sex.

There is no official contraception program. The most common method is the use of the condom. The Soviet brand is referred to as "galoshes," describing the thickness and low-grade rubber with which the condoms are made and their uneven dimensions. There is a lively black market in Western condoms. The other common method is the use of the diaphragm. The pill and the IUD are unknown. Contraception, then, is a rather haphazard affair. Consequently, abortion is the most common method of birth control.

Prostitution is illegal but flourishing. Exhibitionism is also at epidemic proportions. According to Stern, college women sometimes have competitions at the close of the day to see who witnessed the most exhibitionists that day. Stern views exhibitionism as one of the few ways people can assert freedom and individuality—perhaps even be rebellious—in a state that tyrannizes them. A similar argument might be made about sex in public places, which is also common, particularly in subways and buses, and the interminable lines in which Soviet citizens wait.

It is possible that Stern's observations are biased in much the same way Freud's were—in his role as physician and sex counselor, Stern saw mainly people seeking help with problems, and he may therefore have overestimated the extent of disturbed sexuality. His labor camp experience also probably did not contribute to observations of healthy sex. What do you, the reader, think? Do Stern's observations meet scientific standards so that they can be believed? Criteria for judging the scientific quality of research are discussed in Chapter 10.

Source: Mikhail Stern. *Sex in the USSR* (1980). New York: Times Books.

poor the dictum is, "Sex is a man's pleasure and a woman's duty." He found this rule to hold for lower-class people in the United States as well as those in England, Puerto Rico, and Mexico.

Thus a composite picture of social-class differences in sexuality emerged at the time the Kinsey data were collected. The lower-class married couple were more likely to have sex in the dark and with some clothing on, and the male came to orgasm quickly. The husband was also more likely to have extramarital sex with a prostitute. Middle- and upper-middle-class couples, on the other hand, were relatively more likely to sleep in the nude and to have sex in the nude with some lighting. They also used a wider variety of sexual techniques, including varied positions (such as woman-on-top) and fellatio and cunnilingus, and the husband was more likely to delay his orgasm (Kinsey et al., 1948).

Fellatio (fuh-LAY-sho): Mouth stimulation of the penis.

Cunnilingus (kun-nih-LING-us): Mouth stimulation of the female genitals.

It may be that the Kinsey findings are now largely of historical interest. More recent data, collected in the 1970s, suggests that the social-class differences found by Kinsey have diminished greatly or have even disappeared (Hunt, 1974). Social-class differences have diminished particularly among the young.

Black Sexuality

The American population is composed of many ethnic groups, and there may be variations among these groups in sexual behavior. Because the data on other ethnic groups are very limited, the focus here will be on the sexuality of black Americans and the ways in which it differs from that of white Americans.

The sexuality of black Americans, of course, is influenced by many of the same factors influencing the sexuality of white Americans, such as the legacies of the Victorian era and the influence of the Judeo-Christian religious tradition. In addition, at least three other factors may act to make the sexuality of blacks somewhat different from that of whites: (1) the African heritage, (2) the forces that acted upon blacks during slavery, and (3) current economic and social conditions, particularly high unemployment among black men.

Given these forces, what are the sexual behaviors and attitudes of blacks now? There do seem to be some areas in which they differ from whites. There is more approval of premarital sex among blacks than among whites. Blacks tend to have less of a double standard concerning sex; sexual experience can be a status symbol or a sign of entering womanhood for the adolescent black girl (Ladner, 1971; Staples, 1972). Consistent with these differences in attitudes, black teenage girls are more likely to engage in premarital intercourse than their white counterparts. In one well-sampled study, 84 percent of black women had engaged in premarital intercourse by age 19, compared with 49 percent of white women (Zelnik and Kantner, 1977). Black teenagers also engage in coitus for the first time at somewhat earlier ages than white teenagers do; in the same study, the average age of first intercourse was 15.6 years for black women and 16.3 years for white women (Zelnik and Kantner, 1977).

Black women tend to be more open than white women about their sexual needs, both in discussion with other women and in their sexual interactions with men. Perhaps as a result, lower-class black women are more likely to have orgasms during premarital sex than lower-class white women (Staples, 1972).

There are also some differences in patterns of contraceptive use between blacks and whites. For example, black teenagers are more likely than whites to use the pill, and white teenagers are more likely than blacks to use the condom and withdrawal (Zelnik and Kantner, 1977).

There are also variations within black culture. Differences exist between the sexual behavior of black men and women that are similar to the differences between the sexual behavior of white men and women. For example, black men are more accepting of premarital sex than black women are. In addition, there are social-class variations; the sexual behavior of middle-class blacks is more similar to that of middle-class whites than it is to that of lower-class blacks (Staples, 1972).

Generally, the differences between blacks and whites in sexual behavior are not large, and they may be related more to social class than to anything else.

The Significance of the Cross-Cultural Studies

What relevance do the cross-cultural data have to an understanding of human sexuality? They are important for two basic reasons. First, they give us a notion of the enormous variation that exists in human sexual behavior, and they help us put our own society's standards and our own behavior in perspective. Second, these studies provide us with impressive evidence concerning the importance of culture and learning in the shaping of our sexual behavior; they show us that human sexual behavior is not completely determined by biology or drives or instincts. For example, the woman of Inis Beag and the woman of Mangaia presumably have vaginas that are similarly constructed and clitorises that are approximately the same size and have the same nerve supply. But the woman of Inis Beag never has an orgasm, and all Mangaian women orgasm.[3] Why? Their cultures are different, and they and their partners learned different things about sex as they were growing up. Learning is the biggest determinant of human sexual behavior, and instincts or drives play only a minor role.

CROSS-SPECIES PERSPECTIVES

Humans are one of many animal species, and all of them display sexual behavior. To put our own sexual behavior in evolutionary perspective, it is helpful to explore the similarities and differences between our own sexuality and that of other species. There is one other motive behind this particular discussion. Some people classify sexual behaviors as "natural" or "unnatural" depending on whether other species do or do not exhibit those behaviors. Sometimes, though, the data are twisted to suit the purposes of the person making the argument, and so there is a need for a less biased view. Let us see exactly what some other species do!

Masturbation

Humans are definitely not the only species that masturbates. Masturbation is found among many species of mammals, and it is particularly common among the primates (monkeys and apes). Male monkeys and apes in zoos can be observed masturbating, often to the horror of the proper folk who have come to see them. At one time it was thought that this behavior might be the result of the unnatural living conditions of zoos. However, observations of free-living primates indicate that they, too, masturbate (e.g., Carpenter, 1942). Techniques include hand stimulation of the genitals or rubbing the genitals against an object. In terms of technique, monkeys and apes have one advantage over humans: their bodies are so flexible that they can perform mouth-genital sex on themselves. A unique form of male masturbation is found among red deer; during the rutting season they move the tips of their antlers through low-growing vegetation, producing erection and ejaculation (Beach, 1976).

Female masturbation is also found among many species besides our own. The prize for the most inventive technique probably should go to the female porcupine. She holds one end of a stick in her paws and walks around while straddling the stick; as the stick bumps against the ground, it vibrates against her genitals (Ford and Beach, 1951). Human females are apparently not the first to enjoy vibrators.

---

[3] I like to use the word "orgasm" not only as a noun but also as a verb. The reason is that alternative expressions, such as "to *achieve* orgasm" and "to *reach* orgasm," reflect our tendency to make sex an achievement situation (an idea to be discussed further in Chapter 9). To avoid this, I use "to have an orgasm" or "to orgasm."

Mouth-Genital Stimulation

Mouth-genital stimulation is also quite natural, judging from the behavior of other species. It is quite common for the male to apply his mouth to the female's genitals, in part because the sex scents, or *pheromones,* she produces stimulate sexual behavior (see Chapter 8). The following quotation describes this practice among chimpanzees (our nearest evolutionary relatives) and points out the pleasure the female apparently receives from it:

> Wendy was turning so that her face was away from Billy and her posterior parts were turned conspicuously towards him. . . . Billy showed interest in the protruding genitalia (and) . . . gradually the manipulations of his free hand became directed more and more (toward them). . . . He picked at them with his fingers and several times took them in his lips. Shortly after this manipulation began it became apparent that Wendy was sexually stimulated. The clitoris became noticeably erect, and I could detect occasional surges as though she were voluntarily increasing the erection. (Bingham, 1928, pp. 98–99)

Observations indicate that it is less common for the female to stimulate the male's genitals with her mouth, although this does occur (Ford and Beach, 1951).

Homosexual Behavior

Homosexual behavior is found in many species besides our own (Beach, 1976). Indeed, observations of other species indicate that our basic mammalian heritage is bisexual; it is composed of both heterosexual and homosexual elements (Ford and Beach, 1951).

Males of many species will mount other males. Anal intercourse has even been observed in some male primates (Erwin and Maple, 1976; Hamilton, 1914; Kempf, 1917). Male porpoises have also been observed repeatedly attempting to insert their penis into the anus of an intended male partner, even though females were available (McBride and Hebb, 1948). Such attempts at anal intercourse, however, have been observed only among captive animals and may not occur among animals in the wild. Females also mount other females. I have two female dogs, and they delight in mounting each other, particularly when company is present.

In species that form long-term bonds or relationships, long homosexual bonds have been observed. For example, Konrad Lorenz (1966) has reported a long-term relationship between two male ducks.

Human Uniqueness

The general trend, as we move from lower species such as fish or rodents to higher species such as primates, is for sexual behavior to be more hormonally (instinctively) controlled among lower species and to be controlled more by the brain (and therefore by learning) in the higher species (Beach, 1947). Thus environmental influences are much more important in shaping primate—especially human—sexual behavior than they are in shaping the sexual behavior of other species.

An illustration of this is provided by studies of the adult sexual behavior of animals that have been raised in deprived environments. If mice are reared in isolation, their adult sexual behavior will nonetheless be normal (King, 1956, cited by Scott, 1964). But the research of the Harlows shows that if rhesus monkeys are reared in isolation, their adult sexual behavior is severely disturbed, to the point where they may be incapable of reproducing (Harlow et al., 1963). Thus environmental experiences are crucial in shaping the sexual behavior of the higher species, particularly humans; for us, sexual behavior is a lot more than just "doin' what comes naturally."

Female sexuality provides a particularly good illustration of the shift in hormonal control from lower to higher species. Throughout most of the animal kingdom, female sexual behavior is strongly controlled by hormones. In virtually all species, females do not engage in sexual behavior at all except when they are in "heat" (estrus), which is a particular hormonal and physiological state. In contrast, human females are capable of engaging in sexual behavior—and actually do engage in it—during any phase of their hormonal (menstrual) cycle. Thus the sexual behavior of the human female is not nearly so much under hormonal control as that of females of other species.

Traditionally it was thought that female orgasm is unique to humans and does not exist in other species. Then some studies found evidence of orgasm in rhesus macaques (monkeys), although under very artificial laboratory conditions involving stimulation of the female by a mechanical penis (Burton, 1970; Zumpe and Michael, 1968). Now a recent study has shown the same physiological responses indicative of orgasm in human females—specifically, increased heart rate and uterine contractions—in stump-tailed macaques as a result of female homosexual activity, and perhaps for heterosexual activity as well (Goldfoot et al., 1980). Thus it seems that humans can no longer claim that they have a corner on the female orgasm market. This has interesting implications for understanding the evolution of sexuality. Perhaps the higher species, in which the females are not driven to sexual activity by their hormones, have the pleasure of orgasm as an alternative incentive.

The Nonsexual Uses of Sexual Behavior

Two male baboons are locked in combat. One begins to emerge as the victor. The other "presents" (the "female" sexual posture, in which the rump is directed toward the other and is elevated somewhat).

Two male monkeys are members of the same troop. Long ago they established which one is dominant and which one is subordinate. The dominant one mounts (the "male" sexual behavior) the subordinate one.

These are examples of the fact that animals sometimes use sexual behavior for nonsexual purposes (Ford and Beach, 1951; Jensen, 1976b). Commonly this is done to signal the end of a fight, as in the first example above. The loser indicates surrender by presenting, and the winner signals victory by mounting. Sexual behaviors can also symbolize an animal's rank in a dominance hierarchy. Dominant animals mount subordinate ones. As another example, male squirrel monkeys sometimes use an exhibitionist display of their erect penis as part of an aggressive display against another male, something that is called *phallic aggression* (Wickler, 1973).

FIGURE 1.6

Sexual behavior may be used for a variety of nonsexual purposes, such as to express aggression. This primitive figure is defying his opponent by sticking out his tongue and his erect penis.

All this is perfectly obvious when we observe it in monkeys. But do humans ever use sexual behavior for nonsexual purposes? Consider the rapist, who uses sex as an expression of aggression against and power over a woman (Holmstrom and Burgess, 1980), or power over another man, in the case of homosexual rape in prisons. Another example is the exhibitionist, who uses the display of his erect penis to shock and frighten women, much as the male squirrel monkey uses this display to shock and frighten his opponent. Humans also use sex for economic purposes; the best examples are prostitutes and gigolos.

Gigolo (JIH-guh-lo): A man who sells his sexual services to women.

There are also less extreme examples. Consider the couple who have a fight and then make love to signal an end to the hostilities.[4] Or consider the woman who goes to bed with an influential—though unattractive—politician because this gives her a vicarious sense of power.

Pediatrician Michael W. Cohen and psychiatrist Stanford B. Friedman (1975) believe that adolescents may use sexual behavior for the following nonsexual purposes:

1. *Peer approval* Sexual activity, particularly for males, can be a means of acquiring status in the peer group, getting the approval of one's peers, showing that one is part of the "in" crowd, or proving one's masculinity. "[It is] my impression that male patients feel under more pressure than ever before to prove themselves through the sex act. Many experience difficulty simply because they are more interested in the statusful than the tender aspects of lovemaking" (Halleck, 1967).
2. *Expression of hostility* Some adolescents feel real hostility toward their parents, and engaging in sexual activity may be one of the few ways they have of expressing it.
3. *Rebellion* Teenagers can also engage in sex to rebel against parents and express independence. Ironically, it is precisely because parents feel that they must enforce rules concerning sex that engaging in sexual activity becomes such an effective way to express rebellion.
4. *Escape* For the teenage girl who finds living conditions at home intolerable, having sex and becoming pregnant is a good way to ensure getting out of her parents' house.

You can probably think of other examples of the nonsexual use of sexual behavior. Humans, just like members of other species, can use sex for a variety of nonsexual purposes (Marmor, 1969).

SUMMARY

"Sexual behavior" was defined as behavior that produces arousal and increases the chance of orgasm. A distinction was made between "sex" (sexual behavior and anatomy) and "gender" (being male or female).

Throughout most of human history, religion was the main source of information concerning sexuality. In the late 1800s and early 1900s, important contributions to the scientific understanding of sex were made by Sigmund Freud, Havelock Ellis, von Krafft-Ebing, and Magnus Hirschfeld. These early researchers emerged from the Victorian era, in which sexual norms were highly rigid; many people's actual behavior, though, violated these norms.

Studies in various human cultures around the world provide evidence of the enormous variations in human sexual behavior. For example, in a few societies kiss-

---

[4] It has been my observation that this practice does not always mean the same thing to the man and to the woman. To the man it can mean that everything is fine again, but the woman can be left feeling dissatisfied and not at all convinced that the issues are resolved. Thus this situation can be a source of miscommunication between the two.

ing is unknown. Frequency of intercourse may vary from once a week in some cultures to three or four times a night in others. One generalization that does emerge is that all societies regulate sexual behavior in some way. Attitudes regarding masturbation, homosexual behavior, and gender roles vary considerably from one culture to the next. The great variations provide evidence of the importance of learning in shaping our sexual behavior.

Even within the United States, sexual behavior varies with social class and ethnic group. Social class differences have diminished in recent decades. Blacks show more approval of premarital sex than whites do, and black women are more likely to engage in premarital intercourse as teenagers than white women are.

Studies of sexual behavior in various animal species show that masturbation, mouth-genital stimulation, and homosexual behavior are by no means limited to humans. They also illustrate how sexual behavior may be used for a variety of nonsexual purposes, such as expressing dominance.

REVIEW QUESTIONS

1. H. Havelock Ellis was an important nineteenth century sex researcher. True or false?
2. A sex survey of Victorian women found that many of them reported having orgasms during marital intercourse. True or false?
3. On Inis Beag, an island off the coast of Ireland, premarital intercourse is common and many babies are born out of wedlock. True or false?
4. Sex education and sex therapy are widely available in the Soviet Union. True or false?
5. The wide variations in sexual behavior found cross-culturally provide evidence of the importance of learning and culture in shaping human sexual behavior. True or false?
6. Homosexual behavior is unknown among animals. True or false?
7. Black women are more likely to engage in premarital sex as teenagers than white women are. True or false?
8. This textbook uses the term "sex" to refer to sexual anatomy and sexual behavior, and the term _____ to refer to the state of being male or female.
9. The early sex researcher Richard von Krafft-Ebing focused on "pathological" sexual behavior. True or false?
10. All societies regulate sexuality in some way, although the exact regulations vary from culture to culture. True or false?

QUESTIONS FOR THOUGHT, DISCUSSION, AND DEBATE

1. In the wide spectrum of sexual practices in different cultures, from the conservatism of Inis Beag to the permissiveness of Mangaia, where would you place the United States today? Are we permissive, restrictive, or somewhere in between? Why?
2. Research indicates that masturbation, mouth-genital stimulation, and homosexual behaviors are present in other species besides humans. What is the significance of that finding?

SUGGESTIONS FOR FURTHER READING

Gay, Peter. (1984). *The bourgeois experience: Victoria to Freud.* Vol. I. *Education of the senses.* New York: Oxford University Press. This well-known historian analyzes sexuality in the Victorian era.

Gregersen, Edgar. (1983). *Sexual practices: The story of human sexuality.* New York: Franklin Watts. Gregersen, an anthropologist, has compiled a vast amount of information about sexuality in cultures around the world. The book also includes a treasure trove of fascinating illustrations.

Mead, Margaret. (1935). *Sex and temperament in three primitive societies.* New York: Morrow. A fascinating description of Mead's investigations of sex and gender in other cultures.

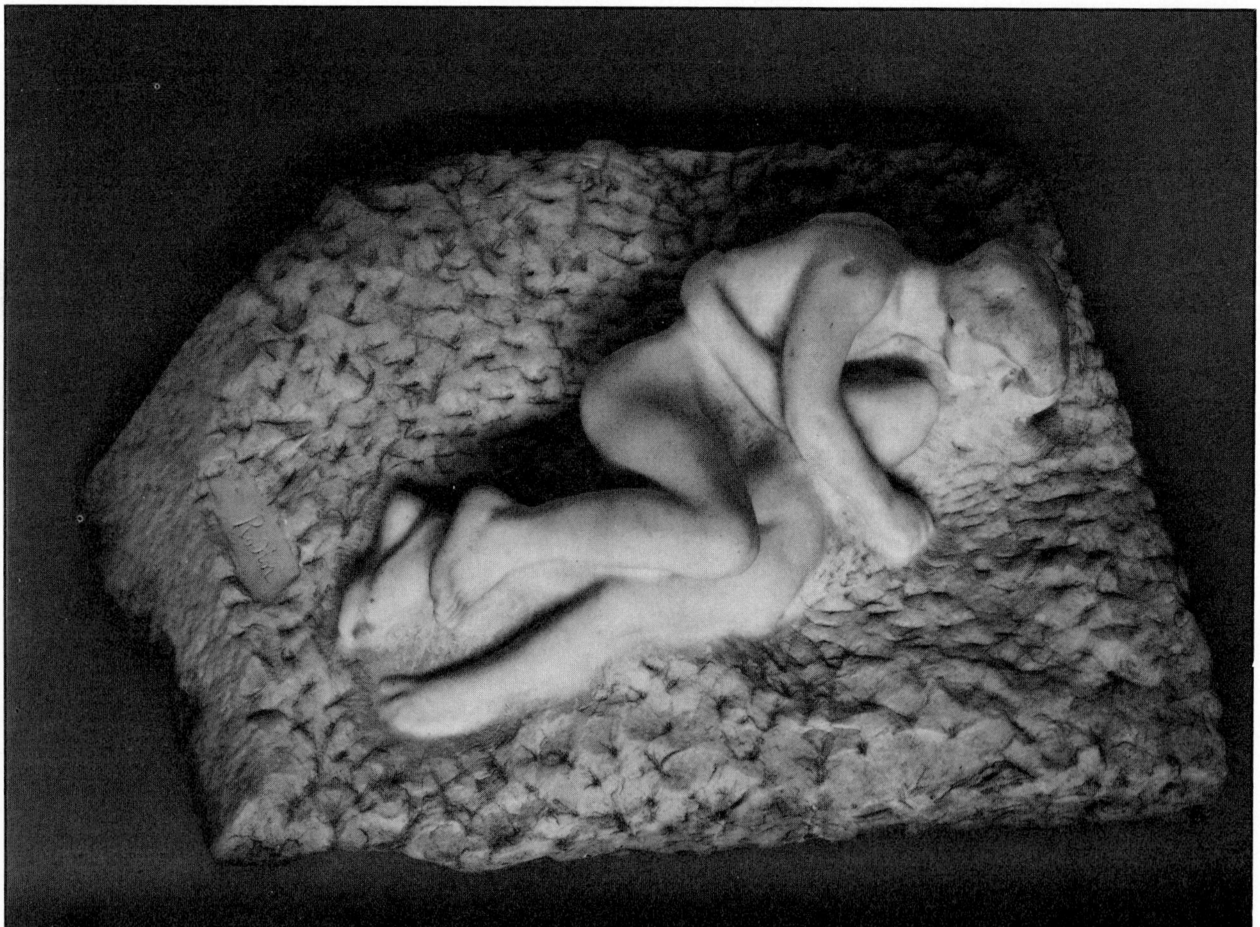

CHAPTER • 2

THEORETICAL PERSPECTIVES ON SEXUALITY

One of the discoveries of psychoanalysis consists in the assertion that impulses, which can only be described as sexual in both the narrower and the wider sense, play a peculiarly large part, never before sufficiently appreciated, in the causation of nervous and mental disorders. Nay, more, that these sexual impulses have contributed invaluably to the highest cultural, artistic, and social achievements of the human mind.*

* *Source:* Sigmund Freud. (1924). *A general introduction to psychoanalysis.* New York: Permabooks, 1953 (Boni & Liveright edition, 1924), pp. 26–27.

On the face of it, sex is at best a peculiar way to reproduce; at worst, it seems profoundly self-defeating.†

†*Source:* Barash, D. P. (1982). *Sociobiology and behavior.* New York: Elsevier, p. 216.

CHAPTER HIGHLIGHTS

I. SOCIOBIOLOGY

II. PSYCHOLOGICAL THEORIES
Psychoanalytic Theory
Learning Theory
Humanistic Psychology

III. SOCIOLOGICAL THEORIES
Functionalism
Conflict Theory
Interactionism
Phenomenology and Ethnomethodology

Imagine, for a moment, a heterosexual couple making love. Imagine, too, that sitting with you in the room, thinking your same thoughts, are Freud, E. O. Wilson (the leader of sociobiology), Albert Bandura (a leading social learning theorist), and Talcott Parsons (a leader in the functionalist school in sociology). The scene you are imagining may evoke arousal and nothing more in you, but your imaginary companions have a rich set of additional thoughts as they view the scene through the special-colored lenses of their own theoretical perspectives. Freud might be marveling at how the biological sex drive, the *libido,* expresses itself so strongly and directly in these people. Wilson, the sociobiologist, is thinking how mating behavior in humans is similar to mating behavior in other species of animals, and how it is clearly the product of evolutionary selection for behaviors that lead to successful reproduction. Bandura might be thinking how sexual arousal and orgasm act as powerful positive reinforcers that will lead the couple to repeat the act frequently, and how they are imitating a technique of neck nibbling that they saw in an X-rated film last week. Finally, Parsons' thoughts may be about the social control of sexuality; this couple is deeply religious and abstained from intercourse until they were married, because of their religious beliefs.

Some of the major theories in the social sciences have had many—and different—things to say about sexuality, and it is these theories that we consider in this chapter.

SOCIOBIOLOGY

Sociobiology: The application of evolutionary biology to understanding the social behavior of animals, including humans.

Sociobiology is a highly controversial new academic discipline. It was heralded by Harvard biologist E. O. Wilson's book, *Sociobiology: The New Synthesis* (1975). Sociobiology is defined as the application of evolutionary biology to understanding the social behavior of animals, including humans (Barash, 1977). Sexual behavior, of course, is a form of social behavior, and so the sociobiologists, often through observations of other species, try to understand why certain patterns of sexual behavior have evolved in humans. Donald Symons has applied sociobiological thinking to human sexuality in his book, *The Evolution of Human Sexuality* (1979).

Evolution: A theory that all living things have acquired their present forms through gradual changes in their genetic endowment over successive generations.

Natural selection: A process in nature resulting in the survival of only those plants and animals that are adapted to their environment.

Before we proceed, we should note that in terms of evolution and natural selection, the thing that counts is producing lots of healthy, viable offspring who will carry on one's genes. It does not matter particularly how clever or talented one is. Advantage is measured in terms of how many of one's genes are passed on to the next generation, and that in turn depends heavily on how many offspring one produces.

How do we select mates? One major criterion is the physical attractiveness of the person (see Chapter 13). The sociobiologist would argue that many of the characteristics we evaluate in judging attractiveness—for example, physique and complexion—are indicative of the health and vigor of the individual. These in turn are probably related to the person's reproductive potential; the unhealthy are less likely to produce many vigorous offspring. Natural selection would favor those individuals preferring mates who would have maximum reproductive success. Thus, perhaps our concern with physical attractiveness is a product of evolution and natural selection. (See Barash, 1977, for an extended discussion of this point and the ones that follow.) We choose an attractive, healthy mate who will help us produce many offspring. Can you guess why the sociobiologist thinks men are attracted to women with large breasts?

From this viewpoint, dating, going steady, getting engaged, and similar customs are much like the courtship rituals of other species. For example, many falcons and eagles have a flying courtship in which objects are exchanged between a pair in midair. The sociobiologist views this courtship as an opportunity for each member of the prospective couple to assess the other's fitness. For example, any lack of speed or coordination would be apparent during the eagle acrobatics. Evolution would favor courtship patterns that permitted individuals to decide on mates who would increase their reproductive success. Perhaps that is exactly what we are doing in our human courtship rituals. The expenditure of money by men on dates indicates their ability to support a family. Dancing permits the assessment of physical prowess, and so on.

The sociobiologists even have an explanation for the double standard—specifically, our relatively permissive attitudes toward male promiscuity and our intolerance for female promiscuity. Sperm are cheap. A man can literally produce millions of them in a day, and he can always produce more. Eggs, in contrast, are far more precious to their owner. Only one can be produced per month, and if certain things happen to it, the result can be a nine-month (or perhaps more accurately, an 18-year) commitment of time and energy. It is therefore no wonder that the female is choosy about whom she has sex with and limits her number of partners compared with the male's number of partners.

Finally, the sociobiologists note that sex is fun. And they have an explanation for why it is fun. Natural selection simply favored individuals who found it to be fun and therefore did it more, and therefore reproduced more.

Many criticisms of sociobiology have been made. Some protest that it ignores the importance of culture and learning in human behavior. However, most sociobiologists would argue that evolution should be recognized as one of several influences on behavior and would not exclude the influence of learning and culture. Other critics resent the biological determinism that it introduces. Further, sociobiologists assume that the central function of sex is reproduction; this may have been true historically, but it probably is not at present. We really do not have sufficient research at this point to do a conclusive evaluation. Until we do have that evidence, sociobiology will remain a provocative source of ideas about human sexuality.

PSYCHOLOGICAL THEORIES

Three of the major theories in psychology are relevant to sexuality: psychoanalytic theory, learning theory, and humanistic psychology.

Psychoanalytic Theory

Psychoanalytic theory: A psychological theory originated by Freud; it contains a basic assumption that part of human personality is unconscious.

Libido (lih-BEE-doh): In psychoanalytic theory, the term for the sex energy or sex drive.

Freud's psychoanalytic theory has been one of the most influential of all psychological theories. Because Freud saw sex as one of the key forces in human life, his theory gives full treatment to human sexuality.

Freud termed the sex drive or sex energy libido, and he saw it as one of the two major forces motivating human behavior (the other being *thanatos,* or the death instinct). Indeed, he felt that much apparently nonsexual behavior is actually motivated by the libido in a process of *sublimation,* whereby the libido is redirected toward higher goals. He thought, for example, that Leonardo da Vinci's interest in painting madonnas resulted from sublimation of his urge for intimacy with his mother, from whom he had been separated at a tender age.

Id, Ego, and Superego

Id: According to Freud, the part of the personality containing the libido.

Ego: According to Freud, the part of the personality that helps the person have realistic, rational interactions.

Freud described the human personality as being divided into three major parts: the id, the ego, and the superego. The id is the basic part of personality and is present at birth. It is the reservoir of psychic energy (including libido) and contains the instincts. Basically it operates on the *pleasure principle;* it cannot tolerate any increase in psychic tensions, and so it seeks to discharge these tensions.

While the id operates only on the pleasure principle and can thus be pretty irrational, the ego operates on the *reality principle* and tries to keep the id in line. The ego functions to make the person have realistic, rational interactions with others.

Superego:
According to Freud, the part of the personality containing the conscience.

Finally, the superego is the conscience. It contains the values and ideals of society that we learn, and it operates on *idealism.* Thus its aim is to inhibit the impulses of the id and to persuade the ego to strive for moral goals rather than realistic ones.

To illustrate the operation of these three components of the personality in a sexual situation, consider the case of a corporate chairman of the board who is at a meeting of the board members; the meeting is also attended by his gorgeous, curvaceous secretary, Miss Luscious. He looks at Miss Luscious, and his id says, "I want to throw her on the table and make love to her immediately. Let's do it!" The ego intervenes and says, "We can't do it now because the other members of the board are also here. Let's wait until 5 P.M., when they're all gone, and then do it." The superego says, "I shouldn't make love to Miss Luscious at all because I'm a married man." What actually happens? It depends on the relative strengths of this man's id, ego, and superego.

The id, ego, and the superego develop sequentially. The id contains the set of instincts present at birth. The ego develops later, as the child learns how to interact realistically with his or her environment and the people in it. The superego develops last, as the child learns moral values.

Erogenous Zones

Erogenous zones (eh-RAH-jen-us):
Areas of the body that are particularly sensitive to sexual stimulation.

Freud saw the libido as being focused in various regions of the body known as erogenous zones (a term that has been used rather loosely by the general public in recent years). An erogenous zone is a part of the skin or mucous membrane which is extremely sensitive to stimulation; manipulating it in certain ways produces feelings of pleasure. The lips and mouth are one such erogenous zone, the genitals are a second, and the rectum and anus are a third. Thus sucking produces oral pleasure, defecating produces anal pleasure, and rubbing the genital area produces genital pleasure.

Stages of Psychosexual Development

Freud believed that the child passes through a series of stages of development. In each of these stages, a different erogenous zone is the focus of the child's striving.

The first stage, lasting from birth to about 1 year of age, is the *oral stage.* The child's chief pleasure is derived from sucking and otherwise stimulating the lips and mouth. Anyone who has observed children of this age knows how they delight in putting anything they can into their mouths. The second stage, which occurs during approximately the second year of life, is the *anal stage.* During this stage, the child's interest is focused on elimination.

Oedipus complex (EH-dih-pus):
According to Freud, the sexual attraction of a little boy for his mother.

The third stage of development, lasting from age 3 to perhaps age 5 or 6, is the *phallic stage.* The boy's interest is focused on his phallus (penis), and he derives great pleasure from masturbating.[1] Perhaps the most important occurrence in this stage is the development of the Oedipus complex, which derives its name from the Greek story of Oedipus, who killed his father and married his mother. In the Oedipus complex, the boy loves his mother and desires her sexually. He hates his father, whom he sees as a rival for the mother's affection. The boy's hostility toward his father grows, but eventually he comes to fear that his father will retaliate by cutting off his prized penis (castration). Thus the boy feels *castration anxiety.* Eventually the castration anxiety becomes so great that he stops desiring his mother and shifts

[1]Masturbation to orgasm is physiologically possible at this age, although males are not capable of ejaculation until they reach puberty.

to identifying with his father, taking on the father's gender role and acquiring the characteristics expected of males by society. Freud considered the Oedipus complex and its resolution to be one of the key factors in human personality development, and thus he saw the desire for incest as being extremely important.

As might be expected from the name of this stage, the girl will have a considerably different, and much more difficult, time passing through it, since she has none of what the stage is all about. For the girl, the stage begins with her traumatic realization that she has no penis, perhaps after observing that of her father or her brother. She feels envious and cheated, and she suffers from *penis envy,* wishing that she too had a wonderful wand. (Presumably she thinks her own clitoris is totally inadequate, or she is not even aware that she has it.) She believes that at one time she had a penis but that it was cut off, and she holds her mother responsible. Thus she begins to hate her mother and shifts to loving her father, forming her version of the Oedipus complex, sometimes called the Electra complex. In part, her incestuous desires for her father result from a desire to be impregnated by him, to substitute for the unobtainable penis. Unlike the boy, the girl does not have a strong motive of castration anxiety for resolving the Oedipus complex; she has already lost her penis. Thus the girl's resolution of the Electra complex is not so complete as the boy's resolution of the Oedipus complex, and for the rest of her life she remains somewhat immature compared with men.

Electra complex (eh-LEK-tra): According to Freud, the sexual attraction of a little girl for her father.

Freud said that following the resolution of the Oedipus or Electra complex, children pass into a prolonged stage known as *latency,* which lasts until adolescence. During this stage, the sexual impulses are repressed or are in a quiescent state, and so nothing much happens sexually. The postulation of this stage is one of the weaker parts of Freudian theory, because it is clear from the data of Kinsey and others that children do continue to engage in sexual behavior during this period.

With adolescence, sexual urges reawaken, and the child passes into the *genital stage.* During this stage, sexual urges become more specifically genital, and the oral, anal, and genital urges all fuse together to promote the biological function of reproduction. Sexuality becomes less narcissistic (self-directed) than it was in childhood and is directed toward other people as appropriate sexual objects.

Of course, according to Freud, people do not always mature from one stage to the next as they should. A person might remain permanently fixated, for example, at the oral stage; symptoms of such a situation would include incessant cigarette smoking and fingernail biting, which gratify oral urges. Most adults have at least traces of earlier stages remaining in their personalities.

Freud on Women

In recent years a storm of criticism of Freudian theory has arisen from feminists. Let us first review what Freud had to say about women and then discuss what feminists object to in his theory.

Essentially, Freud argued that the female is biologically inferior to the male because she lacks a penis. He saw this absence as a key factor in her personality development. The penis envy she feels as a result of her biological deficiency causes her to develop the Electra complex. Yet she never adequately resolves this complex, and she is left, throughout her life, with feelings of jealousy and inferiority, all because of her lack of a penis. As Freud said, "Anatomy is destiny."

Freud believed that female sexuality is inherently passive (as opposed to the active aggressiveness of the male). He also felt that female sexuality is masochistic; in seeking intercourse, the female is trying to bring pain on herself, since childbirth, which may result, is painful and since intercourse itself may sometimes be painful.

The following quotation from Marie Bonaparte, an early follower of Freud, will illustrate the psychoanalytic position:

> Throughout the whole range of living creatures, animal or vegetable, passivity is characteristic of the female cell, the ovum whose mission is to *await* the male cell, the active mobile spermatozoan to come and *penetrate* it. Such penetration, however, implies infraction of its tissue, but infraction of a living creature's tissue may entail destruction: death as much as life. Thus the fecundation of the female cell is initiated by a kind of wound; in its way, the female cell is primordially "masochistic." (1953, p. 79)

Freud also originated the distinction between *vaginal orgasm* and *clitoral orgasm* in women. During childhood little girls rub their clitorises to produce orgasm (clitoral orgasm). Freud believed, though, that as they grow to adulthood they need to shift their focus to having orgasm during heterosexual intercourse, with the penis stimulating the vagina (vaginal orgasm). Thus, not only did he postulate two kinds of orgasm for women, but he also maintained that one kind was better (more mature) than the other. The evidence that Masters and Johnson have collected on this issue will be reviewed in Chapter 8; suffice it to say for now that there seems to be little or no physiological difference between the two kinds of orgasm. Thus, asserting that the vaginal orgasm is more mature makes no sense, and most adult women orgasm as a result of clitoral stimulation.

Feminists understandably object to several aspects of Freud's theory. A chief objection is to the whole notion that women are anatomically inferior to men because they lack a penis. What is so intrinsically valuable about a penis that makes it better than a clitoris, a vagina, or a pair of ovaries? Similarly, feminists find the assertion that women are inherently passive, masochistic, and narcissistic to be offensive. Is it not likelier that men simply have higher status in our culture than women do and that women's feelings of jealousy or inferiority result from these cultural status differences? Feminists argue that psychoanalytic theory is essentially a male-centered theory which may have bad effects on women, particularly when it is used on a woman who seeks psychotherapy from a therapist who uses a psychoanalytic approach.

Evaluation of Psychoanalytic Theory

From a scientific point of view, one of the major problems with psychoanalytic theory is that most of its concepts cannot be evaluated scientifically to see whether they are accurate. Freud postulated that many of the most important forces in personality are unconscious, and thus they cannot be studied by any of the usual scientific techniques.

Another criticism is that Freud derived his data almost exclusively from his work with patients who sought therapy from him. Thus, his theory may provide a view not so much of the human personality as of the *disturbed* human personality.

Finally, many modern psychologists feel that Freud overemphasized biological determinants of behavior and instincts and that he gave insufficient recognition to the importance of the environment and learning.

Nonetheless, Freud did make some important contributions to our understanding of human behavior. He managed to rise above the Victorian era of which he was a part and teach that sex is an important part of personality (although he may have overestimated its importance). His notion that all behavior is motivated is also important, and his recognition that humans pass through stages in their psychological development was a great contribution. Perhaps most important from the perspective of this text, Freud took sex out of the closet; he brought it to the attention of the general public and suggested that we could talk about it and that it was an appropriate topic for scientific research.

Learning Theory

While psychoanalytic and sociobiological theories are based on the notion that much of human sexual behavior is biologically controlled, it is also quite apparent that much of it is learned. Some of the best evidence for this point comes from studies of sexual behavior across different human societies, that were considered in Chapter 1. Here the various principles of modern learning theory will be reviewed, because they can help us understand our own sexuality.

Operant Conditioning

Operant conditioning (OP-ur-unt): The process of changing the frequency of a behavior (the operant) by following it with reinforcement (which will make the behavior more frequent in the future) or punishment (which should make the behavior less frequent in the future).

Operant conditioning, a concept that is often associated with the psychologist B. F. Skinner, refers to the following process: A person performs a particular behavior (the operant). That behavior may be followed by either a reward or a punishment. If a reward follows, the person will be likely to perform the behavior again in the future; if a punishment follows, the person will be less likely to repeat the behavior. Thus if a behavior is repeatedly rewarded, it may become very frequent, and if it is repeatedly punished, it may become very infrequent or even be eliminated.

Some rewards are considered to be primary reinforcers; that is, there is something intrinsically rewarding about them. Food is one such primary reinforcer, and sex is another. Rats, for example, can be trained to learn a maze if they find a willing sex partner at the end of it. Thus sexual behavior plays dual roles in learning theory: it can itself be a reward, but it can also be the behavior that is rewarded or punished.

Other rewards are conditioned reinforcers. For example, there is nothing inherently rewarding about receiving a $10 bill for some work you have done; only through learning or conditioning have you come to realize that such a piece of paper is valuable and to feel that it is a reward. Yet another category is social reinforcers, such as praise or a compliment from another person.

Simple principles of operant conditioning can help explain some aspects of sex (McGuire et al., 1965). For example, if a woman repeatedly experiences pain when she has intercourse (perhaps because she has a vaginal infection), she will probably want to have sex infrequently or not at all. In operant conditioning terms, sexual intercourse has repeatedly been associated with a punishment (pain), and so the behavior becomes less frequent.

What other principles of operant conditioning are useful in understanding sexual behavior? One principle is that reinforcements are most effective in shaping behavior when they occur immediately after a behavior and that the longer they are delayed after the behavior has occurred, the less effective they become. As an example of that principle, consider the male homosexual who continues to engage in homosexual behavior with his lover even though, because of this, his colleagues at work have rejected him and he is even in danger of being fired. Since he is being punished for the behavior, why does he persist in it? The delay-of-reinforcement principle might explain the situation as follows: Every time he engages in homosexual behavior, he enjoys it and finds it rewarding; this occurs immediately. These immediate rewards are effective in encouraging him to continue the behavior, and the punishments, which may not occur until a week after the behavior, are not effective in eliminating it.

Another principle that has emerged in operant conditioning studies is that, compared with rewards, punishments are not very effective in shaping behavior. Often, as in the case of the child who is punished for taking an illicit cookie, punishments do not eliminate a behavior but rather teach the person to be sneaky and engage in it without being caught. As an example, parents, particularly in earlier times in our culture, punished children for masturbating, and yet most of those children continued to masturbate. Punishment is simply not very effective in eliminating behavior. Still using masturbation as an example, children may instead learn to do it under circumstances (such as in a bathroom with the door locked) in which they are not likely to be caught.

Behavior Modification

Behavior modification: A set of operant conditioning techniques used to modify human behavior.

Behavior modification involves a set of techniques, based on principles of operant conditioning, that are used to change or modify human behavior. These techniques have been used to modify everything from problem behaviors of children in the classroom to the behavior of schizophrenics. In particular, these methods can be used to modify problematic sexual behaviors—sexual dysfunctions such as impotence (see Chapter 20) or deviant sexual behavior such as child molesting. Behavior modification methods differ from more traditional methods of psychotherapy such as psychoanalysis in that the behavioral therapist considers only the problem behavior and how to modify it using learning-theory principles; the therapist does not worry about a depth analysis of the person's personality to see, for example, what unconscious forces might be motivating the behavior.

One example of a behavior modification technique that has been used in modifying sexual behavior is aversion therapy (Barlow, 1973). In *aversion therapy,* the problematic sexual behavior is punished using an aversive method. For example, a child molester might be shown pictures of children; if he responds with sexual arousal, he receives an electric shock. Trials are repeated until he no longer feels aroused when he sees a child's picture.

Social Learning

Social learning theory (Bandura, 1969; Bandura and Walters, 1963) is a somewhat more complex form of learning theory. It is based on principles of operant conditioning, but it also recognizes how greatly the learning process is influenced by interactions with other people. In particular, social learning theory postulates two processes at work besides conditioning: *imitation* and *identification.* Identification (the concept here is similar to the one in psychoanalytic theory) and imitation are useful in explaining the development of gender identity, or one's sense of maleness or femaleness. For example, it seems that a little girl acquires many characteristics of the female role by identifying with her mother and imitating her, as when she plays at dressing up after observing her mother getting ready to go to a party. Because most sexual behaviors in our society are kept rather private and hidden, imitation and identification have less of a chance to play a part. However, some of the more open forms of sexuality may be learned through imitation. In high school, for example, the sexiest girl in the senior class may find that other girls are imitating her behaviors and the way she dresses. Or a boy might see a movie in which the hero's technique seems to "turn women on"; then he tries to use this technique with his own dates.

Humanistic Psychology

Humanistic psychology: The study of people as whole persons, aiming at enriching human life.

Humanistic psychologists such as Carl Rogers and Abraham Maslow are concerned with making psychology and psychotherapy more human and with considering indi-

FIGURE 2.1

Luke and Laura? Children may acquire sexual behaviors by imitating models they see on TV or in the movies.

Self-actualization: A striving toward growth and self-fulfillment.

viduals as whole people. A key concept in humanistic psychology is self-actualization, a process of continually growing so as to realize one's own inherent potentialities. As Rogers says, "The organism has one basic tendency and striving—to actualize, maintain, and enhance the experiencing organism" (1951, p. 487).

Humanistic psychologists view sex and love as means of self-actualization. As Abraham Maslow put it:

> It is quite characteristic of self-actualizing people that they can enjoy themselves in love and in sex. Sex very frequently becomes a kind of game in which laughter is quite as common as panting. It is not the welfare of the species, or the task of reproduction, or the future development of mankind that attracts people to each other. The sex life of healthy people, in spite of the fact that it frequently reaches great peaks of ecstasy, is nevertheless also easily compared to the games of children and puppies. It is cheerful, humorous, and playful. (1954, pp. 251–252)

Humanistic psychologists also recognize that some forms of sex, such as impersonal sex, may not be at all self-actualizing but rather may leave the individual feeling alienated.

Encounter groups (or *T groups* or *sensitivity training*) are one of the more visible signs of the human potential movement, which was spawned by humanistic psychology. Such groups are supposed to promote the participants' self-actualization by making them more aware of their own feelings and those of others and by enabling them to relate to others more openly. Some groups emphasize touching or nudity—which the media have capitalized on in discussing this movement—and encourage participants to explore their sexual feelings honestly. By touching, people recognize their need for touching. Adults often repress their need for touching and then confuse that need with sexuality; they think they need copulation when they really need cuddling (Forer, 1972). Thus learning to touch and to be aware of one's needs for touching is often an important part of encounter groups.

SOCIOLOGICAL THEORIES

Sociologists have proposed a number of major theories that are useful in understanding various aspects of sexuality (for a detailed discussion of sociological theories, see Ritzer, 1983).

Functionalism

Structural-functionalism: A sociological theory that views society as an interrelated set of structures that function together to maintain society.

Functionalism, also called structural-functionalism, is a theory that views society as an interrelated set of parts (structures) that operate (function) together harmoniously. Structures are social units that include the family and institutions such as the legal system and religious organizations. Functionalists then look at how different structures function to maintain and preserve society. They focus on social order and stability and assume that societies are in a state of equilibrium. They study the ways in which societies maintain that equilibrium.

Functionalists focus on how societies preserve order and avoid chaos. Thus functionalists study how societies *regulate* things. Chief among those processes to be regulated is sexuality. As we noted in Chapter 1, anthropologists have found that all societies regulate sexuality. Societies regulate sexuality in various ways, through laws, religious beliefs, and norms, and functionalists are interested in studying these regulatory processes. Indeed, one recent article reviewing sociological research on sexuality was titled "The Social Control of Sexuality" (DeLamater, 1981).

FIGURE 2.2

According to the sociological theory of functionalism, the family is important in maintaining a stable society, and sexuality serves a function in helping to preserve families.

Functionalists also look at the functions of sexuality in society. Certainly the family is important in maintaining a cohesive, stable society, and sexuality and long-term love relationships are helpful in preserving stable families. To continue themselves, societies also need to provide some encouragement or permission for heterosexual activity and some means for people to find heterosexual partners—otherwise there would be no subsequent generation.

Other functions must occur for societies to continue. Food, shelter, and clothing must be provided and children cared for. One of the ways societies make sure that this happens is by creating *roles* that divide up the labor. Among these is the division of labor by gender, creating *gender roles.* Thus, in a nonindustrial society, food has to be obtained and children cared for. According to the functionalists, it is efficient for such societies to divide that labor by gender and have men responsible for hunting and women responsible for child care. Functionalists, then, would see gender roles as functional and efficient for societies.

Functionalism is associated with the writings of such sociologists as Emile Durkheim, Talcott Parsons, and Robert Merton. It has been the dominant theory in sociology for most of this century, although in the last two decades it has declined in popularity.

Conflict Theory

Conflict theory:
A sociological theory that focuses on conflicts within society.

In contrast to functionalism, which focuses on social stability, conflict theory looks at the process of social change. It is associated with such writers as C. Wright Mills, Lewis Coser, and Ralf Dahrendorf and has its origins in the writings of Karl Marx.

According to conflict theory, there will always be conflicts in society over the control of economic resources and power. As one group tries to gain more control, social change occurs. At the macro-level conflict theorists might look at conflicts among large social groupings, such as social class conflict, conflict among whole

FIGURE 2.3

Sociological conflict theorists are interested in conflict, such as the conflict between homosexuals and heterosexuals, and how social change results.

societies as occurs in war, or conflict between males and females. At the micro-level, conflict theorists might look at conflicts among individuals; an example would be conflict within a family that might lead to marital rape.

In the realm of sexuality, conflict theorists are particularly interested in the gay liberation movement, which represents a conflict between homosexuals and heterosexuals; and the women's movement, representing the conflict between females and males. It might consider the social change produced by the gay rights movement, including legal challenges in the courts and changed attitudes among many people. It might consider how Anita Bryant's attack on homosexuals united the gay community as it had never been before. It also might analyze the general sexual revolution of the last few decades, the new norms it has produced, and the kinds of conflicts that produced it.

Interactionism

Interactionism: A sociological theory that focuses on interactions between people.

Both functionalism and conflict theory tend to focus on the macro-level, the level of whole societies or classes of people. In contrast, interactionism focuses on interactions at the micro-level, among pairs or in small groups of people. Here we will consider two versions of interactionism: symbolic interactionism and the dramaturgical perspective.

Symbolic interactionism is a school of thought founded by George Herbert Mead. His thought began with behaviorist psychology which emphasizes the observable behavior of people. According to behaviorism, our behavior is a direct response to the behavior of others. Mead advanced the idea that the important thing was the symbolic meaning that one person attaches to another person's or their own observable behavior. That is, our own behavior is a response to what we think the other's behavior means, and there is considerable meaning beyond a particular concrete behavior. Therefore his theory is considerably different from behaviorism in interactionism's emphasis on thought and mind.

As an example of the importance of symbolic meanings attached to behaviors, imagine a male touching a female's shoulder. If the male is a father and the female is his daughter, we might symbolically interpret that action as being comfort extended by a father to a daughter who has just scraped her knee while roller-skating. If, instead, the male is a boss and the female is his secretary, we might see the touch as symbolizing the boss's power and status relative to his secretary, and it would be strange or impertinent for the secretary to touch the boss's shoulder (Henley, 1973; Goffman, 1967). Yet a third possibility is that both the male and the female are in a singles bar, in which case the symbolic meaning to us—and to them—is that the touch is a sexual invitation.

Symbolic interactionists are interested in the process of *socialization,* although they understand it somewhat differently from other social scientists. Symbolic interactionists regard socialization as one way in which children and adults learn particular thought patterns; that is, they learn their culture's consensus on the symbolic meaning of various behaviors. For example, most children in our culture are quickly socialized not to masturbate in public. In symbolic interaction terms, they have learned that the symbolic meaning most people attach to public masturbation is "bad."

Another school of interactionist thought is Erving Goffman's *dramaturgical view.* According to Goffman, in our everyday interactions with others we are much like actors in a drama. Our behavior and theirs is governed by unspoken rules or scripts. Just as actors behave differently when they are onstage and offstage, so we are likely to behave differently in our public and private lives. George, a 35-year-old married man, masturbates in private about once per week. Yet in public he never masturbates, and he *acts* as though he is a devout nonmasturbator.

According to Goffman, when we are in public—that is, when we are interacting with others—we are actors who try to put our best foot forward; that is, we are always trying to create favorable impressions. When we feel that we are not creating a good impression, we are likely to engage in *face-saving,* maneuvers designed to make us look good when we otherwise might not. An example can be found in a dramaturgical analysis of people's behavior at a singles dance (Berk, 1977). A woman usually arrives at these dances with another woman friend. This is face-saving because she wants to appear to be a proper woman with a chaperone, not a woman looking for casual sex.

One of Goffman's concepts is that of *role distance,* which is the extent to which people distance themselves from their role or embrace it (Goffman, 1961). All of us occupy numerous roles; we throw ourselves wholeheartedly into a few and distance ourselves in varying degrees from the rest. As an example, consider the homosexual role. Some male homosexuals—such as some gay activists—are close to the homosexual role and find it important in defining themselves. Other male homosexuals—particularly those who are "in the closet"—put miles of distance between themselves and the homosexual role.

Scripts:
What we have learned to be appropriate sequences of behavior.

Closely related to Goffman's idea of dramaturgy is the concept of scripts, originated by sex researchers John Gagnon and William Simon (1973; Gagnon, 1977) and by Eric Berne in his transactional analysis (1970). It is their contention that sexual behavior (and virtually all human behavior, for that matter) is scripted much as is a play in a theater. That is, sexual behavior is a result of elaborate prior learning that teaches us an etiquette of sexual behavior. According to this concept, little in human sexual behavior is spontaneous. Instead, we have learned an elaborate script that tells us who, what, when, where, and why we do what we do sexually. For example, the "who" part of the script tells us that sex should occur with someone of the opposite gender, of approximately our own age, of our own race, and so on. Even the sequence of sexual activity is scripted. *Scripts,* then, are plans that people carry around in their heads for what they are doing and what they are going to do; they are also devices for helping people remember what they have done in the past (Gagnon, 1977, p. 6). Scripts, of course, vary from one culture to another, as we saw in Chapter 1.

One study attempted to identify the sequence of sexual behaviors that is scripted for males and females in a heterosexual relationship in our culture (Jemail and Geer, 1977). Subjects were given 25 sentences, each describing an event in a heterosexual interaction. They were asked to rearrange the sentences in a sequence that was "most sexually arousing" and then to do it again to indicate what was "the most likely to occur." There was a high degree of agreement among subjects about what the sequence should be. There was also high agreement between males and females. The standard sequence was kissing, hand stimulation of the breast, hand stimulation of the genitals, mouth-genital stimulation, intercourse, and orgasm. Does it sound familiar? Interestingly, not only is this the sequence in a sexual encounter, it is also the sequence that occurs as a couple progress in their relationship. These results suggest that there are culturally defined sequences of behaviors that we all have learned, much as the notion of "script" suggests.

Can you imagine a young man, on the first date, attempting mouth stimulation of the young lady's genitals before he has kissed her? The idea seems amazing, perhaps humorous, perhaps shocking. Why? Because the young man has performed Act IV befor Act I.

Phenomenology and Ethnomethodology

Phenomenology: A theory that focuses on people's subjective experience.

Phenomenology and *ethnomethodology* are two of the newest schools of sociological theorizing. Like interactionism, their focus is the micro-level—interactions among individuals—rather than the macro-level of society or social classes. Although phenomenology and ethnomethodology differ somewhat from each other, they have some defining features in common. Both are critical of traditional sociology's emphasis on scientific objectivity in theories and in research. Phenomenology and ethnomethodology claim that it is legitimate—indeed, important—to study the nature of people's *subjective* experiences. They accuse traditional sociology of imposing its own sense of reality on the social world; phenomenologists and ethnomethodologists want, instead, to get at how people truly, subjectively, experience their social interactions. They do not want to distort that subjective experience by using a carefully, objectively worded questionnaire that does not allow the participant to express how he or she truly feels. They also share the belief that people are active and creative in constructing their own social interactions and their own reality. Both see people's *consciousness,* which is surely subjective, as valid and important to study.

Phenomenology has produced few empirical studies and instead has produced theoretical thought-pieces, analyzing the subjective aspects of consciousness. Doubtless this approach has applications in sexuality—for example, understanding people's own conscious, subjective understandings of their own sexuality and how that understanding contributes to their sexual interactions with others. But such applications have not yet appeared; therefore our discussion of phenomenology is relatively brief.

Ethnomethodology focuses on the techniques (methods) that people use in coping with their everyday world. Harold Garfinkel originated this school of thought. Ethnomethodology has produced a great deal of empirical research, some of which is clearly relevant to understanding sexuality.

One of the classic kinds of studies to come out of ethnomethodology is the *breaching* study (Garfinkel, 1967). Here the experimenter essentially becomes a troublemaker, by violating or breaching some common norm of social interaction, and observing how people respond. For example, in one study experimenters violated interpersonal distance norms by standing too close to another person, to the point where their noses were practically touching. Reactions to the invasion were extreme, including anger and embarrassment. This norm violation was terribly upsetting to people. Such studies show how important cultural norms and role definitions are in guiding our behavior and helping us cope with everyday life. When norms are violated, we react with anger or embarrassment.

Ethnomethodologists have also analyzed naturally occurring conversations between people. In one study, the openings of telephone conversations were investigated (Schegloff, 1979). They fell into a common form of organization, with each person providing verbal cues allowing the other person to recognize who was on the other end of the line. At the same time, the content of individual conversations and the exact cues varied a great deal. Such studies illustrate the view of the ethnomethodologists that people are active and creative in constructing their social interactions, a view much different from functionalism or conflict theory, which looks at larger units of society and views the individual as passive and controlled by these larger units. Applying this approach to sexuality, it is intriguing to imagine an analysis of openings of sexual interactions, analagous to the analysis of the openings of telephone conversations. For a married couple, for example, what is the typical exchange of words or body language that initiates sex?

SUMMARY

Various theoretical perspectives on sexuality were reviewed. Sociobiologists view human sexual behaviors as the product of natural selection in evolution, and thus view these behavioral patterns as being genetically controlled.

Among the psychological theories, Freud's psychoanalytic theory views the sex energy, or libido, as a major influence on personality and behavior. Freud introduced the concepts of erogenous zones and psychosexual stages of development. Learning theory emphasizes how sexual behavior is learned and modified through reinforcements and punishments according to principles of operant conditioning. Behavior modification techniques—therapies based on learning theory—are used in treating sexual variations and sexual dysfunctions. Humanistic psychologists see self-actualization as the most important process in human life; sex and love may contribute to self-actualization.

Among the sociological theories, structural-functionalism views society as consisting of many interrelated structures that function together; the family is an important structure maintaining the stability of society, and sexuality is one factor that holds the family together. Societies also regulate sexuality in order to maintain the society's stability. Conflict theorists look at conflicts among various segments of society and how such conflicts produce social change. Symbolic interactionists look at the behaviors of people in small groups and see as important the symbolic meaning people attach to those observable behaviors. Goffman's dramaturgical approach views us, in our social interactions, as being like actors in a play, following scripts, behaving differently onstage and offstage. Phenomenologists and ethnomethodologists have reacted against the objective, scientific approach of other sociological theories; they wish, instead, to study people's subjective experiences. Ethnomethodologists study the ways in which people cope with their everyday world, as in the breaching experiments.

REVIEW QUESTIONS

1. _____ is the term for the theory that applies evolutionary theory to social behaviors such as sexual behavior.
2. Freud termed the sex energy or sex drive _____.
3. According to Freud, the three major parts of the personality are the id, the ego, and the superego. True or false?
4. Freud used the term _____to refer to the stage of development following the phallic stage and lasting until adolescence.
5. Freud believed that women could have either of two kinds of orgasms, vaginal orgasm or clitoral orgasm. True or false?
6. According to learning theory, teenagers are in the genital stage of development. True or false?
7. According to social learning theory, imitation is a powerful force shaping our sexual behaviors. True or false?
8. The gay liberation movement and the conflict between heterosexuals and homosexuals would be a topic studied by sociologists who are part of the symbolic interactionism school. True or false?
9. According to the notion of scripts, we have been socialized to believe that the appropriate sequence of sexual behaviors is kissing before engaging in intercourse. True or false?
10. The importance of the family and sexuality in holding together society is emphasized by social learning theory. True or false?

QUESTIONS FOR THOUGHT, DISCUSSION, AND DEBATE

1. Compare and contrast how a sociobiologist, a psychoanalyst, and a sociologist would explain why people engage in premarital intercourse.
2. Of the theories described in this chapter, which do you think provides the most insight into human sexuality? Why?
3. Compare how a sociobiologist and a social learning theorist would explain why most child care is done by women.

SUGGESTIONS FOR FURTHER READING

Freud, S. *A general introduction to psychoanalysis.* (1943). Garden City, NY: Garden City Publishing. (Original in German, 1917). Good for the reader who wants a basic introduction to Freud. For a good one-chapter summary, see Hall, C. S., and Lindzey, G. (1970). *Theories of personality.* (2nd ed.) New York: Wiley.

Symons, Donald. (1979). *The evolution of human sexuality.* New York: Oxford University Press. A sociobiological analysis of sexuality.

Yorburg, Betty. (1982). *Introduction to sociology.* New York: Harper & Row. This basic sociology text gives a good introduction to sociological theories with numerous applications in the area of sexuality.

CHAPTER • 3

SEXUAL ANATOMY

All the body image problems are just heightened when you narrow your sights to your genitals. Even people who don't feel particularly sensitive about how they look to the man on the street feel shy or nervous when confronting their own or another's sexual anatomy. The endless taboos on sex in this society and the misguided romanticism of the airbrush mentality keep people from really looking at their sex organs. . . . To integrate your sex into yourself in a positive way, you have to have a clear picture of your external genitals. You also have to know what goes on inside your body sexually.*

* *Source:* Patricia Raley. (1976). *Making love.* New York: Dial Press, p. 84.

CHAPTER HIGHLIGHTS

I. FEMALE SEXUAL ORGANS
   - External Organs
   - Internal Organs
   - The Breasts
   - The Pelvic Exam

II. MALE SEXUAL ORGANS
   - The Penis
   - The Scrotum and Testes
   - Sperm
   - Other Internal Structures

One outgrowth of the feminist movement, the women's health movement, has emphasized that women need to know more about their bodies. Actually, that is a good principle for everyone to follow. The current trend is away from the elitist view that only a select group of people—physicians—should understand the functioning of the body and toward the view that everyone needs more information about his or her own body. The purpose of this chapter is to provide basic information about the structure and functions of the parts of the body that are involved in sexuality and reproduction. Some readers may anticipate that this will be a boring exercise. Everyone, after all, knows what a penis is and what a vagina is. But even today, we find some bright college students who think a woman's urine passes out through her vagina. And how many of you know what the epididymis and the seminiferous tubules are? If you don't know, keep reading. You may even find out a few interesting things about the penis and the vagina that you were not aware of.

FEMALE SEXUAL ORGANS

The female sexual organs can be classified into two categories: the *external organs* and the *internal organs.*

External Organs

Vulva (VULL-vuh): The collective term for the external genitals of the female.

The external genitals of the female consist of the clitoris, the mons pubis, the inner lips, the outer lips, and the vaginal opening (see Figure 3.1). Collectively, they are known as the vulva ("crotch"; other terms such as "cunt" and "pussy" may refer either to the vulva or to the vagina—slang, alas, is not so precise as scientific language).

The Clitoris

Clitoris (KLIT-or-is): A small, highly sensitive sexual organ in the female, found in front of the vaginal entrance.

The clitoris (***klit'-or-is,*** in slang "man in the boat") is an extremely sensitive organ which is exceptionally important in female sexual response. It is a small knob of tissue situated externally, in front of the vaginal opening and the urethral opening. Like the penis, the clitoris is composed of two parts: The *shaft* and the tip or *glans* (see Figure 3.2). The glans is visible, protruding like a small lump. The shaft dis-

FIGURE 3.1

The external genitals of the female.

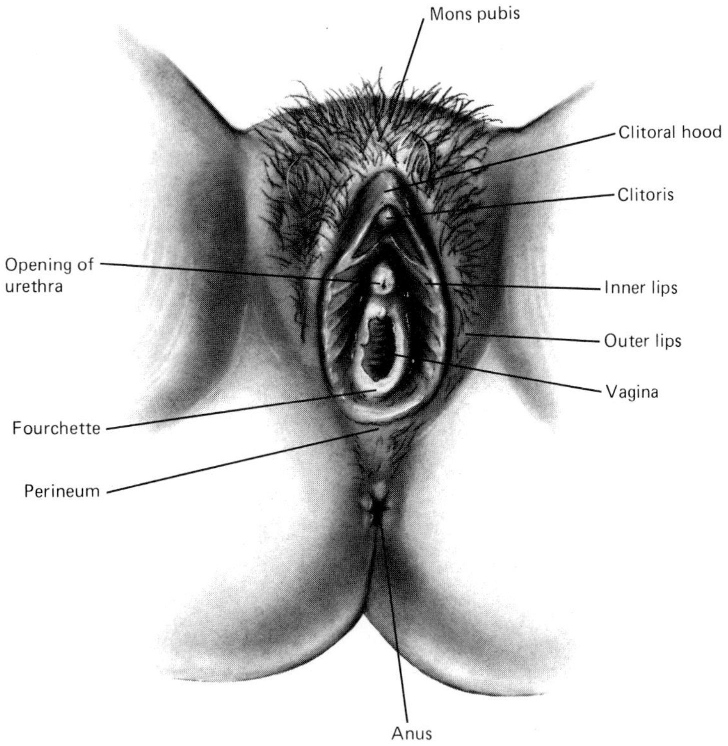

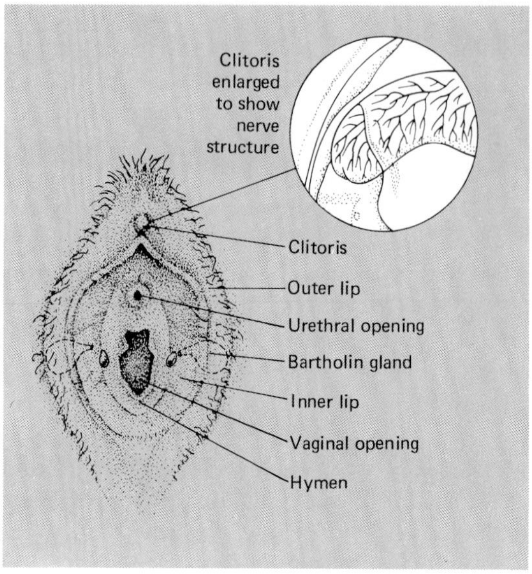

FIGURE 3.2

The structure of the clitoris and its nerve supply.

appears into the body beneath the *clitoral hood,* a sheath of tissue that passes around the clitoris and is an extension of the inner lips.

As will be discussed in Chapter 4, female sexual organs and male sexual organs develop from similar tissue; thus we can speak of the organs of one gender as being *homologous* (in the sense of developing from the same source) to the organs of the other gender. The female's clitoris is homologous to the male's penis; that is, both develop from the same embryonic tissue. The clitoris has a structure similar to that of the penis in that both have a shaft and a glans. The clitoris varies in size from one woman to the next, much as the penis varies in size from man to man. Also, the clitoris, like the penis, is erectile. Its erection is possible because its internal structure contains *corpora cavernosa* that fill with blood, as the similar structures in the penis do. The corpora cavernosa and the mechanism of erection will be considered in more detail in the discussion of the male sexual organs. Like the penis, the clitoris has a rich supply of nerve endings, making it very sensitive to touch (see Figure 3.2). It is more sensitive to erotic stimulation than any other part of the female body.

FIGURE 3.3

The shape of the vulva varies widely from one woman to the next.

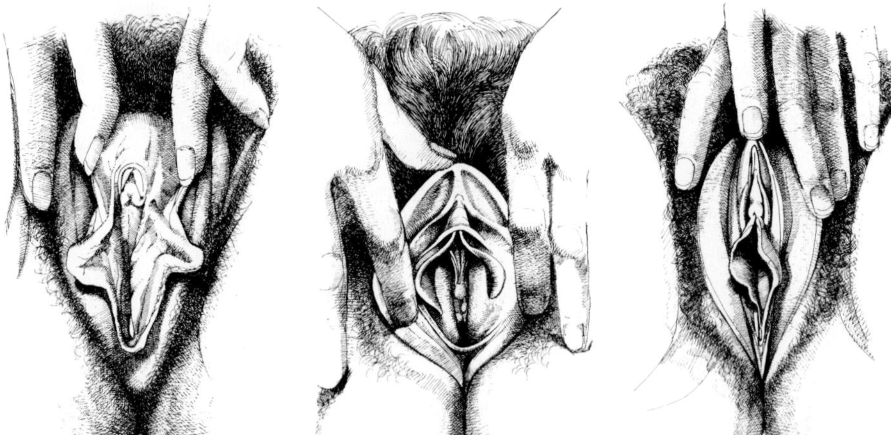

The clitoris is unique in that it is the only part of the sexual anatomy with no known reproductive function. All the other sexual organs serve dual sexual-reproductive functions. For example, not only is the vagina used for sexual intercourse, but it also receives the sperm and serves as the passageway through which the baby travels during childbirth. The penis not only produces sexual arousal and pleasure but also is responsible for ejaculation and impregnation. The clitoris clearly has an important function in producing sexual arousal. Unlike the other sexual organs, however, it appears to have no direct function in reproduction.

At various times in history and in various cultures, the clitoris has been subjected to mutilation. *Clitoridectomy*[1]—the surgical removal of the clitoris—is rare but has been practiced in the Middle East and in some parts of Africa and Latin America. It is still done in Kenya and some parts of Egypt. It was also advocated and practiced by some physicians in the United States during the Victorian era, ostensibly to cure women who were "compulsive masturbators." The existence of the practice in this country is a commentary on the repressive attitudes of the Victorians toward sexuality and their particularly repressive attitudes toward female sexuality.

The Mons

Mons pubis (PYOO-bis): The fatty pad of tissue under the pubic hair.

In outward appearance, the more obvious parts of the vulva are the mons pubis, the inner lips, and the outer lips. The mons pubis (also called the *mons* or the *mons veneris,* for "mountain of Venus") is the rounded, fatty pad of tissue, covered with pubic hair, at the front of the body. It lies on top of the pubic bones (which come together in the center at a point called the *pubic symphysis*) and is the most visible part of the female sexual organs.

The Labia

Outer lips: Fatty pads of tissue lying on either side of the vaginal entrance.

Inner lips: Thin folds of skin lying on either side of the vaginal entrance.

The outer lips (or *labia majora,* for "major lips") are rounded pads of tissue lying along both sides of the vaginal opening; they are covered with pubic hair. The inner lips (or *labia minora,* for "minor lips") are two hairless folds of skin lying between the major lips and running right along the edge of the vaginal opening. Sometimes they are folded over, concealing the vaginal opening until they are spread apart. The inner lips extend forward and come together in front, forming the clitoral hood. The inner and outer lips are well supplied with nerve endings and thus are also important in sexual stimulation and arousal.

Bartholin's Glands

Bartholin's glands: Two tiny glands located on either side of the vaginal entrance.

A pair of small glands, Bartholin's glands, lie just inside the inner lips. Their functioning is relatively unimportant, except that they sometimes become infected.[2] *Skene's glands* are located nearby and, similarly, usually attract attention only when infected.

---

[1]A related practice is *infibulation,* which refers to sewing the vagina closed; it is practiced mainly in Eastern Africa (Gregersen, 1983).

[2]And there is a limerick about them:

There was a young man from Calcutta
Who was heard in his beard to mutter,
"If her Bartholin glands
Don't respond to my hands,
I'm afraid I shall have to use butter."

Actually, there is a biological fallacy in the limerick. Can you spot it? If not, see Chapter 8.

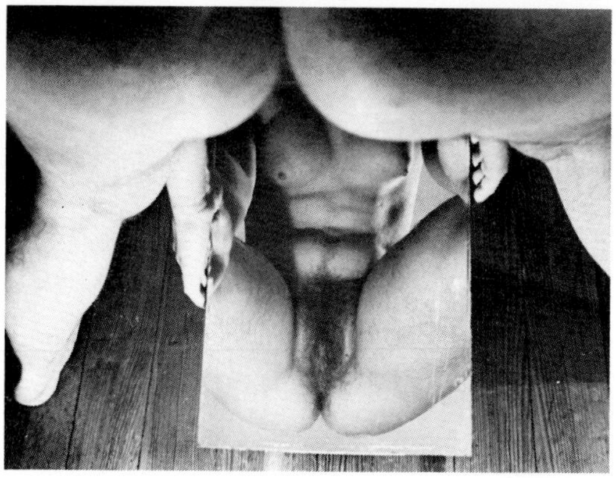

FIGURE 3.4

Body education: The mirror exercise lets women see their own genitals.

Perineum (pair-ih-NEE-um):
The skin between the vaginal entrance and the anus.

Introitus:
Another word for the vaginal entrance.

A few more landmarks should be noted (Figure 3.1). The place where the inner lips come together behind the vaginal opening is called the *fourchette.* The area of skin between the vaginal opening and the anus is called the perineum. The vaginal opening itself is sometimes called the introitus. Notice also that the urinary opening lies about midway between the clitoris and the vaginal opening. Thus urine does not pass out through the clitoris (as might be expected from analogy with the male) or through the vagina, but instead through a separate pathway, the *urethra,* with a separate opening.

What You See Is What You Get

One important difference between the male sex organs and the female sex organs—and a difference that might have some important psychological consequences—is that the female's external genitals are much less visible than the male's. A male can view his genitals directly either by looking down at them or by looking into a mirror while naked. Either of these two strategies for the female, however, will result at best in a view of the mons. The clitoris, the inner and outer lips, and the vaginal opening remain hidden. Indeed, many adult women have never taken a direct look at their own vulva. The mirror, however, makes this possible. The genitals can be viewed either by putting a mirror on the floor and squatting over it (see Figure 3.4) or by standing up and putting one foot on the edge of a chair, bed, or something similar and holding the mirror up near the genitals. I recommend that all women use a mirror to identify on their own bodies all the parts shown in Figure 3.1. The female genitals need not remain mysterious to their owner.

The Hymen

Hymen (HYE-men):
A thin membrane that may partially cover the vaginal entrance.

Before the internal structures are discussed, one other external structure deserves mention: the hymen. The hymen ("cherry," "maidenhead") is a thin membrane which, if present, is situated at the vaginal opening. The hymen may be present in a number of different conditions (see Figure 3.5), although it generally has some openings in it; otherwise the menstrual flow would not be able to pass out.[3] At the time of first intercourse, the hymen, if present, is broken or stretched as the penis moves into the vagina. This may cause bleeding and possibly some pain. Typically,

[3]The rare condition in which the hymen is a tough tissue with no opening is called *imperforate hymen* and can be corrected with fairly simple surgery.

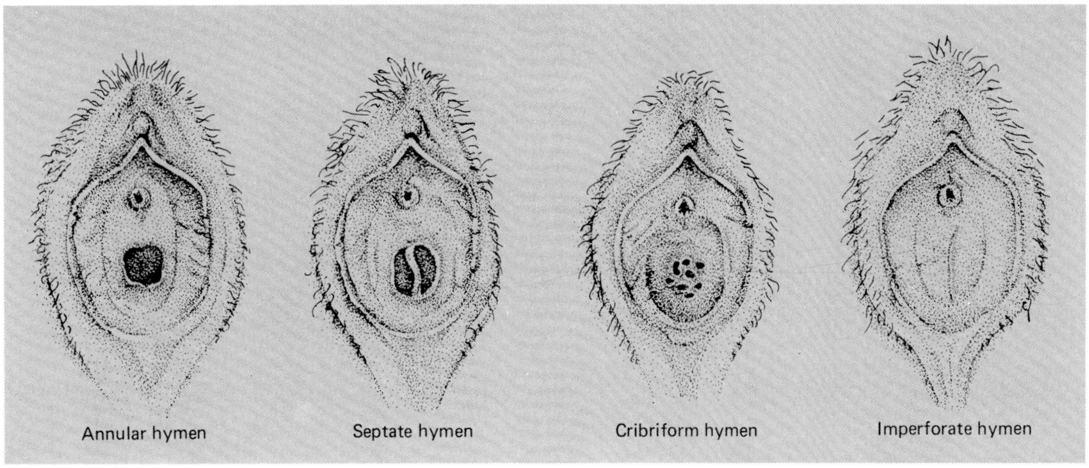

FIGURE 3.5

There are several types of hymens.

though, it is an untraumatic occurrence and goes unnoticed in the excitement of the moment. For a woman who is very concerned about her hymen and what will happen to it at first coitus, there are two possible approaches. A physician can cut the hymen neatly so that it will not tear at the time of first intercourse, or the woman herself can stretch it by inserting a finger into the vagina and pressing on it repeatedly (Lanson, 1975).

The hymen, and its destruction at first intercourse, has captured the interest of people in many cultures. In Europe during the Middle Ages, the lord might claim the right to deflower a peasant bride on her wedding night before passing her on to her husband (the practice is called *droit du seigneur* in French and *jus primae noctis* in Latin). The hymen has been taken as evidence of virginity. Thus bleeding on the wedding night was proof that the bride had been delivered intact to the groom; the parading of the bloody bed sheets on the wedding night, a custom of the Kurds of Arabia, is one of the most obvious rituals based on this belief. In other cultures the destruction of the mysterious hymen has been considered dangerous. In one Australian tribe, the task was accomplished by two old women a week before the wedding. If, at that time, the girl's hymen was discovered not to be in mint condition, she might be tortured or even killed.

These practices rest on the assumption that a woman without a hymen is not a virgin. However, we now know that this is not true. Some females are simply born without a hymen, and others may tear it in active sports such as horseback riding. Unfortunately, this means that some women have been humiliated unjustly for their lack of a hymen.

Internal Organs

The internal sex organs of the female consist of the vagina, the uterus, a pair of ovaries, and a pair of oviducts or fallopian tubes (see Figures 3.6 and 3.7).

The Vagina

Vagina (vuh-JINE-uh): The barrel-shaped organ in the female into which the penis is inserted during intercourse and through which a baby passes during birth.

The vagina is the organ into which the penis is inserted during intercourse, and it receives the ejaculate. It is also the passageway through which the baby travels during birth, and so it is sometimes called the *birth canal.* In the resting state, the vaginal barrel is about 8 to 10 centimeters (3 to 4 inches) long and tilts slightly

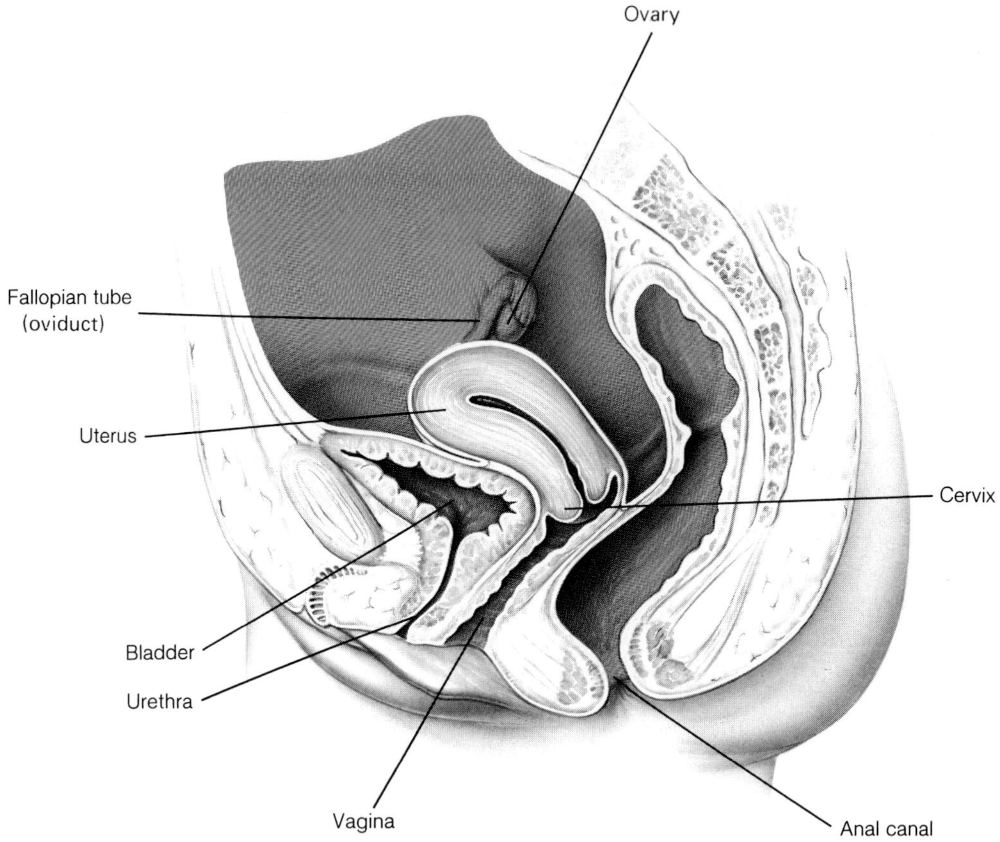

FIGURE 3.6

Internal sexual and reproductive organs of the female, side view.

backward from the bottom to the top. At the bottom it opens to the vaginal opening, or *introitus.* At the top it connects with the cervix (the lower part of the uterus). It is a very flexible, tube-shaped organ that works somewhat like a balloon. In the "resting" state its walls lie against each other like the sides of an uninflated balloon; during arousal it expands like an inflated balloon, allowing space to accommodate the penis.

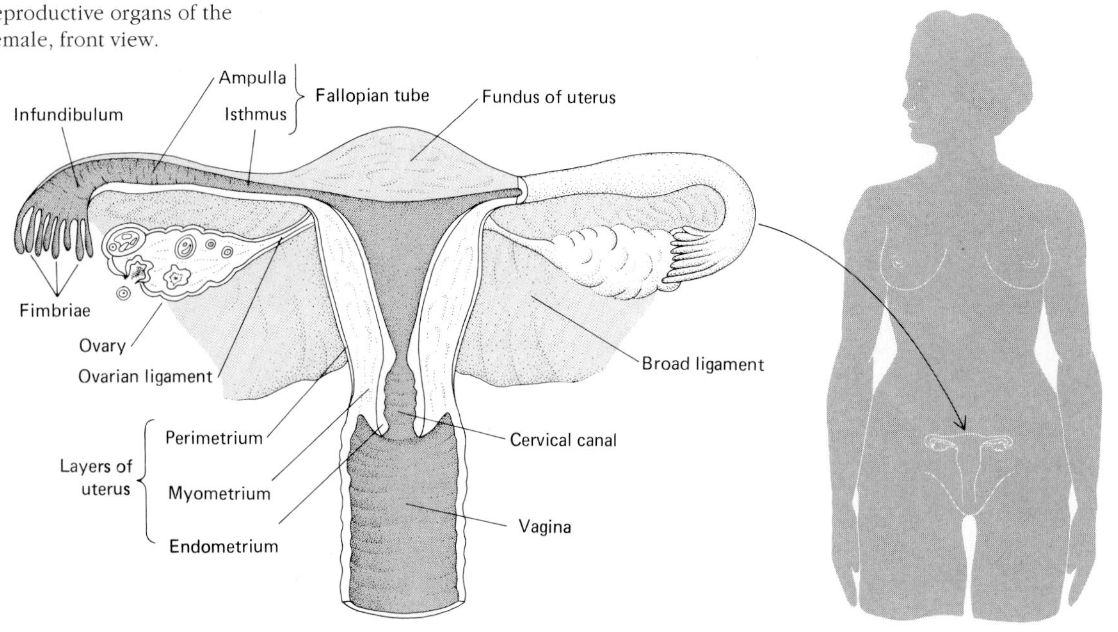

FIGURE 3.7

Internal sexual and reproductive organs of the female, front view.

The walls of the vagina have three layers. The inner layer, the *vaginal mucosa,* is a mucous membrane similar to the inner lining of the mouth. The middle layer is muscular, and the outer layer forms a covering. The walls of the vagina are extremely elastic and are capable of expanding to the extent necessary during intercourse and childbirth, although with age they become thinner and less flexible.

The nerve supply of the vagina is mostly to the lower one-third, near the introitus. That part is sensitive to erotic stimulation. The upper two-thirds of the vagina contains almost no nerve endings and is therefore very insensitive except to feelings of deep pressure.

The number of slang terms for the vagina (for example, "beaver," "cunt") and the frequency of their usage testify to its power of fascination across the ages. One concern has been with size: whether some vaginas are too small or too large. As has been noted, though, the vagina is highly elastic and expandable. Thus, at least in principle, any penis can fit into any vagina. The penis is, after all, not nearly so large as a baby's head, which manages to fit through the vagina.

The part of the vagina which is most responsible for the male's sensation that it is "tight," "too tight," or "too loose" is the introitus. One of the things that can stretch the introitus is childbirth; indeed, there is a considerable difference between the appearance of the vulva of a woman who has never had a baby (*nulliparous*) and the vulva of a woman who has (*parous*) (see Figure 3.8).

FIGURE 3.8

Appearance of the vulva of a woman who is a virgin; a woman who has had intercourse but has not had a baby (nulliparous); and a woman who has had a baby (parous).

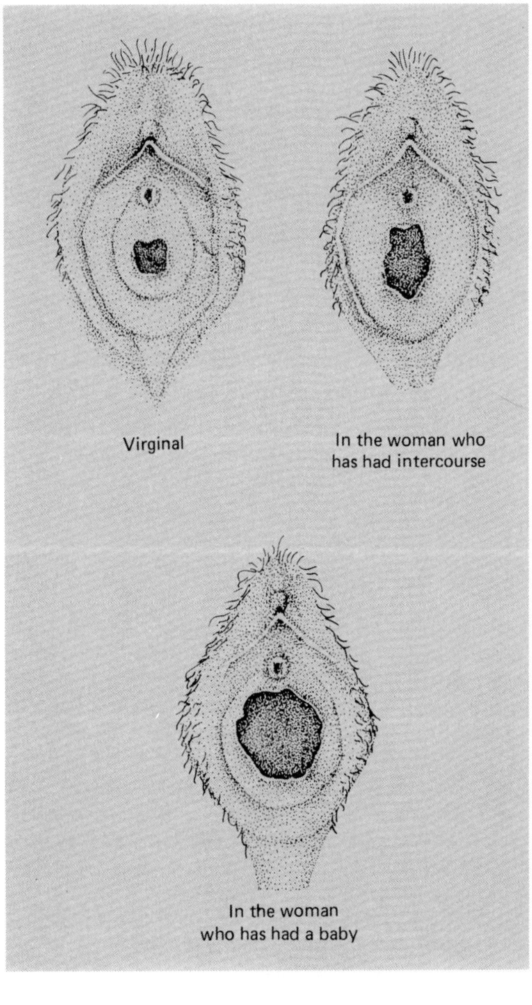

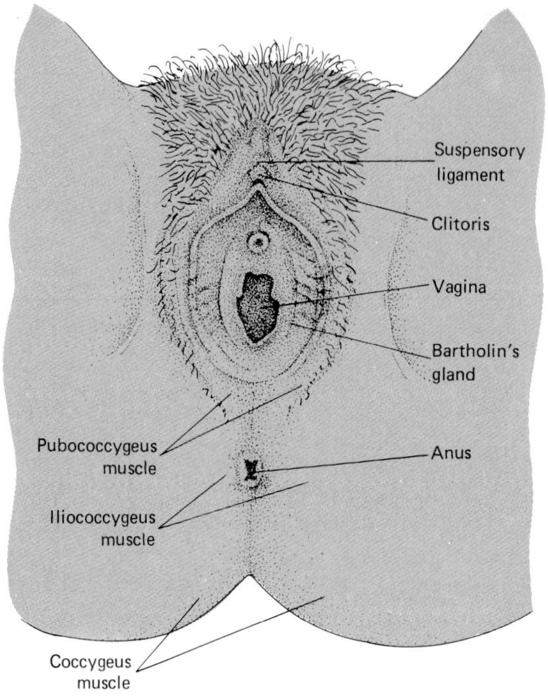

FIGURE 3.9

Muscles on the floor of the pelvis. Note particularly the pubococcygeal muscle, which women may want to exercise (see Chapter 20).

Pubococcygeal muscle (pyoo-bo-cox-ih-GEE-ul): A muscle around the vaginal entrance.

Surrounding the vagina, the urethra, and the anus is a set of muscles called the *pelvic floor muscles* (see Figure 3.9). One of these muscles, the pubococcygeal muscle, is particularly important. It may be stretched during childbirth, or it may simply be weak. However, it can be strengthened through exercise, and this is recommended by sex therapists (see Chapter 20) as well as by many popular sex manuals and magazines.

Because the introitus is highly sensitive, both to pleasure and to pain, and because it is surrounded with muscles, it may reflect a woman's psychological response to sex. If a woman responds to arousal with fear or anxiety, the muscles may tighten, making it difficult for the penis to enter the vagina. In extreme cases, the muscles become so tight that intercourse is impossible, a condition known as *vaginismus* (see Chapter 20). On the other hand, a very expansive, and relaxed introitus also has some disadvantages in that it may not produce enough sensation for the male. Exercising the pubococcygeal muscle should correct this problem

The vagina has also provoked some anxieties. Some people believe that the penis can be trapped inside the vagina and that the man will be unable to withdraw it. This does occur in dogs. The dog's penis expands inside the vagina, creating a "locking" effect, and separation is impossible until the erection is gone. This does not occur in humans, however. There are also many myths among primitive peoples that the vagina is lined with teeth (*vagina dentata*), thorns, or other dangerous objects that can damage the penis. For example, the Pomo Indians of California have a myth in which a young girl has thorns surrounding her vagina, which her intended husband must break off before marrying her.

The Uterus

Uterus (YOO-tur-us): The organ in the female in which the fetus develops.

The uterus (womb) is about the size of a fist and is shaped somewhat like an upside-down pear. It is usually tilted forward and is held in place by ligaments. The narrow lower third is called the *cervix* and opens into the vagina. The top is the *fundus,* and the main part is the *body.* The entrance to the uterus through the cervix is very narrow, about the size of a straw, and is called the *os* (or cervical canal). The major function of the uterus is to hold and nourish the developing fetus.

The uterus, like the vagina, consists of three layers. The inner layer, or *endometrium,* is richly supplied with glands and blood vessels. Its state varies according to the age of the woman and the phase of the menstrual cycle. It is the endometrium which is sloughed off at menstruation and creates most of the menstrual discharge. The middle layer, the *myometrium,* is muscular. The muscles are very strong, creating the strong contractions of labor and orgasm, and are also highly elastic; they are capable of stretching to accommodate a 9-month-old fetus. The outer layer—the *perimetrium* or *serosa*—forms the external cover of the uterus.

The Fallopian Tubes

Fallopian tube (fuh-LOW-pee-un): The tube extending from the uterus to the ovary; also called the oviduct.

Extending out from the sides of the upper end of the uterus are the fallopian tubes, also called the *oviducts* ("egg ducts") or *uterine tubes* (see Figure 3.7). It is these tubes that are tied in the tubal ligation (see Chapter 7). The fallopian tubes are extremely narrow and are lined with hairlike projections called *cilia.* The fallopian tubes are the pathway by which the egg leaves the ovaries and the sperm reach the egg. Fertilization of the egg typically occurs in the infundibulum, and the fertilized egg travels the rest of the way through the tube to the uterus. The infundibulum curves around toward the ovary; at its end are numerous fingerlike projections called *fimbriae* which extend toward the ovary.

The Ovaries

Ovaries: Two organs in the female that produce eggs and sex hormones.

The ovaries are two organs about the size and shape of an unshelled almond; they lie on either side of the uterus. The ovaries have two important functions: they produce eggs (ova), and they manufacture the female sex hormones, *estrogens* and *progesterone.*

Each ovary contains numerous follicles. A *follicle* is a capsule that surrounds an egg (not to be confused with hair follicles, which are quite different). It is estimated that a female is born with about 400,000 immature eggs. Beginning at puberty, one or several of the follicles mature during each menstrual cycle. When the egg has matured, the follicle moves to the surface of the ovary, bursts open, and releases the egg. The ovaries do not actually connect directly to the fallopian tubes. The egg is released into the body cavity and apparently reaches the tube as a result of some mysterious attraction for the fimbriae. If the egg does not reach the tube, it may be fertilized outside the tube, resulting in an abdominal pregnancy (see the section on ectopic pregnancy in Chapter 6). There have also been cases recorded of women who, although they are missing one ovary and the opposite fallopian tube, have nonetheless become pregnant. Apparently, in such cases the egg migrates to the tube on the opposite side.

The Breasts

Though they are not actually sex organs, the *breasts* deserve some mention here because of their erotic and reproductive significance. The breast consists of about

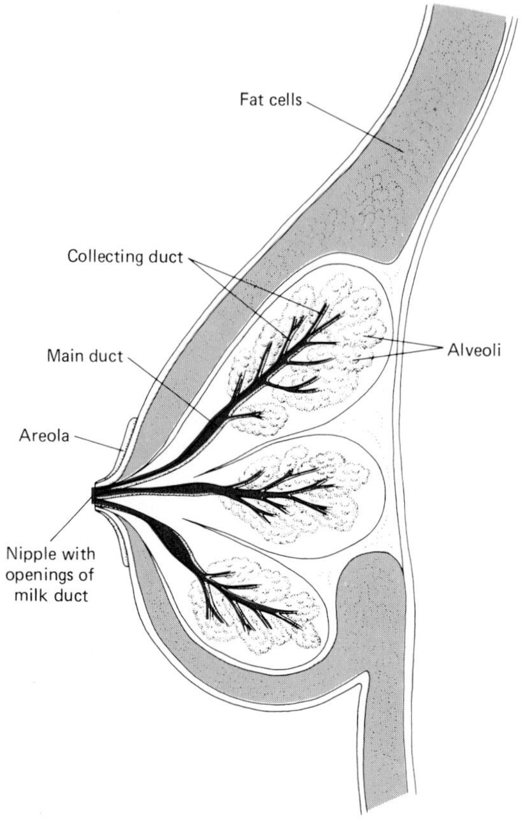

FIGURE 3.10

The internal structure of the breast.

15 or 20 clusters of *mammary glands,* each with a separate opening to the nipple, and of fatty and fibrous tissue which surrounds the clusters of glands (see Figure 3.10). The nipple, into which the milk ducts open, is at the tip of the breast. It is richly supplied with nerve endings and therefore very important in erotic stimulation. The nipple consists of smooth muscle fibers; when they contract, the nipple becomes erect. The area surrounding the nipple is called the *areola.*

There is wide variation among women in the size and shape of the breasts. One thing is fairly consistent, though. Few women are satisfied with the size of their breasts. Most women think they are either too small or too large, and almost no woman thinks hers are just right. It is well to remember that there are the same number of nerve endings in small breasts as in large breasts. It follows that small breasts are actually more erotically sensitive per square inch than large ones (McCary, 1973).

Breasts may take on enormous psychological meaning; they can be a symbol of femininity or a means of attracting men. Ours is a very breast-oriented culture, and men in the United States may develop a nearly overpowering interest in, and attraction to, women's breasts.

The Pelvic Exam

All adult women should have a checkup every one to two years that includes a thorough pelvic exam. Among other things, such an exam is extremely important in the detection of cervical cancer, and early detection is the key to cure (see Chapter 21).

Some women neglect to have the exam because they feel anxious or embarrassed about it; however, having regular pelvic exams can be a matter of life and death. Actually, the exam is quite simple and need not cause any discomfort. The following is a description of the procedures in a pelvic exam (Boston Women's Health Book Collective, 1976).

First, the physician inspects the external genitals, checking for irritations, discolorations, bumps, lice, adhesions to the clitoris, skin lesions, and unusual vaginal discharge. Then there is an internal check for *cystoceles* (bulges of the bladder into the vagina) and *rectoceles* (bulges of the rectum into the vagina), for pus in the Skene glands, for cysts in the Bartholin glands, and for the strength of the pelvic floor muscles and abdominal muscles. There is also a test for stress incontinence; the physician asks the patient to cough and checks to see whether urine flows involuntarily.

Next comes the speculum exam. The *speculum* is a metal (sometimes plastic) instrument that is inserted into the vagina to hold the vaginal walls apart so as to permit examination (see Figure 3.11). Once the speculum is in place (it should be prewarmed to body temperature if it is metal), the physician looks for any unusual signs, such as lesions, inflammation, or unusual discharge from the vaginal walls, and for any signs of infections or damage to the cervix. The physician then uses a small metal spatula to scrape a tiny bit of tissue from the cervix for the Pap test for cervical cancer. If done properly, this should be painless. A smear of discharge should also be taken to check for gonorrhea.

If the woman is interested in seeing her own cervix, she can ask the doctor to hold up a mirror so that she can view it through the speculum. Indeed, some women's groups advocate that women learn to use a speculum and give themselves regular exams with it; early detection of diseases would thus be much more likely. (For a more detailed description, see Boston Women's Health Book Collective, 1976).

Next, the physician does a bimanual vaginal exam. She or he slides the index and middle fingers of one hand into the vagina and then, with the other hand, presses

FIGURE 3.11

The pelvic exam. (*a*) The speculum in place for a pelvic exam. The Ayre spatula is used to get a sample of cells for the Pap test. (*b*) The bimanual pelvic exam.

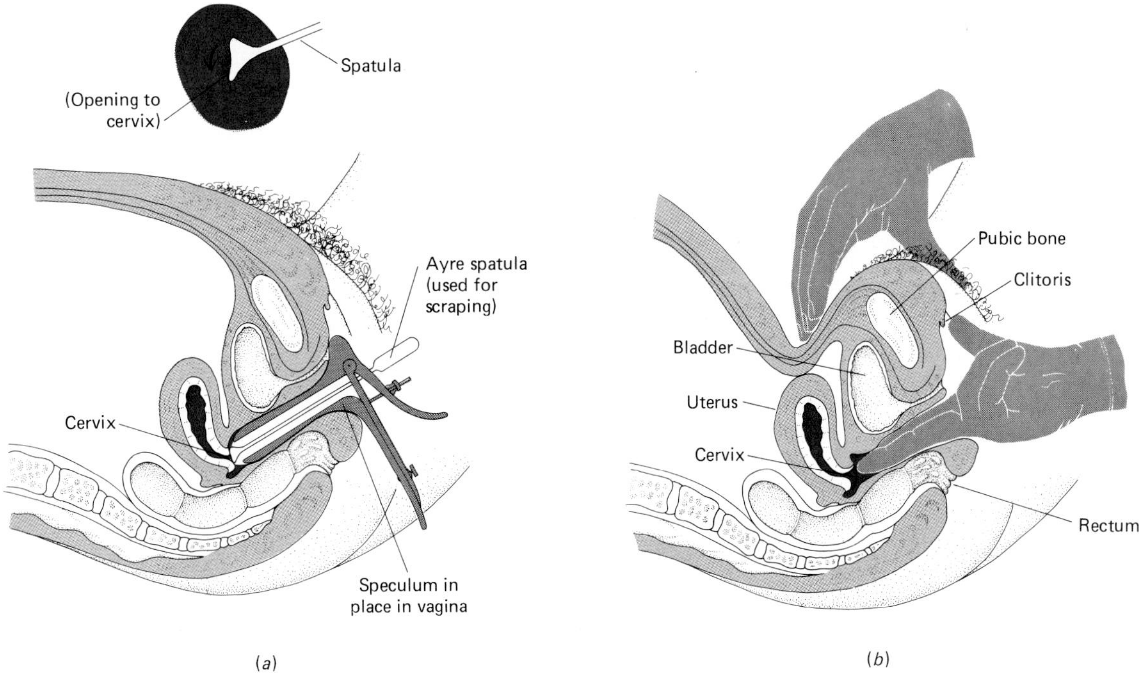

down from the outside on the abdominal wall (Figure 3.11). The physician then feels for the position of the uterus, tubes, and ovaries and for any signs of growths, pain, or inflammation.

Finally, the physician may also do a recto-vaginal exam by inserting one finger into the vagina and one into the rectum; this provides further information on the positioning of the pelvic organs.

Once again, it is important to emphasize that these are not painful procedures and that having them performed regularly is extremely important to a woman's health.

MALE SEXUAL ORGANS

Externally, the most obvious parts of the male sexual anatomy are the penis and the scrotum, or scrotal sac, which contains the testes (see Figure 3.12).

The Penis

Penis:
The male external sexual organ, which functions both in sexual activity and in urination.

The penis (phallus, "prick," "cock," and many other slang terms too numerous to list) serves important functions in sexual pleasure, reproduction, and elimination of body wastes by urination. It is a tubular organ with an end or tip called the *glans.* The opening at the end of the glans is the *meatus,* or *urethral opening,* through which urine and semen pass. The part of the penis that attaches to the body is called the *root,* and the main part of the penis is called the *body* or *shaft.* The raised ridge separating the glans from the body of the penis is called the *corona,* or *coronal*

FIGURE 3.12

The male sexual and reproductive organs, side view.

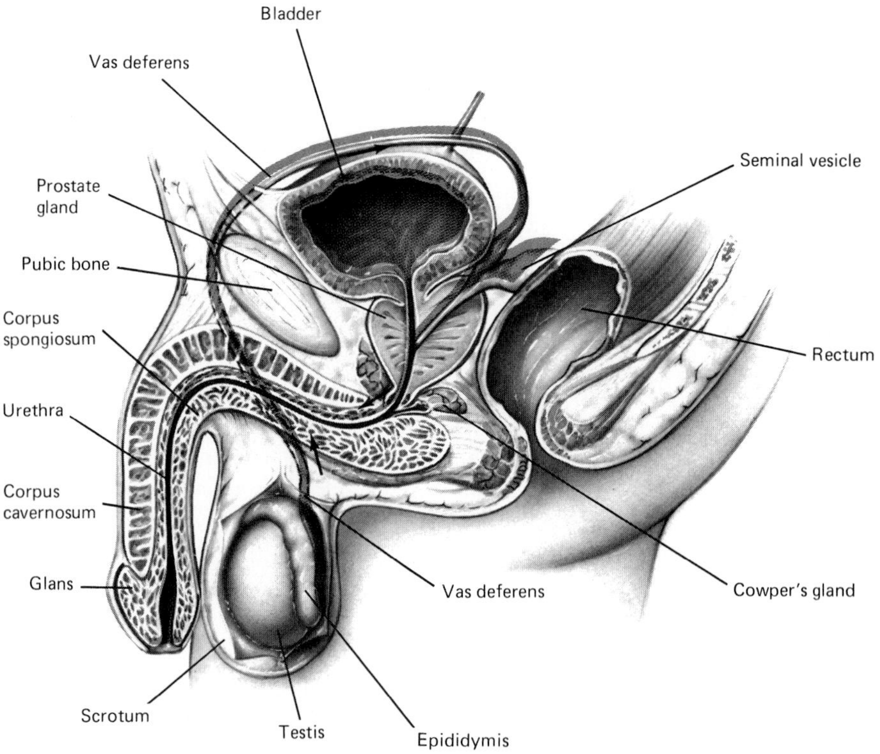

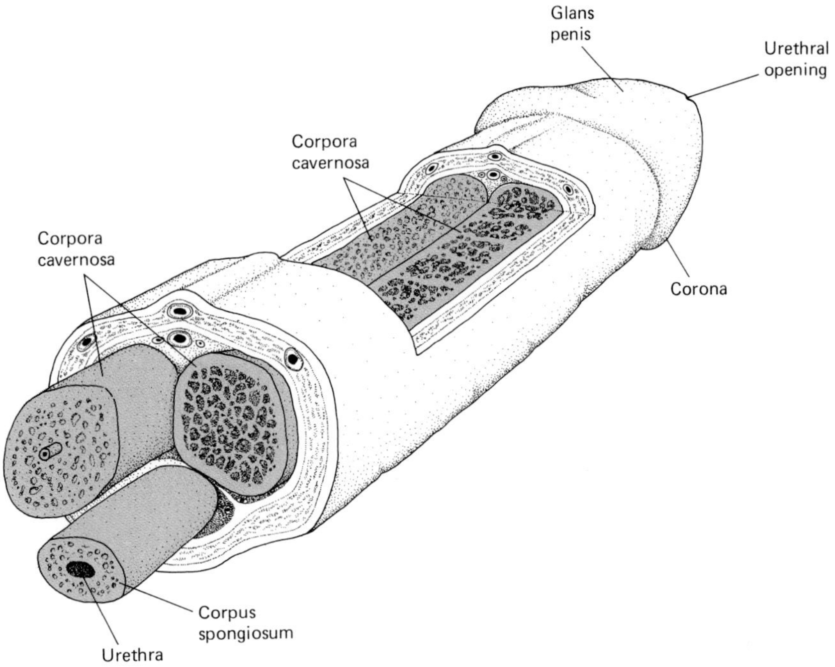

FIGURE 3.13

The internal structure of the penis.

ridge. While the entire penis is sensitive to sexual stimulation, the glans and corona are by far the most sexually excitable region of the male anatomy.

Internally, the penis contains three long cylinders of spongy tissue running parallel to the *urethra,* which is the pathway through which semen and urine pass (see Figure 3.13). The two spongy bodies lying on top are called the corpora cavernosa and the single one lying on the bottom of the penis is called the corpus spongiosum (the urethra runs through the middle of it). During erection, the latter one can be seen as a raised column on the lower side of the penis. As the names suggest, these bodies are tissues filled with many spaces and cavities, much like a sponge. They are richly supplied with blood vessels and nerves. In the flaccid (unaroused, not erect) state, they contain little blood. *Erection,* or *tumescence,* occurs when they become filled with blood (engorged) and expand, making the penis stiff.

Corpora cavernosa: Spongy bodies running the length of the penis.

Corpus spongiosum: A spongy body running the length of the penis.

Contrary to popular belief, the penis does not contain a muscle, and no muscle is involved in erection. Erection is purely a vascular phenomenon; that is, it results entirely from blood flow. It is also commonly believed that the penis of the human male contains a bone. This is not true either. In some other species—for example, dogs—the penis does contain a bone, which aids in intromission (inserting the penis into the vagina). In human males, however, there is none, and a man must accomplish intromission purely on the strength of his own erection.

The skin of the penis is hairless and is arranged in loose folds, permitting expansion during erection. The foreskin, or *prepuce,* is an additional layer of skin which forms a sheathlike covering over the glans; it may be present or absent in the adult male, depending on whether he has been circumcised (see Figure 3.14). Under the foreskin are small glands (Tyson's glands) which produce a cheesy substance called *smegma.* The foreskin is easily retractable,[4] and its retraction is extremely important

Foreskin: A layer of skin covering the glans or tip of the penis in an uncircumcised male; also called the prepuce.

[4]In a rare condition, the foreskin is so tight that it cannot be pulled back; this is called *phimosis* and requires circumcision.

for proper hygiene. If it is not pulled back and the glans washed thoroughly, the smegma may accumulate, producing a very unpleasant smell.

Circumcision: Surgical removal of the foreskin of the penis.

Circumcision refers to the surgical cutting away or removal of the foreskin. Circumcision is practiced widely throughout the world and, when parents so choose, is done to infants in the United States within a few days after birth.

Typically, circumcision is done for hygienic reasons and religious reasons. Hygienic reasons lie behind its practice in the United States. The hygienic argument is that removal of the foreskin permits much better cleansing of the penis; thus smegma and bacteria will not have a tendency to accumulate, as they may when the foreskin is present.

Circumcision may also be practiced for ritualistic and religious reasons. Circumcision has been a part of Jewish religious practice for thousands of years. It symbolizes the covenant between God and the Jewish people and is done on the eighth day after birth, according to scriptural teaching (Genesis 17:9–27). In some cultures circumcision may be done at puberty as an initiation ritual, or *rite de passage.* The ability of the young boy to stand the pain may be seen as a proof of manhood.

A particularly exotic mutilation of the penis occurs in a surgical ritual known as *subincision.* In this operation, which is common among primitive tribes, especially those in central Australia, a slit is made on the lower side of the penis along its entire length and to the depth of the urethra. Urine is then excreted at the base rather than at the tip.

Some proponents of circumcision extend the health arguments and say that circumcision may help reduce the risk of cancer. There is some evidence that cancer of the cervix is less frequent among wives of circumcised men than among wives of uncircumcised men (Weiner et al., 1951; but see Hand, 1970). The scientific data,

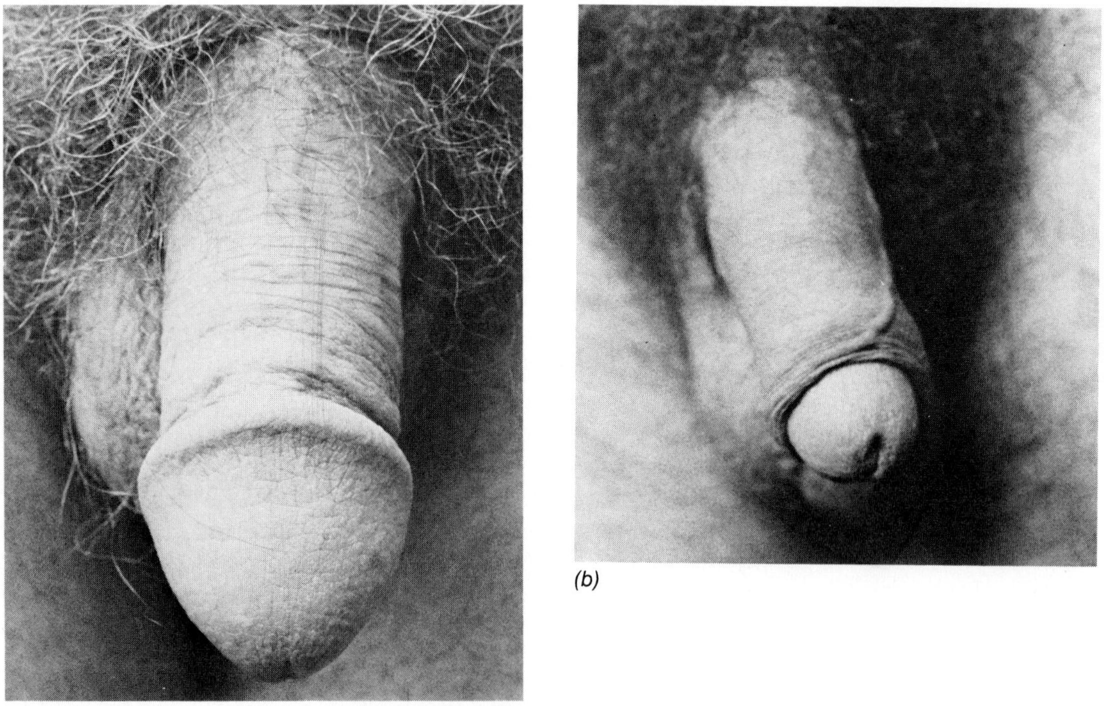

(a) (b)

FIGURE 3.14

(*a*) A circumcised penis and (*b*) an uncircumcised penis, showing the foreskin.

however, are not nearly adequate enough to allow one to conclude that circumcision reduces the risk of cancer or that lack of circumcision increases it.

In the 1980s, an anticircumcision movement has gained momentum. Its proponents argue that circumcision does not have any of the health benefits mentioned earlier, and that it does entail some health risk as well as psychological trauma (for a complete statement of the anticircumcision position, see Wallerstein, 1980.).

Other arguments have focused on whether the circumcised or the uncircumcised male receives more pleasure from sexual intercourse. In fact, Masters and Johnson (1966) have found that there is no difference in excitability between the circumcised and the uncircumcised penis.

To say the least, the penis has been the focus of quite a lot of attention thoughout history. In some cultures, the attention has become so pronounced that the male genitals have actually become the object of religious worship (phallic worship). Not surprisingly, the male genitals were often seen as symbols of fertility and thus were worshipped for their powers of procreativity. In ancient Greece, phallic worship centered on Priapus, the son of Aphrodite (the goddess of love) and Dionysus (the god of fertility and wine). Priapus is usually represented as a grinning man with a huge penis.

In contemporary American society, phallic concern often focuses on the size of the penis. It is commonly believed that a man with a large penis is a better lover than the man with a small penis and can satisfy a woman more. Masters and Johnson (1966), however, have found that this is not true. While there is considerable variation in the length of the penis from one man to the next—the average penis is generally somewhere between 6.4 centimeters (2.5 inches) and 10 centimeters (4 inches) in length when flaccid (not erect)—there seems to be a tendency for the small penis to grow more in erection than the one that starts out large. As a result, there is little correlation between the length of the penis when flaccid and the length when erect. As the saying has it, "Erection is the great equalizer." The average erect penis is about 15 centimeters (6 inches) long; as indicated, there tends to be somewhat less variation in the length of the erect penis than in the length of the flaccid one, although erect penises longer than 33 centimeters (13 inches) have been measured (Dickinson, 1949). Further, as Masters and Johnson note, the vagina has relatively few nerve endings and is relatively insensitive. Hence penetration to the far reaches of the vagina by a very long penis is not essential and may not even be noticeable. Many other factors are more important than penis size in giving a woman pleasure (see Chapters 9 and 20).

Phallic concern has also included an interest in the variations in the shape of the penis when flaccid and when erect, as reflected in this famous limerick:

There was a young man of Kent
Whose kirp in the middle was bent.
To save himself trouble
He put it in double,
And instead of coming, he went.

Phallic concern has also been expressed in psychological theory, the best example being in psychoanalytic theory. According to Freud, concern for the penis and a related castration anxiety are the key factors in male psychological development, leading to the resolution of the Oedipus complex, increased independence from parents, and increased psychological maturity. All this from such a small part of the body! (Indeed, the theory even says that the key factor in female psychological development is the *lack* of a penis.)

The Scrotum and Testes

Scrotum (SKROH-tum):
The pouch of skin that contains the testes in the male.

Testes:
The pair of glands in the scrotum that manufacture sperm and sex hormones.

Seminiferous tubules (sem-ih-NIFF-ur-us):
Tubes in the testes that manufacture sperm.

Interstitial cells (int-er-STIH-shul):
Cells in the testes that manufacture testosterone.

The other major part of the external genitals in the male is the scrotum; this is a loose pouch of skin, lightly covered with hair, which holds the testes ("balls" or "nuts" in slang[5]). The testes themselves are considered part of the internal genitals.

The testes[6] are the *gonads,* or reproductive glands, of the male, and thus they are analogous to the female's ovaries. Like the ovaries, they serve two major functions: they manufacture germ cells (sperm), and they manufacture the male sex hormone, *testosterone.* Both testes are about the same size, although the left one usually hangs lower than the right one.

In the internal structure of the testes, three parts are important: the seminiferous tubules, the interstitial cells, and the epididymis, which is really a structure adjacent to the testis (see Figure 3.15). The seminiferous tubules carry out the important function of manufacturing and storing sperm, a process called *spermatogenesis.* They are a long series of threadlike tubes curled and packed densely into the testes. There are about 1000 of these tubules, and it is estimated that if they were stretched out end to end, they would be several hundred feet in length.

The interstitial cells (or *Leydig's cells*) carry out the second important function of the testes, the production of the male sex hormone, testosterone. These cells are found in the connective tissue lying between the seminiferous tubules. The cells lie close to the blood vessels in the testes and pour the hormones they manufacture directly into the blood vessels. Thus the testes are endocrine glands.

Each testis is surrounded by a tight, whitish sheath (the *tunica albuginea*). In addition to encapsulating the testis, the sheath also extends into it, dividing it into sections, much like a grapefruit; each section is filled with seminiferous tubules. It is this sheath which is responsible for the problem of sterility caused by mumps in the adult male. When the virus invades the testes, it causes them to swell. The tunica albuginea is tight, however, and does not permit expansion. The delicate tubules are thus crushed, which impairs their sperm-producing function. Mumps is not a problem in the female because the ovaries are not enclosed in a comparable tight sheath.

One of the clever tricks that the scrotum and testes perform, as any male will testify, is that they can move up and close to the body or down and away from the body. These changes are brought about mainly by temperature (although emotional factors may also produce them). If a man plunges into a cold lake, the scrotum will shrivel and move close to the body. If the man is working in an extremely hot place, the scrotum will hang down and away from the body. This mechanism is important because the testes should remain at a fairly constant body temperature, slightly lower than normal body temperature. This constancy of temperature is necessary to protect sperm, which may be injured by extremes of temperature. Thus if the air is cold, the testes move closer to the body to maintain warmth, but if the air is too hot,

---

[5]That reminds me of another limerick:

There once was a pirate named Gates
Who thought he could rhumba on skates.
  He slipped on his cutlass
  And now he is nutless
And practically useless on dates.

[6]"Testes" is from the root meaning "witnesses" and comes from the same root as "testimony" does. It is derived from the ancient custom of placing the hand on the genitals when taking an oath. The singular of "testes" is "testis."

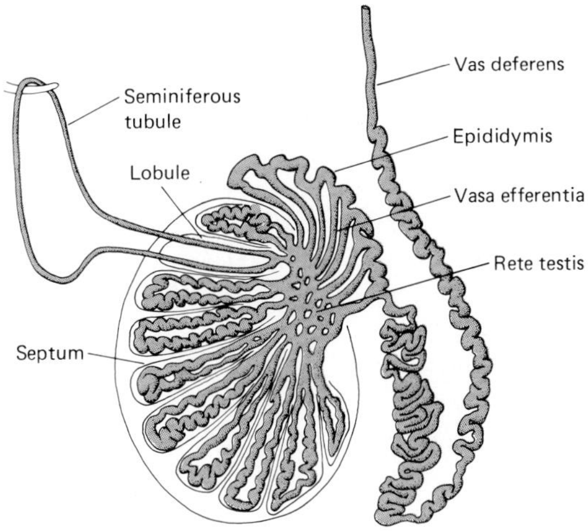

FIGURE 3.15

Schematic cross section of the internal structure of the testis.

they move away from the body to keep cool. The mechanics of this movement are made possible by the *dartos muscle,* which forms the middle layer of the scrotum. It contracts or relaxes reflexively, thereby moving the testes up or down.

Many people believe that taking hot baths, wearing tight athletic supporters, or having a high fever can cause infertility. Indeed, in some countries the men take long, hot baths as a method of contraception. Such a practice has some basis in biological fact, because sperm can be destroyed by heat. However, as a method of contraception, this practice has not been particularly effective. In one study, it was found that the use of a special jockstrap raised the temperature of the scrotum by nearly 1°C (1.7°F) and that wearing the device daily for seven weeks caused about a 25 percent reduction in the number of sperm produced (Robinson and Rock, 1967). Thus such practices might decrease a man's fertility somewhat, but they are far from 100 percent effective as contraceptives. On the other hand, men with problems of infertility can sometimes cure them by getting out of their tight jockstraps and jockey shorts.

Sperm

Sperm:
The mature male reproductive cell, capable of fertilizing an egg.

Following manufacture in the seminiferous tubules, the male germ cells go through several stages of maturation. At the earliest stage, the cell is called *spermatogonium.* Then it becomes a *spermatocyte* (first primary and then secondary) and then a *spermatid.* Finally when fully mature, it is a *spermatozoan,* or sperm. *Spermatogenesis,* the manufacture of sperm, occurs continuously in the adult human male. An average ejaculate contains about 300 million sperm.

A mature sperm is very tiny—about 60 microns, or 60/10,000 millimeter (0.0024 inch), long—and consists of a head, a neck, a mid-piece, and a tail. A normal sperm carries 23 chromosomes in the head. This 23 is half the normal number in the other cells of the human body. When the sperm unites with the egg, which also carries 23 chromosomes, the full complement of 46 for the offspring is produced.

Human cells contain two sex chromosomes: XX in the female and XY in the male (see Chapter 4). Because germ cells contain only half of the full number, they contain only one sex chromosome. Thus each egg contains one X chromosome. A sperm may contain either an X chromosome or a Y chromosome.

After the sperm are manufactured in the seminiferous tubules, they proceed into

Epididymis (ep-ih-DIH-dih-mus): Highly coiled tubules located on the edge of the testis, where sperm mature.

Vas deferens: The tube through which sperm pass on their way from the testes and epididymis, out of the scrotum, and to the urethra.

the *rete testes,* a converging network of tubes on the surface of the testis toward the top. The sperm then pass out of the testis and into a single tube, the epididymis. The epididymis is a long tube (about 6 meters, or 20 feet, in length) coiled into a small crescent-shaped region on the top and side of the testis. The sperm may be stored in the epididymis, in which they ripen and mature, possibly for as long as six weeks.

At the end of the epididymis, the sperm pass into another tube, the vas deferens, or *ductus deferens* (it is the vas which is cut in a vasectomy—see Chapter 7). The vas passes up and out of the scrotum and then follows a peculiar circular path as it loops over the pubic bone, travels across beside the urinary bladder, and then turns downward toward the prostate. As the tube passes through the prostate, it narrows, and at this point is called the *ejaculatory duct.* The ejaculatory duct then opens into the *urethra,* which has the dual function of conveying sperm and conveying urine; sperm move, via the urethra, out through the penis.

Apparently sperm have little motility (capability of movement) of their own while in the epididymis and vas. Not until they mix with the secretions of the prostate and seminal vesicles are they capable of movement on their own. It is thought that, up to this point, they are conveyed by the cilia and by contractions of the epididymis and vas.

Other Internal Structures

The *seminal vesicles* are two saclike structures which lie above the prostate, behind the bladder, and in front of the rectum. They empty their contents into the ejaculatory duct to combine with the sperm. Their exact function has been debated. It was once assumed that they stored the sperm, but it is now thought that they secrete a fluid which activates the sperm's motility.

Prostate: The gland in the male, located below the bladder, that secretes most of the fluid in semen.

The prostate lies below the bladder and is about the size and shape of a chestnut. It is composed of both muscle and glandular tissue. The prostate secretes a milky alkaline fluid which composes the major portion of the semen, or ejaculate. It is thought that the alkalinity of the secretion provides a favorable environment for the sperm and helps prevent their destruction by the acidity of the vagina. The prostate is fairly small at birth, enlarges at puberty, and typically shrinks in old age. It may become enlarged enough so that it interferes with urination, in which case surgery is required. Its size can be determined by rectal examination.

Cowper's glands: Glands that secrete substances into the male's urethra.

Cowper's glands, or the *bulbourethral glands,* are located just below the prostate and empty into the urethra. During sexual arousal, these glands secrete a small amount of a clear alkaline fluid, which appears as a droplet at the tip of the penis before ejaculation occurs. It is thought that the function of this secretion is to neutralize the acidic urethra, allowing safe passage of the sperm. Generally it is not produced in sufficient quantity to serve as a lubricant in intercourse. About 20 to 25 percent of the time, the fluid contains some stray sperm (Stone, 1931). Thus a woman may become pregnant from the sperm in this fluid even though the man has not ejaculated.

SUMMARY

The important external organs of the female are the clitoris, the mons, the inner lips, the outer lips, and the vaginal opening. The clitoris is an extremely sensitive organ and is very important in female sexual response. Another important external structure is the hymen, which has taken on great symbolic significance as a sign of virginity, although its absence is not a reliable indicator that a woman is not a virgin. The important internal structures are the vagina, which receives the penis during intercourse; the uterus, which houses the developing fetus; the ovaries, which produce eggs and manufacture sex hormones; and the fallopian tubes which convey the egg to the uterus. The breasts of the female also function in sexual arousal and may have great symbolic significance.

The important external sexual organs of the male are the penis and the scrotum. The penis contains three spongy bodies which, when filled with blood, produce an erection. Circumcision, or surgical removal of the foreskin of the penis, is a debated practice in the United States. The scrotum contains the testes, which are responsible for the manufacture of sperm (in the seminiferous tubules) and sex hormones (in the interstitial cells). The temperature of the testes is important and is regulated by the contraction and relaxation of the dartos muscle in the scrotum. Sperm pass out of the testes during ejaculation via the vas deferens, the ejaculatory duct, and the urethra. The prostate manufactures most of the fluid that mixes with the sperm to form semen. Cowper's glands and the seminal vesicles also contribute secretions.

REVIEW QUESTIONS

1. The most sexually sensitive organ in the female is the _____.
2. The _____ is a membrane stretching over the vaginal entrance in some virgins.
3. The pubococcygeal muscle is a muscle that supports the uterus, keeping it in place. True or false?
4. The inner layer of the uterus is termed the endometrium. True or false?
5. The ovaries manufacture the sex hormones _____ and _____.
6. The spongy bodies, the corpora cavernosa and the corpus spongiosum, run the length of the penis. True or false?
7. _____ is the term for the surgical removal of the foreskin or prepuce.
8. Testosterone is manufactured in the seminiferous tubules in the testes. True or false?
9. After passing out of the testes and epididymis, sperm move to the vas deferens. True or false?
10. Most of the fluid in semen is manufactured by an organ the size and shape of a chestnut, termed the _____.

QUESTION FOR THOUGHT, DISCUSSION, AND DEBATE

1. Form two groups of students to debate the following: Resolved: Circumcision should not be performed routinely. You can draw on many resources to provide evidence for your debate, including interviews with doctors and nurses, library materials (books and journal articles on the effects of circumcision), and interviews with parents of infants.

SUGGESTIONS FOR FURTHER READING

Boston Women's Health Book Collective. (1984). *The new our bodies, ourselves.* (3rd ed.) New York: Simon & Schuster. A good, easy-to-read source on female biology and sexuality.

Diagram Group. (1976). *Man's body: An owner's manual.* New York: Paddington Press, (Bantam Books paperback). A comprehensive book on men's health, including sexuality.

Netter, F. H. *Reproductive system.* (1965). The Ciba Collection of Medical Illustrations. Vol. 2. Summit, N.J.: Ciba. Generally considered to be the best set of illustrations of the sexual and reproductive anatomy available. Also includes brief explanations.

CHAPTER • 4

SEX HORMONES AND SEXUAL DIFFERENTIATION

An Odd Gastropod

The snail is a hermaphrodite:
It has beneath its shell
The organs we ascribe to males,
And female parts as well.

When courting snails pair off for love,
Do they embrace as gays?
Or Lesbians? Or two of each
That join in wondrous ways?

The puzzle that I ponder most
Is, do their dual features
Provide them half or twice the fun
Enjoyed by other creatures?*

* *Source:* Milton Hildebrand. (1979). *Laugh and love.* Hicksville, NY: Exposition Press, p. 134.

CHAPTER HIGHLIGHTS

One of the marvels of human biology is that the complex and different male and female anatomies—males with penis and scrotum; females with vagina, uterus, and breasts—arise from a single cell, the fertilized egg, which varies only in whether it carries two X chromosomes (XX) or one X and one Y (XY). Many of the structural differences between males and females arise before birth, during the prenatal period, in a process called *prenatal sexual differentiation.* Further differences also develop during puberty. It is this process of sexual differentiation—both prenatally and during puberty—which will be examined in this chapter. First, however, another biological system, the endocrine (hormonal) system, needs to be considered; particular attention will be given to the sex hormones, which play a major role in the differentiation process.

Prenatal period (pree-NAY-tul):
The nine months from conception to birth.

SEX HORMONES

Hormones:
Chemical substances secreted by the endocrine glands into the bloodstream.

Testosterone:
A hormone secreted by the testes in the male (and also present at lower levels in the female).

Androgens:
The group of "male" sex hormones, one of which is testosterone.

Estrogens (ESS-troh-jens):
The group of "female" sex hormones.

Progesterone (pro-JES-tur-ohn):
A "female" sex hormone secreted by the ovaries.

Pituitary gland (pih-TOO-ih-tair-ee):
A small endocrine gland located on the lower side of the brain next to the hypothalamus; the pituitary is important in regulating levels of sex hormones.

Hypothalamus (hy-poh-THAL-ah-mus):
A small region of the brain that is important in regulating many body functions, including sex hormones.

Hormones are powerful chemical substances manufactured by the *endocrine glands* and secreted directly into the bloodstream. Because they go into the blood, their effects are felt fairly rapidly and at places in the body quite distant from the place in which they were manufactured. The most important sex hormones are testosterone (one of a group of hormones called androgens) in the male and estrogens and progesterone in the female. The thyroid, the adrenals, and the pituitary are examples of endocrine glands. We are interested here in the sex glands: the testes in the male and the ovaries in the female. The pituitary gland and a closely related region of the brain, the hypothalamus, are also important because the pituitary regulates the other glands, in particular the testes and ovaries. Because of its importance, the pituitary has been called the "master gland" of the endocrine system. The pituitary is a small gland, about the size of a pea, which hangs down from the lower side of the brain. It is divided into three lobes: the anterior lobe, the intermediary lobe, and the posterior lobe. The anterior lobe is the one that interacts with the gonads. The hypothalamus is a region at the base of the brain just above the pituitary (see Figure 4.1); it plays a part in regulating many vital behaviors such as eating, drinking, and sexual behavior,[1] and it is important in regulating the pituitary.

These three structures, then—hypothalamus, pituitary, and gonads (testes and ovaries)—function together. They influence such important sexual functions as the menstrual cycle, pregnancy, the changes of puberty, and sexual behavior. Because

[1]One psychologist summarized the functions of the hypothalamus as being the four F's: fighting, feeding, fleeing, and, ahem, sexual behavior.

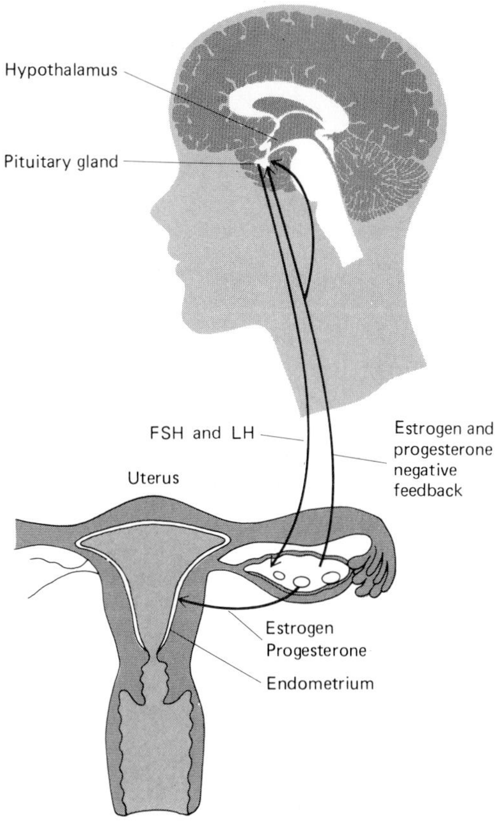

FIGURE 4.1

The hypothalamus-pituitary-gonad feedback loop in women, which regulates production of the sex hormones.

these systems are, not surprisingly, somewhat different in males and in females, the sex hormone systems in the male and in the female will be discussed separately.

Sex Hormone Systems in the Male

The pituitary and the testes both produce hormones. The important hormone produced by the testes is *testosterone*. Testosterone, the "male" sex hormone, has important functions in stimulating and maintaining the secondary sex characteristics (such as beard growth), maintaining the genitals and their sperm-producing capability, and stimulating the growth of bone and muscle.

The pituitary produces several hormones, two of which are important in this discussion: follicle-stimulating hormone (FSH) and luteinizing hormone (LH; also called *interstitial-cell-stimulating hormone* [ICSH] in the male). These hormones affect the functioning of the testes. LH (ICSH) controls the amount of testosterone production, and FSH controls sperm production.

Follicle-stimulating hormone (FSH): A hormone secreted by the pituitary; it stimulates follicle development in females and sperm production in males.

Luteinizing hormone (LH): A hormone secreted by the pituitary; it regulates estrogen secretion and ovum development in the female. In the male, it is called ICSH (interstitial-cell-stimulating hormone).

Gn-RH (gonadotropin-releasing hormone): A hormone secreted by the hypothalamus that regulates the pituitary's secretion of hormones.

Testosterone levels in males are relatively constant. These constant levels are maintained because the hypothalamus, pituitary, and testes operate in a negative feedback loop (Figure 4.2). The levels of testosterone are regulated by a substance called Gn-RH (gonadotropin-releasing hormone), which is secreted by the hypothalamus. (FSH levels are similarly regulated by Gn-RH.) The system comes full circle because the hypothalamus is sensitive to the levels of testosterone present, and thus testosterone influences the output of Gn-RH.

This negative feedback loop operates much like a thermostat-furnace system. If a room is cold, certain changes occur in the thermostat, and it signals the furnace to turn on. The action of the furnace warms the air in the room. Eventually the air becomes so warm that another change is produced in the thermostat, and it sends a signal to the furnace to turn off. The temperature in the room then gradually falls until it produces another change in the thermostat, which then turns on the furnace,

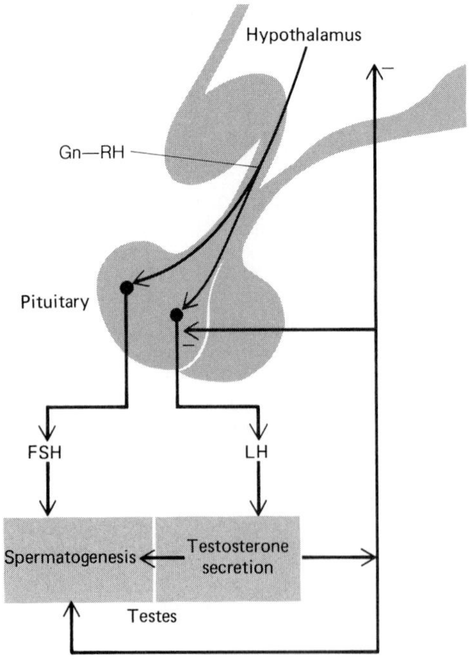

FIGURE 4.2

Schematic diagram of hormonal control of testosterone secretion and sperm production by the testes. The negative signs indicate that testosterone inhibits LH production, both in the pituitary and in the hypothalamus.

and the cycle is repeated. This is a *negative* feedback loop because *rises* in temperature turn *off* the furnace, whereas *decreases* in temperature turn *on* the furnace.

The hypothalamus, pituitary, and testes form a similar negative feedback loop, ensuring that testosterone is maintained at a fairly constant level, just as the temperature of a room is kept fairly constant. The pituitary's production of LH stimulates the testes to produce testosterone. But when testosterone levels get high, the hypothalamus reduces its production of Gn-RH; the pituitary's production of LH is then reduced, and the production of testosterone by the testes consequently decreases. When it has fallen, the hypothalamus again increases production of Gn-RH, and the process starts again.

While the level of testosterone in men is fairly constant, there is probably some cycling, with variations according to the time of the day and possibly according to the time of the month (see Chapter 5).

Inhibin:
A substance secreted by the testes, which regulates FSH levels.

A great deal of interest has been sparked recently by the discovery of a substance called inhibin (Moodbidri et al., 1980; Hafez, 1980). Although it has been clear for some time that there is a negative feedback loop between testosterone levels and LH levels, it has not been clear what regulates FSH levels. Inhibin is a substance produced by the testes (or perhaps by the sperm themselves) which appears to serve exactly that function—it acts to regulate FSH levels in a negative feedback loop.

Interest in inhibin has been so great not only because it is a kind of "missing link" in our understanding of sex hormone control but also because it shows great promise, at least theoretically, as a male contraceptive. That is, if inhibin suppresses FSH production, then sperm production in turn should be inhibited. Developments in this field in the 1990s should be interesting.

Sex Hormone Systems in the Female

The ovaries produce two important hormones, *estrogen*[2] and *progesterone*. The functions of estrogen include bringing about many of the changes of puberty (stimulating the growth of the uterus and vagina, enlarging the pelvis, and stimulating breast growth). Estrogen is also responsible for maintaining the mucous membranes of the vagina and stopping the growth of bone and muscle, which accounts for the smaller size of females as compared with males.

In adult women the levels of estrogen and progesterone fluctuate according to the various phases of the menstrual cycle (see Chapter 5) and during various other stages such as pregnancy and menopause. The levels of estrogen and progesterone are regulated by the two pituitary hormones, FSH and LH. Thus the levels of estrogen and progesterone are controlled by a negative feedback loop of the hypothalamus, pituitary, and ovaries, similar to the negative feedback loop in the male (see Figure 4.3). For example, as shown in the right side of Figure 4.3, increases in the level of Gn-RH increase the level of LH, and the increases in LH eventually produce increases in the output of estrogen; finally, the increases in the level of estrogen inhibit (decrease) the production of Gn-RH and LH.

The pituitary produces a third hormone, *prolactin,* which plays a role in stimulating secretion of milk by the mammary glands after a woman has given birth to a child.

The female sex hormone system functions much like the male sex hormone sys-

[2]"Estrogen" actually refers to a group of hormones and might more properly be called "estrogens," much as we refer to "androgens."

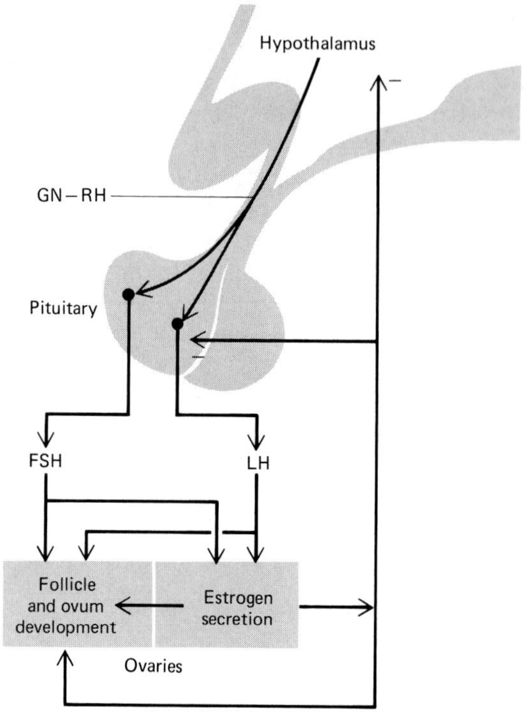

FIGURE 4.3

Schematic diagram of hormonal control of estrogen secretion and ovum production by the ovaries (during the follicular phase of the menstrual cycle). Note how similar the mechanism is to the one in the male (Figure 4.2).

tem, except that the female system is, in two senses, somewhat more complex: the ovaries produce two major hormones (unlike the testes, which produce only one), and the levels of hormones fluctuate in females, whereas levels are fairly constant in males.

The functioning of the female sex hormone system and the menstrual cycle will be considered in more detail in Chapter 5.

PRENATAL SEXUAL DIFFERENTIATION

Sex Chromosomes

As noted above, at the time of conception the future human being consists only of a single cell, the fertilized egg. The only difference between the fertilized egg that will become a female and the fertilized egg that will become a male is the sex chromosomes carried in that fertilized egg. If there are two X chromosomes, the result will normally be a female; if there is one X and one Y, the result will normally be a male. Thus, while incredibly tiny, the sex chromosomes carry a wealth of information which they transmit to various organs throughout the body, giving them instructions on how to differentiate in the course of development.

Occasionally, individuals receive at conception a sex chromosome combination other than XX or XY. Such abnormal sex chromosome complements may lead to a variety of clinical syndromes, such as Klinefelter's syndrome.

The single cell divides repeatedly, becoming a two-celled organism, then a four-celled organism, then an eight-celled organism, and so on. By the time the embryo is 28 days of age (postconception), it is about 1 centimeter (less than 1/2 inch) long, but the male and female embryo are still identical, save for the sex chromosomes; that is, the embryo is still in the undifferentiated state. However, by the fifth or sixth week after conception some basic structures have been formed that will eventually become either a male or a female reproductive system. At this point, the embryo has a pair of gonads (each gonad has two parts, an outer cortex and an inner medulla), two sets of ducts (the *Müllerian ducts* and the *Wolffian ducts*), and rudimentary external genitals (the *genital tubercle,* the *genital folds,* and the *genital swelling*) (see Figure 4.4).

FIGURE 4.4

Development of the male and female genitals from the undifferentiated stage. This occurs during prenatal development. Note homologous organs in the female and male.

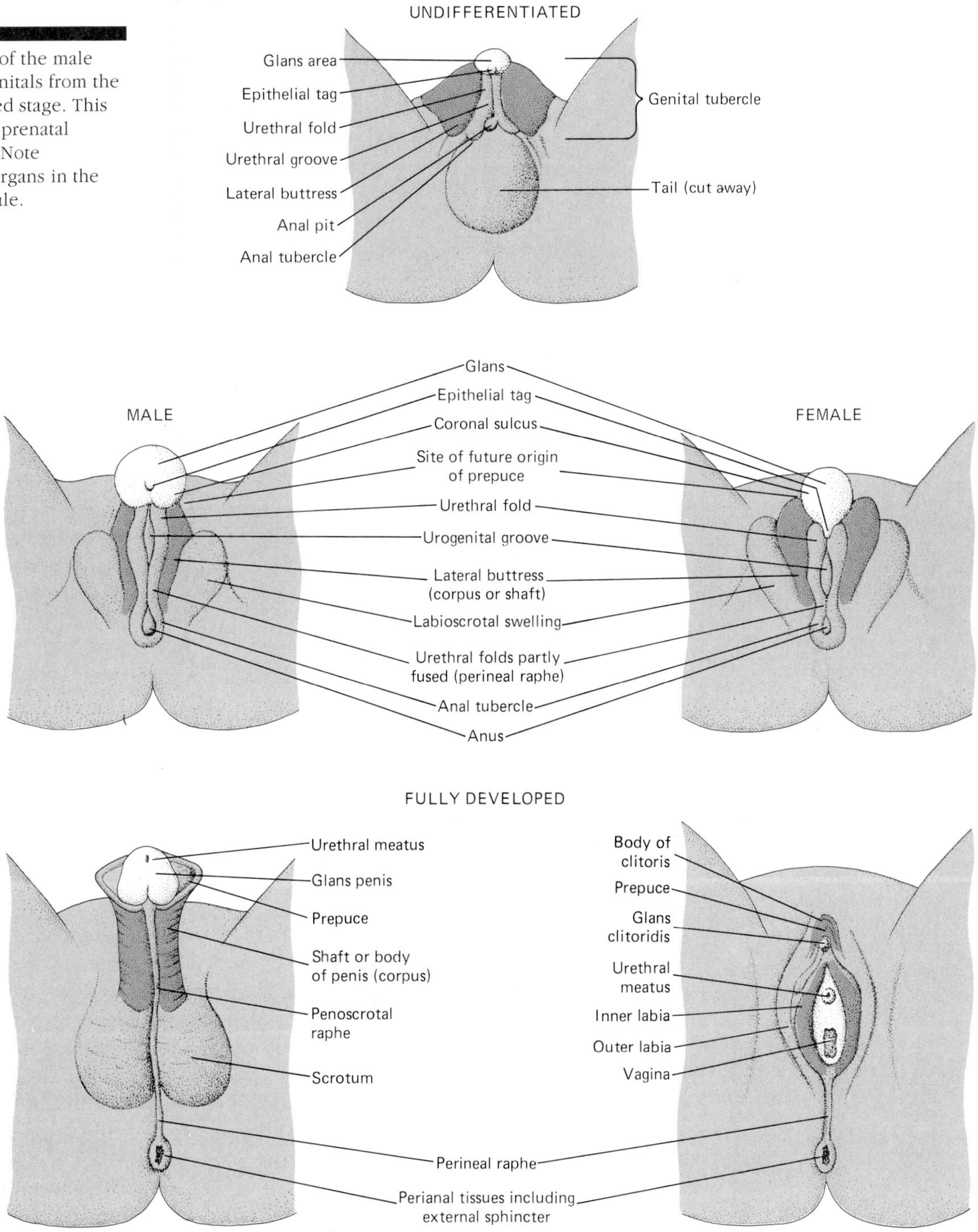

Gonads

Around the seventh week after conception, the sex chromosomes direct the gonads to begin differentiation. In the male, the undifferentiated gonad develops into a testis at about 7 weeks. In the female, the process occurs somewhat later, with the ovaries developing at around 11 or 12 weeks.

There has been a good deal of speculation about the exact mechanisms by which the presence of XX chromosomes causes ovaries to develop. Basically, it appears that the presence or absence of a Y chromosome is critical. If no Y chromosome is present, ovaries differentiate, and female development occurs; if a Y is present, testes differentiate, and male development occurs. Apparently, the Y chromosome produces a substance which induces the differentiation of testes (Jost, 1970).

Hormones and the Internal and External Genitals

Once the ovaries and testes have differentiated, they begin to produce different sex hormones, and these hormones then direct the differentiation of the rest of the internal and external genital system (see Figure 4.4).

Müllerian ducts: Ducts found in both male and female fetuses; in males they degenerate and in females they develop into the fallopian tubes, the uterus, and the upper part of the vagina.

Wolffian ducts: Ducts found in both male and female fetuses; in females they degenerate and in males they develop into the epididymis, the vas, and the ejaculatory duct.

In the female the Wolffian ducts degenerate, and the Müllerian ducts turn into the fallopian tubes, the uterus, and the upper part of the vagina. The tubercle becomes the clitoris, the folds become the inner lips, and the swelling develops into the outer lips.

In the male the testes secrete *Müllerian inhibiting substance,* which causes the Müllerian ducts to degenerate, and the Wolffian ducts turn into the epididymis, the vas deferens, and the ejaculatory duct. The tubercle becomes the glans penis, the folds form the shaft of the penis, and the swelling develops into the scrotum.

The mechanism by which the internal and external genitals differentiate has been the subject of much research. The principle seems to be parallel to that for differentiation of gonads; it appears that the presence or absence of the testes and their hormone production is critical. The testes of the male fetus secrete androgens, which stimulate the development of male structures, and a second substance, the Müllerian inhibiting substance which suppresses the development of the Müllerian ducts. Thus if the hormonal output of the testes is present, male structures develop. If it is absent, female structures develop.

By four months after conception, the gender of the fetus is clear from the appearance of the external genitals (Figure 4.4).

Descent of the Testes and Ovaries

As the developmental changes are taking place, the ovaries and testes are changing in shape and position. At first, the ovaries and testes lie near the top of the abdominal cavity. By the tenth week they have grown and have moved down to the level of the upper edge of the pelvis. The ovaries remain there until after birth; later they shift to their adult position in the pelvis.

The male testes must make a much longer journey, down into the scrotum via a passageway called the *inguinal canal.* Normally this movement occurs around the seventh month after conception. After the descent of the testes, the inguinal canal is closed off.

Two problems in this process may occur. First, one or both testes may have failed to descend into the scrotum by the time of birth, a condition known as *undescended*

Cryptorchidism: Undescended testes; the condition in which the testes do not descend to the scrotum as they should during prenatal development.

testes, or cryptorchidism This occurs in about 2 percent of all males. In most of these cases, the testes do descend by puberty, and so only about 1 in 500 adult men has undescended testes. If the testes do not descend spontaneously, however, the condition must be corrected by surgery or hormonal therapy. The optimum time for doing this is before age 5. Otherwise, if both testes have failed to descend, the man would be sterile because, as was discussed in Chapter 3, the high temperature of the testes inside the body would inhibit the production of sperm. Undescended testes are also more likely to develop cancer.

The second possible problem occurs when the inguinal canal does not close off completely. It may then reopen later in life, creating a passageway through which loops of the intestine may enter the scrotum. This condition is called *inguinal hernia* and can be remedied by simple surgery.

Brain Differentiation

Yes, there are differences between male and female brains (MacLusky and Naftolin, 1981). The differences are found in the hypothalamus, and they result from a differentiation process in prenatal development much like the differentiation process that creates reproductive-system differences (Money and Ehrhardt, 1972). Once the gonads have differentiated, if testosterone is produced, the hypothalamus differentiates in the male direction; if testosterone is absent, the differentiation is in the female direction.

Anatomically, the consequences of this differentiation are that the cells and the neural circuits of the hypothalamus differ somewhat for males and females. Physiologically, an important consequence is that beginning in puberty, the female hypothalamus directs a cyclic secretion of sex hormones, creating the menstrual cycle; the male hypothalamus directs a relatively acyclic, or constant, production of sex hormones.

The brain differentiation probably also has some consequences in terms of behavior, most notably sexual behavior, and aggressive behavior and possibly other behaviors as well. Unfortunately, most of the research on this point has been done with animals, and so there is some debate over whether the effects also occur in humans. This research will be discussed in detail in Chapter 8.

TABLE 4.1

HOMOLOGOUS AND ANALOGOUS ORGANS OF THE MALE AND FEMALE REPRODUCTIVE SYSTEMS

	Homologous Organs		Analogous Organs	
Embryonic Source	**In the Adult Male**	**In the Adult Female**	**In the Adult Male**	**In the Adult Female**
Gonad (medulla plus cortex)	Testes (from medulla)	Ovaries (from cortex)	Testes (from medulla)	Ovaries (from cortex)
Genital tubercle	Glans penis	Clitoris	Glans penis	Clitoris
Genital swelling	Scrotum	Outer lips		
Müllerian duct	Degenerates, leaving only remnants	Fallopian tubes; uterus, part of vagina		
Wolffian duct	Epididymis, vas deferens, seminal vesicles	Degenerates, leaving only remnants		
Urethral primordia	Prostate, Cowper's glands	Skene's glands, Bartholin's glands	Prostate, Cowper's glands	Skene's glands, Bartholin's glands

Homologous organs (huh-MOLL-uh-gus): Organs in the male and female that develop from the same embryonic tissue.

Analogous organs: Organs in the male and female that have similar functions.

Homologous Organs

The preceding discussion of sexual differentiation highlights the fact that although adult men and women appear to have very different reproductive anatomies, their reproductive organs have similar origins. When an organ in the male and an organ in the female both develop from the same embryonic tissue, the organs are said to be homologous When the two organs have similar functions, they are said to be analogous Table 4.1 summarizes the major homologies and analogies of the male and female reproductive systems. For example, ovaries and testes are both homologous (they develop from an indifferent gonad) and analogous (they produce germ cells and sex hormones.)

JOHN MONEY, HERMAPHRODITES, AND THE EIGHT VARIABLES OF GENDER

Gender is not a simple matter, a fact which is apparent from the preceding discussion. Most people, however, assume that it is. That is, people typically assume that if a person is female, she will be feminine; will think of herself as a woman; will be sexually attracted to men; will have a clitoris, vagina, uterus, and ovaries; and will have sex chromosomes XX. The parallel assumption is that all males are masculine; think of themselves as male; are sexually attracted to women; have a penis, testes, and scrotum; and have sex chromosomes XY.

A major research program of the last several decades, conducted at Johns Hopkins University by the psychologist John Money and his colleagues, challenges these assumptions and provides a great deal of information about sexuality and gender and their development. (For an excellent summary of this research, see Money and Ehrhardt, 1972.) Before the results of this research are discussed, however, some background information is necessary.

First, it is important to understand the distinctions among the eight variables of gender.[3]

1. *Chromosomal gender* XX in the female; XY in the male
2. *Gonadal gender* Ovaries in the female; testes in the male
3. *Hormonal gender* Estrogen and progesterone in the female; testosterone in the male
4. *Internal accessory organs* Uterus and vagina in the female; prostate and seminal vesicles in the male
5. *External genital appearance* Clitoris and vaginal opening in the female; penis and scrotum in the male
6. *Assigned gender* The announcement at birth, "It's a girl" or "It's a boy," based on the appearance of the external genitals; the gender the parents and the rest of society believe the child to be; the gender in which the child is reared
7. *Gender identity* The person's private, internal sense of maleness or femaleness—which is expressed in personality and behavior—and the integration of

[3]The first six variables in this list are based on Money's six variables of sex. The last two were added for completeness and clarity. The distinction between the terms "gender" and "sex," discussed in Chapter 1, is being maintained here.

FIGURE 4.5

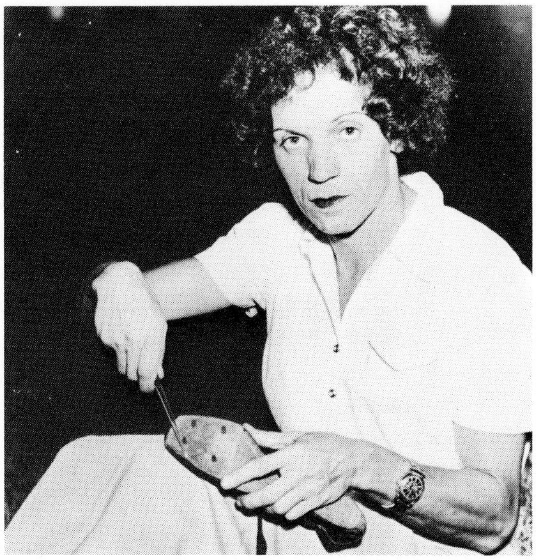

The death, in 1980, of Stella Walsh, aged 69, attracted widespread publicity. Walsh had been a star in women's track competition in the 1930s, winning five gold, one bronze, and three silver medals in international competition. She won the gold medal in the 100-meter dash in the 1932 Olympics, running it in a record 11.9 seconds. She continued on in many events, winning the national pentathlon championship in 1954 at the age of 43. The coroner's report at her death revealed some startling findings, however. Genetically, she was a mosaic—that is, some of the cells in her body contained the male sex chromosome combination (XY) and some contained the female sex chromosomes (XX). Anatomically, she had male sex organs, but they were nonfunctional. Her hair was balding. Yet she had been raised and lived as a female. Unfortunately, the research and treatments of John Money and others were not available in her childhood and certainly her case would be handled differently today. She was married to a man in 1956 for two months. Her former husband, in an interview, said that they had sex a couple of times, always with the lights out. At the time of her death, Walsh was employed by the city of Cleveland in a coaching-type job for the recreation department at a salary of $10,000, the highest one she ever attained.

this sense with the rest of the personality and with the gender roles prescribed by society

8. *Choice of sexual partner* Sexual attraction to members of the same gender, members of the other gender, or both

These variables might be subdivided into biological variables (the first five) and psychological variables (the last three). The discussion that follows will be concerned chiefly with the first seven of these variables. Variable 8, choice of sexual partner, will be discussed in Chapter 16.

In most cases, of course, all variables 1 through 7 are in agreement in an individual. That is, in most cases the person is a "consistent" female or male. If the person is a female, she has XX chromosomes, ovaries, a uterus and vagina, and a clitoris; she is reared as a female; and she thinks of herself as a female. If the person is a male, he has the parallel set of appropriate characteristics.

However, as a result of a number of "accidents" during the course of prenatal sexual development and differentiation, the gender indicated by one or more of these variables may disagree with the gender indicated by others. When the contradictions are among several of the biological variables (1 through 5), the person is called a pseudohermaphrodite or a *hermaphrodite.*[4] Biologically, the gender of such a person is ambiguous; the reproductive structures may be partly male and partly female, or they may be incompletely male or incompletely female. It is these individuals upon whom Money's research is based.

Pseudohermaphrodite: An individual who has a mixture of male and female reproductive structures, so that it is not clear whether the individual is a male or a female.

A number of syndromes can cause pseudohermaphroditism, some of the most common being the adrenogenital syndrome, progestin-induced hermaphroditism, and the androgen insensitivity syndrome. In the *adrenogenital syndrome,* a genetic female develops ovaries normally as a fetus; later in the course of prenatal development, however, the adrenal gland begins to function abnormally (as a result of a recessive genetic condition unconnected with the sex chromosomes), and an excess amount of androgens is produced. Prenatal sexual differentiation then does not fol-

[4]The term "hermaphrodite" is taken from Hermaphroditos, the name of the mythological son of Hermes and Aphrodite. The latter was the Greek goddess of love.

F • O • C • U • S 4.1

TWO CASE HISTORIES FROM THE JOHNS HOPKINS CLINIC

The two individuals discussed below are interesting because both are genetic females (both with the adrenogenital syndrome), and yet one eventually became a female with a female gender identity, while the other eventually became a male with a male gender identity.

The first member of the pair was reared as a girl but was actually announced as a boy at birth because of the appearance of the genitals (Figure 4.6). The correct diagnosis was established by the age of 2 months, and a sex reannouncement was decided upon. The parents were counseled on how to make such an announcement within the family and the community, and they accomplished this successfully. Today it is known that the first stage of surgical feminization could have been done immediately, but at the time it was delayed until the age of 2 years as a precaution against surgically induced trauma. After the surgery, the child had an unremarkable childhood medically, except for the fact that she took cortisone pills daily. Her breast development began at the age of 13, and menstruation did not begin until age 20.

During childhood, she developed behaviorally as a girl with tomboyish tendencies. In adolescence, academic and career interests had priority over dating and romance. There was no romantic inclination toward either boys or girls, but rather a projection of boyfriends and marriage into the future. The girl was attractive and feminine.

The second member of the pair was diagnosed at birth as a male with a hypospadiac phallus and undescended testes. Three stages of surgical masculinization ended in failure because urine backed up into the internal vagina and caused infection. At age 3½ a correct diagnosis was made, and the case was referred to Johns Hopkins. At this time, being in a hospital again terrified the child. He said that a nurse would cut off his "wee-wee" and that his baby sister had had hers cut off. His terror abated when, with clay and water, he was shown how an imperfect penis could be repaired.

low the normal female course. As a result, the external genitals are partly or completely male in appearance; the labia are partly or totally fused (and thus there is no vaginal opening), and the clitoris is enlarged to the size of a small penis (see Figure 4.6). Hence at birth these genetic females are often identified as males. *Progestin-induced hermaphroditism* is a similar syndrome which resulted from a drug, progestin, which was at one time given to pregnant women to help them maintain the pregnancy if they were prone to miscarriage. (The drug is no longer prescribed because of the effects described below.) As the drug circulated in the mother's bloodstream, the developing fetus was essentially exposed to a high dose of androgens. (Progestin and androgens are quite similar biochemicals, and in the body the

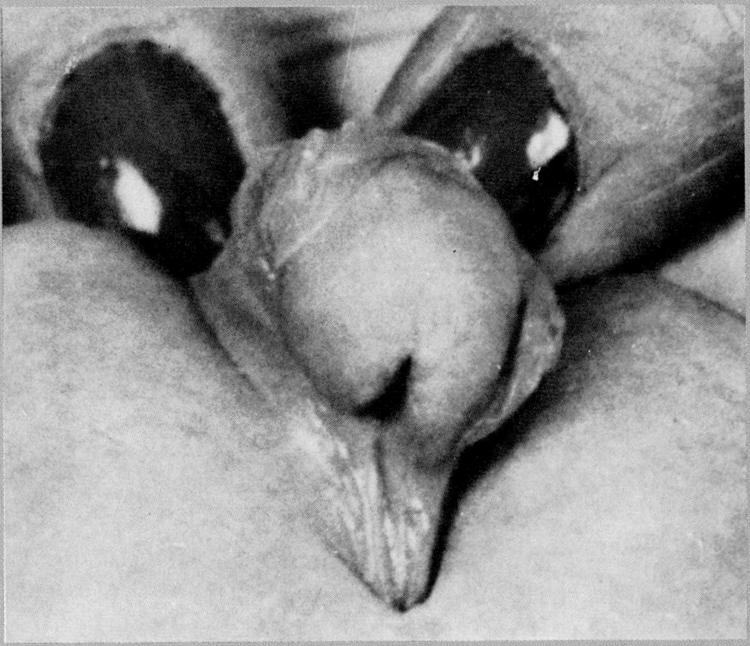

FIGURE 4.6

The appearance, at birth, of the genitals of a pseudo-hermaphrodite. She was a genetic female and was surgically corrected and reared as a female. The appearance of the genitals of a genetic female who is surgically corrected and reared as a male is similar.

It was decided to allow him to continue living as a boy. The appropriate surgery was done, and he was given cortisone therapy during childhood. At the time of puberty, masculinization was induced by androgen therapy. Artificial testes were implanted in the empty scrotum.

Unfortunately, as the boy approached adolescence, his family life was tortured. His parents fought. The mother won points by reminding her husband that he was not the father of this particular child, and the boy heard what she said.

In adolescence the boy was an academic underachiever, and he tended to seek the company of quasi-delinquents, with whom he could achieve status as a rebel. He was accepted by the other boys as one of them. He was not overly aggressive. Psychosexually, all his romantic feelings and approaches were directed toward girls, despite his trepidation at the prospect of attempting intercourse with a penis that was too small and with prosthetic testes that could be recognized on touching as not soft enough.

Thus, although both members of the pair were genetically and anatomically identical at birth, one eventually became a female functioning adequately in the female role, while the other became a male functioning adequately in the male role.

Source: John Money and Anke Ehrhardt. *Man and woman, boy and girl.* Baltimore: Johns Hopkins, 1972, pp. 154–156.

progestin acted like androgen.) In genetic females this produced an abnormal, masculinized genital development similar to that found in the adrenogenital syndrome. The reverse case occurs in *androgen insensitivity syndrome.* In this syndrome a genetic male produces normal levels of testosterone; however, as a result of a genetic condition, the body tissues are insensitive to the testosterone, and prenatal development is feminized. Thus the individual is born with the external appearance of a female: a small vagina (but no uterus) and undescended testes.

Several important findings have emerged from Money's studies of these individuals. First, the research provides good evidence of the great complexity of sex and gender and their development. Many variables are involved in gender and sex, and many steps are involved in gender differentiation, even before birth. Because the process is complex, it is very vulnerable to disturbances, creating conditions such as hermaphroditism. Indeed, the research serves to question our basic notions of what it means to be male or female. In the adrenogenital syndrome, is the genetic female who is born with male external genitals a male or a female? What makes a person male or female? Chromosomal gender? External genital appearance? Gender identity?

A second important result from this research has to do with gender identity and how it develops. There has been a debate over whether gender identity is biologically programmed in an individual or environmentally produced through learning. Money argues an environmentalist position. As evidence, he cites cases of matched pairs of pseudohermaphrodites (see Focus). If such a child is assigned to be a female and is reared as a female (with appropriate corrective surgery and hormone therapy), she adjusts well in the female role and has a female gender identity. If a child with the identical syndrome at birth is assigned to be a male and is reared accordingly (once again with surgical and hormonal treatment), he adjusts well to the male role and has a male gender identity. Thus, Money argues that the human is "psychosexually neutral" at birth and that gender identity is produced by the environment and learning.

However, there do seem to be some limitations to the arbitrariness with which gender can be assigned or reassigned by the environment. Gender reassignment can be done very successfully, as the case histories indicate, up to the age of about 18 months. After that time, reassignment is difficult (and in most cases impossible) and causes serious problems of adjustment, apparently because the child begins forming a strong concept of his or her own gender identity at around 18 months of age (Kohlberg, 1966; Money and Ehrhardt, 1972). Once this basic concept is formed, it is essentially irreversible. Attempts at reassignment are futile.

Money's research and conclusions could be criticized on two grounds. First, in all the cases given as evidence, sex reassignment was supplemented by appropriate surgical or hormonal therapy. That is, the individual's biology was modified to correspond to the assigned gender. Hence it is not reasonable to say that gender can be environmentally assigned independent of biological gender characteristics. Second, it is difficult to know how relevant the abnormal cases that Money studied are to an understanding of the normal process of acquiring a gender identity.

Nonetheless, Money's data do provide impressive evidence on abnormalities of prenatal sexual differentiation, on the complexity of sex and gender, and on the environmental determinants of gender identity.

Diamond's Biased Interaction Model

Reproductive biologist Milton Diamond (1965, 1979) has proposed a model in opposition to Money's environmentalist theory of the determination of gender identity. According to Diamond's *biased interaction model,* gender identity and sexuality are influenced by environmental forces, but this influence is significantly affected by the individual's biological makeup, specifically genes and hormones. Diamond does not deny environmental forces. Rather, he claims that gender identity and sexuality are an outcome of an interaction between biology and environment, with biology biasing the interaction. Thus, according to his position, it is not surprising that the vast majority of people have a gender identity that agrees with their genetic gender and their hormonal gender.

As evidence for his position, Diamond cites the criticisms of Money's environmentalist work noted above. In particular, successful sex reassignment, as in the cases discussed in the Focus, is accompanied not only by environmental changes but by biological changes as well (hormone therapy and surgery to change anatomy). This biological therapy may have been essential to the success of their change in gender identity.

Diamond also cites both animal studies and human studies indicating the effect of biological factors in determining gender identity. One classic study was of an accidental experiment in a small community in the Dominican Republic (Imperato-McGinley et al., 1974). Due to a genetic-endocrine problem, a large number of genetic males were born who, at birth, appeared to be females. They had a vaginal pouch instead of a scrotum and a clitoris-sized penis. The uneducated parents were unaware that there were any problems, and these genetic males were treated as typical females. At puberty, a spontaneous biological change caused a penis to develop. Significantly, their psychological orientation also changed. Despite rearing as females, their gender identity switched to male, and they developed heterosexual interests. Thus all the forces of environment to that point had no effect when biology changed. Biology definitely biased the outcome of their gender identity, just as Diamond's biased interaction model would predict.

PUBERTY

Puberty:
The time during which there is sudden enlargement and maturation of the gonads, other genitalia, and secondary sex characteristics, so that the individual is capable of reproduction.

Puberty is not a point in time, but rather a process. It is the stage in life during which the body changes from that of a child into that of an adult, with secondary sexual characteristics and the ability to reproduce sexually. Puberty can be scientifically defined as the time during which there is sudden enlargement and maturation of the gonads, other genitalia, and secondary sex characteristics, leading to reproductive capacity (Tanner, 1967). It is the second important period—the other being the prenatal period—during which sexual differentiation takes place. Perhaps the most important single event in the process is the first ejaculation for the male and the first menstruation for the female, although the latter is not necessarily a sign of reproductive capability, since girls typically do not produce mature eggs until a year or two after the first menstruation.

The physiological process which underlies puberty in both genders is a marked increase in the level of sex hormones. Thus the hypothalamus, pituitary, and gonads control the changes.

Adolescence is a socially defined period of development which bears some relationship to puberty. Adolescence represents a psychological transition from the behavior and attitudes of a child to the behavior, attitudes, and responsibilities of an adult. In the United States it corresponds roughly to the teenage years. Modern American culture has an unusually long period of adolescence. A century ago, adolescence was much shorter; the lengthening of the educational process has served to prolong adolescence. In some cultures, in fact, adolescence does not exist; the child shifts to being an adult directly, with only a *rite de passage* in between.

Before describing the changes that take place during puberty, two points should be noted. First, the timing of the pubertal process differs considerably for males and females. Girls begin the change around 8 to 12 years of age, while boys do so about two years later. Girls reach their full height by about age 16, while boys continue growing until about age 18 or later. Mother Nature's capriciousness in allowing males and females to be out of step with each other at this stage creates no small number of crises for the adolescent. Girls are interested in boys long before boys are aware that girls exist. A girl may be stuck with a date who barely reaches her armpits, while the boy may have to cope with someone who is better qualified to be on the basketball team than he is.

Second, there are large individual differences (differences from one person to the next) in the age at which the processes of puberty take place. Thus there is no "normal" time to begin menstruating or growing a beard. Accordingly, age ranges are given in describing the timing of the process.

Changes in the Female

The first sign of pubescence in the female is the beginning of breast development, which generally starts at around 8 to 13 years of age. The ducts in the nipple area swell, and there is a growth of fatty and connective tissue, causing the nipples to project forward and the small, conical buds to increase in size. These changes are produced by increases in the levels of the sex hormones by a mechanism that will be described below.

As the growth of fatty and supporting tissue increases in the breasts, a similar increase takes place at the hips and buttocks, leading to the rounded contours that distinguish adult female bodies from adult male bodies. Individual females have unique patterns of fat deposit, and so there are also considerable individual differences in the resulting female shapes.

Another visible sign of pubescence is the growth of pubic hair, which occurs shortly after breast development begins. About two years later, axillary (underarm) hair appears.

Body growth increases sharply during pubescence, approximately during the age range of 9.5 to 14.5 years. The growth spurt for girls occurs about two years before the growth spurt for boys (Figure 4.7). This is consistent with girls' general pattern of maturing earlier than boys. Even prenatally, girls show an earlier hardening of the structures that become bones. One exception to this pattern is in fertility; boys produce mature sperm earlier than girls produce mature ova.

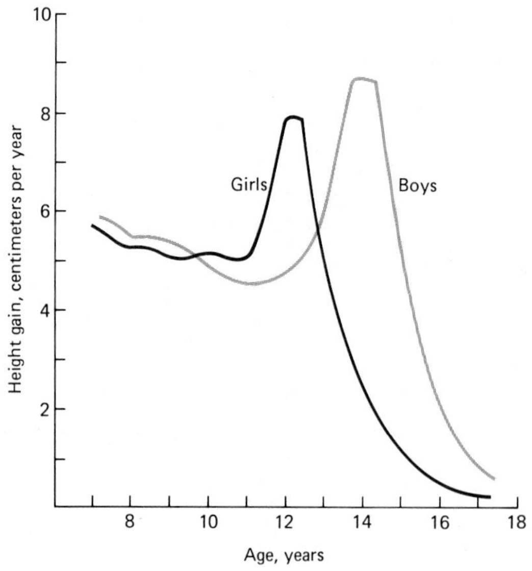

FIGURE 4.7

The adolescent spurt of growth for boys and girls. Note that girls experience their growth spurt earlier than boys do.

Menarche (MEN-ar-key): First menstruation.

Estrogen eventually applies the brakes to the growth spurt in girls; the presence of estrogen also causes the growth period to end sooner in girls, thus accounting for the lesser height of adult women as compared with adult men.

At about 13 years of age, the menarche (first menstruation) occurs. The girl, however, is not capable of becoming pregnant until ovulation begins, typically about two years after the menarche. The first menstruation is not only an important biological event but also an important psychological one. Various cultures have ceremonies recognizing its importance. In Orthodox Jewish families, the mother slaps the girl on the face. In other families, it is a piece of news that spreads quickly to the relatives. Girls themselves display a wide range of reactions to the event, ranging from negative ones, such as fear, shame, or disgust, to positive ones, such as a sense of pride, maturity, and womanliness. Some of the most negative reactions occur when the girl has not been prepared for the menarche, which is still the case in a surprisingly large number of families.

Parents who are concerned about preparing their daughters for the first menstruation should remember that there is a wide range in the age at which it occurs. It is not unusual for a girl to start menstruating in the fifth grade, and instances of the menarche during the fourth grade, while rare, do occur. The youngest mother on record was a 5-year-old Peruvian Indian girl who gave birth to a healthy baby by cesarean section in 1939. Despite her youth, she was sexually mature, and physicians confirmed that she had menstruated since she was perhaps 1 month old. The youngest set of parents on record was a Chinese couple who were blessed with a son in 1910. The father was 9; the mother was 8.

The age at which girls begin to menstruate has been dropping steadily for the last several centuries (Figure 4.8). For example, in Germany the average age at the menarche was 16.6 years in 1795 and 14.5 years in 1920 (Sexual maturity and climate, 1961). In the United States the aveage age was 13.5 in the 1930s and dropped to somewhat less than 13 in the mid-1960s. The indication now, though, is that the trend is leveling off.

What determines the age at which a girl first menstruates? One explanation is the

FIGURE 4.8

Girls today begin menstruating considerably earlier than girls a century ago did.

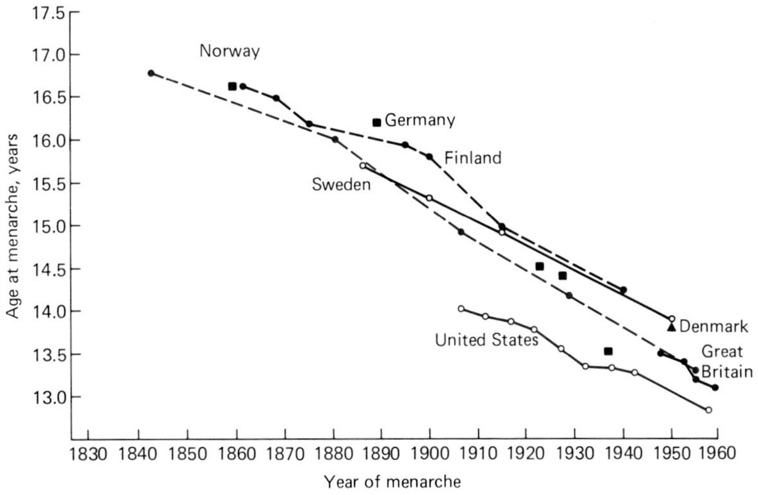

percent body fat hypothesis (Fishman, 1980; Frisch and McArthur, 1974). During puberty, deposits of body fat increase in females. According to the percent body fat hypothesis, the percentage of body weight that is fat has to rise to a certain level for menstruation to occur for the first time and in order for it to be maintained. Thus, very skinny adolescent girls would tend to be late in the timing of first menstruation. The percent body fat hypothesis also helps to make sense of two related phenomena: the cessation of menstruation in anorexics and the cessation of menstruation in women joggers. *Anorexia nervosa* refers to a condition in which the person—most commonly an adolescent girl—engages in compulsive, extreme dieting, perhaps to the point of starving herself to death. As anorexia progresses, the percentage of body fat declines and menstruation ceases. It is also fairly common for women who are joggers, and all women who exercise seriously to the point where their body fat is substantially reduced, to cease menstruating. For both anorexics and female joggers, it seems that when the percentage of body fat falls below a critical value, the biological mechanisms controlling the menstrual cycle shut off the functions producing menstruation.

Before we leave the topic of jogging, I should note that there is some evidence that serious exercise also affects the male reproductive system. One study of male distance runners found that their testosterone levels were only about 68 percent as high, on the average, as a control group's testosterone levels (Wheeler et al., 1984). There are some reports of male long-distance runners complaining of a loss of sex drive, but it is unclear whether it results from reduced testosterone levels or from the perpetual feelings of fatigue they have from their intensive training (Wheeler et al., 1984).

Other body changes during puberty include a development of the blood supply to the clitoris, a thickening of the walls of the vagina, and a rapid growth of the uterus, which doubles in size between the tenth and the eighteenth years. The pelvic bone structure grows and widens, contributing to the rounded shape of the female and creating a passageway large enough for an infant to move through during birth. Once again, there are large individual differences in the shape of the pelvis, and it is important for the physician to identify shapes that may lead to problems in childbirth.

The dramatic changes that occur during pubescence are produced, basically, by the endocrine system and its upsurge in sex hormone production during puberty. The process begins with an increase in secretion of FSH by the pituitary gland. FSH in turn stimulates the ovaries to produce estrogen. Estrogen is responsible for many of the changes that occur; it stimulates breast growth and the growth of the uterus and vagina.

Adrenal gland (uh-DREE-nul):
An endocrine gland located just above the kidney; in the female, it is the major producer of androgens.

Another endocrine gland involved in pubertal changes is the adrenal gland which is located just above the kidney. In the female, the adrenal gland is the major producer of androgens (male sex hormones), which exist at low levels in females. Adrenal androgens stimulate the growth of pubic and axillary hair and may be related to the female sex drive. They also may be related to the development of *acne,* a distressing problem of adolescence that is caused by a clogging of the sebaceous (oil-producing) glands, resulting in pustules, blackheads, and redness on the face and possibly the chest and back. Generally it is not severe enough to be a medical problem, although its psychological impact may be great. In order to avoid scarring, severe cases should be treated by a physician, the treatment typically being ultraviolet light and/or antibiotics.

Another problem for some girls during puberty is a temporary period of overweight or obesity. If the weight gain is not excessive and lasts for only a short period, there is no cause for concern.

Changes in the Male

As noted above, puberty begins at about 10 or 11 years of age in boys, about two years later than it does in girls.

The physical causes of puberty in boys parallel those in girls. They are initiated by increased production of FSH and LH by the pituitary. Recall that LH is called ICSH (interstitial-cell-stimulating hormone) in males because it stimulates the interstitial cells of the testes to produce testosterone. At the beginning of puberty, the increase in ICSH stimulates the testes to produce testosterone, which is responsible for most of the changes of puberty in the male.

The first noticeable pubertal change in males is the growth of the testes and scrotal sac, which begins at around 10 to 13 years of age as a result of testosterone stimulation. The growth of pubic hair begins at about the same time. About a year later the penis begins to enlarge, first thickening, and then lengthening. This change also results from testosterone stimulation. Then as the testes enlarge, their production of testosterone increases even more; thus there is rapid growth of the penis, testes, and pubic hair at ages 13 and 14.

The growth of facial and axillary hair begins about two years after the beginning of pubic-hair growth. The growth of facial hair begins with the appearance of fuzz on the upper lip; adult beards do not appear until two or three years later. Indeed, by age 17, 50 percent of American males have not yet shaved. These changes also result from testosterone stimulation, which continues to produce growth of facial and chest hair beyond 20 years of age.

Erections increase in frequency. The organs that produce the fluid of semen, particularly the prostate, enlarge considerably at about the same time the other organs are growing. By age 13 or 14 the boy is capable of ejaculation. Previously, he was able to have orgasms, but they were not accompanied by ejaculation.[5] By about age 15, the ejaculate contains mature sperm, and the male is now fertile. The pituitary hormone FSH is responsible for initiating and maintaining the production of mature sperm.

Beginning about a year after the first ejaculation, the boy begins having nocturnal emissions, or "wet dreams." For the boy who has never masturbated, a wet dream may be his first ejaculation.

At about the same time penis growth occurs, the larynx ("voice box") also begins to grow in response to testosterone. As the larynx enlarges, the boy's voice drops, or "changes." Typically the transition occurs at around age 13 or 14. Because testosterone is necessary to produce the change in voice, castration before puberty results in a male with a permanently high voice. This principle was used to produce the castrati, who sang in the great choirs of Europe during the eighteenth century. They began as lovely boy sopranos, and their parents or the choirmaster, hating to see their beautiful voices destroyed in puberty, had them castrated so that they

---

[5]Note that orgasm and ejaculation are two separate processes, even though they generally occur together, at least in males after puberty. But orgasm may occur without ejaculation, and ejaculation may occur without orgasm.

TABLE 4.2

SUMMARY OF THE CHANGES OF PUBERTY AND THEIR SEQUENCE

Note the similarities and differences between boys and girls.

Girls			Boys		
Characteristic	Age of First Appearance (Years)	Major Hormonal Influence	Characteristic	Age of First Appearance (Years)	Major Hormonal Influence
1. Growth of breasts	8–13	Pituitary growth hormone, estrogens, progesterone, thyroxine	**1.** Growth of testes, scrotal sac	10–13.5	Pituitary growth hormone, testosterone
2. Growth of pubic hair	8–14	Adrenal androgens	**2.** Growth of pubic hair	10–15	Testosterone
3. Body growth	9.5–14.5	Pituitary growth hormone, adrenal androgens, estrogens	**3.** Body growth	10.5–16	Pituitary growth hormone, testosterone
4. Menarche	10–16.5	Hypothalamic releasing factors, FSH, LH, estrogens, progesterone	**4.** Growth of penis	11–14.5	Testosterone
			5. Change in voice (growth of larynx)	About the same time as penis growth	Testosterone
5. Underarm hair	About two years after pubic hair	Adrenal androgens	**6.** Facial and underarm hair	About two years after pubic hair	Testosterone
6. Oil- and sweat-producing glands (acne occurs when glands are clogged)	About the same time as underarm hair	Adrenal androgens	**7.** Oil- and sweat-producing glands, acne	About the same time as underarm hair	Testosterone

Source: After B. Goldstein. (1976). *Introduction to human sexuality.* New York: McGraw-Hill, pp. 80–81.

remained permanent sopranos. Female bodies are not the only ones that have been mutilated for strange reasons! Contrary to popular belief, castration in adulthood will not produce a high voice because the larynx has already grown.

Like the age at which the menarche takes place, the average age at which the voice changes has declined over the last several centuries. For example, at the time of the eighteenth-century Bach Boys' Choir in Leipzig, voice change occurred, on the average, at age 18 (one assumes that castrati were excluded from the calculations). In London in 1959, it occurred on the average at age 13.3 years (Sullivan, 1971).

A great spurt of body growth begins in males at around 11 to 16 years of age (Figure 4.7). Height increases rapidly. Body contours also change. While the changes in girls involve mainly the increase in fatty tissue in the breasts and hips, the changes in boys involve mainly an increase in muscle mass. Eventually testosterone brings the growth process to an end, although it permits the growth period to continue longer than it does in females.

Puberty brings changes and also problems. As noted previously, one of them is acne, which affects boys more frequently than girls. Gynecomastia (breast enlargement) may occur temporarily in boys, creating considerable embarrassment. About 80 percent of boys in puberty experience this problem, which is probably caused by small amounts of female sex hormones produced by the testes. Obesity may also be a temporary problem, although it is more frequent in girls than boys.

In various cultures around the world, puberty rites are performed to signify the boy's passage to manhood. In the United States the only remaining vestiges of such ceremonies are the Jewish bar mitzvah and, in Christian churches, confirmation. In a sense, it is unfortunate that we do not give more formal recognition to puberty. Puberty rites probably serve an important psychological function in that they are a formal, public announcement of the fact that the boy or girl is passing through an important and difficult period of change. In the absence of such rituals, the young person may think that his or her body is doing strange things and may feel very much alone. This might be particularly problematic for boys, who lack an obvious sign of puberty like the first menstruation (the first ejaculation is probably the closest analogy) to help them identify the stage they are in.

SUMMARY

The sex hormone systems in males and females were discussed in the first section. The major sex hormones are testosterone, which is produced by the male's testes, and estrogen and progesterone, which are produced by the female's ovaries. Levels of the sex hormones are regulated by two hormones secreted by the pituitary: FSH (follicle-stimulating hormone) and LH (luteinizing hormone, or, in the male, interstitial-cell-stimulating hormone [ICSH]). The gonads, pituitary, and hypothalamus regulate one another's output through a negative feedback loop. Inhibin is a recently discovered substance that regulates FSH levels.

Next the process of prenatal sexual differentiation was considered. At conception males and females differ only in the sex chromosomes (XX in females and XY in males). As the fetus grows, the chromosomes direct the gonads to differentiate into the testes or ovaries. Different hormones are then produced by the gonads, and these stimulate further differentiation of the internal and external reproductive structures as well as differentiation of the hypothalamus. A male organ and a female organ which derive from the same embryonic tissue are said to be homologous to each other.

An important distinction between the eight variables of gender arises from John Money's research on hermaphrodites. Pseudohermaphroditism is generally the result of various accidents that occur during the course of prenatal sexual differentiation. Money's work has important implications for an understanding of the environmental determinants of the development of gender identity. Diamond has proposed an alternative biased interaction model.

Finally, the other great period of sexual differentiation, puberty, was considered. Puberty is initiated and characterized by a great increase in the production of sex hormones. Pubertal changes in both males and females include body growth, the development of pubic and axillary hair, and increased output from the oil-producing glands. Changes in the female include breast development and the beginning of menstruation. Changes in the male include growth of the penis and testes, the beginning of ejaculation, and a deepening of the voice.

REVIEW QUESTIONS

1. The ____ is the region of the brain that works together with the pituitary and gonads to regulate sex hormone levels.
2. The pituitary manufactures FSH and LH. True or false?
3. The hypothalamus produces Gn-RH. True or false?
4. In the female, during prenatal sexual differentiation, the Müllerian ducts degenerate, leaving the Wolffian ducts. True or false?
5. Differences between male and female brains are found in the ____.
6. The testes in the male are homologous to the ____ in the female.
7. The adrenogenital syndrome results in hermaphroditism. True or false?
8. From his research, John Money has concluded that gender identity is determined by genetic and hormonal factors. True or false?
9. "Menarche" refers to a teenage girl who has stopped menstruating. True or false?
10. The percent body fat hypothesis has been used to explain the age at which a girl first menstruates. True or false?

QUESTION FOR THOUGHT, DISCUSSION, AND DEBATE

1. Does the evidence support Money's position that gender identity is environmentally determined?

SUGGESTIONS FOR FURTHER READING

Money, John, and Ehrhardt, Anke. (1972). *Man and woman, boy and girl.* Baltimore: Johns Hopkins. An excellent, detailed summary of John Money's important research. Also contains a great deal of other information on sexuality.

Netter, F. H. (1965). *Endocrine system.* The Ciba Collection of Medical Illustrations. Vol. 4. Summit, N.J.: Ciba. The best set of medical illustrations of the endocrine system available, with some commentary as well.

Tanner, J. M. (1962). *Growth at adolescence.* (2nd ed.) Oxford: Blackwell Scientific Publications. The classic work on the changes of puberty.

Turner, C. D., and Bagnara, J. T. (1976). *General endocrinology.* Philadelphia: Saunders. A good endocrinology text.

CHAPTER • 5

MENSTRUATION AND MENOPAUSE

It [menstruation] makes me very much aware of the fact that I am a woman, and that's something very important to me. . . . It's also a link to other women. I actually enjoy having my period. I feel like I've been cleaned out inside.

—M. P. W.

Menstruation is a pain in the vagina.

—S. B. P.

Menopause, it's the best form of birth control. Face it graciously and brag about it. It's great.

—S. F.

Menopause, can I get through it without collapse? Men don't have that damned inconvenience and discomfort. God must have been a man—a woman would have done a better job on women's bodies.

—B. B. W.*

* *Source:* Paula Weideger. (1976). *Menstruation and menopause.* New York: Knopf, pp. 4–5.

CHAPTER HIGHLIGHTS

Women's sexual and reproductive lives have a rhythm of changes much like that of the seasons. And, as is true of the seasons, there are some tangible signs that mark the shifts, the two most notable being menstruation and menopause. As the women quoted on the previous page testify, these events are not only biological but psychological as well, and the psychological responses to them may range from very positive to very negative. This chapter deals with the biology and psychology of menstruation and menopause.

BIOLOGY AND THE MENSTRUAL CYCLE

The menstrual cycle is regulated by fluctuating levels of sex hormones which produce certain changes in the ovaries and uterus. The hormone cycles are regulated by means of the negative feedback loops discussed in Chapter 4.

It is important to note that humans are nearly unique among species in having a menstrual cycle. Only a few other species of apes and monkeys also have menstrual cycles. All other species of mammals (for example, horses and dogs) have *estrous* cycles. There are several differences between estrous cycles and menstrual cycles. First, in animals that have estrous cycles, there is no menstruation; there is either no bleeding or only a slight spotting (as in dogs), which is not a real menstruation. Second, the timing of ovulation in relation to bleeding (if there is any) is different in the two cycles. For estrous animals, ovulation occurs while the animal is in "heat," or estrus, which is also the time of slight spotting. That is, dogs ovulate at about the time of bleeding. In the menstrual cycle, however, ovulation occurs about midway between the periods of menstruation. A third difference is that female animals with estrous cycles engage in sexual behavior only when they are in heat, that is, during the estrous phase of the cycle. Females with menstrual cycles are capable of engaging in sexual behavior throughout the cycle. It is important to note these differences because some people mistakenly believe that women's cycles are like those of a dog or cat, when in fact the cycles are quite different.

The Phases of the Menstrual Cycle

The menstrual cycle has four phases, each characterized by a set of hormonal, ovarian, and uterine changes (see Figure 5.1). Because menstruation is the easiest phase to identify, it is tempting to call it the first phase; biologically, though, it is actually the last phase (although in numbering the days of the menstrual cycle, day 1 is counted as the first day of menstruation because it is the most identifiable day of the cycle).

Hormones and What Happens in the Ovaries

Follicular phase (fuh-LIK-you-lur): The first phase of the menstrual cycle, beginning just after menstruation, during which an egg matures in preparation for ovulation.

Ovulation: Release of an egg from the ovaries; the second phase of the menstrual cycle.

The first phase of the menstrual cycle is called the follicular phase (it is sometimes called the *proliferative phase* or the *preovulatory phase*). At the beginning of this phase, the pituitary secretes relatively high levels of FSH (follicle-stimulating hormone). As the name of this hormone implies, its function is to stimulate follicles in the ovaries. At the beginning of the follicular phase, it signals one follicle (occasionally more than one) in the ovaries to begin to ripen and bring an egg to maturity. At the same time, the follicle secretes estrogen. As the egg matures, it moves, enclosed in the follicle, toward the surface of the ovary.

The second phase of the cycle is ovulation, which is the phase during which the follicle ruptures open, releasing the ripened egg. By this time, estrogen has risen to a high level, which inhibits FSH production, and so FSH has fallen back to a low level. The high levels of estrogen also stimulate the hypothalamus to produce LH-releasing factor, which causes the pituitary to begin production of LH (luteinizing hormone).[1] A surge of LH and FSH causes ovulation.

[1]This may seem to contradict a statement made in Chapter 4, that high estrogen levels cause a decline in LH. It appears that both of these effects may occur, but at different times in the menstrual cycle (Vander et al., 1975). There seem to be two centers in the hypothalamus, one of which produces a negative feedback between estrogen and LH, the other of which produces a positive feedback between the two.

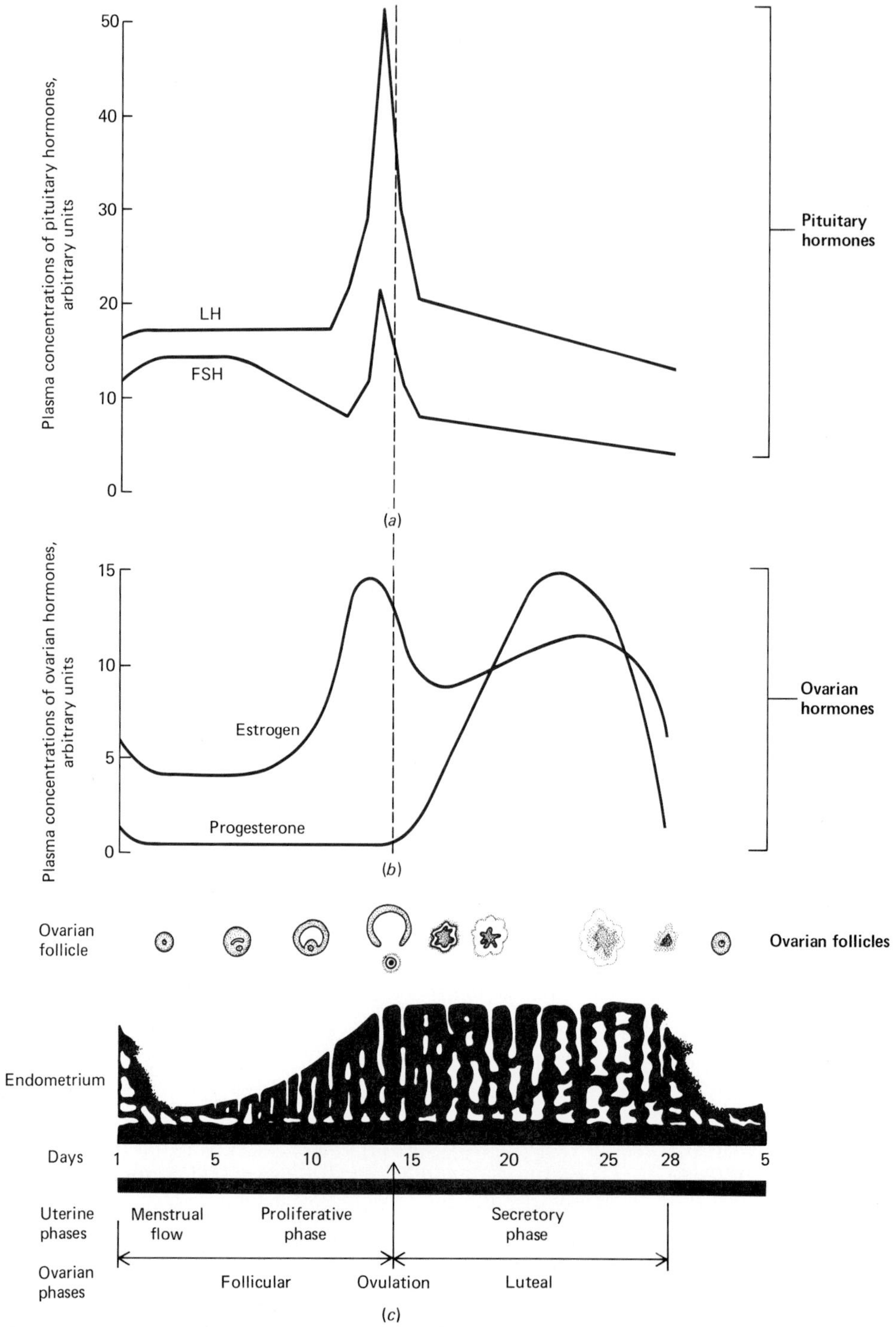

FIGURE 5.1

The biological events of the menstrual cycle. (*a*) Levels of hormones produced by the pituitary. (*b*) Hormones produced by the ovaries. (*c*) Changes in follicles in the ovary and the endometrium of the uterus.

Luteal phase (LOO-tee-uhl):
The third phase of the menstrual cycle, following ovulation.

Corpus luteum:
The mass of cells remaining of the follicle after ovulation; it secretes progesterone.

The third phase of the cycle is called the luteal phase (sometimes also called the *secretory phase* or the *postovulatory phase*). After releasing an egg, the follicle, under stimulation of LH, turns into a glandular mass of cells called the corpus luteum[2] (hence the names "luteal phase" and "luteinizing hormone"). The corpus

[2]*Corpus luteum* is Latin for "yellow body." The corpus luteum is so named because the mass of cells is yellowish in appearance.

luteum manufactures progesterone; thus progesterone levels rise during the luteal phase. But high levels of progesterone also inhibit the pituitary's secretion of LH, and as LH levels decline, the corpus luteum degenerates. Thus the corpus luteum's output leads to its own eventual destruction. And with this degeneration also comes a sharp decline in estrogen and progesterone levels at the end of the luteal phase. The falling levels of estrogen stimulate the pituitary to begin production of FSH, and the whole cycle begins again.

Menstruation: The fourth phase of the menstrual cycle, during which the endometrium of the uterus is sloughed off in the menstrual discharge.

The fourth and final phase of the cycle is menstruation. Physiologically, menstruation is a shedding of the inner lining of the uterus (the endometrium), which then passes out through the cervix and the vagina. During this phase, estrogen and progesterone levels are low, and FSH levels are rising. Menstruation is apparently triggered by the sharp decline in estrogen and progesterone levels at the end of the luteal phase.

What Happens in the Uterus

This brings us to the changes that have been occurring in the uterus while the ovaries and endocrine system were going through the four phases described above. During the first, or follicular, phase, the high levels of estrogen stimulate the endometrium of the uterus to grow, thicken, and form glands that will eventually secrete substances to nourish the embryo; that is, the endometrium proliferates (hence the alternative name for this first phase, the "proliferative phase"). During the luteal phase, the progesterone secreted by the corpus luteum stimulates the glands of the endometrium to start secreting the nourishing substances (hence the name "secretory phase"). If the egg is fertilized and the timing goes properly, about six days after ovulation the fertilized egg arrives in a uterus that is well prepared to cradle and nourish it.

The corpus luteum will continue to produce estrogen and progesterone for about 10 to 12 days. If pregnancy has not occurred, its hormone output declines sharply at the end of this period. The uterine lining thus cannot be maintained, and it is shed, resulting in menstruation. Immediately afterward, a new lining starts forming in the next follicular phase.

The menstrual fluid itself is a combination of blood (from the endometrium), degenerated cells, and mucus from the cervix and vagina. Normally the discharge for an entire period is only about 2 ounces (4 tablespoons). Most commonly the fluid is absorbed with sanitary napkins, which are worn externally, or tampons, which are worn inside the vagina.

Toxic shock syndrome: A sometimes fatal disease associated with tampon use during menstruation.

In 1980 a disturbing discovery was made that toxic shock syndrome, sometimes abbreviated TSS (Todd et al., 1978; Price, 1981) was associated with tampon use. It was particularly associated with Rely brand tampons, and they were withdrawn from the market. Toxic shock syndrome is caused by the bacterium *Staphylococcus aureus,* and tampon use seems to encourage an abnormal growth of the bacteria. Symptoms of toxic shock syndrome include high fever (102°F or greater) accompanied by vomiting or diarrhea; any woman who experiences these symptoms during her period should discontinue tampon use immediately and see a doctor. Toxic shock syndrome leads to death in approximately 10 percent of cases, although its incidence is low and has decreased, apparently in part with a decline in the number of women using tampons as a result of publicity over TSS. It is now recommended that women change tampons frequently, at least every 6 to 8 hours during their periods (although the effectiveness of this is debated), and that they not use tampons continuously throughout a menstrual period.

Length and Timing of the Cycle

How long is a normal menstrual cycle? Generally anywhere from 20 to 36 or 40 days is considered within the normal range. The average is about 28 days, but somehow this number has taken on more significance than it deserves. There is enormous variation from one woman to the next in the average length of the cycle, and for a given woman there can be considerable variation in length from one cycle to the next. In one study, more than 2000 women were asked to give their cycle lengths. Fewer than 13 percent had cycles that varied in length, from the shortest to the longest cycle, by less than 6 days; the remaining 87 percent had variations of 7 days or more (Chiazze et al., 1968). Ninety-five percent of the cycles were between 15 and 45 days long. As Dr. S. Leon Israel has commented, "The absolutely regular cycle is so rare as to be either a myth or a medical curiosity" (1967).

What is the timing of the various phases of the cycle? In a perfectly regular 28-day cycle, menstruation begins on day 1 and continues until about day 4 or 5. The follicular phase extends from about day 5 to about day 13. Ovulation occurs on day 14, and the luteal phase extends from day 15 to the end of the cycle, day 28 (see Figure 5.1). But what if the cycle is not one of those perfect 28-day ones? In cycles that are shorter or longer than 28 days, the principle is that the length of the *luteal* phase is relatively constant. That is, the time from ovulation to menstruation is always 14 days, give or take only a day or two. It is the follicular phase which is of variable length. Thus, for example, if a woman has a 44-day cycle. she ovulates on about day 30. If she has a 22-day cycle, she ovulates on about day 8.

Some women report that they can actually feel themselves ovulate, a phenomenon called *Mittelschmerz* ("middle pain"). The sensation described is a cramping on one or both sides of the lower abdomen, lasting for about a day, and it is sometimes confused with appendicitis.

It is also true that ovulation does not occur in every menstrual cycle. That is, menstruation may take place without ovulation. When this happens the woman is said to have an *anovulatory cycle.* Such cycles occur once or twice a year in women in their twenties and thirties and are faily common among girls during puberty and among women during the menopausal period.

Other Cyclic Changes

Two other physiological processes that fluctuate with the menstrual cycle also deserve mention: the cervical mucus cycle and the basal body temperature cycle. The cervix contains glands that secrete mucus throughout the menstrual cycle. One function of the mucus is to protect the entrance to the cervix, helping to keep bacteria out. These glands respond to the changing levels of estrogen during the cycle. As estrogen increases at the start of a new cycle, the mucus is alkaline, thick, and viscous. When LH production begins, just before ovulation, the cervical mucus changes markedly. It becomes even more alkaline, thin, and watery. Thus the environment for sperm passage is most hospitable just at ovulation. After ovulation, the mucus returns to its former viscous, less alkaline state. If a sample of mucus is taken just before ovulation and is allowed to dry, the dried mucus takes on a fern-shaped pattern. After ovulation, during the luteal phase. that fernlike patterning will not occur. Thus the "fern test" is one method for detecting ovulation.

A woman's *basal body temperature,* taken with a thermometer either orally or rectally, also fluctuates with the phases of the menstrual cycle. Basically, the pattern is the following: The temperature is low during the follicular phase and may take a dip on the day of ovulation; on the day after ovulation it rises noticeably, generally by 0.4°F or more, and then continues at the higher level for the rest of the cycle

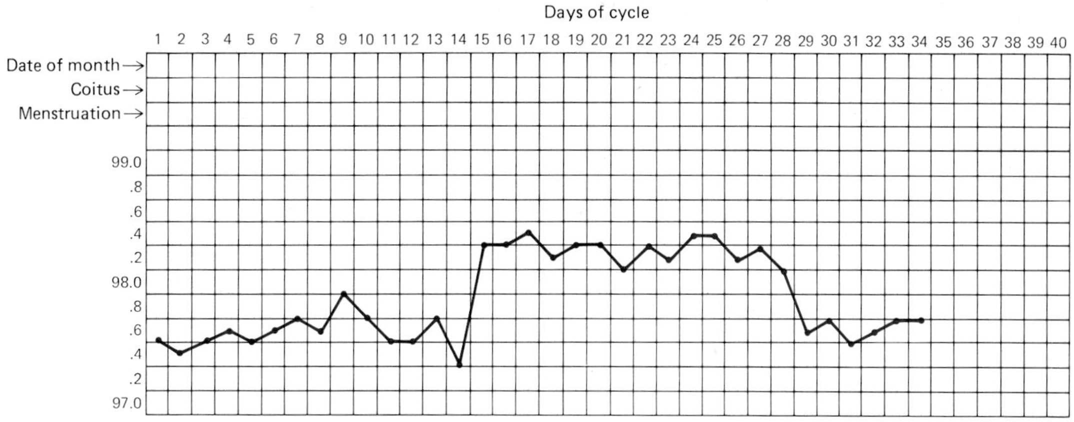

FIGURE 5.2

A basal body temperature graph. Note the dip in temperature, indicating ovulation on day 14.

(Figure 5.2). Progesterone raises body temperature, and the higher temperature during the luteal phase is due to the increased production of progesterone during that time. As the saying goes, "Where there's progesterone, there's heat." This change in basal body temperature is important when a couple are using the rhythm method of birth control (Chapter 7), and also when a woman is trying to determine the time of ovulation so that she may become pregnant (Chapter 6).

Menstrual Problems

Dysmenorrhea (dis-men-oh-REE-uh): Painful menstruation.

The most common menstrual problem is dysmenorrhea (painful menstruation). Almost every woman experiences at least some menstrual discomfort at various times in her life, but the frequency and severity of the discomfort vary considerably from one woman to the next. Cramping pains in the pelvic region are the most common symptom, and other symptoms may include headaches, backaches, nausea, and a feeling of pressure and bloating in the pelvis.

Prostaglandins: Chemicals secreted by the uterus that cause the uterine muscles to contract; they are a likely cause of painful menstruation.

Although the exact causes of dysmenorrhea are unknown, the current leading theory involves prostaglandins, hormonelike substances produced by many tissues of the body, including the lining of the uterus (Budoff, 1980). Prostaglandins can cause smooth muscle to contract and can affect the size of blood vessels. Women with severe menstrual pain have unusually high levels of prostaglandins. The high levels cause intense uterine contractions, which in turn choke off some of the uterus's supply of oxygen-carrying blood. Prostaglandins may also cause greater sensitivity in nerve endings. The combination of the uterine contractions, lack of oxygen, and heightened nerve sensitivity produces menstrual cramps.

Household remedies for painful menstruation are available and may be helpful to some women. Aspirin appears to be the best, and cheapest, painkiller available, and it can help to relieve menstrual pain. Exercise and keeping in good shape may also help. A somewhat more provocative remedy suggested by, among others, Masters and Johnson is masturbation. This makes good physiological sense because part of the discomfort of menstruation—the pressure and bloating—results from pelvic edema (a congestion of fluids in the pelvic region). During sexual arousal and orgasm, pelvic congestion increases. After orgasm, the congestion dissipates (see Chapter 8). Thus orgasm, whether produced by masturbation or some other means, should help to relieve the pelvic edema which causes menstrual discomfort. And it's a lot more fun than taking medicine!

Recently the FDA approved mefenamic acid (an antiprostaglandin drug) for use in the treatment of menstrual pain. The drug is sold with brand names such as Naprosyn and Anaprox. Its use was discovered by Dr. Penny Wise Budoff (1980); 85 percent of the women tested so far have reported significant relief from menstrual pain and symptoms such as nausea, vomiting, dizziness, and weakness. Interestingly, a traditional cure for cramps, aspirin, is also an antiprostaglandin.

A menstrual problem which may be mistaken for dysmenorrhea is *endometriosis.* As noted previously the endometrium is the lining of the uterus; it grows during each menstrual cycle and is sloughed off in menstruation. Endometriosis occurs when the endometrium grows in a place other than the uterus. Common sites include the ovaries, fallopian tubes, rectum, bladder, vagina, vulva, cervix, and lymph glands. The symptoms vary, depending on the location of the growth, but very painful periods that last an unusually long time are the most common. Endometriosis is fairly serious and should be treated by a physician; if left untreated, it may lead to sterility. Hormones are generally used in treatment, but if the problem is severe, surgery may be required.

Amenorrhea:
The absence of menstruation.

Another menstrual problem is amenorrhea, or the absence of menstruation. It is called *primary amenorrhea* if the girl has not yet menstruated by about age 18. It is called *secondary amenorrhea* if she has had at least one period. Amenorrhea has received considerable attention from physicians because, while rare, it is a symptom of infertility. Some of the causes of amenorrhea include pregnancy, congenital defects of the reproductive system, hormonal imbalance, cysts or tumors. disease, stress, and emotional factors related to puberty. Amenorrhea resulting from jogging and from anorexia was discussed in Chapter 4.

PSYCHOLOGICAL ASPECTS OF THE MENSTRUAL CYCLE

It is part of the folk wisdom of our culture that women experience fluctuations in mood over the phases of the menstrual cycle. In particular, women are supposed to be especially cranky and depressed just before and during their periods. This notion is reflected in advertisements for drugs to relieve menstrual discomforts saying that "Sally is blue" at "that time of the month." An extreme of this belief was voiced by Dr. Edgar Berman, Hubert Humphrey's personal physician, who, a few years ago, stated publicly that he believed that women were unfit to hold high public office, such as the presidency, because of their "raging hormonal influences." In France, if a woman commits a crime during her premenstrual period, she may use the fact in her defense, claiming "temporary impairment of sanity."

What is the scientific evidence concerning the occurrence of such fluctuations in mood, and, if they do occur, what causes them?

Fluctuations in Mood: Is Sally Blue?

In 1931, R. T. Frank gave the name "premenstrual tension" to the mood changes that may occur during the three or four days immediately preceding menstruation (about days 24 to 28 of the cycle). Symptoms of premenstrual tension include depression, anxiety. irritability, fatigue, headaches, and low self-esteem. Since the time of Frank's early work, a great many data have been collected on moods during the premenstural period and on whether moods fluctuate during the cycle.

The results seem to indicate a basic pattern. On the average, mood is positive around the time of ovulation (mid-cycle) and is negative premenstrually. For example, in one study, mood was measured by means of a projective technique in which subjects told stories at regular intervals throughout the cycle; the stories were then scored for the amount of anxiety shown in them (Bardwick, 1971; Ivey and Bardwick, 1968). The results indicated that self-confidence and self-esteem are high at ovulation, while anxiety about death, mutilation, and separation are high premenstrually. The following examples illustrate these shifts.

One woman at ovulation said:

> We took our skis and packed them on top of the car and then we took off for up north. We used to go for long walks in the snow, and it was just really great, really quiet and peaceful.

The same woman showed mutilation anxiety in this story told premenstrually:

> [The car] came around a curve and did a double flip and landed upside down. I remember this car coming down on my hand and slicing it right open and all this blood was all over the place. Later they thought it was broken because every time I touched the finger, it felt like a nail was going through my hand.

Another woman expressed a positive mood at ovulation in this story:

> Talk about my trip to Europe. It was just the greatest summer of my life. We met all kinds of terrific people everywhere we went, and just the most terrific things happened.

But the same woman showed hostility premenstrually:

> Talk about my brother and his wife. I hated her. I just couldn't stand her. . . . I used to do terrible things to separate them.

Premenstrual syndrome (PMS):
A combination of severe physical and psychological symptoms, such as depression and irritability, occurring just before menstruation.

The term premenstrual syndrome (PMS) is used to refer to those cases in which the woman has a particularly severe combination of physical and psychological symptoms premenstrually; these symptoms may include tension, depression, irritability, backache, and water retention (Dalton, 1979).

Evidence of the premenstrual syndrome comes from statistics indicating that a large proportion of the criminal acts of violence and suicides committed by women take place during the four premenstrual and four menstrual days of the cycle (Dalton, 1964). It has been found that 45 percent of the female industrial workers who call in sick do so during this period and that 46 percent of the women admitted to psychiatric care are admitted on one of these eight days; also, 52 percent of female accident-emergency admissions occur during the eight premenstrual and menstrual days. In addition, 54 percent of the children brought to a clinic with minor colds were brought during their mothers' eight premenstrual and menstrual days, perhaps indicating an increase in the mother's anxiety at this time (Dalton, 1966).

The evidence concerning mood fluctuation and the premenstrual syndrome has not been accepted without challenge. Of the numerous criticisms that have been made (Parlee, 1973), three deserve special mention here. First, much of the evidence depends on subjective reports of mood and symptoms, which are probably not very reliable. Second, the research has not given sufficient consideration to coping mechanisms; most women do not dissolve into tears and confine themselves to bed for the eight premenstrual and menstrual days of each month. It seems likely that women develop mechanisms for coping with the symptoms. Third, the interpretation of the direction of the differences might be questioned. The typical interpretation is that women show a psychological "deficit" premenstrually, as compared with the "normal" state at ovulation and during the rest of the cycle. However, the opposite interpretation might also be made: that women are "normal" premenstrually and are unusually well-adjusted psychologically at mid-cycle. What defines "normal" or "average" mood, then? Men's moods? Support for a reinterpretation might come from the statistics on violent crimes committed by women. While it is true that women are somewhat more likely to commit crimes during the eight premenstrual and menstrual days, even during this period they are far less likely to commit crimes than men are. Thus women might be considered to experience "normal" or typical moods (comparable to men's moods) during the premenstrual and menstrual days and to have feelings of unusual well-being around ovulation (see also Sommer, 1973).

Taking into account the criticisms and available evidence, it might be reasonable to conclude the following:

1. Women do, on the average, experience some fluctuations in mood over the phases of the menstrual cycle.
2. Present evidence does not clearly indicate how the direction of the shifts should be interpreted—whether women are unusually "low" premenstrually or unusually "high" around the time of ovulation.
3. There is a great deal of variation from one woman to the next in the size of these shifts and the way they are expressed. Some women experience no shifts or shifts so slight that they are not noticeable, while others may experience large shifts. It would be interesting to know how many do show mood fluctuations and how many do not. Unfortunately, the studies that have tried to provide this information themselves show substantial variation in their conclusions (Hyde and Rosenberg, 1976). It appears that about 50 to 75 percent of all women show some mood fluctuation, while at least 25 percent show no fluctuation. It is important to make a distinction between women who have full-blown PMS and women who experience no fluctuation in mood over the cycle, or only experience moderate cycles in mood.

Dr. Katharina Dalton (1979), an expert in treating menstrual problems, advocates the use of *progesterone therapy* in the treatment of PMS. The effectiveness of progesterone in treating PMS is being debated in the medical community. Those studies that are well-controlled show progesterone to be no more effective than a placebo (sugar pill) (Abplanalp, 1983). Currently, then, there is no known medical cure for PMS (Abplanalp, 1983).

Fluctuations in Performance: Can Sally Be President?

So far the discussion has concentrated on fluctuations in psychological characteristics such as depression, anxiety, and low self-confidence. However, in some situations performance is of more practical importance than mood. For example, is a woman secretary's clerical work less accurate premenstrually and menstrually? Is a woman athlete's coordination or speed impaired during the premenstrual-menstrual period?

The available data do not provide evidence of fluctuations in performance with the phases of the menstrual cycle (Sommer, 1973). Thus there is no substantial evidence indicating that the kinds of performance required in a work situation fluctuate over the menstrual cycle.

Fluctuations in Sex Drive

Another psychological characteristic that has been investigated for fluctuations over the cycle is women's interest in, or desire for, intercourse—what might be called the "sex drive." Observations of female animals that have estrous cycles indicate that sexual behavior depends a great deal on cycle phase and the corresponding hormonal state. Females of these species engage in sexual behavior enthusiastically when they are in the estrous, or "heat," phase of the cycle and do not engage in sexual behavior at all during any other phase. This makes good biological sense, since the females engage in sex precisely when they are fertile.

Human females, of course, engage in sexual behavior throughout the menstrual cycle. But might there still remain some subtle cycling in drive, expressed, perhaps, in fluctuations in frequency of intercourse? The women in Kinsey's sample (Kinsey et al., 1953) reported the greatest feelings of sexual arousal during the premenstrual period. Generally there seem to be two peaks in the frequency of intercourse, one just before menstruation and one just after menstruation (Udry and Morris, 1968; Gold and Adams. 1981). Of course, these fluctuations may have nothing to do with hormones; rather, the high frequency of intercourse just after menstruation may just be a compensation for deprivation during menstruation (Gold and Adams, 1981) and the high frequency before menstruation might result from anticipated deprivation. Also, one should be cautious about using frequency of intercourse as a measure of a woman's sex drive. Intercourse requires some agreement between the female and the male, and thus reflects not only her desires but his as well. One study investigated autosexual activity (masturbation, fantasy, and so on) in addition to intercourse, and found that the frequency of autosexual activity actually increased during menstruation, while the frequency of intercourse decreased (Gold and Adams, 1981). Thus there seems to be little correspondence between hormonal fluctuations over the menstrual cycle and fluctuations in sex drive.

What Causes the Fluctuations in Mood: Why Is Sally Blue?

The answer to the question of what causes mood fluctuations during the menstrual cycle (if such fluctuations do occur) resolves down to a nature-nurture, or biology-environment, controversy. That is, some investigators argue that the mood fluctuations are caused by biological factors—in particular, fluctuations in levels of hormones—while others argue that environmental factors such as menstrual taboos and cultural expectations are the cause.

On the biology side, changes in mood appear to be related to changes in hormone levels during the cycle. The fact that depression is more frequent in women premenstrually, at menopause, and postpartum (after having a baby) and among those using birth control pills suggests that there is at least some relationship between sex hormones and depression (S. L. Smith, 1975). The exact hormone-mood relationship is not known, though. Theories of hormonal causes of premenstrual tension involving the following factors have been proposed: (1) absolute amount of estrogen; (2) absolute amount of progesterone; (3) the estrogen-progesterone ratio, or estrogen-progesterone balance; (4) hypersensitivity of some individuals to estrogen levels; and (5) withdrawal reactions to either estrogen or progesterone (during all the premenstrual, postpartum, and menopausal periods, hormone levels are dropping rapidly). Research has not determined which, if any, of these factors is the real cause, though each has some data in its favor. Neither is it known exactly what the mechanism is by which hormones influence mood. The likeliest explanation would involve the effects of estrogen and progesterone on brain neurotransmitters (substances that are involved in the transmission of nerve impulses) such as norepinephrine and dopamine (for a review, see Ruble et al., 1980).

Critics of the hormone point of view note that causality is being inferred from correlational data. That is, the data show simply a correlation between cycle phase (hormone levels) and mood. From this, it is unwarranted to infer that the hormone levels cause the mood shifts. Another equally reaonable interpretation of the data might be that moods influence hormone levels and cycle phase. For example, a bout of depression might bring on menstruation.

A study that answers this objection partially was done by psychologist Karen Paige (1971). She used a manipulation of hormone levels—birth control pills—and studied mood fluctuations resulting from the manipulation. The spoken stories of 102 married women were obtained on days 4, 10, and 16 and two days before menstruation during one cycle, and they were scored using the technique mentioned previously. The subjects fell into three groups: (1) those who were not taking oral contraceptives and never had; (2) those who were taking a combination pill (combination pills provide a steady high dose of both estrogen and progestin, a synthetic progesterone, for 20 or 21 days—see Chapter 7 for a more complete discussion); and (3) those who were taking sequential pills (which provide 15 days of estrogen followed by five days of estrogen plus progestin, which is a fluctuation similar to the natural cycle but at higher levels). The hormone levels across the cycles of the women in these three groups are shown in Figure 5.3. Paige found that the nonpill women experienced statistically significant variation in their anxiety and hostility levels over the menstrual cycle, which was in agreement with findings from previous studies. Women taking the sequential pill showed the same mood change that nonpill women did. This agrees with the predicted outcome, since their artificial hormone cycle is similar to the natural one. Most important, combination-pill women, whose hormone levels are constant over the cycle, showed *no* mood shifts over the cycle; their hostility and anxiety levels were constant. This study therefore provides evidence that fluctuations in hormone levels over the menstrual cycle cause mood fluctuations and that when hormone levels are constant, mood is constant.

Those arguing the other side—that the fluctuations are due to cultural forces—note the widespread cultural expectations and taboos surrounding menstruation (for reviews, see Novell, 1965; Stephens, 1961; Weideger, 1976). In many nonindustrialized cultures—for example, some American Indian groups—women who are menstruating are isolated from the community and may have to stay in a menstrual hut at the edge of town during their period. Often the menstrual blood itself is thought to have supernatural, dangerous powers, and the woman's isolation is considered necessary to the safety of the community. Among the Lele of the Congo, for example:

> A menstruating woman was a danger to the whole community if she entered the forest. Not only was her menstruation certain to wreck any enterprise in the forest that she might undertake, but it was thought to produce unfavorable conditions for men. Hunting would be difficult for a long time after, and rituals based on forest plants would have no efficacy. Women found these rules extremely irksome, especially as they were regularly short-handed and later in their planting, weeding, harvesting, and fishing. (Douglas, 1970, p. 179)

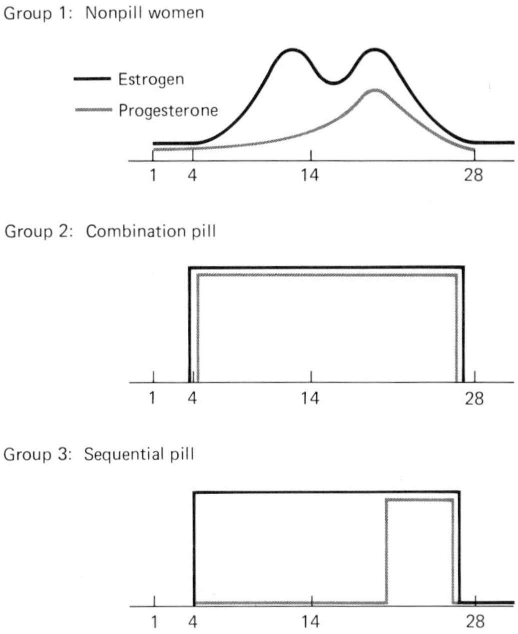

FIGURE 5.3

Hormone levels over the menstrual cycle for the three groups of women in Paige's study (see text for further explanation).

Lest one think that such practices occur only among primitive people, it should be noted that they are present in our own culture as well. For example, the following passage is from the Old Testament:

> When a woman has a discharge of blood which is her regular discharge from her body, she shall be in her impurity for seven days, and whoever touches her shall be unclean until the evening. . . . And whoever touches her bed shall wash his clothes, and bathe himself in water, and be unclean until the evening; whether it is the bed or anything upon which she sits, when he touches it he shall be unclean until the evening. (Leviticus 15:19–23)

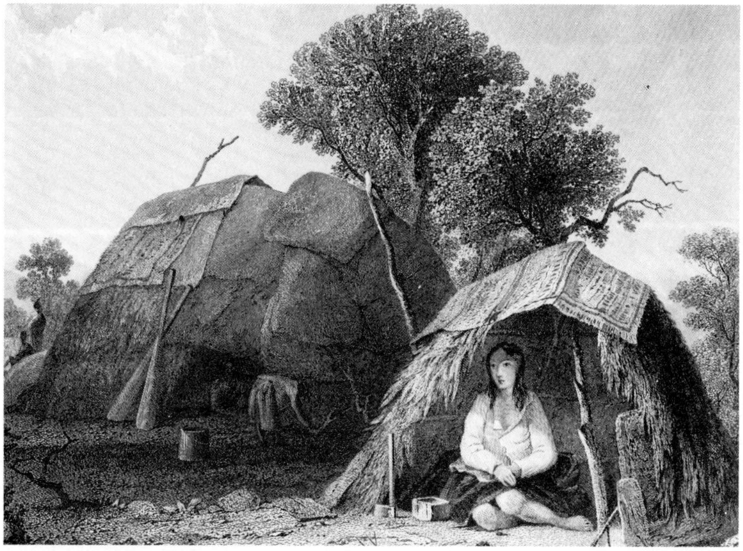

FIGURE 5.4

A Navaho menstrual hut. Some argue that women's negative attitudes around the time of menstruation are due to cultural taboos regarding menstruation.

Even closer to home, the Parks Department issues the following warning:

> "Special precautions apply to women. For their protection, women should refrain from wilderness travel during their menstrual periods. Bears and other large carnivores have attacked women in this physiological condition." (Weideger, 1976, p. 226)

Among the most common menstrual taboos are those prohibiting sexual intercourse with a menstruating woman. For example. the continuation of the passage from Leviticus quoted above is:

> And if any man lies with her, and her impurity is on him, he shall be unclean seven days; and every bed on which he lies shall be unclean. (Leviticus 15:24)

Couples who violated the taboo could be stoned. To this day, Orthodox Jews abstain from sex during the woman's period and for seven days afterward. At the end of this time the woman goes to the mikvah (ritual bath) to be cleansed, and only after this cleansing may she resume sexual relations.

There is evidence that these "primitive" or "archaic" practices are actually widespread in our modern culture as well. For example, a 1972 survey of 960 California families showed that half the men and women had *never* had intercourse during the woman's menstrual period (Paige, 1973). No wonder women get depressed around the time of menstruation!

Advocates of the cultural explanation argue, then, that women become anxious and depressed around the time of menstruation because of the many cultural forces, such as menstrual taboos, that create negative attitudes toward menstruation. Further, women's expectations may play a role. It is a well-documented phenomenon that people's expectations can influence their behavior. Our culture is filled with teachings that women are supposed to behave strangely just before and during their periods—for example, the drug company ads that explain why "Sally is blue." Thus, according to this line of reasoning, women are taught that they should be depressed around the time of menstruation, and because they expect to become depressed, they become depressed.

Surely such forces do exist in our culture. But is there any evidence that they really do have an effect on women's moods and behavior? Another study by Karen Paige (1973) does provide some evidence. She obtained information on the menstrual experiences of 298 unmarried college women and then separated the subjects into three groups depending on their religious background: Protestant, Catholic, and Jewish. The Catholics showed extreme fluctuations in anxiety level over the cycle. while Protestants showed no fluctuation. Among the Jewish women, those who accepted the ban on sexual intercourse during menstruation were the most likely to have menstrual difficulties. Thus, while all the women presumably had similar hormone cycles, whether they experienced fluctuations in mood appeared to depend on their cultural background.

Psychologist Diane Ruble (1977) did a clever experiment to determine whether subjects' culturally induced expectations influence their reporting of premenstrual symptoms. College student subjects were tested on the sixth or seventh day before the onset of their next menstrual period. They were told that they would participate in a study on a new technique for predicting the expected date of menstruation using an electroencephalogram (EEG), a method that had already been successfully tested with older women. After the EEG had been run (it actually wasn't), the subject was informed of when her next period was to occur, depending on which of three experimental groups she had randomly been assigned to: (1) the subject was told she was "premenstrual" and her period was due in one or two days; (2) the subject was told she was "intermenstrual" or "mid cycle" and her period was not expected for at least a week to ten days; or (3) she was given no information at all about the predicted date of menstruation (control group). The women then completed a self-report menstrual distress questionnaire. The results indicated that subjects who had been led to believe they were in the premenstrual phase reported significantly more water retention, pain, and changes in eating habits than did subjects who had been led to believe they were around mid-cycle. (In fact, subjects in these groups did not differ significantly in when their periods actually arrived.) There were no significant differences between the groups in ratings of negative moods, however. This study indicates that probably because of learned beliefs, women overstate the changes in body states that occur over the menstrual cycle. When they think they are in the premenstrual phase, they report more problems then when they think they are at mid-cycle.

This nature-nurture argument will not be easily resolved, particularly because there is good evidence for both points of view. Perhaps the best solution is to say that some women probably do experience mood shifts caused by hormonal and possibly other physical factors and that for many others, slight biological influences are magnified by cultural influences. Premenstrual hormonal state may act as a sort of "trigger." It may, for example, provide a state conducive to depression; and if the environment provides further stimuli to depression, the woman becomes depressed.

CYCLES IN MEN

The traditional assumption, of both lay people and scientists, has been that monthly biological and psychological cycles are the exclusive property of women. The corollary assumption has been that men experience no such monthly cycles. These assumptions are made, at least in part, because men have no obvious signs like menstruation to call attention to the fact that some kind of periodic change is occurring.

Recently there has been an interest in discovering whether men might not experience subtle monthly hormone cycles and corresponding psychological cycles. As early as 1897, it had been observed that bleeding from lung hemorrhages, hemorrhoids, and hyperemia of the liver is periodic, in both women and men (cited in Delaney et al., 1976, pp. 212–213). Epileptic attacks appear to follow a monthly cycle in men (Delaney et al., 1976, p. 213).

In one early study, male industrial workers did appear to have periodic emotional cycles, with an average cycle length of about five weeks. Individual cycle lengths varied from three to nine weeks and were remarkably consistent (Hersey, 1931).

One interesting applied study found some evidence of behavioral cycles in men (cited in Ramey, 1972). The Omi Railway Company of Japan operates more than 700 buses and taxis. In 1969 the directors became concerned about the high losses resulting from accidents. The company's efficiency experts studied each man working for the company to determine his monthly cycle pattern of mood and efficiency. Then schedules were adjusted to coincide with the best times for the drivers. Since then, the accident rate has dropped by one-third.

In another study, the testosterone levels of 20 men were studied for a period of 60 days (Doering et al., 1975). The majority of the men had identifiable testosterone cycles ranging in length from 3 to 30 days, with many clustered around 21 to 23 days. A psychological test to measure the men's moods was also administered (Doering et al., 1978). Although testosterone levels were not correlated with several kinds of moods such as anxiety, high testosterone levels were correlated with depression.

Other researchers have also found cycles in men's emotional states (Parlee, 1978). Thus, the preliminary evidence indicates that men do experience mood cycles. Undoubtedly there will be increased research on this topic in the next decade.

MENOPAUSE

Biological Changes

Menopause:
The cessation of menstruation in middle age.

The *climacteric* is a period lasting about 15 or 20 years (from about ages 45 to 60) during which a woman's body makes the transition from being able to reproduce to not being able to reproduce; the climacteric is marked particularly by a decline in the functioning of the ovaries. But climacteric changes occur in many other body tissues and systems as well. Menopause (the "change of life," the "change") refers to one specific event in this process, the cessation of menstruation; this occurs, on the average, during a two-year period beginning at around age 47 (with a normal menopause occurring anywhere between the ages of 35 and 60).

Biologically, as a woman grows older, the pituitary continues a normal output of FSH and LH; however, as the ovaries age, they become less able to respond to the pituitary hormones. Thus the major biological change during the climacteric is the aging of the ovaries with an accompanying decline in the output of their two major products: eggs and the sex hormones estrogen and progesterone. More specifically, the ovaries become less capable of responding to FSH by maturing and releasing an egg. The hormonal changes of menopause involve a decline in estrogen and progesterone levels and hormonal imbalance.

Physical symptoms of menopause include "hot flashes" or "hot flushes," headaches, dizziness, heart palpitations, and pains in the joints. A probable long-range effect of the decline in estrogen levels is *osteoporosis* (porous and brittle bones, which may lead to "dowager's hump"). The hot flash is probably the best known of the symptoms. Typically it is described as a sudden wave of heat from the waist up. The woman may get red and perspire a lot; when the flush goes away, she may feel chilled and sometimes may shiver. The flashes may last from a few seconds to half an hour and may occur several or many times a day. They may also occur at night, causing insomnia, and the resulting perspiration can actually soak the sheets.

Do all women experience these menopausal symptoms? In a survey of 638 women aged 45 to 55, conducted in London in 1964–1965, 30 to 50 percent of the women reported experiencing dizziness, palpitations, insomnia, depression, headache, or weight gain, and most of these women reported experiencing several of these symptoms rather than just one. About 50 percent of the women experienced hot flashes and half of the 50 percent said the flashes were acutely uncomfortable (McKinlay and Jeffreys, 1974). It is generally estimated that only about 10 percent of all women suffer severe distress at menopause. Thus it might be concluded that at least as many as 50 percent (perhaps 80 to 90 percent) of all women suffer some of these uncomfortable menopausal symptoms, only about 10 percent are severely affected, and a sizable proportion—at least 10 percent and perhaps as many as 50 percent—display none of these symptoms.

Estrogen-replacement therapy (ERT) is available and may be helpful to many menopausal women, particularly for relief of physical discomfort such as hot flashes. However, the therapy needs to be carefully administered by a physician, and its benefits need to be weighed against its potential risks (for a good review and evaluation, see Hammond and Maxson, 1982). There is some evidence linking it to cancer of the uterus. On the other hand, estrogen replacement protects women from osteoporosis ("brittle bones"), which may cause broken hips, which may lead to death. More elderly women die annually from broken hips than from endometrial cancer (Budoff, 1981). In one study. women aged 40 to 69 were followed yearly for 5 years; the women taking replacement estrogen had a death rate much *lower* than those not taking estrogen (Bush et al., 1983). Thus, on balance, estrogen replacement may be relatively safe.

Sexuality and Menopause

During the climacteric, physical changes also occur in the vagina. The lack of estrogen causes the vagina to become less acidic which leaves it more vulnerable to infections. Estrogen is also responsible for maintaining the mucous membranes of the vaginal walls. With a decline in estrogen, there is a decline in vaginal lubrication during arousal, and the vaginal walls become less elastic. Either or both of these may make intercourse painful for the woman. Several remedies are available, including estrogen-replacement therapy and the use of artificial lubricants. Unfortunately. some women do not communicate their discomforts to their husbands or physician and instead suffer quietly and develop an aversion to sex. The topic of sexuality and the elderly will be discussed in more detail in Chapter 12. Suffice it to say here that no physical changes occur during menopause or the climacteric that prevent women from having intercourse or cause them to have a reduced sex drive. Indeed, some women report that intercourse is even better after menopause, when the fear of pregnancy no longer inhibits them.

Psychological Changes

Psychological problems of menopause include depression, irritability, anxiety, nervousness, crying spells, inability to concentrate, and feelings of suffocation. In rare cases, the depression may be extremely severe (*involutional melancholia*) in a woman who has no previous history of mental problems. It is estimated that about 10 percent of women suffer from serious depression during menopause. Less severe depression during menopause is more common.

These psychological symptoms, though, involve a subtle problem of interpretation similar to the one mentioned in conjunction with the premenstrual-tension syndrome. Women are said to have "more" problems during menopause. More than what? More than men? More than at other times in their own lives? Investigating the latter question, psychologists Bernice Neugarten and Ruth Kraines (1965) studied symptoms among women of different age groups. They found that adolescents and menopausal women reported the largest number of problematic symptoms. Postmenopausal women reported the smallest number of problematic symptoms; apparently, menopause does not permanently "wreck" a woman. Among the adolescents, psychological symptoms were the most common (for example, tension), while among the menopausal women, physical symptoms such as hot flashes were most common. Menopausal women showed an increase in only five categories of psychological symptoms: headache, irritability, nervousness, feeling blue, and feelings of suffocation (the latter being associated with hot flashes). Thus menopause may not be the worst time of a woman's life psychologically; probably it is not so bad as adolescence.

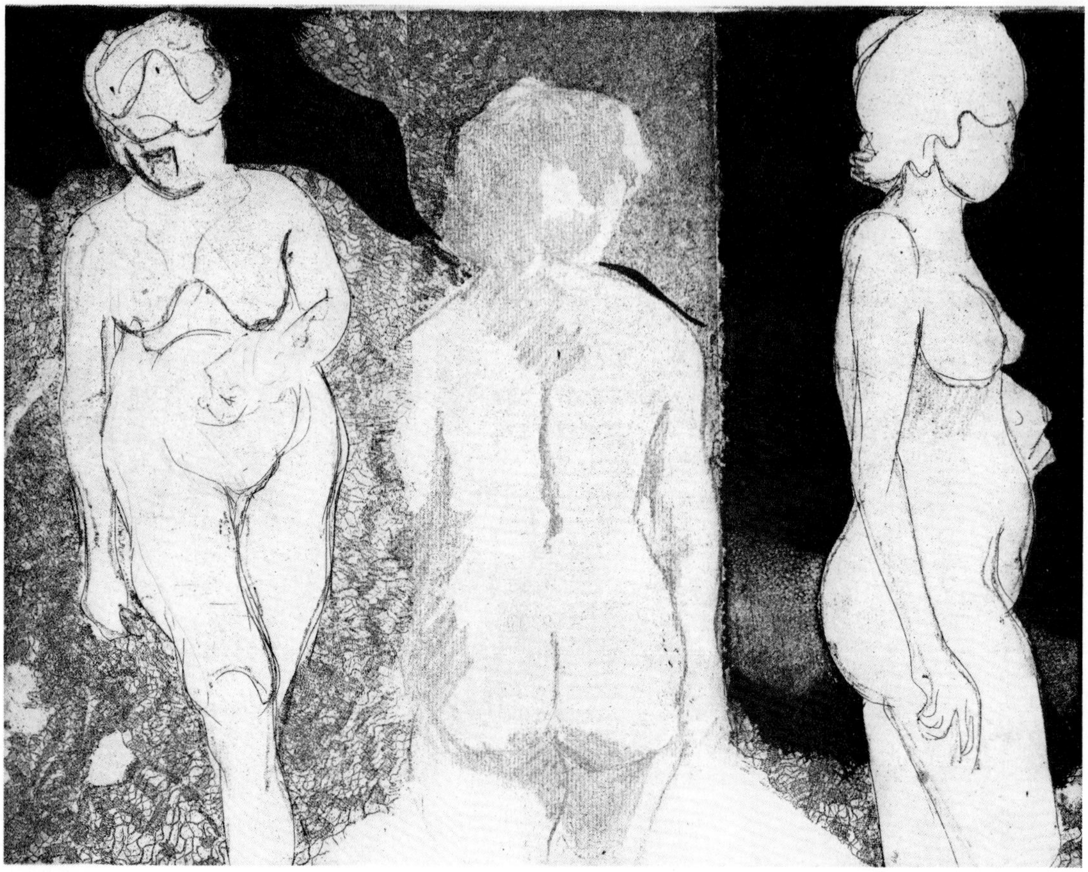

FIGURE 5.5

at menopause.

at menopause

my body is the grapevine that grows and lengthens
brown rope trained to obey the seasons
but ripening comes to an end
there will be no more fruit
no great purple triangles juices bursting the rich skins

(the seasons turn over, the harvesting ends)

my body is growing a new happiness a pungent joy
hard sinews hold up the ancient arbor
touch leaves shade the destroying sun
people shelter beneath me like birds my roots send
more roots into the kind earth, never has the earth been kinder

(the seasons turn over, the fragrances blend)

my body is the grapevine that grows and grows

Mary Winfrey, Whittier, Calif.

What Causes the Symptoms?

The difficulties associated with menopause are attributed to biology (in particular, hormones) by some and to culture and its expectations by others.

From the biological perspective, the symptoms of menopause appear to be due to the woman's hormonal state. In particular, the symptoms appear to be related either to low estrogen levels or to hormonal imbalance. The former hypothesis, called the *estrogen-deficiency theory,* has been the subject of the most research. Proponents of this theory argue that the physical symptoms, such as hot flashes, and the psychological symptoms, such as depression, are caused by declining amounts of estrogen in the body. It is also worth noting that hormonally, the period is similar to the premenstrual period, with its declining estrogen levels, and that the psychological symptoms are also similar: depression and irritability.

The best evidence for the estrogen-deficiency theory comes from the success of estrogen-replacement therapy. Physicians may prescribe estrogen either in its natural form, Premarin, or in a synthetic form such as Stilbestrol, Progynon, or Meprane. Estrogen-replacement therapy is very successful in relieving low-estrogen menopausal symptoms like hot flashes, sweating, cold hands and feet, osteoporosis, and vaginal discharges. It may also relieve psychological symptoms such as irritability and depression (see Bardwick, 1971, for a review). The success of this therapy suggests that low estrogen levels cause menopausal symptoms and that raising estrogen levels relieves the symptoms.

On the other hand, advocates of the environmental point of view note the cultural forces that may act to produce psychological stress in women around the time of menopause. The aging process itself may be psychologically stressful in our youth-oriented culture. The menopausal years remind a woman forcefully that she is aging. Menopause also means that the woman can no longer bear children; for women who have a great psychological investment in motherhood, this can be a difficult realization.

We also have a strong cultural bias toward expecting menopausal symptoms. Thus any quirk in a middle-aged woman's behavior is attributed to the "change." It simultaneously becomes the cause of, and explanation for, all the problems and complaints of the middle-aged woman. Given such expectations, it is not surprising that the average person perceives widespread evidence of the pervasiveness of menopausal symptoms. Ironically, idiosyncrasies in women of childbearing age are blamed on menstruation, while problems experienced by women who are past that age are blamed on the *lack* of it.

Sociologist Pauline Bart (1971) did an important study of depression in middle-aged woman and its cultural causes. Middle-aged women are likely to be afflicted with the problem of the "empty nest"; the children have left home to work or get married, leaving the woman alone with her husband in an empty house. Bart believes that the empty-nest syndrome is the major source of depression in middle-aged women. Loss of role, according to Bart, can cause depression. That is. a person's major role is a major source of identity, and if this role or identity is taken away, depression results. For many adult women, the mother role is their major role and the major definer of their identity. When their children leave home, the mother role and identity leave with them, leading to depression. Interestingly. Bart found that it is not the "rebels"—masculine women or career women—who suffer most from depression in middle age, but rather the traditional, overprotective, "supermother" or "Jewish mother" type. This finding is perfectly consistent with Bart's theory, because the supermother has the greatest investment in the mother role. Because most of her identity is defined by it, she has more to lose when the children leave home. In cross-cultural research, Bart also found that in some cultures a woman's status does not decline in middle age and may even increase at that time; in these cultures, middle-aged women have a low depression rate. This finding provides strong evidence that the "menopausal" symptom of depression is due not to the biological factor of declining hormone levels but rather to cultural factors.

However, sociologist Lillian B. Rubin (1979) has challenged the whole notion of the empty-nest syndrome and questions whether there is substantial depression in the mid-life period for women. Her results are based on a study of 160 women, a cross section of white mothers aged 35 to 54, from the working, middle, and professional classes. To be included in the sample, they had to have given up work or careers after a minimum of three years and to have assumed the traditional role of housewife and mother for at least 10 years after the birth of their first child. Therefore this group should be most prone to the empty-nest syndrome. Typically these women said, "My career was my child." Contrary to the notion of the empty nest, Rubin found that although some women were momentarily sad, lonely, or frightened, they were not depressed in response to the departure of their children. The predominant feeling of every woman except one was a feeling of relief. As one woman put it,

> Lonesome? God, no! From the day the kids are born, if its's not one thing, it's another. After all those years of being responsible for them, you finally get to the point where you want to scream: "Fall out of the nest already, you guys, will you? It's time." (Rubin, 1979, p. 13)

Rather than experiencing an immobilizing depression, most of the women found new jobs and reorganized their daily lives. This research leads one to question whether women do have substantial problems with depression around mid-life or the time of menopause.

In agreement with Rubin's thesis, one recent review concluded that there was good evidence that menopause does *not* increase the rate of depression (Weissman and Klerman, 1977).

MALE MENOPAUSE

Biological Changes

In the technical sense, men do not experience a "menopause"; never having menstruated, they can scarcely cease menstruating. However, men do experience a very gradual decline in the manufacture of both testosterone and sperm by the testes, a mild version of the climacteric process in women, although viable sperm may still be produced at age 90.

One of the most common physical problems for men at this age is enlargement of the prostate gland, which is believed to be related to changes in hormone levels. Prostate enlargement occurs in 10 percent of men by age 40 and 50 percent of men who reach age 80. Enlargement of the prostate causes urination problems; there is difficulty in voluntarily initiating urination, as well as frequent nocturnal urination. These symptoms are usually remedied by surgery to remove the part of the gland pressing against the urethra. Nonsurgical treatment is not effective. Administration of female sex hormones causes shrinkage of prostate cancer but does not reduce benign (noncancerous) prostate enlargement. Contrary to a number of myths, prostate enlargement is not caused by masturbation or excessive sexual activity. The

FIGURE 5.6

Is there a male mid-life crisis? Factors such as the aspiration-achievement gap may produce psychological transitions in the middle-aged man.

infection and inflammation resulting from venereal disease, though, can cause prostate enlargement.

Psychological Changes

Research in the last decade has focused on the notion of a "male mid-life crisis," whether men experience one in their forties, and what its nature is (Levinson, 1978; Lowenthal et al., 1975; see review by Brim, 1976). Major themes that emerge from that research are discussed below.

One theme is the *aspiration-achievement gap.* Most human beings have a desire to feel good about themselves based on their achievements. For men, this positive sense of self comes mainly from their job or career. Around age 40 many men recognize that there is an aspiration-achievement gap, that is, that their actual achievements have not matched the high aspirations and goals they set for themselves when they were in their twenties. How does the man resolve this aspiration-achievement gap for himself? For many, perhaps the majority, there is a gradual reconciliation, with aspirations being reduced until they are at a realistic, attainable level, and the man emerges feeling good about himself. For some. the reconciliation is not easy and there is a crisis and depression.

According to Erik Erikson (1950), one of the major tasks of adult development is a resolution of the *stagnation versus generativity* conflict. Most people seem to have a deep-seated desire to feel a sense of personal growth, or generativity, in their lives. At age 40, when the only thing that seems to be growing is the waistline, it may be difficult to feel a sense of generativity, and stagnation may set in. This crisis may be positively resolved by having a continual sense of generativity in adulthood, often by finding growth in other sources, such as the growth of one's children or grandchildren. Single men or gay men with no children can gain a sense of generativity in many other ways, such as taking an interest in fostering the careers of their younger coworkers.

Relationships within the man's family shift during the mid-life period (Brim, 1976). The children grow and leave home, leaving the husband and wife alone together. Although it is a popular stereotype that this is a difficult time in marriage. causing many divorces, the data actually indicate that married couples on the average rate the postparental period as one of the happiest in their lives (Brim, 1976). The man's own parents may become increasingly dependent on him, requiring a transformation of that relationship. And the man's wife, freed from child-care responsibilities, may seek education, a career, or a more active involvement in a job she already has, once again requiring renegotiation of the marital relationship.

Systematic, well-sampled research indicates that men in their forties—compared with groups of men aged 25 to 39 and 50 to 69—do show significantly higher depression scores and more alcohol and drug use; on the other hand, their levels of anxiety are no higher, and they report no less life satisfaction or happiness (Tamir, 1982). Thus it seems that men in their forties have some problems, but the problems are probably not much worse than the problems men face at other ages.

It is important that the complaints of middle-aged men and women be recognized and that they be considered legitimate complaints. It is also important to note how many of these crises of middle age lead to satisfactory resolution, in which the person makes a positive alteration in her or his life.

SUMMARY

Biologically, the menstrual cycle is divided into four phases: The follicular phase, ovulation, the luteal phase, and menstruation. Corresponding to these phases, there are changes in the levels of pituitary hormones (FSH and LH) and in the levels of ovarian hormones (estrogen and progesterone). as well as changes in the ovaries and the uterus. A fairly common menstrual problem is dysmenorrhea, or painful menstruation. Toxic shock syndrome has been found to be associated with the use of tampons during the menstrual period.

Research indicates that some, though probably not all, women experience changes in mood over the phases of the menstrual cycle. For those who experience such changes, mood is generally positive around the middle of the cycle (that is, around ovulation), while negative moods characterized by depression and irritability are more likely just before and during menstruation. The latter phenomenon is the premenstrual-tension syndrome. On the other hand, research indicates that there are no fluctuations in performance over the cycle. There is evidence suggesting that fluctuations in mood are related to changes in hormone levels, but data are also available suggesting that mood fluctuations are related to cultural factors. Research attempting to document whether men experience monthly biological and/or psychological cycles is now in progress.

The climacteric is the period in middle age during which the functioning of the ovaries (both hormone and egg production) declines gradually. One symptom of this process is menopause, the cessation of menstruation. Physical symptoms, such as hot flashes, during this period probably result from declining levels of estrogen and may be relieved by estrogen-replacement therapy; psychological problems, such as depression, may not be so common as is generally believed. When they occur, they may be related either to the decline of estrogen or to cultural factors, such as the empty-nest syndrome.

Men experience a much more gradual decline in the functioning of their gonads.

They may experience a psychological crisis of middle age parallel to that experienced by women.

REVIEW QUESTIONS

1. The phase of the menstrual cycle following menstruation is called the luteal phase. True or false?
2. Toxic shock syndrome is caused by an abnormal growth of a Staphylococcus bacterium in the vagina. True or false?
3. A woman's basal body temperature generally takes a dip on the day of ovulation and then shows a noticeable rise on the day after ovulation. True or false?
4. _____ are the hormonelike substances that are thought to be responsible for menstrual cramps.
5. The premenstrual syndrome consists of physical and psychological symptoms, including tension, depression, irritability, backache, and headache. True or false?
6. Well-controlled scientific studies show that progesterone is highly effective in curing PMS. True or false?
7. Research indicates that some women experience mood shifts over the phases of the menstrual cycle, but some women do not experience such mood shifts. True or false?
8. _____ has been shown to be effective in treating the physical symptoms of menopause, as well as protecting women from osteoporosis.
9. Challenging the notion of the empty-nest syndrome, one sociologist found in interviews with middle-aged women that their predominant feeling about the departure of their children was relief. True or false?
10. One major theme of the male mid-life crisis is the aspiration-achievement gap. True or false?

QUESTIONS FOR THOUGHT, DISCUSSION, AND DEBATE

1. Are women's fluctuations in mood over the menstrual cycle caused by biological factors or by environmental/cultural factors?
2. Is there a male mid-life crisis? If so, what are its "symptoms," and what causes it?

SUGGESTIONS FOR FURTHER READING

Paige, Karen E. (1973, April). Women learn to sing the menstrual blues. *Psychology Today,* p. 41. A thought-provoking article on the negative attitudes in our culture toward menstruation.

Parlee, Mary B. (April 1978.) The rhythms in men's lives. *Psychology Today,* 82–91. This article discusses research on possible monthly cycles in men's moods.

Rubin, Lillian B. (1979). *Women of a certain age: The midlife search for self.* New York: Harper & Row. This describes Rubin's provocative research and her conclusion that the empty nest is more pleasure than pain.

Weideger, Paula. (1976). *Menstruation and menopause: The physiology and psychology, the myth and the reality.* New York: Knopf. A detailed discussion of menstruation and menopause, and especially of the taboos and superstitions surrounding them. Weideger has some biases, but the book is basically excellent and written for the general public.

CHAPTER • **6**

CONCEPTION, PREGNANCY, AND CHILDBIRTH

I realized I was pregnant the same night I became pregnant. I lay there all night. I'd had a very active sex life, and it was the first time I had ever felt this way. I wasn't expecting to get pregnant, but I felt different that night.

Being pregnant meant I was a woman. I was enthralled with my belly growing. I went out right away and got maternity clothes.

I was lying on my stomach and felt—something, like someone lightly touching my deep insides. Then I just sat very still and for an alive moment felt the hugeness of having something living growing in me. Then I said no, it's not possible, it's too early yet, and then I started to cry. . . . That one moment was my first body awareness of another living thing inside me.

When I was about six months pregnant, and Dick was starting school again, I was home alone, isolated for days at a time. My nightmares and daydreams started around then. Really terrible fears of the baby being deformed. All my life I've always been the good girl. I knew I wasn't really good. I knew I had bad thoughts, but I was never allowed to express them. So I thought that my baby's deformities would be the living proof of the ugliness and badness in me.

I thought it would never end. I was enormous. I couldn't bend over and wash my feet. And it was incredibly hot.*

* *Source:* Boston Women's Health Book Collective. (1973). *Our bodies, ourselves.* New York: Simon & Schuster, pp. 166–167, 170–171.

CHAPTER HIGHLIGHTS

I. CONCEPTION

II. DEVELOPMENT OF THE CONCEPTUS

III. THE STAGES OF PREGNANCY

IV. SEX DURING PREGNANCY

V. NUTRITION

VI. EFFECTS OF DRUGS TAKEN DURING PREGNANCY

VII. BIRTH

VIII. NATURAL CHILDBIRTH

IX. AFTER THE BABY IS BORN: THE POSTPARTUM PERIOD

X. BREAST-FEEDING

XI. PROBLEM PREGNANCIES

XII. INFERTILITY

Chapter 4 described the remarkable biological process by which a single fertilized egg develops into a male or a female human being. This chapter is about some equally remarkable processes involved in creating human beings: conception, pregnancy, and childbirth.

Sperm Meets Egg: The Incredible Journey

On about day 14 of an average menstrual cycle the woman ovulates. The egg is released from the ovary into the body cavity. Typically it is then picked up by the fimbriae (long fingerlike structures at the end of the fallopian tube—see Figure 6.1) and enters the fallopian tube. It then begins a leisurely trip down the tube toward the uterus, reaching it in about five days, if it has been fertilized. Otherwise, it disintegrates in about 48 hours. The egg, unlike the sperm, has no means of moving itself and is propelled by the cilia (hairlike structures) lining the fallopian tube. The egg has begun its part of the journey toward conception.

Meanwhile, the woman has been having intercourse. The man has an orgasm and ejaculates inside the woman's vagina. The sperm are deposited in the vagina, there to begin their journey toward the egg. Actually they have made an incredible trip even before reaching the vagina. Initially they were manufactured in the seminiferous tubules of the testes (see Chapter 3). They then collected and were stored in

FIGURE 6.1

Sexual intercourse, showing the pathway of sperm and egg from manufacture in the testes and ovary to conception, which typically occurs in the fallopian tube.

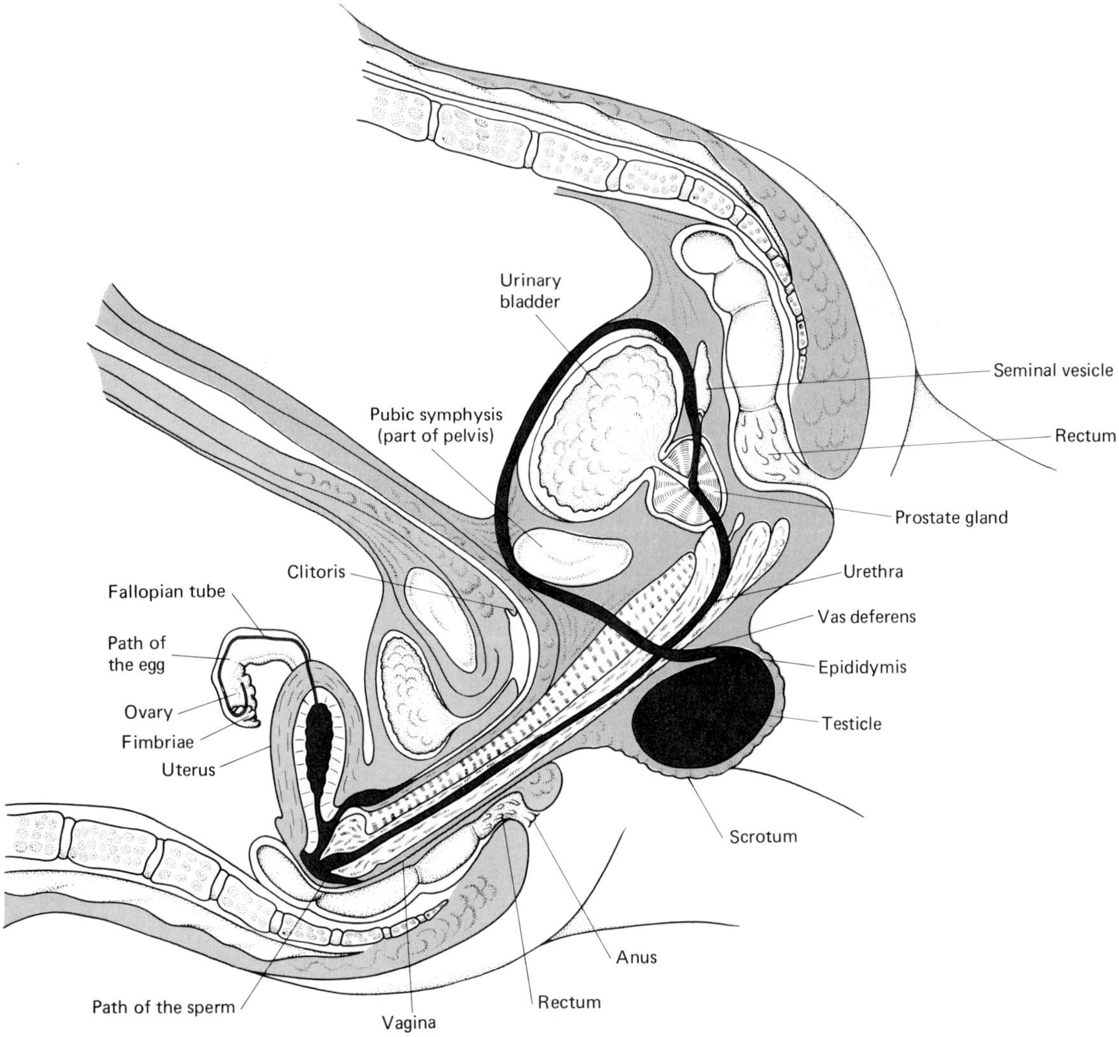

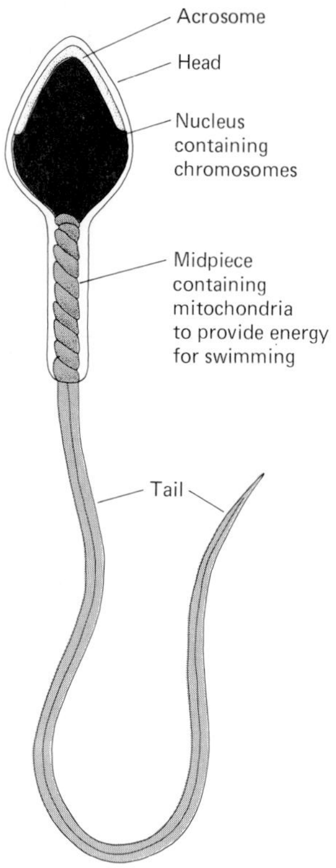

FIGURE 6.2

The structure of a mature human sperm.

the epididymis. During ejaculation they moved up and over the top of the bladder in the vas deferens; then they traveled down through the ejaculatory duct, mixed with seminal fluid, and went out through the urethra.

The sperm is one of the tiniest cells in the human body. It is composed of a *head,* a *midpiece,* and a *tail* (see Figure 6.2). The head is about 5 microns long, and the total length, from the tip of the head to the tip of the tail, is about 60 microns (about 2/1000 inch, or 0.06 millimeter). The chromosomal material, which is the sperm's most importat contribution when it unites with the egg, is contained in the nucleus, which is in the head of the sperm. The midpiece contains mitochondria, which are tiny structures in which chemical reactions occur that provide energy. This energy is used when the sperm lashes its tail back and forth. The lashing action (called *flagellation*) propels the sperm forward.

A typical ejaculate has a volume of about 3 milliliters, or about a teaspoonful, and contains about 300 million sperm. Although this might seem to be a wasteful amount of sperm if only one is needed for fertilization, the great majority of the sperm never get even close to the egg. Some of the ejaculate, together with the sperm in it, may flow out of the vagina as a result of gravity. Other sperm may be killed by the acidity of the vagina, to which they are very sensitive. Of those that make it safely into the uterus, half swim up the wrong fallopian tube (the one containing no egg).

But here we are, several hours later, with a hearty band of sperm swimming up the fallopian tube toward the egg, against the currents that are bringing the egg down. Sperm are capable of swimming 1 to 3 centimeters (about 1 inch) per hour, although it has been documented that sperm may arrive at the egg within 1 to 1½ hours after ejaculation, which is much sooner than would be expected, given their swimming rate. It is thought that muscular contractions in the uterus may help speed them along. By the time a sperm reaches the egg, it has swum approximately 3000 times its own length (this would be comparable to a swim of over 3 miles for a human being).

Contrary to the popular belief that conception occurs in the uterus, typically it occurs in the outer third (the part near the ovary) of the fallopian tube. Of the original 300 million sperm, only about 2000 reach the tube containing the egg. The egg is surrounded by a thin, gelatinous layer called the *zona pellucida.* While the exact mechanism that permits one and only one sperm to enter the egg is unknown, it is thought that the sperm swarm around the egg and secrete an enzyme called hyaluronidase (produced by the acrosome located in the head of the sperm—see Figure 6.2); this enzyme dissolves the zona pellucida, permitting one sperm to penetrate the egg.[1] Conception has occurred.

Hyaluronidase:
An enzyme secreted by the sperm that allows it to penetrate the egg.

Zygote:
A fertilized egg.

The fertilized egg, called the zygote, continues to travel down the fallopian tube. About 36 hours after conception, it begins the process of cell division, by which the original one cell becomes a mass of two cells, then four cells, then eight cells, and so on. About five to seven days after conception, the mass of cells implants itself in the lining of the uterus, there to be nourished and grow. For the first eight weeks of gestation the *conceptus* (product of conception) is called an *embryo;* from then until birth it is called a *fetus.*

Improving the Chances of Conception: Making a Baby

While this topic may seem rather remote to the average college student, whose principal concern is probably *avoiding* conception, some couples do want to have a baby. The following are points for them to keep in mind.

The whole trick, of course, is to time intercourse so that it occurs around the time of ovulation. To do this, it is necessary to determine when the woman ovulates. If she is that idealized woman with the perfectly regular 28-day cycle, then she ovulates on day 14. But for the vast majority of women, the time of ovulation can best be determined by keeping a *basal body temperature chart.* To do this, the woman takes her temperature every morning immediately upon waking (that means before getting up and moving around, having a cigarette, or drinking a cup of coffee). She then keeps a graph of her temperature (like the one shown in Figure 5.2). During the preovulatory phase, the temperature will be relatively constant (the temperature is below 98.6°F because temperature is low in the early morning). On the day of ovulation the temperature drops, and on the day following ovulation it rises sharply, by 0.4°F to 1.0°F above the preovulatory level. The temperature should then stay at that high level until just before menstruation. The most reliable indicator of ovulation is the rise in temperature the day after it occurs. From this, the woman can determine the day of ovulation, and that determination should be consistent with menstruation occurring about 14 days later. After doing this for a couple of cycles, the woman should have a fairly good idea of the day in her cycle on which she ovulates.

Sperm live inside the woman's body for about 48 hours.[2] The egg is capable of

---

[1]Thus while only one sperm is necessary to accomplish fertilization, it appears that it is important for him to have a lot of his buddies along to help him get into the egg. Therefore, maintaining a high sperm count seems to be important for conception.

[2]But do not assume this if you are concerned with *contraception.* A few recent reports indicate that they may survive for 5 or even 10 days.

being fertilized for about the first 12 to 24 hours after ovulation. Allowing the sperm some swimming time, this means that intercourse should be timed right at ovulation or one or two days before.

Assuming you have some idea of the time of ovulation, how frequent should intercourse be? While more may be merrier, more is not necessarily more effective. The reason for this is that it is important for the man's sperm count to be maintained. It takes a while to manufacture 300 million sperm—at least 24 hours. And, as was discussed earlier, maintaining a high sperm count appears to be important in accomplishing the task of fertilizing the egg. For purposes of conceiving, then, it is probably best to have intercourse about every 24 to 48 hours, or about four times during the week in which the woman is to ovulate.

It is also important to take some steps to ensure that once deposited in the vagina, the sperm get a decent chance to survive and to find their way into the fallopian tubes. Position during and after intercourse is important. For purposes of conceiving, the best position for intercourse is with the woman on her back (man-on-top, or "missionary," position—see Chapter 9). If the woman is on top, much of the ejaculate may run out of the vagina because of the pull of gravity. After intercourse, she should remain on her back, possibly with her legs pulled up and a pillow under her hips, preferably for about a half hour to an hour. This allows the semen to remain in a pool in the vagina, which gives the sperm a good chance to swim up into the uterus. Because sperm are very sensitive to the pH (acidity-alkalinity) of the vagina, this factor also requires some consideration. Acidity kills sperm. Douching with commercial preparations or with acidic solutions (such as vinegar) should be avoided. If anything, the woman may want to douche before intercourse with a slightly basic solution made by adding 2 or 3 tablespoons of baking soda to a quart of water. Finally, lubricants and/or suppositories should not be used; they may kill sperm or block their entrance into the uterus.

DEVELOPMENT OF THE CONCEPTUS

For the nine months of pregnancy, two organisms—the conceptus and the pregnant woman—undergo parallel, dramatic changes. The changes that occur in the developing conceptus will be discussed in this section; a later section will be ahout the changes that take place in the pregnant woman.

Typically the nine months of pregnancy are divided into three equal periods of three months, each called *trimesters.* Thus the first trimester is months 1 to 3, the second trimester is months 4 to 6, and the third (or last) trimester is months 7 to 9.

The Embryo and Its Support Systems

We left the conceptus, which began as a single fertilized egg cell, dividing into many cells as it passed down the fallopian tube, finally arriving in the uterus and implanting itself into the uterine wall.

During the embryonic period of development (the first eight weeks) most of the fetus's major organ systems are formed in processes that occur with amazing speed. The inner part of the ball of cells implanted in the uterus now differentiates into two layers, the endoderm and the ectoderm. Later a third layer. the mesoderm, forms between them. The various organs of the body differentiate from these layers. The *ectoderm* will form the entire nervous system and the skin, as well as derivatives of it such as hair and the lens of the eye. The *endoderm* differentiates into the digestive system—from the pharynx, to the stomach and intestines, to the rectum—and the respiratory system. The muscles, skeleton, connective tissues, and reproductive and circulatory systems derive from the *mesoderm.* Fetal development generally proceeds in a cephalocaudal order. That is, the head develops first, and the lower body last. For this reason, the head of the fetus is enormous compared with the rest of the body (see Figure 6.3).

Meanwhile, another group of cells has differentiated into the *trophoblast,* which has important functions in maintaining the embryo and which will eventually become the placenta.

Placenta (plah-SEN-tuh): An organ formed on the wall of the uterus through which the fetus receives oxygen and nutrients and gets rid of waste products.

The placenta is the mass of tissues that surrounds the conceptus early in development and nurtures its growth. Later it moves to the side of the fetus. The placenta has a number of important functions, perhaps the most important of which is that it serves as a site for the exchange of substances between the woman's blood and the fetus's blood. It is important to note that the woman's circulatory system and the fetus's circulatory system are completely separate. That is, with only rare exceptions, the woman's blood never circulates inside the fetus; nor does the fetus's blood circulate in the woman's blood vessels. Instead, the fetus's blood passes out of its body through the umbilical cord to the placenta. There it circulates in the numerous *villi* (tiny fingerlike projections in the placenta). The woman's blood circulates around the outside of these villi. Thus there is a membrane barrier between the two blood systems. Some substances are capable of passing through this barrier, while others are not. Oxygen and nutrients can pass through the barrier, and thus the woman's blood supplies oxygen and nutrients to the fetus, providing substitutes for breathing and eating. Carbon dioxide and waste products similarly pass back from the fetal blood to the woman's blood. Some viruses and other disease-causing organisms can pass through the barrier, including those for German measles (rubella) and syphilis. But other organisms cannot pass through the barrier; thus the woman may have a terrible cold, but the fetus will remain completely healthy. Various drugs can also cross the placental barrier, and the woman should therefore be careful about drugs taken during pregnancy (see the section on drugs during pregnancy, below).

Another major function of the placenta is that it secretes hormones. The placenta produces large quantities of estrogen and progesterone. Many of the physical symptoms of pregnancy may be caused by these elevated levels of hormones. Another hormone manufactured by the placenta is human chorionic gonadotropin (HCG). HCG is the hormone that is detected in pregnancy tests.

Human chorionic gonadotropin (HCG): A hormone secreted by the placenta; it is the substance detected in pregnancy tests.

Umbilical cord: The tube that connects the fetus to the placenta.

The umbilical cord is formed during the fifth week of embryonic development. The fully developed cord is about 55 centimeters (20 inches) long. Normally, it contains three blood vessels: two arteries and one vein. Some people believe that the fetus's umbilical cord attaches to the woman's navel; actually, the umbilical cord attaches to the placenta, thereby providing for the interchanges of substances described above.

Amniotic fluid: The watery fluid surrounding a developing fetus in the uterus.

Two membranes surround the fetus, the *chorion* and the *amnion.* the amnion being the innermost. The amnion is filled with a watery liquid called amniotic fluid, in which the fetus floats and can readily move. It is the amniotic fluid that is sampled when an amniocentesis is performed (see below). The amniotic fluid maintains the fetus at a constant temperature and, most important, cushions the fetus against possible injury. Thus the woman can fall down a flight of stairs, and the fetus will remain undisturbed. Indeed, the amniotic fluid might be considered the original waterbed.

Fetal Development during the First Trimester

In a sense, the development of the fetus during the first trimester is more remarkable than its development during the second and third trimesters, for it is during the first trimester that the small mass of cells implanted in the uterus develops into a fetus with most of the major organ systems present and with recognizable human features.

By the third week of gestation, the embryo appears as a small bit of flesh and is about 0.2 centimeters (1/12 inch) long. During the third and fourth weeks, the head undergoes a great deal of development. The central nervous system begins to form, and the beginnings of eyes and ears are visible. The backbone is constructed by the end of the fourth week. A "tail" is noticeable early in embryonic development but has disappeared by the eighth week.

From the fourth to the eighth weeks, the external body parts—eyes, ears, arms, hands, fingers, legs, feet, and toes—develop (see Figure 6.3*c*, following page 136). By the end of the tenth week they are completely formed. Indeed, by the tenth week, the embryo has not only a complete set of fingers but also fingernails.

By the end of the seventh week, the liver, lungs, pancreas, kidneys, and intestines have formed and have begun limited functioning. The gonads have also formed, but the gender of the fetus is not clearly distinguishable until the twelfth week.

At the end of the twelfth week (end of the first trimester) the fetus is unmistakably human and looks like a small infant. It is about 10 centimeters (4 inches) long and weighs about 19 grams (2/3 ounce). From this point on, development consists mainly of enlargement and differentiation of structures that are already present.

Fetal Development during the Second Trimester

Around the end of the fourteenth week, the movements of the fetus can be detected ("quickening"). By the eighteenth week, the woman has been able to feel movement for two to four weeks, and the physician can detect the fetal heartbeat. The latter is an important point, because it helps the physician determine the length of gestation. The baby should be born about 20 weeks later. If it is born in the twenty-third week, it weighs less than 1000 grams (2 pounds) and has about 1 in 10,000 chance of survival, given expert care (Behrman and Rosen, 1976).

The fetus first opens its eyes around the twentieth week. By about the twenty-fourth week, it is sensitive to light and can hear sounds in utero. Arm and leg movements are vigorous at this time, and the fetus alternates between periods of wakefulness and sleep.

Fetal Development during the Third Trimester

At the end of the second trimester the fetus's skin is wrinkled and covered with downlike hair. At the beginning of the third trimester, fat deposits form under the skin; these will give the infant the characteristic chubby appearance of babyhood. The downlike hair is lost.

A baby born at the end of the seventh month has a 50 percent chance of survival. It is a misconception that babies born during the seventh month are more likely to live than those born during the eighth month. The closer to full term, the better the chance of survival. Thus a baby born at the end of the eighth month has a 90 to 95 percent chance of survival; for one born at the end of nine months, the chance of survival is 99 percent.

During the seventh month the fetus turns in the uterus to assume a head-down position. If this turning does not occur by the time of delivery, there will be a *breech presentation.*

The fetus's growth during the last two months is rapid. At the end of the eighth month it weighs an average of 2500 grams (5 pounds, 4 ounces). The average full-term baby weighs 3300 grams (7.5 pounds) and is 50 centimeters (20 inches) long. According to the *Guinness Book of World Records,* in 1961 Mrs. Saadet Cor, of Turkey, gave birth to the largest normal baby ever born; it weighed 24 pounds, 4 ounces. The smallest baby ever to survive was Marion Chapman, who was born in 1938 in England. She weighed 10 ounces. The birth took place without the help of a physician.

THE STAGES OF PREGNANCY

The First Trimester (The First 12 Weeks)

Symptoms of Pregnancy

For most women, the first symptom of pregnancy is a missed menstrual period. Of course, there may be a wide variety of reactions to this event. For the teenager who is not married or for the married woman who feels that she already has enough children, the reaction may be negative—depression, anger, and fear. For the woman who has been trying to conceive for several months, the reaction may be joy and eager anticipation.

In fact, there are many other reasons besides pregnancy why a woman may have a late period or miss a period; illness or emotional stress may delay a period, and women occasionally skip a period for no apparent reason.

It is also true that a woman may continue to experience some cyclic bleeding or spotting during pregnancy. It is not particularly a danger sign, except that in a few cases it is a symptom of a miscarriage.

If the woman has been keeping a basal body temperature chart, this can provide a very early sign that she is pregnant. If her temperature rises abruptly at about the time ovulation would normally occur and then stays up for more than two weeks—say, about 3 weeks—the chances are fairly good that she is pregnant. The increased temperature results from the high level of progesterone manufactured by the corpus luteum and, later, the placenta.

Other early symptoms of pregnancy are tenderness of the breasts—a tingling sensation and special sensitivity of the nipples—and nausea and vomiting (called "morning sickness," although these symptoms may actually happen anytime during the day). More frequent urination, feelings of fatigue, and a need for more sleep are other early signs of pregnancy.

Pregnancy Tests

A pregnancy test may be done by a physician, at a Planned Parenthood or Family Planning clinic, or at a medical laboratory.

The most widely used pregnancy test is an immunologic test based on detecting the presence of HCG (human chorionic gonadotropin, secreted by the placenta) in the woman's urine. It can be done in a matter of minutes to a few hours and is very accurate. It involves mixing a drop of urine with certain chemicals, either on a slide or in a tube. If HCG is present, the mixture will coagulate and the test for pregnancy is positive (the woman is pregnant).

The laboratory tests for pregnancy are 98 percent accurate. A laboratory test may produce a false negative (tell the woman she is not pregnant when she really is) if it is done too early or if errors are made in processing. Also, some women simply do not show positive signs in the tests or do not do so until the second or third test. The presence of HCG can be detected as early as the third week of pregnancy (one week after the missed period), but the tests are not highly accurate until the sixth or eighth week of pregnancy.

A new test, called the *beta subunit HCG radioimmunoassay,* was developed recently and is 99 percent accurate. It measures HCG in a blood sample and is sensitive enough to detect a pregnancy eight days after conception or five days *before* the missed period. It is highly accurate and is becoming increasingly available.

It is important that early, accurate pregnancy tests be available and that women make use of them. This is true for several reasons. A woman needs to know that she is pregnant as early as possible so that she can see a physician and begin getting good prenatal care. She also needs to know so that she can get the nutrition she requires during pregnancy (see the section on nutrition, below). And if she does not want to carry the baby to term, she needs to know as soon as possible, because abortions are much safer and simpler when performed in the first trimester than when done in the second trimester.

A recent development is the *home pregnancy test,* sold under various brand names as e.p.t. (for "early pregnancy test"), AcuTest, Answer, and Predictor. These are all urine tests designed to measure the presence of HCG; they cost around $10. They can be used about nine days after a missed menstrual period should have begun. Their charm lies in their convenience and the privacy of getting the results. The major problem with them is that they have a very high rate—20 percent—of false negatives, that is, telling the woman she is not pregnant when she actually is (Carpenter, 1979). This compares with an error rate of 1 percent for laboratory tests. The home pregnancy tests also have a 3 percent rate of false positives. To guard against false negatives, the manufacturers recommend repeating the test one week later if the results are negative the first time, although this increases the cost to around $20. The reason that a high rate of false negatives is so serious is that it leads a pregnant woman to think she is not pregnant, and thus she might take drugs that would harm the fetus, and she will not begin getting prenatal care; such dangerous conditions as ectopic pregnancy might therefore go undetected. The tests also require a certain amount of coordination and care in performing. All in all, they are probably not as good an idea as they seem, although improvements in them may be made in the near future.

Hegar's sign:
A sign of pregnancy based on a test done by a physician, in which a softening of the uterus is detected.

At around the sixth to eighth weeks, pregnancy can also be detected by a pelvic exam. The physician looks for Hegar's sign which is a pronounced softening of the isthmus of the uterus (the middle part of the uterus, between the cervix and the body of the uterus). The exam is performed by placing one hand on the abdomen and two fingers of the other hand in the vagina. A change in the color of the cervix, from pale pink to a bluish hue, is another sign of pregnancy at this time.

The signs of pregnancy may be classified as *presumptive signs, probable signs,* and *positive signs.* Amenorrhea, breast tenderness, nausea, and so on, are presumptive signs. The pregnancy tests discussed above all provide probable signs. Three signs are interpreted as positive signs, that is, as definite indications of pregnancy: (1) beating of the fetal heart, (2) active fetal movement, and (3) detection of a fetal skeleton by x-ray (this is done only rarely because of the dangers involved). These signs cannot be detected until the fourth month.

Once the pregnancy has been confirmed, the woman generally is very interested in determining her expected delivery date (called EDC for a rather antiquated expression, "expected date of confinement"). The EDC is calculated using *Nägele's rule*. The rule says to take the date of the first day of the last menstrual period, subtract three months, add seven days, and finally add one year. Thus if the first day of the last menstrual period was September 10, 1986, the expected delivery date would be June 17, 1987: subtracting three months from September 10 gives June 10, adding seven days yields June 17, and adding one year gives June 17, 1987. Nägele's rule works fairly well; 39 percent of infants are born within five days of the predicted date, and 55 percent are born within 10 days of it (Burger and Koromopai, 1939, cited in Hellman and Pritchard, 1971).

Physical Changes

The basic physical change that takes place in the woman's body during the first trimester is the large increase in the levels of hormones, especially estrogen and progesterone, which are produced by the placenta. Many of the other physical symptoms of the first trimester arise from these endocrine changes.

The breasts swell and tingle. This results from the development of the mammary glands, which is stimulated by hormones. The nipples and the area around them (areola) may darken and broaden.

There is often a need to urinate more frequently. This is related to changes in the pituitary hormones that affect the adrenals, which in turn change the water balance in the body so that more water is retained. The growing uterus also contributes by pressing against the bladder.

Bowel movements may become irregular because the high levels of progesterone relax the smooth muscle of the rectum and also because the growing uterus exerts pressure on the rectum. Also, if the woman reduces her activity because of feelings of fatigue, which are common during the first trimester, this may contribute to constipation.

Some women experience morning sickness—feelings of nausea, perhaps to the point of vomiting, and of revulsion toward food or its odor. The nausea and vomiting may occur on waking or at other times during the day. The exact cause of this is not known. One theory is that the high levels of estrogen irritate the stomach. The rapid expansion of the uterus may also be involved. While these symptoms are quite common, it is also true that about 25 percent of pregnant women experience no vomiting at all.

Vaginal discharges may also increase at this time, partly because the increased hormone levels change the pH of the vagina and partly because the vaginal secretions are changing in their chemical composition and quantity.

The feelings of fatigue and sleepiness are probably related to the high levels of progesterone, which is known to have a sedative effect.

Psychological Changes

Our culture is full of stereotypes about the psychological characteristics of pregnant women. It is supposed to be a time of happiness and calm; radiant contentment is said to emanate from the woman's face, making this a good time for her to be photographed. Pregnant women are also seen as somewhat irrational, demanding, and dependent—capable, for example, of sending their husbands to the refrigerator for dill pickles and ice cream at midnight.

Actually, the data suggest that the situation is much more complex than this (see review by Sherman, 1971). A woman's emotional state during pregnancy appears to vary according to a number of factors: her attitude toward the pregnancy (whether she wanted to be pregnant), her social class, her general life adjustment, conflict in the marriage, and stage of pregnancy. The positive emotions noted above are probably a result of the traditional assumption in our culture that all babies are wanted and that all women want babies. However, with increased concern over population size, growing acceptance of methods of contraception, and decreased emphasis on fertility, it has become increasingly recognized that pregnancy may not always be a good thing. These changes in values may make pregnant women feel freer to acknowledge their negative feelings.

Depression and fatigue are not at all uncommon during the first trimester; they may be partly the result of morning sickness. But there is great variation in pregnant women's emotional state. Happiness is more common among those who want to be pregnant, whereas depression is more common among those who do not. Women of lower socioeconomic status are more likely to have negative feelings (although this may be explained by the fact that there are more unwanted pregnancies among women in the lower social classes). Women who have made a generally good life adjustment tend to feel more positive at this time than women with a history of adjustment problems. Finally, negative emotions are commoner when there is a conflict in the marriage.

Myra Leifer (1980) did an intensive study of 19 women, all pregnant for the first time. They were interviewed once during each trimester of pregnancy, on the third day after giving birth, and at six to eight weeks postpartum, and a questionnaire was mailed to them at seven months postpartum. Her general findings were that rather than being a time of calm and bliss, pregnancy was, for most of the women in her sample, difficult and turbulent. She also found that emotional changes during pregnancy and postpartum were strongly related to the emotional support and help the woman received from her husband. The women tended to be emotionally labile (have mood shifts) and to have anxieties. Specifically, in the first trimester anxieties centered on worries about miscarriage. In the first trimester, only the four women for whom the pregnancy was unplanned expressed overall negative emotions. The other women were either positive or ambivalent (had mixed feelings) during the first trimester.

The Second Trimester (Weeks 13 to 26)

Physical Changes

During the fourth month, the woman becomes aware of the fetus's movements ("quickening"). Many women find this to be a very exciting experience.

The woman is made even more aware of the pregnancy by her rapidly expanding belly. There are a variety of reactions to this. Some women feel that it is a magnificent symbol of womanhood. and they rush out to buy maternity clothes and wear them before they are even necessary. Other women feel awkward and resentful of their bulky shape and may begin to wonder whether they can fit through doorways and turnstiles.

Most of the physical symptoms of the first trimester, such as morning sickness, disappear, and discomforts are at a minimum. Physical problems at this time include constipation, hemorrhoids (caused by the pressure of the pelvic organs on the blood vessels of the rectum), and nosebleeds (caused by increased blood volume). Edema—water retention and swelling—may be a problem in the face, hands, wrists, ankles, and feet; it results from increased water retention throughout the body.

Edema (eh-DEE-muh): Excessive fluid retention and swelling.

Colostrum: A watery substance that is secreted from the breast at the end of pregnancy and during the first few days after delivery.

By about mid-pregnancy, the breasts, under hormonal stimulation, have essentially completed their development in preparation for nursing. Beginning about the nineteenth week, a thin amber or yellow fluid called colostrum may come out of the nipple, although there is no milk yet.

Psychological Changes

While the first trimester can be relatively tempestuous, particularly with morning sickness, the second trimester is generally a period of relative calm and well-being. The discomforts of the first trimester are past, and the tensions associated with the close approach of delivery are not yet present. Research shows that women's emotions are more positive during this stage than during the other stages (Sherman, 1971). Leifer (1980) found that the second trimester was the high point psychologically—there was the most happiness and pride in pregnancy. Fears of miscarriage diminished as the women could feel fetal movements, and there was an intense feeling of relief that the fetus was alive.

The Third Trimester (Weeks 27 to 38)

Physical Changes

The uterus is very large and hard now. The woman is increasingly aware of her size and of the fetus, which is becoming more and more active. In fact, some women are kept awake at night by its somersaults and hiccups.

The extreme size of the uterus puts pressure on a number of other organs, causing some discomfort. There is pressure on the lungs, which may cause shortness of breath. The stomach is also being squeezed, and indigestion is common. The navel is pushed out. The heart is being strained because of the large increase in blood volume, the strain peaking at about the thirtieth week and declining from then until labor. Most women feel low in energy (Leifer, 1980).

The weight gain of the second trimester continues. Most physicians recommend about 22 to 27 pounds of weight gain during pregnancy. The average infant at birth weighs 7.5 pounds; the rest of the weight gain is accounted for by the placenta (about 1 pound), the amniotic fluid (about 2 pounds), enlargement of the uterus (about 2 pounds), enlargement of the breasts (1.5 pounds), and the additional fat and water retained by the woman (8 or more pounds). Physicians restrict the amount of weight gain because of the incidence of complications such as high blood pressure and strain on the heart is much higher in women who gain an excessive amount of weight. Also, excessive weight gained during pregnancy can be very hard to lose afterward.

The woman's balance is somewhat disturbed because of the large amount of weight that has been added to the front part of her body. She may compensate for this by adopting the characteristic "waddling" walk of the pregnant woman, which can result in back pains.

Braxton-Hicks contractions: Contractions of the uterus during pregnancy that are not part of actual labor.

The uterus tightens occasionally in painless contractions called Braxton-Hicks contractions; these are not part of labor. It is thought that these contractions help to strengthen the uterine muscles, preparing them for labor.

In a first pregnancy, around two to four weeks before delivery the baby turns, and the head drops into the pelvis. This is called *lightening, dropping,* or *engagement.* Engagement usually occurs during labor in women who have had babies before.

Some women are concerned about the appropriate amount of activity during pregnancy—whether some things constitute "overdoing it." Traditionally physicians and textbooks have warned of the dangers of physical activities and have tried to discourage them. It appears now, however, that such restrictions were based more on superstition than on scientific fact. Current thinking holds that for a healthy pregnant woman, moderate activity is not dangerous and may actually be psychologically beneficial. Modern methods of childbirth encourage sensible exercise for the pregnant woman so that she will be in shape for labor (see the section on natural childbirth, below). The matter, of course, is highly individual. But one recent Olympic swimmer placed third in her event while 3½ months pregnant, and it was reported that 10 of the 25 Soviet women Olympic champions of the Sixteenth Olympiad in Melbourne, Australia, were pregnant (Bruser, 1969).

Psychological Changes

While the second trimester is relatively sunny, the third trimester may be somewhat stressful psychologically. The incidence of mild emotional disturbances increases, particularly during the last six weeks (Sherman, 1971). During the last month women often become very impatient, feeling as if they are in a state of suspended animation and really wanting to get on with it.

The birth of the baby becomes an ever-nearer reality. With that comes some anxieties. Notable among these are worries that the baby will be deformed or defective in some way, an anxiety that may be reflected in the woman's dreams at this time and in her waking fantasies. The woman may also wonder, especially if it is a first child, whether she will be a good mother and whether anything will happen to her during delivery. Leifer (1980) found increases during the third trimester in anxiety about the delivery and about possible deformity of the baby.

The Father's Role in Pregnancy

Couvade and Sympathetic Pregnancy

Occasionally some husbands may experience nausea and vomiting along with their pregnant wives. This reaction is called *sympathetic pregnancy.*

In some cultures this phenomenon takes a more dramatic form, known as *couvade.* In the couvade, the husband retires to bed while his wife is in labor. He suffers all the pains of delivery, moaning and groaning as she does. Couvade is still practiced in parts of Asia, North and South America, and Oceania (Mead and Newton. 1967).

The Father-to-Be

In modern American culture many men expect to devote substantial amounts of time and energy to fathering, unlike the distant fathers of yesteryear. In fact, it has even been claimed that there is a "father instinct" (Biller and Meredith, 1975). Although some men choose to remain in the background, many choose to be actively involved in the pregnancy and the parenting (Antle, 1978). Early in the pregnancy, first-time fathers may recall their own childhood and relationship to their father, and may need to resolve any mixed emotions they still have about that relationship. In one study, 70 percent of expectant fathers were initially ambivalent about fathering, but their feelings gradually became more positive, in anticipation of satisfactions to be derived from being fathers (Obzrut, 1976). In the same study, the fathers reported engaging in many activities in preparation for becoming fathers. Many reported attending parenting classes, planning father-child activities, observing and talking to other fathers, and daydreaming about the baby. Most of these activities, of course, parallel those done by expectant mothers. It has been theorized that men who display this active involvement will do best in the father role after the baby is born (Antle, 1978).

SEX DURING PREGNANCY

Many women are concerned about whether it is safe or advisable for them to have sexual intercourse while they are pregnant, particularly during the latter stages of the pregnancy. Traditionally, physicians were concerned that intercourse might (1) cause an infection or (2) precipitate labor prematurely or cause a miscarriage (for a review on sexuality and pregnancy, see White and Reamy, 1982).

Masters and Johnson (1966) have investigated sexual intercourse during pregnancy. They state emphatically that given a normal, healthy pregnancy, intercourse can continue safely at least until four weeks before the baby is due. (This is an individual matter, however, and should be decided in consultation with a physician; some women are clearly high-risk cases, for whom intercourse is inadvisable.) Masters and Johnson find that the woman is usually sufficiently recovered three weeks after birth for coitus to be safe, and the woman's sexual interest also generally returns at about that time.

However, a recent analysis of 27,000 pregnancies occurring between 1959 and 1966 indicated that infections of the amniotic fluids and subsequent death of the baby were more frequent among women who had intercourse in the month before delivery compared with those who abstained (Naeye, 1979). Criticisms of the study have been made, and one should probably not rush out to urge abstinence by pregnant women. A reasonable recommendation is for women who have a history of miscarriage or whose cervix has begun to dilate to avoid intercourse and orgasm during the last trimester (Herbst, 1979).

Physicians' pronouncements aside, the available data indicate that women continue to have intercourse, and do so at a near-normal rate, until well into the third trimester. As the data in Table 6.1 indicate, intercourse continues through the second trimester with essentially the same frequency as before pregnancy. There is a slight decrease during the seventh and eighth months, but not until the last month do substantial numbers of women report abstaining from intercourse. Indeed, Masters and Johnson found an increased sexual interest during the second trimester, which is probably related to the passing of the nausea and fatigue of the first trimester and the positive feelings associated with the second trimester.

Of course, during the latter stages of pregnancy, the woman's shape makes intercourse increasingly awkward. The missionary position is probably best abandoned at this time. The side-to-side position (see Chapter 9) is probably the position best suited to the special problems of intercourse during the late stages of pregnancy. Couples should also remember that there are many ways of experiencing sexual

TABLE 6.1

PERCENTAGE OF WOMEN HAVING VARIOUS FREQUENCIES OF COITUS AT DIFFERENT STAGES OF PREGNANCY

Number of Acts of Coitus per Week	Baseline One Year before Conception, %	First Trimester, %	Second Trimester, %	Seventh Month, %	Eighth Month, %	Ninth Month, %
None	0	2	2	11	23	59
One	7	11	16	23	29	19
Two to five	81	78	77	63	46	23
Six or more	12	9	5	2	2	1

Source: N. Wagner and D. Solberg. (1974). Pregnancy and sexuality. *Medical Aspects of Human Sexuality,* **8**(3), 44–79.

pleasure and orgasm besides having intercourse—mutual masturbation or oral-genital sex[3] may be a good alternative for the very pregnant woman.

One of the best guides in this matter is the woman's own feelings. If intercourse becomes uncomfortable for her, it should be discontinued until it does feel more comfortable.

NUTRITION

During pregnancy, another living being is growing inside the woman, and she needs lots of energy, protein, vitamins, and minerals at this time. Therefore, diet during pregnancy is extremely important. If the woman's diet is good, she has a much better chance of remaining healthy during pregnancy and of bearing a healthy baby; if her diet is inadequate, she stands more of a chance of developing one of a number of diseases during pregnancy herself and of bearing a child whose weight is low at birth. Babies with low birth weights do not have as good a chance of survival as babies with normal birth weights. According to a study done in Toronto, mothers in a poor-diet group had four times as many serious health problems during pregnancy as a group of mothers whose diets were supplemented with highly nutritious foods. Those with the poor diets had seven times as many threatened miscarriages and three times as many stillbirths; their labor lasted five hours longer on the average (Newton, 1972).

The recommended diet for a pregnant woman is shown in Table 6.2. It is particularly important that she get enough protein, folic acid, iron, calcium, and vitamins A, B, C, D, and E. Protein is important for building new tissues. Folic acid is also important for growth; symptoms of folic acid deficiency are anemia and fatigue. Iron is important for the blood that circulates to the placenta, from which the fetus draws off additional iron for itself. Muscle cramps, nerve pains, uterine ligament pains, sleeplessness, and irritability may all be symptoms of a calcium deficiency. Sometimes even an excellent diet does not provide enough iron, calcium, or folic acid, in which case their intake should be supplemented with pills.

EFFECTS OF DRUGS TAKEN DURING PREGNANCY

We are such a pill-popping culture that we seldom stop to think about whether we should take a certain drug. The pregnant woman, however, needs to know that when she takes a drug, not only does it circulate through her body, but it may also circulate through the fetus. Because the fetus develops so rapidly during pregnancy, drugs may have severe consequences, including producing serious malformations. Drugs that produce such defects are called teratogenic.[4] An example that attracted much attention in the early 1960s was the drug thalidomide, a tranquilizer; if taken early in pregnancy, it resulted in babies with grotesque deformities such as flipper-like appendages where there should have been arms and legs. Of course, not all drugs can cross the placental barrier, but many can. The drugs that pregnant women should be cautious in using are discussed below.

Teratogenic:
Producing defects in the fetus.

[3]There is, however, some risk associated with cunnilingus for the pregnant woman, as discussed in Chapter 9.

[4]"Teratogenic" is from the Greek words *teras,* meaning "monster," and *genic,* meaning "cause."

TABLE 6.2

RECOMMENDED DAILY DIET FOR THE PREGNANT WOMAN

Foods	Serving Size	Number of Servings
Protein foods		
Animal	Meat, poultry, fish, 2 oz.	2
Plant	Legumes, 1 c. cooked;	1
	nut butters, ¼ c.; nuts, ½ c.; seeds, ½ c.; tofu, 1 c.	1
Milk, cheese, etc.	Milk, 1 c.; cheddar cheese, 1½ oz; cottage cheese, 1½ c.; yogurt, 1 c.; tofu, 1 c.	4
Breads and cereals (whole-grain preferable)	Bread, 1 slice; rice, ½ c.; pasta, ½ c.; ready-to-eat cereal, ¾ c.	4
Vitamin-C rich fruits and vegetables	Orange juice, 4 oz.; tomato juice, 12 oz.; ½ grapefruit or canteloupe; strawberries, ¾ c.	1
Dark green vegetables	Broccoli, spinach, collards, turnip or mustard greens, kale, dark green lettuce (e.g., romaine), 1 c. raw or ¾ c. cooked	1
Other fruits and vegetables, including yellow ones high in vitamin A	Carrots, yams, squash, corn, ½ c.	1
Fat and oils	Oil (not palm or coconut), margarine, mayonnaise, or salad dressing, 1 tbsp.	2

	Amounts	
Essential Nutrients	Nonpregnant Adult	Increase during Pregnancy
Calories	2000	+300
Protein (g)	44	+30
Vitamin A (μg RE)	800	+200
Vitamin D (μg)	5	+5
Vitamin E (μg α TE)	8	+2
Vitamin C (mg)	6	+20
Thiamine (mg)	1.0	+0.4
Riboflavin (mg)	1.2	+0.3
Niacin (mg NE)	13	+2
Vitamin B_6 (mg)	2	+0.6
Folacin (μg)	400	+400
Vitamin B_{12} (μg)	3	+1
Calcium (mg)	800	+400
Phosphorous (mg)	800	+400
Magnesium (mg)	300	+150
Iron (mg)	18	+30–60
Zinc (mg)	15	+5
Iodine (μg)	150	+25

Source: Williams, E. R., and Caliendo, M. A. (1984). *Nutrition.* (2nd ed.) New York: McGraw-Hill.

Antibiotics

Long-term use of antibiotics by the woman may cause damage to the fetus. Tetracycline may cause stained teeth and bone deformities. Gentamycin, kanamycin, neomycin, streptomycin, and vincomycin all may cause deafness. Nitrofurantoin may cause jaundice. Some drugs given in the treatment of tuberculosis can cause jaundice, and those taken by diabetics may cause various fetal anomalies.

Addictive Drugs

Alcohol consumed by the woman circulates through the fetus. Alcoholic women can give birth to babies who have alcohol on their breath; the babies then have withdrawal symptoms for the first few days after they are born—scarcely a pleasant introduction to life outside the womb. Excessive amounts of alcohol lead to vitamin depletion and biochemical imbalance, and to low-birth-weight babies, premature birth, or even intrauterine death.

Fetal alcohol syndrome (FAS):
Serious disease in the newborn of an alcoholic mother.

The pattern of physical malformations that occur in the offspring of women who abuse alcohol during pregnancy has been termed the fetal alcohol syndrome (FAS) (for reviews, see Abel, 1980; Clarren and Smith, 1978). Among the characteristics of the syndrome are both prenatal and postnatal growth deficiencies, a small brain, small eye openings, and joint, limb, and heart malformations. Perhaps the most serious effect is mental retardation. About 85 percent of children with the FAS score two or more standard deviations below the mean on intelligence tests—that would be an IQ of about 70 or below. Indeed, two experts concluded that "maternal abuse of alcohol during gestation . . . appears to be the most frequent known teratogenic cause of mental deficiency in the Western world" (Clarren and Smith, 1978, p. 1066).

Current research indicates that the fetus is at risk for the FAS if the mother's consumption of alcohol is six or more drinks per day. It is also clear that women who drink moderately may have children who are affected to some degree (Abel, 1980). Unfortunately, "safe" limits for alcohol consumption during pregnancy have not been established.

Heroin addiction and morphine addiciton lead to similar problems (Householder et al., 1982). The babies are born smaller than average and undergo withdrawal symptoms after birth. In infancy their symptoms include irritability, hyperactivity, and sleep and feeding disturbances. The psychological problems persist into childhood. Methadone can also cause problems in the baby.

Steroids

Synthetic hormones such as progestin can cause masculinization of a female fetus, as discussed in Chapter 4. Corticosteroids are linked with jaundice, low birth weights, cleft palate, and stillbirth. Excessive amounts of vitamin A are associated with cleft palate. Excesses of vitamin D, B^6, and K have also been associated with fetal defects. A potent estrogen, diethylstilbestrol (DES), has been shown to cause cancer of the vagina in girls whose mothers took the drug while pregnant (Herbst, 1972). (DES pops up in a number of places. It is used in the "morning-after" pill and as a diet supplement to fatten cattle, the latter use having recently been prohibited because of the possible dangers of ingesting too much DES.)

Others

According to the U.S. Public Health Service, maternal smoking during pregnancy exerts a retarding influence on fetal growth indicated by decreased infant birth weight and increased incidence of prematurity (see Peterson et al., 1965; Ravenholt and Levinski, 1965; Yerushalmy, 1964; for a review, see Coleman et al., 1979). A study of 28,000 children found that those children whose mothers smoked heavily during pregnancy were almost twice as likely to be hyperactive and impulsive when they were 6 years old than were the children of nonsmoking mothers; the children of smoking mothers also had lower IQs and less developed motor skills (Dunn et al., 1977).

Some antihistamines may produce malformations. Even plain aspirin may cause damage.

Although not classified as a drug, x-rays deserve mention here, since they can damage the fetus, particularly during the first 42 days after conception.

In 1980 the FDA issued a warning that caffeine—which is not only in coffee and tea but also cola drinks and cocoa and stay-awake drugs—may be linked to birth defects (Lecos, 1980). The warning was based on a study in which pregnant rats were fed caffeine. The rats who were given doses equivalent to 12 to 24 cups of coffee per day in humans gave birth to offspring with missing toes. In the case of rats who were given doses equivalent to two cups of coffee per day in humans, the offspring after birth did not grow as fast as normal.

Unfortunately, we have no information available yet on any possible effects of using marijuana during pregnancy (Leavitt, 1974). It is known, though, that the psychoactive chemical in marijuana crosses the placental barrier (Harbison and Mantilla-Plata, 1972; Idänpään-Heikkilä et al., 1969). There is some scanty evidence that use of LSD during pregnancy may cause chromosome damage to the infant (Dishotsky et al., 1971) and increases the risk of spontaneous abortion (McGlothlin et al., 1970).

Probably the best rule for the pregnant woman considering using a drug is, "When in doubt, don't."

BIRTH

The Beginning of Labor

There are a few signs that labor is about to begin, although these vary considerably from one woman to the next. There may be a discharge of a small amount of bloody mucus (the "bloody show"). This is the mucus plug that was in the cervical opening during pregnancy, its purpose being to prevent germs from passing from the vagina up into the uterus. In about 10 percent of all women the membranes containing the amniotic fluid rupture (the bag of waters bursts), and there is a gush of warm fluid down the woman's legs. Labor usually begins within 24 hours after this occurs. More commonly, though, the amniotic sac does not rupture until the end of the first stage of labor.

The Braxton-Hicks contractions may increase before labor and actually may be mistaken for labor. Typically they are distinct from the contractions of labor in that they are very irregular.

The biological mechanism that initiates and maintains labor is not well understood. For years it was thought that oxytocin, or possibly declining levels of progesterone, were responsible. However, currently it is thought that *prostaglandins* are the critical substance. They are known to cause strong uterine contractions at any time during pregnancy; and aspirin, which inhibits prostaglandin manufacture, can delay the onset of labor (Pritchard and MacDonald, 1980).

The Stages of Labor

Labor is typically divided into three stages, although the length of the stages may vary considerably from one woman to the next. The whole process of childbrith is sometimes referred to as *parturition.*

First-Stage Labor

Effacement:
A thinning out of the cervix during labor.

Dilation:
An opening up of the cervix during labor; also called dilatation.

First-stage labor:
The beginning of labor during which there are regular contractions of the uterus; the stage lasts until the cervix is dilated 8 centimeters (3 inches).

Transition:
The difficult stage of labor following first stage, during which the cervix dilates from 8 to 10 centimeters (3 to 4 inches).

First-stage labor begins with the regular contractions of the muscles of the uterus. These contractions are responsible for producing two changes in the cervix, both of which must occur before the baby can be delivered. These changes are called effacement (thinning out) and dilation (opening up). The cervix must dilate until it has an opening 10 centimeters (4 inches) in diameter before the baby can be born.

First-stage labor itself is divided into three stages: early, late, and transition. In *early first-stage labor,* contractions are spaced far apart, with perhaps 15 to 20 minutes between them. A contraction typically lasts 45 seconds to a minute. This stage of labor is fairly easy, and the woman is quite comfortable between contractions. Meanwhile, the cervix is effacing and dilating.

Late first-stage labor is marked by the dilation of the cervix from 5 to 8 centimeters (2 to 3 inches). It is generally shorter than the early stage, and the contractions are more frequent and more intense.

The final dilation of the cervix from 8 to 10 centimeters (3 to 4 inches) occurs during the transition stage, which is both the shortest and the most difficult. The contractions are very strong, and it is during this stage that women report pain and exhaustion.

The first stage of labor can last anywhere from 2 to 24 hours. It averages about 12 to 15 hours for a first pregnancy and about 8 hours for later pregnancies. (In most respects, first labors are the hardest, and later ones are easier.) The woman is usually told to go to the hospital when the contractions are 4 to 5 minutes apart. Once there, she is put in the labor room for the rest of first-stage labor.

Second-Stage Labor: Delivery

Second-stage labor:
The stage during which the baby moves out through the vagina and is delivered.

The second stage of labor begins when the cervix is fully dilated and the baby's head (or whichever part comes first, if the baby is in some other position) begins to move into the vagina, or birth canal. It lasts from a few minutes to a few hours and is generally much shorter than the first stage.

During this stage, many women feel an urge to push or bear down, and if done properly, this may be of great assistance in pushing the baby out. With each contraction the baby is pushed farther along.

Episiotomy (ih-PEE-see-ah-tuh-mee):
An incision made in the skin just behind the vagina, allowing the baby to be delivered more easily.

When the baby's head has traversed the entire length of the vagina, the top of it becomes visible at the vaginal entrance; this is called *crowning.* It is at this point that many physicians perform an episiotomy (see Figure 6.4), in which an incision or slit is made in the perineum, the skin just behind the vagina. Most women do not feel the episiotomy being performed because the pressure of the baby against the pelvic floor provides a natural anesthetic. The incision is stitched closed after the baby is born. The reason physicians give for performing the episiotomy is that if it

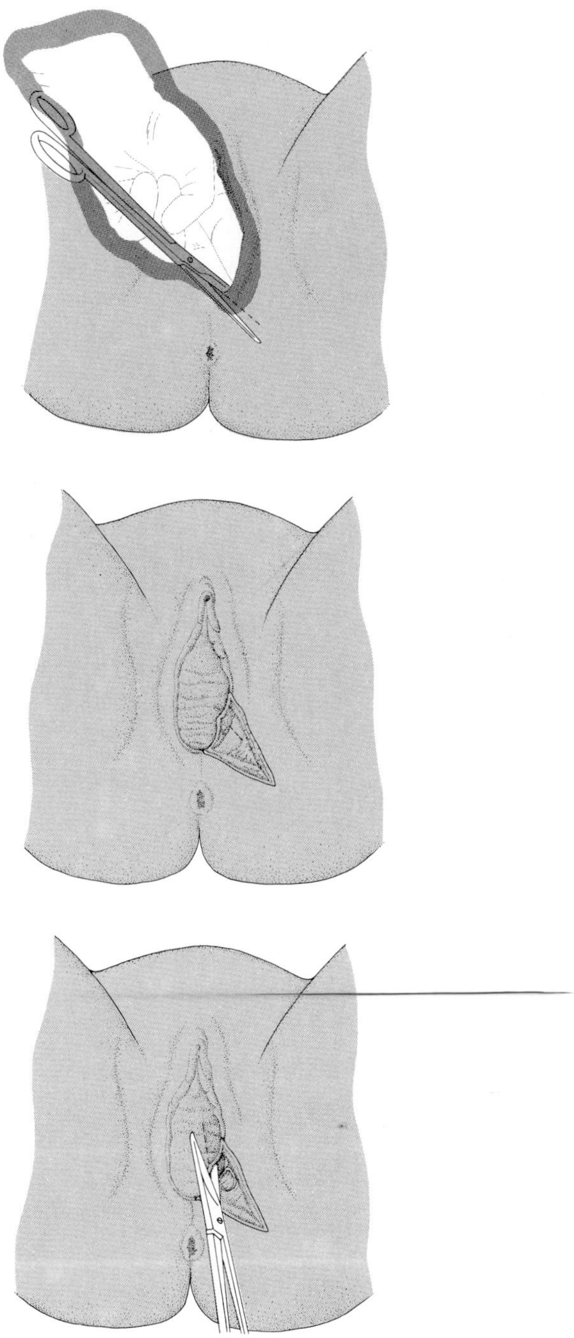

FIGURE 6.4

Episiotomy.

is not done, the baby's head may rip the perineum; a neat incision is easier to repair than a ragged tear, and the tear may go much deeper and damage more tissue. But the use of the episiotomy has been questioned by feminists, who claim that it is unnecessary and is done merely for the doctor's convenience, while causing the woman discomfort later as it is healing. They note that episiotomies are not performed in western European countries, where delivery still takes place quite nicely.

The baby is finally eased completely out of the mother's body. The physician removes any mucus that may be in the baby's mouth, and the infant has usually

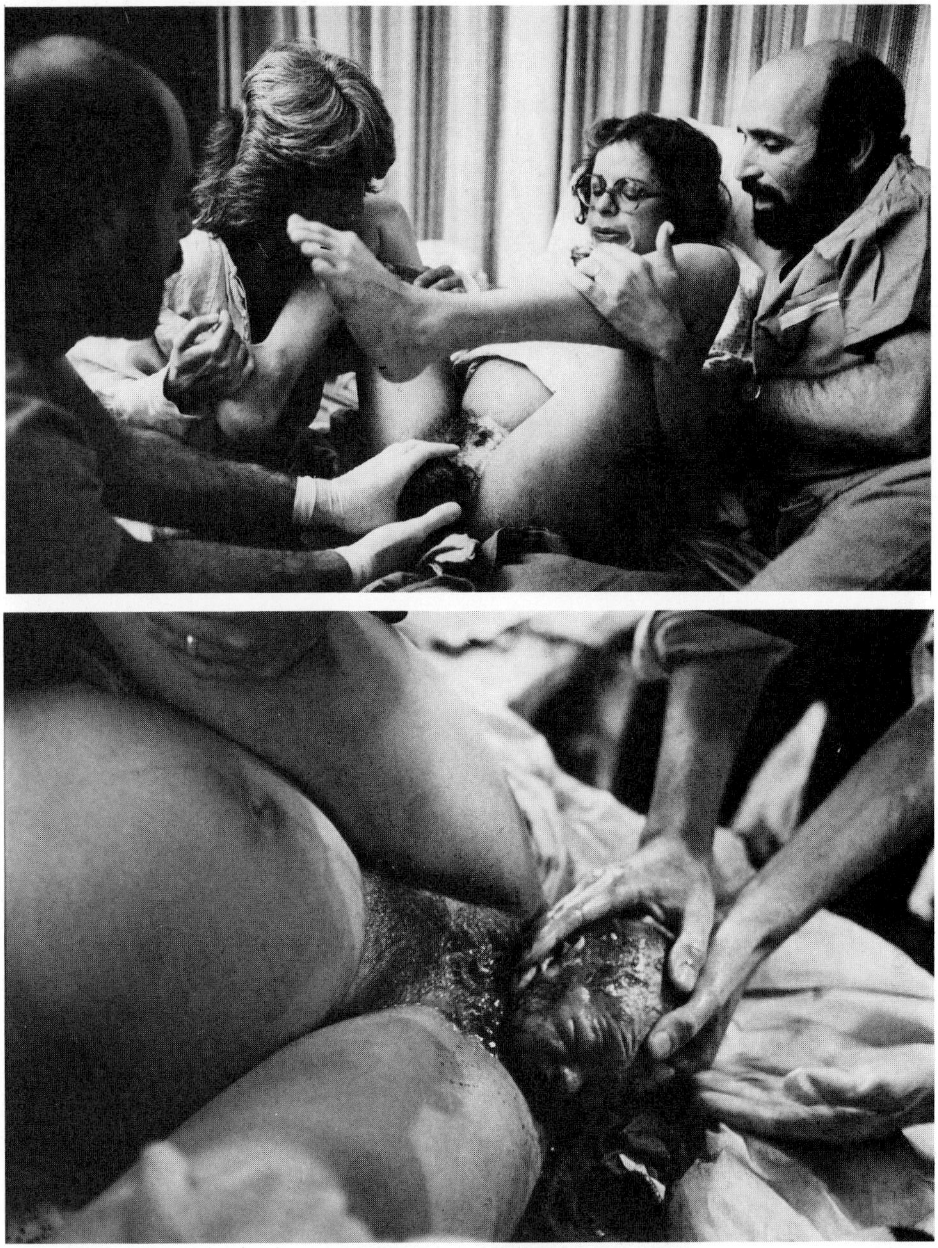

FIGURE 6.5

Stage two labor (*a*) baby's head crowning (*b*) then moving out.

begun crying by this time. At this point, the baby is still connected to the mother by the umbilical cord, which runs from the baby's navel to the placenta, and the placenta is still inside the mother's uterus. As the baby takes its first breath of air, the functioning of its body changes dramatically. Blood begins to flow to the lungs, there to take on oxygen, and a flap closes between the two atria (chambers) in the heart. This process generally takes a few minutes, during which time the baby changes from a somewhat bluish color to a healthy, pink hue.

At this point, the baby no longer needs the umbilical cord, which is clamped and cut off about 7 centimeters (3 inches) from the body. The stub gradually dries up and falls off.

To avoid the possibility of gonorrhea or other eye infection, drops of silver nitrate or a similar drug are placed in the baby's eyes (see Chapter 21).

(a) Ovulation, the release of the egg from the ovary

(b) Fertilization of the egg by a sperm

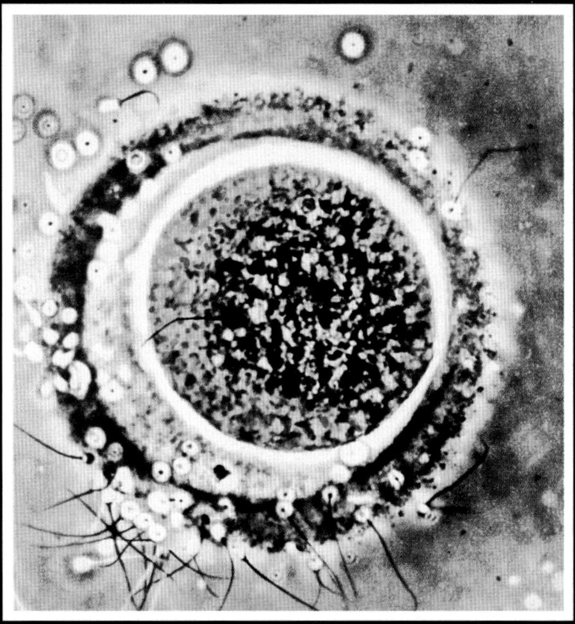

(c) A fetus six weeks after conception

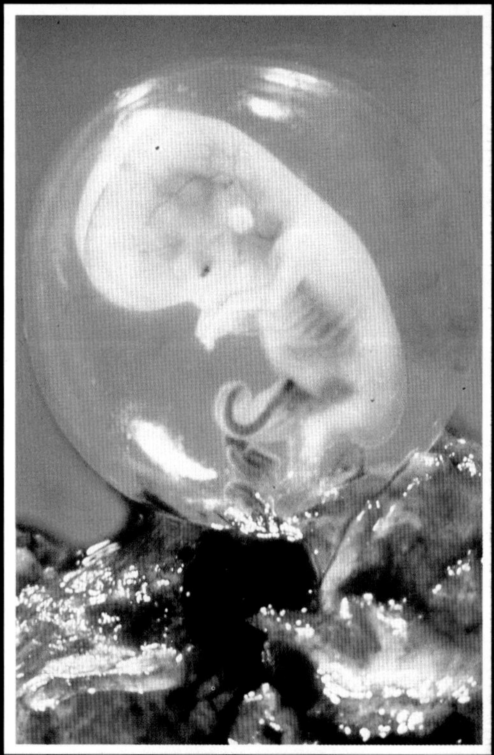

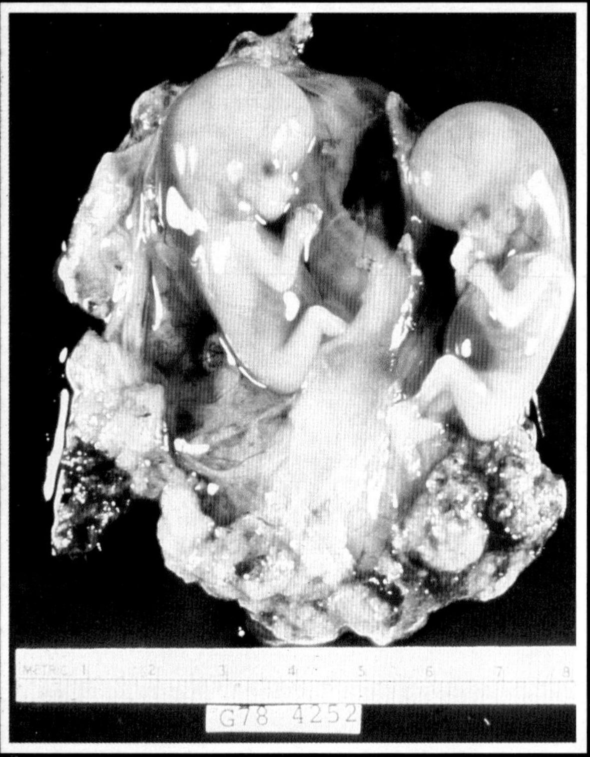

(d) Twins at approximately 10 weeks of age

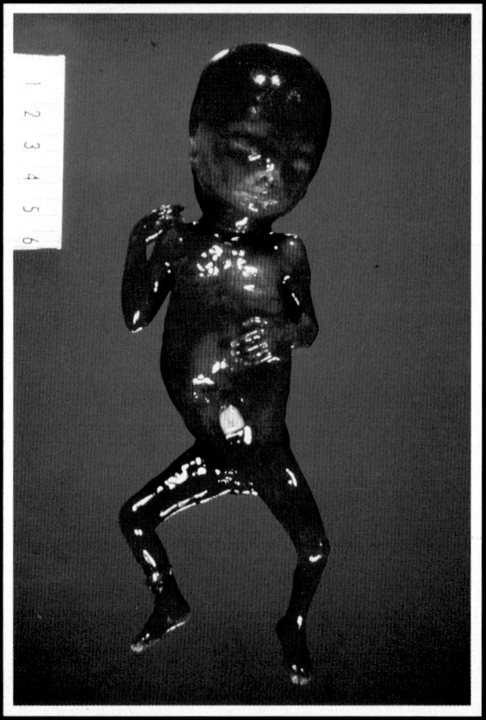

(e) A fetus at approximately 17 weeks (4 months) of age

(f) A fetus at approximately 8 months, showing the umbilical cord and placenta

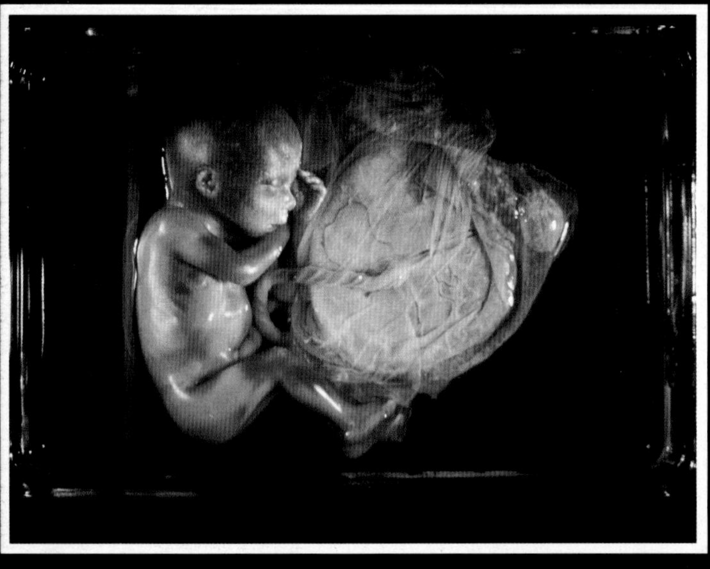

(g) A fetus at approximately 8 months

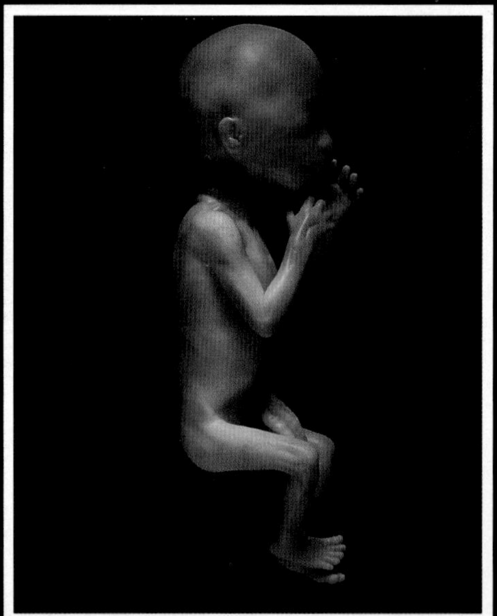

Third-Stage Labor

Third-stage labor: The stage during which the afterbirth is expelled.

During the third stage of labor, the placenta detaches from the walls of the uterus, and the afterbirth (placenta and fetal membranes) is expelled. This stage may take from a few minutes to an hour. Several contractions may accompany the expulsion of the placenta. The episiotomy and/or any tears are sewn up.

Positions of the Fetus

As was noted earlier, in most cases the fetus rotates into a head-down position inside the uterus during the last trimester of pregnancy, and the head emerges first at birth. Such normal presentations occur most often, but the baby may also be born in a number of other positions (see Figure 6.6).

Cesarean Section (C Section)

Cesarean section (C section): A method of delivering a baby surgically, by an incision in the abdomen.

Cesarean section is a surgical procedure for delivery; it is used when normal vaginal birth is impossible or undesirable. Cesarean section may be required for a number of different reasons: if the baby is too large or if the mother's pelvis is too small to allow the baby to move into the vagina; if the labor has been very long and hard and the cervix is not dilating or if the mother is nearing the point of total exhaustion; if the umbilical cord *prolapses* (moves into a position such that it is coming out through the cervix ahead of the baby), if there is an Rh incompatibility (see below); or if there is excessive bleeding or the mother's or the infant's condition takes a sudden turn for the worse.

In the cesarean section, an incision is made through the abdomen and through the wall of the uterus. The physician lifts out the baby and then sews up the uterine wall and the abdominal wall.

Cesarean deliveries account for about 15 percent of all deliveries in the United States, which is a rate considerably higher than in some western European countries. Contrary to popular opinion, though, it is not true that once a woman has had one delivery by cesarean she must have all subsequent deliveries by the same method. Normal vaginal births are possible after cesareans (Whiteside et al., 1983), although often the same conditions are present in later deliveries that ncessitated the first cesarean, making it necessary again in the later deliveries. It is also quite possible for a woman to have two or three cesarean deliveries.

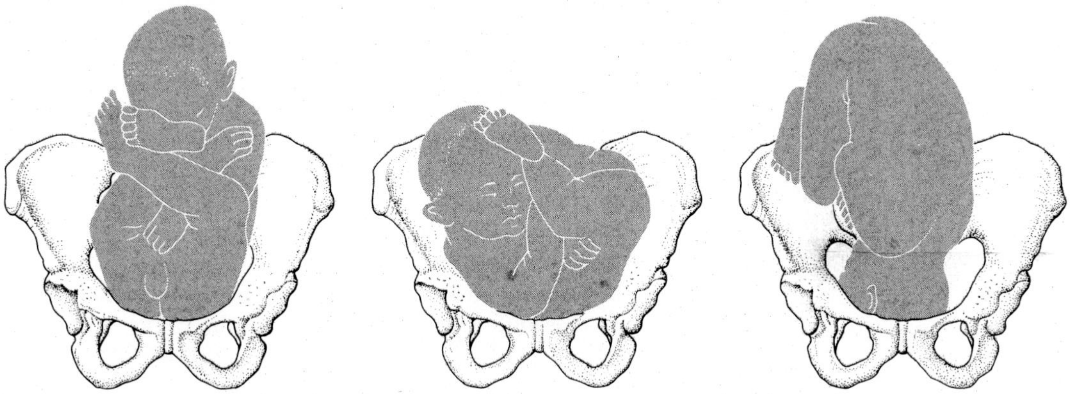

(*a*) (*b*) (*c*)

FIGURE 6.6

Possible positions of the fetus during birth. (*a*) A breech presentation (4 percent of births). (*b*) A transverse presentation (fewer than 1 percent). (*c*) A normal, head-first or cephalic presentation (96 percent of births).

With modern surgical techniques, the rate of complications from such a delivery is extremely low. The recovery period, of course, is somewhat longer than that after a vaginal birth, usually requiring five or six days in the hospital, compared with one or two for a normal vaginal delivery.

NATURAL CHILDBIRTH

The term "natural childbirth" was coined by the English obstetrician Grantly Dick-Read in his book *Childbirth without Fear,* published in 1932. He postulated that fear causes tension and that tension causes pain. Thus to eliminate the pain of childbirth, he recommended a program consisting of education (to eliminate the woman's fears of the unknown) and the learning of relaxation techniques.

Lamaze method: A method of "prepared" childbirth.

Another, similar method—more properly called *prepared childbirth* or the Lamaze method—has become extremely popular in the United States.

The Lamaze Method

A French obstetrician, Fernand Lamaze, developed a technique that he called a *psychoprophylactic* method of childbirth ("psycho" = "mind"; "prophylactic" = "prevention"—or a mental way of preventing pain) after observing women in Russia undergoing labor with apparently no pain. The technique became extremely popular in France and was introduced in the United States by Marjorie Karmel (who had her first baby in Paris while under the care of Dr. Lamaze) in her book *Thank You, Dr. Lamaze,* published in 1959. The method has become very popular in the last decade in the United States, and prepared childbirth classes are now offered in most areas of the country.

The two basic techniques taught in the Lamaze approach are *relaxation* and *controlled breathing.* The woman learns to relax all the muscles in her body. Knowing how to do this has a number of advantages, including conservation of energy during an event that requires considerable endurance and, more important, avoidance of the tension that increases the perception of pain. The woman also learns a series of controlled breathing exercises, which she will use to help her get through each contraction.

Some other techniques are taught as well. One, called *effleurage,* consists of a light, circular stroking of the abdomen with the fingertips. There are also exercises to strengthen specific muscles, such as the leg muscles, which undergo considerable strain during labor and delivery. Finally, because the Lamaze method is based on the idea that fear and the pain it causes are best eliminated through education, the Lamaze student learns a great deal about the processes involved in pregnancy and childbirth.

One other important component of the Lamaze method is the requirement that the woman be accompanied during the classes and during childbirth itself by her husband (or by some other person who serves as "coach" if she is unmarried or if the husband cannot participate). The husband or coach serves an important function and plays an integral role in the woman's learning of the techniques and her use of them during labor. He (we shall assume that it is the father) is present in both the labor room and the delivery room. He times contractions, checks on the woman's state of relaxation and gives her feedback if she is not relaxed, suggests breathing patterns, helps elevate her back as she pushes the baby out, and generally provides encouragement and moral support. Aside from the obvious benefits to the woman,

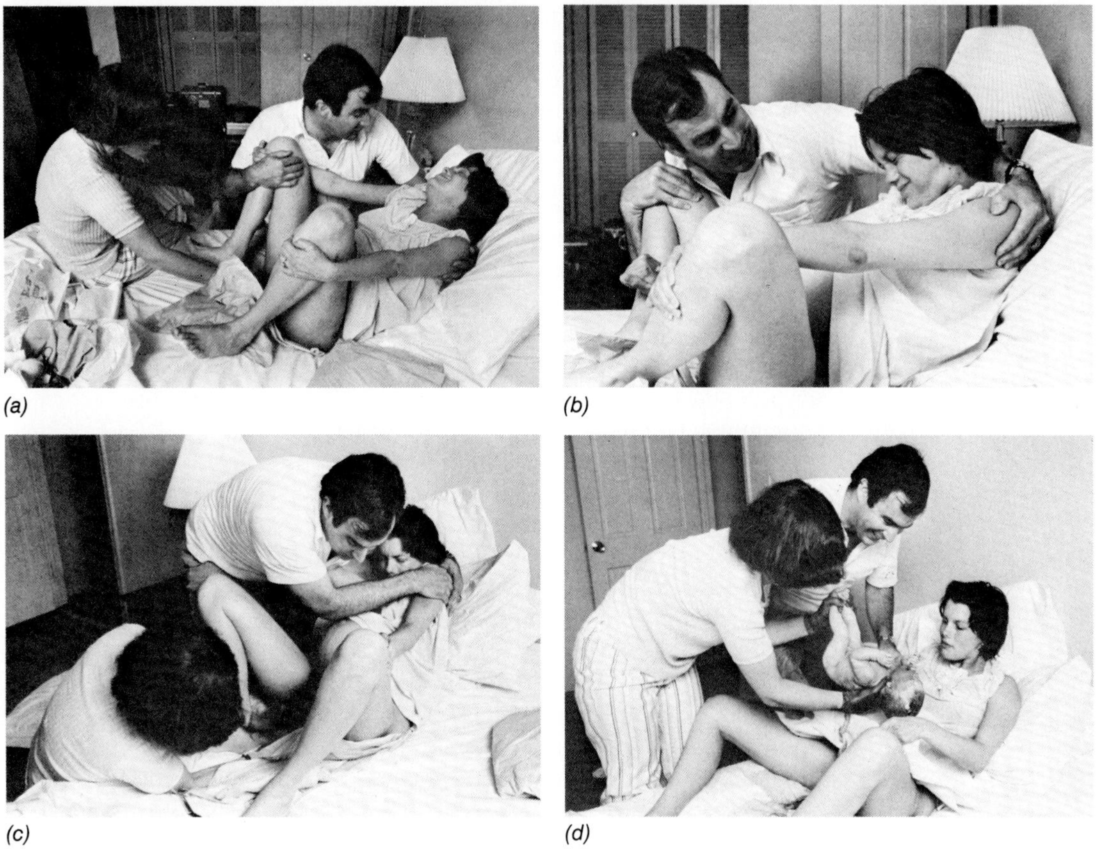

FIGURE 6.7

A home birth.

this principle of the Lamaze method represents real progress in that it allows the man to play an active role in the birth of his own child and to experience more fully one of the most basic and moving of all human experiences, a privilege men have been denied too long.

One common misunderstanding about the Lamaze method is that it is "natural" childbirth, that is, that the use of anesthetics is prohibited. In fact, the Lamaze method is more flexible than that. Its goal is to teach each woman the techniques she needs to control her labor so that she will not need an anesthetic; however, her right to have an anesthetic if she wants one is affirmed. The topic of anesthetics in childbirth, which has become quite controversial in recent years, is discussed below.

A number of studies indicate that childbirth training, such as Lamaze, has several desirable results, including reduction in the length of labor, decreased incidence of birth complications, a decrease in the use of anesthetics, a more positive attitude after birth, increased self-esteem, and an increased sense of being in control (e.g., Felton and Segelman, 1978; Zax et al., 1975). Research also shows that the effects are due to the childbirth training itself rather than to preexisting attitudes (Huttel et al., 1972).

The Use of Anesthetics in Childbirth

Throughout most of human history, childbirth has been "natural"; that is, it has taken place without anesthetics and in the woman's home or other familiar surroundings. The pattern began to change about 200 years ago, at the time of the Revolutionary War, when male physicians rather than midwives started to assist during birth (Wertz and Wertz, 1977). The next major change came around the middle of the nineteenth century, with the development of anesthetics for use in surgery. When their use in childbirth was suggested, there was some opposition from physicians, who felt they interfered with "natural" processes, and some opposition from the clergy, who argued that women's pain in childbirth was prescribed in the Bible, quoting Genesis 3:16: "In sorrow thou shalt bring forth children." Opposition to the use of anesthetics virtually ceased, however, when Queen Victoria gave birth to a child under chloroform anesthesia in 1853. Since then, the use of anesthetics has become routine (too routine, according to some) and extremely effective, and women may now bear children with only minimal discomfort. Before discussing the arguments for and against the use of anesthetics, let us briefly review some of the common techniques of anesthesia used in childbirth.

Tranquilizers (such as Valium) or narcotics may be administered when labor becomes fairly intense. They relax the woman, and she may even fall asleep between contractions. Barbiturates (Nembutal or Seconal) are administered to put the woman to sleep. Scopolamine may sometimes be used for its amnesic effects; it makes the woman forget what has happened, and thus she has no memory afterward of any pain during childbirth. Some general analgesics (pain relievers), such as nitrous oxide, may be given by inhalation. General anesthetics such as ether may also be administered. Regional anesthetics, which numb only the specific region of the body that is painful, are used most commonly. An example is the pudendal block (named for the pudendum, or vulva), in which an injection numbs only the external genitals. Other examples are spinal anesthesia (a "spinal"), in which an injection near the spinal cord numbs the entire birth area, from belly to thighs, and the caudal block and epidural anesthesia, which are both administered by injections in the back and produce similar regional numbing.

Recently, the routine use of anesthetics has been questioned by some. Proponents of the use of anesthetics argue that with modern technology, women no longer need to experience pain during childbirth and that it is therefore silly for them to suffer unnecessarily. Opponents argue that anesthetics have a number of well-documented dangerous effects, on both the mother and infant. All anesthetics in the mother's body pass through the placenta to the infant. Thus while they have the desired effect of depressing the mother's central nervous system, they also depress the infant's nervous system. Research indicates that babies born under anesthesia have sluggish respiration and poor muscle tone, alertness, and sucking ability compared with the characteristics of infants born with no anesthesia (Boston Women's Health Book Collective, 1976; MacFarlane et al., 1978). Thus the effects on the infant are moderately to extremely harmful. There are also negative effects on the mother. Anesthetics prevent her from using her body as effectively as she might to help push the baby out. If administered early in labor, anesthetics may inhibit uterine contractions and thus slow cervical dilation, and they can therefore prolong labor. They also numb a woman to experiencing one of the most fundamental events of her life.

Perhaps the best resolution of this controversy is to say that a pregnant woman should participate in prepared childbirth classes and should use the techniques during labor. If, when she is in labor, she discovers that she cannot control the pain and wants an anesthetic, she should feel free to request it and to do so without guilt; the anesthetic should then be administered with great caution.

Home Birth versus Hospital Birth

In the last decade, home birth has become increasingly popular. Either a physician or a nurse-midwife may assist in a home birth. Advocates of home birth argue that the atmosphere in a hospital—with all of its forbidding machines, rules and regulations, and general lack of comfort and "homeyness"—is stressful to the woman and detracts from what should be a joyous, natural human experience. Further, hospitals are meant to deal with illness, and the delivery of a baby should not be viewed as illness. Birth at home should be more relaxed and less stressful; friends and other children are allowed to be present. There are some studies that indicate that—for uncomplicated pregnancies—home delivery is as safe as hospital delivery (Wertz and Wertz, 1977; Hahn and Paige, 1980).

On the other side of the argument, if unforeseen emergency medical procedures are necessary, home birth may be downright dangerous for the mother, the baby, or both. Further, hospital practices in labor and delivery have changed radically in the last decade, particularly with the increased popularity of the Lamaze method; thus hospitals are not the forbidding, alien environments they once were. Most hospitals, for example, allow fathers to be present for the entire labor and delivery, and many even allow the father to be present in the operating room during cesarean deliveries. Some hospitals are even creating birthing centers which contain a set of homelike rooms, with comfortable beds and armchairs, that permit labor and delivery to occur in a relaxed atmosphere, while being only a minute away from emergency equipment if it is required.

For a woman who wants to do a home birth, careful medical screening is essential. Only women with normal pregnancies and anticipated normal deliveries should attempt a home birth. A qualified physician or nurse-midwife must be part of the planning. Finally, there must be access to a hospital in case of an unanticipated emergency.

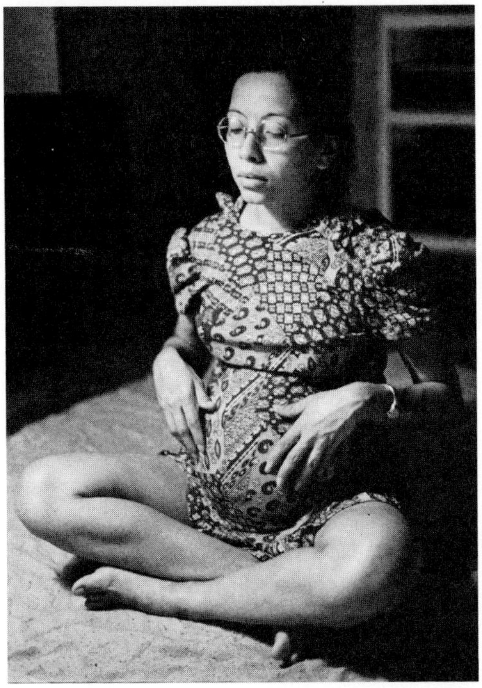

FIGURE 6.8

Practice and concentration are essential in preparing a Lamaze childbirth.

AFTER THE BABY IS BORN: THE POSTPARTUM PERIOD

Physical Changes

With the birth of the baby, the woman's body undergoes a drastic physiological change. During pregnancy the placenta produces high levels of both estrogen and progesterone. When the placenta is expelled, the levels of these hormones drop sharply, and thus the postpartum period is characterized by low levels of both estrogen and progesterone. The levels of these hormones gradually return to normal over a period of a few weeks to a few months. Other endocrine changes include an increase in hormones associated with breast-feeding (discussed below).

In addition, the body undergoes considerable stress during labor and delivery, and the woman may feel exhausted. Discomfort from the episiotomy is common in the first postpartum weeks (Leifer, 1980).

Psychological Changes

For the first one or two days after parturition, the woman typically remains in the hospital. For the first two days, women often feel elated; the long pregnancy is over, they have been successful competitors in a demanding athletic event and are pleased with their efforts, and the baby is finally there, to be cuddled and loved.

Within a couple of days after delivery, many women experience depression and periods of crying. These mood swings range from mild to severe. In the mildest type, *maternity blues* or "baby blues," the woman experiences sadness and periods of crying, but this mood lasts only 24 to 48 hours (Hopkins et al., 1984). Between 50 percent and 80 percent of women experience mild baby blues postpartum. Mild to moderate postpartum depression is experienced by approximately 20 percent of women and typically lasts 6 to 8 weeks (Hopkins et al., 1984). Postpartum depression is characterized by a depressed mood, insomnia, tearfulness, feelings of inadequacy and inability to cope, irritability, and fatigue. Finally, the most severe disturbance is *postpartum depressive psychosis;* fortunately, it is rare, affecting only 0.01 percent of women following birth (Hopkins et al., 1984).

Postpartum depression: Mild to moderate depression in women following the birth of a baby.

It appears that many factors contribute to this depression (see, for example, R. E. Gordon et al., 1965). Being in a hospital in and of itself is stressful as noted previously. Separation from the baby, which is sometimes required for the first 12 to 24 hours in the hospital, may also contribute to depression (Klaus et al., 1972). Once the woman returns home, another set of stresses faces her. She has probably not yet returned to her normal level of energy, and yet she must perform the exhausting task of caring for a newborn infant. For the first several weeks or months she may not get enough sleep, rising several times during the night to tend to a baby that is crying because it is hungry or sick, and she may become exhausted. Clearly she needs help and support from her husband and friends at this time. Some stresses vary depending on whether this is a first child or a later child. The first child is stressful because of the woman's inexperience; while she is in the hospital she may become anxious, wondering whether she will be capable of caring for the infant when she returns home. In the case of later-born children, and some firstborns, the mother may become depressed because she did not really want the baby. In one study, 80 percent of the women were happy about their first one or two children, but only 31 percent were happy about the fourth child or later children (E. M. Gordon, 1967). It is not surprising that a woman might become depressed after the birth of a child she did not want. It is hoped that with the improvement of contraceptive technology and the increased availability and acceptability of abortions, the percentage of undesired pregnancies will decline.

Of course, physical stresses are also present during the postpartum period; hormone levels have declined sharply, and the body has been under stress. Thus it appears that postpartum depression is caused by a combination of physical and social factors.

Another view of the psychological aspects of pregnancy and the postpartum period has been proposed by psychoanalyst Grete Bibring and her colleagues (1961), who studied pregnant women over a 10-year period. Bibring and her colleagues see the pregnancy-postpartum period as a developmental stage, a time of maturational crisis, the resolution of which leads to emotional growth. Perhaps, then, we should begin to think of pregnancy and the postpartum period as normal parts of the process of adult development.

Attachment to the Baby

While much of the traditional psychological research focused on the baby's developing attachment to the mother, more recent interest has been about the development of the mother's attachment (bond) to the infant. Leifer's study (1980) showed clearly that this process begins even before the baby is born; during pregnancy, most women in her sample developed an increasing sense of the fetus as a separate individual and developed an increasing emotional attachment to it. In this sense, pregnancy is something of a psychological preparation for motherhood.

It is possible that there is a kind of "critical period" during the first hours or days postpartum for the mother to form an attachment to the baby. For example, one study found that mothers given more contact with their babies in the first three days postpartum, compared with mothers given the normal contact in the hospital, seemed to have stronger bonds to their babies, with the effects lasting two years (Klaus and Kennell, 1970, 1976). But it is also true that fathers present at the birth show more intense attachments to their infants (Peterson et al., 1979). There is also evidence that the mother's attachment develops gradually over several months postpartum (Leifer, 1980). Therefore, one cannot conclude that maternal feelings have been biologically programmed and spontaneously appear after a couple of days of exposure to the infant. Nonetheless, hospitals are becoming increasingly sensitive to the needs of both mother and father to have extended contact with their newborn.

BREAST-FEEDING

Biological Mechanisms

Two hormones, both secreted by the pituitary, are involved in lactation (milk production). One, *prolactin,* stimulates the breasts to produce milk. Prolactin is produced fairly constantly for whatever length of time the woman breast-feeds. The other hormone, *oxytocin,* stimulates the breasts to eject milk. Oxytocin is produced reflexively by the pituitary in response to the infant's sucking of the breast. Thus sucking stimulates nerve cells in the nipple; this nerve signal is transmitted to the brain, which then relays the message to the pituitary, which sends out the messenger oxytocin, which stimulates the breasts to eject milk.

Actually, milk is not produced for several days after delivery. For the first few days, the breast secretes colostrum, discussed earlier, which is high in protein and is

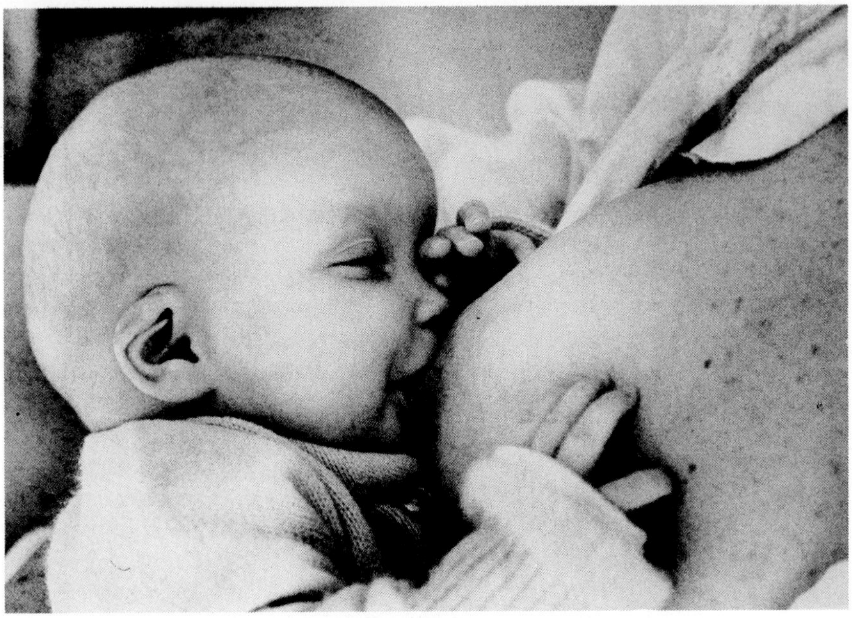

FIGURE 6.9

Breast-feeding.

believed to give the baby a temporary immunity to infectious diseases. Two or three days after delivery, true lactation begins; this may be accompanied by pain for a day or so because the breasts are swollen and congested.

It is also important to note that, much as in pregnancy, substances ingested by the mother may be transmitted through the milk to the infant. The nursing mother thus needs to be cautious about using alcohol and other drugs.

Psychological Aspects

Although bottles for artificially feeding babies were known in Egypt and a few other places as early as the first century, they were used by only a small minority of very wealthy women. Thus throughout most of human history, the vast majority of babies have been breast-fed. By the 1950s and 1960s, however, the majority of babies in the United States were bottle-fed.

Public health officials viewed the decline in breast-feeding with alarm, because breast milk is the ideal food for a baby and has even been termed the "ultimate health food." It provides the baby with the right mixture of nutrients, it contains antibodies that protect the infant from some diseases, it is free from bacteria, and it is always the right temperature. Thus there is little question that it is superior to cow's milk and commercial formulas.

The evidence indicates that the percentage of infants who are breast-fed rose steadily during the 1970s. In 1980, 54 percent were breast-fed initially and 25 percent were still breast-fed at five to six months of age (Martinez and Nalezienski, 1981). This contrasts with 1971, when only 5 percent of babies were still breast-fed at five to six months of age.

From the mother's point of view, breast-feeding has several advantages. Women who breast-feed find that their sexual responsiveness returns sooner after childbirth, compared with women who do not breast-feed (Masters and Johnson, 1966).[5] Some

---

[5]If you are a psychology student, you might want to note that these data are correlational. In view of this, can you infer that breast-feeding *causes* a quicker return of sexual desire? How else might one interpret the data? Why are the data correlational rather than experimental?

women report sexual arousal during breast-feeding, and a few even report having orgasms. Unfortunately, this sometimes produces anxiety in the mother, leading her to discontinue breast-feeding. However, there is nothing "wrong" with this arousal, and it appears to stem from activation of hormonal mechanisms. Clearly, from an adaptive point of view, if breast-feeding is important to the infant's survival, it would be wise for Nature to design the process so that it is rewarding to the mother.

Other advantages from the mother's point of view include a quicker shrinking of the uterus to its normal size and a slightly reduced likelihood of becoming pregnant again immediately. The return of normal menstrual cycles is delayed, on the average, in women who breast-feed, compared with those who do not. This provides some period of rest between pregnancies. However, it is important to note that a woman can become pregnant again after parturition but before she has had her first menstrual period. As was discussed in Chapter 5, ovulation precedes menstruation; thus a woman may ovulate and conceive without having a period. Therefore, a woman should not count on breast-feeding as a means of contraception.

The La Leche League, an organization devoted to breast-feeding, has done much to encourage women to breast-feed their babies and has helped to spread information on breast-feeding. The organization tends to be a bit militant in its advocacy of breast-feeding, however. A few women are physically unable to breast-feed, while some others feel psychologically uncomfortable with the idea. And breast-feeding can be very inconvenient for the woman who works full-time. While breast-feeding has some of the important advantages noted above, long-term studies comparing breast-fed children with bottle-fed children have found no significant differences between them (Schmitt, 1970). What appears to be more important than the method of feeding is the quality of the relationship between the mother and infant and the feelings that the mother communicates to the baby:

> A baby raised in a loving home can grow up to be a healthy, psychologically secure individual no matter how he receives his nourishment. While successful nursing is a beautiful, happy experience for both mother and child, the woman who nurses grudgingly because she feels she *should* will probably do more harm to her baby by communicating her feelings of resentment and unhappiness, than she would if she were a relaxed, loving, bottle-feeding mother. (S. Olds and Eiger, 1973, p. 18)

PROBLEM PREGNANCIES

Ectopic Pregnancy

Ectopic pregnancy: A pregnancy in which the fertilized egg implants somewhere other than the uterus.

Ectopic (misplaced) pregnancy occurs when the fertilized egg implants someplace other than the uterus. Most commonly, ectopic pregnancies occur when the egg implants in the fallopian tube (tubal pregnancy; Schenker and Evron, 1983). In rare cases, implantation may also occur in the abdominal cavity, the ovary, or the cervix.

About 1 pregnancy in every 200 is a tubal pregnancy (Hellman and Pritchard, 1971). Tubal pregnancy may occur if, for one reason or another, the egg is prevented from moving down the tube to the uterus, as when the tubes are obstructed as a result of a gonorrheal infection, for example.

Early in tubal pregnancy, the fertilized egg implants in the tube and begins development, forming a placenta and producing the normal hormones of pregnancy. The woman may experience the early symptoms of pregnancy, such as nausea and amenorrhea, and think she is pregnant; or she may experience some bleeding which she mistakes for a period, and think that she is not pregnant. It is therefore quite difficult to diagnose a tubal pregnancy early.

A tubal pregnancy may end in one of two ways. The embryo may spontaneously abort and be released into the abdominal cavity, or the embryo and placenta may continue to expand, stretching the tube until it ruptures. Symptoms of a rupture include sharp abdominal pain or cramping, dull abdominal pain and possibly pain in the shoulder, and vaginal bleeding. Meanwhile, hemorrhaging is occurring, and the woman may go into shock and, possibly, die; thus it is extremely important for a woman displaying these symptoms to see a doctor quickly.

Abdominal pregnancy, in which the fertilized egg implants in the abdominal cavity, is much rarer and occurs in less than 1 pregnancy in 4000 (Hellman and Pritchard, 1971). Often it is a secondary result of a tubal pregnancy in which the embryo was released into the abdominal cavity, where it again implanted. Occasionally abdominal pregnancies carry on to term, and the infant must be removed by cesarean section; there is a high risk of hemorrhaging in such cases, however.

Pseudocyesis (False Pregnancy)

Pseudocyesis:
False pregnancy, in which the woman displays the signs of pregnancy but is not actually pregnant.

In pseudocyesis, or *false pregnancy,* the woman believes that she is pregnant and shows the signs and symptoms of pregnancy without really being pregnant. She may stop menstruating and have morning sickness. She may begin gaining weight, and her abdomen may bulge. The condition may persist for several months before it goes away, either spontaneously or as a result of psychotherapy. In rare cases it persists until the woman goes into labor and delivers nothing but air and fluid. Readers may be familiar with the character Honey in Edward Albee's *Who's Afraid of Virginia Woolf?* (played by Sandy Dennis in the movie version), who had a false pregnancy. Pseudocyesis is an interesting example of the extent to which a psychological state (emotional factors) can have an effect on a person's physical state.

Toxemia

Toxemia:
A serious disease of pregnancy, marked by severe edema and high blood pressure.

Metabolic toxemia of late pregnancy is a disease with several stages. The first is called *preeclampsia.* The symptoms of mild preeclampsia are severe edema (fluid retention and swelling), high blood pressure, and protein in the urine. Toxemia usually does not appear until after the twentieth to twenty-fourth week of pregnancy, that is, late in pregnancy. In severe preeclampsia, the earlier symptoms persist, blood pressure is dangerously high, and the woman also experiences vision problems, abdominal pains, mental dullness, and severe headaches. In the most severe stage, *eclampsia,* the woman has convulsions, goes into a coma, and may die.

It seems likely that toxemia results from malnutrition, although no one really knows what causes it. Toxemia seems to be related to socioeconomic factors, which probably determine whether a pregnant woman receives adequate nutrition (Eastman, 1968). This argues for the importance of proper diet during pregnancy. It also emphasizes the importance of proper medical care during pregnancy, because toxemia can be managed well during its early stages and death typically occurs only when the woman is receiving no medical care.

Illness during Pregnancy

As was discussed in a previous section, certain substances such as drugs can cross the placental barrier from the woman to the fetus, causing damage. Similarly, certain viruses may pass from the woman to the fetus and cause considerable harm, particularly if the illness occurs during the first trimester of pregnancy. The best-known example is rubella, or German measles. If a woman gets German measles during the first month of pregnancy, there is a 50 percent chance that the infant will be born deaf or mentally deficient or with cataracts or congenital heart defects. The risk then declines, and by the third month of pregnancy the chance of abnormalities is about 10 percent. While most women have an immunity to rubella because they had it when they were children, a woman who suspects that she is not immune can receive a vaccination that will give her immunity; she should do this well before she becomes pregnant.

Herpes simplex is also *teratogenic,* that is, capable of producing defects in the fetus. Symptoms of herpes simplex are usually mild: cold sores or fever blisters. Herpes genitalis (see Chapter 21) is a form of herpes simplex in which sores may appear in the genital region. Usually the infant contracts the disease by direct contact with the sore; delivery by cesarean section can prevent this. Women with herpes genitalis also have a high risk of spontaneously aborting.

Other diseases, such as influenza and the common cold if complicated by pneumonia, may also cause complications in pregnancy. Pregnant women are thus advised to avoid situations in which they may be exposed to diseases.

Birth Defects

As has been noted, a number of factors, such as drugs taken during pregnancy and illness during pregnancy, may cause defects in the fetus. Other causes include genetic defects (for example, phenylketonuria [PKU], which causes retardation) and chromosomal defects (for example, Down's syndrome, or mongolism, which causes retardation).

About 250,000 babies with significant birth defects are born in the United States each year (about 7 percent of all babies born). A "significant birth defect" is one that has an adverse effect on the future mental and/or physical health and well-being of the person. The problem will affect 1 family in every 10 (Fulton, 1974).

In most cases, families have simply had to learn, as best they could, to live with a child who had a birth defect. Now, however, amniocentesis (combined with abortion) and genetic counseling are available to help prevent some of the sorrow, provided that abortion is ethically acceptable to the parents.

Amniocentesis (am-nee-oh--sen-TEE-sus): A test done to determine whether a fetus has birth defects; done by inserting a fine tube into the woman's abdomen in order to obtain a sample of amniotic fluid.

The technique of amniocentesis involves inserting a fine tube through the pregnant woman's abdomen and removing some amniotic fluid, including cells sloughed off by the fetus, for analysis. The technique is capable of providing an early diagnosis of most chromosomal abnormalities, some genetically produced biochemical disorders, and sex-linked diseases carried by females but affecting males (hemophilia and muscular dystrophy). If a defect is discovered, the woman may then decide to terminate the pregnancy with an abortion.

Amniocentesis should be performed between the fourteenth and sixteenth weeks of pregnancy. This timing is important for two reasons. First, if a defect is discovered and an abortion is to be performed, it should be done as early as possible (see Chapter 7). Second, there is a 1 percent chance that the amniocentesis itself will cause the woman to lose her baby, and the risk becomes greater as the pregnancy progresses.

Because amniocentesis itself involves some risk, it is generally thought (although the matter is controversial) that it should be performed only on women who have a high risk of bearing a child with a birth defect. A woman is in that category (1) if

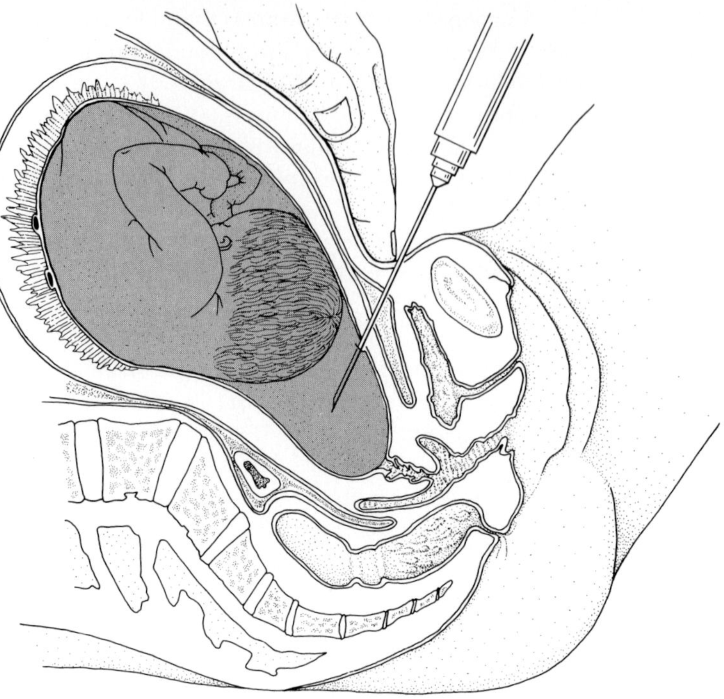

FIGURE 6.10

Amniocentesis. The needle collects a sample of amniotic fluid, containing cells sloughed off by the fetus which can then be analyzed for indicators of birth defects.

she has already had one child with a genetic defect; (2) if she believes that she is a carrier of a genetic defect, which can usually be established through genetic counseling; and (3) if she is over 40, in which case she has a greatly increased chance of bearing a child with a chromosomal abnormality.

Of course, amniocentesis (when followed by abortion) raises a number of serious ethical questions, some of which will be discussed in later chapters. However, it is important to note the extreme psychological stress to which families of children with birth defects are often subjected.

Rh Incompatibility

The Rh factor is a substance in the blood; if it is present, the person is said to be Rh positive (Rh+); if it is absent, the person is said to be Rh negative (Rh−). The Rh factor is genetically transmitted, with Rh+ being dominant over Rh−.

The presence or absence of the Rh factor does not constitute a health problem except when an Rh− person receives a blood transfusion and when an Rh− woman is pregnant with an Rh+ fetus (which can happen only if the father is Rh+). A blood test is done routinely early in pregnancy to determine whether a woman is Rh−. Fortunately, about 85 percent of whites and 93 percent of blacks are Rh+; thus the problems associated with being Rh− are not very common.

If some Rh+ blood gets into Rh− blood, the Rh− blood forms antibodies as a reaction against the Rh factor in the invading blood. Typically, as has been noted, there is little interchange between the woman's blood and the fetus's; the placenta keeps them separate. However, during parturition there can be considerable mixing of the two. Thus during birth, the blood of an Rh+ baby causes the formation of antibodies in an Rh− woman's blood. During the next pregnancy, some of the woman's blood enters the fetus, and the antibodies attack the fetus's red cells. The baby may be stillborn, severely anemic, or retarded. Thus there is little risk for an Rh− woman with the first pregnancy because antibodies have not yet formed; however, later pregnancies can be extremely dangerous.

Fortunately, fairly adequate techniques for dealing with this situation have been developed. An injection of a substance called *Rhogam* prevents the woman's blood from producing antibodies. If necessary the fetus or newborn infant may get a transfusion.

Miscarriage (Spontaneous Abortion)

Miscarriage:
When a pregnancy terminates before the fetus is viable, as a result of natural causes (not medical intervention).

Miscarriage, or *spontaneous abortion,* occurs when a pregnancy is terminated through natural causes, before the conceptus is viable (capable of surviving on its own). It is not to be confused with *induced abortion,* in which a pregnancy is terminated by mechanical or medicinal means (what is commonly called *abortion*—see Chapter 7), or with *prematurity,* in which the pregnancy terminates early, but after the infant is viable.

It is estimated that 10 percent of all pregnancies end in spontaneous abortion (Hellman and Pritchard, 1971). If anything, this is probably an underestimate, since very early spontaneous abortions may not be detected. The woman may not know that she is pregnant, and the products of the miscarriage are mistaken for a menstrual period. Thus the true incidence may be closer to 15 or 20 percent or perhaps as high as 50 percent.

Most spontaneous abortions (75 percent) occur during the first trimester of pregnancy. The first sign that a woman may miscarry is vaginal bleeding or "spotting." If the symptoms of pregnancy disappear and the woman develops abdominal cramps, the fetus is usually expelled.

Studies indicate that most spontaneous abortions occur because the conceptus was defective. Studies of spontaneously aborted fetuses indicate that about 50 percent showed abnormalities that were incompatible with life; for example, many had gross chromosomal abnormalities. Thus, contrary to popular belief, psychological and physical traumas are not common causes of miscarriage. In fact, spontaneous abortions seem to be functional in that they naturally eliminate many defective fetuses.

Prematurity

A major complication during the third trimester of pregnancy is premature labor and delivery of the fetus. Because the date of conception cannot always be accurately determined, prematurity is usually defined in terms of the birth weight of the infant; an infant weighing less than 2500 grams (5½ pounds) is considered premature. However, physicians have recently become concerned more with the functional development of the infant than with the weight. It is estimated that about 7 percent of the births in the United States are premature.

Prematurity is a cause for concern because the premature infant is much less likely to survive than the full-term infant. It is estimated that more than half of the deaths of newborn babies in the United States are due to prematurity. Premature infants are particularly susceptible to respiratory infections, and they must receive expert care. Prematurity may also cause damage to an infant who survives.

Maternal factors such as poor health, poor nutrition, heavy smoking, and syphilis are associated with prematurity. Young teenage mothers, whose bodies are not yet ready to bear children, are also very susceptible to premature labor and delivery. However, in over 50 percent of the cases, the cause of prematurity is unknown (Hellman and Pritchard, 1971).

INFERTILITY

It is estimated that 12 percent of all couples in the United States are involuntarily childless. When fertile couples are purposely attempting to conceive a child, about 50 percent succeed in the first month, and about 80 percent succeed in the first six months (Novak et al., 1975). Most doctors consider a couple infertile if they have not conceived after a year of "trying." The term "sterility" refers only to an individual who has an absolute factor preventing procreation.

Causes of Infertility

Contrary to popular opinion, a couple's infertility is not always caused by the woman; it is estimated that in about 40 percent of infertile couples, male factors are responsible (Speroff et al., 1973).

Causes in the Female

The most common causes of infertility in the female are (1) failure to ovulate, (2) blockage of the fallopian tubes, and (3) cervical mucus, called "hostile mucus," that does not permit the passage of sperm. Age may also be a factor; fertility declines in women after 35 years of age, the decline being especially sharp after age 40. Some cases of infertility in women can be successfully treated using "fertility drugs" such as Clomid.

Causes in the Male

The most common causes of infertility in the male are (1) low sperm count (often due to varicoceles, which are varicose veins in the testes and can generally be remedied by surgery) and (2) low motility of the sperm, which means that the sperm are not good swimmers.

Combined Factors

In some situations a combination of factors in both the man and the woman causes the infertility. For example, there may be an immunologic response. The woman may have an allergic response to the man's sperm, causing her to produce antibodies that destroy the sperm, or the man may produce the antibodies himself. A couple may also simply lack knowledge; they may not know how to time intercourse correctly so that conception will take place, or they may lack other important information.

Psychological Aspects

It is important to recognize the psychological stress to which an infertile couple may be subjected. Their marriage may be strained. Because the male role is defined partly in our society by the ability to father children, the man may feel that his masculinity or virility is in question. Similarly, the female role is defined largely by the ability to bear children and be a mother, and the woman may feel inadequate in her role as a woman. Historically, in most cultures fertility has been encouraged, and indeed demanded; hence pressures on infertile couples were high, leading to more psychological stress. For example, among Orthodox Jews, failure to conceive is grounds for a divorce. As emphasis on population control increases in our society and as childlessness[6] becomes an acceptable and more recognized option in marriage, some of the psychological stresses on the infertile couple may lessen.

SUMMARY

The first section traced the journey of the sperm, which are manufactured in the testes and ejaculated out through the vas deferens and urethra into the vagina. Then they begin their swim through the cervix and uterus and up a fallopian tube to meet the egg, which has already been released from the ovary and has found its way into the end of the tube. When the sperm and egg unite in the fallopian tube, conception occurs. The single fertilized egg cell then begins dividing as it travels down the tube, and finally it implants in the uterus. Techniques for improving the chances of conception were suggested.

The development of the embryo, and then of the fetus, was traced during the nine months of prenatal development. The placenta, which is important in transmitting substances between the woman and the fetus, develops early. The fetus is connected to the placenta by the umbilical cord. The most remarkable development of the fetus occurs during the first trimester (first three months), when most of the major organ systems are formed and when human features develop.

Next, pregnancy was considered from the woman's point of view. Early signs of pregnancy include amenorrhea, tenderness of the breasts, and nausea. The most common pregnancy test is designed to detect HCG in the urine; this test is very accurate by the sixth to eighth weeks of pregnancy. Physical changes during the first trimester are mainly the result of the increasing levels of estrogen and progesterone produced by the placenta. Despite cultural myths about the radiant contentment of the pregnant woman, some women do have negative feelings during the first trimester. During the second trimester the woman generally feels better, both physically and psychologically. During the third trimester she is very much aware that the baby will arrive soon.

Despite many people's concerns, sexual intercourse is generally quite safe during pregnancy.

Nutrition is exceptionally important during pregnancy because the woman's body has to supply the materials to create another human being. Pregnant women also must be very careful about ingesting drugs because some can penetrate the placental barrier and enter the fetus, possibly causing damage.

---

[6]Semantics can make a big difference here. Many couples who choose not to have children prefer to call themselves "child-free" rather than "childless."

Labor is typically divided into three stages. During the first stage, the cervix undergoes effacement and dilation. During the second stage, the baby moves out through the vagina. The placenta is delivered during the third stage. Cesarean section is a surgical method of delivering a baby.

The Lamaze method of "natural" childbirth has become very popular; it emphasizes the use of relaxation and controlled breathing to control contractions and minimize the woman's discomfort. Anesthetics may not be necessary, which seems desirable, since they are potentially dangerous to the infant.

During the postpartum period, hormone levels are very low, and postpartum depression may arise from a combination of this hormonal state and the many environmental stresses on the woman at this time.

Two hormones are involved in lactation; prolactin and oxytocin. Breast-feeding has a number of psychological as well as health advantages, although the nature of the relationship between mother and infant appears to be more important than whether the baby is bottle-fed or breast-fed.

Problems of pregnancy were discussed: ectopic (misplaced) pregnancy, pseudocyesis (false pregnancy), toxemia, illness (such as German measles), a defective conceptus, Rh incompatibility, spontaneous abortion, and prematurity.

Finally, the causes of infertility were discussed.

REVIEW QUESTIONS

1. If an egg is not fertilized, it disintegrates about ten days after ovulation. True or false?
2. It is possible for several sperm to penetrate the egg and fertilize it simultaneously, which is how twins and triplets occur. True or false?
3. Approximately 90 percent of cases of infertility are caused by problems with the woman's reproductive system. True or false?
4. The ______ is the mass of tissue lying beside the fetus that serves important functions in allowing nutrients and oxygen to pass from the mother's blood to the baby's blood.
5. During pregnancy, the placenta manufactures a hormone called ______, which is the substance detected in pregnancy tests.
6. Most of the major organ systems of the body develop during the first three months of fetal development. True or false?
7. Braxton-Hicks contractions indicate that labor has begun. True or false?
8. Drugs taken during pregnancy—including aspirin. antibiotics, and alcohol—may cause damage to the developing fetus. True or false?
9. "Dilation" and "effacement" refer to changes in the cervix that occur during first-stage labor. True or false?
10. The Lamaze method is a method of prepared childbirth in which the woman learns relaxation techniques and controlled breathing to help control the pain of childbirth. True or false?

QUESTIONS FOR THOUGHT, DISCUSSION, AND DEBATE

1. Taking the point of view of a pregnant woman, which would you prefer to have, a home birth or a hospital birth? Why?
2. For those readers who are men, what role would you envision for yourself in parenting if you had a child? Do you feel that you are adequately prepared for that role? For those readers who are women, what role would you ideally like an imaginary husband to take in the parenting of your imaginary children?

SUGGESTIONS FOR FURTHER READING

Arms, Suzanne. (1975). *Immaculate deception: A new look at women and childbirth in America.* Boston: Houghton Mifflin. A provocative, critical analysis of modern childbirth practices in the United States.

Leboyer, F. (1975). *Birth without violence.* New York: Random House. Argues that we make the newborn's introduction to the world traumatic and suggests ways to make it more friendly.

Nilsson, A. L., et al. (1965). *A child is born.* Boston: Seymour Lawrence. Contains exceptional photographs of prenatal development.

Pritchard, J. A. and MacDonald, P. C. (1980). *Williams obstetrics.* (16th ed.) New York: Appleton Century-Crofts. One of the standard obstetrics texts. Not exactly pleasant bedtime reading, but an excellent reference source on technical details.

CHAPTER • 7

BIRTH CONTROL AND ABORTION

For a short time I worked in an abortion clinic. One day I was counseling a woman who had come in for an abortion. I began to discuss the possible methods of contraception she could use in the future (she had been using rhythm), and I asked her what method she planned to use after the abortion.

"Rhythm," she answered. "I used it for eleven months and it worked!"*

* *Source:* Paula Weideger (1976). *Menstruation and menopause.* New York: Knopf, p. 42.

CHAPTER HIGHLIGHTS

I. THE PILL

II. THE IUD

III. THE DIAPHRAGM

IV. THE CONDOM

V. SPERMICIDES

VI. THE SPONGE

VIII. WITHDRAWAL

IX. THE RHYTHM METHOD

X. STERILIZATION

XI. PSYCHOLOGICAL ASPECTS: ATTITUDES TOWARD CONTRACEPTION

XII. ABORTION

XII. NEW ADVANCES

The average student of today grew up in the pill era and simply assumes that highly effective methods of contraception are available. It is sometimes difficult to remember that this has been true only for about the last three decades and that previously contraception was a hit-or-miss affair at best. Contraception is less controversial than it once was (except for the issue of side effects), and yet as recently as 1965 the use of contraceptives was illegal in Connecticut (see the Supreme Court decision in the case of *Griswold v. Connecticut,* 1965).

Today there is a variety of reasons for an individual's use of contraceptives. Many women desire to space pregnancies at least two years apart, knowing that that pattern is better for their health and for the health of their babies. Most couples want to limit the size of their family—usually to two or three children. Unmarried persons typically wish to avoid pregnancy. In some cases a couple knows, through genetic counseling, that they have a high risk of having a child with a birth defect and they therefore wish to prevent pregnancy. And in this era of successful career women, many women feel that it is essential to be able to control when and if they have children.

At the level of society as a whole, there are also important reasons for encouraging the use of contraceptives. There are 1,200,000 adolescent pregnancies annually in the United States and they constitute a major social problem. On the global level, the problem of overpopulation is serious; most experts believe that we must limit the size of the American population as well as assisting other countries in limiting theirs.

In this chapter we discuss various methods of birth control, how each works, how effective they are, what side effects they have, and their relative advantages and disadvantages.

THE PILL

Combination pills: Birth control pills that contain a combination of estrogen and progestin (progesterone).

With combination birth control pills such as Ortho-Novum, Loestrin, and Ovcon, the woman takes a pill that contains an estrogen and progestin (a synthetic progester-

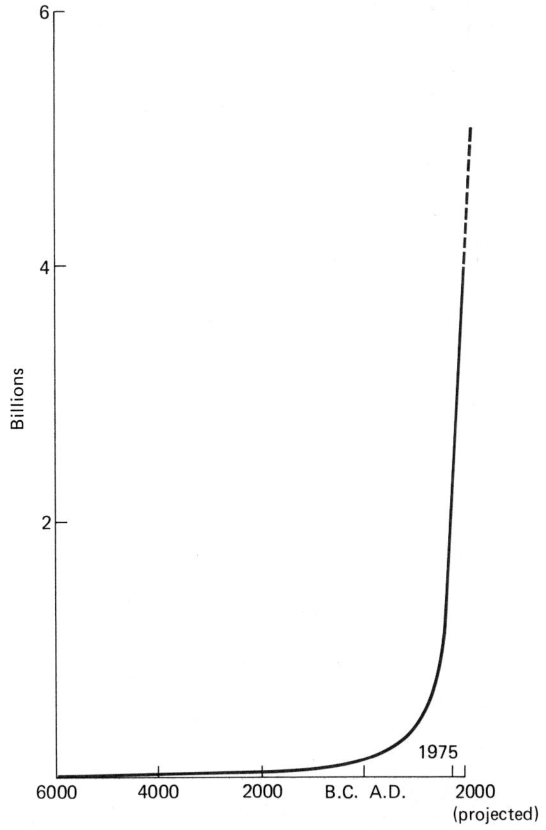

FIGURE 7.1

The growth of the world population from 6000 B.C. to 1975, with a projection to the year 2000. Reducing the population problem is one major reason for using birth control.

F · O · C · U · S 7.1

MARGARET SANGER—BIRTH CONTROL PIONEER

Margaret Higgins Sanger (1883–1966) was a crusader for birth control in the United States; in accomplishing her goals, she had to take on a variety of opponents, including the United States government, and she served one jail term.

She was born in Corning, New York, the daughter of a tubercular mother who died young after bearing 11 children. Her father was a free spirit who fought for women's suffrage. After caring for her dying mother, she embarked on a career in nursing and married William Sanger in 1900.

She became interested in women's health and began writing articles on the subject. Later these were published as books entitled *What Every Girl Should Know* (1916) and *What Every Mother Should Know* (1917).

Perhaps her strongest motivation came from her work as a nurse. All her patients were poor maternity cases on New York's lower East Side. Among these women, pregnancy was a "chronic condition." Margaret Sanger saw them, weary and old at 35, resorting to self-induced abortions, which were frequently the cause of their deaths. Frustrated at her inability to help them, she renounced nursing:

> I came to a sudden realization that my work as a nurse and my activities in social service were entirely palliative and consequently futile and useless to relieve the misery I saw all about me.

She determined, instead, to "seek out the root of the evil." Though she was often accused of wanting to lower the birthrate, she instead envisioned families, rich and poor alike, in which children were wanted and given every advantage.

Impeding her work was the Comstock Act of 1873 (see Chapter 23), which classified contraceptive information as obscene and made it illegal to send it through the mail. In 1914 she founded the National Birth Control League, launching the birth control

one), both at doses considerably higher than natural levels, for 20 or 21 days. Then she takes no pill for seven days, after which she repeats the cycle.

How It Works

The pill works mainly by preventing ovulation. Recall that in a natural menstrual cycle, the low levels of estrogen during and just after the menstrual period trigger the pituitary to produce FSH, which stimulates the process of ovulation (see Chapter

FIGURE 7.2

Margaret Sanger, a pioneer of the birth control movement.

movement in the United States. Though her magazine, *Woman Rebel,* obeyed the letter of the law and did not give contraceptive information, she was nonetheless indicted on nine counts and made liable to a prison term of 45 years.

Margaret Sanger left the United States on the eve of the trial. She toured Europe, and in Holland she visited the first birth control clinics to be established anywhere. There she got the idea of opening birth control clinics in the United States. Meanwhile, the charges against her had been dropped.

She returned to the United States and, in 1916, opened a birth control clinic in Brooklyn. The office was closed by the police after nine days of operation, and Margaret Sanger was put in jail for 30 days. However, on appeal, her case was upheld by the courts, and in 1918 a decision was handed down allowing doctors to give contraceptive information to women for the "cure and prevention of disease."

The birth control movement was gaining followers, and the first National Birth Control Conference was held in 1921 in New York; it was attended by doctors, scientists, and lay supporters. In 1931, the Pope approved the rhythm method for use by Roman Catholics.

Women in Canada were also at the forefront of the birth control movement in that country. In Hamilton, Ontario, Mary Elizabeth Hawkins organized the Hamilton Birth Control Society in 1932. Dr. Elizabeth Bagshaw, one of Hamilton's few female physicians at the time, served the clinic for the next thirty-odd years. Providing information about birth control was technically illegal in Canada, too, at the time, unless it served "the public good," and an Ottawa social worker was actually charged (and acquitted in 1937) for her family planning activity.

Margaret Sanger's role in getting birth control information to American women and in making it legal for them to use the information is unquestioned. Heywood Broun once remarked that Margaret Sanger had no sense of humor. She replied, "I am the protagonist of women who have nothing to laugh at."

Sources: Current Biography, (1944). P. Van Preagh. (1982). The Hamilton birth control clinic: In response to need. *News/Nouvelles, Journal of Planned Parenthood Federation of Canada,* 3(2).

4). The woman starts taking the birth control pills on about day 5 of the cycle. Thus just when estrogen levels would normally be low, they are artificially made high. This high level of estrogen inhibits FSH production, and the message to ovulate is never sent out. The high level of progesterone inhibits LH production, further preventing ovulation.

The progestin provides additional backup effects. It keeps the cervical mucus very thick, making it difficult for sperm to get through, and it changes the lining of the uterus in such a way that even if a fertilized egg arrived, implantation would be unlikely.

When the estrogen and progestin are withdrawn after day 21, the lining of the uterus disintegrates, and withdrawal bleeding or menstruation occurs. although the flow is typically reduced because the progestin has inhibited development of the endometrium.

Hormonally, the action of the pill produces a condition much like pregnancy, when hormone levels are also high, preventing further ovulation and menstrual periods. Thus it is not too surprising that some of the side effects of the pill are similar to the symptoms of pregnancy.

Effectiveness

Before the effectiveness of the pill is discussed, several technical terms that are used in communicating data on effectiveness need to be defined. If 100 women use a contraceptive method for one year, the number of them who become pregnant during that year is called the failure rate or *pregnancy rate*. That is, if 5 women out of 100 become pregnant during a year of using contraceptive A, then A's failure rate is 5 percent. *Effectiveness* is 100 minus the failure rate; thus contraceptive A would be said to be 95 percent effective. We can also talk about two kinds of failure rate; theoretical failure rate and actual failure rate. Theoretical failure rate is the failure rate under hypothetical conditions in which the method is used perfectly. Actual failure rate is the failure rate when people actually use the method, and thus it includes not only failures due to the contraceptive itself but also failures due to improper use, as when a woman forgets to take a pill.

Failure rate:
The pregnancy rate occurring using a particular contraceptive method; the percentage of women who will be pregnant after a year of use of the method.

Theoretical failure rate:
The failure rate of a contraceptive method when it is used perfectly.

Actual failure rate:
The failure rate of a contraceptive method when people actually use it.

The use of combination pills is the most effective method of birth control short of sterilization. The theoretical failure rate is 0.34 percent (that is, the method is essentially 100 percent effective), and the actual failure rate is 2 percent. Failures occur primarily as a result of forgetting to take a pill for two or more days. If a woman forgets to take a pill for one day, she should simply take two the next day; this does not appear to increase the pregnancy risk appreciably. If she forgets for two days, she should take two pills on each of the next two days; however, the chances of pregnancy are now increased. If she forgets for three or more days, she should switch to some other method of birth control for the remainder of that cycle.

Side Effects

You may have seen various reports in the media on the dangerous side effects of birth control pills. Some of these reports are no more than scare stories with little or no evidence behind them. On the other hand, there are some well-documented risks associated with the use of the pill, and women who are using it or who are contemplating using it should be aware of them.

The most serious side effect associated with use of the pill appears to be a slight but significant increase in problems of blood clotting (thromboembolic disorders). Women who use the pill have a higher chance than nonusers of developing blood clots (thrombi). Often these form in the legs, and they may then move to the lungs. There may also be clotting or hemorrhaging in the brain (stroke). The clots may lead to pain, hospitalization, and (in rare cases) death. The risk of death is somewhat less than 3 per 100,000 per year for women on the pill, as compared with 0.4 per 100,000 women per year among nonusers. Symptoms of blood clots are severe headaches, sudden blurring of vision, severe leg or chest pains, and shortness of breath.

There have been many emotional reports in the media of the pill causing cancer; the scientific data, however, do not provide evidence that the pill causes cancer of the cervix, uterus, or breast. However, the pill may aggravate already existing cancer, although there is some evidence that it may retard the growth of benign breast lumps and that it is protective against ovarian cancer and endometrial cancer (Ramcharan et al., 1980; Hatcher et al., 1984). And while some of the studies have looked at effects after fairly long periods of time, there is a need for studies of even longer-term effects, since it is known that cancer-causing agents (carcinogens) may not show their effects for as much as 20 years.

For some women, the pill can cause an increase in blood pressure; thus it is important to have regular checkups so that this can be detected if it occurs. The pill increases the risk of gallbladder disease. For women who have taken it more than five years, the risk of benign liver tumors increases (Hatcher et al., 1980). These tumors can cause death due to bleeding if they rupture. Although these problems are relatively rare, they underline the importance of the doctor's giving a thorough examination before prescribing birth control pills and of the woman's having regular checkups while using them.

FIGURE 7.3

Birth control devices: (*a*) birth control pills, (*b*) diaphragm and spermicidal jelly (note that diaphragms come in different sizes), (*c*) IUDs, (*d*) contraceptive foam with applicator, (*e*) condoms.

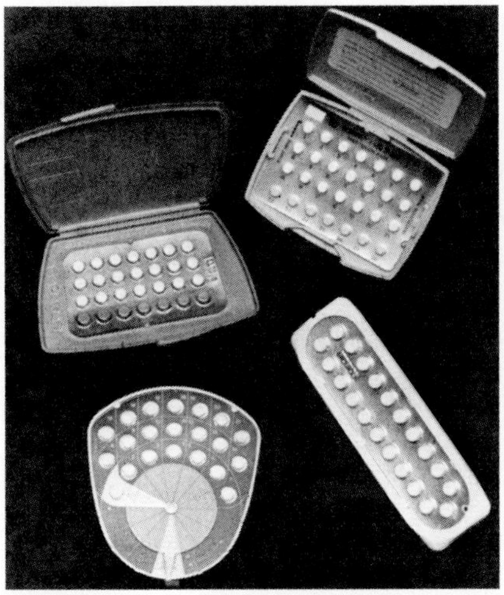

(a)

(b)

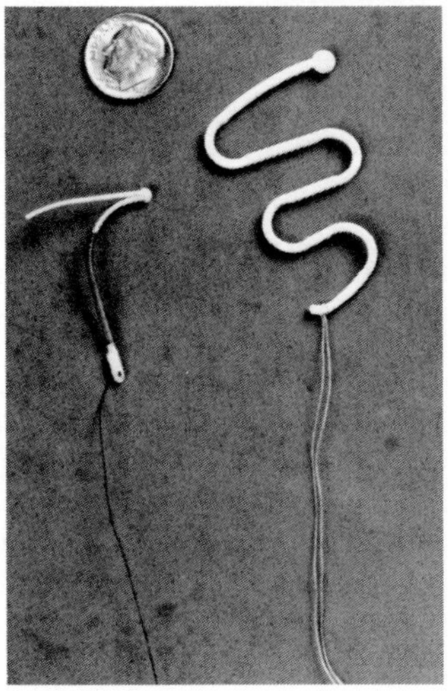

(c)

(d)

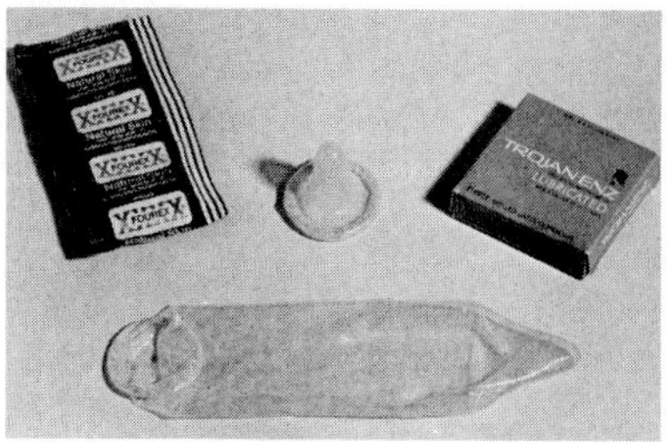

(e)

The pill increases the amount of vaginal discharge and the susceptibility to vaginitis (vaginal inflammations such as monilia and trichomonas—see Chapter 21) because it alters the chemical balance of the lining of the vagina. Women on the pill have in increased susceptibility to gonorrhea, probably for similar reasons.

The pill may cause some nausea, although this almost always goes away after the first month or two of use. Some brands of pills can also cause weight gain, by increasing appetite or water retention, but this can often be reversed by switching to another brand.

Finally, there may be some psychological effects. About 20 percent of women on the pill report increased irritability and depression, which become worse with length of time used. These side effects are probably related to the progesterone in the pill; switching to a different brand may be helpful. There may also be changes in sexual desire. Some women report an increase in sexual interest, mainly because they are now free of the fear of pregnancy. But other women report a decrease in sexual desire as well as a decrease in vaginal lubrication, a loss of sensitivity of the vulva, and decreased ability to have orgasms. Once again, switching brands may be helpful.

Because of the side effects discussed above, the following women should *not* use the pill (Hatcher et al., 1984): those with poor blood circulation or excess blood clotting; those who have had a heart attack or who have coronary artery disease; those with hepatitis or other liver diseases; those with undiagnosed abnormal genital bleeding; those with cancer of the breast; those with cystic fibrosis or sickle-cell anemia (the latter because of the blood-clotting problems); nursing mothers (the pill tends to dry up the milk supply, and the hormones may be transmitted through the milk to the baby); pregnant women (prenatal doses of hormones, as has been noted, can damage the fetus); and women over 40, particularly if they are cigarette smokers (because the risk of heart attack is considerably higher in this group). However, most women in the last category probably plan on having no more babies anyway. A better alternative would probably be some form of sterilization, either a tubal ligation for her or a vasectomy for her husband. Neither should the pill be prescribed for teenagers with irregular or infrequent menstrual periods.

Well, after all this discussion, just how dangerous is the pill? It seems that this depends on who you are and on how you look at it. If you have blood-clotting problems, the pill is extremely dangerous to you; if you have none of the contraindications listed above, it is very safe. One's point of view and standard of comparison also matter. While a death rate of 3 per 100,000 from clotting disorders sounds high, it is important to consider that one alternative to the pill is intercourse with no contraceptive, and that can mean pregnancy, which has a set of side effects and a death rate all its own. Thus while the death rate for the pill is 3 per 100,000, the death rate for pregnancy and delivery is 14 per 100,000. And while the pill may precipitate diabetes, diabetes may also be precipitated by pregnancy. Thus in many ways the pill is no more dangerous than the alternative, pregnancy, and may even be safer. Another possible standard of comparison is drugs that are commonly taken for less serious reasons. Aspirin, for example, is routinely used for headaches. Recent reports indicate that aspirin has side effects, and thus the birth control pill may be no more dangerous than drugs we take without worrying much.

A study of 16,638 women from 1969 to 1977 indicates that the pill may be even less dangerous than previous studies indicated (Ramcharan et al., 1980). In particular, there was no significant difference in death rates for pill users and nonusers. It is difficult to rationalize these findings with the earlier discussions of increased risk for certain problems. Perhaps the pill protects one against as many problems as it creates. Or it may be that the risk of the serious problems—such as thromboembolisms, high blood pressure, and gallbladder disease—is still so low even while taking the pill that it does not produce very significant effects even in a study of 16,000 women.

The pill does have some serious potential dangers, particularly for high-risk individuals, but for many others it is an extremely effective means of contraception that poses little or no danger.

Advantages and Disadvantages

The pill has a number of advantages. It is essentially 100 percent effective if used properly. It does not interfere with intercourse, as some other methods—the diaphragm, the condom, and foam—do. It is not messy. Some of its side effects are also advantages; it reduces the amount of menstrual flow and thus reduces premenstrual tension and cramps. Indeed, it is sometimes prescribed for the noncontraceptive purpose of regulating menstruation and eliminating cramps. Iron-deficiency anemia is also less likely to occur among pill users. It can clear up acne. And the pill has a protective effect against some rather serious things, including pelvic inflammatory disease (PID), and ovarian and endometrial cancer (Hatcher et al., 1984).

The side effects of birth control pills, discussed above, are of course major disadvantages. Another disadvantage is the cost, which is about $11 a month (or as little as $2 to $4 per month through a Planned Parenthood clinic) for as long as they are used. They also place the entire burden of contraception on the woman. In addition, taking them correctly is a little complicated; the woman must understand when they are to be taken, and she must remember when to take them and when not to take them. This would not be too taxing for the average college student, but for an illiterate peasant woman in an underdeveloped country who thinks the pills are to be worn like an amulet on a chain around the neck or for the mentally retarded (they need contraceptives too), presently available birth control pills are too complicated to use them correctly.

One other criticism of the pill is that for a woman who has intercourse only infrequently (say, once or twice a month or less), it represents contraceptive "overkill"; that is, the pill makes her infertile every day of the month (with the side effects of taking it every day), and yet she needs it only a few days each month. Women in this situation might consider a method, such as the diaphragm, that is used only when needed.

Reversibility

When a woman wants to become pregnant, she simply stops taking pills after the end of one cycle. Among women who do this, 60 to 75 percent become pregnant within three months, and 90 percent become pregnant within a year. This is essentially the same rate as for women who have never taken the pill. Therefore, the pill does not seem to affect the fertility of a woman after she stops taking it.

Other Kinds of Pills

To this point, the discussion has centered chiefly on the *combination pill,* so named because it contains both estrogen and progestin. This variety of pill is by far the most widely used, but there are many kinds of combination pills and several kinds of pills other than combination ones.

Combination pills vary from one brand to the next in the dosages of estrogen and progestin. The dose of estrogen is important because higher doses are more likely to induce bloodclotting problems. According to experts, only those drugs containing 50 micrograms or less of estrogen should be used; brands fulfilling that requirement include Ortho-Novum 1/50, Norinyl 1/50, Demulen, Norlestrin 1, Norlestrin 2.5, Ovral, Ovcon 50 (Hatcher et al., 1984). Because of concerns about side effects due to the estrogen in the pill, current pills have considerably lower levels of estrogen than early pills; for example, Ortho-Novum 1/50 has one-third the amount of estrogen of the early pill Enovid 10. High-progestin brands are related to symptoms such as vaginitis and depression. Thus, depending on what side effects the woman wants to avoid, she can choose a brand for its high or low estrogen or progesterone level. (See Hatcher et al., 1980, p. 36, for a list of symptoms related to dosages of estrogen and progestin.)

Another variation of the combination pill is the 28-day pill. There are 28 pills in every package. The first 21 pills that the woman takes are regular combination pills, and the last seven are placebos (they contain no drugs). The purpose of this is simply to help the woman use the pills properly, the idea being that it is easier to remember to take a pill every day than to remember to take one each day for 21 days and then none for seven days; also, the seven placebos eliminate confusion about when to start taking pills again.

Biphasic pill:
A birth control pill containing a steady level of estrogen and two phases of progesterone, one at a low level and one at a high level. Intended to mimic more closely women's natural hormonal cycles.

A biphasic pill (Ortho-Novum 10/11) was introduced in 1982. It contains a steady level of estrogen as the combination pill does, but there are two phases in the levels of progesterone, a lower level for the first 10 days, followed by a higher level for the last 11 days. The idea is to reduce total hormone exposure and provide a cycle more similar to the natural one. It is too early to know much about the effectiveness or side effects of the biphasic pill. There is also a new triphasic pill (Upton, 1983).

Progestin-only pills (such as Micronor, Nor-Q-D, and Ovrette) have been developed recently. They are sometimes called *mini-pills.* The pills contain only a low dose of progestin and no estrogen, and they were designed to avoid the estrogen-related side effects of the standard pills. The woman takes one beginning on the first day of her period and every day thereafter, at the same time each day. Although no one is exactly sure how they work, hypotheses include the following: changes in the cervical mucus such that sperm cannot get through, inhibition of the egg's ability to travel down the tube, inhibition of the sperm's ability to penetrate the egg, inhibition of implantation, and inhibition of ovulation. Progestin-only pills have a theoretical failure rate of 1 to 4 percent, which is considerably higher than that of combination pills, although much of the failure occurs during the first six months of use. They were originally developed to avoid the side effects of the estrogen in combination pills; their major side effect seems to be that they produce very irregular menstrual cycles. Some of the side effects of combination pills have also been reported. Unfortunately, the progestin-only pill has not been in use long enough (it has been marketed since January 1973) for researchers to be certain of all its side effects.

Morning-after pill:
A pill containing a high dose of DES, which can be used in emergency situations for preventing pregnancy after intercourse has occurred.

The morning-after pill was approved for emergency use (for example, after a rape) by the U.S. Food and Drug Administration (FDA) in 1973. It contains a high dose (25 milligrams) of a potent estrogen, diethylstilbestrol (DES), and is taken twice a day for five days, beginning no more than 72 hours after the act of intercourse and preferably within 24 hours. It should be stressed that it is for emergency use only, because of its serious side effects; about 16 percent of women taking it develop severe nausea and vomiting. Possible side effects if it is taken by a pregnant woman were noted in Chapter 6. Therefore it cannot be considered a method of birth control for regular use.

THE IUD

Intrauterine device (IUD): A plastic device sometimes containing metal that is inserted into the uterus for contraceptive purposes.

The intrauterine device, or IUD (sometimes also called *intrauterine contraceptive device* [IUCD]), is a small piece of plastic; it comes in various shapes. Metal or a hormone may also be part of the device. Some IUDs were named after their inventors, for example, the Lippes loop. An IUD is inserted into the uterus by a doctor or nurse practitioner (see Figure 7.4) and then remains in place until the woman wants to have it removed. One or two plastic strings hang down from the IUD through the cervix, enabling the woman to check to see whether it is in place.

The basic idea for the IUD has been around for some time. In 1909 Richter reported on the use of an IUD made of silkworm gut. In the 1920s the German physician Ernst Grafenberg reported data on 2000 insertions of silk or silver wire rings. In spite of the high effectiveness he reported (98.4 percent), his work was poorly received. Not until the 1950s, with the development of plastic and stainless-steel devices, did the method gain much popularity. Currently 60 million women worldwide are using IUDs, 40 million of them in the People's Republic of China (Population Information Program, 1982).

How It Works

No one is really sure how the IUD works, but the data clearly show that it does. The hypothesis that is currently favored is that the IUD prevents implantation of the egg

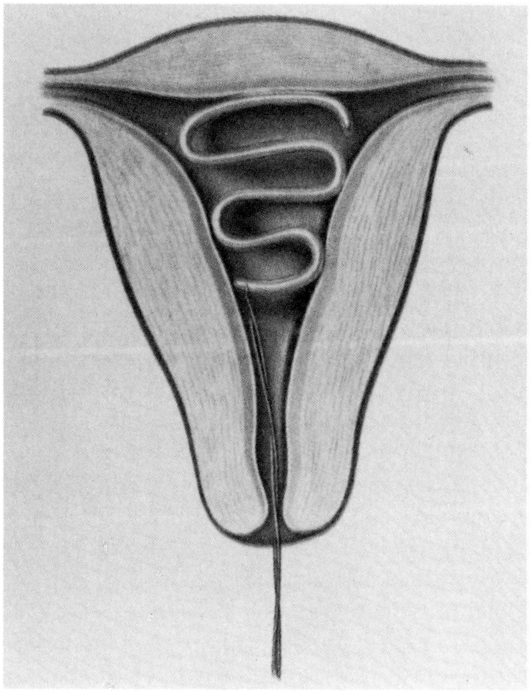

FIGURE 7.4

An IUD (Lippes loop) in place in the uterus. Note the strings hanging down through the cervix to the vagina; they enable the woman to check to make sure the device is in place.

in the uterus. Studies on humans have shown that the IUD produces no systemic effects such as changing levels of hormones. The ovaries and oviducts of women with IUDs function normally. Sperm and eggs have been found in the tubes of women with IUDs, indicating that ovulation proceeds normally and that sperm are not blocked from the tubes. Thus it appears, by the process of elimination, that the action is localized in the uterus. The IUD may produce a continual slight inflammation that keeps implantation from occurring, perhaps by preventing proper development of the endometrium or perhaps by exerting a lethal influence on the fertilized egg.

The small amount of copper that is added to some of the devices (for example, the Copper "7" and the Copper "T") is thought to have an additional contraceptive effect. It seems to alter the functioning of the enzymes involved in implantation.

The Progestasert-T releases progesterone directly into the uterus. One effect is to reduce the endometrium. This results in reduced menstrual flow and reduced risk of anemia, thus overcoming the two undesirable side effects of other IUDs.

Effectiveness

The IUD is extremely effective and is second only to the pill (and sterilization) in effectiveness. Pregnancy rates for the various types now in use range from 0.5 to 5 percent. The rate for the large Lippes loop is about 3 percent. The copper devices have a slightly lower pregnancy rate. The 3 percent failure rate is for the first year of use; after that, the failure rate is lower. Most failures occur during the first three months of use, either because the IUD is expelled or for other, unknown reasons. Thus some physicians recommend that a backup method, such as foam, be used during the first three months. Expulsion is most likely in women who have had no children, in younger women, and in women who are menstruating. The expulsion rate is about 2 to 6 percent during the first year.

The IUD can be made essentially 100 percent effective when combined with another method such as a contraceptive foam or a condom.

Side Effects

Pelvic inflammatory disease (PID):
Infection of the pelvic organs such as the fallopian tubes.

There are two serious possible side effcts of the IUD. One is uterine perforation. This occurs in only about 1 woman in 1000 (Hatcher et al., 1980), but it can be fatal. It is caused mainly by improper insertion, and thus women should exercise care in choosing a physician or clinic when obtaining an IUD. The other serious effect is pelvic inflammatory disease (PID—e.g., uterine or tubal infection). The IUD seems to aggravate already existing pelvic infections, and so it should not be used by a woman who has such an infection or a history of such infections. PID may create a blocking of the fallopian tubes, thus causing infertility. The risk of infertility due to blocked fallopian tubes among women who have never had a baby is 2.6 times higher in women who have used an IUD than in women who have never used one (Daling et al., 1985). The risk is particularly high—nearly 7 times as great in women who have used the Dalkon Shield (now withdrawn from the market). The use of copper-containing IUDs does not seem to increase the rate of infertility.

The most common side effects of IUDs are cramping and abdominal pain, irregular bleeding, and increased menstrual flow. Anemia may result. These symptoms occur in 10 to 20 percent of women using IUDs and are most likely immediately after insertion. These side effects are a major reason for requests for IUD removal.

There is no evidence that the IUD causes cancer.

Because of the possible side effects, women with the following conditions should not use an IUD: pregnancy, endometriosis, venereal disease, vaginal or uterine infection, pelvic inflammatory disease, too small uterus, excessively heavy menstrual flow and/or cramping, bleeding between periods, fibroid growths, uterine deformities, disorders requiring use of anticoagulant drugs, cardiac disease, anemia, and sickle-cell disease (Boston Women's Health Book Collective, 1976).

Advantages and Disadvantages

All the side effects discussed above are disadvantages of the IUD. Another disadvantage is the cost; some private physicians in large cities charge as much as $100 for an IUD plus insertion. Planned Parenthood clinics generally charge much less, and some even perform the service free. Even at the high rates, though, the IUD is a cheap means of contraception over a long period of use, since the cost is incurred once only (except in the case of devices containing copper or progesterone, which must be replaced every year or two).

Although the failure rate of the IUD is low, it is not zero, and this is another major disadvantage. In a group of 100 women using the IUD for a year, about two will become pregnant. Those women who absolutely do not want to become pregnant should use either a backup method, at least around the time of ovulation, or a different method entirely.

Once inserted, the IUD is perfectly simple to use. The woman has only to check periodically to see that the strings are in place. Thus it has an advantage over methods like the diaphragm or condom in that it does not interrupt intercourse in any way. It has an advantage over the pill in that the woman does not have to remember to use it. For these reasons, it has been very popular in underdeveloped nations.

Contrary to what some people think, the IUD does not interfere with the use of a tampon durng menstruation; nor does it have any effect on intercourse.

Reversibility

When a woman who is using an IUD wants to become pregnant, she simply has a physician remove the device. She can become pregnant immediately.

THE DIAPHRAGM

Diaphragm: A cap-shaped rubber contraceptive device that fits inside a woman's vagina over the cervix.

The **diaphragm** is a circular, dome-shaped piece of thin rubber with a rubber-covered rim of flexible metal (see Figure 7.5). It is inserted into the vagina and, when properly in place, fits snugly over the cervix. In order for it to be used properly, a contraceptive cream or jelly (such as Delfen) must be applied to the diaphragm. The cream is spread on the rim and the inside surface (the surface that fits against the cervix). The diaphragm may be inserted up to 6 hours before intercourse; it must be left in place for at least 6 hours afterward and may be left in for as long as 16 hours.

Use of the diaphragm was the earliest of the highly effective methods of contraception for women. It was popularized in a paper in 1882 by the German researcher Mensinga, and it was the mainstay of contraception until about 1960. Many readers may safely assume that their own parents managed to limit their number of children to two to three by careful use of the diaphragm.

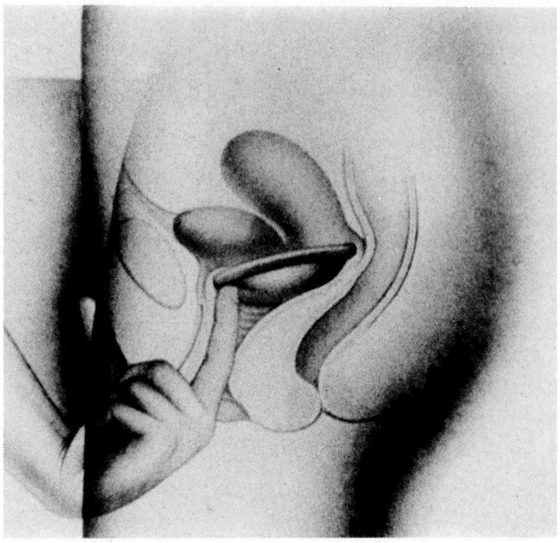

FIGURE 7.5

A diaphragm properly inserted.

How It Works

The primary action of the diaphragm itself is mechanical; it simply blocks the entrance to the uterus so that sperm cannot swim up into it. The spermicidal cream kills any sperm that manage to get past the barrier. Any sperm remaining in the vagina die after about eight hours (for this reason, the diaphragm cannot be removed until six to eight hours after intercourse).

Effectiveness

The theoretical failure rate of the diaphragm, plus cream or jelly, is about 3 percent. Thus, used properly, it is extremely effective; "used properly" means using it every time, using cream or jelly every time, and leaving it in long enough. The actual failure rate has been estimated to be about 17 percent. Most failures are due to improper use; the woman may not use it every time, or she may not use cream or jelly. Even with perfectly proper use, there is still a 2 to 3 percent failure rate. For example, Masters and Johnson have shown that the expansion of the vagina during sexual arousal (see Chapter 8) may cause the diaphragm to slip. To get closer to 100 percent effectiveness, the diaphragm can be combined with a condom around the time of ovulation.

Because the fit of the diaphragm is so important to its effectiveness, it is important that the woman be individually fitted for one by her physician. She must be refitted after the birth of a child, an abortion, extreme weight gain or loss, or any similar occurrence that would alter the shape and size of the vagina.

Side Effects

The diaphragm has few side effects, one being the possible irritation of the vagina or the penis; this is caused by the cream or jelly and can be relieved by switching to another brand. The only other side effect is the rare occurrence of toxic shock syndrome (TSS) that has been reported in women who left the diaphragm in place for more than 24 hours. Therefore users should be careful not to leave the diaphragm in place for much more than the necessary six to eight hours, especially during menstruation.

Advantages and Disadvantages

Some people feel that the diaphragm is undesirable because it must be inserted just before intercourse and therefore ruins the "spontaneity" of sex. People with this attitude, of course, should not use the diaphragm as a means of birth control, since they probably will not use it all the time, in which case it will not work. However, a student of mine told me that she and her boyfriend make the preparation and insertion of the diaphragm a ritual part of their foreplay; he inserts it, and they both have a good time! Couples who maintain this kind of attitude are much more likely to use the diaphragm effectively.

Some women dislike touching their genitals and sticking their fingers into their vagina. Use of the diaphragm is not a good method for them.

The diaphragm requires some thought and presence of mind on the woman's part. She must remember to have it with her when she needs it and to have a supply of cream or jelly. She also needs to avoid becoming so carried away with passion that she forgets about it or decides not to use it.

A disadvantage is that the cream or jelly may leak out after intercourse.

The cost of a diaphragm is about $13 plus the cost of the office visit and the cost of the spermicidal cream. With proper care, a diaphragm should last about two years, and thus it is not expensive.

The major advantages of the diaphragm are that it has no major side effects and, when used properly, is extremely effective. For this reason, women who are worried about the side effects of the pill or the IUD should seriously consider the diaphragm as an alternative.

Reversibility

If a woman wishes to become pregnant, she simply stops using the diaphragm. Its use has no effect on her later chances of conceiving.

THE CONDOM

Condom:
A male contraceptive sheath that is placed over the penis.

The condom ("rubber," "prophylactic," "safe") is a thin sheath that fits over the penis. It comes rolled up in a little packet (see Figure 7.3) and must be unrolled before use. It may be made of latex ("rubber") or of the intestinal tissue of lambs ("skin"). The widespread use of the modern condom, both for contraception and for protection against venereal disease (VD), dates from about 1843, when vulcanized rubber was developed; however, the use of a sheath to cover the penis has been known throughout most of recorded history.[1] Casanova (1725–1798) was one of the first to popularize it for its contraceptive value as well as its protective value.

---

[1]Condoms have also been the stimulus for humor throughout history, an example being this limerick:

There was a young man of Cape Horn
Who wished he had never been born
  And he wouldn't have been
  If his father had seen
That the end of the rubber was torn.

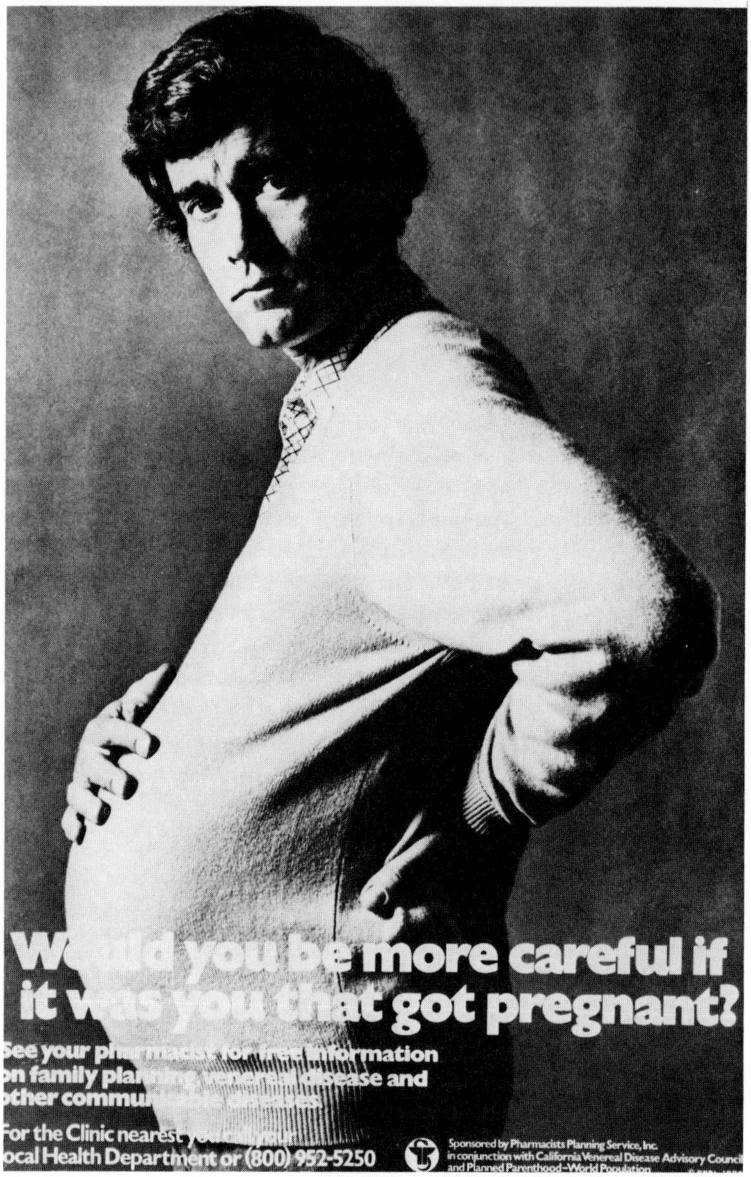

FIGURE 7.6

Male responsibility is a key issue in birth control.

To be effective, the condom must be used properly. It must be unrolled onto the erect penis before the penis ever enters the vagina—*not* just before ejaculation, since long before then some drops containing a few thousand sperm may have been produced. There are two kinds of condoms: those with plain ends and those with a protruding tip that catches the semen. If a plain-ended one is used, about ½ inch of air-free space should be left at the tip to catch the ejaculate. Care should be taken that it does not slip during intercourse. After the man has ejaculated, he must hold the rim of the condom against the base of the penis as he withdraws. It is best to withdraw soon after ejaculation, while the man still has an erection, in order to minimize the chances of slippage.

Condoms may be either lubricated or unlubricated. Some further lubrication for intercourse may be necessary. A contraceptive foam or jelly works well and provides additional protection. A sterile lubricant such as K-Y jelly may also be used.

Consumer Reports (October 1979) did laboratory tests of condoms and surveyed readers about their experiences with condom use. Among the most popular latex brands were Nuform and Trojans Plus; a popular skin condom was Fourex Capsuled. If you want a more detailed evaluation of individual brands, you should consult the *Consumer Reports* article.

How It Works

The condom simply catches the semen and thus prevents it from entering the vagina. A new condom coated inside and outside with a spermicide—Ramses Extra—was introduced recently. The spermicide kills sperm and thus provides double protection.

Effectiveness

Condoms are actually much more effective as a contraceptive than most people think. The theoretical failure rate is only about 2 percent. The actual failure rate is about 10 percent, but many failures result from improper or inconsistent use. The FDA controls the quality of condoms carefully, and thus the chances of a failure due to a defect in the condom itself are small.

Combined with a contraceptive foam or cream or a diaphragm, the condom is close to 100 percent effective.

Side Effects

The condom has no side effects.

Advantages and Disadvantages

One disadvantage of the condom is that it must be used at the time of intercourse, raising the old "spontaneity" problem again. If the couple can make an enjoyable ritual of putting it on together, this problem can be minimized.

Some men complain that the condom reduces their sensation and thus lessens their pleasure in intercourse ("It's like taking a shower with a raincoat on"). This can be a major disadvantage. On the other hand, with condoms, as with many other things, you get what you pay for. The more expensive "skins" provide more sensation than the less expensive "rubbers." The reduction in sensation, however, may be an advantage for some; for example, it may help the premature ejaculator.

There are several advantages to condoms. Their use is the only contraceptive method presently available for men except sterilization. They are cheap (around $1.25 to $1.50 for three), they are readily available without prescription at a drugstore, and they are fairly easy to use, although the man (or woman) must plan ahead so that one will be available when it is needed. Finally, it is one of the few contraceptive devices that also provide some protection against sexually transmitted diseases, an important consideration in our VD epidemic era.

Reversibility

The method is easily and completely reversible. The man simply stops using them if conception is desired.

SPERMICIDES

Spermicide (SPERM-ih-side):
A substance that kills sperm.

Contraceptive foams (Delfen, Emko), creams, and jellies are all classified as spermicides, that is, sperm killers. They come in a tube or a can, along with a plastic applicator. The applicator is filled and inserted into the vagina; the spermicide is then pushed out into the vagina near the cervix with the plunger. Thus it is inserted much as a tampon is. It must be left in for six to eight hours after intercourse. One application provides protection for only one act of intercourse.

Spermicides are not to be confused with the various feminine hygiene products (vaginal deodorants) on the market. The latter are not effective as contraceptives.

How They Work

Spermicides consist of a spermicidal chemical in an inert base, and they work in two ways: chemical and mechanical. The chemicals in them kill sperm, while the inert base itself mechanically blocks the entrance to the cervix so that sperm cannot swim into it.

Effectiveness

Actual failure rates for spermicides can be as high as 25 percent. Put simply, they are not very effective. Foams tend to be more effective, and creams and jellies less so. Spermicidal tablets and suppositories are also available, and they are the least effective. Spermicides are highly effective only when used with a diaphragm or a condom.

Side Effects

Traditionally it has been thought that spermicides have no side effects except that they may occasionally irritate the vagina or penis. However, a recent large-scale study suggests otherwise (Jick et al., 1981). The study compared infants born to mothers who had obtained (and presumably used) a spermicide in the ten months before conception, with a comparison group. The incidence of certain birth defects—including limb deformities and chromosomal defects (such as Down's syndrome, which leads to retardation)—was 2.2 percent in the spermicide group, compared with 1.0 percent in the control group. Spontaneous abortions were also about twice as frequent in the spermicide group as in the control group. It is uncertain how spermicides might have such effects. It is possible that they damage sperm, but the sperm are still capable of producing conception. Another possibility is that they are absorbed into the woman's bloodstream and then go on to damage the egg. Or it is possible that, when used after a conception has occurred, they damage the embryo or fetus. The study has been criticized (Hatcher et al., 1984) and it is too early to conclude that spermicides should be banned. But it is clear that there is a need for more research and for more alertness from consumers.

Advantages and Disadvantages

The major advantage of spermicides is that they are readily available, without prescription, in any drugstore. Thus they can be used as a stopgap method until the woman can see a physician and get a more effective contraceptive. Foam and some brands of creams and jellies also help prevent venereal disease.

Their major disadvantage is that by themselves, they are not very effective. They also interrupt the spontaneity of sex, although only very briefly. Some women dislike the sensation of the spermicide leaking out after intercourse, and some are irritated by the chemicals. Finally, most people find that they taste terrible, and so their use interferes with oral sex.

THE SPONGE

Contraceptive sponge: A polyurethane sponge containing a spermicide, which is placed in the vagina for contraceptive purposes.

The vaginal contraceptive sponge was approved by the FDA in 1983. It is marketed under the brand name Today. It is made out of polyurethane and is shaped rather like a large mushroom cap (see Figure 7.7). It is inserted into the vagina in a similar way as the diaphragm. The hollow side fits against the cervix, and the side with the woven loop is on the outside so that the loop can be used for removing it. It should be moistened with water before inserting it and it can be left in place for up to 24 hours. It provides protection if there are multiple acts of intercourse while it is in place. After use it is discarded. It comes in a single size and is available over the counter, without prescription.

How It Works

The sponge works in three ways. First, it contains a spermicide, which kills sperm. Second, because it fits over the cervix, it provides a mechanical barrier to sperm swimming into the uterus. Finally, as a sponge, it soaks up semen, trapping sperm inside it.

Effectiveness

The actual failure rate of the sponge is about 17 percent (Hatcher et al., 1984), making it somewhat less effective than the diaphragm.

Side Effects

Some women are allergic to the spermicide in the sponge. About 6 percent of women in a U.S. study had such difficulty removing the sponge that they discontin-

FIGURE 7.7

The contraceptive sponge.

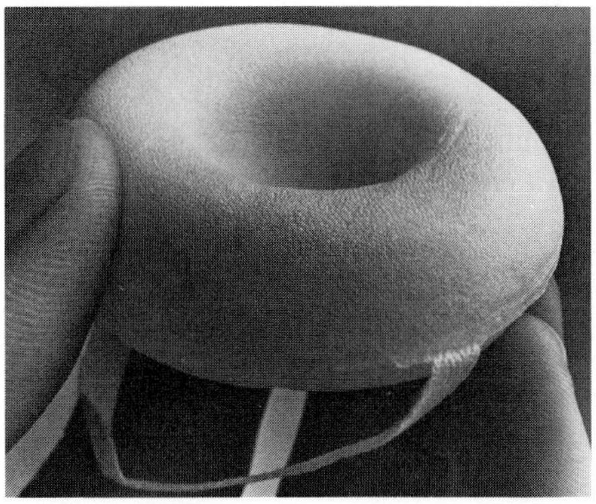

ued using it, and a few found it uncomfortable. Some women also find that it absorbs their vaginal lubrication so that they have a problem with vaginal dryness during sexual intercourse.

Advantages and Disadvantages

The main advantage of the sponge is that it is available over the counter, without prescription, and thus it is a good stopgap method until a woman can see a physician for a more effective, prescription contraceptive. It can be inserted well before intercourse, so that it does not interrupt lovemaking.

The major disadvantage is its high failure rate. Also, costing more than $1 per sponge, it is a rather expensive method for a woman who has intercourse frequently.

DOUCHING

Douching (DOOSH-ing): Flushing out the inside of the vagina with a liquid.

Some people believe that douching (flushing the vagina with a liquid) with any one of a variety of solutions is an effective contraceptive technique. A popular rumor among teenagers is that douching with Coca-Cola will prevent pregnancy. Unfortunately, while it is true that acidic solutions will kill sperm, it takes only a minute for some of the sperm to reach the cervical mucus; once there, they are free to continue moving up into the uterus, and no douching solution will reach them. The woman would have to be a championship sprinter to get herself up and douched soon enough. And the douche itself may even push some sperm up into the uterus. Douching, therefore, is just not effective as a contraceptive method.

WITHDRAWAL

Withdrawal: A method of birth control in which the man withdraws his penis from the vagina before he has an orgasm.

Withdrawal (coitus interruptus, "pulling out") is probably the most ancient form of birth control. (A reference to it is even found in Genesis 38:8–9, in the story of Onan; hence it is sometimes called *onanism,* although this term is also sometimes used for masturbation.) Withdrawal is still widely used throughout the world. The man withdraws his penis from the vagina before he has an orgasm and thus ejaculates outside the vagina.

Effectiveness

Withdrawal is not very effective as a method of birth control. The failure rate is somewhere around 20 to 25 percent. Failures occur for several reasons: The few drops of fluid that come out of the penis during arousal may carry enough sperm for conception to occur; if ejaculation occurs outside the vagina but near or on the vulva, sperm may still get into the vagina and continue up into the uterus; and sometimes the man simply does not withdraw in time.

Side Effects

Withdrawal produces no direct physical side effects. However, over long periods of time, it may contribute to producing sexual dysfunctions in the man, such as premature ejaculation, and also sexual dysfunction in the woman.

Advantages and Disadvantages

The major advantage of withdrawal is that it is the only last-minute method; it can be used when nothing else is available, although if the situation is this desperate, one might consider abstinence as an alternative. Obviously, withdrawal requires no prescription, and it is completely free.

One major disadvantage is that withdrawal is not very effective. In addition, it requires exceptional motivation on the part of the man, and it may be very psychologically stressful to him. He must constantly maintain a kind of self-conscious control. The woman may worry about whether he really will withdraw in time, and the situation is certainly less than ideal for her to have an orgasm.

THE RHYTHM METHOD

Rhythm method:
A method of birth control that involves abstaining from intercourse around the time when the woman ovulates.

Rhythm (fertility awareness) is the only form of "natural" birth control and is therefore the only method officially approved by the Roman Catholic Church. It requires simply abstaining during the woman's fertile period (around ovulation). There are actually several rhythm methods, depending on how the woman's fertile period is determined.

The Calendar Method

Calendar method:
A type of rhythm method of birth control in which the woman determines when she ovulates by keeping a calendar record of the length of her menstrual cycles.

The calendar method is the simplest rhythm method. It is based on the assumption that ovulation occurs about 14 days before the onset of menstruation. It works best for the woman with the perfectly regular 28-day cycle. She should ovulate on day 14, and almost surely on one of days 13 to 15. Three days are added in front of that period (previously deposited sperm may result in conception), and two days are added after it (to allow for long-lasting eggs); thus the couple must abstain from day 10 to day 17. Thus even for the woman with perfectly regular cycles, eight days of abstinence are required in the middle of each cycle.

The woman who is not perfectly regular must keep a record of her cycles for at least six months, and preferably a year. From this she determines the length of her shortest cycle and the length of her longest cycle. The preovulatory safe period is then calculated by substracting 18 from the number of days in the shortest cycle, and the postovulatory safe period is calculated by substracting 11 from the number of days in the longest cycle (see Table 7.1). Thus for a woman who is somewhat irregular—say, with cycles varying from 26 to 34 days in length—a period of abstinence from day 8 to day 23 (a total of 16 days) would be required.

The Basal Body Temperature Method

Basal body temperature method:
A type of rhythm method of birth control in which the woman determines when she ovulates by keeping track of her temperature.

A somewhat more accurate method for determining ovulation is the basal body temperature (BBT) method. The principle behind this was discussed in Chapters 5 and 6. The woman takes her temperature every day immediately upon waking. During the preovulatory phase her temperature will be at a fairly constant low level. On the day of ovulation it drops (although this does not always occur), and on the day after ovulation it rises sharply, staying at that high level for the rest of the cycle. Intercourse would be safe beginning about three days after ovulation. Some of the psychological stresses involved in using this method have been noted previously. As a form of contraception, the BBT method has a major disadvantage in that it deter-

TABLE 7.1

DETERMINING THE FERTILE PERIOD USING THE CALENDAR METHOD*

Shortest Cycle (Days)	Day Fertile Period Begins	Longest Cycle (Days)	Day Fertile Period Ends
22	4	23	12
23	5	24	13
24	6	25	14
25	7	26	15
→ 26 →	(8)	27	16
27	9	28	17
28	10	29	18
29	11	30	19
30	12	31	20
31	13	32	21
32	14	33	22
		→ 34 →	(23)
		35	24

Example: If a woman's cycles vary in length from 26 days to 34 days, she can be fertile any time between days 8 and 23 of the cycle, and she must therefore abstain from day 8 to day 23.

*See text for further explanation.

Source: After E. Havemann. (1967). *Birth control.* New York: Time-Life, p. 23.

mines safe days only *after* ovulation; theoretically, according to the method, there are no safe days before ovulation. Thus the BBT method is probably best used in combination with the calendar method, which determines the preovulatory safe period; the BBT method determines the postovulatory safe period.

Cervical mucus method: A type of rhythm method of birth control in which the woman determines when she ovulates by checking her cervical mucus.

The Cervical Mucus (Ovulation) Method

Another rhythm method was developed by Drs. Evelyn and John Billings (Billings et al., 1974). Their method is based on variations over the cycle in the mucus produced by the cervix. It works in the following way:

There are generally a few days just after menstruation during which no mucus is produced and there is a general sensation of vaginal dryness. This is a relatively safe period. Then there are a number of days of mucus discharge around the middle of the cycle. On the first days, the mucus is white or cloudy and tacky. The amount increases, and the mucus becomes clearer, until there are one or two *peak days,* when the mucus is like raw egg white—clear, slippery, and stringy. There is also a sensation of vaginal lubrication. Ovulation occurs within 24 hours after the last peak day. Abstinence is required from the first day of mucus discharge until four days after the peak days. After that the mucus, if present, is cloudy or white, and intercourse is safe.

The Billingses believe that women can be taught to use this method very effectively.

Sympto-thermal method: A type of rhythm method of birth control combining both the basal body temperature and the cervical mucus method.

The Sympto-Thermal Method

The sympto-thermal method combines two rhythm methods in order to produce better effectiveness. The woman records changes in her cervical mucus (symptoms) as well as her basal body temperature (thermal). The combination of the two should give a more accurate determination of the time of ovulation.

Other Methods

Because of the view of some Roman Catholics that rhythm is the only acceptable method of birth control, as well as the concern of many others about side effects from the pill and the IUD, scientists have devoted considerable effort to trying to develop more effective rhythm methods (or, essentially, better methods of determining ovulation). One such method is a litmus-type test for detecting changes in cervical secretions. Another method tests for changes in saliva. These methods are still in the experimental stages, however.

Effectiveness

The effectiveness of the rhythm method varies considerably, depending on a number of factors, but basically it is not a very effective method (giving rise to its nickname, "Vatican roulette," and a number of old jokes like, "What do they call people who use the rhythm method?" Answer: "Parents"). The failure rate is somewhere between 15 to 25 percent with an average of about 19 percent; there tend to be fewer failures when the woman's cycle is very regular and when the couple are highly motivated and have been well instructed in the methods.

On the other hand, the effectiveness of the rhythm method depends partly on one's purpose in using it: whether for preventing pregnancy absolutely or for spacing pregnancies. If absolute pregnancy prevention is the goal (as it would be, for example, for an unmarried teenager), the method is just not effective enough. But if the couple simply wish to space pregnancies farther apart than would occur naturally, the method will probably accomplish this. Knowing when the woman's fertile times occur can also improve the effectiveness of other methods of contraception.

Advantages and Disadvantages

For many users of the rhythm method, its main advantage is that it is considered an acceptable method of birth control by the Roman Catholic Church.

The method has no side effects except possible psychological stress, and it is cheap. It is easily reversible. It also helps the woman become more aware of her body's functioning. Finally, the method requires cooperation from both partners, which may be considered either an advantage or a disadvantage.

Its main disadvantages are its high failure rate and the psychological stress it may cause. Periods of abstinence of at least eight days, and possibly as long as two or three weeks, are necessary, which is an unacceptable requirement for many couples. Actually, the rhythm method would seem best suited to people who do not like sex very much.

A certain amount of time, usually at least six months, is required to collect the data needed to make the method work. Thus one cannot simply begin using it on the spur of the moment.

Finally, a risk associated with the method has been discovered recently. When the method fails and a pregnancy occurs, there is an unusually high percentage of defective babies born as a result (Berger, 1980; Iffy and Wingate, 1970). Apparently this occurs because such pregnancies are a result of intercourse *after* the "safe" period, and thus an overripe egg is fertilized; this creates a high incidence of chromosomal defects and abnormal development.

STERILIZATION

Sterilization:
A surgical procedure by which an individual is made sterile, that is, incapable of reproducing.

Sterilization is a surgical procedure whereby an individual is made permanently sterile, that is, unable to reproduce. Sterilization is a rather emotion-laden topic for a number of reasons. It conjures up images of government-imposed programs of *involuntary* sterilization in which groups of people—possibly the mentally retarded, criminals, or members of some minority group—are sterilized so that they cannot reproduce. (The following discussion deals only with voluntary sterilization used as a method of birth control for those who want no more children or who want no children at all.) Some people confuse sterilization with castration, though the two are quite different. This is also an emotional topic because sterilization means the end of one's capacity to reproduce, which is very basic to gender roles and gender identity. The ability to impregnate and the ability to bear a child are very important in our cultural definitions of manhood and womanhood. It is hoped that as gender roles become more flexible in our society and as concern about reproduction is replaced by a concern for limiting population size, the word "sterilization" will no longer be so frightening.

Most physicians are conservative about performing sterilizations; they want to make sure that the patient has made a firm decision on his or her own and will not be back a couple of months later wanting to have the procedure reversed. The physician has an obligation to follow the principle of "informed consent." This means explaining the procedures involved, telling the patient about the possible risks and advantages, discussing alternative methods, and answering any questions the patient has. Only after the patient has been so informed should the doctor obtain her or his written consent to have the surgery performed.

Despite this conservatism, both male sterilization and female sterilization have become increasingly popular as methods of birth control, and the number performed per year has risen phenomenally since 1969. Among white couples married 15 to 19 years, 4 percent had vasectomies in 1965, compared with 20 percent in 1975 (Westoff and Jones, 1977). The total number of sterilized adults in the United States is now estimated to be about 11 million (Forrest and Henshaw, 1983). Sterilization is the most common method of birth control for married couples over 30 years of age (Presser and Bumpass, 1972).

Male Sterilization

Vasectomy (vas-EK-tuh-mee):
A surgical procedure for male sterilization involving severing of the vas deferens.

The male sterilization operation is called a vasectomy,[2] so named for the vas deferens, which is tied or cut (see Figure 7.8). It can be done in a physician's office under local anesthesia and requires only about 20 minutes to perform. The physician makes a small incision on one side of the upper part of the scrotum. The vas is then separated from the surrounding tissues, tied off, and cut. The procedure is then repeated on the other side, and the incisions are sewn up. For a day or two the man may have to refrain from strenuous activity and be careful not to pull the incision apart.

---

[2]As someone has said, "Vasectomy is never having to say you're sorry."

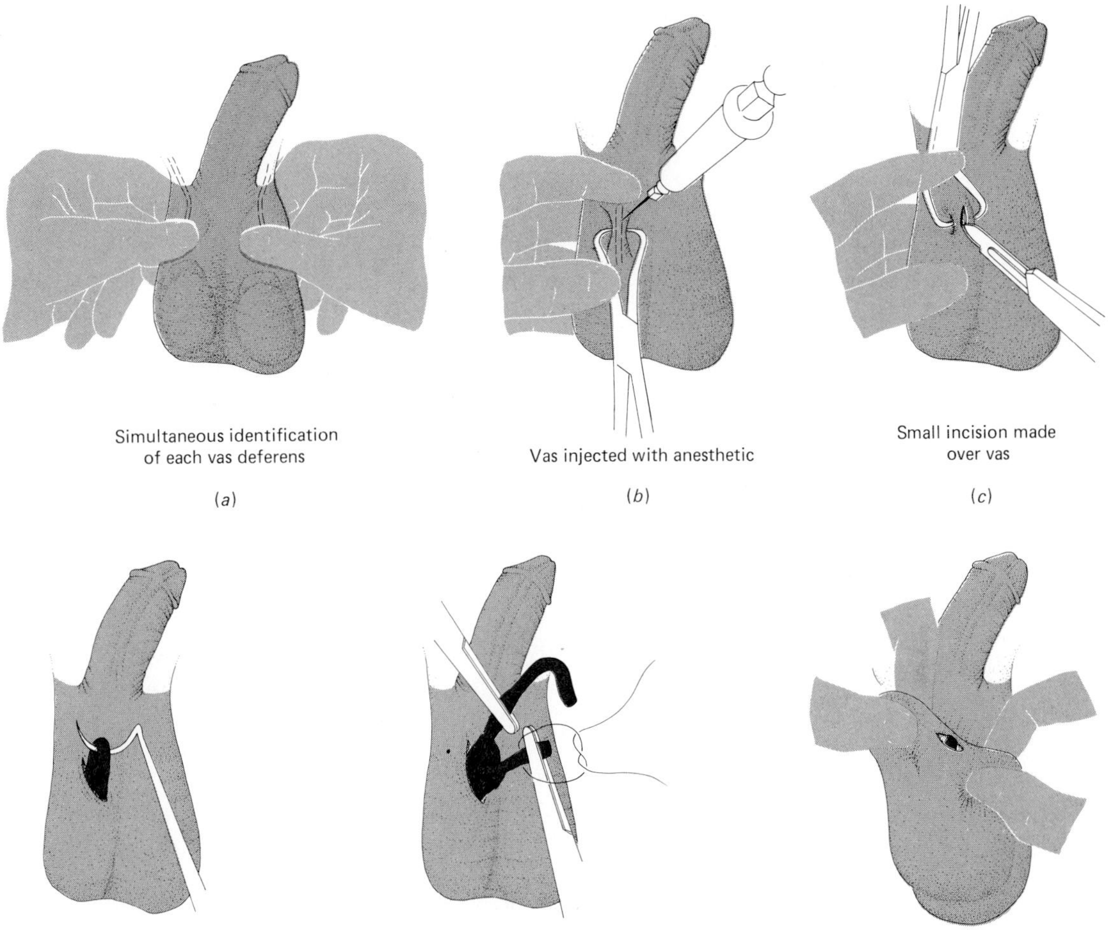

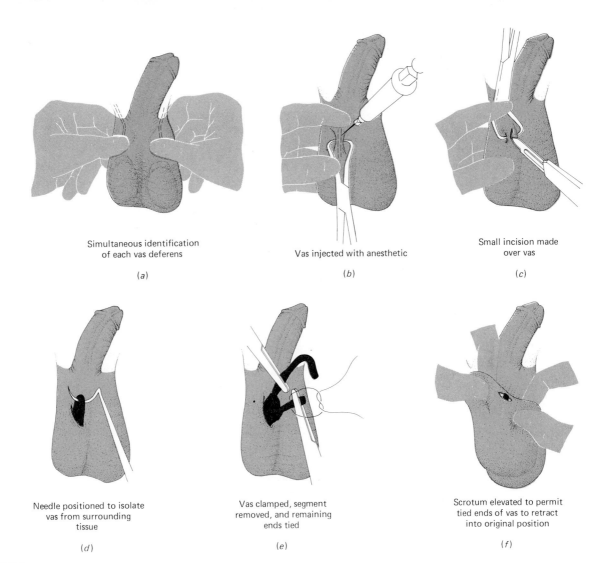

Simultaneous identification of each vas deferens

(*a*)

Vas injected with anesthetic

(*b*)

Small incision made over vas

(*c*)

Needle positioned to isolate vas from surrounding tissue

(*d*)

Vas clamped, segment removed, and remaining ends tied

(*e*)

Scrotum elevated to permit tied ends of vas to retract into original position

(*f*)

FIGURE 7.8

The procedure for doing a vasectomy.

Typically, the man can return to having intercourse within a few days. It should not be assumed that he is sterile yet, however. There may still be some stray sperm lurking in his ducts beyond the point of the incision. All sperm are generally gone in two or three months, and their absence should be confirmed by semen analysis. Until this confirmation is made, an additional method of birth control should be used.

Misunderstandings about the vasectomy abound. In fact, a vasectomy creates no physical changes that interfere with erection. Neither does it interfere in any way with sex hormone production; the testes continue to manufacture testosterone and secrete it into the bloodstream. Men with vasectomies will not develop high-pitched voices! Neither does a vasectomy interfere with the process or sensation of ejaculation. As was noted earlier, virtually all the fluid of the ejaculate is produced by the prostate and seminal vesicles, and the incision is made long before that point in the duct system. Thus the ejaculate is completely normal, except that it does not contain any sperm.

How It Works

The vasectomy makes it impossible for sperm to move beyond the cut in the vas. Thus the vasectomy prevents sperm from being in the ejaculate.

Effectiveness

The vasectomy is essentially 100 percent effective; it has a failure rate of 0.15 percent. Failures occur because stray sperm are still present during the first few months after surgery, because the physician did not successfully sever the vas, or because the ends of the vas have grown back together.

Side Effects

The physical side effects of the vasectomy are minimal. In about 5 percent of cases, there is a minor complication from the surgery, such as inflammation of the vas (Gould, 1974).

Some psychologically based sexual problems such as impotency may arise. Thus the man's attitude toward having a vasectomy is extremely important.

Reversibility

Quite a bit of effort has been devoted to developing techniques for reversing vasectomies and to developing vasectomy techniques that are more reversible. At present, reversibility rates range from 20 to 60 percent (Hatcher et al., 1984). In making a decision about whether to have a vasectomy, it should be assumed that it is irreversible.

A silicone rubber valve that could be implanted in the vas is currently being investigated; if the patient desired to reverse his sterilization, the valve could be reopened in simple surgery (Brueschke et al., 1979).

It appears, however, that after a vasectomy some men begin forming antibodies to their own sperm. Because these antibodies destroy sperm, they might contribute further to the irreversibility of the vasectomy.

Advantages and Disadvantages

The major advantages of the vasectomy are its effectiveness and its minimal health risks. Once performed, it requires no further thought or planning on the man's part. As a permanent, long-term method of contraception, it is very cheap. The operation itself is simple—much simpler than the female sterilization procedures—and requires no hospitalization or absence from work. Finally, it is one of the few methods that allow the man to assume contraceptive responsibility.

The first hint of possible health risks associated with a vasectomy came recently (Clarkson and Alexander, 1980). It was discovered that a vasectomy increases the risk of atherosclerosis (hardening of the arteries) in two species of monkeys. Apparently this is due to the formation of the antisperm antibodies as a result of the presence of sperm in the body following a vasectomy. These antibodies appear to injure the blood vessels, contributing to a buildup of deposits in them. However, a recent study of vasectomized men showed no higher rate of heart attacks for that group compared with a nonvasectomized control group (Walker et al.. 1981). Thus most experts believe that vasectomies create no increased risk of atherosclerosis.

The permanency of the vasectomy may be either an advantage or a disadvantage. If permanent contraception is desired, the method is certainly much better than something like birth control pills, which must be used repeatedly. But if the couple change their minds and decide that they want to have another child, the permanency is a distinct disadvantage. Some men put several samples of their sperm in a frozen sperm bank so that artificial insemination can be performed if they do decide to have another child after a vasectomy.

Another disadvantage of the vasectomy is the various psychological problems that might result if the man sees sterilization as a threat to his masculinity or virility. However, long-term studies of vasectomized men provide no evidence of such psychological problems (Population Information Program, 1983). In studies done around the world, the majority of vasectomized men say that they have no regrets about having had the sterilization performed, that they would recommend it to others, and that there has been no change or else an improvement in their happiness and sexual satisfaction in marriage. Fewer than 5 percent of vasectomized men report psychological problems such as decreased libido or depression, and this rate is no higher than in control samples of unvasectomized men.

Finally, if a married couple use the vasectomy as a permanent method of birth control, the woman is not protected if she has intercourse with someone other than her husband.

Female Sterilization

Several surgical techniques are used to sterilize a woman: laparotomy, laparoscopy, culpotomy, and culdoscopy. These techniques differ in terms of the type of procedure used and the path of entry. All are performed under local or, more commonly, general anesthesia, and all involve blocking the fallopian tubes in some way so that sperm and egg cannot meet.

Tubal ligation: A surgical method of female sterilization; also called salpingectomy.

The tubal ligation or *salpingectomy* ("having the tubes tied") is the most common method of female sterilization. A small section is cut out of each fallopian tube, and the ends of each tube are tied off at the incision. The tubes may be reached through a small incision in the abdomen, in which case the procedure is called a *laparotomy.* Another avenue is through an incision made at the end of the vagina, in which case the procedure is called a *culpotomy* (the end of the vagina, the part past the cervix, is called the cul-de-sac; hence the name "culpotomy").

A more recent procedure is the *endoscopy.* A small tube, with lights and a mirror in it, is inserted to enable the physician to locate the fallopian tubes, which are cauterized (burned) with a small instrument. If entry is through the abdomen, the procedure is called a *laparoscopy,* and if entry is through the vagina, it is called a *culdoscopy.* One other variation involves inserting the instrument through the vagina and the uterus, in which case the procedure is called a *uteroscopy* or *hysteroscopy.*

These female sterilization procedures do not interfere with the ovaries, and therefore the production of sex hormones continues normally; thus a tubal ligation does not bring on premature menopause or cause the woman to grow a beard. Some of the misunderstandings concerning female sterilization procedures arise from confusion of these procedures with hysterectomy (surgical removal of the uterus) or oophorectomy (surgical removal of the ovaries, which does impair hormonal functioning). These latter two operations do produce sterility, but they are generally performed for purposes other than sterilization, for example, removal of tumors.

How It Works

All the female sterilization procedures make it impossible for the egg to move down the fallopian tube toward the uterus. They also prevent sperm from reaching the egg.

Effectiveness

These procedures are essentially 100 percent effective. The failure rate of 0.05 percent may be due to an occasional rejoining of the ends of the fallopian tubes.

Side Effects

Occasionally there are side effects arising from the surgery, such as infections, hemorrhaging, and problems related to the anesthetic. Generally, only 1 to 2 percent of women undergoing the surgery experience complications. A small percentage of women have long-term side effects including menstrual problems (dysmenorrhea or irregular cycles) or benign breast lumps (Vorherr et al., 1983).

Reversibility

The operations are essentially irreversible, although occasionally it has been possible to rejoin the ends of the tube. In deciding whether to have such an operation, it should be assumed that it is irreversible.

Advantages and Disadvantages

Female sterilization has some of the same advantages as male sterilization in terms of effectiveness, permanence, and cheapness when used for long-term contraception.

Compared with male sterilization methods, the methods of female sterilization currently used are somewhat more complex. A hospital stay may be required, although generally the procedures can be performed on an outpatient basis; the surgery is also somewhat more serious, and so complications are more likely.

PSYCHOLOGICAL ASPECTS: ATTITUDES TOWARD CONTRACEPTION

It is a favorite old saying among the Planned Parenthood crowd that contraceptives are only as effective as the people who use them. That is, no contraceptive method is effective if it is not used or if it is used improperly. Thus the user is at least as important as all the technology of contraception.

Each year in the United States one million teenagers (mostly unmarried) become pregnant; 30,000 of those pregnancies happen to girls 15 years of age and younger (Byrne, 1983). Approximately 16 percent of teenage women become premaritally pregnant (Zelnik and Kantner, 1980). It is not an overstatement, then, to say that teenage pregnancy is at epidemic proportions. Approximately 37 percent of these unwanted pregnancies are terminated by abortion (Zelnik and Kantner, 1980), 50 percent result in live births (to single teenagers or to couples joined in "shotgun" matrimony) and the remainder end in miscarriage.

If we are to understand this problem and take effective steps to solve it, we must understand the psychology of contraceptive use and nonuse. A number of researchers have been investigating this issue.

According to Donn Byrne (1983), a social psychologist, there are five steps involved in effective contraception:

1. The person must acquire and remember accurate information about contraception.
2. The person must acknowledge that there is a likelihood of engaging in sexual intercourse. Contraceptive preparation, of course, makes sense only if one has

TABLE 7.2

PERCENTAGE OF U.S. WOMEN AGED 15 TO 44 REPORTING THE USE OF VARIOUS METHODS OF CONTRACEPTION, 1982*

Method	Percentage Using Method
Sterilization	21†
Pill	18
IUD	4
Condom	8
Spermicide	3
Diaphragm	3
Withdrawal	2
Rhythm	1
Douche and other	<1
Sexually active and using nothing	6
Not sexually active	33

*Canadian data show an essentially similar pattern, with the pill and sterilization being quite popular, and condoms, diaphragms, the IUD, and spermicides being runners up (Badgley et al., 1977).

†Of the 21 percent who report sterilization, 12 percent are tubal ligations and 9 percent are vasectomies.

Source: Jacqueline D. Forrest and Stanley K. Henshaw. (1983, Aug.). What U.S. women think and do about contraception. *Family Planning Perspectives,* **15**(4), pp. 157–166.

some expectations of having intercourse. Gender-role socialization has made it particularly difficult for women to acknowledge such expectations.

3. The person must obtain the contraceptive. This may involve a visit to a doctor or to a drugstore or Planned Parenthood clinic.
4. The person must communicate with his or her partner about contraception. Otherwise, both may assume that the other will take care of things.
5. The person must actually use the method of contraception.

According to Byrne's analysis, a number of psychological factors can intervene in any of these five steps, making the person either more likely or less likely to use contraceptives effectively. These factors include attitudes and emotions, information, expectations, and fantasies.

Erotophobia: Feeling guilty and fearful about sex.

Erotophilia: Feeling comfortable with sex, lacking in feelings of guilt and fear about sex.

Attitudes and emotions play an important role. One particular dimension is *erotophilia-erotophobia* (Byrne, 1983; Fisher et al., 1983; Byrne, 1977). Erotophobes don't discuss sex, have sex lives that are influenced by guilt and fear of social disapproval, have intercourse infrequently with few partners, and are shocked by sexually explicit films. Erotophiles are just the opposite—they discuss sex, they are relatively uninfluenced by sex guilt, they have intercourse more frequently with more partners, and they find sexually explicit films to be arousing. Research shows that erotophiles are more likely to be consistent, reliable contraceptive users. At every one of the five steps of contraceptive use, the erotophobes are more likely to fail. Research shows that they have less sex information than erotophiles do, and that, when exposed to the same sex information, erotophobes learn less than erotophiles do (Fisher et al., 1983). Because of their fearfulness, erotophobes are less likely to acknowledge that intercourse may occur, which makes contraceptive planning difficult. Erotophobes also have more difficulty going to a doctor or a drugstore to obtain contraceptives. Erotophobes don't discuss sex or contraception very much, and therefore effective communication with their partner is unlikely to occur. And finally, erotophobes have trouble with the final step of actually using the contraceptive. An erotophobic male isn't going to be thrilled about pulling out a condom. An erotophobic female won't be thrilled with inserting a diaphragm or thinking about sex every day as she takes her pill.

Information is also an important factor in contraceptive use and nonuse. People who lack information about contraceptives and their correct use can scarcely use them effectively.

Expectations play an important role. When thinking about sex and contraception, people have some expectations about how likely it is that intercourse will result in pregnancy. Research shows that many people think that the chance is zero or close to it, expressing the expectation that "It can't happen to me." (see Focus 7.2). People with that expectation are unlikely to use contraceptives.

Although it is generally recognized that *fantasy* is an important part of sexual expression, only recently have scientists realized that fantasy may play an important role in contraceptive behavior (Byrne, 1983). Most of us have fantasies about sexual encounters, and we often try to make our real-life sexual encounters turn out like the "scripts" of our fantasies. An important shaper of our fantasies is the media. Through movies, television, and romance novels, we learn idealized techniques for kissing, holding, lovemaking. But the media's idealized versions of sex almost never include a portrayal of the use of contraceptives. When Captain Frank Furillo and lawyer Joyce Davenport of *Hill Street Blues* hop into bed together, they never show Frank reaching for a condom or Joyce's nightly routine of taking her pill. Thus our fantasy sex, shaped by the media, lacks contraception as part of the script. One exception occurred in the movie *Saturday Night Fever.* John Travolta, lying on top of a willing young woman in the back seat of a car, asks her if she is using a contraceptive. When she replies that she isn't, he zips his pants up and leaves. If teenagers saw lots of instances of their heroes and heroines behaving responsibly about contraception, it would probably influence their behavior. But right now that is not what the media gives them.

What are the solutions? Can this new research and theorizing on the social psychology of contraceptive use be applied to reducing the teenage pregnancy problem? The most direct solution would involve better programs of sex education in the schools. Many districts have no sex education programs, and those that do often skip the important issue of contraception, fearing that it is too controversial. Sex education programs would need to include a number of components that are typically missing (Gross and Bellew-Smith, 1983). These include legitimizing presex communication about sex and contraception; legitimizing the purchase and carrying of contraceptives; discussion of how one weighs the costs and benefits of pregnancy, contraception, and abortion; legitimizing noncoital kinds of sexual pleasure, such as masturbation and oral-genital sex; and encouraging males to accept equal responsibility for contraception.

ABORTION

Abortion:
The termination of a pregnancy.

In the past decade, abortion (the termination of a pregnancy) has been a topic of considerable controversy in North America. Feminist groups talk of the woman's right to control her own body, while members of Right-to-Life groups speak of the unborn fetus's rights. In 1973, the United States Supreme Court made two landmark decisions that essentially decriminalized abortion by denying the states the right to regulate early abortions. Since then, the number of abortions performed each year has risen steadily.

In other countries, policies on abortion vary widely. It is legal and widely practiced in the Soviet Union and Japan, parts of eastern and central Europe, and South America. The use of abortion in the underdeveloped nations of Africa and Asia is limited because of the scarcity of medical facilities.

This section will be about methods of abortion and the psychological aspects of abortion; the ethical and legal aspects will be discussed in Chapters 22 and 23.

Abortion Procedures

There are several methods of abortion; which one is used depends on how far the pregnancy has progressed.

Vacuum Curettage

Vacuum curettage: A method of abortion that is performed during the first trimester.

The vacuum curettage method (also called *vacuum suction,* and *vacuum aspiration* can be performed during the first trimester of pregnancy and up to 20 weeks from the beginning of the last menstrual period (LMP). It is done on an outpatient basis with a local anesthetic. The procedure itself takes only about 10 minutes, and the woman stays in the doctor's office, clinic, or hospital for a few hours.

The woman is prepared as she would be for a pelvic exam, and an instrument is inserted into the vagina; the instrument dilates (stretches open) the opening of the

FIGURE 7.9

A vacuum-suction abortion.

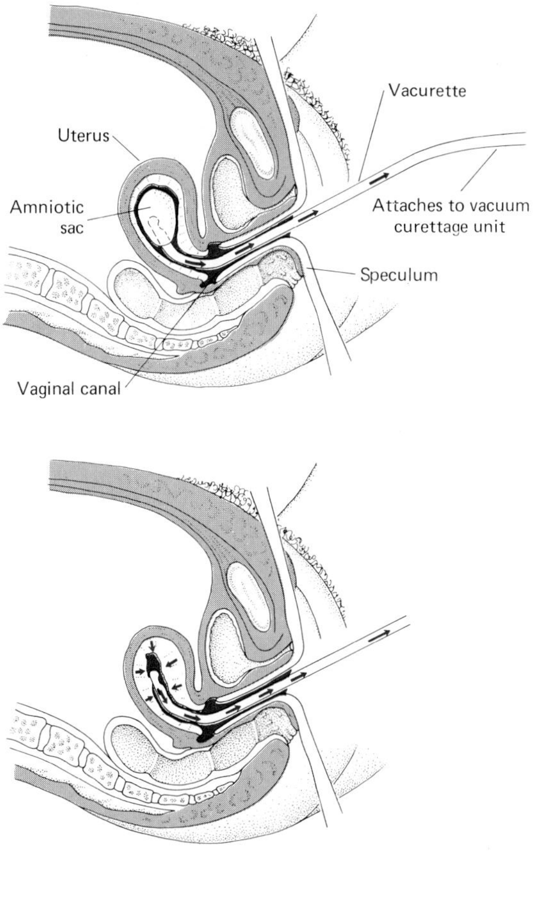

F · O · C · U · S 7.2

THE SOCIAL PSYCHOLOGY OF CONTRACEPTION: TAKING CHANCES

In California in 1971–1972, more than 2 out of 10 pregnancies were terminated by abortion. This raises the following question: Why should women who have readily available, highly effective contraceptives as an option choose not to use them and instead undergo the expensive and possibly humiliating or traumatic experience of abortion, or of unwanted pregnancy? Sociologist Kristin Luker set out to answer this question. To do so, she collected data at an abortion clinic in northern California, analyzing the medical records of 500 women seen at the clinic and doing in-depth interviews with 50 women undergoing abortions at the clinic. As a result, she developed a theory of the social psychology of contraceptive use (and nonuse) among women.

Prior to Luker's work, there were two prevailing theories about why women have unwanted pregnancies. The first theory, held widely by family planning agencies, is that women have unwanted pregnancies because they lack knowledge about or access to contraceptives. The second theory, growing out of psychoanalytic thought, holds that women have adequate contraceptive skills but fail to use them because of internal psychological conflict. The first theory was inadequate to explain the cases of the women Luker studied, since over half of them had previously used a prescription method (usually the pill), and 86 percent had used some method of birth control in the past; further, the majority of them displayed some or considerable birth control information when interviewed. Clearly the women had skills that they did not use. This makes the second theory seem more reasonable. However, Luker also rejected that theory. First, she argued that the data upon which this theory is based are biased, since the psychiatrist typically sees only the unwanted pregnancies that lead to severe disturbance. Second, this theory ignores social influences on contraceptive behavior, which are enormous.

As an alternative, Luker developed a theory in which unwanted pregnancy results from "contraceptive risk-taking" behavior which is the result of a conscious decision-making process. As such, the unwanted pregnancy is not indicative of neurotic conflict or irrationality; instead, it becomes an analyzable process much like the decision not to fasten one's seat belt when driving. According to Luker's theory, the woman engages in a cost-benefit analysis (although she might not be able to articulate it) in which she weighs the costs and benefits of contraception, the costs of pregnancy, and the possible benefits of pregnancy. The woman must assess the probability of pregnancy (which is actually unknown, even to the scientist), and she generally decides that it is very low. Thus if there are many costs associated with contraception, or many benefits associated with pregnancy, the woman begins to engage in risk taking.

What are the costs of contraception? First there are a number of social-psychological costs. Using, and planning to use, contraceptives involves acknowledging that one is a sexually active woman, and this is difficult for many women, even today. Using a contraceptive such as the pill signals that one is always sexually available, and this decreases the woman's right to say "no." Some methods, particularly using foam and using the diaphragm, decrease the spontaneity of sex, and this is a psychological cost. Second, there are structurally created costs—women must call for an appointment with a physician for some methods, and they may be told that no appointments are available for several weeks. They are expected to have high motivation and use abstinence, or call repeatedly for appointments. Even the "drugstore" methods (foam, condoms) involve going into the store and openly acknowledging to the world—or at least the people in the store—that one is sexually active. Third, there may be costs to the relationship—the woman may fear negative reaction from the man if she uses a contraceptive such as foam or a diaphragm, or rejection if she asks him to use a condom. Finally, there are biological-medical costs, particularly fears of side effects from the pill. The most frequent concern of women in the study was potential weight gain from using the pill.

Luker also points out that benefits to pregnancy may be anticipated. Pregnancy is proof of womanhood, and this may be particularly important in a society with a fluctuating view of gender roles. Pregnancy may enhance one's feeling of self-worth, proving that one is a valuable person who can produce children. Unarguably, pregnancy is a proof of fertility, and some women may feel a need for this proof—fully two-thirds of the women interviewed said that their gynecologists had told them they would have trouble getting pregnant because of problems in their reproductive system. Pregnancy can be a way of accomplishing things with significant others such as parents, perhaps rebelling against them or gaining independence. Pregnancy may force the man to define the relationship more clearly—perhaps going from living together to marriage. Finally, the pure excitement of risk taking itself may be fun for some—the Evel Knievels of contraception.

Given all this, the woman, according to Luker, weighs the costs and benefits and often decides to take risks. The costs and benefits, of course, vary from one woman to the next at different times in a woman's life. The costs of pregnancy to a single college student are probably far greater than they are to a married woman with two children who would rather have no more. Risk taking, if successful, may foster more risk taking—"If I got away with it once, I surely can again." And so the cycle goes, eventually ending in an unwanted pregnancy. But the costs of this failure are not terribly high now, with the legalization and availability of abortion. Accordingly, some women leave the abortion clinic with no plans to use an effective method in the future, and the risk taking begins again.

On a more hopeful note, Luker argues that the more aware women become of their decision-making process, the more effective they will become in using contraceptives to achieve the goals they truly desire.

Source: Kristin Luker. (1975). *Taking chances: Abortion and the decision not to contracept.* Berkeley: University of California Press.

cervix. A nonflexible tube is then inserted into this opening until one end is in the uterus. The other end is attached to a suction-producing apparatus, and the contents of the uterus, including the fetal tissue, are sucked out.

The vacuum curettage is becoming the most common method of early (first-trimester) abortion because it is simple and entails little risk. There are minor risks of uterine perforation, infection, hemorrhaging, and failure to remove all the fetal material.

Dilation and Curettage

The *dilation and curettage* (D and C), or *dilatation and curettage,* is similar to the vacuum curettage, but it must be done in a hospital under a general anesthetic. It is also done from 8 to 20 weeks LMP.

As in the vacuum curettage, the cervical opening is dilated. Then a sharp metal loop, attached to the end of a long handle (the curette), is inserted into the uterus; it is used to scrape out the uterine contents.

The vacuum curettage is now the most common first-trimester abortion technique. The D and C used to be the method of choice, and it still is for some physicians because they are familiar with the technique, since it is also used as a nonabortion gynecological procedure. In the latter case it is used for scraping out the uterine contents in the treatment of infertility and menstrual problems. Thus if someone tells you she was in the hospital for a D and C, you cannot necessarily assume that she was having an abortion.

The vacuum curettage is considered preferable to the D and C because the latter requires hospitalization (and is therefore more expensive) and a general anesthetic. It also causes more discomfort, and the risks of complications such as uterine perforation, infection, and hemorrhaging are greater.

Yet a third procedure is the D and E (dilation and evacuation). It is used especially from 15 to 18 weeks LMP. It is somewhat similar to the D and C and vacuum curettage, except that the procedures are a bit more complicated because the fetus is relatively large by 15 to 18 weeks LMP.

Induced Labor

Saline-induced abortion: A method of abortion done in the late second trimester, involving inducing labor by injecting a saline solution into the amniotic sac.

Prostaglandin abortion: A method of abortion done in the late second trimester, involving inducing labor by injecting prostaglandins into the amniotic sac.

During the late part of the second trimester, abortion is usually performed by inducing labor and a miscarriage. The most commonly used version of this method is the saline-induced abortion A fine tube is inserted through the abdomen into the amniotic sac inside the uterus. Some amniotic fluid is removed through the tube, and an equal amount of saline solution is injected into the amniotic sac. Within several hours, the solution has caused labor to begin. The cervix dilates, and the fetus is expelled through the contractions of labor. A variation on this technique is the prostaglandin method. Prostaglandins (hormonelike substances that cause contractions) are injected into the amniotic sac (or intravenously or by means of a vaginal suppository) and cause labor.

Induced labor is the method used most often for abortion if pregnancy has progressed late into the second trimester. This method is both more hazardous and more costly ($350 to $750) than the previous methods. The most serious complications of the saline-induced method are shock and possibly death (if the technique is done carelessly and the saline solution gets into a blood vessel) and a bleeding disorder, although these are rare. The prostaglandin method has several advantages over the saline method: it induces labor more quickly, and the labor itself is shorter. The chances of excessive bleeding and retained placenta are higher with the prostaglandin method, however, and there is also the risk that the cervix may tear as a result of too rapid dilation. There is also some chance that a live fetus will be expelled. Less serious side effects such as nausea, vomiting, and diarrhea are more common with the prostaglandin method.

Traditionally it was thought that abortions should not be performed during weeks 13 to 15, because the uterus was too soft and the procedure was dangerous; the recommended procedure from 16 weeks on was saline-induced abortion. However, data indicate that the D and E is safe through weeks 13 to 15 and is safer than saline-induced abortion through week 20 (Center for Disease Control, 1976).

Hysterotomy

Hysterotomy: A surgical method of abortion done in the late second trimester.

Hysterotomy is a surgical method of abortion that can be done from 16 to 24 weeks LMP. Essentially, a cesarean section is performed, and the fetus is removed. Hysterotomy is more serious and more expensive (around $1000) than the other methods, and there is a greater risk of complications. It is done only rarely, but it may be useful if the pregnancy has progressed to the late second trimester and the woman's health is such that the induction methods should not be used.

Other Methods

There are several other abortion methods, but they are not widely used in North America either because they are still in the developmental stages or because they have not gained acceptance here.

Several mechanical methods of stimulating the uterus to induce abortion have been developed and are used widely in Japan (Manabe, 1969). They are simple to perform and inexpensive, but they have not become popular in the United States because they are associated with more blood loss and a greater chance of infection.

Early abortion is done as soon as a positive pregnancy test is obtained up to eight weeks LMP. It is very similar to the vacuum curettage method, described above, except that a flexible tube is inserted through the cervix without dilating it, and the uterine contents are sucked out. The procedure can be done without an anesthetic. This method is not yet widely used.

Menstrual regulation (also called *endometrial aspiration, preemptive abortion,* and *menstrual extraction*) is a similar technique. The uterine contents are sucked out before the period is due and before pregnancy has been confirmed.

Psychological Aspects

In light of the controversies surrounding abortion and the complex ethical issues it raises, it might be expected that the whole experience of becoming pregnant and having an abortion would be a traumatic one and that the stresses involved might cause some psychological disturbance in the woman.

However, according to the research that has been done on legal abortion, the experience is not traumatic (Greer et al., 1976; see the review by Osofsky and Osofsky, 1972). Indeed, most women feel relieved and happy after an abortion. Fewer than 10 percent of women experience psychological problems afterward, and most of these women had problems before the pregnancy and abortion. However, most of the studies have looked at women *after* abortion, when they do indeed feel relieved; the research may not capture the complex and sometimes agonizing feelings that may occur in the weeks in which the woman makes the decision to have an abortion.

Research in this area raises several interesting questions. Women generally

TABLE 7.3

SUMMARY OF HEALTH RISKS ASSOCIATED WITH LEGAL ABORTION

Death*	
3.2 deaths per 100,000 legal abortions:	
Suction method	1.7 per 100,000
Induced labor	16.9 per 100,000
Hysterotomy	60.8 per 100,000
Normal childbirth	14.0 per 100,000
Complications†	
All methods combined	13.1 per 100 women
Suction	7.3 per 100 women
D and C	11.1 per 100 women
Saline	26.3 per 100 women
Hysterotomy	23.1 per 100 women

*Based on 635,237 abortions, Center for Disease Control, 1977.

†Including excessive bleeding, infection, uterine perforation, retained tissue, and minor complications.

Sources: Family Planning Digest, 1974, **5**(3), p. 12; C. Tietze and S. Lewit (1971). Early complications of abortion under medical auspices: A preliminary report. *Studies in Family Planning,* **2**(7), 137.

appear well adjusted after having an abortion, but well adjusted compared with what? That is, what is the appropriate control or comparison group? One comparison group that has been studied is women who requested an abortion but were denied it. Women in this group have a much higher rate of disturbance than women who have had abortions. Another group that has been studied is children who were born because an abortion request was denied. They, too, show a high incidence of psychiatric disturbance (Forssman and Thuwe, 1966).

Men and Abortion

Only women become pregnant, and only women have abortions, but where do men enter the picture? Do they have a right to contribute to the decision to have an abortion? What are their feelings about abortion?

Sociologist Arthur Shostak and his colleagues (1984) surveyed 1,000 male "abortion veterans." The most common reaction from the men was a sense of helplessness. Although most men are used to being in control, in this situation they are not, and the feeling of powerlessness is difficult for them. Most of the men also felt isolated, angry at themselves and their partners, and fearful of emotional and physical damage to the woman. Most of them tried to hide their stress and remain unemotional. Nonetheless, 26 percent thought of abortion as murder, and 81 percent said they thought about the child who might have been born. However, few men wanted to be able to overrule the woman's decision; they only wanted to share in it.

Although counseling for women undergoing abortion is a standard procedure, counseling is rarely available for the men who are involved. Given Shostak's findings, it is clear that such counseling is badly needed.

NEW ADVANCES

According to some, a really good method of contraception is not yet available. The highly effective methods either are permanent (sterilization) or have associated health risks (the pill). Other, safer methods (such as the condom and the diaphragm) have appreciable failure rates. Most of the methods are for women, not men. Because of the dissatisfaction with the currently available methods, contraception research continues. A few of the more promising possibilities for the future are discussed below.

Male Methods

Several possibilities for male contraception are being explored (see, for example, Sciarra et al., 1975). One is the use of hormones in a "male pill" that would stop spermatogenesis (much as the pill inhibits ovulation in women). Both testosterone and progesterone accomplish this. Unfortunately, the hormones that have been tested so far inhibit not only sperm production but also sex drive, and therefore they are considered unacceptable. Theoretically at least, sperm production and hormone production are separate processes, and so it should be possible to stop sperm production without affecting sex drive.

On the basis of the principle that the testes must be slightly cooler than body temperature for sperm to survive, scientists are experimenting with the possibility of using *ultrasound* to warm the testes and thus destroy sperm (Arehart-Treichal, 1974). They envision a small device that could be kept in one's bathroom, rather like a Water Pik, for convenient application of ultrasound treatment. A major drawback might be that it would cause deformed sperm and defective genetic material, increasing the incidence of birth defects.

Chinese scientists have done large-scale studies on the use of *gossypol* as a male contraceptive (National Coordinating Group on Male Antifertility Agents, 1978; Peyster, 1979). Gossypol is derived from the cotton plant. The Chinese accidentally discovered in the 1950s that cooking with cottonseed oil could cause infertility and that the effect seemed to be stronger in men. Gossypol appears to be capable of reducing the sperm count to zero, and a study of 4000 men over a period of six months indicated that it was 99.89 percent effective in preventing pregnancy. Unfortunately, by U.S. standards the drug is rather toxic (it has been used as a pesticide), and so it is unlikely that the FDA will approve it for use in the United States.

Female Methods

Cervical cap: A method of birth control involving a rubber cap that fits snugly over the cervix.

There is much recent interest in a cervical cap, although it is not yet approved by the FDA. The cervical cap is similar to the diaphragm but is somewhat different in shape, fitting more snugly over the cervix (see Figure 7.10). The advantage is that it can be left in place longer. Research is focusing on the development of a one-way valve for it that would permit menstrual fluid to get out but prevent sperm from getting in.

A *vaginal ring,* shaped like a diaphragm and containing hormones, should be on the market shortly. When it contains progestin, it apparently does not suppress ovulation but rather affects the cervical mucus, making it impenetrable to sperm.

The cervical cap.

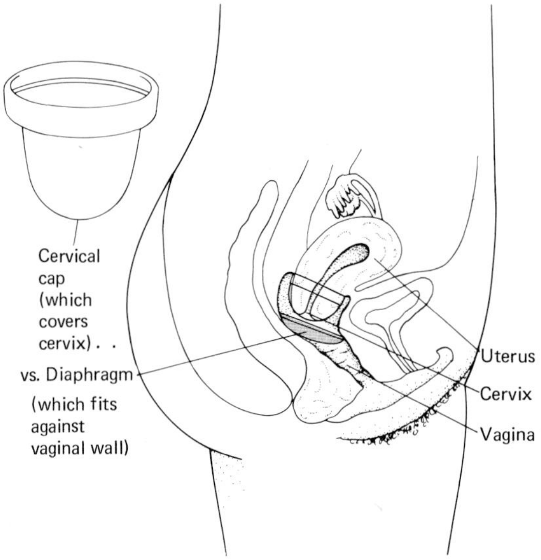

FIGURE 7.10

The cervical cap.

Analogous to the reversible valve in the vas, the possibility of improved reversibility of the female sterilization procedure is being explored. One promising lead is to inject a fast-setting latex substance into the tubes to block them; a line is attached to this "plug" so that it can be pulled out if it is desired for the woman to become pregnant.

The possibility of long-acting progestins—either in the form of shots or implants—is being explored. Both are used widely in other countries, but neither has been approved by the FDA for use in this country. For the injectable method, DMPA (Depo-Provera) is injected ("The Shot") in a three-month or a six-month dose. It is highly effective, with a failure rate of less than 1 percent. With the implant method, a capsule that slowly releases a progestin is inserted under the skin, usually in the arm. Its effects can last for up to seven years, and the method is reversible when the capsule is removed.

Methods for Either Men or Women

An immunologic approach might be used on either women or men. Since some cases of infertility are caused by the formation of antibodies that destroy sperm (see Chapter 6), it would seem that if antibody formation could be stimulated, it would work as a contraceptive, although it would probably be a permanent method. Other immunologic methods, such as immunizing the woman against placental hormones so that implantation will not occur, are also being explored (Hatcher et al., 1976).

A contraceptive nasal spray for either men or women is being investigated (Bergquist et al., 1979). The spray contains a hypothalamic releasing factor (GnRH). It reduces the production of gonadotropins (pituitary hormones) and thus prevents ovulation in women, and speculatively, sperm production in men. Perhaps a common question of the future between men and women will be "Did you take a sniff today?"

F • O • C • U • S
7.3

A BRIEF SUMMARY OF THE DEVELOPMENT OF SOPHISTICATED METHODS OF CONTRACEPTION

Late 1700s	Casanova (1725–1798) popularizes and publicizes use of the sheath, or "English riding coat."
1798	Malthus urges "moral restraint" or abstinence.
1840s	Goodyear vulcanizes rubber. Production of rubber condoms soon follows.
1883	Mensinga invents the diaphragm.
1893	Harrison performs the first vasectomy.
1909	Richter uses the intrauterine silkworm gut.
1910–1920	Margaret Sanger pioneers in New York City; the term "birth control" is coined.
1930	Graffenberg publishes information documenting his 21 years of experience with the ring (silver and copper) and catgut as IUDs.
1930–1931	Knaus and Ogino elucidate "safe and unsafe" periods of the woman's menstrual cycle: the rhythm method.
1934	Corner and Beard isolate progesterone.
1937	Makepeace demonstrates that progesterone inhibits ovulation.
1950s	Abortions are utilized extensively in Japan.
1950–1960	Hormonal contraceptive research results in FDA approval of the use of the pill as a contraceptive in 1960.
1960s	Many Western nations liberalize abortion laws. Modern IUDs become available. Contraceptive sterilization becomes more acceptable. The laparoscopic tubal ligation technique is developed.
1973	The United States Supreme Court rules on abortion. The first "mini-pill," or low-dose progestin pill, wins FDA approval. The Shot is provided in over 50 nations.

Source: Robert A. Hatcher et al. (1976). *Contraceptive technology,* 1976–1977. (8th ed.) New York: Irvington.

SUMMARY

Table 7.4 provides a comparative summary of the various methods of birth control discussed in this chapter.

TABLE 7.4

SUMMARY OF INFORMATION ON METHODS OF BIRTH CONTROL AND ABORTION

Method	Effectiveness Rating	Theoretical Failure Rate, %	Actual Failure Rate, %	Death Rate (per 100,000 Women)	Yearly Costs*	Advantages	Disadvantages
Birth control pills	Excellent	0.34	2	0.3–3.0	$130	Highly effective, not used at time of coitus, improved menstrual cycles	Cost, possible side effects, must be taken daily
IUD	Excellent	1–3	5	0.3–2.0	$50†	Requires no memory or motivation	Side effects, may be expelled
Condom	Very good	2	10	1.7†	$52	Easy to use, protection from VD	Interference with coitus, continual expense
Diaphragm with cream or jelly	Very good	3	17	3.0†	$50	No side effects, inexpensive	Aesthetic objections
Vaginal foam	Fair	3	22	3.4†	$49	Easy to use, availability	Messy, continual expense
Sponge	Fair	6	17		$200	Availability	Continual expense
Withdrawal	Fair	9	20–25		None	No cost	Requires high motivation
Rhythm	Poor to fair	13	19		None	No cost, accepted by Roman Catholic Church	Requires high motivation, prolonged abstinence, not all women can use
Unprotected intercourse	Poor	90	90	14‡	None§		
Legal abortion, first trimester	Excellent	0	0	3.2	$200–$400	Available when other methods fail	Expense, moral or psychological unacceptability
Sterilization, male	Excellent	<0.15	0.15		$150¶	Is permanent and highly effective	Is permanent, psychological complications
Sterilization, female	Excellent	0.04	0.05		$200¶	Is permanent and highly effective	Is permanent, expense, psychological complications

*Based on 150 acts of intercourse.

†Based on a cost of $75 for the IUD plus the cost of the insertion by the physician, and the assumption that the IUD will be used for two years.

‡Based on the death rate for pregnancies resulting from the method.

§But having a baby is expensive.

¶These are one-time-only costs.

Sources: R. A. Hatcher, et al. (1984). *Contraceptive technology,* 1984–1985. New York: Irvington. L. Hellman. (1969). Oral contraceptives: Safety and complications. In A. Rubin (Ed.), *Family planning today.* Philadelphia: Davis.

REVIEW QUESTIONS

1. Combination birth control pills contain the hormones _____ and _____.
2. The birth control pill works mainly by preventing ovulation. True or false?
3. Cancer is the major health risk associated with the use of the birth control pill. True or false?
4. The IUD is inserted into the uterus and appears to work by preventing implantation of the fertilized egg. True or false?
5. The actual failure rate of the IUD is about 25 percent. True or false?
6. In order to be highly effective, the diaphragm must be used with a spermicidal cream or jelly. True or false?
7. The contraceptive sponge is 99 percent effective in preventing pregnancy. True or false?
8. The calendar method, the basal body temperature method, and the cervical mucus method are all variations on the _____ method of birth control.
9. Two highly effective methods of birth control that can be used by men are _____ and _____.
10. According to the research of Byrne, erotophobes are more likely than erotophiles to be consistent, reliable users of contraceptives. True or false?

QUESTIONS FOR THOUGHT, DISCUSSION, AND DEBATE

1. Do you think you are an erotophobe or an erotophile? In what ways do you think your erotophobia or erotophilia has affected or will affect your use of birth control?
2. Debate the following topic. Resolved: The birth control pill is a safe and effective method of birth control for most women.
3. On your campus, as on all campuses, students probably are inconsistent in their use of birth control or use nothing even though they are sexually active. Design a program to improve birth control practices on your campus.

SUGGESTIONS FOR FURTHER READING

Byrne, Donn. (1977, July). A pregnant pause in the sexual revolution. *Psychology Today.* 67–68. An insightful discussion regarding the reasons why sexually active teenagers fail to use contraceptives.

Ehrlich, Paul R., and Ehrlich, Anne H. (1972). *Population, resources, environment.* (2nd ed.) San Francisco: Freeman. A highly informative discussion of the population problem. Paul Ehrlich is one of the foremost population and ecology experts in the country.

Fleishman, N., and Dixon, P. L. (1973). *Vasectomy, sex, and parenthood.* Garden City, N.Y.: Doubleday. A thorough discussion of vasectomy from a provasectomy point of view.

Luker, Kristen. (1984). *Abortion and the politics of motherhood.* Berkeley, University of California Press. A sociological analysis of the women who are in the prochoice and prolife camps of the abortion debate. The book is both sympathetic and insightful.

Montreal Health Press. (1979). *A book about birth control.* Montreal: MHP. One of the best sources of information on birth control for the lay person, originated by a student society at McGill University. Available for 50 cents from Montreal Health Press, P.O. Box 1000, Station G, Montreal, Quebec H2W 2N1, Canada.

CHAPTER · 8

THE PHYSIOLOGY OF SEXUAL RESPONSE

Here are some colors of different people's orgasms: champagne, all colors and white and gray afterward, red and blue, green, beige and blue, red, blue and gold. Some people never make it because they are trying for plaid.*

* *Source:* Eric Berne. (1970), *Sex in human loving.* New York: Simon & Schuster, p. 238.

CHAPTER HIGHLIGHTS

I. THE FOUR STAGES OF SEXUAL RESPONSE
   Excitement
   Plateau
   Orgasm
   Resolution

II. OTHER FINDINGS OF THE MASTERS AND JOHNSON RESEARCH
   Clitoral Orgasm versus Vaginal Orgasm
   Multiple Orgasm in Women

III. ALTERNATIVES TO THE MASTERS AND JOHNSON MODEL
   Kaplan: Biphasic Model
   Zilbergeld and Ellison: Five-Component Model

IV. HORMONAL AND NEURAL CONTROL OF SEXUAL BEHAVIOR
   The Brain, the Spinal Cord, and Sex
   Hormones and Sex

V. PHEROMONES

This chapter is about the way the body responds during sexual arousal and orgasm and also the mechanisms behind these responses. This information is very important in developing good techniques of lovemaking (see Chapter 9) and in analyzing and treating sexual dysfunctions such as premature ejaculation (see Chapter 20). Important though the topic is, it had not been investigated scientifically before the work of Masters and Johnson.

THE FOUR STAGES OF SEXUAL RESPONSE

The Masters and Johnson research on the physiology of sexual response began in 1954 and culminated in 1966 with the publication of *Human Sexual Response,* which reported data on 382 women and 312 men observed in over 10,000 sexual cycles of arousal and orgasm. (A discussion and critique of the Masters and Johnson research techniques is presented in Chapter 10.)

According to Masters and Johnson, there are four stages of sexual response, which they call *excitement, plateau, orgasm,* and *resolution.* (This does not mean, of course, that a person makes a noticeable shift from one stage to another, as if he or she were shifting gears in a car. Rather, the stages flow together, and the differentiation into four stages is simply for convenience in describing what occurs.)

Vasocongestion (vay-so-con-JES-tyun): An accumulation of blood in the blood vessels of a region of the body, especially the genitals; a swelling or erection results.

Myotonia (my-oh-TONE-ee-ah): Muscle contraction.

The two basic physiological processes that occur during these stages are vasocongestion and myotonia. Vasocongestion occurs when a great deal of blood flows into the blood vessels in a region, in this case the genitals, as a result of dilation of the blood vessels in the region. Myotonia occurs when muscles contract, not only in the genitals but also throughout the body. Let us now consider in detail what occurs in each of the stages.

Excitement

Excitement: The first stage of sexual response, during which erection in the male and vaginal lubrication in the female occur.

The excitement phase is the beginning of erotic arousal. The basic physiological process that occurs during excitement is vasocongestion. This produces the obvious arousal response in the male, erection. Erection results when the corpora cavernosa and the corpus spongiosum fill (becoming engorged) with blood (see Figure 8.1). Erection may be produced by direct physical stimulation of the genitals, by stimulation of other parts of the body, or by erotic thoughts. It occurs very rapidly, within a few seconds of the stimulation, although it may take place more slowly as a result of a number of factors, including age, intake of alcohol, and fatigue.

The most obvious response of the woman in the excitement phase is the lubrication of the vagina. Although this response might seem much different from the male's, actually they both result from the same physiological process: vasocongestion. Masters and Johnson found that vaginal lubrication results when fluids seep through the semipermeable membranes of the vaginal walls, producing lubrication as a result of vasocongestion in the tissues surrounding the vagina. This response to arousal is also rapid, though not quite so fast as the male's; lubrication begins 10 to 30 seconds after the onset of arousing stimuli.[1] Some sex manuals advise that the appearance of lubrication serves as a good indicator to the man that the woman is "ready" for intercourse; the lubrication, however, signals only the beginning of arousal. Many other changes must also occur before the woman is close to orgasm.

Several other physical changes occur in women during the excitement phase. The glans of the clitoris (the tip) swells. This results from engorgement of its corpora cavernosa and corpus spongiosum and thus is quite similar to erection in the male.

The nipples become erect; this results from contractions of the muscle fibers (myotonia) surrounding the nipple. The breasts themselves swell and enlarge some-

[1]Before the Masters and Johnson research, it was thought that the lubrication was due to secretions of Bartholin's glands, but it now appears that these glands contribute little if anything. At this point, you might want to go back to the limerick about Bartholin's glands in Chapter 3 and see whether you can spot the error in it.

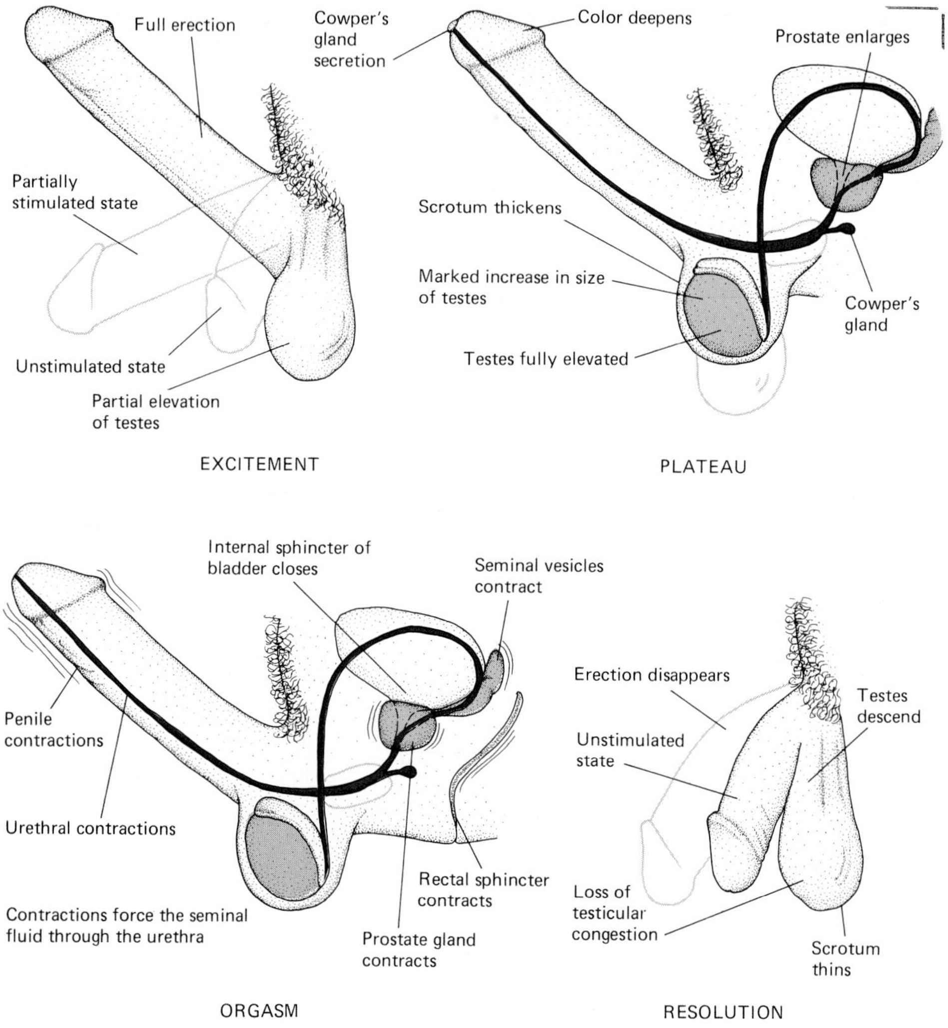

FIGURE 8.1

Internal changes in the female sexual response cycle.

what in the late part of the excitement phase (a vasocongestion response). Thus the nipples may not actually look erect but may appear somewhat flatter against the breast because the breast has swollen. Many males also have nipple erection during the excitement phase.

In the unaroused state the inner lips are generally folded over, covering the entrance to the vagina, and the outer lips lie close to each other. During excitement the inner lips swell and open up (a vasocongestion response). The outer lips move apart a bit and flatten out.

The vagina shows an important change during excitement. Think of the vagina as being divided into two parts, an upper (or inner) two-thirds and a lower (or outer) one-third. In the unaroused state the walls of the vagina lie against each other, much like the sides of an uninflated balloon. During the excitement phase, the upper two-thirds of the vagina expands dramatically (see Figure 8.2), in what is often called a "ballooning" response; that is, it becomes more like an inflated balloon. Clearly this is functional in accommodating the entrance of the penis. The cervix and uterus also pull up during excitement, creating a "tenting effect" in the vaginal walls (Figure 8.2) and making a larger opening in the cervix, which probably allows sperm to move into the uterus more easily.

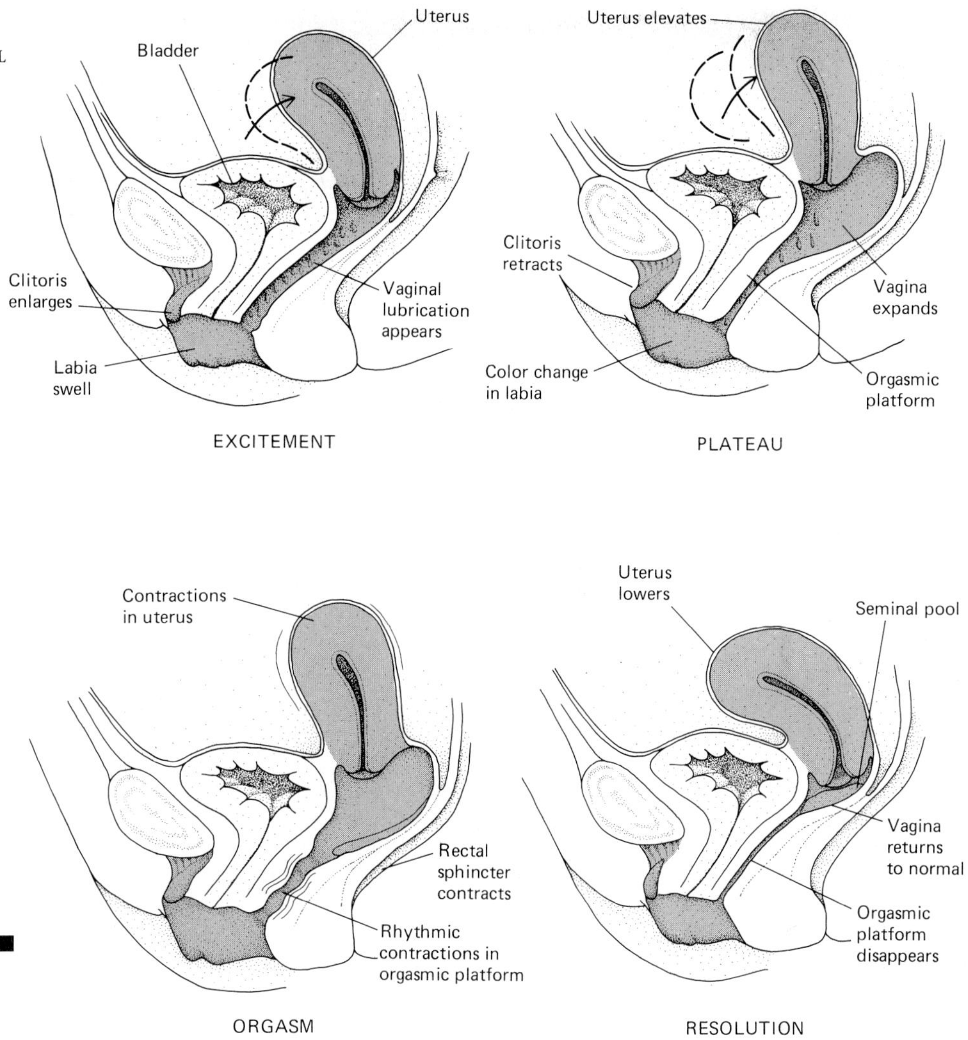

FIGURE 8.2

External and internal changes in the male sexual response cycle.

During excitement a "sex flush" may appear on the skin of both men and women, though more commonly of women. The sex flush resembles a measles rash; it often begins on the upper abdomen and spreads over the chest. It may also appear later in the sexual response cycle.

Other changes that occur in both men and women include an increase in pulse rate and in blood pressure.

In men, the skin of the scrotum thickens. The scrotal sac also tenses, and the scrotum is pulled up and closer to the body (Figure 8.1). The spermatic cords shorten, elevating the testes.

Plateau

Plateau:
The second stage of sexual response, just before orgasm.

During the plateau phase, vasocongestion reaches its peak. In men, the penis is completely erect, although there may be fluctuations in the firmness of the erection. In addition, the coronal ridge at the edge of the glans swells. The testes are so engorged with blood that they may be 50 percent larger than in the unaroused state. They are pulled up even higher and closer to the body. A few drops of fluid, prob-

F · O · C · U · S 8.1

WILLIAM MASTERS AND VIRGINIA JOHNSON

William Howell Masters was born in Cleveland in 1915. He attended Hamilton College in Clinton, New York, graduating in 1938 with a B.S. degree. At Hamilton he specialized in science courses, and yet he managed to play on the varsity football, baseball, basketball, and track teams and to participate in the Debate Club. The college yearbook called him "a strange, dark man with a future . . . Has an easy time carrying three lab courses but a hard time catching up on lost sleep. . . . Bill is a boy with purpose and is bound to get what he is working for." His devotion to athletics persisted, and in 1966 a science writer described him as "a dapper, athletically trim gynecologist who starts his day at 5:30 with a two-mile jog."

He entered the University of Rochester School of Medicine in 1939, planning to train himself to be a researcher rather than a practicing physician. In his first year there he worked in the laboratory of the famous anatomist Dr. George Washington Corner. Corner was engaged in research on the reproductive system in animals and humans, which eventually led to important discoveries about hormones and the reproductive cycle. He had also published *Attaining Manhood: A Doctor Talks to Boys about Sex* and the companion volume, *Attaining Womanhood.*

The first-year research project that Corner assigned to Masters was a study of the changes in the lining of the uterus of the rabbit during the reproductive cycle. Thus his interest was focused early on the reproductive system.

Masters was married in 1942 and received his M.D. in 1943. He and his wife had two children, born in 1950 and 1951.

After Masters received his degree, he had to make an important decision: To what research area should he devote his life? Apparently his decision to investigate the physiology of sex was based on his shrewd observation that almost no prior research had been done in the area and that he thus would have a good opportunity to make some important scientific discoveries. In arriving at the decision, he consulted with Dr. Corner. He was aware of Kinsey's progress and also of the persecution he had suffered; thus Corner advised Masters not to begin the study of sex until he had established himself as a respected researcher in some other area, was somewhat older, and could conduct the research at a major university or medical school.

Masters followed the advice. He completed his internship and residency and then established himself on the faculty of the Washington University School of Medicine in St. Louis. From 1948 to 1954 he published 25 papers on various medical topics, especially on hormone-replacement therapy for postmenopausal women.

In 1954 he began his research on sexual response at Washington University, supported by grants from the U.S. Public Health Service. The first paper based on that research was published in 1959, but the research received little attention until the publication, in 1966, of *Human Sexual Response* and, in

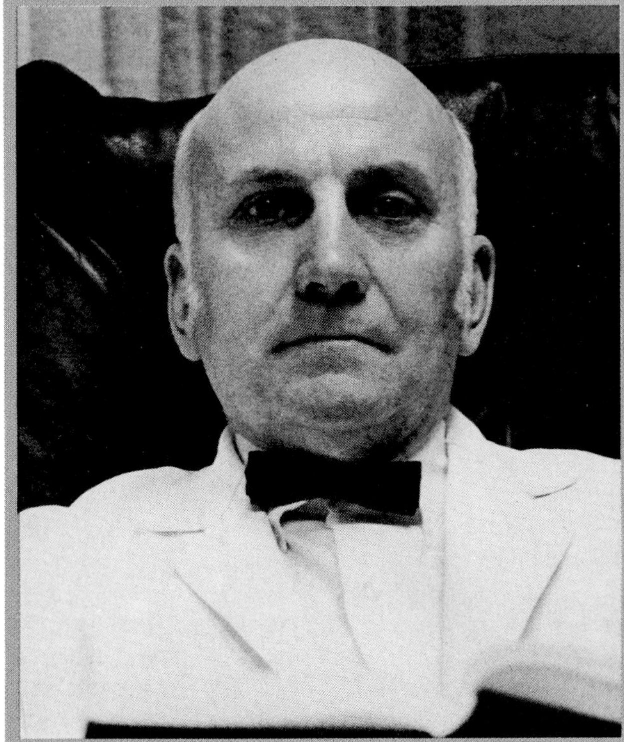

FIGURE 8.3

William H. Masters.

FIGURE 8.4

Virginia Johnson.

1970, of *Human Sexual Inadequacy* (to be discussed in Chapter 20), both of which received international acclaim.

In 1964 he founded the Reproductive Biology Research Foundation, now called the Masters and Johnson Institute, near the medical school, where the research continues today.

Virginia Johnson was born Virginia Eshelman in 1925 in the Missouri Ozarks. She was raised with the realistic attitude toward sex that rural children often have, as well as many of the superstitions that have grown up in that area. She began studying music at Drury College but transferred to Missouri University, where she studied psychology and sociology. She was married in 1950 and had two children, one in 1952 and the other in 1955. Shortly after that, she and her husband separated, and she went to the Washington University placement office to find a job. Just at that time, Masters had put in a request for a woman to assist him in research interviewing, preferably a married woman with children who was interested in people. Mrs. Johnson was sent over to him, and she has been a member of the research team and therapy team since 1957.

Following the divorce of Masters and his first wife, he and Virginia Johnson were married.

Source: Ruth Brecher and Edward Brecher (Eds.). (1966). *An analysis of human sexual response.* New York: Signet Books, New American Library.

ably secreted by Cowper's glands, appear at the tip of the penis. Although they are not the ejaculate, they may contain active sperm.

In both women and men there is a further increase in the rate of breathing, in pulse rate, and in blood pressure.

Orgasmic platform: The thickening of the walls of the outer third of the vagina that occurs during the plateau stage of sexual response.

In females, the most notable change during the plateau phase is the formation of the orgasmic platform. This is a swelling or thickening of the tissues surrounding the outer third of the vagina (Figure 8.2). Thus the size of the vaginal entrance actually becomes smaller, and there may be a noticeable increase in gripping of the penis.

Another change is the elevation of the clitoris. The clitoris essentially retracts or draws up into the body.

Other changes include a further swelling of the breasts and an enlargement of the uterus. Finally, the color of the inner lips changes, from bright red to a deep wine color in women who have had children and from pink to bright red in women who have not. This last change indicates that orgasm is close. If proper stimulation continues and other conditions are right, the woman will have an orgasm soon after the color change.

Essentially, then, the processes of the plateau phase are a continuation of the basic process—vasocongestion and myotonia—of the excitement phase. Both processes continue to build until there is sufficient tension for orgasm.

Orgasm

Orgasm: The third stage of sexual response; an intense sensation that occurs at the peak of sexual arousal and is followed by release of sexual tensions.

In the male, orgasm consists of a series of rhythmic contractions of the pelvic organs at 0.8-second intervals. Actually, male orgasm occurs in two stages. In the preliminary stage, the vas, seminal vesicles, and prostate contract, forcing the ejaculate into a bulb at the base of the uretha (Figure 8.1). Masters and Johnson call the sensation in this stage one of "ejaculatory inevitability" ("coming"); that is, there is a sensation that ejaculation is just about to happen and cannot be stopped. And, indeed, it cannot be, once the man has reached this point. In the second stage the urethral bulb and the penis itself contract rhythmically, forcing out the semen.

In both males and females, there are sharp increases in pulse rate, blood pressure, and breathing rate during orgasm.[2] Muscles contract throughout the body. The face may be contorted in a grimace; the muscles of the arms, legs, thighs, back, and buttocks may contract; and the muscles of the feet and hands may contract in "carpopedal spasms." Generally, of course, in the passion of the moment, one is not really aware of these occurrences, but an aching back or buttocks may serve as a reminder the next day.

The process of orgasm in females is basically similar to that in males. It is a series of rhythmic muscular contractions of the orgasmic platform. The contractions generally occur at about 0.8-second intervals; there may be three or four in a mild orgasm or as many as a dozen in a very intense, prolonged orgasm. The uterus also contracts rhythmically, with the contractions moving in waves from the top of the uterus down toward the cervix. Other muscles, such as those around the anus, may also contract rhythmically.

Female orgasm is a funny thing. As with love, you can almost never get anyone to give you a solid definition of what it is. Instead, people usually fall back on,

[2]With all the current attention to aerobics and exercising the heart, I have yet to hear anyone suggest orgasm aerobics. It seems to me that it should work. Jazzercise, watch out. Here comes sexercise!

"You'll know what it is when you have one." This evasiveness is probably related to several factors, most notably that female orgasm leaves no tangible evidence of its occurrence like ejaculation; indeed, the very existence of female orgasm has sometimes been questioned (for a clever satire on this point, see Raphael, 1973). Also, women often do not reach orgasm as quickly as men do, a point to be discussed in more detail in Chapter 15. In fact, some women, particularly young women, probably think they are having an orgasm when they are not; they have never had an orgasm, and they mistake intense arousal for orgasm.

Just what does orgasm in the female feel like? The main feeling is a spreading sensation that begins around the clitoris and then spreads outward through the whole pelvis. There may also be sensations of falling or opening up. The woman may be able to feel the contraction of the muscles around the vaginal entrance. The sensation is very intense and is more than just a warm glow or a pleasant tingling. In one study, college men and women gave written descriptions of what an orgasm felt like to them (Vance and Wagner, 1976). Interestingly, a panel of experts (medical students, obstetrician-gynecologists, and clinical psychologists) could not reliably figure out which of the descriptions were written by women and which by men. This suggests that the sensations are quite similar for males and females.

Some of the men in my classes have asked me how they can tell whether a woman has really had an orgasm. Their question in itself is interesting. In part it reflects a cultural skepticism about female orgasm. There is obvious proof of male orgasm: ejaculation. But there is no similar proof of female orgasm. The question also reflects the fact that men know that women sometimes "fake" orgasm. Faking orgasm is a complex issue. Basically, it probably is not a very good idea, because it is dishonest. On the other hand, one needs to be sympathetic to the variety of reasons why women do it. It is often difficult for women to reach orgasm, and our culture currently places a lot of emphasis on everyone's having orgasms. Thus the woman may feel that she is expected to have an orgasm, and realizing that it is unlikely to happen this time, she "fakes" it in order to meet expectations. She may also do it to please her partner.[3] But back to the question: How can one tell? There really is not any very good way. From a scientific point of view, a good method would be to have the woman hooked up to an instrument that registers pulse rate; there is a sudden sharp increase in the pulse rate at orgasm, and that would be a good indicator. I doubt, though, that most men have such equipment available, and I am even more doubtful about whether most women would agree to be so wired up. Probably rather than trying to check up on each other, it would be better for partners to establish good, honest communication and avoid setting up performance goals in sex, points that will be discussed further in later chapters.

Resolution

Resolution: The fourth stage of sexual response, in which the body returns to the unaroused state.

Following orgasm is the resolution phase, during which the body returns physiologically to the unaroused state. Orgasm triggers a massive release of muscular tension and of blood from the engorged blood vessels. These are the basic processes that occur during resolution. Resolution, then, repesents a reversal of the processes that built up during the excitement and plateau stages.

[3]Indeed, many of the old sex manuals, as well as physicians' textbooks, counseled women to fake orgasm. For example: "It is good advice to recommend to the women the advantage of innocent simulation of sex responsiveness, and as a matter of fact many women in their desire to please their husbands learned the advantage of such innocent deception" (Novak and Novak, 1952, p. 572).

The first change in women is a reduction in the swelling of the breasts. As a result, the nipples may appear to become erect, since they seem to stand out more as the surrounding flesh moves back toward the unstimulated size. This may provide the kind of sign wanted by those who are concerned about proof of female orgasm. In women who develop a sex flush during arousal, this disappears rapidly following orgasm.

In the 5 to 10 seconds after the end of the orgasm, the clitoris returns to its normal position, although it takes longer for it to shrink to its normal size. The orgasmic platform relaxes and begins to shrink. The ballooning of the vagina diminishes, and the uterus shrinks.

The resolution phase generally takes 15 to 30 minutes, but it may take much longer—as much as an hour—in women who have not had an orgasm. This latter fact helps to account for the chronic pelvic congestion that Masters and Johnson observed in prostitutes (see Chapter 10). The prostitutes frequently experienced arousal without having orgasms. Thus there were repeated buildups of vasocongestion without the discharge of it brought about by orgasm. The result was a chronic vasocongestion in the pelvis. A mild version of this occurs in some women who engage in sex but are not able to have orgasms, and it can be quite uncomfortable.

In both males and females, there is a gradual return of pulse rate, blood pressure, and breathing rate to the unaroused levels during resolution.

In men, the most obvious occurrence in the resolution phase is the loss of erection in the penis. This happens in two stages, the first occurring rapidly but leaving the penis still enlarged (this first loss of erection probably results from an emptying of the corpora cavernosa) and the second occurring more slowly, as a result of the slower emptying of the corpus spongiosum and the glans. The scrotum and testes return to their unstimulated size and position.

Refractory period (ree-FRAK-toh-ree): The period following orgasm during which the male cannot be sexually aroused.

During the resolution phase, men enter into a refractory period, during which they are refractory to further arousal; that is, they are incapable of being aroused again, having an erecton, or having an orgasm. The length of this refractory period varies considerably from one man to the next; in some it may last only a few minutes, and in others it may go on for 24 hours. The refractory period tends to become longer as men grow older.

Women do not enter into a refractory period, making possible the phenomenon of multiple orgasm in women, to be discussed below.

OTHER FINDINGS OF THE MASTERS AND JOHNSON RESEARCH

A number of other important findings on the nature of sexual response have emerged from the Masters and Johnson research, two of which will be discussed here.

Clitoral orgasm: Freud's term for orgasm in the female resulting from stimulation of the clitoris.

Vaginal orgasm: Freud's term for orgasm in the female resulting from stimulation of the vagina in heterosexual intercourse; Freud considered vaginal orgasm to be more mature than clitoral orgasm.

Clitoral Orgasm versus Vaginal Orgasm

Some people believe that women can have two kinds of orgasm: clitoral orgasm and vaginal orgasm The words "clitoral" and "vaginal" are not meant to imply that the clitoris has an orgasm or that the vagina has an orgasm. Rather, they refer to the locus of stimulation: an orgasm resulting from clitoral stimulation versus an orgasm resulting from vaginal stimulation. The whole notion of the distinction was originated by Sigmund Freud. Freud believed that in childhood little girls masturbate and thus have orgasms by means of clitoral stimulation, or clitoral orgasms. He thought that as women grow older and mature, they ought to shift from having orgasms as a result of masturbation to having them as a result of heterosexual intercourse, that is, by means of vaginal stimulation. (Freud's self-interest as a male in this matter is rather transparent!) Thus the vaginal orgasm was considered "mature" and the clitoral orgasm "immature" or "infantile," and not only did there come to be two kinds of orgasm, but also one was "better" (that is, more mature) than the other. (For a review of the clitoral orgasm–vaginal orgasm controversy, see Brown, 1966.)

Freud's formulation is of more than theoretical interest, since it has had an impact on the lives of many women. Many have undertaken psychoanalysis and spent countless hours agonizing over why they were not able to achieve the elusive vaginal orgasm and why they enjoyed the immature clitoral one so much. Women who could have orgasm only through clitoral stimulation were called "vaginally frigid" or "fixated" at an infantile stage.

According to the results of Masters and Johnson's research, though, the distinction between clitoral and vaginal orgasms does not make sense. This conclusion is based on two findings. First, their results indicate that all female orgasms are physiologically the same, regardless of the locus of stimulation. That is, an orgasm always consists of contractions of the orgasmic platform and the muscles around the vagina, whether the stimulation is clitoral or vaginal. Indeed, they found a few women who could have orgasm purely through breast stimulation, and that orgasm was the same as the other two, consisting of contractions of the orgasmic platform and the muscles around the vagina. Thus physiologically there is only one kind of orgasm. (Of course, this does not mean that psychologically there are not different kinds; the experience of orgasm during intercourse may be quite different from the experience of orgasm during masturbation.) Second, Masters and Johnson found that clitoral stimulation is almost always involved in producing orgasm. Because of the way in which the inner lips connect with the clitoral hood, the movement of the penis in and out of the vagina creates traction on the inner lips, which in turn pull the clitoral hood so that it moves back and forth, stimulating the clitoris. Thus even the purely "vaginal" orgasm results from quite a bit of clitoral stimulation.

It seems that clitoral stimulation is usually the "trigger" to orgasm and that the orgasm itself occurs in the vagina and surrounding tissues.

It is unfortunate that the distinction between clitoral and vaginal orgasms persists, since it has no scientific basis. That is, there is no physiological difference between orgasms occurring during intercourse and those occurring as a result of clitoral stimulation during masturbation.

Multiple Orgasm in Women

Traditionally it was believed that orgasmically, women behaved like men in that they could have one orgasm and then would enter into a refractory period before they could have another. According to the Masters and Johnson research, however, this is not true; rather, women do not enter into a refractory period, and they can have multiple orgasms within a short period of time. Actually, women's capacity for multiple orgasms was originally discovered by Kinsey in his interviews with women (Kinsey et al., 1953; see also Terman et al., 1938). The scientific establishment, however, dismissed these reports as another instance of Kinsey's unreliability.

Multiple orgasm: Having several orgasms within a short period of time.

Kinsey estimated that about 13 percent of all women have multiple orgasms. The Masters and Johnson research, though, suggests that many more women, perhaps most, are capable of having multiple orgasms if properly stimulated (though the Masters and Johnson data are not good for estimating percentages—see Chapter 10).

The term "multiple orgasm," then, refers to having one orgasm after another within a short period of time. They do not differ physiologically from single orgasms except that there are many of them. Each is a "real" orgasm, and they are not minor experiences. One nice thing, though, is that the later ones generally require much less effort than the first one. The first one may require quite a bit of stimulation, but subsequent ones can often be triggered by less than a minute of stimulation.

How does multiple orgasm work physiologically? Immediately following an orgasm, both males and females move into the resolution phase. In this phase, the male enters into a refractory period, during which he cannot be aroused again.[4] But the female does not enter into a refractory period. That is, if she is stimulated again, she can immediately be aroused and move back into the excitement or plateau phase and have another orgasm.

Multiple orgasm, of course, is more likely to result from hand-genital or mouth-genital stimulation than from intercourse, since most men do not have the endurance to continue thrusting for such long periods of time. Regarding capacity, Masters and Johnson found that women in masturbation might have 5 to 20 orgasms. In some cases, they quit only when physically exhausted. When using a vibrator, less effort is required, and some women were capable of having 50 orgasms.

It should be noted that some women who are capable of multiple orgasm are completely satisfied with one, particularly in intercourse, and do not wish to continue. We should be careful not to set multiple orgasm as another of the many goals in sexual performance.

It is also worth noting that there is more variability in female orgasm patterns than there is in male orgasm patterns (Masters and Johnson, 1966, p. 5).

ALTERNATIVES TO THE MASTERS AND JOHNSON MODEL

Some experts disagree with Masters and Johnson's model of sexual response proceeding in four successive stages. Two alternative models are presented here.

Kaplan: Biphasic Model

Biphasic model: Kaplan's model of sexual response in which there are two phases: vasocongestion and muscular contractions.

On the basis of her work in sex therapy (discussed in Chapter 20), Helen Singer Kaplan (1974) has proposed a biphasic model of sexual response. Rather than thinking of the sexual response as having successive stages, she prefers to conceptualize it as having two relatively independent phases or components: *vasocongestion* of the genitals and the reflex *muscular contractions* of the orgasm phase.

There are a number of justifications for this approach. First, the two phases are controlled by different parts of the nervous system. Vasocogestion—producing erection in the male and lubrication in the female—is controlled by the parasympathetic division of the autonomic nervous system. In contrast, ejaculation (and presumably orgasm in the female) is controlled by the sympathetic division. Second, the two phases or components involve different anatomical structures, blood vessels for vasocongestion and muscles for the contractions of orgasm. Third, vasocongestion and orgasm differ in their susceptibility to being disturbed by injury, drugs, or age. For example, the refractory period following orgasm in the male lengthens with age.

[4]Some experts, however, believe that some men are capable of having multiple orgasms (e.g., Zilbergeld, 1978).

Accordingly, there is a decrease in the frequency of ejaculation with age. In contrast, the capacity for erection is relatively unimpaired with age, so that an elderly man may have nonejaculatory sex several times a week, with a firm erection, although he may have an orgasm only once a week. Fourth, the reflex of ejaculaion in the male can be brought under voluntary control by most men, but the erection reflex generally cannot. Finally, the impairment of the vasocongestion response and impairment of the orgasm response produce different disturbances (sexual dysfunctions). Erection problems in the male are caused by an impairment of the vasocongestion response, whereas premature ejaculation and retarded ejaculation are disturbances of the orgasm response. Similarly, many women show a strong arousal and vasocongestion response yet have trouble with the orgasm component of their sexual response.

Thus, Kaplan's biphasic model seems to be useful both for understanding the nature of sexual response and for understanding and treating disturbances in it. More recently, Kaplan (1979) has elaborated her work into a triphasic model, adding a *desire phase* to the two phases discussed above. Her work on disorders of sexual desire will be discussed in Chapter 20.

Zilbergeld and Ellison: Five-Component Model

Zilbergeld and Ellison's (1980) basic criticism of the Masters and Johnson model is that it ignores the cognitive and subjective aspects of sexual response. That is, Masters and Johnson focus almost entirely on the physiological aspects of the response, ignoring what the person is thinking and feeling emotionally. This would not be such a problem except that there can be major discrepancies between physiological response and subjective feelings. Men can have erections without feeling the least bit aroused sexually. People can also feel highly aroused or desirous of having sex, yet they have no erection or vaginal lubrication.

Zilbergeld and Ellison feel that two particularly important subjective factors have been ignored: sexual desire and arousal. They define sexual desire as being how frequently the person wants to have sex—whether ten times per day, once a week, or once every six months. Arousal refers to how excited or turned on one gets during sex; it is purely subjective and can be assessed only by self-report, not by any physiological measures.

Sexual desire:
How frequently one wants to have sex.

Arousal:
The feeling of being excited or turned on during sex.

Having added these concepts to understanding sexual response, Zilbergeld and Ellison proposed a *five-component model* of sexual response. The five components, each of which is related to the others but also fairly autonomous, are as follows:

1. Interest or desire
2. Arousal
3. Physiological readiness (vaginal lubrication/swelling and erection)
4. Orgasm
5. Satisfaction (how one evaluates or feels about what has occurred)

Zilbergeld and Ellison feel that their own model, compared with the Masters and Johnson conceptualization, is more useful in understanding sexual dysfunctions and in treating them. Sex therapists are seeing increasing numbers of cases of problems of sexual desire (see Chapter 20). These cannot be accounted for by the Masters and Johnson model, yet the Zilbergeld and Ellison model makes it clear which component—desire—is disturbed.

In sum, then, Zilbergeld and Ellison feel that the subjective aspects of sex—particularly desire, arousal, and satisfaction—are essential components of the sexual response.

Note that in both Zilbergeld and Ellison's model and Kaplan's triphasic model, there is increased emphasis on the *psychological* aspects of sexual response, compared with the exclusively *physiological* focus of Masters and Johnson's model. As the saying has it, the greatest erogenous zone is the brain.

HORMONAL AND NEURAL CONTROL OF SEXUAL BEHAVIOR

Up to this point we have focused on the genital responses that occur during sexual activity. We have not yet considered the neural and hormonal mechanisms that make this possible; they are the topic of the following section.

The Brain, the Spinal Cord, and Sex

The brain and the spinal cord both have important interacting functions in sexual response. First, the relatively simple spinal reflexes involved in sexual response will be discussed; then the more complex brain mechanisms will be considered.

Spinal Reflexes

Several important components of sexual behavior, including erection and ejaculation, are controlled by fairly simple spinal cord reflexes (see the lower part of Figure 8.5). A reflex has three basic components: the *receptors,* which are sense organs that detect stimuli and transmit the message to the spinal cord (or brain); the *transmitters,* which are centers in the spinal cord (or brain) that receive the message, interpret it, and send out a message to produce the appropriate response; and the *effectors,* which are organs that respond to the stimulation. The reflex jerking away of the hand when it touches a very hot object is a good example.

Mechanism of Erection

Erection is produced by a spinal reflex with a similar mechanism. Tactile stimulation (stroking or rubbing) of the penis (the receptor) or nearby regions such as the scrotum or inside of the thighs produces a neural signal which is transmitted to an "erection center" in the sacral, or lowest, part of the spinal cord (there may also be another erection center higher in the cord). This center then sends out a message via the parasympathetic division of the nervous system to the muscles (the effectors) around the walls of the arteries in the penis. In response to the message, the muscles relax; the arteries then expand, permitting a large volume of blood to flow into them, and erection results. Further, the valves in the veins and the compression of the veins, caused by the swelling in the tissue around them, reduce the blood flow out (H. D. Weiss, 1973).

The existence of this reflex is confirmed by the responses of men who have had their spinal cords severed, as a result of accidents, at a level above that of the reflex center. They are capable of having erections and ejaculations produced by rubbing their genitals, although it is clear that no brain effects can be operating, since signals from the brain cannot move past the point at which the spinal cord was severed. (In fact, they cannot "feel" anything because neural signals cannot be transmitted up

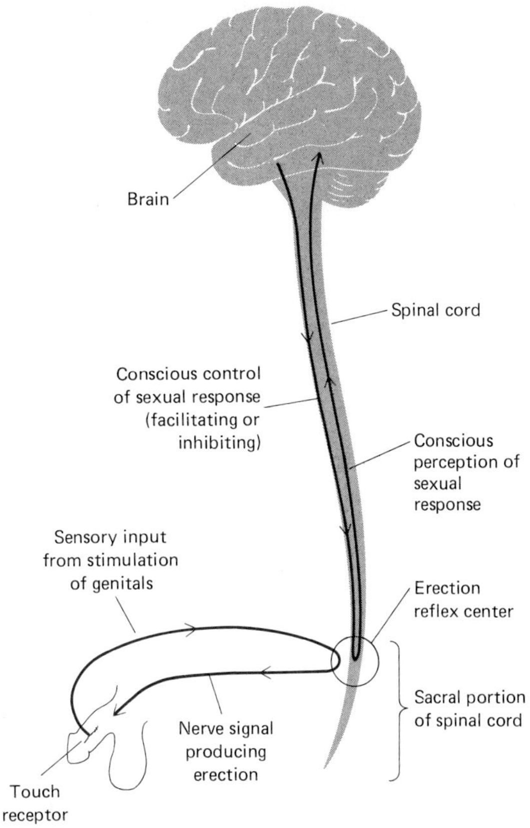

FIGURE 8.5

Nervous system control of erection. Note both the reflex center in the spinal cord and brain control.

the spinal cord either.) Thus it appears that erection can be produced simply by tactile stimulation of the genitals, which triggers the spinal reflex.

It is clear that erection may also be produced by conditions other than tactile stimulation of the genitals; for example, fantasy or other purely psychological factors may produce erection. This points to the importance of the brain in producing erection, a topic that will be discussed in more detail below.

Mechanism of Ejaculation

The ejaculation reflex is much like the erection reflex, except that the ejaculation center is located higher in the spinal cord, the sympathetic division of the nervous system is involved (as opposed to the parasympathetic division in the erection reflex), and the response is muscular, with no involvement of the blood vessels. In the ejaculation reflex, the penis responds to stimulation by sending a message to the "ejaculation center," which is located in the lumbar portion of the spinal cord. A message is then sent out via the nerves in the sympathetic nervous system, and this message triggers the contractions of the muscles in the internal organs involved in ejaculation.

It is clear that ejaculation can often be controlled voluntarily. This fact highlights the importance of brain influences on the ejaculation reflex.

Retrograde ejaculation: A condition in which orgasm in the male is not accompanied by an external ejaculation; instead, the ejaculate goes into the urinary bladder.

The three main problems of ejaculation are premature ejaculation, retarded ejaculation, and retrograde ejaculation. Premature ejaculation, which is by far the most common problem, and retarded ejaculation will be discussed in Chapter 20. Retrograde ejaculation occurs when the ejaculate, rather than going out through the tip

F • O • C • U • S 8.2

SEXUALITY AND THE HANDICAPPED

It is commonly believed that the person in a wheelchair is sexless. The physically handicapped are thought not to be interested in sex, much less to be capable of engaging in sexual activity. Such ideas are perpetuated by novels such as *Lady Chatterley's Lover,* in which a woman who is sexually frustrated because of her husband's paralysis turns to another man.

About 10 percent of adults in the United States have a physical handicap that imposes a substantial limitation on their activities. Given a chance to express themselves, these people emphasize the importance of their sexuality and sex drive, which may be unaltered by their disability (Richardson, 1972).

Just what can physically handicapped people do sexually? Space does not permit a complete enumeration of all types of physical disabilities and their consequences for sexuality. Instead, the discussion will concentrate on one illustrative example: spinal-cord injury. The reader who is interested in further information may consult excellent reviews by Cole (1975) and Higgins (1978). They form the basis for the following discussion.

Spinal-cord-injured people are becoming increasingly common, with the rising numbers of high-speed car crashes and motorcycle accidents, surfboard accidents, civilian gunshot wounds, and injuries sustained during war.

Paraplegia (paralysis of the lower half of the body on both sides) and quadriplegia (paralysis of the body from the neck down) are both caused by injuries to the spinal cord. Many able-bodied people find it difficult to understand what it feels like to be par-

of the penis, empties into the bladder (Greene et al., 1970). A "dry orgasm" results, since no ejaculate is emitted. This problem can be caused by some illnesses, by tranquilizers and drugs used in the treatment of psychoses, and by prostate surgery. The mechanism that causes it is fairly simple (see Figure 8.6). Two sphincters are involved in ejaculation: an internal one, which closes off the entrance to the bladder during a normal ejaculation, and an external one, which opens during a normal ejaculation, allowing the semen to flow out through the penis. In retrograde ejaculation, the action of these two sphincters is reversed; the external one closes, and thus the ejaculate cannot flow out through the penis, and the internal one opens, permitting the ejaculate to go into the bladder. The condition itself is quite harmless, although some men are disturbed by the lack of sensation of emitting semen.

alyzed. Imagine that your genitals and the region around them have lost all sensation. You would not know they were being touched unless you saw it happen. Physical orgasm is impossible. For the male, no matter how erotic his thoughts, no erection occurs. Further, there is loss of bladder and bowel control, which may produce embarrassing problems if sexual activity is attempted.

However, these limitations do not rule out sexual activity completely, and many people with spinal-cord injuries have satisfying sex lives. Exactly what the person can and cannot do depends on the location and extent of the damage to the spinal cord. There are erection and ejaculation reflex centers located in the lower part of the spinal cord. If these have been destroyed, of course, neither erection nor ejaculation is possible. But more commonly, the cord has been severed at some level above these centers. This makes it impossible for nerve stimulation from the brain to reach the erection center, and so erotic thoughts can no longer produce erection. However, reflex erection as a result of stimulation of the genitals is still quite possible. Thus many spinal-cord-injured men experience the same sexual responses as able-bodied men—including erection, elevation of the testes, and increases in heart rate—except that they generally cannot ejaculate; nor can they feel the physical stimulation. In various studies the percentage of men with spinal-cord injuries who are able to have erections ranges between 50 and 90 percent (Higgins, 1978). Generally, fewer are able to ejaculate, the percentages ranging from 0 to 50.

Spinal-cord-injured women generally experience the same sexual responses as able-bodied women, including engorgement of the clitoris and labia, erection of the nipples, and increases in heart rate. However, vaginal lubrication and orgasm generally do not occur, although they may in some cases. Amenorrhea may occur after injury, but there is generally a return to normal menstrual cycling. Further, such women ovulate and are quite capable of becoming pregnant and carrying a baby to term.

Because sexuality in our culture is currently so orgasm-oriented, orgasm problems among spinal-cord-injured people may appear to be devastating. But many of these handicapped people report that they have been able to cultivate a kind of "psychological orgasm" that is as satisfying as the physical one. Fantasy is a perfectly legitimate form of sexual expression that has not been ruled out by their injury.

There are three general points to be made about sexuality and the handicapped: (1) They generally do have sexual needs and desires; (2) they are often capable of sexual response quite similar to that of able-bodied people; and (3) there is a real need for more information—and communication—about what people with various handicaps can and cannot do sexually.

For more information on all types of handicaps, see Stewart's *The Sexual Side of Handicap* (1979).

Mechanisms in Women

Unfortunately, there is no comparable research on similar reflex mechanisms of arousal in women. Generally it is assumed that since the basic processes of sexual response (vasocongestion and myotonia) are similar in males and females and since their genital organs are derived from the same embryonic tissue (and thus have similar nerve supplies), reflexive mechanisms in women are similar to those in men. That is, since the lubrication response in women results from vasocongestion, it is similar to erection in the male, and thus it might be expected to be controlled by a similar spinal reflex. This is purely speculative, though, since there is no research on the subject.

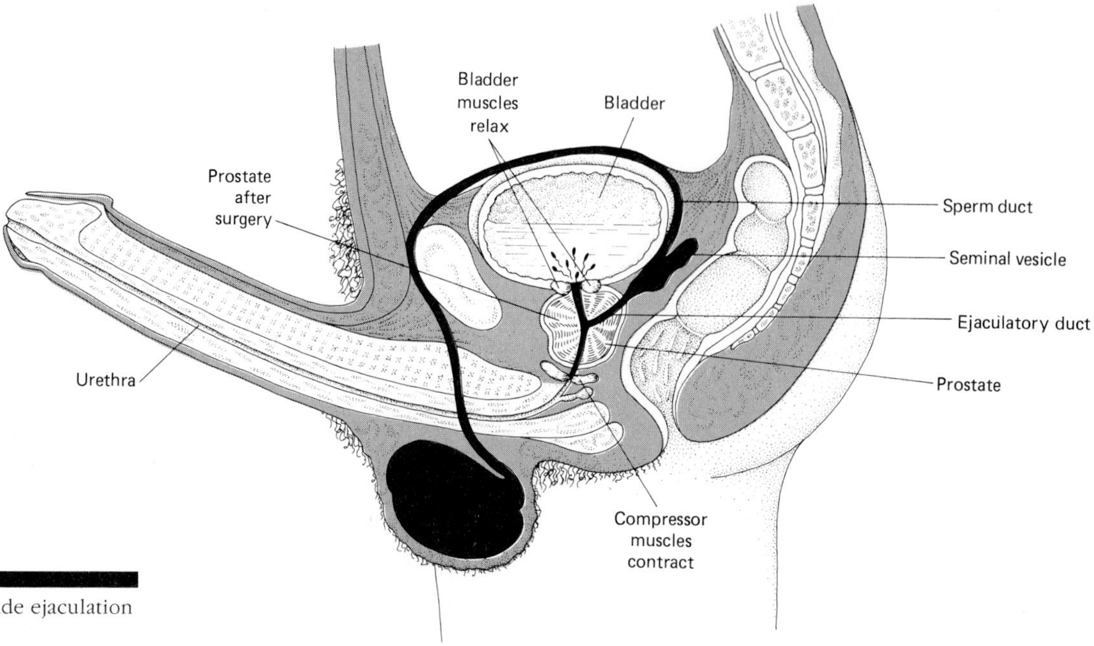

FIGURE 8.6

How a retrograde ejaculation occurs.

Gräfenberg spot (GRAY-fen-berg) or G-spot: A small gland on the front wall of the vagina, emptying into the urethra, which has been hypothesized to be responsible for female ejaculation.

Recent research suggests the possibility that there is such a thing as *female ejaculation* (Perry and Whipple, 1981; Addiego et al., 1981; Belzer, 1981). The research has discovered fluid spurting out of the urethra during orgasm; chemically, the fluid is like the seminal fluid of vasectomized men—that is, semen without the sperm. The organ responsible seems to be the Gräfenberg spot (or *G-spot*), also called the female prostate. It is located on the top side of the vagina (with the woman lying on her back, which is the best position for finding it), about halfway between the pubic bone and the cervix (see Figure 8.7). Stroking it produces an urge to urinate, but if the stroking continues for a few seconds more, it begins to produce sexual pleasure. Perry and Whipple argue that continued stimulation of it produces a *uterine orgasm,* characterized by deeper sensations of uterine contractions than the clitorally induced vulvar orgasm investigated in the Masters and Johnson research. Their ideas are sure to raise the whole clitoral-vaginal orgasm controversy again, although from a different research base. Perry and Whipple also find that not every woman ejaculates, but it is important to recognize that some women do. Our firm notions of male-female differences are constantly challenged!

But Perry and Whipple's results are also being challenged. In one study, two gynecologists examined 11 women, 6 of whom said they were ejaculators (Goldberg et al., 1983). The gynecologists found an area fitting the description of the G-spot

FIGURE 8.7

G-spot: Hypothesized to produce ejaculation in some women.

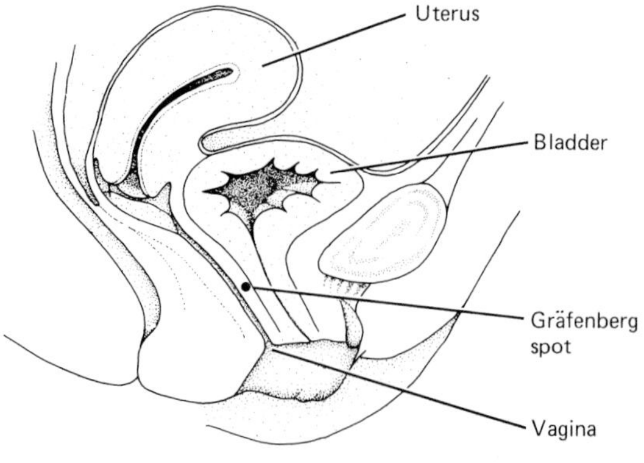

in 4 of the women, but 2 of them were ejaculators and 2 were not. Chemical analysis of the fluid ejaculated by the 6 ejaculators did not find it to be chemically like male semen; chemically it was like urine. Thus the study gave some support to the existence of a G-spot, but it gave no support to the hypothesis that some females ejaculate. In my judgment, it will take another ten years of research, by many independent investigators, before we will really be able to sort out what the G-spot is and does.

Brain Control

As was noted above, it is clear that sexual responses are controlled by more than simple spinal reflexes. Sexual responses may be brought under voluntary control, and they may be initiated by purely psychological forces, such as fantasy. Environmental factors, such as having been taught as a child that sex is dirty and sinful, may also affect one's sexual response. All these phenomena point to the critical influence of the brain and its interaction with the spinal reflexes in producing sexual response (see Figure 8.5).

Brain control of sexual response is complex and only partly understood at the present time. It appears that the most important influences come from a set of structures called the limbic system (see Figure 8.8) (MacLean, 1962). The limbic system forms a border between the central part of the brain and the outer part (the cerebral cortex); it includes the amygdala, the hippocampus, the cingulate gyrus, the fornix, and the septum. The thalamus, the hypothalamus, the pituitary, and the reticular formation are not properly part of the limbic system, but they are closely connected to it.

Limbic system: A set of structures in the interior of the brain, including the amygdala, hippocampus, and fornix; believed to be important for sexual behavior in both animals and humans.

Several lines of evidence point to the importance of the limbic system in sexual behavior. In experiments with monkeys, an electrode was inserted into various regions of the brain to deliver electrical stimulation. It was discovered that stimulation of some areas of the brain would produce an erection. In particular, three "erection centers" were found in the limbic system, including one in the septal region. For obvious reasons, little of this research has been done with humans. But in one study, stimulation of the septal region of the limbic system produced orgasm in two human subjects (Heath, 1972).

Klüver-Bucy syndrome: A syndrome of hypersexuality discovered in monkeys that had had the temporal lobes of the brain destroyed.

The existence of a phenomenon called the Klüver-Bucy syndrome provides further evidence of the importance of the limbic system in sexuality. If the temporal lobes of the brain (the lobes at the side of the brain) of monkeys are destroyed, they become highly erotic and hypersexual (as well as very tame); this is the Klüver-Bucy

FIGURE 8.8

The limbic system of the brain, which is important in sexuality.

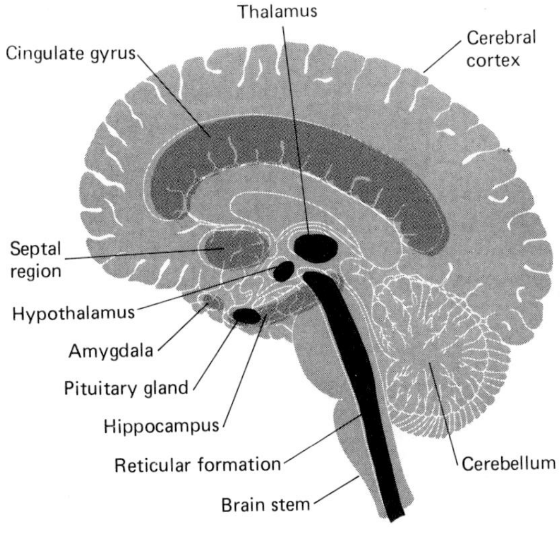

syndrome. When the temporal lobes are destroyed, the amygdala and the hippocampus, among other things, are destroyed; since they are important structures in the limbic system, the hypersexuality that results from their destruction further implicates the limbic system in the control of sexual response.

The thalamus (see Figure 8.8), a structure closely related to the limbic system, also appears to be involved. For example, electrical stimulation of the thalamus produces ejaculation.

Structures in the central part of the brain, then, particularly the structures of the limbic system and the thalamus, are important in influencing sexual response. It is very significant that centers controlling certain other functions—most notably pleasure, olfaction (the sense of smell), and aggression—are located very close to the sex centers and are connected to them.

The important work of the physiological psychologist James Olds (Olds, 1956; Olds and Milner, 1954) established the existence of "pleasure centers" in the brain. Electrodes were implanted in various regions of the brains of rats and were wired so that a rat could stimulate its own brain by pressing a lever. When the electrodes were placed in certain regions—in particular, the septal region and the hypothalamus—the rats would press the lever thousands of times per hour and would forgo food and sleep and endure pain in order to stimulate these regions. The location of these pleasure centers so close to the sex centers may explain why sexual experiences are so intensely pleasurable.

The study of humans noted above also points to an association between the sex centers and the pleasure centers (Heath, 1972). Electrodes were placed in the brains of two human subjects for therapeutic purposes (one male psychiatric patient and one female epileptic). When the stimulation was to certain areas, the subjects reported it as being very pleasurable; these areas were essentially the same as the pleasure centers found in the brains of animals. When the stimulation was delivered to the septal region or the amygdala (both in the limbic system), the pleasure was sexual in nature. In addition to the subjects' reports of sexual arousal and pleasurable sexual feelings, the male subject stimulated himself almost insatiably (as many as 1500 times per hour) and begged to be allowed to stimulate himself a few more times whenever the apparatus was taken away.

There are also "rage," or "aggression," centers in the brain, the stimulation of which throws the animal into a rage so that it will attack any object in the cage. These centers are located in the hypothalamus and, like the pleasure centers, are close to the sex centers; the closeness of the two may explain the association of sex and aggression in phenomena such as rape, competition over mates, and sadomasochism (MacLean, 1962).

The brain centers for sex are also close to the olfactory centers. This brings us to the topic of pheromones and their role in sexual behavior, which will be discussed later in the chapter.

Hormones and Sex

The sex hormones are another important physiological force that interacts with the nervous system to influence sexual response.

Organizing versus Activating Effects

Endocrinologists generally make a distinction between the organizing effects of hormones and the activating effects of hormones (Feder, 1984). As was seen in Chapter

Organizing effects of hormones:
Effects of sex hormones early in development, that result in a permanent effect on the brain or reproductive system.

Activating effects of hormones:
Effects of sex hormones in adulthood, resulting in the activation of behaviors, especially sexual behaviors and aggressive behaviors.

4, hormones present during prenatal development may have important influences on the hypothalamus and on the genitals (creating male or female genitals). Hormone effects such as these are called organizing effects because they cause a relatively permanent change in the organization of some structure, whether in the nervous system or the reproductive system. Typically there are "critical periods" during which these hormone effects may occur.

It has also been known for some time that if an adult male mouse or rat is castrated (has the testes removed, which removes the source of testosterone), it will cease engaging in sexual behavior (and also will be less aggressive). If that animal is then given injections of testosterone, it will start engaging in sex again. Hormone effects such as these are called activating effects because they activate (or deactivate) certain behaviors.

The organizing effects of sex hormones on sexual behavior have been well documented. In a classic experiment, testosterone was administered to pregnant female guinea pigs. The female offspring that had been exposed to testosterone prenatally[5] were, in adulthood, incapable of displaying female sexual behavior (in particular, lordosis, which is a sexual posturing involving arching of the back and raising of the hindquarters so that the male's intromission is possible) (Phoenix et al., 1959). It is thought that this occurred because the testosterone "organized" the brain tissue (particularly the hypothalamus) in a male fashion. These female offspring were also born with masculinized genitals, and thus their reproductive systems had also been organized in the male direction. But the important point here is that the prenatal doses of testosterone had masculinized their sexual behavior. Similar results have been obtained in experiments with many other species as well.

These hormonally masculinized females in adulthood displayed mounting behavior, a male[6] sexual behavior. When they were given testosterone in adulthood, they showed about as much mounting behavior as males did. Thus the testosterone administered in adulthood *activated* male patterns of sexual behavior.

The analogous experiment on males would be castration at birth, followed by administration of ovarian hormones in adulthood. When this was done with rats, female sexual behavior resulted; these males responded to mating attempts by other males essentially in the same way females do (Harris and Levine, 1965). Apparently their brain tissue had been organized in a female direction during an early, critical period when testosterone was absent, and the female behavior patterns were activated in adulthood by administration of ovarian hormones.

It thus seems that males and females initially have capacities for both male and female sexual behaviors; if testosterone is present early in development, the capacity for exhibiting female behaviors is suppressed. Sex hormones in adulthood then activate the behavior patterns that were differentiated early in development.

One question that might be raised is: How relevant is this research to humans? Generally the trend is for the behavior of lower species to be more under hormonal control and for the behavior of higher species to be more under brain (neural) control. Thus human sexual behavior is probably less under hormonal control than rat sexual behavior; human sexual behavior is more controlled by the brain, and thus

---

[5]Note the similarity of these experiments to John Money's observations of human hermaphrodites (Chapter 4).

[6]The term "male sexual behavior" is being used here to refer to a sexual behavior that is displayed by normal males of the species and either is absent in females of that species or is present at a much lower frequency. Normal females do mount, but they do so less frequently than males do. "Female sexual behavior" is defined similarly.

F • O • C • U • S 8.3

CASTRATION OR INCARCERATION?

In 1983, Judge C. Victor Pyle delivered a controversial sentence in a rape case: The defendants could choose 30 years in prison or castration. The three men had been convicted of a brutal gang rape of an 80-pound woman, after which she required a transfusion of 4 pints of blood and five days of hospitalization.

The sentence raises a host of questions, some of them legal, some within the province of the sciences. Legally, the castration sentence will surely be protested on the grounds that it is cruel and unusual punishment. What purpose did the judge have in mind when he assigned the castration sentence? Was he simply being punitive and letting the punishment fit the crime? Or did he view castration as a solution that would ensure that the men would never commit rape again? The scientific data become pertinent in addressing this last point.

Would castration (surgical removal of the testes, technically known as *bilateral orchidectomy*) prevent a man from committing rape? When the testes are removed, the man is left with little or no natural testosterone in his body. Numerous experiments with lower animals have demonstrated that the effect of

FIGURE 8.9

Judge C. Victor Pyle.

learning and past experiences, which are stored in the brain, are more likely to have a profound effect. For example, it is estimated that only about 20 percent of cases of human sexual dysfunction (e.g., impotence) are caused by physical factors; the rest are due to psychological factors (see Chapter 20).

Let us now consider in more detail the known activating effects of sex hormones on the sexual behavior of adult humans.

this reduced level of testosterone is a sharply reduced sex drive and the virtual elimination of sexual behavior. However, the effects in humans are not so clear, because we are not as hormone-dependent as other species. There are documented cases of castrated men continuing to engage in sexual intercourse for years after the castration. Thus, castration may reduce sexual behavior in humans, but the effects are not completely predictable. Further, testosterone is available artificially, either by pill or by injection, so that the men might secretly obtain replacement testosterone even when their natural testosterone had been removed.

The discussion up to this point has focused on rape as a form of sexual behavior. Yet many experts in the field believe that rape is better conceptualized as an aggressive or violent crime that happens to be expressed sexually. Thus, the scientific question may be restated from "Does castration eliminate sexual behavior," to "Does castration eliminate aggressive behavior?" Here, too, there are numerous experiments documenting—in other species—that castration, by lowering testosterone levels, greatly reduces aggressive behavior. But once again, the hormone effects are not as clear or consistent in humans. Thus, castration might be effective in reducing sexual or aggressive behaviors and thus might reduce the chance of the men committing rape again, but such effects could not be guaranteed.

Other biological treatments for rapists are being explored. One is injections of the drug Depo-Provera, which has also been used experimentally as a form of birth control for women. In male sex offenders, Depo-Provera is thought to be a kind of "chemical castration" because its effect is to reduce sharply the levels of testosterone in the body. It seems clear that Depo-Provera should be only part of the treatment, which should also include intensive psychotherapy. In one treatment program combining Depo-Provera and psychotherapy, after 3½ years only 15 percent of the men had repeated their offense, compared with rates as high as 85 percent for men who are only imprisoned. Yet some authorities believe that Depo-Provera is dangerous, possibly increasing the risk of cancer and suicidal depression.

Two questions remain for scientists. What role does testosterone play in sexual behavior and in aggressive behavior in humans? And, will biological therapies be effective in stopping rapists from repeating their crime?

Sources. Michael S. Serrill. (1983, Dec. 12). Castration or incarceration? *Time,* p. 70.

Nikolaus Heim. (1981). Sexual behavior of castrated sex offenders. *Archives of Sexual Behavior,* **10**, pp. 11–20.

Robert T. Rubin, June M. Reinisch, and Roger F. Haskett. (1981). Postnatal gonadal steroid effects on human behavior. *Science,* **211**, pp. 1318–1324.

Depo-Provera (DEH-poh-proh-VARE-uh): A drug containing synthetic hormones; used as an experimental form of birth control in women, as well as in treating male sex offenders.

Testosterone and Libido

Testosterone has well-documented effects on libido in humans. In men deprived of their main source of testosterone by castration or by illness, there is a dramatic decrease in sexual behavior in some, but not all, cases (Feder, 1984). Libido and potency are rapidly lost if a man is given an antiandrogen drug. Thus testosterone seems to have an activating effect in maintaining sexual behavior in the adult male.

However, in cases of castration, sexual behavior may decline very slowly and may be present for several years after the source of testosterone is gone; this points to the importance of experience and brain control of sexual behavior in humans.

Recently it has been demonstrated that androgens are related to libido in women also (Feder, 1984). If all sources of androgen in women are removed (the adrenals and the ovaries), women lose sexual desire. On the other hand, androgens are sometimes used in the treatment of low-libido states in women, although their use is limited by their tendency to have masculinizing side effects.[7]

PHEROMONES

Pheromones (FARE-oh-mones): Biochemicals secreted outside the body that are important in communication between animals and that may serve as sex attractants.

There has been a great deal of interest recently in the role that pheromones play in sexual behavior. Pheromones are somewhat like hormones. Recall that hormones are biochemicals that are manufactured in the body and secreted into the bloodstream to be carried to the organs that they affect. Pheromones, on the other hand, are biochemicals that are secreted outside the body. Thus, through the sense of smell, they are an important means of communication between animals. Often the pheromones are contained in the animal's urine. Thus the dog that does "scent marking" is actually depositing pheromones. Some pheromones appear to be important in sexual communication, and some have even been called "sex attractants."

Much of the research on pheromones has been done with mice and demonstrates the importance of pheromones in sexual and reproductive functioning. For example, exposure to the odor of male urine induces estrus (ovulation and sexual behavior) in female mice (the *Whitten effect*). If a female mouse copulates with a male and conceives and is then exposed to the odors of a strange male mouse, the pregnancy is aborted, presumably because implantation is prevented (the *Bruce effect*).

It appears that testosterone is critical to the male pheromones' ability to have these effects on females. If a male mouse is castrated, its urine will not induce estrus or block pregnancy (Bruce, 1969).

Pheromones present in female urine also have an influence on male sexual behavior. An early study demonstrated that male rats can tell the difference between the odor of estrous females and that of females not in estrus and that the males prefer estrous females (LeMagnen, 1952). Similar phenomena have been demonstrated in male dogs, stallions, bulls, and rams (Michael and Keverne, 1968). The ovarian hormones estrogen and progesterone are critical to the female pheromones' ability to have an effect on males (Beach and Merari, 1970).

The sense of smell (olfaction) seems to be essential in order for pheromone effects to occur. Removal of the olfactory bulbs (a part of the brain important in olfaction) severely inhibits sexual behavior in both males and females (Bronson, 1968).

Some research has been done on pheromones in primates. It has been found, for example, that estrogen treatment of a female rhesus monkey sexually excites the males in her cage (Herbert, 1966). If the males' sense of smell is blocked, they no longer are sexually excited.

---

[7]Lest the reader be distressed by the thought that women's considerably lower levels of testosterone might mean that they have lower sex drives, it should be noted that the sensitivity of cells to hormone levels is critical. Women's cells may be more sensitive to testosterone than men's are. Thus for women, a little testosterone may go a long way.

What relevance does all this have for humans? Humans are not, by and large, "smell animals." Olfaction is not particularly important for us, especially compared with other species. We tend to rely mostly on vision and, secondarily, hearing. Compare this with a dog's ability to get a wealth of information about who and what has been in a park simply by sniffing around for a few minutes. On the other hand, humans do seem to be capable of developing remarkable senses of smell; Helen Keller reportedly could recognize all people she met by their scents.

Nonetheless, humans do not depend heavily on their sense of smell. Does this mean that pheromones have no influence on our sexual behavior? Evidence is beginning to accumulate suggesting that humans produce and respond to pheromones much as other species do.

A classic study of the "exaltolide phenomenon" demonstrated the importance of hormones in the sense of smell (LeMagnen, 1952). Exaltolide is a synthetic compound with a musklike odor. The pheromones present in the urine of other species have a musky odor, and there are musklike odors in human urine. Thus, this compound may be quite similar to pheromones. Exaltolide can be perceived by adult women, but not by girls before puberty or by males. Further, the study demonstrated that the ability to perceive the smell of this compound varied according to the phase of the menstrual cycle; women are most sensitive to it around the time of ovulation. These results with exaltolide seem to be quite comparable to the findings from research on pheromones in nonhumans.

Researchers are now speculating that human pheromones exist and that they play an important role in sexual behavior (Comfort, 1971). Indeed, pheromones may be exactly the "body chemistry" that attracts people to each other. It has been speculated that human pheromones are produced by the sweat glands of the armpits and by the prepuce of the male's penis and the female's clitoris. It should be noted that perfumes with musky scents have become quite popular and presumably increase sexual attractiveness, perhaps because they smell like pheromones. The perfume industry has eagerly tried to capitalize on the pheromone research; indeed, there is a perfume on the market called "Pheromone."

One exciting advance in this research has been the identification, in the vaginal secretions of 50 women, of chemicals known to be sex-attractant pheromones in monkeys (Michael et al., 1974). The peak in production of these volatile fatty acids is just before and during ovulation. In another study, subjects rated the pleasantness of the odor of vaginal secretions at various stages of the menstrual cycle (Doty et al., 1975). The results indicate that the secretions are more pleasant around ovulation. In sum, it appears that there are the most pheromones around ovulation and that pheromones have the pleasantest smell around ovulation, exactly when it would be expected from an evolutionary perspective. That is exactly when the pheromones would promote intercourse, which would encourage reproduction, and that is exactly what natural selection tries to encourage. At the very least, it seems clear that humans do produce pheromones.

It should be noted that the smell of pheromones would not necessarily have to be consciously perceived in order for it to have an effect. The olfactory system can respond to odors even when they are not consciously perceived. Thus, pheromones that we are not even aware of may have important influences.

If these speculations about the effects of pheromones on human sexual behavior are correct, our "hyperclean" society may be destroying the scents that attract people to each other. The normal genital secretions (assuming reasonable cleanliness to eliminate bacteria) may contain sex attractants. The feminine hygiene deodorants may destroy precisely the odors that "turn men on."

Future research on human pheromones should be interesting indeed.

SUMMARY

William Masters and Virginia Johnson conducted an important program of research, beginning in the 1950s, on the physiology of human sexual response. They found that two basic physiological pocesses occur during arousal and orgasm: vasocongestion and myotonia. They divide the sexual response cycle into four stages: excitement, plateau, orgasm, and resolution.

Their research indicates that there is no physiological distinction between clitoral and vaginal orgasms in women, which refutes an early idea of Freud's. They have also provided convincing evidence of the existence of multiple orgasm in women.

Alternatives to Masters and Johnson's model are Kaplan's two-component (vasocongestion and muscular contraction) model and Zilbergeld and Ellison's model. The latter emphasizes subjective aspects of sexual response (desire and arousal).

The nervous system and sex hormones are important in sexual response. The nervous system functions in sexual response by a combination of spinal reflexes (best documented for erection and ejaculation) and brain influences (particularly of the limbic system). There is new evidence that some women ejaculate. Hormones are important to sexual behavior, both in their influences on prenatal development (organizing effects) and in their stimulating influence on adult sexual behavior (activating effects). Testosterone seems to be important for maintaining libido in both men and women.

Pheromones are biochemicals secreted outside the body that play an important role in sexual communication and attraction.

REVIEW QUESTIONS

1. According to Masters and Johnson, the four stages of sexual response are, in order, _____, _____, _____, and _____.
2. According to Masters and Johnson, the two basic physiological processes that occur during sexual arousal are _____ and myotonia.
3. According to Masters and Johnson, vaginal lubrication in the female is caused by vasocongestion. True or false?
4. Masters and Johnson have documented the fact that there are two kinds of orgasm in the female, vaginal orgasm and clitoral orgasm. True or false?
5. Only men are capable of multiple orgasm. True or false?
6. Erection in the male is produced by a simple spinal reflex. True or false?
7. It has been hypothesized that a small organ, called the _____, is responsible for ejaculation in some women.
8. If female guinea pig fetuses are exposed to testosterone prenatally, they are born with masculinized genitals and hypothalamus and show male sexual behaviors; this demonstrates the activating effects of hormones. True or false?
9. _____ are biochemicals secreted outside the body that may serve a role as sex attractants.
10. When Judge Pyle sentenced three convicted rapists to prison or castration, he made a wise decision because research has proven that castration prevents men from committing rape in the future. True or false?

QUESTION FOR THOUGHT, DISCUSSION, AND DEBATE

1. Debate the following topic. Resolved: Castration is an appropriate and effective treatment for convicted rapists.

SUGGESTIONS FOR FURTHER READING

Bermant, G., and Davidson, J. M. (1974). *Biological bases of sexual behavior.* New York: Harper & Row. A thorough analysis of biological (neural, hormonal) influences on sexual behavior, concentrating mostly on animal research. The book was intended as a text for advanced undergraduates.

Raphael, Bette-Jane. (1973, Oct. 25) The myth of the male orgasm. *Village Voice.* (Reprinted in *Psychology Today,* January 1974.) A marvelous satire on male scientists' skepticism about the female orgasm.

White, David. (1981, Sept.) Pursuit of the ultimate aphrodisiac. *Psychology Today,* **15**, 9–12. An evaluation of current scientific evidence on human pheromones.

[redacted]

CHAPTER • **9**

TECHNIQUES OF AROUSAL AND COMMUNICATION

Lust is more abstract than logic; it seeks (hope triumphing over experience) for some purely sexual, hence purely imaginary, conjunction of an impossible maleness with an impossible femaleness.*

* *Source:* C. S. Lewis. (1958). *The allegory of love.* New York: Oxford University Press, p. 196.

CHAPTER HIGHLIGHTS

I. EROGENOUS ZONES

II. ONE-PERSON SEX

III. TWO-PERSON SEX

IV. APHRODISIACS

V. ARE INTERCOURSE AND ORGASM THE GOAL?

VI. FROM INEXPERIENCE TO BOREDOM

VII. COMMUNICATION AND SEX

We live in the era of sex manuals. Books like *Everything You Always Wanted to Know about Sex . . .* , *The Joy of Sex, The Sensuous Woman,* and *The Sensuous Man,* as well as numerous feature articles and advice columns in magazines like *Playboy,* give us information on how to produce bigger and better orgasms in ourselves and our partners. The "read-all-about-it" boom has produced not only benefits but also problems. It may turn our attention so much to mechanical techniques that we forget about love and the emotional side of sexual expression. The sex manuals may also set up impossible standards of sexual performance that none of us can meet. On the other hand, we live in a society that has a history of leaving the learning of sexual techniques to nature or to chance, in contrast to some "primitive" societies in which adolescents are given explicit instruction in methods for producing sexual pleasure. For human beings, sexual behavior is a lot more than "doin' what comes naturally"; we all need some means for learning about sexual techniques, and the sex manuals may help to fill that need.

The purpose of this chapter is to provide information on techniques of arousal, while attempting to avoid making sex too mechanical or setting up unrealistic performance standards. It also focuses on skills for communicating in a relationship.

EROGENOUS ZONES

Erogenous zones (eh-RAH-jen-us): Areas of the body that are particularly sensitive to sexual stimulation.

While the notion of erogenous zones originated in Freud's work, the term is now part of our general vocabulary and refers to parts of the body which are sexually sensitive; stroking them or otherwise stimulating them produces sexual arousal. The genitals and the breasts are the most obvious examples. The lips, neck, and thighs are generally also erogenous zones. But even some rather unlikely regions—such as the back, the ears, the stomach, and the feet—can also be quite erogenous. One person's erogenous zones can be quite different from another person's. Thus it is impossible to give a list of sure "turn-ons." The best way to find out is to communicate with your partner, either verbally or nonverbally.

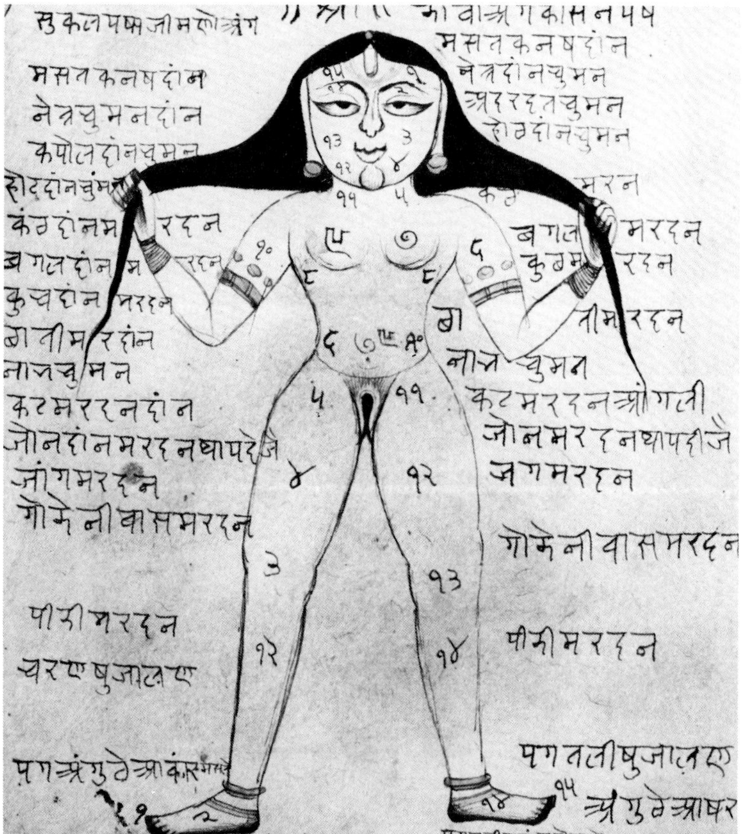

FIGURE 9.1

Erotic miniature painting from India (eighteenth century) showing the sensitive parts of the female body, which were believed to vary during each day of the lunar month.

ONE-PERSON SEX

Autoeroticism: Sexual self-stimulation, for example, masturbation.

It does not necessarily take two to have sex. One can produce one's own sexual stimulation. Sexual self-stimulation is called autoeroticism.[1] The best examples are masturbation and fantasy.

Masturbation

Masturbation: Hand stimulation of either one's own or another's genitals.

The term masturbation can refer either to hand stimulation of one's own genitals or to hand stimulation of another's genitals. Here the term "hand-genital stimulation" will be reserved for stimulation of another's genitals and the term "masturbation" for self-stimulation, either with the hand or with some object, such as a pillow or a vibrator. Masturbation is a very common sexual behavior; almost all men and the majority of women masturbate to orgasm at least a few times during their lives, and many do so frequently. The techniques used by males and females in masturbation are interesting in part because they provide information to their partners concerning the best techniques to use in lovemaking.

Techniques of Female Masturbation

Most commonly women masturbate by manipulating the clitoris and the inner lips (Hite, 1976; Kinsey et al., 1953, pp. 158, 189). They may rub up and down or in a circular motion, sometimes lightly and sometimes applying more pressure to the clitoris. Some prefer to rub at the side of the clitoris, while a few stimulate the glans of the clitoris directly. The inner lips may also be stroked or tugged. One woman described her technique as follows:

> I use the tips of my fingers for actual stimulation, but it's better to start with patting motions or light rubbing motions over the general area. As excitement increases I begin stroking above the clitoris and finally reach a climax with a rapid, jerky circular motion over the clitoral hood. Usually my legs are apart, and occasionally I also stimulate my nipples with the other hand. (Hite, 1976, p. 20)

This finding is in distinct contrast to what many men imagine to be the techniques of female masturbation; the male pictures the woman inserting a finger, a banana, or a similar object into the depths of the vagina (Kinsey et al., 1953). In fact, this is not often done; by far the most common method is clitoral and labial manipulation. Of the women in Kinsey's sample who masturbated, 84 percent used clitoral and labial manipulation; inserting fingers or objects into the vagina was the second most commonly used technique, but it was practiced by only 20 percent of the women.

Other techniques used by women in masturbation include breast stimulation, thigh pressure exerted by crossing the legs and pressing them together rhythmically to stimulate the clitoris, and pressing the genitals against some object, such as a pillow, or massaging them with a stream of water while in the shower. A few women (about 2 percent in Kinsey's sample) are capable of using fantasy alone to produce orgasm.

[1]For those of you who are interested in the roots of words, "autoeroticism" does not refer to sex in the back seat of a car. The prefix "auto" means "self" (as in "autobiography"); hence self-stimulation is autoeroticism.

Techniques of Male Masturbation

Almost all males report masturbating by hand stimulation of the penis. Generally the activity is accomplished as quickly as possible, taking only a minute or two (Kinsey et al., 1948, p. 509).

Most men use the technique of circling the hand around the shaft of the penis and using an up-and-down movement to stimulate the shaft and glans. Because the penis produces no natural lubrication of its own, some men like to use a form of lubrication, such as soapsuds while showering. The tightness of the grip, the speed of movement, and the amount of glans stimulation vary from one man to the next. Most increase the speed of stimulation as they approach orgasm, slowing or stopping the stimulation at orgasm because further stimulation would be uncomfortable (Masters and Johnson, 1966). At the time of ejaculation, they often grip the shaft of the penis tightly. Immediately after orgasm, the glans and corona are hypersensitive, and the man generally avoids further stimulation of the penis at that time (Sadock and Sadock, 1976).

Fantasy

Fantasy:
Mental images that are usually pleasant and unrestrained by reality.

Fantasies are another form of self-stimulation, or autoeroticism. Sexual fantasies can occur by themselves or during masturbation or sexual intercourse with another person.

Fantasy during Masturbation

Approximately 80 percent of men and 80 percent of women who masturbate fantasize at least some of the time while doing so (Hunt, 1974, p. 91). Fantasies are, therefore, quite common.

The exact content of fantasies is highly individual, but some general themes are quite common. Table 9.1 summarizes some of the themes of fantasies during masturbation that were reported by the respondents in the Hunt survey (see Chapter 10 for a discussion of this study). Common themes include having intercourse with a loved one or with strangers (sometimes movie stars such as Robert Redford or Bo

TABLE 9.1

COMMON THEMES OF FANTASIES WHILE MASTURBATING

	Number of People Having That Type of Fantasy	
Theme of Fantasy	Males, %	Females, %
1. Having intercourse with a loved one	75	80
2. Having intercourse with a stranger	47	21
3. Having sex with more than one person at the same time	33	18
4. Doing sexual things one would never do in reality	19	28
5. Being forced to have sex	10	19
6. Forcing someone to have sex	13	3
7. Having sex with someone of the same gender	7	11

Source: Morton Hunt. (1974). *Sexual behavior in the 1970s.* Chicago: Playboy Press, pp. 91–93.

Derek), engaging in group sex, being forced to or forcing someone to have sex, or doing other things that would not actually happen in reality. Heterosexuals typically have heterosexual fantasies, and homosexuals have homosexual fantasies, but there may be some crossing over; for example, a heterosexual may sometimes have homosexual fantasies.

As Table 9.1 indicates, the themes of fantasies differ somewhat for males and females, though there are considerable similarities. The differences might be summarized as follows: Males' fantasies tend to involve situations in which they are powerful and aggressive and are engaged in impersonal sex, while females' fantasies are more likely to involve romance or being forced to have sex (Barclay, 1973; DeLora and Warren, 1977; Shope, 1975). Here is an adolescent male's description of one of his favorite fantasies during masturbation:

> We would be riding in the back seat of the car, and I would reach over and fondle her breasts. She would reach into my pants and begin to caress my penis and finally suck me off. (Jensen, 1976a, p. 144)

This is the fantasy of a 20-year-old female:

> The bedside table light was on as I entered the room. Its dimmed light cast lavender shadows on my soft, pink, nylon negligee, which revealed just a hint of my body beneath. He smiled as he lay in bed with his naked body half concealed by covers. With only a motion, he picked up the covers for me to join him. As I slipped beneath the covers I felt his warm body surround me. Our lips met, and our embraces grew tighter. A short time later he loosened my bow, and the nightgown fell away. Crazy, wonderful shivers went through my body, and we kissed for quite some time. Perhaps with the fear that his body weight might hurt me or perhaps with satisfaction, he moved and once again lay beside me on the bed very calmly. (Shope, 1975, pp. 215–216)

The content of male and female sexual fantasies seems to be influenced by cultural stereotypes of male and female sexuality.

Fantasy during Two-Person Sex

Fantasies are also a means of self-stimulation to heighten the experience of sex with another person. Particularly in a long-term, monogamous relationship, sexual monotony can become a problem; fantasies are one way to introduce some variety and excitement, without violating an agreement to be faithful to the other person. It is important to view such fantasies in this way, rather than as a sign of disloyalty to, or dissatisfaction with, one's sexual partner.

Fantasies during two-person sex are generally quite similar to the ones people have while masturbating. In a study of married women, 65 percent said they fantasized while having sex with their husbands (Hariton, 1973; see also S. Fisher, 1973). The following were the seven most common themes of their fantasies, listed in order of frequency, beginning with the most common:

1. Thinking of an imaginary lover
2. Imagining being overpowered or forced to surrender
3. Pretending to be engaging in something that is wicked or forbidden
4. Imagining being in a different place, such as a car, a motel, a beach, or the woods
5. Reliving a previous sexual experience

6. Imagining myself delighting many men
7. Imagining observing myself or others having sex

The fantasies were not a sign of poor marital relations; the women who fantasized reported better sexual relationships with their husbands than the women who did not fantasize. Diane is an example:

> Diane is happily married. Yet she finds sexual foreplay with her husband more exciting if she imagines herself a harem slave displaying her breasts to an adoring sheik. While having intercourse, she sometimes envisions making love in the back seat of a car or in an old-fashioned house during a group orgy. She likes to imagine being forced by one man after another. In one favorite scene she goes to a drive-in movie and is raped by a masculine figure whose face is a "blur." (Hariton, 1973, p. 39)

Vibrators, Dildos, and Such

Various sexual devices, such as vibrators and dildos, are used by some people in masturbation or by couples as they have sex together. Such devices are sold in "sex supermarkets" and through the mail.

Dildo: An artificial penis.

Both male and female artificial genitals can be purchased. A dildo is an artificial penis; it can be inserted into the vagina or the anus. Dildos are used by women in masturbation (although, as was noted in the previous section, this is not very common), by lesbians, by male homosexuals or heterosexuals, and by heterosexual couples. Artificial vaginas, and even inflatable replicas of the entire female body, can also be purchased.

Vibrators are generally shaped like a penis; there are models with a cord that plugs into an electric socket and also battery-operated, cordless models. Women may use them to masturbate, stimulating the clitoral and mons area, or they may insert them into the vagina. Males may use them to stimulate the genitals or the anus. They are used either in masturbation or during sex with another person. They can be purchased in "respectable" stores (where they are euphemistically called "face massagers," for example), in sex supermarkets, and by mail.

Body oils are also increasingly popular for sexual use. In fact, their use has been encouraged by experts in the field; for example, Masters and Johnson and other sex therapists recommed them for the touching or sensate focus exercises that they prescribe for their patients in sex therapy (see Chapter 20). Oils have a sensuous quality that heightens erotic feelings. Further, if you are being stroked or massaged for an extended period of time, the oil helps ensure that the part of your body that is being stimulated will not end up feeling like a piece of wood that has been sandpapered. Oils can be used either while masturbating or while having sex with another person. The sex stores sell them in a variety of exotic scents, but plain baby oil will also do nicely.

TWO-PERSON SEX

When most of us think of techniques of two-person sex, the image that flashes across our mind generally reflects several assumptions. One assumption is that one of the people is a male and the other a female, that is, that the sex is heterosexual. This reflects a belief that heterosexual sex is normative. Further, we tend to assume that the male is supposed to do certain things during the act and that the female is supposed to do certain other things. He, for example, is supposed to take the initiative in deciding what techniques are used, while she is to follow his lead. Although there is nothing particularly evil in these assumptions, they do tend to impose some limitations on our own sexual expression and to make some people think that their own sexual behavior is "not quite right." Therefore, an attempt to avoid these assumptions will be made in the sections that follow.

Kissing

Kissing (or what we might call, technically, "mouth-mouth stimulation") is an activity that virtually everyone in our culture has engaged in (Kinsey et al., 1953). In simple kissing, the partners keep their mouths closed and simply touch each other's lips. In deep kissing ("French kissing"), both people part their lips slightly and insert their tongues into each other's mouths (somehow these clinical descriptions do not make it sound like as much fun as it is). There are endless variations on these two basic approaches, such as nibbling at the partner's lips or tongue or sucking at the lips; they depend only on your imagination and personal preference. There are also plenty of other regions of the body to kiss: the nose, the forehead, the eyelids, the earlobes, the neck, the breasts, the genitals, and even the feet, to give a few examples.

Touching

Enjoying touching and being touched is essential to sexual pleasure. Caressing or massaging, applied to virtually any area of the body can be exciting. The regions that are exciting vary a great deal from one person to the next and depend on how the person is feeling at the moment; thus it is important to communicate what sort of touching is most pleasurable to you. (For specific exercises on touching and being touched, see Chapter 20.)

As was noted earlier, one of the best ways to find out how to use your hand in stimulating the genitals of another person is to find out how that person masturbates.

Hand Stimulation of the Male Genitals

As a technique of lovemaking, hand stimulation of the male genitals can be used as a pleasurable preliminary to intercourse, as a means of inducing orgasm itself, or as a means of producing an erection after the man has had one orgasm and wants to continue for another round of lovemaking ("rousing the dead").

Alex Comfort, in *The Joy of Sex,* recommends the following technique:

> If he isn't circumcised, she will probably need to avoid rubbing the glans itself, except in pursuit of very special effects. Her best grip is just below the groove, with the skin back as far as it will go, and using two hands—one pressing hard near the root, holding the penis steady, or fondling the scrotum, the other making a thumb-and-first-finger ring, or a whole hand grip. She should vary this, and, in prolonged masturbation, change hands often. (1972, p. 118)

As a good technique for producing an erection he also mentions rolling the penis like dough between the palms of the hands. Firm pressure with one finger midway between the base of the penis and the anus is another possibility.

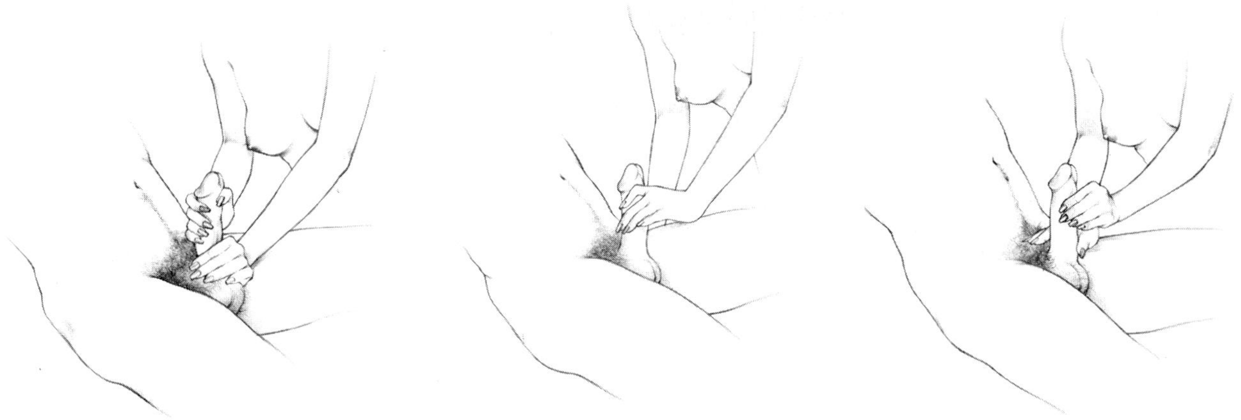

FIGURE 9.2

Techniques of hand stimulation of the penis.

One of the things that make hand stimulation most effective is for the man's partner to have a playful delight in, and appreciation of, the man's penis. Most men think their penis is pretty important. If the partner cannot honestly appreciate it and enjoy massaging it, hand stimulation might as well not be done.

Hand Stimulation of the Female Genitals

The hand can be used to stimulate the woman's genitals to produce orgasm, as a preliminary method of arousing the woman before intercourse, or simply because it is pleasurable.

Generally it is best, particularly if the woman is not already aroused, to begin with gentle, light stroking of the inside of the thighs and the inner and outer lips, moving to light stroking of the clitoris. As she becomes more aroused, the stimulation of the clitoris can become firmer. There are several rules for doing this, though. First, remember that the clitoris is very sensitive and that this sensitivity can be either exquisite or painful. Some care has to be used in stimulating it; it cannot just be manipulated like a piece of Silly Putty. Second, the clitoris should never—except, perhaps, for some light stroking—be rubbed while it is dry, for the effect can be more like sandpaper stimulation than sexual stimulation. If the woman is already somewhat aroused, lubrication can be provided by touching the fingers to the vaginal entrance and then spreading that lubrication on the clitoris. If she is not aroused or does not produce much vaginal lubrication, saliva works well too. Moisture makes the stimulation not only more comfortable but also more sensuous. Third, some women find direct stimulation of the clitoral glans to be painful in some states of arousal. These women generally prefer stimulation on either side of the clitoris instead.

With those caveats in mind, the clitoris can be stimulated with circular or back-and-forth movements of the finger. The inner and outer lips can also be stroked, rubbed, or tugged. These techniques, if done with skill and patience, can bring the woman to orgasm. Another technique that can be helpful in producing orgasm is for the partner to place the heel of the hand on the mons, exerting pressure on it while moving the middle finger in and out of the vaginal entrance. Another rule should also be clear by now: The partner needs to have close-trimmed nails that do not have any jagged edges. This is sensitive tissue we are dealing with.

So far, this chapter has been focused on tactile (touch) sensations in sexual arousal. However, the other senses—vision, smell, and hearing—can also make contributions.

Sights

The things that you see while making love can contribute to arousal. Men seem, in general, to be more turned on by visual stimuli; many men have mild fetishes (see Chapter 17 for more detail on fetishes) and like to see their partners wearing certain types of clothing. Perhaps in the next few years, as female sexuality becomes more liberated, women will become more interested in visual turn-ons. A good rule here, as elsewhere, is to communicate with your partner to find out what he or she would find arousing.

The decor of the room can also contribute to visual stimulation. Furry rugs, placed on the floor or used as a bedspread, are sensuous both visually and tactilely. Large mirrors, hung either behind the bed or on the ceiling above it, can be a visual turn-on, since they allow you to watch yourself make love. Candlelight is soft and contributes more to an erotic atmosphere than an electric light, which is harsh, or complete darkness, in which case there is no visual stimulation at all.

Perhaps the biggest visual turn-on comes simply from looking at your own body and your partner's body.

Smells

Odors can be turn-ons or turn-offs. The odors of a body that is clean, having been washed with soap and water, are themselves natural turn-ons. They do not need to be covered up with anything like "intimate deodorants."[2] In a sense, the odor of your skin, armpits, and genitals is your "aroma signature," and these natural odors can be quite arousing (Comfort, 1972).

A body that has not been washed or a mouth that has not been cleaned or has recently been used for smoking can be a real turn-off. Ideally, the communication between partners is honest and trusting enough so that if one offends, the other can simply request that the appropriate clean-up be done.

Burning incense is also popular as an additional form of odor stimulation during lovemaking.

Sounds

Music—whether your preference is for disco or Brahms's Fourth—can contribute to an erotic atmosphere. Another advantage of playing music is that it helps muffle the sounds of sex, which can be important if you live in an apartment with thin walls or if you are worried about your children hearing you.

---

[2]With the increased popularity of mouth-genital sex, some women worry that the scent of their genitals might be offensive. The advertisements for feminine hygiene deodorant sprays prey upon those fears. These sprays should not be used because they may irritate the vagina (*Consumer Reports,* January 1972). And besides, there is nothing offensive about the odor of a vulva that has been washed; some people, in fact, find it arousing.

Genital-Genital Stimulation: Positions of Intercourse

Coitus: Sexual intercourse; insertion of the penis into the vagina.

One of the commonest sexual techniques involves the insertion of the penis into the vagina; this is called coitus[3] or *sexual intercourse.*

The couple may be in any one of a number of different positions while engaging in this basic sexual activity. Ancient love manuals and other sources illustrate many positions of intercourse (see Figure 9.3).

[3]From the Latin word *coire,* meaning "to go together."

FIGURE 9.3

Positions of intercourse shown on modern Asian playing cards.

Some authorities state that there are only four positions of intercourse. Personally, I prefer to believe that there are an infinite number. Consider how many different angles your arms, legs, and torso may be in, in relation to those of your partner, and all the various ways in which you can intertwine your limbs—that's a lot of positions. I trust that given sufficient creativity and time, you can discover them all for yourselves. I would agree, though, that there are a few basic positions and a few basic dimensions along which positions can vary. One basic variation depends on whether the couple face each other (face-to-face position) or whether one partner faces the other's back (rear-entry position); if you try the other obvious variation, a back-to-back position, you will quickly find that you cannot accomplish much that way. The other basic variation depends on whether one partner is on top of the other or whether the couple are side by side. Let us consider four basic positions that illustrate these variations. As Julia Child often does, I'll give you the basic recipes and let you decide on the embellishments.

Man-on-Top

The face-to-face, man-on-top position ("missionary" position—see Figure 9.4) is the one used most frequently by couples in the United States. Indeed, Kinsey, commenting from his 1940s perspective, said:

> Nearly all coitus in our English-American culture occurs with the partners lying face to face, with the male above the female. There may be as much as 70 percent of the population which has never attempted to use any other position in intercourse. (Kinsey et al., 1948, p. 578)

Surveys in the 1970s, however, indicate that people are using much more of a variety of positions now (Hunt, 1974).

In the man-on-top position (which used to be called "male-superior," an unacceptable term today) the man and woman stimulate each other until they are aroused, he has an erection, and she is producing vaginal lubrication. Then he

FIGURE 9.4

The man-on-top position of intercourse.

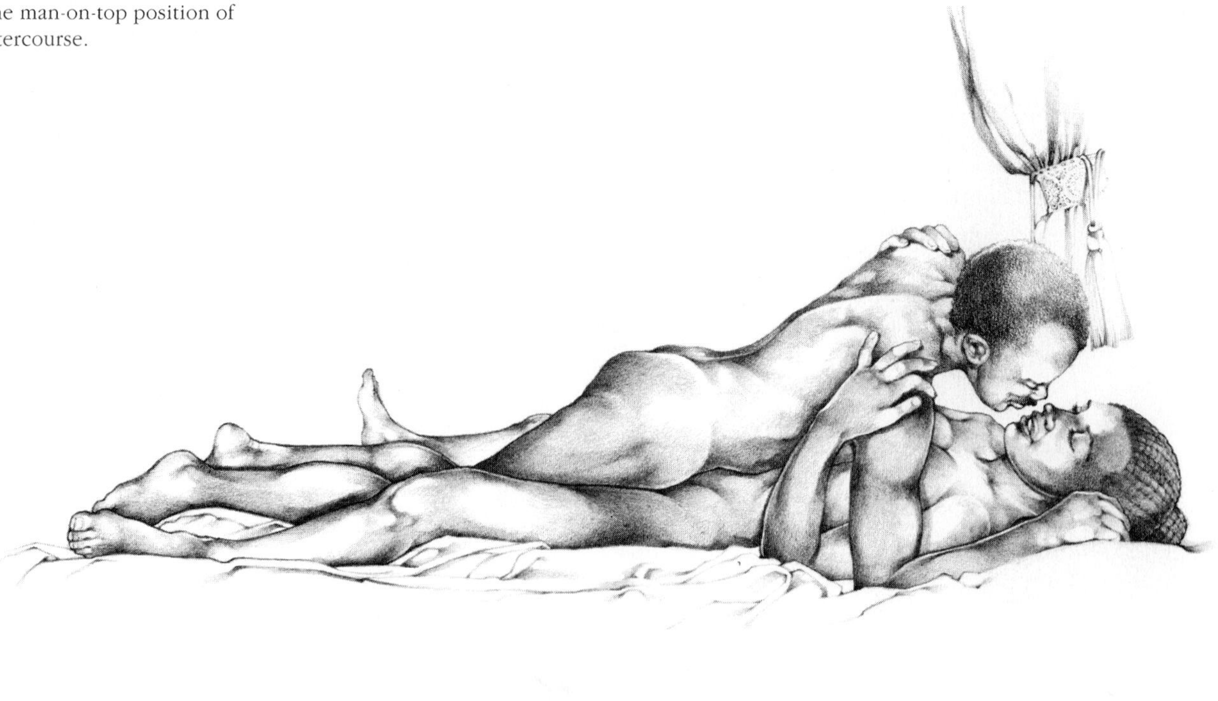

moves on top of her as she spreads her legs apart, either he or she spreads the vaginal lips apart, and he inserts his penis into her vagina. He supports himself on his knees and hands or elbows and moves his penis in and out of the vagina (pelvic thrusting). Some men worry that their heavy weight will crush the poor woman under them; however, because the weight is spread out over so great an area, most women do not find this to be a problem at all, and many find the sensation of contact to be pleasurable.

The woman can have her legs in a number of positions that create variations. She may have them straight out horizontally, a position that produces a tight rub on the penis but does not permit it to go deeply into the vagina. She may bend her legs and elevate them to varying degrees, or she may hook them over the man's back or over his shoulders. The last approach permits the penis to move deeply into the vagina. The woman can also move her pelvis, either up and down or side to side, to produce further stimulation.

The man-on-top position has some advantages and some disadvantages. It is the best position for ensuring conception, if that is what you want to ensure. It leaves the woman's hands free to stroke the man's body (or her own, for that matter). The couple may feel better able to express their love or to communicate other feelings, since they are facing each other. This position, however, does not work well if the woman is in the advanced stages of pregnancy or if either she or the man is extremely fat. Sex therapists have also found that it is not a very good position if the male wants to control his ejaculation; the woman-on-top position is better for this (see Chapter 20).

Woman-on-Top

There are a number of ways of getting into the woman-on-top position (Figure 9.5). You can begin by inserting the penis into the vagina while in the man-on-top position and then rolling over. Another possibility is to begin with the man on his back; the woman kneels over him, with one knee on either side of his hips. Then his hand or her hand guides the erect penis into the vagina as she lowers herself onto it. She then moves her hips to produce the stimulation. Beyond that, there are numerous variations, depending on where she puts her legs. She can remain on her knees, or she can straighten out her legs behind her, putting them outside his legs or between them. Or she can even turn around and face toward his feet.

This position has a number of advantages. It provides a lot of clitoral stimulation, and the woman can control the kind of stimulation she gets; thus many women find it the best position for them to have an orgasm. It is also a good position for the man who wants to delay his ejaculation, and for this reason it is used in sex therapy. This position is also a good one if the man is tired and it seems advisable for the woman to supply most of the movement. Further, the couple face each other, facilitating better communication, and each has the hands free to stroke the other.

Rear-Entry

In the rear-entry position, the man faces the woman's back. One way to do this is to have the woman kneel with her head down; the man kneels and inserts his penis into her vagina (Figure 9.6). (This is sometimes called the "dog position," because it is the manner in which dogs and most other animals copulate.) Another possibility is for the woman to lie on her stomach, raising her hips slightly so that the man can insert his penis while kneeling over her. Rear-entry can also be accomplished when the couple are in the side-to-side position (see below).

In this position the man's hands are free to stimulate the woman's clitoris or any

FIGURE 9.5

The woman-on-top position of intercourse.

other part of her body. The couple, however, do not face each other, and some couples dislike this aspect of the position. A small amount of air may enter the vagina when this position is used, producing interesting noises when it comes out.

Side-to-Side

In the side-to-side position, the man and woman lie beside each other, either face to face or in a rear-entry position (Figure 9.7). There are many variations beyond this, depending on where the arms and legs go—so many, in fact, that no attempt will be made to list them. One should be aware, though, that in this position an arm or a leg can get trapped under a heavy body and begin to feel numb, and shifting positions is sometimes necessary.

The side-to-side position is good for leisurely or prolonged intercourse or if one or both of the partners are tired. It is also good for the pregnant and the obese. At least some hands are free to stimulate the clitoris, the scrotum, or whatever.

Other Variations

Aside from the variations in these basic positions that can be produced by switching the position of the legs, there are many other possibilities for variations. For example, the man-on-top position can be varied by having the woman lie on the edge of a bed with her feet on the floor while the man kneels on the floor. Or the woman can lie on the edge of a table while the man stands (don't forget to close the curtains first). Both these positions produce a somewhat tighter vagina and therefore more stimulation for the penis. Or the man can sit on a chair and insert the penis as the woman sits on his lap, using either a face-to-face or a rear-entry approach. Or, with both partners standing, the man can lift the woman onto his erect penis as she wraps her legs around his back, or she can put one leg over his shoulder (you have to be pretty athletic to manage this one, however).

Mouth-Genital Stimulation

One of the most striking features of the sexual revolution of the last few decades is the increased popularity of mouth-genital, or oral-genital, techniques (Hunt, 1974). There are two kinds of mouth-genital stimulation ("going down on" one's partner): cunnilingus and fellatio.

Figure 9.6

The rear-entry position of intercourse.

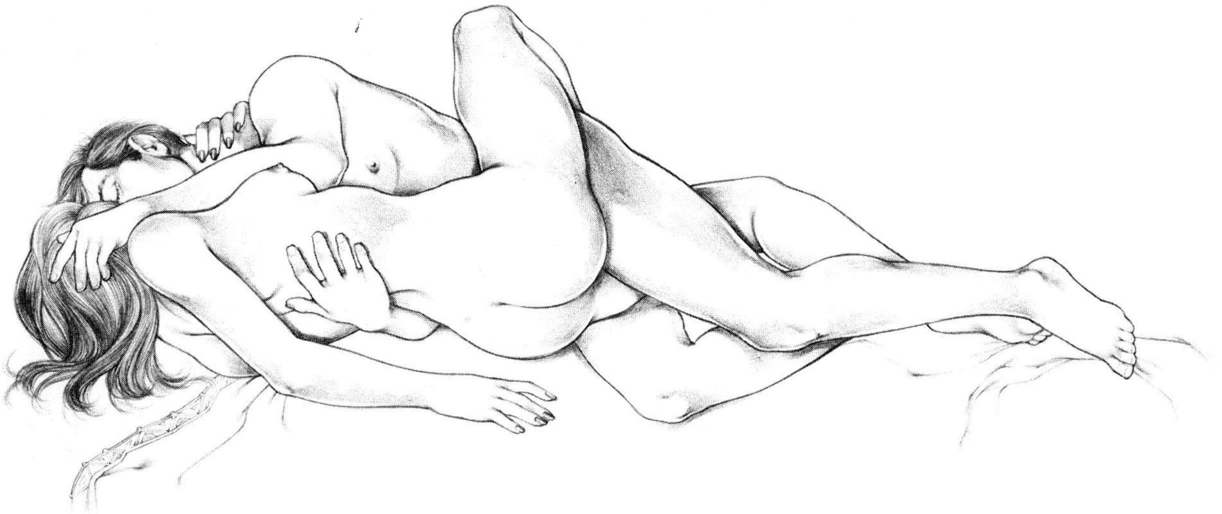

FIGURE 9.7

The side-to-side position of intercourse.

Cunnilingus (cun-ih-LING-us): Mouth stimulation of the female genitals.

Cunnilingus

In cunnilingus, or "eating" (from the Latin words *cunnus,* meaning "vulva," and *lingere,* meaning "to lick"), the woman's genitals are stimulated by her partner's mouth. Generally the focus of stimulation is the clitoris, and the tongue stimulates it and the surrounding area with quick darting or thrusting movements, or the mouth can suck at the clitoris. A good prelude to cunnilingus can be kissing of the inner thighs or the belly, gradually moving to the clitoris. The mouth can also suck at the inner lips, or the tongue can stimulate the vaginal entrance or be inserted into the vagina. During cunnilingus, some women also enjoy having a finger inserted into the vagina or the anus for added stimulation. The best way to know what she wants is through communication between partners, either verbally or nonverbally.

Many women today are enthusiastic about cunnilingus and say that it is the best way, or perhaps the only way, for them to have orgasm. Such responses are well within the normal range of female sexuality. As one woman put it:

> A tongue offers gentleness and precision and wetness and is the perfect organ for contact. And, besides, it produces sensational orgasms. (Hite, 1976, p. 234)

Cunnilingus poses no health problems; in fact, some health experts say that the vagina is cleaner (has fewer bacteria) than the mouth, and few people worry about the health risks associated with kissing. One exception should be noted, though. Some women enjoy having their partner blow air forcefully into the vagina. While this technique is not dangerous under normal circumstances, when used on a pregnant woman it has been known to cause death (apparently as the result of air getting into the uterine veins), damage to the placenta, and embolism (Sadock and Sadock, 1976). Thus it should not be used on a pregnant woman.

Cunnilingus can be performed by either heterosexual couples or lesbian couples.

Fellatio

Fellatio (feh-LAY-shoh): Mouth stimulation of the male genitals.

In fellatio[4] ("sucking," "a blow job") the man's penis is stimulated by his partner's mouth. The partner licks the glans of the penis, its shaft, and perhaps the testicles.

[4]"Fellatio" is from the Latin word *fellare,* meaning "to suck." Women should not take the "sucking" part too literally. The penis, particularly at the tip, is a delicate organ and should not be treated like a straw in an extra-thick milkshake.

The penis is gently taken into the mouth. If it is not fully erect, an erection can generally be produced by stronger sucking combined with hand stimulation along the penis. After that, the partner can produce an in-and-out motion by moving the lips down toward the base of the penis and then back up, always being careful not to scrape the penis with the teeth. Or the tongue can be flicked back and forth around the tip of the penis or along the corona.

To bring the man to orgasm, the in-and-out motion is continued, moving the penis deeper and deeper into the mouth and perhaps also using the fingers to encircle the base of the penis and give further stimulation. Sometimes when the penis moves deeply toward the throat, it stimulates a gag reflex, which occurs anytime something comes into contact with that part of the throat. To avoid this, the partner should concentrate on relaxing the throat muscles while firming the lips to provide more stimulation to the penis.

When a couple are engaged in fellatio, the big question in their minds may concern ejaculation. The man may, of course, simply withdraw his penis from his partner's mouth and ejaculate outside it. Or he may ejaculate into it, and his partner may even enjoy swallowing the ejaculate. The ejaculate resembles partially cooked egg white in texture; it does not have a very distinctive flavor but often leaves a salty aftertaste. Because some people have mixed feelings about having the semen in their mouths, it is probably a good idea for the couple to discuss ahead of time (or during the activity) what they plan to do.

Most men find fellatio to be a highly stimulating experience, which no doubt accounts for the high frequency with which prostitutes are asked to do it. Enjoyment of fellatio is certainly within the normal range of male sexuality.

Fellatio can be performed by either heterosexuals or male homosexual couples.

Sixty-nining: Simultaneous mouth-genital stimulation; also called "soixante-neuf."

Sixty-Nining

Fellatio and cunnilingus can be performed simultaneously by both partners. This is often called sixty-nining[5] because the numerals "69" suggest the position of the two

[5]If you want to be elegant and impress your friends, you can call it *soixante-neuf,* which is just "sixty-nine" in French.

FIGURE 9.8

Simultaneous mouth-genital stimulation in the sixty-nine position.

bodies during simultaneous mouth-genital sex. Sixty-nining may be done either side to side or with one person on top of the other, each with the mouth on the other's genitals (Figure 9.8).

Simultaneous mouth-genital sex allows both people to enjoy the pleasure of that stimulation at the same time. It can give a feeling of total body involvement and total involvement between partners. Some couples, however, feel that this technique requires doing too many things at once and is more complicated than enjoyable. For example, the woman may be distracted from enjoying the marvelous clitoral stimulation she is receiving because she has to concentrate at the same time on using her mouth to give good stimulation to the penis. If sixty-nining is done in the man-on-top position, some women also feel that they have no control over the movement and that they may be choked.

Anal Intercourse

Anal intercourse: Insertion of the penis into the partner's rectum.

In anal intercourse the man inserts his penis into his partner's rectum (Morin, 1981). In legal terminology it is sometimes called sodomy (although this term may also refer to other things such as intercourse with animals), and it is sometimes referred to as having sex "Greek style." It may be done by either heterosexual couples or male homosexual couples.

Anal intercourse is somewhat more difficult than penis-in-vagina intercourse because the rectum has no natural lubrication and because it is surrounded by fairly tight muscles. The man should therefore begin by moistening the partner's anus, either with saliva or with a sterile surgical lubricant such as K-Y jelly (*not* Vaseline). He should also lubricate his penis. He then inserts it gently into the rectum and begins controlled pelvic thrusting. It is typically done in the rear-entry position or in the man-on-top position. The more the partner can relax, the less uncomfortable it is; if it is done properly, it need involve no pain. While some heterosexual couples find the idea repulsive, others delight in it. Some women report orgasm during anal intercourse, particularly when it is accompanied by hand stimulation of the clitoris. Gay men also report orgasms from anal intercourse, primarily due to stimulation of the prostate.

Anal intercourse may be chosen if the woman is having a particularly heavy menstrual flow, if her vagina is very loose and the man wants more stimulation, or simply if more variety in sexual techniques is desired.

Anilingus (AY-nih-ling-us): Mouth stimulation of the partner's anus.

Another variation is anilingus (*feuille de rose* in French, "rimming" in slang), in which the tongue and mouth stimulate the anus. The anus may also be stimulated by the hand, and some people report that having a finger inserted into the rectum near the time of orgasm provides a heightened sexual sensation. Anilingus carries with it some risk of getting either hepatitis or *E. coli* infections.

Although anal intercourse is basically safe, one health risk should be noted. The penis should never be inserted into the vagina after anal intercourse unless it has been washed thoroughly. The reason for this is that the rectum contains bacteria which do not belong in the vagina and which can cause a dandy case of vaginitis if they happen to get there.

Techniques of Gays and Lesbians

Some people have difficulty imagining exactly what gays do in bed; after all, the important ingredients for sex are one penis and one vagina, aren't they?

Interfemoral intercourse: A sexual technique used by male homosexuals in which one man moves his penis between the thighs of the other.

Tribadism (TRY-bad-izm): A sexual technique in which one woman lies on top of another and moves rhythmically in order to produce sexual pleasure, particularly clitoral stimulation.

The preliminaries consist, as they do for heterosexuals, of kissing, hugging, and petting. Male homosexuals engage in mutual masturbation, oral-genital sex (fellatio), and, less frequently, anal intercourse (also called *sodomy* in legal terminology in the United States and *buggery* in England). Male homosexuals sometimes also engage in interfemoral intercourse, in which one man's penis moves between the thighs of the other. Lesbians engage in mutual masturbation, oral-genital sex (cunnilingus), and a practice called tribadism ("dry hump"), in which heterosexual intercourse is imitated, with one partner lying on top of the other and making thrusting movements so that both receive genital stimulation. According to *The Gay Report,* this is a common practice (Jay and Young, 1979). A rare practice is the use of an artificial penis, or dildo, by one person to stimulate the other. Of course, dildos are also used by heterosexual women in masturbation, although they probably appear much more frequently in men's fantasies than they do in women's hands.

An important point to note about these practices is that they are all behaviors in which heterosexuals also engage. That is, homosexuals do the same things sexually that heterosexuals do. The only thing that is distinctive about the homosexual act is that both partners are of the same gender.

Masters and Johnson (1979), in their laboratory studies, have done direct observations of the lovemaking techniques of gays, and compared them with those of straights. They found that, in masturbation techniques, there were no differences. However, in couple interactions there were some substantial differences. The major one was that homosexuals "took their time"—that is, they seemed not to have any goal orientation. Heterosexual couples, on the other hand, seemed to be performance-oriented—they seemed to strive toward a goal of orgasm for each. In the initial approach to stimulating the female, heterosexuals and lesbians began with holding and kissing, but this only lasted about 30 seconds for the heterosexuals, who quickly moved on to genital stimulation. Lesbians, on the other hand, spent more time in holding and kissing and then went on to a long period of breast stimulation, which sometimes resulted in orgasm in the absence of genital stimulation. This breast stimulation was a major difference between heterosexual and homosexual techniques. Lesbians also appeared to communicate more with each other. In the initial approach to stimulating the male, gays did extensive stimulation of the nipples, generally producing erection; such a technique was rare among heterosexuals (only with 3 of 100 couples). Homosexuals were also much more likely to stimulate the frenulum (the area of the penis on the lower side, just below the corona). Homosexuals also used a "teasing technique" in which the man brings his partner near orgasm, then relaxes the stimulation, then increases the stimulation again, and so on, essentially prolonging the pleasure. Among heterosexuals, the husband's most frequent complaint was that the wife did not grasp the shaft of the penis tightly enough. Masters and Johnson argue that heterosexuals can learn from homosexuals; the technique of gays benefits from stimulating another body like their own.

APHRODISIACS

Is There a Good Aphrodisiac?

Aphrodisiac (ah-froh-DIZ-ih-ak): A substance that increases sexual desire.

An aphrodisiac is something—such as a food, a drug, or a perfume—that excites sexual desire. Throughout history people have searched for the "surefire" aphrodisiac. Before arousing your hopes, I should note that the search has been unsuccessful; there is no known substance that works well as an aphrodisiac.

One popular idea is that oysters are an aphrodisiac. This notion appears to be an example of the idea that foods that resemble sexual organs have sexual powers. For example, bananas resemble the penis and have been thought to be aphrodisiacs; perhaps oysters are thought to have such powers because of their resemblance to the testes (MacDougald, 1961). Another example is the Chinese belief that powdered rhinoceros horn is an aphrodisiac (perhaps this is also the origin of the term "horny"). Oysters, however, contain no substances that can in any way influence sexual functioning (Neiger, 1968).

Doubtless some substances gain a continued reputation as aphrodisiacs because simply believing that something will be arousing can itself be arousing. Thus the belief that a bull's testicles ("prairie oysters") or peanuts or clams have sexual powers may produce a temporary improvement in sexual functioning, not because of the chemicals contained in them but because of a belief in them (McCary, 1973).

Alcohol also has a reputation as an aphrodisiac. The effects of alcohol on sexual functioning will be discussed in Chapter 20. Briefly, drinking small quantities of alcohol may, for some people, decrease psychological inhibitions and therefore increase sexual desire. Moderate to large quantities, however, rapidly lead to an inability to function sexually.

Users of marijuana report that it acts as a sexual stimulant. Probably this is due, in part, to the fact that marijuana produces the sensation that time is being stretched out, thus prolonging and intensifying sensations, including sexual sensations. There is no scientific documentation of the aphrodisiac effects of marijuana except for the reports of users. Possible negative effects of marijuana on sexual functioning are discussed in Chapter 20.

Unfortunately, some of the substances that are thought to enhance sexual functioning are quite dangerous. For example, cantharides (Spanish fly) has a reputation as an aphrodisiac, but it is poisonous (Craven and Polak, 1954; Nickolls and Teare, 1954; for further information, see Kaplan, 1974; Leavitt, 1974).

Amyl nitrate ("poppers") is popular among some homosexuals and some heterosexuals. Users report that it produces heightened sensations during orgasms (Everett, 1975). Probably it acts by dilating the blood vessels in the genitals. It may, however, have side effects, including dizziness, headaches, fainting, and, in rare cases, death; thus it can be dangerous (Louria, 1970).

Butyl nitrite—sold under such trade names as Rush, Locker Room, Climax, and Discorama—is a chemical relative of amyl nitrate. It is used to heighten sexual pleasure, and it is sometimes used in disco dancing. Although no deaths have been reported from inhaling it, there are two reported deaths from swallowing it (UPI, 1981).

Anaphrodisiacs

Anaphrodisiac (an-ah-froh-DIZ-ih-ak): A substance that decreases sexual desire.

Just as people have searched for aphrodisiacs, so they have sought anaphrodisiacs substances or practices that would diminish sexual desire. Cold showers are reputed to have such effects, as is potassium nitrate (saltpeter). The latter contains nothing that decreases sexual drive, but it does act as a diuretic; it makes the person want to urinate frequently, which may be distracting enough so that he or she is not much interested in sex.

There has been some medical interest in finding drugs that would decrease sex drive for use in treating aggressive sexual offenders. One such drug is cyproterone acetate. There have been reports of its successful use in England, Germany, and Switzerland, as well as the United States, but it is too soon to know whether it is truly effective and lacking in side effects (Associated Press, 1971; Intelligence Report, 1971).

Other drugs that may lead to a loss of sexual functioning are discussed in Chapter 20.

ARE INTERCOURSE AND ORGASM THE GOAL?

Traditionally in our culture it has been the belief that a sexual encounter should "climax" with intercourse and orgasm, at least orgasm for the man. In our modern era of multiple orgasms for women and general sexual liberation, the view that intercourse is the important part of sex and that orgasm is the goal toward which both must strive is pervasive. This belief system is reflected in the term "foreplay," which implies that activities like hand stimulation of the genitals, kissing, and mouth-genital sex are only preliminaries that take place before intercourse, the latter being "real sex." Similar beliefs are reflected in a commonly used phrase, "achieving orgasm," as if orgasm were something to be achieved like a promotion on the job.[6]

Psychologist Rollo May feels that men particularly, by concentrating on "achieving" orgasm and *satisfying* their desire, miss out on the more important part of the sexual experience: prolonging the feeling of desire and pleasure, building it higher and higher. As he puts it:

> The pleasure in sex is described by Freud and others as the reduction of tension [orgasm]; in eros, on the contrary, we wish not to be released from the excitement but rather to hang on to it, to bask in it, and even to increase it. (1974, pp. 71–72)

Marc Feigen Fasteau, a men's liberation leader, argues that although orgasm is good, a larger part of pleasure is building up to orgasm:

> What the masculine disdain for feeling makes it hard for men to grasp is that the state of desire . . . is one of the best perhaps *the* best, part of the experience of love. (1974, p. 31)

Another one of the "goals" of sex that has emerged recently is the simultaneous orgasm. Some people consider this an event to be worked for rather than a pleasant thing that sometimes happens.

The legacy of the Protestant ethic in our culture is that our achievement drives now seem to be channeled into our sexual behaviors (see Focus 9.1). There is nothing intrinsically wrong with expressing achievement drives in sex, except that anytime there is an achievement situation, there is also the potential for a failure. If she does not have an orgasm or if he cannot get an erection, the couple feel as if the whole experience was a disaster. The problem with setting up sexual goals, then, is that the possibility of sexual failures or sexual dysfunctions is also being set up.

The best approach is probably to enjoy all the various aspects of lovemaking for themselves, rather than as techniques for achieving something, and to concentrate on sex as a feast of the senses, rather than as an achievement competition.

---

[6]To avoid this whole notion, I never use the phrase "to achieve orgasm" in this book. Instead, I prefer "to have an orgasm" or simply "to orgasm." Why not turn it into a verb so that we will not have to work at achieving it?

F · O · C · U · S
9.1

THE PROTESTANT ETHIC: SEX AS WORK

Sociologist Philip Slater has argued that the old Protestant ethic—work hard and become successful—is alive and well in modern American sexual attitudes. According to him, we turn sex into work and then work hard to become successful at it.

Our discussions of sex tend to focus on orgasm rather than on pleasure in general. Orgasm is the observable "product," and we are concerned with how many orgasms we can produce or have, much as a plant manager is concerned with how many cans of soup are produced on the assembly line each day.

The emphasis on "simultaneous orgasm" may express how clock-oriented we are. It is important for us to have things running on schedule and happening at exactly the right time, and so orgasms must also be timed perfectly.

We tend to use the term "adequacy" in relation to sex and to set standards of sexual performance, much as we would set standards of work performance on the job. Ironically, according to current definitions of "adequacy," a man is considered adequate if he can delay his orgasm, whereas a woman is considered adequate if she can make hers happen faster. Why does the same standard not apply to both? The answer has to do with our concept of orgasm as a "product" and with our concern about timing.

Slater also argues that work (on the job) and sex are natural enemies. The more a person becomes dedicated to work and the more time she or he spends on it, the greater the inroads on the sex life. This is substantiated in a study of successful executives, government officials, and professionals (*Sex and the Significant Americans,* by John Cuber and Peggy Harroff). For those in the study, sex was brief and perfunctory. Their commitment to work left little time for, or interest in, sex.

One might even speculate that the more we see sex as work and apply performance standards to it, the more "failures"—sexual dysfunctions—we shall have.

As Slater put it:

> The preoccupation in Western sexual literature with orgasm seems to be a natural extension of the Protestant work ethic in which nothing is to be enjoyed for its own sake except striving.
>
> The antithetical attitude would be to view orgasm as a delightful interruption in an otherwise continuous process of generating pleasurable sensations. (1973, p. 134)

Source: P. E. Slater. (1973, Dec.). Sexual adequacy in America. *Intellectual Digest,* pp. 132–135. See also George W. Albee. (1977). The Protestant ethic, sex, and psychotherapy. *American Psychologist,* **32**, pp. 150–161.

FROM INEXPERIENCE TO BOREDOM

Some people, after an initial lack of experience with sex, shift rather quickly to becoming bored with it, with perhaps only a brief span of self-confident, pleasurable sexuality in between. Most of us, of course, are sexually inexperienced early in our lives, and most of us feel bored with the way we are having sex at times. How do we deal with these problems?

Sexual Inexperience

In our culture we expect men to be "worldly" about sex—to have had experience with it and to be skillful in the use of sexual techniques. A man or a boy who is sexually inexperienced (perhaps a virgin) or who has had only a few sexual experiences, with little opportunity to practice, may have a real fear about whether he will be able to "perform" (the achievement ethic again) in a sexual encounter. With the sexual revolution has come an increasing expectation that women also should have a bag of sexual tricks ready to use, and so they, too, are increasingly expected to be experienced.

How can one deal with this problem of inexperience? First, it is important to question society's assumption that one should be experienced (see, for example, Glassberg, 1970). Everyone has to begin sometime, and there is absolutely nothing wrong with inexperience. Second, there are many good books and articles on sexual techniques that are definitely worth reading, although it is important to be selective, since a few of these may be more harmful than helpful. This chapter should be a good introduction; you also might want to consult *The Joy of Sex, More Joy of Sex,* or any of the self-help manuals listed at the end of Chapter 20, particularly Raley's *Making Love.* Do not become slavishly attached to the techniques you read about in books, though; they should serve basically as a stimulus to your imagination, not as a series of steps that must be followed. Third, communicate with your partner. Because individual preferences vary so much, no one, no matter how experienced, is ever a sexual expert with a new partner. The best way to please a partner is to find out what that person likes, and communication may accomplish this better than prior experience. A later section in this chapter gives some specific tips on communication. Interestingly, one study found that the best sexual predictor of relationship satisfaction was not frequency of sex or techniques but mutual agreement on sexual issues (Markman, personal communication).

Boredom

The opposite problem to inexperience is the feeling of boredom in a long-term sexual relationship. Boredom, of course, is not always a necessary consequence of having sex with the same person over a long period of time. Certainly there are couples who have been married for 40 or 50 years and who continue to find sexual expression exciting. Unfortunately, the major sex surveys have not inquired about the phenomenon of boredom, and thus it is not possible to estimate the percentage of people who eventually become bored or who experience occasional fits of boredom. However, such experiences are surely common. As someone once said, a rut is no place to be making love. How can we deal with the problem of boredom?

Communication can help in this situation, as it can in others. Couples sometimes evolve a routine sexual sequence that leads to boredom, and sometimes that sequence is not really what either person wants. By communicating to each other what they really would like to do and then doing it, two people can introduce some variety into their relationship. The various love manuals can also give ideas on new techniques. Finally, a couple's sexual relationship often mirrors the other aspects of their relationship, and sexual boredom may sometimes mean that they are generally bored with each other. Rejuvenating the rest of the relationship—perhaps taking up a hobby or a sport together or going on a good vacation, during which they really try to build their relationship in general—may do wonders for their sexual relationship.

One might also question the meaning of "boredom." Perhaps our expectations for sexual experience are too high. Encouraged by the media, we tend to believe that every time we have intercourse, the earth should move. We do not expect that every meal we eat will be fantastic or that we will always have a huge appetite and enjoy every bite. Yet we do tend to have such expectations with regard to sexuality. Perhaps when boredom seems to be a problem, it is not the real issue; rather, the problem may be unrealistically high expectations.

COMMUNICATION AND SEX

Consider the following situation:

> Sam and Donna have been married for about three years. Donna had not had intercourse with anyone but Sam before marriage, and she had never masturbated. Since they've been married, she has had orgasms only twice during intercourse, despite the fact that they make love three or four times per week. She has been reading some magazine articles about female sexuality, and she is beginning to think that she should be experiencing more sexual satisfaction. As far as she knows, Sam is unaware that there is any problem. Donna feels lonely and a bit sad.

What should Donna do? She needs to communicate with Sam. They apparently have not communicated much about sex in the last three years, and they need to begin. The following sections will discuss the relationship between sex, communication, and relationships and provide some suggestions on how to communicate effectively.

Communication and Building a Good Relationship

A good deal of research has looked at differences in communication patterns between nondistressed (happy) married couples and distressed (unhappy, seeking marital counseling) married couples. This research shows, in general, that distressed couples tend to have communication deficits (Markman and Floyd, 1980). Research also shows that couples seeking therapy for sex problems have poor communication patterns compared with nondistressed couples (Zimmer, 1983). Of course, there are many other factors that contribute to marital or relationship conflict, or sex problems, but poor communication patterns are certainly among them. The problem with this research is that it is correlational (see Chapter 10 for a discussion of this problem in research methods)—in particular, we cannot tell whether poor communication causes unhappy marriages or whether unhappy marriages create poor communication patterns.

An elegant longitudinal study designed to meet this problem provides evidence that unrewarding, ineffective communication precedes and predicts later relationship problems (Markman, 1979; 1981). Dating couples who were planning marriage were studied for 5½ years. The more positively couples rated their communication interactions at the beginning of the study, the more satisfaction they reported in their relationship when they were followed up 2½ years later and 5½ years later.

On the basis of this notion that communication deficits cause relationship problems, marriage counselors and marital therapists often work on teaching couples better communication skills. Research shows that this training is effective (e.g., Jacobson, 1978; Wampler 1982). After training to improve communication skills, couples show improved communication and report more satisfaction in their relationships.

One such program is Relationship Enhancement Therapy (Guerney, 1977). The purpose of RE programs is to increase the psychological and emotional satisfaction that can be derived from intimate relationships; this is accomplished in large part by communication skills training. The goal is to develop an empathic relationship in which the participants have compassionate understanding of their own and the other's thoughts, needs, and feelings, and good communication is essential to doing so. RE programs are probably better viewed as education rather than therapy, and they can be used for enrichment with happily married couples, for therapy with distressed couples, and for "preventive medicine" training with premarital couples (Ginsberg and Vogelsong, 1977). The goal of communication skills training with premarital couples is to establish good communication early in the relationship, trying to prevent relationship problems later on (Gottman and Floyd, 1980).

All in all, it is clear that good communication patterns are important in developing and maintaining good intimate relationships. The sections that follow will describe some of the skills that are involved in good communication. They are techniques that are often recommended by therapists. These ideas arise from extensive programs of research comparing distressed and nondistressed couples (e.g., Gottman et al., 1976) to see exactly how the happy, nondistressed couple communicate differently from the unhappy one; the ideas are also based on the experiences of marital therapists.

Be an Effective Communicator

Back to Donna and Sam: One of the first things to do in a situation like Donna's is to decide to talk to one's partner, admitting that there is a communication gap. Then the issue is to resolve to communicate, and particularly to be an *effective* communicator. Suppose Donna begins by saying,

You're not giving me any orgasms when we have sex. **(1)**

FIGURE 9.9

Sam gets angry and walks away. Donna meant to communicate that she wasn't having any orgasms, but Sam thought she meant that he was a lousy lover. It is important to recognize the distinction between intent and impact in communicating (Gottman et al., 1976). Intent is what you mean. A good communicator is one whose impact matches her or his intent. Donna wasn't an effective communicator in the above example because the impact on Sam was considerably different from her intent.

Intent:
What the speaker means.

Impact:
What someone else understands the speaker to mean.

Effective communicator:
A communicator whose impact matches his or her intent.

Many people value spontaneity in sex, and this attitude may extend to communicating about sex. It is best to recognize that to be an effective communicator, it may be necessary to plan your strategy (Langer and Dweck, 1973). It often takes some thinking to figure out how to make sure that your impact matches your intent. Planning also allows you to make sure that the timing is good—that you are not speaking out of anger, or that your partner is not tired or preoccupied with other things (Brenton, 1972).

Finally, we ought to recognize that it is going to be harder for Donna to broach this subject than it would be to ask Sam why he didn't take out the garbage as he had promised. It is hard for most people to talk about sex, particularly sexual problems, with their partners.[7] Ironically, in the last few decades public communication about sex has become relatively open, but private communication remains difficult (Brenton, 1972). That doesn't mean that Donna can't communicate. But she shouldn't feel guilty or stupid because it is difficult for her. And she will be better off if she uses some specific communication skills and has some belief that they will work. The sections that follow suggest some skills that are useful in being an effective communicator and how to apply these to sexual relationships.

Leveling and Editing

Leveling:
Telling your partner what you are feeling by stating your thoughts clearly, simply, and honestly.

Leveling means that you tell your partner what you are feeling by stating your thoughts clearly, simply, and honestly (Gottman et al., 1976). It is really the first step in communication and is often the hardest. In leveling keep in mind that the purposes are:

1. To make communication clear
2. To clear up what partners expect of each other
3. To clear up what is pleasant and what is unpleasant
4. To clear up what is relevant and what is irrelevant
5. To notice things that draw you closer or push you apart (Gottman et al., 1976)

Editing:
Censoring or not saying things that would be deliberately hurtful to your partner or that are irrelevant.

When you begin to level with your partner, you also need to do some editing. Editing involves censoring (not saying) things that would be deliberately hurtful to your partner or that would be irrelevant. You must take responsibility for making your communication polite and considerate. Leveling, then, should not mean a "no holds barred" approach. Ironically, research indicates that married people are ruder to each other than they are to strangers (Gottman et al., 1976).

[7]In fact, a survey of students in human sexuality courses at two universities indicated that sexual "pleases" and "displeases" are the most difficult topics to talk about with one's partner. Further, women seem more aware of problems in this aspect of the relationship than men are (Markman, personal communication).

FIGURE 9.10

Donna may be so disgruntled about her lack of orgasms that she's thinking of having an affair to jolt Sam into recognizing her problem, or perhaps in order to see if another man would stimulate her to orgasm. Donna is probably best advised to edit out this line of thought and concentrate on the specific problem: her lack of orgasms. If they can solve that, she won't need to have the affair anyway.

The trick is to balance leveling and editing. If you edit too much, you may not level at all, and there will be no communication. If you level too much and don't edit, the communication will fail because your partner will respond negatively, and things may get worse rather than better.

Good Messages

"I" language: Speaking for yourself, using the word "I"; not mind reading.

One tip that couples communication experts give is to use I language (e.g., Brenton, 1972). That is, speak for yourself, not your partner (Miller et al., 1975). By doing this you focus on what you know best—your own thoughts and feelings. "I" language is less likely to make your partner defensive. If Donna were to use this technique, she might say,

I feel a bit unhappy because I don't have orgasms very often when we make love. **(2)**

Notice that she focuses specifically on herself. There is less cause for Sam to get angry than there was in message 1.

One of the best things about "I" language is that it avoids mind reading (Gottman et al., 1976). Suppose Donna says,

> I know you think women aren't much interested in sex, but I really wish I had more orgasms. **(3)**

Mind reading:
Making assumptions about what your partner thinks or feels.

She is engaging in mind reading That is, she is making certain assumptions about what Sam is thinking. She assumes that Sam believes women aren't interested in sex or having orgasms. Research shows that mind reading is more common among distressed couples than among nondistressed couples (Gottman et al., 1977). Worse, she doesn't *check out* her assumptions with Sam. The problem is that she may be wrong, and Sam may not think that at all. "I" language helps avoid this by focusing on me and what I feel rather than on what my partner is doing or failing to do. Another important way to avoid mind reading is by giving and receiving feedback, a technique to be discussed in a later section.

Documenting:
Giving specific examples of the issue being discussed.

Documenting is another important component of giving good messages (Brenton, 1972). In documenting you give specific examples of the issue. This is not quite so relevant in Donna's case, because she is talking about a general problem, but even here, specific documenting can be helpful. Once Donna has broached the subject, she might say,

> Last night when we made love, I enjoyed it and felt very aroused, but then I didn't have an orgasm, and I felt disappointed. **(4)**

Now she has gotten her general complaint down to a specific situation that Sam can remember.

Suppose further that Donna has some idea of what Sam would need to do to bring her to orgasm: he would have to do more hand stimulation of her clitoris. Then she might do specific documenting as follows:

> Last night when we made love, I enjoyed it, but I didn't have an orgasm, and then I felt disappointed. I think what I needed was for you to stimulate my clitoris with your hand a bit more. You did it for a while, but it seemed so brief. I think if you had kept doing it for two or three minutes more, I would have had an orgasm. **(5)**

Now she has not only documented to Sam exactly what the problem was, but she has given a specific suggestion about what could have been done about it, and therefore what could be done in the future.

Another technique in giving good messages is to offer *limited choices* (Langer and Dweck, 1973). Suppose Donna begins by saying,

> I've been having trouble with orgasms. Could we discuss it? **(6)**

The trouble with this approach is that a "no" from Sam is not really an acceptable answer to her because she definitely wants to discuss the problem. Yet she set up the question so that he could answer by saying "no." To use the technique of limited choices she might say,

> I've been having trouble with orgasms when we make love. Would you like to discuss it now, or would you rather wait until tomorrow night? **(7)**

Now, either answer he gives will be acceptable to her; she has offered a set of acceptable limited choices.[8] She has also shown some consideration for him by recognizing that he might not be in the mood for such a discussion now and would rather wait.

Breaking the Ice: Sex Manuals

As we have already noted, one of the most difficult things about situations like Donna and Sam's is just getting the communication started—breaking the ice. One possible approach is to suggest reading a sex manual together as an icebreaker. For example, Donna could go out and buy a copy of *The Joy of Sex,* bring it home, and suggest to Sam that they read and discuss it together. When they get to the section on hand stimulation, it may be easier for Donna to raise the subject of her own desire for hand stimulation of the clitoris.

A side benefit of this approach is that Donna and Sam may find out about some techniques that they weren't aware of or had been afraid to do. For example, Donna may have secret thoughts that cunnilingus would be nice and might help her to have orgasms, but she is afraid to mention it to Sam because she thinks he would be repulsed by the idea. Sam might be thinking that Donna might enjoy cunnilingus, but he is afraid to bring up the subject, fearing that she may be shocked. Note that they have both been doing some mind reading. When they get to the section on mouth-genital sex in the manual, their discussion may be able to clear up some of their assumptions. And Donna may even be able to learn some more about what Sam would like sexually.

Nonverbal communication: Communication not through words, but through the body, e.g., eye contact, tone of voice, touching.

Body Talk: Nonverbal Communication

Often the precise words we use are not so important as the way we say them. Tone of voice, expression on the face, position of the body, whether you touch the other person—all are important in conveying the message.

As an example, take the sentence "So you're here." If it is delivered "So *you're* here" in a hostile tone of voice, the message is that the speaker is very unhappy that you're here. If it is delivered "So you're *here*" in a pleased voice, the meaning may be that the speaker is glad and surprised to see you here in Ohio, having thought you were in Europe. "So you're here" with a smile and arms outstretched to initiate a hug might mean that the speaker has been waiting for you and is delighted to see you.

Suppose that in Donna and Sam's case, the reason Donna doesn't have more orgasms is that Sam simply doesn't stimulate her vigorously enough. During sex, Donna has adopted a very passive, nearly rigid posture for her body. Sam doesn't stimulate her more vigorously because he is afraid that he might hurt her, and he is sure that no lady like his wife would want such a vigorous approach. The response

---

[8]The technique of limited choices is useful in a number of other situations, including dealing with children. For example, when my 2-year-old has finished watching *Sesame Street* and I want the TV turned off, I don't say, "Would you turn the TV off?" (she might say "no"), but, rather, "Do you want to turn off the TV, or would you like me to?" Of course, sometimes she evades my efforts and says "no" anyway, but most of the time it works.

FIGURE 9.11

(*a*) A couple with good body language (good eye contact and body position); (*b*) A couple with poor body language (poor eye contact and body position)

(or rather nonresponse) of her body confirms his assumptions. Her body is saying "I don't enjoy this. Let's get it over with." And that's exactly what she's getting. To correct this situation, she might adopt a more active, encouraging approach. She might take his hand and guide it to her clitoris, showing him the kind of firm way she likes to have it rubbed. She might place her hands on his hips and press to indicate how deep and forceful she would like the thrusting of his penis in her vagina to be. She might even take the daring approach of using some verbal communication and saying "That's good" when he becomes more vigorous.

The point is that in communicating about sex, we need to be sure that our nonverbal signals help to create the impact we intend rather than one that we don't intend. It is also possible that nonverbal signals are confusing communication and need to be straightened out. Checking out is a technique for doing this which will be discussed in a later section.

Interestingly, research shows that distressed couples differ from nondistressed couples more in their nonverbal communication than in their verbal communication (Gottman et al., 1977; Vincent et al., 1979). For example, even when a person from a distressed couple is expressing agreement with his or her spouse, that person is more likely to accompany the verbal expressions of agreement with negative nonverbal behavior. Distressed couples are also more likely to be negative listeners—while listening the individuals are more likely to display frowning, angry, or disgusted facial expressions, or tense or inattentive body postures. Once again, it is not only what we say verbally but how we say it, and how we listen nonverbally, that makes the difference.

Listening

Up to this point, we have been concentrating on techniques for you to use in sending messages about sexual relationships. But, of course, communication is a two-way street, and you and your partner will exchange responses. It is therefore important for you and your partner to gain some skills in listening and responding constructively to messages. The following discussion will suggest such techniques.

One of the most important things is that you must really *listen.* That means more than just removing the headphones from your ears. It means actively trying to understand what the other person is saying. Often people are so busy trying to think of their next response that they hardly hear what the other person is saying. Good listening also involves positive nonverbal behaviors, such as maintaining eye contact with the speaker and nodding one's head when appropriate.

Paraphrasing: Saying, in your own words, what you thought your partner meant.

The next step, after you have listened carefully, is to give *feedback.* This often will involve the technique of paraphrasing, that is, repeating in your own words what you thought your partner meant. Suppose, in response to Donna's initial statement, "You're not giving me any orgasms when we have sex," Sam hadn't walked away angrily. Instead, he tried to listen and then gave her feedback by paraphrasing. He might have responded,

> I hear you saying that I'm not very skillful at making love to you, and therefore you're not having orgasms. **(8)**

At that point, Donna would have had a chance to clear up the confusion she had created with her initial message, because Sam had given her feedback by paraphrasing his understanding of what she said. At that point she could have said, "No, I think you're a good lover, but I'm just not having any orgasms, and I don't know why. I thought maybe we could figure it out together." Or perhaps she could have said, "No, I think you're a good lover. I just wish you'd do some of the things you do more, like rubbing my clitoris."

It's also a good idea to *ask for feedback* from your partner, particularly if you're not sure whether you're communicating clearly.

Check Out Sexy Signals

One of the problems with verbal and nonverbal sexual communications is that they are often ambiguous. It is therefore important to check them out—ask the communicator exactly what she or he means—before proceeding.

Sue is at the office Christmas party. While she is in conversation with three people, one of them, Howard, puts his arm around her shoulder and gives her a quick hug. How should she interpret that? Is it a gesture of camaraderie and the goodwill of the Christmas spirit? Is he being patronizing, putting his arm around her shoulder as if she were a little girl? Or is he issuing an invitation to have sex at his place after the party? And what will it mean if she gives him a hug back? Is she spreading more Christmas cheer, or is she saying, "Sure, I'd like to go back to your place."

The problem is that most of us are very reticent about checking out the meaning in situations like this. Somehow we assume that we ought to know exactly what the person meant, and we are dumb or naive if we don't. It is important to recognize that many "sexy signals" like putting an arm around someone's shoulder are ambiguous; we need to make some effort to clear them up. But probably Sue would feel very awkward saying, "Excuse me, did that hug mean you want to have sex, or are you just being friendly?"

Probably Sue's best bet in this case is just to ignore the hug. But what if Howard continues to keep close to her for the next hour and starts raising his eyebrows? At that point she had better do some explicit checking out of his meaning. It's important to her to do that before she says "OK—let's go to your place now" because Howard may just be too shy to talk to anyone else and may have a muscle twitch around his eyebrows. It's also important for her to do some checking out before she gets angry at Howard for propositioning her if she's a married woman. The best rule here is not to make any assumptions about the meaning of ambiguous messages unless you have checked them out with the sender.

Validating

Validation:
Telling your partner that, given his or her point of view, you can see why he or she thinks a certain way.

One good technique in communication is validation (Gottman et al., 1976). This means that you communicate to your partner that, given his or her point of view, you can see why he or she thinks a certain way. It doesn't mean that you agree with your partner or that you're giving in. It simply means that you recognize your partner's point of view as legitimate, given his or her set of assumptions, which may be different from yours.

Suppose that Donna and Sam have gotten into an argument about cunnilingus. She wants him to do it and thinks it would bring her to orgasm. He doesn't want to do it because he finds the idea repulsive and because he believes no real man would do such a thing. If Donna tried to validate Sam's feelings, she might say,

> I can understand the way you feel about cunnilingus, especially given the way you were brought up about sex. **(9)**

Sam might validate Donna's feelings by saying,

> I understand how important it is for you to have an orgasm. **(10)**

Validating hasn't solved their disagreement, but it has left the door pleasantly open so that they can now make some progress.

Drawing Your Partner Out

Suppose it is Sam who initiates the conversation rather than Donna. Sam has noticed that Donna doesn't seem to get a lot of pleasure out of sex, and he would like to find out why and see what they can do about it. He needs to draw her out. He might begin by saying,

> I've noticed lately that you don't seem to be enjoying sex as much as you used to. Am I right about that? **(11)**

That much is good because he's checking out his assumption. Unfortunately, he's asked a question that leads to a "yes" or "no" answer, and that can stop the communication. So, if she replies "yes," he'd better follow it up with an *open-ended* question like

> Why do you think you aren't enjoying it more? **(12)**

If she can give a reasonable answer, good communication should be on the way. One of the standard—and best—questions to ask in a situation like this is

> What can we do to make things better? **(13)**

Fighting Fair

Fighting fair: A set of rules designed to make arguments constructive rather than destructive.

Even if you use all the techniques described above, you may still get into arguments with your partner. Arguments are a natural part of a relationship and are not necessarily bad. Given that there will be arguments in a relationship, it is useful if you and your partner have agreed to a set of rules called fighting fair (Bach and Wyden, 1969) so that the arguments may help and won't hurt.

Here are some of the basic rules for fighting fair that may be useful to you (Brenton, 1972):

1. Don't make sarcastic or insulting remarks about your partner's sexual adequacy. It generates resentment, opens you to counterattack, and is just a dirty way to fight.
2. Don't bring up the names of former spouses, lovers, boyfriends, or girlfriends to illustrate how all these problems didn't happen with them. Stick to the issue: your relationship with your partner.

FIGURE 9.13

Arguments are not necessarily bad for a relationship, but it is important to observe the rules for "fighting fair."

3. Don't play amateur psychologist. Don't say things like "The problem is that you're a compulsive personality" or "You acted that way because you never resolved your Oedipus complex." You really don't have the qualifications (even after reading this book) to do that kind of psychologizing. Even if you did, your partner would not be apt to recognize your expertise in the middle of an argument, thinking, quite rightly, that you're probably biased at the moment.
4. Don't threaten to tell your parents or run home. This involves ganging up on your partner or retreating like a child.
5. If you have children, don't bring them into the argument. It is too stressful emotionally to force them to take sides between Mom and Dad.

Take Responsibility for Your Own Pleasure

Self-awareness is essential to good couple communication (Miller et al., 1975). Up to this point, we have been assuming that if only Sam would change his technique a little bit, Donna would have her orgasm. The problem with this is that Donna is not taking responsibility for her own sexual pleasure; instead, she is expecting Sam to produce her orgasm for her. This isn't very effective, and it isn't fair to Sam.

The first step in taking responsibility for your own sexual pleasure is to get to know your own body and its responsiveness better. The exercise in Focus 9.2 is designed to help you do that. Once you have this knowledge, your responsibility is to communicate it to your partner.

Positive Communication

We have been concentrating on negative communications, that is, communications where some problem or complaint needs to be voiced. It is also important to communicate positive things about sex (Miller et al., 1975). If that was a great episode of lovemaking, or the best kiss you've ever experienced, say so. A learning theorist would say that you're giving your partner some positive reinforcement. Social psychologists' research shows that we tend to like people better who give us positive reinforcements (see Chapter 13). Recognition of the strengths in a relationship offers the potential for enriching it (e.g., Miller et al., 1975; Otto, 1963). And if you make a habit of positive communications about sex, it will be easier to initiate the negative ones, and they will be better received.

Most communication during sex is limited to muffled groans, or "Mm-m's," or an occasional "Higher, Harry" or "Did you, Diane?" It might help your partner greatly if you gave frequent verbal and nonverbal feedback such as "That was great" or "Let's do that again." That would make the positive communications and the negative ones far easier.

Research shows that nondistressed couples make more positive and fewer negative communications than distressed couples (Birchler et al., 1975; Billings, 1979). Not only do the happy couples make more positive communications; they are more likely to respond to a negative communication with something positive (Billings, 1979). Distressed couples, on the other hand, are more likely to respond to negative communicating with more negative communicating, escalating into conflict. We might all take a cue from the happy couples and make efforts not only to increase our positive communications but even to make them in response to negative comments from our partner.

F · O · C · U · S 9.2

A PERSONAL GROWTH EXERCISE: GETTING TO KNOW YOUR OWN BODY

Most experts on sexual communication agree that before you can begin to communicate your sexual needs to your partner, you must get to know your own body and its sexual responsiveness. This exercise is designed to help you do that. Set aside some time for yourself, preferably 30 minutes or more. You'll need privacy and a mirror, preferably a full-length mirror.

1. Undress and stand in front of the mirror. Relax your body completely.
2. Take a good look at your body, top to bottom. Look at the colors, the curves, the textures. Take your time doing this. Try to discover things you haven't noticed before. What pleases you about your body? What don't you like about your body? Can you say these things aloud?
3. Look at your body. What parts of it influence how you feel about yourself sexually?
4. Run your fngers slowly over your body, head to toe. How does it feel to you? Are some parts soft? Are some sensitive? Are you hurrying over some places? Why? How do you feel about doing this?
5. Explore your genitals. *If you're a man,* look at them. Do you like the way they look? Now explore your genitals with your fingers. Gently stroke your penis, scrotum, and the area behind the scrotum. Pay close attention to the various sensations you're producing. Which areas feel particularly good when they're stroked? Try different kinds of touching—light, hard, fast, slow. Which kind feels best? If you get an erection, that's OK. Just take your time and learn as much as you can. Are there differences in sensitivities between the aroused state and the unaroused state? *If you're a woman,* take a hand mirror and look at your genitals. Do you like the way they look? Now explore your genitals with your fingers. Touch your outer lips, inner lips, clitoris, vaginal entrance. Which areas feel particularly good? Try different kinds of touching—light, hard, fast, slow. Which kind feels best? If you get aroused, that's OK. Are there differences in sensitivities between the aroused state and the unaroused state? Just take your time and learn as much as you can.
6. Now you're ready to communicate some new information to your partner!

For more exercises like this, see Zilbergeld's *Male Sexuality* (1978) and Heiman, LoPiccolo, and LoPiccolo's *Becoming Orgasmic: A Sexual Growth Program for Women* (1976).

Sources: Brenton (1972), Heiman et al. (1976), Zilbergeld (1978).

Symmetrical communicating relationship: A relationship in which both partners take equal responsibility for communication.

A Symmetrical Communicating Relationship

Research shows that a symmetry or equality in partner communication and in other areas of the relationship contributes to satisfaction and growth in the relationship (Miller et al., 1975). In particular:

1. Couples in which both husband and wife use high levels of disclosure (leveling) in communicating report higher levels of marital satisfaction than couples in which one or both partners use low disclosure (Corrales, 1974).

2. Couples in which both members are highly accurate at understanding the other's view on a number of issues are more satisfied than couples in which one or both partners are low in accuracy (Corrales and Miller, cited in Miller et al., 1975).
3. A number of studies show that couples with equalitarian power structures are higher in marital satisfaction than are couples with other kinds of power structures (Lu, 1952; Blood and Wolfe, 1960; Rainwater, 1965; Corrales, 1974).

In a word, if communication is to be good, it must be mutual.

SUMMARY

Sexual pleasure is produced by stimulation of various areas of the body; these are the erogenous zones.

Sexual self-stimulation, or autoeroticism, includes masturbation and sexual fantasies. Women typically masturbate by rubbing the clitoris and surrounding tissue and the inner and outer lips. Men generally masturbate by circling the hand around the penis and using an up-and-down movement to stimulate the shaft. Many people have sexual fantasies while masturbating. Common themes of these fantasies are having intercourse with a loved one or a stranger and having sex with several people simultaneously. Similar sexual fantasies are also common while having intercourse.

An important technique in two-person sex is hand stimulation of the partner's genitals. A good guide to technique is to find out how the partner masturbates. Touching other areas of the body and kissing are also important. The other senses—sight, smell, and hearing—can also be used in creating sexual arousal.

While there are infinite varieties in the positions in which one can have intercourse, there are four basic positions: man-on-top (the "missionary" position), woman-on-top, rear-entry, and side-to-side.

There are two kinds of mouth-genital stimulation: cunnilingus (mouth stimulation of the female genitals) and fellatio (mouth stimulation of the male genitals). Both are engaged in frequently today and are considered highly pleasurable by many people. Gays and lesbians use techniques similar to those of straights (e.g., hand-genital stimulation and oral-genital sex). Homosexuals, though, seem less goal-oriented, take their time more, and communicate more than heterosexuals do.

Anal intercourse involves inserting the penis into the rectum.

An aphrodisiac is a substance that arouses sexual desire. There is no known reliable aphrodisiac, and some of the substances that are popularly thought to act as aphrodisiacs can be dangerous to one's health.

We have a tendency in our cuture, perhaps a legacy of the Protestant ethic, to view sex as work and to turn sex into an achievement situation, as witnessed by expressions such as "achieving orgasm." Such attitudes make sex less pleasurable and may set the stage for sexual failures or sexual dysfunctions.

We must all face the problem of being sexually inexperienced at some time in our lives; many people also face the problem of boredom in a long-term sexual relationship.

Some specific tips for being a good communicator were given: leveling and editing, using "I" language, avoiding mind reading, documenting your points with specific examples, offering limited-choice questions, breaking the ice by using sex manuals, being aware of nonverbal communication, listening carefully, giving feedback by paraphrasing, checking out sexy signals, and validating. It is important to draw your partner out and to fight fair. Taking responsibility for your own sexual pleasure and emphasizing positive communications are other good techniques. An equal pattern of communication between partners is related to marital satisfaction.

REVIEW QUESTIONS

1. The most common technique of female masturbation involves inserting a dildo or similar object into the vagina. True or false?
2. The majority of both men and women fantasize while they masturbate. True or false?
3. The man-on-top position of intercourse works well for a woman in the late stages of pregnancy. True or false?
4. The scientific term for mouth stimulation of the female genitals is _____.
5. Following anal intercourse, it is safe to insert the penis into the vagina. True or false?
6. Masters and Johnson, in their research on the lovemaking techniques of homosexuals and heterosexuals, found that the gays took their time and were less goal-oriented. True or false?
7. Research shows that couples seeking therapy for sex problems have poor communication patterns compared with nondistressed couples. True or false?
8. _____ is the term for telling your partner what you are feeling by stating your thoughts clearly, simply, and honestly.
9. The use of "I" language is considered to be a poor technique in couple communication. True or false?
10. A good technique in couple communication is validation, which involves communicating to your partner that, given his or her point of view, you can see why he or she thinks a certain way. True or false?

QUESTIONS FOR THOUGHT, DISCUSSION, AND DEBATE

1. If you are involved in a long-term relationship, think about the kind of communication pattern you have with your partner. Do you use the methods of communication recommended in this chapter? If not, do you think that there are areas in which you could change and improve? Would your partner cooperate in attempts to improve your communication pattern?
2. What do you think about sexual fantasizing? Is it harmful, or is it a good way to enrich one's sexual expression? Are your ideas consistent with the results of the research discussed in this chapter?

SUGGESTIONS FOR FURTHER READING

Comfort, Alex. (1972). *The joy of sex.* New York: Crown. (Simon & Schuster paperback.) Probably the best of the current crop of sex manuals. (And now, *More joy of sex.*)

Goleman, Daniel, and Bush, Sherida. (1977, Oct.). The liberation of sexual fantasy. *Psychology Today,* **11**, 48–53 and 104–107. Psychologists' views on the pros and cons of fantasy.

Gottman, John, Notarius, Cliff, Gonso, Jonni, and Markman, Howard. (1976). *A couple's guide to communication.* Champaign, Ill.: Research Press. Offers a good, complete guide and specific suggestions to help couples enhance their communication.

Vatsyayana. *The kama sutra.* (1963). (R. F. Burton and F. F. Arbuthnot, Trans.). New York: Putnam. The classic Eastern love manual.

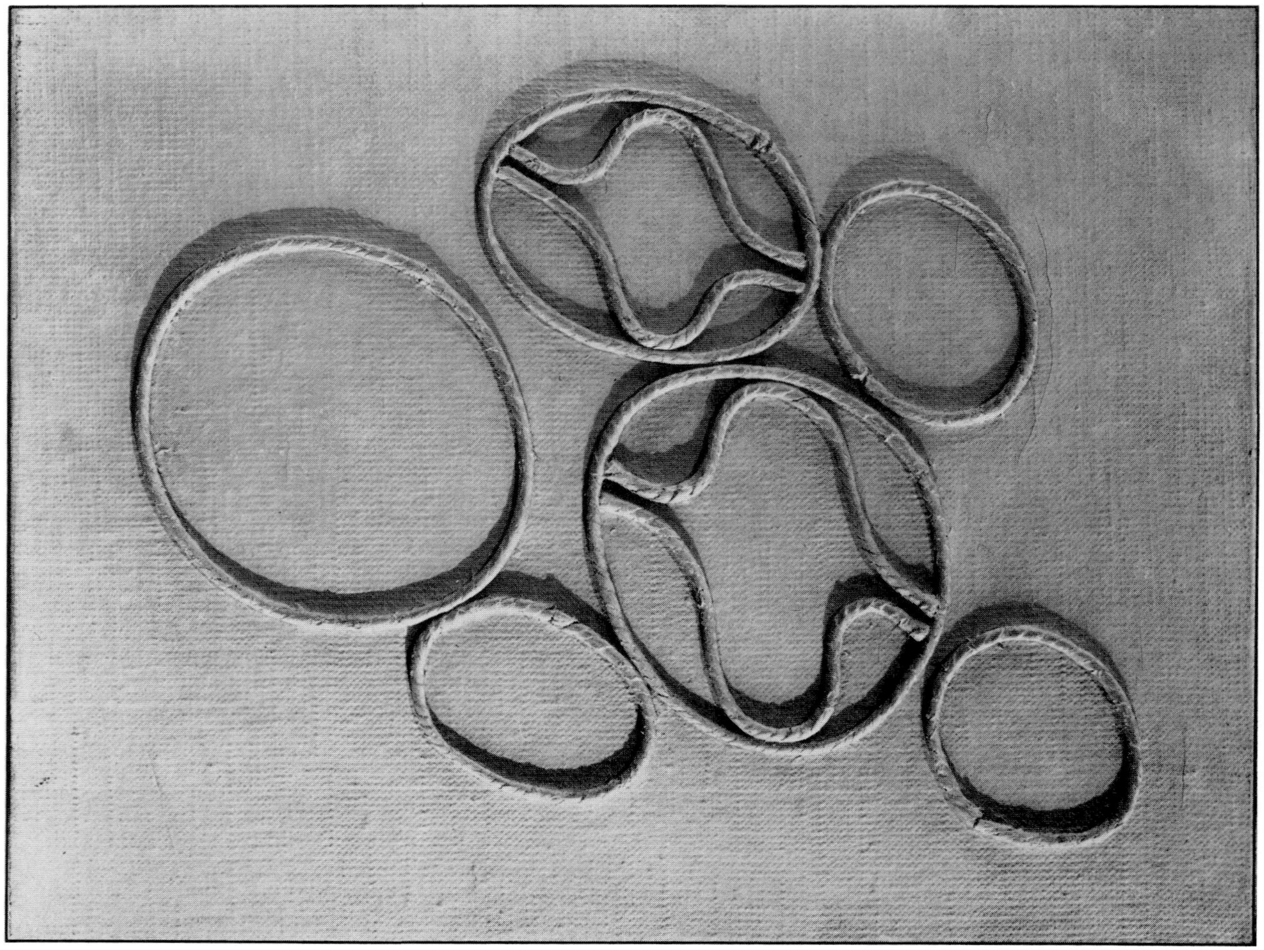

Jean Arp: *Leaves and Navels*, 1929. Collection, The Museum of Modern Art, New York.

CHAPTER • 10

SEX RESEARCH

According to the Kinsey Report
Every average man you know,
Much prefers to play his favorite sport,
When the temperature is low,
But when the thermometer goes way up,
And the weather is sizzling hot,
  Mr. Adam
  For his madam
  Is not.
    'Cause it's too darn hot.*

Source: Kiss Me Kate, a musical comedy. (1973). Music and lyrics by Cole Porter; book by Sam and Bella Spewack. New York: Knopf.

CHAPTER HIGHLIGHTS

In the last few decades, sex research has become increasingly common, and the names of Kinsey and of Masters and Johnson have become household words. Just exactly what do sex researchers do, and how valid are their conclusions? Those are the topics that will be discussed in this chapter.

There are many different types of sex research, but basically the techniques vary in terms of the following: (1) whether they rely on people's self-reports of their sexual behavior or whether the scientist actually observes the sexual behavior directly; (2) whether large numbers of people are studied (surveys) or whether a small number or just a single individual is studied (in laboratory studies or case studies); (3) whether the studies are conducted in the laboratory or in the field; and (4) whether sexual behavior is studied simply as it occurs naturally or whether some attempt is made to manipulate it experimentally.

Examples of studies using all these techniques will be considered and evaluated later in the chapter. First some issues in sex research—objections frequently made to studies that have been done—will be discussed.

It is important to have some knowledge of the techniques of sex research and their limitations. This knowledge will help you evaluate the studies that are cited as evidence for various conclusions in later chapters and will also help you decide how willing you are to believe these conclusions. Perhaps more important, this knowledge will help you evaluate future sex research. The knowledge we have of sexuality at present is based on relatively few studies. Many more will be done in the future. The information in this chapter should help you understand and evaluate sex research that appears 10 or 20 years from now.

ISSUES IN SEX RESEARCH

Sampling

Population: A group of people a researcher wants to study and make inferences about.

Sample: A part of a population.

Probability sampling: An excellent method of sampling in research, in which each member of the population has a known probability of being included in the sample.

Random sampling: An excellent method of sampling in research, in which each member of the population has an equal chance of being included in the sample.

Problem of refusal or nonresponse: The problem that some people will refuse to participate in a sex survey, thus making it impossible to have a random sample.

One of the first steps in conducting sex research is to identify the appropriate population of people to be studied. Does the population in question consist of all adult human beings, all adults in the United States, all adolescents in the United States, all people guilty of sex crimes, or all married couples who engage in swinging? Generally, of course, the scientist is unable to get data for all the people in the population, and so a sample is taken.

At this point, things begin to get sticky. If the sample is a random or representative sample of the population in question and if it is a reasonably large sample, then results obtained from it can safely be generalized to the population that was originally identified. That is, if one has really randomly selected 1 out of every 50 adolescents in the United States, then the results obtained from that sample are probably true of all adolescents in the United States. One technique that is sometimes used to get such a sample is probability sampling.[1] But if the sample consists only of adolescents with certain characteristics—for example, only those whose parents would agree to let them participate in sex research—then the results obtained from that sample may not be true of all adolescents. Sampling has been a serious problem in sex research.

Typically, sampling proceeds in three phases: the population is identified, a method for obtaining a sample is adopted, and the people in the sample are contacted and asked to participate. The scientific techniques of the second phase—obtaining a sample—are by now fairly well developed and should not be a problem in future research, provided investigators use them. What is perhaps the thorniest problem, though, occurs in the last phase: getting the people identified for the sample to participate. If any of the people refuse to participate, then the nice probability sample is ruined. And generally in sex research, rather large numbers of people will refuse to participate; this is called the problem of refusal (or nonresponse). As a result, the researcher is essentially studying volunteers, that is, people who volun-

[1]A detailed discussion of probability sampling is beyond the scope of this book. For a good description of this method as applied to sex research, see Cochran et al. (1953). A random sample is one example of a probability sample.

Volunteer bias: A problem in sex surveys caused by some people refusing to participate, so that those who are in the sample are volunteers who may in some ways differ from those who refuse to participate.

teer to be in the research. Therefore, this problem is also called volunteer bias. Even in Hunt's carefully designed study (to be discussed later in this chapter), the response rate was only about 20 percent. The problem of refusal in sex research is very difficult, since there is no ethical way of forcing people to participate when they do not want to.

The problem of volunteer bias would not be so great if those who refused to participate were identical in their sexual behavior to those who participated. But it seems likely that those who refuse to participate differ in some ways from those who agree to, and that leads to a biased sample. Evidence suggests that volunteers who participate in sex research tend to be more liberal politically and more experienced sexually than those who do not participate (Kaats and Davis, 1971; Maslow and Sakoda, 1952; but see Barker and Perlman, 1975).

Reliability of Self-Reports of Sexual Behavior

Most sex researchers have not directly observed the sexual behavior of their subjects. Instead, most have relied on respondents' self-reports of their sexual practices. The question is: How accurately do people report their own sexual behavior? There are several ways in which inaccuracies may occur. These are discussed below.

Purposeful distortion: Purposely giving false information in a survey.

Purposeful Distortion

If you were an interviewer in a sex research project and a 90-year-old man said that he and his wife made love twice a day, would you believe him, or would you suspect that he might be exaggerating slightly? If a 35-year-old woman told you that she had never masturbated, would you believe her, or would you suspect that she had masturbated but was unwilling to admit it?

Respondents in sex research may, for one reason or another, give self-reports that are distortions of reality. These distortions may be in one of two directions. People may exaggerate their sexual activity (a tendency toward "enlargement"), or they may minimize their sexual activity or hide the fact that they have done certain things ("concealment"). Unfortunately, we do not know whether most people tend toward enlargement or concealment.

Distortion is a basic problem when using self-reports. To minimize distortion, subjects must be impressed with the fact that because the study will be used for scientific purposes, their reports must be as accurate as possible. They must also be assured that their responses will be completely anonymous; this is necessary, for example, so that a politician would not be tempted to hide a homosexual history or an extramarital affair for fear that the information could be used to blackmail him.

But even if all respondents were very truthful and tried to give as accurate information as possible, two factors might still cause their self-reports to be inaccurate: memory and ability to estimate.

Memory

Some of the questions asked in sex surveys require respondents to recall what their sexual behavior was like many years before. For example, some of the data we have on sexual behavior in childhood come from the Kinsey study, in which adults were asked about their childhood sex behavior. This might involve asking a 50-year-old man to remember at what age he began masturbating and how frequently he masturbated when he was 16 years old. It may be difficult to remember such facts accurately. The alternative is to ask people about their current sexual behavior, although getting data like this from children raises serious ethical and practical problems.

"*Another of those damned sex surveys, I suppose.*"

FIGURE 10.1

Sex researchers have tried to devise some ingenious methods of overcoming the problems of self-reports.

Ability to Estimate

One of the questions Kinsey asked was: How long, on the average, do you spend in precoital foreplay? If you were asked this question, how accurate a response do you think you could give? It is rather difficult to estimate time to begin with, and it is even more difficult to do so when engaged in an absorbing activity. The point is that in some sex surveys people are asked to give estimates of things that they probably cannot estimate very accurately. This may be another source of inaccuracy in self-report data (Levitt, 1983).

Interviews versus Questionnaires

In the large-scale sex surveys, two methods of collecting data have been used. Either interviewers question people directly about their sexual behavior, or people are given a questionnaire which they complete themselves. Each of these methods has some advantages when compared with the other.

The advantage of the personal interview is that the interviewer can establish rapport with the respondent and, it is hoped, convince that person of the research's worth and of the necessity for being honest. An interviewer can also vary the sequence of questions, depending on the person's response. For example, in the Kinsey interviewing procedure, if a person mentioned having had a homosexual experience, this would be followed by a series of questions about the experience; however, those questions would be omitted if the person reported having had no homosexual experiences. It would be hard to get this kind of flexibility in a printed questionnaire. Finally, interviews can be administered to persons who cannot read or write.

Questionnaires are much less costly, since they do not require hiring interviewers to spend the many hours necessary to interview subjects individually. Although it might seem that respondents would be more honest in answering a questionnaire because they are more anonymous, the actual evidence indicates that questionnaires and interviews yield equally valid self-reports (DeLamater, 1982). Questionnaires are less subject to the problem of responses being influenced by extraneous factors, such as the personality of the interviewer or a grimace from the interviewer when a particular behavior is reported.

Self-Reports versus Direct Observations

As has been noted, one of the major ways of classifying techniques of sex research is according to whether the scientist relied on people's self-reports of their behavior or observed the sexual behavior directly.

The problems of self-reports have been discussed above. In a word, self-reports may be inaccurate. Direct observations—such as those done by Masters and Johnson in their work on the physiology of sexual response—have a major advantage over self-reports in that they are accurate. No purposeful distortion or poor memory can intervene. On the other hand, direct observations have their own set of problems. They are expensive and time-consuming, with the result that generally a rather small sample of subjects is studied. Further, obtaining a random or representative sample of the population is even more difficult than in survey research. While many people are reticent about completing a questionnaire concerning their sexual behavior, even more would be unwilling to come to a laboratory where their sexual behavior would be observed by a scientist or where they would be hooked up to recording instruments while they engaged in sex. Thus results obtained from the unusual group of volunteers who would be willing to do this might not be generalizable to the rest of the population. One study showed that volunteers for a laboratory study of male sexual arousal were less guilty, less sexually fearful, and more sexually experienced than nonvolunteers (Farkas et al., 1978; for similar results with females, see Wolchik et al., 1983).

Direct observations of sexual behavior in the laboratory, such as those made by Masters and Johnson, also involve one other major problem: Is sexual behavior in the laboratory the same as sexual behavior in the privacy of one's own bedroom? For example, might sexual response in the laboratory be somewhat inhibited?

Extraneous Factors

Various extraneous factors may also influence the outcomes of sex research. For example, people report more sexual feelings to an interviewer of their own gender than to an interviewer of the opposite gender (Walters et al., 1962). Generally, respondents are most open with interviewers who are of their own gender (Benney et al., 1956; J. Ehrlich and Riesman, 1961). Thus such extraneous factors as the gender or age of the interviewer may influence the outcome of sex research. Questionnaires do not get around these problems, since such simple factors as the wording of a question may influence the results. For example. if a question reads "On the average, how many times do you have intercourse per month?" the estimates of frequency of intercourse that are obtained will not be the same as if the question had read "On the average, how many times do you have intercourse per day?" Thus sex researchers must be careful to control these extraneous factors so that they influence the results as little as possible.

Ethical Issues

In recent years, scientists as well as lay people have become more aware of the ethical problems involved in doing research. Such ethical problems are particularly difficult in sex research, because people are more likely to feel that their privacy has been invaded when you ask them about sex than when you ask them to name their favorite presidential candidate or memorize a list of words. The ethical standards of most scientific organizations—such as the American Psychological Association and the American Sociological Association—involve two basic princples: informed consent and protection from harm (see, for example, American Psychological Association, 1973).

Informed Consent

Informed consent: An ethical principle in research, in which subjects have a right to be informed, before participating, of what they will be asked to do in the research.

According to the principle of informed consent, subjects have a right to be told, before they participate, what the purpose of the research is and what they will be asked to do. They may not be forced to participate or be forced to continue. An investigator may not coerce people to be in a study, and it is the scientist's responsibility to see to it that all subjects understand exactly what they are agreeing to do. In the case of children who may be too young to give truly informed consent, it is usually given by the parents.

The principle of informed consent was adopted by scientific organizations in the 1970s, and thus it was violated in some of the older sex studies, as will be discussed later in this chapter.

Protection from Harm

Investigators should minimize the amount of physical and psychological stress to those participating in their research. Thus, for example, if an investigator must shock subjects during a study, there should be a good reason for doing this. Questioning people about their sexual behavior may be psychologically stressful to them and might conceivably harm them in some way, and thus sex researchers must be careful to minimize the stress involved in their procedures. The principle of *anonymity* of response is important to ensure that subjects will not suffer afterward for their participation in research.

A Cost-Benefit Approach

Cost-benefit approach: An approach to analyzing the ethics of a research study, based on weighing the costs of the research (the subjects' time, stress to subjects, and so on) against the benefits of the research (gaining knowledge about human sexuality).

Considering the possible dangers involved in sex research, is it ever ethical to do such research? Officials in universities and government agencies sponsoring sex research must answer this question for every proposed sex research study. Typically they use a cost-benefit approach. That is, stress to subjects should be minimized as much as possible, but some stresses will remain; they are the cost. The question then becomes: Will the benefits that will result from the research be greater than the cost? That is, will the subjects benefit in some way from participating, and will science and society in general benefit from the knowledge resulting from the study? Do these benefits outweigh the costs? If they do, the research is justifiable; otherwise, it is not.

As an example, Masters and Johnson considered these issues carefully and they feel that their subjects benefited from being in their research; they have collected data from former subjects that confirm this belief. Thus a cost-benefit analysis would suggest that their research is ethical, even though their subjects may be temporarily stressed by it. Even in such an ethically questionable study as Laud Humphreys's study of the tearoom trade (discussed in a Focus in Chapter 16), the potential cost to the subjects must be weighed against the benefits that accrue to society from being informed about this aspect of sexual behavior.

F · O · C · U · S 10.1

ALFRED C. KINSEY

Alfred C. Kinsey was born in 1894 in New Jersey, the first child of uneducated parents. In high school he did not date, and a classmate recalled that he was "the shyest guy around girls you could think of."

His father was determined that Kinsey become a mechanical engineer. From 1912 to 1914 he tried studying mechanical engineering at Stevens Institute, but he showed little talent for it. At one point he was close to failing physics, but a compromise was reached with the professor, who agreed to pass him if he would not attempt any advanced work in the field! In 1914 Kinsey made the break and enrolled at Bowdoin College to pursue his real love: biology. Because this went against his father's wishes, Kinsey was put on his own financially; the only economic help he received from his parents after that was a single suit costing $25.

FIGURE 10.2

Alfred C. Kinsey.

What Do Subjects Say About Ethics?

Psychologist Paul Abramson (1977) attempted to collect empirical data relevant to the problems of ethics in sex research. He administered standard sex research procedures to undergraduate volunteers; they filled out a questionnaire about their past sexual behavior, they completed a personality inventory on sexual attitudes, they read an erotic story and rated their arousal, they were observed in a waiting room with sexually explicit magazines, they responded to double entendres (words with double meanings, one of which is sexual), and they were tested for retention of information on reproductive biology. Afterward, subjects reported that they felt that their participation had been constructive and void of negative aftereffects. Thus this study suggests that volunteer subjects do not view their participation as having

In 1916 he began graduate work at Harvard. There he developed his interest in insects, specializing in gall wasps. Even while a graduate student he wrote a definitive book on the edible plants of eastern North America.

In 1920 he went to Bloomington, Indiana, to take a job as assistant professor of zoology at Indiana University. That fall he met Clara McMillen, whom he married six months later. They soon had four children.

With his intense curiosity and driving ambition, Kinsey quickly gained academic success. He published a high school biology text in 1926, and it received enthusiastic reviews. By 1936 he had published two major books on gall wasps; they established his reputation as a leading authority in the field and contributed not only to knowledge of gall wasps but also to genetic theory.

Kinsey came to the study of human sexual behavior as a biologist, not as a social reformer. His shift to the study of sex began in 1938, when Indiana University began a "marriage" course; Kinsey chaired the faculty committee teaching it. Part of the course included individual conferences between students and faculty, and these were Kinsey's first sex interviews. When confronted with teaching the course, he also became aware of the incredible lack of information on human sexual behavior. Thus his research resulted in part from his realization of the need of people, especially young people, for sex information. In 1939 he made his first field trip to collect sex histories in Chicago. His lifetime goal was to collect 100,000 sex histories.

His work culminated with the publication of the Kinsey reports in 1948 *(Sexual Behavior in the Human Male)* and 1953 *(Sexual Behavior in the Human Female).* While the scientific community generally received them as a landmark contribution, they also provoked hate mail.

In 1947 he founded the Institute for Sex Research (known popularly as the Kinsey Institute) at Indiana University. It was financed by a grant from the Rockefeller Foundation and, later, by book royalties. But in the 1950s Senator Joseph McCarthy, the communist baiter, was in power. He made a particularly vicious attack on the institute and its research, claiming that its effect was to weaken American morality and thus make the nation more susceptible to a communist takeover. Under his pressuring, support from the Rockefeller Foundation was terminated.

Kinsey's health began to fail, partly as a result of the incredible work load he set for himself, partly because he was so involved with the research that he took attacks personally, and partly because he saw financial support for the research collapsing. He died in 1956 at the age of 62 of heart failure, while honoring a lecture engagement when his doctor had ordered him to convalesce.

Fortunately, by 1957 McCarthy had been discredited, and the grant funds returned. The Institute was headed by Dr. Paul Gebhard, an anthropologist who had been a member of the staff for many years. The Institute continues to do research today; it also houses a large library on sex and an archival collection including countless works of sexual art.

Sources: P. Gebhard. The Institute. In M. S. Weinberg (Ed.). (1976). *Sex research: Studies from the Kinsey Institute.* New York: Oxford University Press, pp. 10–22. C. V. Christensen. (1971). *Kinsey: A biography.* Bloomington: Indiana University Press.

harmed them; instead, they feel good about having contributed something to knowledge in this area.

Having considered some of the problems with sex research—though these problems are by no means limited to sex research and are common in most research on human behavior—let us proceed to examine some of the studies that have been done.

THE MAJOR SEX SURVEYS

In the major sex surveys, the data were collected from a large sample of people by means of questionnaires or interviews. The best known of these studies are those done by Kinsey.

Sampling

Kinsey and his colleagues interviewed a total of 5300 males, and their responses were reported in *Sexual Behavior in the Human Male;* 5940 females contributed to *Sexual Behavior in the Human Female.* Though some blacks were interviewed, only interviews with whites were included in the publications. The interviews were conducted between 1938 and 1949.

Initially, Kinsey was not much concerned with sampling issues. His goal was simply to collect sex histories from as wide a variety of people as possible. He began collecting interviews on the university campus and then moved to collecting others in large cities, such as Chicago.

Later he became more concerned with sampling issues and developed a technique called *100 percent sampling.* In this method he contacted a group, obtained its cooperation, and then got every one of its members to give a history. Once the cooperation of a group had been secured, peer pressure assured that all members would participate. Unfortunately, while he was successful in getting a complete sample from such groups, the groups themselves were by no means chosen randomly. Thus among the groups from which 100 percent samples were obtained were 2 sororities, 9 fraternities, and 13 professional groups. About one fourth of the sex histories came from these 100 percent samples.

In the 1953 volume, Kinsey said that he and his colleagues had deliberately chosen not to use probability sampling methods because of the problems of nonresponse. This is a legitimate point. But as a result, we have almost no information on how adequate the sample was.

As one scholar observed, the sampling was haphazard but not random (Kirby, 1977). For example, there were more subjects from Indiana than from any other state. Generally, the following kinds of subjects were overrepresented in the sample: college students, young people, well-educated people, Protestants, people living in cities, and people living in Indiana and the northeast. Underrepresented groups included manual laborers, less well-educated people, older people, Roman Catholics, Jews, members of racial minorities, and people living in rural areas.

Interviewing

While scientists generally regard Kinsey's sampling methods with some dismay, his interviewing techniques are highly regarded. The interviewers made every attempt to establish rapport with the people they spoke to, and they treated all reports matter-of-factly. They were also skillful at phrasing questions in language that was easily understood. Questions were worded so as to encourage subjects to report anything they had done. For example, rather than asking "Have you ever masturbated?" the interviewers asked "At what age did you begin masturbating?" Thus the burden of denial was placed on the subject. They also developed a number of methods for crosschecking a subject's report so that false information would be detected. Wardell Pomeroy recounts an example:

> Kinsey illustrated this point with the case of an older Negro male who at first was wary and evasive in his answers. From the fact that he listed a number of minor jobs when asked about his occupation and seemed reluctant to go into any of them [Kinsey] deduced that he might have been active in the underworld, so he began to follow up by asking the man whether he had ever been married. He denied it, at which Kinsey resorted to the vernacular and inquired if he had ever "lived common law." The man admitted he had, and that it had first happened when he was 14.

> "How old was the woman?" [Kinsey] asked.
> "Thirty-five," he admitted, smiling.
> Kinsey showed no surprise. "She was a hustler, wasn't she?" he said flatly.
> At this the subject's eyes opened wide. Then he smiled in a friendly way for the first time, and said, "Well, sir, since you appear to know something about these things, I'll tell you straight."
> After that, [Kinsey] got an extraordinary record of this man's history as a pimp. . . . (1972, pp. 115–116)

Strict precautions were taken to ensure that responses were anonymous and that they would remain anonymous. The data were stored on IBM cards, but using a code that had been memorized by only a few people directly in the project, and the code was never written down. They had even made contingency plans for destroying the data in the event that the police tried to demand access to the records for the purposes of prosecuting people.[2]

Over 50 percent of the interviews were done by Kinsey himself, and the rest by his associates, whom he trained carefully.

Put simply, the interviewing techniques were probably very successful in minimizing purposeful distortion. However, other problems of self-report remained: the problems of memory and of inability to estimate some of the numbers requested.

Checking for Accuracy

Kinsey and his colleagues developed a number of methods for checking on the accuracy of subjects' self-reports.

Test-retest reliability: A method for testing whether self-reports are reliable or accurate; subjects are interviewed (or given a questionnaire) and then interviewed a second time sometime later to determine whether their answers are the same both times.

They did retakes of the histories of 162 men and women, with a minimum of 18 months between the two interviews (in technical language, the correlation between the two reports estimates the test-retest reliability). Any discrepancies between the two histories would be accounted for by memory problems, purposeful distortion, and various chance factors. The results indicated a high degree of agreement between the first and second interviews for all measures. Correlations greater than .95 between the first and second interviews were obtained for reports of incidence of masturbation, extramarital coitus, and homosexual activity. Thus these data indicate that the self-reports were highly reliable.

Another method for checking accuracy is to interview a husband and a wife independently; their reports on many items should be identical and can thus be used as a check for accuracy. Kinsey did exactly this for 706 couples. The results indicated that reports of objective facts—such as the number of years they had been married, how long they were engaged, and how much time elapsed between their marriage and the birth of their first child—showed perfect or near-perfect agreement between spouses. However, as was noted earlier in this chapter, some other questions required much more subjective responses or estimates of things that might be difficult to estimate. On such items, there was less agreement between spouses. For example, the correlation between husband's and wife's estimate of the average frequency of intercourse early in marriage was only about .50 (this was the lowest correlation obtained). Even with these subjective reports, though, husbands and wives showed a fairly high degree of agreement.

---

[2]From today's vantage point, Kinsey's fears were not so unrealistic. In a recent highly publicized case, police subpoenaed a psychologist who was studying heavy marijuana users and demanded that he divulge their names. The psychologist was faced with a choice between violating the anonymity of his subjects and being jailed for contempt. He chose the latter. Such actions by the police seriously jeopardize the integrity of scientific research.

Thus from the available data it appears that the self-reports varied from being fairly accurate (on the subjective items, such as reports of frequencies) to highly accurate (on items such as vital statistics and incidences of activities).

How Accurate Are the Kinsey Statistics?

When all is said and done, how accurate are the statistics presented by Kinsey?

The American Statistical Association appointed a blue-ribbon panel to evaluate the Kinsey reports (Cochran et al., 1953; for other evaluations, see Terman, 1948; Wallin, 1949). While they generally felt that the interview techniques had been excellent, they were dismayed by Kinsey's failure to use probability sampling, and they concluded, somewhat pessimistically:

> In the absence of a probability-sample benchmark, the present results must be regarded as subject to systematic errors of unknown magnitude due to selective sampling (via volunteering and the like). (Cochran et al., p. 711)

However, they also felt that this was a nearly insoluble problem for sex research; even if a probability sample were used, refusals would create serious problems:

> In our opinion, no sex study of a broad human population can expect to present incidence data for reported behavior that are *known* to be correct to within a few percentage points. . . . If the percentage of refusals is 10 percent or more, then however large the sample, there are no statistical principles which guarantee that the results are correct to within 2 or 3 per cent. (Cochran et al., 1953, p. 675)

It is possible, then, that the Kinsey statistics are very accurate, but there is no way of proving it.

The statisticians who evaluated Kinsey's methods felt that four of his findings might have been particularly subject to error: (1) generally high levels of sexual activity, and particularly the high incidence of homosexuality; (2) little difference between older and younger generations; (3) a strong relationship between sexual activity and social class; and (4) the relationship between sexual activity and changes in social class. All these conclusions might have been seriously influenced by discrepancies between reported and actual behavior and by sampling problems.

Kinsey's associates felt that the most questionable statistic was the incidence of male homosexuality. Wardell Pomeroy commented, "The magic 37 percent of males who had one or more homosexual experience was, no doubt, overestimated." (1972, p. 466).

In sum, it is impossible to say how accurate the Kinsey statistics are; they may be very accurate, or they may contain serious errors. Probably the single most doubtful figure is the high incidence of homosexuality. Also, at this point the Kinsey survey is 40 years old, and so we need to look to more recent research.

The Hunt Survey

In the early 1970s the Playboy Foundation commissioned a large-scale sex survey. Its purpose was threefold: (1) to get up-to-date data on sexual behavior, (2) to collect modern data that could be compared with Kinsey's to see whether sexual behavior had changed over 30 years, and (3) to collect data that would be more accurate than Kinsey's as a result of the use of better sampling procedures. The results were written up by Morton Hunt, a professional journalist who had specialized in writing popularized versions of scientific studies, and published in a book entitled *Sexual Behavior in the 1970s.* This study will be referred to as the "Hunt survey"; it is sometimes called the "*Playboy* survey," although that name implies a bias in the data that is probably not present.

Sampling

The Playboy Foundation commissioned the Research Guild, an independent research organization, to devise a sampling method, design a questionnaire, and collect the data.

To obtain the sample, the Research Guild chose 24 cities throughout the United States. In each city, names were chosen at random from the telephone book. The researchers called these people and asked them to participate anonymously in small, private panel discussions of present trends in American sexual behavior, for the benefit of behavioral researchers; no mention was made of filling out a questionnaire. Of those contacted, 20 percent came for the discussions. After the discussions had been held, the participants were asked to complete the questionnaire. Of those present, 100 percent cooperated. Thus 20 percent of the originally identified sample contributed data, for a total of 2026 subjects. All data were collected in 1972.

According to Hunt, the sample closely paralleled the U.S. population aged 18 and over. It consisted of 982 males and 1044 females; 90 percent were white, and 10 percent were black;[3] 71 percent were married, 25 percent had never been married, and 4 percent had previously been married but were not married at that time. In terms of other major characteristics, such as age, education, occupation, and urban-rural background, the sample was fairly similar to the U.S. population.

On the other hand, because the sample was obtained via the telephone book, certain groups of people were excluded: the very poor and those in institutions such as prisons and colleges. (Kinsey, in contrast, made a special point of collecting data in such institutions.) And 80 percent of the original sample refused to participate—a very high refusal rate. Unfortunately, we have no idea of what differences there might have been between the 20 percent who agreed to participate and the 80 percent who did not.

While Hunt's sampling techniques were probably more adequate than Kinsey's, one ethical issue should be raised. The principle of informed consent was violated because subjects were not told, at the time they were recruited, that they would be asked to fill out a questionnaire on their own sexual behavior. Often, unfortunately, there is a trade-off between ethics and sampling adequacy in sex research.

The Questionnaire

There were four versions of the questionnaire used in Hunt's study. One was geared to unmarried males; one, to unmarried females; one, to married males; and one, to married females. The questionnaire asked for between 1000 and 1200 items of information covering the individual's background, sex education, sex history, and sex attitudes. It covered most of the areas covered in Kinsey's study and also went beyond it in some areas; for example, there were questions about anal sex and about attitudes.

The relative merits of questionnaires versus the kinds of interviews Kinsey used were discussed earlier in this chapter.

---

[3]When comparing his results with Kinsey's, Hunt dropped the blacks from his sample because the Kinsey report did not include blacks.

The 2000 questionnaire responses were supplemented by 200 in-depth interviews that were similar to Kinsey's. Quotations from those interviews are sprinkled throughout Hunt's book; they provide a more personal view of people's sexuality than statistics do.

Comparing Kinsey and Hunt

Hunt's sample was considerably smaller than Kinsey's. However, in terms of providing estimates of the sexual behavior of Americans, the Hunt study was probably at least as accurate as the Kinsey study (and possibly more accurate), because the Hunt sample was probably better than the Kinsey sample in the sense of being closer to a random sample of the United States population. (I say "probably" because we still do not know about the 80 percent who did not participate.)

The Sexual Revolution

It is a popular notion that there has been a "sexual revolution" (which might be called a "copulation explosion") in the United States in the last two decades or so. Comparing the Hunt data and the Kinsey data can give us some idea of whether sexual behavior changed in the approximately 30 years from Kinsey's research to Hunt's.

According to Hunt's comparison of the two sets of data, there have been major changes. In particular, premarital intercourse is considerably more common, gender differences are now smaller, and social-class differences have shrunk.

In the chapters that follow, frequent references will be made to changes in sexual behavior in the last several decades, with the evidence for these changes coming from a comparison of the Kinsey data and the Hunt data.

The Magazine Surveys

A number of large-scale surveys have been conducted through magazines. For example, *Psychology Today* included a 100-item sex questionnaire in its July 1969 issue. Over 20,000 readers responded, and the results were published in the July 1970 issue (Athanasiou et al., 1970). *Redbook* included a questionnaire about female sexuality in its October 1974 issue (Levin and Levin, 1975). *Redbook* did another survey in February 1980 and *Ladies Home Journal* did one in June, 1982. Let us consider, as a typical example, a survey by *McCall's.*

The McCall's Survey

McCall's magazine printed a survey on marriage, love, and sex in its August 1979 issue and reported the results in January 1980 (Gittelson, 1980).

In terms of sample size, the response was enormous; questionnaires were returned by more than 20,000 women. However, in sex research, as in some other aspects of sexuality, bigger is not always better. A carefully chosen probability sample of 1000 is much better than a highly selective sample of 20,000, and the McCall's sample gives evidence of having been such a selective sample. First, only *McCall's* readers were surveyed, and not every woman reads *McCall's.* Among others, this omits all women who cannot or do not read. Second, only those who voluntarily returned the questionnaire were included; presumably, women who felt very uncomfortable about sex or who were not married or in some other permanent relationship were less likely to respond. Confirming this argument, 82 percent of the respondents were married, whereas nationally the percentage is only 70.

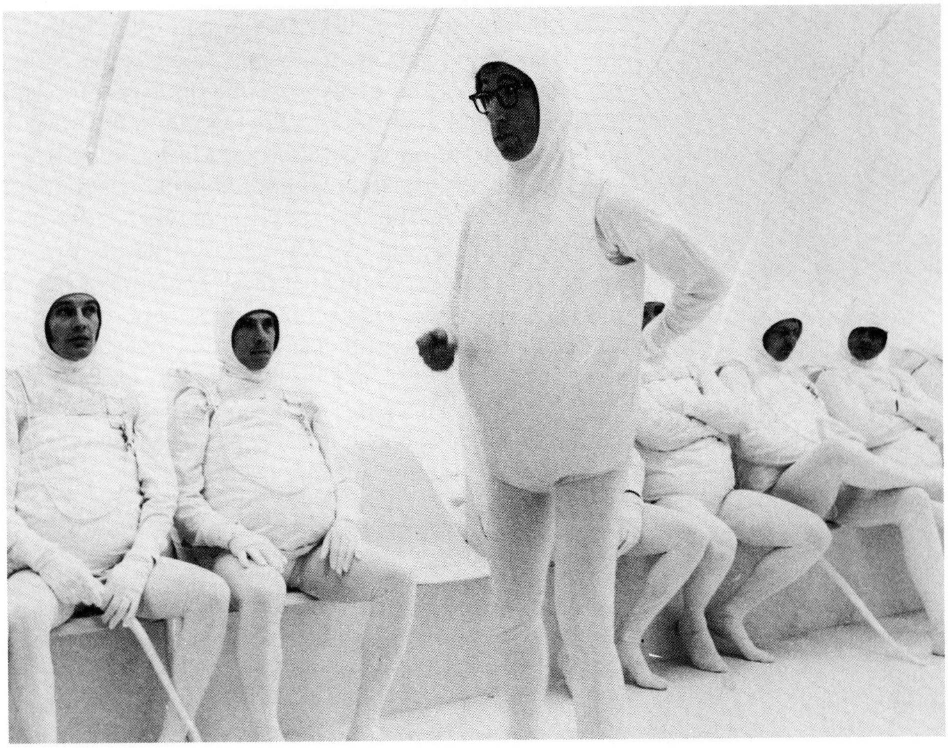

FIGURE 10.3

One of the visible signs of the sexual revolution of the past few decades is the more open treatment of sexuality by the media. Here Woody Allen and fellow sperm await blast-off in the film *Everything You Always Wanted to Know about Sex but Were Afraid to Ask.*

As an example of the problems associated with selective samples, one of the questions asked what was most important to them now. The leading response—from 61 percent—was "the feeling of being close to someone." Only 17 percent answered "my job." Should we infer from this that only 17 percent of U.S. women feel that their job is most important to them? Of course not. The likelier explanation is that happy housewives read *McCall's* and happy career women don't.

For these reasons, the statistics from the *McCall's* survey characterize only the 20,000 women who responded; it would not be legitimate to infer that they characterize U.S. women in general.

I could continue with more examples of magazine surveys, but the general conclusion should be clear by now. Although they may appear impressive because of the large number of respondents, they actually are poor in quality because the sample is seriously biased.

Probability Samples

As has been noted, one of the biggest problems with the major sex surveys is sampling. A few investigators have conquered this problem and have actually obtained probability samples in sex surveys. Perhaps the two best examples are the studies by Westoff (1974) and by Kantner and Zelnik (1972; Zelnik and Kantner, 1977).

The National Fertility Studies

As part of the National Fertility Studies, Charles Westoff (1974) studied a national probability sample of married women of reproductive age. In 1965, a probability sample of 4603 women were interviewed face to face. The same questions were asked in interviews in 1970, with a sample of 5432.

Most of the questions asked were not explicitly about sexual behavior. Generally, they dealt with more neutral topics, such as the number and spacing of children. Because most of the items were thus not very threatening, it was probably more feasible to get a good probability sample in this study than in a study that was just about sexual behavior. On the items concerning sex, such as the question about average frequency of intercourse per week, it was possible to determine the refusal rate. On that question, the refusal rate was 4.8 percent in 1965 and 7.8 percent in 1970. Thus the refusal rate was low, and statistics reported in this study should be highly accurate (assuming that those responding were accurate in their answers).

The median frequency of intercourse reported by the women in this sample was 7 times per 4 weeks in 1965 and 8.2 times per 4 weeks in 1970. This study provides some of the best evidence on increased frequency of some sexual behaviors, such as marital intercourse, in recent years. The evidence is good because it is based on two excellent and comparable samples taken five years apart. Nonetheless, the problems of self-report remain.

The Kantner and Zelnik Survey

In 1971, John Kantner and Melvin Zelnik conducted a study based on a national probability sample of the 15- to 19-year-old female population of the United States. A total of 4611 young women were interviewed. The study provides particularly good information on premarital sexual behavior among females and on contraceptive use among young unmarried women (Kantner and Zelnik, 1972, 1973). It provides excellent data on differences between blacks and whites in sexual behavior, since 1479 blacks were interviewed. It also provides interesting analyses of how various social factors, such as social class and religion, are related to varying patterns of sexual behavior. Kantner and Zelnik conducted a parallel survey in 1976, and a comparison of the results of the two studies provides good information on increases in premarital sex and contraceptive use in the 1970s (Zelnik and Kantner, 1977).

The major virtue of these studies is that the sampling was excellent. The studies had some limitations, however. Because only young women between the ages of 15 and 19 were interviewed, it was impossible to reach any conclusions about male-female differences or about people who are older or younger. This is a particular problem for the data on premarital sex, since some young women do not begin engaging in it before their twenties.

Another limitation is that the studies relied on self-reports. In the 1976 survey, however, Kantner and Zelnik used a new research method, called the *randomized response technique.* Space does not permit a detailed explanation; suffice it to say that it enables the researcher to estimate how accurate people are being in their self-reports. Kantner and Zelnik used this method on one of the most sensitive questions—and therefore the one likeliest to yield inaccurate self-reports—namely whether the respondent had ever had intercourse. According to self-reports, 42 percent of the women had; the estimate of the true incidence, by use of the randomized response technique, was 44 percent. This result indicates that the self-reports were highly accurate. Perhaps we can, after all, place a good deal of confidence in self-report studies.

STUDIES OF SPECIAL POPULATIONS

In addition to the large-scale studies of the U.S. population discussed above, several studies of special populations have been done. Particularly worthy of mention are Sorensen's study of adolescents, the Bell, Weinberg, and Hammersmith study of homosexuals and heterosexuals, and the Jay and Young study of homosexuals.

Sorensen: Adolescents

R. C. Sorensen conducted a major survey of adolescents and their sexual behavior in 1972; the results were published in a book entitled *Adolescent Sexuality in Contemporary America,* commonly known as the "Sorensen report."

Sampling

Using randomization techniques, Sorensen obtained an initial sample of 2042 households in urban, suburban, and rural areas; 839 adolescents (aged 13 to 19) lived in those households. This initial method of sampling was excellent, and it omitted only those adolescents living in college dormitories and institutions such as reformatories.

Sorensen then required written permission to participate from all parents. He received cooperation from the parents of 60 percent of the adolescents. This left 508 adolescents eligible on the basis of parental consent. Their consent to participate was then requested, and 393 (77 percent) agreed to participate. The adolescents thus showed a high response rate.

In sum, Sorensen tried to strike a balance between getting a good sample and maintaining high ethical standards of informed consent. Nonetheless, the nonresponse rate was high—53 percent—which limits the precision of the statistics in the study.

The Questionnaire

All the adolescents filled out a self-administered questionnaire with a researcher present; this maximized rapport and the chance for researchers to explain any items that were difficult to understand. The items had been developed on the basis of 200 interviews with adolescents, the purpose being to ensure that the language used in the items was understandable to persons in this age group. In addition, items that might have proved stressful or harmful, such as questions about anal intercourse, were eliminated.

When each questionnaire was completed, it was immediately placed in an envelope and mailed, thus assuring anonymity.

Jay and Young: Homosexuals

In 1977, professional writers Karla Jay and Allen Young undertook a large-scale questionnaire survey of gays in the United States. They published the results in a book entitled *The Gay Report* (1979).

They printed their questionnaire as a 16-page booklet, with separate forms for gay men and lesbians. It contained about 100 multiple-choice items and about 28 open-ended questions (for example, "Tell us about the importance of sex in your life. Do you feel that too much or too little importance is placed on sex by you or by others, and why do you feel that way?"). Jay and Young used these open-ended questions to allow gays to express themselves more freely, arguing that gays are often alienated by the scientific methods used by scientists. One such alienating technique, they feel, is asking the same question in several different ways, a standard technique used to assess the reliability of self-reports. As Jay and Young put it, "We approached this survey as writers and editors, with a commitment to *communication,* not to social science" (1979, p. 12).

They printed about 95,000 copies of their questionnaire and sent them to people on the mailing lists of gay organizations. In addition, several gay newspapers and magazines printed the questionnaire. Jay and Young estimated that about 400,000 gay men and 100,000 lesbians saw the questionnaire. They received completed questionnaires from 4,400 gay men and 1,000 lesbians, for a 1 percent response rate. Finally, they took only a random subsample of 250 questionnaires completed by lesbians and 419 questionnaires completed by male homosexuals to analyze for their book.

In evaluating *The Gay Report* one must recognize that the sampling problems are tremendous, much as they are in the case of *The Hite Report* (on female sexuality; see Chapter 15). One simply cannot take the results to be representative of all gays in the United States. However, as we shall see below, even in a carefully conducted study such as that of Bell, Weinberg, and Hammersmith, one still does not get a representative sample. A second point is that Jay and Young were so busy not alienating their respondents that they totally ignored issues of reliability and validity of response, something Bell and his colleagues handled better. Nonetheless, Jay and Young's point about not alienating respondents in surveys is well taken.

The real merit of the book lies in the countless first-person quotes from respondents that describe the gay experience so vividly.

Bell, Weinberg, and Hammersmith: Homosexuals and Heterosexuals

Under the sponsorship of the Kinsey Institute at Indiana University, Alan Bell, Martin Weinberg, and Sue Hammersmith conducted a major survey of homosexuals and heterosexuals, reporting the results in their book *Sexual Preference* (1981). As the title of the book implies, their goal was to find out what factors determine people's sexual preference, whether heterosexual or homosexual.

The data came from face-to-face interviews with 979 homosexual women and men and 477 heterosexual women and men, all living in the San Francisco Bay Area. Although the sampling has an obvious geographical limitation, Bell and his colleagues justified their choice of working in the Bay Area as permitting them to obtain a large sample of homosexuals who could be open enough to cooperate and participate in the research. In order to contact prospective subjects, recruiters—half of them gay themselves—visited locations such as gay bars; recruiting was also done by posters, ads in local newspapers, television spots, and referral by persons already interviewed for the study. There would be no comparable recruiting methods for heterosexuals, so they were obtained by a random sampling technique.

The interview contained 200 questions and took three to five hours. The questions focused on a wide variety of events in the subject's childhood and adolescence, the goal being to use the responses to test the various theories that have been proposed to explain why people become homosexual—or heterosexual. In several cases, two questions on the same topic appeared at different places in the interview, so that an individual's answers could be checked for reliability. Some of the respondents were reinterviewed six months after the original interview, again to check for the reliability of the self-reports. Bell and his colleagues reported no specific results of these reliability checks, but they appeared to be satisfied with the results.

They used a statistical technique called path analysis to analyze the data. I would have to go too far afield from our discussion of sexuality to explain path analysis here, but briefly, it is a statistical technique that allows one to make conclusions about causal factors from correlational data. Bell and his colleagues wanted to test various hypotheses about experiences and environmental factors that might cause homosexuality, yet their survey data were clearly correlational, so path analysis is a good solution. The results of this study will be discussed in detail in Chapter 16; to summarize them briefly here, they found that the usual environmental factors that have been used to explain homosexuality—parent-child relationship, parental identification, early heterosexual trauma—are not confirmed by their data.

In evaluating this study, one can see that it was done more carefully and according to better scientific standards than the Jay and Young *Gay Report.* The interviewing seems to meet the same high standards as the earlier Kinsey report. There are internal checks for reliability, although the method of self-report is still used, and there might be problems of memory for events that occurred years ago, in childhood. Although the sampling was done carefully, it is still problematic. The sample could not be considered random or representative of all gays in the United States. It omits all those who are outside the "San Francisco scene." And it omits covert gays, those who do not frequent bars or parties, and are not willing to be open enough to participate in a research interview. This research raises the point that studies of special populations defined by their sexual behavior—such as homosexuals or bisexuals or fetishists—are essentially impossible to do in any kind of representative fashion. It is impossible to identify all the people in the population in the first place, and therefore it is impossible to sample them properly. In contrast, samples of the general population, such as Kinsey's or Hunt's, are more feasible to obtain, though not easy.

LABORATORY STUDIES USING DIRECT OBSERVATIONS OF SEXUAL BEHAVIOR

The numerous problems associated with using self-reports of sexual behavior in scientific research have been discussed. The major alternative to using self-reports is to make direct observations of sexual behavior in the laboratory. These direct observations overcome the major problems of self-reports: purposeful distortion, inaccurate memory, and inability of subjects to estimate correctly or describe certain aspects of their behavior. The outstanding example of this approach is Masters and Johnson's work on the physiology of sexual response.

Masters and Johnson: The Physiology of Sexual Response

William Masters began his research on the physiology of sexual response in 1954 (R. Brecher and Brecher, 1966). No one had ever studied human sexual behavior in the laboratory before. Thus Masters had to develop all the necessary research techniques from scratch. He began by interviewing 118 female prostitutes (as well as 27 male prostitutes working for a homosexual clientele). They gave him important preliminary data in which they "described many methods for elevating and controlling sexual tensions and demonstrated innumerable variations in stimulative techniques," some of which were useful in the later program of therapy for sexual dysfunction.

Meanwhile, Masters began setting up his laboratory and equipping it with the necessary instruments: an electrocardiograph to measure changes in heart rate over the sexual cycle, an electromyograph to measure muscular contractions in the body during sexual response, and a pH meter to measure the acidity of the vagina during the various stages of sexual response.

The prostitutes helped with the initial "dry runs" of the apparatus. But Masters soon realized that they would not be satisfactory subjects for his research. In particular, they had a variety of pathological conditions in their pelvic organs, making them unsuitable for research on normal sexual response.

Sampling

Masters made a major breakthrough when he decided that it was possible to recruit normal subjects from the general population and have them engage in sexual behavior in the laboratory, where their behavior and physiological responses could be carefully observed, measured, and recorded. This approach had never been used before, as even the daring Kinsey had settled for subjects' verbal reports of their behavior.

Most of the subjects were obtained from the local community simply by word of mouth. Masters let it be known in the medical school and university community that he needed volunteer subjects for laboratory studies of human sexual response. Some subjects volunteered because of their belief in the importance of the research, and others were referred by their own physicians. Some, of course, came out of curiosity or because they were exhibitionists; they were weeded out in the initial interviews. Subjects were paid for their hours in the laboratory, as is typical in medical research, and so many young medical students and graduate students participated because it was a way to earn money. Some of the subjects were women who had been patients of Dr. Masters. When they heard he needed volunteers, they wanted to help, and they brought their husbands along as well.

Initially, all subjects were given detailed interviews by the Masters and Johnson team. Subjects who had histories of emotional problems or who seemed uncomfortable with the topic of sex either failed to come back after this interview or were eliminated even if they were willing to proceed. Subjects were also assured that the anonymity and confidentiality of their participation would be protected carefully.

In all, 694 people participated in the laboratory studies reported in *Human Sexual Response.* The men ranged in age from 21 to 89, while the women ranged from 18 to 78. A total of 276 married couples participated, as well as 106 women and 36 men who were unmarried when they entered the research program. The unmarried subjects were helpful mainly in the studies that did not require sexual intercourse, for example, studies of the ejaculatory mechanism in males and of the effects of sexual arousal on the positioning of the diaphragm in the vagina.

Certainly the group of people Masters and Johnson studied were not a random sample of the population of the United States. In fact, one might imagine that people who would agree to participate in such research would be rather unusual. The data indicate that they were more educated than the general population, and the sample was mostly white, with only a few blacks participating. Probably paying the subjects helped, since this attracted some participants who simply needed the money. The sample omitted two notable types of people: those who are not sexually experienced or do not respond to sexual stimulation and those who are unwilling to have their sexual behavior studied in the laboratory. Strictly speaking, the results Masters and Johnson obtained might not generalize to such people.

But just exactly how critical is this sampling problem to the validity of the research? Masters and Johnson were not particularly concerned about sampling because of their assumption that the processes they were studying are normative; that is, they work in essentially the same way in all people. This assumption is commonly made in medical research. For example, a researcher who is studying the digestive process typically does not worry that the sample is composed of all medical students, since the assumption is that digestion works the same way in all human beings. If this assumption is also true for the physiology of sexual response, then all people respond similarly, and it does not matter that the sample is not random. Whether this assumption is correct remains to be seen, but it does not appear to be too unreasonable. The sampling problem, however, does mean that Masters and Johnson cannot make statistical conclusions on the basis of their research; for example they cannot say that X percent of all women have multiple orgasms. Any percentages they calculate would be specific to their subjects and might not generalize to the rest of the population.

In defense of their sampling techniques, even if they had identified an initial probability sample, they would still almost surely have had a very high refusal rate, probably higher than in survey research, and the probability sample would have been ruined. At present, this seems to be an unsolvable problem in this type of research.

Data Collection Techniques

After they were accepted for the project, subjects then proceeded to the laboratory phase of the study. First, they had a "practice session," in which they engaged in sexual activity in the laboratory in complete privacy, with no data being recorded and with no researchers present. The purpose of this was to allow the subjects to become comfortable with engaging in sexual behavior in a laboratory setting. Interestingly, males had a higher "failure rate" (inability to have orgasm) under these conditions than females did.

The physical responses of the subjects were then recorded during sexual intercourse, masturbation, and "artificial coition." Masters and Johnson made an important technical advance with the development of the artificial coition technique. It involves the woman stimulating herself with an artificial penis constructed of clear plastic; it is powered by an electric motor, and the woman can adjust the depth and frequency of the thrust. There is a light and a recording apparatus inside the artificial penis, and thus motion picture records can be made of the changes occurring inside the vagina.

Measures such as these avoid problems of distortion possible in self-reports. They also answer much different questions. That is, it would be impossible from such measures to tell whether the person had had any homosexual experiences or how frequently he or she masturbated. Instead, they measure how the body responds to sexual stimulation, with a kind of accuracy and detail that would be impossible to obtain through self-reports.

Two problems also deserve mention. One has to do with the problems of laboratory studies: Do people respond the same sexually in the laboratory as they do in the privacy of their own homes? Another problem is that the Masters and Johnson results have never been replicated, that is, independently confirmed by other investigators. Although most scientists believe that Masters and Johnson's results are correct, the scientific method nonetheless demands that they be independently confirmed. It is hoped that this will be done soon.

Ethics

Masters and Johnson have been concerned with the ethical implications of their research. They were careful to use the principle of informed consent. Potential subjects were given detailed explanations of the kinds of things they would be required to do in the research, and they were given ample opportunity at all stages to withdraw from the research if they so desired. Further, Masters and Johnson eliminated from the subject pool people who appeared too anxious or distressed during the preliminary interviews.

It is also possible that participating in the research itself might have been harmful in some way to the subjects, perhaps damaging their future ability to respond sexually. Masters and Johnson have been particularly concerned with the long-term effects on their subjects of participating in the research. Accordingly, they make follow-up contacts with the subjects at five-year intervals. In no case has a subject reported developing a sexual dysfunction (for example, impotence). In fact, many of the couples report specific ways in which participating in the research has enriched their marriages. Thus the available data seem to indicate that such research does not harm the subjects and may in some ways benefit them, not to mention the benefit to society that results from gaining information in such an important area.

In sum, direct observations of sexual behavior of the type done by Masters and Johnson have some distinct advantages but also some disadvantages, compared with survey-type research. The research avoids the problems of self-reports and is capable of answering much more detailed physiological questions than self-reports could. But the research is costly and time-consuming, making large samples impossible; further, a high refusal rate is probably inevitable, and thus probability samples are impossible.

Masters and Johnson: Homosexual Behavior

Even more daring than the Masters and Johnson study of the physiology of sexual response was their study of homosexual behavior, *Homosexuality in Perspective* (1979). Essentially, they repeated the 1966 study, but this time with gays as subjects. That is, gay men and women volunteers came into the laboratory and engaged in sexual acts; their behavior was observed, and their physiological responses were recorded.

PARTICIPANT-OBSERVER STUDIES

Participant-observer study: A research method in which the scientist becomes part of the community to be studied and makes observations from inside the community.

A common research method, used by anthropologists and sociologists, is the participant-observer technique. In this type of research, the scientist actually becomes a part of the community to be studied, and she or he makes observations from inside the community. In the study of sexual behavior, the researcher may be able to get direct observations of sexual behavior combined with interview data.

Examples of this type of research are studies of sexual behavior in other cultures, such as those done in Mangaia and Inis Beag, which were discussed in Chapter 1. Two other examples are Laud Humphreys's study of the tearoom trade and Bartell's study of swinging.

Humphreys: The Tearoom Trade

Sociologist Laud Humphreys (1970) did a participant-observer study of impersonal homosexual sex in public places such as rest rooms. The study is discussed in detail in a Focus in Chapter 16. Briefly, Humphreys acted as a lookout while men engaged in homosexual acts in public rest rooms; his job was to sound a warning if police or other intruders approached. This permitted Humphreys to make direct observations of the sexual behavior. He also got the license-plate numbers of the men involved, traced them, and later interviewed them in their homes under the pretext of taking a routine survey.

Humphreys got a wealth of information from the study, but in so doing he violated most of the ethical principles of behavioral research. He had no informed consent from his subjects; they were never even aware of the fact that they were subjects in research, much less of the nature of the research. Thus this study has been quite controversial.

Bartell: Swinging

Anthropologist Gilbert Bartell (1970) did a participant-observer study of swinging (a married couple having sex with another person or another couple). He and his wife contacted swinging couples by responding to ads that swingers had placed in newspapers. They took the role of "baby swingers"—a couple who are swinging for the first time—but they also state that they did not misrepresent themselves and informed all subjects that they were anthropologists interested in knowing more about swinging. In addition, they attended a large number of swingers' parties and large-scale group sexual activities and made observations in that context.

Sampling is often a problem in studies of special groups such as this one, since it is difficult to get any kind of a random sample of people who engage in a particular kind of sexual behavior. In this particular case the problem was made somewhat less difficult because many such contacts are made through newspaper ads, to which the researchers could respond. This method permitted studying only current swingers; it did not allow sampling of people who had engaged in swinging but had stopped for one reason or another (Kirby, 1977). There is also some question as to how honest the respondents were, since swingers are doing something that they take great pains to hide; in fact, Bartell cited specific examples of distortion in reports of information on such things as age and interests.

Ethically, it was easy to preserve anonymity, since swingers go to great lengths to preserve their own anonymity; even with one another, they use first names only. Bartell obtained some kind of informed consent, since he told his subjects that he was doing research; in other, similar studies, however, researchers have posed as swingers, have not divulged the fact that data were being collected, and therefore have seriously misled their subjects.

EXPERIMENTAL SEX RESEARCH

Correlational study: A study in which the researcher does not manipulate variables, but rather studies naturally occurring relationships (correlations) among variables.

All the studies discussed so far had one thing in common: they all were studies of people's sexual behavior as it occurs naturally, conducted by means of either self-reports or direct observations. Data obtained from such studies are correlational in nature; that is, at best they can tell us that certain factors are related. They cannot tell us what *causes* various aspects of sexual behavior.

As an example, Kinsey found that women who masturbated to orgasm before marriage were more likely to have a high consistency of orgasm in marriage than women who did not. From this it would be tempting to conclude that practice in masturbating to orgasm causes women to have more orgasms in heterosexual sex. Unfortunately, this is not a legitimate conclusion to draw from the data, since many other factors might also explain the results. For example, it could be that some women have a higher sex drive than others; this high sex drive causes them to masturbate and also to have orgasms in heterosexual sex. Therefore, the most we can conclude is that masturbation experience is related to (or correlated with) orgasm consistency in marital sex.

Experiment: A type of research study in which one variable (the independent variable) is manipulated by the experimenter while all other factors are held constant; the research can then study the effects of the independent variable on some measured variable (the dependent variable); the researcher is permitted to make causal inferences about the effects of the independent variable on the dependent variable.

An alternative method in behavioral research that allows us to determine the causes of various aspects of behavior is the experiment. According to the technical definition of "experiment," one factor must be manipulated while all other factors are held constant. Thus any differences among the groups of people who received different treatments on that one factor can be said to be caused by that factor. For obvious reasons, most experimental research is conducted in the laboratory.

One example of experimental sex research is Julia Heiman's study of male and female responses to erotic materials, which is discussed in Chapter 15. As an example of experimental sex research here, let us consider a study of male-female differences in response to reading erotic stories, conducted by German researchers Gunter Schmidt, Volkmar Sigusch, and Siegrid Schäfer at the University of Hamburg (1973). Their subjects were 120 male and 120 female university students who volunteered to participate in an experiment involving "psychosexual stimulation." All the subjects read erotic stories that included explicit descriptions of oral-genital sex, coitus, and orgasm. Half of the subjects, however, read stories in which the characters were very affectionate with each other, while the other half read stories that were comparable except that the affection component was missing. Immediately after reading a story, subjects rated how arousing it had been on a scale from 1 to 9 (note that this was a self-report technique). Subjects also reported their physiological arousal (erection, vaginal lubrication, and so on). Thus the study could assess experimentally whether stories in which the characters were affectionate with each other were more arousing than those in which they were not. It could also assess whether males and females differed in their responses. Subjects also filled out a form 24 hours after the experiment in which they reported their actual sexual activity during those 24 hours.

The stories with the affection component were rated as being significantly more arousing than the stories without it. Thus we can conclude (at least if we believe the subjects' self-reports) that affection between characters in an erotic story *causes* people to be somewhat more aroused than they would be otherwise.

Interestingly, it was women who reported an increase in coital activity in the 24 hours after reading the story, as compared with the 24 hours before reading it.

Experimental sex research permits us to make much more powerful statements about the causes of various kinds of sexual phenomena. For example, the study just discussed provides much more convincing evidence that affection in an erotic story makes it arousing than would be provided by a survey in which people were asked, "Do you find erotic stories more arousing when the characters show affection to each other or when they do not?" Laboratory studies avoid the problems of memory in much of the self-report data in survey research, but much of the experimental research, including the study described here, still does rely on self-reports. Experimental sex research is time-consuming and costly, and it can generally be done only on very restricted samples of subjects. Further, it cannot address some of the most interesting, but most complex, questions in the field of sexual behavior, such as what factors cause people to develop heterosexual or homosexual preferences.

SOME STATISTICAL CONCEPTS

It was Kinsey who pioneered the approach of using statistics to describe people's sexual behavior, and this approach is now quite common. Therefore, before you can understand the reports of sex research, you must understand some basic statistical concepts.

Average

Mean:
The average of subjects' scores.

Suppose we get data from a sample of married couples on how many times per week they have sexual intercourse. How can we summarize the data? One way to do this is to compute some average value for all the subjects; this will tell us how often, on the average, these people have intercourse. In sex research, the number that is usually calculated is either the mean or the median; both of these give us an indication of approximately where the average value for that group of subjects is. The mean is simply the average of the scores of all the subjects. The *median* is the score that splits the sample in half, with half of the subjects falling below that score and half falling above.

Variability

In addition to having an indication of the average for the sample of subjects, it is also interesting to know how much variability there was from one subject to the next in the numbers reported. That is, it is one thing to say that the average married couple in a sample had intercourse three times per week, with a range in the sample from two to four times per week, and it is quite another thing to say that the average was three times per week, with a range from 0 to 15 times per week. In both cases the mean is the same, but in the first there is little variability, and in the second there is a great deal of variability. These two alternatives are shown graphically in Figure 10.4. There is great variability in virtually all kinds of sexual behavior.

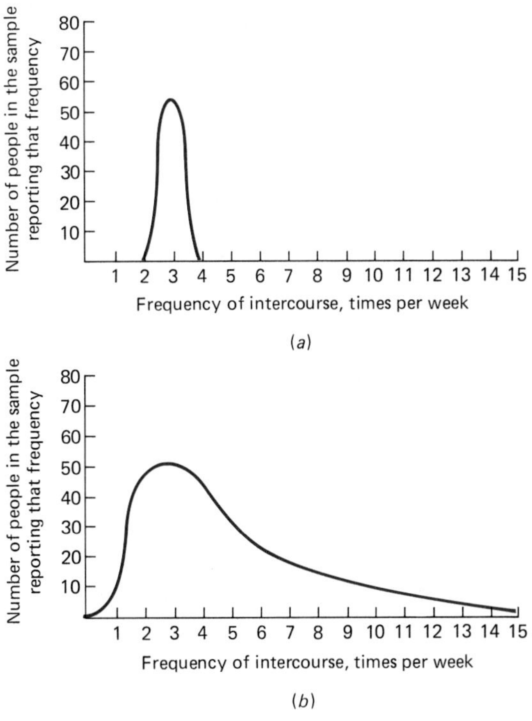

FIGURE 10.4

Two hypothetical graphs of the frequency of intercourse for married couples in a sample. In both, the average frequency is about three times per week, but in (*a*) there is little variability (almost everyone has a frequency between two and four times per week), while in (*b*) there is great variability (the frequency ranges from 0 to 15 or 20 times per week). For most sexual behavior, the graph looks like (*b*); there is great variability.

Average versus Normal

It is interesting and informative to report the average frequency of a particular sexual behavior, but this also introduces the danger that people will confuse "average" with "normal." That is, there is a tendency, when reading a statistic like "The average person has intercourse twice per week," to think of one's own sexual behavior, compare it with that average, and then conclude that one is abnormal if one differs much from the average. If you read that statistic and your frequency of intercourse is only once a week, you may begin to worry that you are undersexed or that you are not getting as much as you should. If you are having intercourse seven times per week, you might begin worrying that you are oversexed or that you are wearing out your sex organs. Such conclusions are a mistake, first because they can make you miserable and second because there is so much variability in sexual behavior that any behavior (or frequency or length of time) within a wide range is perfectly normal. Don't confuse average with normal.

Another version of this phenomenon is called "medical students' disease." As they read about each new disease, medical students tend to begin seeing the symptoms in themselves and to decide that they are afflicted with it. The best way to avoid such problems is not to take the statistics you read in this book too personally.

Incidence versus Frequency

Incidence:
The percentage of people giving a particular response.

Frequency:
How often a person does something.

In sex statistics, the terms "incidence" and "frequency" are often used. Incidence refers to the percentage of people who have engaged in a certain behavior. Frequency refers to how often people do something. Thus we might say that the incidence of masturbation among males is 95 percent (95 percent of all males masturbate at least once in their lives), while the average frequency of masturbation among males between the ages of 16 and 20 is about once per week.

A closely related concept is that of cumulative incidence (or accumulative incidence). If we consider a sexual behavior according to the age at which each person in the sample first engaged in it, the *cumulative incidence* refers to the percentage of people who have engaged in that behavior before a certain age. Thus the cumulative incidence of masturbation in males might be 10 percent by age 11, 25 percent by age 12, 80 percent by age 15, and 95 percent by age 20. Graphs of cumulative incidence always begin in the lower left-hand corner and move toward the upper right-hand corner. An example of a cumulative-incidence curve is shown in Figure 10.5.

FIGURE 10.5

A cumulative-incidence curve for masturbation in males. From the graph, you can read off the percentage of males who report having masturbated by a given age. For example, about 82 percent have masturbated to orgasm by age 15.

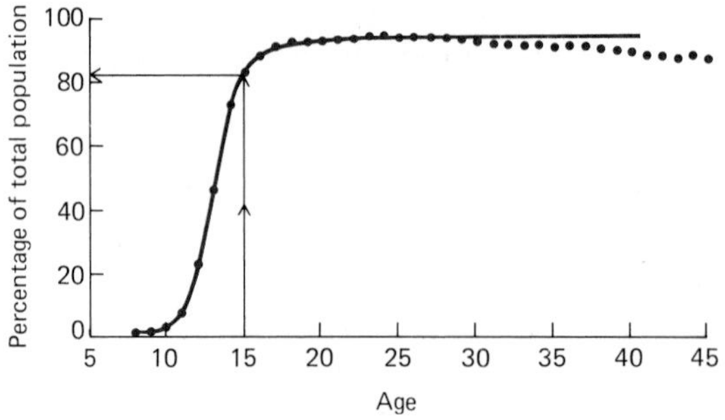

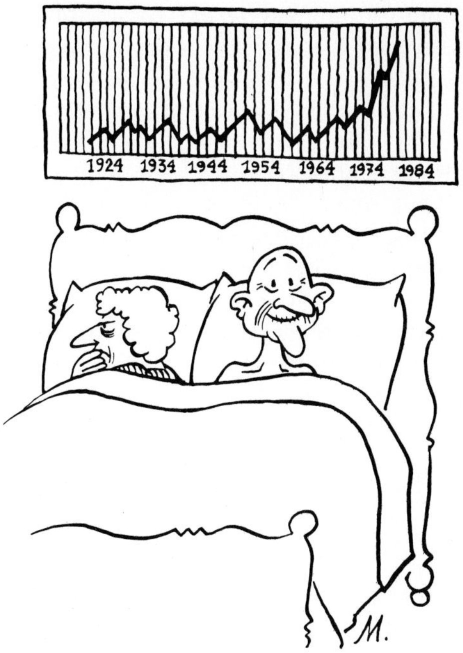

FIGURE 10.6

SUMMARY

This chapter reviewed the major methods that have been used in sex research and the problems and merits associated with each; the goal was to help readers better evaluate the sex research that has been done and to aid them in developing skills for understanding and evaluating the sex research that will be done in the future.

Ideally, sex research should employ random sampling or probability sampling techniques; this is generally not possible because many persons refuse to participate in sex research.

Large-scale surveys of sexual behavior generally rely on subjects' self-reports, which may be inaccurate because of purposeful distortion, problems of memory, or inability to estimate some of the information requested. Direct observations of sexual behavior avoid these problems, but they lead to an even more restricted sample of subjects. They also answer questions that are somewhat different from those answered by surveys.

In all behavioral research, the ethical principles of informed consent and protection from harm must be observed, although historically some sex researchers have not done this.

Two major sex surveys are Kinsey's large-scale interview study of the sexual behavior of Americans, done during the 1940s, and a similar study done by Morton Hunt in 1972. Two other large surveys have been done, one through *McCall's* magazine and the other through *Psychology Today;* the samples in these studies, however, were so restricted that we cannot draw any general conclusions from them. Two surveys have used probability samples: the Westoff study of married women and the Kantner and Zelnik study of young unmarried women.

Studies of special populations include Sorensen's study of adolescents, the Bell, Weinberg, and Hammersmith study of homosexuals and heterosexuals, and the Jay and Young survey of gays.

In participant-observer studies, the scientist becomes a part of the community to be studied, and he or she uses a combination of direct observations and interviewing. Examples are studies of sexual behavior in other cultures, Humphreys's study of the tearoom trade, and Bartell's study of swinging.

In experimental sex research, the goal is to discover what factors cause various aspects of sexual behavior.

The following statistical terms were introduced: "average," "variability," "incidence," and "frequency."

REVIEW QUESTIONS

1. Random sampling or probability sampling is important in doing a good sex survey, but these techniques have been used in only a few studies. True or false?
2. Volunteer bias is a problem in sex research. True or false?
3. Purposeful distortion and memory problems may create problems with the reliability of self-reports in sex research. True or false?
4. One alternative to self-reports that helps overcome some of their problems is the method of _____, which was used by Masters and Johnson.
5. Kinsey's sampling techniques were excellent; his interviewing techniques were also excellent. True or false?
6. The most questionable statistic in the Kinsey report was the incidence of homosexuality. True or false?
7. Magazine surveys, such as those conducted by *Psychology Today* and *McCall's,* provide a good, rich source of information about human sexuality. True or false?
8. _____ is the term for the type of study in which the researcher becomes a part of the community being studied and thus observes it from the inside, as in the studies of swingers.
9. Kinsey's research would properly be termed an experiment. True or false?
10. If someone says "Approximately 67 percent of people engage in premarital intercourse," this is a statement about frequency. True or false?

QUESTIONS FOR THOUGHT, DISCUSSION, AND DEBATE

1. Find a recent sex survey in a magazine. Evaluate the quality of the study, using concepts you have learned in this chapter.
2. Of the research techniques in this chapter—surveys, laboratory studies using direct observations, participant observer studies, experiments—which do you think is best for learning about human sexuality? Why?

SUGGESTION FOR FURTHER READING

Bentler, P. M. and Abramson, P. R. (1981). The science of sex research: Some methodological considerations. *Archives of Sexual Behavior,* **10**, 225–251. This article takes up where the present chapter leaves off, and offers many excellent suggestions on research methods for sex researchers.

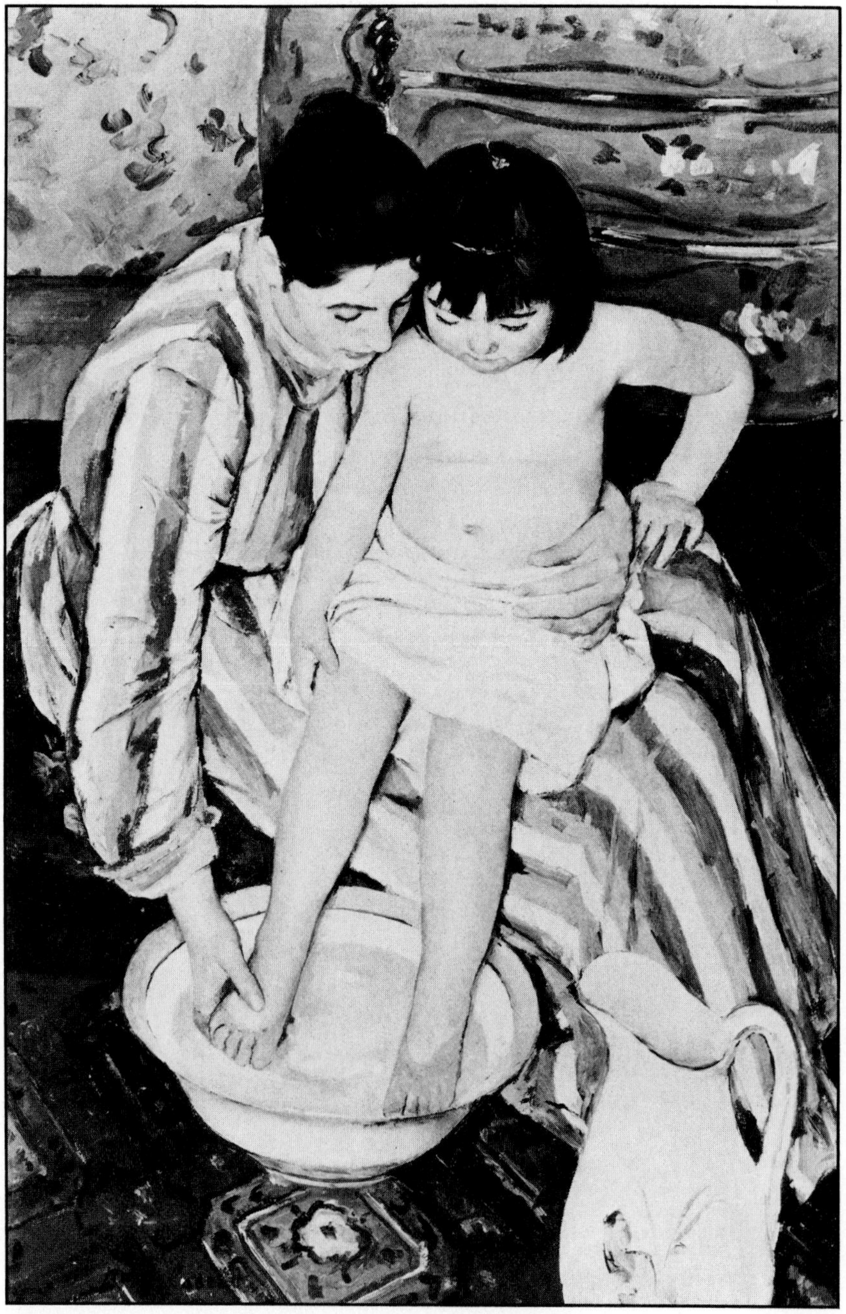

CHAPTER • 11

SEXUALITY AND THE LIFE CYCLE: CHILDHOOD AND ADOLESCENCE

My friend said to me, "If you show me yours, I'll show you mine." I said, "All right," but that we should go into the garage where no one would see us. I knew or thought that if someone caught us, we'd both be in real trouble. I don't remember what brought on this fear, but he seemed to have the same idea. So we went into the garage, and that was the first time I ever remember seeing a boy's penis. Many more incidents of sexual interest and exploration took place with this same playmate. . . .*

* *Source:* Female respondent quoted in Eleanor S. Morrison et al. (1980). *Growing up sexual.* New York: Van Nostrand.

CHAPTER HIGHLIGHTS

Stop for a moment and think of the first sexual experience you ever had. Some of you will think of the first time you had sexual intercourse, while others will remember much earlier episodes, like "playing doctor" with the other kids in the neighborhood. Now think of the kind of sex life you had, or expect to have, in your early twenties. Finally, imagine yourself at 65 and think of the kinds of sexual behavior you will be engaging in then.

In recent years, scientists have begun thinking of human development as a process that occurs throughout the lifespan. This represents a departure from the Freudian heritage, in which the crucial aspects of development were all thought to occur in childhood. This

Lifespan development: Development from birth through old age.

chapter and Chapter 12 are based on the newer lifespan or "life-cycle" approach to understanding the development of our sexual behavior throughout the course of our lives. The things you were asked to remember and imagine about your own sexual functioning at the beginning of this chapter will give you an idea of the sweep of this development.

DATA SOURCES

What kinds of scientific data are available on the sexual behavior of people at various times in their lives? Two of the basic sources we have are the Kinsey reports (Kinsey et al., 1948, 1953) and the Hunt study (1974). Comparing the reults of Kinsey's survey and Hunt's survey can give us an idea of how much the sexual behavior of young people has changed in the last several decades. The scientific techniques used by Kinsey and Hunt were discussed and evaluated in Chapter 10; since there are limitations to their studies, your evaluation of them may affect how much you are willing to accept the data presented in this chapter and in Chapter 12.

In both the Kinsey studies and the Hunt study, adult subjects were questioned about their childhood sexual behavior, and their responses form some of the data to be discussed in this chapter. These responses may be even more problematic than some of the other kinds of data from those studies, though. For example, a 50- or 60-year-old man is asked to report on his sexual behavior at age 10. How accurately will he remember things that happened 40 or 50 years ago? Surely there will be some forgetting. Thus the data on childhood sexual behavior may be subject to errors that result from being asked to recall things that happened a very long time ago.

An alternative would be to interview children about their sexual behavior or perhaps even to observe their sexual behavior. Few researchers have done either. The reasons are obvious; such a study would be exceptionally difficult and would involve serious ethical problems. Might a child be harmed by being interviewed about his or her sexual behavior? Could a child truly give informed consent to participate in such a study?

In a few studies children have been questioned directly about their sexual behavior. Kinsey interviewed 432 children, aged 4 to 14, and the results of the study were published after his death by Elias and Gebhard (1969). Several studies of adolescent sexual behavior have also been done. Particularly notable is the survey done by Sorensen (1973), popularly known as the "Sorensen report," and the study by Kantner and Zelnik of young unmarried women (1972, 1973). Sociological studies of premarital sexual behavior have been done by Robert Bell (1966), by Ira Reiss (1967), and, most recently, by John DeLamater and Patricia MacCorquodale (1979; see Focus 11.1).

The studies of child and adolescent sexual behavior have all been surveys, and they have used either questionnaires or interviews. No one has made systematic, direct observations of children's sexual behavior.

INFANCY (0 to 2 YEARS)

A century ago it was thought that sexuality was something that magically appeared at puberty. Historically, we owe the whole notion that children—in fact, infants—have sexual urges and engage in sexual behavior to Sigmund Freud.

The capacity of the human body to show a sexual response is present from birth. Male infants, for example, get erections. Indeed, boy babies are sometimes born with erections. In a study of nine male babies aged 3 to 20 weeks, erection was observed at least once daily in seven of the nine (Halverson, 1940). Indeed, ultrasound studies indicate that reflex erections occur in the male fetus for several months before birth (Masters et al., 1982). Vaginal lubrication has been found in baby girls in the 24 hours after birth (Masters et al., 1982).

Masturbation

Infants have been observed masturbating, that is, fondling their own genitals. There is some question as to how conscious they are of what they are doing, but at the least they seem to be engaging in some pleasurable, sexual self-stimulation. Toward the end of infancy, erotic feelings become more definitely centered in the genitals, and periods of definite sex play can be observed (Ribble, 1955, p. 26). Ford and Beach (1951), on the basis of their survey of sexual behavior in other cultures, noted that if permitted, most boys and girls will progress from absentminded fingering of their genitals to systematic masturbation by ages 6 to 8. In fact, in some cultures adults fondle infants' genitals to keep them quiet, a remarkably effective pacifier.

Orgasms from masturbation are possible even at this early age, although before puberty boys are not capable of ejaculation. Kinsey reported that 32 percent of boys under 1 year of age were able to have orgasms. He also reported on 23 girls, 3 years old and younger, who had orgasms as a result of masturbation (Kinsey et al., 1948, 1953).

Masturbation is a normal, natural form of sexual expression in infancy. It is definitely not a sign of pathology, as some previous generations believed. Indeed, in one study comparing infants who had optimal relationships with their mothers and infants who had problematic relationships with their mothers, it was the infants with the optimal maternal relationships who were more likely to masturbate (Spitz, 1949).

FIGURE 11.1

Infant masturbation.

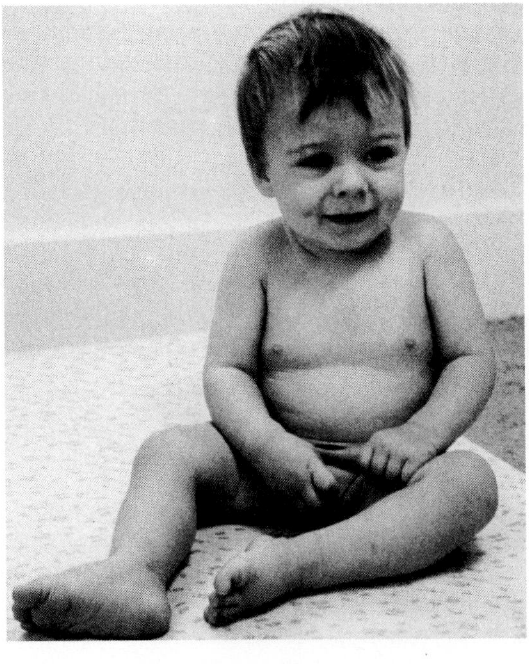

Infant-Infant Sexual Encounters

Infants and young children are very self-centered (what the psychologist Jean Piaget calls *egocentric*). Even when they seem to be playing with another child, they may simply be playing alongside the other child, actually in a world all their own. Their sexual development parallels the development of their other behaviors. Thus their earliest sex is typically one-person sex—masturbation. Not until later do they develop social, two-person sex, either heterosexual or homosexual.

Nonetheless, particularly in later infancy, there may be some infant-infant encounters, either affectionate or sexual.

Nongenital Sensual Experiences

Many of the sensual experiences that infants and young children have are diffuse and not easily classified as masturbation or as heterosexual or homosexual activity. For example, as Freud noted, infants delight in putting things in their mouths. Thus sucking at the mother's breast, or sucking on his or her own fingers, may be a sensuous experience for the infant.

Being cuddled or rocked can be a warm, sensuous experience. Indeed, the infant's experiences in such early intimate encounters might influence her or his reactions to intimacy and cuddling in adulthood. It seems that some infants are cuddlers and some are noncuddlers (Schaffer and Emerson, 1964). Cuddlers enjoy physical contact. Noncuddlers, unlike cuddlers, show displeasure and restlessness when they are handled or held. As soon as they are old enough to do so, they show resistance to such situations or crawl or walk away from them. Cuddling and noncuddling seem to be basically different personality patterns. It would be interesting to know whether these patterns remain consistent into adulthood.

Attachment

Attachment: A psychological bond that forms between an infant and the mother, father, or other care giver.

The quality of the relationship with the parents at this age can be very important to the child's capacity for later sexual and emotional relationships. In psychological terms, an attachment (or bond) forms between the infant and the mother, father, or other care giver. The bond begins in the hours immediately following birth and continues throughout the period of infancy (Higham, 1980). Later, other attachments form to other familiar people. These are the individual's earliest experiences with love and emotional attachment. It seems likely that the quality of these attachments—whether they are stable and satisfying or unstable and frustrating—affects the person's capacity for emotional attachments in adulthood.

We have little direct evidence supporting this last point. However, a classic study of attachment in infant monkeys by Harlow (1959) provides some suggestive evidence. Infant monkeys were reared not by their own mothers but by cloth or wire "surrogates." In adulthood, these monkeys showed seriously disturbed sexual behavior. Presumably their early lack of attachment to their mother had severe consequences for their later sexuality.

Knowing about Boy-Girl Differences

By age 2 or 2½, children know what gender they are. They know that they are like the parent of the same gender and different from the parent of the opposite gender

FIGURE 11.2

Harlow's study of infant monkeys reared not by their own mothers but by surrogates is a classic. In adulthood, these monkeys showed disturbed sexual behavior, presumably as a result of being deprived of an early attachment to their mothers.

and from other children of the opposite gender. At first, infants think that the difference between girls and boys is a matter of clothes or haircuts. But by age 2½ there may be at least some vague awareness of differences in the genital region and differences in positions during urination (Martinson, 1973).

EARLY CHILDHOOD (3 to 7 YEARS)

Between the ages of 3 and 7, there is a marked increase in sexual interest and activity, just as there is an increase in activity and interest in general.

Masturbation

Children increasingly gain experience with masturbation during childhood, although certainly not all children masturbate during this period. In a study of college students, 15 percent of the males and 20 percent of the females recalled that their first masturbation experiences occurred between ages 5 and 8 (Arafat and Cotton, 1974).

Children also learn during this period that masturbation is something that one does in private.

Heterosexual Behavior

By the age of 4 or 5, children's sexuality has become more social. There is some heterosexual play. Boys and girls may hug each other or hold hands, in imitation of adults. "Playing doctor" can be a popular game at this age. It generally involves no more than exhibiting one's own genitals, looking at those of others, and perhaps engaging in a little fondling or touching.

When I was six years old, I consciously experienced my first erection with a neighborhood girl of the same age. My curiosity increased when I saw only a small glimpse of her genital area when we played "doctor" and my desire to know more about the female sex increased tremendously. One day after school, the girl came over to my house. We proceeded up to my bedroom where I told her, "You can see me if I can see you." After she agreed, we both pulled down our pants. She asked me what my penis was. I told her that it was my "weiner," and that she didn't have one—only boys had "weiners." I then proceeded to touch my "weiner" to her "doop" (rear). This contact lasted for only a short time, yet I noticed for the first time that my penis was stiff. I had previously seen my friend's penis become erect as we played "doctor," but my penis becoming stiff was something I had never consciously experienced before. (Martinson, 1973, p. 31)

By about the age of 5, children have formed a concept of marriage—or at least of its nongenital aspects. They know that a member of the opposite gender is the appropriate marriage partner, and they are committed to marrying when they get older (Broderick, 1966). They practice marriage roles as they "play house."

Homosexual Behavior

During late childhood and preadolescence, sexual play with members of one's own gender may be more common than sexual play with members of the opposite gen-

FIGURE 11.3

Between the ages of 3 and 7 there is a marked increase in sexual interest.

der (Martinson, 1973). Generally the activity involves no more than touching the other's genitals (Broderick, 1966a). One girl recalled:

> I encountered a sexual experience that was confusing at kindergarten age. . . . Some afternoons we would meet and lock ourselves in a bedroom and take our pants off. We took turns lying on the bed and put pennies, marbles, etc. between our labia. . . . As the ritual became old hat, it passed out of existence. (Martinson, 1973, p. 39)

Sex Knowledge and Interests

At age 3 or 4, children begin to have some notion that there are genital differences between males and females, but their ideas are very vague. Not until they are 5 or 6 or 7 do they have a clear idea of what the true differences are (Martinson, 1973). Children generally react to their discovery of genital differences calmly, though of course there are exceptions.

At age 3, children are very interested in different postures for urinating. Girls attempt to urinate while standing. Children are also very affectionate at this age. They enjoy hugging and kissing their parents and may even propose marriage to the parent of the opposite gender (Martinson, 1973).

At age 4, children are particularly interested in bathrooms and elimination. Games of "show" are also common at this age.

Games of show become less common at age 5, as children become more modest. Generally children have well-developed principles of modesty and privacy by age 6 or 7. Children at this age are also becoming aware of the social restrictions on sexual expression. A woman recalled:

> When I was six years old I climbed up on the bathroom sink and looked at myself naked in the mirror. All of a sudden I realized I had three different holes. I was very excited about my discovery and ran down to the dinner table and announced it to everyone, "I have three holes!" Silence. "What are they for?" I asked. Silence even heavier than before. I sensed how uncomfortable everyone was and answered for myself. "I guess one is for pee-pee, the other for doo-doo and the third for ca-ca." A sigh of relief; no one had to answer my question. But I got the message—I wasn't supposed to ask "such" questions, though I didn't fully realize what "such" was about at that time. (Boston Women's Health Book Collective, 1976, p. 40)

It is important to remember that children's sex play at this age is motivated largely by curiosity and is part of the general learning experiences of childhood. One man illustrated this well as he recalled:

> As a child I experienced several incidents of homosexual exhibitions, many heterosexual exhibitions, and several instances of heterosexual play. This exploratory stage was experienced chiefly between the ages of four to seven. A secluded spot would be secured for purposes of observing and touching the opposite sex's genitals. This happened repeatedly with two girls, one older and one younger. Initiation for each experience seemed to be about fifty percent my effort. . . . At the age of six or seven my friend (a boy) and I had a great curiosity for exploring the anus. It almost seemed *more like scientific research.* (Martinson, 1973, p. 40, italics added)

PREADOLESCENCE (8 to 12 YEARS)

Preadolescence is a period of transition between the years of childhood and the years of puberty and adolescence.

Freud used the term "latency" to refer to the preadolescent period following the resolution of the Oedipus complex. He believed that the sexual urges go "underground" during latency and are not expressed. The evidence indicates, however, that Freud was wrong and that children's interest in and expression of sexuality remain lively throughout this period, perhaps more lively than their parents are willing to believe. For many, "sexual awakening" does not occur until the teens, but for others, it is a very real and poignant part of preadolescence (Martinson, 1973).

At around age 9 or 10, the first bodily changes of puberty begin: the formation of breast buds in girls and the growth of pubic hair. An increased self-consciousness about the body develops, to the point where the child may feel uncomfortable about being seen nude by the parent of the opposite gender. All this marks the transition to adolescence.

Masturbation

During preadolescence, more and more children gain experience with masturbation. Of the women in the Kinsey study, 8 percent recalled masturbating to orgasm by age 10, and 12 percent said they had done so by age 12.[1] The comparable figures for males are 2 percent by age 10 and 21 percent by age 12 (Kinsey et al., 1948, 1953). These data, as well as those on adolescence, indicate that boys generally start masturbating earlier than girls do.

Interestingly, boys and girls learn about masturbation in different ways. Typically boys are told about it by their peers, they see their peers doing it, or they read about it; girls, on the other hand, most frequently learn about masturbation through accidental self-discovery (Kinsey et al., 1953). One man recalled:

> An older cousin of mine took two of us out to the garage and did it in front of us. I remember thinking that it seemed a very strange thing to do, and that people who were upright wouldn't do it, but it left a powerful impression on me. A couple of years later, when I began to get erections, I wanted to do it, and felt I shouldn't, but I remembered how he had looked when he was doing it, and the memory tempted me strongly. I worried, and held back, and fought it, but finally I gave in. The worry didn't stop me, and doing it didn't stop my worrying. (Hunt, 1974, p. 79)

The more recent data collected by Hunt suggest that children begin masturbating at earlier ages now than they did in Kinsey's time and that this change is particularly marked among girls. A comparison of the Kinsey and Hunt data, as well as data from two other studies, is given in Table 11.1. Notice that about twice as many girls reported having masturbated to orgasm by age 13 in the recent studies, compared with the number in the Kinsey study, done a generation ago. Boys still masturbate earlier, on the average, but the gap has closed somewhat.

Heterosexual Behavior

There is generally little heterosexual behavior during the preadolescent period, mainly because of the social division of males and females into separate groups.

However, children commonly hear about sexual intercourse for the first time during this period. Their reactions to this new information are an amusing combination of shock and disbelief—particularly disbelief that their parents would do such a thing. A college woman recalled:

---

[1]These are cumulative-incidence figures, to use the terminology introduced in Chapter 10.

TABLE 11.1

COMPARATIVE DATA FROM DIFFERENT STUDIES ON THE AGE AT WHICH CHILDREN BEGIN TO MASTURBATE

Note that children today, especially girls, begin masturbating at an earlier age than children a generation ago.

	Number Who Had Masturbated by Age 13			
	Kinsey (1948, 1953), %	Hunt (1974), %	Arafat and Cotton (1974), %*	Ramsey (1943), %†
Males	45	63	49	85
Females	15	33	32	

*Based on a sample of 300 college students in the New York area.

†Based on interviews with boys. The statistic given is the percentage of 13-year-olds who reported having masturbated. It is interesting that the percentage based on direct questioning of boys is so much higher than percentages based on adults' recall.

One of my girlfriends told me about sexual intercourse. It was one of the biggest shocks of my life. She took me aside one day, and I could tell she was in great distress. I thought she was going to tell me about menstruation, so I said that I already knew, and she said, "No, this is *worse!*" Her description went like this: "A guy puts his thing up a girl's hole, and she has a baby." The hole was, to us, the anus, because we did not even know about the vagina and we knew that the urethra was too small. I pictured the act as a single, violent and painful stabbing at the anus by the penis. Somehow, the idea of a baby was forgotten by me. I was horrified and repulsed, and I thought of that awful penis I had seen years ago. At first I insisted that it wasn't true, and my friend said she didn't know for sure, but that's what her cousin told her. But we looked at each other, and we knew it was true. We held each other and cried. We insisted that "my parents would never do that," and "I'll never let anyone do it to me." We were frightened, sickened, and threatened by the idea of some lusty male jabbing at us with his horrid penis. (From a student essay)

For some preadolescents, too, heterosexual activity occurs in an incestuous relationship, whether brother-sister or parent-child. This topic is discussed in detail in Chapter 18.

Homosexual Behavior

According to one authority, the number of females who have homosexual encounters increases steadily, from about 6 percent at age 5 to 33 percent at adolescence; approximately 60 percent of males engage in homosexual play during preadolescence (Reevy, 1967).

It is important to understand this homosexual activity as a normal part of the sexual development of children. In preadolescence, children have a social organization that is essentially homosocial. That is, boys play separately from girls, and thus children socialize mainly with members of their own gender. This separation begins at around age 8. According to one study of children's friendship patterns, the segregation reaches a peak at around 10 to 12 years of age. At ages 12 to 13 children are simultaneously the most segregated by gender and the most interested in members of the opposite gender (Broderick, 1966b). Some of the social separation of the genders during preadolescence is actually comical; boys, for example, may have been convinced that girls have "cooties" and that they must be very careful to stay away from them. Given that children are socializing almost exclusively with other members of their own gender, sexual exploring at this age will likely be homosexual in nature.

Homosocial:
A general form of social groupings in which males play and associate with other males, and females play and associate with other females; that is, the genders are separate from each other.

These homosexual activities generally involve masturbation, exhibitionism, and the fondling of others' genitals. Boys, for example, may engage in a "circle jerk," in which they masturbate in a group.

Girls do not seem so likely to engage in such group homosexual activities, perhaps because the spectacle of them masturbating is not quite so impressive or perhaps because they already sense the greater cultural restrictions on their sexuality and are hesitant to discuss sexual matters with other girls. In any case, as noted above, boys seem to do their sexual exploring with a gang, while girls do it alone.

Dating

There is some anticipation of adolescent dating in the socializing patterns of preadolescents.

Group dating and heterosexual parties emerge first among preadolescents. Boys, particularly, are slow in adjusting to the behavior expected of them, and they may be more likely to roughhouse than to ask a girl to dance.

Kissing games are popular at parties, reaching their peak of popularity among children aged about 10 to 13 (Broderick, 1966b). There may also be some pairing off for "making out," which generally involves no more than kissing at this age. Genital fondling is not common (Martinson, 1973).

The first paired dating generally begins around the age of 12 or 13. It may consist simply of walking to a movie or going bowling together. At age 12, 48 percent of the boys and 57 percent of the girls in one study were dating (Broderick, 1966b). At 13, the figure was 69 percent for both. Typically, though, boys and girls at this age date only a few times a year.

Going steady also starts at this age, although often the activity centers more on symbols, such as an exchange of rings or bracelets, than it does on any real dating (Martinson, 1973).

Of course, these patterns are averages for American preadolescents. There is great variability within American culture, and in some other cultures boys and girls may already be married by age 13.

FIGURE 11.4

Group dating and heterosexual parties emerge during preadolescence; but girls' earlier growth spurts make for amusing height combinations.

Sexual Values

Preadolescents tend to be sexually conservative, while adolescents become increasingly liberal (Schoof-Tams et al., 1976). For example, in regard to premarital intercourse, 11-year-olds generally favor abstinence; they see intercourse as proper in marriage. Later in adolescence, the precondition for intercourse will shift to love rather than marriage.

ADOLESCENCE (13 to 19 YEARS)

A surge of sexual interest occurs around puberty and continues through adolescence (which is equated here roughly with the teenage years, ages 13 to 19). This heightened sexuality may be caused by a number of factors, including bodily changes and an awareness of them, rises in levels of sex hormones, and increased cultural emphasis on sex and rehearsal for adult gender roles. We can see evidence of this heightened sexuality particularly in the data on masturbation.

Masturbation

According to the Kinsey data, there is a sharp increase in the incidence of masturbation for boys between the ages of 13 and 15. This is illustrated in Figure 11.5. Note that the curve is steepest between the ages of 13 and 15, indicating that most boys begin masturbating to orgasm during that period. By age 15, 82 percent of the boys in Kinsey's study had masturbated. Many girls also begin masturbating at around that age, but note that the curve on the graph is flatter for them, indicating that many girls do not begin masturbating until later. Thus the increase in their masturbation behavior is much more gradual than boys' and continues past adolescence.

As was noted in a previous section, more recent data suggest that children and adolescents begin to masturbate earlier today than they did a generation ago, and thus the Kinsey data probably need to be pushed back about one or two years. However, the general shape of the curves still seems to hold.

Boys typically masturbate two or three times per week, whereas girls do so about once per month (Hass, 1979).

One man recalled his adolescent experiences with masturbation and the intense feelings involved as follows:

> When I was fourteen I was like Portnoy—always rushing off to the bathroom when the urge came over me. I did it so much that my dick would get swollen and sore, but even that didn't stop me. By the time I was nineteen I was screwing, but there'd be times

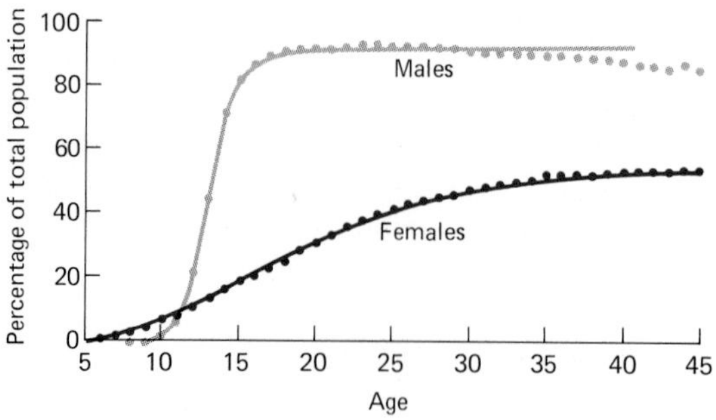

FIGURE 11.5

Cumulative incidence of males and females who have masturbated to orgasm, according to Kinsey's data.

> when I wouldn't be able to get anything, and I'd go back to jacking off—and then I felt really guilty and ashamed of myself, like I was a failure, like I had a secret weakness. (Hunt, 1974, p. 95)

Interestingly, the frequency of masturbation among boys decreases during periods when they are having sexual intercourse; among girls, however, this situation is accompanied by an increased frequency of masturbation (Sorensen, 1973).

Attitudes toward Masturbation

Attitudes toward masturbation have undergone a dramatic change in this century. As a result, adolescents are now given much different information about masturbation, and this may affect both their behavior and their feelings about masturbation.

For example, a popular handbook, *What a Boy Should Know,* written in 1913 by two doctors, advised its readers:

> Whenever unnatural emissions are produced . . . the body becomes "slack." A boy will not feel so vigorous and springy; he will be more easily tired. . . . He will probably look pale and pasty, and he is lucky if he escapes indigestion and getting his bowels confined, both of which will probably give him spots and pimples on his face. . . .
>
> The results on the mind are the more severe and more easily recognized. . . . A boy who practices this habit can never be the best that Nature intended him to be. His wits are not so sharp. His memory is not so good. His power of fixing his attention on whatever he is doing is lessened. . . . A boy like this is a poor thing to look at. . . .
>
> . . . The effect of self-abuse on a boy's character always tends to weaken it, and in fact, to make him untrustworthy, unreliable, untruthful, and probably even dishonest. (Schofield and Vaughan-Jackson, 1913, pp. 30–42)

Masturbation, in short, was believed to cause everything from warts to insanity.

Attitudes toward masturbation are now considerably more positive, and few people would now subscribe to notions like those expressed above. Currently only about 15 percent of young people believe that masturbation is wrong (Hunt, 1974, p. 74). Indeed, masturbation is now recommended as a remedy in sex therapy. As psychiatrist Thomas Szasz said, the shift in attitudes toward masturbation has been so great that in a generation it has changed from a disease to a form of therapy.

While approval of masturbation is now explicit, people can still have mixed feelings about it. An example of a lingering negative attitude is that of the man quoted previously who likened his adolescent masturbation to Portnoy's,[2] accompanied as it was by feelings of guilt and shame. Among the adolescents interviewed by Sorensen (1973), few felt guilty about masturbation, but many felt defensive or embarrassed about it.

Homosexual Behavior

According to the Kinsey data, 3 percent of adolescent girls and 22 percent of adolescent boys have at least one homosexual experience resulting in orgasm. In many cases the person has only one or a few homosexual experiences, partly out of curiosity, and the behavior is discontinued. Such adolescent homosexual behavior does not seem to be predictive of adult homosexual orientation.

---

[2]Of the novel *Portnoy's Complaint,* which poignantly and humorously describes an adolescent male's masturbation.

Currently, about 11 percent of adolescent males and 6 percent of adolescent females report having had homosexual experiences, and 25 percent say they have been approached for a homosexual experience. Of those who have had homosexual experiences, 24 percent had their first experience with a younger person, 39 percent with someone of their own age, 29 percent with an older teenager, and 8 percent with an adult (Sorensen, 1973). Thus there is no evidence that adolescent homosexual experiences result from being seduced by adults; most such encounters take place between peers.

There are some discrepancies between the figures from the Sorensen report and those from the Kinsey report. These discrepancies may be due to changes in the climate of our society that took place between 1940 and the 1970s, or they may be due to memory inaccuracies among the adults in the Kinsey study who were asked to recall their adolescent behaviors. The data indicate that there has been no increase in the incidence of premarital homosexual behavior in recent years (DeLamater and MacCorquodale, 1979). It seems safe to conclude from these studies, taken together, that about 10 percent of adolescents have homosexual experiences, with the percentages being somewhat higher for boys than for girls.

Teenagers can be quite naive about homosexual behavior and societal attitudes toward it. In some cases, they have been taught that heterosexual sex is "bad"; having been told nothing about homosexual sex, they infer that it is permissible. In some cases, homosexual relationships naively develop from a same-gender friendship of late childhood and adolescence. One woman recalled:

> When I was a junior and senior in high school I had an intense friendship with Jan, a girl in my school. We wrote notes and went on walks and climbed trees, sharing dreams, reciting poems that we liked, and talking about coming back to the school in later years to teach together. We vowed lifelong love and friendship, but physically we could express the energy that was between us only by clowning around, bumping into each other—and once when she was asleep I kissed her hair. The intensity of my friendship with Jan made my family uneasy—I remember comments about seeing too much of one person. Their uneasiness got to me a little, because I was a bit uncomfortable with my strong pit-of-the-stomach feelings about her anyway. I remember being shy about undressing with her in the room, although I undressed with other friends without thinking about it. Then during the summer after we graduated, having not seen Jan for several weeks, I was leafing through a psychology book and found a section that talked about the intense, bordering-on-homosexual friendship of young girls.
>
> Before long I had labeled it as a silly, childishly intense friendship. I made no efforts to see her when we both went to college, for I figured we had nothing in common.
>
> I think our feelings grew more intense as we tried to repress their sexual side. So I pulled away from Jan because I couldn't handle the natural sexual part of my feelings and affection for her. (Boston Women's Health Book Collective, 1976, p. 64)

Heterosexual Behavior

Toward the middle and end of the adolescent years, more and more young people engage in heterosexual sex, with more and more frequency. Thus heterosexual behavior gains prominence and becomes the major source of sexual outlet.

In terms of the individual's development, the data indicate that there is a very regular progression from kissing, through French kissing and breast and genital fondling, to intercourse and oral-genital contact; this generally occurs over a period of four or more years (DeLamater and MacCorquodale, 1979).

FIGURE 11.6

Sexuality in early adolescence is often playful and unsophisticated.

PREMARITAL SEX[3]

One of the most dramatic changes to occur in sexual behavior and attitudes in recent decades is in the area of premarital sexual behavior.

How Many People Have Premarital Intercourse?

On the basis of his data collected in the 1940s, Kinsey concluded that about 33 percent of all females and 71 percent of all males have premarital intercourse by the age of 25.

[3]Note that the very term "*pre*marital sex" contains some hidden assumptions, most notably that marriage is normative and that proper sex occurs in marriage. Thus, sex among never-married (young) persons is considered *pre*marital—something done before marrying. A more neutral term would be "nonmarital sex," although it fails to distinguish between premarital sex, extramarital sex, and postmarital sex.

TABLE 11.2

PERCENTAGES OF PEOPLE WHO HAD ENGAGED IN PREMARITAL INTERCOURSE, ACCORDING TO THE KINSEY REPORT AND THE HUNT REPORT

	Kinsey (1948, 1953)	Hunt (1974)
Males (by age 25)	71	97
Females (by age 25)	33	67

F • O • C • U • S 11.1

A SOCIOLOGICAL ANALYSIS OF PREMARITAL SEXUAL BEHAVIOR

Sociologists John DeLamater and Patricia MacCorquodale (1979) conducted a large-scale survey and detailed analysis of patterns of premarital sexuality. They interviewed both students and nonstudents between the ages of 18 and 23 in Madison, Wisconsin. They obtained an initial random sample of 1141 students at the University of Wisconsin. They attempted to interview all these people, obtaining an 82 percent response rate. Nonstudents were contacted by a probability sample of residences in the telephone directory; they had a 63 percent response rate. Data for a total of 1376 respondents were analyzed. The study is notable because it is recent, because it included both students and nonstudents, and because it used excellent sampling techniques and had a good response rate, except that the nonstudent response rate was a bit lower than would be desirable. It is difficult to know to what extent the results are limited to Madison, Wisconsin, and whether they would be generalizable to other areas of the country.

The data on the sexual experience of the respondents are summarized in the table.

Respondents also answered a number of other questions, and analyses of the answers permitted the authors to come to some conclusions regarding what factors are most strongly related to premarital sexual expression.

One of the most important factors appeared to be sexual ideology or attitudes. That is, those with the most liberal attitudes had the most premarital sexual experience. DeLamater and MacCorquodale argued that this occurs because ideology forms the basis for self-control. That is, the individual's standards specify the type of relationship, in terms of emotional commitment, which is necessary before particular behaviors are appropriate. Confirming this notion, the variable most closely related to the respondents'

The Hunt data collected in 1972, indicate a much higher incidence of premarital coitus, particularly for females (see Table 11.2).[4] It appears that virtually all males and over two-thirds of all females engage in premarital intercourse.

[4]The Kantner and Zelnik study (1972), which used better scientific techniques than the Kinsey and Hunt studies (see Chapter 10), also found an apparent increase in the incidence of premarital sex, compared with Kinsey's data. Kantner and Zelnik found that in 1971, 46 percent of women had had premarital sex by age 19; Kinsey found that about 19 percent had done so by age 19. Indeed, Kantner and Zelnik even found an increase in the incidence of premarital intercourse from 1971 to 1976 (Zelnik and Kanter, 1977). In comparison with the 1971 finding that 46 percent of the 19-year-olds had had intercourse, 55 percent had done so in 1976. The trend continued for data collected in 1979 (Zelnik and Kantner, 1980). Unfortunately, since the Kantner and Zelnik survey did not include any women over age 19, it does not enable us to determine how many women eventually have premarital sex.

PERCENTAGES OF RESPONDENTS WHO HAD EVER ENGAGED IN A BEHAVIOR

	Male		**Female**	
	Student	**Nonstudent**	**Student**	**Nonstudent**
Necking	97	98	99	99
French kissing	93	95	95	95
Breast fondling	92	92	93	93
Male fondling of female genitals	86	87	82	86
Female fondling of male genitals	82	84	78	81
Genital apposition	77	81	72	78
Intercourse	75	79	60	72
Male mouth contact with female genitals	60	68	59	67
Female mouth contact with male genitals	61	70	54	63

current behavior was the emotional quality of their current relationship.

How are the person's attitudes shaped? DeLamater and MacCorquodale found that parents, and sometimes religion, are early shapers of ideology. Later, close friends and dating partners become more important, while the influence of parents wanes. As peers become more important influences, the young person's standards typically become more permissive.

Contrary to what one might expect, the results indicated that a number of psychological variables—self-image, self-esteem, body image, sense of internal or external control, and gender-role definitions—were *un*related to premarital sexual behavior.

Finally, the results indicated increased similarities between women and men and a decline of the double standard, as other recent surveys have found. One of the few differences that remains, though, is that women still require greater emotional commitment before they are accepting of premarital intercourse. This may cause conflicts in some relationships.

DeLamater and MacCorquodale concluded that it is the couple and the nature of their relationship—rather than variables such as social class or religion—that are essential to understanding premarital sexuality.

It is tempting to make causal inferences from these data—for example, that permissive attitudes *cause* increased premarital sexual experience. It is important to remember that these data are correlational in nature and that causality cannot be inferred. Nonetheless, this study provides good evidence of what factors are most related to premarital sexual patterns, and these findings can be confirmed by later research.

Source: John DeLamater and Patricia MacCorquodale. (1979). *Premarital sexuality: Attitudes, relationships, behavior.* Madison: University of Wisconsin Press.

To summarize, the trends in premarital intercourse in the last two decades are in the direction of: (1) more adolescents engaging in premarital intercourse; (2) a greater increase in incidence for females, thereby narrowing the gap between males and females; and (3) intercourse occurring at somewhat earlier ages (Hopkins, 1977).

First Intercourse

The adolescents in the Sorensen report described their emotional reactions to their first act of intercourse. Contrary to what one might expect, girls generally attached less significance to it than boys did. However, positive reactions—such as feelings of maturity and joy—were about twice as common among boys as among girls. Girls more often said they felt such emotions as guilt, sorrow, and disappointment. Most typically, the immediate reaction of males was to feel excitement, while females typically felt afraid. Unfortunately, the boy usually did not realize that the girl was having a negative reaction (Sorensen, 1973).

Peggy Lee syndrome: The feelings of disappointment experienced by teenage girls at first intercourse when it is not as thrilling as they expected.

The typical female reaction to first intercourse has been described as the Peggy Lee syndrome (named for her song "Is That All There Is?"). Despite our culture's romanticized high expectations that the first intercourse experience will be like firecrackers popping on the Fourth of July, it turns out to be much less thrilling than that for most females. For example, a sample of college women, recalling their experience of first intercourse, on the average gave it only a 3.9 on a pleasure scale (1 = didn't experience pleasure at all, 7 = strongly experienced pleasure) (Weis, 1983).

Sex with a Prostitute

A generation ago, premarital sex with a prostitute was fairly common among males, and many young men received their sexual initiation in this manner. Among the noncollege men over age 35 in the Hunt study 20 percent had had their first intercourse with a prostitute (Hunt, 1974, p. 145). Now, however, having premarital sex with a prostitute is much less common. This can be seen by comparing the percentages of men under 35 in Hunt's study who had ever had sex with a prostitute with the percentages of men over 35 who had ever done so (see Table 11.3). From these data it appears that only about half as many men now have premarital sex with prostitutes as was the case a generation ago. Further, those who do have such contacts have far fewer of them. Sex with prostitutes is one of the few sexual behaviors to show a decline between the time of the Kinsey study and the time of the Hunt study.

Techniques in Premarital Sex

Paralleling the increase in the incidence of premarital intercourse is an increase in the variety of techniques that are used in premarital sex. One of the most dramatic changes has been the increased use of oral-genital techniques. In the Kinsey sample, 33 percent of the males had experienced fellatio premaritally, and 14 percent had engaged in cunnilingus. In the Hunt survey, 72 percent of the males had engaged in fellatio premaritally, and 69 percent had performed cunnilingus (Hunt, 1974, p. 166). In my classes, I generally find that about 5 percent of the women students have engaged in fellatio and/or cunnilingus but not in intercourse—I suspect because some have discovered that mouth-genital sex cannot cause pregnancy. Young people today also use a greater variety of positions, not just the standard man-on-top (Hunt, 1974, p. 167).

Doubtless some of this increased variety in techniques is a result of today's "performance ethic" in sexual relations, which was discussed in Chapter 9. Adolescents and young adults may feel pressured to be gold medalists in the sexual Olympics. One man said:

> Sometimes I'm really good; I can make a girl have orgasms until she's about half dead. But if I don't like the girl, or if I'm not feeling confident, it can be hard work—and sometimes I can't even cut the mustard, and that bothers me a lot when that happens. (Hunt, 1974, p. 163)

TABLE 11.3

PERCENTAGES OF MARRIED MALES WHO HAD EVER HAD PREMARITAL INTERCOURSE WITH A PROSTITUTE

	Age of Respondents	
Education of Respondents	**Under 35, %**	**35 and over, %**
High school or less	30	61
Some college or more	19	52

Source: Morton Hunt. (1974). *Sexual behavior in the 1970s.* Chicago: Playboy Press, p. 144.

Attitudes toward Premarital Intercourse

Abstinence:
A standard in which premarital intercourse is considered wrong, regardless of the circumstances.

Permissiveness with affection:
A standard in which premarital intercourse is considered acceptable if it occurs in the context of a loving, committed relationship.

Permissiveness without affection:
A standard in which premarital intercourse is acceptable even if there is no emotional commitment.

Double standard:
A standard in which premarital intercourse is considered acceptable for males but not for females.

Attitudes toward premarital intercourse have also undergone marked changes, particularly among young people.

Sociologist Ira L. Reiss (1960) has distinguished between four kinds of standards for premarital coitus:

1. Abstinence Premarital intercourse is considered wrong for both males and females, regardless of the circumstances.
2. Permissiveness with affection Premarital intercourse is permissible for both males and females if it occurs in the context of a stable relationship that involves love, commitment, or being engaged.
3. Permissiveness without affection Premarital intercourse is permissible for both males and females, regardless of emotional commitment, simply on the basis of physical attraction.
4. Double standard Premarital intercourse is acceptable for males but is not acceptable for females. The double standard may be either "orthodox" or "transitional." In the orthodox case, the double standard holds regardless of the couple's relationship, while in the transitional case, sex is considered acceptable for the woman if she is in love or if she is engaged.

Historically in the United States, the standard has been either abstinence or the double standard. However, today, particularly among young people, the standard is one of permissiveness with affection.

We can see evidence of this new standard, and of the shift it represents from standards of previous generations, by comparing the data on current attitudes toward premarital intercourse among respondents in the Hunt study (1974) with results from older surveys. These data are shown in Table 11.4. Note that in surveys conducted in both 1937 and 1959, few people approved of premarital intercourse, and there was some evidence of a double standard in that some people felt that premarital intercourse was acceptable for men only. By 1972, though, the majority of respondents felt that premarital intercourse was acceptable if there was strong affection between the people, and particularly if they were engaged. There is still some evidence of a double standard, in that somewhat more people approve of premarital coitus for men than for women. Note also that women tend to have somewhat more conservative standards; fewer of them approve of premarital coitus. The dominant view that emerges, though, is that premarital intercourse is acceptable if there is strong affection, and that is precisely the standard of "permissiveness with affection" that Reiss described.

TABLE 11.4

PERCENTAGES OF PEOPLE AGREEING THAT PREMARITAL INTERCOURSE IS ACCEPTABLE, 1937, 1959, 1972

"Do you think it is all right for either or both parties to a marriage to have had previous sexual intercourse?"

	1937, %	1959, %
All right for both	22	22
All right for men only	8	8
All right for neither	56	54
Don't know or refused to answer	14	16

Percentages Agreeing That Premarital Coitus Is Acceptable, 1972

	Male Respondents, %	**Female Respondents, %**
For a man:		
Where strong affection exists	75	55
Couple in love, but not engaged	82	68
Couple engaged	84	73
For a woman:		
Where strong affection exists	66	41
Couple in love, but not engaged	77	61
Couple engaged	81	68

Source: Morton Hunt. (1974). *Sexual behavior in the 1970s.* Chicago: Playboy Press, pp. 115–116.

Among young people, attitudes toward premarital intercourse vary considerably with age. The attitudes of adolescents up to 17 years of age toward premarital intercourse differ considerably from those of young adults over age 18 (R. R. Bell, 1966, p. 66). Many readers will recall that they disapproved of premarital intercourse while they were in high school but changed their minds when they entered college.

Motives for Having Premarital Intercourse

The adolescent respondents in the Sorensen study (1973) commonly mentioned a need to search for new experience and a desire to escape from tensions as reasons for engaging in premarital coitus. Other reasons included using it as a means of communication, as a sign of maturity, and as a way of handing out rewards or punishments (perhaps rewarding a boyfriend or punishing parents—recall the nonsexual uses of sexual behavior). Some respondents said they engaged in premarital intercourse simply because it was expected by the peer group. Challenging parents or society and deriving physical pleasure were not commonly mentioned as reasons for engaging in premarital intercourse. As homosexuality receives more publicity and as adolescents become anxious about it, having premarital sex may also be a means of "proving" one's heterosexuality (R. R. Bell, 1966).

Nonetheless, one should not overestimate the importance teenagers attach to sex. When asked to rank what was most important to them, teenagers listed doing well in school and friendships first and second, and sex sixth in a list of six (Hass, 1979).

Rampant Promiscuity?

Promiscuity (prah-miss-CYOO-ih-tee): Undiscriminating, casual sexual relations with anyone.

Some members of our society are concerned that today's young people have no standards at all and are engaging in rampant promiscuity (undiscriminating, casual sexual relations with anyone and everyone). These concerns are encouraged by flashy newspaper and magazine articles about the sexual scene in high schools and on college campuses.

Is all this true? Not really, according to the available data. First, although the standard for acceptable sex in the previous generation was marriage, this generation has not abolished standards completely. Instead a new standard has been substituted, and it is based on the quality (not the legality) of the relationship between the two people—its stability and the emotional commitment involved. This standard of permissiveness with affection is scarcely a license for casual or impersonal sex. Second, the number of premarital partners is generally small. Among those women who engage in premarital intercourse, most have only one partner, whom they eventually marry. Studies indicate that 54 percent have only one partner, and for about 50 percent this partner is their fiancé (Hunt, 1974, pp. 151–152; see also Kantner and Zelnik, 1972). Typically, men have about six premarital partners (Hunt, 1974), scarcely an orgy.

The present generation has probably done little more than change the time sequence of things. For their parents, the appropriate sequence was to fall in love, get married, and have intercourse; for young people today, the sequence is to fall in love, have intercourse, and get married. Some have even argued that the trend in the 1980s is toward increased conservatism in sexual attitudes and behaviors, a point to be discussed in the last chapter of this book.

Dating, Going Steady, Getting Engaged

The social forces that have produced changes in premarital sexual behavior and standards are complex. But among them seems to be a change in courtship stages—in the processes of dating, going steady, and getting engaged. Dating and going steady occur much earlier now than in previous generations. As psychologist Albert Ellis has commented:

> [The] most significant change in American courtship procedures and its sex dance during the last ten years (from 1950 to 1960) is the enormous increase in dating, and especially in going steady, among teen-agers (twelve-to fifteen-year-olds) that has taken place. (1962, p. 84)

Dating earlier and going steady earlier create both more of a demand for premarital sex and more of a legitimacy for it. For many, sexual intimacy is made respectable by going steady (R. R. Bell, 1966). As Ira Reiss noted, "No other dating custom is quite so central to the understanding of teen-age sexual codes as going steady."

Serial monogamy: A premarital sexual pattern in which there is an intention of being faithful to the partner, but the relationship may end and the person will then move on to another partner.

Sorensen (1973) found the most common premarital sexual pattern to be serial monogamy without marriage. In such a relationship there is an intention of being faithful, but the relationship is of uncertain duration. Of those in the sample who had premarital intercourse, 40 percent were serial monogamists. Though they averaged about four partners, nearly half of them had had only one partner, and about half of them had been involved in their current relationship for a year or more.

F • O • C • U • S
11.2

COHABITING IN COLLEGE: GOING VERY STEADY

In the stricter days of 1968, a Barnard College sophomore named Linda LeClair became an overnight celebrity after the public revelation that she was living off campus with a former Columbia University student. Linda's battle with school authorities made front-page news in *The New York Times* and other papers across the country.

Since then, a number of researchers have investigated the phenomenon of cohabitation ("living together") among college students, finding that it is an important contemporary living pattern.

Estimates of the number of students who cohabit vary from 10 percent at small liberal arts colleges that do not permit off-campus housing or overnight visits to 35 percent at large state universities that permit off-campus housing and have 24-hour visiting privileges.

An intensive study of cohabitation at Cornell University indicated that there was no significant difference in academic performance between cohabitants and noncohabitants. Neither did the two groups differ in their desire to marry eventually.

The sexual aspects of cohabitation should not be overdramatized. In most cases, of course, the couple have a full sexual relationship. But in about 10 percent of the cases, the couple lived together for three months or more before having intercourse. (This is a more general phenomenon in premarital sex; a couple may literally "sleep together" for some time before they begin having intercourse.) The motives for cohabitation seem to be more emotional than sexual.

In the Cornell study, the students gave a number of reasons for cohabiting: the loneliness of a large university, the superficiality of the "dating game," a search for more meaningful relations with others, the emotional satisfaction of living and sleeping with someone who cares about you, a desire to try out a relationship before marriage, and widespread doubts about the very institution of marriage. The single most important reason cited for choosing to live with someone was "emotional attachment to each other." Most of the relationships were monogamous.

For those who had not cohabited, the reason seemed to be more often lack of opportunity than ethical standards.

In most cases, though, living together was not a purposeful act based on a carefully made decision. Initially, most cohabitation relationships were drifted into, with the couple sleeping together more and more often.

The students in the Cornell study definitely did not see the relationship as a "trial marriage." They did not consider themselves married in any sense of the word, and very few of them saw marriage as a viable alternative to their present situation. Instead, they were engaged in a living out of what used to be called "going steady."

Cohabitation, of course, is also common beyond the college years. In 1980 there were 1.6 million unmarried couples living together in the United States, triple the number in 1970. Because people are postponing the age at which they marry, from 1975 to 1980 there was a decline in the number of married people in the under-25 age group, but a substantial increase in the number who were cohabiting.

Sources: Eleanor D. Macklin. (1974). Cohabitation in college: Going very steady. *Psychology Today,* **8**(6), 53–59. Graham B. Spanier. (1983). Married and unmarried cohabitation in the United States: 1980. *Journal of Marriage and the Family,* **45**, 277–288.

Conflicts

We are currently in an era of transition between a restrictive sexual ethic and a permissive one. In such circumstances, conflicts are bound to arise. One is between parents and children, as parents hold fast to conservative standards while their children adopt permissive ones.

These conflicts within our society are mirrored in the messages of the mass media. As Albert Ellis describes the situation:

> Premarital sex relations today are widely believed to be bad, silly and pointless; *but* thoroughly enjoyable; *but* normal and natural; *but* necessary for healthful living; *but* smart, gay, and sophisticated; *but* romantically permissible and thrilling; *but* adventurous and exciting; *but* inevitable in this all-too-fleshy world, and so on. (1962, p. 29)

Listening to such messages while growing up, it is no wonder adolescents may sometimes feel conflicts about premarital sex.

Young people may also experience conflicts between their own behaviors and their attitudes or standards. Behaviors generally change faster than attitudes do (R. R. Bell, 1966). As a result, people may engage in premarital sex while still disapproving of it. Feelings of guilt or anxiety can result. Generally with time, such conflicts are smoothed out. Among married women looking back on their premarital sexual experiences, 77 percent saw no reason to regret having had premarital coitus (Kinsey et al., 1953).

HOW SEXUALITY AIDS IN PSYCHOLOGICAL DEVELOPMENT

Erik Erikson, whose work represents a major revision of Freudian theory, has postulated a theory of psychosocial development according to which we experience crises at eight different stages of our lives (Erikson, 1950, 1968). Each one of these crises may be resolved in one of two directions. Erikson notes that social influences are particularly important in determining the outcomes of these crises.

The stages postulated by Erikson are listed in Table 11.5. Note that the outcomes of several of them may be closely linked to sexuality. For example, in early childhood there is a crisis between autonomy and shame, and later between initiative and guilt. The child who masturbates at age 5 is showing autonomy and initiative. But if the parents react to this activity by severely punishing the child, their actions may produce shame and guilt. Thus they may be encouraging the child to feel ashamed and consequently to suffer a loss of self-esteem.

In adolescence, the crisis is between identity and role confusion. Gender roles are among the most important; in later adolescence the person may emerge with a

TABLE 11.5

ERIKSON'S STAGES OF PSYCHOSOCIAL DEVELOPMENT

Approximate Stage in the Life Cycle	Crisis
Infancy	Basic trust vs. mistrust
Ages 1½ to 3 years	Autonomy vs. shame and doubt
Ages 3 to 5½ years	Initiative vs. guilt
Ages 5½ to 12 years	Industry vs. inferiority
Adolescence	Identity vs. role confusion
Young adulthood	Intimacy vs. isolation
Adulthood	Generativity vs. stagnation
Maturity	Ego integrity vs. despair

stable, self-confident sense of manhood or womanhood or, alternatively, may feel in conflict about gender roles. A choice of career is extremely important in this developing sense of identity, and gender roles influence career choice. A sexual identity also emerges—whether, for example, one is heterosexual or homosexual, popular or unpopular.

In young adulthood, the crisis is between intimacy and isolation. Sexuality, of course, can function in an important way as people develop their capacity for intimacy.

For adolescents particularly, sexuality is related to accomplishing important developmental tasks (A. P. Bell, 1974a). Among these are:

1. Becoming independent of parents. Sexuality is a way of expressing one's autonomy and one's independence from parents. The adolescent boy who masturbates, for example, may be expressing a need to cut the apron strings that tie him to his mother—as you know if you have read *Portnoy's Complaint.*
2. Establishing a viable moral system of one's own. For many adolescents, some of the most critical moral decisions of their lives made independently of parents are in the area of their own sexual conduct. A personal ethical system emerges.
3. Establishing an identity—in particular, a sexual identity.
4. Developing a capacity for establishing an intimate relationship with another person and sustaining it.

Thus we can see that sexuality is an integral part of our psychological development.

SUMMARY

A capacity for sexual response is present from infancy. According to Kinsey's data, about 10 percent of children have masturbated to orgasm by age 10, although recent studies indicate that children begin masturbating at somewhat earlier ages now than a generation or so ago. Children also engage in some heterosexual play, as well as some homosexual activity.

During adolescence there is an increase in sexual activity. By age 15, nearly all boys have masturbated. Girls tend to begin masturbating somewhat later than boys, and fewer of them masturbate. Attitudes toward masturbation are considerably more permissive now than they were a century ago. About 10 percent of adolescents have homosexual experiences to orgasm, with the figure being slightly higher for boys than for girls.

Today the majority of males and the majority of females have premarital sex. This is a considerable increase over the incidence reported in the Kinsey studies, done a generation ago. Adolescents today are also considerably more likely to use a variety of sexual techniques, including mouth-genital sex.

The prodominant sexual standard today is one of "permissiveness with affection"; that is, sex is seen as acceptable outside marriage, provided there is an emotional commitment between the partners. The evidence does not support the notion that teenagers today are engaging in rampant promiscuity.

Following Erik Erikson's theory, experiences with sexuality can serve important functions in a person's psychological development. They may be important, for example, in the process of becoming independent of parents and in establishing a viable moral system.

REVIEW QUESTIONS

1. Several investigators have been able to do studies of children's sexual behavior using the method of direct observation. True or false?
2. Children do not begin masturbating until 10 or 11 years of age. True or false?
3. The results of Harlow's experiments indicate that monkeys that did not have normal attachments to their mothers in infancy showed seriously disturbed sexual behavior in adulthood. True or false?
4. The majority of both males and females engage in premarital intercourse. True or false?
5. One of the few sexual behaviors to show a decline in incidence in the last few decades is sex with a prostitute. True or false?
6. DeLamater and MacCorquodale, in their sociological analysis of premarital sexual behavior, concluded that the particular couple and the nature of their relationship are the most important factors in determining whether people engage in premarital intercourse. True or false?
7. According to sociologist Ira Reiss, the current standard under which most adolescents believe that intercourse is acceptable is termed "permissiveness without affection." True or false?
8. Sorenson uses the term ____ to describe the premarital sexual pattern in which there is an intention of being faithful to the partner, but the relationship may end and the person will then move on to another partner.
9. In a study of couples cohabiting in college, the single most important reason cited for living together was a desire for frequent and reliable sex. True or false?
10. Sexuality may aid in psychological development, including establishing a moral system of one's own and establishing an intimate relationship with another person. True or false?

QUESTIONS FOR THOUGHT, DISCUSSION, AND DEBATE

1. Do you think cohabitation is a good, adaptive lifestyle for young adults today? What are its advantages? What are its disadvantages?
2. Does "permissiveness with affection" characterize the standard for premarital intercourse among those 18- to 22-year-olds you know?

SUGGESTIONS FOR FURTHER READING

McCormick, Naomi B. (1979). Come-ons and put-offs: Unmarried students' strategies for having and avoiding intercourse. *Psychology of Women Quarterly,* **4**, 194–211. An interesting discussion of college students' reported techniques for inviting or avoiding intercourse, and how these techniques relate to gender-role stereotypes.

Morrison, Eleanor S., et al. (1980). *Growing up sexual.* New York: Van Nostrand. A fascinating view of sexual development with many first-person quotes, based on student autobiographies for a human sexuality course.

Simon, William, and Gagnon, John. (1969). Psychosexual development. *Transaction,* **6** (5). Reprinted in E. S. Morrison and V. Borosage (Eds.). (1977). *Human sexuality.* (2nd ed.) Palo Alto: Mayfield. A sociological approach to understanding sexual development.

CHAPTER • **12**

SEXUALITY AND THE LIFE CYCLE: ADULTHOOD

Grow old along with me!
The best is yet to be.

—Robert Browning

CHAPTER HIGHLIGHTS

I. MARITAL SEX
   - Frequency of Marital Intercourse
   - Techniques in Marital Sex
   - Masturbation in Marriage
   - Attitudes toward, and Satisfaction with, Marital Sex
   - Sexual Patterns in Marriage
   - Sex and the Two-Career Family

II. EXTRAMARITAL SEX
   - How Many People Engage in Extramarital Sex?
   - Attitudes toward Extramarital Sex
   - Consensual Extramarital Sex
   - Factors Related to Extramarital Sex
   - Equity and Extramarital Sex

III. SEX AND THE SINGLE PERSON
   - The Never-Married
   - The Divorced and the Widowed

IV. SEX AND THE SENIOR CITIZEN
   - Physical Changes
   - Attitudes about Sex and the Elderly
   - Sexual Behavior of the Elderly

This chpater will continue to trace the development of sexuality across the lifespan by considering sexuality in adulthood. The discussion will include sexuality in marriage and outside marriage (extramarital sex, postmarital sex, and sex among the never-married), as well as sex among the elderly.

MARITAL SEX

Despite all the talk in the 1970s about the end of the institution of marriage, it is clear from a 1980s perspective that the institution has survived, although perhaps now in more varied forms; indeed, there seems to be a reawakening of interest in intimacy and forming relationships (Scanzoni, 1982).

About 80 to 90 percent of all people in the United States marry, and of those who divorce, a high percentage remarry (Gagnon, 1977). In our society, marriage is also the context in which sexual expression has the most legitimacy. Therefore, sex in marriage is one of the commonest forms of sexual expression for adults.

Frequency of Marital Intercourse

It appears that the average American couple have coitus about two or three times per week when they are in their twenties, with the frequency gradually declining to about once per week for those aged 45 and over.

The precise data on this point from the Hunt, Kinsey, and Westoff studies are shown in Table 12.1. Several things can be noted from that table. First, there has been an increase in the frequency of marital sex in the last few decades. In every age group, the people in Hunt's study reported a higher average frequency of intercourse than the people in Kinsey's study. Second, the frequency of intercourse declines with age; however, even among those over 55, the frequency is still about once per week.

It is important to note that there is wide variability in these average frequencies. For example, about 8 to 12 percent of couples in their twenties report not engaging in intercourse at all, and another 5 to 10 percent report doing so less than once per month (Wilson, 1975). Data from a major, recent survey of American couples also confirm this wide variability, as shown in Figure 12.1 (Blumstein and Schwartz, 1983).

As was noted in Chapter 10, there may be serious problems with the Kinsey and Hunt data because of inadequacies in the sampling methods used. Recall that Westoff's (1974) study of married women used a probability sample and therefore probably provides better data. Note in Table 12.1 that the frequencies reported by the women in Westoff's study are generally lower than those reported by the people in Hunt's study, although the data were collected only two years apart. This suggests that Hunt's sample may indeed have been biased toward including people who were more sexually active than the general population.

The Westoff data also provide the best evidence of an increase in the frequency of marital intercourse in recent decades. In that study, a national probability sample of women were interviewed in 1965, and another probability sample were inter-

TABLE 12.1

MARITAL COITUS: FREQUENCY PER WEEK (MALE AND FEMALE ESTIMATES COMBINED), 1938–1949 AND 1970s

1938–1949 (Kinsey)		1972 (Hunt)		1970 (Westoff)	
Age	Median Frequency per Week	Age	Median Frequency per Week	Age	Mean Frequency per Week
16–25	2.45	18–24	3.25	20–24	2.5
26–35	1.95	25–34	2.55	25–34	2.1
36–45	1.40	35–44	2.00	35–44	1.6
46–55	0.85	44–54	1.00		
56–60	0.50	55 and over	1.00		

Sources: Morton Hunt. (1974). *Sexual behavior in the 1970s.* Chicago: Playboy Press, table 30, p. 191. Charles Westoff. (1974). Coital frequency and contraception. *Family Planning Perspectives,* **6**(3), pp. 136–141.

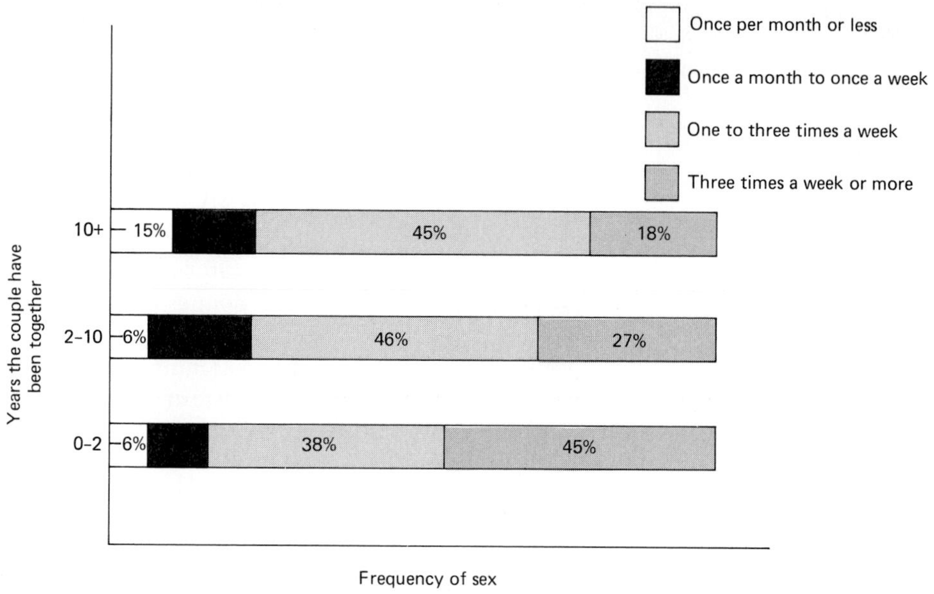

FIGURE 12.1

There is a wide variety in the frequency with which married couples have sex (Blumstein and Schwartz, 1983).

viewed in 1970. There was indeed an increase in reported frequency of coitus—even during that brief five-year period—from an average of 1.7 times per week in 1965 to 2.0 times per week in 1970. This finding confirms the general direction of the changes that occurred between the time the Kinsey report appeared and the time Hunt conducted his survey. The problems of self-report, of course, remain in the Westoff data.

Techniques in Marital Sex

Married couples now use—or at least say they use— a greater variety of sexual techniques than couples in the previous generation.

Couples today generally spend a longer time lovemaking than couples in previous generations. The women in the Kinsey sample estimated that the average duration of foreplay was about 12 minutes (Kinsey et al., 1953, p. 364). Generally the figure was somewhat higher among college-educated persons and considerably lower among those with less education. Further, about 75 percent of the men orgasmed within two minutes after inserting the penis into the vagina (Kinsey et al., 1948, p. 580). In the Hunt sample, the average duration of foreplay, among both the college-educated and the non-college-educated, was about 15 minutes (Hunt, 1974, p. 201); thus there has been a particularly substantial increase in the duration of foreplay among the non-college-educated. The reported duration of actual coitus (from insertion of the penis to the male's orgasm) increased to a median of about 10 minutes in the Hunt study.

Married couples today use a wider variety of positions during coitus than couples in past decades. For example, the female-on-top position is now used, at least occasionally, by about 75 percent of married couples, as compared with about 35 percent in Kinsey's sample (Hunt, 1974, p. 202). Experimentation with different positions is particularly common among younger couples.

The increased popularity of mouth-genital techniques is one of the most dramatic changes in marital sex to have occurred since the time of the Kinsey study. Data on

TABLE 12.2

MOUTH-GENITAL TECHNIQUES IN MARITAL SEX, ACCORDING TO THE KINSEY STUDIES AND THE HUNT STUDY

Respondents	Percentage of Marriages in Which Fellatio Is Used		Percentage of Marriages in Which Cunnilingus Is Used	
	Kinsey (1939–1949)	Hunt (1972)	Kinsey	Hunt
Males with a high school education	15	54	15	56
Males with a college education	43	61	45	66
Females with a high school education	46	52	50	58
Females with a college education	52	72	72	72

Source: Morton Hunt. (1974). *Sexual behavior in the 1970s.* Chicago: Playboy Press, p. 198. Copyright © 1974 by Morton Hunt. Reprinted by permission of Playboy Press.

this point are shown in Table 12.2. Cunnilingus and fellatio are now used in the majority of marriages, and they are particularly common among the college-educated.

Hunt notes that there has been a comparable change in attitudes toward various sex techniques that is particularly noticeable among the young:

> Among our older interviewees there were a number who, after a party at which they drank a great deal, or after some erotically stimulating event, might occasionally use fellatio, cunnilingus or even anal play, though ordinarily they felt squeamish about such acts or hesitant about suggesting them to their spouses. In contrast, most of the younger interviewees spoke as if they thoroughly enjoyed oral practices and took them as a matter of course, including them very frequently and naturally in their foreplay; a substantial minority, moreover, said that they also used manual-anal play anywhere from occasionally to fairly often. (1974, p. 200)

Negotiations

Before these techniques themselves are executed, there is typically a "mating dance" between the man and the woman. Sexual scripts are played out in marriage as in other aspects of sex (J. H. Gagnon, 1977, pp. 208–209). Deciding to have intercourse involves some preliminary negotiations, which are often phrased in indirect or euphemistic language, in part so that the person's feelings can be salvaged if her or his partner is not interested. For example. the husband may say, "I think I'll go take a shower" or "I think I'll go take a nap" (that means "I want to, do you?"). The wife may respond with, "I think I'll take one too" (that means "yes") or "The kids will be home any moment" or "I have a headache" (that means "no"). Or conversely, she may put on a lot of his favorite perfume and parade around in front of him (that is *her* offer). He may respond with, "I had an exhausting day at work" (his "no") or "I'll meet you upstairs" (his "yes"). To avoid some of the risk of rejection inherent in such negotiations, some couples simply ritualize sex so that both understand when it will and when it will not occur—Thursday night may be their time, or perhaps Sunday afternoon.

A recent survey of married couples found that, for 33 percent of them the husband and wife are about equally likely to initiate sex; for 51 percent the husband is more likely to be the initiator, and in only 16 percent of the couples is the wife usually the initiator (Blumstein and Schwartz, 1983). Thus there is some evidence of liberation (the couples where both are initiators), but traditional roles persist, with the majority of couples having the male in the initiating role. Women seem to be particularly careful not to initiate sex when they believe their spouse is feeling psychologically vulnerable. The traditional gender-typing of initiation patterns may also be related to how people deal with a refusal. If the man initiates and the woman refuses, he can simply attribute it to her lesser sexual appetite, according to traditional stereotypes. If the woman initiates and the man refuses, she has no stereotype to rescue her, and she is likely to conclude that he is not interested in *her* (Blumstein and Schwartz, 1983). Therefore men may have easier ways of dealing with refusal.

Masturbation in Marriage

Many adults continue to masturbate even though they are married and have ready access to heterosexual sex. This behavior is perfectly normal, although it often evokes feelings of guilt and may be done secretly.

Recent data indicate that about 72 percent of young husbands masturbate, with an average frequency of about twice a month. About 68 percent of young wives do so, with an average frequency of slightly less than once a month (Hunt, 1974, p. 86).

Masturbation in marriage, of course, can serve a variety of distinctly nonsexual purposes. For example, it can be used as an expression of anger or hostility toward a spouse who has not furnished the expected sexual satisfaction.

But masturbation can also serve very legitimate sexual needs in marriage. It can be a way of remaining faithful to a spouse when husband and wife are separated or cannot have sex for some reason such as illness.[1] As one man expressed it:

> Whenever I travel, it takes about a week until I can't stand it anymore. I lie there at night trying to sleep, and the damn thing won't go away, and I tell myself, "It's either do it or go out on the town." But I'm not that kind of guy, so I do it, and I feel better—and also a little worse. (Hunt, 1974, p. 96)

Masturbation can also be a pleasant adjunct to marital sex. One young man said:

> My wife and I have a great sex relationship, and always have had since before we were married. But we both still masturbate, because it seems a pleasant thing to do and because sometimes the urge comes over each one of us at times when we're alone—I'm away most of the day in the laboratory or the library, and she works at the (TV) studio until after midnight. I may suddenly have a momentary desire to ejaculate, and I run into the bathroom and do it. Or I may read something and it makes me fantasize having sex with some strange voluptuous woman—a belly dancer maybe. Incidentally, I never have had intercourse with any woman other than my wife, so I enjoy these fantasies. There's nothing secret about it—I tell my wife if I've done it during the day, and she tells me if she has. It doesn't diminish our lovemaking at all, although sometimes one or the other of us isn't as eager as we might be—but then, sometimes it does just the opposite, because we try out with each other some of the exotic things we've been fantasizing. (Hunt, 1974, p. 98)

---

[1]An old Navy saying has it, "If your wife can't be at your right hand, let your right hand be your wife."

Attitudes toward, and Satisfaction with, Marital Sex

The majority of married people today express satisfaction with their marital sex. Unfortunately, Kinsey did not collect data on attitudes or satisfaction, and so we have no basis for saying that attitudes or satisfaction has changed since the previous generation. But let us consider the current data.

In the Hunt sample, about two-thirds of the married men reported that marital coitus in the last year was "very pleasurable." When one adds to this the group who described it as "mostly pleasurable," the percentage expressing general satisfaction with marital coitus is about 99 percent among those in the younger age groups and 94 percent among those over 45.

About 60 percent of the married women under 45 rated marital coitus as "very pleasurable." After adding in those who rated marital sex as "mostly pleasurable," the percentages are 88 percent for those under 25, 93 percent for those aged 35 to 44, 91 percent for those aged 45 to 54, and 83 percent for those over 55. Note that the highest reported satisfaction among women is not in the youngest age group but rather in the 35- to 44-year-old age group. Note also that women express slightly less satisfaction with marital sex than men do but that both groups are generally satisfied.

Sexual Patterns in Marriage

Sexual patterns can change during the course of a marriage: after 10 or 20 years of marriage they may be quite different from what they were during the first year. One stereotype is that sex becomes duller as marriage wears on, and certainly there are some marriages in which that happens. But there are also those in which the process is exactly the opposite—in which there is a gradual awakening of the sexuality of both partners over the course of the marriage. In other marriages, sexual patterns remain remarkably constant over the years. The following descriptions illustrate the diversity of patterns. First, the words of a man for whom marital sex has become less intense than it apparently once was:

> We do it maybe once a week now, or less. The underlying reason for the slowdown is that we're both pretty busy. It's not that we don't enjoy sex. We do, but I have a lot of meetings, and I get home late and she's asleep, and anyway I'm tired. I would perhaps enjoy a bit more activity, but I'm not discontented about it in any way. . . . Mostly, she does have orgasm—not that we ever discuss it, but I feel pretty sure she does. . . . Our typical sex act is about like this: I'll roll over and decide I'd like a little action. Sometimes it's very rapid—a minute or so—but sometimes it goes on longer, ten minutes, say, half before I put it in, half inside. (Hunt, 1974, p. 220)

A woman described the growth of sexuality in her marriage as follows:

> After we'd been married a while, we felt there was a lot happening that we didn't understand, so I asked my husband if him and I should try to read up on it. So we went out and bought three books, and through them we found all different ways of caressing, and different positions, and it was very nice because we realized that these things weren't dirty. Like I could say to my husband, "Around the world in eighty days" and he'd laugh and we'd really go at it, relaxed and having fun. (Hunt, 1974, p. 183)

Finally, a middle-aged man described a consistent pattern of excitement in marital sex:

> I love my sex, and I've got a wife that loves it just as much as me. Our first five years of married life it was every day with us, and sometimes twice a day because my job would allow me to stop off at home at lunchtime for a quickie. Nowadays, even after twenty years of marriage, it's still about three times a week—and with the kids finally all in school, we've even started up again on the lunchtime business once in a while. Most of the time, naturally, it's in the evening, after the kids are in bed. My wife puts some of that damned perfume on and I know right away that she wants it tonight, and that really gets me going. . . . She can wiggle that ass of hers around like you wouldn't believe, and any position I want to use, she couldn't care less. . . . And sometimes I kid her about stuff I've seen in some stag movie the boys have been showing down at the garage, and would you believe she often wants me to *show* her how it went? After all these years? (Hunt, 1974, pp. 225–226)

Segregated conjugal (KON-joo-gul) role relationships: A marriage relationship in which the husband and wife function independently, having different and separate interests and activities.

Joint conjugal role relationship: A marriage relationship in which husband and wife engage in activities together or perhaps alternate who does a particular task.

Sociologists make a distinction between segregated conjugal role relationships and joint conjugal role relationships (Rainwater, 1965). In the segregated relationship, each person has different interests and activities in the nonsexual area of his or her life and pursues these independently, showing little interest in the other's concerns. In the joint relationship, the husband and wife carry out their acivities together, or they may take turns performing a given function. Sexual patterns tend to be different in these two types of marriage. Couples in highly segregated relationships generally report less sexual satisfaction than those in joint relationships. In the segregated relationship, moreover, the husband is considerably more likely to find sex satisfying than the wife is.

Segregated and joint role relationships vary according to social class. Joint relationships are more common among upper-middle-class couples, while segregated relationships are more common among those in the lower class. Sexual satisfaction shows a comparable social-class variation; reported satisfaction is higher among middle- and upper-class couples than among those in the lower class.

Sex and the Two-Career Family

In our busy, achievement-oriented society, is it possible that work commitments—particularly with the increased incidence of wives holding jobs—may interfere with a couple's sex life? One couple, both of whom are professionals, commented to me that they actually have to make an appointment with each other to make love.

While there has been little scientific research on this topic, there is some evidence that patterns of marital sexuality are related to the wife's working (Westoff, 1974). As it turns out, the couple's frequency of intercourse is related not only to the fact that the woman has a job but also to her motivation for having it. Women who work for reasons other than money have a higher frequency of coitus than women who do not work or who work mainly to earn money. Career-motivated women have the highest frequency of coitus of any of the groups of women. Thus there is no evidence that a woman's commitment to a career will damage the expression of marital sexuality.

EXTRAMARITAL SEX

Extramarital sex: Sex between a married person and someone other than that person's spouse; adultery.

The term extramarital sex refers to sex between a married person and someone other than that person's spouse.[2] We can distinguish between three types of extramarital sex, each of which has different implications for the people involved (Clanton,

[2]The more traditional—and nastier—term for this is "adultery."

Clandestine (klan-DES-tin) extramarital sex: An extramarital relationship that is concealed from the spouse.

Consensual (kun-SEN-shoo-ul) extramarital sex: Extramarital sexual activity in which the spouse knows about the activity and may even approve of it.

Ambiguous extramarital sex: Extramarital sex in which the spouse knows about the activity but pretends not to.

1973): (1) clandestine extramarital sex, in which the extramarital relationship is concealed from the spouse ("clandestine" means "secret"); (2) consensual extramarital sex, in which the spouse knows about the extramarital activity and may even approve of it ("consensual" means "by mutual consent"); and (3) ambiguous extramarital sex, in which the spouse knows about the extramarital relationship but pretends not to know. Consensual extramarital sex is relatively rare in our culture, as will be seen below, and most extramarital sex is either clandestine or ambiguous.

How Many People Engage in Extramarital Sex?

Approximately one-half of all married men have extramarital sex at some time in their lives, compared with about one-quarter of all women. The relevant data are shown in Table 12.3. Several points should be noted from the table:

1. Men are more likely to report engaging in extramarital sex than women are.
2. Approximately 50 percent of all males and about 25 percent of all females engage in extramarital sex at least once.
3. Although the incidence of extramarital sex for males seems to be holding constant, there is some indication that the incidence for females has increased in the 1970s and 1980s, and some experts believe that the rate for females is approaching the rate for males (Thompson, 1983).

A 1980s survey confirms this trend for increasing numbers of females to engage in extramarital sex, finding a higher incidence of extramarital sex in the youngest group of wives (Blumstein and Schwartz, 1983). This may be due to their rejection of the double standard; the young woman of today may believe that if extramarital sex is all right for her husband, it is for her, too.

How are we to evaluate the incidence figures shown in Table 12.3? Some—particularly the 69 percent of female readers of *Cosmopolitan* having extramarital sex—clearly suffer from sampling bias. Female readers of *Cosmo* are a highly select group. However, if one discounts the magazine-sample surveys, the remaining figures are

TABLE 12.3

INCIDENCE OF EXTRAMARITAL SEX IN 11 STUDIES

Study	Married Men (%)	Married Women (%)
Kinsey (1948, 1953)	50	26
Athanasiou et al. (1970)*	40	36
Johnson (1970)	20	10
Hunt (1974)	41	18
Bell et al. (1975)	—	26
Tavris and Sadd (1975)†	—	39
Maykovich (1976)	—	32
Pietropinto and Simenauer (1976)	47	—
Yablonsky (1979)	47	
Wolfe (1980)‡	—	69
Hite (1981)	66	—

*sample of *Psychology Today* readers

†sample of married female *Redbook* readers

‡sample of married female *Cosmopolitan* readers

Source: Anthony P. Thompson. (1983). Extramarital Sex: A review of the research literature. *Journal of Sex Research, 19,* Table 1, pp. 5–6.

probably best regarded as minimums, because of the problems of self-reports. Extramarital sex is one of those socially disapproved behaviors that people are likely not to report in a survey. For example, in one study 30 percent of the subjects initially reported extramarital sex, but during intensive psychotherapy an additional 30 percent revealed extramarital sexual activities (Green et al., 1974).

As I noted above, most extramarital sex tends to be clandestine or ambiguous. Swinging, which is a form of consensual extramarital sex, was reported by only 2 percent of the males and less than 2 percent of the females in the Hunt study (1974, p. 271); even in the *Redbook* survey, which generally reported very high levels of sexual activity, only 4 percent of the women said they had engaged in swinging (Levin and Levin, 1975, p. 44).

For women, at least, there is no indication that extramarital sex is casual or promiscuous. In one survey, of those married women who had extramarital sex, 43 percent had done so with only one partner (Blumstein and Schwartz, 1983).

Attitudes toward Extramarital Sex

While attitudes toward premarital sex have changed substantially during the last several decades, attitudes toward extramarital sex have apparently remained relatively unchanged; most people in the United States disapprove of extramarital sex. In the Hunt survey, about 75 percent of the women and over 60 percent of the men agreed with the statement "Mate-swapping is wrong." Between 80 and 98 percent of both women and men said that they would object if their spouse engaged in sexual activity with someone else.

One of the best predictors of extramarital sexual permissiveness is premarital sexual permissiveness (Thompson, 1983). That is, the person who had a liberal or approving attitude about premarital sex is also likely to hold a liberal or approving attitude toward extramarital sex. On the other hand. attitudes toward extramarital sex are not very good predictors of extramarital sexual behavior (Thompson, 1983). That is, the person who approves of extramarital sex is not more likely to actually engage in extramarital sex than the person who disapproves of it. Therefore, we have to look to factors other than attitudes in trying to understand why people engage in extramarital sex; some of these other factors are discussed later in this section.

Because our society condemns extramarital sex, the individual who engages in it typically has confused, ambivalent feelings. A 45-year-old physician described his extramarital affair and the complex emotions it involved:

> She was twenty years younger than I and very seductive, and she had this fantastic, longlegged, high-breasted body. She took the initiative one afternoon when she was the last one in my office, and I couldn't stop myself; it just happened, right then and there, on the waiting-room couch—the first time for me, after fifteen years of marriage. At first I was all torn up about it, but I couldn't give it up. It made me feel totally different—younger and more attractive then I had in twenty years, completely reawakened inside. A young girl, so sexy and so marvelous to look at and touch, wanting me! It went on for months. I'd meet her and have relations with her at least once or twice a week, usually at her place. sometimes at my office after hours. And now listen to the funny part—she was *no* good at all, sexually. Despite all her sexiness, she was frigid, and she'd lie there obviously getting nothing out of it. So even though I'd enjoy the whole situation and the buildup, when it came to the actual act I'd do it in a minute or two and get it over with. And still, for months I couldn't break it off; I felt as if I were hooked on some drug. (Hunt, 1974, p. 286)

Consensual Extramarital Sex

As was noted above, most extramarital sex is kept secret. Unfortunately, there has been little research on that type of extramarital sexual activity, precisely because the participants are so careful to hide it. Therefore, this section will concentrate on consensual extramarital sex, which has been the subject of more research.

Open Marriage

Nena and George O'Neill's book *Open Marriage* (1972) was a best-seller, presenting the possibility for a new, open attitude toward marital and extramarital sex.

The O'Neills argued that traditional marriage—what they call closed marriage—is rigid and limiting to the partners and that it is no longer a realistic pattern in our society. Closed marriage is based on principles of exclusivity and possession and on a belief that the partners can control each other; it also assumes that things will remain forever unchanged. It does not encourage the partners to grow.

Open marriage: A marriage in which the partners are committed to their own and each other's growth and extramarital sex may be seen as acceptable or even desirable.

Open marriage, on the other hand, is defined as a relationship in which the partners are committed to their own and to each other's growth (N. O'Neill and O'Neill, 1976). In order for growth to take place, the partners must be able, from time to time, to rewrite their marriage "contract," the contract being a set of verbalized and nonverbalized understandings about what each person will do and will not do. In a closed marriage, the contract specifies monogamous sex, that is, that the partners will have sex with no one but each other. In open marriage, the partners may rewrite their contract to permit extramarital sex. Contracts can be completely open, or they can have varying degrees of openness. A "compartmentalized" contract, for example, may allow the marriage to be open on Thursday nights only; on Thursday night, the husband is free to play poker with the boys, the wife can play bridge with the girls, or both partners can have sex with whomever they wish.

Thus, while extramarital sex has traditionally been viewed as destructive to marriage, the O'Neills feel that it can lead to the growth of the marriage and of the spouses. One of the most useful aspects of the O'Neills' work is that it highlights the fact that we all have expectations for our own and our spouse's behavior in marriage and that these expectations can periodically be revised—the contract rewritten—in a way that is satisfactory to both partners.

Swinging

Swinging: A form of consensual extramarital sex in which married couples exchange partners with each other.

One form of such a renegotiated contract occurs in swinging. In swinging, married couples exchange partners with other married couples, with the knowledge and consent of all involved.[3]

Swingers may find their partners in several ways. Most commonly they advertise, either in a sensational tabloid, such as the *National Enquirer,* or in a swinger's magazine, such as *Swinger's Life* or *Kindred Spirits.* The following is an example:

> New Orleans, young couple, 28 and 32. She a luscious red head, 5'7", 36-26-38. He, 5'9", 175, well built. Enjoy all cultures.[4] Attractive couple main interest, but will consider extremely attractive single girls and men. Photo required to reply. (Bartell, 1970, p. 115)

---

[3]Swinging was originally called "wife-swapping." However, because of the sexist connotations of that term and the fact that women were often as eager to swap husbands as men were to swap wives, the more equitable "mate-swapping" or "swinging" was substituted.

[4]In this context, "cultures" refers to various sexual techniques. Mouth-genital sex, for example, would be "French culture."

FIGURE 12.2

A swingers' party? Initially a swingers' party looks much like other parties and swingers are much like everyone else except for their pattern of sexual behavior.

The descriptions in such advertisements are not always accurate; generally they tend to minimize age and maximize the mammary measurement of the woman (Bartell, 1970). Swingers may also meet partners at swinger's bars or "sodalities"—clubs or organizations of swingers. In some cases, couples are referred by other couples. Finally, in rare cases, a couple may try to convert a nonswinging couple.

There are three forms of swinging: simple swinging with another couple (either open or closed), swinging at parties (open or closed), and three-way swinging (Bartell, 1970; for a critique of the Bartell study, see Chapter 10). In *closed swinging,* the two couples meet and exchange partners, and each pair goes off separately to a private place to have intercourse, returning to the meeting place at an agreed-upon time. In *open swinging,* the pairs get back together for sex in the same room for at least part of the time. In 75 percent of the cases, this includes the two women having sex with each other, although male homosexual sex almost never occurs (Bartell, 1970; Gilmartin, 1975).

Swinging parties are held at the home of an organizer. At the closed party there are certain regulations concerning behavior; for example, nudity may be prohibited in the central party room, or only one couple may be permitted in a bedroom at a time. An open party is similar, but there are fewer regulations. Nudity is permitted anywhere in the house, and participants are free to form large groups for mass sex (Bartell, 1970).

Finally, a couple may sometimes swing with just one other person rather than another couple. In the majority of cases, the extra person is a female (Bartell, 1970).

Swingers may vary from those seeking purely sexual experiences to those wanting to form lasting relationships or friendships (Gilmartin, 1975). However, most swingers stress emotional noninvolvement with the other couple, and the norm is not to engage in sex with the same couple more than once (Bartell, 1970; Gilmartin, 1975). Swinging couples typically engage in swinging only about once every two weeks, and thus it is scarcely an obsession (Gilmartin, 1975).

What kind of people are swingers? In the nonsexual areas of their lives, they are quite ordinary—perhaps even dull. Although they describe themselves in their ads as exciting people with many interests, in fact they engage in few activities and have few hobbies. As one researcher observed, "These people do nothing other than swing and watch television" (Bartell, 1970, p. 122). Though one might expect, from their sexual behavior, that these people would be liberal, they are traditional or conservative in other areas of their lives. In one study conducted during the 1968 presidential campaign, 60 percent of the swingers studied backed George Wallace (Bartell, 1970).

Husbands tend to initiate swinging, but wives typically become the enthusiasts (Bartell, 1970; Gilmartin, 1975). Particularly in swinging at parties, the man's biological sexual capacity may limit him, compared with a woman. He goes to a party, and suddenly he is in a situation that he may have fantasized about since his youth—a roomful of naked women with whom he is permitted to have intercourse. But the pressure is on him to "perform," which may cause anxiety, and the anxiety may cause failure. Even if he "succeeds" with the first few women, he will eventually run out of steam long before the women do. Thus by the end of a swinging party, the only activity still going on may be homosexual activity between the women; 65 percent of the women in one study said they enjoyed their homosexual encounters with other women to the point where they preferred them to heterosexual encounters with males (Bartell, 1970). Thus some men can have very negative experiences at a swinging party.

Factors Related to Extramarital Sex

Sociologists have tried to determine what factors are most related to, or perhaps even cause, extramarital sexual activity. One analysis suggested that two factors were particularly critical: *alienation* and *opportunity* (Whitehurst, 1972). That is, the more alienated a man feels, the more likely he is to engage in extramarital sex. Similarly, opportunity, particularly as it occurs in some work settings, is also important.

In another large-scale analysis, it was found that childhood socialization variables were essentially unrelated to patterns of extramarital sex (Edwards and Booth, 1976). This is a rather interesting point, because it argues against the usual assumption that social learning in childhood is an important influence on adult sexual behavior. Instead, the pattern that emerged was that the greater the strain and conflict in the marriage, the lower the frequency of marital intercourse; and as marital sex becomes less frequent, extramarital affairs become more likely to occur.

Situational variables: Factors that occur in a specific situation (rather than personality variables or life history variables) that influence behavior.

Notice that both these analyses point to situational variables—opportunity for extramarital sex, the situation of conflict in one's marriage—as the most important determiners of extramarital sexual activity.

Let us now consider an even more detailed theoretical analysis of factors contributing to extramarital sex.

Equity and Extramarital Sex

Equity theory: A theory in social psychology that argues that people mentally calculate the benefits and costs for them in a relationship, and thereby feel that the relationship is equitable or inequitable; their behavior is then affected by whether they feel there is equity or inequity and they will act to restore equity if there is inequity.

Equity theory is a social-psychological theory designed to predict and explain many kinds of human relations (Walster, Walster, and Berscheid, 1978). In particular, it has been applied to predicting patterns of extramarital sex (Walster, 1978).

The basic idea in equity theory is that in a relationship, people mentally tabulate their inputs to it and what they get out of it (benefits or rewards); then they calculate whether these are equitable or not. In an equitable relationship between person A and person B, it would be true that

$$\text{Rewards}_A - \text{Inputs}_A = \text{Rewards}_B - \text{Inputs}_B$$

In a traditional marriage, the wife's inputs might include her beauty, keeping a charming house, cooking good meals, and so on. The husband's inputs might include his income and his pleasant temperament. His rewards from the relationship might include feeling proud when he is accompanied by his beautiful wife, enjoying her cooking, and so on. Notice that this is not an egalitarian relationship in the modern sense; however, it is an equitable relationship (as defined by equity theory) because both partners derive equal benefits from it.

According to equity theory, if individuals perceive a relationship as inequitable (they feel they are not getting what they deserve), they become distressed. The more inequitable the relationship, the more distressed they feel. In order to relieve the distress, they make attempts to restore equity in the relationship. For example, people who feel they are putting too much into a relationship and not getting enough out of it might let their appearance go, or not work as hard to earn money, or refuse sexual favors, or refuse to contribute to conversations. The idea is that such actions would restore equity.

If these equity processes do occur, it seems logical that they might help to explain patterns of extramarital sex. That is, engaging in extramarital sex would be a way of restoring equity in an inequitable relationship. Social psychologist Elaine Walster (1978) tested this notion. Her prediction was that people who felt underbenefited in their marriages (that is, they felt that there was an inequity and that they were not getting as much as they deserved) would be the ones to engage in extramarital sex. Confirming this notion, subjects who felt they were underbenefited began engaging in extramarital sex earlier in their marriages and had more extramarital partners than did people who felt equitably treated or overbenefited. Apparently, feeling that one is not getting all one deserves in a marriage is related to engaging in extramarital sex. (As an aside, equitable marriages were rated as happier than inequitable ones)

Walster and her colleagues (Walster, Walster, and Traupmann, 1978) have also applied equity theory to patterns of premarital sex, although the theoretical predictions did not work out so well in that case.

The more interesting point, deserving of further research, is that whether we feel a relationship is equitable or not may affect our patterns of sexual activity both in and out of the relationship.

SEX AND THE SINGLE PERSON

Although most adults in our society do marry, there are still many single adults—the never-married, the divorced, and the widowed—who have sexual needs and seek to express them.

The Never-Married

The person who passes age 25 without getting married gradually enters a new world (J. H. Gagnon, 1977). The social structures that supported dating—such as college—are gone, and most people of the same age are married. Dating and sex are no longer geared to mate selection, and by the time a person is 25 or 30, it no longer seems reasonable to call her or his sexual activity "premarital sex."

The attitudes of singles about their status vary widely. Some plan never to get married; they find their lifestyle exciting and enjoy its freedom. Others are desperately searching for a spouse, with the desperation increasing as the years wear on.

At one extreme, there is the *singles scene.* It is institutionalized in such forms as singles' apartment complexes and singles' bars. The singles group, of course, is composed of the never-married as well as the divorced and the widowed. The singles' bar is a visible symbol of the singles scene. It functions in many ways like a gay bar (J. H. Gagnon, 1977). Everyone is there for a similar purpose: to meet Mr. or Ms. Right. However, most will settle for a date, and it is fairly well understood that coitus will be a part of the date. The singles' bar is somewhat like a meat market; the people there try to display themselves to their best advantage and are judged and chosen on the basis of their physical appearance—and perhaps rejected for too high a percentage of fat.

Many singles, however, do not go to singles' bars. Some are turned off by the idea; some feel that they cannot compete, that they are too old, or that they are not attractive enough; and some live in rural areas where they have no access to such places.

Unfortunately, the major studies of sexual behavior have focused primarily on premarital sexual behavior and only to a lesser extent on postmarital sexual behavior. Researchers have neglected the never-married adult, who deserves more attention in future studies.

The Divorced and the Widowed

Divorced and widowed people are in a somewhat unusual situation in that they are used to regular sexual expression and suddenly find themselves in a situation in which the socially acceptable outlet for that expression—marital sex—is no longer available. Partly recognizing this dilemma, our society places few restrictions on postmarital sexual activity, although it is not so much approved as marital sex (Gebhard, 1968).

Divorced and Widowed Women

Most divorced women, but fewer widowed women, return to having an active sex life. Data collected between 1939 and 1956 showed that 82 percent of divorced women had postmarital coitus and that 43 percent of widowed women did (Gebhard, 1968). In the recent Hunt study, only about 10 percent of divorced women did not engage in postmarital sex.

The lower incidence of postmarital sex among widows, compared with divorcées, is due in part to the fact that widows are, on the average, older than divorcées. But even when matched for age, widows are still less likely to engage in postmarital sex. There are probably several reasons for this (Gebhard, 1968). Widows are more likely to be financially secure than divorced women and therefore have less motivation for engaging in sex as a prelude to remarriage. They have the continuing social support system of in-laws and friends, and so they are less motivated to seek new friendships. There is also a belief that a widow should be loyal to her dead husband, and having a sexual relationship with another man is viewed as disloyalty. Many widows believe this or tell themselves that they will "never find another one like him."

Most widowed or divorced women who have postmarital sex begin such relationships within a year after the death or divorce. While most women who have premarital sex do so with only one partner, the fiancé, most women who have postmarital sex have multiple partners. In one study only 16 percent of widowed and 12 percent of divorced women had sex with only the fiancé (Gebhard, 1968). Divorced women average about four partners per year (Hunt, 1974).

Divorced and widowed women who return to having an active sex life generally express great satisfaction with it. Indeed, these women have a higher frequency of orgasm in postmarital sex than they did in marital sex (Gebhard, 1968; Hunt, 1974).

Divorced and Widowed Men

Virtually all divorced and widowed men return to an active sex life (Gebhard, 1968; Hunt, 1966). Indeed, 100 percent of the divorced men under 55 in the Hunt study had sexual intercourse during the past year.

It is a popular stereotype that these men have a wild sex life. On the basis of his data, however, Kinsey felt that this was not true. For example, in his sample, only 2 percent of married men over 50 were not having sex at all, whereas 18 percent of divorced and widowed men were not (Kinsey et al., 1948, p. 280). However, the more recent Hunt study found that widowed and divorced men actually have sex slightly more frequently than married men of the same age. Thus the sexual liberation of recent years seems to have affected not only premarital sex but also postmarital sex. Men average eight partners per year in postmarital sex, about twice as many as women do (Hunt, 1974).

In summary, virtually all divorced women and somewhat fewer widowed women engage in postmarital sex; virtually all divorced and widowed men do so, with little distinction between the divorced and widowed.

The Divorce Subculture

Morton and Bernice Hunt (1977) have done an intensive study of the divorce experience, based on questionnaires completed by 984 people, plus 200 depth interviews. We will focus on their findings about sexual relationships here.

Within a couple of months of the divorce, the divorced person typically goes out on the "first date." Although divorced individuals may be in their thirties or forties and think of themselves as mature, the first date makes them strangely anxious. Essentially, they are "second-time beginners." The problem is that they do not know the rules of the dating game among formerly marrieds (FMs). They have never been an FM before. And worse, rules for dating and sex have changed a great deal since they were dating as teenagers.

Anxiety-provoking though this early dating is, it serves two important functions. First, it socializes the individuals into the norms of the FM world. They quickly learn the rules and expectations. Second, early dating fosters an important kind of self-appraisal. Having been married for a number of years, the individuals have no idea how they will be responded to by potential dates. How will they do on the dating market? Most make positive, self-affirming discoveries about themselves. Demoralized by the divorce, they find that members of the opposite gender do find them attractive.

They typically move into a phase of "dating around," which is the norm among FMs. Most quickly discover, to their surprise, that the sexual scene among FMs is even more open and fast-paced than it is among young singles. Most are surprised at how common it is for men to suggest intercourse with a woman they know only casually and are dating for only the first or second time. About 60 percent of the women surveyed said that most men they had dated made some kind of serious sexual approach on the first or second date. The median frequency of intercourse is about twice per week.

It seems, from the Hunts' work, that dating around (and sleeping around) is essentially a developmental stage after divorce. The individuals eventually move out of it into a reconstruction phase, in which they again form a deeper, more committed relationship and begin to reintegrate sex with emotion. Once again, we see that sex can serve important developmental functions.

SEX AND THE SENIOR CITIZEN

When Freud suggested that young children, even infants, have sexual thoughts and feelings, his ideas met with considerable resistance. When, 50 years later, researchers began to suggest that elderly men and women also have sexual thoughts and feelings, there was similar resistance (Pfeiffer et al., 1968). This section deals with the sexual behavior of elderly men and women, the physical changes they undergo, and the attitudes that influence them.

Physical Changes

As part of their research on the physiology of sexual response, Masters and Johnson (1966) observed the sexual behavior of elderly men and women in order to document the physical changes that take place in the later years. What follows is based mainly on their work.

Changes in the Female

There is a gradual decline in the functioning of the ovaries around menopause, and with this comes a gradual decline in the production of estrogen (see Figure 12.4). Because of the decline in estrogen, several changes take place in the sexual organs.

FIGURE 12.3

Affection, romance, and sex are not just for the young.

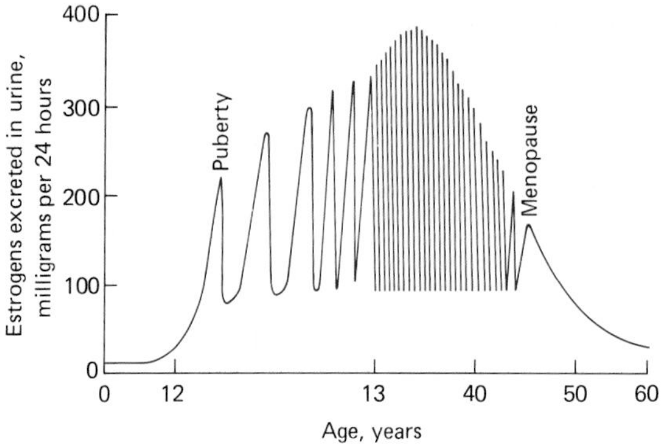

FIGURE 12.4

Levels of estrogen production in women across the lifespan.

The walls of the vagina, which are thick and elastic during the reproductive years, become thin and inelastic (this condition is called, depressingly, *senile vagina,* and irritations to the vagina that may result are called *senile vaginitis*). Because the walls of the vagina are thinner, they cannot absorb the pressures from the thrusting penis as they once did, and thus nearby structures—such as the bladder and the urethra—may be irritated. As a result, elderly women may have an urgent need to urinate immediately after intercourse. Further, the vagina shrinks in both width and length, and the labia majora also shrink; thus there is a constriction at the entrance to the vagina, which may make penile insertion somewhat more difficult, and the vagina may be less able to accommodate the size of a fully erect penis.

By about five years after menopause, the amount of vaginal lubrication has decreased noticeably. Intercourse can then become somewhat more difficult and painful.

Because of hormonal imbalance, the contractions of the uterus that occur during orgasm can become painful, to the point where the woman avoids intercourse. Nonetheless, the woman has the same physical capacity for orgasm at 80 that she did at 30.

Lest these changes sound discouraging, it is important to realize that there are a number of ways to deal with them successfully. Some women's physicians prescribe estrogen-replacement therapy for them after menopause; with these added doses of estrogen, the changes described above are minimized or may not occur at all. A simple measure is to use a sterile surgical lubricant as a substitute for vaginal lubrication.

It also appears that these changes are related in part to sexual activity or, rather, to the lack of it. Among the women in the Masters and Johnson study, those who had intercourse infrequently (once a month or less) and who did not masturbate regularly had difficulty accommodating the penis when they attempted intercourse. The three women over 60 in their studies whose vaginas expanded well to accommodate the penis and who produced adequate lubrication had all maintained regular intercourse once or twice a week. For this reason and others, Masters and Johnson stress the importance of regular sexual activity in maintaining an active sex life among the elderly, a point which will be discussed in more detail later.

Thus it appears that the continuing of sexual activity depends more on the opportunity for such activity and on various psychological factors than it does on any physical changes, a point that holds true for both men and women.

Hysterectomy (hiss-tur-EK-tuh-mee): Surgical removal of the uterus.

Some people believe that a hysterectomy means the end of a woman's sex life. In fact, sex hormone production is not affected as long as the ovaries are not

Oophorectomy (OH-uh-fuh-REK-tuh-mee): Surgical removal of the ovaries.

removed (surgical removal of the ovaries is called oophorectomy or ovariectomy). The majority of women report that hysterectomy has no effect on their sex life. However, approximately one-third of women who have had hysterectomies report problems with sexual response (Zussman et al., 1981). There are two possible physiological causes for these problems. If the ovaries have been removed, hormonal changes may be responsible; specifically, the ovaries produce androgens, and they may play a role in sexual response. The other possibility is that the removal of the cervix, and possibly the rest of the uterus, is an anatomical problem if the cervix serves as a trigger for orgasm.

Changes in the Male

Testosterone production declines gradually over the years (see Figure 12.5). A major change is that erections occur more slowly. It is important for men to know that this is a perfectly natural slowdown so that they will not jump to the conclusion that they are becoming impotent. It is also important for women to know about this so that they will use effective techniques of stimulating the man and so that they will not mistake slowness for lack of interest.

Morning erections also become less frequent, declining from about two per week in the early thirties to about 0.5 per week at the age 70 (Kinsey et al., 1948, p. 230).

For men, the refractory period lengthens with age; thus for an elderly man, there may be a period of 24 hours after an orgasm during which he cannot get an erection. (Note that women do not undergo a similar change; women do not enter into a refractory period and are still capable of multiple orgasm at age 80.) Other signs of sexual excitement—the sex flush and muscle tension—diminish with age.

The volume of the ejaculate gradually decreases, and the force of ejaculation lessens. The testes become somewhat smaller, but viable sperm are produced by even very old men. Ninety-year-old men have been known to father children.

One advantage is that middle-aged and elderly men may have better control over ejaculation than young men; thus they can prolong coitus and may be better sexual partners.

Despite these physical changes, though, Masters and Johnson conclude that there need be no time limit on sexual expression for either men or women.

FIGURE 12.5

Levels of testosterone production in men across the lifespan.

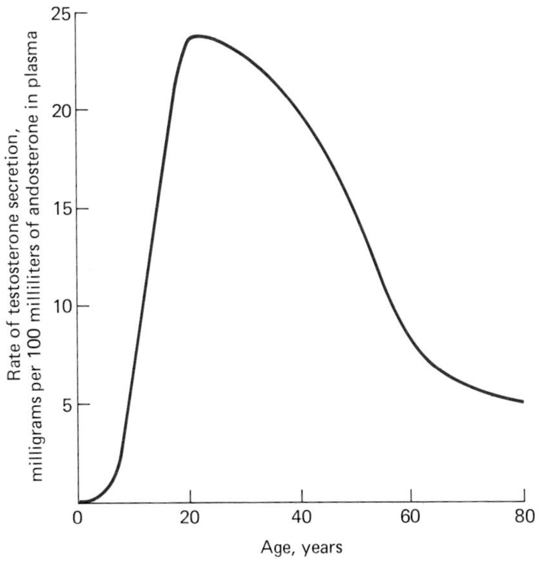

Prostatectomy (pros-tuh-TEK-tuh-mee): Surgical removal of the prostate.

Some people believe that prostate surgery or removal of the prostate (prostatectomy) means the end of a man's sex life. It is true that the volume of the ejaculate will decrease. Prostatectomy can cause damage to the nerves supplying the penis, creating erection problems. In other cases, retrograde ejaculation may result. Whether there are such problems depends on which of several available methods of surgery is used.

Attitudes about Sex and the Elderly

Our society has a negative attitude toward sexual expression among the elderly. Somehow it seems indecent for two 70-year-old people to have sex with each other, and even more indecent for a 70-year-old to masturbate. These negative attitudes become particularly obvious in nursing homes, where staff members frequently frown on sexual activity among the residents. Men and women are segregated into separate rooms, and even married couples may be separated; patients may have their hands tied to a wheelchair or bed in order to prevent them from masturbating. Somehow what is "virility" at 25 becomes "lechery" at 65 (I. Rubin, 1965).

A group of undergraduates at Brandeis University were asked to complete the sentence "Sex for most old people. . . ." Almost all of them gave responses like "negligible," "unimportant," or "past" (Golde and Kogan, 1959).

Cross-cultural research indicates that the sexual behavior of the elderly is related to these cultural expectations (Winn and Newton, 1980). The elderly continue to be sexually active in 70 percent of societies and in precisely those societies where they are expected to be sexually active. Indeed, in 22 percent of societies, women are expected to become more uninhibited about sexuality when they become old.

Why does our society have such negative attitudes toward sex among the elderly? In part, these attitudes are due to the fact that ours is a youth-oriented culture. We value youth, and the physical characteristics that are considered "sexy" are youthful ones, such as a trim, firm body and smooth skin. It is therefore hard to believe that someone with old, wrinkled skin could be sexually active. Our negative attitudes may be a holdover from the belief that sex was for reproductive purposes only—those past the age of reproduction should therefore not engage in it (Pfeiffer, 1975). The incest taboo may also be involved in our negative attitudes. We tend to identify old people with our parents or grandparents, and we find it hard to think of them as sexual beings. This factor is made worse because many parents take great pains to hide their sexual activity from their children.

These attitudes affect the way elderly people are treated, and the elderly may even hold such attitudes themselves. One remedy that has been proposed for these negative attitudes is a "coming out of the closet"; as one 67-year-old commented,

> The common view that the aging and aged are nonsexual, I believe, can only be corrected by a dramatic and courageous process—the *coming-out-of-the-closet* of sexually active older women and men, so that people can see for themselves what the later years are really like. (Brecher, 1984, p. 21)

Various specific misunderstandings may influence sexuality. For example, a man may believe that sex will precipitate a heart attack or, if he has already had a heart attack, that it will bring on another one. Of patients who were sexually active before a heart attack, only 25 percent resumed sexual activity after the heart attack (Papadopoulos, 1978). The lack of sexual activity was caused by medical or physiological factors in only a few cases; in most, it was created by fears and misinformation. Most authorities agree, though, that the benefits of sexual activity for the cardiac patient outweigh any potential dangers (Hellerstein and Friedman, 1969).

Although Masters and Johnson found that the heart rate accelerated during sexual intercourse, another study showed that the mean heart rate during orgasm was only 117 beats per minute, which is about that attained during many common forms of daily exercise (Hellerstein and Friedman, 1969). It is about the equivalent of climbing two flights of stairs at a moderate pace. Thus the demands on the heart are not unreasonable. Unfortunately, many physicians neglect to discuss the issue with cardiac patients, who then may simply assume that sex is dangerous or forbidden. Even more unfortunate is the fact that there are only three or four studies on the potential problem of the "coital coronary" (see review by Derogatis and King, 1981), so physicians have little solid evidence to convey to their patients.

One interesting study of male coronary patients found that two-thirds had a sexual dysfunction (most commonly erectile dysfunction, less commonly premature ejaculation) *before* the heart attack (Wabrek and Burchell, 1980). This puts the incidence of dysfunction after a heart attack in better perspective. The authors suggested that there might be complex interactions between sexual dysfunction, stress, and heart attacks. That is, severe stress might precipitate both a sexual dysfunction and a heart attack. Or a bout of sexual dysfunction might be the stress that precipitated the heart attack. We need more research on the relationship between coronary problems and sex problems.

Some men also mistakenly believe that sexual activity saps their "vital strength." In some cases men may believe that they can have only a fixed number of orgasms during their life (as a woman has a fixed number of ova) and therefore adopt a strategy of saving them now so that they will have some left later on. One woman wrote:

> My husband has reached the age of sixty-five. He has decided that, in order to ensure a longer life and health, he will no longer engage in sex activity. He is convinced that intercourse and the emission of semen are quite debilitating, particularly in his years. (I. Rubin, 1966, p. 258).

Ideas such as this, as well as factors such as illness or hospitalization, may lead to a period of sexual inactivity. But being sexually inactive is one of the most effective ways of diminishing sexuality. In one study of elderly people, 75 percent were sexually inactive. When they were reinterviewed three to four years later, only 14 percent of the inactive group had returned to sexual activity; the rest had remained inactive (Pfeiffer et al., 1968). Thus it seems unlikely that an old person will return to sexual activity after a period of inactivity.

In agreement with these findings, Masters and Johnson emphasize that two factors are critical in maintaining sexual capacity in old age:

1. Good physical and mental health. An excellent study confirms this notion (Persson, 1980). A representative sample of 70-year-olds in one town in Sweden were selected, and 85 percent agreed to participate in the detailed interviews. In the entire sample, 46 percent of the men and 16 percent of the women still had sexual intercourse; when only those who were currently married were considered, the figures rose to 52 percent for men and 36 percent for women. For both men and women, those who continued to have sexual intercourse had better mental health as rated by a psychiatrist and more positive attitudes toward sexual activity among the aged.

2. Regularity of sexual expression. As was noted earlier, they even have evidence that some physical changes of the sex organs in old age are related to sexual inactivity. As the saying goes, "If you don't use it, you lose it."

Apparently some elderly people have caught on to this fact. As one 80-year-old husband said of his relationship with his 75-year-old wife,

> My wife and I both believe that keeping active sexually delays the aging pocess . . . if we are troubled with an erection or lubrication, we turn to oral methods or masturbation of each other. We keep our interest alive by a great deal of caressing and fondling of each other's genitals. We feel it is much better to wear out than to rust out. (Brecher, 1984, p. 33)

Various other factors that may lead to sexual problems for the elderly man include (1) the monotony of a repetitious sexual relationship (usually boredom with the wife), (2) preoccupation with his job, (3) mental or physical fatigue, (4) overindulgence in food and particularly in alcohol, and (5) fear of "failure" (I. Rubin, 1966).

Nutrition is very important in maintaining one's sexual capacity (LeWitter and Abarbanel, 1973). In one study of men with nutritional deficiencies, two-thirds had definitely impaired libido and potency (Biskind, 1947).

Women's beliefs about menopause may influence their sexuality in the later years. Some believe that menopause means the end of sex. "I was afraid we couldn't have sexual relations after the menopause," said one woman, "and my husband thought so, too" (I. Rubin, 1966, p. 256). Certainly such attitudes could lead to diminishing, or even a cessation, of sexual activity. Probably in a few cases, women who never really enjoyed sex use menopause as an excuse to stop having intercourse. On the other hand, some women who spent their younger years worrying about getting pregnant find menopause to be a liberating experience; their sexual activity may actually increase.

Reformers urge us to change our attitudes about sex and the senior citizen. Nursing homes particularly need to revise their practices; even such simple changes as knocking before entering a patient's room would help (people masturbate, you know). Other reforms would include making provisions for spouses to stay overnight and allowing married—or unmarried—couples to share a bedroom. Indeed, some experts even advocate sex as a form of therapy for persons in nursing homes (Rice, 1974):

> Sex relations can provide a much needed and highly effective resource in the later years of life, when so often men face the loss of their customary prestige and self-confidence and begin to feel old, sometimes long before they have begun to age significantly. The premature cessation of sexual functioning may accelerate physiological and psychological aging since disuse of any function usually leads to concomitant changes in other capacities. After menopause, women may find that continuation of sexual relations provides a much needed psychological reinforcement, a feeling of being needed and of being capable of receiving love and affection and renewing the intimacy they earlier found desirable and reassuring. (L. K. Frank, 1961, pp. 177–178)

Sexual Behavior of the Elderly

While sexual behavior and sexual interest do decline somewhat with age, there are still substantial numbers of elderly men and women who have active sex lives, even when in their eighties.

In interviews, 40 to 65 percent of a group of active, healthy people between the ages of 60 and 71 reported engaging in sexual intercourse with some frequency; about 10 to 20 percent of those aged 78 and over reported doing so (Pfeiffer et al., 1968). Yet there did not seem to be any age beyond which all people are sexually inactive.

Some elderly people do, for various reasons, stop having intercourse after a certain age. For women, this occurs most often in the late fifties and early sixties, while it occurs somewhat later for men (Pfeiffer et al., 1968). Contrary to what one might expect, though, when a couple stop having intercourse, the husband is most frequently the cause; both wives and husbands agree that this is true. In some cases, the husband has died (and we can hardly blame him for that), but even excluding those cases, the husband is still most frequently the cause. Thus the decline in female sexual expression with age may be directly related to the male's decline (Kinsey et al., 1953). Death of the spouse is more likely to put an end to intercourse for women than it is for men, in part because women are less able to remarry (Lobsenz, 1974; Pfeiffer et al., 1968).

A recent survey—the largest one to date on sexuality and the elderly—provides rich detail on sexual patterns among the elderly (Brecher et al., 1984). The study was sponsored by Consumers Union, the nonprofit organization that publishes the magazine *Consumer Reports.* In the November 1977 issue of *Consumer Reports,* a notice appeared requesting cooperation from men and women born before 1928, and thus over 50 years of age at the time. Readers were asked to write in to obtain a questionnaire on personal relationships—family, social, and sexual—during the later years of life. Over 10,000 questionnaires were mailed out in response, and 4246 were returned. Although earlier, in Chapter 10, I concluded that magazine surveys are of little value because of severe problems of sampling bias, this study stands out. It is one of the few important sources of information concerning sex and the elderly, a topic about which there is a real shortage of knowledge. The problem of a nonrandom and volunteer-biased sample remains. Specifically, elderly people who are sick, in nursing homes, or whose sight has failed so that they cannot read, are highly unlikely to have responded to the survey. Thus we must regard this as a survey of elderly people who are above average in health, activity, and intelligence and who are doubtless more sexually active than sick or disabled persons.[5] In a sense, the survey gives a view of the richest potential of sexuality in the later years.

Some statistics from the survey are summarized in Table 12.4. Notice that, even among respondents over 70 years of age, 33 percent of the women and 43 percent of the men still masturbate (see also Catania and White, 1982). And 65 percent of the married women and 59 percent of the married men over 70 years old report that they continue to have sex with their spouse.

The questionnaire also contained questions about patterns of extramarital sexuality and homosexuality. The results indicated that 8 percent of the wives and 24 percent of the husbands had engaged in extramarital sex at least once after age 50. For the entire sample 13 percent of the men and 8 percent of the women had had a homosexual experience at some time in their lives, and 4 percent of the men and 2 percent of the women had engaged in homosexual activity after the age of 50.

What we see from this survey, then, is that, among older people who are healthy and active and have regular opportunities for sexual expression, sexual activity in all forms—including masturbaton and homosexual behavior—continues past 70 years of age. The sexuality of the elderly has indeed come out of the closet.

---

[5]For a discussion of sexuality among residents of nursing homes, see White (1982).

TABLE 12.4

SEXUAL ACTIVITY IN A SAMPLE OF ELDERLY PERSONS

All Respondents	In Their 50s	In Their 60s	70 and Over
Women			
Orgasms when asleep or while waking up	26%	24%	17%
Women who masturbate	47%	37%	33%
Frequency of masturbation among women who masturbate	0.7/week	0.6/week	0.7/week
Wives having sex with their husbands	88%	76%	65%
Frequency of sex with their husbands	1.3/week	1.0/week	0.7/week
Men			
Orgasms when asleep or while waking up	25%	21%	17%
Men who masturbate	66%	50%	43%
Frequency of masturbation among men who masturbate	1.2/week	0.8/week	0.7/week
Husbands having sex with their wives	87%	78%	59%
Frequency of sex with their wives	1.3/week	1.0/week	0.6/week

Source: Edward M. Brecher and the Editors of Consumer Reports Books. (1984). *Love, Sex, and Aging.* Mount Vernon, NY: Consumers Union, p. 316.

SUMMARY

Married couples today report engaging in sexual intercourse more frequently than couples several decades ago. Currently, couples in their twenties have sex about two or three times a week, on the average, with the frequency declining to about once per week for those aged 45 and over. Married couples today also tend to use a wide variety of techniques other than intercourse in the man-on-top position, including intercourse in other positions and oral-genital sex. Many people continue to masturbate even though they are married. Most people today—both women and men—express general satisfaction with their marital sex life.

Sexual patterns in marriage, however, show great variability. In part these variations are related to the husband's and the wife's relative roles in nonsexual aspects of the marriage. Sexual satisfaction tends to be greater among those with conjoint relationships than among those with highly segregated relationships.

About 40 to 50 percent of all married men and 20 percent of all married women engage in extramarital sex at some time. Extramarital sex is disapproved of in our society and is generally carried on in secrecy. In a few cases, it is agreed that both husband and wife can have extramarital sex, as in open marriage and swinging. Equity theory may be helpful in understanding patterns of extramarital sex.

Single adults—whether never-married, widowed, or divorced—generally do engage in sexual activity. Virtually all widowed and divorced men return to an active sex life, as do most divorced women and about half of widowed women. A particular set of sexual norms characterizes the divorce subculture.

While sexual activity declines somewhat with age, it is perfectly possible to remain sexually active into one's eighties or nineties. When a couple stop having intercourse, most often it is the husband who is the cause. Problems with sex or the cessation of intercourse may be related to physical factors. In women, declining estrogen levels result in a thinner, less elastic vagina and less lubrication; in men, there is lowered testosterone production, combined with slower erections and longer refractory periods. Psychological factors can also be involved, such as the belief that the elderly cannot or should not have sex. Masters and Johnson emphasize that two factors are critical to maintaining sexuality in old age: good physical and mental health and regularity of sexual expression.

REVIEW QUESTIONS

1. In general, the frequency of marital intercourse declines with age. True or false?
2. One of the greatest changes in marital sex during the last few decades is the increased popularity of mouth-genital sex. True or false?
3. Masturbation is rare among married adults—only about 10 percent of husbands and wives report that they still engage in masturbation. True or false?
4. Most extramarital sex is clandestine, that is, secret. True or false?
5. People's attitudes toward extramarital sex have changed in the last several decades, so that by the 1980s a majority of Americans approved of extramarital sex. True or false?
6. _____ refers to married couples exchanging sexual partners with other married couples, with the knowledge and consent of all involved.
7. According to equity theory, people who feel they are in equitable marriages are more likely to engage in extramarital sex than those who are in inequitable marriages. True or false?
8. Most divorced women, but fewer widowed women, return to having an active sex life. True or false?
9. According to cross-cultural research, in societies in which the elderly are expected to be sexually active, they are. True or false?
10. According to Masters and Johnson, the most important factors in maintaining sexual capacity in old age are good physical and mental health and _____.

QUESTIONS FOR THOUGHT, DISCUSSION, AND DEBATE

1. What is your response when you see an elderly couple expressing affection physically with each other, perhaps kissing or holding hands? Why do you think you respond that way?
2. What is your opinion about extramarital sex? Is it ethical or moral? What are its effects on a marriage—does it destroy marriage or improve it, or perhaps have no effect?
3. If you are currently in a relationship, apply equity theory to your relationship. Do you feel that it is equitable or inequitable? If you view it as inequitable, what effects does that have on your behavior?

SUGGESTIONS FOR FURTHER READING

Brecher, Edward M. (1984). *Love, sex, and aging.* Mount Vernon, NY: Consumers Union. This large-scale survey offers a liberated view of sexuality in the elderly.

Kaplan, Helen S., and Sager, Clifford J. (1971, June). Sexual patterns at different ages. *Medical Aspects of Human Sexuality,* **5**, 10–23. A good, readable discussion of female and male sexual patterns over the lifespan.

CHAPTER • 13

LOVE AND ATTRACTION

To be in love is merely to be in a state of perceptual anesthesia—to mistake an ordinary young man for a Greek god or an ordinary young woman for a goddess.*

* *Source:* H. L. Mencken. (1919). *Prejudices.* (First Series.) New York: Knopf, p. 16.

We made love, Your Honor. He didn't have any and neither did I. So we made some. It was good.†

†Julie in Lois Gould, *Such good friends.*

CHAPTER HIGHLIGHTS

The lyrics to the old song, "Love and marriage, love and marriage, go together like a horse and carriage," might today be rewritten as "Love and sex, love and sex, go together. . . ." The standard of today is that sex is appropriate if one loves the other person (see Chapter 11), and sex seems to be the logical outcome of a loving relationship. Therefore, it seems important in a text on sexuality to spend some time considering that emotion that we link so closely to sex: love.

Love is one of those things that people seem to feel uncomfortable about defining. Perhaps when you were an adolescent, you were curious about love and asked an adult, "What is love?" or "How can you tell when

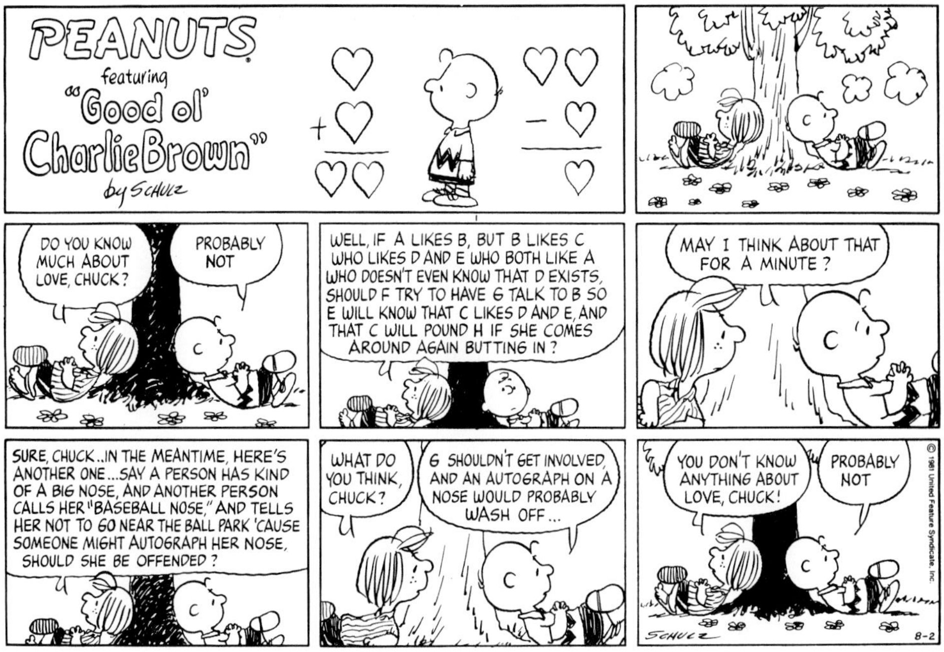

FIGURE 13.1

Communicating about love is often difficult.

you're in love?" Adults in this situation have a tendency to give answers like "It's not something you can define, but you'll know when you're in it." Such a response is not very scientific, nor is it very informative. This chapter will provide a bit deeper understanding of what love really is. First, various theoretical views of the nature and meaning of love will be discussed; then the research that has been done on love and attraction will be reviewed.

THEORETICAL VIEWS

The Greeks

Our language is rather limited in that we have only one word, "love," to express a wide variety of feelings and relationships. "Love" can mean everything from a mother's love for her child to the kind of love that leads quickly to an intense affair that burns itself out after a week. Sometimes we seek to express these various kinds of love by adding modifers, such as "brotherly" love or "passionate" love.

The ancient Greeks had a much richer vocabulary that allowed them to express more precisely the different kinds of love that exist. They had four different words, all of which translate to "love": eros (AIR-ohs), agape (AH-gah-pay), philia (FIL-ee-ah), and storge (STORE-gay).

Eros refers to passionate love or erotic love; it is the kind of love we refer to when we say that we are "in love." Storge means affection, particularly the kind of affection that parents feel toward their children or that ch'ldren feel toward their parents. Philia means solid friendship. Agape refers to a kind of selfless, giving love.

Eros (AIR-ohs): The Greeks' term for passionate or erotic love.

Storge (STORE-gay): The Greeks' term for affection.

Philia (FILL-ee-uh): The Greeks' term for friendship or liking.

Agape (AH-gah-pay): The Greeks' term for a giving, self-sacrificing love.

C. S. Lewis

The British writer C. S. Lewis (author of *The Screwtape Letters*), writing from a Christian perspective, has expanded on the Greeks' concepts of different kinds of love in his book entitled *The Four Loves* (1960).

Lewis uses the term "affection" for what the Greeks would have called *storge*. Affection is the kind of warm feeling that a parent has when cuddling a baby. Lewis says that we see this affection in:

> . . . the mere ease and ordinariness of the relationship (free as solitude, yet neither is alone) as it wraps us round. No need to talk. No need to make love. No needs at all except perhaps to stir the fire. (1960, p. 57)

Affection is a nondiscriminating love; indeed, it may even fail to discriminate among species, since it is probably the way you feel about your dog or cat. It is also a humble love and is rather like the feeling one has about soft slippers or some favorite old clothes; they do not give one much status, but they are loved affectionately nonetheless. According to Lewis, affection does not expect too much, turns a blind eye to faults, and revives easily after quarrels.

Philia, or friendship, is, in a sense, the least physical of the loves. It does not raise your pulse rate or make you blush or turn pale. Indeed, some people probably never experience true friendship. Lewis contrasts friendship with eros: lovers are face to face, absorbed in each other; friends stand shoulder to shoulder, absorbed in some common interest. Because of this aspect of friendship, Lewis argues that in a strictly gender-role-stereotyped society, true friendship rarely exists between a man and a woman. They have none of the things in common that make for friendship. Lewis sees as the critical definer of friendship the following question: "Do you see the same truth?" (As we will discuss in a later section, the social psychologist rephrases this to ask, "Do you have similar attitudes?")

Eros is "being in love," or the kind of love that lovers are "in." Lewis uses the term "Venus" to refer to the specifically sexual aspect of eros. But eros is more than Venus or lust. In lust, the person wants only another body to have sex with. In eros, one wants a specific person, the beloved. One of the characteristics of eros is preoccupation; the person is scarcely able to think of anything other than the beloved and longs to be with the beloved when they are separated. However, eros does not always produce happiness:

> For it is the very mark of Eros that when he is in us we had rather share unhappiness with the Beloved than be happy on other terms. (Lewis, 1960, p. 150)

Finally, Lewis uses the word "charity" as a translation of *agape.* In doing this, he means charity in its older sense, not in its modern sense, which has a connotation of condescension. Charity is a basic feeling of goodness and decency toward the other. As he says, "charity suffers long and is kind and forgives."

Whether or not one agrees with the categorizations of love proposed by Lewis, the important point is that there are many different kinds of love.

Maslow: B-love and D-love

B-love (Being-love): Maslow's term for an unneeding, unselfish love between two self-actualized people.

D-love (Deficiency-love): A selfish love between two people that arises because of their psychological needs.

The psychologist Abraham Maslow, founder of humanistic psychology, distinguishes between B-love and D-love (1968). B-love (short for Being love) is an unneeding, unselfish love for another. In contrast, D-love (short for Deficiency love) is a need for love, a selfish love. Maslow clearly believes that B-love is better than D-love. As he says, "B-love is, beyond the shadow of a doubt, a richer, 'higher,' more valuable subjective experience than D-love" (1968, p. 43).

Maslow believes that some people are B-lovers and some are D-lovers. He views B-lovers as far more healthy and self-actualizing:

> B-lovers are more independent of each other, more autonomous, less jealous or threatened, less needful, more individual, more disinterested, but also simultaneously more eager to help the other toward self-actualization, more proud of his triumphs, more altruistic, generous and fostering. (1968, p. 43)

Thus D-love is the kind of love that arises between two people because of their psychological needs; each seems to satisfy some needs that the other has. B-love occurs between two self-actualized people who are independent and yet appreciative of each other.

Fromm: *The Art of Loving*

Psychoanalyst Erich Fromm developed his ideas about love in his book *The Art of Loving* (1956). As the title of the book implies, Fromm believes that loving is an art, something that one must learn about and practice. He also emphasizes that love is something one *does,* not a state one is *in.* Thus, he would say "I love," not "I am in love."

Fromm believes that a central problem of human existence is a sense of separateness or isolation from others. This sense of separateness causes anxiety. We therefore have a basic need to overcome the sense of separateness, and loving—establishing a union with another person—is one of the best ways of doing this. Sexual experiences themselves help to conquer the sense of separateness, but Fromm believes that they do so only temporarily unless there is love too.

Fromm distinguishes between immature love, which is characterized by a symbiotic[1] union between two people, and mature love, which he believes to be one of the most important human emotions:

> In contrast to symbiotic union, mature *love is union under the condition of preserving one's integrity,* one's individuality. *Love is an active power in man:* a power which breaks through the walls which separate man from his fellow men, which unites him with others; love makes him overcome the sense of isolation and separateness, yet it permits him to be himself, to retain his integrity. In love the paradox occurs that two beings become one and yet remain two. (1956, p. 17)

Fromm says that mature love is characterized by care, responsibility, respect, and knowledge of the loved person.

Fromm disagrees with Freud, who saw sexual desire as being a drive to discharge energy. Fromm instead views sexual desire as a basic need for love and union, a desire to overcome the sense of separateness. One of the basic kinds of separateness that exist among humans is the separateness between men and women, and Fromm believes that heterosexual lovemaking is a means of overcoming it.

Fromm distinguishes between brotherly love, motherly love, erotic love, and self-love. Most relevant for this discussion are his ideas about erotic love.

Fromm says that erotic love is:

> . . . the craving for complete fusion, for union with one other person. It is by its very nature exclusive and not universal; it is also perhaps the most deceptive form of love

[1]"Symbiotic" is a term with origins in biology; it refers to a relationship between two organisms in which each essentially lives off the other. They are highly dependent on each other, and neither could survive without the other.

> there is. . . . Erotic love, if it is love, has one premise. That I love from the essence of my being—and experience the other person in the essence of his or her being. (1956, pp. 44, 47)

Thus Fromm sees erotic love as exclusive—something one can do with only one other person at a time—because it is a total fusion with the other person. He also believes that erotic love is fairly permanent; this idea is tied up with his notion that love is something one does, not a state one is in:

> To love somebody is not just a strong feeling—it is a decision, it is a judgment, it is a promise. If love were only a feeling there would be no basis for the promise to love each other forever. A feeling comes and it may go. How can I judge that it will stay forever, when my act does not involve judgment and decision? (1956, p. 56)

Thus Fromm views erotic love as a craving for total union with the other, which is exclusive and enduring.

John Alan Lee: Lovestyles

On the basis of his research, sociologist John Alan Lee (1974, 1977) believes that there are three basic types of love, and he uses Greek and Latin words to distinguish them: eros, storge, and ludus.

Eros, according to his view, is a powerful attraction to the physical appearance of the loved person. The erotic lover often has an ideal partner in mind, and it may be "love at first sight" when he or she meets that person. Erotic lovers cultivate a variety of sexual techniques so that they will continually delight in each other's bodies.

Ludus (LOO-dus): Lee's term for playful, casual love.

Ludus refers to playful love. For ludic lovers, love is a pleasant pastime; however, they refuse to get too involved, to become dependent on the beloved, or to let the beloved become too attached to them. Because of their low commitment, ludic lovers may have more than one lover at a time. They also show little interest in improving sexual techniques, since they find it easier to get a new partner than to work out problems in an old relationship.

Storge is "love without fever, tumult or folly, a peaceful and enchanting affection." It is the kind of love that sneaks up unnoticed in a relationship; storgic lovers remember no special point in the relationship when they "fell" in love. Because the relationship develops gradually, sex typically does not occur for some time. Storge is the kind of quiet affection expressed by the lyrics to the song "I've Grown Accustomed to Her Face." Storge also tends to be a very stable love that can last through crises in the relationship and even through long separations.

Lee sees these three basic types of love as being analogous to the three primary colors: red, yellow, and blue. Just as new colors are produced by combining primary colors—orange is a mixture of red and yellow, for example—so other types of love result from blendings of the three basic types. For example, in *mania,* which may be viewed as a combination of eros and ludus, love is an obsession. In mania, the person is consumed with thoughts of the beloved, may feel furious jealousy, and may suffer from symptoms such as agitation, sleeplessness, and loss of appetite. The manic lover alternates between feelings of ecstasy and despair. Manic lovers have the passion of eros but play the games of ludus. Needless to say, this is the sort of stuff that makes for great novels and plays.

Pragma: Lee's term for practical love, in which the person consciously tries to find a lover with a certain set of desirable characteristics.

Pragma is a kind of practical love; it combines the compatibility of storge with the game playing of ludus. The pragmatic lover consciously tries to find a lover who has a certain set of characteristics that are thought desirable. Once a good match is

(a)

(b)

FIGURE 13.2

Various kinds of love. (*a*) Companionship in an egalitarian love relationship, or storge, to use Lee's terminology. (*b*) Romantic love, or eros, to use Lee's terminology. (*c*) Playful love, or ludus, to use Lee's terminology.

(c)

found, pragmatic love may grow over the years. It is the kind of love that existed for centuries when marriages were arranged by persons other than the couple themselves.

Agape, the classic Christian view of love, is altruistic, undemanding, never jealous, and always kind and patient. It seems to represent a combination of storge and eros.

Of what practical significance are these ideas? Lee believes that conflicts arise when two different types of lovers are paired with each other. People often think that it is the quantity of love that is the problem—the old complaint is "you don't love me enough"—but instead there may be a mismatch of the types of lovers. For example, suppose we have a ludic man and a storgic woman. He feels that she is trying to trap him into a commitment when he just wants to have some fun. She wants to develop a slow, lasting relationship and accuses him of playing games just to get her to go to bed with him. They have a conflict. According to Lee, two lovers of the same type are most compatible.

RESEARCH ON LOVE

Measuring Love

So far the discussion has focused on theoretical definitions of various kinds of love. As we noted earlier, different people may mean different things when they use the word "love." One of the ways that psychologists define terms is by using an operational definition. In an operational definition a concept is defined by the way it is measured. Thus, for example, "IQ" is sometimes defined as the kinds of abilities that are measured by IQ tests. "Job satisfaction" can be defined as a score on a questionnaire that measures one's attitudes toward one's job. Operational definitions are very useful because they are precise and because they help clarify exactly what a scientist means by a complex term such as "love" or "aggression."

Operational definition: Defining some concept or term by how it is measured, for example, defining intelligence as those abilities that are measured by IQ tests.

Psychologist Zick Rubin (1970) has used the operational-definition approach to study love. That is, he has constructed a paper-and-pencil test to measure romantic love. (He also constructed another test to measure "liking.") Basically, Rubin sees love as an attitude one has toward another person. Thus the items on the scale involve reporting feelings about a specific person. Some items from Rubin's love scale and liking scale are shown in the Focus. Subjects rate each item on a scale from 1 to 9 to indicate how much they agree with it. If you feel that you are in love with someone, you might want to think of how you would answer the questions, keeping that person in mind.

The content of the love items seems to imply that there are three major components of romantic love:

1. *Affiliative and dependency needs* For example, "If I could never be with _____, I would feel miserable."
2. *A predisposition to help* For example, "I would do almost anything for _____."
3. *Exclusiveness and absorption* For example, "I feel very possessive toward _____."

In contrast, liking seems to involve respect and admiration.

Rubin administered the questionnaire to a group of dating couples at the University of Michigan. He found that loving and liking were only moderately corre-

F · O · C · U · S 13.1

SOME ITEMS FROM A LOVE SCALE AND A LIKING SCALE

LOVE-SCALE ITEMS

These items measure how much you love a person.

1. I would do almost anything for _____.
2. If I could never be with _____, I would feel miserable.
3. If I were lonely, my first thought would be to seek _____ out.

LIKING-SCALE ITEMS

These items measure how much you like a person.

1. I would highly recommend _____ for a responsible job.
2. In my opinion, _____ is an exceptionally mature person.
3. _____ is the sort of person whom I myself would like to be.

Source: Zick Rubin. (1970). Measurement of romantic love. *Journal of Personality and Social Psychology,* **16**, p. 267. Each item is ranked on a scale from 1 (not at all true; disagree completely) to 9 (definitely true; agree completely).

lated. That is, we seem to have some tendency to like the person we love, but not a very strong tendency. Love scores did, however, tend to be highly correlated with subjects' estimates of the likelihood that they would eventually marry this dating partner. Rubin also found that the love scores of men (for their girlfriends) were almost identical to the love scores of women (for their boyfriends). That is, there was no evidence that either men or women had a stronger tendency to feel more loving toward their partners. There was, however, a tendency for women to like their boyfriends more than men liked their girlfriends.

Using this instrument, Rubin was able to do further investigations of love relationships. For example, he found that couples who were strongly in love (both had high scores on the love scale) spent more time gazing into each other's eyes than couples who were only weakly in love (both had low scores on the love scale).

Rubin (1973) found some evidence that interfaith couples loved each other more strongly than same-faith couples. This may be an example of the "Romeo and Juliet effect" (R. Driscoll et al., 1972): the more parents object to a relationship, the stronger the love becomes.

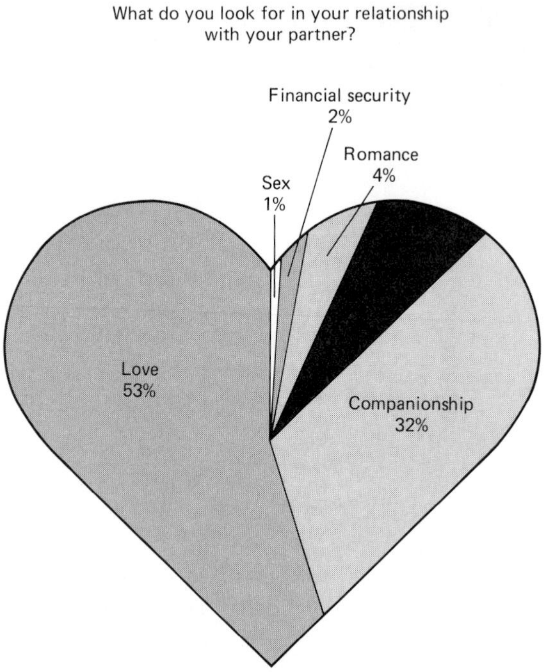

FIGURE 13.3

Psychology Today surveyed its readers on the topic of love. These are the responses to the question, "What do you look for in your relationship with your partner?" Notice that "love" came in first, and "companionship" second.

Rubin's research is a good example of the way psychologists study an important but complex topic—such as love—scientifically.

Love as a Relationship Develops

As a romantic relationship progresses, the nature of the love typically changes. The early part of a relationship is generally characterized by passionate love, but there is a gradual switch to companionate love (Driscoll et al., 1972; Cimbalo et al., 1976). The transformaton tends to occur when the relationship is between 6 and 30 months old (Walster and Walster, 1978).

Some may find this a rather pessimistic commentary on romantic love. But it may be, instead, that this is a good way for relationships to develop. Passionate love is probably necessary to hold a relationship together in the early stages, while conflicts are being resolved. But once we move past that, most of us find that what we really need is a friend—someone who shares our interests, who is happy when we succeed, and who sympathizes when we fail—and that is just what we get with companionate love.

Gender Differences

The stereotype is that women are the romantics—they yearn for love, fall in love more easily, cling to love. Do the data support this idea?

In fact, research measuring love in relationships indicates that just the opposite is true. Men hold a more romantic view of male-female relations than women do (Hobart, 1958). They fall in love earlier in a relationship (Kanin et al., 1970; Rubin et al., 1981). Men also cling longer to a dying love affair (Hill et al., 1976; Rubin et al., 1981). Indeed, three times as many men as women commit suicide after a disastrous love affair (Walster and Walster, 1978).

In a word, it seems that men are the real romantics.

Love and Adrenalin

Two-component theory of love:
Berscheid and Walster's theory that two conditions must exist simultaneously for passionate love to occur: physiological arousal and attaching a cognitive label ("love") to the feeling.

Social psychologists Ellen Berscheid and Elaine Walster (1974) have proposed a two-component theory of love. According to their theory, passionate love occurs when two conditions exist simultaneously: (1) the person is in a state of intense *physiological arousal,* and (2) the situation is such that the person applies a particular *label*—"love"—to the sensations being experienced. Their theory is derived from an important theory and experiment conducted by psychologist Stanley Schachter (1964); it will be described first.

The Schachter and Singer Study

Suppose that your heart is pounding and your palms are sweating. What emotion are you experiencing? Love? Anger? Fear? Embarrassment? Sexual arousal? As it turns out, it may be any of these. Psychologists have discovered that a wide variety of strong emotions produce similar physiological states (pounding heart and sweating palms) and that what differentiates these emotions is the way we interpret or label what we are experiencing. Schachter's (1964) two-component theory of emotion says just this: that an emotion consists of a physiological state of arousal plus a cognitive or mental labeling of it as a particular emotion.

Schachter and Singer (1962) demonstrated this phenomenon in a classic experiment in which they manipulated both the physiological arousal of subjects and the labeling of emotions. Male college-student volunteers were the subjects. When they arrived at the laboratory, they were told that they were participating in a study designed to measure the effects of a new vitamin, Suproxin, on vision. Physiological arousal was manipulated using the drug epinephrine (adrenalin). Epinephrine stimulates the sympathetic nervous system, producing an arousal state including increased heart rate and increased rate of breathing. Subjects were in one of four groups (see Table 13.1). Subjects in the *informed group* received an injection of Suproxin (really adrenalin) and were told to expect the exact effects of adrenalin: pounding heart, flushed face, and so on. Subjects in the *misinformed group* also received the adrenalin injection, but they were told to expect a wrong set of side effects: numbness, itching, and a slight headache. Subjects in the *ignorant group* received the injection of adrenalin but were given no information about the side effects. Finally, subjects in the *placebo group* were given an injection that contained no drug and were told nothing about side effects.

After receiving the injections, the subjects were put in a waiting room for 20 minutes. An accomplice of the experimenters was also in the waiting room. It was his job to create a situation that would lead the subjects to apply a certain label to their feelings of arousal. Half of the subjects were in the *euphoria* condition. The accomplice behaved in a deliriously happy way; among other things, he shot paper airplanes and danced wildly with a hula hoop. The other half of the subjects were in the *anger* condition. The accomplice and the subjects were asked to fill out forms. The questions began innocuously but gradually became insulting. The accomplice became increasingly angry; finally he threw the questionnaire on the floor and stomped out shouting, "I'm not wasting any more time. I'm getting my books and leaving."

TABLE 13.1

THE SCHACHTER-SINGER EXPERIMENT

Group	Injection	Expectations	Resulting State	Model	Effects
Informed	Adrenalin	Told precise side effects of adrenalin	Not bewildered Aroused	Euphoric Angry	No effect No effect
Ignorant	Adrenalin	Told nothing about side effects	Bewildered Aroused	Euphoric Angry	Euphoric Angry
Misinformed	Adrenalin	Misled about side effects	Bewildered Aroused	Euphoric	Euphoric
Placebo	Neutral solution	Told nothing about side effects	Not bewildered Not aroused	Euphoric Angry	No effect No effect

The experimenters watched the interaction from behind a one-way mirror and rated the kind of emotion the subjects expressed. The subjects also rated themselves as to the kind of emotions they felt.

Schachter and Singer made the following predictions for the outcomes of the study: Subjects in the informed group are aroused, but they can easily explain it, and so they should not be susceptible to the accomplice's suggestions of emotion. Subjects in the misinformed and ignorant groups, however, are aroused, but they have no easy way to explain it. These subjects should seek a label for their emotional state and will use the one provided by the accomplice. Finally, subjects in the placebo group are not aroused, and so they are not likely to think they are experiencing strong emotions, regardless of the accomplice's behavior.

The results turned out exactly as predicted (Table 13.1) Subjects in the misinformed and ignorant groups felt either euphoric or angry, depending on the accomplice's behavior. Subjects in the informed and placebo groups were unaffected by the accomplice.

On the basis of these results, Schachter (1964) proposed his two-component theory of emotion: that an emotion consists of a physiological arousal state plus the labeling of it as a particular emotion (for a critical evaluation of the theory, see Reisenzein, 1983). Berscheid and Walster have applied this to the emotion of "love." What they suggest is that we feel passionate love when we are aroused and when conditions are such that we believe it is love that we are feeling.

Evidence on Berscheid and Walster's Theory

Several experiments provide evidence for Berscheid and Walster's theory.

In one study, male subjects exercised vigorously by running in place; that produced the physiological arousal response of pounding heart and sweaty palms (White et al., 1981). Afterward they rated their liking for an attractive woman, who actually was a confederate of the experimenters. Subjects in the running group said they liked the woman significantly more than did subjects who were in a control condition and had not exercised. This result is consistent with Berscheid and Walster's theory. The effect is called the misattribution of arousal; that is, in a situation like this, the men misattribute their arousal—which is actually due to exercise—to their liking for the attractive woman.

Misattribution of arousal: When one is in a state of physiological arousal (e.g., from exercising or being in a frightening situation), attributing these feelings to be love or attraction to the person present.

FIGURE 13.4

The misattribution of arousal. If people are physically aroused (e.g., by jogging), they may misattribute this arousal to love or sexual attraction, if the situation suggests such an interpretation.

Another study suggests that fear can increase a man's attraction to a woman (Dutton and Aron, 1974; see also Brehm et al., cited in Berscheid and Walster, 1974). An attractive female interviewer contacted male passersby either on a fear-arousing suspension bridge or on a non-fear-arousing bridge. The fear-arousing bridge was constructed of boards attached to cables and had a tendency to tilt, sway, and wobble; the handrails were low, and there was a 230-foot drop to rocks and shallow rapids below. The "control" bridge was made of solid cedar; it was firm, and there was only a 10-foot drop to a shallow rivulet below. The interviewer asked subjects to fill out questionnaires that included projective test items. These items were then scored for sexual imagery.

The men in the suspension-bridge group should have been in a state of physiological arousal, while those in the control-bridge group should not have been. In fact, there was more sexual imagery in the questionnaires filled out by the men in the suspension-bridge group, and these men made more attempts to contact the attractive interviewer after the experiment than the subjects on the control bridge. Intuitively, this might seem to be a peculiar result: that men who are in a state of fear are more attracted to a woman than men who are relaxed. But in terms of the Berscheid and Walster two-component theory, it makes perfect sense. The fearful men were physiologically aroused, while the men in the control group were not. And according to this theory, arousal is an important component of love or attraction.[2]

Now, of course, if the men had been approached by an 80-year-old woman or a

---

[2]According to the terminology of Chapter 10, note that the Schachter and Singer study and the Dutton and Aron study are both examples of *experimental* research.

crippled woman or a child, probably their responses would have been different. In fact, when the interviewer in the experiment was male, the effects discussed above did not occur. Society tells us what the appropriate objects of our love, attraction, or liking are. That is, we know for what kinds of people it is appropriate to have feelings of love or liking. For these men, feelings toward an attractive woman could reasonably be labeled "love" or "liking," while such labels would probably not be attached to feelings for an 80-year-old woman. Thus in this experiment subjects were provided with a situation in which "love" or "liking" was a reasonable label for their feelings; however, only the suspension-bridge group also had the physiological arousal that is necessary to create the emotion. Our society generally encourages people to attach the label "love" to a wide variety of confused feelings (Walster and Berscheid, 1974).

The physical arousal that is important for love need not always be produced by unpleasant or frightening situations. Pleasant stimuli, such as sexual arousal or praise from the other person, may produce arousal and feelings of love. Indeed, Berscheid and Walster's theory does an excellent job of explaining why we seem to have such a strong tendency to associate love and sex. Sexual arousal is one method of producing a state of physiological arousal, and it is one that our culture has taught us to label as "love." Thus both components necessary to feel love are present: arousal and a label (see, for example, Stephan et al., 1971).

INTERPERSONAL ATTRACTION

What causes you to be attracted to another person? Social psychologists have done extensive research on interpersonal attraction. The major results of this research are discussed below.

Birds of a Feather

We tend to like people who are similar to us. We are attracted to people who are approximately the same as we are in terms of economic and social status, ethnicity, intelligence, and attitudes (Byrne, 1971; Laumann, 1969; Vandenberg, 1972).

Social psychologist Donn Byrne (1971) has done numerous experiments demonstrating that we are attracted to people whose attitudes and opinions are similar to ours. In these experiments, Byrne typically has subjects fill out an opinion questionnaire. They are then shown a questionnaire that was supposedly filled out by another person and are asked to rate how much they think they would like that person. In fact, the questionnaire was filled out to show either high or low agreement with the subject's responses. Subjects report more liking for a person whose responses are similar to theirs than for one whose responses are quite different.

Folk sayings are sometimes wise and sometimes foolish. The interpersonal-attraction research indicates that the saying "Birds of a feather flock together" contains some truth.

"Hey, Good-Lookin'"

We also tend to be attracted to people who are physically attractive, that is, "good-looking" (Berscheid and Walster, 1974). For example, in one study snapshots were taken of college men and women (Berscheid et al., 1971). A dating history of each subject was also obtained. Judges then rated the attractiveness of the men and women in the photographs. For the women there was a fairly strong relationship between attractiveness and popularity; the women judged attractive had had more dates in the last year than the less attractive women. There was some relationship between appearance and popularity for men, but it was not so marked as it was for women. In general, then, we are most attracted to good-looking people. However, this phenomenon is somewhat modified by our own feelings of personal worth, as will be seen in the next section.

The Interpersonal Marketplace

Although this may sound somewhat callous, whom we are attracted to and pair off with depends a lot on how much we think we have to offer and how much we think we can "buy" with it (see, for example, Rubin, 1973, pp. 67ff.). Generally, the principle seems to be that women's worth is based on their physical beauty, whereas men's worth is based on how successful they are. There is a tendency, then, for beautiful women to be paired with wealthy, successful men.

Data from many studies document this phenomenon. In one study, high school yearbook pictures of 601 males and 745 females were rated for attractiveness (Udry and Eckland, 1984). The subjects were followed up 15 years after graduation and measures of education, occupation status, and income were obtained. Females who were rated the most attractive in high school were significantly more likely to have husbands who had high incomes and were highly educated (see also Elder, 1969). Interestingly, for males, the relationship was the reverse; the least attractive males had the most education and the highest occupational status.

In another study, women students were rated on their physical attractiveness (Rubin, 1973, p. 68). They were then asked to complete a questionnaire about what kinds of men they would consider desirable dates. A man's occupation had a big effect on his desirability as a date. Men in high-status occupations—physician, lawyer, chemist—were considered highly desirable dates by virtually all the women. Men in low-status occupations—janitor, bartender—were judged hardly acceptable by most of the women. A difference emerged between attractive and unattractive women, however, when rating men in middle-status occupations—electrician, bookkeeper, plumber. The attractive women did not feel that these men would be acceptable dates, whereas the unattractive women felt that they would be at least moderately acceptable. Here we see the interpersonal marketplace in action. Men with more status are more desirable. But how desirable the man is judged to be depends on the woman's sense of her own worth. Attractive women are not much interested in middle-status men because they apparently think they are "worth more." Unattractive women find middle-status men more attractive, presumably because they think such men are reasonably within their "price range."

From the Laboratory to Real Life

The phenomena discussed so far—feelings of attraction to people who are similar to us and who are good-looking—have been demonstrated mainly in psychologists' laboratories. Do these phenomena occur in the real world?

Donn Byrne and his colleagues (1970) did a study to find out whether these results would be obtained in a real-life situation. They administered an attitude and personality questionnaire to 420 college students. Then they formed 44 "couples."

F · O · C · U · S 13.2

JEALOUSY

Jealousy is an unpleasant emotion that is often associated with love and with sexual relationships. Traditionally in the United States, jealousy has been considered a normal, even necessary, emotion; it has been viewed as strengthening monogamy and marriage. Recently, though, young people interested in radical lifestyles have expressed the view that jealousy is a threat to a relationship and reflects the insecurity of the two people and the weakness of their bond.

Psychologists Gordon Clanton and Lynn G. Smith have studied jealousy and have provided some insights into its nature and how we can cope with it. They believe that there are two basic types of jealousy. The mild and relatively harmless form is a feeling of being left out. Suppose you are at a party and you see your date talking animatedly with someone else. You feel a twinge of jealousy mainly because you feel excluded and wish you were a part of the interaction. This kind of jealousy passes quickly. The more serious form of jealousy is related to a fear of loss, and it becomes a persistent fear. What do you fear losing? You may fear loss of face; what will all the other women think when they see your husband flirting openly with someone else? Perhaps you fear loss of control—not being in command of the relationship or your own future or perhaps facing the prospect of no dates for some time. Finally, you may fear the loss of your partner and the love and affection that person provides. Basically, Clanton and Smith see jealousy as a sort of instinctive reaction to a threat to oneself or to a relationship.

Clanton and Smith believe that jealousy is an emotion we begin experiencing early in life and that our

For half of the couples, both people had made very similar responses on the questionnaire; for the other half of the couples, the two people had made very different responses. The two people were then introduced and sent to the student union on a "Coke date." When they returned from the date, an unobtrusive measure of attraction was taken—how close they stood to each other in front of the experimenter's desk. The subjects also evaluated their dates on several scales.

The results of the study confirmed those from previous experimental work. The couples who had been matched for similar attitudes were most attracted to each other, and those with dissimilar attitudes were not so attracted to each other. The students had also been rated as to their physical attractiveness both by the experimenter and by their dates, and greater attraction to the better-looking dates was reported. In a follow-up at the end of the semester, those whose dates were similar to them and were physically attractive were more likely to remember the date's name and to express a desire to date the person again in the future. Thus in an experiences with it as we grow up shape the way we react in jealousy-provoking situations when we are adults. From earliest infancy, we are dependent on our mother and feel jealous when we have to share her with someone else—our father or siblings. Later, we feel sibling rivalry and have another experience of jealousy. How our parents handle these situations may have a great deal to do with our later tendencies toward jealousy. For example, if your parents tried to make you feel loved and wanted when you cried because your mother was sharing her attentions with a sibling, you may develop a low propensity to jealousy. If they punished you severely for behaving that way, you may develop tendencies to repress jealousy. And if they reacted by depriving you of your mother's attentions even more, you may develop a deep sense of insecurity and jealousy in adulthood.

Clanton and Smith believe that we have a choice in dealing with our own jealousy: we can react in an insecure, defensive manner, or we can react in a secure, constructive way. The following two reactions illustrate the difference. The first one is defensive:

> His interest in her confirms my suspicion that he is on the make. I never did trust him. Her interest in him shows she is dissatisfied with me. He's quite attractive. I guess she's grown tired of me. And he's so attentive to her, so appreciative. I guess I've come to take her for granted. No wonder she's so turned on by his courtesies. They want to go to the opera together, and I feel left out. I wonder what other excuses they'll find to spend time together. Maybe she'll take time away from me to be with him. Maybe I'll have to cook dinner and take care of the kids while she's off at the "opera." If I can't count on my own wife, what the hell can I count on?

This is a constructive reaction:

> His interest in her confirms her attractiveness. I'm proud of her. Her interest in him shows she is alert and alive. I'm glad for that. An inert partner, no matter how secure the relationship, is a bad deal. He's like me in some ways, so I am affirmed by her choice of him. He's different from me in some ways, which suggests she has some needs that I don't meet. I must consider these needs carefully and try to find out if I could do a better job of meeting them. But I realize I cannot meet all of her needs without violating my own autonomy, so I must work to become glad she has other friends who can fulfill her in ways I do not and would rather not. Thank God, she's found someone who wants to go to the opera with her. I want to be reassured that our relationship means as much to her as it does to me, but I won't demand that she renounce all others in order to demonstrate that to me.

Source: Gordon Clanton and Lynn G. Smith. (1977). The self-inflicted pain of jealousy. *Psychology Today,* **10**(10), p. 44.

experiment that was closer to real life and real dating situations, the importance of similarity and physical appearance was again demonstrated.

The Girl Next Door

There is also evidence that we tend to be more attracted to people with whom we have had contact many times than we are to people with whom we have had little contact (Rubin, 1973). This has been demonstrated in laboratory studies in which the amount of contact between subjects was varied. At the end of the session, subjects gave higher "liking" ratings to those with whom they had had much contact and lower ratings to those with whom they had had little contact (Saegert et al., 1973). Mere repeated exposure to someone seems to make us like that person. Thus, there does seem to be a "girl-next-door" or "boy-next-door" phenomenon; we tend to be attracted to people with whom we have had much contact, to whom we have been exposed, and with whom we are familiar.

Playing Hard-to-Get

The traditional advice that has been given to girls—by Ann Landers and others—is that boys will be more attracted to them if they play hard-to-get. Is there any scientific evidence that this is true?

In fact, two experiments provide no support for this kind of strategy; according to these experiments, playing hard-to-get does not work (Walster et al., 1973). In one of these experiments, college men were recruited for a computer-dating program. They were given the phone number of their assigned date and were told to phone her and arrange a date from the experimenters' laboratory; after they phoned her, they assessed their initial impressions of her. In fact, all the men were given the same telephone number—that of an accomplice of the experimenters. For half of the men, she played easy-to-get; she was delighted to receive the phone call and to be asked out. With the other half of the men, she played hard-to-get; she accepted the date with reluctance and obviously had many other dates. The results failed to support the hard-to-get strategy: the men had equally high opinions of the hard-to-get and easy-to-get woman.

The same experimenters reported an ingenious field experiment in which a prostitute played either hard-to-get or easy-to-get with her clients and then recorded the clients' responses, such as how much they paid her. Once again, the hard-to-get hypothesis was not supported; the men seemed to like the easy-to-get and the hard-to-get prostitute equally well.

The experimenters were faced with the bald fact that a piece of folk wisdom just did not seem to be true. They decided that they needed a somewhat more complex hypothesis. They hypothesized that it is not the woman who is generally hard-to-get or generally easy-to-get who is attractive to men but rather the one who is *selectively hard-to-get.* That is, she is easy-to-get for you, but she is hard-to-get for other men or unavailable to them. A computer-dating experiment supported this notion; the selectively hard-to-get woman was the most popular with men.

In practical terms, this means that if a woman is going to use hard-to-get strategies, she had better use them in a skillful way. It seems that the optimal strategy would be to give the impression that she has many offers for dates with others but refuses them, while being delighted to date the young man in question.

Interestingly, in all the research discussed, it is always the woman who is playing hard-to-get and the man who is rating her. This reflects cultural gender-role stereotypes, in which it is the woman's role to do things like play hard-to-get. What we do not know is how men's use of hard-to-get strategies would affect the way women perceive them.

Byrne's Law of Attraction

It is a rather commonsense idea—and one that psychologists agree with—that we tend to like people who give us reinforcements or rewards and to dislike people who give us punishments. Social psychologist Donn Byrne (cited in Walster and Walster, 1978) has actually formulated this mathematically:

$$Y = m\left[\frac{\Sigma R}{\Sigma R + \Sigma P}\right] + k$$

The Y stands for attraction, R for reinforcements, and P for punishments; m and k are just constants. Essentially what the formula says is that our attraction to another person is proportionate to the number of reinforcements that person gives us relative to the total number of reinforcements plus punishments the person gives us. Or, simplified even more, we like people who are frequently nice to us and seldom nasty.

Research repeatedly shows that we do tend to like those who give us more rewards. In fact, these effects have even been found with the preschool crowd. In a nursery school, the children who give the most positive reinforcement to others tend to be the most popular.

These effects also work if we even *associate* another person with reinforcements or punishments. In one study, young people were asked to meet a stranger (Griffitt, 1970). In half the meetings, the couple met in a cool, comfortable room. In the other half, they met in an uncomfortably hot room. Those who met in the comfortable surroundings later liked each other more than did those who met in the unpleasant environment.

These findings have some practical implications (Walster and Walster, 1978). If you are trying to get a new relationship going well, make sure you give the other person some positive reinforcement. Also, make sure that you have some good times together, so that you *associate* each other with rewards. Do not spend all your time stripping paint off old furniture or cleaning out the garage. And do not forget to keep the positive reinforcements (or "strokes," if you like that jargon better) going in an old, stable relationship.

Evaluating the Interpersonal-Attraction Research

Much of the research discussed in this section is an investigation not so much of love as of first impressions, or of attraction in the early stages of a relationship. Thus many of the results might not be true of long-term, deeply committed relationships. On the other hand, first impressions have a lot to do with casual dating, and casual dating is the usual prelude to serious relationships. In this way, first impressions may influence whom we eventually come to love.

AN AFTERTHOUGHT

Senator William Proxmire, watchdogging the spending of federal funds for research, has been very critical of research on sex and love. According to him, the last thing we need to do is understand love (Schaffer, 1977).

Personally, I think that it is one of the first things we should try to understand, and I hope that much more research will be done in this area. As Abraham Maslow put it, "We *must* understand love; we must be able to teach it, to create it, to predict it, or else the world is lost to hostility and to suspicion" (1970, p. 181).

SUMMARY

The Greeks had a richer vocabulary than we do for describing the various kinds of love. Their terms included eros (erotic or passionate love), storge (affection), philia (friendship), and agape (selfless love). C. S. Lewis has expanded on these four different kinds of love.

Abraham Maslow distinguishes between B-love, or Being love (a high, unselfish form of love), and D-love, or Deficiency love (a kind of love based on dependency or needs). Erich Fromm sees loving as an art; it is something we must learn and practice and something we do rather than a state we are in. Sociologist John Alan Lee believes that there are three basic kinds of love: eros (passionate physical attraction), ludus (playful love), and storge (long-lasting affection). According to him, mania, pragma, and agape are other types of love that result from the blending of the three basic types.

Zick Rubin has constructed a scale to measure romantic love and another scale to measure liking. This makes it possible to do further scientific research on love. Research indicates that love shifts from passionate to companionate as a relationship progresses. Research also indicates that men are more romantic and fall in love earlier in a relationship.

Berscheid and Walster have hypothesized that there are two basic components of romantic love: being in a state of physiological arousal and attaching the label "love" to the feeling.

Research on interpersonal attraction suggests that we tend to be attracted to people who are similar to us (in terms of attitudes, intelligence, and social status) and to people who are physically attractive. We also tend to be attracted to people whom we believe to be "within reach" of us, depending on our sense of our own attractiveness or desirability. Mere exposure to another person also seems to facilitate attraction. Playing hard-to-get seems to work only if the person is able to convey the sense of being selectively hard-to-get. We tend to be attracted to those who give us positive reinforcements.

REVIEW QUESTIONS

1. _____ is the Greeks' term for passionate love or erotic love.
2. Maslow uses the term B-love for an unselfish love for another. True or false?
3. Erich Fromm, in *The Art of Loving,* argues that love is something one does, not a state one is in. True or false?
4. According to John Alan Lee's research on lovestyles, conflicts in relationships often occur because one partner is more in love than the other. True or false?
5. As a relationship progresses, there is usually a shift from companionate love to passionate love, occurring when the relationship is between 6 and 30 months old. True or false?
6. Research indicates that men fall in love earlier in a relationship than women do, and that men cling longer to a dying love affair. True or false?
7. According to Berscheid and Walster's two-component theory, passionate love exists when two conditions exist simultaneously: _____ and attaching a cognitive label ("love") to the experience.
8. In the Schachter experiment on emotions, the subjects who received injections of adrenalin, were informed of its precise side effects, and were then exposed to an angry model, themselves experienced anger. True or false?

9. In one experiment, male subjects engaged in vigorous running in place and then met an attractive woman; they liked her significantly more than did a control group of subjects who didn't exercise. This effect is called the ______.

10. Research indicates that we are more attracted to people whose attitudes are similar to ours than to people whose attitudes are different. True or false?

QUESTIONS FOR THOUGHT, DISCUSSION, AND DEBATE

1. If you are currently in love with someone, how would you describe the kind of love you feel, using the various terms discussed in this chapter?
2. Do you agree with Senator Proxmire that the federal government should not be funding research on love? Why or why not?

SUGGESTIONS FOR FURTHER READING

Peele, Stanton, and Brodsky, Archie. (1975). *Love and addiction.* New York: New American Library. A provocative book in which the authors argue that love is much like a physical addiction to heroin or a similar drug.

Walster, Elaine, and Berscheid, Ellen. (1971). Adrenalin makes the heart grow fonder. *Psychology Today,* **5**(1), 46. Presents Walster and Berscheid's two-component theory of romantic love.

Walster, Elaine, and Walster, G. William. (1978). *A new look at love.* Reading, Mass.: Addison-Wesley. A beautifully written book that explains social psychologists' research on love and attraction and the practical implications of this research.

CHAPTER · 14

GENDER ROLES

What are little girls made of?
Sugar and spice and everything nice,
and that's what little girls are made of.
What are little boys made of?
Snips and snails and puppy dog tails,
and that's what little boys are made of.
—Children's rhyme

The great mind must be androgynous.
—Samuel Taylor Coleridge

CHAPTER HIGHLIGHTS

I. GENDER ROLES AND STEREOTYPES

II. GROWING UP FEMALE

III. GROWING UP MALE

IV. MALE-FEMALE PSYCHOLOGICAL DIFFERENCES

V. IMPACT OF GENDER ROLES ON SEXUALITY

VI. A NEW TREND: ANDROGYNY

VII. TRANSSEXUALISM

A baby is born. What is the first statement made about it? "It's a boy" or "It's a girl," of course. Sociologists tell us that gender is one of the most basic of status characteristics. That is, in terms of both our individual interactions with people and the position we hold in society, gender is exceptionally important. Consider, for example, the consternation we typically feel when we see a long-haired (or sometimes a short-haired) person in a baggy shirt and jeans whose gender is not apparent. We do not know how to interact with this person, and we feel quite flustered, not to mention curious, until we can ferret out some clue as to whether the person is a male or a female.

GENDER ROLES AND STEREOTYPES

Gender role:
A cluster of socially defined expectations that people of one gender are expected to fulfill.

Stereotype:
A set of expectations for an individual, based on that individual's membership in some category (e.g., male or female, heterosexual or homosexual).

One of the basic ways societies codify this emphasis on gender is through gender roles.[1] A gender role is a cluster of socially or culturally defined expectations that people of one gender are expected to fulfill.

A closely related phenomenon is stereotyping, in which we essentially prejudge someone, expecting the person to behave in a certain way or to have certain characteristics because that person is a male or a female. Stereotypes, like many other things, have both advantages and disadvantages. One of the basic advantages (and probably the reason why people have such a tendency to stereotype) is that stereotypes give us information in situations where we would otherwise have none. For example, if you meet a man whom you have never met before, you probably assume that he has a job, and that gives you a starter for conversation. Statistically, your chances of being right are fairly good. Similarly, you might assume that a women whom you meet for the first time is a full-time housewife and mother.[2] Once again, you have a good chance of being correct, although not so good a chance as with the man. Somehow, it is comforting to "know" these things about people with whom we are not really acquainted. But the problem with such assumptions is that they are not always correct. The man may be unemployed, and the woman may have an exciting career. One of the disadvantages of gender-role stereotypes, then, is that they lead to false assumptions about people. Another problem is that they tend to restrict people's opportunities. For example, a high school girl may have the ability to become an electrical engineer, but she may not even consider that as a possible career because she believes that only men are electrical engineers. Similarly, a high school boy who would make a good nurse might reject the possibility because he thinks nursing is only for women or because he fears that he would be teased and ridiculed if he decided to pursue that career.

Socialization:
The ways in which society conveys to the individual its expectations for his or her behavior.

Many adult women and men, though, do behave as gender roles say they should. Why does this happen? Psychologists and sociologists believe that it is a result of gender-role socialization. Socialization refers to the ways in which society conveys to the individual its expectations for his or her behavior. Socialization occurs especially in childhood, as children are taught to behave as they will be expected to in adulthood. Socialization may involve several processes. Children may be rewarded for behavior that is appropriate for their gender ("What a little man he is"), or they may be punished for behavior that is not appropriate to their gender ("Nice young ladies don't do that"). The adult models they imitate—whether these are parents of the same gender, teachers, or women and men on television—also contribute to their socialization. In some cases, simply telling children what is expected of males and females may be sufficient for role learning to take place. Socialization, of course, continues in adulthood, as society conveys its norms of appropriate behavior for adult women and men.

Who (or what) are society's agents in accomplishing this socialization? Certainly parents have an early, important influence, from buying dolls for girls and footballs or baseball bats for boys to giving boys more freedom to explore (Block, 1983). The parents' own conformity to their roles, which children may imitate, is also important. Parents are not the only socializing agents, though. The peer group can have a big

---

[1]The distinction between sex and gender will be maintained in this chapter. Male-female roles—and thus gender roles—are being discussed here.

[2]As a result of the women's movement, however, many people realize that this is not always an accurate assumption. Thus, they do not know what to assume about a woman, which can be awkward.

impact in socializing for gender roles, particularly in adolescence. Other teenagers can be extremely effective in enforcing gender-role standards; for example, they may ridicule or shun the boy whose behavior is effeminate. Thus peers can exert great pressure for gender-role conformity.

The media can also be important as socializing agents. For example, popular songs, despite all their counterculture pretensions, portray very stereotypical roles for males and females. In two studies of the lyrics of popular songs, it was found that males, who were the more frequent topics of the songs, were portrayed as sexually aggressive, nonconforming, rigid, egotistical, and adventurous; females were typically portrayed as sensitive, passive, insecure, and dependent. Further, in the songs, males were considerably more likely to be politically active and to use drugs (Chafetz, 1974, pp. 43–46). Preadolescents listening to these lyrics can scarcely be expected to miss the lessons the songs teach about what males are supposed to be like and what females are supposed to be like. While movies seem to be showing some trend away from portraying people only in stereotypical roles, television—both the programs and the commercials—continues to be blatant in portraying stereotyped gender roles (Kalisch and Kalisch, 1984; Mamay and Simpson, 1981; McArthur and Resko, 1976). For example, in one study of television commercials, it was found that virtually all men who did the selling used either a "factual" or "aggressive sales-pitch" approach, whereas women who did the selling typically used either "seductive" or "soft-spoken" approaches. Two-thirds of the commercials aimed at females took place in a domestic setting (Chafetz, 1974). Some advertisers are trying to avoid traditional stereotyping—as in the commercial showing the mother who is a dentist—but traditional roles still seem to prevail.

Children's textbooks and readers are also important socializing influences, and they show females and males in very stereotyped roles (Weitzman et al., 1972; Women on Words and Images, 1972). Women and girls are portrayed more frequently in restrictive, boring, passive, supportive, or downright stupid roles, while boys are portrayed as being unrealistically brave (for example, a small boy singlehandedly wrestling an alligator).

Finally, children may themselves be the agents of their own socialization. Once children have formed concepts of gender and know whether they are boys or girls, they typically acquire a very strong motivation to adopt their gender role (Kohlberg, 1966). That is, children actively seek out information about their gender role and then try to behave as they think boys or girls are supposed to behave. Thus, not only are gender roles imposed on children by society, but children also strive to learn them.

The following sections will be more specific about the gender-role pressures that males and females experience while growing up. First, though, it should be noted that while gender roles themselves are universal (Rosaldo, 1974)—that is, all societies have gender roles—the exact content of these roles varies from one culture to the next, from one ethnic group to another, and from one social class to another. For example, Margaret Mead (1953) studied several cultures in which gender roles

FIGURE 14.1

Children are very interested in achieving adult gender roles.

are considerably different from those in the United States. One such group is the Mundugumor of New Guinea. In that culture both females and males are extremely aggressive.

Gender-role expectations may change over the lifespan. Teenagers have fairly rigid concepts of gender roles (J. F. Adams, 1973), and young married couples, particularly those with small children, may follow very stereotyped roles (the woman takes care of the home and children, and the husband is the breadwinner). However, as people reach retirement age, there may be a considerable shifting of roles. After retiring, the husband may spend his time in the home, doing the marketing, cleaning, and cooking. As people get older, they are increasingly likely to be single, because of divorce or the death of a spouse, and thus they are more likely to assume both the male and the female roles (earn a living and take care of a home).

Having noted these gender-role variations, let us discuss the effect of gender roles on people as they grow up male or female. The role standards discussed will be mainly those of the white middle-class in the United States. There are several reasons for this. First, most of the research has been done on this group. Second, white middle-class culture has an overwhelming impact on our culture as a whole through its domination of the media (television and children's readers, for example). Finally, limitations of space do not permit a fuller discussion of the gender roles present in other cultures. As you read the following sections, you should keep in mind the effects that gender roles might have on sexuality.

GROWING UP FEMALE

Stereotypes about Women

Stereotypes, by definition, are pervasive in any culture, and so we are all aware of the stereotypes about women in American society—that they are passive, unaggressive, not intellectually inclined, emotional, nurturant, and irresponsible with money, for example.

Psychologists have studied gender-role stereotypes in the United States (Ruble, 1983; Broverman et al., 1972; Rosenkrantz et al., 1968). To do this, they simply asked people to name the characteristics on which the average man and the average woman differ. They found that there is a high degree of consensus on the ways in which men and women differ and that this consensus still exists not only among adults in the general population but also among college students. The feminine traits that are considered desirable fall into a general category of "warmth" and "expressiveness." Feminine traits that are not valued include characteristics such as emotionality and lack of competitiveness.

Heterosexuality is another important part of gender roles. The "feminine" woman is expected to be sexually attractive to men and, in turn, to be attracted to them. Women who violate any part of this—for example, gay women—are viewed as violators of gender roles and are considered masculine (Storms et al., 1981).

Keeping in mind the content of these stereotypes about women and their potential impact on developing children (and perhaps also on adults), let us look at what happens to females as they grow up.

Infancy and Early Childhood

While boys and girls are quite similar in their behavior in infancy and early childhood, there are some marked differences. One is aggression. As soon as children are old enough to behave aggresively (around age 2 to 3), girls are less aggressive than boys (Hyde, 1984; Maccoby and Jacklin, 1974). Another difference that appears early is in toy preference. By 2 years of age, boys and girls have different toy preferences, and by the age of 3 or 4, girls show a preference for playing at housekeeping and caring for babies (dolls), stringing beads, and sewing. It is not clear exactly why this occurs. It may be related to the different kinds of toys that adults give to children and a tendency for children to play with things they are familiar with, or it may result from the child's developing sense of gender identity and a corresponding desire to behave the way a "little woman" or a "little man" should (Maccoby and Jacklin, 1974).

There is evidence that, beginning in infancy, parents treat girls and boys differently (Block, 1983). Parents are less responsive and less attentive to girl babies, and female infants are given less freedom to explore. Female babies are also held less and given less physical stimulation. Also, in infancy and early childhood, girls are given different toys than boys are; girls are more likely to be given gender-typed toys such as dolls and cooking equipment (Bell and Carver, 1980; Seavey et al., 1975).

Childhood

In childhood, girls' school achievement is generally better than boys'. Their grades are better, and they are less frequently made to repeat a grade and are more frequently permitted to "skip" a grade. Girls' adjustment to school is also better than boys' (e.g., Werry and Quay, 1971).

In childhood, the forces of gender-role stereotyping become more prominent. Parents emphasize gender roles increasingly as children get older (Block, 1983). Teachers and the schools also become agents of socialization. For example, girls get less attention from teachers than boys do (Block, 1983). And play, both at school and after school, becomes gender-segregated, with boys playing in all-boys' groups and girls playing in all-girls' groups.

Television programming and advertising messages must make girls increasingly aware that women are housewives and mothers (but rarely lawyers) and nurses (but rarely doctors) and that their chief concern—and potential source of embarrassment if they do not meet the standards—is whether they will be diligent and wise enough to avoid "ring around the collar."

While it is true that socialization exerts an increasing force, it is also true that girls, at least at this stage, actually appear to have more freedom than boys do in regard to gender roles (Hartley, 1959). It is quite permissible, especially now, for girls to play baseball and climb trees; it is still relatively taboo for boys to play with dolls. Being a tomboy is tolerated; being a sissy is not.

Adolescence

Gender-role socialization forces are much stronger in adolescence than they were at earlier ages, and they may actually be stronger during this period than at any other stage of life. The peer group exerts tremendous pressures for conformity, and most adolescents meekly obey. Interestingly, corresponding to this increased socialization pressure, some psychological gender differences (for example, mathematical ability) appear for the first time in adolescence.

Femininity-achievement incompatibility: The notion, in our culture, that one cannot be both feminine and an achiever.

A principle that the adolescent girl becomes increasingly aware of is the femininity-achievement incompatibility (Horner, 1972; Hyde, 1985). The notion is that in our culture, one cannot be both feminine and an achiever. Achievement is somehow perceived as reducing one's femininity, and the truly feminine female is not an achiever. This puts the female in a double bind; achievement is a valued human characteristic, and one that she was rewarded for in elementary school, and yet it is now incompatible with her gender role. As Margaret Mead put it, "Every step forward as a human being is a step backward as a woman." Of course, it is important to emphasize that this is simply an arbitrary rule of our culture—there is nothing intrinsically incompatible about femininity and achievement. Nonetheless, the belief is a strong one.

An important psychological task of late adolescence is to begin to form an adult identity (Erikson, 1950, 1968). For the male, adult identity will be defined mainly in occupational terms (see below), and so he begins preparing himself for this future identity—for example, being a doctor or a farmer—in late adolescence. For adult women, though, identity is defined not by a career but rather by the wife-mother role. Thus in late adolescence many girls actually seek to postpone their identity formation so that they will be able to adapt their identity to that of the as-yet-unknown husband (Angrist, 1969). And rather than seeking a unique identity, the girl seeks popularity.

Adulthood

For most adult women, the wife-mother role is the major source of identity. Even today, college women tell me tht they are preparing themselves to be teachers or social workers or nurses so that they will have "something to fall back on." That is, the wife-mother role, rather than the career, is expected to be the major focus of adulthood; the career will be for use in emergencies, such as widowhood or divorce.

If she defines her identity through the wife-mother role, the woman does not form a unique sense of personal identity; rather, she defines her identity in terms of others. She is Mrs. John Smith; that is, she is not Mary Smith but rather John Smith's wife. At PTA meetings she may say that she is "Jimmy's mother," in this case defining her identity through her child.

It is true that increasing numbers of women are holding jobs outside the home. In 1981, women made up 43 percent of the labor force. Among women aged 18 to 64 about 62 percent held paying jobs (U.S. Department of Labor, 1982). However, it is important to note that most women work not for personal satisfaction but rather because they must. That is, many women work because they are single (divorced or widowed) and have to support a family, or at least themselves, or because their husband's income is not adequate to support the family.

Working women may often be caught in a double bind. In adulthood the femininity-achievement incompatibility is rerun under a new format, the work-mother incompatibility. That is, it is widely believed in our society that the children of working mothers suffer and that a woman cannot both be a good mother and hold a job. Thus working mothers may be told that any problems their children have are due to their working, despite the fact that there is no evidence that the children of working mothers suffer psychological damage (Hoffman, 1974). Nonetheless, working women may feel a tension between the demands of their work and the demands of being a housewife and mother.

Middle and Old Age

A well-known phenomenon of middle age is the depression that some women suffer as a result of the "empty-nest syndrome" (Bart, 1971). When the woman is about 50, usually the last child has left home—to go to college, to go to work, or to get married—and she is left with an "empty nest." Recent research, however, challenges these notions. In interviews with middle-aged women, the predominant feeling when the last child left home was not depression but relief (Rubin, 1979). Perhaps the empty nest is not a miserable place to be but a free place.

Widowhood may contribute to problems. Widows by far outnumber widowers in the United States; it has been estimated that the ratio of widows to widowers is 4 to 1 (Berardo, 1968). That is, in most marriages the man dies first. Statistics indicate that the average age of widowhood is 56 and that half of the women over 65 are widows (Berardo, 1968; U.S. Department of Commerce, 1973). The preponderance of widows is a result of two factors: the tendency of women to marry men older than themselves and the greater longevity of women. But the fact remains that many women spend the last 15 or so years of their lives as widows. This can make an empty nest even emptier and can also create financial problems and other emotional strains, as well as a celibate lifestyle.

The loss of attractiveness that occurs in middle and old age may also be stressful. Ours is a youth-oriented culture, and women's status in adolescence and adulthood is so heavily determined by their physical attractiveness that the loss of this attractiveness may lead to a fear—and perhaps a realistic one—that they will no longer be valued or loved as much.

Evidence of the effects of these stresses and the continuing ambivalence in the lives of women can be seen in the data on male-female ratios in mental illness. Studies consistently indicate that more adult women than men are mentally ill, as measured by the number in psychotherapy (Chesler, 1972; Gove and Tudor, 1973). There are approximately twice as many women in psychotherapy as there are men.

Lest we be overwhelmed with the stresses affecting middle-aged women, it is important to note that many women successfully resolve the crisis of middle age (Rubin, 1979). A woman and her husband may rediscover each other after years of being preoccupied with the children, or she may decide to get a job for the first time or go back to school. Such changes in her life may give her a great deal of satisfaction.

Who ends up happier—women who remain in the home exclusively or career women? The answer seems to depend on when in their lives you look at them. One study of college graduates indicated that in their twenties, the full-time housewives are happier. They enjoy raising small children and may be getting creative satisfaction from the role of housewife. Career women may be enduring the stresses of building up a career and trying to mesh that with the role of wife and mother. On the other hand, in their forties, women who are employed have higher self-esteem (Birnbaum, 1976). They are now reaping the benefits of satisfaction and identity built up in their careers, while those who have not worked are suffering from the empty-nest syndrome. Indeed, research indicates that "supermothers"—those who devote themselves exclusively to their children—are most likely to suffer from the empty-nest syndrome (Bart, 1971), while working mothers have found additional sources of identity and thus have less to lose when their children leave home.

GROWING UP MALE

Stereotypes about Men

We are all aware of the stereotypes about men that are prevalent in American culture: that they are aggressive, athletic, successful, unemotional, brave, and instantly aroused by attractive women.

Research on gender-role stereotypes finds a consensus about the traits of men in our culture (Rupple, 1983; Broverman et al., 1972). The traits that are valued in men fall into a general "competency" category, including traits like independence, objectivity, competitiveness, logicalness, and skill in business. That is, a key expectation for men in our culture is that they be competent and possess the characteristics that go along with competence.

It is important to note that sexuality itself is important in defining gender roles. For example, in one survey, 48 percent of the women felt that a "real man" should be a skilled lover (Tavris, 1977). Even in bed, men are required to be competent.

Keeping these stereotypes in mind, let us look at what happens in the process of growing up male.

Infancy and Early Childhood

As noted earlier in this chapter, some gender differences appear early. By about age 2, boys are more aggressive than girls. From infancy, boys are more active than girls, although this difference between them tends to be smaller than the difference related to aggression (Block, 1983). The rate of hyperactivity is also far higher in boys than in girls. The most common estimate is that among hyperactive children the ratio of males to females is about 6:1; in other words about 86 percent of hyperactive children are male (Wright et al., 1979).

Boys' toy and game preferences become gender-typed early, too. By the age of 3 or 4, boys already prefer activities such as carpentry and toys such as guns, trucks, tractors, and fire engines over "girls'" toys and activities (Maccoby and Jacklin, 1974).

Childhood

Boys do not do so well in school as girls, and they have more adjustment problems and are more often referred to psychologists (Andrews and Cappon, 1957; Dreger et al., 1964; Spivack and Spotts, 1965; Werry and Quay, 1971). This may be the result of a number of factors. First, the vast majority of elementary school teachers are women, and so the boy may not have a teacher who understands him or with whom he can identify, as the girl does. Research, however, does not confirm this hypothesis. Comparisons of classrooms with male teachers and classrooms with female teachers indicate that there are few differences—either in academic achievement or measures of adjustment—between boys in these two kinds of classrooms (Gold and Reis, 1982; Pleck, 1981). A second possibility is that, because young boys are developmentally immature, compared with girls, and since entrance to kindergarten is often based on age rather than readiness, many boys may enter kindergarten or first grade before they are ready to do the work that will be demanded of them. This may lead to failure, frustration, and the formation of emotional blocks that prevent them from learning when they are mature enough. A third possible source of boys' school problems is their greater aggressiveness. Teachers generally frown on displays of aggressiveness, and thus boys may quickly become classified as "behavior problems." Further, the aggressiveness may interfere with their attention and therefore with their learning.

Boys become increasingly aware of society's expectations for them. On television they see that men frequently shoot each other and they learn that men must always be brave, even in situations where anyone with any sense would be afraid. They see that to be respected, a man must be a doctor or a lawyer or a police officer.

Boys also learn quickly that they should not show emotion and that they must not cry even if they feel terrible. While the stereotype of the unemotional man may have some advantages over the stereotype of the "hysterical" woman, many men resent the fact that their emotions were "shut off" when they were children and say that they really wish they could cry.

Adolescence

Gender roles become increasingly prominent in adolescence. While the adolescent girl must prove herself in the area of popularity and attractiveness, boys must prove themselves in athletics (Pleck and Sawyer, 1974). The message is that to be a "big man on campus"—and get all the rewards that this entails, including the admiration of girls—the adolescent boy must be a successful athlete, especially in the glamour sports—football and basketball. As the lyrics of a popular song go, "You've got to be a football hero to get the love of a beautiful girl."

The problem with this, of course, is that not all, or even most, boys can be football heroes; in fact, only a few in any class can be. What about the boy who is uncoordinated, overweight, or small for his age? The message from society is that he is less of a man because he is a "failure" at athletics. However, the benefits of the pressure toward athletics should also be recognized. The athletic training boys get at this age encourages their competitiveness, and competitiveness is probably an important factor in attaining job success in adulthood.

Late in adolescence, boys begin to realize the necessity of preparing for an occupation. Some boys may become concerned about grades for the first time and begin to realize that to be a success, they have to go to college. Others may cultivate a hobby, such as working on cars, which they have found enjoyable and which will prepare them for an occupation.

Adulthood

Provider role: The role in which men are expected to be breadwinners, providing financially for the wife and children.

One of the major roles for adult men is the provider role (Pleck, 1981; Bernard, 1981). That is, men are supposed to be breadwinners, providing for their wife and children. Historically that might have meant building a log cabin and shooting wild game for dinner. But in the capitalistic, commercial culture of the twentieth-century United States, the provider role has been transformed into the *good provider role* (Pleck, 1981; Bernard, 1981). That is, the man is expected to provide for his family by earning money, and the more, the better. Thus not only are men expected to hold jobs, but they are also expected to be successful at them (Tavris, 1977). Yet because in our society success is defined by comparison with others, not all men can be successes. Are they then also failures as men? Margaret Mead said, "Women are unsexed by success, men are unsexed by failure." The pressure may become a great burden and a source of stress. As a slogan of men's liberation has it, "We're more than just success objects."

Another major adult role for men is the *father role* (Pleck, 1981). Although this aspect of men's lives was traditionally overlooked in psychological research, psychologists have recently become much more interested in fatherhood: what effects fathers have on their children, and what the stresses or satisfactions of the father role are for men. For example, research indicates that fathers can be as competent in caring for infants and as responsive to them as mothers are (Parke, 1979). The evidence also indicates that not only women, but men as well, rate marriage and the family as more satisfying to them than work (Campbell et al., 1976).

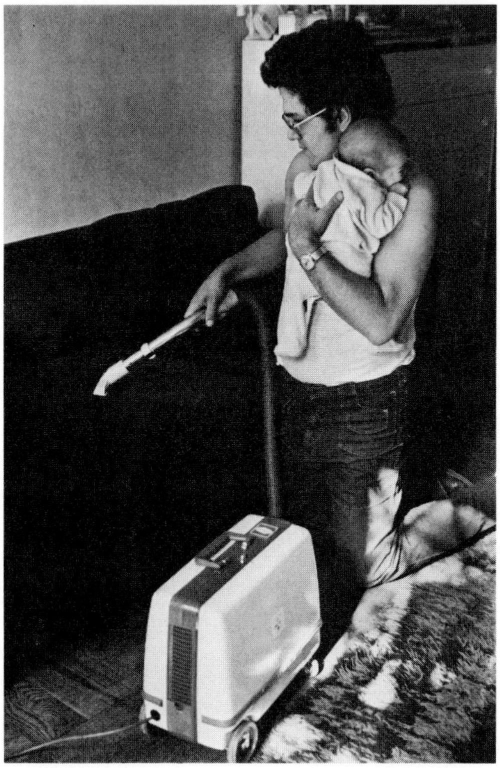

FIGURE 14.2

Men of the 1980s are much more interested in fulfilling the father role. Research indicates that men can be as competent in caring for infants and as responsive to them as mothers are.

Middle and Old Age

Middle age is a period of reassessment for most men. At around age 50, many realize that their lives are more than half over. It is no longer realistic to suppose that they will suddenly become successful in the next few years if they have not been successful in the past. Middle-aged men must assess whether they have accomplished the goals they set for themselves when they were 20. Success is critical in the male role, and middle-aged men must assess whether they have achieved it. As noted in Chapter 4, a kind of "male menopause" may result, in which the man may become depressed or discontented as he appraises his life and accomplishments.

Until recently, most men had to retire at age 65. (New legislation has raised the age of compulsory retirement to 70). For some, retirement may be a liberating experience; they can pursue hobbies for which they never had time before. Others, however, find the adjustment very difficult. They suddenly have vast amounts of unstructured time available, and they have no idea how to use it. Further, their ability to earn money was important to them, and they can no longer do this.

Though gender roles can be fairly rigid in adolescence and young adulthood, they may often relax and even be reversed in middle and old age. With the children grown, the woman is less restricted to the wife-mother role. And in some marriages, because the husband is older than the wife, he may retire while she is still working. Thus she becomes the breadwinner, and he spends all day at home.

This discussion has pointed out some of the forces that act upon females and males as they grow up in their respective roles. Feminists note the stresses associated with women's low status, their restriction from high achievements, and the demand that they be wives and mothers. Men's liberationists argue that while women's low status does involve stresses, there are also stresses involved in always having to be at the top.

Current thinking among psychologists tends to support both of these points of view. More traditional psychological thought, extending from the 1930s to the 1960s, tended to be accepting and even encouraging of gender roles. Conformity to gender roles and a strong sense of gender identity were thought to be essential to good adjustment (Pleck, 1981). In the 1970s and 1980s, however, psychologists have shifted their thinking and their research toward the belief that gender roles are actually sources of stress or strain for people (Pleck, 1981); the view now is that the best-adjusted people may be those who manage to surmount gender roles and become androgynous, a topic to be discussed later in this chapter. That is, the view has shifted away from thinking that masculinity is best for men and femininity is best for women, toward thinking that androgyny is best for everyone.

MALE-FEMALE PSYCHOLOGICAL DIFFERENCES

The discussion so far has centered on the gender roles and socialization forces present in our society. It is not too unreasonable to assume that these forces have some effect on people's behavior and personalities. What psychological differences between males and females result?

Personality

As has been noted, males and females differ in *aggressiveness* (Maccoby and Jacklin, 1974; this difference as well as others discussed here are documented in detail in that volume). Males are more aggressive than females. This is true for virtually all indicators of aggression (physical aggression such as fighting, verbal aggression, and fantasy aggression). It is also true at all ages; as soon as children are old enough to perform aggressive behaviors, boys are more aggressive, and adult males dominate the statistics on violent crimes. In some situations, it is possible for women to be as aggressive as men, but it is very rare for women to be more aggressive than men (Frodi et al., 1977). The gender difference in aggression tends to be largest among preschoolers but it gets smaller with age, so that gender differences in adults' aggression are small (Hyde, 1984).

Another difference is in *self-esteem* (Block, 1983, 1976). Females tend to have lower self-esteem and less confidence in their own abilities to succeed at future tasks. For example, if a group of college students take their first examination for a course and immediately afterward they are asked to estimate how many points they will get on the test, females give lower estimates than males do (Berg and Hyde, 1976; Maccoby and Jacklin, 1974), presumably indicating that they have less self-confidence in their own abilities. Of course, when we think of the stereotypes of women as being dumb and irrational and of men as being competent and logical, it is hardly surprising that women have less self-confidence in their own abilities.

Females' lesser aggressiveness and lower self-esteem may have far-reaching consequences; these differences might help to explain, for example, why there are relatively few women in high-prestige careers. Both aggressiveness and self-confidence are usually necessary for success in such occupations. These differences also may have important consequences for sexuality, as will be discussed below.

Abilities

While there are no gender differences in general intelligence (IQ), there are a number of gender differences in more specialized intellectual abilities. Females tend to

FIGURE 14.3

In the United States, there are few women in positions of power and prestige. (*a*) The M.I.T. faculty in 1900. (*b*) The United States Supreme Court in 1984.

(a)

(b)

do better than males in most tests of verbal abilities, from low-level ones, such as spelling tests, to complex ones, such as tests involving analogies and creative writing. Males, on the other hand, are superior to females in mathematical ability and spatial ability. Recent analyses, however, indicate that these differences are small (Hyde, 1981).

Communication Styles

A number of scholars have noted that men and women differ in their styles of communicating, both verbally and nonverbally (Mayo and Henley, 1981; Deaux, 1976; Key, 1975; Lakoff, 1973).

Women and men tend to use language differently. For example, women enunciate more precisely; they are more likely to say "working," while men are likely to say "workin'." Men are more likely than women to use swearwords and dirty words, although this difference may have narrowed in the last few years. Many of my female students have exceptionally colorful vocabularies.

In terms of total talking time, men consistently outdistance women. This is a good example of a stereotype—women as constant talkers—that turns out not to be true in reality. Men actually spend more time talking than women do. Men are also more likely to interrupt than women are (McMillan et al., 1977).

Self-disclosure: Telling personal information to another person

Social psychologists have also found gender differences in studies of self-disclosure In these studies, people are brought into a laboratory and are asked to disclose personal information either to friends or to strangers. Women are much more willing to disclose information than men are, at least in situations like these (Cozby, 1973; Jourard and Lasakow, 1958).

Norms about self-disclosure are changing, though. Traditional gender roles favored emotional expressiveness for females, but emotional repressiveness and avoiding of self-disclosure for males. There is a new, emerging ethic, though, of good communication and openness which demands equal self-disclosure from males and females (Rubin et al., 1980). Research with college students who are dating couples confirms the emergence of this new norm; the majority of both males and females reported that they had disclosed their thoughts and feelings fully to their partners (Rubin et al., 1980). However, women revealed more in some specific areas, particularly their greatest fears. And couples with egalitarian attitudes disclosed more than couples with traditional gender-role attitudes. Thus the traditional expectation that men should not express their feelings seems to be shifting to a new expectation that they be open and communicative.

In studies of nonverbal communication, or "body language," gender differences have also been found. Men are more likely to touch others, while women are more likely to be touched (Henley, 1973a, 1973b). Men and women also differ in their reactions to being touched. In one ingenious study, the effects of being touched briefly, in an accidental way, were studied (J. D. Fisher et al., 1975). The investigators arranged to have library clerks (both male and female) either touch or not touch the hands of students who were checking out books. Soon after the student left the checkout desk, he or she was approached by an experimenter with a questionnaire concerning the library and its personnel. Women who had been briefly touched by the clerk reported feeling more positive than women who had not, and they reacted more favorably toward both the clerk and the library. However, being touched seemed to have no effect on the men's feelings. This study suggests, then, that being touched may be a more positive experience for women than it is for men.

There is a related finding from studies of interpersonal space. These studies indicate that American men prefer greater distances between themselves and another person than American women do (Deaux, 1976). For example, at public exhibits women stand closer to other women than men do to other men. Women also sit closer together when they are in an experimental laboratory.

Not only are there gender differences in nonverbal behaviors, there are also gender differences in people's ability to understand the nonverbal behaviors of others. The technical phrase for this is "decoding nonverbal cues"—that is, the ability to read others' body language correctly. It might be measured, for example, by accuracy of interpreting facial expressions. Research shows that women are better than men at decoding such nonverbal cues (Hall, 1978). Certainly this is consistent with the gender-related expectation of greater interpersonal sensitivity for women.

What are the implications of these gender differences in communication styles for sexuality? For example, if men are unwilling to disclose personal information about themselves, might this not hamper their ability to communicate their sexual needs to their partners (Jourard, 1971)? If women react more favorably to being touched than men do, might this suggest that women enjoy this aspect of sex and that men might be relatively hampered in their enjoyment of being touched sexually? Further research in this area should be intriguing.

Gender Similarities

Most of the research and the textbooks on gender roles, as well as most courses in the subject, tend to be based on the assumption that psychological gender differences are pervasive, that is, that men and women have quite different kinds of personalities. This notion is also quite popular among lay people; for example, in cartoons and on television, as well as in real life, we often see a man shaking his head over his inability to understand women. Their minds work so differently, after all.

Just how different are the minds of men and women? Although differences have been found to exist in personality and communication styles, as was discussed above, for the vast majority of psychological characteristics, there are no gender differences. Therefore, gender similarities seem to be the rule, not gender differences (Hyde, 1985). Although men and women think and behave differently in some ways, for the most part they are very similar. As the British author Dorothy Sayers put it:

Gender similarities: The notion that males and females are more similar than different.

> The first thing that strikes the careless observer is that women are unlike men. They are "the opposite sex"—(Though why "opposite" I do not know; what is the "neighboring sex"?). But the fundamental thing is that women are more like men than anything else in the world. (1946, p. 116)

When I bring up this notion of gender similarities, some people invariably start clucking fondly, remembering the good old days when "women were women and men were men," or they mouth phrases like "Vive la différence." That is, some people think that the more different men are from women, the better a place the world is to live in. I don't agree. I think that the real basis for understanding, communication, and enjoyment between men and women is their similarities, not their differences, particularly in the area of sexuality. If a woman and a man have totally different motives, attitudes, thoughts, desires, and goals with regard to sex, it may be very difficult for them to establish the kind of communication and understanding that is so important to a good mutual sexual experience.

A conceptual distinction will be made here between gender-role stereotypes, psychological gender differences that have been determined empirically to exist ("real" differences), and the causes of gender differences, whether they be biological or environmental. Gender-role stereotypes are simply the way most people think that males and females should be psychologically. The nature of these stereotypes has been reviewed in previous sections. When data are collected on how males and females behave, the stereotypes turn out to be true for some behaviors ("real" differences) but not for others. For example, there is a stereotype that males are more aggressive than females. The data show that males are actually more aggressive than females. Therefore, this stereotype turns out to be a real difference. But there is also a stereotype that women are less intelligent than men, while data show that there are no gender differences in IQ. In this case, the stereotype turns out not to be true. Finally, if a gender difference is found for some behavior, it requires one more step of analysis—and a very difficult one—to determine whether the difference is biologically caused or environmentally caused, or both. For example, because there is a well-documented gender difference in aggression, we cannot automatically infer that it is biologically caused (e.g., by sex hormones); nor can we automatically decide that it is produced by environmental factors (e.g., socialization). Gender differences may be caused by biological factors, environmental factors, or both.

IMPACT OF GENDER ROLES ON SEXUALITY

Because gender roles and sexuality interact so closely, it seems likely that the content of gender roles has some effect on sexuality. Some of the more salient aspects of gender roles that may affect sexuality are discussed below. The reader may want to speculate about other aspects of gender roles that may affect sexuality.

Aggressive versus Passive

Certainly, one stereotype that exists in our culture is that males are aggressive (especially in the physical sense), while females are unaggressive or passive. Of course, an individual couple may not conform to these stereotypes, but if they do, what effects do these stereotypes have on them when they come together to have sex? The male may think that he has to play the aggressive role in bed just as he would on the football field. As a result, he may think that he should be strong and perhaps even rough (he may think that women want to be treated that way), that he should initiate the sexual activity, and that he should control the sequence of techniques that are used. Gentleness might seem incompatible with this masculine role. Gender role playing might even affect the positions that he thinks are appropriate in intercourse. For example, he might think that the man-on-top position is the best and that the woman-on-top position is unacceptable because a "real man" would not be on the bottom (the winner of a fight is always on top, isn't he?).

A woman who conforms strongly to the female role of passivity may feel that she should not initiate sex and that she should not take an active part in the lovemaking. Carried to an extreme, female passivity can lead to the "dead-fish" approach to experiencing sexuality. A belief in passivity in women is related to orgasm problems (Barbach, 1975).

Aroused versus Unaroused

Another stereotype is that men are easily provoked to high levels of arousal, while it is almost impossible to arouse women. (As one popular but incompetent columnist of pop psychology put it, "Men are 100 percent sexual; women are 0 percent sexual.") The data on whether this is a real difference or just a stereotype will be discussed in Chapter 15. Here the emphasis will be on what conformity to this stereotype might mean for sexuality.

For a man, the "aroused" role may lead him to believe that he should always be aroused by any attractive woman and that arousal should always come easily and quickly (Zilbergeld, 1978). Failures in either respect might be interpreted as inadequacy in the masculine role. It may also lead the man or his dates to expect that he will always want sex to be part of a date, even though he may just be interested in having a good time or establishing a friendship. Some of the men in my classes tell me, "I feel like I'm expected to at least *try* to get every woman I date to go to bed with me."

For a woman, conformity to the "unaroused" stereotype may also lead to the dead-fish approach. The woman may believe that it is not appropriate for her to be easily aroused, and so she does not become aroused, or she tries to hide arousal when it occurs. But there may also be a price for lack of conformity to this role. The woman who is easily aroused and who expresses it, perhaps by initiating sex, may have her behavior interpreted as an indication that (1) she is not feminine, (2) she is a threat to men and wants to take away their prerogatives, or (3) she is an oversexed slut.

Of course, gender roles are changing and have become less rigid in the last decade. But this change may carry with it problems of its own, since expectations may not be clear. For example, a woman may honestly express her sexual interest, believing that this is now acceptable, only to have her interest interpreted as being an indication that she is "easy." Stereotypes like the saint-slut dichotomy for women die hard. And it has been argued that the shift from the old stereotype of man as a sexual animal to the new one of man as a competent lover is but a superficial one (Gross, 1978). In the old role, the man was supposed to make conquests of as many women as possible. In the new role, the man sticks to one woman but makes as many orgasms in her as possible. In both cases, the performance demand is clear.

Emotional versus Unemotional

Another stereotype is that women are emotional, while men are not emotional or should not express emotion if they feel it. For example, one of the first rules of socialization enforced on boys is that they must not cry. Conformity to this stereotype might lead a man to believe that sex should be purely physical for him and that he should not express emotion (love and tenderness) or become emotionally committed (the "love 'em and leave 'em" philosophy). This stifling of emotional expression may lead him to have sexual experiences that are less fulfilling than they might be (Gross, 1978). On the other hand, a violation of the stereotype that men are not emotional—for example, self-disclosure or an expression of tenderness—might be interpreted by some women as an indication that the man is not masculine or that he is poorly adjusted (Chaikin and Derlega, 1976). Thus nonconformity may also carry a cost, although most women appreciate emotional expressiveness in a man (Tavris, 1977).

Androgyny:
A combination of both masculine and feminine characteristics in an individual.

A NEW TREND: ANDROGYNY

One of the most exciting areas of recent research on gender roles is that of psychological androgyny (Bem, 1974; Heilbrun, 1973). Androgyny[3] refers to a combination of both feminine and masculine traits in a single individual. Thus if a person is androgynous, he or she possesses both masculine and feminine characteristics.

The traditional research on gender roles and masculinity-femininity has been based on the assumption that all (or at least most) males are masculine and that all (or most) females are feminine; it was also assumed that females are not masculine and that males are not feminine. Further, it was assumed that the more masculine a person was, the less feminine that person would be, and vice versa. That is, if a woman learned how to repair cars, for example, that would make her more masculine and therefore less feminine. Similarly, if a man took up cooking, that made him more feminine and therefore decreased his masculinity.

But human beings are not that simple. Many men have a lot of masculine qualities but also some "feminine" interests and talents as well, and many women possess both feminine traits and masculine traits. As the psychologist Walter Mischel has expressed it:

> When we observe a woman who seems hostile and fiercely independent some of the time but passive, dependent, and feminine on other occasions, our reducing valve usually makes us choose between the two syndromes. We decide that one pattern is in the service of the other, or that both are in the service of a third motive. She must be a really castrating lady with a facade of passivity—or perhaps she is a warm, passive-dependent woman with a surface defense of aggressiveness. But perhaps nature is bigger than our concepts and it is possible for the lady to be a hostile, fiercely independent, passive, dependent, feminine, aggressive, warm, castrating person all-in-one. Of course which of these she is at any particular moment would not be random and capricious—it would depend on who she is with, when, how, and much, much more. But each of these aspects of her self may be a quite genuine and real aspect of her total being. (1969, p. 1015)

Once this complexity is acknowledged, we can go beyond the simple idea that people can be filed into one of two categories: masculine or feminine. We can then recognize that there are at least four kinds of individuals: those who are very masculine (and they will not necessarily all be males), those who are very feminine (and they will not necessarily all be females), those who are really neither very masculine nor very feminine, and those who are both masculine and feminine, the last group being the androgynous people.

Psychologist Sandra Bem has done some important research that provides information on androgyny and androgynous people. The first step in her work was the construction of the Bem Sex Role Inventory, or BSRI (Bem, 1974), a paper-and-pencil test that measures a person's degree of androgyny. The BSRI contains 20 "masculine" items (for example, "aggressive," "ambitious," "willing to take risks") and 20 "feminine" items (for example, "affectionate," "loves children," "yielding"), as well as 20 "neutral" items (for example, "happy"). Items were included in the masculine list on the basis of the criterion that in a preliminary study, subjects rated them as being significantly more desirable for males than for females in American society. A parallel criterion was used for the feminine items. To take the BSRI, sub-

[3]From the Greek roots *andro,* meaning "man" (as in "androgens"), and *gyn,* meaning "woman" (as in "gynecologist").

jects indicate, for each item on a seven-point scale, the extent to which the item characterizes them. Each person then gets both a masculinity score (average score on the masculine items) and a femininity score (average score on the feminine items). A person is considered androgynous if she or he has both a high masculinity score and a high femininity score. Bem finds that about one-third of the subjects in her college samples are androgynous.

Armed with the BSRI and its ability to detect androgynous people, Bem proceeded to see how androgynous people compare with strongly gender-typed people. She began with the assumption that gender roles constrict people and keep them from enjoying and doing well at certain kinds of activities, namely, activities supposedly reserved for the other gender. She believes that androgynous people are more liberated and do not allow gender roles to stifle their behavior. She tested these assumptions in several studies. For example, in one study subjects were under pressure to conform in their judgments on how funny some jokes were (Bem, 1975). Those who refused to conform would be showing the "masculine" trait of independence. As predicted, masculine subjects and androgynous subjects of both sexes showed significantly more independence than feminine subjects, who were more likely to conform. In another study, subjects listened to a student who poured out a list of troubles in adjusting to college life (Bem et al., 1976). The subjects were scored for their responsiveness to, and sympathy toward, the talker; this was a measure of their nurturance, nurturance being a "feminine" characteristic. As predicted, feminine subjects and androgynous subjects of both sexes were significantly more nurturant to the troubled student than the masculine subjects were.

These two studies, taken together, suggest that androgynous people have the flexibility to exhibit either masculine or feminine behaviors, depending on what the situation calls for; they can be independent when pressured to conform, and they can be nurturant to an unhappy person. On the other hand, the highly masculine person may do well in a situation that requires masculine behavior but may not do so well when feminine behavior is required; similarly, feminine people do well in situations that require feminine behavior but may not be able to function when masculine behavior is necessary. The results then serve to question the traditional assumption that very masculine men and very feminine women are well adjusted (Taylor and Hall, 1982). Instead, the results suggest that those who are androgynous, and thus transcend gender roles, are better able to function effectively in a wider range of situations.

What implications does androgyny have for sexual behavior? The ways in which gender roles might limit our abilities to respond sexually were discussed in a previous section. Androgyny may represent a new vision not only of personality but also of sexuality. Because androgynous people have both masculine and feminine behaviors in their bag of tricks, they should be more flexible and comfortable in their sexuality. For example, an androgynous person, whether male or female, should feel comfortable initiating sex but should also feel comfortable when the other person initiates sex. An androgynous person should be happy with a position in intercourse in which he or she is on top, as well as with a position in which she or he is on the bottom. An androgynous person would enjoy both the physical aspects of sex and the emotional aspects. Perhaps this androgyn, who integrates both masculinity and femininity, represents the vision of a truly liberated sexuality.

Is there any evidence that these speculations are true? Several recent studies have looked at the relationship between gender-typing (whether one is androgynous or traditionally gender-typed) and sexual attitudes and behaviors. Three studies show positive results for androgynous people. In one, the results indicated that androgynous women have orgasms more frequently than feminine women (Radlove, 1983).

In another study, androgynous women reported more sexual satisfaction than feminine women did (Kimlicka et al., 1983). And in the third study, androgynous subjects (both male and female) were less likely to stereotype the sexual behavior of others (Garcia, 1982). In yet another study, androgynous females were more comfortable with sex than feminine females, and androgynous males were more comfortable with sex than masculine males, just as Bem would predict (Walfish and Myerson, 1980). However, males were considerably more comfortable than females, so that masculine males were still considerably more comfortable with sex than were androgynous females. That is, it seemed that gender had a much stronger effect than did gender-typing. Similar results were found in two other studies (Allgeier, 1981; Allgeier and Fogel, 1978). In one, college student subjects viewed slides of couples having intercourse in either the traditional man-above position or the woman-above position (Allgeier and Fogel, 1978). They then rated their attitudes toward the individuals in the slides. Females were more negative about the woman-above position than were males. Gender typing (androgynous versus stereotyped) was unrelated to attitudes about the woman-above position.

Thus, in sum, the studies on androgyny and sexuality produce mixed results. Some show the flexibility and benefits to sexuality Bem would predict, yet others show no difference between androgynous subjects and traditionally gender-typed subjects. Probably we should not set our expectations for androgyny too high. It probably will not be the cure to all of the sexual woes of our society. But it might help. And it may be that androgyny and changing gender roles will make their impact last in the area of sexuality, where we are most vulnerable, or where the rewards of relinquishing traditional behaviors are not obvious (Allgeier, 1981).

There is evidence that people's attitudes about gender roles have changed in the last 10 or 20 years. One study administered the Attitude toward Women Scale to samples of college students in 1972, 1976, and 1980 (Helmreich et al., 1982). There was a large and significant shift toward more liberal, egalitarian attitudes from 1972 to 1976. However, from 1976 to 1980 there was no significant change in male attitudes, and females' attitudes actually changed slightly in the conservative direction. Thus it appears that there were substantial shifts toward approval of equality in gender roles, occurring in the early to mid-1970s, but this trend seems to have leveled off.

TRANSSEXUALISM

Transsexual: A person who believes he or she is trapped in a body of the wrong gender.

Gender dysphoria (dis-FOR-ee-uh): Unhappiness with one's gender; another term for transsexualism.

Male-to-female transsexual: A person who is born with a male body but who has a female identity and wishes to become a female biologically in order to match her identity.

Many texts include transsexualism in the chapter on sexual variations or deviations. However, I have included it in the chapter on gender because it is fundamentally a problem of gender, and more specifically, a problem of gender identity.

A transsexual is a person who believes that he or she is trapped in the body of the wrong gender. This condition is also known as gender dysphoria, meaning unhappiness or dissatisfaction with one's gender. Transsexuals are the candidates for the sex-change operations that have received so much publicity, beginning with the case of Christine Jorgenson. The term "transsexual" is used to refer to the person both before and after the operation. There are, of course, two kinds of transsexuals: those with male bodies who think they are females (called male-to-female transsexuals) and those with female bodies who think they are males (called *female-to-male transsexuals*). Male-to-female transsexuals have been more likely to seek help at clinics and have more often been given sex-reassignment surgery, in part because the surgery required in such cases is easier. Accordingly, most of the discussion that follows will focus on male-to-female transsexuals.[4]

Keeping in mind the distinction between sex and gender, it is important to note that transsexualism is a problem not of sexual behavior but of gender and gender identity. That is, the transsexual is preoccupied not with some specific kind of sexual behavior but rather with wanting to be a female when her body is male. Sex, of course, is involved insofar as being sexually attracted to a member of the opposite gender (which is expected in our society) is concerned. But I also know of one transsexual who has never engaged in any sexual activity beyond kissing since she had surgery to make her a female. She is delighted with the results of the surgery and loves being a woman, but she is not particularly interested in sex. One male-to-female transsexual expressed her motivation for having a sex-change operation as follows:

> I did it for the psychological thing. . . . I need the reassurance that I am a woman. I don't have a man to make love to me and I don't care. . . . I wanted to be a woman, whether the sex part was successful or not. I wanted to be of one sex, dress like one, act like one. . . . Well, mentally I always thought of myself as a woman. I don't even remember thinking of myself as a man. (Kando, 1973, p. 96)

References to transsexuals are found in much of recorded history, although of course they are not referred to by that modern, scientific term (Green, 1966). Philo, the Jewish philosopher of Alexandria, described them as follows: "Expending every possible care on their outward adornment, they are not ashamed even to employ every device to change artificially their nature as men into women. . . . Some of them . . . craving a complete transformation into women . . . have amputated their generative members." The American Indians had an institutionalized role for men who dressed as women and performed the functions assigned to women. Transsexualism is therefore by no means a phenomenon of modern, industrialized cultures.

Psychologically the transsexual is, to put it mildly, in an extreme conflict situation (Levine et al., 1976). The body says, "I'm a man," but the mind says, "I'm a woman." The person may understandably react with fright and confusion. Believing herself truly to be a female, she may try desperate means to change her body accordingly. Particularly in the days before the sex-change operation was performed, or among people who were unaware of it, self-castrations have been reported. The woman I mentioned above ate large quantities of women's face cream containing estrogens to try to bring about the desired changes in her body.

The Sex-Change Operation

Sex-change operation: The surgery done on transsexuals to change their anatomy to the other gender.

Gender reassignment is rather complex and proceeds in several stages (Roberto, 1983). In this country, the surgery was first performed at the Johns Hopkins Hospital in Baltimore. The Stanford University School of Medicine also pioneered. More recently, the procedure has been performed at many other hospitals.

The first step in the process is very careful counseling and psychiatric evaluation. It is important to establish that the person is a true transsexual, that is, someone

[4]Because this kind of transsexual thinks of himself as a female, he prefers to be called "she," and to simplify matters in this discussion, "she" will be used to refer to the transsexual. Otherwise, figuring out which pronoun to use would be extremely difficult.

whose gender identity does not match her body type. Some people mistakenly seek gender reassignment; for example, a man who is simply poorly adjusted, unhappy, and not very successful might think that things would go better for him if he were a woman. Sometimes schizophrenics display such confused gender identity that they might be mistaken for transsexuals. It is important to establish that the person is a true transsexual before going ahead with a procedure that is fairly drastic.

The next step is hormone therapy. The male-to-female transsexual is given estrogen and must remain on this for the rest of her life. The estrogen gradually produces some feminization. The breasts enlarge. The pattern of fat deposits becomes feminine; in particular, the hips become rounded. Balding, if it has begun, stops. Secretions by the prostate diminish, and eventually there is no ejaculate. Erections become less and less frequent, a phenomenon with which the transsexual is pleased, since they were an unpleasant reminder of the unwanted penis. The female-to-male transsexual is given androgens, which bring about a gradual masculinization. A beard may then develop, to varying degrees. The voice deepens. The pattern of fat deposits becomes more masculine. The clitoris enlarges, although not nearly to the size of a penis, and becomes more erectile. The pelvic bone structure, of course, cannot be reshaped, and breasts do not disappear except with surgery.

Next comes the "real life test," which is the requirement that the person live as a member of the new gender for a period of one or two years. This is done to ensure that the person will be able to adjust to the role of the new gender; once again, the idea is to be as certain as possible that the person will not regret having had the operation. Some transsexuals, even before consulting a physician, spontaneously enter this "transvestite" stage in their efforts to become women. Problems may arise, though. Cross-dressing is illegal in many cities, and they may be arrested.

The final step is the surgery itself (transsexuals refer to it simply as "the operation"). For the male-to-female transsexual, the penis and testes are removed, but without severing the sensory nerves of the penis. The external genitalia are then reconstructed to look as much as possible like a woman's (see Figure 14.5). Next, an artificial vagina—a pouch 15 to 20 centimeters (6 to 8 inches) deep—is constructed. It is lined with the skin of the penis so that it will have sensory nerve endings that can respond to sexual stimulation. For about six months afterward, the vagina must be dilated with a plastic device so that it does not reclose. Other cosmetic surgery may also be done, such as reducing the size of the Adam's apple.

The female-to-male change is more complex and generally less successful. A penis and scrotum are constructed from tissues in the genital area (see Figure 14.4). The penis, unfortunately, does not have erectile capacity; in some cases a rigid silicone tube is implanted in the penis so that it can be inserted into a vagina, making coitus possible. Some female-to-male transsexuals choose not to have genital surgery and just go through breast removal and possibly hysterectomy.

What Causes Transsexualism?

Scientists have not found a definite cause of transsexualism. One speculation is that it might be due to some prenatal exposure to hormones of the wrong gender, causing improper brain differentiation. There is no direct evidence supporting this idea, though, and so it must remain speculative at present.

Two studies have investigated hormone levels in transsexuals before gender reassignment, one in male-to-female transsexuals and the other in female-to-male transsexuals (J. R. Jones, 1972; Migeon et al., 1968). In both studies the hormone levels were found to be within the normal range for the individuals' "original" gender (not

FIGURE 14.4

Female-to-male transexual surgery. (*a*) A penile shaft is made from abdominal skin and fat and is skin grafted. The labia majora are incised (colored line) and closed over the clitoris to form a "scrotum." (*b*) Two months later the penile shaft is ready for detachment from the abdomen. A fan of abdominal skin has been partially released and resutured in preparation for final release and construction of the penile head. (*c*) The release is now complete and the penile head constructed from the smooth abdominal skin. Note the "urethral dimple" in the tip of the head: This is not functional as the patient must still sit to urinate. Silicone testicles have also been inserted into the "scrotum." Also a temporary silicone rod has been inserted down the hollow center of the penile shaft to allow this patient to "have an erection." This is removed most of the time and is used only for intercourse.

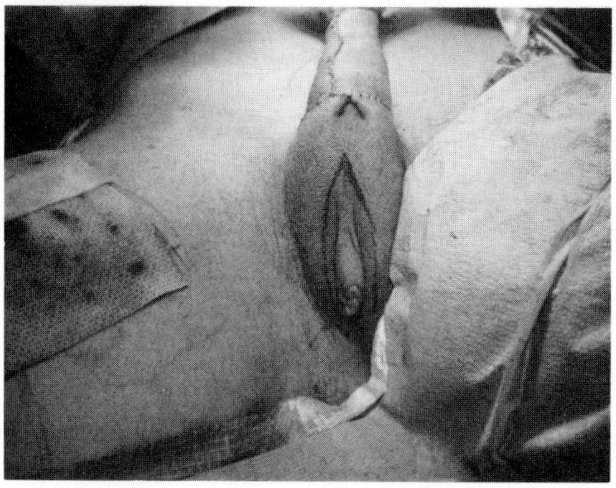

(a)

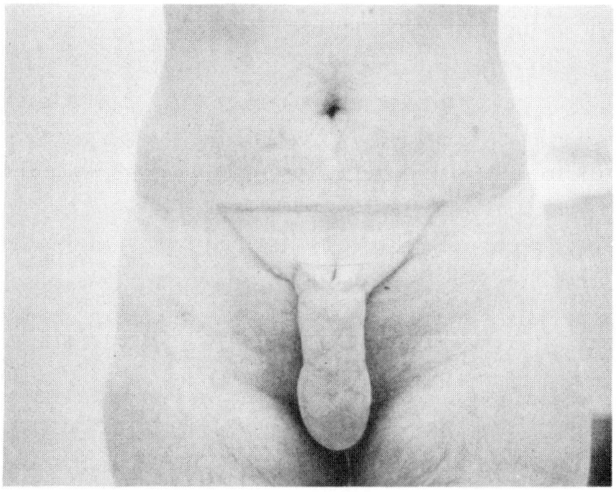

(b)

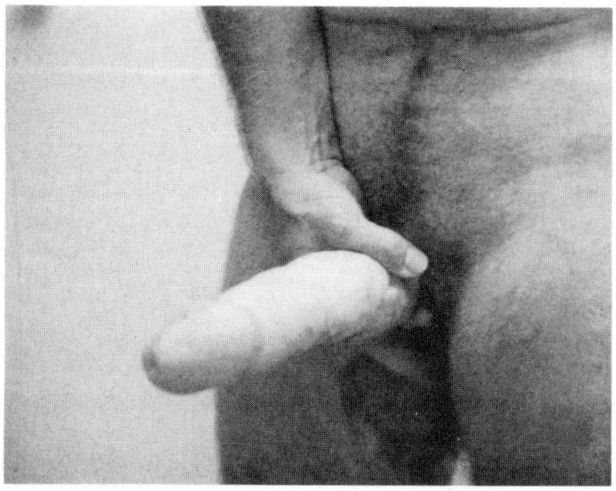

(c)

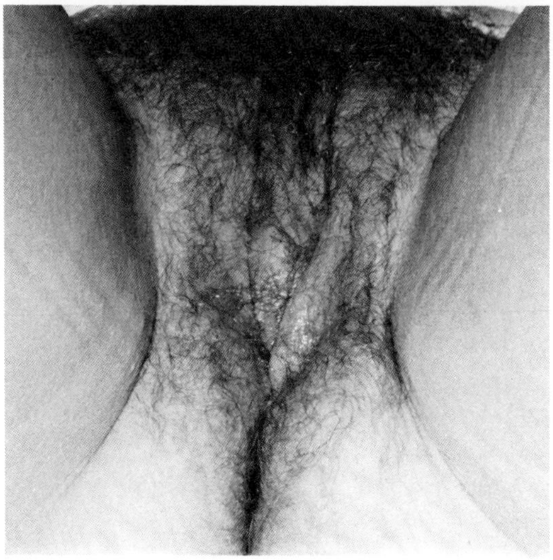

FIGURE 14.5

The genitals following transsexual surgery. Male-to-female transsexual.

the gender to which they wanted to be reassigned), suggesting that transsexualism does not result from a hormonal imbalance.

One idea for which there is some supporting evidence is that transsexualism results from early learning experiences. In one sample of 17 male-to-female transsexuals, all had had their gender treated inappropriately or ambiguously from infancy to puberty by their parent or parents (J. P. Driscoll, 1971; see also Green, 1975). Though they had the bodies of boys, they had been given girls' toys or had been dressed in girls' clothing. Feminine behavior, such as putting on the mother's high heels when guests were present, had been rewarded as "cute." When the interviewer asked whether they had been reared as boys or girls, one responded, "I was raised as a girl by my mother and aunts. My sex was discovered by a school nurse when I was six." It seems likely that such early learning experiences would be critical in giving the child a gender identity that is incongruent with her body. On the other hand, there are transsexuals who had no such learning experiences; thus learning theory does not seem adequate to explain every case.

By the time these transsexuals were of school age, they hated gym class and were labeled "freaks" by their peers. Not surprisingly, problems of adjustment arose. In adulthood, transsexuals often have trouble holding steady jobs, at least in part because they are so preoccupied with their gender problem.

In the early days of sex-change surgery, male-to-female transsexuals accounted for the great majority of cases, outnumbering female-to-male transsexuals by a ratio of 3:1 (Green, 1975). Several explanations for this lopsided ratio were offered: Perhaps male prenatal development is more complex and error-prone, or perhaps the problem is that preschool boys spend so much more time with their mothers than with their fathers. Currently, however, male-to-female and female-to-male transsexuals are seeking help at clinics in a ratio of about 1:1 (Roberto, 1983), thus removing the need for explanations of discrepancies in male and female rates.

Other Issues

The phenomenon of transsexualism raises a number of interesting psychological, legal, and ethical questions for our contemporary society.

One case that attracted attention is that of Dr. Renée Richards, formerly Richard Raskind, a physician who had her gender reassigned to that of a woman. When she was a man, she was a successful tennis player. In 1976 she attempted to enter a women's tennis tournament. The women players protested that she was not a woman, and she protested that she was. Officials subsequently decided to use the bucchal smear test for gender, which is also the one used in the Olympics. In this test a sample of cells is scraped from the inside of the mouth and is stained. If the sex chromosomes are XX, a Barr body should be present and will show up under the stain; if the chromosomes are XY, the Barr body should be absent. The test is therefore one of genetic gender. Dr. Richards protested that this was not the appropriate test to be used on her. Psychologically she is a female, she has female genitals, and she functions socially as a female, and she feels that these are the appropriate criteria. She does, though, have a male pelvic bone structure and other bone structures that are masculine, and these may have important consequences for athletic performance. The issue will require some time to settle. But the important question it raises is: What should the criteria be for determining a person's gender? Should it be chromosomal gender (XX or XY) as tested by the bucchal smear? Should it be the gender indicated by the external genitals? Should it be psychological gender identity?

Bucchal smear: A test of genetic sex, in which a small scraping of cells is taken from the inside of the mouth, stained, and examined under a microscope.

Barr body: A small, black dot appearing in the cells of genetic females; it represents an inactivated X chromosome.

Another question that might be raised concerns religious groups that do not permit women to become members of the clergy. Is a male-to-female transsexual, for example, qualified to be a priest before "the operation" but not after? Is the female-to-male transsexual qualified to be a priest by virtue of having had a sex-change operation?

Another problem arises in classifying the sexual behavior of the transsexual. For example, many male-to-female transsexuals perfer to engage in sex with men, even before gender reassignment. Is that sexual behavior homosexual (it is between two

FIGURE 14.6

Transsexual Renée Richards before the sex-change operation (left) as tennis player Richard Raskind and following transsexual surgery (right) as a female tennis player.

men), or is it heterosexual (because one of them thinks she is a woman)? Or is the behavior homosexual before surgery and heterosexual after surgery?

The transsexual also encounters a number of practical problems following gender reassignment. Official records, such as the social security card, must be changed to show not only the new name but also the new gender. Sometimes a new birth certificate is issued and the old one is sealed away. However, when the person reaches retirement age, it is not clear whether she should receive social security benefits beginning at age 62, the proper age for females, or age 65, the age for males. If the person was married before the sex change, often—though not always—the spouse must be divorced. Changing one's gender is, to say the least, a complicated process.

In the next decade, as more transsexuals are discovered and studied scientifically, they should be able to give us, through their own personal accounts, new insights into the nature of sex and gender. For example, most of us have wondered, at some time, how members of the opposite gender feel during sexual intercourse. The transsexual is in a unique position for giving us information on this question.

Criticisms of Sex-Change Surgery

A number of criticisms of sex-change surgery for transsexuals have been raised. One of these comes from a study by Johns Hopkins researcher Jon Meyer (1979). He did a follow-up study of the adjustment of 50 transsexuals, 29 of whom received surgery, 21 of whom did not. His conclusion, much publicized, was that there were no significant differences in the adjustment of the two groups. If that is the case, then transsexual surgery is unnecessary and should not be done.

Then criticisms of Meyer's study appeared (e.g., Fleming et al., 1980). Meyer's adjustment scale was somewhat peculiar and involved debatable values. Basically, Meyer calculated an adjustment score for each transsexual on the basis of positive or negative points assigned to various behaviors the individual might have engaged in. For example, being arrested earned −1 point. Having a high-level job earned + 3 points. Cohabiting with a "gender appropriate" person earned a +1, but cohabiting with a "gender inappropriate" person earned −1, and so on. How were these numerical values assigned? Arbitrarily, it appears. And it certainly is a strong value statement to say that cohabiting with a "gender inappropriate" person (presumably someone of one's own gender) is as bad as being arrested. Further, Meyer ignored any kind of affective data, that is, the person's own reported feelings of happiness or adjustment. In short, if Meyer's measurement of adjustment is questionable, then his conclusion that there are no differences in adjustment between operated and unoperated transsexuals is also questionable.

After the Meyer study and also criticisms of it, some clinics ceased doing transsexual surgery, but most continue to do it. Almost surely we will see more attempts in the future to treat transsexualism with psychotherapy rather than surgery, but these methods remain to be worked out (see, e.g., Barlow et al., 1978). Unfortunately, attempts to use psychotherapy, such as psychoanalysis, as an alternative to surgery have generally been unsuccessful (Roberto, 1983). That is, trying to change the gender identity to match the anatomy—rather than the reverse as in the sex-change operation—does not seem to work very well. In contrast, adjustment of transsexuals has been shown to be significantly better following surgery (Fleming et al., 1981; Blanchard et al., 1983).

In another vein, Janice Raymond has offered a feminist ethical critique in her book *The Transsexual Empire: The Making of the She-Male* (1979). She argues that transsexualism itself is the product of a gender-role-stereotyped society. If we did not have two strictly defined roles, it would not be necessary for people to attempt drastic steps such as surgery to move from one to the other. They would simply behave as they pleased. It is ironic, as she notes, that at a time when gender-role stereotypes and their restrictiveness are being questioned by society, the transsexual movement goes in the opposite direction, defining gender in anatomical terms and assuming that roles should be sharply divided. Finally, Raymond questions the ethics involved in the enormous medical empire (some call it a $10 million per year growth industry) that has grown up around transsexual surgery. She raises the issues of unnecessary surgery and mutilation of the body.

One interesting empirical study bears on Raymond's critique. The Bem Sex Role Inventory, which measures androgyny, was administered to 72 self-defined transsexuals, all presurgery (Fleming et al., 1980). The results indicated that the female-to-male transsexuals had a gender-role pattern nearly identical to that of male college students—35 percent were masculine and 35 percent were androgynous. Male-to-female transsexuals showed a higher percentage of feminine people (60 percent) than college women do, but 22 percent still fell into the androgynous category. These results question Raymond's (and others') assumption that the transsexual is an overly gender-typed person—there are many who are androgynous. The results reaffirm the notion that transsexualism is an issue of gender identity, not of stereotyped role behaviors.

Nonetheless, Raymond's points about values and ethics involved in transsexualism and surgery for it are worth considering.

SUMMARY

One of the most basic ways we categorize people is by gender. Along with this categorization go a set of expectations for people of each gender (gender roles) and a set of practices in the culture that teach people to conform to their role (socialization).

Various forces act on females as they grow up. Gender-role stereotypes surely act upon them, such as the beliefs that women are talkative, emotional, and dependent. Parents begin treating daughters and sons differently in infancy and continue to do so in childhood and adolescence. One concept learned by adolescents that helps bring about some of the differences is that of femininity-achievement incompatibility. In adulthood, most women define their identity in terms of their roles as wife and mother, although increasing numbers work outside the home. Aging may be stressful to women in our culture.

Boys are influenced by stereotypes that say they should be aggressive, unemotional, self-confident, and so on. In childhood, boys are more aggressive than girls, and boys also have more problems in school. Athletic ability is important in adolescence. In adulthood, the good-provider role and the father role are important to men.

While, for the most part, males and females are quite similar, there are some differences in their behavior. Males are more aggressive and have higher self-esteem than females. Men and women also have somewhat different styles of communication.

It seems likely that gender roles influence the way people behave sexually, leading men, for example, to take an aggressive role and women a passive role.

Research on androgyny (the combination of both masculine and feminine characteristics in one individual) suggests that it may provide a good alternative to being simply masculine or simply feminine. It also may permit a liberation in sexuality, although the evidence on this point is mixed.

Transsexuals—those people who seek sex-reassignment surgery—represent an interesting variation in which gender identity does not match anatomy.

REVIEW QUESTIONS

1. Gender differences in aggression and in toy and game preferences appear as early as the preschool years. True or false?
2. Parents tend to treat boy and girl infants differently; parents are less attentive to girl babies and girl babies are given less freedom to explore. True or false?
3. Research on gender-role stereotypes indicates that "masculine" traits generally fall into a competency category, including independence, objectivity, competitiveness, and logicalness. True or false?
4. There are more hyperactive girls than hyperactive boys. True or false?
5. Traditionally, psychologists believed that gender roles were stressful to people, but in the 1970s and 1980s, psychologists shifted to viewing gender-role conformity as good for psychological adjustment. True or false?
6. Men are experiencing a shift from the traditional norm that they not express their feelings, to a new expectation that they be open and communicative in their relationships. True or false?
7. One stereotype for men is that they should always be easily and quickly aroused by an attractive woman. True or false?
8. _____ is the term for a combination of both feminine and masculine traits in an individual.
9. _____ is the term for a person who feels trapped in a body of the wrong gender.
10. Research indicates that the adjustment of transsexuals is significantly better following surgery than it was before surgery. True or false?

QUESTIONS FOR THOUGHT, DISCUSSION, AND DEBATE

1. Do you think that transsexual surgery is the appropriate treatment for transsexuals? Why or why not?
2. Recalling from your childhood, do you think you were socialized in a stereotyped masculine or feminine way? What impact do you think those socialization experiences have on your current sexual attitudes and behaviors?

SUGGESTIONS FOR FURTHER READING

Allgeier, Elizabeth R. and McCormick, Naomi B. (1983). *Changing boundaries: Gender roles and sexual behavior.* Palo Alto: Mayfield. This is an interesting collection of essays by experts, on the impact of gender roles and sexuality.

Bem, Sandra. (1975). Androgyny vs. the tight little lives of fluffy women and chesty men. *Psychology Today,* **9**(4), 58. An interesting description of Bem's research on androgyny.

Chafetz, Janet S. (1978). *Masculine/feminine or human? An overview of the sociology of sex roles.* (2nd ed.) Itasca, Ill.: F. E. Peacock. An excellent introduction to the sociological approach to gender roles.

Doyle, James A. (1983). *The male experience.* Dubuque, Iowa: Wm. C. Brown. This is a good introduction to all of the new scholarship on men and the male role.

Gross, Alan E. (1978). The male role and heterosexual behavior. *Journal of Social Issues,* **34**(1), 87–107.

Hyde, Janet S. (1985). *Half the human experience: The psychology of women.* (3rd ed.) Lexington, Mass.: Heath. I am not in a very good position to give an objective appraisal of this book, but, for what it's worth, I think it is an interesting, comprehensive summary of what is known about the psychology of women.

Morris, Jan. (1974). *Conundrum.* New York: New American Library.

Left, Wilhelm Lehmbruck: *Standing Youth*, 1913. Collection, The Museum of Modern Art, New York. Right, Wilhelm Lehmbruck, *Kneeling Woman*, 1911. Collection, The Museum of Modern Art, New York.

CHAPTER · 15

FEMALE SEXUALITY AND MALE SEXUALITY

Hoggity higgamous,
   men are polygamous,
Higgity hoggamous,
   women monogamous.

–Dorothy Parker

CHAPTER HIGHLIGHTS

I. DATA ON MALE-FEMALE DIFFERENCES IN SEXUALITY
   - Orgasm Consistency
   - Desire for Sex and Motives for Having Intercourse
   - Masturbation
   - Arousal to Erotica

II. WHY THE DIFFERENCES?
   - Biological Factors
   - Cultural Factors
   - Other Factors

III. BEYOND THE YOUNG ADULTS

IV. THE FUTURE
   - Gender Similarities
   - The "New Impotence"?
   - Greater Sex Drive in Women?

There is a widespread belief in our culture that male sexuality and female sexuality are quite different from each other. The Dorothy Parker jingle above expresses one of the ways in which they are thought to differ. In fact, some authors of textbooks on sexuality apparently believe that male sexuality and female sexuality are so different that they discuss them in entirely separate chapters.

Are these stereotypes simply outmoded cultural beliefs that do not exist in reality? Just how different are male sexuality and female sexuality? This chapter will try to answer these questions by examining the available scientific evidence.

DATA ON MALE-FEMALE DIFFERENCES IN SEXUALITY

In the sections that follow, the discussion will focus on areas of sexuality in which there is some evidence of male-female differences. As will be pointed out, there are some differences, but they are in a rather small number of areas—masturbation especially and, to a lesser extent, orgasm consistency in intercourse. There is a danger in focusing on these differences to the point of forgetting about gender similarities. Gender similarities will be discussed later in the chapter. You should keep in mind that males and females are in many ways quite similar in their sexuality—for example, in the physiology of their sexual response (Chapter 8)—while considering the evidence on male-female differences that follows.

Orgasm Consistency

There is evidence that males and females differ in the consistency with which they orgasm during heterosexual intercourse. Women, on the average, seem to be less consistent at having orgasms—at least during coitus—than men are. Investigators have repeatedly found that about 30 percent of married women never have orgasms or do so only occasionally during intercourse with their husbands (for example, Kinsey et al., 1953; Terman, 1951). Kinsey estimated that the average married female in his sample had orgasms about 75 percent of the time during intercourse with her husband (Kinsey et al., 1953, p. 375). Kinsey believed that males orgasmed 100 percent of the time, or so close to it that he did not bother to tabulate comparable statistics for them. He found, further, that about 36 percent of the women in his sample had never had an orgasm before marrying. These data generally reflect the phenomenon that it is harder for females to orgasm. In fact, one book on female sexuality contains a chapter entitled "The Struggle for Orgasm" (Kronhausen and Kronhausen, 1964), and it expresses how some women feel—as if they have to struggle to have an orgasm. One woman said:

> I don't think I've ever really experienced an orgasm. In any event, not the way I've read about them. My husband's clitoral stimulation usually leads to a climax for me but never during vaginal stimulation. I keep hoping and working at it. Sometimes I tend to think maybe I'm not supposed to experience a vaginal climax. Sometimes it bothers my husband more than it does me. He really feels badly that I don't experience the same type of pleasure he does. Sometimes I think we work at it too hard and sometimes we think we're getting closer to it, but I never experience anything physically ecstatic. (Hite, 1976, pp. 131–132)

The irony of this, of course, is that women are struggling to have their orgasms as quickly as possible, while men are struggling to delay theirs as long as possible.

More recent surveys seem to indicate a trend toward women having orgasms with greater consistency during marital sex. In the Hunt survey (1974), only about 10 to 15 percent of the women reported having orgasms seldom or never.[1] This increased consistency of orgasm might be related to a number of factors, including the increased variety of techniques—such as cunnilingus—that are used in marital sex now. The trend generally seems to be in the direction of diminishing what formerly

---

[1]Interestingly, the Hunt survey also found some evidence of orgasm inconsistency in men. In that sample, 8 percent of the men 45 and over, 7 percent of the men between 25 and 44, and 15 percent of those under 25 failed to have orgasms a quarter of the time or more during coitus.

was a large gender difference in orgasm consistency, but the difference remains to some extent.

Desire for Sex and Motives for Having Intercourse

In a 1920 survey, two-thirds of the wives reported that they desired intercourse less frequently than their husbands did (cited by R. R. Bell, 1966, p. 137). Though Kinsey provided no direct data on the point, he noted that early in marriage many husbands desired intercourse more frequently than their wives did, although the pattern was often reversed in middle age (Kinsey et al., 1953, p. 353). Traditionally, then, there appeared to be a gender difference in desire for intercourse, with men wanting it more frequently than women did. The "I have a headache" syndrome appeared to be fairly common among women in those studies.

In the recent Hunt survey, though, less than 5 percent of the wives said they wished marital intercourse was less frequent (Hunt, 1974). Thus it seems that the "I have a headache" syndrome is mostly a thing of the past. In fact, in the recent *Redbook* survey, one-third of the wives said that they wished they had intercourse *more* frequently than they did.

There is a stereotype that men and women differ in their motives for having sex. Men—at least according to the stereotype—are more interested in the physical aspects of sex and have a "love 'em and leave 'em" attitude. Women, on the other hand, are thought to be most interested in love and romance and to be concerned with the interpersonal more than the physical aspects of the relationship. Recognizing that there were no studies directly testing this stereotype, Jan Carroll, Kari Volk, and I surveyed 249 undergraduates about their motives for having sex (Carroll et al., 1985). The levels of sexual experience among these never-married men and women were relatively similar: 94 percent of the males and 80 percent of the females had engaged in sexual intercourse. However, their motives and attitudes were considerably different. When asked, "For you, is an emotional involvement a prerequisite for participating in sexual intercourse?" 45 percent of the females responded "Always," compared with only 8 percent of the males. Consistent with stereotypes, males and females gave considerably different responses to the question "What are your motives for having sexual intercourse?" Females emphasized love and emotional commitment, as in the following examples:

> Emotional feelings that were shared, wonderful way to express LOVE!!
> My motives for sexual intercourse would all be due to the love and commitment I feel for my partner.

Contrast those responses with the following typical responses from males:

> Need it.
> To gratify myself.
> When I'm tired of masturbation. (Carroll et al., 1985, p. 137)

Clearly males—at least in the college years—emphasize physical needs and pleasure as their motives for intercourse, whereas females emphasize love, relationships, and emotional commitment. No wonder there is some conflict in relationships between women and men!

Masturbation

One striking gender difference that emerged in the Kinsey studies was in masturbation. In that sample, 92 percent of the males had masturbated to orgasm at least once in their lives, as compared with 58 percent of the females. Not only did fewer women masturbate, but also, in general, those who did masturbate had begun at a later age than the males. Virtually all males said they had masturbated before age 20 (most began between ages 13 and 15), but substantial numbers of women reported masturbating for the first time at age 25, 30, or 35.

Unlike some other gender differences in behavior—which were present in the older Kinsey study but which seem to have evaporated by the time of the more recent Hunt study—gender differences in masturbation still seem to be a very real phenomenon. Hunt (1974) found that 94 percent of the males and 63 percent of the females in his sample had masturbated to orgasm at least once. These percentages are very close to those found by Kinsey a generation before. Hunt found that both boys and girls in his study appeared to have begun masturbating earlier than those in Kinsey's study, but girls still began later than boys.

One question we must ask, though, is whether this is a real gender difference or just an inaccuracy induced by using self-reports. In our culture, particularly in previous decades, more restrictions have been placed on female sexuality than on male sexuality. It might be that these restrictions have discouraged females from ever masturbating. On the other hand, they might simply lead females not to report masturbating. That is, perhaps women do masturbate but are simply more reticent about reporting it than males are. Someone once said that 99 out of 100 people masturbate, and the hundredth is a liar. Are one-third of all women liars, or are they nonmasturbators?

There are, of course, no data to answer that question directly. However, a comparison of the Kinsey data and the Hunt data can provide a clue. In the time intervening between these two studies, presumably restrictions against female sexuality lessened to some extent. A likely consequence of this change is that women began to feel freer to admit that they engaged in various forms of sexual behavior; for exam-

FIGURE 15.1

Female masturbation: Surveys consistently show that fewer females than males masturbate. Females who do not masturbate are missing an important experience of learning about their own sexuality.

ple, many more women report that they engage in premarital sex and in oral-genital sex now than at the time of the Kinsey study. Yet the percentage of women who say they masturbate has remained relatively constant (58 percent in the Kinsey study and 63 percent in the Hunt report.) This suggests that the women in Hunt's study would have felt free to say that they masturbated if they really did; after all, they were willing to say that they engaged in premarital sex and oral-genital sex. Thus we can conclude that those who said they did not masturbate were being honest. In the absence of direct evidence, though, this reasoning is purely speculative.

The data suggest, then, that there is a substantial gender difference in the incidence of masturbaion (Clement et al., 1984); virtually all males masturbate to orgasm, while about one-third of all women never do.

Arousal to Erotica

Traditionally in our society most erotic material—sexually arousing pictures, movies, or stories—has been produced for a male audience. The corresponding assumption presumably has been that women are not interested in such things. Does the scientific evidence bear out this notion?

Kinsey found that the females in his sample were considerably less likely than the males to report responses to erotic materials. For example, about half of the males reported having been aroused at some time by erotic stories; although almost all the women had heard such stories, only 14 percent had been aroused by them. These data are often cited as evidence that women are not so easily aroused as men.[2]

Studies done in the last decade, however, have provided little evidence that males and females differ in their arousal to erotic materials. For example, in one study the responses of 128 male and 128 female university students to erotic slides and movies were studied (Schmidt and Sigusch, 1970). The slides and movies showed petting and coitus. In several tests for gender differences, either there were no differences, or the differences were small, with about 40 percent of the females reporting a stronger arousal response than the average male. All the females and almost all the males reported genital responses to the slides and movies. And women—not men—showed an increase in petting and coitus in the 24 hours after seeing the erotic stimuli. Therefore, there seems to be little basis for saying that women are not erotically responsive to such materials.

An interesting study by psychologist Julia Heiman (1975, 1977; for a similar study with similar results, see Steinman et al., 1981) provides a good deal of insight into the responses of males and females to erotic materials. Her subjects were sexually experienced university students, and she studied their responses as they listened to tape recordings of erotic stories. Not only did Heiman obtain subjects' self-ratings of their arousal, as other investigators have done, but she also got objective measures of their physiological levels of arousal. To do this, she used two instruments: a penile strain gauge and a photoplethysmograph (Figure 15.2). The penile strain gauge (my students have dubbed this the "peter meter") is used to get a physiological measure of arousal in the male; it is a flexible loop that fits around the base of the penis. The photoplethysmograph measures physiological arousal in the female;

Penile strain gauge: A device used to measure physiological sexual arousal in the male; it is a flexible loop that fits around the base of the penis.

Photoplethysmograph (foh-toh-pleth-ISS-moh-graf): An acrylic cylinder that is placed inside the vagina in order to measure physiological sexual arousal in the female.

[2]Actually, though, the Kinsey data were not that simple. Kinsey noted wide variability in women's responses and speculated that perhaps one-third of all women are as erotically responsive as the average male. Further, there were no gender differences in certain behaviors; for example, about the same number of females as males reported having been aroused by erotic literary materials.

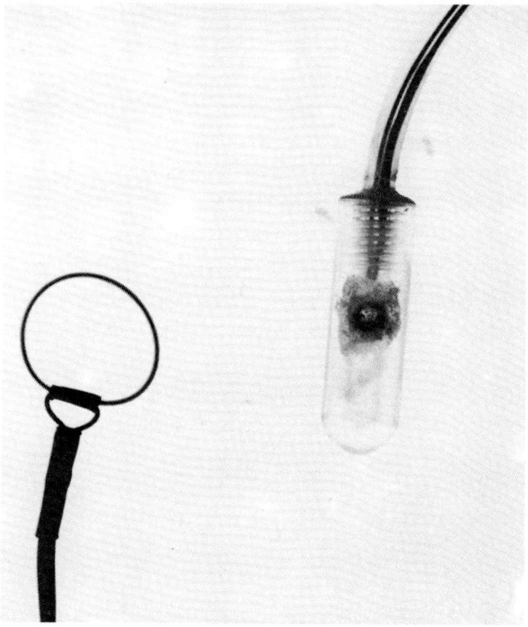

FIGURE 15.2

Two devices used to measure physiological sexual response in males and females. The penile strain gauge (left) consists of a flexible band that fits around the base of the penis. The photoplethysmograph (right) is an acrylic cylinder, containing a photocell and light source, which is placed just inside the vagina.

it is an acrylic cylinder, about the size of a tampon, that is placed just inside the entrance to the vagina. Both instruments measure vasocongestion in the genitals, which is the major physiological response during sexual arousal (see Chapter 8). These physiological measures are a great advance, since they are not subject to the errors or distortions that may occur when subjects simply rate their own arousal.

Subjects heard one of four kinds of tapes. There is a stereotype that women are more turned on by romance, while men are more aroused by "raw sex." The tapes varied according to which of these kinds of content they contained. The first group of tapes was *erotic;* they included excerpts from popular novels giving explicit descriptions of heterosexual sex. The second group of tapes was *romantic;* a couple were heard expressing affection and tenderness for each other, but they did not actually engage in sex. The third group of tapes was *erotic-romantic;* they included erotic elements of explicit sex and also romantic elements. Finally, the fourth group of tapes served as a *control;* a couple were heard engaging in conversation but nothing else. The plots of the tapes also varied according to whether the male or the female initiated the activity and whether the description centered on the female's physical and psychological responses or on the male's. Thus the tapes were male-initiated or female-initiated and female-centered or male-centered. Three important results emerged from the study:

1. Explicit heterosexual sex (the erotic and erotic-romantic tapes) was most arousing, both for women and for men. The great majority of both males and females responded most, both physiologically and in self-ratings, to the erotic and erotic-romantic tapes. Women, in fact, rated the erotic tapes as more arousing than men did. Neither men nor women responded—either physiologically or in self-reports—to the romantic tapes or to the control tapes (except for a couple of men who were aroused by a discussion of the relative merits of an anthropology major versus premed—ah, well).
2. Both males and females found the female-initiated, female-centered tape to be most arousing. Perhaps the female-initiated plot was most arousing because of its somewhat forbidden or taboo nature.

3. Women were sometimes not aware of their own physiological arousal. Generally there was a high correlation between self-ratings of arousal and objective physiological measures of arousal, both for men and for women. When men were physically aroused, they never made an error in reporting this in their self-ratings—it is pretty hard to miss an erection. But when the women were physically aroused, about half of them failed to report it in their self-ratings. (One might assume that women who were sophisticated enough to volunteer for an experiment of this nature and who were willing to insert a photoplethysmograph into their vagina would not suddenly become bashful about reporting their arousal; that is, it seems likely that these women honestly did not know when they were physically aroused.)

In sum, then, Heiman's study indicates that males and females are quite similar in their responses to erotic materials but that women can sometimes be unaware of their own physical arousal. This study, however, dealt only with the preliminary stages of arousal; perhaps women vary in the point at which they recognize arousal.

WHY THE DIFFERENCES?

The previous section reviewed the evidence on differences between male and female sexuality. Two differences—the lower percentage of females, compared with males, who masturbate and the higher percentage of females who do not have orgasms during intercourse—seem to be fairly well documented and in need of explanation.[3] Other stereotyped gender differences, such as differences in response to erotic materials, are not well documented by current data and thus are not in need of explanation. What factors, though, lead some women not to masturbate and not to orgasm during intercourse? Many different possible explanations have been suggested by a wide variety of scholars; these will be considered below.

Biological Factors

There has been some speculation that gender differences in sexuality are created by two biological factors: anatomy and hormones (see, for example, Bardwick, 1971).

Anatomy

The male sexual anatomy is external and visible and has a very obvious response: erection. When the male is nude, he can easily see his sexual organs, either by looking down or by looking in a mirror. The female sexual organs, in contrast, are hidden. The nude female looks down and sees nothing except pubic hair (which really is not very informative); she looks in a full-length mirror and sees the same thing. Only by doing the mirror exercise described in Chapter 3 can she get a good view of her own genitals. Further, the female's genitals do not have an obvious arousal response like the male's erection. As a result, she may be less aware of her own arousal, a notion that is supported by Heiman's research.

The anatomical explanation, then, is that because the woman's genitals are not in plain view and because their arousal response is less obvious than that of the

[3]Unfortunately, both these differences could be interpreted as indicating that women have less of a sexual capacity than men; see, for example, Focus 15.1.

man's genitals, she is less likely to masturbate and less likely to develop her full sexual potential. If this explanation is correct, or at least part of the answer, could anything be done to help women develop their sexuality? Perhaps parents could show their daughters the mirror exercise at an early age and encourage them to become more aware of their own sexual organs. It is also possible that parents should discuss the idea of masturbation with their daughters.

Hormones

The hormonal explanation rests on the finding that testosterone is related to sexual behavior. This evidence was reviewed in Chapter 4. Basically, the evidence comes from studies in which male animals are castrated (have their source of testosterone removed), with the result that their sexual behavior disappears, presumably reflecting a decrease in sex drive. If replacement injections of testosterone are given, the sexual behavior returns.

Females generally have lower levels of testosterone in their tissues than males do. Human females, for example, have about one-sixth the level of testosterone in their blood that human males do (Salhanick and Margulis, 1968).

The hormonal explanation, then, is that if testosterone is important in activating sexual behavior and if females have only one-sixth as much of it as males have, this might result in a lower level of sexual behavior such as masturbation in women, or a lower "sex drive."

There are several problems with this logic. First, it may be that cells in the hypothalamus or the genitals of women are more sensitive to testosterone than the comparable cells in men; thus a little testosterone may go a long way in women's bodies (Sherfey, 1966). Second, while testosterone activation of sexual behavior has been fairly well established in animals, such effects are not so well documented in humans, and they may not be nearly so strong. Thus it would be a mistake to make an inference to human males and females from studies done on animals.

Cultural Factors

Our culture has traditionally placed tighter restrictions on women's sexuality than it has on men's, and vestiges of these restrictions linger today. It seems likely that these restrictions have acted as a damper on female sexuality, and thus they may help to explain why some women do not masturbate or do not have orgasms.

One of the clearest examples of the differences in restrictions on male and female sexuality is the double standard. The double standard says, essentially, that the same sexual behavior is evaluated differently, depending on whether a male or a female engages in it. An example is premarital sex. Traditionally in our culture, premarital sex has been more acceptable for males than for females. Indeed, premarital sexual activity might be a status symbol for a male but a sign of cheapness for a female.

Double standard: The evaluation of male behavior and female behavior according to different standards; used specifically to refer to holding more conservative, restrictive attitudes toward female sexuality.

These different standards have been reflected in behavior. For example, the Kinsey data, collected in the 1940s, indicated that over twice as many males (71 percent) as females (33 percent) had premarital sex. Apparently, society's message got through to young women of that era. Most of them managed to keep themselves chaste before marriage, while their male contemporaries tended to get the experience that was expected of them.

Generally there seems to be less of a double standard today than there was in former times. For example, as the data in Chapter 11 indicate, people now approve

F · O · C · U · S
15.1

DIFFERENT EQUALS LESS: FEMALE SEXUALITY IN SEX MANUALS

Sociologists Michael Gordon and Penelope Shankweiler did an interesting study of the way female sexuality is discussed in marriage and sex manuals. These manuals are important both because they reflect the thoughts of the society in which they are written and because they sell widely and may influence many people's thinking.

The content of a group of old sex manuals, published in the 1800s, reflects the understanding of sex at that time; it was seen as a procreative necessity. Female sexual desire was thought to be virtually nonexistent:

> As a general rule, a modest woman seldom desires any sexual gratification for herself. She submits to her husband, but only to please him; and, but for the desire of maternity, would far rather be relieved from his attentions. The married woman has no wish to be treated on the footings of a mistress. (Hayes, 1869, p. 227)

By the early years of the twentieth century, a change in thinking had occurred. Sex was now seen, in the context of marriage, not only as right and proper but also as an important part of married life.

of premarital sex for females about as much as they do for males. In Hunt's sample, 82 percent of the men felt that premarital sex was acceptable for males when the couple are in love, and 77 percent felt that it was acceptable for females under the same circumstances (Hunt, 1974). Interestingly, the females in the sample seemed to believe in a double standard more than the males did.

This change in attitudes is reflected in behavior. A much higher percentage of women report having engaged in premarital sex now than in Kinsey's time. In the Hunt sample, among respondents aged 18 to 24, 95 percent of the males and 81 percent of the females had had premarital sex. Thus there is much less of a difference between males and females now than there was a generation ago; the vast majority of both males and females are now engaging in premarital sex. Premarital sex still remains somewhat more common among males, though.

The decline of the double standard may help to explain why some of the gender differences found in older studies of sex behavior have disappeared in more recent studies. When cultural forces do not make such a distinction between male and female, males and females become more similar in their sexual behavior.

Female sexuality was now acknowledged. But women, supposedly, did not experience sexual desires until they were married, and then only when these were brought to the surface by the husband:

> No doubt women differ greatly, but in every woman who truly loves there lies dormant the capacity to become vibrantly alive in response to her lover, and to meet him as a willing and active participant in the sacrament of marriage. (Gray, 1922, p. 145)

Indeed, sex came to be seen as such an important part of marriage that by the 1930s, a "cult of mutual orgasm" had developed.

In the 1950s, the books still gave advice based on the notion that the wife entered into marriage a virgin, while the husband was furtively experienced. But by the 1960s the manuals began to acknowledge and be less critical of the fact that women did engage in premarital sex.

Extramarital sex was still overwhelmingly rejected in these books, and the major concern was with improving marital sex so as to avert this eventuality. The "gourmet" sex books, such as *Sex for Advanced Lovers,* are in this vein of rejuvenating marital sex. Hedonism within the context of marriage seems to be the current norm.

In these recent sex manuals, female sexuality is generally treated as "equal but different." Men are presented as sexually simple creatures whose desire is as easily satisfied as it is aroused. Women are seen as requiring love and slow, gentle stimulation. The Masters and Johnson evidence that women have multiple orgasms is not discussed, in terms of either technique or the possible implication that women may have greater sexual potential than men.

The assumption still remains that the man must exercise the leadership and initiative in the relationship. Even the supposedly liberated *Sensuous Woman* gives the following advice to female readers:

> In lovemaking your body is your instrument. You shouldn't settle for less than the best. An Arthur Rubenstein or Van Cliburn is not going to select a clunky, unresponsive, out-of-tune piano on which to perform his artistry. ("J," 1969, p. 28)

Thus, though the gourmet approach to sex encourages a more active role for the woman, it still has not altered the fundamental assumption that the man must take the initiative.

Source: M. Gordon and P. J. Shankweiler. (1971). Different equals less: Female sexuality in recent marriage manuals. *Journal of Marriage and the Family,* **33**, pp. 459–466.

Gender roles are another cultural force that may contribute to differences in male and female sexuality, as was discussed in Chapter 14. Gender roles dictate proper behavior for females and males in sexual interactions—that is, they specify the script. For example, there is a stereotype of the male as the aggressor and the female as the passive object of his advances; surely this does not encourage the woman to take active steps to bring about her own orgasms. As a result of such stereotypes, the male has borne the whole weight of responsibility, both for his response and for the woman's response, and women have not been encouraged to take responsibility for producing their own pleasure.

Marital and family roles may play a part. When children are born, they can act as a damper on the parents' sexual relationship. The couple lose their privacy when they gain children. They may worry about their children bursting through an unlocked door and witnessing the "primal scene." Or they may be concerned that their children will hear the sounds of lovemaking. Generally, though, the woman is assigned the primary responsibility for child rearing, and so she may be more aware of the presence of the children in the house and more concerned about possible

F · O · C · U · S 15.2

FEMALE SEXUALITY: THE HITE REPORT

The Hite Report, published in 1976, received a great deal of publicity as providing a new view of female sexuality. The book is based on a survey of women conducted by Shere Hite, who holds an M.A. in history.

Hite's questionnaire consisted of open-ended (as opposed to multiple-choice) questions about female sexuality; respondents could make their answers as detailed as they wished. For example, one question read, "Please give a graphic description or a drawing of how your body could best be stimulated to orgasm." Hite mailed the questionnaires to women's groups, including chapters of the National Organization for Women and abortion-rights groups, and to university women's centers. Notices were also placed in *The Village Voice* and in *Mademoiselle, Bride's,* and *Ms.* magazines, as well as in church newsletters

FIGURE 15.3

Shere Hite, author of *The Hite Report.*

harmful effects on them of witnessing their parents engaging in sex. Once again, her worry and anxiety do not contribute to her having a satisfying sexual experience.

A related point is that a couple typically have sex in their own home or apartment; at least for the traditional homemaker, this is her place of work. Her homemaking responsibilities may then intrude into her sexual expression. For example, one hears of men complaining that their wives leap up in the middle of lovemaking to go and turn off the oven because they think the roast is overcooking. This understandably hurts a man's feelings, and it cannot be doing a thing to help the woman have an orgasm. The woman whose ear is cocked to hear whether a baby is crying or whose nose is sniffing to smell whether dinner is burning is not the woman who has an orgasm.

and women's newsletters, telling readers that they could write in to request copies of the questionnaire. *Oui* magazine ran a copy of the questionnaire, and an early paperback by Hite included a copy and requested that readers send replies. Beginning in 1972, Hite distributed over 100,000 copies of the questionnaire. Completed replies were received from 3019 women (a 3 percent response rate).

Hite's study has some of the same problems present in other survey-type sex research, such as the Kinsey reports and the Hunt survey; for example, only people who were willing to have their sexual behavior surveyed were included as subjects, and the data were based on people's self-reports of their sexual behavior (which may not be accurate) rather than on actual observations of behavior. The study had an additional bias: because the questionnaires were distributed so heavily through feminist groups, the sample was probably composed of a high percentage of feminists. It was certainly not a random sample of women in the United States, and it was most probably not a representative sample of them, either. There are few Kinsey-type percentages in the book; this was a wise decision on Hite's part, since because of the biased sample, the percentages would have been limited to the sample of 3019 respondents and could not have been generalized any further.

One interesting finding emerged in the report. Hite asked, "Do you regularly achieve [sic!] orgasm during intercourse without separate massaging of the clitoris?" Only 26 percent of the respondents said "yes." Unfortunately, because of the peculiarities of the sampling techniques used, one could not infer that only 26 percent of all American women would have answered "yes" to this question. The low percentage is nonetheless interesting.

The Hite study is prescientific. Its main value lies in the countless direct quotations that constitute the major part of the text of the book. Some are sad, some are happy, and some are poignant. Examples have been scattered in various chapters of the present text, and so one will suffice here:

> The Sexual Revolution tells me I am abnormal if I don't desire to make it with every Tom, Dick, or Jane that I see. I am only free to say yes. (Hite, 1976, p. 312)

In reading *The Hite Report,* some women may recognize themselves, and men may learn more about female sexuality.

Source: Shere Hite. (1976). *The Hite Report.* New York: Macmillan.

Other Factors

A number of other factors, not easily classified as biological or cultural, may also contribute to differences between male and female sexuality.[4]

Women get pregnant and men do not. Particularly in the days before highly effective contraceptives were available, pregnancy might be a highly undesirable consequence of sexuality for a woman. Thinking that an episode of lovemaking might result in a nine-month pregnancy and another mouth to feed could put a damper on anyone's sexuality. Even today, pregnancy fears can be a force (Rubenstein, 1983). For example, research in the 1970s indicated that 75 percent of sexually

[4]Other possible causes of orgasm problems in women are discussed in Chapter 20.

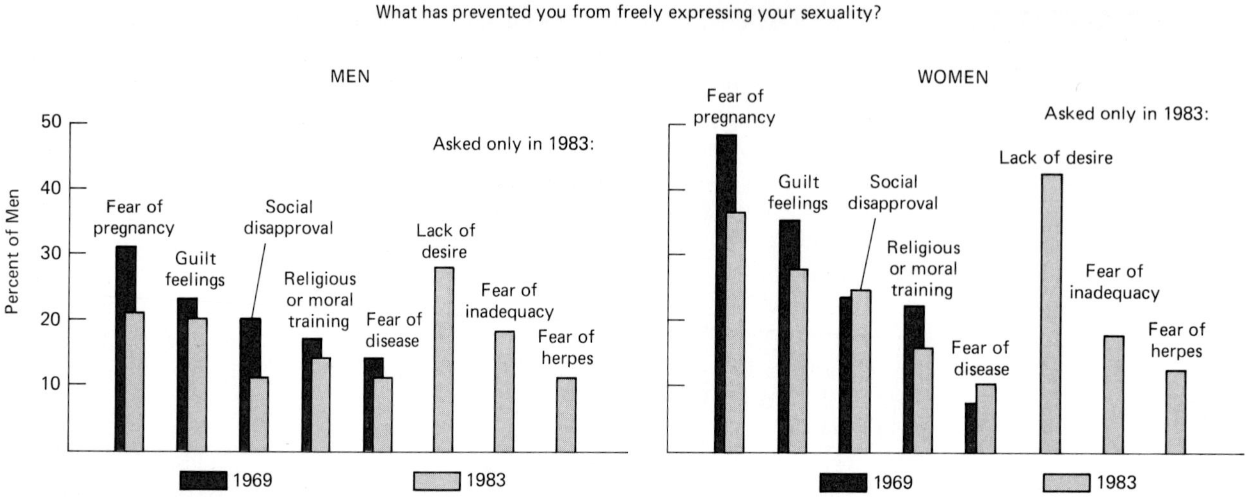

FIGURE 15.4

In 1969 and again in 1983 *Psychology Today* surveyed its readers on the topic of love. These are the responses of men and women to the question, "What has prevented you from freely expressing your sexuality?" Notice that women are more likely to report being affected by fear of pregnancy, guilt feelings, and social disapproval.

active single girls used contraceptives not at all or only occasionally (Teen-Age Sex, 1972). A woman who is worried about whether she will become pregnant—and, if she is not married, about whether others will find out that she has been engaging in sexual activity—is not in a state conducive to the enjoyment of sex, much less the experience of orgasm (although this scarcely explains why women do not masturbate).

Ineffective techniques of stimulating the woman may also be a factor. Kinsey found, for example, that women could masturbate to orgasm about as quickly as men could. This suggests that it is no harder for women to orgasm than it is for men, since they do it with about equal ease when they masturbate (and presumably they give themselves about ideal stimulation when they masturbate). The commonest techniques of intercourse, with the penis moving in and out of the vagina, may provide good stimulation for the male but not for the female, since she is not getting sufficient clitoral stimulation. As Kinsey concluded:

> Some 45 percent of all those females in the sample who had ever masturbated reported that they usually reached orgasm in three minutes or less, and another 25 percent in something between four and five minutes. . . . Many of those who took longer to reach orgasm did so deliberately in order to prolong the pleasure of the activity and not because they were incapable of responding more quickly.
>
> These data on the female's speed in reaching orgasm provide important information on her basic sexual capacities. There is a widespread opinion that the female is slower than the male in her sexual responses, but the masturbatory data do not support that opinion. The average male may take something between two and three minutes to reach orgasm unless he deliberately prolongs his activity. . . . It is true that the average female responds more slowly than the average male in coitus, but this seems to be due to the ineffectiveness of the usual coital techniques. (Kinsey et al., 1953, pp. 163–164.)

Perhaps the problem, then, is that women are expected to orgasm as a result of intercourse, when that is not a very effective technique for producing orgasms in women.

There may also be a relationship between the data on women not masturbating and the data on women not orgasming. Childhood and adolescent experiences with masturbation are important early sources of learning about sexuality. Through these experiences we learn how our bodies respond to sexual stimulation and what the most effective techniques for stimulating our own bodies are. This learning is important to our experience of adult, two-person sex. Perhaps the women who do not masturbate, and who are thus deprived of this early learning experience, are the same ones who do not have orgasms in sexual intercourse. This is exactly what Kinsey's data suggested—that women who masturbate to orgasm before marriage are more likely to orgasm in intercourse with their husbands.[5] For example, 31 percent of the women who had never masturbated to orgasm before marriage had not had an orgasm by the end of their first year of marriage, while only 13 to 16 percent of the women who had masturbated had not had orgasms in their first year of marriage (Kinsey et al., 1953, p. 407). There seems to be a possibility, then, that women's lack of experience with masturbation in adolescence is related to their problems with having orgasms during intercourse. One woman spoke of how she discovered masturbation late and how this may be related to her orgasm capacity in heterosexual sex:

> I thought I was frigid, even after three years of marriage, until I read this book and learned how to turn myself on. After I gave myself my first orgasm, I cried for half an hour, I was so relieved. Afterwards, I did it a lot, for many months, and I talked to my doctor and to my husband, and finally I began to make it in intercourse. (Hunt, 1974, pp. 96–97)

Not only may women's relative inexperience with masturbation lead to a lack of sexual learning, but it also may create a kind of "erotic dependency" on men. Typically, boys' earliest sexual experiences are with masturbation, which they learn how to do from other boys. More important, they learn that they can produce their own sexual pleasure. Girls typically have their earliest sexual experiences in heterosexual petting. They therefore learn about sex from boys. Their early learning experiences are with boys, and they learn that their sexual pleasure is produced by the male. As sex researcher John Gagnon commented:

> Young women may know of masturbation, but not know *how* to masturbate—how to produce pleasure, or even what the pleasures of orgasm might be. . . . Some young women report that they learned how to masturbate after they had orgasm from intercourse and petting, and decided they could do it for themselves. (1977, p. 152)

And Betty Dodson, in her book *Liberating Masturbation,* says:

> Masturbation is the way we discover our eroticism, the way we learn to respond sexually, the way we learn to love ourselves and build self-esteem. Sex is like any other skill—it has to be learned and practiced. When a woman masturbates, she learns to like her own genitals, to enjoy sex and orgasm, and furthermore, to become proficient and independent about it. (1974, cited in Gagnon, 1977, p. 161)

Once again, these ideas might lead to a recommendation that girls be given information about masturbation. It is also possible that as women begin having as much premarital sexual experience as men, their orgasmic response will become more consistent.

Numerous factors that may contribute to shaping male and female sexuality have been discussed. My own feeling is that a combination of several of these factors produces the differences that do exist. I think that the early differences in experi-

---

[5]Note that this is in direct contradiction to the old-fashioned advice given in manuals that suggested that "getting hooked" on masturbation might impair later marital sexuality; if anything, just the reverse is true.

F · O · C · U · S 15.3

MALE SEXUALITY: TWO REPORTS

Following close on the heels of *The Hite Report* on female sexuality came two reports on male sexuality: *Beyond the Male Myth* and *Male Sexuality*.

Psychiatrist Anthony Pietropinto and writer Jacqueline Simenauer, apparently feeling that the Hite report was antimale and wanting to provide a more accurate picture of male sexuality, conducted a survey of men for *Beyond the Male Myth*.

The authors commissioned an independent research organization to conduct the study. A questionnaire was developed consisting of 40 multiple-choice items and 4 open-ended questions. The sampling proceeded as follows: Field agents were sent to numerous communities; there they approached men in shopping centers, in office-building complexes, at tennis clubs, on college campuses, and at airports and bus depots and asked them to complete the questionnaire. Responses were obtained from 4066 men; the agents "estimated" that half the men approached agreed to participate. While this method of sampling may seem better than Hite's, a probability sample of American men was not initially identified, and the nonresponse rate was still high. Therefore, the percentages given in this study may be no more true of American men than Hite's percentages are true of American women.

Some interesting findings emerged from the study:

In response to the question "How do you feel about being in love?" 38 percent of the men said that love was the most important thing in their lives.*

*The responses may have been influenced by the alternatives listed in the multiple-choice items. For example, on this question respondents were forced to choose from among answers describing various degrees of enthusiasm about love. Their responses might have been different had they been asked to list what was most important to them, given choices of love, power, money, success, sex, etc. Many of the alternatives on the multiple-choice items in this survey seem arbitrary.

ences with masturbation are very important. Although these differences may result from differences in anatomy, they could be eliminated by giving girls information on masturbation. Women may enter into adult sexual relationships with a lack of experience in the bodily sensations of arousal and orgasm, and they may also be unaware of the best techniques for stimulating their own bodies. Put this lack of experience together with various cultural forces, such as the double standard and ineffective techniques of stimulation, and it is not too surprising that some women do have problems having orgasms.

The majority of the men (60 percent) said they were irritated most by a woman who seemed cold or uninterested while having sex. Few of them (less than 5 percent) said they were irritated by a woman who made the first advance, by a woman who made demands, or by a woman who seemed "too easy."

About 47 percent of the men reported cheating on a wife or steady girlfriend at least once.

About 32 percent of the men said they would prefer to marry a virgin. The percentage varied with the age of the man, but even among those aged 18 to 29, it was 25 percent.

The two most frequent responses to the question "What could your partner do to make you more excited?" were "be more active" (34 percent) and "use more oral sex" (24 percent).

Bernie Zilbergeld wrote *Male Sexuality* on the basis of his experience as a sex therapist and psychotherapist. He argues that the media have taught us a Fantasy Model of Sex, which is ultimately detrimental to men. He captures this idea in his chapter title "It's Two Feet Long, Hard as Steel, and Can Go All Night," describing the Fantasy Model of the erect penis. The Fantasy Model of Sex creates unrealistic expectations and performance pressures on men. Zilbergeld discusses a number of cultural myths based on the Fantasy Model. Here are some of them:

Myth 1. Men should not have, or at least not express, certain feelings. They are only allowed aggressiveness, anger, joviality, a sense of being in control. They are not allowed tenderness, sensuality, vulnerability. This cripples them for emotional relationships, and women need to understand this.

Myth 4. A man always wants and is always ready to have sex. This is simply not always true. Men need to acknowledge that sometimes they are just too tired, or whatever, to be interested in sex, and they need to learn how to refuse a partner. Women have had a lot of practice at this; men need to learn how.

Myth 7. Sex requires an erection. This is based on the assumption that real sex equals intercourse. As Zilbergeld puts it:

> The erection is considered by almost all men as the star performer in the drama of sex, and we all know what happens to a show when the star performer doesn't make an appearance. The whole show is cancelled or, to be a bit more accurate, the planned performance gives way to an impromptu tragedy. . . . (p. 53)

Men need to learn that the penis is not the only sexual part of their bodies, and that many very enjoyable forms of sexual behavior require no erection at all. That relieves a lot of performance pressure.

My choice for the best of these books is Zilbergeld's *Male Sexuality.* It is not based on a quick, slipshod survey. Rather it is based on the author's experiences as a sex therapist. That, of course, may bias his views insofar as he sees people having problems and seeking therapy. But his observations are nonetheless insightful.

Sources: Anthony Pietropinto and Jacqueline Simenauer. (1977). *Beyond the male myth.* New York: Times Books. Bernie Zilbergeld. (1978). *Male sexuality.* New York: Bantam Books.

BEYOND THE YOUNG ADULTS

One of the problems with our understanding of gender differences in sexuality is that so much of the research has concentrated on college students or other groups of young adults (as is true of much behavioral research). For example, Schmidt and Sigusch used college students as subjects in their studies of male-female differences in arousal response to erotic materials, as did Heiman in her research. Using this population may provide a very narrow view of male-female differences; they are considered during only a very small part of the lifespan.

Female sexuality and male sexuality change in their nature and focus across the lifespan. For example, it is a common belief in our culture that men reach their sexual "peak" at around age 19, whereas women do not reach theirs until they are 35 or 40. There is some scientific evidence supporting this view. Kinsey found, for example, that women generally had orgasms more consistently at 40 than they did at 25.

Psychiatrist Helen Singer Kaplan, a specialist in therapy for sexual dysfunctions, has advanced an interesting view of differences between male sexuality and female sexuality across the lifespan (Kaplan and Sager, 1971). According to her analysis, the teenage male's sexuality is very intense and almost exclusively genitally focused. As the male approaches age 30, he is still highly interested in sex, but not so urgently. He is also satisfied with fewer orgasms, as opposed to the adolescent male, who may have four to eight orgasms per day through masturbation. With age the man's refractory period becomes longer. By the age of 50, he is typically satisfied with two orgasms a week, and the focus of his sexuality is not so completely genital; sex becomes a more sensuously diffuse experience, and there is a greater emotional component.

In women, the process is often quite different. Their sexual awakening may occur much later; they may, for example, not begin masturbating until age 30 or 35. While they are in their teens and twenties, their orgasmic response is slow and inconsistent. However, by the time they reach their mid-thirties, their sexual response has become quicker and more intense, and they orgasm more consistently than they did during their teens and twenties. They initiate sex more frequently than they did in the past. Also, the greatest incidence of extramarital sex for women occurs among those in their late thirties. Vaginal lubrication takes place almost instantaneously in women in this age group.

Men, then, seem to begin with an intense, genitally focused sexuality and only later develop an appreciation for the sensuous and emotional aspects of sex. Women have an early awareness of the sensuous and emotional aspects of sex and develop the capacity for intense genital response later. To express this in another way, we might use the terminology suggested by Ira Reiss: person-centered sex and body-centered sex Adolescent male sexuality is body-centered, and the person-centered aspect is not added until later. Adolescent female sexuality is person-centered, and body-centered sex comes later.

Person-centered sex: Sexual expression in which the emphasis is on the relationship and emotions between the two people.

Body-centered sex: Sexual expression in which the emphasis is on the body and physical pleasure.

It is important to remember, though, that these patterns may be culturally, rather than biologically, produced. In some other cultures—for example, Mangaia in the South Pacific (see Chapter 1)—females have orgasms 100 percent of the time during coitus, even when they are adolescents.

THE FUTURE

The data indicate that major changes in sexual behavior have occurred in the last several decades and that these changes have affected female and male sexuality. Will there be further changes in the future, and if so, what will they be?

Gender Similarities

A comparison of the Kinsey data and the Hunt data suggests that there has been a trend toward gender similarities in sexual behavior recently. A survey of West German university students conducted in 1966 and again in 1981 confirms the trend toward gender similarities (Clement et al., 1984). That is, male sexual behavior and female sexual behavior are becoming more similar than they were in former times. For example, premarital sex used to be much more common among males than among females, but now it is quite common among both.

It seems reasonable to expect that this trend toward gender similarities will continue. One of the best pieces of data to use for making projections into the future concerns the youngest age group (aged 18 to 24) in the Hunt (1974) survey. In that group, 95 percent of the males and 81 percent of the females had had premarital sex. This suggests that in the future nearly everyone, both males and females, will have premarital sex. Under those circumstances, there can scarcely be a double standard.

A similar trend toward gender similarities in the 18- to 24-year-old age group is also indicated by the data on extramarital sex. While that behavior traditionally was much more common among males, the data from the youngest age group suggest that women are catching up; in that group, 32 percent of the males and 24 percent of the females had engaged in extramarital sex.

The trend toward gender similarities, though, is not limited to females' becoming more like males. Male sexuality is also changing and is showing some tendency to move in the direction of female patterns. For example, as noted earlier, some males now experience problems having orgasm in intercourse (Hunt, 1974). Men are now much less likely to have sex with prostitutes than they were a generation ago (Hunt, 1974). Males are generally less promiscuous than they were, and their premarital sexual relations tend to center on one partner (Schmidt, 1977).

Although the trend is toward gender similarities in *behavior,* the evidence suggests that substantial gender differences remain in *attitudes,* and it may be that these differences will not disappear. In data collected in the 1980s, females are still considerably more disapproving of casual sex than males are (Carroll et al., 1985). And patterns of sexual behavior are still most related to dominance in men, but to love and affection in women (Keller et al., 1982).

The "New Impotence"?

Some magazines have been carrying articles on the "new impotence." The idea is that with the rise of the women's liberation movement, a sexually liberated, sexually demanding woman has emerged and that some men feel so threatened by this situation that they have become impotent. To give some data supporting this view, some psychotherapists and sex therapists feel that they are seeing a sharp rise in the number of men seeking help for problems of impotence (Ginsberg et al., 1972).

Does the sexual liberation of women create impotence in men? There really are not any good scientific data on either side of this argument, and so I will simply offer my own opinion. I think that the apparent rise in cases of impotence is largely illusory. There have probably always been numerous cases of impotence; they appear to be more frequent now because of all the publicity given to sex therapy. Men probably now feel that it is more socially acceptable to admit they are having a problem with impotence and to seek therapy for it. Thus I doubt that more men are now impotent; there are simply more of them who are willing to ask for help with the problem. Masters and Johnson (1970) report that they treated many cases of impotence during the 1960s and felt that sexual dysfunctions were quite common, and this was before the women's movement was really rolling. I agree with Masters and Johnson, who feel that men stand to gain much from the women's movement (1974).

Greater Sex Drive in Women?

Masters and Johnson, among others, have speculated that women acutally have an innately stronger sex drive than men have, in direct opposition to the sterotype that women's sex drive is weaker (Masters and Johnson, 1966; see also Sherfey, 1966). As evidence, they cite the insatiable sex drive of female primates in estrus. A female chimpanzee, when in estrus, "presents" herself to one male after the next, perhaps copulating with a dozen in an hour. She appears to be nearly insatiable. Could it be that human females, who are capable of having sex at any phase in their cycle, are continuously insatiable? Another piece of evidence that is cited is the capacity of women to have multiple orgasms. Unlike men, who enter into a refractory period following orgasm, women may have one orgasm after another, which might suggest a greater, not a smaller, sexual capacity than men's. The argument then goes that in prehistoric, primitive human societies, the powerful sex drive of women created havoc—not to mention making the men feel insecure—and therefore societies instituted restrictions on female sexuality to bring it more in line with male sexuality; that explains the restrictions on female sexuality that persist to the present day. Since there are really no scientific data on this point, the whole idea is purely speculative, though intriguing. Perhaps, as restrictions on female sexuality lessen, future generations will regard women as having the greater sex drive.

SUMMARY

The evidence indicates that there is a gender difference in masturbation. While virtually all men masturbate, a sizable number—perhaps one-third—of all women never do. There is also some tendency for women to be less consistent than men in having orgasms during intercourse, although this gender difference has decreased in recent years. Gender differences in other aspects of sexuality—such as desire for sex, motives for having intercourse, and arousal to erotic materials—are not so well documented, or else the differences that existed a generation ago have evaporated in recent years. For the most part, then, males and females are now quite similar in their sexuality.

Julia Heiman's study of arousal to erotic stories suggests that women and men are about equally aroused by similar erotic stories but that women may sometimes not be aware of their own early stages of physical arousal.

Numerous factors may contribute to creating male-female differences in orgasm consistency and masturbation. Biological factors include anatomy (the male's genitals are more observable, and his arousal is more obvious) and hormones (males have higher testosterone levels than females). Cultural factors include the double standard and gender roles. Other factors include pregnancy fears in women, women's distraction by household and child-rearing responsibilities, and the use of ineffective techniques in stimulating the female. Because many women do not masturbate in childhood or adolescence, they miss this important sexual learning experience, which may contribute to later inconsistency in orgasm.

Patterns of gender differences in sexuality change over the lifespan. Males' sexuality is genitally focused in adolescence and early adulthood; it acquires the sensuous and emotional components later. Females' sexuality in adolescence and early adulthood is focused more on the emotional aspects of sex; the capacity for intense genital response develops later, around the ages of 35 to 40.

It seems reasonable to expect present trends toward gender similarities in sexual behavior to continue into the future.

REVIEW QUESTIONS

1. The data indicate that there are differences between males and females in orgasm consistency and in the incidence of maturbation. True or false?
2. Among college students, women emphasize love as their motive for engaging in premarital intercourse, whereas men emphasize the satisfaction of physical needs. True or false?
3. According to Kinsey _____ percent of males and _____ percent of females masturbate to orgasm at least once in their lives.
4. The photoplethysmograph is a device that measures physiological sexual arousal in the male. True or false?
5. Heiman's research on male and female response to erotic materials indicates that both males and females are most aroused by erotic, physical descriptions of sex, but females are sometimes unaware of their own arousal. True or false?
6. Today, a majority of teenage girls use effective methods of contraception, allowing them to be sexually uninhibited. True or false?
7. According to the Hite report, the majority of U.S. women need clitoral stimulation in order to have an orgasm during sexual intercourse. True or false?
8. The Hite report used excellent sampling techniques and interviewing techniques. True or false?
9. According to the Kinsey data, women who had not masturbated to orgasm before marriage were considerably more likely not to have had an orgasm in their first year of marriage than were women who had masturbated. True or false?
10. Zilbergeld uses the phrase "It's two feet long, hard as steel, and can go all night" to describe the ideal penis according to the Fantasy Model of Sex. True or false?

QUESTIONS FOR THOUGHT, DISCUSSION, AND DEBATE

1. Get together a group of men and women. Then separate into subgroups, one composed entirely of men, the other of women. Each group writes a list of questions they have always wanted to ask a member of the other gender. Then have the groups come together and ask and answer the questions for each other.
2. Do you think there is still a double standard for male and female sexuality today? Why?

SUGGESTIONS FOR FURTHER READING

Heiman, Julia R. (1975). The physiology of erotica: Women's sexual arousal. *Psychology Today,* **8**(11), 90–94. A report on Heiman's interesting research on women's and men's arousal response to erotic materials, discussed in this chapter.

Zilbergeld, Bernie. (1978). *Male sexuality.* New York: Bantam Books paperback. An authoritative, insightful, highly readable discussion of male sexuality. Includes many self-help exercises.

CHAPTER • 16

SEXUAL ORIENTATION: GAY, STRAIGHT, OR BI?

The homosexual today is kind of like the invisible man. But what most people don't realize is that homosexuals are all around. They're not just somewhere "out there." They are in one's own family—they could be one's doctor, one's minister, one's friend, husband, wife, whatever. People don't like to think about this, but it is so. There are a lot of homosexuals, a group of people, in fact, numbering into the millions, and they're not going to stay invisible forever.

—Dr. Martin Hoffman*

* *Source:* Quoted in Bettie Wysor. (1974). *The lesbian myth.* New York: Random House, p. 125.

CHAPTER HIGHLIGHTS

I. STEREOTYPES AND DISCRIMINATION
   Attitudes toward Homosexuality
   Stereotypes about Gays
   Gays as a Minority Group

II. THE GAY LIFESTYLE
   Coming Out
   Gay Relationships
   The Gay Subculture

III. HOW MANY PEOPLE ARE GAY, STRAIGHT, OR BI?

IV. SEXUAL ORIENTATION: IMPLICATIONS FOR ADJUSTMENT
   Sin and the Medical Model
   Research Results
   Therapy for Homosexuality

V. WHY DO PEOPLE BECOME HOMOSEXUAL OR HETEROSEXUAL?
   Biological Theories
   Learning Theory
   Interactionist Theory
   Sociological Theory
   Empirical Data

VI. BISEXUALITY

In June 1969, in response to police harassment, homosexuals rioted in a bar in Greenwich Village, in perhaps the first open group rebellion of homosexuals in history. Gay liberation was born. Since then, the public has been forced into an awareness of an issue—sexual orientation—that it had previously preferred to ignore. Gay liberationists proclaim that gay is good and that homosexuals are not "sick" and should not be treated differently from the way heterosexuals are treated. Meanwhile, the average American charitably maintains that homosexuals are sick (but can be cured).

Homosexual:
A person who has sexual relations with a member of the same gender.

Lesbian:
A female homosexual.

Gay:
Homosexual; now used to refer to male homosexuals.

Straight:
Heterosexual; that is, a person who has sexual relations with a member of the opposite gender.

Homophile:
A person who likes or loves members of his or her own gender.

Most of us want to know more about sexual orientation. The purpose of this chapter is to try to provide a better understanding of people's sexual orientations, whether homosexual, heterosexual, or bisexual.

First, though, some terms need to be defined. A homosexual is a person who has sexual relations with a member of the same gender (although, as will be seen later in the chapter, this is much too simple a definition). The word is derived from the Greek root *homo,* meaning "same" (not the Latin word *homo,* meaning "man"). The term "homosexual" may be applied in a general way to homosexuals of both genders or specifically to male homosexuals. The term lesbian, which is used to refer to female homosexuals, can be traced to the great Greek poet Sappho, who lived on the island of Lesbos (hence "lesbian") around 600 B.C. She is famous for the love poetry that she wrote to other women. Sappho was actually married, apparently happily, and had one daughter, but her homosexual feelings were the focus of her life.

Several other terms are also used in conjunction with homosexuality. Gay liberationists prefer the term gay to "homosexual" because the latter emphasizes the sexual asects of the lifestyle and can be used as a derogatory label, since there are so many negative connotations to homosexuality.[1] A heterosexual is then referred to as straight. Currently, the term "gay" is generally used for male homosexuals and "lesbian" for female homosexuals.

The term homophile is also used to mean someone who loves people of the same gender; like the word "gay," it does not have the sexual connotations of the term "homosexual." There are, of course, a number of derogatory slang terms for homosexuals, such as "queer," "fairy," "dyke," and "faggot" or "fag."

STEREOTYPES AND DISCRIMINATION

Your sexual orientation has implications for the attitudes people have toward you. First, there is the stereotype that all people are heterosexual, that heterosexuality is the norm. Further, just as there are sterotypes about other minority groups—for example, the stereotype that all blacks are stupid and lazy—so there are stereotypes about homosexuals. In this section we will examine some of these stereotyped ideas and attitudes and compare them with the scientific data.

Attitudes toward Homosexuality

First, it is important to note what may be a fairly obvious point, namely, that most Americans disapprove of homosexuality. In a national survey 72 percent of the sample believed that homosexual relations were "always wrong" (Nyberg and Alston, 1976). In a national probability sample of U.S. adults, three-quarters of the respondents woud deny a homosexual the right to be a minister, schoolteacher, or judge, and two-thirds approved of barring homosexuals from medical practice and government employment (Levitt and Klassen, 1974). In the same sample, 45 percent voiced the belief that homosexuals seek out sexual contacts with children, and nearly 50

[1]It is wise to have a good vocabulary on topics such as this. My husband had an aunt, a single lady, who frequently invited a pair of single young men who lived across the hall from her to her parties. The men were fairly open about their homosexuality. Aunt Mary, while an otherwise sophisticated person, was unaware of the usage of the term "gay." Greeting them at her party, she typically complimented them on their appearance by saying, in a loud voice, "My, how gay you look."

percent believed that homosexuality is such a corrupt force that it could cause the downfall of civilization. Finally, 60 percent expressed the view that homosexuality was a sickness but that it could be cured.

The intensity of these negative attitudes is illustrated in the following comments taken from letters to the editor written in response to a 1975 *Time* magazine cover story on homosexuality:

> Disgusting, repulsive, lowbrow, nauseating. I'm no Victorian, but those individuals should crawl into a hole—and take *Time* with them.
>
> From time immemorial we have recognized yellow fever, malaria, syphilis, leprosy, perversion, degeneracy, garbage, and homosexuality in about that order. There need be no change.

But one writer offered a rather profound thought:

> Only in the armed forces can you be highly decorated for killing thousands of your fellow men and be drummed out of the corps if you dare to love one.

Has the gay liberation movement succeeded in changing the negative attitudes of Americans? Apparently not. Table 16.1 shows the results of a national survey in which the same questions were asked in 1973 and again in 1984. As you can see in that table, the percentage of people who believe that homosexual behavior is always wrong remained essentially unchanged from 1973 to 1984.

Homophobia: A strong, irrational fear of homosexuals; negative attitudes and reactions to homosexuals.

Some experts believe that many Americans' attitudes toward homosexuals can best be described as homophobic (Fyfe, 1983; Hudson and Ricketts, 1980). Homophobia may be defined as a strong, irrational fear of homosexuals and, more generally, to fixed, negative attitudes and reactions to homosexuals (Fyfe, 1983). Other terms, such as "homonegativism," are also used to describe these negative attitudes.

In a thought-provoking illustration of the psychological impact of society's attitudes toward homosexuality on the gay person, the authors of a psychology text ask the reader to imagine that being anxious is as taboo as being gay:

> Imagine for a moment that you are an anxious person and that being anxious is against the law. You must try to hide your fears from others. Your own home may be a safe place to feel anxious, but a public display of apprehension can lead to arrest or at least to social ostracism. At work one day an associate looks at you suspiciously and says, "That's funny, for a crazy moment there I thought you were anxious." "Heck no," you exclaim a bit too loudly, *"not me."* You begin to wonder if your fellow worker will report his suspicions to your boss. If he does, your boss may inform the police or will at least change your job to one that requires less contact with customers, especially with those who have children. (Davison and Neale, 1974, p. 293)

But we should also recognize the other side of the coin. As we can see both from the quotations from *Time* and from the statistics in Table 16.1, some Americans are tolerant of, or supportive of homosexuals. For example, about half of Americans approve of an overt homosexual teaching in a college or university. Thus Americans are a strange mixture of bigots and supporters on the issue of homosexuality. As one woman said,

> I really don't feel that I've ever been oppressed as a lesbian or suffered any abuse. I've been careful who I've told, but those people have been really accepting. (Jay and Young, 1979, p. 716)

TABLE 16.1

ATTITUDES OF ADULT AMERICANS TOWARD HOMOSEXUALITY, 1973 AND 1984.

Question and Responses	Percent of Sample 1973	Percent of Sample 1984
1. Are sexual relations between two adults of the same sex:		
Always wrong	74	73
Almost always wrong	7	5
Wrong only sometimes	8	7
Not wrong at all	11	14
2. Should an admitted homosexual man be allowed to teach in a college or university?		
Yes	49	59
No	51	41

Source: J. A. Davis and T. Smith. (1984). *General Social Surveys, 1972–1984: Cumulative data.* New Haven: Yale University, Roper Center for Public Opinion Research.

Stereotypes about Gays

In addition to negative attitudes, many Americans have stereotyped ideas about homosexuals.

The Swish and the Dyke

One such stereotype is that all male homosexuals are effeminate; they are supposed to be limp-wristed, have a swishy walk, and talk with a lisp. The corresponding stereotype about the lesbian is that she is masculine; she has short hair and wears a man-tailored suit. Because people have these stereotyped ideas, they believe that it is easy to spot homosexuals and that it is always obvious who is a gay and who is a straight. In fact, these stereotypes are far from the truth, and people's abilities to spot homosexuals are not nearly so good as they think they are. In contrast to stereotypes a study of male university athletes found that 40 percent of them had engaged in homosexual behavior to orgasm in the last two years (Garner and Smith, 1977). Most gay people look and behave just like everybody else. Except for a small percentage of cases, it is impossible to tell a homosexual simply by appearance and mannerisms. Kinsey estimated that only about 15 percent of male homosexuals could be identified by their appearance. This is particularly true now because recent fashions in clothing have been stolen in part from gays: women now wear pants frequently. Mustaches are much in style for male gays, as they are for male straights.

The belief that male homosexuals are feminine and that lesbians are masculine represents a confusion of two important concepts: *gender identity* (masculine or feminine) and *sexual orientation* (heterosexual or homosexual). The gay person differs from the majority in choice of sexual partner because he or she makes the homosexual choice, but the gay person does not typically differ from the majority in gender identity (Storms, 1980). That is, the male homosexual chooses a partner of the same gender, but his identity is quite definitely masculine. He thinks of himself as male and has no desire to be a female. The same holds true for the lesbian; while she makes a homosexual choice of sexual partner, she is quite definitely a woman and typically has no desire to be a man (Wolff, 1971). (Interestingly, this confusion of the concepts of choice of sexual partner and gender identity also occurs in some of the scientific theories about homosexuality to be discussed later in this chapter.)

FIGURE 16.1

(*a*) In 1978, Harvey Milk, a gay activist, was an elected member of San Francisco's Board of Supervisors, representing a district including many gays. Milk fought for gay rights throughout the state of California, and was supported by San Francisco's mayor, George Moscone. On November 17, 1978, Dan White, himself a former supervisor, entered City Hall and fired shots that killed both Milk and Moscone. White confessed within hours. In May 1979, a jury declined to convict White of first degree murder, instead finding him guilty of voluntary manslaughter, a lesser offense carrying a reduced jail sentence. The gay community, as well as many sympathetic supporters, were shocked and furious. A protest march and the White Night Riot ensued. The entire incident symbolizes the ambivalent progress achieved by gay liberation: a gay liberationist can be elected to an important public office, but he is then murdered. (*b*) Victims and killer—San Francisco Mayor George Moscone (center), Milk (left), Dan White (right). White is a former city police officer, firefighter, and city supervisor.

The Role-Playing Stereotype

Another common stereotype is that in their relationships, homosexuals role-play heterosexual roles: that in a pair of male homosexuals, one will assume the dominant role and the other the submissive role, and that in a lesbian couple, one will play the male role ("butch") and the other the female role ("femme"). In the sexual act itself, some people believe that the inserter is playing the active (or masculine) role, while the insertee is playing the passive (or feminine) role. While such role playing does occur to some extent, in fact it is far from typical.

In regard to sexual practices most homosexuals engage in all forms of behavior and do not restrict themselves to one or another role. One study of a group of male homosexuals (Hooker, 1965) found that 46 percent practiced all forms of sexual activity and varied their roles (inserter or insertee), depending on the preference of the partner, a wish for variety, and so on. Only 20 percent of the sample showed a distinct preference for given activities and for a particular role. Homosexual partners often switch roles during the sex act or engage in mutual oral-genital stimulation, further calling into question the notion that one plays the male role and one the female role.

In regard to role playing outside the sexual act itself, the practice seems to be far from typical (Peplau, 1981). In *The Gay Report* sample, 56 percent of the lesbian respondents had never played such roles, and an additional 23 percent had done so only infrequently (Jay and Young, 1979). The comparable statistics for the male homosexuals were 47 percent and 23 percent. Thus only a minority of gays engage in role playing with any substantial frequency. Del Martin and Phyllis Lyon, gay activists and cofounders of the Daughters of Bilitis, observe that for lesbians such role playing occurs mainly among those new to the gay scene. When first entering the lesbian lifestyle, women attempt to set up a relationship based on the only model they have available, that of heterosexual relations. Unfortunately, this role playing leads to all the problems inherent in heterosexual roles—dominance and submissiveness, inequality in decision making, and so on. Thus, these roles are generally discarded as the relationship progresses and matures (Martin and Lyon, 1972). With the combined influences of gay activism and a generalized questioning of gender roles in our culture, the incidence of this role playing seems to be even more on the decline.

The Child-Molester Stereotype

Another common belief is that male homosexuals are child molesters. If an elementary school teacher or even a high school teacher is discovered to be a homosexual, there is an instant public outcry demanding that he be fired, based on the belief that he will try to seduce all the young boys in the school. Strangely, the same people who worry about this never seem to worry that hetereosexual male teachers will try to seduce young girls, although that seems to be just as logical a possibility. Actually, most child molesting is done by heterosexual men to little girls; 80 percent of child molesting is in that category, and only 20 percent is homosexual (McCaghy, 1971). According to *The Gay Report,* 93 percent of the male homosexuals had never had sex with someone 12 or under, and 77 percent had never had sex with anyone between 13 and 15. The comparable statistics for lesbians were 98 percent and 94 percent (Jay and Young, 1979). Further, most adolescents are initiated into homosexual activity not by an adult but rather by another teenager (Sorensen, 1973). Therefore, there is no reason to assume that a given homosexual is a child molester.

Jokes about Gays

Jokes are one reflection of society's negative attitudes toward homosexuals and of the fact that homosexuals have not been accepted as much by the general public as other minorities have. It is no longer considered acceptable for television comedians to make jokes about the stupidity or dishonesty of blacks or the mercenary qualities of Jews; formerly such jokes were common, but now they are extremely rare. Jokes about homosexuals are very common, though, and in a sense homosexuals have become the new minority. Recently on a single one-hour variety program, I counted five separate derogatory jokes about homosexuality—the standard routine about limp wrists and lisps.

People make jokes about things that make them uncomfortable, and so the frequency of these jokes reflects people's homophobia. But jokes may also have an effect on the people about whom they are made. When gay people hear entertainers make jokes about their way of life, this must at least make them uncomfortable and might even encourage them to believe the stereotypes incorporated in the jokes. Jokes may represent a particularly insidious form of stereotyping because the ideas conveyed in them are not subject to rational and open debate: who would argue with the content of a joke? Thus they contribute to a kind of nonconscious ideology (Bem and Bem, 1970) that teaches that gays are limp-wristed, swishy, silly, and generally the object of public ridicule. It would be interesting to do an analysis of the content of jokes on television to see how many jokes ridicule homosexuals and to see whether the frequency of such jokes declines in the future if people come to accept homosexuality more.

Gays as a Minority Group

From the foregoing, it is clear that gay people are the subject of many stereotypes, just as other minorities are. They also have several other things in common with members of other minority groups. First, they suffer from job discrimination. Just as blacks and women have been denied access to certain jobs, so too have homosexuals. Homosexuality is grounds for a dishonorable discharge from the armed forces, and there are many cases in which this rule has been applied (Martin and Lyon, 1972; Williams and Weinberg, 1971).[2] Homosexuality has also been grounds for firing a person from federal employment and for denial of a security clearance. The reason commonly given for the latter two rules is that homosexuals are susceptible to being blackmailed and therefore cannot be put in situations in which they have access to sensitive information. Actually, many heterosexuals might also be susceptible to blackmail because of their sexual activities—for example, the married man who is having an affair—although such factors are not grounds for denial of security clearance. In fact, in one sample 90 percent of lesbians and 86 percent of male homosexuals had never been the object of blackmail or threats of blackmail (Jay and Young, 1979). In addition, as homosexuals become more open, they will be less subject to blackmail.

There is an important way in which homosexuals differ from other minorities, though. In the case of most other minorities, appearance is a fairly good indicator of minority-group status. It is easy to recognize a black or a woman, for example, but one cannot tell simply by looking at a person what his or her sexual practices are. Thus, homosexuals, unlike other minorities, can hide their status. There are certain advantages to this. It makes it fairly easy to get along in the heterosexual world—to "pass." However, it has the disadvantage of encouraging the person to live a lie and to deny her or his true identity; not only is this dishonest, but it may also be psychologically stressful.

---

[2]The case of Leonard Matlovitch, which challenged this practice, attracted wide attention. Matlovich, an Air Force sergeant who was decorated with a Bronze Star and a Purple Heart for his service in Vietnam, openly declared his homosexuality and challenged the right of the Air Force to discharge him. His lawyers hoped that his case would reach the Supreme Court and that the Court would make a landmark ruling on the rights of homosexuals. (See Chapter 23 for a complete discussion.)

Lest the picture seem bleak for the homosexual, it should also be noted that there are some advantages to being a homosexual. For example, lesbians claim that other women are better lovers; many men, they say, have a shaky knowledge of female anatomy and an even shakier knowledge of how to stimulate it. The female knows her own body and how to stimulate it best. Indeed, it has been reported that lesbians have greater orgasm consistency than heterosexual women (Kinsey et al., 1953). And Masters and Johnson (1979) hold the opinion that gays are better at lovemaking than straights.

THE GAY LIFESTYLE

Covert homosexual: A homosexual who is "in the closet," who keeps his or her sexual orientation a secret.

Overt homosexual: A homosexual who is "out of the closet," who is open about his or her homosexuality.

In understanding the gay lifestyle. it is important to recognize that there is a wide variety of gay experiences. One of the most important aspects of this variability is whether the person is covert (in the closet) or overt (out of the closet) about his or her homosexuality. The covert homosexual may be heterosexually married, have children, and be a respected professional in the community, spending only a few hours a month engaging in secret homosexual behavior. The overt homosexual, on the other hand, may live almost entirely within a homosexual community, particularly if he or she lives in a large city like New York or San Francisco where there is a large gay subculture, and may have relatively few contacts with heterosexuals. The lifestyle of gay males also differs considerably from that of gay females, probably as a result of the different roles assigned to males and females in our society and the different ways that males and females are reared. In addition, there is more discrimination against male homosexuals than there is against lesbians. For example, it is considered quite natural for two women to share an apartment, but if two men do so, eyebrows are raised.

The lifestyles of homosexuals are thus far from uniform. They vary according to whether one is male or female and overt or covert about the homosexuality and also according to social class, occupation, personality, and a variety of other factors.

TABLE 16.2

SOME SLANG TERMS FROM THE GAY SUBCULTURE

Term	Meaning
In the closet	Keeping one's homosexuality hidden, not being open or public
Coming out	Coming out of the closet, or becoming open about one's homosexuality
Queen	An effeminate male homosexual
Nellie	An effeminate male homosexual
Closet queen	A homosexual who is covert or in the closet
Drag queen	A male homosexual who dresses in women's clothing ("drag")
Butch	A masculine male homosexual or a masculine lesbian
Dyke	A masculine lesbian
Femme	A feminine lesbian
Trick	A casual sexual partner
Cruising	Looking for a sexual partner
Tearoom	A public restroom where gay men engage in casual sex

FIGURE 16.2

A "leather bar," named TY's, on Christopher Street in New York.

Coming Out

As I noted earlier, there are significant variations in the gay experience depending on whether or not one is out of the closet. Being in the closet has some real disadvantages. One lesbian commented,

> I hate being in the closet. It's so boring having people ask if I have a boyfriend. I feel like putting the most horrified look possible on my face, and as if I'm deeply insulted exclaim, "I beg your pardon? I certainly hope not!" If I were sure of a job and safe living conditions, everyone would be fully informed that I am gay. I am seriously contemplating getting a T-shirt with "Support Gay Liberation" inscribed on it. (Jay and Young, 1979, p. 75).

Coming out: The process of acknowledging to oneself, and then to others, that one is homosexual.

The process of coming of out of the closet, or coming out, involves acknowledging to oneself, and then to others, that one is homosexual (Coleman, 1982). The person is very vulnerable during this stage. Whether the person experiences acceptance or rejection from friends and others to whom he or she comes out, can be critical to self-esteem.

Following the period of coming out, there is a stage of exploration, in which the person experiments with the new sexual identity; they make contact with the gay and lesbian community and practice new interpersonal skills. Following the stage of exploration, there is typically a stage of forming first relationships. These relationships are often short-lived and characterized by jealousy and turbulence, much like many heterosexual dating relationships. Finally, there is the integration stage, in which the person becomes a fully functioning member of society and is capable of maintaining a long-term, committed relationship (Coleman, 1982).

Gay Relationships

Social scientists used to spend their time trying to figure out how many people are gay, or whether homosexuals are mentally ill or not. Today there is a recognition that homosexuals do form relationships—often long-term, committed ones—and current research focuses on understanding the nature of gay relationships.

In their study *Homosexualities,* sex researchers Alan Bell and Martin Weinberg (1978) concluded that homosexual people could be classified into five categories, depending on the kinds of relationships they formed: close-coupled, open-coupled, functional, dysfunctional, and asexual. The typology appeared to work both for male homosexuals and for lesbians.

Close-coupled:
Gay couples who are in a faithful, monogamous relationship.

Open-coupled:
Gay couples who are in a nonmonogamous relationship.

Functional:
Bell and Weinberg's term for gay men who are not in a relationship but who have a high level of sexual activity and are satisfied with their lifestyle.

Dysfunctional:
Bell and Weinberg's term for gay men who are not in a relationship but who have a high level of sexual activity and are dissatisfied with their lifestyle.

The close-coupled people are essentially the happily married couples of the gay world. The individuals live together with their sexual partner on a fairly permanent basis. They tend to have few sexual problems, a low number of different partners (indicating that they are fairly monogamous) but a high rate of sexual activity, and a low amount of cruising. The open-coupled individuals are in a quasi-marriage, like the close-coupled individuals, but the open-coupled individuals had a high number of sexual partners (indicating that they are not monogamous), and they tended to have more sexual problems and do more cruising. The functional people are "single"; they had a high number of different partners and a high level of sexual activity, but they had few sexual problems and little regret over their homosexuality. They are essentially the happy singles of the gay world. The dysfunctional subjects were also single and had a high number of partners, but they had many sexual problems and expressed regret over their homosexuality. Their problems had to do mainly with concerns that they were not sexually adequate and difficulties in having

FIGURE 16.3

A gay male couple.

TABLE 16.3

PERCENTAGES OF BELL AND WEINBERG'S (1978) GAY RESPONDENTS FALLING INTO THEIR FIVE CATEGORIES

	Male Homosexuals	Female Homosexuals
Close-coupled	10	28
Open-coupled	18	17
Functional	15	10
Dysfunctional	12	5
Asexual	16	11
Other (not classified)	29	29

Asexual: Engaging in little or no sexual activity.

orgasms, finding suitable sexual partners, and maintaining affection for their partner. Finally, the asexual people were single; they were low in sexual activity and number of partners and did little cruising. They had more sexual problems (mostly related to difficulties in finding sexual partners) and lower levels of sexual interest; they had more regret over their homosexuality and tended to be more covert.

About 71 percent of the Bell and Weinberg sample could be classified into these categories. Thus future research may uncover other types of gay lifestyles to describe those who did not fit into one of the above five categories. The number of males and females in each category is shown in Table 16.3. Notice that the number of respondents in all categories is fairly even, except that a high number of lesbians are close-coupled, and few lesbians are dysfunctional.

When you hear the term "couple," what do you think of? Most likely a heterosexual married couple, or perhaps a heterosexual dating couple. Sociologists Philip Blumstein and Pepper Schwartz (1983) took an innovative approach in their major study, *American Couples*. They defined "couples" to include heterosexual married couples, heterosexual cohabiting couples, gay male couples, and lesbian couples. They found that many of the characteristics and problems of gay couples are similar to those of heterosexual couples. For example, the frequency of sex declines when the couple have been in the relationship for more than 10 years; this occurs for gay male couples, lesbian couples, and heterosexual married couples. For gay and lesbian couples, there are sometimes problems involved in who initiates sex, just as there are for straight couples. Among heterosexual couples, it is typically the man who initiates; among gay couples, the more emotionally expressive partner is the one who initiates sex.

In their relationships, lesbians attach great importance to emotional expressiveness, as do heterosexual women (Peplau and Amaro, 1982). For example, "being able to talk about my most intimate feelings" is rated as highly important by lesbians. Lesbians also tend to place a high value on equality in their relationships. In research on satisfaction in relationships, the most satisfying lesbian relationships are those in which the partners are equally committed, they are equally "in love," and there is equality of power between the two (Peplau, Padesky, and Hamilton, 1982).

In regard to satisfaction in relationships, comparisons of matched samples of lesbians, gay men, and heterosexuals indicate that lesbians and gay men rate their relationships as highly satisfying. There are no significant differences among lesbians, gay men, and heterosexuals in their satisfaction in the relationship, or in the love they feel for the partner (Peplau and Amaro, 1982). Thus, the research makes it clear—contrary to stereotypes that homosexuals specialize in promiscuous sex and one-night stands—that gay men and lesbians do form satisfying long-term relationships.

A major contribution to this new research on gay relationships is a study of male couples done by psychiatrist David McWhirter and psychologist Andrew Mattison

(1984). They interviewed 312 gay men in 156 couples. On the average, the couples had been together 8.9 years; in fact, 8 of the couples had been together for 30 or more years, another striking contradiction to the stereotype that gay men are incapable of forming long-term relationships. Mattison and McWhirter came to the conclusion that gay couples pass through six identifiable stages as their relationship progresses through the years.

Stage 1, Blending, occurs in the first year they are together. This stage, according to Mattison and McWhirter, is characterized by merging, limerance, equalizing of the partnership, and a high level of sexual activity. In merging, the two separate men are joining together to form a couple. "Limerance" refers to the sense that one is falling in love, romantically and passionately. The men also work to equalize the relationship. Gender-role socialization in our culture assures that men are brought up to be providers; when two men form a couple, they must work out new models, in which they share and equalize the work of providing.

Stage 2, Nesting, occurs in the second and third years of the relationship. It is characterized by homemaking, finding compatibility, a decline of limerance, and ambivalence. Stage 2 begins with a feeling of homemaking, a desire to make a home for the two of them together, to fix things up, to feather the nest. As one participant in the study said, "After a while I really wanted *our* home. You know, a place we were proud of, where we could have friends and family. We had a lot of fun fixing it up together" (1984, p. 41). This stage is also characterized by a decline of limerance, the passion and romance of the first stage. Because limerance declines, there are new efforts to find compatibility in the relationship; differences and flaws in the partner were ignored in the passion of Stage 1, but they can no longer be covered up in Stage 2, and so compatibility becomes an issue. As one man commented on this stage,

> It was real gradual, like I would feel aggravated which I had never felt before when he changed the TV channel, or I'd want want to be alone in the bedroom and he'd follow me in, or suddenly I couldn't stand the noise he made chewing his food. I just wasn't floating on air as often as before. I got real scared thinking I was falling out of love. (1984, p. 52)

Because there is continued attraction to the partner, but also a recognition of flaws and problems, this stage is characterized by ambivalence, or mixed feelings.

Stage 3, Maintaining, occurs in the fourth and fifth years and is a time of the reappearance of the individual, taking risks, dealing with conflict, and establishing traditions. In contrast to the first two stages, where the emphasis was on oneness and togetherness, individuality and independence become important in the third stage, as the partners discover that too much togetherness can lead to stagnation. Because the relationship is longer and more stable than it was, the partners are willing to take risks, perhaps confessing dissatisfactions that they had covered up before. Couples in this stage also evolve their own characteristic ways of dealing with conflicts in the relationship, such as compromise or establishing some fixed roles for each. The couple also begins establishing traditions—such as customs at Christmas or birthdays—that enrich the relationship and increase the sense that it is permanent.

Stage 4, Building, occurs in the sixth through the tenth year of the relationship. It is characterized by collaborating, increasing productivity, establishing independence, and a sense of the dependability of the partners. In collaborating the couple works together, whether it involves finishing each other's sentences because they know the other's thoughts so well, or opening a business together. Because the rela-

F · O · C · U · S 16.1

A GAY COUPLE: TOM AND BRIAN

Tom and Brian have been living together as lovers for three years. Tom is 29, and Brian is 22; they live in a medium-sized midwestern city.

Tom grew up in a Roman Catholic family and attended parochial schools. His father was killed in an automobile accident when Tom was 4 days old. His mother remarried when he was 8 years old; though he gets along well with his stepfather, he feels that he has never had a real father. When asked why he thought he was gay, he said he felt it was because of the absence of a father in his early years.

After graduating from high school, Tom joined the Army and served in Vietnam and Germany. His first sexual experience was with a Japanese prostitute. Though he enjoyed the physical aspects of sex with her, he felt that something was missing emotionally. When he was 23, after returning to the United States, he had his first homosexual experience with someone he met at a bar.

Tom had sex with about 20 different men before meeting Brian, including one with whom he had a long-term relationship. He is currently a student at a technical college and is working toward a career in electronics.

Brian also grew up in a Roman Catholic family and attended parochial schools. He has always gotten along well with both his parents and his four siblings, and he recalls his childhood as being uneventful. He realized he was gay when he was in his early teens, but he chose to ignore his feelings and instead tried to conform to what society expected of him. He had a girlfriend when he was in high school. After he graduated from high school, he took a job; he had his first homosexual experience when he was 18 with a man he met at work. He currently works as a salesperson at Penney's. He had sex with eight different men before meeting Tom. He has never had intercourse with a woman.

Brian and Tom have not discussed their homosexuality directly with their families. Both think their parents may have some vague suspicions, but the parents apparently prefer not to have to confront the situation directly and instead prefer to think of their sons as just being "roommates." Both Brian and Tom wish they could be more honest about their gayness with their parents. However, they also do not want to hurt them, and so they have not pressed the matter.

Their relationship with each other is exclusive; that is, they have an agreement that they will be faithful to each other and that neither will have sex with anyone else. Both of them said they would feel hurt if they found out that the other had been seeing someone else on the sly. They both consider casual sex unfulfilling and want to have a real relationship with their sexual partner.

Household chores are allocated depending on who has the time and inclination to do them. Both like to cook, and so they share that duty about equally, as they do the laundry. Tom is good at carpentry, and therefore he tends to do things of that sort.

Tom and Brian feel that the greatest problem in their relationship is lack of communication, which sometimes creates misunderstandings and arguments. Brian feels that the greatest joy in their relationship is the security of knowing that they love each other and can count on each other. Tom agrees, and he also says that it is important to him to know that there is someone who really cares about him and loves him.

Source: Based on an interview conducted by the author.

tionship is now stable it is a source of strength for the individuals, and they are increasingly productive, whether the productivity involves going back to school to get a new degree or starting a new hobby like gardening. The sense of stability and dependability in the relationship also allows more independence for both.

Stage 5, Releasing, occurs from the eleventh through the twentieth year of the relationship. Its characteristics are trusting, merging of money and possessions, constricting, and taking each other for granted. Although there has always been trust in the relationship, it is greater and more salient now. Possessions and money are merged, and the couple no longer worries about who is paying for what or whether they are paying equally for the groceries; it is "our" money. There is often some constriction at this time, perhaps involving less of a social life for the couple, or one or both members going through a mid-life crisis. The partners also tend to take each other for granted.

Stage 6, Renewing, occurs after the couple have passed 20 years in the relationship, and it is characterized by achieving security, shifting perspectives, restoring the partnership, and remembering. Couples who move on to this stage and restore the partnership must take some active steps to move beyond the tendency to take each other for granted that occured in Stage 5. As one respondent said,

> I almost lost him after his heart attack, and somehow we learned. We learned to take better care of ourselves, and we remembered to take better care of each other. I say "I love you" every night before we go to sleep now. And I mean it. We had stopped that ten years ago. It seemed like kid stuff, I suppose. But, I'll tell you, it's good medicine. (McWhirter and Mattison, 1984, p. 110)

Couples in this stage typically feel a sense of security, both in their relationship and also in financial terms. Having pooled two male incomes and having had no dependents for 20 or more years, they are likely to have accumulated a good deal of money. Couples in this stage are also storytellers, remembering the many good times they have had together.

Because McWhirter and Mattison interviewed only gay male couples, they claim their stage theory only for that population. But it may well be that heterosexual couples and lesbian couples go through the same stages as their relationships progress. Only much more long-term research on relationships will be able to test those possibilities. Yet the thing that strikes me about all the research on gay relationships is how similar they are—in their satisfactions, loves, joys, and conflicts—to heterosexual relationships.

The Bars

Gay bar:
A cocktail lounge catering to gay men or lesbians.

Gay bars are an important aspect of the gay social life. These are cocktail lounges that cater exclusively to gays. Drinking, perhaps dancing, socializing, and the hope of finding a sexual partner for the evening are the important elements. Some gay bars look just like any other bar from the outside, while others may have names—for example, The Open Closet—that indicate to the alert who the clientele is. Bars are typically gender-segregated—that is, they are for either male homosexuals or lesbians—although a few are mixed. There are far more bars for gay males than for gay females. Typically, the atmosphere is different in the two, the male bars being more for picking up sexual partners, and the female bars being more for talking and socializing. Lest the reader be unduly shocked at the none-too-subtle nature of pick-up bars, it is well to remember that there are many bars—singles' bars—that serve precisely the same purpose for heterosexuals.

The Baths

Baths: Clubs for gay men that offer an opportunity for casual sex.

For some men, another feature of the gay lifestyle is the baths (or "steam baths" or "tubs"). The baths are clubs with many rooms in them, generally including a swimming pool or a whirlpool, as well as rooms for dancing, watching television, and socializing; most areas are dimly lit. On entering, the man rents a locker or a room, where he leaves his clothes; then he proceeds with a towel wrapped around his waist. When a sexual partner has been found, they go to one of a number of small rooms, furnished with beds, where they can engage in sexual activity. The baths feature impersonal sex, since a partner can be found and the act completed without the two even exchanging names, much less making any form of emotional commitment. Generally there is also an "orgy room," where people can engage in group sex.

One ethnographer described a scene as follows:

> This popular Tenderloin bath has a TV room which is essentially an orgy room after 8:00 P.M. On the third floor, up a short flight of stairs, it is a very dimly lit room with benches around the walls. Two couples were kissing, standing in the middle of the room with several men standing around watching. On the benches several people were fondling each other. All at once everyone in the room moved over to the west wall. A young black man was performing fellatio on a very young blond man. Soon almost everyone in the room was rubbing against the other in what was much like some tribal initiation ceremony. After the young white man ejaculated, he and the black youth embraced. The atmosphere in the room at that point was more brotherly than sexual. (Bell and Weinberg, 1978, p. 240)

Large cities generally have a number of baths, and there are several chains, one of the largest being The Club. Interestingly, baths seem to be almost exclusively a male phenomenon. Once again, lest the reader be shocked at the blatant searches for sexual partners, it is well to remember that similar forms of impersonal sex occur among heterosexuals, for example, in massage parlors. In addition, heterosexual baths have opened in New York (Plato's Retreat). It is also important to remember that there is great variability from one homosexual to the next in how important the baths are to his lifestyle. I know a 42-year-old man who has been exclusively gay since he was 13 and who has never been in the baths. For others, the baths may become a focal point in their lives. Some gay males leave work at 5 P.M. on Friday, spend the entire weekend inside the baths, and do not leave again until they return to work on Monday morning. The baths can also serve as a kind of "home away from home" for the traveler; they can serve as a hotel, and they provide a way to meet new people in a strange city.

The Tearoom Trade

Tearoom trade: Impersonal sex in public places such as restrooms.

A related aspect of the gay lifestyle is the "tearoom trade." This phenomenon was studied by sociologist Laud Humphreys and is reported in an important book entitled *Tearoom Trade: Impersonal Sex in Public Places* (see the Focus on the ethics of sex research). As the title of the book implies, the "tearoom trade" refers to impersonal sexual acts in places like public rest rooms. Typically the man enters the rest room and conveys to another man who is already there an interest in having sex. He may do this by making certain signals while urinating or by making tapping sounds while in one of the stalls, for example. The sexual act is generally performed in a stall and may be accomplished without a single word being exchanged. The activity engaged in is typically fellatio, which can be done rapidly and with a mini-

F • O • C • U • S 16.2

THE ETHICS OF SEX RESEARCH: THE TEAROOM TRADE

Sociologist Laud Humphreys's study entitled *Tearoom Trade: Impersonal Sex in Public Places* (1970) is a classic in the field of sexuality. In light of recent concern on the part of both scientists and the general public about ethical standards in research, however, his methods of data collection appear somewhat questionable. Important issues are raised about the difficulty of doing good sex research within ethical bounds.

In the tearoom-trade situation, a third person generally serves as a "lookout" who watches for the police or other intruders while the other two engage in sex. To obtain his data, Humphreys became a lookout. Not only did he observe the behaviors involved in the tearoom trade, but he also wrote down the license-plate numbers of the participants. He then traced the numbers through government records and thus was able to get the addresses of the persons involved and to obtain census information about the neighborhood in which they lived. He also went to the homes of the people and administered a questionnaire (which included questions on sexual behavior) to them under the pretense of conducting a general survey.

The research provided some important data, particularly on the extent to which these sexual practices are engaged in by "respectable" citizens. Humphreys, of course, maintained the complete anonymity of the subjects in his report of the research. However, the ethical problems are still numerous. Was there invasion of privacy, particularly when Humphreys entered someone's home and obtained personal information under false pretenses? Was there a problem of deceiving subjects, and particularly of not "debriefing" them (explaining the true purpose of the research) afterward? Would the people have consented to being involved with the research had they known its true purpose? Could Humphreys have obtained good data within the bounds of ethics? On the other hand, these clearly negative aspects of the study have to be weighed against the benefits to society from knowing more about this form of sexual behavior.

Source: Laud Humphreys. (1970). *Tearoom trade: Impersonal sex in public places.* Chicago: Aldine.

mum of encumbrance, which is important in case the police or others intrude. The police have been very concerned with eliminating this behavior. There is some justification for their attempts, since the behavior is done in public rather than in private and may therefore be a nuisance to the innocent person who happens on the scene. Police efforts to eliminate the phenomenon, though, have met with little success.

Humphreys's book provoked quite a controversy, not only because of the topic but also because of his findings that many of the men who engaged in this behavior were heterosexually married men, some of them respected leaders in the community. Apparently, the tearoom trade served a need for quick, impersonal sex, and the behavior of choice was homosexual. But the notion that "heterosexual," respectable men could engage in homosexual behavior was shocking to many. Indeed, many gays find the tearoom trade to be shocking.

Gay Liberation

Certainly in the last two decades the gay liberation movement has had a tremendous impact on the gay lifestyle. In particular, it has encouraged homosexuals to be more overt and to feel less guilty about their behavior. Gay liberation meetings and activities provide a social situation in which gay people can meet and discuss important issues rather than simply playing games as a prelude to sex, which tends to be the pattern in the bars. Gay liberation meetings also provide an opportunity to discuss common experiences, thereby producing some consciousness raising. In addition, they provide a political organization that can attempt to bring about legal change, combat police harassment, and fight cases of job discrimination, as well as do public relations work. The National Gay Task Force[3] is the central clearinghouse for all these groups; it can provide information on local organizations.

Publications

Among other accomplishments the gay liberation movement has succeeded in founding numerous gay newspapers and magazines. These have many of the same features as other newspapers: forums for political opinions, human-interest stories, and fashion news. In addition, the want-ads sections feature advertisements for sexual partners; similar ads for homosexual and heterosexual partners can be found in underground newspapers such as the *Berkeley Barb.* Probably the best-known gay newspaper is *The Advocate,* published in Los Angeles and circulated throughout the United States. *The Ladder* is a publication of the Daughters of Bilitis, the largest organization of lesbians. There are also several publications that list all the gay bars and baths by city in the United States, which is handy for the traveler or for those newly arrived on the gay scene.

HOW MANY PEOPLE ARE GAY, STRAIGHT, OR BI?

Most people believe that homosexuality is rare. What percentage of people in the United States are gay? As it turns out, the answer to this question is complex. Basically, it depends on how one defines "a homosexual" and "a heterosexual."

One source of information we have on this question is Kinsey's research (see Chapter 10 for an evaluation of the Kinsey data). Kinsey found that about two-thirds of all males have a homosexual experience in childhood (prior to age 15); such behavior, however, did not appear to be a predictor of adult homosexual behavior. Excluding this childhood behavior, Kinsey found that 37 percent of all males have at least one homosexual experience to orgasm in adulthood (Table 16.4). This is clearly a large percentage, and it indicates that homosexuality is not so rare as many people think. Indeed, it was this statistic, combined with some of the findings on premarital sex, that led to the furor over the Kinsey report. The comparable figure

---

[3]The National Gay Task Force, 80 Fifth Avenue, New York, NY 10011; (212) 741-1010. See the Appendix at the end of this book for a list of other organizations dealing with various aspects of sexuality.

TABLE 16.4

PERCENTAGES OF PEOPLE IN THE KINSEY DATA WITH VARYING AMOUNTS OF HOMOSEXUAL AND HETEROSEXUAL EXPERIENCE

Rating	Males (%)	Females (%)
0 Exclusive heterosexuality	63	87
1–6 At least one same-gender experience leading to orgasm	37	13
6 Exclusive homosexuality	4	2

Source: A. C. Kinsey, W. B. Pomeroy, C. E. Martin, and P. H. Gebhard. (1953). *Sexual behaviors in the human female.* Philadelphia: Saunders.

for females was 13 percent. Kinsey's collaborators later felt that the 37 percent figure for males was too high and that 25 to 33 percent might have been more accurate (e.g., Pomeroy, 1972).

After reading these statistics, though, one is still left wondering how many people are homosexuals. As Kinsey soon realized in trying to answer this question, it depends on how you count. A prevalent notion is that like black and white, homosexual and heterosexual are two quite separate and distinct categories. This is what might be called a *typological conceptualization* (see Figure 16.4). Kinsey made an important scientific breakthrough when he decided to conceptualize homosexuality and heterosexuality not as two separate categories but rather as variations on a continuum (Figure 16.4, section 2). The black and white of heterosexuality and homosexuality have a lot of shades of gray in between: people who have had both some heterosexual and some homosexual experience, in various mixtures. To accommodate all these varying degrees of homosexual and heterosexual experience, Kinsey constructed a scale running from 0 (exclusively heterosexual) to 6 (exclusively homosexual), with the midpoint of 3 indicating equal amounts of heterosexual and homosexual experience. The percentages of people he found falling into these categories are shown in Table 16.4. Several important points emerge from the data. First, while the percentages of people who are exclusively homosexual are rather small (about 4 percent of all males and about 2 percent of all females), the number

FIGURE 16.4

Three ways of conceptualizing homosexuality and heterosexuality.

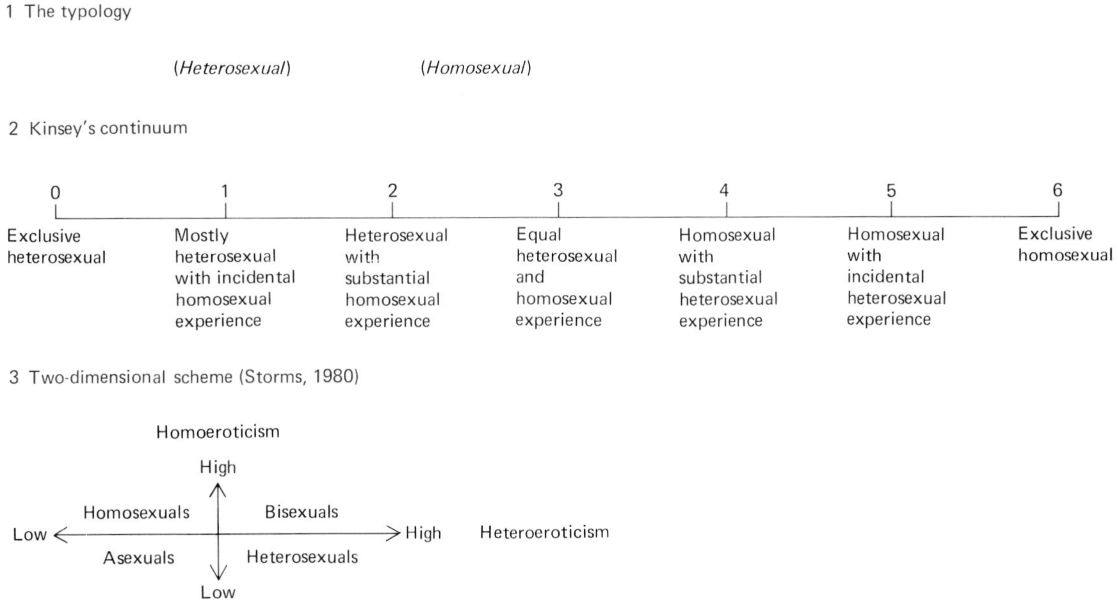

of people who have had at least some homosexual experience (ratings of 1 to 6) is large: about 37 percent of males and 13 percent of females.[4] Quite a lot of people have engaged in at least some homosexual behavior. About 63 percent of the males and 87 percent of the females in Kinsey's sample claimed exclusive heterosexuality. It is also true that although the percentages for exclusive homosexuality are small, the 4 percent of males who are exclusively homosexual represents about 2 million Americans, a substantial number.

Second, it should also be noted in Table 16.4 that the incidence of homosexuality among men is considerably higher than the incidence among women. About three times as many males as females have a homosexual experience to orgasm in adulthood. Other studies have essentially confirmed this result; homosexuality appears to be two to three times as common among males as among females.

In light of these data on behavior, when is a person a homosexual? If you have had one homosexual experience, does that make you a homosexual, or do you have to have had substantial homosexual experience (say, a rating of 2 or 3 or higher)? Or do you have to be exclusively homosexual to be a homosexual? Kinsey dealt with this problem in part by devising the scale, but he also made another important point. He argued that we should not talk about "homosexuality" but rather about "homosexual behavior." "Homosexuality," as we have seen, is exceedingly difficult to define. "Homosexual behavior," on the other hand, can be scientifically defined as a sexual act between two people of the same gender (Kinsey collected data not only on acts culminating in orgasm but also on arousal responses to members of the same gender). Therefore, we can talk more precisely about people who have engaged in varying amounts of homosexual behavior or who have had varying amounts of homosexual experience, thereby avoiding the problem of deciding exactly when a person is a homosexual, which is difficult, if not impossible, to do.

Recently it has been suggested that Kinsey's one-dimensional scale is too simple (Storms, 1980). The alternative is to form a two-dimensional scheme, much like the two-dimensional scheme for recognizing androgyny as an alternative to masculinity-femininity (discussed in Chapter 14). The idea here is to have one scale for heteroerotocism (the extent of one's arousal to members of the opposite gender), ranging from low to high, and another for homoeroticism (extent of arousal to members of one's own gender), ranging from low to high (see Figure 16.4, section 3). Thus if one is high on both heteroeroticism and homoeroticism, one is a bisexual; the person high on heteroeroticism but low on homoeroticism is heterosexual; the person high on homoeroticism and low on heteroeroticism is homosexual; and finally, the person who is low on both scales is asexual. This scheme allows even more complexity in describing homosexuality and heterosexuality than Kinsey's scale did.

Chapter 10 included a discussion of Hunt's 1972 survey of sexual behavior comparable to Kinsey's. It indicated substantial increases in certain behaviors, most notably premarital sex. Interestingly, this survey provided no evidence that homosexuality is increasing. Hunt's statistics are similar to Kinsey's; Hunt estimated that about 20 to 25 percent of males have an overt homosexual experience in adulthood, as do about 10 percent of married women and 20 percent of single women. Studies from other countries, such as Sweden and Germany, also indicate that about 2 to 4 percent of the adult male population is exclusively homosexual. Thus the incidence of homosexuality appears to be fairly stable both over time and across cultures.

The answer to the original question—How many people are homosexual and

---

[4]For females, this figure depended quite a bit on marital status. Kinsey estimated that only about 3 percent of married women, but 26 percent of single women, have overt homosexual experiences.

how many are heterosexual?—is complex. Probably about 75 percent of men and 85 percent of women are exclusively heterosexual. About 2 percent of men and slightly less than 1 percent of women are exclusively homosexual. And the remaining 25 percent of men and 15 percent of women have had varying amounts of both heterosexual and homosexual experience.

SEXUAL ORIENTATION: IMPLICATIONS FOR ADJUSTMENT

As I noted earlier, many Americans consider the homosexual to be sick. Is this really true? Do psychologists and psychiatrists agree that homosexuals are poorly adjusted or deviant? Does research on homosexuality confirm the notion that the homosexual is sick? What are the implications of sexual orientation for a person's adjustment?

Sin and the Medical Model

Actually, the belief that homosexuality is a sickness is something of an improvement over previous beliefs about homosexuality. Before this century, the dominant belief in Europe and the United States was that homosexuality was a sin or a heresy. During the Inquisition, those accused of being heretics were also frequently accused of being homosexuals and were burned at the stake. Indeed, in those times, all mental illness was regarded as a sin. In the twentieth century, this view was replaced by the medical model, in which mental disturbance, and homosexuality in particular, is viewed as a sickness or illness. This view is widely held now by the general public.

Medical model: A theoretical model in psychology and psychiatry in which mental problems are thought of as sickness or mental illness; the problems in turn are often thought to be due to biological factors.

Psychiatrist Thomas Szasz and others are critical of the medical model. In his well-known writing on "the myth of mental illness," Szasz argues that the medical model is now obsolete and that we need to develop a more humane and realistic way of dealing with mental disorders and variations from the norm. He has argued the case particularly for homosexuality (Szasz, 1965). Gay liberationists have joined in, saying that they do not like being called "sick" and that this is just another form of persecution of homosexuals.

Research Results

Theoretical and rhetorical approaches to the question are clearly diverse. What do the scientific data say? Once again, the answers provided by the data are complex and depend on the assumptions of the particular investigator and the research design used. Basically, three kinds of research designs have been used, representing progressive sophistication and changing assumptions about the nature of homosexuality (see Rosen, 1974, for a review).

Clinical Studies

The first, and earliest, approach was clinical; homosexuals who were in psychotherapy were studied by the investigator (usually the therapist). He or she looked for disturbances in their current adjustment or in past experiences or homelife. The data were then reported in the form of a case history of a single individual or a report of common factors that seemed to emerge in studying a group of homosexuals (for example, Freud, 1920; see also the review by Rosen, 1974). These clinical studies provided evidence that the homosexual was sick or abnormal; she or he typically was found to be poorly adjusted and neurotic. But the reasoning behind this research was clearly circular. The homosexual was assumed to be sick, and then evidence was found supporting this view.

Studies with Control Groups

The second group of studies made significant improvements over the previous ones by introducing control groups. The question under investigation was rephrased. Rather than "Do homosexuals have psychological disturbances?" (after all, most of us have some problems) it became "Do homosexuals have more psychological disturbances than heterosexuals?" The research design then involved comparing a group of homosexuals in therapy with a group of randomly chosen heterosexuals not in therapy or perhaps with a group of heterosexuals matched with the homosexuals on some variables like age and education. These studies tended to agree with the earlier ones in finding more problems of adjustment among the homosexual group than among the heterosexual group (Rosen, 1974). The homosexuals tended to make more suicide attempts, to be more neurotic, and to have more disturbed family constellations. Once again, though, it became apparent that there were some problems with this research design. It compared a group of people in therapy with a group of people not in therapy and found, not surprisingly, that the people in therapy had more problems. It, too, was circular in assuming that homosexuals were abnormal (in therapy) and that heterosexuals were normal (not in therapy) and then finding exactly that. Of course, the investigator used the homosexuals in therapy as subjects at least in part because they were convenient, but this does not help to make the results any more accurate.

Nonpatient Research

Nonpatient research: Research in which groups of heterosexuals and homosexuals are compared, neither group being patients in psychotherapy.

A major breakthrough came with the third group of studies, which involved nonpatient research. In these studies, a group of homosexuals not in therapy (nonpatients) were compared with a group of heterosexuals not in therapy. The nonpatient homosexuals were generally recruited through homophile organizations, advertisments, or word of mouth. The results of these studies are mixed, but the general results seem to indicate that nonpatient homosexuals do not differ from nonpatient heterosexuals in their adjustment (see the review by Rosen, 1974). As a psychiatrist who has reviewed the literature on adjustment differences between homosexual and heterosexual women concluded, "The only difference between the lesbian and other women is the choice of love object" (Rosen, 1974, p. 65; see also Siegelman, 1979; and for similar results with male homosexuals, see Evans, 1970; J. H. Gagnon and Simon, 1973; Green, 1972).

Bell and Weinberg (1978) found similar results in their study. Lesbians and heterosexual women did not differ on most measures of psychological adjustment. Gay men were somewhat less self-accepting and more lonely, depressed, and tense than straight men. However, Bell and Weinberg's analysis of the variety of types of homosexual experience is helpful in understanding this difference. It is mostly the dysfunctionals and asexuals who are less well off psychologically. Among men, close-coupleds cannot be distinguished from heterosexuals on adjustment measures, and they actually scored higher on happiness. It seems clear that homosexuality per se does not cause adjustment difficulties—of more importance may be failure or success at establishing a long-term relationship with a partner.

Psychologist Evelyn Hooker did an important study that sheds considerable light on the question of differences in adjustment between heterosexuals and homosexuals. The assumption that the homosexual is sick or poorly adjusted implies that there are considerable psychological differences between heterosexuals and homosexuals. If this is the case, such differences should be indicated on standard personality tests. Hooker (1957) obtained data on 30 overt, nonpatient male homosexuals and on a group of 30 male heterosexuals matched for age, education, and IQ. The homosexuals were exclusively homosexual, except for three who had had very minimal heterosexual experience. The heterosexuals, similarly, were exclusively heterosexual, except for three who had each had one homosexual experience. Hooker administered the Rorschach, a projective test, to all subjects. The Rorschach was used because it is considered a good measure of total personality and is sometimes used in the "diagnosis" of homosexuality. In the first phase of the experiment, the Rorschach responses were arranged in random order and were given to two highly skilled clinicians for interpretation. The clinicians assigned an adjustment rating from 1 (superior) to 5 (maladjusted) to each profile. According to these ratings, there were no differences in the adjustment of the homosexuals as compared with that of the heterosexuals; about two-thirds of each group were well adjusted. In the second phase, the clinicians received the profiles in the matched pairs and were asked to identify which of each pair was the heterosexual and which was the homosexual. One clinician identified 17 of the 30 pairs correctly, while the other was accurate for 18 of the 30. Since one would expect accuracy for 15 of the 30 merely by chance, the clinicians did not do better than chance in identifying the homosexuals and the heterosexuals. Apparently, even the skilled clinician cannot tell the gay

FIGURE 16.5

Gay social issues: (*a*) Lesbian mothers want the right to keep their children; (*b*) the right to adoption—David Frater (right) has been permitted to adopt a teenage son.

(*a*)

(*b*)

from the straight without a scorecard. The notion that the homosexual has a disturbed personality receives no support in the results of this study.

While research fails to provide evidence that the homosexual is less well adjusted than the heterosexual, gay activist psychologist Mark Freedman has argued that homosexuals are *better* adjusted than heterosexuals. In the face of social pressures against them, gays may engage in "centering"—an intense developing of one's personal identity. In one study comparing lesbians with matched controls, the lesbians were higher on autonomy, spontaneity, and sensitivity to one's own needs and feelings (M. Freedman, 1975). A similar study found lesbians to be more independent, resilient, and self-sufficient (Hopkins, 1969). Freedman also believes that gays deal better with gender roles. Lesbians, for example, are better at accepting their own natural aggressiveness and assertiveness. Gay men are better at expressing tenderness. Finally, the process of coming out may encourage better self-knowledge as well as candor. According to personality tests such as the Minnesota Multiphasic Personality Inventory (MMPI), gays tell fewer lies than straights (M. Freedman, 1975; Horstman, 1972). Thus, according to Freedman, gays are healthier than straights.

On the basis of these studies, it must be concluded that the evidence does not support the notion that the homosexual is "sick" or poorly adjusted. This position has received official professional recognition by the American Psychiatric Association. Prior to 1973, the APA had listed homosexuality as a disorder under Section V, "Personality Disorders and Certain Other Nonpsychotic Mental Disorders," in its authoritative *Diagnostic and Statistical Manual of Mental Disorders.* In 1973, the APA voted to remove homosexuality from that listing; thus it is no longer considered a psychiatric disorder.

Therapy for Homosexuality

Related to the question of whether homosexuality is a sickness is the issue of whether the homosexual should receive psychotherapy (Coleman, 1982; Davison, 1982). The psychologist's or psychiatrist's answer to this question would depend on which one of a number of theoretical models (to be discussed in the next section) he or she operated under. A psychoanalyst, for example, would probably consider homosexuality to be abnormal and would recommend psychoanalysis to "cure" it.

Sexual dissatisfaction: Masters and Johnson's term for homosexuals who are unhappy with their sexual orientation and seek therapy to become heterosexual.

Masters and Johnson (1979) use the term sexual dissatisfaction to refer to homosexuals who seek therapy to become heterosexual. They treated 54 males and 13 females for this, using behavioral techniques similar to those described in Chapter 20. The report of the results of this therapy created much of the controversy over their book on homosexuality. Traditionally, psychologists have achieved a cure rate of only 10 to 20 percent in "converting" gays to straights. Masters and Johnson, however, reported a failure rate of 21 percent immediately after therapy and 28 percent five years after therapy, translating to a 72 percent success rate. It was this high success rate that created the controversy over the book. If one can change gays into straights, this has enormous implications in many areas—for example, a school principal might order a homosexual teacher to get therapy and become a heterosexual or be fired.

This research is subject to much the same criticism as that made in Chapter 20. For example, Masters and Johnson often do not define clearly what they mean by a "success" or "failure." Low motivation has often been pinpointed as the cause of the traditional low success rate for therapy for sexual dissatisfaction; Masters and Johnson carefully screened applicants for therapy and probably kept only those with very high motivation. And many of their "homosexuals" might more accurately have been described as bisexuals.

This whole concept of therapy for homosexuality, however, conflicts with the conclusion made earlier that homosexuality is not abnormal. If there is nothing wrong with homosexuality, trying to "cure" it makes no sense. Ethical issues are raised as well: should a person be changed from a homosexual to a heterosexual against his or her will? Perhaps the best resolution to this problem is that if a person freely requests therapy to help stop being a homosexual because the homosexual behavior is causing emotional distress, then the person should receive it, particularly in light of the fact that living as a homosexual in our society is difficult and that this alone might be sufficient reason for seeking therapy (but see Davison, 1976). Otherwise, there is no need for therapy.

WHY DO PEOPLE BECOME HOMOSEXUAL OR HETEROSEXUAL?

A fascinating psychological question is: Why do people become homosexual or heterosexual? Several theoretical answers to this question, as well as the results of empirical research on it, are discussed below. You will notice that the older theorists and researchers considered it their task to explain homosexuality; more recent investigators, realizing that heterosexuality needs to be explained as well, are more likely to consider it their task to explain sexual orientation.

Biological Theories

There has been some speculation that homosexuality might be caused by biological factors. The likeliest candidates for these biological causes are endocrine imbalance, prenatal doses of inappropriate hormones, and genetic factors.

Hormonal Imbalance

Investigating the possibility that endocrine imbalance is the cause, many researchers have tried to determine whether the testosterone ("male" hormone) levels of male homosexuals differ from those of male heterosexuals. Recent studies fail to find any hormonal differences between male homosexuals and male heterosexuals (see Rose, 1975; Meyer-Bahlburg, 1980). Of the 12 studies of testosterone levels in male homosexuals published since 1971, 8 found no significant differences between heterosexuals and homosexuals, 2 found heterosexuals to have higher levels of testosterone, and 2 found homosexuals to have higher levels (Gartrell, 1982).

Despite these results, some clinicians have attempted to cure male homosexuality by administering testosterone therapy (Glass and Johnson, 1944). This therapy fails; indeed, it seems to result in even more homosexual behavior than usual. This is not an unexpected result, since, as was seen in Chapter 8, androgen levels seem to be related to sexual responsiveness. As a clinician friend of mine replied to an undergraduate male who was seeking testosterone therapy for his homosexual behavior, "It won't make you heterosexual; it will only make you horny."

Other, more complex kinds of hormonal differences between heterosexuals and homosexuals are also being explored (e.g., Gladue et al., 1984); however, it is too early to be able to conclude much from these studies.

Virtually all these hormone studies have been done on male homosexuals. The two available studies on lesbians did find higher testosterone levels and lower estrogen levels among them than among a control group of heterosexual women (Loraine et al., 1971; Gartrell et al., 1977). The results have not been replicated yet, and so they should be viewed cautiously.

Prenatal Hormone Exposure

Another speculation about a possible biological cause is that homosexuality develops as a result of an exposure to inappropriate hormones during the prenatal period (Dörner, 1976). As was seen in Chapter 4, exposure to inappropriate hormones during fetal development can lead a genetic female to have male genitals, or a genetic male to have female genitals. It has been suggested that a similar process might account for homosexuality (and also for transsexualism—see Chapter 17). Direct evidence for this hypothesis has not been produced, and the indirect evidence is weak and contradictory (Gartrell, 1982; Ehrhardt et al., 1985), so this hypothesis must remain tentative.

Despite the flimsiness of the evidence for this theory, a program of psychosurgery derived from it was begun in West Germany. The idea was that inappropriate prenatal hormone exposure would have its effect on the hypothalamus, so that destruction of the corresponding part of the hypothalamus would "cure" homosexuality. A number of homosexuals were given this treatment, but a heated controversy arose, and there has been a moratorium on the surgery (Meyer-Bahlburg, 1980).

Genetic Factors

Franz Kallman (1952a, 1952b) has argued that there is a genetic predisposition to homosexuality, and he has provided data to support his claim. He found perfect concordance for homosexuality among all the identical-twin pairs he studied (that is, if one was a homosexual, so was the other). Among nonidentical twins the degree of concordance was not statistically significant. Numerous criticisms of this study could be made. The identical twins were all reared together, and thus they shared not only common genes but also a common environment. Therefore, environmental factors might explain the similarities. Further, nonidentical twins are not genetically unrelated; they share, on the average, half of their genes. Hence if homosexuality were genetic, one would expect a moderate degree of concordance for them. Other investigators have failed to replicate Kallman's findings (Heston and Shields, 1968). Thus the genetic explanation for homosexuality is not generally accepted. Indeed, from a geneticist's point of view, the genetic hypothesis about homosexuality makes little sense. If homosexuality were genetically controlled, one could hardly imagine a trait against which natural selection would act more strongly. Suppose that Mr. X carries the gene or genes for homosexuality and is therefore a homosexual. Because he is a homosexual he will not have children, and therefore his genes will not be passed on to the next generation. Thus genes for homosexuality, if they existed, would quickly be removed from circulation. This does not argue against the possibility of a genetic predisposition to bisexuality, however. The bisexual would engage in homosexual behavior but would also engage in heterosexual behavior and, through the heterosexual behavior, could reproduce and pass the genes on.

In conclusion, there is little evidence supporting any of the biological hypotheses—hormonal imbalance, prenatal hormone exposure, or genetic factors—regarding the causes of homosexuality (Gartrell, 1982). In a sense, these biological explanations were doomed to failure from the very beginning, since they assume that homosexual and heterosexual are two distinct diagnostic categories and then attempt to explain why a person becomes a member of the homosexual category. But as has already been noted, heterosexual and homosexual are not two separate categories, and thus the basic assumption of the biological approaches is open to question.

Psychoanalytic Theory

Freudian Theory

Since Freud believed sex to be the primary motivating force in human behavior, it is not surprising that he concerned himself with sexual orientation and its development (his classic work on the subject is *Three Essays on the Theory of Sexuality,* published in 1910).

Polymorphous perverse: Freud's term for the infant's indiscriminate, undifferentiated sexuality.

According to Freud, the infant is polymorphous perverse; that is, the infant's sexuality is totally undifferentiated and is therefore directed at all sorts of objects, both appropriate and inappropriate. As the child grows up and matures into an adult, sexuality is increasingly directed toward "appropriate" objects (members of the other gender), while the desire for "inappropriate" objects (for example, members of the same gender) is increasingly repressed. Therefore, according to Freud. the homosexual is fixated at an immature stage of development.

Negative Oedipus complex: Freud's term for the opposite of the Oedipus complex; in the negative Oedipus complex the child loves and sexually desires the parent of the same gender and identifies with the parent of the opposite gender.

According to Freud, homosexuality also stems from the negative Oedipus complex In the (positive) Oedipus complex, discussed in Chapter 2, the child loves the parent of the opposite gender but eventually gives this up and comes to identify with the parent of the same gender, thereby acquiring a sense of gender identity. In the negative Oedipus complex, things are just the opposite: the child loves the parent of the same gender and identifies with the parent of the opposite gender. For example, in the negative Oedipus complex, a little boy would love his father and identify with his mother. In the process of maturation, once again, the child is supposed to repress this negative Oedipus complex. The homosexual person, however, fails to repress it and remains fixated on it. Thus according to Freud, for example, a woman becomes a homosexual because of a continuing love for her mother and identification with her father. In Freud's view, homosexuality is a continuation of love for the parent of the same gender.

Consistent with Freud's belief that the infant is polymorphous perverse was his belief that all humans are inherently bisexual; that is, he believed that all people have the capacity for both heterosexual and homosexual behavior. Thus he viewed homosexuality as very possible, if not desirable. This notion of inherent bisexuality also led to the concept of the *latent homosexual,* the person with a repressed homosexual component.

Bieber's Research

Because Freud had such a great influence on psychiatric thought, he inspired a great deal of theorizing and research, in particular on homosexuality. Irving Bieber and his colleagues (1962) did one of the more important of these psychoanalytically inspired studies. They compared 106 male homosexuals with 100 male heterosexuals; all the subjects were in psychoanalysis, which makes the results somewhat questionable. The family pattern that Bieber and his colleagues tended to find among the homosexuals was that of a dominant mother and a weak or passive father. The mother was both overprotective and overly intimate. Bieber thus originated the concept of the homoseductive mother as an explanation of male homosexuality. This family pattern, according to Bieber, has a double effect: the man later fears heterosexual relations both because of his mother's jealous possessiveness and because her seductiveness produced anxiety. Bieber thus suggested that homosexuality results, in part, from fears of heterosexuality. While Bieber's findings on the homoseductive mother have received a great deal of attention, a more striking find-

Homoseductive mother: Bieber's term for the mother who is seductive toward her son, traumatizing the boy and turning him into a homosexual.

ing in his research was of a seriously disturbed relationship between the homosexual male and his father (Bieber, 1976). The fathers were described as detached and/or openly hostile; thus the homosexual son emerged into adulthood hating and fearing his father and yet deeply wanting the father's love and affection.

Wolff's Research

Charlotte Wolff, a British psychiatrist, has carried out a similar program of research and theorizing about the origins of lesbianism (1971). She studied over 100 non-patient lesbians, comparing them with a control group of heterosexual women matched for family background, profession, and social class. The family characteristics that were more frequent among the homosexual women than among the heterosexual women were a rejecting or indifferent mother and a distant or absent father. Wolff theorized that lesbianism results from the girl's receiving inadequate love from the mother; as a result, she continues, throughout her life, to seek that missing love in other women. Secondarily, because her father was distant or absent, she may not have learned to relate to men.

Evaluation of Psychoanalytic Theories

Psychoanalytic theories of the genesis of homosexuality clearly operate under the assumption that homosexuality is deviant or abnormal. As Irving Bieber writes:

> We consider homosexuality to be a pathologic, bio-social, psycho-sexual adaptation to pervasive fears surrounding the expression of heterosexual impulses. (Bieber et al., 1962, p. 22).
>
> All psychoanalytic theories assume that adult homosexuality is psycho-pathologic. (Bieber et al., 1962, p. 18)

Actually, in his later writings Freud came to consider homosexuality to be within the normal range of variation of sexual behavior; this view, however, appears not to have had much of an impact, compared with that of his earlier writings on the subject. Psychoanalytic theory could thus be criticized for the abnormality assumption, since, as has been seen, there is no strong evidence for the notion that the homosexual is poorly adjusted.

The psychoanalytic approach can also be criticized for its confusion of the concepts of "gender identity" and "choice of sexual partner." As was previously noted, the homosexual differs from the heterosexual in choice of sexual partner but not in gender identification: the male homosexual generally has a masculine identification, and the lesbian has a feminine identification. Psychoanalytic theory, however, assumes that the homosexual not only makes an inappropriate object choice but also has an abnormal gender identification—that the male homosexual has not identified with his father and has therefore not acquired a masculine identity and that the lesbian has not identified with her mother and has therefore not acquired a feminine identity. This basic assumption of abnormal gender identification is not supported by the data and is therefore another basis for criticizing psychoanalytic theories of homosexuality.

Learning Theory

Behaviorists emphasize the importance of learning in the development of sexual orientation. They note the prevalence of bisexual behavior both in other species and in young humans, and they argue that rewards and punishments must shape the individual's behavior into predominant homosexuality or predominant heterosexuality. The assumption, then, is that humans have a relatively amorphous, undifferentiated pool of sex drive which, depending on circumstances (rewards and punishments), may be channeled in any of several directions. In short, people are born sexual, not heterosexual or homosexual. Only through learning does one of these behaviors become more likely than the other. For example, a person who has early heterosexual experiences that are very unpleasant might develop toward homosexuality. Heterosexuality has essentially been punished and therefore becomes less likely. This might occur, for instance, in the case of a girl who is raped at an early age; her first experience with heterosexual sex was extremely unpleasant, and so she avoids it and turns to homosexuality. Parents who become upset about their teenagers' heterosexual activities might do well to remember this notion; punishing a young person for engaging in heterosexual behavior may not eliminate the behavior but rather rechannel it in a homosexual direction.

Another possibility, according to a learning-theory approach, is that if early sexual experiences are homosexual and pleasant, the person may become a homosexual. Homosexual behavior has essentially been rewarded and therefore becomes more likely.

The learning-theory approach treats homosexuality as a normal form of behavior and recognizes that heterosexuality is not necessarily inborn but must also, like homosexuality, be learned. There is a problem with the learning theory approach, however (Whitam, 1977). The rewards in our society go overwhelmingly to heterosexuality. Society gives few rewards to homosexuality, and often punishes it. Why, then, does anyone become homosexual? While human sexual behavior is no doubt determined in part by reinforcement contingencies, it probably also has much more complex determinants which are not yet understood.

Interestingly, though, preliminary research indicates that children who grow up with a homosexual parent are not themselves likely to become gay (Green, 1978). In this sense, then, homosexuality is not "learned" from parents.

Interactionist Theory

Storms: Maturation Rates

Psychologist Michael Storms (1981; see also Bermant, 1972) has proposed a theory of the development of erotic orientation in which the rate of sexual maturation in adolescence is seen as the critical factor. According to this theory, most people develop the sex drive in early adolescence, around the ages of 12 to 15. It is at that time that certain stimuli (e.g., a member of the same or the opposite gender) become conditioned to be arousing or erotic. As we descussed in Chapter 11, homosocial patterns (same-gender friendships and groups) predominate in preadolescence, reaching a peak at around age 12. Heterosexual interactions begin to emerge after that time, and most people have begun heterosexual dating by age 15. According to Storms, homosexuality results when individuals have an early maturing sex drive, at about age 12 when they are still in homosocial groupings, so that erotic conditioning is more likely to focus on members of their own gender with whom they spend time, since heterosexuality has not yet emerged as an alternative. Those whose sex drive emerges later are already immersed in a heterosexual culture of dating and friendships, so that they eroticize heterosexual experiences.

Supporting Storms's theory, data show that homosexual women are earlier sexual maturers than heterosexual women, as measured by age of beginning to masturbate, age of earliest feelings of sexual arousal, and age of first sexual fantasizing (Goode and Haber, 1977; Saghir and Robins, 1973).

This theory provides an explanation for why there are more men than women who have engaged in homosexual activity and who are exclusively homosexual: the sex drive in males emerges earlier, as evidenced by the earlier appearance and more frequent masturbation of adolescent males (see Chapter 11). Thus males are more likely to experience the development of the sex drive while they are still in homosocial groupings. Females are more likely to experience the emergence of their sex drive later, after heterosexuality has become the norm in their lives.

In terms of the nature-nurture controversy, Storms's theory can be viewed as an interactionist theory. That is, it integrates biological factors (biological maturation of the sex drive) with environmental factors (social patterns and interactions). One virtue of Storms's theory is that it is not based on an assumption that homosexuality is pathological. Rather, it seeks to explain both homosexuality and heterosexuality in terms of maturational patterns. The theory is very recent and so it will take some time to accumulate enough data to determine its strengths and weaknesses.

Sociological Theory

Sociologists emphasize the effects of *labeling* in explaining homosexuality. The label "homosexual" has a big impact in our society. If you are a heterosexual, suppose that someone said to you, "I think that you are a homosexual." How would you react? Your immediate reaction would probably be negative: anger, anxiety, and embarrassment. The label "homosexual" has derogatory connotations and may even be used as an insult. This reflects our society's negative attitudes toward homosexuality.

A clever experiment demonstrated the effects of labeling someone a homosexual. Half of the subjects (all men) were led to believe that a particular member of their group was a homosexual. For the other half of the subjects (the control group), the man was not labeled. Subjects in the experimental group, in which the man was labeled, rated him as being significantly less clean, softer, more womanly, more tense, more yielding, more impulsive, less rugged, more passive, and quieter (Karr, 1978). Thus labeling a person a homosexual does influence people's perception of that person.

But the label "homosexual" may also act as a self-fulfilling prophecy. Suppose that a young boy—possibly because he is slightly effeminate, because he is poor in sports, or for no reason at all—is called a "homosexual." He reacts strongly and becomes more and more anxious and worried about his problem. He becomes painfully aware of the slightest homosexual tendency in himself. Finally he convinces himself that he is a homosexual. He begins engaging in homosexual behavior and associates with a gay group. In short, a homosexual has been created.

Sociologists also emphasize the importance of *roles* in explaining human behavior. Homosexuality might be a role people play, much like the male role or the female role (Goode, 1981; McIntosh, 1968; M. S. Weinberg and Williams, 1974). This view helps explain the apparent ease with which many homosexuals pass for heterosexuals in the straight world. They simply play the heterosexual role in certain situations and the homosexual role in others. Actually, there are two homosexual roles (Goode, 1981). One is the derogatory role ascribed to gays in American culture—limp wrists and so on. The other is the homosexual role defined by the gay subculture. In the developmental process of coming out, both these roles are important in shaping the gay person's identity.

FIGURE 16.6

Victor/Victoria: Homosexuality has received more open coverage in recent movies.

Empirical Data

Theoretical positions on the origins of sexual orientation are many and varied. Some of the various explanations that have been proposed for lesbianism alone include:

> . . . fear of growing up and assuming adult responsibilities; fear of dominance and destruction; fear of rejection; fear of the opposite sex; fear of castration and of the penis; the desire to conquer and possess the mother; neurotic dependency; heterosexual trauma (including rape); seduction in adolescence by an older female; first sexual experience with someone of the same sex and finding it pleasurable; tomboy behavior in early childhood; prolonged absence of the mother; masturbation with resulting clitoral fixation; social factors (such as heterosexual taboos and unisexual, all female, groups); and physical factors (genetic, constitutional, and endocrine abnormalities). (Rosen, 1974, p. 8)

Do any of these proposed explanations have a basis in fact? Unfortunately, most of the investigators who have collected data on the previous experiences of homosexuals have operated from a particular theoretical conviction; they then tended to obtain data supporting the theory in which they believed. Many of the early studies also have the problems of design mentioned in the discussion of whether homosexuality is abnormal. Many of the studies have been of either the first type (homosexuals in therapy, with no comparison group) or the second type (homosexuals in therapy compared with heterosexuals). Thus results of those studies should be interpreted cautiously.

Further, when studies do find differences between homosexuals and heterosexuals, the factors are generally not common enough among the homosexuals to make them the "explanation" of homosexuality. A good example is Charlotte Wolff's (1971) study of lesbians. Mothers of lesbians were more frequently indifferent or negligent, but indifference was characteristic of only 27 percent of the mothers of lesbians (as compared with 10 percent of the mothers of controls), and negligence was characteristic of only 10 percent of the mothers of lesbians (as compared with 0 percent of the mothers of controls). Hence, while maternal negligence and indifference are more common among lesbians, they certainly do not explain all cases of lesbianism.

The most comprehensive recent study of the causes of sexual orientation was done by Alan Bell, Martin Weinberg, and Sue Hammersmith, of the Kinsey Institute (1981). They interviewed 979 homosexual men and women and a comparison sample of 477 heterosexual men and women, all in San Francisco. The interviews, which took three to five hours, included approximately 200 questions about the person's childhood and adolescence; the questions were designed specifically to allow the researchers to test all of the major theories that have been proposed as explanations for the development of homosexuality. In general, their results indicated that all of the environmental explanations are inadequate and are not supported by the data. Specifically, they concluded that:

1. The notion that disturbed parental relationships are influential—as proposed in psychoanalytic theory—is grossly exaggerated. Parental relationships seem to make little or no difference in whether one becomes heterosexual or homosexual.
2. The sociologists' notion that homosexuality results from labeling by others received no support from the data.
3. The notion—proposed by learning theory—that homosexuality results from early unpleasant heterosexual experience received no support. For example, lesbians were no more likely to have been raped than heterosexual women were.
4. The idea—proposed by learning theory—that homosexuality might result from a boy or girl being seduced by an older member of their own gender (an early positive homosexual experience) also was not supported.

Having shot down all the standard theories, Bell, Weinberg, and Hammersmith did reach some positive conclusions. Two are especially important.

1. Sexual preference seems to be determined before adolescence. This would be important if, for example, it was discovered that the high school football coach was gay. According to Bell and his colleagues, parents and the principal should not worry that he will be a "bad influence" on the team members; their sexual preference is already determined.
2. There is likely a biological basis for homosexuality. The researchers reached this conclusion because none of the standard environmental explanations was supported by the data. They actually collected no biological data (e.g., measuring hormone levels). Thus this conclusion amounts to no more than speculation, although it received a great deal of publicity.

In summary, when all the studies in this area are surveyed, no single factor emerges consistently as a cause of male homosexuality or of lesbianism (the two might have different causes). To be blunt, we do not know what causes homosexuality. But there may be a good theoretical lesson to be learned from this somewhat frustrating statement. It has generally been assumed not only that homosexuals form a distinct category (which, as has already been seen, is not very accurate) but also that they form a homogeneous category, that is, that all homosexuals are fairly similar. Probably this is not true. Probably there are many different kinds or "types" of homosexuals. Indeed, one psychologist, expressing this notion, has suggested that we should refer not to "homosexuality" but rather to "the homosexualities" (A. P. Bell, 1974b; Bell and Weinberg, 1978). If this is the case, then one would not expect a single "cause" of homosexuality but rather many causes, each corresponding to its type. The next step in research, then, should be to identify the various types of homosexuals—not to mention the various kinds of heterosexuals—and the different kinds of development that lead to each.

BISEXUALITY

Here is a riddle: What is like a bridge that touches both shores but doesn't meet in the middle? The answer: Research and theories on sexual orientation (MacDonald, 1982; you'll have to admit that this is classier than the average riddle). The point of the riddle is that scientists, as well as lay people, focus on heterosexuals and homosexuals, ignoring all the bisexuals in between.

Bisexual:
A person who has sex sometimes with men and sometimes with women.

A bisexual is a person who has sex sometimes with men and sometimes with women, that is, sometimes with a member of the same gender and sometimes with a member of the opposite gender. Such a person is clearly not exclusively heterosexual or exclusively homosexual. He or she is called *bisexual* or, in slang, "ac-dc" (alternating current-direct current). Some scientists also call such a person ambisexual

Ambisexual:
Another term for bisexual.

Bisexuality has become something of a fad, particularly on the East and West coasts. In some large cities there are "bi" bars, where one can see both same-gender and opposite-gender pairs dancing together and having a good time.

Bisexuality is really not at all rare; in fact, it is far more common than exclusive homosexuality (if a "bisexual" is defined as a person who has had at least one sexual experience with a male and one with a female). For example, earlier in this chapter it was noted that about 75 percent of all males are exclusively heterosexual and that about 2 percent are exclusively homosexual. That leaves a large number, perhaps 25 percent, who are bisexual according to the definition stated above.

The proponents of bisexuality argue that it has some strong advantages. It allows more variety in one's sexual and human relationships than either exclusive heterosexuality or exclusive homosexuality. The bisexual does not rule out any possibilities and is open to the widest possible variety of experiences, characteristics which are highly valued by today's young people.

On the other hand, the bisexual may be viewed with suspicion or downright hostility by the gay community (Blumstein and Schwartz, 1976). Radical lesbians refer to bisexual women as "fence sitters," saying that they betray the lesbian cause because they can pretend to be heterosexual when it is convenient and homosexual when is it convenient. Some gays even argue that there is no such thing as a true bisexual.

A consideration of the phenomenon of bisexuality will help illuminate several theoretical points and also provide some insights into homosexuality and heterosexuality. First, though, several concepts need to be clarified. A distinction has already been made between sex (sexual behavior) and gender (being male or female) and between gender identity (the male's association with the male role and the female's association with the female role) and choice of sexual partner (heterosexual, homosexual, or bisexual). To this, the concept of sexual identity should be added; this refers to one's self-label or self-identification as a heterosexual, homo-

Sexual identity:
One's self-identity as homosexual, heterosexual, or bisexual.

sexual, or bisexual.[5] Sexual identity, then, is the person's concept of herself or himself as a heterosexual, homosexual, or bisexual.

Strangely, there may be contradictions between people's sexual identity (which is clearly subjective) and their actual choice of sexual partners viewed objectively. Sociologists Philip Blumstein and Pepper Schwartz (1974) have conducted perhaps the largest program of research on bisexuals, and they have provided some good examples of these contradictions. For example, one of their subjects identified herself as a lesbian, and yet occasionally she sleeps with men. Objectively, her choice of sexual partners is bisexual, but she sees herself as a lesbian. More common are persons who think of themselves as heterosexuals but who engage in both heterosexual and homosexual sex. A good example of this is the tearoom trade—the successful, heterosexually married men in gray flannel suits who occasionally stop off at a public rest room to have another male perform fellatio on them. Once again, the behavior is objectively bisexual, in contradiction with the heterosexual identity. Another example is the group of women who claim to have bisexual identities but who have experienced only heterosexual sex, and never homosexual sex. These women, often as a result of feminist beliefs, claim bisexuality as an ideal which they are capable of attaining at some later time. Once again, identity contradicts behavior.

Just as we recognized a diversity of types of homosexuals, so there is a diversity of bisexuals (MacDonald, 1982). Some bisexuals, referred to as 50:50 bisexuals, have equal preferences for men and for women. Other bisexuals have a preference for one gender but are accepting of sex with the other gender. Some bisexuals are sequentially bisexual, whereas others are simultaneously bisexual; that is, some have only one lover at a time, sometimes a man and sometimes a woman, whereas other bisexuals have both a male and a female lover at the same time. And finally, some bisexuals are transitory bisexuals, passing through a bisexual phase on the way to becoming exclusively homosexual or heterosexual, whereas others are enduring bisexuals, maintaining their bisexual preferences throughout their lifespan.

The available data on bisexual development (see the Focus about a bisexual woman) suggest several important points. First, they argue for the importance of late-occurring experiences in the shaping of one's sexual behavior and identity. As has been seen, most of the research on the development of homosexuality rests on the assumption that it is somehow determined by pathological conditions in childhood. Yet some females, as the story of the woman in the Focus illustrates, have their first homosexual encounter at age 30 or 40. It is difficult to believe that these behaviors were determined by some pathological conditions to which such women were exposed at age 5. Human behavior can be modified at any time through the lifespan. Deprivation homosexuality, or situational homosexuality, is also a good example of this. A heterosexual man who enters prison may engage in homosexual behavior and then return to heterosexuality after his release. Once again, it seems likelier that such a man's homosexual behavior was determined by his circumstances (being in prison) than by some problem with his Oedipus complex 20 years before. Unlike gender identity, which seems to be fixed in the preschool years, sexual identity continues to evolve throughout one's lifetime (Riddle, 1978). This contradicts Bell, Weinberg, and Hammersmith's assertion that sexual orientation is determined before adolescence. I think it is still an open question when sexual preference is determined.

Deprivation homosexuality: Homosexual activity that occurs in certain situations, such as prisons, when people are deprived of their regular heterosexual activity.

---

[5]Clearly, the term "sexual identity" is not being used here the way it is generally used, which is to refer to one's sense of maleness or femaleness (for which the term "gender identity" is used in this book). However, it seems important to be able to talk about a person's sense that he or she is a heterosexual or a homosexual, and "sexual identity" seems the most likely term to use for that purpose.

F · O · C · U · S 16.3

JOAN, A BISEXUAL WOMAN

Joan, a professional woman in her middle thirties, considered herself exclusively heterosexual until about four years ago. Until that time she had never had homosexual fantasies or feelings, but she had been generally liberal about "sexual alternatives" and believed in equal rights for homosexuals. Four years ago, however, Joan became active in the women's liberation movement and developed closer friendships with some of the women with whom she worked. None of these relationships was sexualized, but her curiosity was aroused by sexual possibilities with women. Her approach to her own potential homosexual behavior was at this time still more intellectual than emotional and was not accompanied by graphic fantasies or feelings of attraction to other women whom she might meet or see in public.

During this period, Joan met another woman in her profession whom she found both intellectually and socially attractive. Vivian was also heterosexual, but she had had a few homosexual experiences. The relationship between the two women became closer, and during an exchange of confidences Joan learned that Vivian had had sexual experiences with women. At this point, Joan began to have sexual fantasies involving Vivian and began to be more overtly physical toward her, but she never crossed the bounds of female heterosexual friendship. The relationship intensified, and intimate discussions about sexuality turned to the possibility of sex between the two women. After about six months of such discussions, they slept together, first having overcome their initial worries concerning the effect that any guilt feelings about their "experimentation" might have on their friendship.

After the first successful sexual experience, Joan and Vivian repeated it approximately once every month for over a year. Vivian, however, continued to think of herself as a heterosexual, while Joan began to feel that she was in love with her friend and to want a more committed relationship. Joan stopped sleeping with Vivian when she realized that Vivian did not agree with her terms for the relationship. The two remained close friends, but Joan looked for someone else who might wish to share a committed relationship. She eventually fell in love with another woman, and an intense romantic and sexual relationship continued for two years. At the present, Joan is unsure of what sexual label to apply to herself, but she prefers "bisexual." At the time of her interview, she had both a male and a female lover.

Source: Philip W. Blumstein and Pepper Schwartz. (1976). Bisexual women. In J. P. Wiseman (Ed.), *The social psychology of sex*. New York: Harper & Row, pp. 154–162.

Second, a question is raised as to whether heterosexuality is really the "natural" state. The pattern in some theories has been to try to discover those pathological conditions which cause homosexuality (for example, a father who is an inadequate role model or a homoseductive mother)—all on the basis of the assumption that heterosexuality is the natural state and that homosexuality must be explained as a deviation from it. As we have seen, this approach has failed; there appear to be multiple causes of homosexuality, just as there are multiple causes of heterosexuality. The important alternative to consider is that bisexuality is the natural state, a point acknowledged both by Freud and by the behaviorists. This chapter will close, then, with some questions. Psychologically, the real question should concern not the pathological conditions that lead to homosexuality but rather the causes of exclusive homosexuality and exclusive heterosexuality. Why do we eliminate some people as potential sex partners simply on the basis of their gender? Why is it that everyone is not bisexual?

SUMMARY

Homosexual behavior is sexual behavior with a member of the same gender; it is considerably more complex to define what a "homosexual" is.

Homosexuals suffer from discrimination and from a number of derogatory stereotypes. The majority of Americans believe that homosexuals are suffering from a curable illness. Although one stereotype is that male homosexuals are effeminate and lesbians are mannish, this is not true; in most cases one cannot tell a homosexual from a heterosexual on the basis of appearance. The belief that male homosexuals tend to be child molesters is also not true. Discrimination against homosexuals can take many forms; gay people may lose their jobs when their sexual practices become known, and derogatory jokes about homosexuals are common.

The gay lifestyle includes gay bars and the baths. It is important to remember, however, that homosexuals are not all identical and that they differ as much among themselves as heterosexuals do. To describe this diversity, Bell and Weinberg say that there are five types of homosexual experience: close-coupled, open-coupled, functional, dysfunctional, and asexual. In regard to satisfaction and love, long-term homosexual relationships are much like long-term heterosexual relationships. Research on long-term gay relationships—some of 20 or more years duration—indicates that there are predictable stages in the development of gay relationships.

In order to describe the homosexual behavior of the people in his sample, Kinsey devised a seven-point scale ranging from 0 (exclusively heterosexual) through 6 (exclusively homosexual), with the midpoint of 3 representing equal amounts of heterosexual and homosexual experience. Probably about 25 percent of males have had a homosexual experience to orgasm (not counting childhood experiences). About 2 percent of males are exclusively homosexual. Among females, about 15 percent have had a homosexual experience to orgasm, and about 1 percent are exclusively homosexual.

Available data do not support the notion that homosexuals are poorly adjusted or "sick." Psychologically, they do not appear to differ substantially from heterosexuals except for their choice of sexual partner. The American Psychiatric Association no longer classifies homosexuality as a mental disorder.

Masters and Johnson have done therapy to change homosexuals to heterosexuals.

In regard to the causes of sexual orientation, biological explanations (endocrine imbalance, prenatal hormone exposure, and genetic factors) are not supported by the data. According to the psychoanalytic view, homosexuality results from a fixation at an immature stage of development and a persisting negative Oedipus complex. Learning theorists stress that the sex drive is undifferentiated and is channeled, through experience, into heterosexuality or homosexuality. Storms's interactionist theory proposes that homosexuality results when the sex drive matures while the preadolescent is still in homosocial groupings; heterosexuality results when the sex drive matures later and heterosexual socializing is the norm. Sociologists emphasize the importance of roles and labeling in understanding homosexuality. Available data do not point to any single factor as a cause of homosexuality but rather suggest that there may be many types of homosexuality ("homosexualities") with corresponding multiple causes.

Bisexuality is more common than exclusive homosexuality. A person's sexual identity may be discordant with his or her actual behavior. Bisexuality may be more "natural" than either exclusive heterosexuality or exclusive homosexuality.

REVIEW QUESTIONS

1. Attitudes toward homosexuality have become more liberal in recent years, so that now a majority of Americans believe that sexual relations between two adults of the same gender are not wrong. True or false?
2. _____ is the term for a strong, irrational fear of homosexuals and to fixed, negative attitudes to homosexuals.
3. Homosexual couples tend to have stereotyped gender roles; for example, in a lesbian couple, one generally plays the butch role and the other plays the femme role. True or false?
4. Approximately _____ percent of child molesting is heterosexual (men molesting girls) and _____ percent is homosexual (men molesting boys).
5. _____ is the term for casual sex in a public place such as a restroom.
6. The process of "coming out" involves acknowledging to oneself and then to others that one is homosexual. True or false?
7. Lesbians and gay men rate their relationships as highly satisfying. True or false?
8. According to Kinsey's scale, someone who is a "3" is exclusively heterosexual. True or false?
9. According to the Kinsey data, approximately 2 to 4 percent of males and 1 to 2 percent of females are exclusively homosexual. True or false?
10. According to nonpatient research, there are no significant differences in adjustment between heterosexuals and homosexuals. True or false?

QUESTIONS FOR THOUGHT, DISCUSSION, AND DEBATE

1. Debate the following topic. Resolved: Homosexuals should not be discriminated against in employment, even in such occupations as high school teaching.
2. Do you feel that you are homophobic, or do you feel that your attitude toward gays is positive? Why do you think your attitudes are the way they are? Are you satisfied with your attitudes or do you want to change them?

SUGGESTIONS FOR FURTHER READING

Clark, Don. (1978). *Loving someone gay.* New York: New American Library paperback. A therapist offers some excellent thoughts for those who are coming out and for friends and spouses of gay men and lesbian women.

Jay, Karla, and Young, Allen. (1979). *The gay report.* New York: Summit Books. A fascinating wealth of information is found in this survey of gays.

Kohn, Barry and Matusow, Alice. (1980). *Barry and Alice.* Englewood Cliffs, N.J.: Prentice-Hall. An autobiography of a bisexual married couple.

Martin, Del, and Lyon, Phyllis. (1972). *Lesbian/woman.* San Francisco: Glide Publications. Two lesbian activists discuss the lesbian lifestyle.

Peplau, Letitia Anne. (1981, Mar.) What homosexuals want in relationships. *Psychology Today,* **15**(3), 28–38. Some sophisticated social-psychological research that goes beyond the stereotypes.

Warren, Patricia. (1974). *The front runner.* New York: Morrow. A novel about a gay male track star and his lover, this has been called the gay *Love Story.* It is really much better than that, however.

Richard Lidner: *The Meeting*, 1953. Collection, The Museum of Modern Art, New York.

CHAPTER • 17

VARIATIONS IN SEXUAL BEHAVIOR

Some men love women, some love other men, some love dogs and horses, and occasionally you find one who loves his raincoat.*

* *Source:* Max Schulman. *I was a teen-age dwarf.*

CHAPTER HIGHLIGHTS

Most lay people, as well as most scientists, have a tendency to classify behavior as normal or abnormal. There seems to be a particular tendency to do this with regard to sexual behavior. Many terms are used for abnormal sexual behavior, including "sexual deviance," "perversion," "sexual variance," and "paraphilias." The term "sexual variations" will be used in this chapter because it is currently favored in scientific circles and because defining exactly what is "deviant" or what is a "perversion" is rather difficult.

In Chapter 16 I argued that homosexuality per se is not an abnormal form of sexual behavior. This chapter will deal with some behaviors that might more justifiably be considered abnormal, and so it seems advisable at this point to consider exactly when a sexual behavior is abnormal. That is, what is a reasonable set of criteria for deciding what kinds of sexual behavior are abnormal?

WHEN IS SEXUAL BEHAVIOR ABNORMAL?

Definitions and Criteria

As we saw in Chapter 1, sexual behavior varies a great deal from one culture to the next. There is a corresponding variation across cultures in what is considered to be "deviant" sexual behavior. Given this great variability, how can one come up with a reasonable set of criteria for what is deviant? Perhaps it is best to begin by considering the way others have defined "deviant" or "abnormal" sexual behavior.

One approach is to use a *statistical definition* (Pomeroy, 1966). According to this approach, a deviant sexual behavior is one that is rare, that is, one that is not practiced by many people. Following this definition, then, standing on one's hands while having intercourse would be considered deviant because it is rarely done, although it does not seem very "sick" in any absolute sense. This definition, unfortunately, does not give us much insight into the deviant person's psychological or social functioning.

In the *sociological approach,* the problem of culture dependence is explicitly acknowledged. A sociologist might define a deviant sexual behavior as a sexual behavior that violates the norms of society. Thus if a society says that a particular sexual behavior is deviant, it is—at least in that society. This approach recognizes the importance of the individual's interaction with society and of the problems that people must face if their behavior is labeled "deviant" in the culture in which they live.

A modern *psychological approach* was stated by Arnold Buss in his text entitled *Psychopathology* (1966). He says, "The three criteria of abnormality are discomfort, inefficiency, and bizarreness." The last of these criteria, bizarreness, has the problem of being culturally defined; what seems bizarre in one culture may seem normal in another. However, the first two criteria are good in that they focus on the discomfort and unhappiness felt by the person with a truly abnormal pattern of sexual behavior and also on inefficiency; for example, if a man has such a fetish for women's undies that he steals them, gets himself arrested, and cannot hold a job, that is inefficient functioning, and the behavior can reasonably be considered deviant.

Buss's definition is the one that will be used in this chapter: A sexual behavior is deviant or abnormal when it is uncomfortable for the person, inefficient, and/or bizarre. A fourth criterion should also be added: that of doing harm, either physically or psychologically, to oneself or others. But it is clearly a complex matter to define "deviant" or "abnormal," and for this reason the less value-laden term "sexual variations" is used in this chapter.

FETISHISM

Fetishism:
When a person becomes sexually fixated on some object other than another human being and attaches great erotic significance to that object.

One form of sexual variation is fetishism. In fetishism, a person becomes sexually fixated on some object other than another human being and attaches great erotic significance to that object. In extreme cases the person is incapable of becoming aroused and having an orgasm unless the fetish object is present. Typically, the fetish item is something closely associated with the body, such as clothing. Inanimate-object fetishes can be roughly divided into two subcategories: media fetishes and form fetishes.

Media Fetishes

Media fetish:
When the fetish object is anything made of a particular substance, such as leather.

In the media fetish, it is the material out of which an object is made that is important in its erotic value. An example would be a leather fetish, in which any leather item is arousing to the person. Media fetishes can be subdivided into hard media fetishes and soft media fetishes. In the hard media fetish, the fetish is for a hard substance, such as leather or rubber. Hard media fetishes may often be associated with sadomasochism (see below). In the soft media fetish, the substance is soft, such as fur or silk.

Form Fetishes

Form fetish:
When the fetish item is an object with a particular shape, such as high-heeled shoes.

In the form fetish, it is the object and its shape that are important. An example would be a shoe fetish, in which shoes are highly arousing (see the Focus). Often shoe fetishists require that the shoes be high-heeled; this fetish may be associated with sadomasochism, in which the fetishist derives sexual satisfaction from being walked on by a woman in high heels. Other examples of form fetishes are fetishes for boots (which also may be associated with sadomasochism), garters, and lingerie (almost all fetishists are men).

The Normal-Abnormal Continuum

Perhaps reading that being aroused by lingerie is deviant has made you rather uncomfortable because you yourself find lingerie arousing. Fetishes are discussed first in this chapter because they provide an excellent example of the continuum from normal to abnormal sexual behavior. That is, normal sexual behavior and abnormal sexual behavior (like other normal and abnormal behaviors) are not two separate categories but rather gradations on a continuum. Many people have mild fetishes—they find things such as silk underwear arousing—and that is well within the range of normal behavior; only when the fetish becomes extreme is it abnormal.

This continuum from normal to deviant behavior might be conceptualized using the scheme shown in Figure 17.1. A mild preference, or even a strong preference, for the fetish object (say, silk panties) is within the normal range of sexual behavior. When the silk panties have become an absolute necessity—when the man cannot become aroused and have intercourse unless they are present—then we have probably crossed the boundary into abnormal behavior. In extreme forms, the silk panties may become a substitute for a female sexual partner, and the man's sexual behavior consists of masturbating with the silk panties present. In these extreme forms, the man may commit burglary or even assault to get the desired fetish object (Karpman, 1954), and this would certainly fit our definition of abnormal sexual behavior.

The continuum from normal to abnormal behavior holds for many of the sexual variations discussed in this chapter, such as voyeurism, exhibitionism, and sadism.

FIGURE 17.1

The continuum from normal to abnormal behavior in the case of fetishes.

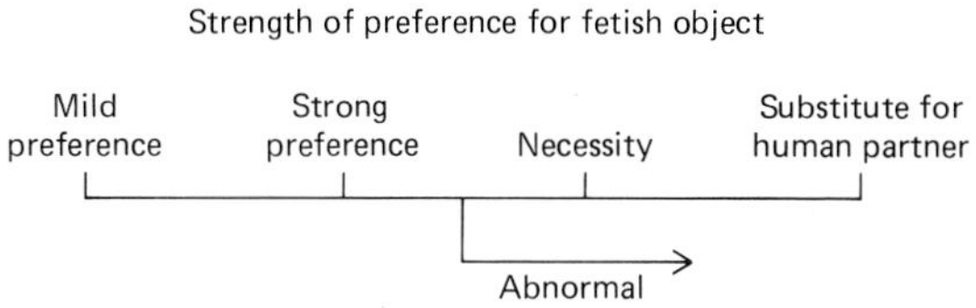

Why Do People Become Fetishists?

Psychologists are not completely sure what causes fetishes to develop. A likely explanation is based on learning theory (see, for example, McGuire et al., 1965). This approach would say that fetishes result from a learned association between the fetish object and sexual arousal and orgasm. In some cases a single learning trial might serve to cement the association. For example, a 12-year-old boy might masturbate to orgasm for the first time while standing on a fuzzy bathroom rug and ever after require fuzzy objects to become aroused. Another example appears to be the shoe fetishist described in the Focus. In this case, shoes were associated with sexual arousal as the result of an early learning experience. There is even an experiment that demonstrated that males could, in the laboratory, be conditioned to become sexually aroused when viewing pictures of shoes (Rachman, 1966).

Whatever the cause, fetishism typically develops early in life. In one sample of rubber fetishists, most of them first recognized their attraction to rubber when they were 4 to 10 years old (Gosselin and Wilson, 1980).

TRANSVESTISM

Transvestism: Deriving sexual gratification from dressing as a member of the opposite gender.

Drag queen: A male homosexual who dresses in women's clothing.

Female impersonator: A man who dresses up as a woman as part of a job in entertainment.

Transvestism ("trans" = "cross"; "vest" = "dressing") refers to dressing as a member of the opposite gender. Cross-dressing may be done by a variety of people for a variety of reasons. As has been noted, transsexuals may go through a stage of cross-dressing in the process of becoming women. Some male homosexuals—the drag queens—dress up as women, and some lesbians dress in masculine clothes ("butch"); these practices, though, are basically caricatures of masculinity and femininity. Female impersonators are men who dress as women, often as part of their jobs as entertainers. For example, comedian Flip Wilson is a female impersonator when he plays the character Geraldine. Finally, some—perhaps many—adolescent boys cross-dress, usually only once or a few times (Green, 1975). This behavior does not necessarily mean a life of transvestism; it may simply reflect the sexual drives, confusions, and frustrations of adolescence.

In contrast to people who engage in the kinds of cross-dressing discussed above, the true transvestite[1] is a person who derives sexual gratification from cross-dressing. Thus transvestism is probably basically a fetish (Pomeroy, 1975) and seems to be quite similar to a clothing fetish. The cross-dressing may often be done in private, perhaps even by a married man without his wife's knowledge.

---

[1]A common abbreviation for transvestism, used both by scientists and by members of the transvestite subculture, is TV. Therefore, if you see an ad in an underground newspaper placed by a person who is a TV, this is *not* someone who has delusions of broadcasting the six-o'clock news but rather a transvestite.

F · O · C · U · S 17.1

A CASE HISTORY OF A SHOE FETISHIST

The following case history is taken directly from *Psychopathia Sexualis,* by von Krafft-Ebing, the great early investigator of sexual deviance. It should give you the flavor of his work.

Case 114. X., aged twenty-four, from a badly tainted family (mother's brother and grandfather insane, one sister epileptic, another sister subject to migraine, parents of excitable temperament). During dentition he had convulsions. At the age of seven he was taught to masturbate by a servant girl. X. first experienced pleasure in these manipulations when the girl happened to touch his member with her shoe-clad foot. Thus, in the predisposed boy, an association was established, as a result of which, from that time on, merely the sight of a woman's shoe, and finally, merely the idea of them, sufficed to induce sexual excitement and erection. He now masturbated while looking at women's shoes or while calling them up in imagination. The shoes of the school mistress excited him intensely, and in general he was affected by shoes that were partly concealed by female garments. One day he could not keep from grasping the teacher's shoes—an act that caused him great sexual excitement. In spite of punishment he could not keep from performing this act repeatedly. Finally, it was recognized that there must be an abnormal motive in play, and he was sent to a male teacher. He then revelled in the memory of the shoe-scenes with his former school-mistress and thus had erections, orgasms, and, after his fourteenth year, ejaculation. At the same time, he masturbated while thinking of a woman's shoe. One day the thought came to him to increase his pleasure by using such a shoe for masturbation. Thereafter he frequently took shoes secretly and used them for that purpose.

Nothing else in a woman could excite him; the thought of coitus filled him with horror. Men did not interest him in any way. At the age of eighteen he opened a shop and, among other things, dealt in ladies' shoes. He was excited sexually by fitting shoes for his female patrons or by manipulating shoes that came for mending. One day while doing this he had an epileptic attack, and, soon after, another while practicing onanism in his customary way. Then he recognized for the first time the injury to health caused by his sexual practices. He tried to overcome his onanism, sold no more shoes, and strove to free himself from the abnormal association between women's shoes and the sexual function. Then frequent pollutions, with erotic dreams about shoes occurred, and the epileptic attacks continued. Though devoid of the slightest feeling for the female sex, he determined on marriage, which seemed to him to be the only remedy.

He married a pretty young lady. In spite of lively erections when he thought of his wife's shoes, in attempts at cohabitation he was absolutely impotent because his distaste for coitus and for close intercourse in general was far more powerful than the influence of the shoe-idea, which induced sexual excitement. On account of his impotence the patient applied to Dr. Hammond, who treated his epilepsy with bromides and advised him to hang a shoe up over his bed and look at it fixedly during coitus, at the same time imagining his wife to be a shoe. The patient became free from epileptic attacks and potent so that he could have coitus about once a week. His sexual excitation by women's shoes also grew less and less.

Source: R. Von Krafft-Ebing. (1886). *Psychopathia sexualis,* p. 288. (Reprinted by Putnam, New York, 1965.)

(a) (b)

FIGURE 17.2

Two examples of cross-dressing. (*a*) A modern female impersonator. (*b*) Edward Hyde (1661–1723), governor of the colonies of New York and New Jersey from 1702 to 1708, who chose to be painted this way while he was governor.

As a result, no one has accurate data on the incidence of transvestism. One authority, though, estimates that more than a million males in the United States are involved in it, if all instances of men getting at least a temporary erotic reward from wearing female clothing are counted (Pomeroy, 1975). The vast majority of transvestites are heterosexuals (Prince and Butler, 1972); most are married and have children (Talamini, 1982).

Transvestism is almost exclusively a male sexual variation; it is essentially unknown among women. There may be a number of reasons for this phenomenon, including our culture's tolerance of women who wear masculine clothing and intolerance of men who wear feminine clothing. The phenomenon illustrates a more general point, namely, that many sexual variations are defined for, or practiced almost exclusively by, members of one gender; the parallel practice by members of the other gender is often not considered deviant. Most sexual variations, with the exception of prostitution, are practiced mainly by males.

Research indicates that there are four basic motivations for men engaging in transvestite activities (Talamini, 1982):

1. *Sexual arousal*—As I noted earlier, transvestism appears to result from a conditioned association between sexual arousal and women's clothing. As one male transvestite commented,

> My older sister had beautiful clothes. When I was thirteen I wanted to see what I looked like when I dressed as a woman. We're about the same height. I put some of her lingerie on and I never had such powerful sexual feelings. It's twenty years later and I still dress up. (Talamini, 1982, p. 20)

2. *Relaxation*—Transvestites report that they periodically need a break from the confining, pressured male role. Dressing up as women allows them to express emotionality and grace, traits that are taboo for men in our society.
3. *Role playing*—Just as many actors derive great satisfaction from playing roles in the theater, so transvestites get a great sense of achievement from being able to pass as women when in public.
4. *Adornment*—Men's clothes are relatively drab, whereas women's are more colorful and beautiful. Transvestites enjoy this sense of being beautiful.

How do the wives and children of the transvestite react to his unusual behavior? In one sample of 50 heterosexual transvestites, 60 percent of the wives were accepting of their husband's cross-dressing (Talamini, 1982). Most of these women commented that otherwise he was a good husband. Some of the wives felt fulfilled being supportive of the husband, and some even helped him in dressing and applying makeup. In the same sample, 13 of the couples had told their children about the cross-dressing. They claimed that the relationship with the children was undamaged and that the children were tolerant and understanding.

Transvestism is one of the harmless, victimless sexual variations, particularly when it is done in private. Like other forms of fetishism, it is a problem only when it becomes so extreme that it is the person's only source of erotic gratification. For the person who is severely disturbed by the problem and wants to be cured of it, aversion therapy appears to be highly effective (Marks and Gelder, 1967). Electrodes are applied to the person's wrists, and mild shocks are delivered as the person fantasizes about cross-dressing or actually cross-dresses. Such aversion therapies have also been used in treating other sexual variations. However, in most cases transvestites are happy with their lifestyle, and such extreme therapy is not necessary.

SADISM AND MASOCHISM

Sadist:
A person who derives sexual satisfaction from inflicting pain on another person.

A sadist is a person who derives sexual satisfaction from inflicting pain on another person. The term "sadism" derives from the name of the historical character the Marquis de Sade, who lived around the time of the French Revolution. Not only did he practice sadism—several women apparently died from his attentions (Bullough, 1976)—but he also wrote novels about these practices (the best known is *Justine*), thus assuring his place in history.

Masochist:
A person who derives sexual satisfaction from experiencing pain.

A masochist is a person who is sexually aroused by experiencing pain. This variation is named after Leopold von Sacher-Masoch (1836–1895), who was himself a masochist and who wrote novels expressing masochistic fantasies. Notice that the definitions of these variations make specific their *sexual* nature; the terms are often loosely used to refer to people who are cruel or to people who seem to bring misfortune on themselves, but these are not the meanings used here.

Bondage:
A type of sadomasochism in which sexual pleasure is derived from feeling restricted, usually by being tied up with ropes.

Though many sadists and masochists trade on physical pain, another version of sadomasochism, bondage, depends on the person's feeling restricted; this is usually done by tying him or her up with ropes. In yet another psychological version, the sadist adopts a "master" role and the masochist a "slave" role. The master then exerts psychic dominance over the slave, who submits.

Sadomasochism is often accompanied by elaborate rituals and gadgetry, such as tight black leather clothing, pins and needles, ropes, whips, and hot wax (Figure 17.4). In the case of the psychological forms, the slave may actually wear a dog's collar and be led around on a leash by the master.

FIGURE 17.3

Sadomasochism in art: Aristotle and Phyllis.

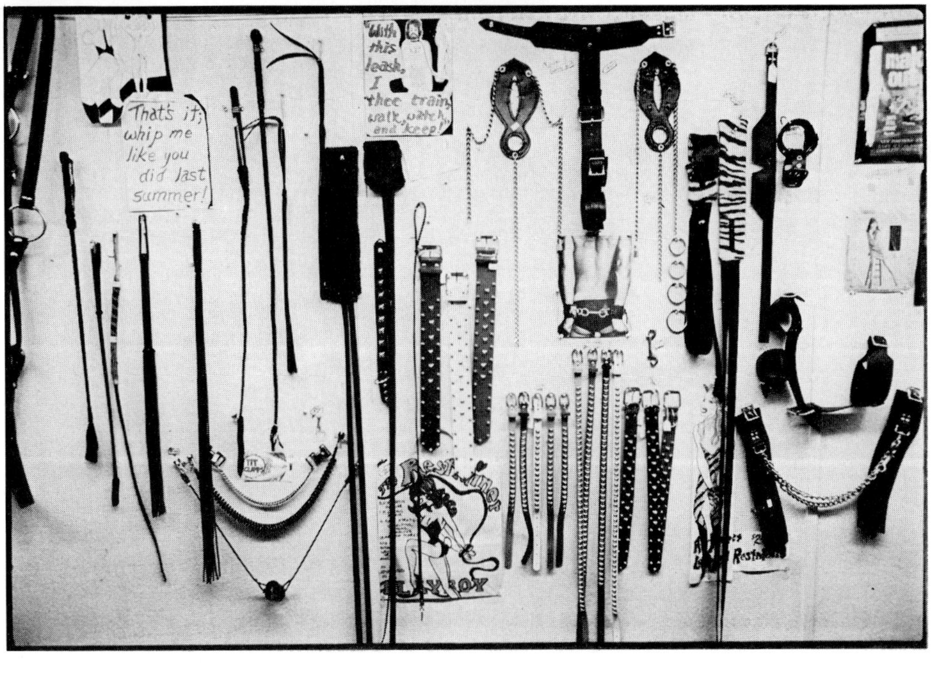

FIGURE 17.4

Some of the paraphernalia used by sadists and masochists and those who enjoy bondage.

Sadism and masochism are, of course, complementary to each other. The sadist needs a masochist for a partner, and vice versa. It appears, though, that the numbers do not work out quite right, since there are more masochists than sadists (Gosselin and Wilson, 1980).

Interestingly, sadists and masochists do not consistently find experiencing pain and giving pain to be sexually satisfying. For example, the masochist who smashes a finger in a car door will yell and be unhappy just like anyone else. Pain is arousing for such people only when it is part of a carefully scripted ritual. As one woman put it,

> Of course, he doesn't *really* hurt me. I mean quite recently he tied me down ready to receive "punishment," then by mistake he kicked my heel with his toe as he walked by. I gave a yelp, and he said, "Sorry love—did I hurt you?" (Gosselin and Wilson, 1980, p. 55)

Sadomasochism (S-M) is a rare form of sexual behavior, although in its milder forms it is probably more common than many people think. Kinsey found that about 10 percent of males and 3 percent of females reported definite or frequent arousal responses to sadomasochistic stories. He also found that 26 percent of females and the same percentage of males had experienced definite or frequent erotic responses as a result of being bitten during sexual activity (Kinsey et al., 1953, pp. 677–678). In the Hunt survey (1974), about 4 to 5 percent of all respondents said they had at some time obtained sexual pleasure from inflicting or receiving pain. Sadistic or masochistic fantasies appear to be considerably more common than real-life sadomasochistic behavior.

The causes of sadism and masochism are not precisely known. Conditioning seems to be one of the likeier explanations. For example, a little boy is being spanked over his mother's knee; in the process, his penis rubs against her knee, and he gets an erection. Or a little girl is caught masturbating and is spanked. In both cases, the child has learned to associate pain or spanking with sexual arousal, possibly setting up a lifelong career as a masochist.

VOYEURISM

Voyeur:
A person who becomes sexually aroused from secretly viewing nudes.

Scoptophilia:
A sexual variation in which the person becomes sexually aroused from others' sexual acts and genitals.

The term voyeur ("Peeping Tom")[2] generally refers to a person who derives sexual pleasure from watching nudes or from watching others have sex. Actually, there are some variations within this category. In scoptophilia, sexual pleasure is derived from observing sexual acts and the genitals; in *voyeurism,* technically, the sexual pleasure comes from viewing nudes, often while the voyeur is masturbating.

Voyeurism appears to be much more common among males than among females, a fact that is reflected in the common name for it, "Peeping Tomism." According to FBI reports, nine men to one woman are arrested on charges of "peeping."

Voyeurism provides another good illustration of the continuum from normal to abnormal behavior. For example, many men find it arousing to watch a nude woman—otherwise there would be no burlesque houses—and this is certainly well within the normal range of behavior. Some women are "crotch watchers," much as men are breast watchers (Friday, 1973, 1975). The voyeurism is abnormal when it replaces sexual intercourse or when the person commits a crime such as breaking and entering to observe others, thereby risking arrest.

Peepers typically want the woman they view to be a stranger and do not want her to know what they are doing (Yalom, 1960). The element of risk is also important;

[2]"Voyeur" comes from the French word *voir,* meaning "to see." "Peeping Tom" comes from the story of Lady Godiva; when she rode through town nude to protest the fact that her husband was raising his tenants' taxes, none of the townspeople looked except one, Tom of Coventry.

while one might think that a nudist camp would be heaven to a peeper, it is not because the elements of risk and forbiddenness are missing (Sagarin, 1973).

Voyeurs generally are not dangerous. Potentially dangerous voyeurs can be identified by the following characteristics: (1) they enter the confines of a building or other structure in order to view their subject, and (2) they draw the attention of their subject to the fact that they are watching (Yalom, 1960).

The voyeur is generally young and a "late bloomer" (R. S. Smith, 1976). He is typically a shy, sexually inadequate person who has difficulty establishing romantic relationships with others. It is rare to find a peeper who has a good sex life (Gebhard et al., 1965; Yalom, 1960).

In one study of arrested peepers, it was found that they were likely to be the youngest child in their family and to have good relationships with their parents but poor relationships with their peers (Gebhard et al., 1965). They had few sisters and few female friends. Few were married. This study, however, points up one of the major problems with the research on sexual variations: much of it has been done only on people who have been arrested for their behavior. The "respectable deviant" who has the behavior under somewhat better control or who is skilled enough or can pull enough strings not to get caught is not studied in such research. Thus the picture that research provides for us of these variations may be very biased.

EXHIBITIONISM

Exhibitionist:
A person who drives sexual gratification from exposing his genitals to others in situations in which this is inappropriate.

The complement to voyeurism is exhibitionism ("flashing"), in which the person derives sexual pleasure from exposing his genitals to others in situations where this is clearly inappropriate.[3] The pronoun "his" is used advisedly, since exhibitionism is defined almost exclusively for men. The woman who wears a dress that reveals most of her bosom is likely to be thought of as attractive rather than deviant. When the male exposes himself, it is considered offensive. Once again, whether a sexual behavior is considered deviant depends greatly on whether the person doing it is a male or a female. Homosexual exhibitionism is also quite rare, and so the prototype we have for exhibitionism is a man exposing himself to a woman. About 35 percent of all arrests for sexual offenses are for exhibitionism (Ellis and Brancale, 1956).

The man generally begins exhibiting himself when he is in his early twenties, although some may begin in adolescence (Blair and Lanyon, 1981). Exhibitionists generally recall their childhoods as being characterized by inconsistent discipline, lack of affection, and little training in appropriate forms of social behavior.

In adulthood, exhibitionists do not seem to be psychiatrically disturbed (Blair and Lanyon, 1981). However, they generally are timid and unassertive and lacking in social skills. They also seem to have trouble recognizing and handling their own feelings of hostility. Many are married, but they do not seem to be gratified with heterosexual sex.

One study indicated that exhibitionists have frequently been arrested previously for other sex offenses such as rape and voyeurism (Gebhard et al., 1965). However, this was a study of arrested exhibitionists, and this pattern might not hold for the more "normal" exhibitionist who doesn't get himself arrested.

---

[3]Here is a classic limerick on exhibitionism:

There was a young lady of Exeter
So pretty. men craned their necks at her.
  One was even so brave
  As to take out and wave
The distinguishing mark of his sex at her.

FIGURE 17.5

Exhibitionism.

The exact causes of exhibitionism are not known, but a behavioristic-learning theory explanation offers some possibilities (Blair and Lanyon, 1981). According to this view, the parents might have subtly (or perhaps obviously) modeled such behavior to the man when he was a child. In adulthood, there may be reinforcements for the exhibitionistic behavior because the man gets attention when he performs it. In addition, the man may lack the social skills to form an adult relationship, or the sex in his marriage may not be very good, so he receives little reinforcement for nondeviant sex.

The behaviorist-learning approach has been used to devise some programs of therapy that have been successful in treating exhibitionists. For example, in one therapy program exhibitionists were shown photos of scenes in which they typically engaged in exhibitionism; simultaneously, an unpleasant-smelling substance was placed at their nostrils (Maletzky, 1974, 1977, 1980). After 11 to 19 twice-weekly sessions of this conditioning and some self-administered home sessions, all but one of the men passed a temptation test in which they were placed in a naturalistic situation with a volunteer female and managed not to flash at her.

Many women, understandably, are alarmed by the exhibitionist. But since the exhibitionist's goal is to produce shock or some other strong emotional response, the woman who becomes extremely upset is gratifying him. Probably the best strategy for a woman to use in this situation is to remain calm and make some remark indicating her coolness, such as suggesting that he should seek professional help for his problem.

NECROPHILIA

Necrophilia:
A sexual variation involving having sexual contact with a dead person.

Necrophilia is sexual contact with a dead person. It is a very rare form of behavior and is considered by experts to be psychotic and extremely deviant. Necrophilia involves deriving sexual gratification from viewing a corpse or actually having intercourse with it; the corpse may be mutilated afterward (Thorpe et al., 1961).

BESTIALITY

Bestiality (bes-tee-Al-ih-tee):
Sexual contact with an animal; also called zoophilia or sodomy.

Bestiality is sexual contact with an animal; this behavior is also called *zoophilia* and *sodomy,* although the latter term is also used to refer to anal intercourse or even mouth-genital sex.

About 8 percent of the males in Kinsey's sample reported sexual experiences with animals. Most of this activity was concentrated in adolescence and probably reflected the experimentation and diffuse sexual urges of that period. Not too surprisingly, the percentage was considerably higher among boys on farms; 17 percent of boys raised on farms had had animal contacts resulting in orgasm. Kinsey found that about 3 to 4 percent of all females have some sexual contact with animals, and thus females appear to be less likely to engage in this behavior than males.

NYMPHOMANIA AND SATYRIASIS

Nymphomania (nim-foh-MANE-ee-uh):
An excessive, insatiable sex drive in a woman.

Satyriasis (sat-ur-EYE-uh-sis):
An excessive, insatiable sex drive in a man.

Hypersexuality:
An excessive, insatiable sex drive in either men or women.

Nymphomania and satyriasis are both conditions in which there is an extraordinarily high level of sexual activity and sex drive, to the point where the person is apparently insatiable and where sexuality overshadows all other concerns and interests. When it occurs in women, it is called nymphomania; in men it is called satyriasis While this definition seems fairly simple, in practice it is difficult to say when a person has an abnormally high sex drive. As was seen in Chapters 11 and 12 there is a wide range in the frequencies with which people engage in coitus; therefore, the range we define as "normal" should also be broad. In real life, the "nymphomania" or "satyriasis" is often defined by the spouse. Some men, for example, might think that it was unreasonable for a wife to want intercourse once a day or even twice a week, and they would consider such a woman a nymphomaniac.[5] Other men might think it would be wonderful to be married to a woman who wanted to make love every day. Labels like "nymphomaniac" can be used as weapons in marital squabbles. Because such terms are so loaded, some scholars think the term hypersexuality is preferable.

The term "nymphomaniac" is used particularly loosely by lay people. A nymphomaniac is more than just a woman who likes sex. True nymphomania is very rare, a point that should be kept in mind when reading the Focus. What defines the true nymphomaniac, then? Probably it is her insatiability and the compulsiveness of her behavior. It is compulsive in the sense that she feels driven to it, even when there may be very negative consequences. She is also never satisfied by the activity and may not be having orgasms, despite all the sexual activity. Similar criteria can be

[4]Satyriasis is named for the satyrs, who were part-human, part-animal beasts in Greek mythology. A part of the entourage of Dionysus, the god of wine and fertility, they were jovial and lusty and have become a symbol of the sexually active male.

[5]Someone once defined a nymphomaniac as a woman that a man can't keep up with.

F · O · C · U · S 17.2

A CASE HISTORY OF NYMPHOMANIA

Mrs. M was a lower-middle-class, attractive, slightly overweight young woman. She was 19 years old and the mother of an 8-month-old child. She was referred to a neurosurgeon by her family physician because she had persistent headaches and lower back pain. No physical causes of these symptoms could be found, and so she was referred to a psychologist for evaluation and psychotherapy. Testing revealed that she was preoccupied with sexual matters, loneliness, suicide, and hostility.

In an initial interview Mrs. M talked readily about her insatiable sexual appetite and her early sexual experiences. She said that she and her husband, aged 20, had sexual relations every night for several hours, or for as long as he could sustain the pace. He was a kind and cooperative man who believed it was his duty to provide his wife with as much sex as she wanted, but he was bewildered by her overwhelming sexual demands and could not understand why she was as sexually hungry after hours of coitus and dozens of orgasms as she had been at the beginning of the activity. On rare occasions, Mrs. M reported, she was relatively sexually satisfied, and following such occurrences her headache would disappear for a day or so.

The dynamics of the case were fairly easy to establish. Mrs. M had begun having sexual intercourse with her stepfather when she was 9 years old. Since

used to define satyriasis. Such cases would meet the criteria for abnormal behavior discussed at the beginning of this chapter: the compulsiveness of the behavior leads it to become extremely inefficent, with the result that it impairs functioning in other areas of the person's life.

Once again, these variations illustrate the extent to which the person's gender is important in defining abnormality. Since the stereotype is that women have a very low sex drive, a woman with a high sex drive is classified as a "nympho," a term that is commonly used. Men, according to the stereotype, have a high sex drive; thus it is scarcely even recognized that a few men might have problems with an abnormally high sex drive, and the term "satyriasis" is rarely used.

CELIBACY

Celibacy: Abstaining from sexual activity.

At the opposite end of the continuum of sexual behavior from nymphomania and satyriasis is celibacy, in which the person abstains totally from sexual activity.

Some religious groups require celibacy of their clergy, as the Roman Catholic Church does for priests. Some religions even demand celibacy from all members her father had left the home when she was 5, she had been deprived of male attention, and that was what she enjoyed about the intercourse with her stepfather. Further, her mother gave her little attention. She continued having coitus with the stepfather two or three times a week for the next seven years. She also discovered that she could win the affection and attention of other older men, and she became sexually involved with two uncles and several quite old men in her neighborhood. Sometimes they initiated the behavior, and sometimes she did.

When Mrs. M was about 14, she began to feel guilty about the sexual involvement with her stepfather and confessed all to her mother. Her mother refused to believe the story and made heated accusations against her, saying that she was a seductress and a generally worthless person. The sexual relationship with the stepfather continued for about two more years. Then she felt so guilty that she broke it off. Not coincidentally, the stepfather left Mrs. M's mother at this time and was never heard from again. It was at this point that Mrs. M developed the headaches, and she was subsequently unsatisfied in all her episodes of intercourse except on rare occasions with her husband.

Her mother became even more rejecting after the departure of the stepfather. Mrs. M managed to seduce or be seduced by most of her mother's suitors. Her headaches continued to worsen. Her mother, jealous over the attention the suitors paid to her daughter, pressured her into moving into her grandparents' home. They, however, were critical of her behavior, and the grandmother was suspicious of the girl's interaction with the grandfather. At this time Mrs. M met her future husband and they were married two months later. For the first time in her life, she was in a warm, affectionate relationship, although she managed to create some friction with her in-laws by being seductive toward her father-in-law.

Over the course of 10 months of psychotherapy, attempts were made to help Mrs. M create a positive self-image and accept her husband's love as sincere and valuable. She made an initial sexual advance to the therapist, but he helped her to see that her seductive behavior with an older man—the therapist—was merely an attempt to prove her worth as a human being. As the therapy progressed and Mrs. M came to understand the causes of her behavior, her frequency of sexual intercourse and the satisfaction she found in it gradually became quite normal.

Source: J. L. McCary. (1972, Nov.). Nymphomania: A case history. *Medical Aspects of Human Sexuality,* **6**, 192–202.

(for example, the Shakers), although such groups have a tendency to die out, not surprisingly. Some radical feminists also advocate celibacy, both as a form of separatism from men and as a way to free their emotional energies so that they can work even more devotedly for women's rights.

One woman expressed her feelings about being celibate:

> I have been celibate for over a year, since the beginning of my involvement with the women's movement, which gave me a lot of support. I work very hard and feel good about working. I have created my own physical environment, building a house, and have provided my own psychological space—a good combination. I masturbate a lot and enjoy it. I feel happy, independent and free to figure out my own expectations of me. (Boston Women's Health Book Collective, 1976, p. 78)

Other people become celibate simply as a result of circumstance; an example would be a widow who chooses not to remarry and not to engage in sexual activity. Yet another pattern is experimental celibacy, in which people experiment with being celibate for a period, just as they may experiment with premarital or homosexual sex.

We commonly speak of the sex "drive," as if it, like hunger, must be satisfied, or a person will die. Yet there is no evidence that celibacy is in any way damaging to one's health, and it is clear that many celibates lead long, happy lives. Celibacy should be recognized as a valid alternative sexual lifestyle, although probably not everyone is suited to it.

Troilism (TROY-uhl-ism): Three people having sex together.

Saliromania: A desire to damage or soil a woman or her clothes.

Coprophilia (cop-roh-FILL-ee-uh): Deriving sexual satisfaction from contact with feces.

Urophilia (YUR-oh-fill-ee-uh): Deriving sexual satisfaction from contact with urine.

RARE SEXUAL VARIATIONS

The sexual variations discussed below are too rare to have had much research devoted to them; they are nonetheless interesting because of their bizarreness.

Troilism, or *triolism,* refers to three people having sex together.

Saliromania is a disorder found mainly in men; there is a desire to damage or soil a woman or her clothes or the image of a woman, such as a painting or statue. The man becomes sexually excited and may ejaculate during the act.

Coprophilia and urophilia are both variations having to do with excretion. In coprophilia the feces are important to sexual satisfaction. In urophilia it is the urine that is important. The urophiliac may want to be urinated on as part of the sexual act.

PREVENTION OF SEXUAL DISORDERS

The misery that many people—e.g., nymphomaniacs—suffer, not to mention the harm they may do to others (e.g., the child molester), is good reason to want to develop programs for preventing sexual disorders (Qualls, 1978). In preventive medicine, a distinction is made between primary prevention and secondary prevention. Applied to the sexual disorders, primary prevention would involve some interventions in home life or other factors in childhood that might prevent problems from developing, or trying to teach people how to cope with crises or stress so that problems do not develop. In secondary prevention, the idea is to diagnose and treat the problem as early as possible, so that difficulties are minimized.

It would be highly advantageous to do primary prevention of sexual disorders—that is, head them off before they even develop. Unfortunately, this is proving to be difficult, for a number of reasons. One problem is in diagnostic categories. The categories for the diagnosis of sexual variations are not nearly so clear-cut as they may seem in this chapter, and multiple diagnoses for a person are not uncommon. That is, a given man might have engaged in incest, pedophilia, and exhibitionism. If it is unclear how to diagnose sexual variations, it is going to be rather difficult to figure out how to prevent them. If one is not sure if there is a difference between chickenpox and measles, it is rather difficult to start giving innoculations.

An alternative approach that seems promising—rather than figuring out ways to prevent each separate variation—is to analyze the *components of sexual development.* Disturbance in one or more of these components in development might lead to different variations. One proposal for these components is as follows (Bancroft, 1978):

1. Gender identity—the sense of maleness or femaleness developed in early childhood
2. Sexual responsiveness—arousal to appropriate stimuli
3. Formation of relationships with others

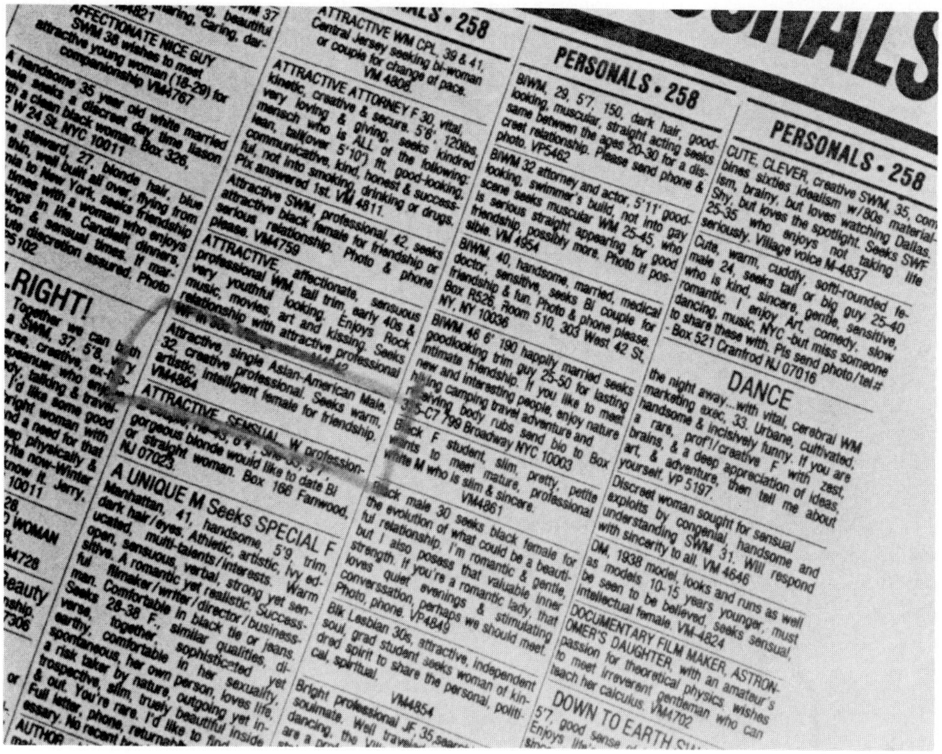

FIGURE 17.6

Top, advertising for sexual partners. Many newspapers and magazines carry "personals."

It seems clear that different developmental components are disturbed in different variations. For example, in transsexualism, it is the first component, gender identity, that is disturbed. In the case of the fetishist, it is the second component, sexual responsiveness to appropriate stimuli, that is disturbed. And in the case of the exhibitionist, it may be that it is the last component, the ability to form relationships, that is disturbed.

The idea would then be to try to assure that as children grow up, their development in each of these three components is healthy. Ideally, sexual variations should not occur then.

Space does not permit us to consider what prevention programs might look like for all the different variations (see Bancroft, 1978, for further discussion), so let us consider one example, transsexualism, in some detail (Green, 1978b; see Chapter 14 for a discussion of transsexualism).

Suppose that we have a typical case of a very feminine boy, Billy, whose parents bring him in for treatment. Billy prefers to dress in girls' clothes, wants to play with dolls and plays house, and dislikes playing with boys because they are too rough. He might be considered a high risk for becoming a transsexual, because virtually all transsexuals recall a sense of being trapped in the wrong body from earliest childhood.

What kind of therapy can be used? Some efforts are made at simple education—making sure Billy understands the anatomical differences between boys and girls, and that one cannot change gender magically. Positive aspects of maleness are emphasized. Male playmates are found who are not rough. Parents are encouraged not to engage in behavior that may reinforce his conflict—for example, commenting that he is cute when dressed up as a girl. The father-son relationship is encouraged, and a male therapist is used so that the boy can identify with him. Finally, intervention may simply be to help the child live with his own atypical behavior.

Such therapy raises a host of ethical issues. Is it right to make a traditional, stereotyped male out of a boy who might simply be androgynous? Is it right to intervene when one is not sure that he will become a transsexual? Indeed, in longitudinal follow-up studies of 26 feminine boys, 14 did become transsexuals, transvestites, or homosexuals, but 12 became heterosexuals. Therefore, one cannot be sure about a feminine 5-year-old. And even if superficial masculine behavior is successfully encouraged, what if a host of conflicts continues to simmer below the surface, creating a more seriously disturbed individual? Richard Green summarizes the complex problems this way:

> It may be argued that to induce intervention (which may be prevention) reinforces societal sexism. Regrettably, to a degree it does. But while we have a responsibility to reduce sexism, we have a responsibility to an individual child caught in the cross fire between sex role idealism and the real world in which he is embedded. (1978b, p. 88)

We have a long way to go in preventing sexual disorders, to say the least.

SUMMARY

It seems reasonable to define "abnormal sexual behavior" as behavior that is uncomfortable for the person, inefficient, bizarre, and/or physically or psychologically harmful to the person or others.

A fetishist is a person who becomes erotically attached to some object other than another human being. Most likely, fetishism arises from conditioning, and it provides a good example of the continuum from normal to abnormal behavior.

The transvestite derives sexual satisfaction from dressing as a member of the opposite gender. Like many other sexual variations, transvestism is more common among men than among women.

The sadist derives sexual pleasure from inflicting pain, while the masochist is sexually excited by experiencing pain.

The voyeur is sexually aroused by looking at nudes or by watching others have sex, while the exhibitionist displays his sexual organs to others. Both are generally harmless.

Nymphomania in women and satyriasis in men are conditions in which there is an extraordinarily high, insatiable sex drive. Both syndromes are very rare. Celibacy, or complete abstinence from sex, is a requirement in some religious communities; there is no evidence that it is damaging to one's health.

The possibility of programs or therapies to prevent sexual variations is being explored, although the topic is complex.

REVIEW QUESTIONS

1. According to a psychological definition, sexual behavior can be considered abnormal if it causes discomfort to the person, if it is bizarre, or if it causes harm to the self or others. True or false?
2. ______ is the term for becoming sexually fixated on some object other than another human being and attaching great erotic significance to that object.
3. Transvestism is considered to be a fetish, because the man becomes sexually aroused from dressing in women's clothes. True or false?
4. A ______ is a person who becomes sexually aroused when experiencing pain.
5. A voyeur is a person who derives sexual gratification from exposing his or her genitals to others. True or false?
6. When a woman has an insatiable sex drive it is termed nymphomania; when a man has an insatiable sex drive it is termed ______.
7. Celibacy poses some health risks, both physically and mentally. True or false?
8. It is rare to find a transvestite who is heterosexually married. True or false?
9. "Bondage" refers to a form of sado-masochism in which the pleasure is derived from one partner tying up the other one with ropes. True or false?
10. A learning theory, behavior modification approach has been successful in treating exhibitionists. True or false?

QUESTIONS FOR THOUGHT, DISCUSSION, AND DEBATE

1. What do you think of the idea about preventing sexual disorders presented at the end of this chapter? Do you think the schools or some other agency should institute a program to screen children, trying to detect those with characteristics that might indicate they would develop a sexual variation later in life, and then do therapy with those children?
2. Of the sexual variations in this chapter, which seems to you to be the most abnormal? Why? Does the one you have chosen fit the criteria for abnormality discussed at the beginning of the chapter?

SUGGESTION FOR FURTHER READING

Brown, Gabrielle. (1980). *The new celibacy.* New York: McGraw-Hill. A study of modern celibacy from a procelibacy point of view.

CHAPTER • 18

SEXUAL COERCION

RAPE POEM

There is no difference between being raped
and being pushed down a flight of cement steps
except that the wounds also bleed inside.

There is no difference between being raped
and being run over by a truck
except that afterward men ask if you enjoyed it.

There is no difference between being raped
and going head first through a windshield
except that afterward you are afraid
not of cars
but half the human race.

—Marge Piercy*

* *Source:* Excerpted from Marge Piercy. (1976). Rape poem. In *Living in the open.* New York: Knopf. Reprinted by permission of Wallace & Sheil Agency, Inc.

CHAPTER HIGHLIGHTS

This chaper is about sexual activity that involves coercion and is not between consenting adults; specifically, we will consider rape, incest and child molestation, and sexual harassment at work and in education. All of these have been highly publicized topics in the last five to ten years, and some good scientific research on them has quickly appeared.

RAPE

In 1982 there were 77,763 cases of reported rape in the United States; that means there were 33.6 reported rapes for every 100,000 women (FBI, 1983). However, according to the FBI, forcible rape is "one of the most underreported crimes." It is generally estimated that only about one rape in every five is reported; that is, about 80 percent go unreported (Amir, 1971, pp. 27–28; FBI, 1973, p. 15). Based on interviews with a random sample of San Francisco women, researchers concluded—after adjusting for age—that there is a 26 percent probability that a woman will be the victim of a completed rape at some time in her life (Russell and Howell, 1983). This is a strikingly high figure. Further, it is considerably higher than the FBI figures on reported rapes, confirming the underreporting of rape.

We will examine what is known about the rape victim, about the rapist, and about what can be done to prevent rape. First, however, some terms need definition. Though the legal definition of rape varies from state to state, the following is typical of the definitions used in the United States (Snelling, 1975):

Rape: Sexual intercourse that occurs without consent, whether by force or fear.

> . . . the perpetration of an act of sexual intercourse with a female, not one's wife, against her will and consent, whether her will is overcome by force or fear resulting from the threat of force, or by drugs or intoxicants; or when, because of mental deficiency, she is incapable of exercising rational judgment; or when she is below an arbitrary "age of consent." (Brownmiller, 1975, p. 368)

The last phrase refers to a specific kind of rape, statutory rape, which is intercourse with a girl who is below the legal age of consent. The idea is that in this particular offense, resistance or will is irrelevant, since the girl is simply too young to make a judgment; therefore, the man is automatically considered to have taken advantage of her. The legal age of consent varies from state to state; in most states, it ranges between 12 and 16 years.

Statutory rape: Intercourse with a girl who is younger than the legal age of consent.

Contemporary efforts at legal reform have led to the rewriting of rape laws. The victim may be referred to as a "person" to include male rape victims. The laws may also be worded so as to permit a wife to prosecute her husband for rape. However, many states have not rewritten their laws, and the definition given above would be typical for them.

Theorectical Views of Rape

To provide a perspective for the discussion that follows, we can distinguish between three major theoretical views of the nature of rape (Albin, 1977):

Victim-precipitated: The view that rape is a result of a woman "asking for it."

1. Victim-precipitated This view holds that a rape is always caused by a woman "asking for it." Rape, then, is basically the woman's fault. This view represents the tendency to "blame the victim."
2. *Psychopathology of rapists* This theoretical view holds that rape is an act committed by a psychologically disturbed man. His deviance is responsible for the crime occurring.
3. *Feminist* Feminist theorists view rapists as the standard (normal) product of gender-role socialization in our culture. They deemphasize the sexual aspects of rape and instead view rape as an expression of power and dominance by men over women.

You personally may subscribe to one of these views. It is also true that researchers in this area have generally based their work on one of these theoretical models, and this may influence their research. You should keep these models in mind as you continue to read the rest of this chapter.

Attitudes toward Rape

Psychologist Hubert Feild (1978) investigated attitudes toward rape among police, rapists, rape-crisis counselors, and citizens from the general population. He began his research by constructing a paper-and-pencil questionnaire that would measure people's attitudes toward rape on a number of different dimensions. Items were ranked on a scale from 1 (strongly agree) to 6 (strongly disagree) and consisted of statements such as "A woman should be responsible for preventing her own rape." Once Feild had developed this attitude scale, he administered it to people from the groups listed above. He obtained a number of interesting results.

In general, there was strong agreement with the following statements: "A woman can be raped against her will" and "A woman should feel guilty following a rape." There was strong disagreement with "A raped woman is a less desirable woman"; "If a woman is going to be raped, she might as well relax and enjoy it"; "Most women secretly desire to be raped"; "It would do some women some good to get raped"; and "Rape serves as a way to put or keep women in their 'place.'" On the other hand, people on the average were fairly neutral (ratings around 3.5) on items such as "Women provoke rape by their appearance or behavior" and "The reason most rapists commit rape is for sex."

There were a number of gender differences in attitudes toward rape, as might be expected. Men indicated to a significantly greater extent that it was a woman's responsibility to prevent rape, that punishment for rape should be harsh, that victims precipitate rape through their appearance or behavior, that rapists are mentally normal, that rapists are not motivated by a need for power over women, that a woman is less attractive as a result of being raped, and that women should not resist during rape. It was also true that attitudes toward rape were correlated with attitudes toward women.

Comfortingly, there was a significant difference between rapists and rape-crisis counselors in their attitudes toward rape. Convicted rapists were more likely to endorse the following views: rape prevention is primarily a woman's responsibility; rape is motivated by a desire for sex; victims are likely to precipitate rape through their appearance or behavior; and rapists are not mentally normal.

Distressingly, however, police officers' views of rape were more similar to the rapists' than they were to the counselors'. No significant differences were found between police and rapists on most dimensions. It was also true that citizens from the general population had attitudes more like those of rapists than those of counselors. The citizens generally seemed to hold a negative view of rape victims.

In another study, judges were interviewed about their attitudes toward rape (Bohmer, 1974). They appeared to divide rape cases into three types. First, there were clear cases of "genuine victims," in which there was no question that a forcible rape had occurred; the attack had been brutal, carried out by a total stranger on an unsuspecting victim. Second, the judges saw some rapes as being "consensual intercourse," in which the woman had "asked for it," for example, by allowing herself to be picked up in a bar. They had a variety of cute expressions for this, including "friendly rape," "felonious gallantry," and "assault with failure to please." Finally, the judges felt that there was a third category, "female vindictiveness," in which the woman was trying to get even with a former husband or boyfriend by accusing him of rape.

Thus, in sum, the research evidence indicates that three groups of people who are very important to the rape victim—the police, judges, and the general population of people with whom she interacts daily—tend to have negative views of her as a rape victim.

Psychological Responses of the Rape Victim

Rape trauma syndrome: The psychological and physical damage that occurs to a woman who has been raped.

One of the largest programs of research on rape victims has been carried out at Boston City Hospital by Ann Wolbert Burgess, a nurse, and Lynda Holmstrom, a sociologist (Burgess and Holmstrom, 1974a, 1974b). They have found that rape is a time of crisis for a woman and that the effects on her adjustment may persist for six months or more. On the basis of their analysis of the responses of 92 victims of forcible rape, they documented the existence of a rape trauma syndrome, which refers to the emotional changes that a woman undergoes following a rape or an attempted rape.

The rape trauma syndrome progresses in two phases: an acute phase and a long-term reorganization phase. The *acute phase* begins immediately after the rape and may last for several weeks. During the first few hours following the rape, women have a wide variety of emotional reactions that may be classified into two basic types: an expressive reaction, in which the woman cries and expresses feelings of fear, anger, anxiety, and tension, and a controlled reaction, in which the woman apparently masks or subdues her feelings and appears calm and composed or subdued. There were many physical reactions during the acute phase, including some that were direct results of the bruises and cuts they had received during the scuffle. Some women who were forced to have oral sex suffered irritation or damage to the throat. Rectal bleeding and pain were reported by the women who had been forced to have anal intercourse. Various irritations of the genitals were also common,[1] as were symptoms of tension such as headaches, sleeplessness, and a feeling of jumpiness. Emotional reactions varied widely, from fear, humiliation, and embarrassment to anger and a desire for revenge. Two feelings were especially prominent: fear and self-blame. Many women reported an overwhelming fear of physical violence and said that they had believed they would be murdered during the attack; these feelings of fear sometimes persisted long after the rape had taken place. Self-blame also occurred, with the woman spending hours agonizing over what she had done to bring on the rape or what she might have done to prevent it: "If I hadn't worn that tight sweater,. . ." "If I hadn't worn that short skirt,. . ." "If I hadn't been stupid enough to walk on that dark street,. . ." "If I hadn't been dumb enough to trust that guy,. . ." This is an example of a tendency on the part of both the victim and others to "blame the victim."

The acute phase is followed by a *long-term reorganization phase.* The rape creates a major disruption in the woman's life. For example, some women are unable to return to work after being raped, particularly if the rape occurred at work (Brodsky, 1976). They may quit their jobs and remain unemployed for some time. The seriousness of these lasting effects is illustrated in the Focus. Many of the women

[1]Tests for venereal disease should routinely be done as part of the hospital treatment of rape victims. Pregnancy tests can be done four to six weeks afterward if the woman's period is late. Another alternative, if pregnancy seems likely, is to administer the morning-after pill immediately, although it has some serious side effects (see Chapter 7).

studied by Burgess and Holmstrom moved during the long-term reorganization phase, sometimes several times; many also changed their telephone number, and some got an unlisted number. These actions seemed to result from a fear that the rapist would find them and attack them again. Some women who had been raped indoors developed fears of being indoors, and some who had been raped outdoors developed fears of being outdoors. Sexual phobias were also common. The women's normal sexual lifestyles were often severely disrupted for long periods. For example, one woman reported, five month after being raped, "There are times I get hysterical with my boyfriend. I don't want him near me; I get panicked" (Burgess and Holmstrom, 1974a, p. 984).

If a woman reports the rape and decides to press charges, the police investigation and the trial itself may be further crises for her. She must recall the traumatic experience in detail. The police and the courts have a history of callous or even abusive treatment of rape victims. The woman may be offered little sympathy, and the police may adopt a cynical attitude, as noted above, suggesting that she agreed to have sex but then changed her mind afterward. The attitudes of the police are not too surprising, for the police officers grew up in a culture that abounds with stereotypes about women, including the one that says that rape is only a situation in which a woman changed her mind. Of course, not all police officers have been guilty of such cynisicm, but too many victims report treatment like this:

> They finally told me they thought I was lying. They said I'd probably been having sex with my boyfriend and probably was afraid I was pregnant. They also theorized that my boyfriend had set me up for it. They wanted to know if he'd ever asked me to have relations with his friends. (Brownmiller, 1975, p. 366)

Or this:

> I went to the police station and said, "I want to report a rape." They said, "Whose?" and I said, "Mine." The cop looked at me and said, "Aw, who'd want to rape you?" (Brownmiller, 1975, p. 364)

The defense lawyer, in attempting to defend the rapist, may try to make it look as if the victim was actually the criminal—that she seduced him and later decided to call it rape, that she is a slut and therefore cannot be raped, and so on. She may be questioned about her prior sexual experiences, the idea being that if she has had premarital or extramarital sex, she is promiscuous and cannot be raped. As one woman expressed it:

> They trotted out my whole past life, made me go through all these changes, while he just sat at the defendant's table, mute, surrounded by his lawyers. Of course that was his right by law, but it looked like I was the one who was on trial. (Brownmiller, 1975, p. 372)

Recently some states have passed "reform" evidence laws, which do not permit the woman's previous sexual experience (except with the alleged rapist) to be a topic during a trial for rape.

Recently, perhaps partly as a result of several excellent television programs dramatizing the plight of the woman who has been raped, many police departments have tried to change their handling of rape victims. Some even have special "rape squads" composed of women police officers who record the woman's story and investigate the case; this spares the woman the embarrassment of describing the incident to a man.

F · O · C · U · S 18.1

A RAPE VICTIM TELLS HER STORY

High school was quite successful for me. I was a member of the group of about twenty who literally ran the school from the administration downward. I had several authoritative positions. The majority of my comrades were also female. This was very unusual, or so it seems, to have the student government of a school of two thousand primarily female. All of my friends went Ivy League or south to college. I was on my way to the University of Virginia as a National Merit Commended Scholar. I had the world by the tail, so I thought. . . .

I arrived there in August, 1978 full of the usual freshmen dreams of success and maybe even love. On October 12, my dreams were shattered. I was raped. My friend, Betsy, and I attended a Toga party that night. I left the party to go outside to cool off from dancing. I thought I was alone. Apparently, I was followed from the party. My rapist caught me in a very dark place, threw me down, knocked me out and raped me.

It would have been to my advantage if I had remained unconscious. But, I regained consciousness just as he was climaxing. At that moment I hated everything that my femininity symbolized. He was deriving the utmost physical pleasure at the cost of my dignity and more importantly, at the cost of my future.

The cuts and bruises healed but the mental torture remained and will always be present. Because of him, I lost a year of my life, I was forced to withdraw from UVA and go home. I was mentally unable to return to school until September, 1979 and am now a year behind my class. That is the least of it. The emotional aspects of it have been crippling.

Because of one single hateful act, I lost my security, my confidence, my trust, and my boyfriend. It was quite a price to pay for someone else's personality flaws. My loss of security arose from my loss of advantages—meaning my position in life. All that I worked to build was destroyed. My very base was blown out from under me. All this because I was the first woman to walk out a door alone. My number was certainly up that night. I had nothing to fall back on after I left UVA.

As a result I lost every ounce of self-confidence I ever had. I had a low opinion of myself because I experienced something which many rape victims experience. I asked myself over and over again if I had "asked for it." For a while, I was convinced that I was a slut and had gotten what I had deserved. This is something which is extremely difficult to overcome. A year and a half later, I still have little self-confidence.

I was once a very trusting person. Now, however, I do not trust men, and I constantly have trouble trusting women. I question people's motives. In the back of my mind, I must feel that everyone has the hate for me that that one person exemplified. It is a very unhealthy and unfair attitude. I realize this but I still judge harshly.

The person who took the brunt of all my inner unrest was my boyfriend of two and a half years. I mistrusted him and lashed out at him once too often because of my own insecurities. He and I gave up trying to regain what was once strong and beautiful because my ability to give and receive as before was lost along with the UVA and National Merit.

I was forced to realize my gender in a very brutal way. I would give anything to replace this experience with having been discriminated against for a job or something like that. But, my fate is mine and no one else but me can repair the damage done. I hope I live long enough to recapture myself. I miss me.

Source: From a student essay.

It also appears that the victim's sense of guilt over the crime contributes to the trauma she experiences. According to a specialist in criminal psychiatry, "The victim who is beaten into almost senselessness may suffer far less emotional trauma than the woman who submits to rape when her life is threatened" (Brussel. 1971, p. 30). That is, emotional noninvolvement between the victim and the criminal helps the victim adjust better afterward. The woman who is beaten unconscious is much less likely than the woman who escapes with only minor scratches to have others imply (or to think in her own mind) that she brought on the attack or that she cooperated or enjoyed it.

To say the least, then, rape is a traumatic experience for many women, and it may have effects lasting six months or more after the attack. In view of this, Burgess and Holmstrom emphasize the need for counseling for rape victims. The counselor provides support and encourages the victim to vent her feelings. The counselor should be with the victim during the hospital procedures and while the police are questioning her and then should provide follow-up counseling; the counselor should also be with the woman during the court procedures, since, as has been noted, they can be extremely traumatic.

Carefully conducted research indicates that rape victims are significantly more depressed than nonvictims, but research also indicates that the adjustment of victims has typically stabilized by four months after the rape (Atkeson et al., 1982; Resick et al., 1981). Thus, although it is important to understand the psychological trauma of rape, it is also important to appreciate the coping strengths of women recovering from it. Most women do not allow themselves to remain permanent victims (see also Gruber et al., 1982; Burgess and Holmstrom, 1979).

Silent Rape Reaction

Silent rape reaction: The psychological responses of a woman when she doesn't tell anyone that she has been raped.

Burgess and Holmstrom (1974a) have also documented the existence of a phenomenon they call the silent rape reaction. As was noted, probably the majority of rapes are not reported. However, not only do some women fail to report the rape to the police, but they also tell no one about it. They, of course, experience the same problems of adjustment that other rape victims do, but they have no way of expressing or venting these feelings. People who do counseling or psychotherapy should be aware of this syndrome. For example, a woman may come for counseling complaining of quite different problems—perhaps inability to have orgasms or anxiety and depression—when her real problem is that she has been raped but is unable to talk about it. Symptoms of this silent rape reaction are similar to those associated with the rape trauma syndrome, described above. Such women should be helped gently to begin to talk about the experience so that they can start to deal with it.

Female Socialization: Creating Rape Victims

How do women become victims of rape? This section will discuss the notion that many of the qualities for which females are socialized make them vulnerable to rape (Russell, 1975; Weis and Borges, 1973).

For example, according to gender-role stereotypes, weakness is feminine, while strength is masculine. As a result, many women think of themselves as being physically weak, and those who do not exercise may actually be weak. This weakness is symbolized in many ways, as when men open doors for women or carry heavy bundles for them. To expect a person who needs such assistance to fight off a 220-pound

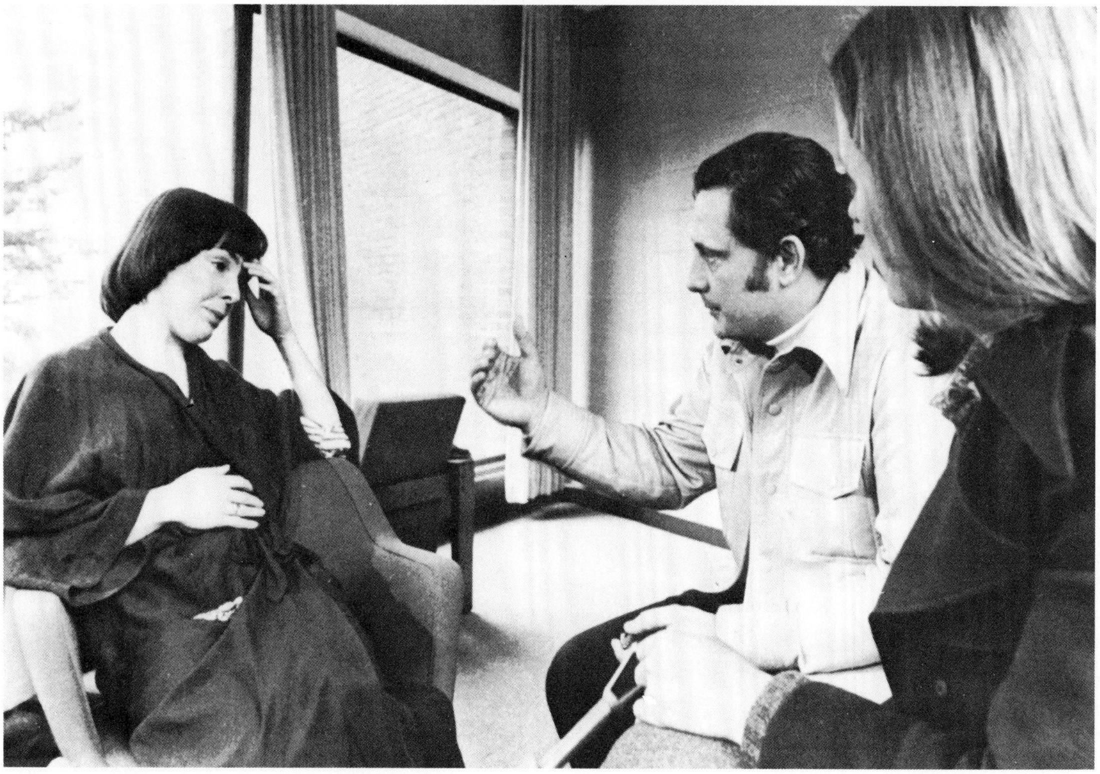

FIGURE 18.1

In a simulation demonstration program a professional model (left) gives a "rape report" in a new police training program at Brandeis University designed to increase police sensitivity and improve rape investigations. The man and woman at the right are both students in the course.

attacker would be silly. Thus, the weakness and passivity for which females are socialized contribute to making them rape victims.

Females are also socialized for nurturance (taking care of others) and altruism (paying attention to the needs of others rather than one's own needs). The woman who has been socialized to be nurturant and who spends her days expressing her gentleness toward her children can scarcely be expected to attempt to gouge out a man's eyes with her fingernails, as some self-defense experts advise. Female altruism has an ironic effect in the rape situation. Some women report the rape but then choose not to press charges because they say they are afraid that the rapist might have to go to jail for a long time[2] or that his reputation will be ruined. Thus, the victim may adopt a nurturant, altruistic attitude toward her attacker, considering his needs and feelings first.

The feelings of altruism that lead to nonreporting are magnified by the fact that in nearly half the cases, the victim knows her attacker at least casually. Statistics indicate that in 53 percent of all cases, the attacker is a total stranger. However, in 30 percent of all cases, the woman and the rapist are slightly acquainted; in 7 percent, they are relatives (father and daughter, brother and sister, uncle and niece, etc.); and in 3 percent, they are not related but have had a previous close association (Mulvihill et al., 1969).

Females are also socialized for a group of qualities that might be called collectively "being ladylike." Ladies are neat and clean and pretty. Some women, immediately after a rape, go home to shower, wash their hair, and change their clothes;

[2]Those who worry about condemning a man to a long jail sentence may be interested to know that the average convicted rapist spends less than four years in jail for the offense (Brownmiller, 1975).

then they proceed to the police station. While their emotional need to get themselves clean is understandable, they have destroyed most of the evidence of the crime, and the skeptical reaction of the police is not surprising. If you look neat and clean and pretty, it is hard to believe that you have just been raped.

Children, and girls especially, are taught to fear sex crimes. They are told never to accept rides with strange men or to take candy from them. Yet the exact nature of the potential danger remains unknown and so the girl may build up an exceedingly great dread of a mysterious crime, perhaps thinking that it would be the worst thing that could happen to her. Thus, when she is attacked, she may be absolutely immobilized with fear. She freezes and is unable to wage an effective counterattack.

The reader can probably think of other examples of qualities that females are socialized for that contribute to making them rape victims. However, the important point is that conformity to traditional standards of femininity makes women more vulnerable to rape, at least when they are in a situation in which a man intends to rape them (Russell, 1975).

The Rapist

What is the profile of the typical rapist? The basic answer to that question is that there is no typical rapist. Rapists vary tremendously from one to the next in occupation, education, marital status, previous criminal record, and motivation for committing the rape.

A few generalizations can be made about rapists. Most are young. According to the FBI *Uniform Crime Reports,* 61 percent are under 25. Many have a tendency to repeat their offense (M. L. Cohen et al., 1971). It is also true that most rapists are not murderers (Selkin, 1975). Probably only about 1 rape in 500 is accompanied by a murder (Brownmiller, 1975).[3] This statistic is important for women who wonder how best to react in a rape situation. Statistically, although the rapist may threaten the woman with violence or murder, he is unlikely to carry through on this and is only using the threat to get her to submit. This may encourage women to resist the attacker rather than submit.

In an attempt to deal with the diversity in the personalities and approaches of rapists, some researchers have developed typologies, or schemes for categorizing rapists. According to one such typology, rapists vary according to whether their aim is primarily aggressive,[4] primarily sexual, or a mixture of the two (Cohen et al., 1971—a case history from this typology is given in Focus 18.2). The trouble with research of this kind is that it is based on reported rapes only, and typically investigates rapists who have been arrested and sent to jail. It seems likely that these rapists are more deviant than those who escape being reported. Thus the research ignores the more common, "normal" rapist—the date rapist, the boss who rapes his secretary.

The Date Rape

Though often not categorized as rape, some acts of coitus on dates involve a great deal of force and could at least be called *sex aggression.*

---

[3]If anything, this is probably an *over*estimate of the number of rapes that end in murder, since rape-murders are almost invariably discovered, whereas the rape in which the woman escapes with minor scratches is likely to go unreported.

[4]It is clear from the statistics that intercourse is not always the goal of the rapist. In one study, vaginal intercourse occurred in less than half the rape cases investigated (Selkin, 1975).

F · O · C · U · S
18.2
CASE HISTORY OF A RAPIST: PHILLIP

Phillip is 25. He is tall and well built, and although his walk, voice, and manner are assertive, he has a boyish smile enhanced by a cowlick and deep blue, guileless eyes.

He was committed to the center four years ago following a sexual assault on a young girl. He was driving along a city road when he saw a girl, whom he did not know. He stopped his car beside her, stepped out, and asked her where she was going. He did not hear her answer and asked again in an angry manner. She turned to walk away, and Phillip felt she was trying to make a fool of him. He believed that she had been interested in him at first but had rejected him when he showed his interest in her. He punched her in the stomach, pulled her into his car, and drove away to a secluded area. After he had parked, he climbed into the back and dragged her over the seat beside him. He undressed her and violently penetrated her. He states that he then withdrew, without having an orgasm, and let her out of the car, threatening to kill her is she made mention of the attack. When he was arrested shortly thereafter, he immediately admitted his guilt.

During the diagnostic interviews he discussed the incident, describing himself as enraged at the time, not sexually excited. He had gone to visit his girlfriend, a "good" girl whom he had been seeing off and on since early adolescence; there had been no sexual activity throughout the courtship. He found her necking on the porch with a black man, and he drove away from her house in a blind rage. He was partially aware as he drove away that he was going to look for someone to attack sexually.

Phillip has had an active sexual life, but only with girls whom he considered "bad." These relationships were short-lived, ending when he was directly confronted with the girls' promiscuity. The relationships were always terminated violently, with Phillip assaulting either the girl or the boyfriend who had replaced him.

Although Phillip has had no history of homosexual experiences, his behavior toward homosexuals indicates the presence of homosexual desires and the tenuousness of their repression. Within the center, he reacted with exaggerated, explosive anger toward homosexual invitations.

Phillip began to have sexual intercourse at age 15 with the girls described above. He remembers his first heterosexual experience as being somewhat traumatic. When he was 9 or 10 years old, he was approached by a girl who engaged him in sexual play, telling him that girls liked this kind of play. Shortly thereafter a neighborhood girl asked him to play with her, and he began to fondle her, believing that this was what she desired. She ran home and told her parents, who in turn called Phillip's father. According to Phillip, his father felt so disgraced that they moved to a different part of town.

Phillip's father was a strict man, the disciplinarian of the family. His mother was a somewhat passive, quiet woman. Their family life was quite stable, with the father working as a machinist for the same company for 25 years. There were two other children in the family, an older sister and a younger brother, both of whom appear to be living normal lives.

Phillip is a very likable young man; he is well thought of by the officers and his fellow patients. His anger appears to be very specific to threats to his sense of independence or challenges to his sense of masculinity.

Phillip dealt at some length in therapy with his self-destructive behavior, showing some awareness of the self-inflicted pain in his relationships.

Source: M. L. Cohen, R. Garofalo, R. Boucher, and T. Seghorn. (1971). The psychology of rapists. *Seminars in Psychiatry,* **3**, pp. 315–317. According to the authors' typology, Phillip is an example of an aggressive-aim rapist.

Incidents of this type were investigated by Eugene J. Kanin (1969). He began by contacting a random sample of unmarried male university students; 95 percent cooperated. Of those who responded, 25 percent reported having performed at least one act of sex aggression, defined as making a forceful attempt at coitus to the point of being disagreeable and offensive to the woman, with the woman responding by fighting or crying, for example. The 87 males who had engaged in such acts reported 181 episodes with 142 females.

The incidents of sex aggression were not confined to cases of casual bar pickups. They occurred in every degree of involvement, from pickups and first dates to couples who dated regularly or were pinned.

In some cases, the sex aggression appears to result from female-male miscommunication. There is a saying among males that "When she says 'no,' she really means 'yes.'" How, then, is a woman supposed to say "no" when she really means it? Such confused communication patterns between men and women can contribute to the date rape, as described in the following example:

> I picked up M and she suggests we go and park and "talk." Talk shifts to "old times." I move over and kiss her. One thing leads to another and I am petting her breasts. M begins to complain about her girdle and removes it. The pace increases to the point where I try to lay her down on the front seat of the car. She resists and I keep going until she suddenly starts fighting and screaming at me. I finally told her to shut up and took her home. She was really sore. (Kanin, 1969)

In this case, the man doubtless interpreted the woman's taking off her girdle as an invitation to intercourse, while she probably in fact took it off because it felt uncomfortable.

In some cases, miscommunication and misunderstanding are so great as to be nearly unbelievable. For example, some rapists have been reported to ask, after the rape, whether the victim had an orgasm (see, for example, the Bibliography entry for the case reported by Anonymous, 1975).

In other cases, the rape appears to be a way for the man to exert social control over the woman. For example, sex aggression was apparently used by some men to punish women whom they perceived as being "teases" or "gold diggers."

A more recent survey of a representative sample of university students yielded similar results (Koss and Oros, 1982). In response to the question "Have you ever been raped?" 6 percent of the women replied "yes." But when the definition was broadened somewhat, percentages went up substantially; 21 percent of the women said that they had had sexual intercourse with a man when they didn't really want to because they had felt pressured by his continual arguments.

The point of both these studies is that such incidents were not found to be rare, but rather are fairly common even in "normal" populations.

Marital Rape

Marital rape: The rape of a woman by her husband.

The possibility that a man could rape his wife was brought to public attention when, in 1978 in Oregon, Greta Rideout brought suit against her husband for marital rape Defining marital rape is complicated by the fact that, in many states, rape laws exclude the possibility of marital rape; the assumption seems to be that sex in marriage is always the husband's "right."

How common is marital rape? In a random sample of San Francisco women, 14 percent of those who had ever been married had been raped by a husband or ex-husband (Russell, 1983).

One phenomenon that emerges from the research is an association between marital violence and marital rape—that is, the man who batters his wife is also likely to rape her. For example, in a study of 137 women who had reported beatings from their husbands, 34 percent reported being raped by their husband (Frieze, 1983). Reflecting the fact that some women are unwilling to define certain acts as marital rape, 43 percent of that sample said that sex was unpleasant because their husband forced them to have sex, a higher percentage than those admitting being raped. The response of the majority of the women was anger toward the husband. However, women who had been raped frequently began to experience self-blame. Marital rape also appeared to have consequences for the marriage: The raped women were more likely to say that their marriages had been getting worse over time.

What are the motivations for a man raping his wife? Three motives emerge in research: anger, power-domination, and sadism (Russell, 1983). In some cases the husband is extremely angry, perhaps in the middle of a family argument, and he expresses his anger toward his wife by raping her. In other cases, power and domination of the wife seem to be the motive—for example, the wife may be threatening to leave him, and he forces or dominates her into staying by rape. Finally, some rapes appear to occur because the husband is sadistic—enjoys inflicting pain—and is a psychiatrically disturbed individual.

The research shows that marital rape is a real and not uncommon phenomenon, that it is associated with wife battering, and that it has negative consequences, both for the woman and for the marriage.

Male Socialization: Creating Rapists

One view is that rapists are created as the result of standard gender-role socialization practices in our culture (Albin, 1977). To remedy the situation, radical changes in gender-role socialization practices would be necessary. The ideas in this section reflect this theoretical view.

A previous section reviewed the argument that many of the characteristics for which we socialize females contribute to making them rape victims. The parallel argument is also informative, namely, that males are socialized for characteristics that contribute to making them rapists (Russell, 1975; Weis and Borges, 1973).

Aggression, dominance, power, and strength are manly. In the study of gender-role stereotypes discussed in Chapter 14, it was found that Americans consider aggression to be a desirable characteristic of males. Having been socialized to be aggressive, it is not surprising that men commit the aggressive crime of rape. Further, rapists may themselves be victims of our culture's confusion of sex and aggression. For example, we often refer to the male as playing the "aggressive" role in sex, suggesting that sex is supposed to have an aggressive component. Sex and aggression are also combined in the sadomasochistic pornography that is so common (see Chapter 19). The rapist's confusion of sex and aggression reflects a confusion existing in our society.

It may be, then, that rape is a means of proving masculinity or self-worth for the male who is insecure in his role (Geis, 1977). For this reason, the statistics on the youthfulness of rapists make sense; youthful rapists may simply be young men who are trying to adopt the adult male role, who feel insecure about doing this, and who commit a rape as proof of their manhood. Further, heterosexuality is an important part of manliness. Raping a woman is a flagrant way to prove that one is a heterosexual. Interestingly, some rapists have a history of passivity, heterosexual inadequacy, and being called "queers" or "pansies" by their peers in adolescence. Rape for them may establish their heterosexual manliness.

The view that pressures of male socialization and a desire to prove masculinity contribute to rape is illustrated well by cases of *gang rape.* Gang rapes are more common than most people think; in one study of reported rapes, 43 percent were done by two or more men (Amir, 1971). A psychologist studied two sets of adolescent gang rapists (Blanchard, 1959). One group of five boys had been out drinking and decided to "scare" some lovers who were parked. With one boy as their leader, they assaulted the couple, raping the girl. When the psychologist studied them individually, they were relatively tame, but when they came together as a group, they immediately began to compete for dominance to see who could find the most sexual symbols in a group of Rorschach cards. The leader, Pete, appeared to be "a very sadistic youngster with a strong need to prove his masculinity." And rape was the way to do it.

Based on a series of samples of male college students at several universities, it was found, on the average, that about 35 percent indicated some likelihood that they would rape a woman if the opportunity was there and they were sure they would not be caught (Malamuth, 1981). This high percentage also supports the notion that rapists are the result of common male socialization practices in our culture.

Cross-cultural research provides further evidence that rape is the product of social learning. As Margaret Mead observed, "Of rape the Arapesh know nothing beyond the fact that it is the unpleasant custom of the Nugum people to the southeast of them" (1935, p. 110). The Arapesh understanding of the nature of males—that they are nurturant, caring, gentle—is totally incompatible with the notion of rape, and so apparently it never occurs.

Other cross-cultural research has found tribes that use rape precisely to punish women and enforce property rights (Chappell, 1976).

Rape, then, does seem to be a product, at least in part, of socialization patterns.

Men Raped by Women

Although it might seem to be a physical impossibility for a woman to rape a man, research shows that men may respond with an erection in emotional states such as anger and terror (Sarrel and Masters, 1982). In one study, 11 male victims of rape by women were interviewed (Sarrel and Masters, 1982). The cases fell into four categories: assault (the rape included physical constraint or threats of physical violence); "baby-sitter" abuse (a young boy is seduced by an older female who is not a relative); incestuous abuse (seduction of a boy by a female relative); and dominance rape (in which no physical violence is used but the male victim is intimidated or terrified). Some cases of female gang rape of males were even discovered. The research found that there was a rape trauma syndrome for men who had been raped which was much like the rape trauma syndrome discussed earlier for female victims. It is important for counselors and others in helping professions to recognize this possibility of male rape victims.

Prison Rape

In most states, rape is legally defined as a crime that has a male offender and a female victim. However, this definition ignores a whole set of "homosexual" rapes of men by other men, many of which, in the United States, occur in prisons (Brownmiller, 1975).

Indeed, it is becoming increasingly apparent that for a male, one of the worst things about going to prison today is the danger of being the object of sexual violence. One case history will suffice as an illustration. In 1973, a 28-year-old Quaker pacifist named Robert A. Martin held a press conference in which he told the story of his experience of prison rape (Aiken, 1973; Stout, 1973). Arrested during a peace demonstration, Martin had chosen to go to jail rather than post a $10 bond. His first week in the District of Columbia jail was uneventful. But then he was transferred to another cellblock. During the first evening recreation period, he was invited into a cell by some other inmates. Then, "My exit was blocked and my pants were forcibly taken off me, and I was raped. Then I was dragged from cell to cell all evening." He was promised protection from further assaults by two of the men. The next night his "protectors" initiated a second round of oral and anal rape, collecting cigarettes from prisoners wanting a turn. When he was given a brief rest to overcome gagging and nausea, he escaped, alerted a guard, and was taken to a hospital; bond was posted for him the next day by a Quaker friend. Where were the guards when all this was going on? No one knows. Martin called the press conference to help prevent others from being subjected to this experience.

A major study on this topic is Daniel Lockwood's *Prison Sexual Violence* (1980), based on interviews with aggressors and targets, as well as members of the prison staff. Readers wanting to pursue this topic should consult that book.

Prison rapes are the most tangible symbol of the dominance hierarchy among prisoners. Those at the bottom of the dominance hierarchy are the objects of this sexual violence, and, interestingly, they are called "girls." Prison rape is a particularly clear example of the way in which rape is an expression of power and aggression.

The Wider Impact of Rape

Up to this point, the discussion has centered on rapists and the impact of rape on the victim. But rape has much broader ramifications in our society, and it affects many people besides the victim. Most women perform a number of behaviors that stem basically from rape fears. For example, a single woman is not supposed to list her full first name in the telephone book, because that is a giveaway that she is alone; rather, she should list a first initial or a man's name. Many women, when getting into their car at night, almost reflexively check the back seat to make sure that no one is hiding there. Most college women avoid walking alone through dark parts of the campus at night. At least once in their lives, most women have been afraid of spending the night alone. If you are a woman, you can probably extend the list from your own experience; however, the point is that most women experience the fear of rape, if not rape itself. Further, this fear restricts their activities.

There is also reason to be concerned about the effects of rape on relationships between men and women. If women see men as potential rapists, how can trusting relationships be built? One authority, advising women on how to avoid being raped, said:

> A woman's first act of resistance should be to refuse to help or be helped by strange men. It is unwise to stop on the street to give a man a light or explain street directions. . . . The safest stance for a woman alone, either on the street or in her home, is to be aloof and unfriendly. (Selkin, 1975, pp. 72, 74).

This may be good advice for avoiding rape, but what does it do to human relationships?

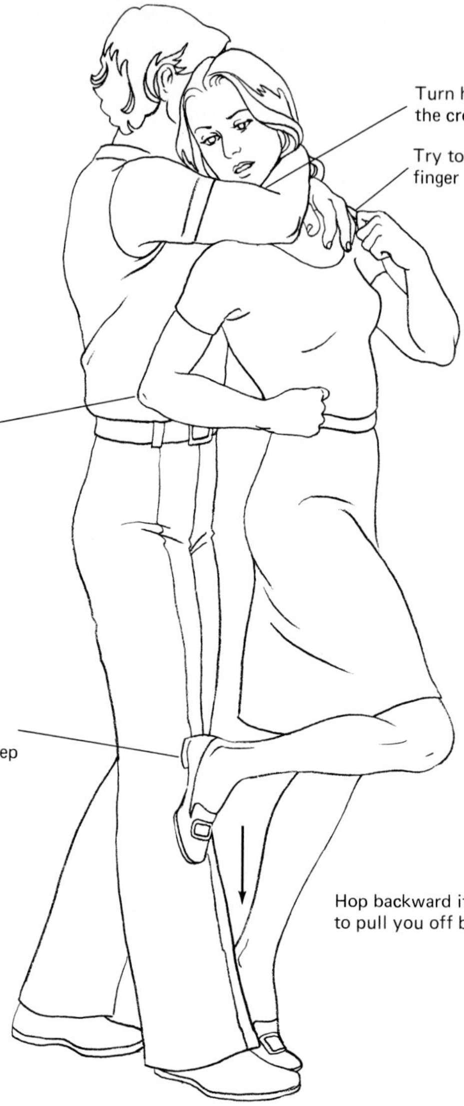
Turn head into
the crook of his arm
Try to pry his little
finger back and break it
Jab elbow into
his solar plexus
Drive heel down
over his kneecap
and onto his instep
Hop backward if he tries
to pull you off balance

FIGURE 18.2

Self-defense suggestions for a woman.

Preventing Rape

Rape is clearly an important problem in our society. What can be done to prevent it? The first answer is self-defense training for women. Many universities, YWCAs, and other organizations now offer self-defense classes for women, and I believe that every woman should take at least one such course. Many techniques are available. Judo (and aikido, which is similar) emphasizes throwing and wrestling. Tae kwon do (Korean karate) emphasizes kicking. Jujitsu uses combinations of these strategies. The exact method the woman chooses is probably not too important, as long as she does know some techniques. Related to this is the importance of getting exercise and keeping in shape; this gives a woman the strength to fight back and the speed to run fast.

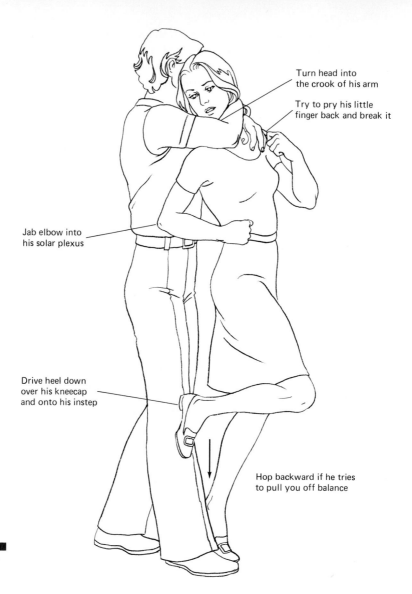

Self-defense, though, is useful to the woman only in defending herself once an attack has been made. Feminists argue that it would be far better if rape could be rooted out at an earlier stage so that attacks never occurred. To do this, our society

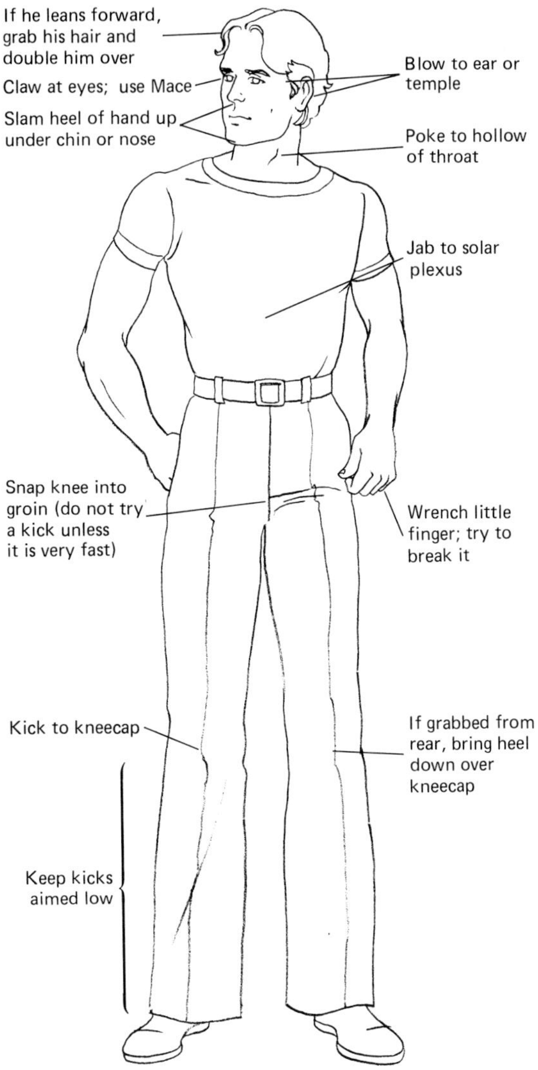
If he leans forward, grab his hair and double him over
Claw at eyes; use Mace
Slam heel of hand up under chin or nose
Blow to ear or temple
Poke to hollow of throat
Jab to solar plexus
Snap knee into groin (do not try a kick unless it is very fast)
Wrench little finger; try to break it
Kick to kneecap
If grabbed from rear, bring heel down over kneecap
Keep kicks aimed low

FIGURE 18.3

Vulnerable spots of a rapist.

would need to make a radical change in the way it socializes males and females. If little boys were not so pressed to be aggressive and tough, perhaps rapists would never develop. If adolescent boys did not have to demonstrate that they are hypersexual, perhaps there would be no rapists. As we noted earlier, rape is unheard of in some societies where males are socialized to be nurturant rather than aggressive (Mead, 1935).

Changes would also need to be made in the way females are socialized, particularly if women are to become good at self-defense. Weakness is not considered a desirable human characteristic, and so it should not be considered a desirable feminine characteristic, especially because it makes women vulnerable to rape. Mothers particularly need to think of the kinds of role models they are providing for their daughters and should consider whether they are providing models of weakness. The stereotype of female weakness and passivity is so pervasive in our society that a complex set of strategies will be required to change it. Girls also need increased experience with athletics as they grow up. This change might have a number of beneficial effects: building strength, speed, and agility in women; building up their confidence in their ability to use their own bodies; and decreasing their fear of rough body contact. All of these should help them defend themselves against rape. While some people think that it is silly for the federal government to rule that girls must have athletic teams equal to boys' teams, it seems quite possible that the abscence of athletic training for girls has contributed to making them rape victims.

Some authors, though, have argued that just changing the way we socialize girls and boys is not enough (Russell, 1975). These socialization practices exist precisely to prepare children for their adult roles, and as long as women and men have substantially different roles, the problem will not be solved.

Finally, for both males and females, we need a adical restructuring of our ideas concerning sexuality. As long as females are expected to pretend to be uninterested in sex and as long as males and females continue to play games on dates, then rape will persist.

INCEST AND CHILD MOLESTATION

Here we discuss two situations in which children are sexually coerced: child molestation (pedophilia) and incest.

Pedophilia

Pedophiliac (peed-oh-FILL-ee-ak):
An adult who engages in or desires sexual contact with a child; a child molester.

The pedophiliac[5] ("child molester") is an adult who engages in or desires sexual contact with a child. Pedophilia is typically regarded as one of the most despicable of sex offenses because of the naive trust of children and because the pedophiliac uses his power and authority as an adult over the child.

How common is child molesting? Kinsey found that 24 percent of the women in his sample had been approached, between the ages of 4 and 13, by males at least 5 years older than they were who made or tried to make sexual contacts. John Gagnon reanalyzed the Kinsey data and estimated that 20 to 25 percent of middle-class and 33 to 40 percent of lower-class female children have experienced some kind of molesting. In a survey of 1800 university students, 30 percent of the men and 35 percent of the women reported having had childhood experiences with sexual deviants (Landis, cited by McCaghy, 1971).

What kind of a person is a child molester? The common stereotype is that he is a dangerous stranger who lurks in the shadows, waiting to pounce on the unsuspecting child. A number of facts contradict this notion, however. In at least one-half to two-thirds of the cases, the molester is a friend, acquaintance, or relative of the child; when he is a relative, a form of incest is involved. In most cases, then, the offender is not a stranger. It is also true that force is rarely used; violence is involved in probably no more than 3 percent of all cases (McCaghy, 1971). Intercourse is rarely attempted; the activity is generally limited to genital fondling (Gebhard et al.. 1965). Finally, in some cases the child may collaborate in or even initiate the contact; this is probably true in about 8 percent of offenses, the percentage being higher for homosexual contacts.

As is true for many other kinds of sexual variation, there is no typical child molester (McCaghy, 1971). Several general categories of child molesters have been

---

[5]Those of you who are interested in the roots of words might mistakenly guess that a pedophiliac is a foot fetishist. The root "ped-," however, refers to "child," as in "pediatrician."

found to exist, though. One is that of the *incestuous molester,* who will be discussed further below. Another category is that of *molesters who work with children,* such as teachers or choirmasters. Though these people apparently do not enter their profession with the intent of molesting, they do have a keen interest in children; they have their contacts with children for whom they have a high regard, seeing the contact as part of a love relationship. Homosexual molesting is quite comon in this category, but many such contacts are collaborative or are initiated by the child. For the *asocial molester,* a third type, the sexual offense is simply one of many crimes he has committed. There are also *aged offenders;* for example, they may be retired men who molest children in their neighborhood. The *career molester* has a history of repeated, deliberate, systematic molesting of children, typically children he does not know. He generally does not use force, but he may have a puppy or monkey with him to lure the child. Finally, the *spontaneous-aggressive molester* uses violence against his victims, who are usually not known to him. Fortunately, this last type is rare.

Generally, child molesters do tend to be from the lower class. In one study, most were between 30 and 40, with an average age of 37 (McCaghy, 1971). Only about 20 percent of child molesters are homosexual offenders (sexual activity between a man and a boy is called pederasty).

Pederasty (PED-ur-as-tee): Sexual contact between a man and a boy.

What effects does the molesting have on the child? Some authorities believe that the molesting itself is not always traumatic for the child (J. H. Gagnon, 1965a; McCaghy, 1971). Often the trauma arises from the highly emotional reaction of the parents or from the police and judicial procedures. While the experience itself is often not traumatic, there are two exceptions to this general rule. The experience may be psychologically damaging to the child if violence or extreme coercion is used. Repeated, serious sexual contacts, particularly if they are with a close relative, may also be very damaging.

It is important for parents to encourage open communication with their children so that the children will confide in them if molesting occurs. If a child does bring such a report to a parent, the parent should not overreact but rather should encourage the child to talk about the incident, while calmly reassuring the child.

Incidence of Incest

Incest: Sexual contact between relatives.

Incest is typically defined as sexual relations between blood relatives, although the definition is often extended to include sex between nonblood relatives, for example stepfather and stepdaughter (Maisch, 1972; Sagarin, 1977).

Traditionally it was thought that incest was a rare and bizarre occurrence. Early research confirmed this notion, indicating that the incidence of incest prosecuted by the police was only about one or two people per million per year in the United States (Weinberg, 1955). The catch, though, is that the overwhelming majority of cases go unreported to authorities and unprosecuted. To get a better idea of the true incidence of incest, it is necessary to do a survey of the general population. In one such survey, 7 percent of the sample had had sexual intercourse with a relative (Hunt, 1974). In a general survey of undergraduates, 15 percent of the females and 10 percent of the males said they had had a sexual experience with a sibling (Finkelhor, 1980). In most cases, the activity was limited to fondling and exhibiting the genitals. Intercourse occurred in only 5 percent of the incidents under age 8 and 18 percent of the incidents over age 13. The point is that incest, particularly if it is defined to include sexual contact other than intercourse, is not at all rare—perhaps 10 percent of people in the United States have been involved as children.

FIGURE 18.4

Incest in art: Lot and his daughter.

I have already mentioned the distinction between father-daughter incest and brother-sister incest. Which is more common? In a study of *reported* incest (reported to the police or other authorities), father-daughter cases were by far the most common: father-daughter cases constituted 78 percent of the sample, 18 percent were brother-sister, 1 percent were mother-son, and the remaining 3 percent were multiple incestuous relationships (Weinberg, 1955). However, in surveys of the *general* population, brother-sister incest is far more common, outnumbering father-daughter incest cases by about 5 to 1 (Gebhard et al., 1965). Thus it appears that brother-sister is actually the most common form, but it is far less likely to be reported to the police than father-daughter incest. Because most research has been done on reported cases, most of the research is on father-daughter incest.

Father-Daughter Incest

What kind of man commits incest with his daughter? The stereotype is that such men are cases of extreme psychopathology. However, extensive reviews of the research literature on incest show that this stereotype is not true (Meiselman, 1978; Herman, 1981). Rather, the man who commits incest appears to be a classical patriarch within his family (Herman, 1981). He is a good provider, but he rules the family. The division of roles is traditional, and the mother is typically a full-time homemaker. She also seems to be somewhat isolated within the family, often because her health is poor. Within these family dynamics, the daughter-victim seems to take on the role of holding the family together and develops a "special" relationship with her father within which the incest occurs.

The sexual activity with his daughter appears to fulfill several needs for the father (Herman, 1981). He has feelings of dependency and a need for nurturance, which he receives in the relationship with his daughter (Justice and Justice, 1979). Doubtless he experiences a sense of power in the act, for he can control it exactly as he wishes and need not fear a rejection of his techniques as he might from a mature woman (Herman, 1981). The excitement coming from the secrecy may be pleasurable. Finally, it has been suggested that the daughter's unhappiness with the sexual activity may contribute to pleasure in men who are basically expressing hostility.

One of the best accounts of the internal dynamics of father-daughter incest is Katherine Brady's autobiography, *Father's Days* (1978).

Psychological Impact on the Victim

Here we must keep in mind the distinction between father-daughter incest and brother-sister incest, because they may produce different effects on their victims.

Many therapists who are experienced with cases of incest feel that the effects of father-daughter incest on the victim are serious and long-lasting, despite the fact that the incidents were not reported and seem to have been repressed (Herman, 1981). Consider the following case:

> A 25-year-old office worker was seen in the emergency room with an acute anxiety attack. She was pacing, agitated, unable to eat or sleep, and had a feeling of impending doom. She related a vivid fantasy of being pursued by a man with a knife. The previous day she had been cornered in the office by her boss, who aggressively propositioned her. She needed the job badly and did not want to lose it, but she dreaded the thought of returning to work. It later emerged in psychotherapy that this episode of sexual harassment had reawakened previously repressed memories of sexual assaults by her father. From the age of 6 until mid-adolescence, her father had repeatedly exhibited himself to her and insisted that she masturbate him. The experience of being entrapped at work had recalled her childhood feelings of helplessness and fear. (Herman, 1981, p. 8)

Unfortunately, research in this area has not yet come to definitive conclusions about the effects on the victim, in part because the issue has been raised so recently and therefore little research has been done, and in part because there are some methodological difficulties in doing the research. Most of the research has been on reported or prosecuted cases, in which father-daughter incest is overrepresented, and in which police and court proceedings may have done as much damage to the victim as the act of incest itself, similar to what may happen with rape victims. Thus most research gives little information on sibling incest and its effects, nor about the less traumatic cases that are never reported to the police or that never lead the victim to seek psychotherapy.

Two studies are worthy of note. In a general survey of 796 undergraduates, 15 percent of the females and 10 percent of the males said they had had a sexual experience with a sibling (Finkelhor, 1980). Among those who had had sibling incest, there was an almost even division between those who felt the experience had been positive for them and those who felt it had been negative. There also seemed to be some long-term effects on sexuality. Women who had had sibling sexual experience had substantially higher levels of current (college-age) sexual activity than did women who had not experienced sibling incest. In addition, those who had had experiences with a much older sibling before they were 9 years of age suffered lowered sexual self-esteem, but those who had had positive experiences after age 9 had heightened sexual self-esteem.

In a second, well-designed study, newspaper advertisements were used to recruit women falling into these three categories: women who were victims of childhood molestation and were seeking therapy for the resulting problems (called the *clini-*

cal group); women who were victims of childhood molestation but felt well-adjusted and not in need of therapy (*nonclinical group*); and a group of women who were not victims of childhood molestation (*control group*) (Tsai et al., 179). As it turned out, 73 percent of the clinical group and 63 percent of the nonclinical group had been molested by their fathers, stepfathers, or grandfathers, so the study essentially became an investigation of father-daughter incest. The resuts showed that the clinical and nonclinical groups differed in a number of ways. The molestation went on for five years, on the average, for the clinical group, whereas it went on for about half that amount of time for the nonclinical group. The molestation also lasted until the girls were older in the clinical group. Attempted intercourse was more common in the clinical group. And finally, women in the clinical group were significantly less satisfied in their current, adult sexual relationships than were women in the nonclinical group, indicating the long-term consequences of being a childhood incest victim. This study is particularly interesting because it shows us some of the factors—long duration of molestation, molestation at older ages, attempted intercourse—that seem to be related to long-term psychological damage in women who are incest victims.

Given the previously cited statistics about the greater frequency of sibling incest. it may seem peculiar that this study found father-daughter and similar forms of incest to account for the great majority of the cases. I think that the answer lies in the fact that the newspaper ad recruiting participants used the term "molestation." An adult woman who was the victim of an incestuous relationship with her stepfather probably realizes that she was the victim of molestation. But sibling incest, particularly for a brother and sister close in age, may not seem to the woman to be "molestation," so such women would be relatively unlikely to respond to newspaper advertisements using that term.

What, then, are the psychological consequences of incest for the victim? Basically I think there is not enough good research to be able to tell right now. But I think the following conclusion is warranted: In some cases incest is highly damaging psychologically to the victim, but it is probably not damaging in every case (Renshaw, 1982). Many factors are probably involved in whether or not it is damaging: whether it is father-daughter or brother-sister incest (father-daughter being the more damaging); the age at which the victim experiences the incest; the age differences between the victim and her brother if it is sibling incest; the extent to which coercion is used, how often the activity is repeated, and the extent to which the family is disrupted by the activity. In short, it depends.

Incest Taboos

Incest taboo:
A social norm forbidding or banning incest.

Taboos against incest have been found in virtually all human societies, although some exceptions have been documented, including the Incan society and the societies of ancient Iran and ancient Egypt (Middleton, 1962; Murdock, 1949; Slotkin, 1947). It is possible that these taboos arose because people noted the harmful effects, either physical or social, of incest.

Genetically, incest may have bad consequences because it leads to inbreeding. In a study done in Japan in which marriages between cousins were compared with marriages of unrelated persons, it was found that the offspring of the cousin marriages did significantly worse in school performance and did worse on tests of physical performance, tests of intelligence, and some measures of health, although on some other measures there were no differences (Schull and Neel, 1965). Incest may also have bad social consequences; it can cause conflict and rivalry within the family, and it may also cause role strain ("Should I behave like a father or a boyfriend to her?" "How can I discipline her when I just had sex with her?").

SEXUAL HARASSMENT

Sexual harassment: Unwanted imposition of sexual requirements in the context of a relationship of unequal power, such as an employer and an employee or a professor and a student.

Because incidents of sexual harassment differ in the degree of offensiveness and coercion, they can be difficult to define, both in a legal-scholarly sense and in a personal sense. Stanford Law School Professor Catharine MacKinnon has proposed this definition: "Sexual harassment, most broadly defined, refers to the unwanted imposition of sexual requirements in the context of a relationship of unequal power." (1979, p. 1). Examples include verbal sexual suggestions or jokes, constant leering or ogling, brushing against your body "accidentally," a friendly pat, squeeze or pinch or arm against you, catching you alone for a quick kiss, the indecent proposition backed by the threat of losing your job, and forced sexual relations (MacKinnon, 1979, p. 2). Sexual harassment may occur in a variety of settings—at work, in education, in psychotherapy, or on the street.

Sexual Harassment at Work

Sexual harassment at work may take a number of different forms. A prospective employer may make it clear that sexual activity is a prerequisite to being hired. Stories of such incidents are rampant among actresses. Once on the job, sexual activity may be made a condition for continued employment, for a promotion, or for other benefits such as a raise. Here is one case:

> June, a waitress in Arkansas, was serving a customer when he reached up her skirt. When she asked her manager for future protection against such incidents, she was harassed by him instead. "They put me on probation," she recalled, "as if I was the guilty one. Then things went from bad to worse. I got lousy tables and bad hours." (Phillips, 1977)

It is clear in such incidents how a person in a position of power can use that power to punish noncompliance with sexual requests.

Surveys indicate that sexual harassment at work is far more common than many people realize. More than 9000 working women responded to a *Redbook* survey on sexual harassment at work (Safran, 1976). Almost 90 percent of them had experienced some form of sexual harassment at work. The experience was reported as being degrading and humiliating, with the woman feeling a sense of helplessness similar to that reported by rape victims. As we discussed in Chapter 10, magazine surveys of this kind tend to have serious problems because the sampling is nonrandom. In a well-sampled survey of over 20,000 members of the federal work force, 42 percent of the women and 15 percent of the men reported having been sexually harassed at work within the preceding two years (Tangri et al., 1982). The preponderance of harassers (78 percent) were male. Both women and men victims reported that the harassment had negative effects on their emotional and physical condition, their ability to work with others on the job, and their feelings about work.

FIGURE 18.5

Sexual harrassment at work: The man has positioned himself so that the woman cannot avoid contact and if he is her supervisor, she may be hesitant to protest.

Although coworkers were reported as the most common harassers of both males and females, women were considerably more likely to have been harassed by a supervisor (37 percent of the cases with a female victim) than men were to have been harassed by a supervisor (14 percent of the cases with a male victim) (Tangri et al., 1982). Thus the power differential component of sexual harassment is more likely to be a factor for female victims.

Sexual harassment at work is more than just an annoyance. Particularly for women, because they are more likely to be harassed by supervisors, it can make a critical difference in career advancement. For the working-class woman who supports her family, being fired for sexual noncompliance is a catastrophe. The power of coercion is enormous.

Sexual Harassment in Education: An A for a Lay

Sexual harassment in education was brought to public attention when, in 1977, women students sued Yale University, complaining of sexual harassment, in the

TABLE 18.1

TYPES OF UNWANTED SEXUAL ATTENTION FROM MALE INSTRUCTORS, REPORTED BY WOMEN STUDENTS AT BERKELEY

Behavior	Examples
Verbal advances	Explicit sexual propositions
Invitations	For dates, to one's apartment
Physical advances	Touching, kissing, fondling breasts
Body language	Leering, standing too close
Emotional come-ons	Writing long letters
Undue attention	Too helpful
Sexual bribery	Grade offered in exchange for affair

Source: D. J. Benson, and G. E. Thomson. (1982). Sexual harassment on a university campus: the confluence of authority relations, sexual interest and gender stratification, **29**, 236–251.

important case *Alexander v. Yale.* The case recognized that sexual harassment of women in education was a possible violation of Title IX of the Civil Rights Act.

A survey of a random sample of undergraduate women at Berkeley found that 30 percent had received unwanted sexual attention from at least one male instructor during their four years in college (Benson and Thomson, 1982; see also Adams et al.. 1983). Table 18.1 shows the types of unwanted sexual attention reported by these women.

When the sexual harassment occured with a professor with whom the woman student had had little previous contact, she generally reported coping with the situation by avoiding the man as much as possible; some of the respondents, for example, reported having their boyfriends pick them up after class (Benson and Thomson, 1982). When the harassment occured after the woman had had a long-term academic relationship with the professor, it appeared to have more devastating effects on her. These women reported experiencing self-doubt and a loss of confidence in their academic ability, as well as disillusionment with male faculty in general.

As with sexual harassment at work, we must realize the serious consequences of such incidents. Women may lose opportunities, miss certain courses, or even be forced out of a graduate degree program because of sexual harassment.

In the wake of the Yale case and others, many universities have set up grievance procedures for sexual harassment cases. An important part of such procedures is that the victim's identity is kept anonymous so that she (or sometimes he) is reasonably protected from reprisals by the faculty member.

SUMMARY

This chapter explored three situations in which power or coercion is used to force sex on an unwilling victim: rape, incest, and sexual harassment.

There are three major theoretical views of rape: victim-precipitated, psychopathology of rapists, and the feminist view.

Rape victims often do not report the crime. Common psychological responses to being raped are fear, guilt, and shame. Research indicates that serious psychological damage lasts around four months, and in some cases, more.

Although rapists vary tremendously, most are young, many repeat the offense, and most are not murderers. Date rape is common, and 14 percent of women who have been married report having been raped by a husband or an ex-husband.

Patterns of gender-role socialization probably contribute to females becoming victims and males becoming rapists.

Brother-sister incest is the most common form of incest, and is less likely to be psychologically damaging than other forms. Father-daughter incest is the second most common form, and is likely to be psychologically damaging to the daughter-victim.

Sexual harassment occurs both at work and in education. The most common pattern is that of a male harasser and a female victim, although the reverse pattern also occurs. Sexual harassment usually occurs in a context of unequal power between the harasser and the victim, as when the harasser is the victim's supervisor or professor. Sexual comments, propositions, and sexual touching all are classified as harassment. The consequences to the victim can be serious.

REVIEW QUESTIONS

1. Based on a random sample of California women, one study concluded that there is a 26 percent chance that a woman will be the victim of a completed rape at some time in her life. True or false?
2. A person who believes that a raped woman is really a slut who got what she was asking for holds the ______view of rape.
3. Research conducted with rape victims indicates that there is a rape trauma syndrome that typically lasts for about ten years following the attack. True or false?
4. The typical rapist is in his forties and hypersexual. True or false?
5. Gender-role socialization is a contributing factor in making women rape victims and men rapists. True or false?
6. The typical motive for a man raping his wife is that they are not having intercourse as frequently as he would like. True or false?
7. "Pedophiliac" is the scientific term for a child molester. True or false?
8. Surveys of the general population indicate that the most common form of incest is father-daughter incest. True or false?
9. Father-daughter incest generally seems to be more psychologically damaging to the victim than brother-sister incest. True or false?
10. A job interviewer promising a woman she will get a job if she has intercourse with him is an example of sexual harassment. True or false?

QUESTIONS FOR THOUGHT, DISCUSSION, AND DEBATE

1. On your campus, what services are available for rape victims? Do these services seem adequate, given what you have read in this chapter about victim responses to rape? What could be done to improve the services?
2. Find out, on your campus, what procedures are available if a student is a victim of sexual harassment by a professor.

SUGGESTION FOR FURTHER READING

Brady, Katherine. (1979). *Father's days.* New York: Dell paperback. This autobiography of an incest victim is both moving and insightful.

CHAPTER • 19

SEX FOR SALE

Last night
A rather trite
Thought occurred to me. Exactly what pleasure
Is there in being a "Lady of Leisure?"
One has to submit (and grit one's teeth) to a great many men
who, when the "fun" is at an end
Pretend
They've "never done this before."
I'm forgetting the "slave":
On bended knee he'll crave
To be allowed to clean your lavatory.
And when you've stripped him
and whipped him
Mercilessly,
Asks: "Do you get many like me?"

—From a poem by Kay, a London prostitute*

Pornography is an expression not of human erotic feeling and desire, and not of a love of the life of the body, but of a fear of bodily knowledge, and a desire to silence eros.†

* *Source:* Wayland Young. (1964). *Eros denied.* New York: Grove Press.
† *Source:* Susan Griffin. *Pornography and silence.* (1981). New York: Harper & Row.

CHAPTER HIGHLIGHTS

*I*n this chapter we consider two ways in which sex can be bought and sold: prostitution and pornography. Both involve complex legal issues and public outrage, but also a steady stream of eager customers.

PROSTITUTION

Prostitute: A person who engages in sexual acts in return for money, and does so in a promiscuous, fairly nondiscriminating fashion.

Prostitutes ("hookers," "whores") engage in sexual acts in return for money. As some social critics have pointed out, though, some marriages and dating arrangements would also fall into this category. Thus one should probably add the conditions that prostitutes are promiscuous and fairly nondiscriminating in their choice of partners. Female prostitution will be discussed first.

Kinds of Prostitutes

There are many kinds of prostitutes; they vary in terms of social class, status, and the lifestyle they have.

Call girl: The most expensive and exclusive category of prostitutes.

The call girl is the Cadillac of prostitutes. She is expensively dressed, lives in an attractive apartment in a good section of town, and probably charges a minimum of $50 for an hour's worth of her services (more if she is classier or is asked to engage in more exotic sexual acts, such as anal intercourse). She can thus earn over $50,000 a year, tax-free. But she does have high business expenses: an expensive wardrobe and apartment, high medical bills for VD prevention, expenses for makeup and hairdressers, high tips for doormen and landlords, and the cost of an answering service.

She obtains her clients through personal referrals and may have many regular customers; thus she maintains close control over whom she services. She may also provide other than sexual services; for example, she may be an attractive companion for a party, or she may be part of a "reward" that businesses provide for executives. The contact is often made over the phone, or perhaps in an expensive bar; the sexual activity may then take place in either her apartment or his.

The call girl is typically from a middle-class background, has more self-discipline than other prostitutes, and is better educated; some are college graduates. The movie *Klute,* starring Jane Fonda, provides a good look into the life of a call girl.

Brothel (BRAH-thul): A house of prostitution, where prostitutes and customers meet for sexual activity.

Other prostitutes work out of brothels. In the 1800s and early 1900s there were many successful brothels in the United States. They varied from clip joints, where the customer's money was stolen by an accomplice while he was sexually occupied, to the sporting houses and mansions. There the women were beautifully dressed, and fine food and liquor were served. The customer could choose his partner in an attractive living room downstairs; the bedrooms were upstairs, and no time limits were imposed on the customer (Bess and Janus, 1976). Brothels have declined in numbers and success since World War II. In the last decade, though, a replacement seems to have cropped up: the massage parlor

Massage parlor: A place where massages, as well as sexual services, can generally be purchased.

Some women sell their sexual services in massage parlors (Velarde and Warlick, 1973). Massage parlors—and massages, of course—are perfectly legal, and so this setup has some advantages over more standard forms of prostitution, which are illegal. Once the customer is inside the private massage room, though, it is understood that he can get whatever services he pays for. Intercourse is not always possible, since massage parlors are not legally permitted to have beds, but fellatio and hand stimulation of the penis (a "local") are quite practical. Here, too, the customer may be fleeced. For example, he may pay for "oral sex" and find he is allowed to talk for several minutes and is then shown out.

Another way in which a veneer of respectability is added to a sex business is through an "escort service," which may actually offer sexual services.

Streetwalker: A lower-status prostitute who walks the streets selling her services.

At the lower end of the status hierarchy is the streetwalker, which is the style of the majority of prostitutes. She sells her wares on the streets of cities. She is generally less attractive and less fashionably dressed than the call girl, and she charges correspondingly less for her services, perhaps as little as $10 for a "quickie." She is more likely to impose strict time constraints on the customer. Because her mode of operation is obvious, she is likely to be arrested, and she is also more likely to be exposed to dangerous clients.

Bar girls are similar to streetwalkers, except that they operate out of working-class bars. A *fleabag* is an old bar girl, perhaps 60 or 70 years old, who caters mostly to skid-row alcoholics and bums.

Baby pro: A young prostitute, generally 16 years of age or younger.

A baby pro is generally younger than 16 years old and works conventions, resorts, and hotels (Shoemaker, 1977). There has been an increasing demand in recent years for this kind of prostitute.

(a)

FIGURE 19.1

The oldest profession. (*a*) Fifteenth-century prostitutes "in the women's house." (*b*) Modern prostitute "working the street."

(b)

Pimps and Madams

Pimp:
A prostitute's companion, protector, and master.

Panderer:
The person who helps the prostitute and client find each other.

Madam:
A woman who manages a brothel.

The pimp ("The Man") is the companion-master of the prostitute. She supports him with her earnings, and in return he gives her companionship and sex, gets her out of jail, and provides her with food, clothing, shelter, and drugs, especially cocaine. He also provides protection against theft and other crimes, since the prostitute is scarcely in a position to go to the police if she is robbed by a customer. The *procurer,* or panderer, helps the prostitute and client find each other. Pimps sometimes, though not always, function as panderers.

The prostitutes working for a pimp are called his "stable," and each is called a "wife." An "outlaw" is a prostitute who has no pimp. Typically, the pimp returns only 5 percent of the prostitute's earnings to her (Sheehy, 1973).

A madam is a woman who manages a brothel. Typically, she is quite intelligent and has excellent financial and social skills. The best-known madam of the 1970s was Xaviera Hollander, who managed a brothel in New York and wrote *The Happy Hooker.*

Psychological Functioning of Prostitutes

Contrary to common belief, most prostitutes are not lesbians; in their private, noncommercial sex lives, most are heterosexual (Gallo and Alzate, 1976; Gebhard, 1969).

Although most prostitutes are of average intelligence, the majority—with the exception of call girls—are not well educated (Bess and Janus, 1976). Given that they are of normal intelligence and sensitivity, they must surely perceive the low esteem in which society holds them. How do they cope with this degrading image of themselves?

According to one study, several rationalizing strategies may be adopted (Jackman et al., 1963). One group of prostitutes become a part of a criminal subculture and adopt its set of values. The prostitute then has a set of counterculture values and is critical of conventional values. She might say that middle-class, conventional mores are hypocritical and boring. A second group of women shift their lives between two worlds. They are middle-class, are often married and have children, and use prostitution as a means of supporting themselves and their families. These women have very conventional values and maintain a strict dissociation between their two worlds. One said:

> I think that I am a good mother who takes care of her children. I love my family very much. I have a normal family life other than being a prostitute. I hope that my husband can find a job and gets to working steadily again so I can be an ordinary housewife. (Jackman et al., 1963, p. 157)

Finally, Jackman and his colleagues described a third group as totally alienated. Their lives have no orientation and seem meaningless, and they have no well-defined set of values.

The Career of a Prostitute

The first step in a prostitute's career is entry. There appear to be many reasons why a woman enters prostitution (Bess and Janus, 1976). One is sheer economics. This factor is particularly likely during war, when prostitution may be the only means of survival. But even in times of peace, prostitution can be economically appealing, particularly for the woman who has no job skills. Why take a boring, restrictive job as a secretary for $150 a week when you can make that much in a day, or even a few hours, as a call girl? A related factor is a dislike of routine and regimen and an attraction for the glamour and excitement of the world of the prostitute. For some women—for example, a poor but very attractive woman—prostitution is a means of attaining upward economic mobility. Some women become prostitutes in order to support a drug addiction. Another category of reasons involves gaining power. For example, a woman who serves as a call girl to famous politicians may think of herself as having access to real political power. As a woman who was involved in one of the Capitol Hill sex scandals uncovered in the 1970s said, "I was only a pillowcase away from the Presidency." Still other women gradually drift into prostitution, perhaps because they have a friend who is a prostitute who encourages them to do it. Rumors that there is a large "white slave" market in the United States are untrue, however; only about 4 percent of prostitutes were actually forced into the profession (Gebhard, 1969).

On entering prostitution, some women—particularly if they want to be call girls—go through an apprenticeship in which they pay an experienced call girl to teach them the skills of the profession (Bryan, 1965). The apprentice learns not only sexual techniques but also how to manage finances, how to control customers, how to avoid being robbed, and how to make contacts.

One problem with prostitution is that it is a short-lived career, in this respect bearing a resemblance to the career of a professional basketball or football player. Even a woman who starts as a high-priced call girl may find herself drifting down in status, either as she ages and begins to show wrinkles or if she gets hooked on alcohol or drugs. In prostitution, seniority is not rewarded.

"Squaring up" or "leaving the life" refers to giving up prostitution. Financially it is a difficult thing to do, particularly for the woman with no job skills; recognizing this, some rehabilitation programs provide job training, as well as a halfway house to integrate the woman back into society (Winick and Kinsie, 1971).

The married prostitute may simply go back to being a housewife. The unmarried woman may escape through marriage, since she may get proposals from her regular customers (Benjamin and Masters, 1964; Young, 1970).

Other reasons for leaving include arrest and the threat of a long-term jail sentence, government agencies' insistence that she give up her children, and the knowledge that a friend was the victim of violence while she worked as a prostitute (Bess and Janus, 1976).

Customers

At the time of the Kinsey research, about 69 percent of all white males had had some experience with prostitutes (Kinsey et al., 1948). The recent Hunt survey, however, found that the use of prostitutes is becoming less common in the under-35 age group, particularly among middle-class males; only 19 percent of the men under 35 with some college education had had premarital intercourse with a prostitute (Hunt, 1974). Thus the use of prostitutes seems to be declining.

Prostitutes refer to their customers as "johns." About 60 percent of the clients are occasional johns; they may be respectable businessmen who seek only occasional contacts with prostitutes, perhaps while on business trips. Others are habitual johns who seek a regular relationship with a prostitute. Some are compulsive johns, who use prostitutes for their major sexual outlet. They are driven to them and cannot stay away. Some of these men are able to function sexually only with prostitutes (Bess and Janus, 1976).

Men use the services of prostitutes for a variety of reasons. Some are married but want sex more frequently than their wives do or want to engage in practices—such as fellatio—that they feel their wives would not be willing to do. Some use prostitutes to satisfy their exotic sexual needs, such as being whipped or having sex with a woman who pretends to be a corpse. The motivation for the unmarried man or the one who is away from home for a long period of time (for example, during a war) may simply be release of sexual tension. Others, particularly adolescents. may have sex with prostitutes to prove their manhood or to get sexual experience. Finally, some men enjoy sex with prostitutes because it is "forbidden."

Male Prostitutes

Gigolo (JIG-uh-loh): A male prostitute who sells his services to women; also refers to professional male escorts.

Hustler: A male prostitute who sells his services to men.

Some male prostitutes serve a heterosexual clientele, selling their services to women; they are called gigolos. They often cater to wealthy, middle-aged women and provide them with escort as well as sexual services. Their approach is generally subtle and romantically flattering to their clients. The character played by Jon Voight in *Midnight Cowboy* made an attempt to support himself in this way.

Hustlers are male prostitutes who cater to a homosexual clientele. Interestingly, some of them consider themselves to be heterosexual, not homosexual (Coombs, 1974). They may have strict rules for their customers to follow, such as only permitting the customer to perform fellatio on them. To indicate their masculinity, they may wear leather jackets and tight jeans. There is some market for "chickens" (young boys) as prostitutes.

Male prostitutes seem to fall into four categories (Allen, 1980). First are the full-time street and bar hustlers, who operate much as do female streetwalkers. Second are full-time call boys or kept boys. They tend to have a more exclusive clientele and to be more attractive and more sexually versatile than the streetwalkers. Surprisingly, by far the largest group was the third: part-time hustlers, who were typically students or individuals employed in another occupation. They generally work at prostitution only when they need money. The part-time hustlers are notable because unlike those in the other groups, they are less likely to come from inadequate families. They also have the best long-term chance for getting an education and a stable job and achieving a good social adjustment. Finally, a fourth group is made up of delinquents; they use prostitution and homosexuality as extensions of other criminal activities, such as assault and robbery. They are taught by older gang members how to pick up homosexuals and then threaten, blackmail, or assault them.

PORNOGRAPHY

A debate over pornography is currently raging. Feminists and fundamentalists (strange bedfellows, indeed!) agree that some kinds of pornography should be made illegal, while civil liberties groups argue that freedom of expression, guaranteed in the Constitution, must be preserved and therefore pornography should not be restricted by law. Meanwhile, Joe Brown goes to his local newsstand, buys his monthly copy of *Playboy,* thinks a little longer about *Hustler,* buys it, too, and strolls back to his apartment for a pleasurable evening's entertainment. Here we will examine what the issues are, paying particular attention to social scientists' research on the effects of pornography on people who are exposed to it. First, we need to clarify some terminology.

Terms

Pornography: Sexually arousing art, literature, or films.

Soft-core pornography: Pornography that is suggestive but not explicit in portraying sexual acts or the genitals.

Hard-core pornography: Pornography that is explicit in depicting sexual acts or the genitals.

Obscenity: Something that is offensive according to accepted standards of decency; the legal term for pornography.

Erotica: Sexually arousing material that is not degrading or demeaning to women. men, or children.

We can distinguish between pornography, obscenity, and erotica. Pornography comes from the Greek word "porneia," which means, quite simply, "prostitution"; in general usage today, it refers to literature, art, film, and so on, that are sexually arousing in nature. Soft-core pornography refers to pornography that is suggestive rather than explicit. Hard-core pornography, in contrast, is explicit in that it shows actual sexual acts or explicit photographs of the genitals.

In legal terminology the word used is "obscenity," not pornography. Obscenity refers to that which is foul, disgusting, or lewd, and it is used as a legal term for that which is offensive to the authorities or to society (Wilson, 1973). The U.S. Supreme Court has had a rather hard time defining exactly what is obscene and what can be regulated legally, a point to be discussed in more detail in Chapter 23.

In the current debate over pornography, some make the distinction between pornography (which is unacceptable to them) and erotica (which is acceptable). For example, sociologist Diana E. H. Russell defines *pornography* as "explicit representations of sexual behavior, verbal or pictorial, that have as a distinguishing characteristic the degrading or demeaning portrayal of human beings, especially women" (Russell, 1980, p. 218). In contrast, erotica is defined as differing from pornography "by virtue of not degrading or demeaning women, men, or children" (Russell, 1980, p. 218). According to this distinction, a movie of a woman being raped would be pornography, whereas a movie of two mutually consenting adults who are both enjoying having sexual intercourse together would be considered erotica, not pornography.

Beyond these definitions given by scholars in the area, it is interesting to see how typical Americans define pornography. Research shows that there is incredible diversity in what people consider pornography. Table 19.1 shows the result of one study on this question. It shows, for example, that 77 percent of Americans would consider a picture of a female performing fellatio on a male to be pornographic, but that means that 23 percent of Americans would not consider that pornographic. And even Leonardo Da Vinci's painting of Christ is considered pornographic by 13 percent of those surveyed (Brown et al., 1978).

Types of Pornography

Pornography is a multimillion dollar business in the United States. Included in that business are a number of products: magazines, films, kiddie porn, and live sex shows.

A large chunk of the pornography market consists of magazines, ranging from *Playboy* and *Penthouse* to *Hustler* and hundreds of others with less well-known names. The soft-core magazines mushroomed beginning in the early 1970s. In the 1980s the market is large and includes both general magazines and those catering to special tastes. For example, some specialize in "pinks"—close-ups of the female genitals, while others feature photographs of lesbian activity.

Most pornography is designed for the heterosexual male reader. Yet in the 1970s *Playgirl* appeared, featuring "beefcake" to please the heterosexual female customer. There is also a large gay pornography business.

TABLE 19.1

PERCENTAGES OF ADULT AMERICANS RATING VARIOUS PHOTOGRAPHS AS PORNOGRAPHIC

Picture Content	Adults Seeing Content as Pornographic (%)
Two nude males petting	79
Female performing fellatio on male	77
Nude male standing with genitals exposed	50
Nude female, side view with pubic hair showing	37
Leonardo Da Vinci's Christ	13
Couple kissing, faces only showing	11

Source: C. Brown et al. (1978). Community standards, conservatism, and judgments of pornography. *Journal of Sex Research*, **14**, 81–95.

Soft-core pornography is a lucrative business, to put it mildly. In 1981, the ten best-selling soft-core magazines had a total monthly circulation of over 16 million, and in 1979 they brought in over $500 million in profit (Serrin, 1981).

Hard-core magazines have a no-holds-barred approach to what they present. Photographs may include everything from vaginal intercourse to anal intercourse, sadomasochism, bondage, and sex with animals.

Here, again, the profit motive is great. The markups may be as high as 600 percent, and it is estimated that there are approximately 20,000 stores in the United States selling hard-core magazines. If run properly, such a business will have as much as $200,000 per year in gross sales (Serrin, 1981). Yet more profit comes from customers who have regular subscriptions for pornographic magazines by mail, and repeat, frequent customers account for a large part of the market.

Although sexually explicit movies were made as early as 1915, only in the last two decades have these films been slick and well produced. The *hard-core film* industry began to emerge in a big way around 1970. Two films were especially important in starting the revolution. *I Am Curious, Yellow,* appearing in 1970, showed sexual intercourse explicitly. In part because it was a foreign film with an intellectual tone, it became fashionable for people, including married couples, to see it. I remember long conversations in the faculty lounge among my psychology professor colleagues about their opinions after seeing it. The other important early film was *Deep Throat,* appearing in 1973. With its humor and creative plot, it was respectable and popular among the middle class. Linda Lovelace, the female star, gained national recognition and later appeared on the cover of *Esquire.*

After the success of *Deep Throat,* there was a rapid appearance of full-length, technically well-done hard-core films. *Deep Throat* had made it clear that there were big profits to be made. It cost $24,000 to make, yet by 1982 it had yielded $25,000,000 in profits ("Video Turns Big Profit," 1982).

Loops are short (10-minute) hard-core films. They are set up in coin-operated projectors in private booths, usually in adult bookstores. The patron can enter and view the film in privacy, and perhaps masturbate while doing so.

In the early 1980s, business declined at X-rated theaters. But this was more than offset by a booming new business: X-rated *videocassettes.* For example, *Deep Throat* became available on cassette in 1977, and, by 1982, 300,000 copies of it had been sold ("Video turns big profit," 1982; Cohn, 1983).

Cable television has also entered the arena, with porn stations in some areas. Needless to say, these are causing considerable controversy. The notion that a 3-year-old might innocently flip the station from *Sesame Street* and discover a man binding a woman in chains and then having intercourse with her does seem offensive at best and dangerous at worst.

FIGURE 19.2

One of the newest innovations in the sex entertainment business is male strippers.

Live sex shows are yet another part of the sex industry. Strip shows, of course, have a long tradition in our culture. They have declined in popularity recently, but the new rage is male strippers, catering to a female audience. In the sex districts of many cities, there are also now live sex shows featuring couples or groups engaging in sexual acts onstage.

Kiddie porn: Pictures or films of sexual acts with children.

Finally, there is kiddie porn, which features pictures or films of sexual acts with children. It is currently viewed as the most reprehensible part of the porn industry, because it produces such an obvious victim, the child model. Children, by virtue of their developmental level, cannot give true informed consent to participate in such activities, and the potential for doing psychological damage to them is great. Many states have recently moved to outlaw kiddie porn, making it illegal to photograph or sell such material; as of 1984, 49 states prohibited the production of child pornography and 36 prohibited its distribution (Burgess, 1984, p. 202).

Again, the profit motives are strong. An advertisement in the magazine *Screw* offered $200 for young girl-child models, and dozens of parents responded. A reporter covering the scene said:

> Some parents appeared in the movie with their children; others merely allowed their children to have sex. One little girl, age 11, who ran crying from the bedroom after being told to have sex with a man of 40 protested, "Mommy I can't do it." "You have to do it," her mother answered. "We need the money." And of course the little girl did. (Anson, 1977)

Some major, well-known films could easily be classified as kiddie porn. *Taxi Driver* featured Jodie Foster as a 12-year-old prostitute. And *Pretty Baby* launched the career of Brooke Shields, playing the role of a 12-year-old brothel prostitute in New Orleans. Brooke herself was 12 years old when the film was made.

The kiddie porn business is extremely secretive, so statistics must be regarded as approximations, but here are some interesting ones (Hurst, 1977; Ditkoff, 1978):

F · O · C · U · S 19.1

ERNIE: A PEDOPHILE AND CHILD PORNOGRAPHER

In a study of child sexual abuse and child pornography, the investigators reported the following description of one offender:

In March 1979 contact was made with Ernie, a northern Indiana man, and arrangements were made to meet with him to share child pornography collections. Ernie arrived at a motel room carrying a small suitcase containing approximately 75 magazines and a metal file box containing twelve super-8-mm movies. The metal box was also filled with numerous photographs. Ernie then began to discuss his collection. He described himself as a pedophile and showed a series of instant photographs he had taken of his 7-year-old niece while she slept. The pictures revealed Ernie's middle finger inserted into the young girl's uncovered genitals, and he described how he had "worked" his finger up into her. Other photographs featured the girl being molested in various ways by Ernie while she remained asleep.

Despite the fact that he had engaged in numerous incidents of child molestation, Ernie had not been discovered because his victims remained asleep. He had molested and exploited both males and females, his own children, grandchildren, and neighborhood children. In order to photograph the uncovered genitals of his sleeping victims, Ernie had devised a string and hook mechanism. The hook was attached to the crotch of the panties, and he would uncover his sleeping victims' genitals as he photographed them with an instant-developing camera.

Ernie displayed his collection with the pride of a hobbyist. He exhibited photographs he had reproduced from magazines; he had reproduced these same photographs repeatedly and had engaged in a child pornography business from his residence.

While displaying his magazines and films, Ernie was arrested. A search warrant was obtained for his residence, and material seized from his one-bedroom apartment filled two pickup trucks. Numerous sexually explicit films, photographs, magazines, advertisements, and children's soiled underwear were confiscated. The panties had been encased in plastic, the child's school photograph featured with the panties. Also confiscated were nine cameras and a projector.

Several months passed before investigators found proof that Ernie had processed, through a central Indiana photographic lab, approximately 1500 photographs per week. It is believed that Ernie sold these pictures at $2 each, grossing an estimated $3000 per week.

Source: Ann W. Burgess. (1984). *Child pornography and sex rings.* Lexington, MA: Lexington Books of D. C. Heath, pp. 26–27.

- Of the $2.5 billion porn industry, about $1 billion is from kiddie porn.
- Each year, 1.2 million children are involved in commercial sex—either prostitution or pornography and often both.
- Most runaways can survive only as prostitutes or by posing for pornography. Each year there are 1 million runaway children.
- Covenant House in New York City shelters 5000 runaways each year. Over 2000 are involved in pornography and prostitution and of this number, 1000 are under 12.

A major study of offenders (the people who produce child pornography) and victims profiled the offender as follows: all of the 69 offenders studied were male. They ranged in age from 20 to 70, with an average of 43. And 38 percent had an already established relationship with the child before the illicit activity began—they were family friends or relatives, neighbors, teachers, or counselors (Burgess. 1984).

Sex ring:
A group of children involved with an adult in sexual acts or producing kiddie porn.

One important part of the child pornography and prostitution business is the sex ring (Burgess, 1984). This refers to cases in which a group of children are involved with an adult, either engaging in sexual acts with the adult or posing as models in the filming of pornographic materials. In the *solo ring* one adult operates alone with a small group of children. In the *syndicated ring* there is a well-structured organization of adults formed for recruiting children, producing the pornography, delivering child prostitution services, and recruiting customers.

A study of 66 children who had been involved in sex rings documented the damaging psychological consequences for the children (Burgess, 1984). Because the child is forced so prematurely into adult sexual activity, there is difficulty integrating the physical, emotional, and psychological aspects of sexuality. Some children deal with the forced physical activity by separating their emotions from the physical aspects of sex. Some repress the events so that they cannot consciously remember their occurrence. Most learn that sex is to be shrouded in secrecy. And some become programmed to use sex to get attention and bolster their failing sense of self-esteem. In the din of public outrage over kiddie porn, we must not forget to care for the quiet child-victims.

Yet we shouldn't leave our discussion of pornography with this most shocking aspect of it; let us instead close the discussion by considering a mating of sex and money that all of us encounter every day—*sex in advertising.* Both subtle and obvious sexual promises are used to sell a wide variety of products. Brooke Shields wants nothing between her and her Calvin Klein jeans. Perfumes promise that they will make women instantly sexually attractive. There is even a brand of coffee now that seems to guarantee a warm, romantic, sensuous evening for the couple who drink it. An important part of the presence of sexuality in the media is advertising.

The Customers

What is known about the customer of pornography? The stereotype is that he is a real sicko, living alone in a rundown apartment, obsessively reading and viewing pornography, and then slinking out to commit sex crimes against women and children. Yet the scientific studies consistently indicate that the average customer of pornography is an educated, middle-class male between the ages of 22 and 34 (Mahoney, 1983). That is, the use of pornography is "typical" or "normal" (in the statistical sense) among males. Whether that fact is good or bad is debatable.

As an example, in one survey of university students 59 percent of the white males and 36 percent of the white females said they went to X-rated movies or read pornographic books (Houston, 1981). Over 5 percent of the females and 9 percent of the males said they did so frequently or very frequently. Repeat customers are a critical part of the success of the porno business.

Feminist Objections to Pornography

Beginning around 1978, feminists became very critical of pornography (e.g., Lederer, 1980; Griffin, 1981; Morgan, 1978). Why would feminists, who prize sexual liberation, be opposed to pornography?

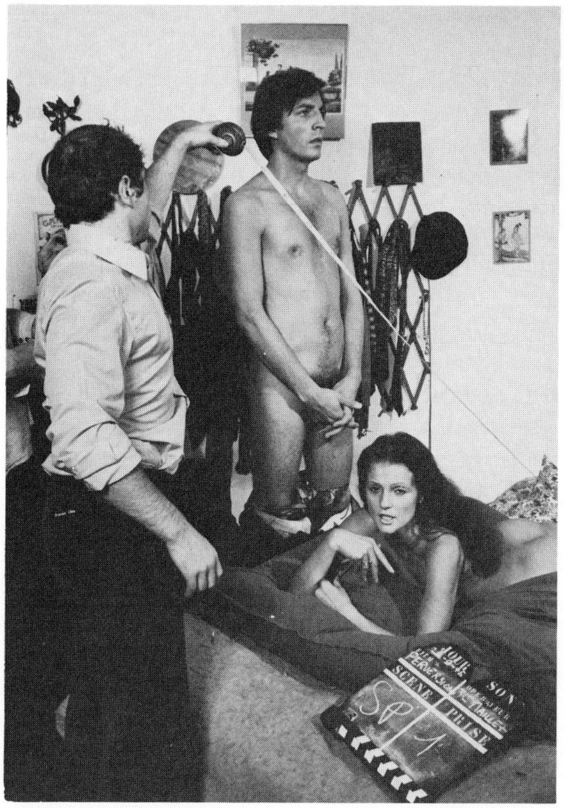

FIGURE 19.3

The making of a porn film.

There are three basic reasons why feminists object to pornography. First, they argue that pornography debases women. In the milder, soft-core versions it portrays women as sex objects whose breasts, legs, and buttocks can be purchased and then ogled. In the hard-core versions women may be shown being urinated upon or being chained. This scarcely represents a respectful attitude toward women. Second, pornography associates sex with violence toward women. As such, it contributes to rape and other forms of violence against women and girls. Robin Morgan puts it bluntly: ". . . pornography is the theory and rape is the practice" (Morgan, 1980, p. 139). This is a point that can be tested with scientific data, and this evidence will be covered in the next section. Third, pornography shows, indeed glamorizes, unequal power relationships between women and men. A common theme in pornography is men forcing women to have sex, and so the power of men and subordination of women is emphasized. Consistent with this point, feminists do not object to sexual materials that portray women and men in equal, humanized relationships—what we have termed *erotica*.

Feminists also note the intimate relationship between pornography and traditional gender roles. Pornography is enmeshed as both cause and effect. That is, pornography in part results from traditional gender roles that make pornography socially acceptable for men to use, and require hypersexuality and aggressiveness as part of the male role. Consistent with the idea that use of pornography is linked to traditional masculinity, one study of androgyny and the use of pornography among college students found that the likeliest users of pornography are traditionally gender-typed, masculine males and androgynous females (Kenrick et al., 1980). Yet the reverse process may also occur—that is, pornography may serve to perpetuate traditional gender roles. By showing dominant males and submissive, dehumanized females, each new generation of adolescent boys is socialized to accept these roles.

The variety of possible effects of pornography on those who use it is summarized in Table 19.2. Some of the assertions summarized above—for example, that violent pornography may predispose men to committing violent crimes against women—can be tested using the methods of social science. A number of social psychologists have been busy collecting data to test such assertions.

Two basic questions can be asked about the effects of pornography: Does it affect the sexual behavior of its users; and does it affect the aggressive or criminal behavior of its users?

In 1967 Congress established the Commission on Obscenity and Pornography, which was charged with investigating these issues; the commission issued its report in 1970 (Commission on Obscenity and Pornography, 1970). The basic conclusion of the report was that pornography did not have bad effects on people. Soon after, there appeared a report of the "Denmark experiment"; Denmark completely legalized pornography, and the result seemed to be a reduction in sex crimes, notably child molestation (Kutchinsky, 1973). Thus most textbooks featured the conclusion that pornography is not harmful.

However, the Report of the Commission on Obscenity and Pornography has been criticized because aggressive-pornographic materials were relatively rare at the time, and thus the materials it investigated were relatively mild and soft-core and did not depict violence (Malamuth, 1984). Aggressive pornography might give much more cause for concern, and there is evidence that it is increasing in frequency. One study analyzed the content of hard-core paperback books published between 1968 and 1974 (Smith, 1976). The results indicated that about one-third of the episodes involved the use of force and it was almost always by a male to coerce a female into an act of unwanted sex. Further, the average number of rape episodes doubled from 1968 to 1974. Another study analyzed pictures and cartoons in *Playboy* and *Penthouse* (Malamuth and Spinner, 1980). About 10 percent of the cartoons were violent, and sexual violence in the pictures increased from 1 percent in 1973 to 5 percent in 1977. An analysis of the covers of pornographic magazines indicated that, in 1981, 17 percent of them featured bondage and domination imagery (Dietz and Evans, 1982). In short, the conclusions of the 1970 commission report may no longer be accurate, and so we turn to more recent studies.

In general, research indicates that pornography—whether violent or not—does not seem to have much of a long-term effect on people's *sexual behavior* (although there may be some short-term increases in arousal lasting from a few minutes to an hour). For example, in one study males were exposed to sexually explicit, but not violent, slides (Brown et al., 1976). In the week afterward there was no significant increase in sexual activity, although there was a large increase in masturbation on the day of exposure. Neither does exposure to aggressive pornography seem to produce increases in sexual arousal, even when the exposure is to five feature-length movies over a period of several weeks (Ceniti and Malamuth, 1981, cited in Malamuth, 1984).

The effect of aggressive pornography on *aggressive behavior* is a different story. Here we do seem to find effects, with violent porn increasing aggressive behavior as well as affecting attitudes and perceptions of violence toward women. For example, in one study male subjects were assigned to one of three experimental conditions: reading aggressive pornography stories with pictures (from *Penthouse,* depicting a male pirate raping a woman); reading nonaggressive pornography with pictures

TABLE 19.2

POSSIBLE CONSEQUENCES OF EXPOSURE TO PORNOGRAPHY

	Sexual	Nonsexual
Criminal or generally regarded as harmful	1. Rape 2. Incest 3. Adultery 4. Dehumanized sexual acts 5. Misinformation about sex 6. Change of individual's values so that deviant or illegal behaviors are thought to be normal	1. Murder 2. Juvenile delinquency 3. Rejection of reality 4. Devaluing of women
Beneficial or helpful	1. Drains off inappropriate or violent sexual urges 2. Pleasure 3. Enhances appropriate sexual expression, such as livening marital sex	

Source: Adapted from the Report of the President's Commission on Obscenity and Pornography (1970). New York: Bantam Books.

(also from *Penthouse,* but showing a loving interaction); or reading a neutral selection (from *National Geographic,* but apparently not one of their selections featuring nude natives). Afterward all subjects were insulted by a woman who was actually a confederate of the experimenter's (Malamuth, 1978, cited in Malamuth, 1984). They were then placed in a situation in which they could aggress against her by delivering electric shocks to her—a standard way psychologists measure aggression—although in fact the shock did not reach her. Those who had been exposed to the aggressive pornography showed significantly higher levels of aggression than those exposed to the nonaggressive pornography. Other studies indicated that exposure to aggressive pornography increases the aggressive behavior of male subjects toward females but not toward males (Donnerstein, 1980, 1983; Donnerstein and Berkowitz, 1981).

Another, more naturalistic study investigated the impact of violent pornography on attitudes about violence against women (Malamuth and Check, 1981). Undergraduates volunteered to participate in a study that was supposedly about movie ratings. They viewed, on two different nights, either (1) the movies *Swept Away* and *The Getaway,* which show sexual aggression against women with "positive" consequences (the woman eventually becomes aroused by the aggressive sex); or (2) neutral feature-length films. The films were part of the university film series. Several days later the students completed a number of attitude scales, including some on sexual attitudes and acceptance of interpersonal violence. The results indicated that exposure to the films that showed sexual aggression with "positive" consequences significantly increased male subjects' acceptance of interpersonal violence against women and increased their acceptance of rape myths. Interestingly, these same increases did not occur for female subjects.

In sum, then, we can conclude that exposure to pornography does not have much of an effect on people's sexual behavior. However, exposure to aggressive pornography does increase males' aggression toward women, as well as affecting males' attitudes, making them more accepting of violence against women.

These are disturbing conclusions. What is the solution? Should pornography be censored or made illegal? Or would that only make it forbidden and therefore more attractive, and still available on a black market? Or should all forms of pornography be legal and readily available, and should we rely on other methods—such as education of parents and students through the school system—to abolish its use? Or should we adopt some in-between strategy, making some forms of pornography—kiddie porn and violent porn—illegal, while allowing free access to erotica? These are important questions for us to discuss and decide as a society. I hope that we will take the most humanizing approach.

SUMMARY

There are several kinds of prostitutes, ranging from call girls to streetwalkers. The career of a prostitute begins with entry, often for economic reasons. There may then be an apprenticeship, followed by a career that is generally short.

Male prostitutes are either gigolos (catering to women) or hustlers (catering to men).

There is a distinction between soft-core pornography (sexually suggestive but not explicit), hard-core pornography (sexually explicit), obscenity (the legal term), and erotica (sexual material that shows men and women in equal, humane relationships). Hard-core films and magazines form a multimillion dollar business. Children—often runaways—are the star-victims in kiddie porn.

Feminists object to pornography on the grounds that it debases women, that it encourages violence against women, and that it features unequal relationships between men and women.

Psychological research generally indicates that pornography has little long-term effect on people's sexual behavior, but that violent pornography can increase men's aggression toward women, as well as creating more tolerant attitudes toward violence against women.

REVIEW QUESTIONS

1. The call girl is the most expensive and exclusive of prostitutes. True or false?
2. The massage parlor is a modern version of a brothel. True or false?
3. The _____ is the companion-master of the prostitute.
4. _____ are male prostitutes who sell their services to women.
5. Hard-core pornography is defined as pornography that includes physical violence. True or false?
6. Feminists distinguish between pornography and erotica, erotica being sexually explicit but not degrading to women, men, or children. True or false?
7. Kiddie porn is considered to be the worst part of the porn industry; it is illegal to produce kiddie porn in virtually all of the states. True or false?
8. The typical customer of pornography is a male in his forties or fifties who is psychiatrically disturbed, usually a psychopath. True or false?
9. In a 1970 report, the President's Commission on Obscenity and Pornography concluded that pornography is not harmful, but the studies available at the time tested only the effects of nonviolent, soft-core pornography. True or false?
10. Malamuth's research indicates that male subjects who are exposed to aggressive pornography are later more aggressive to women than are a control group of males. True or false?

QUESTION FOR THOUGHT, DISCUSSION, AND DEBATE

1. What is your position on the issue of censoring pornography? Do you think that all pornography should be illegal? Or should all pornography be legal? Or should some kinds—such as kiddie porn and violent porn—be illegal? What reasoning led you to your position?

SUGGESTIONS FOR FURTHER READING

Donnerstein, Edward and Linz, Daniel. (1984, Jan.). Sexual violence in the media: A warning. *Psychology Today,* 14–15. This article discusses Donnerstein and others' research on the harmful effects of violent pornography.

Malamuth, Neil and Donnerstein, Edward. (1984). *Pornography and sexual aggression.* New York: Academic Press. An excellent collection of articles by experts on the effects of pornography.

Sheehy, Gail. (1973). *Hustling: Prostitution in our wide-open society.* New York: Delacorte Press. An inside look at prostitution written by a well-known journalist.

CHAPTER • **20**

SEXUAL DYSFUNCTION AND SEX THERAPY

We have nothing to fear but fear itself.

—Franklin Delano Roosevelt

CHAPTER HIGHLIGHTS

I. KINDS OF SEXUAL DYSFUNCTION

II. WHAT CAUSES SEXUAL DYSFUNCTION?

III. TWO MODELS OF THERAPY

IV. THE MASTERS AND JOHNSON SEX THERAPY PROGRAM

V. OTHER THERAPIES

VI. SEX THERAPY FOR GAYS

VII. CRITIQUES OF SEX THERAPY

VIII. SOME PRACTICAL ADVICE

Sexual dysfunctions such as premature ejaculation in men and inability to have orgasms in women have been the cause of a great deal of mental anguish, not to mention marital discord. Psychoanalysts, psychiatrists, and psychologists have for years used long-term therapy to treat sexual dysfunctions; however, a new era in understanding and treatment was ushered in with the publication, in 1970, of *Human Sexual Inadequacy,* by Masters and Johnson. This book reported not only their research on sexual dysfunctions and the causes of these dysfunctions but also their rapid-treatment program of therapy for such disorders. The work of Masters and Johnson, as well as that of others currently working in the field, will be discussed in this chapter.

Sexual dysfunction: A problem with sexual response that causes a person mental distress.

First, though, it is necessary to define the term "sexual dysfunction." A sexual dysfunction (the prefix "dys-" means "impaired") is any one of various disturbances or impairments of sexual functioning. A synonym might be "sexual malfunctioning." Examples are inability to get an erection (erectile dysfunction) in the male and inability to have an orgasm (orgasmic dysfunction, or anorgasmia) in the female. This definition seems fairly simple; as will be seen in the following sections, however, in practice it can be difficult to determine exactly when something is a sexual dysfunction.

No one knows exactly how many people have sexual dysfunctions. We know only about those who seek some kind of treatment for the problem, and they may be few in number compared with those who have a dysfunction but suffer quietly and never seek therapy, as a result of either ignorance or embarrassment. According to Masters and Johnson (1970), "A conservative estimate would indicate half the marriages [in this country] as either presently sexually dysfunctional or imminently so in the future." While this may be a slight overestimate, it seems safe to say that many Americans either have a sexual dysfunction or are affected by one in their partner and that perhaps an even more sizable number of people are affected by occasional instances of sexual dysfunction; most men, for example, occasionally experience problems in getting an erection.

In this section, the various kinds of sexual dysfunctions will be discussed: erectile dysfunction (impotence), premature ejaculation, and retarded ejaculation in men; orgasmic dysfunction and vaginismus in women; and painful intercourse and problems of sexual desire, which may occur in men or women.

KINDS OF SEXUAL DYSFUNCTION

Erectile Dysfunction (Impotence)

Erectile (eh-REK-tile) dysfunction: The inability to have or maintain an erection.

Primary erectile dysfunction: Cases of erectile dysfunction in which the man has never had an erection sufficient to have intercourse.

Secondary erectile dysfunction: Cases of erectile dysfunction in which the man at one time was able to have satisfactory erections, but now no longer does.

Erectile dysfunction (also called *impotence*) is the inability to have an erection or to maintain one. As a result, the man is not able to engage in penis-inside-vagina intercourse (or anal intercourse, for that matter), since an erection, at least a moderate one, is necessary for the penis to be inserted into the vagina. Masters and Johnson further classify cases of erectile dysfunction into primary erectile dysfunction and secondary erectile dysfunction. Primary erectile dysfunction refers to cases where the man has never been able to have intercourse; secondary erectile dysfunction refers to cases where the man has difficulty getting or maintaining an erection but has been able to have vaginal or anal intercourse at least once. Masters and Johnson classify a man as secondarily dysfunctional if he has erection problems 25 percent or more of the time in sexual encounters.

Among men seeking sex therapy, erectile dysfunction is common, and secondary cases are more common than primary ones. It has been estimated that half of the general male population has experienced occasional episodes of erectile dysfunction, and this is certainly well within the range of normal sexual response (Kaplan, 1974). Erectile difficulties affect men of all ages, from teenagers to the elderly.

One problem of terminology is present. The word "impotence," which is often used, certainly carries negative connotations (the word means "lack of power"). A man who has erection problems has enough trouble without having people call him "impotent" besides. Further, the term is often confused with others, such as "sterility." There are many sterile men who do not have erectile dysfunction; they get fine, hard, lasting erections, but they just do not produce enough viable sperm to cause pregnancy. Conversely, many men with erectile dysfunction produce fine sperm and will be able to impregnate a woman as soon as they are able to have erections. The term "erectile dysfunction" is preferable to "impotence," since it gives a precise description of the problem but does not have the negative connotations.

Psychological reactions to erectile dysfunction may be severe. It is undoubtedly one of the most embarrassing things that can happen to a man. Depression may follow from repeated episodes. The situation is also embarrassing to the man's partner.

The causes of erectile dysfunction and its treatment will be discussed later in the chapter.

Premature Ejaculation

Premature ejaculation: A sexual dysfunction in which the man ejaculates too soon and he feels he cannot control when he ejaculates.

Premature ejaculation (*ejaculatio praecox,* in medical terminology, or "PE," if you want to be on familiar terms with it) occurs when the man ejaculates too soon or is not able to postpone ejaculation long enough. In extreme cases, ejaculation may take place so soon after erection that it occurs before the penis can even be inserted into the vagina. In other cases, the man is able to delay the ejaculation to some extent, but not as long as he would like or not long enough for his partner to have an orgasm.

While the definition given above—ejaculating prematurely or too soon—seems simple enough, in practice it is much more difficult to define when a man is a premature ejaculator. What should the precise criterion for "too soon" be? Should the man be required to last for 30 seconds after erection? For 12 minutes? The definitions used by authorities in the field vary widely. One source defines "prematurity" as the occurrence of orgasm less than 30 seconds after the penis has been inserted into the vagina. Another group has extended this to 1½ minutes; a third uses the criterion of ejaculation before there have been 10 pelvic thrusts. Masters and Johnson define premature ejaculation as inability to delay ejaculation long enough for the woman to have an orgasm at least 50 percent of the time. This last definition is interesting in that it stresses the importance of the interaction between the two partners; however, it carries with it the problem of how easily the woman is stimulated to orgasm. Psychiatrist Helen Singer Kaplan (1974) believes that the key to defining the premature ejaculator is the absence of voluntary control of ejaculation; that is, the premature ejaculator has little or no control over when he ejaculates, and this is what causes the problem. One of the best definitions, though, is self-definition; if a man finds that he has become greatly concerned about his ejaculatory control or that it is interfering with his ability to form intimate relationships, or if a couple agree that it is a problem in their relationship, then a dysfunction is present.

Premature ejaculation is a common dysfunction in the general male population but men are probably not so likely to seek therapy for it as they are for erectile dysfunction. Premature ejaculation is particularly common among young men who have a very high sex drive and have simply not yet learned to control ejaculation.

Like erectile dysfunction, premature ejaculation may create a host of related psychological problems. Because the ability to postpone ejaculation and the ability to "satisfy" a woman are so important in our concept of a man who is a competent lover, premature ejaculation can cause a man to become anxious about his masculinity and sexual competence. Further, the condition may affect his partner and create friction in the relationship. The woman may be frustrated because she is not having a satisfying sexual experience either.

The negative psychological effects of premature ejaculation are illustrated by a young man in one of my sexuality classes who handed in an anonymous question.

He described himself as a premature ejaculator and said that after several humiliating experiences in intercourse with dates, he was now convinced that no woman would want him in that condition. He now did not have the courage to ask for dates, and so he had stopped dating. Basically, he wanted to know how the women in the class would react to a man with such a problem. The question was discussed in class, and most of the women agreed that their reaction to his problem would depend a great deal on the quality of the relationship they had with him. If they cared deeply for him, they would be sympathetic and patient and help him overcome the difficulty. The point is, though, that the premature ejaculation had created problems so severe that the young man not only had stopped having sex but also had stopped dating.

Retarded Ejaculation

Retarded ejaculation:
A sexual dysfunction in which the male cannot have an orgasm, even though he is highly aroused and has had a great deal of sexual stimulation.

Retarded ejaculation (*ejaculatio retardata*) is the opposite of premature ejaculation. The man is unable to ejaculate, even though he has a solid erection and has had more than adequate stimulation. Masters and Johnson call this syndrome "ejaculatory incompetence," although this term has the disadvantage of the negative connotations of the word "incompetence." The severity of the problem may range from only occasional problems ejaculating to a history of never having experienced an orgasm. In the most common version, the man is incapable of ejaculating into the woman's vagina but may be able to ejaculate as a result of hand or mouth stimulation.

In the original Masters and Johnson report, retarded ejaculation appeared to be a fairly rare condition, accounting for only 17 of the 448 cases of male sexual dysfunction. However, other authorities now believe that in its mild forms, retarded ejaculation may be fairly common, at least as judged by the number of people seeking therapy for it (Kaplan, 1974; Munjack and Kanno, 1979).

Retarded ejaculation, to say the least, is a frustrating experience for the man. One would think that his partner, though, would be in an enviable position, being made love to by a man with a long-lasting erection that is not terminated by orgasm. In fact, though, some women react negatively to this condition in their partners, seeing the man's failure to ejaculate as a personal rejection. Some men, anticipating these negative reactions, have adopted the practice of "faking" orgasm.

Let us now turn to some of the sexual dysfunctions in women.

Orgasmic Dysfunction

Orgasmic dysfunction:
A sexual dysfunction in which the woman is unable to have an orgasm.

Anorgasmia:
Another term for orgasmic dysfunction; the term "preorgasmic" is also used.

Primary orgasmic dysfunction:
Cases of orgasmic dysfunction in which the woman has never in her life had an orgasm.

Orgasmic dysfunction (or anorgasmia) in women is the condition of being unable to have an orgasm. The more commonly used term for this situation is "frigidity," but Masters and Johnson reject this term because of its derogatory connotations, substituting the more neutral term "orgasmic dysfunction."[1] Like some other sexual dysfunctions, cases of orgasmic dysfunction may be classified as primary or secondary. Primary orgasmic dysfunction refers to cases where the woman has never in her life experienced an orgasm (Andersen, 1983); *secondary orgasmic dysfunction* refers to cases where the woman had orgasms at some time in her life but no longer

[1] The term "frigidity" is ambiguous, since it is used to refer to women who are unable to have orgasms and also to refer to women who show a total lack of sexual responsiveness and do not even become sexually aroused. The scientific term for this latter condition is "general sexual dysfunction."

Situational orgasmic dysfunction: Cases of orgasmic dysfunction in which the woman is able to have an orgasm in some situations (e.g., while masturbating) but not in others (e.g., while having sexual intercourse).

does so. Situational orgasmic dysfunction refers to cases in which the woman has orgasms in some situations but not others. Some therapists also prefer the term *preorgasmic,* suggesting that the woman has not yet learned to have orgasms, but will be able to.

Once again, though, these definitions become more complicated in practice than they are in theory. Consider the case of the woman who has orgasms as a result of masturbation or of hand or mouth stimulation by a partner but who does not have orgasms in vaginal intercourse (what might be called "coital orgasmic inadequacy"). Is this really a sexual dysfunction? The notion that it is a dysfunction can be traced back to Freud's distinction between clitoral orgasms and vaginal orgasms and his belief that "mature" women should be able to have vaginal orgasms (see Chapter 2); both of these ideas have been debunked by Masters and Johnson. It can also probably be traced to beliefs that there is a "right" way to have sex—with the penis inside the vagina—and a corresponding "right" way to have orgasms. However, survey data indicate that this condition is quite common among women and may even characterize the majority of women (see Chapter 15). Some authorities (for example, Kaplan, 1974) consider such a condition to be well within the normal range of female sexual response. Perhaps the woman who orgasms as a result of manual or oral stimulation, but not penile thrusting, is simply having orgasms when she is adequately stimulated and is not having them when she is inadequately stimulated. Thus there is some doubt as to whether "coital orgasmic inadequacy" is a dysfunction or an inadequacy at all and a corresponding doubt about whether it requires therapy.

On the other hand, there should be room for self-definition of dysfunctions. If a woman has this coital orgasmic inadequacy, is truly distressed that she is not able to have orgasms during vaginal intercourse, and wants therapy, then it might be appropriate to classify her condition as a dysfunction and provide therapy for it, simply because she herself sees it as a problem (Zeiss et al., 1977). The therapist, however, should be careful to explain to her the issues and problems of definition raised above, in order to be sure that her request for therapy stems from her own dissatisfaction with her sexual responding rather than from a casual reading of Freud. Therapy in such cases probably is best viewed as an "enrichment experience" rather than "fixing a problem."

Orgasmic dysfunctions in women are quite common. They accounted for the vast majority—342 out of 371—of cases of female sexual dysfunction reported by Masters and Johnson. Surveys such as those of Kinsey and Hunt (see Chapter 10) indicate that orgasmic dysfunction is quite common among women but that secondary orgasmic dysfunctions are probably more common than primary ones. These surveys indicate that probably about 10 percent of all women have never had an orgasm and that an additional 20 percent have orgasms only irregularly.

In recent years, particularly with the advent of the "Playboy ethic," female orgasm has come to be highly prized, and multiple orgasm may even be expected. In view of these pressures, it is not surprising that the woman who has difficulty having orgasms feels inadequate. Further, her partner may feel guilty if he cannot stimulate her to orgasm. Thus orgasmic dysfunctions in women are a cause for concern.

Vaginismus (Vaj-in-IS-mus): A sexual dysfunction in which there is a spastic contraction of the muscles surrounding the entrance to the vagina, in some cases so severe that intercourse is impossible.

Vaginismus

Vaginismus[2] is a spastic contraction of the outer third of the vagina; in some cases it is so severe that the entrance to the vagina is closed, and the woman cannot have

[2]The suffix "-ismus" means "spasm."

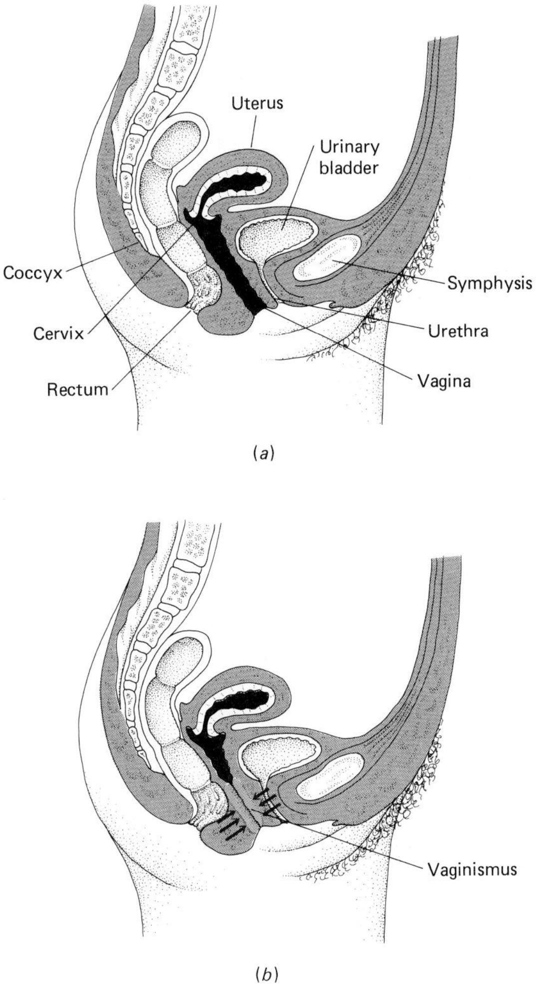

FIGURE 20.1

Vaginismus. (*a*) A normal vagina and other pelvic organs, viewed from the side, and (*b*) Vaginismus, or involuntary constriction of the outer third of the vagina.

intercourse (see Figure 20.1). Vaginismus and dyspareunia (see below) may be associated. That is, if intercourse is painful, one result may be spasms that close off the entrance to the vagina.

Vaginismus is not a very common sexual dysfunction. It accounted for only 29 (9 percent) of the 371 cases of sexual dysfunction reported by Masters and Johnson. Unfortunately, because the problem is rare and because it is often not discussed in the medical literature, physicians may fail to diagnose it or may misdiagnose it as something else, such as a small hymen.

Painful Intercourse

Dyspareunia (dis-pah-ROO-nee-uh): Painful intercourse.

Painful intercourse, or dyspareunia, is often thought to be only a female problem, but it may affect males too. In women, the pain may be felt in the vagina, around the vaginal entrance and clitoris, or deep in the pelvis. In men, the pain is felt in the penis. To put it mildly, dyspareunia decreases one's enjoyment of the sexual experience and may even lead one to abstain from sexual activity.

While complaints of occasional pain during intercourse are fairly common among women, persistent dyspareunia was not very common among the cases reported by Masters and Johnson. Painful intercourse may be related to a variety of physical causes, to be discussed below.

Problems of Sexual Desire

Low sexual desire:
A sexual dysfunction in which there is a lack of interest in sexual activity; also termed "inhibited sexual desire."

Sexual desire or *libido* refers to a set of feelings that lead the individual to seek out sexual activity or to be pleasurably receptive to it (Kaplan, 1979). When sexual desire is inhibited, so that the individual is not interested in sexual activity, the sexual dysfunction is termed ***inhibited sexual desire*** or low sexual desire (LoPiccolo, 1980). People with inhibited sexual desire typically manage to avoid situations that will evoke sexual feelings. If, despite their best efforts, they find themselves in an arousing situation, they experience a rapid "turn-off" so that they feel nothing. The turn-off may be so intense that they report negative, unpleasant feelings; others simply report *sexual anesthesia,* that is, no feeling at all, even though they may respond to the point of orgasm.

The identification of low sexual desire as a sexual dysfunction by sex therapists is relatively recent. It arose from the study of patients who were failures with traditional sex therapy. Typically these patients had been misdiagnosed into one of the categories discussed earlier, and therapy was unsuccessful. Therapists came to realize that they were seeing a new, and increasingly frequent, disorder of desire rather than excitement or orgasm (e.g., Kaplan, 1979; LoPiccolo, 1980). Indeed, statistics indicate that low sexual desire is probably the most common dysfunction now. A survey of a "normal" (nonpatient) population indicated that 35 percent of the women and 16 percent of the men complained of disinterest in sex (Frank et al., 1978).

As with other dysfunctions, there are complex problems of definition. There are many circumstances when it is perfectly normal for a person's desire to be inhibited. For example, one cannot be expected to find every potential partner attractive. Kaplan (1979) recounts an example of a couple consisting of a shy, petite woman and an extremely obese (350 pounds, 5 feet 3 inches tall), unkempt man. He complained of her lack of desire, but one can hardly blame her, nor would one want to classify her as having a sexual dysfunction. One cannot expect to respond sexually at all times, in all places, and with all persons.

Discrepancy of sexual desire:
A sexual dysfunction in which the partners have considerably different levels of sexual desire.

It is also true that the individual's absolute level of sexual desire is often not the problem—rather, the problem is a discrepancy between the partners' levels (Zilbergeld and Ellison, 1980). That is, if one partner wants sex less frequently than the other partner wants it, there is a conflict. This problem is termed a discrepancy of sexual desire.

Because recognition of this dysfunction is relatively recent, there is little agreement in the field about definition or diagnosis. However, it seems likely that low sexual desire will turn out not to be a single category (LoPiccolo, 1980). Rather, it represents a single symptom that can be caused by many factors. The following have been implicated as determinants of desire problems: hormones, psychological factors (particularly anxiety and/or depression), and cognitive factors (not having learned to perceive one's arousal accurately or having limited expectations for one's own ability to be aroused) (LoPiccolo, 1980).

WHAT CAUSES SEXUAL DYSFUNCTION?

There are many causes of sexual dysfunction, varying from person to person and from one dysfunction to the next. Three general categories of factors may be related to sexual dysfunctions: organic causes, drugs, and psychological causes.

Organic causes of sexual dysfunction:
Physical factors, such as disease, that cause sexual dysfunctions.

Organic Causes

About 10 to 20 percent of cases of sexual dysfunction result directly from organic (physical) factors. Because of this, a thorough physical examination may be suggested. It is useless to apply behavioral therapy such as that developed by Masters and Johnson if the dysfunction is a result of a physical condition, such as infection. Some specifc organic factors that are known to cause sexual dysfunctions are discussed below.

Erectile Dysfunction

Most cases of erectile dysfunction appear to be due to psychological rather than physical factors. For example, only 7 of the 213 cases of secondary erectile dysfunction reported by Masters and Johnson (3.2 percent) were found to have a physiological cause. Supporting this, the administration of testosterone is ineffective in treating males with erectile dysfunction (Benkert et al., 1979). Nonetheless, a number of physical conditions can cause erectile dysfunction.

Any severe illness may cause erection problems as well as loss of libido. Diseases associated with the heart and the circulatory system are particularly likely to be associated with the condition, since erection itself depends on the circulatory system. Any kind of vascular pathology (problems in the blood vessels supplying the penis) can produce erection problems (Tordjman et al., 1980). Erection depends on a great deal of blood flowing into the penis via the arteries, with a simultaneous constricting of the veins so that it cannot flow out as rapidly as it is coming in. Thus damage to either these arteries or veins may produce erectile dysfunction.

There is some association of erectile dysfunction with diabetes mellitus (Jensen, 1981). Either diabetes or a prediabetic condition may cause erectile dysfunction, although the exact mechanism by which this happens is not known. In fact, erectile dysfunction may in some cases be the earliest symptom of a developing case of diabetes. The incidence of erectile dysfunction among diabetic men is about two to five times higher than the incidence in the general population (Marmor, 1976b). Of course, this by no means suggests that all diabetic men have erectile dysfunction; indeed, the majority do not.

Any disease or accident that damages the lower part of the spinal cord may cause erectile dysfunction, since that is the location of the erection reflex center (see Chapter 8).

Erectile dysfunction may also result from severe stress or fatigue. Some diseases of, or defects in, the genitals or reproductive tract may create erectile dysfunction. Finally, some—though not all—kinds of prostate surgery may cause the condition.

One of the easiest ways to separate cases that are physically caused from cases that are psychologically caused is by noting the presence or absence of morning erections. If a man regularly wakes with an erection, it is clear that there is no physical impairment. (For a more detailed discussion, see Marshall et al., 1981.)

Premature Ejaculation

Premature ejaculation is almost always caused by psychological, rather than physical, factors (Kaplan,1974). Particularly in the man who has never been able to control his ejaculating, the causes are almost invariably psychological. In cases of secondary dysfunction, though, in which the man at one time had ejaculatory control but later lost it, physical factors may occasionally be involved. A local infection such as prostatitis may be the cause, as may a degeneration in the related parts of the nervous system, which may occur in degenerative neural disorders such as multiple sclerosis.

An intriguing explanation for premature ejaculation is provided by the sociobiologists (Hong, 1984). Their idea is that rapid ejaculation has been selected for in the process of evolution—what we might call "survival of the fastest." Focusing on monkeys and apes, the argument is that copulating and ejaculating rapidly would be advantageous in that the female would be less likely to get away and the male would be less likely to be attacked while he was copulating, by other sexually aroused males. Thus males who ejaculated quickly were more likely to survive and to reproduce. Interestingly, among chimpanzees, our nearest evolutionary relatives, the average time from intromission (insertion of the penis into the vagina) to ejaculation is 7 seconds (Tutin and McGinnis, 1981). In modern U.S. society, of course, rapid ejaculation is not particularly advantageous and might even lead a man to have difficulty finding female partners. Nonetheless, according to the sociobiologists, there are still plenty of genes for rapid ejaculation hanging around from natural selection occurring thousands of years ago.

Retarded Ejaculation

Retarded ejaculation may be caused by various diseases attacking the nervous system (Munjack and Kanno, 1979), by Parkinson's disease, and by diabetes. It is most commonly caused, though, by psychological factors.

Orgasmic Dysfunction in Women

Orgasmic dysfunction in women may be caused by an extremely severe illness, by general ill health, or by extreme fatigue. Most cases of orgasmic dysfunction, though, are caused by psychological factors. They may also be a result of the loss of libido that occurs in severe depressions.

Hormonal factors are usually *not* the cause of orgasmic dysfunction in women, and treatment with estrogen is generally not effective (Marmor, 1976a).

Painful Intercourse

Dyspareunia in women is often caused by organic factors (Marmor, 1976a; Wabrek and Wabrek, 1975). These include:

1. *Disorders of the vaginal entrance* Intact hymen or irritated remnants of the hymen; painful scars, perhaps from an episiotomy; or infection of the Bartholin glands
2. *Irritation or damage to the clitoris*
3. *Disorders of the vagina* Vaginal infections; allergic reactions to douches, creams, jellies, or the latex in condoms and diaphragms; a thinning of the vaginal walls (senile vaginitis), which occurs naturally with age; or scarring of the roof of the vagina, which may occur after hysterectomy
4. *Pelvic disorders* Pelvic infection, endometriosis, tumors, cysts, or a tearing of the broad ligaments supporting the uterus

Masters and Johnson found 11 patients suffering from dyspareunia due to torn ligaments. Five of the cases had resulted from childbirth, three from illegal abortion, and three from gang rape.

F · O · C · U · S 20.1

A CASE OF ORGASMIC DYSFUNCTION IN A WOMAN

Mr. and Mrs. F were referred for treatment six years after they were married. He was 29, and she was 24. They had one child, a girl, 3 years old.

Mrs. F came from a family of seven children; she remembers growing up in a warm. loving environment, with harried but happy parents.

Mr. F had a much different background. He was an only child who had been overindulged by his devoted parents. He began masturbating in his early teens, and he had a number of heterosexual experiences, including one relationship in which he had intercourse with his fiancée for six months before he broke the engagement.

The school years were uneventful for both Mr. and Mrs. F. When they first began dating, each was interested in someone else, but their mutual interest increased rapidly, and a courtship developed. They had intercourse regularly during the three-month period before their marriage.

During the courtship, Mr. F made every social decision, and he continued to exercise total control in the marriage. He insisted on making all decisions and was consistently concerned only with his own demands, paying little or no attention to his wife's needs. As a result, constant friction developed between the two.

Mrs. F did not have an orgasm before she was married. Afterward, she did have an orgasm on several occasions as a result of manual stimulation by her husband, but never during coitus. As the personal friction between the two increased, she found herself less and less responsive during coitus, although she occasionally had orgasms through manual stimulation. Pregnancy intervened at this time, distracting her for a year, but after that the problem became distressing to her and most embarrassing to her husband. He seemed to worry as much about his image as a sexually effective male as he did about his wife's frustration. Mrs. F's lack of sexual response was considered a personal affront by her uninformed husband.

Mr. F sent her to authorities to do something for "her" sexual inadequacy several times. The thought that the situation might have been in any way his responsibility was utterly foreign to him. When they were referred to Masters and Johnson for therapy, he at first refused to join her in treatment on the grounds that it was "her" problem. When he was told that the problem would not be accepted for treatment unless both partners cooperated, Mr. F grudgingly consented to participate.

According to Masters and Johnson's analysis, this was a case of secondary orgasmic dysfunction resulting from the woman's lack of identification with, or rejection of, her partner.

Source: William H. Masters and Virginia E. Johnson. (1970). *Human sexual inadequacy.* Boston: Little, Brown, pp. 243–344.

TABLE 20.1

DRUGS THAT MAY DECREASE LIBIDO OR IMPAIR SEXUAL RESPONSE

Painful intercourse in men can also be caused by a variety of organic factors. For an uncircumcised man, poor hygiene may be a cause; if the penis is not washed thoroughly, material may collect under the foreskin, causing infection. Proper hygiene practices require that the man frequently retract the foreskin completely and wash the penis thoroughly with soap and water. Phimosis, a condition in which the foreskin cannot be pulled back, can also cause painful intercourse. An allergic reaction to vaginal douches, creams, jellies, and foams may also be involved. Vaginal infections may cause irritation, as may gonorrhea. Finally, various prostate problems may cause pain on ejaculation.

Vaginismus

Vaginismus generally results when a woman has learned to associate pain or fear with intercourse (Kaplan, 1974). In some cases vaginismus is a result of prior episodes of painful intercourse, which may itself be caused by organic factors; in such cases, vaginismus may be considered to be caused indirectly by the same physical factors that cause dyspareunia.

Drugs

Some drugs may have side effects causing sexual dysfunctions (A.M. Freedman, 1976; Kaplan, 1979; Abel, 1985). For example, the drugs used in treating peptic ulcers may cause erectile dysfunction, and those used to treat allergies may in some cases decrease libido in women and erection capacity in men. A list of drugs that may decrease libido or impair sexual response is provided in Table 20.1.

The effects of illicit (illegal) drugs on sexual response vary widely. For example, some stimulants taken intravenously are powerful sexual stimulants (Rylander, 1969). One addict was quoted as saying that a shot of phenmetrazine "goes straight from the head to the scrotum." The opiates, on the other hand, can severely depress sexual behavior (Abel, 1985; Hollister, 1975; Isbell, 1965). In one report, nearly half of the 100 heroin addicts studied had erectile dysfunction (Chein et al., 1964, p. 166; see also Cushman, 1972; H. Jones and Jones, 1977). Because of their tendency to sharpen experiences, hallucinogens, such as LSD and marijuana, may increase the enjoyment of sexual activity.

Marijuana

Most users report that smoking marijuana enhances sexual pleasure and increases sexual desire; sensations of touch and taste are particularly enhanced (Weller and Halikas, 1984). In a survey of 200 marijuana users, 44 percent said that their sexual desires were increased, and frequent users agreed that enjoyment was also enhanced (Goode, 1970; Halikas et al., 1971; see also Tart, 1970).

A study of the potential effects of marijuana on sexual responding, conducted at the Masters and Johnson Institute, received a great deal of publicity (Kolodny et al., 1974). The study compared the levels of testosterone in the blood of 20 men, aged 18 to 28, who smoked marijuana frequently (they smoked at least four days per week

Drug	How It Is Thought to Affect Sexual Functioning	Some Common Medical Indications*
	Drugs That Act on the Brain†	
1. Sedatives		
Alcohol and barbiturates	Depress CNS activity in a single large dose; long-term heavy use leads to neural damage	Sedatives and hypnotics (sleep inducers)
Narcotics Heroin Morphine Codeine paregoric	General depression of the CNS plus depression of the sex centers. In high doses, produce impotence and inhibit orgasm	Analgesics (pain relievers); methadone used in treatment of narcotic addiction; control of coughing, diarrhea
2. Antiandrogens	Oppose the stimulating action of androgen on the brain and sexual organs	
Estrogen	May decrease libido in women and decrease erections in men	Replacement therapy in postmenopausal women; birth control; men with prostatic cancer; after urinary-tract surgery, used to prevent erection
Cyproterone acetate	Decreases sexual arousal	Experimental—used in treatment of compulsive sexual disorders
Adrenal steroids Cortisone ACTH		Allergies and inflammatory disorders
	Drugs That Act on the Genitals‡	
1. Anticholinergic drugs Banthine Probanthine Atropine Quaternary ammonium compounds	Inhibit the parasympathetic nerves and so may cause erectile dysfunction	Peptic ulcers, dyskinesias, glaucoma and other eye problems
2. Antiadrenergic drugs Phentolamine Ergo alkaloids Guanethidine (Ismelin)	Inhibit the sympathetic nerves and so may cause ejaculatory problems; may also diminish libido and erection	Hypertension (high blood pressure) and other vascular disorders
Methyl dopa (Aldomet)	Erectile dysfunction is a frequent complication; some women report loss of orgasm and decreased arousability	
	Miscellaneous	
Disulfiram (Antabuse)	Occasional erectile dysfunction and delay of ejaculation reported	Alcohol abuse
Chlorphentermine (presate)	Occasional erectile dysfunction reported	Weight reduction
Antihistamines	Continuous use may interfere with sexual activity	Colds and allergies
Monoamine oxidase inhibitors (MAO) or tricyclics	Ejaculation problems; erection problems; anorgasmia in women	Depression

*"Medically indicated" means that a physician may prescribe it for the condition.

†These primarily decrease desire and the sexual responses.

‡These block the nerves controlling the smooth muscles and blood vessels of the genital organs.

Sources: Helen S. Kaplan. (1979). *Disorders of sexual desire.* Ernest L. Abel. (1985). *Psychoactive drugs and sex.* New York: Plenum. James S. Woods. Drug effects on human sexual behavior. In N. F. Woods (Ed.). (1975). *Human sexuality in health and illness.* St. Louis: Mosby. Kolodny, R. C., Masters, W. H., and Johnson, V. E. (1979). Drugs and sex. In R. C. Kolodny et al. *Textbook of sexual medicine.* Boston: Little, Brown.

for a minimum of six months before the study) with the testosterone levels in the blood of 20 other men, matched for age, who had never smoked marijuana. All subjects used no other drugs at the time of the study, and none had ever used "hard" drugs. The investigators found that the smokers had significantly lower testosterone levels than nonsmokers. Further, testosterone levels were related to frequency of usage. Heavy smokers (10 or more joints per week) had significantly lower testosterone levels than light smokers (9 or fewer joints per week). Heavy smokers also had significantly lower sperm counts than light smokers. Two of the smokers (as compared with none of the nonsmokers) had erection problems. Finally, three of the smokers stopped smoking for two weeks; their testosterone levels rose considerably during that time (by 57 and 141 percent). This study raises serious questions about the effects of marijuana use on sexual and reproductive functioning, since testosterone is so important to both. On the other hand, the study suggests that the results are quickly reversible when use is discontinued. We should also be cautious about sounding an alarm before the results have been replicated by other investigators; at least one other study failed to find the same results (Mendelsohn et al., 1974; see also E. M. Brecher, 1975). But another study found a 66 percent reduction in sperm count after one month of marijuana use (Hembree et al., 1976). At the very least, these studies indicate a need for more research in this area.

Alcohol

The effects of alcohol vary considerably. A small amount of alcohol may reduce anxiety and inhibitions, thereby improving sexual responsiveness. A large amount of alcohol, however, acts as a depressant and may therefore prevent sexual arousal, thereby causing sexual dysfunction. Alcoholics, who are exposed to repeated high doses of alcohol, frequently have sexual dysfunctions, particularly erectile dysfunction (H. Jones and Jones, 1977). As one alcoholic put it, "I started out Early Times, but quickly wound up as Old Grandad" (Lemere and Smith, 1973).

Psychiatric Drugs

Some of the drugs used in treating psychiatric disorders may also affect sexual functioning. For example, "dry orgasm," an orgasm in which the man produces no ejaculate, may be a side effect of some of the drugs used in the treatment of schizophrenia (Mitchell and Popkin, 1983). Tranquilizers and antidepressants, while producing some cases of sexual dysfunction, often help improve sexual responding as a result of their improvement of the person's mental state. (For a more complete discussion, see Abel, 1985; Kaplan, 1979; Leavitt, 1974.)

Psychological Causes

The psychological sources of sexual dysfunction have been categorized into immediate causes and prior learning (Kaplan, 1974). Prior learning refers to the things that people learned earlier—for example, in childhood—which now inhibit their sexual response. Immediate causes are various things that happen in the act of lovemaking itself that inhibit the sexual response.

Prior learning: Things that people learned earlier—for example, in childhood—that now affect their sexual response.

Immediate causes: Various factors that occur in the act of lovemaking that inhibit sexual response.

Immediate Causes

The following five factors have been identified as immediate causes of dysfunction: (1) anxieties such as fear of failure, (2) the constructing of barriers to the experience of erotic pleasure, (3) failure of the partners to communicate, (4) failure to engage in effective, sexually stimulating behavior, and (5) negative thoughts.

Anxiety during intercourse can be a source of sexual dysfunction. Anxiety may be caused by fear of failure, that is, fear of being unable to perform. But anxiety itself can block sexual response. Often anxiety can create a vicious circle of self-fulfilling prophecy in which fear of failure produces a failure, which produces more fear, which produces another failure, and so on. For example, a man may have one episode of erectile dysfunction, perhaps after drinking too much at a party. The next time he has sex, he anxiously wonders whether he will "fail" again. His anxiety is so great that he cannot get an erection. At this point he is convinced that the condition is permanent, and all future sexual activity is marked by such intense fear of failure that erectile dysfunction results. The prophecy is fulfilled.

Similarly, anxiety in a woman may block arousal. If she is not aroused, she does not produce vaginal lubrication, and the result can be painful intercourse.

Fears of failure can also be created by a demand for performance by the partner. For example, some cases of erectile dysfunction apparently began when the woman demanded intercourse but the man did not feel aroused and therefore did not get an erection. Following that failure, anxiety built up in anticipation of future failures. Such a process is illustrated by the case history presented in Focus 20.3. Demands for performance, of course, are generally harder on men than they are on women; to engage in intercourse, the man must be aroused and have an erection, and it is painfully obvious when this does not occur. Arousal is not an absolute necessity for a woman to have intercourse, though. The parallel demand for performance in women is the demand that they have orgasms. Once again, if the woman is unable to meet this demand, the result is anxiety and fear of failure, which further inhibit her response.

While a desire to please one's partner is generally a good thing in lovemaking, it can create anxiety if carried to an extreme. For example, a man may obsessively wonder whether he is using the right techniques to stimulate his partner; a woman may anxiously worry that her breasts are not large enough to please her partner. Such compulsive desires to please are often rooted in insecurity and fears of rejection. While many people in sex therapy need to be taught to be more sensitive to their partner's needs, people in the desire-to-please category need the opposite training; they need to learn the value of temporary selfishness and of enjoying one's own sexual experience.

Spectatoring: Masters and Johnson's term for acting as an observer or judge of one's own sexual performance; hypothesized to contribute to sexual dysfunction.

Constructing barriers to the experience of erotic feelings is another way to produce sexual dysfunction. Spectatoring, a term coined by Masters and Johnson, is one of the most common of these barriers. The person behaves like a spectator or judge of his or her own sexual "performance." People who do this are constantly (mentally) stepping outside the sexual act in which they are engaged to evaluate how they are doing, mentally commenting. "Good job," or "Lousy," or "Could stand improvement." Since a full sexual response requires abandonment to the experiencing of erotic feelings, this compulsive evaluation inhibits sexual response.

Failure to communicate is one of the most important causes of sexual dysfunction. Many people expect their partners to have ESP concerning their own sexual needs. You are the leading expert in the field of what feels good to you, and your partner will never know what turns you on unless you make this known, either verbally or nonverbally. But many people do not communicate their sexual desires. For example, a woman who needs a great deal of clitoral stimulation to have an orgasm may never tell her partner this; as a result. she does not get the stimulation she needs and consequently does not have an orgasm.

Another immediate cause of sexual dysfunction is a *failure to engage in effective, sexually stimulating behavior.* Often this is a result of simple ignorance. For example, some couples seek sex therapy because of the wife's failure to have orgasms; the therapist soon discovers that neither the husband nor wife is aware of the location of the clitoris, much less of its fantastic erotic potential. Often such cases can be cleared up by simple educational techniques.

One final immediate cause is the conjuring up of *negative thoughts.* That is, in the sexual situation, the individuals focus their attention on unattractive features of the partner—his bad breath, her fat thighs—or of themselves—"My breasts are too small to be attractive." Essentially, such persons turn themselves off, although they typically are not conscious that they are doing so. This immediate cause is typical of cases of inhibited sexual desire (Kaplan, 1979).

Prior Learning

The other major category of psychological sources of sexual dysfunction is prior learning and experience. This includes various things that were learned or experienced in childhood, adolescence, or even adulthood.

In some cases of sexual dysfunction, the person's first sexual act was a very traumatic experience. An example would be a young man who could not get an erection the first time he attempted intercourse and was laughed at by his partner. Such an experience sets the stage for future erectile dysfunction. Rape is another traumatic experience that may lead to sexual dysfunction.

Seductive parents may contribute to early traumatic sexual experiences. A parent may be seductive or may force the child to engage in intercourse; the child is in no position to refuse, but she or he feels terribly guilty. Once again, sex becomes associated with psychic pain, laying the groundwork for a lack of sexual responsiveness later.

In other cases of sexual dysfunction, the person grew up in a very strict, religious family and was taught that sex was dirty and sinful. Such a person may grow up thinking that sex is not pleasurable, that it should be gotten over as quickly as possible, and that it is for purposes of procreation only. To say the least, such learning inhibits the enjoyment of a full sexual response.

Another source of dysfunction originating in the family occurs when parents punish children severely for sexual activity such as masturbation. An example is the little girl who is caught masturbating, is punished severely, and is told never to "touch herself" again; she obeys, and in adulthood she finds that she cannot have an orgasm through masturbation or as a result of manual stimulation by her partner.

Parents who teach their children the double standard may also contribute to sexual dysfunction, particularly in their daughters. Women whose sexual response is inhibited in adulthood often have a history of being taught, when they were children, that no nice lady is interested in sex or enjoys it.

We should, though, note one major problem with the evidence of Masters and Johnson and others on these factors as causes of sexual dysfunction: the evidence comes from clinical data. This means that a group of people seeking therapy for their sexual problems were studied; certain factors emerged as common in their life histories, and it was therefore concluded that those factors must cause sexual dysfunction. The problem is that no data were collected on a comparison group of people who were functioning adequately in their sex lives to see whether those "causes" were also common in their histories. A classic example of this problem in logic is the following: A psychiatrist studies a group of schizophrenic patients and finds that every single one of them had a mother. The psychiatrist concludes that having a mother must cause schizophrenia. Had the psychiatrist also studied a comparison group of normal people, she or he would have discovered that they all had mothers too and that having a mother is therefore not a very likely cause of schizophrenia. We might apply this same critique to the statement that sexual dysfunction is caused by strong religious teachings. While strong religious teachings were common in the backgrounds of many of the patients with sexual dysfunctions, it might be that such a factor is also common among those who function quite well sexually; religious homes were, after all, quite common 30 or 40 years ago.

One study on female orgasm capacity provides some information that is relevant here. A large sample of adult women filled out a questionnaire about their own sexual behavior; they also provided other background information on such things as how religious they were (S. Fisher, 1973). The results indicated that the extent to which a woman was religiously devout had no relationship to her orgasm capacity. Similar results have been obtained in other studies (e.g., Kinsey et al., 1953). In fact, in a survey done by *Redbook* magazine (see Chapter 10). the results indicated that the most religious women were actually happier with their sex lives than those who were less religious or not at all religious. These findings seem to contradict Masters and Johnson.

The point is that the conclusions made by Masters and Johnson and other sex therapists concerning the causes of sexual dysfunction are not based on very good evidence. Our knowledge of exactly what factors in a person's past experience contribute to making that person sexually dysfunctional is highly speculative at the present time, and further research is needed.

Relationship Conflict

Although Masters and Johnson and others using similar forms of sex therapy concentrate on treating the immediate and prior-learning causes of dysfunction, there are some other, more complex causes that are also worth considering. One of these is disturbances in the relationship between the two partners. If there is severe discord in marriage, sexual dysfunction may develop. Anger and hating one's sexual partner do not create an optimal environment for sexual enjoyment. Sex can also be used as a weapon to hurt a partner; for example, a woman can hurt her husband by refusing to engage in a sexual behavior that he enjoys. Sexual dysfunction, then, may be one of many symptoms of marital discord.

Intrapsychic Conflict

Intrapsychic conflict: Psychological conflicts, often unconscious, that are believed by psychoanalysts to be the cause of sexual dysfunction.

In contrast to Masters and Johnson and other behavior therapists who view sexual dysfunction as a simple result of learning, Freudian analysts view sexual dysfunction as a result of unconscious intrapsychic conflict. The idea is that while humans have a strong craving for sexual expression, they also have unconscious anxieties about it and are afraid that they will be punished for engaging in sex. Put the two together, and you have conflict.

According to Freud, much of this conflict originates in childhood. specifically in the Oedipus complex. Resolving the Oedipus complex—identifying with the same-gender parent and repressing the incestuous sexual desires for the parent of the opposite gender—is essential for attaining mature, good adjustment. Sexual problems in adulthood result when an unresolved Oedipus complex, which has lain dormant for years, is reactivated. For example. an adult man is about to make love to a woman; suddenlv, however, old castration anxieties are evoked, and he loses his erection. According to Freud, all sexual problems are caused by an unresolved Oedipus complex.

It follows from this theoretical model that sexual dysfunctions could be cured only by intensive, long-term psychoanalysis designed to uncover these unconscious, unresolved conflicts.

The success of the Masters and Johnson rapid-treatment program using behavior therapy provides evidence against the psychoanalytic model; according to Freud, their therapy techniques should not be successful. On the other hand, they do have a failure rate—at least 20 percent, and higher for certain dysfunctions—and it is likely that those who fail in their treatment program are precisely the people whose dysfunction is caused by intrapsychic conflict. Accordingly, some therapists, such as Helen Singer Kaplan (1974, 1979), use a joint approach, combining the Masters and Johnson behavior therapy with psychotherapy for intrapsychic conflicts.

Fear of Intimacy

The fear of intimacy represents a peculiar blend of immediate causes, prior learning, and intrapsychic conflict, as documented by Helen Singer Kaplan (1979).

Some people actually seem to be fearful of intimacy—that is, of a deep emotional closeness to another person. Indeed, some people appear to fear intimacy more than they do sex. They would prefer to watch TV or talk about the weather or have sex rather than engage in a truly intimate, emotionally vulnerable, and trusting conversation with another person. If such persons are single, they typically progress in a relationship to a certain degree of closeness and then lose interest. This pattern is repeated with many partners. The fear of intimacy may be a result of negative or disappointing intimate relationships—particularly with the parents—in early childhood. The fear of intimacy causes a person to draw back from a sexual relationship before it becomes truly fulfilling.

TWO MODELS OF THERAPY

In the treatment of psychological problems, including sexual problems, there are two basic theoretical models that may be used, each leading to a different type of therapy. These are the psychoanalytic approach and the behavioral approach (see, for example, Meissner, 1980; Fensterheim and Kantor, 1980).

Psychoanalytic therapy: A system of therapy originated by Freud, based on uncovering and resolving unconscious conflicts.

Psychoanalytic Approach

The assumption of psychoanalysts is that sex problems are caused by unconscious intrapsychic conflict, often the result of childhood experiences. Following this assumption, sex problems can be cured only by long-term (perhaps several years), intensive psychotherapy designed to uncover the unconscious conflicts, gain insight into them, and resolve them. Often the problems are seen to be the result of a lack of resolution of the Oedipus complex. The idea is that if the unconscious conflicts are resolved, the problem sexual behavior should disappear.

This psychodynamic approach was essentially the only form of therapy available for sexual dysfunctions until the mid-1960s, with the advent of the Masters and Johnson work.

Behavior therapy: A system of therapy based on learning theory, in which the focus is on the problem behavior and how it can be modified or changed.

Behavioral Approach

In contrast to the psychoanalytic approach is the behavioral approach, or behavior therapy, with its roots in behaviorism and learning theory. The basic assumption is that sex problems are the result of learning in the past and that they are maintained by ongoing reinforcements and punishments (the immediate causes). It follows that these problem behaviors can be unlearned by new conditioning. Note that the focus is on the problem *behavior* and how to recondition it. There is no concern whatsoever with the unconscious or with intrapsychic conflicts.

THE MASTERS AND JOHNSON SEX THERAPY PROGRAM

The Format and Basic Principles

Masters and Johnson operate out of a behavior therapy model because they see sexual dysfunction as a learned behavior rather than a psychiatric illness. If sexual dysfunction is learned, it can be unlearned. Thus Masters and Johnson use a two-week, rapid-treatment program of intensive therapy. The therapy consists mainly of discussions and specific behavioral exercises, or "homework assignments." The sequence of events in the two-week therapy program is outlined in the Focus.

One of the most basic goals of Masters and Johnson's therapy is to eliminate goal-oriented sexual performance. Many patients believe that in sex they must perform and achieve certain things. If sex is an achievement situation, it also can become the scene of failure, and it is perceived failures that lead people to believe they have a sexual problem. Spectatoring contributes to the problem.

Sensate focus exercise: A part of sex therapy developed by Masters and Johnson, in which one partner caresses the other, the other communicates what is pleasurable, and there are no performance demands.

In part, Masters and Johnson eliminate the couple's goal-oriented attitude toward sex by forbidding, from the beginning of therapy, any sexual activity not explicitly ordered by the therapists. Then they assign exercises, such as the sensate focus exercise, that reduce the demands on the patients. As the patients successfully complete these, they are given assignments in which the sexual components are gradually increased. The couple continue to chalk up successes until eventually they are having intercourse and the dysfunction has disappeared. Masters and Johnson operate on the notion that adequate sexual functioning is quite natural and that all they must do in therapy is remove unnatural impediments to sexual functioning. For example, as they put it, a man is born with the capacity to have an erection. His first erection did not happen because he tried to make it happen; he simply found himself with it. Sexual response is natural, and after impediments to it have been removed, the couple should begin to enjoy satisfying sexual responses.

One distinctive feature of the Masters and Johnson therapy format is that both members of the couple must participate in therapy. For example, a man cannot simply come to the therapists with a problem of erectile dysfunction and be treated. His wife must participate also. There are two reasons behind this requirement. First, many of the therapy techniques, such as the "homework" exercises, require the cooperation of the other partner as well as some training of the partner. For example, the "squeeze technique" is used in treating premature ejaculation, but it must be performed by the man's partner, and thus she must be trained to do it. The second reason for the requirement that both persons participate in therapy is that each is almost invariably affected by the other's dysfunction and thus needs therapy as well. For example, the wife of a man with erection problems is probably having some difficulties with orgasm herself and thus will benefit from therapy. The husband of a woman who has orgasmic dysfunction may be feeling that he is inadequate as a lover, and thus the therapy will help him also. As Masters and Johnson put it, "There is no such thing as an uninvolved partner in any marriage in which there is some form of sexual inadequacy" (1970, p. 2). They believe that it is the couple and their relationship that are the real patients in therapy.

F · O · C · U · S
20.2
THE SCHEDULE OF TREATMENT IN THE MASTERS AND JOHNSON THERAPY PROGRAM

DAY 1

1. *The initial interview* Both therapists meet with the couple to explain their commitments to the program and the procedure for the first few days. The rule that both partners must participate in the therapy is explained. Patients are told that they should not have intercourse or engage in any other sexual activity until told to do so by the therapists.
2. *The first history-taking interview* The female therapist interviews the woman, and the male therapist interviews the man. They collect information on the sexual problem and on the patients' sexual functioning. Life history data are also collected: the patient's childhood and family relationships, sexual experiences, marital relationships, and what is sensuous to the patient.

DAY 2

The second history-taking interview The female therapist interviews the husband, and the male therapist interviews the wife. Sensitive areas are probed. The motivation of the patients for seeking therapy is discussed; for example, did one partner drag the other one there?

DAY 3

1. *Medical examination* In order to rule out physical causes of the dysfunction, a complete medical history is taken of each patient, and a physical examination and diagnostic laboratory tests are performed.
2. *Round table discussion* Both therapists and both patients participate in a round table discussion. The therapists summarize the findings of the history-taking interviews, and the patients correct any errors. The therapists present the probable causes of the dysfunction. Spectatoring is discussed.
3. *Homework assignment: sensate focus* The patients are instructed to complete two periods of sensate focusing before the therapy session the next day. The genitals and breasts, though, are "out of bounds" for stroking at this stage. The "getting" partner tells the "giving" partner when any stimulation is unpleasant.

DAY 4

1. *Discussion of actions and reactions to the homework assignment.*
2. *Discussion of the anatomy of the genital organs.*
3. *Homework assignment: sensate focus* The couple are again instructed to complete two sensate focus sessions, this time extending stimulation to the breasts and genitals. Also, this time the "getting" partner guides the hand of the "giving" partner to show personal preferences concerning how and where she or he likes to be touched.

DAYS 5 TO 14

Homework assignments are given to treat the specific dysfunction. The exercises vary, depending on the dysfunction (see text for further discussion).

Source: Fred Belliveau and Lin Richter. (1970). *Understanding human sexual inadequacy.* New York: Bantam.

Surrogate (SIR-oh-get): An extra member of a sex therapy team who serves as a sexual partner for the client, allowing the client to do the prescribed exercises if no other partner is available.

The requirement that both persons participate in the therapy raises one problematic issue, however. Should therapy be denied to the married person who has a sexual dysfunction but whose spouse absolutely refuses to participate? Or should a single person who has no steady relationship but who nonetheless has a sexual dysfunction also be denied therapy? One strategy that Masters and Johnson developed for dealing with such people was the use of a surrogate, or a third member of the therapy team who served as a sexual partner for the patient during the two-week therapy program. The surrogates were a group of volunteers carefully chosen by Masters and Johnson. They were not prostitutes; rather, they were people who were sincerely concerned with helping those with sexual dysfunctions. In fact, one of the female surrogates was a physician. The use of surrogates proved to be effective, judged by the success rate for people in this type of therapy, which was the same as the success rate for married couples in therapy. The use of surrogates did attract considerable publicity, though, and it remains a controversial practice to the present day, as well as opening up a confused mass of legal difficulties, such as the possibility of being charged with prostitution. Nonetheless, the use of surrogates does seem to be a reasonable solution to the problem of treating certain people who otherwise would be denied sex therapy.

Other therapists are exploring other techniques—such as masturbation therapy, biofeedback, and hypnosis—for persons without partners.

Basic Therapy Techniques

Masters and Johnson use several basic techniques in therapy. The sequence of these techniques is outlined in the Focus. Notice that the therapy begins with a set of standard exercises for the first four or five days and then proceeds to a special set of exercises for the specific dysfunction and the set of conditions that produced it.

One of the basic techniques used is simple education. Masters and Johnson give the couple thorough instruction in the anatomy and physiology of the male and female sexual organs. Some couples, for example, have no idea of what or where the clitoris is. There is also an opportunity to clear up some of the misunderstandings that either the man or the woman may have had since childhood. For example, a man with problems of erectile dysfunction may have learned as a child that men can have only a fixed number of orgasms in their lifetime. As he approaches middle age, he starts to worry about whether he may have used up almost all his orgasms, and this inhibits his sexual response. It is important for such men to learn that nature has imposed no such quota on them.

The *sensate focus* exercises are perhaps the most important of the Masters and Johnson therapy techniques. They are based on the notion that touching and being touched are important forms of sexual expression and that touching is also an important form of communication; for example, a touch can express affection, desire, understanding, or lack of caring. In the exercises, one member of the couple plays the "giving" role (touches the other), while the other person plays the "getting" role (is touched by the other). The giving partner is instructed to massage or fondle the other, while the getting partner is instructed to communicate to the giver what is most pleasurable. Thus the exercise fosters communication between the two. The couple then switch roles after a certain period of time. At the beginning, the giver is not to stroke the genitals or breasts but may touch any other area. As the couple progress through the exercises, they are instructed to begin touching the genitals and breasts. These exercises also encourage the persons to focus their attention or concentrate on the sensuous pleasures they are receiving. Many people's sexual response is dulled because they are distracted; for example, they are thinking about what to cook for dinner, or they are spectatoring on their own performance. The sensate focus exercises train people to focus on their sexual experience, thereby increasing their pleasure.

Masters and Johnson combine these basic therapy techniques with specific treatments for specific dysfunctions. These specific treatments will be discussed later in the chapter.

Even with the use of these exercises, though, the Masters and Johnson therapy program still requires quite a bit of clinical skill and insight on the part of the therapists. In addition to prescribing exercises, they must, for example, be able to understand the feelings of the patients and to get the partners to understand each other's feelings. These are not simple or mechanical procedures.

The Success Rate

Masters and Johnson have collected data on the success and failure rates of their therapy. In *Human Sexual Inadequacy* they reported on the treatment of 790 individuals. Of these, 142 were still dysfunctional at the end of the two-week therapy program. This yields a failure rate of 18 percent, or *a success rate of 82 percent.* While the failure rate ran around 18 percent for most dysfunctions, there were two exceptions: therapy for premature ejaculation had a very low failure rate (2.2 percent), and therapy for primary erectile dysfunction had a very high failure rate (40.6 percent). That is, premature ejaculation seems to be quite easy to cure, whereas primary erectile dysfunction is rather difficult. In addition, research shows that there are significant increases in couples' communication skils by the end of the two-week therapy program (Tullman et al., 1981). Masters and Johnson's success rate is impressive and is considerably higher than the success rate in many forms of traditional psychotherapy, although some have questioned their results, as we shall see later in this chapter.

Masters and Johnson have also been able to follow up 226 people five years after therapy. The former patients were interviewed about their current sexual functioning. After the five years, the failure rate had risen to only about 25.5 percent; that is, the therapy seems to have lasting effects, and few people seem to develop their old problems again afterward.

OTHER THERAPIES

While Masters and Johnson have dominated the field of sex therapy, they are by no means the only sex therapists; nor is their method of treatment the only one available. Other kinds of therapeutic approaches are discussed below.

Variations of the Masters and Johnson Method

One of the problems with the Masters and Johnson treatment program is that it is expensive. In 1984. the two-week treatment program cost $5000, although reduced fees or free care are available to people with low incomes. Thus a number of people have developed variations on their program with the goal of making treatment available more cheaply to more people. Having two therapists essentially doubles the price of the therapy, and so some people use a single therapist, apparently with good results. Others have explored group therapy, in which five or ten people, all with the same dysfunction, are treated together in a group (see, for example, Schneidman and McGuire, 1976; Zilbergeld, 1975). Therapy for a group with a mixture of dysfunctions has also been explored (Leiblum et al., 1976). The Masters and Johnson program is also expensive because it requires taking off two weeks from work, traveling to St. Louis, and staying in a motel for two weeks. Many therapists have therefore changed from the two-week, rapid-treatment program to a format of one or two sessions per week for 10 or 15 weeks. Many major-medical health insurance programs now cover psychiatric treatment and therefore sex therapy, which makes cost somewhat less of a problem for many people.

Specific Treatments for Specific Problems

Squeeze Technique

Squeeze technique: A form of sex therapy for premature ejaculation, in which the partner squeezes the man's penis, stopping his orgasm just when he felt he was about to orgasm.

A method that Masters and Johnson and others use to treat premature ejaculators is the squeeze technique. The woman sits on the bed with her back against the backboard, propped by pillows. The man lies on his back, facing her, with his feet outside her thighs (Figure 20.2). The woman caresses his genitals until he gets an erection. When he has a full erection, she holds his penis between the thumb and first two fingers of her hand. The thumb is placed on the lower surface of the penis, just below the corona, and the two fingers are placed on the opposite side of the penis, one above the coronal ridge and the other below it. When he feels that ejaculation is about to happen, he tells her, and she then squeezes the penis fairly hard for 3 to

FIGURE 20.2

Techniques for treating premature ejaculation. (*a*) The squeeze technique and (*b*) the position the couple use while doing the squeeze technique.

4 seconds. This causes the man to lose his urge to ejaculate. He may also lose some of his erection. After waiting 15 to 30 seconds, the woman again stimulates him to a full erection, squeezes, and so on. The couple may thus engage in 15 to 20 minutes of continuous sex play, and the man gradually gains some control over his ejaculation. Lest this technique sound like cruel and unusual punishment. it should be noted that the squeeze, when done properly, does not hurt.

After the man has gained some control with this method, the couple assume the woman-on-top position (see Figure 20.3), and he inserts his penis into her vagina; however. no pelvic thrusting is permitted. If the man feels that he is about to ejaculate, the woman simply raises her body and uses the squeeze technique. After there is control in this situation, the man is instructed to begin some pelvic thrusting. As he gradually gains more control, they may proceed to the side-to-side position for intercourse and finally to the man-on-top position.

The squeeze technique is actually a variant on the *stop-start technique,* which was originally devised by Dr. James Semans (1956) and is used by Dr. Helen Singer Kaplan and others. The woman uses her hand to stimulate the man to erection. Then she stops the stimulation. Gradually he loses his erection. She then starts stimulation again, he gets another erection, she stops, and so on. Dr. Kaplan finds that this procedure is less uncomfortable than the squeeze technique and that couples respond better to it in the treatment of premature ejaculation.

Masturbation

One interesting form of behavior therapy for women with orgasmic dysfunction has been developed: masturbation (LoPiccolo and Lobitz, 1972; Andersen, 1983). The data indicate that masturbation is the technique most likely to produce orgasm in

FIGURE 20.3

The woman-on-top position is used in treating sexual dysfunctions in both women and men.

FIGURE 20.4

A position used in treating female sexual dysfunction.

women. Kinsey found that the average woman reaches orgasm 95 percent of the time when masturbating, as opposed to 73 percent of the time in intercourse. Masters and Johnson found that masturbation produces the most intense orgasm in women. Masturbation therefore seems to be a likely treatment for women with primary orgasmic dysfunction. The therapists, of course, must first deal with the patient's negative attitude toward masturbation. Following this, they use a nine-step (one per week) program to treat the dysfunction:

1. The woman is instructed to do the mirror exercises (see Chapter 3) and to begin a program of Kegel exercises.
2. The woman is instructed to explore her genitals by touch.
3. The woman again explores her genitals by touch, this time trying to find the most pleasurable, sensitive area (this is almost invariably the clitoris).

4. The woman stimulates the area she found to be pleasurably sensitive.
5. If the woman has not yet had an orgasm, she is instructed to increase the intensity and duration of her self-stimulation and to use fantasy in addition.
6. If the woman still has not had an orgasm, she stimulates herself with a vibrator.
7. Once the woman is having orgasms, her husband is integrated into her sexual experience. The first step in this process is for her to masturbate in his presence.
8. He then stimulates her manually.
9. They have intercourse while he stimulates her manually.

Masturbation is sometimes recommended as therapy for men (Zilbergeld, 1978).

Kegel Exercises

Kegel (KAY-gul) exercises: A part of sex therapy for women with orgasmic dysfunction, in which the woman exercises the muscles surrounding the vagina; also called pubococcygeal or PC muscle exercises.

One technique that is used with women is the Kegel exercises, named for the physician who devised them (Kegel, 1952). They are designed to exercise and strengthen the *pubococcygeal muscle,* or PC muscle, which runs along the sides of the entrance of the vagina (see Figure 3.8 in Chapter 3). The exercises are particularly helpful for women who have had this muscle stretched in childbirth and for those who simply have poor tone in the muscle. The woman is instructed first to find her PC muscle by sitting on a toilet with her legs spread apart, urinating, and stopping the flow of urine voluntarily. The muscle that stops the flow is the PC muscle. After that, the woman is told to contract the muscle 10 times during each of six sessions per day. Gradually she can work up to more.[3] The most important effect of these exercises is that they seem to increase women's sexual pleasure by increasing the sensitivity of the vaginal area (Messé and Geer, 1985). They also permit the woman to stimulate her partner more, and they are a cure for women who have problems with involuntarily urinating as they orgasm. Kegel exercises are sometimes also used with men.

Marital Therapy

While the above approaches are essentially all forms of behavior therapy, based on a learning-theory model, another approach is marital therapy. Marital therapy rests on the assumption that sexual dysfunction is caused by a problem in the marital relationship, that is, that the dysfunction is a symptom of interpersonal conflict between the husband and wife. In marital therapy, the relationship between them is treated, with the goal of reducing the antagonisms and tensions in the marriage. The idea is that as the marital relationship improves, the sexual dysfunction should disappear.

Individual Psychotherapy

If one believes that sexual dysfunction is caused by intrapsychic conflict, the appropriate form of therapy is psychotherapy or psychoanalysis. The idea is that the sexual

[3]Students should recognize the exciting possibilities for doing these exercises. For example, they are a good way to amuse yourself in the middle of a boring lecture, and no one will ever know you are doing them.

dysfunction is a symptom of poor adjustment or a disordered personality. The therapy would then treat the person's individual adjustment, with the goal of trying to resolve conflicts. The idea is that sexual functioning should improve as adjustment improves.

David Reuben, in his popular *Everything You Always Wanted to Know about Sex,* voices this viewpoint when he says, "The only effective treatment for total orgasmic impairment is psychotherapy, because the condition is a psychiatric one. The sexual difficulty is simply a manifestation of a deeper emotional dysfunction" (1969, p. 129).

Kaplan: Psychosexual Therapy

Psychosexual therapy: A form of sex therapy advocated by Helen Singer Kaplan, in which both behavior therapy exercises (like Masters and Johnson's) and psychotherapy are combined.

Prominent sex therapist Helen Singer Kaplan (1974, 1979) advocates the combining of psychotherapy with the Masters and Johnson type of behavioral sex therapy into what she calls psychosexual therapy for the treatment of sexual dysfunctions (see also Hartman and Fithian, 1974). That is, she assigns specific sexual exercises, but she also believes that the symptoms may have deeper roots, and thus in psychotherpy she confronts the patient's resistances, unconscious conflicts, and so on.

Her analyses of the outcomes of sex therapy indicate that some dysfunctions, such as orgasmic dysfunction in women, are relatively easy to cure using the Masters and Johnson approach. Problems of sexual desire, however, fall at the opposite end of the spectrum and have a very low success rate with behavior therapy. Psychosexual therapy, combining behavioral exercises with a heavy focus on psychotherapy aimed at developing insight into unconscious conflicts, is necessary for such persons.

FIGURE 20.5

Prominent sex therapist Dr. Helen Singer Kaplan advocates a combination of behavior therapy and psychotherapy for the treatment of sexual dysfunctions.

F · O · C · U · S 20.3

A CASE OF ERECTILE DYSFUNCTION

Mr. X was a handsome and successful 30-year-old businessman who had been divorced two years earlier. He and his fiancée, who was 26 years old, were planning to be married shortly.

The chief complaint was erectile dysfunction. The man was easily aroused and had an erection quickly upon commencing sex play. Almost invariably, though, his erection diminished when he was about to begin coitus. His fiancée had no sexual difficulty; she was easily aroused and orgastic on clitoral stimulation.

Neither had a history of psychiatric problems. In fact, they seemed to be very well adjusted individuals. Their relationship also seemed to be excellent.

In his prior marriage, which had lasted five years and produced two children, Mr. X had experienced no sexual difficulty. He and his wife had intercourse two or three times per week, and he invariably functioned well. His wife left him because she was in love with and wished to marry a close friend of the family.

The divorce was very traumatic for Mr. X. He became depressed and was left with deep feelings of insecurity. He kept wondering why his wife had left him and whether he was inferior to the other man.

Biofeedback

Biofeedback: Various techniques whereby individuals receive some feedback (such as a graph on a video screen) on biological changes in their body, to which they would normally not be very sensitive.

The use of biofeedback in the treatment of sexual dysfunctions is beginning to be explored. Biofeedback refers to various techniques whereby individuals receive some kind of feedback (usually visual, such as a graph on a video screen, or auditory, such as clicking sounds) on biological changes that are occurring in their body and to which they would normally not be very sensitive. As an example of an application in sex therapy, in one study 30 men with erectile dysfunction had penile strain gauges placed on them in the laboratory (Reynolds, 1980). They were instructed to concentrate on thoughts that would produce erections. Any increase in erection showed up on a graph that they could see and produced increases in the rate of clicking sounds. They also saw 90 seconds of an erotic film if they showed erection increases. The results did indicate improved erection in the laboratory, although the investigator concluded that the therapeutic value of biofeedback in cases of erectile dysfunction had yet to be firmly established.

The uses of biofeedback will doubtless be explored with great interest in the next few years.

Eight months after the separation he went to a party and met a woman who wanted to have sex with him right there. On her urging, they went to an upstairs room (which did not have a lock) and attempted to have intercourse on the floor. He became excited and erect, but for the first time in his life, he lost his erection. He tried to regain it, but his effort was of no avail.

Mr. X reacted to this experience with alarm. He felt depressed and extremely humiliated and embarrassed. He never saw this woman again. One month later he tried to make love to another woman, but again he lost his erection when the memory of his previous failure intruded into his mind. From then on the problem escalated. He met his fiancée shortly thereafter, but initially he avoided making love to her because he anticipated failure. Later, when they became more intimate, he confessed his problem to her. They attempted to have sex, but in most instances Mr. X was unable to function. Questioning revealed that he was preoccupied with thoughts about whether he would fail during lovemaking. He continued to feel humiliated and feared rejection, despite his fiancée's reassurance and sensitivity.

According to psychiatrist Helen Singer Kaplan's analysis, this was a case in which performance anxiety (an immediate cause) produced secondary erectile dysfunction.

In therapy Mr. X responded very readily to methods designed to dispel his performance anxiety. Initially, intercourse was forbidden. During this time he and his fiancée engaged in mutual caressing. This proved most pleasurable to both. They then proceeded to gentle, teasing genital stimulation. Specifically, the woman stimulated the penis until it was erect. Then she stopped. When the erection abated, she resumed stimulation. This was repeated several times, still without orgasm for him.

Meanwhile, in the sessions with the therapist, Mr. X was told to stop watching the process of his erection and worrying about his "performance." He was confronted with the destructive effects of his spectatoring and his performance anxiety. In addition, the therapist was able to work through the dynamics of his reactions to his former wife's rejection of him, which seemed to be related to his current problems. The therapy thus combined elements of behavior therapy and psychotherapy, and is an example of Kaplan's psychosexual therapy.

Treatment proceeded to a successful conclusion.

Source: Helen S. Kaplan. (1974). *The new sex therapy.* New York: Brunner/Mazel, pp. 128–129

Hypnosis

Daniel Araoz (1982) and other therapists use hypnosis in treating cases of sexual dysfunction. Hypnosis can be used in a number of different ways in sex therapy. It can be used in diagnosing the problem; that is, it can be used to uncover the original source of the problem, perhaps in childhood, which the client knows subconsciously but not consciously. In hypnosis, the client can recall early scenes that created the dysfunction. Hypnosis can also be used to transfer relaxation. As we saw in an earlier section, anxiety is a common cause of sexual dysfunctions. Under hypnosis, the client can be encouraged to relax while imagining a very pleasant, peaceful situation; then the client is told to transfer this relaxation to a sexual scene. Posthypnotic suggestion can also be used. For example. in one case a woman was not able to become sexually aroused, much less have an orgasm, a condition known as general sexual dysfunction or sexual unresponsiveness. Under hypnosis she was asked to recall early sexual interactions in which she felt pleasurably aroused. Then she was given the posthypntoic suggestion to feel the same pleasure and sexual excitement when in a sexual situation with her partners.

Surgical Therapy: The Inflatable Penis

Penile prosthesis (prahs-THEE-sis): A surgical treatment for erectile dysfunction, in which inflatable tubes are inserted into the penis.

For severe cases of erectile dysfunction, surgical therapy is possible. The surgery involves implanting a prosthesis into the penis (see Figure 20.6). A sac or bladder of water is implanted in the lower abdomen, connected to two inflatable tubes running the length of the corpus spongiosum, with a pump in the scrotum. Thus the man can literally pump up or inflate his penis so that he has a full erection.

The surgery takes approximately one and a half hours and requires only one incision, where the penis and scrotum meet. The total cost of the treatment is about $10,000.

It should be emphasized that this is a radical treatment and it should be reserved only for those cases that have not been cured by sex therapy. Typically it should be a case of primary erectile dysfunction that is due to organic factors such as diabetes. The patient must understand that the surgery itself destroys some portions of the penis, so that a natural erection will never again be possible. Although the treatment is radical and should be used conservatively, it is a godsend for some men who have been incapable of erection because of organic difficulties. Indeed, more than a dozen children have been born as a result of this surgery, to men who had previously been incapable of intercourse.

Which Therapy Is Best?

At the present time we have no definitive evidence on which of the three basic therapy approaches—behavior therapy (the Masters and Johnson program being an example), marital therapy, or individual psychotherapy—is the "right" one for treating sexual dysfunction. (For a critical review, see Sotile and Kilmann, 1977.) The success of the Masters and Johnson program argues for the assumptions and methods of behavior therapy. But probably there is no "right" method. Marital therapy

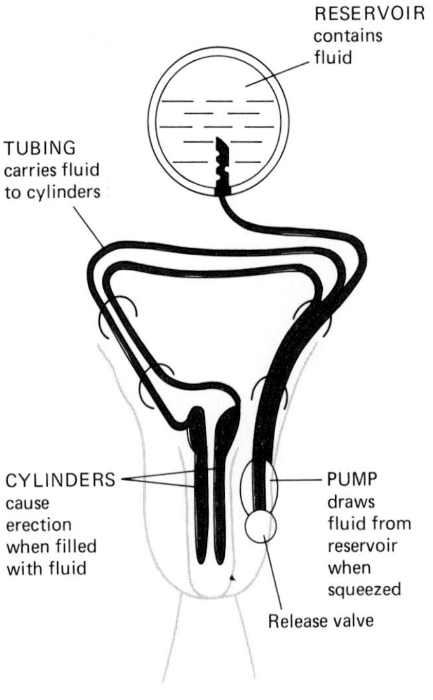
RESERVOIR
contains
fluid
TUBING
carries fluid
to cylinders
CYLINDERS
cause
erection
when filled
with fluid
PUMP
draws
fluid from
reservoir
when
squeezed
Release valve

FIGURE 20.6

A surgically implanted prosthesis can be used in treating erectile dysfunction.

or psychotherapy may be just what is needed by people who are not helped in the Masters and Johnson program. Indeed, many therapists who use techniques like those of Masters and Johnson refuse to treat people with severe adjustment problems or those whose marital relationships are severely disturbed; such people may be referred for marital therapy or psychotherapy. It may also be desirable to combine behavior therapy with marital therapy or psychotherapy—what Kaplan calls psychosexual therapy—when this seems appropriate, a practice illustrated in Focus 20.3.

SEX THERAPY FOR GAYS

Masters and Johnson were among the first to write about the notion that gays might have problems with erection or orgasm. Thus they initiated a program of therapy for gays, using the same methods as were described earlier for heterosexuals. They reported the results in their 1979 book on homosexuality (see also McWhirter and Mattison, 1980).

They treated 57 homosexual men for erectile dysfunction. At the five-year follow-up, four of them were categorized as failures, leading to a 7 percent failure rate or a 93 percent success rate. This is phenomenally high. Notice that it is higher than the success rate for heterosexuals. Masters and Johnson speculated that they obtained a higher success rate with homosexuals for two reasons: (1) they are treating two people who have the same body—this leads to intrinsic advantages in communication and knowing what techniques will be most effective; and (2) there is less performance pressure for erection in male homosexuals, since intercourse is not required. Nonetheless, they noted that the pattern of casual sex that is common with gay men does impose some serious performance pressures, and they cited instances in which the man's unwillingness to give up casual sex created a failure in therapy.

They also treated 27 lesbians for anorgasmia. At the five-year follow-up, only two were classified as failures, once again for a 93 percent success rate. This, too, is higher than the success rate in treating heterosexual women. However, Masters and Johnson note that lesbians have no demand for orgasm from intercourse—which is generally hardest for heterosexual women—so that essentially the lesbians have an easier criterion to meet.

These results are promising in opening up the topic of the possible need for sex therapy among gays.

CRITIQUES OF SEX THERAPY

In 1980, two important critiques of sex therapy, and of Masters and Johnson's work in particular, were published. It is interesting to note that these did not appear until a full 10 years after the publication of *Human Sexual Inadequacy* in 1970. Why did a critical assesment take so long? Probably partly because everyone was so enthusiastic about the successes of Masters and Johnson, and partly because their previous work on the physiology of sexual response had established them as respected scientists.

Psychologists Bernie Zilbergeld and Michael Evans (1980) have done an extensive critique of the research methods used by Masters and Johnson in evaluating the success of their sex therapy. Zilbergeld and Evans concluded that there are a number of substantial problems. In brief, the criticisms suggest that we really do not know what the success rate of Masters and Johnson's therapy is, and it is almost surely lower than 80 percent. A discussion of the specific criticisms follows.

First, Masters and Johnson never actually reported a *success* rate for the therapy. Instead, they reported a *failure* rate of about 20 percent. Thus, most people have concluded, as I did earlier in the chapter (and you probably thought it was logical as you read it), that that implies a success rate of about 80 percent. But Masters and Johnson say that this is not the case. That is, that 80 percent apparently includes a mixture of clear successes and cases that are ambiguous as to whether they are successes or failures—in short. they have 80 percent nonfailures, but that does not mean 80 percent successes.

Further, Masters and Johnson never defined what they meant by a "success" in therapy. This is an important point. How improved does a person have to be to be counted as a success? Suppose a woman seeks help for anorgasmia; she has never had an orgasm. By the end of therapy, she is able to have orgasms from a vibrator, but not from hand stimulation or mouth stimulation by her partner, nor by intercourse. Is that a success? How would Masters and Johnson have classified her? We cannot tell from their book.

Masters and Johnson did define what they meant by failure: "Initial failure is defined as indication that the two-week rapid treatment phase has failed to initiate reversal of the basic symptomatology of sexual dysfunction." (This will give you a flavor of Masters and Johnson's writing style and will help explain why people have often accepted their results without reading the original book.) The problem is that this, too, is vague—for example, how would we classify the anorgasmic woman described above?

Zilbergeld and Evans initiated their critical appraisal after finding that they and other sex therapists were unable to get success rates as dramatic as the ones Masters and Johnson reported. The obvious possibility is that other sex therapists have been using definitions of therapy success that are much stricter and more precise than the definition used by Masters and Johnson.

Masters and Johnson did not report clearly how the initial population of patients for therapy was chosen. They said that they rejected some people from therapy, but they did not specify who made the decision, how the decision was made, and how many people were thus rejected. It seems quite possible that Masters and Johnson weeded out the most difficult cases, leaving themselves with the easier ones and a high success rate.

With their five-year follow-up of patients, Masters and Johnson reported an amazingly low relapse rate of 7 percent, but other sex therapists find much higher relapse rates. Once again, Masters and Johnson did not specify their criterion for relapse clearly, and so it is hard to evaluate or replicate the 7 percent figure.

Masters and Johnson were also somewhat misleading about the duration of their therapy. They described it as two weeks of rapid treatment. Other therapists typically find that patients need more sessions than that. What Masters and Johnson failed to highlight is the fact that patients were instructed to call Masters and Johnson if they ran into problems; in addition, there were regularly scheduled telephone calls between the couple and the cotherapists. Essentially, a couple could get a great deal more than two weeks of therapy.

Finally, Masters and Johnson never discussed the possible harmful effects of their therapy. They made fleeting references to a couple of cases where the therapy apparently ended in divorce, but they made no systematic attempt to assess problems of this sort. Their five-year follow-up was of "successes" only, not failures. It seems likely that the failures were precisely those who might have been harmed, yet there is no information on them.

In contrast to the scientific criticisms by Zilbergeld and Evans is the criticism by psychiatrist Thomas Szasz. In his book *Sex by Prescription* (1980) he criticizes the philosophical basis of sex therapy. Szasz has long been an outspoken critic of psychotherapy. He is particularly critical of the medical model in dealing with psychological problems (see, for example, his classic *The Myth of Mental Illness*). His essential argument is that psychologists and psychiatrists take people who have problems in living, or perhaps freely chosen alternative lifestyles, and classify them as "sick" or "mentally ill" (the medical model) and in need of therapy. Although the professionals may think they are being helpful, they may do more harm than good. For example, once persons are classified as "sick," the implication is that they need a psychologist to fix them up; it might be better for them simply to make active efforts to solve their own problems. As Szasz puts it:

> Among all the medical specialties, psychiatry is the only one whose job it is to stigmatize people with moral judgments camouflaged as diagnoses and to imprison them under the guise of treatment. (1980, p. 125)

Applying this thinking to the sex therapy field, Szasz argues that the sex therapists have essentially created a lot of illnesses by creating the (somewhat arbitrary) diagnostic categories of the sexual dysfunctions. For example, the man who cannot have intercourse because he cannot manage an erection is termed "impotent," yet the man who cannot bring himself to perform cunnilingus is not regarded as having any dysfunction. Why should the first problem be an "illness" and the second one not? A man who ejaculates rapidly is termed a "premature ejaculator" and considered in need of therapy, but what exactly is wrong with ejaculating rapidly? Szasz believes that instead of regarding the sexual dysfunctions as diseases, it would be better to see them as individuals' solutions to various life situations.

Szasz criticizes Masters and Johnson for presenting their work as medical and scientific; he believes that it is moral and political and laden with values. For example, Masters and Johnson claim that homosexuality is not a disease but that nonetheless they can cure it in two weeks. Further, there is a confusion of science and ethics. For example, Masters and Johnson claim that their finding of the same physiology of sexual response in homosexuals as in heterosexuals should improve public opinion about homosexuals. But the physiology of homosexuals is in fact irrelevant to the question of whether homosexuality is ethical or sinful.

Szasz also points to a circularity of evidence in Masters and Johnson's work. Their theory (that sexual dysfunctions are learned and maintained by simple immediate causes and can therefore be unlearned) is used as support for the kind of therapy they administer. But then the success of the therapy (which, as we saw above, is being questioned) is used as a justification of the theory.

Szasz summarizes his arguments as follows:

> I do not deny that sexual problems exist or are real. . . . I maintain only that such problems—including sexual problems—are integral parts of people's lives. . . .
>
> As some of the examples cited in the book illustrate, one medical epoch's or person's sexual problem may be another epoch's or person's sexual remedy. Today, it is dogmatically asserted—by the medical profession and the official opinion-makers of our society—that it is healthy or normal for people to enjoy sex, that the lack of such enjoyment is the symptom of a sexual disorder, that such disorders can be relieved by appropriate medical (sex-therapeutic) interventions, and that they ought, whenever possible, to be so treated. This view, though it pretends to be scientific, is, in fact, moral or religious: it is an expression of the medical ideology we have substituted for traditional religious creeds. (1980, pp. 164–165)

There is one final bit of negative evidence on sex therapy in general, and the

Masters and Johnson variety in particular. Recent experimental studes have tested some of Masters and Johnson's basic assumptions and found evidence contradicting those assumptions (Barlow et al., 1983; Lange et al., 1981). For example, two of Masters and Johnson's basic assumptions are that anxiety causes sexual dysfunctions (and therefore therapy to reduce anxiety will cure them) and that a performance orientation causes sexual dysfunctions. In one experiment, David Barlow and his colleagues (1983) trained male subjects to expect electric shocks when a signal light was on. All subjects had a penile strain gauge placed on them to measure the strength of erections. Then, in one condition, the subjects viewed an erotic film and the signal light came on. In a second condition, subjects viewed the film and the warning light came on, but they were told that they would be shocked only if they did not get an erection of a certain size. In a third condition, subjects were not threatened with shock. The idea is that the threat of shock should create anxiety, and the threat of shock unless there is an erection should create a performance demand. Interestingly, when men were threatened with shock unless they achieved an erection, they showed the greatest erection response; those threatened with shock had the next greatest erection response, and those who were not threatened with shock showed the least erection response. That is, those who were anxious and had demands for performance actually showed the greatest sexual response, directly contradicting Masters and Johnson's ideas. What can one conclude from this study? It seems to make sense that many cases of sexual dysfunction are related to anxiety, yet this experimental study finds just the opposite effect. Perhaps anxiety works like alcohol—at low levels anxiety increases sexual response but at high levels inhibits it. Or it may depend on the person—for some people, anxiety might be sexually stimulating whereas for others it might be sexually inhibiting.

Where do these criticisms leave us? In my opinion they do not completely invalidate the work of Masters and Johnson or other sex therapists. Rather, they urge us to be cautious. We probably cannot expect cure rates as high as Masters and Johnson claimed; the 63 percent found by Kaplan (1979) may be more realistic. The relapse rate is probably higher than Masters and Johnson claimed. Their rapid, behavioral treatment probably works well with the "easy" dysfunctions; the harder dysfunctions will require longer and deeper therapy. Finally, we must be sensitive to the values expressed in labeling something or someone "dysfunctional."

SOME PRACTICAL ADVICE

Avoiding Sexual Dysfunction

Since I was raised by a father who worked for the National Safety Council, I learned well their motto: "Prevention Is Better than Cure." It seems to me that this principle could be applied not only to accidents but also to sexual dysfunction. That is, people could use some of the principles that emerge from sex therapists' work to avoid having sexual dysfunctions in the first place. I think the following are some principles of good sexual mental health:

1. Communicate with your partner. Don't expect him or her to be a mind reader concerning what is pleasurable to you. One way to do this is to make it a habit to talk to your partner while you are having sex; verbal communication then does not come as a shock. Some people, though, feel uncomfortable talking at such times; nonverbal communication, such as placing your hand on top of your partner's and moving it where you want it, works well too (see Chapter 9 for more detail).

2. Don't be a spectator. Don't feel as if you are putting on a sexual performance that you constantly need to evaluate. Concentrate as much as possible on the giving and receiving of sensual pleasures. not on how well you are doing.
3. Don't set up goals of sexual performance. If you have a goal, you can fail. and failure can produce dysfunctions. Don't set your heart on having simultaneous orgasms or, if you are a woman, on having five orgasms before your partner has one. Just relax and enjoy yourself.
4. Be choosy about the situations in which you have sex. Don't have sex when you are in a terrific hurry or are afraid you will be disturbed. This produces anxiety, and anxiety can produce dysfunction, as in the case of a man whose first sexual experiences were "quickies" in the back seats of cars and who became a premature ejaculator as a result. Also be choosy about who your partner is. Trusting your partner is essential to good sexual functioning; similarly, a partner who really cares for you will be understanding if things don't go well and will not laugh or be sarcastic.
5. "Failures" will occur. They do in any sexual relationship. What is important is how you deal with them. Don't let them ruin the relationship. Instead, try to think, "How can we make this turn out well anyhow?"

Choosing a Sex Therapist

Unfortunately, most states do not have licensing requirements for sex therapists (most states do have requirements for marriage counselors and psychologists). Particularly with the popularizing of Masters and Johnson's work, quite a few quacks have hung out shingles saying "Sex Therapist," and many states make no attempt to regulate this. Some of these "therapists" have no more qualifications than having had a few orgasms themselves.

On the other hand, Masters and Johnson are not the only sex therapists in the land; even if they were, they could not possibly treat everyone with dysfunctions. So how do you go about finding a good, qualified sex therapist? Your local medical association or psychological association can provide a list of psychiatrists or psychologists and may be able to tell you which have special training in sex therapy. There are also professional organizations of sex therapists. The American Association of Sex Educators, Counselors, and Therapists (Washington, D.C.) certifies sex therapists.

SUMMARY

In men, the major kinds of sexual dysfunction are erectile dysfunction, premature ejaculation, and retarded ejaculation; in women, the major dysfunctions are orgasmic dysfunction and vaginismus. Dyspareunia and sexual desire problems may occur in men or women. Masters and Johnson reported on these dysfunctions and the way they treat them in their important book *Human Sexual Inadequacy* (1970).

Sexual dysfunction may be caused by a variety of organic (physical) factors such as some illnesses, infections, and damage to the spinal cord. Certain drugs may also create problems of sexual functioning. Most cases. though, are caused by various psychological factors. Some of these are immediate causes—anxieties about failure, spectatoring, and failure to communicate. Others may result from prior experiences such as an early traumatic sexual experience. Other theorists believe that relationship discord or intrapsychic conflict may cause dysfunctions.

Masters and Johnson's program is a kind of behavior therapy based on the assumption that sexual dysfunction is learned and can therefore be unlearned. One of their major goals in therapy is the elimination of goal-directed sexual performance. They require that both husband and wife participate in therapy.

Some of the therapy techniques they use are education, sensate focus exercises, Kegel exercises, and the squeeze technique. Their overall success rate in therapy is about 80 percent.

Others have developed variations of the basic Masters and Johnson techniques, often in an effort to reduce the cost of the therapy. Marital therapy and psychotherapy, which are based on different theoretical models, are two other approaches to treating sexual dysfunction. Sex therapy for gays is being explored.

Criticisms of Masters and Johnson's work question their high reported success rate, focusing on their lack of definition of what actually constitutes a "success" or "failure" in therapy, their lack of specification of whom they accepted and whom they rejected for therapy, and their lack of consideration of the possible harmful effects of therapy. Szasz rejects the medical model of sexual dysfunction.

REVIEW QUESTIONS

1. ____ is the proper term for the inability to have an erection or maintain one.
2. Orgasmic dysfunction or anorgasmia in women is the condition of being unable to have an orgasm. True or false?
3. According to sex therapists, the most common sexual dysfunction now is low sexual desire. True or false?
4. Approximately 75 percent of cases of sexual dysfunction are caused by organic (physical) factors. True or false?
5. A large quantity of alcohol acts as a depressant and can thus cause sexual dysfunction. True or false?
6. ____ is Masters and Johnson's term for acting as an observer or judge of one's own sexual performance, thus contributing to sexual dysfunction.
7. The Masters and Johnson approach to sex therapy can be classified as psychoanalytic. True or false?
8. Masters and Johnson use sensate focus exercises to reduce performance demands on their clients and encourage communication. True or false?
9. Masturbation is one part of therapy recommended for women with orgasmic dysfunction. True or false?
10. Masters and Johnson's research on the effectiveness of their program of sex therapy has been criticized on several grounds, including the fact that they never define what they mean by a "success" in therapy. True or false?

QUESTIONS FOR THOUGHT, DISCUSSION, AND DEBATE

1. When (if) you engage in sexual activity with a partner, do you feel that you are under pressure to perform and do you feel you engage in spectatoring? If so, what can you do to change the pattern?
2. Considering the prior learning causes of sexual dysfunction that Masters and Johnson speak about, what are the implications for parents who want to raise sexually healthy children? Could parents do certain things that would avoid or prevent sexual dysfunctions for their children?

SUGGESTIONS FOR FURTHER READING

Barbach, Lonnie G. (1975). *For yourself: The fulfillment of female sexuality.* Garden City, N.Y.: Doubleday. Provides good information for women with orgasmic dysfunction, based on the author's program of group therapy for sexually dysfunctional women.

Francoeur, Robert. (1983, July). Drugs that screw up sex. *Forum.* (Reprinted in O. Pocs (Ed.), (1985). *Human Sexuality 85/86* Guilford, CT: Dushkin. pp. 52–54.) A thought-provoking article on common prescription drugs that can create sexual dysfunctions.

Kilmann, Peter R. and Mills, Katherine H. (1983). *All about sex therapy.* New York: Plenum. These two recognized therapists have written this book to educate the general public about sex therapy. Helpful for those considering sex therapy.

[redacted]

CHAPTER • 21

SEXUALLY TRANSMITTED DISEASES

I did not know what venereal disease was, only that you could die from it. It was some mysterious disease that you contracted from "doing it too much" and since masturbation, as far as I knew, was just like "doing it," when the soap dried out the skin on my penis to the point that it was itchy and flaky, I thought I was a goner!*

* *Source:* From a student essay.

CHAPTER HIGHLIGHTS

I. GONORRHEA

II. CHLAMYDIA AND NGU

III. GENITAL HERPES

IV. SYPHILIS

V. PUBIC LICE

VI. AIDS

VII. OTHER DISEASES THAT ARE SEXUALLY TRANSMITTED

VIII. PREVENTING STD

IX. OTHER INFLAMMATIONS

X. CANCER OF THE SEX ORGANS

As long as you and your partner have never had sex with anyone else and have sex only with each other, there is no risk of sexually transmitted disease (STD, also known as venereal disease or VD). But if you or your partner starts to have sex with someone else or if your partner has had previous partners, the risk of STD is introduced. Your health is very important, and a good way to ruin it or cause yourself a lot of suffering is to have an untreated case of STD (one of the possible results is sterility). Consequently, it is very important to know the symptoms of the various kinds of STD so that you will seek treatment if you develop any of them. Also, there are some ways to prevent STD or at least reduce your chances of getting it, and these are certainly worth knowing about. Finally, after you have read some of the statistics on how many people contract STD every year and on your chances of getting it, you may want to modify your sexual behavior somewhat. If you love, love wisely.

This chapter will be about not only diseases spread primarily through sexual intercourse but also other diseases of the sexual organs.

GONORRHEA

Gonorrhea (gon-uh-REE-uh): A sexually transmitted disease that usually causes symptoms of a puslike discharge and painful, burning urination in the male, but is frequently asymptomatic in females.

Historical records indicate that gonorrhea ("the clap," "the drip") is the oldest of the sexual diseases. Its symptoms are described in the Old Testament, Leviticus 15 (about 1500 B.C.). The Greek physician Hippocrates (400 B.C.) believed that gonorrhea resulted from "excessive indulgence in the pleasures of Venus," the goddess of love (hence the name "venereal" disease). Albert Neisser identified the bacterium that causes it, the gonococcus *(Neisseria gonorrhoeae),* in 1879.

Gonorrhea has always been a particular problem during wars, when it spreads rapidly among the soldiers and the prostitutes they patronize. In this century, a gonorrhea epidemic occurred during World War I, and gonorrhea was also a real problem during World War II. Then, with the discovery of penicillin and its use in treating gonorrhea, the disease became much less prevalent in the 1950s; indeed, public health officials thought that it would be virtually eliminated.

Gonorrhea is now once again at epidemic proportions. In 1971 there were 620,000 *reported* cases of gonorrhea in the United States; however, since public health officials believe that only about 25 percent of the cases are reported, it is estimated that there were about 2.5 million cases (Millar, 1972).[1] In 1982 there were approximately 1 million reported cases (Centers for Disease Control, 1983a). Thus to say that there is an "epidemic" does not seem to be an exaggeration.

The current epidemic seems to be due to a number of factors. One factor is the shift in contraceptive practices from 1950 to 1970. The condom, which provides some protection against gonorrhea. has been replaced by the pill. Also, increased sexual permissiveness has probably contributed. If everyone were completely monogamous, there would be no STD; it is spread only when a person has intercourse with an infected person and then has intercourse with someone else.

Symptoms

Most cases of gonorrhea result from penis-in-vagina intercourse. In the male, the gonococcus invades the urethra, producing gonococcal urethritis (inflammation of the urethra). White blood cells rush to the area and attempt to destroy the bacteria, but the bacteria soon win the battle. In most cases, symptoms appear three to five days after infection, although they may appear as early as the first day or as late as two weeks after infection. Initially a thin, clear mucous discharge seeps out of the

[1]These statistics are even more remarkable when one realizes that gonorrhea is not 100 percent contagious. For example, the chances of a man catching it from one act of intercourse with an infected woman are between 20 and 50 percent (Hooper et al., 1978); that is, you do not always get it. Thus an even greater number of people were exposed to it, but some were lucky and did not contract it. (I debated for a long time over whether to mention that statistic. I fear it will create an "it can't happen to me" attitude. But don't count on it. And remember that the more times you have intercourse with an infected partner, the greater your chances of getting the disease on one of those occasions.)

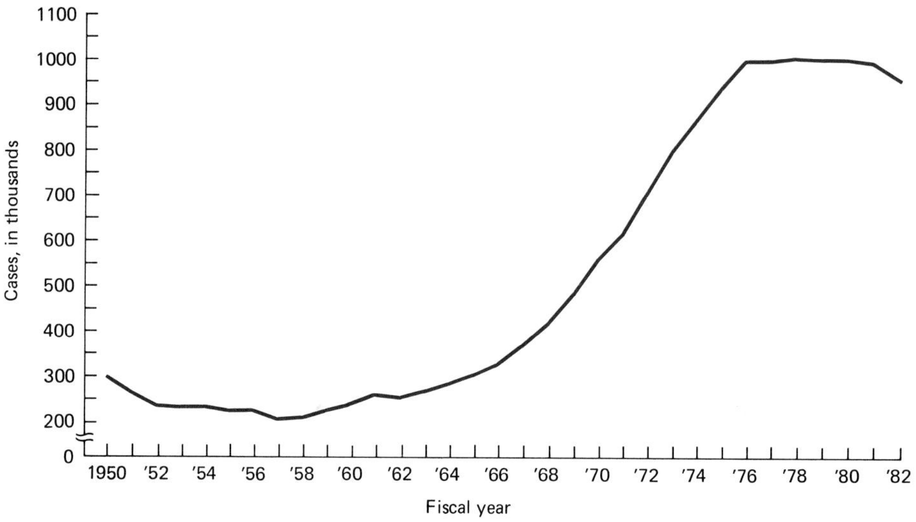

FIGURE 21.1

Reported cases of gonorrhea in the United States, 1950 to 1982. Note how sharply the number rose during the 1960s and 1970s, although rates leveled off in the early 1980s.

meatus (the opening at the tip of the penis). Within a day or so it becomes thick and creamy and may be white, yellowish, or yellow-green. This is often referred to as a "purulent" (puslike) discharge. The area around the meatus may become swollen. There is a painful burning sensation when urinating, and the urine may contain pus or blood. In some cases, the lymph glands of the groin become enlarged and tender.

Because the early symptoms of gonorrhea in the male are painful and obvious, most men seek treatment immediately and are cured. If the disease is not treated, however, the urethritis spreads up the urethra, causing inflammations in the prostate (prostatitis), seminal vesicles (seminal vesiculitis), urinary bladder (cystitis), and epididymis (epididymitis). Pain on urination becomes worse and is felt in the whole penis. Then these early symptoms may disappear as the disease spreads to the other organs. If the epididymitis is left unteated, it may spread to both testicles, and the resulting scar tissue may cause sterility.

Asymptomatic (ay-simp-toh-MAT-ik): Having no symptoms.

Asymptomatic gonorrhea (gonorrhea with no symptoms) does occur in males, but its incidence is low (Handsfield et al., 1974). In some studies, though, as many as 50 percent of men with gonorrhea have been asymptomatic or have had only slight symptoms (Handsfield et al., 1974). This high rate is due to the fact that these men do not seek treatment and the disease is quite persistent if it is not treated. These asymptomatic carrier males are an important source of transmission of the disease to women.

About 60 to 80 percent of women infected with gonorrhea are asymptomatic during the early stages of the disease. Many women are unaware of their infection unless they are told by a male partner. Therefore, it is extremely important for any male who is infected to inform all his contacts.

The gonorrheal infection in the woman invades the cervix. Pus is discharged, but the amount may be so slight that it is not noticed. When present, it is yellow-green and irritating to the vulva, but it is generally not heavy (it is not to be confused with normal cervical mucus, which is clear or white and nonirritating. or with discharges resulting from the various kinds of vaginitis—discussed later in this chapter—which are irritating but white). Although the cervix is the primary site of infection, the inflammation may also spread to the urethra, causing burning pain on urination (not to be confused with cystitis.)

If the infection is not treated, the Bartholin glands may become infected and, in rare cases, swell and produce pus. The infection may also be spread to the anus and rectum, either by a heavy cervical discharge or by the menstrual discharge.

Pelvic inflammatory disease (PID): An infection and inflammation of pelvic organs in the female, such as the fallopian tubes and the uterus.

Because so many women are asymptomatic in the early stages of gonorrhea, many receive no treatment, and thus there is a high risk of serious complications. In about 30 percent of women who go untreated, the gonococcus moves up into the uterus, often during the menstrual period. From there it infects the fallopian tubes, causing *salpingitis*.[2] The tissues become swollen and inflamed, and thus the condition is also called pelvic inflammatory disease (PID—although PID can be caused by diseases other than gonorrhea). The major symptom is pelvic pain and, in some cases, irregular or painful menstruation. If the salpingitis is not treated, scar tissue may form. blocking the tubes and leaving the woman sterile. Indeed, untreated gonorrhea is one of the commonest causes of sterility in women. If the tubes are partially blocked, so that sperm can get up them but eggs cannot move down, ectopic pregnancy can result, since the fertilized egg is trapped in the tube.

In rare cases, in both males and females, the gonococcus may enter the bloodstream and travel to the joints, causing *gonococcal arthritis,* or to the heart valve.

There are three other major sites for nongenital gonorrhea infection: the mouth and throat, the anus and rectum, and the eyes. If fellatio is performed on an infected person, the gonococcus may invade the throat. (Cunnilingus is unlikely to spread gonorrhea, and mouth-to-mouth kissing rarely does.) Such an infection is often asymptomatic; the typical symptom, if there is one, is a sore throat. Rectal gonorrhea is contracted through anal intercourse and thus affects both women in heterosexual relations and, more commonly, men in homosexual relations. Symptoms include some discharge from the rectum and itching, but many cases are asymptomatic. Gonorrhea may also invade the eyes. This occurs only rarely in adults, when they touch the genitals and then transfer the bacteria-containing pus to their eyes by touching them. This eye infection is much more common in newborn infants *(gonococcal ophthalmia neonatorum).* The infection is transferred from the mother's cervix to the infant's eyes during birth. For this reason, most states require that silver nitrate, or erythromycin or some other antibiotic, be put in every newborn's eyes to prevent any such infection. If left untreated, the eyes become swollen and painful within a few days, and there is a discharge of pus. Blindness was a common result in the preantibiotic era.

Diagnosis

In males, the physician can generally make a "clinical diagnosis" by inspecting the genitals and the discharge; absolute confirmation, however, must be based on a laboratory analysis of the discharge. A sample is obtained by inserting a swab about ½ inch up the urethra (this causes some pain, but it is not severe).

The simplest laboratory test of the discharge is performed by wiping the coated swab across a microscope slide. The slide is then treated with Gram stain, and the gonococcus should show up, stained by the dye. Unfortunately, this test is somewhat inaccurate for men and highly inaccurate for women. The alternative is a somewhat more complex, time-consuming test, in which the bacteria are grown ("cultured") by wiping the swab onto a medium on a culture plate. After 24 to 48 hours, under appropriate conditions, the bacteria have multiplied so that the colonies are

---

[2] "Salpinx" is another name for the fallopian tubes.

visible to the naked eye as grayish dots.These bacteria are then Gram stained and subjected to other chemical tests to determine whether they are the gonococcus.

If gonorrhea is suspected in the throat, a swab should be taken and cultured using the same technique. Male homosexuals who suspect that they may have rectal gonorrhea should request that a swab be taken from the rectum, since most physicians will not automatically think to do this.

The penis and testes should also be examined for signs of swelling and soreness.

In females, the vulva is first inspected for inflammations. Then a speculum is inserted into the vagina, and a sample of the cervical discharge is obtained by inserting a cotton-tipped swab into the cervix, a procedure that may be uncomfortable but is usually painless. This discharge is then culturd as decribed above. A pelvic examination should also be performed. Pain during this exam may indicate salpingitis. Women who suspect throat or rectal infection should request that samples be taken from those sites as well.

Treatment for gonorrhea should not be started until these tests have been performed.

At the present time there is no good blood test for gonorrhea available, as there is for syphilis. This is unfortunate, since a blood test would permit routine diagnosis, especially in asymptomatic cases and in pregnant women.

Treatment

The treatment of choice is 3.5 grams of ampicillin[3] and 1.0 gram of probenecid taken orally or 4.8 million units of procaine penicillin G administered by two shots into the buttocks, plus 1.0 gram of probenecid taken orally. This large dose is essential to ensure that all the bacteria are killed so that resistant strains will not develop. This treatment is extremely effective. If complications are present, penicillin is still the treatment of choice, although the dose may have to be larger.

For people who are allergic to penicillin, the treatment of choice is tetracycline taken orally. However, tetracycline should not be given to pregnant women; instead, erythromycin is used. One advantage of treatment with tetracycline is that it will simultaneously cure a chlamydia infection (discussed in the next section) if it is also present.

Routine dosing with penicillin in the absence of a diagnosis of gonorrhea is unwise, since it may contribute to the development of resistant strains and to allergic reactions in the individual.

CHLAMYDIA AND NGU

Chlamydia (klah-MIH-dee-uh):
An organism causing a sexually transmitted disease; the symptoms in males are a thin, clear discharge and mild pain on urination; females are frequently asymptomatic.

Nongonococcal urethritis (non-gon-oh-COK-ul yur-ith-RITE-is):
An infection of the male's urethra usually caused by chlamydia; also called NGU.

Chlamydia trachomatis is an organism that is spread by sexual contact and infects the genital organs of both males and females. The female is said to have a chlamydia infection. Men with a chlamydia infection in the urethra are said to have nongonococcal urethritis. NGU (also known as *nonspecific urethritis* or NSU). NGU is any inflammation of the male's urethra that is not caused by a gonorrhea infection. (For a review, see Felman and Nikitas, 1981.) *Chlamydia trachomatis* is one organism known to cause it, but it may be caused by several other organisms.

---

[3]This dose is 8 to 10 times larger than the dose required 20 years ago. Some physicians are expressing concern that the buttocks may not be able to accept the dosages required in the future.

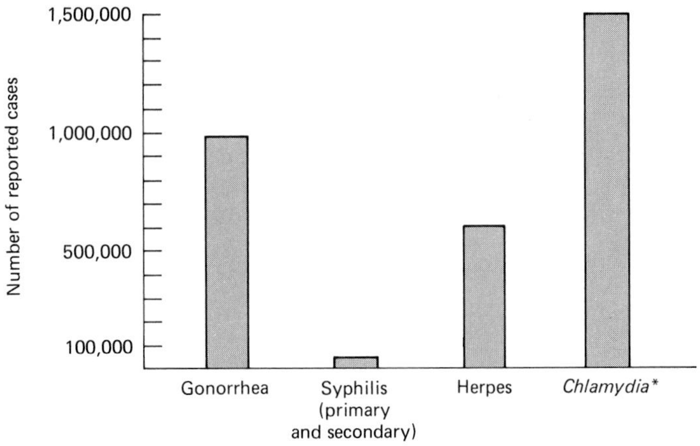

FIGURE 21.2

Comparing the rates of various sexually transmitted diseases, 1982.
(*Because chlamydia is not a reportable disease, this is an estimate based on experts' belief that it is 1.5 times more common than gonorrhea.)

Recent statistics indicate that NGU has become one of the major sexually transmitted diseases, In Great Britian, there are about twice as many cases of NGU per year as there are cases of gonorrhea in men. Unfortunately, NGU is not a legally "reportable" disease in the United States, and so we do not have accurate figures. However, the Center for Disease Control estimates that between 800,000 and 1 million cases of NGU occurred in the United States in 1978, with approximately the same number of or slightly fewer cases of male gonorrhea in the same year. Therefore, the two most common STDs in the United States today are chlamydia and gonorrhea, with herpes coming in third (see Figure 21.2). NGU is more prevalent in higher socioeconomic groups and among university students. Thus when a man consults a physician because of a urethral discharge, his chances of having NGU are about as good as his chances of having gonorrhea. It is important that the correct diagnosis be made, since NGU does not respond to penicillin.

The main symptoms are a thin, usually clear discharge and mild discomfort on urination. The symptoms are somewhat similar to the symptoms of gonorrhea in the male. However, gonorrhea tends to produce more painful urination and a more profuse, puslike discharge. Diagnosis is made from a scraping of cells from the genitals; a chemical test is then done which is both fast and accurate (Boffey, 1984).

NGU is treated with tetracycline or erythromycin, since, as noted above, it does not respond to penicillin. Poorly treated or undiagnosed cases may lead to a number of complications: urethral damage, epididymitis (infection of the epididymis), Reiter's syndrome, and proctitis in men who have had anal intercourse. Female partners of men with NGU are likely to harbor the *Chlamydia* and may experience the following complications if not treated: damage to the cervix, salpingitis (infection of the fallopian tubes), pelvic inflammatory disease, and possibly infertility. A baby born to an infected mother may develop pneumonia or an eye infection. It is essential to treat female partners, both so that they do not suffer complications and so that they do not reinfect the man.

GENITAL HERPES

Genital herpes (HERpees): A sexually transmitted disease, the symptoms of which are small, painful bumps or blisters on the genitals.

Herpes genitalis has received quite a bit of publicity. It is a disease of the genital organs caused by the herpes simplex virus Type II in 85 percent of the cases, and otherwise by the Type I virus (Gunby, 1983). Herpes simplex Type I usually causes symptoms on parts of the body: cold sores and fever blisters, for instance. It is thought that herpes genitalis is transmitted by sexual intercourse, although there are people who have it whose only sexual partner does not. Herpes simplex Type I may be transmitted to the genitals during oral-genital sex (Gunby, 1983).

The symptoms are small, painful bumps or blisters on the genitals. In women, they are usually found on the vaginal lips; in men, they usually occur on the penis. They may be found around the anus if the person has had anal intercourse. The blisters burst and are extremely painful. They heal on their own in about three weeks in the first episode of infection. The virus continues to live in the body, however. It may remain dormant for the rest of the person's life. But the symptoms may recur unpredictably so that the person repeatedly undergoes 7- to 14-day periods of sores. The disease may also be transmitted from a pregnant woman to the fetus. Some children recover, but others develop a brain infection that rapidly leads to death.

With an estimated 600,000 new cases of herpes per year (Gunby, 1983), it approaches gonorrhea and chlamydia in frequency (see Figure 21.2). This does not count recurrent cases, which may number 5 million to 10 million per year.

Unfortunately, there is not yet any known drug that kills the virus. In short, once you have genital herpes, you have it for the rest of your life. Researchers are pursuing two solutions: drugs that would cure symptoms in someone who is already infected, and vaccinations that would prevent herpes. One recent breakthrough is the discovery of the drug acyclovir, which prevents or reduces the recurring symptoms, although it does not actually "cure" the disease (Saral et al., 1981). Acyclovir in ointment form was approved by the FDA in 1982; when applied early in a person's first episode of the disease, it speeds up the healing process and the disappearance of the symptoms. Acyclovir in intravenous and capsule forms is also being explored; this use seems to reduce pain and swelling in the recurrent episodes (Gunby, 1983). Other drugs—and even the use of lasers—are also being investigated.

As to a vaccine that would prevent herpes, Dr. Bernard Roizman at the University of Chicago has used gene-splicing techniques to produce a form of the virus that could be used as a vaccine (Gunby, 1983). If testing goes well, the vaccine might be generally available by the late 1980s.

The major long-term risk associated with the disease is cervical cancer. Women who have been exposed to herpes genitalis have an increased risk of getting cervical cancer and should have a Pap smear every six months.

Because there is as yet no known cure for herpes, and because it is very common, there are enormous psychological consequences to the disease. One man commented on how his recurrent attacks contributed to the breakup of a serious relationship:

> A lot of the time I couldn't be sexual. She saw it as a way of rejecting her. I withdrew emotionally and she didn't understand. Finally, she moved out. I felt guilty, asexual. (*Time,* August 2, 1982)

And a psychiatrist commented, "As time goes on there is a 'leper' effect, and some patients describe convictions of their own ugliness, contamination or even dangerousness."

SYPHILIS

Syphilis (SIFF-ih-lis): A sexually transmitted disease that causes a chancre to appear in the primary stage.

There has been considerable debate over the exact origins of syphilis. The traditional theory has been the "Columbian theory," which states that syphilis was

FIGURE 21.3

Symptoms of some common sexually transmitted diseases.

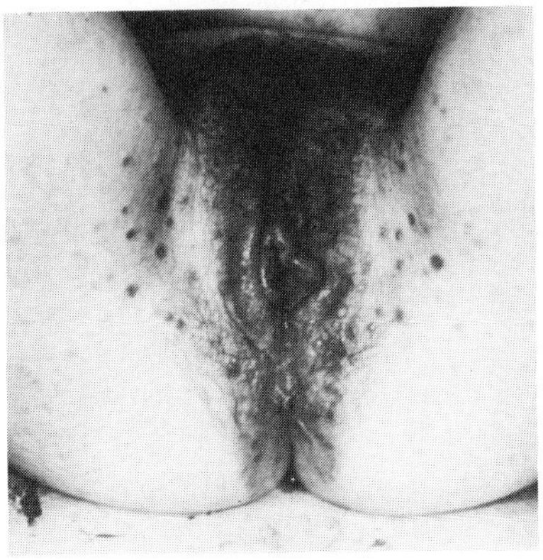

(a) The skin rash characteristic of secondary stage syphilis

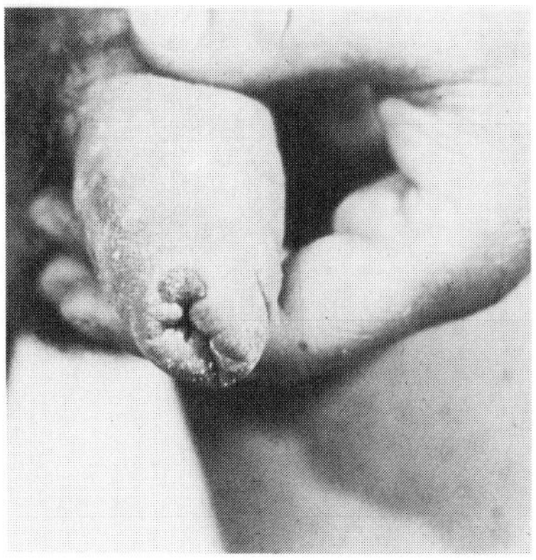

(b) The chancre characteristic of primary stage syphilis

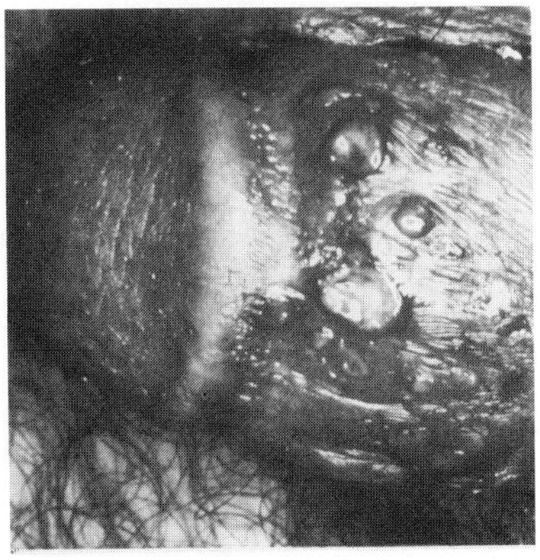

(c) The ulcers remaining after herpes blisters burst

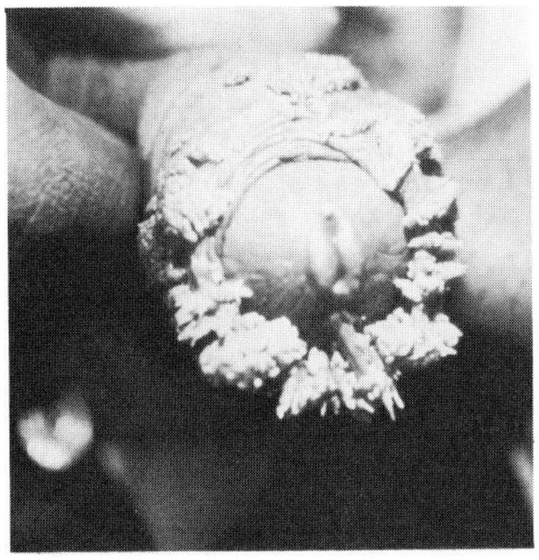

(d) Venereal warts

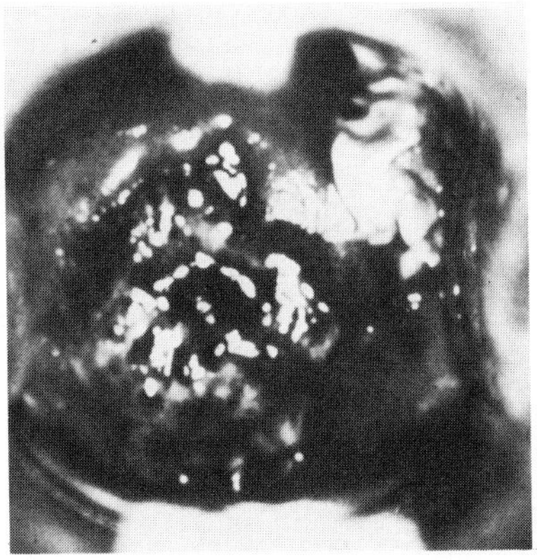

(e) Herpes infection of the cervix

brought back to Europe by Columbus and his crew after their first voyage to the West Indies in 1493. In 1495, King Charles VIII of France besieged the city of Naples, which was defended by mercenaries, many of them from the port cities of Spain. The armies were struck by a strange new disease, which soon ended the fighting. The French army, on its way home, spread the disease throughout Europe. The disease, called "The Great Pox," became a pandemic by 1500.

An alternative theory concerning the origin of syphilis is the "pre-Columbian" or "evolutionary" theory (Hackett, 1963; Rosebury, 1971). According to this theory. syphilis is not a disease itself but one form of the disease treponematosis, the other forms being yaws, endemic syphilis, and pinta. All are caused by the same organism (see below), but the disease takes on different forms as it evolves with humans in different environments and societies. According to this theory, yaws was present from the time of the evolution of the first humans in tropical Africa. Indeed, a disease resembling yaws can still be found in African monkeys and apes. Yaws is a childhood disease affecting the skin, and it is spread by skin contact. It is still common in some tropical areas. As humans migrated to the cooler, drier parts of North Africa and Asia, the skin became less cozily moist. Then the treponemata organism, which is actually rather delicate, retreated to the remaining moist areas of the body—the underarms, mouth, nostrils, crotch, and anus—and endemic syphilis developed. Later, the organism retreated again, this time to the safe, moist areas of the genitals and rectum. Transmission then was by sexual intercourse.

There is some evidence in support of each of these theories (Catterall, 1974). In support of the Columbian theory, syphilis damage has been found in the bones of Indians from the pre-Columbian period in the Americas, while no similar damage has been found in the bones of Egyptians before that time (although this point has been disputed—Rosebury, 1971). Further, the disease is not described in the writings of Europeans before the time of Columbus. Supporters of the evolutionary theory point to the fact that the organisms causing yaws and syphilis are indistinguishable.

Whatever the precise origin of the disease, its naming seems to have been a good example of "it wasn't my fault." The French called it "the Naples disease." In Naples it was called "the French disease." And in England it was called "the Spanish disease." (Although one person commented profoundly that it was really "the disease of him who has it.") It received the name we use today in 1530, when an Italian physician, Fracastoro, wrote a poem about a shepherd boy named Syphilis who was afflicted with the French disease as punishment for violating the will of the sun god. The poem was widely read, and the name stuck.

For the next few centuries there was considerable confusion about venereal diseases. It was thought that gonorrhea and syphilis were a single disease. In a famous bit of experimentation, John Hunter (1728–1793) attempted to differentiate between the two by inoculating himself with some pus from a patient suffering from gonorrhea. Unfortunately, the patient also had syphilis, and so Hunter developed symptoms of both diseases. Thus the experiment caused further confusion, not to mention Hunter's death. In 1837 the two diseases were finally distinguished by Philip Ricord.

The organism causing syphilis was identified by the German scientists Shauddin and Hoffman in 1905. The bacterium they identified is called *Treponema palidum* (*T. pallidum,* if you want to be on cozy terms with it). It is spiral-shaped and is thus often called a *spirochete* (see Figure 21.4). In 1906, Wassermann, Neisser, and Bruck described a test for diagnosing syphilis; this was known as the *Wassermann test* or *Wassermann reaction.* This test has been replaced by more modern blood tests, but the "Wassermann" label hangs on.

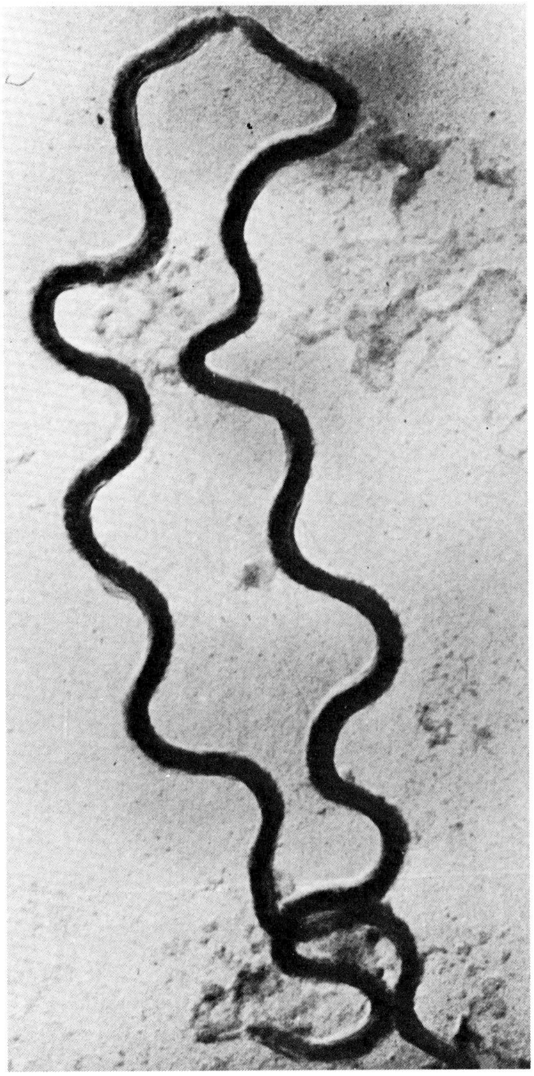

FIGURE 21.4

Treponema pallidum, the spiral-shaped organism that causes syphilis.

The incidence of syphilis, unlike that of gonorrhea, has not increased dramatically in the last decades. Thus statements about the "VD epidemic" refer to gonorrhea, chlamydia, and herpes, not syphilis. There were 33,600 reported cases in 1982, compared with 960,600 reported cases of gonorrhea (Centers for Disease Control, 1983a). Although the disease is not nearly so common as gonorrhea and is not increasing in frequency, the effects of syphillis are much more serious than those of gonorrhea. In most cases, gonorrhea causes only discomfort and, sometimes, sterility; syphilis can kill.

Symptoms

Chancre (SHANK-er): A painless, ulcerlike lesion with a hard, raised edge that is a symptom of syphilis.

The major early symptom of syphilis is the chancre. It is a round, ulcerlike lesion with a hard, raised edge, resembling a crater (see Figure 21.3). One of the distinctive things about it is that although it looks terrible. it is painless. The chancre appears about three to four weeks (as early as ten days or as late as three months) after intercourse with the infected person. The chancre appears at the point where the bacteria entered the body. Typically, the bacteria enter through the mucous membranes of the genitals as a result of intercourse with an infected person. Thus in men the chancre often appears on the glans or corona of the penis, or it may appear anywhere on the penis or scrotum. In women, the chancre often appears on the cervix, and thus the woman does not notice it and is unaware that she is infected (Nature's sexism again; this may be a good reason for a woman to do the pelvic self-exam with a speculum as described in Chapter 3). The chancre may also appear on the vaginal walls or, externally, on the vulva.

If oral sex or anal intercourse with an infected person occurred, the bacteria can also invade the mucous membranes of the mouth or rectum. Thus the chancre may appear on the lips, tongue, or tonsils or around the anus.

Finally, the bacteria may enter through a cut in the skin anywhere on the body. Thus it is possible (though this happens rarely) to get syphilis by touching he chancre of an infected person. The chancre would then appear on the hand at the point where the bacteria entered through the break in the skin.

The progress of the disease once the person has been infected is generally divided into four stages: primary-stage syphilis, secondary-stage syphilis, latent syphilis, and late (tertiary) syphilis. The phase described above, in which the chancre forms, is primary-stage syphilis. If left untreated, the chancre goes away by itself within one to five weeks after it appears. This marks the end of the primary stage. The important thing to remember is that the disease has not gone away just because the chancre has healed. The disease has only gone underground.

Primary stage syphilis: The first few weeks of a syphilis infection during which the chancre is present.

By the time the chancre has appeared, the bacteria are well into the bloodstream and have circulated throughout the body. Beginning one to six months after the original appearance of the chancre, a generalized body rash develops, marking the beginning of secondary-stage syphilis. The rash is very variable in its appearance, the most distinctive feature being that it does not itch or hurt. It generally appears as raised bumps on various parts of the body. When the rash appears on the palms of the hands or the soles of the feet, it is a particularly distinctive symptom of syphilis. On white skin the bumps are first cherry- or ham-colored and then become coppery or brown. On black skin the bumps are grayish blue. In the moist areas the bumps may form large growths called *condylomata lata.* When these break, a thick fluid oozes out; this fluid is highly infectious because it contains many of the bacteria.

Secondary stage syphilis: The second stage of syphilis, occurring several months after infection, during which the chancre has disappeared and a generalized body rash appears.

Hair loss may also occur during the secondary stage. Other symptoms of secondary syphilis are a sore throat; headaches; loss of appetite; nausea; constipation; pain in the bones, muscles, or joints; and a low, persistent fever. For this reason, syphilis is sometimes called "the great imitator." since its symptoms in the secondary and later stages look like those of so many other diseases.

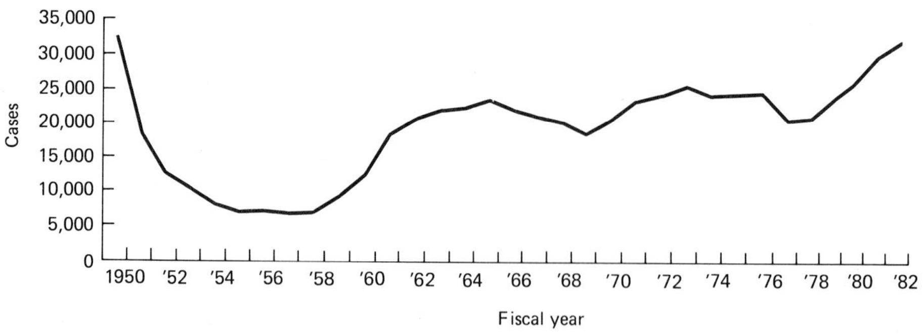

FIGURE 21.5

Reported cases of primary and secondary syphilis in the United States, 1950 to 1982.

Usually the symptoms are troublesome enough that the person seeks medical help. With appropriate treatment in this stage, the disease can still be cured, and there will be no permanent effects.

Even without treatment, the secondary-stage symptoms go away in two to six weeks, leading people to believe mistakenly that the disease has gone away. Instead, it has entered a more dangerous stage.

Latent (LAY-tent) stage syphilis:
The third stage of syphilis, which may last for years, during which symptoms disappear although the person is still infected.

After the symptoms of the secondary stage have disappeared, the disease is in the latent stage, which may last for years. While there are no symptoms in this stage, *T. pallidum* is busily burrowing into the tissues of the body, especially the blood vessels, central nervous system (brain and spinal cord), and bones. After the first year or so of the latent stage, the disease is no longer infectious, except that a pregnant woman can still pass it on to the fetus.

Late syphilis:
The fourth and final stage of syphilis, during which the disease does damage to major organs of the body such as the lungs, heart, or brain; also called tertiary stage syphilis.

About half of the people who enter the latent stage remain in it permanently, living out the rest of their lives without further complications. The remaining half, however, move into the dangerous *late (tertiary-stage) syphilis.* There are three major kinds of late syphilis. In *benign late syphilis,* the skin, muscles, digestive organs, liver, lungs, eyes, or endocrine glands may be affected. The characteristic effect is the formation of a *gumma*—a large, destructive ulcer—on the affected organ. With prompt treatment, the gumma can heal and the patient recovers completely. In *cardiovascular late syphilis* the heart and major blood vesses are attacked; this occurs 10 to 40 years after the initial infection. Cardiovascular syphilis can lead to death. In *neurosyphilis* the brain and spinal cord are attacked, leading to insanity and paralysis, which appear 10 to 20 years after infection. Neurosyphilis may be fatal.

Congenital (kun-JEN-ih-tul) syphilis:
A syphilis infection in a newborn baby resulting from the mother having a syphilis infection.

If a pregnant woman has syphilis, the fetus may be infected when the bacteria cross the placental barrier, and the child gets congenital (from birth) syphilis. The infection may cause early death of the fetus (spontaneous abortion), or severe illness at or shortly after birth. It may also lead to late complications which only show up at 10 or 20 years of age. Women are most infectious to their baby when they have primary or secondary stage syphilis, but they may transmit the infection to the fetus in utero as long 8 years after the mother's initial infection. If the disease is diagnosed and treated before the fourth month of pregnancy, the fetus will not develop the disease. For this reason, a syphilis test is done as a routine part of the blood analysis in a pregnancy test.

Diagnosis

Syphilis is somewhat difficult to diagnose because, as noted above, its symptoms are like those of many other diseases.

The physical exam should include inspection not only of the genitals but also of the entire body surface. Women should have a pelvic exam so that the vagina and the cervix can be checked for sores. If the patient has had anal intercourse, a rectal exam should also be performed.

If a chancre is present, some of its fluid is taken and placed on a slide for inspection under a dark-field microscope. If the person has syphilis, *T. pallidum* should be present, with its characteristic shape (Figure 21.4).

The commonest tests for syphilis are the blood tests, which can be used either for individual diagnosis or for mass screening (as with everyone who obtains a marriage license). The VDRL (named for the Venereal Disease Research Laboratory of the U.S. Public Health Service, where the test was developed) is the most frequently used of these blood tests, all of which are based on antibody reactions. The VDRL is fairly accurate, cheap, and easy to perform. However, it has some limitations. It does not give accurate results until at least four to six weeks after the person has been infected. Even then, it correctly diagnoses only about 75 percent of the cases of primary syphilis; in the other 25 percent it gives a "false negative." It is completely accurate in detecting secondary syphilis. The VDRL may give a "false positive" in the case of people who have recently had diseases like measles or chicken pox and in the case of drug addicts.

Treatment

The treatment of choice for syphilis is penicillin. *T. pallidum* is actually rather fragile, and so the large doses used in the treatment of gonorrhea are not necessary in the treatment of syphilis; however, the bacteria may survive for several days, and therefore a long-acting penicillin is used. The recommended dose is two shots of benzathine penicillin, of 1.2 million units each, one in each of the buttocks. Latent, late, and congenital syphilis require larger doses.

For those allergic to penicillin, tetracycline is the recommended treatment, but it should not be given to pregnant women.

Follow-up exams should be performed to make sure that the patient is completely cured.

PUBIC LICE

Pubic lice: Tiny lice that attach themselves to the base of pubic hairs and cause itching; also called crabs or pediculosis pubis.

Pubic lice ("crabs" or pediculosis pubis) are tiny lice that attach themselves to the base of pubic hairs and there feed on blood from their human host. They are about the size of a pinhead and, under magnification, resemble a crab (see Figure 21.6). They live for about 30 days, but they die within 24 hours if they are taken off a human host. They lay eggs frequently, the eggs hatching in seven to nine days. Crabs are transmitted by sexual contact, but they may also be picked up from sheets. towels, sleeping bags, or toilet seats. (Yes, Virginia, there are some things you can get from toilet seats.)

The major symptom of pubic lice is an itching in the region of the pubic hair, although some people do not experience the itching. Diagnosis is made by finding the lice or the eggs attached to the hairs.

FIGURE 21.6

A pubic louse, enlarged.

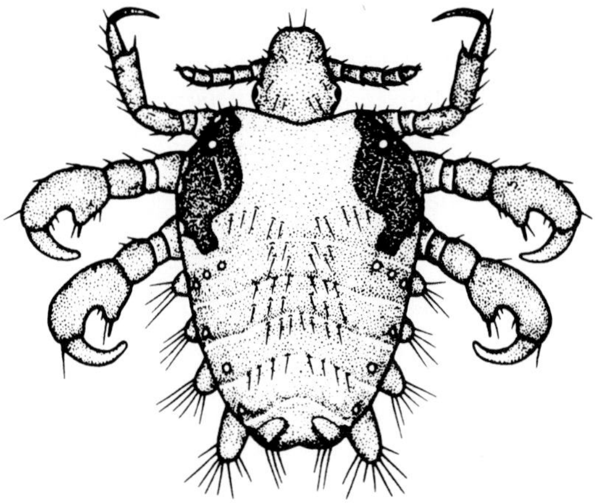

Pubic lice are treated with the drug gamma benzene hexachloride, which is available by prescripion only as a cream, lotion, or shampoo under the brand name Kwell (Kwellada in Canada). A-200 Pyrinate is also effective and is available without prescription. Both kill the lice. After treatment, the person should put on clean clothing. Since the lice die within 24 hours, it is not necessary to disinfect clothing that has not been used for over 24 hours. However the eggs can live up to six days, and in difficult cases it may be necessary to boil or dry-clean one's clothing (Hatcher et al., 1980).

AIDS

In 1981, a physician in Los Angeles reported a mysterious and frightening new disease identified in several gay men. Within two years, the number of cases escalated sharply to the point where it could be called an epidemic, the gay community had become both frightened and outraged, and Washington had funded a major public health effort aimed at understanding and eradicating the disease.

Acquired immune-deficiency syndrome (AIDS): A sexually transmitted disease that destroys the body's natural immunity to infection so that the person is susceptible to and may die from diseases such as pneumonia or cancer.

Pneumocystis carinii (noo-moh-SIST-is kah-RIN-ee-eye) pneumonia: A form of pneumonia that may cause death and to which AIDS victims are particularly susceptible.

Kaposi's sarcoma (KAP-oh-seez sar-coh-muh): A rare form of skin cancer to which AIDS victims are particularly susceptible.

The disease was named *AIDS,* an abbreviation for acquired immune deficiency syndrome As the name implies, the disease destroys the body's natural system of immunity to diseases. Once AIDS has destroyed an individual's immune system, opportunistic diseases may take over the body, and the person usually dies within a few months to a few years. The two most common of these diseases found in AIDS patients are one form of pneumonia (Pneumocystis carinii pneumoniaor *PCP)* and a rare form of cancer (Kaposi's sarcomaor *KS)* that produces purplish lesions on the skin. Both are killers.

As of April 1985, approximately 9000 cases of AIDS had been reported, and more than 4000 of those diagnosed with AIDS had died.

Although the disease has most often been found in gay or bisexual men, they are not the only victims. Of those diagnosed as having AIDS, 71 percent are gay or bisexual men, 17 percent are men or women who abuse intravenous drugs (usually heroin addicts), 5 percent are natives of Haiti living in the United States, and 1 percent are persons with hemophilia. In the remaining category are some women who are heterosexual sex partners of bisexual men or men in the other high-risk categories (Fox and Lipton, 1983).

Not all gay men are equally at risk for the disease. Contracting AIDS seems to be most related to having a large number of different sexual partners and to engaging in anal intercourse (Darrow, 1984).

The psychological impact on gays in many cases has been enormous.

> In Manhattan . . . a WABC-TV crew refused to enter the Gay Men's Health Crisis office to cover a story on AIDS. . . . Said one of the technicians: "Look, nobody knows anything about AIDS. What makes them so cocksure I'm not going to get it from a sweaty palm?" One of the homosexuals in the office had a question: "Do you understand now that we're treated like lepers?" (*Time,* July 4, 1983, p. 56)

Some have termed AIDS the "gay plague," ignoring the fact that there are documented cases of exclusive heterosexuals contracting it. At a time when gay activists have put so much effort into changing public opinion about homosexuality, AIDS seems to be adding new fuel to the fire of homophobia.

HTLV-3: Human T-cell leukemia/lymphoma virus, the virus thought to cause AIDS.

A major breakthrough came in 1984 when Dr. Robert Gallo, of the National Institutes of Health, announced that he had identified the virus causing AIDS. A French team simultaneously announced the same discovery. The virus is named *HTLV-3*

F · O · C · U · S 21.1

AN AIDS VICTIM TELLS HIS STORY

Last March, I was diagnosed as having AIDS. This altered my life so profoundly that seven months later I am still struggling to adjust to the change.

Perhaps my reaction was different from most AIDS patients. Because we are all individuals, I am sure that every person so diagnosed reacts differently. No one can fully understand another's anguish in such circumstances. Nevertheless, let me recount my personal experience, although cautioning against accepting it as "normal" for all other AIDS patients.

Suspecting that the purple spots that appeared on the inside of my thighs might be Kaposi's sarcoma, I tried to prepare myself for the news that would be given by my doctor.

The doctor was very compassionate, saying that this was probably the worst news I had ever received in my life, and he was right. All of my mental preparation was insufficient to thwart the tidal wave of emotion that swept over me as I received what, at the time, I regarded as a death sentence. I went home that evening in the company of my lover, Michael, feeling the weight of two worlds—mine and his—on my shoulders.

Wanting to protect him not only from the possibility of contracting the disease himself, but also from the difficulties that I knew were ahead for me, I asked him to leave me. He refused, reminding me that we were in this together.

I have always considered myself an independent person, tough enough to brave everything life had to throw at me. In fact, I took pride in my ability to "tough things out"—alone, if necessary. And that was the way I wanted it. Eventually we were able to cry together, although I still feel ashamed and weak at such emotional displays.

The Whitman-Walker Clinic in Washington has provided counseling services which I have found very valuable. My counselor is a professional who understands that being depressed is not so bad, but is rather a normal mental experience.

because it is similar to a previously identified virus *HTLV* (for human T-cell leukemia/lymphoma virus), which causes a form of leukemia and lymphoma. Now that the virus has been identified—although further tests are needed to confirm it positively as the cause of AIDS—intensive research efforts are being directed at developing a vaccination against AIDS, and at developing a simple and cheap blood test for AIDS. A blood test that detects antibodies to the HTLV-3 virus was developed in 1985 and it should be useful in testing of blood supplies collected for medical use. Because AIDS has been found in people receiving blood transfusions, there has been concern about the safety of the nation's blood supply, and a blood test would allow routine screening of all blood that is collected.

It is also extremely difficult for me to make others understand that I do not want sympathy. It is demeaning and humiliating to me when I perceive that someone feels sorry for me. Friends can be supportive, understanding, and helpful without pitying me.

For those of you with friends with AIDS, please remember that this is no time for an "out of sight, out of mind" philosophy. When your friends are too ill to participate in your life as they did before, don't just forget them. Remember, this is when they need you the most and, if you can, respond to that need.

Four months prior to my diagnosis, I ran the Marine Corps Marathon in about four hours. Struggling to maintain my physical conditioning through all the emotional and physical realities, plus the debilitating treatments, has called upon all of my resources. It is difficult for me to run even two miles now, although I continue to do so. When I am on intravenous medication, I try to ride a stationary bicycle that has been placed in my room at the hospital.

The first [treatment] began in April—treatments with Alpha Interferon. The protocol required 10 daily injections, 10 days of rest, and then 10 more daily injections. The side effects were both physically and emotionally devastating. Within two hours of the first injection, I had severe chills, followed by high fever. The evening of the first injection, my fever climbed to 104 degrees, and there were a few hours when I scarcely remember anything. Over the 30-day course of treatment, I noticed myself becoming profoundly more fatigued and depressed.

It was at this point that I finally realized what was going to happen to me—I was going to die. From the first moment of that realization to this day, it is not the act of passing from life to death that frightens me but the events that lead up to that point. The body and physical abilities of which I have been so proud and for which I have worked so hard are deteriorating with cancer and weakness.

I am convinced that to give up is to die. For this reason I submit my body and my life to further experimentation because there simply isn't anything else to do. For those of us already afflicted, it is a matter of holding on until research efforts are successful. That is our hope. Although there are discouraging moments, we cannot—we will not—lose sight of that hope.

To those of you not afflicted goes the task of ensuring that our cause is not forgotten by the politicians and civic leaders responsible for allocating funds to carry on the research that feeds our hopes. To you is assigned the work of keeping our plight in the public eye so that those who would ignore the problem in the hope that it will go away, or those who would declare it to be a problem afflicting only a single segment of our society, cannot accomplish what people of good conscience know is patently wrong. It is up to you to correct the public's misperception, fostered by often insensitive media representation, that all AIDS patients are ignoble, drug-abusing people who are undeserving of attention, let alone the benefits of a worldwide quest to save them from a devastating disease.

We are not bad people. We are merely gay, and that is no reason to regard us with disdain. Those of us physically unable to carry on this message look to you for champions.

[Note: Tony Ferrara died on June 4, 1984.]

Source: Ferrara, Anthony J. (1984). My personal experience with AIDS. *American Psychologist*, **39**, 1285–1287.

Until vaccinations against AIDS are available, a number of measures are recommended to reduce the chances of contracting it. Gay men are being advised to use condoms when having sex, to avoid anal intercourse, and to limit themselves to fewer sex partners or to a single, exclusive relationship. There is evidence that the fear of AIDS and these recommendations are making substantial changes in the gay lifestyle. Several bathhouses in San Francisco have closed for lack of business, and those that remain are struggling along with a fraction of the patrons they had 10 years ago.

FIGURE 21.7

AIDS: Gays have mobilized to provide information on AIDS and support for its victims.

OTHER DISEASES THAT ARE SEXUALLY TRANSMITTED

Genital warts: A sexually transmitted disease causing warts on the genitals.

Genital warts are cauliflowerlike warts appearing on the genitals, usually around the urethral opening of the penis, the shaft of the penis, or the scrotum in the male, and on the vulva, the walls of the vagina, or the cervix in the female (Margolis, 1984). Typically they appear one to two months after intercourse with an infected person, although they may appear as late as nine months later. They are caused by a papilloma virus, similar to the one that causes common skin warts. Cases of genital warts have increased in recent years, so that they account for about 1 million visits to physicians' offices annually (Margolis, 1984).

Diagnosis can generally be made simply by inspecting the warts, because their appearance is distinctive. Treatment consists of painting on a solution of podophyllin in alcohol. The warts then dry up and fall off within a few days or weeks. There is cause for medical concern over genital warts because they have been linked to cervical cancer.

Other sexually transmitted diseases include *chancroid, lymphogranuloma venereum* (LGV), and *granuloma inguinale,* but these are also all found mostly in the tropics and are rare in the United States.

PREVENTING STD

While most of the literature one reads concentrates on the rapid diagnosis and treatment of STD, prevention would be much better than cure, and there are some ways in which one can avoid getting STD, or at least reduce one's chances of getting it. The most obvious, of course, is limiting yourself to a monogamous relationship or abstaining from sexual activity. This would not be an acceptable strategy to some of you, but some of the following may be.

The condom, in addition to being a decent contraceptive, gives good protection against gonorrhea and some protection against syphilis. With increasing disillusionment over birth control pills and the rise of the STD epidemic, the condom may again become popular. Contraceptive foams, creams, and jellies (for example, Delfen foam, Emko foam, and Ortho cream) help to kill STD bacteria.

Some simple health precautions are also helpful. Successful prostitutes, who need to be careful about STD, take such precautions. Washing the genitals before intercourse helps remove bacteria. This may not sound like a romantic prelude to lovemaking, but prostitutes make a sensuous game out of soaping the man's genitals. You can do this as part of taking a shower or bath with your partner. The other important technique is inspecting your partner's genitals. If you see a chancre or a discharge, put on your clothes and leave (do not fall for the "it's only a pimple" routine). This technique may sound a little crude or embarrassing, but it seems to me that if you are intimate enough with someone to make love with that person, you ought to be intimate enough to look at her or his genitals. Once again, if you are cool about it, you can make this an erotic part of foreplay.

Urinating both before and after intercourse helps to keep bacteria out of the urethra.

Finally, each person needs to recognize that it is his or her social responsibility to get early diagnosis and treatment and not to have sex until the disease is cured. Probably the most important responsibility is that of informing prospective partners if one has STD and of informing past partners if one discovers that one has it. Because so many women are asymptomatic for gonorrhea, it is particularly important for men to take the responsibility for informing their female partners if they find that they have the disease.

OTHER INFLAMMATIONS

Vaginitis (vaj-in-ITE-is): An irritation or inflammation of the vagina, usually causing a discharge.

Vaginitis (vaginal inflammation or irritation) is very common among women and is endemic in college populations. Three kinds of vaginitis, as well as cystitis (inflammation of the urinary bladder and proctatitis), will be considered here. Strictly speaking, vaginitis is not always a venereal disease because it is generally not transmitted by sexual contact; it is, however, a common inflammation of the sex organs.

Monilia

Monilia (Moh-NILL-ee-uh): A form of vaginitis causing a thick, white discharge; also called candida or yeast infection.

Monilia (also called *candida, yeast infection, fungus,* and *moniliasis*) is a form of vaginitis caused by the yeast fungus *Candida albicans. Candida* is normally present in the vagina, but if the delicate environmental balance there is disturbed (for example, if the pH is changed), the growth of *Candida* can get out of hand. Conditions that encourage the growth of *Candida albicans* include long-term use of birth control pills, menstruation, diabetes or a prediabetic condition, pregnancy, and long-term doses of antibiotics such as tetracycline. It is not a sexually transmitted disease, although intercourse may aggravate it.

The major symptom is a thick, white, curdlike vaginal discharge, found on the vaginal lips and the walls of the vagina. The discharge can cause extreme itching, to the point where the woman is not interested in having intercourse. Because monilia can be very uncomfortable, physicians need to take their patients' complaints about it seriously.

Treatment is by the drug nystatin (Mycostatin or other drugs) in vaginal suppositories. The problem sometimes resists treatment, though. Women, especially those who have frequent bouts of monilia, may want to take some steps to prevent it (see Focus 21.2).

If a woman has monilia while she is pregnant, she can transmit it to her baby during birth. The baby gets the yeast in its digestive system, a condition known as *thrush.* Thrush can also result from oral-genital sex.

Trichomoniasis

Trichomoniasis (trick-oh-moh-NY-us-is): A form of vaginitis causing a frothy white or yellow discharge with an unpleasant odor.

Trichomoniasis ("trich") is caused by a single-celled organism, *Trichomonas vaginalis;* it has four strands protruding from it that whip back and forth, propelling it.

Trichomoniasis can be passed back and forth from the man to the woman, and so it is technically a venereal disease (for this reason, it is important for the man as well as the woman to be treated), but it can also be transmitted by such means as toilet seats and washcloths. As with gonorrhea, some women are asymptomatic.

The symptom is an abundant, frothy, white or yellow vaginal discharge which irritates the vulva and also has an unpleasant smell. There are usually no symptoms in the male.

It is extremely important that accurate diagnoses of the different forms of vaginitis be made, since the drugs used to treat them are different, and since the long-term effects of untreated trichomoniasis can be bad (see below). A drop of the vaginal discharge should be put on a slide and examined under a microscope. If the infection is trichomoniasis, then *Trichomonas vaginalis* should clearly be present. Cultures can also be grown.

The treatment of choice is metronidazole (Flagyl) taken orally, although Nader's health research group has raised some questions about its safety (see also *Medical Letter,* June 20, 1975).

If left untreated for long periods of time, trichomoniasis may cause damage to the cells of the cervix, making them more susceptible to cancer.

Nonspecific Vaginitis

Nonspecific vaginitis: A form of vaginitis caused by an anaerobic bacterium.

Nonspecific vaginitis occurs when there is a vaginal infection, with accompanying discharge, but it is not a case of monilia or trichomoniasis. This diagnosis can be made only when microscopic examination of the discharge, as well as other laboratory tests, has eliminated all the other common causes of vaginitis (trichomoniasis, monilia, gonorrhea) as possibilities. A distinctive symptom is often the foul odor of the discharge. The cause is an anaerobic bacterium. Treatment is by Flagyl taken orally (Hatcher et al., 1980).

F · O · C · U · S 21.2

PREVENTING VAGINITIS

The following steps help to prevent vaginitis:

1. Wash the vulva carefully and dry it thoroughly.
2. Do *not* use feminine hygiene deodorant sprays. They are not necessary, and they can irritate the vagina (*Consumer Reports,* January 1972).
3. Wear cotton underpants. Nylon and other synthetics retain moisture, and vaginitis-producing organisms thrive on moisture. Consider cutting out the center panel in the crotch of panty hose, even in those with cotton crotches, which still do not allow much air to circulate.
4. Avoid wearing pants that are too tight in the crotch; they increase moisture and may irritate the vulva. Loose-fitting clothes are best, since they permit air to circulate.
5. Keep down the amount of sugar and carbohydrates in your diet.
6. Wipe the anus from front to back so that bacteria from the anus do not get into the vagina. For the same reason, never go immediately from anal intercourse to vaginal intercourse. After anal intercourse, the penis must be washed before it is put into the vagina.
7. Douching with a mildly acidic solution (1 or 2 tablespoons of vinegar in a quart of water) can help to prevent vaginitis.

Cystitis

Cystitis (sis-TY-tis): An infection of the urinary bladder in women, causing painful, burning urination.

Cystitis is an infection of the urinary bladder that occurs almost exclusively in women. In most cases it is caused by the bacterium *Escherichia coli.* The bacteria are normally present in the body (in the intestine), and in some cases, for unknown reasons, they get into the urethra and the bladder. Sometimes frequent, vigorous sexual intercourse will irritate the urethral opening, permitting the bacteria to get in. For this reason, it used to be called "honeymoon cystitis," since many women got it on their honeymoons. But with the demise of the virgin bride and the "wedding night," the name no longer seems appropriate.

The symptoms are a desire to urinate every few minutes, with a burning pain on urination. The urine may be hazy or even tinged with red; this is caused by pus and blood from the infected bladder. There may also be backache. Diagnosis can usually be made simply on the basis of these symptoms. A urine sample should be taken and analyzed, though, to confirm that *E. coli* is the culprit.

Treatment is usually with a sulfa drug (such as Gantrisin, ampicillin, or other drugs) taken orally.[4] The drug may include a dye that helps relieve the burning sensation on urination, and the dye turns the urine bright orange-red. If the cause is a bacterium other than *E. coli,* ampicillin is typically prescribed.

If cystitis is left untreated (which it seldom is, since the symptoms are so unpleasant), the bacteria may get up to the kidneys, causing a kidney infection, which is dangerous.

To prevent cystitis or prevent recurring bouts of it, drink lots of water and urinate frequently, especially just before and after intercourse. This will help flush any bacteria out of the bladder and urethra.

Prostatitis

Prostatitis (pros-tuh-TY-tis): An infection or inflammation of the prostate gland.

Prostatitis is an inflammation of the prostate gland. As with cystitis in women, the infection is usually caused by the bacterium *E. coli.* The symptoms are fever, chills, pain around the anus and rectum, and a need for frequent urination. It may produce sexual dysfunction, typically painful ejaculation. In some cases, proctatitis may be chronic (long-lasting) and may involve no symptoms, or only lower-back pain. Antibiotics are used in treatment.

CANCER OF THE SEX ORGANS

Cancer in most cases is not a sexually transmitted disease, but it is a disease that can affect the sex organs.

Breast Cancer

Cancer of the breast is the most common form of cancer in women. It is rare, though not unheard of, in women under 25, and a woman's chances of developing breast cancer increase every year after that age. About 1 out of every 11 American women (9 percent) has breast cancer at some time in her life. Every year, 35,000 women in this country die of breast cancer (American Cancer Society, 1980).

Diagnosis

Because of the statistics cited above, it is extremely important for women to do a breast self-exam regularly (see Focus 21.3). The exam should be done once a month. For purposes of remembering to do it, one strategy might be to do it on the first day of the menstrual period. Unfortunately, the exam should not be done at that time because there tend to be natural lumps in the breast during the premenstrual and menstrual phases. Ideally, the exam should be done at about mid-cycle, around the time of ovulation. It is extremely important to do the self-exam once a month because the earlier breast cancer is detected, the better the chances of a complete recovery with proper treatment. Physicians say that the woman is the best detector of a lump in her breast because she can do the exam frequently and can become

[4]Sulfa drugs can be dangerous to black people. About 10 to 14 percent of American blacks have an inherited enzyme deficiency called *glucose-6-phosphate-dehydrogenase* (G6PD). Sulfa administered to such people can cause hemolytic anemia, which can cause death. A simple test can detect G6PD, and blacks should refuse to take sulfa drugs unless they have been tested and are sure that they do not have G6PD.

familiar with the feel of her own breasts, which makes her better able to detect lumps.

Unfortunately, psychological factors can interfere with this process. Many women do not do the self-exam because they are afraid they will find a lump; thus one can go undetected for a long time, making recovery less likely. Some other women do the self-exam, but when they discover a lump, they become so frightened that they do nothing about it. First Lady Betty Ford did a great service to the women of the nation when, in 1974, she announced that a lump had been detected in her breast and that she would have surgery for it. In doing so, she brought the subject "out of the closet" so that it could be discussed. She also alerted millions of women to the importance of doing the self-exam, probably saving many lives.

Perhaps knowing a bit more about the realities of breast lumps and the surgery that is performed when they are discovered will help dispel some of the fears surrounding the subject of breast cancer. There are three kinds of breast lumps: *cysts* (fluid-filled sacs, also called *fibrocystic disease* or *cystic mastitis*), *fibroadenomas,* and *malignant tumors.* The important thing to realize is that 80 percent of breast lumps are cysts or fibroadenomas and are benign, that is, not dangerous. Therefore, if you find a lump in your breast, the chances are fairly good that it is not malignant; of course, you cannot be sure of this until a doctor has made a diagnosis.

Once you have discovered a lump, you should see a doctor immediately. One of several diagnostic procedures may then be carried out. Until recently, surgery was routinely done to remove any lump. However, several preliminary diagnostic techniques are now in use that reduce the need for surgery. One is *needle aspiration,* in which a fine needle is inserted into the breast; if the lump is a cyst, the fluid in the cyst will be drained out. If the lump disappears after this procedure, then it was a cyst; the cyst is gone, and there is no need for further concern. If the lump remains, it must be either a fibroadenoma or a malignant tumor. Several other procedures can then be used to determine whether it is malignant: thermography, mammography, and xeroradiography. *Thermography* detects heat variations over the body. Because malignant cells multiply rapidly, they produce heat, which should show up on the thermograph. The advantage of this method is that it does not involve x-rays and the dangers they entail, but it also has a very high rate of "false positives" (telling a woman that a benign tumor is malignant or spotting lumps that do not exist). Basically, *mammography* involves taking an x-ray of the breast. *Xeroradiography* is a refinement of this technique; there is less exposure to x-rays, the test is processed more efficiently, and there is a higher degree of accuracy. Both of these x-ray techniques are highly accurate, although some errors are still made. Their major advantage, though, is that they are capable of detecting tumors that are so small that they cannot yet be felt; thus they can detect cancer in very early stages, making recovery more likely. For this reason, some experimental mass-screening programs, in which women were given yearly mammograms routinely, were begun a few years ago. In 1976, Dr. Lester Breslow of U.C.L.A. provided data suggesting that mammograms themselves may cause breast cancer (see also Breast Cancer, 1976). The question is: Which is more dangerous—having yearly mammography or not detecting breast cancer until a later stage? The National Cancer Institute has issued guidelines saying that routine mammography should not be performed on women aged 35 to 50 unless they are high-risk cases.

Most physicians feel that the only definitive way to differentiate between a fibroadenoma and a malignant tumor is to do an *excisional biopsy.* A small slit is made in the breast, and the lump is removed. A pathologist then examines it to determine whether it is cancerous. If it is simply a fibroadenoma, it has been removed, and there is no further need for concern.

F · O · C · U · S

21.3

THE BREAST SELF-EXAM

(a) In the shower: Examine your breasts during a bath or shower; your hands glide more easily over wet skin. With your fingers flat, move your hand gently over every part of each breast. Use your right hand to examine the left breast, your left hand for the right breast. Check for any lump, hard knot, or thickening. *(b) Before a mirror:* Inspect your breasts with your arms at your sides. Next, raise your arms high overhead. Look for any changes in the contour of each breast, a swelling, a dimpling of the skin, or changes in the nipple. Then rest your palms on your hips and press down firmly to flex your chest muscles. The left and right breasts will not exactly match—few women's breasts do. Regular inspection shows what is normal for you and will give you confidence in your examination. *(c) Lying down:* To examine your right breast, put a pillow or folded towel under your right shoulder. Place your right hand behind your head—this distributes the breast tissue more evenly on the chest. With your left hand, fingers flat, press gently in small circular motions around an imaginary clock face. Begin at the outermost top of your right breast for 12 o'clock, then move to 1 o'clock and so on around the circle back to 12. A ridge of firm tissue in the lower curve of each breast is normal. Then move in an inch, toward the nipple. Keep circling to examine *every part of your breast,* including the nipple. This requires at least three more circles. Now slowly repeat the procedure on your left breast, with a pillow under your left shoulder and your left hand behind your head. Notice how your breast structure feels. Finally squeeze the nipple of each breast gently between your thumb and index finger. Any discharge, clear or bloody, should be reported to your doctor immediately.

Mastectomy

Radical mastectomy (mast-ECT-uh-mee):
A surgical treatment for breast cancer in which only the lump and a small bit of surrounding tissue are removed; also called lumpectomy.

Quadrectomy:
A surgical treatment for breast cancer in which the entire breast, as well as underlying muscles and lymph nodes are removed.

Several forms of surgery may be performed when the lump is malignant (radiation therapy, chemotherapy, and hormone therapy may also be used). The most serious is radical mastectomy, in which the entire breast and the underlying muscle (pectoral muscle) and the lymph nodes are removed. Advocates of this procedure argue that if the cancer has spread to the adjoining lymph nodes, the procedure ensures that all the affected tissue is removed. The disadvantage of the procedure is that there may be difficulty in arm movement following the removal of the pectoral muscles. In *modified radical mastectomy* the breast and lymph nodes, but not the muscles, are removed. In *simple mastectomy* only the breast (and possibly a few lymph nodes) is removed. In quadrectomy, or *lumpectomy,* only the lump itself and a small bit of surrounding tissues are removed. The breast is thus preserved, and silicone-envelope implants can restore it to its original shape. Current research indicates that in cases of early breast cancer lumpectomy or quadrantectomy (removing the quarter of the breast where the lump is) followed by radiation therapy are as effective as

FIGURE 21.8

Techniques used in the breast self-exam.

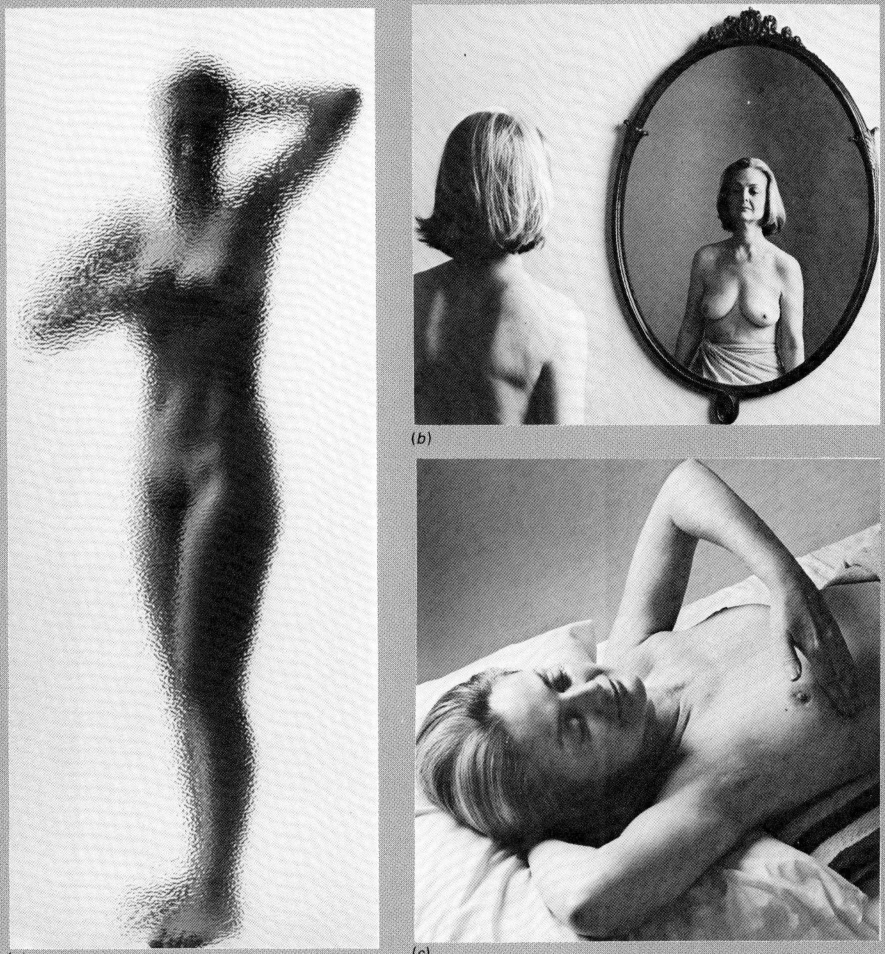

(a) (b) (c)

the old-fashioned radical mastectomy (Veronesi et al., 1981; Henahan, 1984), and obviously much preferable. (See *Consumer Reports,* January 1981, for a discussion of the relative merits of various treatments.)

Psychological Aspects

A lot more is involved in the subject of breast cancer and mastectomy than technical details about diagnosis and surgery. The psychological impact of breast cancer and mastectomy can be enormous (for an excellent review see Meyerowitz, 1980). There seem to be two sources of the trauma: finding out that one has cancer of any kind is traumatic, and the amputation of the breast is additionally stressful.

The typical emotional response of the mastectomy patient is depression, often associated with anxiety and anger. These responses are so common that they can be considered normal. The woman must make a number of physical adaptations, including different positions for sleeping and lovemaking and a change to less revealing clothing. It is common for women to have difficulty showing their inci-

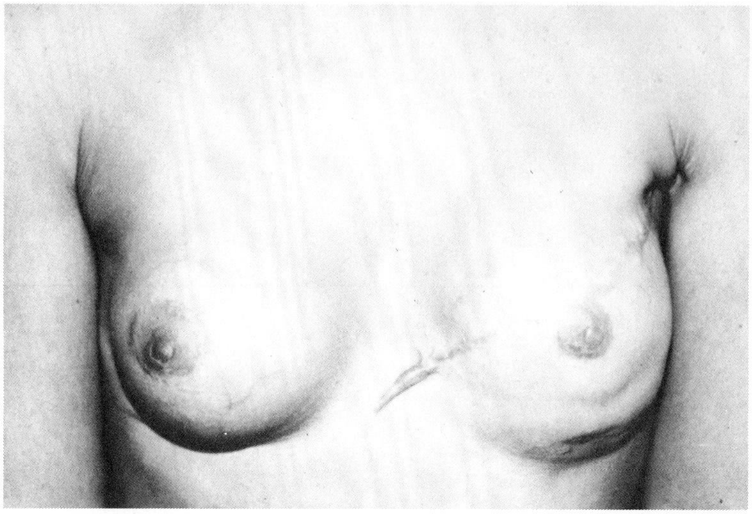

FIGURE 21.9

Appearance of a breast reconstructed after a mastectomy.

sions to their sexual partners. Marital tensions and sexual problems increase. The woman experiences a fear of recurring cancer and its treatment and of death, as well as concerns about the mutilation of mastectomy and loss of femininity. Our culture is very breast-oriented, and a woman who has defined her identity in terms of her beauty and voluptuous figure has a more difficult time adjusting.

Often these emotional responses last for a year. However, the evidence indicates that the experience of breast cancer and its treatment need not have permanent psychological effects. Long-term studies indicate that women gradually adapt to the stresses they have experienced. Gradually they return to their precancer level of psychological functioning.

It is extremely important for a mastectomy patient and her husband to have some form of counseling available to them. In many towns the American Cancer Society has organized support groups for mastectomy patients; these are composed of women who have themelves had mastectomies and who are willing to share their experiences and provide emotional support to mastectomy patients.

Causes

Unfortunately, no one yet knows what causes breast cancer. The likeliest candidate currently seems to be a particular virus. It is not clear, if a virus is the cause, how it is transmitted, but there is some evidence that it is transmitted from mother to infant during breast-feeding (Lanson, 1975). This would help explain the fact that women whose mothers had breast cancer are themselves more likely to develop it than women whose mothers did not, although this also implicates genetic factors. A great deal of research is currently being focused on this problem.

Cancer of the Cervix

Cancer of the cervix and entire uterus is the third most common form of cancer in women; about 2 to 3 percent of all women develop it at some time in their lives. In the next 12 months, 11,000 American women will die of uterine cancer, and another 54,000 new cases will be detected (American Cancer Society, 1980).

The exact causes of cervical cancer are unknown, but, as in the case of breast cancer, a virus is suspected. A number of pieces of data lead to this conclusion. First, there are the apparent connections between cervical cancer and the herpes simplex virus and the virus causing genital warts. noted earlier in this chapter. There also seems to be an association between heterosexual intercourse and cervical cancer; the greater the number of partners, the greater the chances of developing cervical cancer. Teenagers who start having intercourse very early seem especially susceptible (Rotkin, 1962, 1973), suggesting that the virus may be spread by intercourse. Cervical cancer is unknown among nuns, and it is rare among other celibate women and among lesbians (F. Gagnon, 1950; Towne, 1955).

If detected in the early stages, cervical cancer is quite curable. Fortunately, there is a good, routine test to detect it, the *Pap test,* which is highly accurate and can detect the cancer long before the woman feels any pain from it. Every woman over the age of 20 should have one done annually. The procedure itself is simple and painless. The woman lies on the examining table with her feet in metal "stirrups." A speculum is inserted into her vagina, and then a sample of the cervical mucus is obtained on a cotton swab. It is smeared on a slide, stained, and inspected under a microscope for signs of any abnormal cells. The results of the test may be either negative (Class 1—normal) or positive (Classes 2 through 5—some sign of abnormality). It is important to know that a positive result does not necessarily mean cancer. Class 2 results generally indicate some sort of infection. Class 3 and 4 results indicate the need for further testing, and Class 5 results indicate a malignancy. Given Class 3, 4, or 5 results, positive confirmation of malignancy should be done by taking a biopsy (surgical removal of a small piece of cervical tissue, which is then examined under a microscope).

Hysterectomy (his-tuh-REK-tuh-mee): Surgical removal of the uterus.

If cervical cancer is confirmed, the treatment is usually a complete hysterectomy, which involves the surgical removal of the entire uterus and cervix (although in some cases, less radical procedures may be possible). The side effects of hysterectomy are minimal, except, of course, for the risks associated with any major surgery. A hysterectomy does not leave the woman "masculinized," with a beard growing and a deep voice developing, because hormone production is not affected; recall that it is the ovaries that manufacture hormones, and they are not removed (except in rare cases where there is evidence that the cancer has spread to them).

Other cancers of the female sexual-reproductive organs include uterine (endometrial) cancer, ovarian cancer, and cancer of the vulva, vagina, and fallopian tubes, but these are all rare in comparison with cervical cancer.

Cancer of the Prostate

Cancer of the prostate is the second most common form of cancer in men (the most common being lung cancer). It is not, however, a major cause of death because it generally affects old men (25 percent of men over 90 have prostate cancer) and because most of the tumors are small and spread only very slowly.

Early symptoms of prostate cancer are frequent urination (especially at night), difficulty in urination, and difficulty emptying the bladder (these are also symptoms of benign prostate enlargement). These symptoms result from the pressure of the prostate growth on the urethra. In the early stages, there may be frequent erections and an increase in sex drive; however, as the disease progresses, there are often problems with sexual functioning.

Preliminary diagnosis of prostate cancer is by a rectal examination, which is simple and causes no more than minimal discomfort. The physician (wearing a lubricated glove) simply inserts one finger into the rectum and palpates (feels) the prostate. All men over 50 should have a rectal exam at least once a year. If the rectal exam provides evidence of a tumor, further laboratory tests can be made as confirmation.

Treatment often involves surgical removal of the prostate, plus some type of hormone therapy. Surgical castration (surgical removal of the testes, which also removes the source of testosterone) is often part of the treatment and appears to halt the disease. Administration of estrogen also seems to be helpful, although it may induce feminine breast development, erectile dysfunction, and loss of sex drive. Because the pituitary controls hormone output, another treatment involves surgical removal of the pituitary *(hypophysectomy).*

Cancer of the penis is another cancer of the male sexual-reproductive system, but it is rare compared with prostate cancer. It seems to be much more common among uncircumcised men than among circumcised men, suggesting that the accumulation of smegma under the foreskin may be related to its cause. Treatment may consist of surgery or radiation therapy.

Cancer of the Testes

Cancer of the testes is not a particularly common form of cancer. About 2500 new cases are diagnosed each year (2 per 100,000 men). However, it tends to be a disease of young men, and it is the most common form of cancer in men between the ages of 29 and 35.

The first sign is usually a painless lump in the testes, or a slight enlargement or change in consistency of the testes. There may be pain in the lower abdomen or groin. Unfortunately, many men do not discover the tumor, or if they do, they do not see a physician soon, so that in most cases the cancer has spread (metastasized) to other organs by the time a physician is consulted. A recent study showed that when the lump was reported early to the physician, the chances for survival were better than 90 percent. However, when the man waited over three months to see a physician, the survival rate dropped to approximately 25 percent ("A Regular Check," 1980).

Diagnosis is made either by the physician's or your examination of the testes and by x-rays. Final diagnosis involves surgical removal of the entire testis. This is also the first step in treatment. Fortunately, the other testicle remains, so that hormone production and sexual functioning can continue unimpaired. An artificial, gel-filled testicle can even be implanted. The nature of further treatment and the patient's chances of survival depend greatly—as they do with breast cancer—on how early the cancer is detected and whether it has spread. If the cancer is detected early, while it is confined to the testicle, its surgical removal is usually the only necessary treatment, and the survival rate is around 90 percent.

The cause of testicular cancer is not known for certain. However, it is fairly certain that an undescended testis or a late-descended testis has a much greater risk of developing cancer. Also, a recent study has suggested that excessive estrogens during embryonic development of the testes may increase the risk of developing testicular cancer (Henderson et al., 1978).

F • O • C • U • S 21.4

THE TESTICULAR SELF-EXAM

Testicular cancer is a disease of young men, occurring mainly in the 20-to-35 age group. Therefore, college-age men should do regular testicular self-exams. The exam takes only about three minutes, once a month.

Do your self-examination after a warm bath or shower when the skin of the scrotum is relaxed. Examine each testicle gently with the fingers of both hands by rolling the testicle between the thumb and fingers to check for any hard lumps. If a lump or a nodule is found, it will usually be on the sides or front of the testicle and should not be confused with the epididymis, which is located on the top and back side of the testicle. The lump may not be malignant, but most lumps are in this age group, and thus you should see a physician promptly.

These are warning signals:

1. A small, hard lump, usually painless, on the front or side of the testicle
2. A heavy feeling in the testicle
3. Discomfort and/or pain in the groin
4. Swelling or tenderness in the breast
5. Accumulation of fluid in the scrotum
6. Enlarged lymph nodes.

See a physician promptly if you have any of these symptoms.

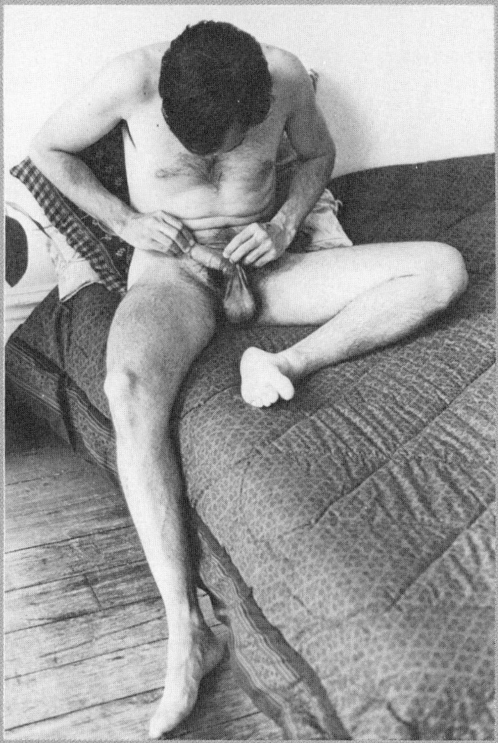

FIGURE 21.10

The technique used in the testicular self-exam.

Source: American Cancer Society. (1978). *Facts on testicular cancer.*

SUMMARY

STD is at epidemic levels in the United States.

Chlamydia and gonorrhea are the commonest of the sexually transmitted diseases. The primary symptoms of gonorrhea in the male, appearing three to five days after infection, are a white or yellow discharge from the penis and a burning pain on urination. The majority of all women with gonorrhea are asymptomatic. Gonorrhea is caused by a bacterium, the gonococcus; it is treated quite successfully with a large injection of penicillin. If left untreated, it may lead to sterility.

Chlamydia may be symptomatic or asymptomatic in women and men. In men, it produces nongonococcal urethritis. NGU has symptoms similar to those of gonorrhea, except the pain on urination is mild. In woman, chlamydia may cause cervicitis, PID, or urethritis.

Genital herpes is a virus infection that produces bouts of painful blisters on the genitals, that may recur for the rest of the person's life. Currently there is no known cure, although the drug acyclovir minimizes the symptoms.

Syphilis is caused by the bacterium *Treponema pallidum*. The first symptom is a chancre, which appears three to four weeks after infection, generally on the sexual organs. The chancre is painless and ulcerlike, with a round, hard rim. Many women do not notice this symptom, since the chancre often appears on the cervix. Diagnosis is made through a blood test. Treatment with penicillin is very successful. If left untreated, the disease progresses past the primary stage to the secondary stage, and then to the latent stage; however, it may reappear as late-stage syphilis, in which various body organs—including the heart, blood vessels, and nervous system—are attacked, leading to death. Congenital syphilis results when the disease is transmitted to the fetus by an infected mother.

Pubic lice are tiny lice that infect the pubic hair; they are spread through sexual contact.

AIDS destroys the body's natural immune system, and leaves the person vulnerable to certain kinds of infections and cancer that lead to death. It is found mostly among gay men, intravenous drug abusers, and Haitians.

Techniques for preventing STD include thorough washing of both partners' genitals before intercourse, urination both before and after intercourse, inspcting the partner's genitals for symptoms like a chancre or urethral discharge, and the use of a condom or contraceptive foam or cream.

Three types of vaginitis (vaginal inflammation), all of which lead to irritating vaginal discharges, are monilia, trichomoniasis, and nonspecific vaginitis. Cystitis is an infection of the urinary bladder in women, leading to frequent, burning urination.

Breast cancer is the commonest form of cancer in women. Most breast lumps are not cancerous but are instead either cysts or fibroadenomas. The usual treatment for those that are cancerous is some form of lumpectomy or mastectomy.

Cancer of the uterus is also fairly common in women. It is extremely important for all adult women to have yearly Pap tests; early detection is the key to cure. If a malignancy is found, the usual treatment is hysterectomy.

Cancer of the prostate is the second most common form of cancer in men, although it spreads very slowly. Symptoms are a frequent need to urinate and difficulty in urination. Hormone therapy is the usual treatment.

Testicular cancer is found mainly among men between the ages of 20 and 35.

REVIEW QUESTIONS

1. Currently, the most common sexually transmitted disease in America is ______.
2. A puslike discharge from the penis and burning, painful urination are symptoms of ______.
3. Gonorrhea is frequently asymptomatic in women, but it is never asymptomatic in men. True or false?
4. If left untreated, gonorrhea in women can cause sterility. True or false?
5. Small, painful bumps or blisters on the genitals are symptoms of ______.
6. Currently there is no known cure for genital herpes. True or false?
7. The chancre is a symptom of secondary stage syphilis. True or false?
8. Pubic lice are tiny lice that attach themselves to the base of pubic hairs and may cause cancer if left untreated. True or false?
9. AIDS is found exclusively among male homosexuals. True or false?
10. The only effective treatment for breast cancer is radical mastectomy. True or false?

QUESTIONS FOR THOUGHT, DISCUSSION, AND DEBATE

1. Contact the student health service on your campus and see whether they are willing to share with you the number of cases of chlamydia, gonorrhea, and herpes they diagnose per year; then share the information with your class.
2. Design a program to reduce the number of cases of sexually transmitted disease on your campus.

SUGGESTIONS FOR FURTHER READING

Boston Women's Health Book Collective. (1984). *The new our bodies, ourselves.* New York: Simon & Schuster. Mentioned in previous chapters, this book contains a much more detailed discussion of breast cancer and cervical cancer than space permitted here.

Kushner, Rose. (1975). *Breast cancer: A personal history and an investigative report.* New York: Harcourt Brace Jovanovich. The author tells of her own experiences with breast cancer and surgery and reviews the important issues surrounding breast cancer and its treatment.

Montreal Health Press. (1977). *VD handbook.* (3rd ed.) Montreal: MHP. One of the best and most thorough discussions of VD available for the lay person. It is available from the same address listed for *Birth Control Handbook* at the end of Chapter 7.

Rosebury, T. (1971). *Microbes and morals.* New York: Viking. A fascinating (really!) discussion of STD. The author is a physician who also happens to be an excellent writer.

Virtus
Honos

CHAPTER · 22

ETHICS, RELIGION, AND SEXUALITY*

Let us say with all possible emphasis that human sexuality is a very good thing. It is part of a man's nature, very central to his personality in the making. It is part of God's creation, a creation which the myth in Genesis tells us God found to be "very good." It is tied in with and expressive of the urgent desire to love, which is deepest and highest in the universe.†

†*Source:* W. Norman Pittenger. *Making sexuality human.* Philadelphia: Pilgrim Press, 1970, pp. 76–77.

*This chapter was contributed by Clark Hyde, M.A., M. Div., an Episcopal priest.

CHAPTER HIGHLIGHTS

I. SEXUALITY IN GREAT ETHICAL TRADITIONS
   Classical Greek Philosophy
   Judaism and the Old Testament
   The New Testament and Christianity
   Humanism
   Sexuality in Other Religions

II. CONTEMPORARY ISSUES IN SEXUAL ETHICS
   Premarital Intercourse
   Extramarital Sex
   Contraception
   Abortion
   Homosexuality

III. TECHNOLOGY AND SEXUAL ETHICS

IV. TOWARD AN ETHICS OF HUMAN SEXUALITY

A college student is very much in love with her boyfriend and wonders whether they ought to begin sleeping together. A corporation executive hears rumors that one of his employees is a homosexual, and he tries to decide what to do about it. A minister is asked to counsel a husband and wife, one of whom is involved in an affair. A presidential candidate is confronted by a right-to-life group demanding support for a constitutional amendment to ban abortion. All these people are facing the need to make decisions which involve sexuality, and they find that issues of values and principles make the decisions difficult. The two principal conceptual frameworks for dealing with questions of value are religion and ethics, which are therefore the topics of this chapter.

Ethics:
A system of moral principles, a way of determining right and wrong.

There are two concerns that give force to our consideration of the religious and ethical aspects of human sexuality. First, there is the scientific concern to describe observable sexual phenomena. Since religion and ethics are important influences on people's behaviors, especially in matters of sex, one cannot fully appreciate why people do what they do without looking at these influences. Second, there is also a personal side to this coin. We are all ethical decision makers; we all have a personal system of values. Each of us must make decisions with respect to our own sexuality. Therefore, we would do well to consider how such decisions are made.

An ethical system is a priority of values, a way of deciding what is most important to us, particularly when there is a conflict between things we value or desire highly. Sexual gratification may be an important value for one person and something to be avoided for another. However, regardless of the importance we attach to sex, we need a way of integrating our sexuality into our patterns of decision making. To do this we use such categories as "right or wrong," "good or bad," "appropriate or inappropriate," and "moral or immoral." These are the kinds of distinctions made in the field of ethics; since we use them every day, we are all practical ethicists.

Religion enters the picture as a source and creator of values, attitudes, and ethics. For believers, religion sets forth an ethical code and provides sanctions (rewards and punishments) that motivate them to obey the rules. When a particular religion is practiced by many people in a society, it helps create culture, which then influences even those who do not accept the religion. Therefore, it is important to study the relationship of religion to sexuality for two reasons. First, it is a powerful influence on the sexual attitudes of many individuals. And second, as a creator of culture, it often forms a whole society's orientation toward human sexuality.

Hedonism:
A moral system based on maximizing pleasure and avoiding pain.

Asceticism:
An approach to life emphasizing discipline and impulse control.

Let us begin by defining some terms that will be useful in discussing ethics, religion, and sexuality. Hedonism and asceticism have to do with one's approach to the physical and material aspects of life in general and to sexuality in particular. The word "hedonism" comes from the Greek word meaning "pleasure" and may be used to refer to the belief that the ultimate goal of human life is the pursuit of pleasure, the avoidance of pain, and the fulfillment of physical needs and desires: "Eat, drink, and be merry, for tomorrow we die." Asceticism, in contrast, holds that there is more to life than its material aspects, which must be transcended to achieve true humanity. Ascetics are likely to view sexuality as neutral at best and evil at worst; they will prize self-discipline, the avoidance of physical gratification, and the cultivation of spiritual values. Orders of monks, found in Eastern religions as well as Christianity, are good examples of institutionalized asceticism, with their affirmation of celibacy, virginity, poverty, and so on.

Legalism:
Ethics based on the assumption that there are rules for human conduct and that morality consists of knowing the rules and learning to apply them.

Situationism:
Ethics based on the assumption that there are no absolute rules, or at least very few, and that each situation must be judged as it is.

Two other terms, legalism and situationism, refer to methods of ethical decision making. As an approach to ethics, legalism concentrates on following some sort of law which comes from a source outside the individual, such as nature or religion. Legalistic ethics sets forth a series of rules and regulations"Do this" and "Don't do that"—and calls for persons to behave according to them. In today's ethical theory, the term "situationism" is usually used to refer to the opposite tendency (the word derives from the title of Joseph Fletcher's book *Situation Ethics*—see the Focus). Situationists would contend that although there may be broad general guidelines for ethical behavior, essentially each ethical decision should be made according to the individual persons and situations involved. Whereas legalism deals in universal laws, situationism decides matters on a case-by-case basis, informed by certain guiding principles, such as love. Classical religious ethical systems—Old Testament Judaism, Roman Catholicism, and Protestant fundamentalism—have tended to be quite legalistic. However, today situationism has become more popular, creating a real ferment in religious ethics, which will be examined later.

F · O · C · U · S 22.1

JOSEPH FLETCHER AND SITUATION ETHICS

Any discussion of situation ethics, which is sometimes called the "New Morality," must deal with the figure of Joseph Fletcher, not because he invented the approach but because he articulated it with great style and clarity. In this sense, Fletcher has become a symbol of an approach and has received much undeserved criticism from those who have not read him but who think they know what he stands for.

When he was professor of Christian ethics at the Episcopal Theological School in Cambridge, Massachusetts, Fletcher wrote *Situation Ethics,* published in 1966. In describing his approach and proposing some cases for thought and discussion, Fletcher wrote:

> In this moral strategy the governing consideration is the situation, with all of its contingencies and exigencies. The situationist enters into every decision-making situation armed with principles, just as the legalist does. But the all-important difference is that his moral principles are *maxims* of general or frequent validity; their validity always depends upon the situation. The situationist is prepared in any concrete case to suspend, ignore, or violate any principle if by doing so he can effect more good than by following it. (pp. 31–34)

Since Fletcher consciously writes against legalism as a valid approach to ethics, his concepts help define a continuum with legalism. Writing in a Christian context, Fletcher makes his guiding imperative love, that is, a firm intent to do good to others. This can be seen in the Six Ethical Propositions of his 1967 work, *Moral Responsibility:*

1. Only one thing is intrinsically good, namely, love: nothing else.
2. The ultimate norm of Christian decisions is love: nothing else.
3. Love and justice are the same thing, for justice is love distributed.
4. Love wills the neighbor's good whether we like him or not.
5. Only the end justifies the means: nothing else.
6. Decisions ought to be made situationally, not prescriptively. (pp. 14–25)

Although Fletcher's principles are explicitly Christian, it would be possible to formulate a nonreligious situational ethic. Joseph Fletcher, his critics, and his supporters have carried on a vigorous debate for the last decade which makes the field of ethics extremely interesting, if a bit confusing.

Of course, few ethical systems are purely hedonistic or ascetic or entirely legalistic or situationist; most lie between these extremes. However, the terms are useful in pointing to tendencies and will be used for that purpose in this chapter. The concluding section will try to put them into perspective and offer some critique of their strengths and weaknesses as approaches to sexual ethics.

SEXUALITY IN GREAT ETHICAL TRADITIONS

With these ways of looking at ethics, especially sexual ethics, as background, let us examine certain great ethical traditions to see how they deal with norms for sexual behavior. Although some attention will be given to non-Western sexual ethics, the thrust of this section will be on ethical traditions of Western culture, primarily because this is a text for American undergraduates, who are part of that culture. We are understandably interested in *our* story, in the world of ideals and practice in which *we* live. That culture can, at the risk of oversimplification, be seen as originating in the confrontation of Greek culture, preserved and developed by the Romans, and Jewish tradition, extended by Christianity in the first three centuries. From that point on, until rather recently, Western culture was Christian, at least officially. Even self-conscious revolts against Christian culture in the West are part of that tradition because of their roots.

Classical Greek Philosophy

During the Golden Age of Greek culture, covering roughly the fifth and fourth centuries B.C., philosophers such as Socrates, Plato, and Aristotle pondered most of the great ethical questions that have continued to interest Western intellectuals. These Athenians regarded the beautiful-and-good as the chief goal of life, and they admired the figure of the warrior-intellectual, who embodied the virtues of wisdom, courage, temperance, justice, and piety.

While nothing in Greek culture rejected sex as evil—the gods and goddesses of Greek mythology are often pictured enjoying it—the great philosophers did develop a kind of asceticism that assumed an important place in Western thought. They thought that virtue resulted from wisdom, and they believed that people would do right if they could, failing to live morally only through ignorance. To achieve wisdom and cultivate virtue, violent passions must be avoided, and these might well include sex. Plato believed that love *(eros)* led toward immortality and was therefore a good thing. However, since this kind of love was rather intellectual and more like friendship than vigorous sexuality, the term "platonic love" has come to mean sexless affection. There was also, among the warrior class, a certain approval of pederasty, that is, a sexual relationship between an older man and a younger one. However, the practice was far from universal and was frequently ridiculed (Brinton, 1959).

Later, Greek philosophy became even more ascetic than in the Golden Age. Epicurus (341–270 B.C.) taught that the goal of life was *ataraxia,* a tranquil state between pleasure and pain in which the mind is unaffected by emotion. The Stoics of the same period valued detachment from worldly anxieties and pleasures and, indeed, a total indifference to either life or death. Sex was seen not necessarily as evil but as less important than wisdom and virtue, something to be transcended to achieve the beautiful-and-good.

Judaism and the Old Testament

The basic source of the Judeo-Christian tradition, which is the religious foundation of Western culture, is the Old Testament of the Bible, which is the basis for Judaism and a major source for Christianity as well. Written between approximately 800 and 200 B.C., the Old Testament has a great deal to say about the place of sexuality in human life and society. However, sexuality and all aspects of life are always seen in religious terms.

To begin, the Old Testament view of sexuality is fundamentally positive. In the Genesis myth of creation we read, "So God created man in his own image, in the image of God he created him; male and female he created them" (Genesis 1:27). Human sexual differentiation is not an afterthought or an aberration; it is part and parcel of creation, which God calls "good." Judaism sees sexuality as a gift to be used responsibly and in obedience to God's will, never as something evil in itself. Looking at the Old Testament as a whole, we can find three themes in this view of sexuality.

First, sex is seen not as just another biological function but as a deep and intimate part of a *relationship* between two people. The very ancient story of Adam and Eve states that "a man leaves his father and cleaves to his wife and the two become one flesh" (Genesis 2:24). Frequently, biblical Hebrew uses the verb "to know" to mean sexual intercourse (as in "Adam knew Eve and she conceived a child"). It also uses the word "knowledge" with this suggestion of deep intimacy, to describe the relationship between God and his people.[1] The use of sexual imagery in describing both marital and divine-human relationships testifies to the positive view of the Old Testament toward sex.

Second, in the Old Testament, sexuality could never be separated from its *social consequences.* Historically, Israel began as a small group of nomadic tribes fighting to stay alive in the near-desert of the Arabian peninsula. Sheer survival demanded that there be enough children, especially males, so that there would be enough herdsmen and warriors.[2] Thus, nonprocreative sex could not be allowed. Further, since the tribes were small and close-knit, sex had to be regulated to prevent jealousy over sexual partners, which could have divided and destroyed the group. It is not surprising, then, that so much of the Old Testament is concerned with laws regarding people living together in society and that these laws often include the regulation of sexual practices.

Finally, the Old Testament sees sexual behavior as an aspect of *national and religious loyalty.*Individual sexual morality significantly affected the moral and religios health of the whole people. This health was threatened when the Israelites settled in what is now the state of Israel, about 1200 to 1000 B.C. Here, they came into contact with the Canaanites, the original inhabitants, and with their culture and religion. The Canaanites were farmers whose chief concern was the fertility of the land. Like the religions of many other ancient Near Eastern peoples, theirs was based on fertility and was acted out in sexual terms. They believed that Baal, the Sky Father, must mate with Asherah (Astarte or Ishtar), the Earth Mother, in order for the crops to grow. They sought to encourage this mating by ritual performance of the sexual act; thus temple prostitutes were very much a part of the Canaanite religion.

Pure Judaism was always under the threat of either apostasy (abandonment for the attractions of the fertility cult) or syncretism (the introduction of elements from other religions). Because of this threat, sexual misconduct was seen not only as an ethical lapse but also as a betrayal of one's nation and religion. Many sexual practices are forbidden by the Old Testament because they were found in Canaanite religion, which meant that they might lead to infidelity to the God of Israel.

Fertility cult:
A form of nature-religion in which the fertility of the soil is sought through various forms of ritual magic, often including ritual sexual intercourse.

It is my contention that the sexual regulations of the Old Testament need to be

[1]See, for example, Hosea, The Song of Solomon, and, in the New Testament, Revelation.

[2]Note that the heart of God's promise to the patriarch Abraham was descendant as numberless as the sand or the stars in the sky (Genesis 13:14–17, among many other places).

seen against this historical background. From the struggle for survival of Israel during the nomadic period, we see laws against illegitimacy and nonprocreative sex, as well as institutions such as polygamy (many wives) and concubinage (slaves kept for childbearing purposes) designed to produce many children. From the confrontation with the fertility cult, Israel derived prohibitions against sexual laxity, nakedness, cultic prostitution, and other such typically Canaanite practices. Both themes are present in this passage from Leviticus 20:10–19:

> If a man commits adultery with his neighbor's wife, both adulterer and adulteress shall be put to death. The man who has intercourse with his father's wife has brought shame on his father. They shall both be put to death; their blood shall be on their own heads . . . A man who has intercourse with any beast shall be put to death, and you shall kill the beast. . . . If a man takes his sister, his father's daughter or his mother's daughter, and they see one another naked, it is a scandalous disgrace. They shall be cut off in the presence of their people. . . . If a man lies with a woman during her monthly period and brings shame upon her, he has exposed her discharge and she has uncovered the source of her discharge; they shall both be cut off from their people.

Adultery and incest are threats to the peaceful life of the group. Not only is bestiality "unnatural," but it is also nonprocreative and may have been a feature of Canaanite religion. The menstrual taboo is typical of many societies (see Chapter 4).

FIGURE 22.1

According to Jewish law, menstruation makes a woman unclean. The period of uncleanness must be ended by a ritual bath, or mikvah, as shown in this medieval woodcut.

It should be noted that all societies have had laws regulating sex (Chapter 1) and that these laws, however exotic they may seem to us, made sense in their historical context and were, for the most part, remarkably humane for the time. The Old Testament is also marked by a great regard for married love, affection, and sexuality; this is in marked contrast to, for example, the Greek view of marriage as an institution for breeding and housekeeping. Old Testament Judaism is highly legalistic but not particularly ascetic in its high regard for responsible sexuality as a good and integral part of human life.

The New Testament and Christianity

As the discussion turns to Christianity, which grew in three centuries from an obscure Jewish sect to the dominant religion in the West, the complex conditions of the Mediterranean world between 100 B.C. and 100 A.D. must be noted. The world in which Christianity developed was one of tremendous ferment in the spheres of philosophy, religion, and morals. Although Stoicism remained popular among intellectuals, ordinary folks preferred various blends of mythology, superstition, and religion. Few people were much concerned with the pursuit of wisdom and virtue. There were many strange cults, often characterized by some sort of dualism. This was the notion that body and spirit were unalterably separate and opposed to each other and that the goal of life was to become purely spiritual by transcending the physical and material side of life. Public morals were notably decadent, and even ethical pagans were shocked by a society in which people prized pleasure above all things, at least those who could afford it (Brinton, 1959).

Dualism: A religious or philosophical belief that matter and spirit are opposed to each other and that the goal of life is to free spirit from the bondage of matter, thus a depreciation of the material world and the physical aspect of humanity.

Revulsion at the excesses of Roman life affected even Judaism, which became markedly more dualistic and antisex by the time of Jesus' birth and the growth of

FIGURE 22.2

The Virgin Mary. During the Middle Ages, a great devotion to the mother of Jesus developed, emphasizing her perpetual virginity, purity, and freedom from all sin.

his Church. That Church's ethical tradition is rooted in Old Testament Judaism and was given its direction by the teachings of Jesus, the writings of St. Paul, and the theology of the Fathers of early Christianity. From these beginnings, Christian ethics has evolved and developed over 2000 years in many and various ways. This makes oversimplification a real danger, and yet it is possible to speak in general terms of a Christian tradition of sexual ethics and morality.

Jesus

It would be very difficult to elaborate a sexual ethic from the teachings of Jesus, since he said almost nothing on the subject. Jesus urged his followers to strive for ethical perfection, and he spoke strongly against pride, hypocrisy, and self-righteousness. Toward humble and penitent sinners, including those whose sins were sexual, the Gospels show him to have been compassionate and understanding (see, for example, his dealings with "fallen women" in John 4:1–30, John 8:53–9:11, and Luke 7:36–50). His ethical teaching is strongly based in the tradition of the Old Testament prophets and includes sexual conduct as a part of a whole moral life of loving God and neighbor.

St. Paul

The task of applying the principles of Jesus in concrete situations fell to St. Paul, the first Christian theologian, whose letters form the earliest part of the New Testament. A complex personality, Paul was very much a child of his time and quite ambivalent in his attitude toward sexuality. Above all, he, along with the whole early Church, expected the *parousia* (Second Coming) of Christ and the end of the world to occur at any time. He therefore advocated celibacy, not necessarily because he was opposed to sex but because in a world that was about to end, the demands of marriage might prove a distraction from prayer, worship, and the proclamation of the Gospel. Like Jesus, Paul opposed all sexual expression outside marriage, and he had a number of harsh things to say about sexual immorality. However, he saw these in the larger context of humanity's total revolt against the will of God. He wrote a good deal, for example, about the "sins of the flesh," but by this he meant all aspects of fallen humanity, such as "immorality, impurity, sorcery, enmity, strife, jealousy, anger, selfishness, paltry spirit, envy, drunkenness, carousing, and the like" (Galatians 5:19–21). Later Christian theologians tended to understand the "sins of the flesh" primarily in sexual terms; thus, from Paul's writings, Christianity acquired a bias against sexuality which goes well beyond what Paul probably intended. Indeed, the New Testament, like the Old Testament, is ambivalent about sexuality.

The Early Christian Church

The "Fathers of the Church," who wrote roughly between 150 and 600 A.D., completed the basic theological shape of the Christian faith. During this time, Christian ethics became increasingly ascetic, partly as a result of its natural tendencies, partly as it assimilated dualistic tendencies from Greek philosophy, partly as a response to the decadence of Roman society, and partly because of the conversion of the Roman Emperor Constantine in 325. This last event ended nearly three centuries of persecution and moved most of the Mediterranean world into the Christian Church by 400. Suddenly part of the "establishment," the Church began to grow corrupt and worldly, and for the first time, the lip-service believer entered the picture.

Serious Christians revolted against this situation by moving to the desert to become monks and hermits, to fast, to pray, and to practice all sorts of self-denial,

Celibate (SEL-ih-bit): A person who remains unmarried, usually for religious reasons. (Celibacy: the practice of remaining celibate.) Sometimes used to refer to abstaining from sexual intercourse, the correct term for which is "chastity."

including, of course, celibacy. From this point on, monasticism and the religious orders became a permanent reform movement within the Church, a vanguard of ascetics calling Christians to greater rigor. Their success can be seen in the twelfth-century requirement that all clergy in the West be celibate, a departure from early church practice.[3] The Fathers of the Church, almost all of whom were celibates, allowed that marriage was good and honorable but thought virginity to be a much superior state. The message could not have been lost on the laity: sexuality, even in marriage, was incompatible with true holiness.

St. Augustine

The most notable of the Western Fathers was St. Augustine (354–430 A.D.), who had had a promiscuous youth and overreacted after his conversion to Christianity.[4] For Augustine, sexuality was a consequence of the Fall, and every sexual act was tainted by concupiscence (from the Latin word *concupisencia,* meaning "lust" or "evil desire of the flesh"). Even sex in marriage was sinful, and in *The City of God* he wrote that "children could not have been begotten in any other way than they know them to be begotten now, i.e. by lust, at which even honorable marriage blushes" (1950 ed., Article 21). The stature of Augustine meant that this negative view of sexuality was perpetuated in subsequent Catholic theology.

St. Thomas Aquinas

During the Middle Ages, these basic principles continued to be elaborated and extended. The most important figure of the period, and even today the basic source of Catholic moral theology, was St. Thomas Aquinas (1225–1274). His great achievement was to synthesize Christian theology with Aristotelian philosophy in such a way as to answer virtually any question a Christian might ask on any topic. Thomas combined reason with divine revelation to arrive at the moral law of the universe, which, as God's intention for creation, is to be obeyed as His will. For example, Thomas believed that sex was obviously intended for procreation and that nonprocreative sex therefore violated the natural law and was sinful, being opposed to both human nature and the will of God.

In the *Summa Theologica,* Thomas devoted a chapter to various sorts of lust and their gravity, treating premarital intercourse (fornication), nocturnal emissions, seduction, rape, adultery, incest, and "unnatural vice," which included masturbation, bestiality, and homosexuality. He asked, "Is simple fornication a grave sin?"

> Beyond all doubt we should hold that simple fornication is a moral sin. . . . To explain, a sin which directly attacks a requirement for human life is deadly. Now simple fornication is an inordinate act of a sort to injure life that may be formed from the intercourse. . . . Now it is evident that the bringing up of a human child requires the care of the mother who nurses him and much more the care of a father, under whose guidance and guardianship his earthly needs are supplied and his character developed. . . . Accordingly, since fornication or intercourse between people who are not committed to one another is outside marriage, which is for the good of the children, it is a mortal sin. (1968 ed., Second Part of the Second Part, Question 154, Article 2)

---

[3]The First Epistle of Timothy, Chap. 3, shows the clear expectation that clergy will be married and fathers.

[4]Byron once remarked that Augustine's youthful escapades, as reported in the *Confessions,* "make the reader envy his transgressions."

Thomas's theological supremacy ensured the triumph of natural law in Western Catholic ethics and has great consequences even today.

The theology of Aquinas was communicated to the ordinary Christian through the Church's canon law which determined when intercourse was or was not sinful. All sex outside marriage was, by definition, a sin. Even within marriage the Church forbade intercourse during certain times in a woman's physiological cycle (during menstruation, pregnancy, and up to 40 days postpartum) as well as on certain holy days, fast days (such as Fridays) and even during whole liturgical seasons (such as Advent and Lent). These rules were "enforced" through the *Penitentials,* guidebooks for priests hearing confessions, which instructed them on how to judge certain sins and what penances to assign for them (Brundage, 1984). All of this communicated to the ordinary person that the Church regarded sex as basically evil, for procreation only, and probably not something one should enjoy!

The Protestants

The Protestant Reformation in the sixteenth century destroyed the Christian unity of Europe and shook the theological foundations of the Catholic Church. However, in matters of sexual ethics there were only rather modest changes. The Protestant churches abandoned clerical celibacy, regarding it as unnatural and the source of many abuses, and placed a higher value on marriage and family life. However, Reformers feared illegitimacy and saw sexuality only in the confines of matrimony. Even then, they were often ambivalent. For example, Martin Luther, who was the founder of the Reformation and was happily married to a former nun, called marriage "a hospital for the sick" and saw its purpose as being to "aid human infirmity and prevent unchastity" (quoted in Thielicke, 1964, p. 136)—scarcely an enthusiastic approach.

A significant contribution of Reformation Protestantism to Christianity was a renewed emphasis on the individual conscience in matters such as the interpretation of the Bible and in ethical decision making. Such an emphasis on freedom and individual responsibility has led to the serious questioning of legalistic ethics and, in part, to today's ethical ferment.

The Reformation also gave rise to Puritanism, an English movement inspired by the French Reformer John Calvin (1509–1564). Calvin and the Puritans followed Augustine in emphasizing the doctrine of "original sin" and the "total depravity" of fallen humanity. This led them to use civil law to regulate human behavior in an attempt to suppress frivolity and immorality. As will be seen in the next chapter, this urge to make people good by law has many sexual applications, although the Puritans were probably no more sexually repressive than other Christians of the time. What we often think of as "Puritan" sexual rigidity is probably more properly referred to as "Victorian." During the reign of Queen Victoria (1819–1901), English society held sexual expression in exaggerated disgust and probably exaggerated its importance. While strict public standards of decency and purity were enforced, many Victorians indulged in the private vices of pornography, prostitution, and the rest. It is against this typically Victorian combination of repressiveness and hypocrisy that many of the twentieth century have revolted, wrongly thinking the Victorian period to be representative of the whole Christian ethical tradition.

It should be noted that across Western history there has been a great deal of consensus in sexual ethics. Sex has been seen as part of God's creation, but a source of temptation which needs to be controlled. Although at various times chastity has been exalted, marriage and the family have always been held in esteem, and sex outside marriage has been condemned in theory, if not in practice. Finally, it is only within this century that sex has been seen as having any "official" purpose beyond procreation.

Current Trends

Today, however, even within the Christian Church the old consensus is breaking down, and sexual ethics is a subject for renewed discussion and argument. The Reformation emphasis on individual conscience calls natural law into question, even within Roman Catholicism. Among Jews, while the Orthodox still live by the rabbinic interpretation of Old Testament law, Conservative and Reform Judaism are in the same flux. Several factors have contributed to this ferment, both within the religious community and outside it.

Modern biblical scholars hold that many of the prohibitions against various sexual practices in the Bible must be seen in historical and cultural context and may not be applicable today. Modern post-Freudian psychology suggests that sexuality is not simply a matter of will and that sexual "misconduct" may not be sin so much as neurosis. Behavioral scientists are likely to stress the importance of sexuality to all human life and to question whether it is a lesser or evil aspect of personality. Technology has made it possible, for the first time in human history, to prevent conception reliably and to terminate pregnancy safely. Theologians and ethicists are still wrestling with this problem, which, for example, blunts the force of natural-law arguments against premarital intercourse, since illegitimate children need not be the result.

However, the Old Morality is not dead, and the New Morality is still in the process of formulation. The controversy can be quite heated, as will be seen in the discussions of specific topics, and a new consensus has not yet been achieved.

Humanism

It would be misleading to suggest that within Western culture, at least since the Renaissance, all ethical thinking has been religious in origin. Many ethicists have quite consciously tried to find a framework for moral behavior that does not rely on divine revelation or any direction from a source outside or beyond human intellect and personality. Nonreligious ethics covers the whole spectrum; however, we can look at a fairly broad mainstream called humanism.

Humanism:
A religious or philosophical system which denies a divine origin for morality and holds that ethical judgments must be made on the basis of human experience and human reason.

Humanistic ethics accepts no supernatural source for direction and insists that values can be found only in human experience in this world, as observed by the philosopher or social scientist. Most humanists would hold that the basic goals of human life are happiness, self-awareness, the avoidance of pain and suffering, and the fulfillment of human needs. Of course, the individual pursuit of these ends must be tempered by the fact that no one lives in the world alone and that some limitation of individual happiness may be required by the common good. Another important humanistic principle is that the individual must make his or her own decisions and accept responsibility for them and their consequences, without appeal to some higher authority, such as God.

In the area of human sexuality, humanism demands a realistic approach to human behavior that does not create arbitrary or unreasonable standards and expectations; it is very distrustful of the legalistic approach. It seeks real intimacy between persons and condemns impersonal and exploitative relationships, though probably not with the vigor that marks religious ethics. It tends to be tolerant, compassionate, and skeptical of claims of absolute value.

Sexuality in Other Religions

While the discussion so far has been mostly concerned with Western culture and the Judeo-Christian tradition, this tradition and this culture certainly do not contain the only possible approaches to sexual ethics. Therefore, it may broaden our outlook if we briefly consider human sexuality in religious traditions outside our own experience. Obviously, this could be the topic for a very large book itself, and the reader will have to be content with a rather brief look at the three non-Western religions with the largest number of adherents: Islam, Hinduism, and Buddhism.

Islam

Geographically, and in terms of its roots, Islam is the closest faith to the Judeo-Christian heritage. It was founded by the Prophet Muhammad, who lived from 570 to 632, in what is now Saudi Arabia. Its followers are called *Moslems (or Muslims),* and its sacred scripture is the Koran. Islam shares some of its basic precepts with a neighboring faith, Judaism, but it has a flavor all its own. Classical Islam values sexuality very positively, and Muhammad saw intercourse, especially in marriage, as the highest good of human life. Islam sanctions both polygamy and concubinage, and the Prophet had several wives. In legend, great sexual prowess is attributed to him, although it may be exaggerated. He opposed celibacy, and Islam has very little ascetic tradition. A male-dominated faith, Islam has a strong double standard but recognizes a number of rights and prerogatives for women as well. Although sex outside either marriage or concubinage is viewed as a sin, Islam can be ethically quite moderate and rather tolerant of sexual sin, including homosexuality. All these aspects combine to create a "sex-positive" religion (Bullough, 1976, p. 205). However, there is a kind of Islamic "puritanism" visble among militant Moslem reformers, such as Iran's Ayatollah Khomeni, which can be quite antisex and antifemale.

FIGURE 22.3

A resurgence of Islamic fundamentalism has attacked the liberalization of sexual practices and gender roles. The regime of the Ayatollah Khomeni is in the vanguard of this movement. In Iran, there has been great repression of women, symbolized by the requirement that they resume the wearing of veils in public.

Hinduism

"Hinduism" is a rather inclusive term which refers to a highly varied complex of mythology and religious practice founded on the Indian subcontinent. Here can be found virtually every approach to sexuality the human species has yet invented. However, certain themes are worth mentioning. In Hinduism, four possible approaches to life are acceptable: Kama, the pursuit of pleasure; Artha, the pursuit of power and material wealth; Dharma, the pursuit of the moral life; and Moksha, the pursuit of liberation through the negation of the self in Nirvana. Kama is notable because it has produced an extensive literature on the achievement of sexual pleasure, notably the *Kama Sutra* of Vatsyayana, a masterpiece of erotic hedonism. This testifies to the highly positive view of sexuality to be found in Hinduism.

However, in contrast, the ways of Dharma and Moksha can be as rigorously ascetic as anything in Christianity. By avoiding all passions, including sex, the follower of these ways of renunciation seeks to pass out of the cycle of continual rebirth to absorption into the godhead. Part of this is *brahmacarya,* or celibacy, which is to be cultivated at the beginning of life (for the purposes of education and discipline) and at the end of life (for the purpose of finding peace). It is interesting to note that in between it is permissible to marry and raise a family, and thus this form of Hinduism makes active sexuality and asceticism possible in the same lifetime (Noss, 1963).

FIGURE 22.4

A yoga master's view of sex: "Sexual life is not unnatural nor condemned by God. Those who are interested in it should get into matrimonial life and experience it in moderation. Overindulgence in anything will be detrimental to both physical and mental health. Others whose interest is in serving God and his creation full-time should stay away from matrimony to avoid personal obligations and to conserve and redirect their sexual, physical and mental energies toward their service." In this statement, Sri Swami Satchidananda summarizes much Hindu teaching on sexuality.

Buddhism

Buddhism was a development of Hinduism; it originated in the life and thought of Guatama (560–480 B.C.) and has been elaborated in many forms since then. There is little discussion of sex in the teachings of the Buddha; his way is generally ascetic and concentrates on the achievement of enlightenment and on escape from the suffering of the world. Two main traditions, Therevada and Mahayana, are found in contemporary Buddhism, and they differ greatly. The ethics of Therevada includes the strict nonindulgence of the desires which bring joy; understanding, morals, and discipline are emphasized. The ethics of Mahayana is more active and directed toward love of others. Both encourage men to live celibate lives as monks. Originally, Buddha sought a "middle way" between extreme asceticism and extreme hedonism, but today the situation is rather like that of medieval Christianity: the masses live ordinary and usually married lives, and the monks cultivate ascetic wisdom.

Tantric Buddhism, found particularly in Tibet, is a form of Buddhism which is of particular interest. There is a devotion to natural energy *(shakti),* and followers are taught that passion can be exhausted by passion. For example, sexual desire can be overcome while satisfying it according to occult knowledge. Sexuality can therefore be used as a means of transcending the limitations of human life. This sexual mysticism is by no means common, but it is one of the various forms which Eastern religion may take (Parrinder, 1980).

CONTEMPORARY ISSUES IN SEXUAL ETHICS

It cannot be said too frequently that human sexuality is a heavily value-laden subject and, therefore, is likely to be the subject of strongly and emotionally held convictions. It is also likely to be the focal point of conflicts in society, if there is no broad consensus as to the norms of sexual behavior. This is clearly the case in contemporary American society. Rapid change in all aspects of life has been the rule for the last several decades, and this change includes the "sexual revolution." This change is perceived by many people as a threat to all they hold dear, and not surprisingly, they respond with fear and anger. The backlash against the more liberal view of sexuality and the greater freedom of sexual behavior which has come about in the last 20 years has resulted in explosive public debate, organized attempts at legislating the Old Morality back into force, and a reassertion of a highly legalistic view of the Judeo-Christian ethic. The debate promises to continue for some time and to generate much heat.

Moralism: A religious or philosophical attitude which emphasizes moral behavior, usually according to strict standards, as the highest goal of human life. Moralists tend to favor strict regulation of human conduct to help make people good.

Pluralism: A philosophical or political attitude which affirms the value of many competing opinions and believes that the truth is discovered in the clash of diverse perspectives. Pluralists, therefore, believe in the maximum human freedom possible.

This debate over the limits, if any, of individual sexual freedom can be seen as the clash between the New Morality and the Old, but let us propose a more helpful model. The Old Morality is, to a great extent, supported by people who believe that there are clearly and objectively defined standards of right and wrong and that a society has a right to insist that all its members conform, at least outwardly, to them. We might call this view moralism, and it has many proponents in the religious community who see the objective standard of morality as deriving from divine Law. Opposed to this view are the proponents of pluralism; they see the question of public morality as being much more complex. Pluralists deny that there are objective standards which everyone can know, and they are likely to contend that truth is to be discovered in the clash of differing opinions and convictions. A society is, therefore, according to this view, wise to allow many points of view to be advocated and expressed. The conscience and rights of the individual are to be stressed over the needs of society for order and uniformity. Pluralists are much less likely than moralists to appeal to either law or religion for the enforcement of their views, and they are more likely to allow freedom to individuals even if society might be endangered by their actions. The debate between moralist and pluralist has been going on for a very long time, both in the religious community itself and throughout American history. It will probably not be settled any time soon.

An illustration of the above can be found in the emergence of a "profamily" position which is rooted in religious conservatism and is increasingly attempting to influence the legislative process. Profamily activists are against the Equal Rights Amendment and other bars to sex discrimination, in favor of an absolute constitutional ban on abortion, against any kind of legal tolerance of the cohabitation of unmarried persons, and in favor of legal discrimination against homosexuals in such things as housing, child custody, and employment.

This position is essentially that of the New Religious Right, a coalition of conservative religious and political groups. Members of this movement, largely but not exclusively fundamentalist Protestants, argue that the New Morality has sapped the moral vigor of American society, leaving the country open to inner decay, Communist infiltration, and divine judgment. Their efforts to enforce their religious convictions by legislation have created one of the most intense church-state controversies of the twentieth century (see Chapter 23). Their position is clearly odious to pluralists and to those who have benefited by the liberalization of laws and attitudes concerning sexuality. These persons and groups will fight to keep what they consider to be gains, while profamily and New Right activists will seek to turn the clock back to what they perceive to have been a healthier and more moral time.

This conflict can be found within most American religious communities today. Even liberal "mainline" Protestant groups, which have tended to accommodate at least some of the New Morality, have been under attack from portions of their own membership on such issues as abortion, premarital sex, and homosexuality. Within the Roman Catholic Church, a less rigorous stance on sexuality has been met with firm opposition from Pope John Paul II, who has vigorously reasserted the traditional condemnation of all sexual activity outside marriage. In *Educational Guidance in Human Love,* a 1983 pamphlet issued by the Vatican for parents and teachers, procreation is seen as the essential purpose of conjugal love; masturbation, extramarital sexual relations, and homosexuality are all described as "grave moral disorders" (*The Christian Century,* 1983, **100**, p. 1177). Reports in the church press of national gatherings of American religious groups reveal a remarkable number of debates related to human sexuality. These debates parallel those in the society at large, and can be illustrated by examining six significant ethical issues.

Premarital Intercourse

About once a quarter, I find myself addressing an undergraduate class in human sexuality on sexual ethics, and invariably the liveliest discussion concerns premarital sexual behavior. The general direction of comments from the class is usually along the lines of "What is so wrong with it after all, if nobody gets hurt?" The implicit assumption, supported by statistics, is that "everybody (or almost everybody) is doing it," and this has led contemporary ethicists to do a good deal of rethinking. This is a typical process in ethics; pastoral considerations—that is, dealing with people as they are—often lead to developments in theology.

The traditional position of the Christian Church is, of course, that sex before marriage is wrong. This is the position of conservative Protestantism and also of Roman

Catholicism. In January 1976, the Congregation for the Doctrine of the Faith, with the support of Pope Paul VI, issued a "Declaration on Certain Questions Concerning Sexual Ethics." It stated:

> Today there are many who vindicate the right to sexual union before marriage, at least in those cases where a firm intention to marry and an affection which is already in some way conjugal in the psychology of the subjects require this completion which they judge to be connatural. . . . This option is contrary to Christian doctrine which states that every genital act must be within the framework of marriage (Sacred Congregation for the Doctrine of the Faith, 1976, p. 11)

This statement reiterates the basic papal encyclical on the subject, Pope Pius XI's *Casti Connubi* of 1930, which forbade premarital intercourse, adultery, birth control, sterilization, abortion, and divorce—in short, all sexual activity outside marriage or not for the purpose of procreation (Pope Pius XI, 1930).

On the other hand, proponents of situation ethics would allow for sexual expression in precisely the situation mentioned in the Vatican "Declaration," that is, where there is commitment and affection. Many ethicists would say that it is the quality of the relationship, not its legal status, that determines whether intercourse is appropriate. Further, there is a concern for helping people form good relationships, and this may allow a certain amount of "experimentation" to be, if not endorsed, at least not vigorously condemned.

Related to this is a concern for personhood, a concern which is broader than simply sexual. Liberal ethicists often argue that the gravest sin consists not in the violation of certain rules but in the violation of persons, that is, the exploitation of other human beings for one's own gratification. Premarital sex may thus be all right if it does not involve the exploitation of one individual by another. Such exploitation can occur within marriage, as well as outside it, as, for example, when a man uses his wife simply for his own pleasure or when a woman "withholds her favors" until her husband promises to give her something she wants. Again, it is the quality of the relationship, and not the legality, which matters most.

In summary, the conservative or legalistic answer to the question of whether premarital intercourse is permissible is a resounding "no." The more liberal answer may be said to be "maybe" or "yes, but." Few ethical thinkers today take the position that either promiscuity or impersonal sex is a good thing, and most would pose fairly hard questions about commitment and intent to an unmarried couple contemplating a sexual relationship.

Extramarital Sex

Adultery:
Voluntary sexual intercourse by a husband or wife to someone not one's spouse, thus, betrayal of one's marriage vows.

The Judeo-Christian traditon has always taken a very dim view of extramarital sex (or adultery, to use the biblical term). In the Old Testament, the penalty for adultery was being stoned to death; in the New Testament, we find that it is the only grounds for divorce which Jesus allows (Matthew 6:21–22). In subsequent Christian theology, adultery is seen in the context of unfaithfulness to God, since marriage is seen as a sacramental—that is, symbolic—sign of God's relationship to his people. Therefore, adultery is regarded as one of the gravest sins possible.

This view has changed little even in today's ethical ferment. Contemporary ethicists regard extramarital sex as the breaking of a trust and the violation of a relationship which must be based on commitment. However, many ethicists would avoid absolute condemnation, in favor of a more understanding approach when extramarital relationships occur. For them, the problem is to help a couple establish a more satisfying relationship, sexually and otherwise, that will eliminate the need for sex outside marriage. Such an approach also recognizes that it often takes two to create such a situation and that an extramarital relationship may be a symptom of problems shared by both persons. Such an approach seeks reconciliation based on forgiveness and love, rather than punishment based on law, and takes seriously the individuality of the persons involved and their circumstances.

Contraception

The situation today with respect to birth control is clearer than the situation with respect to some of the other topics dealt with here. Roman Catholics and Orthodox Jews oppose any "artificial" means of contraception; other Jews and most Protestants favor responsible family planning by married couples. Moreover, most ethicists would suggest that unmarried persons who are sexually active ought to be using some means to prevent pregnancy.

Those who oppose birth control for religious reasons see it as being contrary to the will of God, against the natural law, or both. Orthodox Judaism cites the biblical injunction to "be fruitful and multiply" (Genesis 1:26) as God's command to his people, not to be disobeyed in any way. Further, some members of other Jewish communities warn that limiting family size threatens the future existence of the Jewish people, and they call for a return to the traditionally large Jewish family.

The Roman Catholic position is best articulated in Pope Paul VI's 1968 encyclical, *Humanae Vitae:*

> Marriage and conjugal love are by their nature ordained toward the begetting and educating of children. . . . In the task of transmitting life, therefore, they are not free to proceed completely at will, as if they could determine in a wholly autonomous way the honest path to follow, but they must conform their activity to the creative intention of God, expressed in the very nature of marriage and by its acts, and manifested by the constant teaching of the Church. (Pope Paul VI, 1968, p. 20)

The encyclical continued the Church's approval of abstinence or "rhythm" as legitimate methods of family planning. *Humanae Vitae* was not enthusiastically accepted by all Catholics, and as noted in Chapter 6, there is evidence to suggest that many Catholic couples, often with the encouragement or tacit approval of their priest, ignore the encyclical and use contraceptives anyway. Nonetheless, the teachings of *Humanae Vitae* has been repeatedly and resoundingly reiterated by Pope John Paul II all over the world.

Those in the religious community who favor the use of contraceptives do so for a variety of reasons. Many express a concern that all children who are born should be "wanted," and they see family planning as a means to this end. Others, emphasizing the dangers that the population explosion poses to the quality and future of human life, the need for a more equitable distribution of natural resources, and the needs of the emerging nations, call for family planning as a matter of justice. Another point of view regards the use of contraceptives as part of the responsible use of freedom required of the believer. In this view, any couple who are unwilling or unready to assume the responsibility of children have an actual duty to use contraceptives. For these groups, the decision to use contraceptives is a highly individual one, and the government must allow each individual the free exercise of his or her conscience.

Abortion

Related to the issue of contraception is the thorny question of abortion, the center of one of the most vigorous ethical debates of our time. Indeed, just how related abortion and contraception are is an issue itself. For the Roman Catholic Church, abortion and contraception are, in intent, the same thing, and for Joseph Fletcher and other liberals, abortion is also seen as a variety of contraception—less desirable, perhaps, but better than unwanted pregnancy. For many other ethicists, abortion and contraception are clearly distinguished, and while advocating contraception, they may question the morality of abortion.

A distinction is often made between therapeutic abortion and abortion on demand. Therapeutic abortion is a termination of pregnancy when the life or mental health of the woman is threatened or in cases of trauma such as rape and incest. Many ethicists are willing to endorse therapeutic abortion as the lesser of two evils but do not sanction abortion on demand, that is, abortion whenever requested by a woman for whatever reason (see, for example, Thielicke, 1964, pp. 226–244).

The leadership of the antiabortion movement clearly comes from the Roman Catholic Church, which sees it as one of the most crucial ethical issues confronting modern society. Catholic theology regards human life as beginning at the moment of conception; therefore, the termination of any pregnancy is murder. Interestingly, for most of its history, the Roman Catholic Church accepted Aristotle's teaching that "ensoulment," that is. the entry into the fetus of its distinctively human soul, took place at 40 days after conception for a male and at 80 or 90 days after conception for a female. Theoretically. this permitted abortions at least until the fortieth day. In 1869, Pope Pius IX eliminated the concept of ensoulment, holding that human life begins at conception and that all abortion is therefore murder (Fulton, 1974). From this, the Catholic political position, as seen in the right-to-life movement, is clear; if you regard abortion as murder, you cannot in good conscience permit your government to allow it. The 1984 presidential campaign was marked by strongly worded statements by a number of bishops who made abortion the primary issue, and by an attack on Democratic Vice-Presidential candidate Geraldine Ferraro, a devout Catholic, for taking a legislative prochoice position.

The Roman Catholic position is shared by Orthodox Jews, the Eastern Orthodox, and conservative Protestants, although some of the latter will allow therapeutic abortions in some cases. Antiabortionists also fear that legal abortion might lead to a general decline in respect for human life and open the door to euthanasia (mercy killing), genocide (the killing of "undesirable" groups), and other threats to life and civilization. An end to legalized abortion is increasingly at the top of the sociopolitical agenda of various theologically conservative groups, not just Roman Catholics.

For those who favor at least some form of abortion under certain circumstances, and this includes most liberal Protestants and Conservative and Reformed Jews, the problem is one of balancing several goods against one another. Human life is good and ought to be preserved, but the *quality* of life is also important. An unborn child may have a right to life, but does it not also have a right to be wanted and cared for? Might not the danger to the well-being of a woman already alive take precedence over the well-being of an unborn fetus? Does not a woman have the right to determine what happens to her own body? Since until quite recently all ethicists were male, ought women to follow rules made by men, who can never be in their situation? Indeed, for many feminists this consideration makes abortion on demand an absolute value.

The pluralist response to abortion is the "prochoice" position, which holds that

F · O · C · U · S
22.2

PROLIFE VERSUS PROCHOICE

The following statements suggest some of the arguments and rhetoric of the two positions in the abortion debate. In reading them it is useful to keep in mind the Gallup poll which has recorded a remarkable constancy of attitude toward abortion over time, and an equally remarkable lack of consensus.

PROLIFE STATEMENTS

Destruction of the embryo in the mother's womb is a violation of the right to live which God has bestowed upon this nascent life. To raise the question whether we are here concerned already with a human being or not is merely to confuse the issue. The simple fact is that God certainly intended to create a human being and that this nascent human being has been deliberately deprived of his life. (Dietrich Bonhoeffer, a Lutheran theologian, in *Ethics,* 1955)

Our opposition to abortion derives from the conviction that whatever is opposed to life is a violation of man's inherent rights, a position that has a strong basis in the history of American law. The U.S. Bill of Rights guarantees the right to life to every American, and the U.N. Declaration of the Rights of the Child, which our nation endorses, affirms that the child, because of his dependent status, should be accorded a special protection under the law before as well as after birth. (National Conference of Catholic Bishops, 1970)

All human beings ought to value every person for his or her uniqueness as a creature of God, called to be a brother or sister of Christ by reason of the incarnation and universal redemption. For us, the sacredness of human life is based on these premises. And it is on the same premises that there is based our celebration of human life—all human life. This explains our efforts to defend human life against every influence or action that threatens or weakens it, as well as our endeavors to make every life more human in all its aspects. (Pope John Paul II, 1979)

PROCHOICE STATEMENTS

. . . laws prohibiting abortion are neither just nor enforceable. They compel women to bear unwanted children or to seek illegal abortions regardlessof the medical hazards and suffering involved. By severely limiting access to safe abortions, these laws have the effect of discriminating against the poor. (United Church of Christ, General Synod, 1971.

TABLE 22.1

THE GALLUP POLL HAS REPEATEDLY SURVEYED AMERICANS ON THEIR ATTITUDES TOWARD ABORTION.

(Notice That There Has Been Little Change Since 1975.)

	1975	1977	1980	1983
Abortion should be:				
Legal under any circumstances	21%	22%	25%	23%
Legal under only certain circumstances	54	55	53	58
Illegal under all circumstances	22	19	18	16
No opinion	3	4	4	3

FIGURE 22.5

The abortion controversy. Profile and prochoice advocates are both adamant about their positions.

The willful termination of pregnancy by medical means on the considered decision of a pregnant woman may on occasion be morally justifiable. Possible justifying circumstances would include medical indications of physical or mental deformity, conception as a result of rape or incest, conditions under which the physical or mental health of either mother or child would be gravely threatened, or the socioeconomic condition of the family. The procedure should be performed only by licensed physicians under optimal conditions, and with appropriate medical consultation and ministerial counseling, preferably with her own minister. (Presbyterian Church in the United States, General Assembly, 1970)

We believe that all should be free to express and practice their own moral judgment on the matter of abortion. We also believe that on this matter, where there is not ethical or theological consensus, and where widely differing views are held by substantial sections of the religious community, the Constitution should not be used to enforce one particular religious belief on those who believe otherwise. (United Methodist Church, Women's Division of the Board of Global Ministries, 1975)

Our belief in the sanctity of unborn human life makes us reluctant to approve abortion. But we are equally bound to respect the sacredness of life and well being of the mother, for whom devastating damage may result from an unacceptable pregnancy. In continuity with past Christian teaching, we recognize tragic conflicts of life with life that may justify abortion. (United Methodist Church, General Conference, 1976)

Sources: The Right to Life Society and the Religious Coalition for Aborton Rights.

since no practical consensus has been reached in society, the government ought to keep out and let the individual woman make up her own mind. Actually, the prochoice coalition includes several different points of view, from a strong proabortion stance to the position of those who have serious ethical qualms about abortion but oppose the legislation of any particular moral view on the subject. The "prolife" position is much more absolute and apparently simple, while the "prochoice" approach is subtle and differentiated. Both positions agree on the sacredness of human life, but are sharply divided on when life begins, how various conflicting interests are to be balanced, and how human life is best preserved and enhanced. The clash between the two is likely to become even more severe as the political climate becomes more conservative. It is a clash about life, law, freedom, and values, and few people are neutral on these great issues (see the Focus).

Homosexuality

Mirroring society as a whole, the religious community is engaged in a vigorous debate on the issue of homosexuality. Despite the overwhelming condemnation of any and all homosexual acts in the Judeo-Christian tradition, many ethicists are reexamining their attitudes on the subject. This change has occurred in part because modern biblical scholarship suggests that scriptural prohibitions of homosexuality may derive from a context that is questionable today and in part because the impact of social science has led some ethicists to question whether homosexuality is truly abnormal and unnatural and therefore against the will of God.

Nonetheless, both the Bible and tradition are uniformly against it.[5] In addition to the story of the destruction of Sodom (Genesis 19:4-11), homosexual practices are included on lists of cultic offenses against God in the Old Testament. In the New Testament, although Jesus made no comment on the subject, St. Paul was unambiguous. He apparently believed that homosexual acts were committed by fundamentally heterosexual people for sheer perverse pleasure. Thus he included them in lists of sexual sins, such as adultery and fornication, which are in opposition to the will of God and symptomatic of human depravity. However, Paul does not seem to have found homosexuality any more dreadful than other sexual sins (Thielicke, 1964).

The Fathers of the early Church strongly condemned homosexuality, partly because of the dreadful morals of the pagan world at that time. They saw it as a crime against nature which might bring down the wrath of God upon the whole community. Aquinas stated that "unnatural vice . . . flouts nature by transgressing its basic principles of sexuality and is in this matter the gravest of sin" (1968 ed., Second Part of the Second Part, Question 154, Article 12). Thielicke notes a similar attitude among Reformation theologians and quotes a seventeenth-century Lutheran, Benedict Carpzov, as listing the following results of homosexuality: "earthquakes, famine, pestilence, Saracens, floods, and very fat voracious field mice" (1964, p. 276).

A strong condemnation of homosexuality is found in most quarters of the Christian community today. However, there are various shadings of this essentially negative approach. Biblical fundamentalists, for example, would be likely to condemn all homosexual activity and see the homosexual person as a sinner needing radical cure. The Roman Catholic Church takes a somewhat different position. It maintains

---

[5]At least this is the conventional understanding, which has recently been challenged by Yale historian John Boswell (see Focus).

that while, as a matter of natural law, homosexual *acts* are not permissible, it is not necessarily sinful to *be* homosexual. Catholic homosexuals are therefore not to be rejected, but they must accept celibacy as the only way to deal with their sexual nature. As stated in the recent Vatican document:

> In the pastoral field these homosexuals must certainly be treated with understanding and sustained in the hope of overcoming their personal difficulties and their inability to fit into society. . . . But no pastoral method can be employed which would give moral justification to these acts on the grounds that they would be consonant with such people. . . . [The] judgment of scripture does not, of course, permit us to conclude that all who suffer from this anomaly are personally responsible for it, but it does attest to the fact that homosexual acts are intrinsically disordered and can in no way be approved (Sacred Congregation for the Doctrine of the Faith, 1976, p. 11)

Various Protestant groups have taken roughly the same stance—that is, being gay per se may not be sinful, but homosexual acts are—and a statement by the 1976 General Conference of the United Methodist Church is typical: "We do not condone the practice of homosexuality and consider this practice incompatible with Christian teaching" (*The Christian Century,* 1976, **93**, p. 557).

Those holding this position are often willing to concede civil rights and liberties to homosexuals, although there are differences in the willingness to press for them. When the Wolfenden report was published (see Chapter 23), the Roman Catholic hierarchy in England endorsed decriminalization of homosexual acts between consenting adults, stating that they were matters for the confessional and not for the courts (Griffin, 1956). While condemning the seduction of minors, prostitution, and force in sexual relations, a number of Protestant groups have arrived at the same conclusion.

There has been a movement in some churches toward a greater acceptance of the homosexual person. The movement began in 1963 when a group of English Friends challenged traditional thinking about sexuality, including homosexuality, in *Toward a Quaker View of Sex.* Since that time, Quakers and Unitarians have been notable for their acceptance not only of the homosexual person but of his or her sexual behavior. as long as it is conscientious. Within virtually all the mainline churches gay caucuses and organizations have been formed in an effort to move religious persons toward greater understanding and tolerance. That some progress has been made can be seen, for example, in a statement of the 1976 General Convention of the Episcopal Church that stated:

> Homosexual persons are children of God who have a full and equal claim with all other persons upon the love, acceptance, and pastoral concern and care of the Church. (Daily of the General Convention, September 15, 1976. p. 1)

Nonetheless, homosexuality remains a deeply divisive issue among Christians and the most common focus of conflict is ordination. In 1977, the Episcopal Bishop of New York ordained a lesbian to the priesthood and provoked a storm of controversy. A vigorous protest led to the adoption, at the 1979 General Convention, of a resolution declaring the practice of homosexuality to be incompatible with the ordained ministry. While 27 bishops signed a statement of dissent, no publicly avowed gay Episcopalian has been ordained since. The 1980s have seen a parade of mainline Protestant denominations—Lutherans, Presbyterians and United Methodists among them—debating and rejecting the ordination of homosexuals. This issue was one of the most explosive at the Bicentennial General Conference of the United Methodist Church in 1984. That body passed legislation requiring all clergy and

FIGURE 22.6

The first lesbian priest. Changing attitudes toward homosexuality in some Christian churches are reflected in the ordination of Ellen Barrett as a priest of the Episcopal Church, shown here with The Right Reverend Paul Moore, Bishop of New York, who ordained her.

candidates for ordination to observe "fidelity in marriage and celibacy in singleness," and added a specific prohibition against the ordination of "self-avowed practicing homosexuals" to its *Book of Discipline* (*The Christian Century,* 1984, **101**, p. 565). At present only the Unitarian-Universalist Association and the United Church of Christ seem willing to ordain openly gay people, and the lines are pretty clearly drawn in other religious groups, at least for now.

Within the gay community, the subject of religion is highly controversial as well. Many gays reject all forms of religion as oppressive and invalid. Gay believers, on the other hand, have a variety of options. They may simply remain in their religious community, sometimes welcomed privately while condemned officially. Others may join a reform movement within their church and work for change. Still others may take an increasingly common path and join a gay religious group. One result of the gay movement has been the establishment of homosexual religious organizations—churches, synagogues, temples, covens, and the like—in which gay people are free to practice their faith without harassment. The largest of these groups, the Universal Fellowship of Metropolitan Community Churches, recently sought unsuccessfully to join the National Council of Churches, the major American organization of Christian bodies (see Figure 22.7).

Meanwhile, within the religious community theological debate and discussion continues. An increasing body of literature challenges the assumption that homosexuality is sinful, or that the Judeo-Christian tradition is necessarily antigay. Among these "revisionists" are historians (such as John Boswell—see Focus), biblical

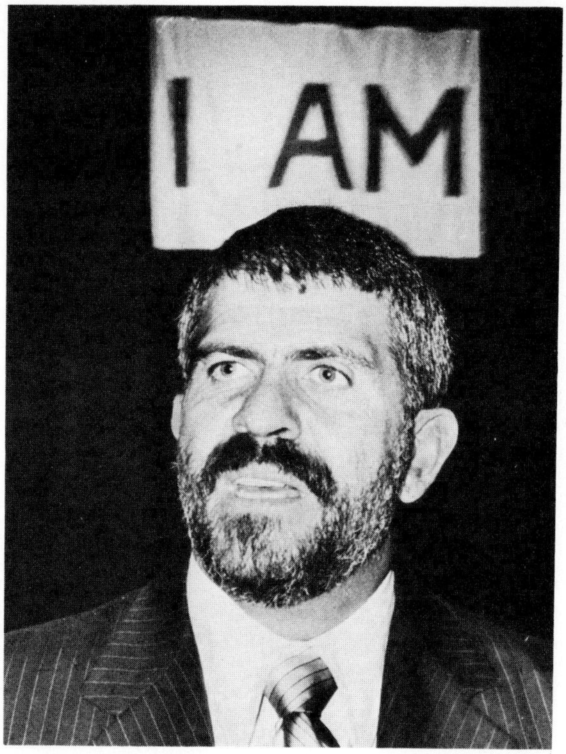

FIGURE 22.7

The Reverend Troy Perry of the Metropolitan Community Church is a spokesperson for issues confronting the homosexual religious community.

scholars, and theologians. These scholars seek to discern positive guidance for homosexuals from the Western religious tradition, and to question the stance taken by official church bodies. Such efforts are sometimes costly, but they have pushed the religious community to reexamine their presuppositions.[6] One such theologian, the Anglican Norman Pittenger, has argued that *any* relationship of mutual respect, concern, and commitment—of love in its fullest sense—is to be valued and supported, whatever the sex of the partners (1970). Virtually all would agree that a person's sexual orientation is an integral part of his or her personhood and can be affirmed as part of God's creation, or, in the words of the Lutheran Helmut Thielicke, "a task to be wrestled with . . . a talent to be invested." (1964, p. 284). Since the issue of homosexuality raises fundamental questions about the nature of creation, the purpose of sexuality, human relationships, and the will of God, it is certain that religious bodies will continue the debate for a long time to come.

TECHNOLOGY AND SEXUAL ETHICS

A major challenge to ethicists in the late twentieth century is the rapid development of technologies that raise new moral issues before the old ones have been resolved, in matters of human sexuality as in anything else. We have already discussed several issues in which technology has played a major role. Although sex outside of marriage is hardly a problem unique to our time, the availabiliy of reliable birth control techniques has probably increased the incidence of pre- and extramarital sex. The

[6]Father John McNeill, a Jesuit, has been forbidden by his order from speaking or writing on the subject of sexuality, since the 1976 publication of his groundbreaking book, *The Church and the Homosexual.*

F · O · C · U · S 22.3

JOHN BOSWELL: A REVISIONIST VIEW OF GAYS AND THE CHURCH

Religion is a powerful creator of culture, the source of attitudes and presuppositions of which we are often not fully aware. Prejudice against homosexual persons is deeply ingrained in Western culture, which is rooted in the Judeo-Christian tradition. Most people within that tradition regard homosexual behavior as deeply sinful and those who practice it as offensive to God. The Bible, the Fathers of the church, church law, and the whole weight of Christian tradition contribute to a rejection of this form of sexuality, and this rejection has strongly influenced the attitudes of Western society for 2000 years.

Or has it? Suddenly, in the late twentieth century, scholars are challenging this generally accepted view of the religious origin of antigay laws and attitudes. The most sweeping study is that by Yale historian John Boswell in *Christianity, Social Tolerance, and Homosexuality* (1980), winner of the 1981 American Book Award for History. Subtitled *Gay People in Western Europe from the Beginning of the Christian Era to the Fourteenth Century,* Boswell's book argues that for centuries the Christian church was relatively neutral toward homosexuality and, when it saw homosexual behavior as sinful, did not regard it as any worse than heterosexual transgressions. Boswell retranslates and analyzes those few passages

fact that millions of people can enjoy vigorous sex lives without ever conceiving children, unless they choose to, has markedly changed the basic moral climate.

The issue of abortion is likewise intensified by technological advances of the past few decades, and will only get more complicated in the future. The developing medical science of neonatology means that fetuses are viable outside the uterus earlier and earlier. Some late-pregnancy abortions produce a fetus that can be kept alive, and hospital staffs are faced with agonizing questions about what should be done in such cases. Traditional ethics suggest that such unwanted children be kept alive, yet this can be incredibly costly and the children are often severely handicapped. Hospitals may find it prudent to limit, or even forbid, second-trimester abortions to deal with the issue. Beyond these problems, new ethical issues seem to be surfacing almost every day.

Another complex of issues arises with efforts to conceive children outside the "normal" process of sexual intercourse. Since traditional sexual ethics have been based on that assumption, there is little guidance from the past. When a couple who are unable to conceive decides on artificial insemination by donor (AID), a certain impersonality is introduced into a traditionally deeply personal life experience, and this is troubling to many ethicists. Analogous problems could arise if ova banking, in the Bible that are supposed to condemn homosexuality and finds them rather ambiguous. He questions whether the New Testament even deals with what we today would call sexual preference, despite the fact that same-sex relationships were common and accepted in first century Greco-Roman society. Surveying the Fathers of the Church, the first great theologians, Boswell finds that very few of them seemed concerned with the problem, and about the others he says:

> Further, it is important to bear in mind in this context that the same fathers of the church—a very vocal minority—who censured homosexual behavior also censured, no less severely, behavior which is today universally accepted by Christian communities. Lending at interest, sexual intercourse during the menstrual period, jewelry or dyed fabrics, shaving, regular bathing, wearing wigs, serving in the civil government or army, performing manual labor on feast days, eating kosher food, practicing circumcision—all were condemned absolutely by various fathers of the church, the same who condemned homosexual behavior and many other activities, due to personal prejudice, misinformation, or an extremely literal interpretation of the Bible. None of these practices is today a matter of controversy within the Christian community, and it seems illogical to claim that it was the opposition of a few influential Christian theorists which caused homosexual practices alone, out of hundreds of proscribed actions, to incur such a powerful and permanent stigma in Western culture. Obviously some more sophisticated analysis is required. (pp. 165–166)

With remarkable scholarship, erudition, and wit, Boswell carries his research through 1400 years, several dead languages, an incredible variety of long-lost documents, and all over Europe. He contends that throughout this period there was a gay subculture that flourished at various times and in various places, that it was known to the Christian church, that clergy and church officials were often part of it, and that it was not infrequently tolerated by religious and civil authorities alike. It was not until the thirteenth century that the whole weight of Western culture finally turned against homosexuality, leading to the situation with which we are so familiar today.

Boswell's work is, by his own admission, provisional and tentative. Certainly it is controversial and not universally accepted. Nonetheless, it is a significant challenge to the conventional wisdom and suggests that the attitude of the Bible and Christian tradition toward homosexuality is rather more complex than has been previously assumed. John Boswell, and other scholars like him, ensure that the church and the gay community will continue dialogue, debate, and struggle for quite some time.

Source: John Boswell (1980). *Christianity, social tolerance, and homosexuality.* Chicago: University of Chicago Press.

FIGURE 22.8

There are ethical issues posed by developing technologies as seen by the question of paternity involving surrogate mother Judy Stiver and her husband Ray (left), of Lansing, Michigan, and Alexander Malahoff who contracted with the Stivers for the birth of the infant "Baby Doe." They appeared on the Phil Donahue show to discuss the controversy—the baby was born with microcephaly. Blood tests show Malahoff is not the father.

now possible through in vitro fertilization (IVF) becomes common (see Chapter 25). Likewise, a couple may conceive a child through IVF but, owing to the inability of the mother to carry the child to term, they may employ a "surrogate" for the pregnancy. How is she to be treated and what ought the "contract" among these parties look like to be fair and ethcial for all? Finally, since it is possible to maintain a fertilized embryo by freezing, and then implant it in a surrogate, some fundamental questions about the nature of parenthood and its responsibilities are raised (McDowell, 1983). All of these intrusions into the way in which children have been conceived and born raise the troubling spectre of humans "playing God" with his most profound of all life's processes. Many ethically sensitive persons are concerned about these issues, but few have any definitive answers.

Another area of concern centers around possible manipulation of the stuff of life itself."Spare" embroyos conceived by IVF could be used in experiments which make Dr. Frankenstein's look like small potatoes indeed. Genetic engineering frightens many ethicists, who are concerned about as yet unknown long-range effects of such experimentation. Further, there is the crucial issue of "who decides" what sort of engineering is appropriate and beneficial. The images of *Brave New World,* in which people are "manufactured" on a sort of scientific assembly line, and Hitlerian eugenics in which "undesireable characteristics" are bred out of the population, have been raised by these technologies. Balancing the very real possibility for improving the quality of life with the dangers of abuse requires wisdom and ethical sensitivity of a high order.

Eugenics:
The "science" of improving the quality of a species by careful selection of the parents, or by other methods of manipulating the process of procreation.

There is no way to stop the development of technology, or its speed, and it would not be desirable. Nonetheless, it is important to recognize that decisions about human life and reproduction ought not to be made on purely scientific grounds. By definition, they have the deepest moral implications, and these implications must be adequately addressed if the essential values of human life are to be preserved.

TOWARD AN ETHICS OF *HUMAN* SEXUALITY

The combined forces of the sexual revolution and the New Morality have strongly attacked the traditional Judeo-Christian sexual ethic as narrow and repressive. This may be true, but it has not yet been proved to everyone's satisfaction that the alternatives proposed are a real improvement upon the Old Morality. Whether the debate will be resolved, and how, remains to be seen. Some of the arguments and possibilities are considered below.

The Old Morality tends to be ascetic and legalistic and, at its worst, reduces ethical behavior to following a series of rules. Its asceticism may downgrade the goodness of human sexuality and negate the very real joys of physical pleasure. A healthy personality needs to integrate the physical side of life and affirm it, and this kind of self-acceptance may be made more difficult by the Old Morality. Further, if morality is simply a matter of applying universal rules, there is no real choice, and human freedom is seriously undermined. In short, opponents of the Old Morality might argue, this approach diminishes the full nature of humanity and impoverishes human life. On the other hand, the traditional approach deserves a few kind words as well. For one thing, with the traditional morality people almost always know where they stand. Right and wrong and good and bad are clearly, if somewhat inflexibly, spelled out. Moreover, asceticism does witness to the fact that the human is more than merely the body.

The New Morality, with its situational approach and tendencies toward hedonism, has its own share of pluses and minuses. It does affirm quite positively the physical and sexual side of human nature as an integral part of the individual. This is helpful, but if it is pushed too far, it can also leave people under no control and thus less than fully human. Situation ethics quite properly calls for an evaluation of every ethical decision on the basis of the concrete aspects of the personalities involved and the context of the decision. Its broad principles of love, respect, and interpersonal responsibility are sound, but it can be argued that situationism does not take sufficiently into account the problem of human selfishness. Dishonesty about our real motives may blind us to the actual effects of our actions, however sincere we profess to be. Futher, situationism is a much less certain guide than the older approach, since so many situations are ambiguous.

There is a middle way between these two extremes, one which may yet prove to be the synthesis that sexual ethics seems to be searching for. This approach would use the traditional principles (laws) as guidelines for actions while insisting that they must be applied in concrete situations and occasionally reworked to conform to changes in the human situation. This approach differs from the Old Morality by stating that ethical principles must be flexible, and it differs from the New Morality by holding that departures from tradition must be based on very strong evidence that the old rules do not apply. For those adopting this position, healthy decision making functions in the tensions between the rigid "thou shalt not" of the legalist and the "do your own thing" of the situationist.

In the specific case of sexual ethics, such a middle-of-the-road approach would affirm the goodness of human sexuality but insist that sexual behavior needs to be regulated on the basis of reason, experience, and conscience. It would accept sexuality as a vital part of human personality, but not the sum total of who we are. Such an approach to sexual ethics would indeed be consistent with what was shown earlier in this chapter to be the heart of the Judeo-Christian tradition, shorn of some of its unnecessary rigidity and distrust of sexuality. If, as is sometimes claimed, the sexual revolution is over, and there is a movement toward relationship and commitment, this might prove to be just the sexual morality that people in our time are looking for.

SUMMARY

It is important to study religion and ethics in conjunction with human sexuality because they frequently provide the framework within which people judge the rightness or wrongness of sexual activity. They give rise to attitudes and approaches which influence the way members of a society regard sexuality, and they are therefore powerful influences on behavior. Religion and ethics may be hedonistic (pleasure-oriented) or ascetic (emphasizing self-discipline). They may be legalistic (operating by rules) or situational (making decisions in concrete situations, with few rules).

In the great ethical traditions, the Greeks tended toward a philosophical asceticism, while the Old Testament had a positive, though legalistic, view of sexuality. Christian New Testament sources are ambivalent about sexuality, with Jesus saying little on the subject and with St. Paul, influenced by the immorality of Roman culture and his expectation of the end of the world, being somewhat negative. Later, Christianity became much more ascetic; this is reflected in the writings of Augustine and

Thomas Aquinas, who also confirmed Catholic moral theology in the natural-law mold. The Protestant Reformation abolished clerical celibacy and opened the door to greater individual freedom in ethics. Today, technological development and new forms of biblical scholarship have led to a wide variety of positions on issues of sexual ethics.

Humanistic ethics rejects external authority, replacing it with a person-centered approach to ethics. A variety of approaches to sexuality can be found in Islam, Hinduism, and Buddhism.

Six ethical issues involving human sexuality have provoked lively debate recently. Among liberals, there is a greater acceptance of premarital intercourse, although the legalistic tradition is firmly against it. Extramarital sex is opposed by virtually all ethicists, but a more compassionate approach is often urged. Contraception is opposed by Roman Catholicism and Orthodox Judaism on scriptural and natural-law grounds, but it is positively valued by many other groups. The issue of abortion involves a very emotional argument on which there are many positions, ranging from adamant opposition on the grounds that it is murder to a view that urges each woman to make her own decision on the matter. Another very vigorous debate is going on today over homosexuality, with some movement away from the traditional view that condemns it absolutely and toward either a qualified approval at least of civil rights and liberties for gay people or a warmhearted acceptance of their sexuality. Developments in the technology of human reproduction are creating complex ethical issues in which there are, as yet, few clear norms.

A possible resolution of the conflict between the Old Morality and the New Morality involves an ethics of *human* sexuality, neither hedonistic nor rigidly ascetic, which takes seriously the historical tradition of ethical thinking while insisting that decisions be made on the basis of the concrete situation.

REVIEW QUESTIONS

1. In *Situation Ethics,* Joseph Fletcher lays down careful rules to follow to live a moral life. True or false?
2. Jewish teaching, as found in the Old Testament of the Bible, is uniformly negative about sex. True or false?
3. Much Christian teaching, from the Apostle Paul through the Middle Ages, favored _____ over marriage for ordinary Christians, and required it for the clergy.
4. Engagement in sexual intercourse and family life at one time in life and extreme asceticism at others is characteristic of the _____religion.
5. A political and religious position found in contemporary society, which opposes abortion, the Equal Rights Amendment, and gay rights, is often called _____.
6. Roman Catholicism opposes all sexual intercourse outside of marriage. True or false?
7. Abortion is uniformly condemned by all religious groups in the United States. True or false?
8. Debate about homosexuality in most religious groups is likely to center around whether or not gay people should be ordained to the ministry. True or false?

9. Technological advances in manipulating conception such as AID and IVF have been warmly welcomed by all members of the religious community. True or false?
10. The ethical position which takes a less legalistic and more positive approach to matters of human sexuality and which affirms current psychological understandings of the subject is often called ____.

QUESTIONS FOR THOUGHT DISCUSSION, AND DEBATE

1. If you are a member of a religious group, investigate your group's beliefs on the issues discussed in this chapter (premarital sex, extramarital sex, contraception, abortion, homosexuality, and technology). Do you agree with those positions? If you are not a member of a religious group, see if you can state a view of sexual ethics that is consistent with your philosophy of life.
2. Seek out a person, group, or written material which takes the opposite of your position on abortion and carefully consider those arguments. What effect does this have on your views?

SUGGESTIONS FOR FURTHER READING

Boswell, John. (1980). *Christianity, social tolerance, and homosexuality.* Chicago: University of Chicago Press. A very sophisticated reassessment of Christian attitudes toward gays, and their place in Western society through the Middle Ages.

Brinton, Crane. (1959). *A history of Western morals.* New York: Harcourt, Brace & World. With remarkable scholarship and great wit, this eminent historian traces Western ethics from the time of the Greeks to the present.

Cox, Harvey (Ed.) (1968). *The situation ethics debate.* Philadelphia: Westminster Press. Fletcher, Joseph. (1966). *Situation ethics.* Philadelphia: Westminster Press. Fletcher, Joseph. (1967). *Moral responsibility: Situation ethics at work.* Philadelphia: Westminster Press. Three very readable books which give the outline of the great debate over the New Morality.

Parrinder, Geoffrey. (1980). *Sex in the world's religions.* New York: Oxford University Press. A superb and concise treatment of the variety of religious approaches to human sexuality. The best short book in the field.

Pittenger, W. Norman. (1970). *Making sexuality human.* Philadephia: Pilgrim Press. A short but well-thought-out work which grounds the New Morality in good theology.

CHAPTER · 23

SEX AND THE LAW*

What the consenting adult does in private has become everybody's business to the precise extent that debate waxes hot over whether it is nobody's business.†

*This chapter was contributed by Clark Hyde, M. A., M. Div.

†*Source:* Herbert Packer. (1968). *The limits of the criminal sanction.* Stanford, Calif.: Stanford University Press, p. 301.

CHAPTER HIGHLIGHTS

One day in the late 1960s, I stood chatting on a Berkeley street corner with David and Ken, who are gay. David leered at his companion and announced in mock conspiratorial tones, "We're going to commit an illegal act." And they were. And so, that day, were a great many other people—gay and straight, male and female, single and married. All would be violating one or another of various state laws telling them, in effect, what they might do, how, where, and with whom. The average citizen might be very surprised by what the law has, over the years and even today, seen fit to regulate in this most private act. Twenty years ago, legal scholar Ralph Slovenko concluded in a massive study that "Americans commonly and regularly engage in sexual practices which are technically forbidden by law" (1965, p. 5). Kinsey estimated that about 95 percent of the males in his sample had engaged in illegal sexual acts (Kinsey et al, 1948, p. 392). The past generation has seen fast-moving and remarkable change in sex laws, and today fewer Americans probably commit crime in the bedroom. Nonetheless, the number of laws regulating sexual behavior is still considerable. This chapter will consider why there are such laws, what sorts of behaviors are affected, how these laws are enforced, how they are changing, and what the future prospects for sex-law reform might be.

WHY ARE THERE SEX LAWS?

To begin, we might well ask why there are laws regulating sexual conduct in the first place. This actually is a very modern question, for throughout most of Western history such laws were taken for granted. Sexual legislation is quite ancient, dating back certainly to the time of the Old Testament (see Chapter 22). Since then, in countries where the Judeo-Christian tradition is influential, attempts to regulate morals have been the rule. Today we are likely to regard sex as a private matter, of concern only to those involved. However, historically it has been seen as a matter which very much affects society and therefore as a fit subject for law.

Even today, certain kinds of sex laws are probably legitimate and necessary. Stanford law professor Herbert Packer argues that the following might be rationally included in law: protection "against force and equivalent means of coercion to secure sexual gratification," "protection of the immature against sexual exploitation," and, although this is somewhat problematic, "the prevention of conduct that gives offense or is likely to give offense to innocent bystanders" (1968, p. 306). It seems obvious that people ought to be free from sexual assault and coercion and that children should not be sexually exploited; individual rights and the interests of society are here in agreement.

However, sex laws have been designed for other purposes which may be more open to question. Historically, the rationale was to preserve the family as the principal unit of the social order by protecting its integrity from, for example, adultery or desertion of a spouse. Sex laws also seek to assure children of a supportive family by prohibiting conduct such as fornication, which is likely to result in out-of-wedlock births. Changing social conditions may call for revision of these statutes, but the principles behind them are understandable.

Fornication: Sex among persons not married to each other.

There is yet another realm of motivation behind sex laws which is highly problematic, and that is the protection of public morals. However, this tends to become a matter of religion, and the constitutional separation of church and state is designed to prevent one religious group from enforcing its tenets on others. The concern for public morality results in laws against any form of nonprocreative sex, for reasons outlined in Chapter 22. Thus there have been laws against homosexual acts, bestiality, and contraception. Religious beliefs as to what is "unnatural," "immoral," or "sinful" have found expression in law, as it was often held that the state had a duty to uphold religion as a pillar of civilized society, using the law to make people good. The example of England is instructive, since American law derives so extensively from English law. Both before and after the Reformation, church and state in England were seen as identical, and the state had an obligation to protect the interests of the Church. A secular state, such as the United States, was unthinkable, and an individual's morals were a matter of public concern. Sin and crime have often been confused in the public mind, and this confusion has found its way into law (Parker, 1983; Katz, 1982).

It can be argued that another principal source of sex laws is *sexism,* which is deeply rooted in Western culture. One scholar has suggested that the history of the regulation of sexual activity could as well be called the "history of the double standard." He goes on to note that:

> The law of marriage and the law controlling sexual expression are really the same question looked at from different angles. Women have always been looked upon as the property of men—whether fathers or husbands. Marriage has frequently in history been a commercial transaction or a way in which the fabric of society could be maintained. The male insistence on chastity was simply an attempt to regularize social relations, to cement dynasties, to ensure the orderly succession of property (particularly real property) and to perpetuate male domination (Parker, 1983, p. 190).

It is probably not coincidental that movement for sex-law reform has gone hand in hand with the movement for the liberation of women.

The American tradition of moralism in politics, the prudery of the Victorian period (during which much of the American legal system came into being), and the zealousness of such individuals as Anthony Comstock (see Focus) combined to provide the United States with an enormous amount of sexual legislation. This legislation reflects a great deal of ambiguity in our attitudes toward sex, which is perhaps unsurprising in such a varied population. It also contrasts with other societies in which the trend since 1800 has been away from such laws. According to one authority, "The United States apparently has more laws on the subject than all of the European countries combined" (Slovenko, 1965, p. 9).[1] The U.S. legal tradition assumes both the right of the state to enforce morals and a consensus in society as to which morals are to be enforced. However, contemporary citizens have come to question the legitimacy of government interference in what they regard as their private affairs. This tension has led to a widespread demand for a radical overhaul of laws that regulate sexual conduct. It all makes for a fascinating, if frustrating, field of study, for law has a way of reflecting the ambiguities and conflicts of society.

WHAT KINDS OF SEX LAWS ARE THERE?

Cataloging the laws pertaining to sexual conduct would be a difficult project. It is possible that no one really knows how many such laws there are, given the large number of jurisdictions in the American legal system. When one considers federal law, the Uniform Code of Military Justice, state laws, municipal codes, county ordinances, and so on, the magnitude of the problem becomes clear. In addition to *criminal* law, portions of civil law that may penalize certain sexual behaviors—such as licensing for professions, personnel rules for public servants, and immigration regulations—must also be considered. Further, these laws are changing all the time, and any list would be obsolete before it went to press. Therefore, what is offered here is not so much a statistical summary of specific sex laws as a look at the *kinds* of laws that are, or have been, on the statute books.[2] The subheadings, all of which contain the word "crime," have been chosen with care, as a reminder that we are discussing legal offenses which can carry with them the penalty of loss of freedom,

---

[1]For a good comparison with another English-based North American legal system, see the history of Canadian sex laws (Parker, 1983).

[2]A general discussion of the kinds of laws may be found in MacNamara and Sagarin, 1977. State-by-state listings appear in Boggan et al., 1983, Mueller, 1980; and Rivera, 1979.

F · O · C · U · S 23.1

ANTHONY COMSTOCK: CRUSADER AGAINST VICE

In any discussion of laws regulating sexual behavior, the name of Anthony Comstock looms large. His zeal for moral reform is reflected in the use of the term "Comstock laws" for the kinds of statutes considered here.

Comstock was born in Connecticut in 1844 and was reared as a strict Puritan Congregationalist; he had a well-developed sense of his own sinfulness—and of others' as well. He served in the Union Army during the Civil War and worked as a dry-goods salesperson. While still a young man, he became very active in the Young Men's Christian Association, seeking the arrest and conviction of dealers in pornography. He helped found the Committee for the Suppression of Vice within the YMCA. This later became an independent society, as his efforts gained him national attention.

Comstock's most noteworthy success was probably a comprehensive antiobscenity bill which passed the United States Congress in 1873. The law prohibited the mailing of obscene matter within the United States, as well as advertisements for obscenity, which included matter "for the prevention of conception." Comstock initiated the passage of a similar law in New York, making it illegal to give contraceptive information verbally, and many other states followed suit. At the same time, Comstock received an appointment as a special agent of the U.S. Post Office, and this gave him the authority personally to enforce the Comstock Law. He did, with a vengeance, claiming at the end of his career to have been personally responsible for the jailing of over 3600 offenders against public decency.

Comstock's energies were directed not only against pornography but also against abortionists, fraudulent advertisers and sellers of quack medicines, lotteries, saloonkeepers, artists who painted nude subjects, and advocates of free love. Among the objects of his wrath were many of the most famous advocates of unpopular opinions of his day. He carried on a crusade against women's movement pioneers Victoria Woodhull and her sister Tennessee Claflin; he helped jail William Sanger, husband of Margaret Sanger, the birth control crusader; he attacked Robert Ingersoll, the atheist; and he tried to prevent the New York production of George Bernard Shaw's play about a prostitute, *Mrs. Warren's Profession.* For the last of these efforts, Shaw rewarded him by coining the word "comstockery."

Anthony Comstock was a controversial figure during his own lifetime and has often been blamed for all legislation reflecting his views. However, it is important to understand that he had a great deal of support from the public, without which he could not have jailed his 3600 miscreants. He will probably go down in history as a symbol of the effort to make people moral by legislation. He died in 1915 shortly after representing the United States at an International Purity Congress.

Anthony Comstock may be long-dead, but comstockery has always been a feature of American society and seems to be making a comeback in the 1980s. He might very well be a patron saint for the Moral Majority.

Source: Heywood Broun and Margaret Leech. (1927). *Anthony Comstock: Roundsman of the Lord.* New York: Boni.

loss of reputation, loss of property, or all of these. However quaint and amusing some of these laws may seem, they are a serious matter.

Crimes of Exploitation and Force

Recalling Packer's suggestions about the kinds of laws that seem to make sense in a pluralistic society, let us begin with those seeking to prevent the use of force or exploitation in sexual relations—chiefly laws against rape and sexual relations with the young. In the past two decades, there has been a movement toward seeing such crimes not so much as sex crimes but as crimes of violence and victimization, with laws being revised to accommodate this different understanding and to protect the victims (see Chapter 18).

Rape:
In the broadest sense, sexual intercourse when one of the parties is unwilling.

For generations, the classical definition of [forcible] rape was:

> The act of sexual intercourse with a female person not the wife of, or judicially separated from bed and board from, the offender, committed without her lawful consent. Emission is not necessary; and any sexual penetration, however slight, is sufficient to accomplish the crime. (Slovenko, 1965, p. 48)

In trials under this definition, the principal issue was the consent of the victim and many states allowed the victim's prior sexual activities to be considered as evidence of her consent, in effect putting the victim on trial. The Model Penal Code of the American Law Institute, attempting to deal with some of the problems of the older definition, proposed this law:

> Rape. A male who has sexual intercourse with a female not his wife is guilty of rape if: (a) he compels her to submit by force or by threat of imminent death, serious bodily injury, extreme pain or kidnapping, to be inflicted on anyone; or (b) he has substantially impaired her power to appraise or control her conduct by administering or employing without her knowledge drugs, intoxicants or other means for the purpose of generating resistance; or (c) the female is unconscious; or (d)the female is less than ten years old. Rape is a felony of the second degree unless (i) in the course thereof the actor inflicts serious bodily injury upon anyone, or (ii) the victim was not a voluntary social companion of the actor upon the occasion of the crime and had not previously permitted him sexual liberties, in which cases the offense is a felony of the first degree. Sexual intercourse includes intercourse per os or per annum [in the mouth or rectum], with some penetration however slight, emission is not required. (MacNamara and Sagarin, p. 31)

Even by this statute, only a woman can be the victim of a rape and a husband cannot be tried for raping his wife, however unwilling she may be. Some states, however, have revised their laws so that a husband can be tried for raping his wife (Mueller, 1980). The 1979 Rideout case in Oregon was the first prosecution under such a law, although the husband was acquitted. Some states have also revised the language of their statutes to eliminate the word rape, choosing instead "criminal sexual assault" which permits prosecution of men for raping men and even of women for raping men (Jaffe and Becker, 1984).

Laws that seek to prevent the sexual exploitation of children and young people are complicated by the issues of consent, coercion, and immaturity, all of which are rather difficult to define. Most states have laws against *statutory rape,* or carnal knowledge of a juvenile. These laws presume that all intercourse by an adult male (normally one over 17 or 18), with any female under a certain age is, by definition, illicit because she cannot give genuine consent. That age, the "age of consent," varies state to state from 12 to 18. Many states have laws that also include a reference to the difference in ages between the male and the female, on the assumption that there is a difference in criminality between a 16-year-old girl having intercourse with her 18-year-old boyfriend and with a man in his thirties or forties (MacNamara and Sagarin, 1977; Mueller, 1980).

There is a great variety of laws against the *sexual abuse of children,* called variously child molestation, carnal abuse of a child, or impairing the morals of a child. These general terms usually cover all sexual contact between adult and child, heterosexual and homosexual, and can include the use of sexual language, exhibitionism, showing pornography to a child, having a child witness intercourse, or taking a child to a brothel or gay bar (MacNamara and Sagarin, 1977). Such statutes attempt to protect children, a reasonable goal, but are often so vague as to be either ineffective or to criminalize innocuous behavior. With the great increase recently in public awareness of the extent of child sexual abuse, it is likely that more precise and effective laws will be developed.

Incest: Sexual relations between persons closely related to each other.

Finally, every state includes laws against incest in its penal code. Although incestuous sexual relations can take place between adults, the law seems far more concerned where children are involved. The nearly universal taboo against incest seems to have as its purpose the guarantee to children that the home will be a place where they can be free from sexual pressure. In many states, penalties against incest are more severe the closer the relationship (Mueller, 1980). Incest laws also seek to prevent the alleged genetic problems of inbreeding. Again, greater public awareness of the extent of incest (see Chapter 18) is likely to lead to a reexamination of laws on the subject.

Criminal Consensual Acts

While it is not hard to see the logic of laws against force and exploitation of the young, many people are amazed to discover the number of sexual acts forbidden to consenting adults. These laws, as has been noted, were designed to protect marriage and the family, but a quick look at the divorce statistics will suggest that they are not doing a very good job.

With respect to heterosexuals, there are a number of laws against fornication (intercourse between unmarried parties), cohabitation (unmarried persons living together), and adultery (intercourse between unmarried persons, at least one of whom is married to someone else). Although these laws have been revised in many states recently, it is remarkable how many were still on the books in 1972, when *Playboy* magazine summarized them (Rhodes, 1972). Twenty-three states forbade fornication, with fines ranging from $10 to $1000 and with jail terms up to a year. Cohabitation was illegal in 26 states and punishable by fines of up to $500 and jail sentences of up to five years. Adultery, in addition to being grounds for divorce in all jurisdictions, was a crime in 41 states; adulterers could be fined as little as $10 and as much as $200 and could be incarcerated for as long as five years.

Miscegenation: Sex between members of different races.

It is also rather disconcerting to realize that as recently as 1965 there were laws in 25 states against miscegenation, that is, against sex between members of different races, married or not (Slovenko, 1965, p. 41). The number of states indicates that such laws were not confined to the Deep South alone. Antimiscegenation laws did not make any distinction between married and unmarried parties; rather, they sought to prevent any sexual contact between whites and blacks. Laws against interracial marriage were invalidated by the United States Supreme Court in the 1967 case of *Loving v. Virginia.*

Besides specifying with whom one might have sex, laws have also attempted to regulate what acts are permissible, even in the case of a legally married couple. Until quite recently, virtually all states had laws prohibiting sodomy, or "crimes against nature."[3] These laws attempt to prohibit "unnatural" sex acts, even among consenting, married, heterosexual adults. Sodomy laws are many and varied, and they differ in terms of specificity, acts prohibited, and severity of the penalties. Sodomy laws are notoriously vague, as if the state legislatures did not wish to turn the statute books into pornography by describing the behaviors they wanted to prevent. The Louisiana law, which is clearer than most, describes sodomy as follows:

> The crime against nature is the unnatural carnal copulation by a human being with another of the same or opposite sex or with an animal. Emission is not necessary, and, when committed by a human being with another, the use of the genital organ of one of the offenders of whatever sex is sufficient to constitute the crime. (Quoted by Slovenko, 1965, p. 82)

From this, the reader is meant to understand that oral-genital and anal-genital acts, as well as bestiality, are forbidden under the rubric of "sodomy." In some jurisdictions, the statute also includes necrophilia, or sex with a dead person.

Crimes of Sexual Orientation

Sodomy: From the alleged homosexuality of the men of Sodom in the Bible, homosexual acts, often expanded to include all "unnatural" sexual acts, especially anal or oral sex.

Although, in theory, most sodomy laws are supposed to prohibit "unnatural acts" between heterosexuals, when they are enforced, which is not very often, the prosecution is almost invariably against gay people. The severity of the penalties of many sodomy laws probably reflects the attitude of legislators toward homosexual behavior. For example, in Georgia, sodomy, defined as "any sex act involving the mouth or anus of one person and the sex organs of another," is a felony punishable by not less than one and not more than *twenty* years in prison (Boggan et al., 1983). This attitude is peculiarly American. Consensual sodomy has been legal in France since the time of Napoleon, is legal throughout Europe and is prohibited by law only in Ireland, Rumania, Yugoslavia, and the Soviet Union (Barnett, 1973).

Sodomy laws are only the tip of the iceberg in a legal structure of discrimination against homosexual persons (Rivera, 1981–82; Rivera, 1979; Boggan et al., 1983). In most places gay persons may be denied private employment. However, the federal civil service regulations forbid such discrimination in public employment, and some state governors have forbidden sexual preference discrimination by executive order. Gays are still denied security clearances and the right to serve in the military. Many professional and occupational licensing requirements have "good character" or morality clauses which seem to invite discrimnation. For example, a number of public school teachers have been dismissed when their homosexuality became known. No right to gay marriage is supported by statute and gay relationships have very little legal support. The homosexuality of a parent is serious disadvantage in child custody proceedings. Homosexual persons may be denied entry to the United States or deported despite long residence.

Some states and municipalities have passed laws and ordinances forbidding discrimination on the basis of sexual orientation, notably in housing and employment,

[3]Beginning with Illinois in 1961, roughly half the states have decriminalized consensual sodomy, either by direct repeal or through a revision of the criminal code, most in the last decade (Boggan et al., 1983; Rivera, 1979). For a complete list of the remaining laws, and their penalties, see Boggan et al., 1983.

(*a*) (*b*)

FIGURE 23.1

Anita Bryant versus the gays and lesbians of Miami. In 1977, a Dade County, Florida, ordinance forbidding discrimination against homosexuals was contested at the polls and defeated by a 2 to 1 margin. (*a*) The leader of the antiordinance forces was singer Anita Bryant, then a fundamentalist Christian and spokesperson for Florida orange juice. Relying on the traditional Christian view of homosexuality for support, Ms. Bryant argued that the ordinance would allow gays to seduce children. Asked why she thought God hates homosexuality, she argued, "Sperm is the most concentrated form of blood. The homosexual (engaging in fellatio) is eating life. That's why God calls homosexuality an abomination." (*b*) Gay Miamians responded in kind to Ms. Bryant in a campaign that drew gay activists from all over the country.

but such laws are few, often unpopular, and subject to repeal by referendum (see Figure 23.1). Surveying this dismal landscape, legal scholar Rhonda Rivera documented

> systematic and pervasive discrimation against homosexual individuals in our courts. . . . Homosexuals are penalized in all aspects of their lives because of their sexual preference. They lose their jobs, their children, and numerous other precious rights as a result of many current judicial policies. (Rivera, 1979, p. 947)

Crimes against Taste

Another broad category of sex offenses can be viewed as crimes against community standards of taste and delicacy. In this company we find laws against exhibitionism, voyeurism, solicitation, disorderly conduct, being a public nuisance, and "general lewdness." These statutes are by and large quite vague and punish acts which are offensive, or *likely* to be offensive, to someone. Over half the states have such laws, and they carry penalties of from 30 days to 5 years in jail, with fines of $5 to $5000 (Boggan et al., 1983; Rosenbleet and Pariente, 1973). As will be seen below, unequal enforcement of these laws, their vagueness, and the difference between what is offensive and what is actually criminal make these statutes suspect.

Exhibitionism:
Showing one's genitals to passersby, indecent exposure.

Voyeurism:
Spying on people engaged in sexual activity.

Crimes against Procreation

As was noted in the Focus on their instigator, the Comstock laws included a ban on the giving of information concerning the prevention of conception. Comstock apparently regarded contraception and abortion as identical. These issues will be discussed more fully in the section on the right to privacy, below; here it will be mentioned only that until recently, abortion was prohibited or severely limited in all jurisdictions, and contraception was prohibited in many. These laws are clear examples of the values of another day enshrined in statute books. They arise from an understanding of procreation as the only legitimate purpose of sex and a belief in the necessity of vigorous propagation of the species. Such laws have been overturned by Supreme Court action, but continuing agitation, at least in the case of abortion, ensures that public debate will continue for some time.

Criminal Commercial Sex

The law has also deemed it illegal to make money from sex, at least in certain circumstances. It is not illegal to sell products with subtle promises of sexual fulfillment, but it is illegal actually to provide such fulfillment, either in direct form (that is, prostitution) or on paper, as in pornography. Since attitudes toward sex are changing, it is not surprising that there are attacks against these last limitations on sexual free enterprise. Both will be treated in greater detail below; first, however, the kinds of laws made on these subjects should be noted.

Prostitution is the exchange of sex for money. Except in Nevada, where counties may allow it, prostitution is illegal in every jurisdiction in the United States, though not in many other countries. The law also forbids activities related to it, such as solicitation, pandering (pimping, procuring), renting premises for prostitution, and enticing minors into prostitution (Perry, 1980). Laws against vagrancy and loitering are also used against prostitutes. However, the prostitute's client is almost never charged or chargeable with a crime. These laws have proved very difficult to enforce, and so the "oldest profession" goes on unabated.

Obscenity: That which is offensive to decency or modesty, or calculated to arouse sexual excitement or lust.

Obscenity will be discussed in more detail in a later section. Suffice it to say here that in most jurisdictions it is a crime to sell material or to present a play, film, or other live performance which is "obscene." That much is fairly simple, although many civil libertarians attack censorship as an infringement on freedom of the press. The real problem comes in deciding *what* exactly is obscene and how that will be determined without doing violence to the First Amendment. So far, no satisfactory answer has been found. Obscenity laws seem to have a twofold basis. First, they attempt to prevent the corruption of morals by materials that incite sexual thoughts and desires. Second, they attempt to ensure that no one will profit by the production and distribution of such materials. Whether either can be done, or is worth doing, is a question that will be taken up in a later section.

SEX-LAW ENFORCEMENT

From the foregoing, it is clear that the law has intruded into areas which the reader may well have thought were his or her own business. We can now ask: How are sex laws enforced? The answer is simple: With *great* inconsistency. Packer estimated that "the enforcement rate of private consensual sex offenders must show incredibly heavy odds against arrest—perhaps one in ten million" (1968, p. 304). The contrast between the number and severity of the laws themselves and the infrequency and capriciousness of their enforcement reflects the ambiguity of society's attitude toward the whole subject.

This contrast leads to serious abuses and to demands for radical reform of sex laws. A summary of the arguments for reform will be presented later in this chapter. First, however, it should be noted that as long as the laws are on the books, the *threat* of prosecution or even of arrest, can exact a great penalty from the "offender." Loss of job, reputation, friendship, family, and so on, can result from the sporadic enforcement of sex laws. For persons engaging in the prohibited acts, especially homosexual persons, the threat of blackmail is ever present. Of course, for those actually convicted on "morals charges," the situation is even worse. That individuals should be subjected to such liabilities for private acts is questionable.

Second, the uneven enforcement of sex laws may have a very bad effect on law enforcement generally. It invites arbitrary and unfair behavior and abuse of discretionary authority by police and prosecutors, and it may even lead them to corruption and extortion. One serious abuse is entrapment, in which an undercover police agent, posing, for example, as a homosexual or a prostitute's potential client, actually solicits the commission of a crime. Since a sexual act between consenting parties means that there is no one to report the act to the authorities, undercover agents must create the crime in order to achieve an arrest for it. Such entrapment hardly leads to respect for the law. Moreover, the knowledge that sex laws are violated with impunity creates a general disrespect for the law, particularly among those who know that they are, strictly speaking, "criminals" under it. If nothing else, the failure of Prohibition ought to demonstrate that outlawing activities of which a substantial proportion of the populaton approves is bad public policy. It may well be said that more violations of the public good result from the enforcement of sex laws than from the acts they seek to prevent.[4] Keeping this in mind, let us turn to the prospects for the future.

TRENDS IN SEX-LAW REFORM

It has been difficult to specify the number and details of certain types of sex laws because change is very rapid in this area. My distaste for these attempts to regulate human behavior leads me to call this "reform," although many in our society would contend that the change is for the worse. Since sex is a topic heavily laden with values, such reform is not likely to be accomplished without a good deal of conflict. This makes it difficult to predict either the precise directions of change or its speed. However, some important legal principles are used to bring about changes in sex laws; these trends in reform are discussed below.

Early Efforts at Sex-Law Reform

In recent years, there have been two landmark efforts to get oppressive sexual legislation off the statute books—one English and one American. In 1954, largely at the instigation of the Moral Welfare Council of the Church of England, a blue-ribbon Committee on Homosexual Offenses and Prostitution was appointed to advise Parliament on possible reform of the laws in these two areas. After much careful research and deliberation, in 1957 the committee issued its report, commonly known by the name of its chairman, J. F. Wolfenden. The recommendations were rather startling, most notably that "homosexual behavior between consenting adults in private be no longer a criminal offense" and that prostitution be decriminalized, leaving laws only against public nuisance (Great Britain Committee on Homosexual Offenses and Prostitution, 1963, p. 187). Essentially, the Wolfenden report concluded that private sex ought to be a private matter, and the British Parliament gradually came to agree with it.

Decriminalization: Removing some act from those prohibited by law, ceasing to define it as a crime.

On this side of the Atlantic, the American Law Institute's Model Penal Code recommended decriminalization of many kinds of sexual behavior previously outlawed. Under the section dealing with sexual offenses, it includes only rape, deviate sexual intercourse by force or imposition, corruption and seduction of minors, sexual assault, and indecent exposure (American Law Institute, 1962, Article 213). With the notable exception of prostitution, which it still makes illegal, the American Law Institute follows the principle that private sexual behavior between consenting

[4]For a good exposition of these and other arguments, see Packer, 1968, pp. 301–306.

adults is not really the law's business. The recommendation of the Model Penal Code has been followed by a few states.

While there are exceptions, a state is more likely to reform its sex laws as part of a complete overhaul of its criminal code than it is to make specific repeal of such laws. The reason for this is political and is grounded in the distinction between legalization and decriminalization.[5] If legislators "legalize" unconventional sexual practices, people are likely to become upset and accuse the state of "condoning" them. It is therefore important to note that what is advocated is decriminalization, that is, ceasing to define certain acts as criminal or removing the penalties attached to them. Decriminalization is morally neutral; it neither approves nor disapproves, and it simply revises the definitions.

A leading symbol of recent efforts to reform sex laws is the case of former Air Force Technical Sergeant Leonard Matlovich. Although an outstanding airman by the evidence of his superiors, in 1975 he was dismissed from the Air Force with a general (less than honorable) discharge after informing the Air Force of his homosexuality. Seeking a test case, Matlovich sued to be reinstated. Federal District Court Judge Gerhard Gesell commended his record but ruled nevertheless that the service had a right to "establish standards of behavior." On appeal, the Court of Appeals reversed the lower court, ordered that Matlovich receive further administrative hearings, and instructed the military to develop a consistent policy on the employment of homosexuals. In 1980, the case was returned to Judge Gesell who found that the Air Force had not sufficiently clarified its policies and ordered Matlovich reinstated. The case was settled out of court when Matlovich agreed to drop the suit in return for an honorable discharge and $160,000 in back pay. Although the case forced the military services to give honorable discharges to homosexual personnel and was a personal vindication for Leonard Matlovich, it did not prove to be the hoped-for "gay *Brown v. Board of Education.*" (For more detail on this case, see McCrary and Gutierrez, 1979–1980.)

Right to Privacy

A legal principle which has been very important in sex-law reform is the constitutional right to privacy. This has come into play chiefly in attacks on sex laws through the courts. Interestingly enough, although the right to privacy is invoked in connection with an amazing variety of matters—criminal records, credit bureaus and banks, school records, medical information, government files, wiretapping, and the 1974 amendment to the Freedom of Information Act, known as the Privacy Act, to name a few—the definitive articulation of the constitutional principle came in a sex-related case (Brent, 1976).

In 1965 the Supreme Court decided the case of *Griswold v. Connecticut* and invalidated a state law under which a physician was prosecuted for providing information, instruction, and medical advice concerning contraception for a married couple. Mr. Justice Douglas stated flatly that "we deal with a right of privacy older than the Bill of Rights, older than our political parties, older than our school system" (*Griswold v. Connecticut,* 1965, p. 486). The problem that Douglas, and the six justices who voted with him, faced was finding the specific provisions of the Constitution which guaranteed this right. Douglas found it not in any actual article of the

---

[5]One exception concerns California, where laws prohibiting adulterous cohabitation, sodomy, and oral copulation were specifically rescinded by the narrowest possible margin in the state senate (*Sexual Law Reporter,* 1975, p. 18).

FIGURE 23.2

Leonard Matlovich initiated a test case on the legality of discrimination against homosexuals in the armed forces.

Bill of Rights but in "penumbras, formed by emanations from those guarantees that help give them life and substance" (*Griswold v. Connecticut,* 1965, p. 484). Critics have found this a splendid example of constitutional double-talk, and the debate over the scope and application of the right to privacy continues. Nonetheless, in invalidating the Connecticut law, the Court defined a constitutional right to privacy which was, in this instance, abridged when a married couple was denied access to information on contraception.

While the decision in the Griswold case declared the marriage bed an area of privacy, in the 1972 case of *Eisenstadt v. Baird,* the Court invalidated a Massachusetts law forbidding the dissemination of contraception information to the unmarried. In doing so, the Court stated that "if the right of privacy means anything, it is the right of the individual, married or single, to be free from unwarranted governmental intrusion into matters as fundamentally affecting a person as the decision whether to bear or beget a child" (*Eisenstadt v. Baird,* 1972, p. 453). Other decisions have established one's home as a protected sphere of privacy which the law cannot invade (Brent, 1976).

The right to privacy was also invoked by the Court in 1973 in one of its most controversial cases, *Roe v. Wade,* which invalidated laws prohibiting abortion. Suing under the assumed name of Jane Roe, a Texas resident argued that her state's law against abortion denied her a constitutional right. The Court agreed that "the right of personal privacy includes the abortion decision" (*Roe v. Wade,* 1973, p. 113). However, it held, by a 7 to 2 margin, that such a right is not absolute and that the state has certain legitimate interests which it may preserve through law, such as the protection of the viable fetus. Nonetheless, the Court declared that a fetus is not a person and therefore not entitled to constitutional protection. The effect of the Roe case, and of related litigation, was to invalidate most state laws against abortion. The Court limited second- and third-trimester abortions to reasons of maternal health but made a woman's right to a first-trimester abortion nearly absolute.

Victimless Crimes

In the past decade, a great deal of legislative change has taken place through the principle of "victimless crimes"—a concept that has broad applicability beyond sexual behavior. It is asserted that when an act does no legal harm to anyone or does not provide a demonstrable victim, it cannot be reasonably defined as a crime. The thrust of the argument is well articulated by University of Chicago Law School Dean Norval Morris:

> Most of our legislation concerning drunkenness. narcotics, gambling and sexual behavior is wholly misguided. It is based on an exaggerated conception of the capacity of the criminal law to influence men and, ironically, on a simultaneous belief in the limited capacity of men to govern themselves. We incur enormous collateral costs for that exaggeration and we overload our criminal justice system to a degree that renders it grossly defective where we really need protection—from violence and depredations on our property. But in attempting to remedy this situation, we should not substitute a mindless "legalization" of what we now proscribe as crime. Instead, regulatory programs, backed up by criminal sanctions, must take the place of our present unenforceable, crime-breeding and corrupting prohibitions. (1973, p. 11)

The victimless-crime argument should appeal not only to the public's sense of privacy but also to its pocketbooks. Crimes in which there is no readily identifiable victim account for over half the cases handled by U.S. courts (Boruchowitz, 1973). If the court dockets could be cleared and law enforcement officers reassigned, protection against violent crimes would be rendered more efficient and less expensive.

The application of the principle to some of the issues disussed above should be obvious. A sexual act performed by consenting adults, whatever it might be, produces neither a victim nor legal harm. The only conceivable end served by criminalizing such an act is the protection of "public morals," which, in a society with many values, seems an end not worth the cost, if it is even possible. If sodomy laws, for example, are removed by a state legislature, the victimless-crime argument is likely to be used, by itself or in combination with an appeal to the right to privacy.

Many scholars and reformers would like to see this right to privacy extended to all private sexual activity among consenting adults. This right to "sexual autonomy" would rest not only on the Constitution but on the general idea of human rights (Richards, 1979). Testing this proposition in the courts gives very mixed results. The highest courts of some states, including the Supreme Courts of New York and Pennsylvania, have struck down as unconstitutional laws against consensual sodomy or "voluntary deviate sexual intercourse," citing the right to privacy (Katz, 1982; Bader, 1981). However, the Supreme Court of the United States summarily affirmed a lower court decision upholding a Virginia antisodomy law in the 1976 decision of *Doe v. Commonwealth Attorney.* This decision was one of several in which the Court

POT
"PORN"
"PERVERSION"
©1976 Chicago Sun-Times
"Be right with you, ma'am, soon as I've brought these lawbreakers to justice."

FIGURE 23.3

A cartoonist's view of victimless crime.

apparently recognized the right of states to legislate against various forms of consensual sexual behavior in the interests of promoting decency and morality. Moreover, the Supreme Court has avoided cases dealing with the activities of homosexuals. (Katz, 1982).

The most common reference to the decriminalization of victimless crimes is with respect to prostitution. Police efforts at curbing the "oldest profession" seem to be ineffective, open to corruption and questionable practices, and tremendously expensive. Since prosecution is normally of the prostitute and not her customer, there seems to be a clear pattern of discrimination against women which violates the constitutional principle of equal protection. Finally, as all manner of adult consensual behavior is decriminalized, the legitimacy of distinguishing between commercial and noncommercial consensual sex has been questioned (Parnas, 1981). It has been suggested that much of the demonstrable harm associated with prostitution, such as the committing of robbery and other crimes by prostitutes and pimps and the connections with organized crime, has resulted *because* the practice is illegal (Caughey, 1974). Further, the argument that prostitution is a leading contributor to the spread of venereal disease seems to lack any basis in fact.[6]

Thus, it has been argued that all would benefit if prostitution were no longer defined as a crime—the prostitute, her patron, the police, and society at large (Parnas, 1981; Rosenbleet and Pariente, 1973). The offensiveness of public solicitation

[6]Studies indicate that no more than 5 percent of the venereal disease in the United States is atrributable to prostitution. Further, the 15- to 30-year-old age group accounts for 84 percent of reported VD, while the 30- to 60-year-old age group accounts for 70 percent of visits to prostitutes (Caughey, 1974).

might be avoided if, as in England, prostitution were allowed to operate as a business rather than as a clandestine affair. If legalized it could be regulated—clients could be protected from disease, prostitutes could be free of victimization by their pimps, a considerable source of police effort and corruption could be eliminated, and the government could even receive tax revenues! Following this line of argument, if prostitution need not necessarily lead to crime, public offense, or the spread of VD, how does its continued criminalization benefit society?

An exception that proves the rule in this argument is the case of child prostitution. Recent attention in the media indicates that the use of juveniles, even very young children, for the sexual gratification of paying adults is a considerable social problem. Statistics are hard to come by, as the trade in child and teenage prostitutes is underground, but especially in large cities there is an appallingly large market for their services. The effects of prostitution on the young are traumatic, degrading, and psychologically crippling (Burgess, 1984). They clearly are *victims* and current efforts to develop more effective laws and enforcement against child prostitution are obviously appropriate (Shouvlin, 1981).

In a society in which crimes of violence and crimes against property endanger everyone, it seems reasonable to expect increasing decriminalization of acts that do not clearly harm people so that police and the courts may be freer to attack crimes that do. In England, the Wolfenden rcommendations were adopted; prostitution is legal, solicitation is regulated, and consensual homosexual activity has been decriminalized. Whether, or how soon, American legislatures will follow this example remains to be seen. Nonetheless, the movement to eliminate victimless crimes is established and seems likely to grow.

The Problem of Obscenity and Pornography

In the entire area of sexual regulation, there is no subject on which there has been more heat and less light generated than that of obscenity and pornography. A substantial portion of the American populace apparently finds pornography offensive and wishes it suppressed. Many others do not share this view and find any form of censorship outrageous and unconstitutional. Antivice crusaders consider "smut" dangerous to the average citizen, and yet few social scientists have found any evidence that it is (see, for example, M. J. Goldstein and Kant, 1975; also Eysenck and Nias, 1978). Legislators are swamped with demands that something be done, while the courts have labored unsuccessfully for years to balance the First Amendment right of freedom of speech with an apparent national desire to outlaw, or at last regulate, pornography. The enormous amount of energy and money spent on the issue suggests that pornography is a problem, but hardly anyone seems to be able to explain why it is a problem or even to define it, and it will probably be a long time before any generally satisfactory resolution can be achieved.

The discussion will begin with a problem of definition. Here it is helpful to distinguish between "pornography" as a popular term and "obscenity" as a legal concept. "Pornography" comes from the Greek word *porneia,* which means, quite simply, "prostitution." In general usage today, it refers to literature, art, film, speech, and so on, that are sexually arousing, or presumed to be arousing, in nature. Pornography may be "soft-core," that is, suggestive, or "hard-core," which usually means that there is explicit depiction of some sort of sexual activity. Pornography, as such, has never been illegal, but obscenity is. The word "obscene" suggests that which is foul, disgusting, or lewd, and it is used as a legal term for that which is offensive to the authorities or to society (Wilson, 1973).

Whatever its origin, obscenity has been the legal issue ever since the Supreme Court decided the Roth case in 1957. The Court explicitly stated that obscenity was not protected by the First Amendment—which guarantees freedom of speech and the press and which, by long-recognized extensions, includes film, pictures, literature, and other forms of artistic expression. However, it also ruled that not all sexual expression is obscene, defining obscenity as material "which deals with sex in a manner appealing to prurient interest" (*U.S. v. Roth,* 1957, p. 487). The Roth decision evoked much controversy, both from those who thought the Court had opened the floodgates of pornography and from civil libertarians who found the definition too limiting of freedom. The Court continued to try to refine the test for obscenity. In the 1966 Memoirs case, obscenity was additionally defined as that which is "utterly without redeeming social value." In the Ginzburg decision the same year, the Court upheld the obscenity conviction of a publisher for "pandering" in his advertising, that is, flagrantly exploiting the sexually arousing nature of his publication. However, none of these tests was persuasive to more than five members of the Court, much less to the public at large.[7]

The next attempt by the Supreme Court to define obscenity came in the 1973 case of *Miller v. California.* Rejecting the "utterly without redeeming social value" test, Chief Justice Burger and the four justices concurring with him proposed the following definition:

> (a) whether "the average person, applying contemporary community standards" would find that the work, taken as a whole, appeals to the prurient interest, (b) whether the work depicts or describes, in a patently offensive way, sexual conduct specifically defined by the applicable state law, and (c) whether the work, taken as a whole, lacks serious literary, artistic, political or scientific value. (*Miller v. California,* 1973, p. 24)

The goals of this decision seem to be to define as obscenity "hard-core pornography" in the popular sense, to require from state statutes precise descriptions of that which is to be outlawed, and to give governments more power to regulate it (Gruntz, 1974). The notable problem in the Miller standards, at least for civil libertarians, is the "contemporary community standards" provision. This allows the local community to determine what is obscene, rather than using national norms. This makes it impossible to predict what a given jury in a particular town might find obscene. For example, a vigorously antismut county prosecutor has kept metropolitan Cincinnati, Ohio, free of adult bookstores, while in Columbus several flourish. Can 120 miles really make that much difference in community standards?!

One important factor which has affected the law on pornography is the extent to which legislators, law enforcement officers, and courts believe that it causes harm to the general population. For evidence, they have often turned to social science, and found a mixture of data and conclusions. Some empirical research in the late 1960s indicated that pornography did little harm and led the Commission on Obscenity to issue a 1970 report which favored the availability of pornography to consenting adults, while keeping it from children and unconsenting adults (Kemp, 1974). Further studies in the 1970s tended to affirm those findings and were consistent with more liberal attitudes on the subject (Eysenck and Nias, 1978).

However, the studies detailed in Chapter 19 and the new feminist critique have led to a reevaluation of the question of the harm in pornography, especially the

[7]Perhaps the frustration of defining obscenity is best expressed by Justice Potter Stewart in *Jacobelis v. Ohio* (1964): "I shall not further attempt to define [hard-core pornography], and perhaps I could not ever succeed in intelligibly doing so. But I know it when I see it" (378 U.S. 197).

more violent kind. Some efforts have been made to put this opposition into law. In 1983, the Minneapolis City Council passed by one vote an ordinance defining certain kinds of pornography to be discriminatory against women and, therefore, illegal. The ordinance was vetoed by the mayor, but a simliar one was passed in Indianapolis a few weeks later. Such ordinances have not yet been tested in the courts, and it will be interesting to see how the idea fares.

Another rising concern is the problem of child pornography, which is widespread and damaging to the young people involved in it (Burgess, 1984). Efforts to stem the tide have not been very effective, but efforts are bound to continue. In the 1982 case of *New York v. Ferber,* the U.S. Supreme Court ruled unanimously that child pornography, whether or not it is obscene under the prevailing legal standards, is not protected by the Constitution. This decision gives states broader latitude in regulating child pornography, based on the state's right to protect children from abuse (Shewaga, 1983). The Court required states to be precise about whether they were proscribing the production, processing, or distribution of child pornography, and to develop clear definitions of what was to be outlawed. Another approach to the problem is to make tougher and more precise laws against child sexual abuse, without which child pornography could not be made. This approach would criminalize the making of child pornography and sidestep the more complicated constitutional issue of distribution and sale (Shouvlin, 1981).

The Supreme Court has not abandoned the Miller test, but the complexity of applying it, and the continuing debate over what is appropriate for Americans to read and view, will undoubtedly keep the matter of pornography, obscenity, and erotica controversial for some time to come.

The Controversy over Reproductive Freedom

An even more convulsive controversy is to be found in the matter of abortion. While the Supreme Court's decision in the Roe case was quite clear and has not been modified, it has been under continuous attack from several quarters, and it seems that the right of a woman to terminate an unwanted pregnancy is not absolute. Congressman Henry Hyde (no relation to the author of this text) has annually proposed a rider to the appropriation bill for the Department of Health and Human Services forbidding the expenditure of any federal money for abortions under Medicaid. The Court ruled the "Hyde amendment" constitutional in the 1980 case of *Harris v. McRae* and poor women have been denied this means of obtaining abortions (Milbauer, 1983).

Another challenge to the availability of abortions has been the introduction of state and municipal laws designed to make them more difficult or more unpleasant to obtain. These laws require parental consent for minors, waiting periods, or informed consent in which women contemplating an abortion are told that life begins at conception and are shown pictures of aborted fetuses. A model ordinance passed in Akron, Ohio, in 1978 permitted second trimester abortions to be done only in hospitals, required detailed "informed consent," mandated a 24-hour waiting period and a counseling session from a doctor, and permitted minors under age 15 to get an abortion only with parental consent or a court order. The Akron ordinance was struck down by a 6 to 3 decision of the Supreme Court in 1983, casting serious doubt on the viability of this antiabortion tactic (Mereson, 1983).

Informed consent: In law, the idea that people must be thoroughly informed about the risks and possible consequences of an action, such as a surgical procedure, so that they can give real consent for it.

With this strong reaffirmation of Roe by the Court, the battle has moved to the floor of Congress, where opponents of abortion have sought various ways to get around the decision. The most notable is the Human Life Amendment to the Constitution, which was defeated in the Senate in 1983, falling 18 votes short of the necessary two-thirds majority. Antiabortion organizations, which prefer to be called

FIGURE 23.4

Jerry Falwell, leader of the Moral Majority, with President Reagan.

"prolife" are well organized and well financed and not likely to give up the fight. They have proved to be an effective lobbying force and have been instrumental in the defeat of a number of legislators who have not supported their cause. They have had a powerful ally in Ronald Reagan, and in the Republican party whose 1980 and 1984 platforms have opposed abortion and called for the passage of the Human Life Amendment. The emphasis on this issue in the 1984 campaign points to continuing, vigorous political controversy over abortion.

A more moderate attack on Roe would eliminate "abortion on demand" but allow it in certain cases. This is the situation in Canada, where abortion has been legal since 1969, but only if it is done (1) in an accredited hospital, (2) with the approval of an abortion committee composed of physicians, and (3) to protect the life or health of the woman. The law does not permit freestanding abortion clinics, but only hospital abortions. However, hospitals are not required to have abortions committees and many do not, which means that few hospitals perform abortions. Since women's "health" is not defined in the law, it may be interpreted restrictively. The effect of these limitations is to make a legal abortion difficult and time consuming to obtain (Morgentaler, 1982).[8]

Some members of the New Right have also attacked other aspects of reproductive freedom. Efforts have been made to eliminate or weaken the funding of family planning organizations by Title X federal funds. One such effort was the so-called squeal rule of 1983. This was a proposed regulation by the Department of Health and Human Services that would have required all federally funded family planning clinics to notify the parents of young people, age 17 and younger, who were given contraceptives. Implementation of the squeal rule was blocked by federal courts in New York and Washington, D. C.

THE FUTURE OF SEX-LAW REFORM

When the first edition of this book was written, it seemed reasonable to assume that reform and revision of sex laws would continue. The right to privacy would even-

[8]Dr. Henry Morgentaler, who has established freestanding abortion clinics in defiance of Canadian law, served a jail sentence for doing so in Quebec, and at this writing is on trial in both Ontario and Manitoba for attempting to establish abortion clinics in those provinces.

tually be extended to homosexual actions; sexual orientation would be increasingly protected by decision and statute; criminal-code revision would continue, quietly dropping sodomy and related offenses from the books; abortion, prostitution, and pornography would be debated, but with less force and fervor. Or so it seemed. However, the prospect for the 1980s seems very different. It may well be proved that the peak of sex-law reform was reached in the previous decade and that a reaction has been provoked which will limit further reform, and perhaps reverse some of what has occurred. The so-called New Right, with its powerful allies in the conservative evangelical sector of the religious community, claims to have scored a great victory in the 1980 election. At the top of its agenda for change, this political force includes the very issues we have considered, especially abortion, homosexuality, pornography, and other perceived threats to the family and public morality.

It seems quite possible, at this writing, that the right to privacy has been taken as far in the sexual sphere as it is likely to go for some time. Although some legal scholars have seen in the right to privacy a means of decriminalizing all adult consensual sexual behavior, the Supreme Court has declined the opportunity do so. Legislative grants of protection to sexual minorities have not fared well, either. With increasingly conservative state legislatures and the prospect of a Supreme Court made much less progressive by Reagan appointees, we may well see a halt to the extension of the right to privacy in sexual matters.

It is likewise to be questioned whether the notion of "victimless crimes" will be persuasive in the future. A significant segment of U.S. society seems determined to use the law to enforce morality, and in such a climate the decriminalization of prostitution and other such acts may not be possible. Further efforts to control pornography are probable as well. All of this illustrates the point made at the beginning of this chapter. Law reflects the tensions, conflicts, and ambiguities of a society in the area of values. Sexuality is value-laden and full of conflicts. Unless there is a greater degree of consensus in our society over the proper role and value of sexuality, legislatures and courts are likely to be battlefields for opposing views and concerns.

SUMMARY

It is reasonable to suggest that laws to protect adults from coercion, children from sexual exploitation, and the public from offensive behavior are justifiable. However, many laws against sexual conduct originated in a desire to promote public morality and perpetuate sexism, and it is hard to justify them.

The laws governing sexual conduct are concerned with crimes of exploitation and force (such as rape, carnal knowledge of a juvenile, and child molestation), various consensual acts (such as fornication, adultery, sodomy, and other "unnatural acts"), laws which discriminate against gays, offenses against public taste (exhibitionism, voyeurism, solicitation, disorderly conduct, lewdness, and the like), crimes against procreation (contraception and abortion), and criminal commercial sex (notably prostitution and obscenity). These laws are often capriciously enforced, and this unequal enforcement has high social costs which may require reform.

Certain trends can be discerned in the reform of such sex laws. The British Wolfenden report and the American Model Penal Code are early examples of proposals to decriminalize much sexual behavior. The legal principle which has accounted for much court action to reform laws against contraception and abortion is the "right to privacy," which has not yet been broadened to include consensual acts by adults. A factor which has influenced legislators, and will probably continue to do so, is the movement for the decriminalization of "victimless crimes." The issue of pornography and obscenity, which includes such problems as definition, conflicting societal values, and actual demonstration of effects, is a confusing one. Abortion remains a volatile and highly controversial matter. Sex-law reform may move more slowly in the 1980s than it did in the previous decade.

REVIEW QUESTIONS

1. The regulation of sexual conduct by law is a fairly new development in American history. True or false?
2. Until recently a husband could not be prosecuted for raping his wife. True or false?
3. By and large, the law allows consenting adults to do in private whatever they want to do. True or false?
4. Laws which, in theory, may apply to many forms of sexual conduct, but which are usually only enforced against homosexuals, are ____ laws.
5. An illegal police tactic frequently used to arrest prostitutes and gays is ____.
6. A number of sex laws have been removed from the statute books by the appeal to the right of privacy or the appropriateness of eliminating victimless crimes. True or false?
7. In legal terms, what is often called pornography is not protected by the Constitution if it can be shown to be ____.
8. Liberal laws on pornography and obscenity have recently been attacked by feminists and those seeking greater protection for children and juveniles. True or false?
9. The Supreme Court has recently undercut the right to abortion which it recognized in the case of *Roe v. Wade.* True or false?
10. The reform of sex laws and the extension of the right of privacy are likely to continue in the future with little controversy. True or false?

QUESTIONS FOR THOUGHT, DISCUSSION, AND DEBATE

1. Find out what sort of laws relate to sexual activity in the state in which you live or go to school. Are there any moves to change those laws?
2. What aspects of human sexuality do you think it is reasonable for the law to regulate?
3. How do you think children can best be protected from sexual abuse and exploitation?

SUGGESTIONS FOR FURTHER READING

Boggan, E. C., Haft, M. G., Lister, D., Rupp, J. H., and Stoddard, T. B. (1983). *The rights of gay people.* (Revised ed.) New York: Bantam Books. Prepared by the American Civil Liberties Union, this is a comprehensive review of the legal problems faced by homosexuals. It also includes a good deal about laws affecting a wide variety of sexual behaviors.

Great Britain Committee on Homosexual Offenses and Prostitution. (1963). *The Wolfenden report.* (American ed.) New York: Stein and Day. Barnett, W. (1973). *Sexual freedom and the Constitution.* Albuquerque: University of New Mexico Press. The classic works—English and American, respectively—which argue for extensive reform of sex laws.

MacNamara, Donal E. J. and Sagarin, Edward. (1977). *Sex, crime and the law.* New York: The Free Press. A systematic treatment of the whole spectrum of sex laws, with discussion of the rationale behind them and possibilities for their reform.

Milbauer, Barbara. (1983). *The law giveth: Legal aspects of the abortion controversy.* New York: Atheneum. A fascinating and detailed account of the issue of abortion in the courts and legislatures.

Balthus: *The Living Room*, 1942. Collection, The Museum of Modern Art, New York.

CHAPTER • 24

SEX EDUCATION

A little girl was taking a shower with her mother. She looked up at her mother, and said, "Mommy, why am I so plain, and you're so fancy?"*

* *Source:* Rosemary Zumwalt. (1976). Plain and fancy: A content analysis of children's jokes dealing with adult sexuality. *Western Folklore,* **35**, p. 258.

CHAPTER HIGHLIGHTS

Children are often curious about sex. That is perfectly normal and good, and it motivates them to learn. The only problem is that adults often do not know what to do about it. This chapter is about concepts and methods that are useful in sex education, both in a formal school curriculum and in informal sex education in the home or some other situation.

IN THE HOME, IN THE SCHOOL, OR SOMEWHERE ELSE?

When concerned parents get together and urge a school system to begin a sex education curriculum, invariably

TABLE 24.1

CHILDREN'S MAIN SOURCES OF SEXUAL INFORMATION

Source	Males, %	Females, %
Friends	59	46
Reading	20	22
Mother	3	16
Father	6	1
School program	3	5
Adults outside the home	6	4
Brothers, sisters	4	6
Others and no answer	7	7

Source: Morton Hunt. (1974). *Sexual behavior in the 1970s.* Chicago: Playboy Press, p. 122. Roughly similar results have been obtained by J. H. Gagnon (1965) and Athanasiou et al. (1970).

some upright citizens of the community raise a protest. They might say that sex education promotes promiscuity, communism, or some other disaster, and they are sure that it should take place only in the home (or possibly the church), but certainly not in the schools.

What these upright citizens overlook is the realistic alternative to sex education in the schools. For most children, the primary source of sex information in childhood is friends (see Table 24.1), and that is the classic case of the blind leading the blind. Mothers come in a poor third, and fathers even further down the list, as actual sources of sex information. Interestingly, young people would prefer to hear about sex from their parents (J. H. Gagnon, 1965b). But—although there are certainly exceptions—many parents handle their children's questions about sex by issuing orders rather than by having a discussion (Libby and Nass, 1971). The following comments from parents exemplify such attitudes toward sex education:

> "I try to keep them from knowing too much."
> "My parents did not tell me about it. I don't discuss it, either."
> "I just tell them to behave and keep their eyes open." (Libby and Nass, 1971, pp. 230, 233)

FIGURE 24.1

Although some parents claim that sex education belongs in the home, it rarely happens there effectively.

The fact is that many children are given no sex education in the home. Rather, they learn about sex in the street, and the result is a massive amount of misinformation. Thus, people who say that sex education should be carried out in the home, not in the school, are not making a sensible argument.

In fact, most parents favor sex education in the schools. According to a Gallup poll, 71 percent of parents are in favor of it (Breasted, 1970). Those who are opposed to sex education constitute a rather small group that makes a great deal of noise, leading one to overestimate their numbers.

Of course. the times are changing, and many of today's parents are precisely the people who participated in the sexual revolution of the 1960s and 1970s. Perhaps they will be better sex educators. But some experts feel these parents are still too unclear about their changing attitudes and lifestyles to be helpful to their children (Roberts et al., 1978).

EFFECTS OF SEX EDUCATION

One argument made by people opposed to sex education in the schools is that it leads to terrible consequences, particularly increases in premarital sex and promiscuity. Is there any scientific evidence backing this assertion? (For comprehensive reviews of the effects of sex education courses, see Voss, 1980; Kilmann et al., 1981).

In 1967 a national probability sample of 1177 college students were interviewed about their current sexual behavior and their previous sources of sex information (Spanier, 1976, 1977). The results indicated that having sex education in the schools had had little effect on the students' premarital sexual activity; current factors—such as dating patterns—seemed to be much more important influences (Spanier, 1976). Thus, the evidence does not support the contention that sex education encourages premarital sexual experimentation.

In contrast, there is evidence that responsible sex education may have a number of desirable effects. A large-scale study of numerous junior high and high school sex education programs indicated that students' knowledge of factual information about sex increased from the beginning to the end of the courses, and that the increased knowledge was maintained five months after the courses (Kirby, 1984). In another well-conducted survey of teenagers in metropolitan areas, those who had had sex education were no more nor less likely to have had sexual intercourse than those who had not had sex education; but sexually active young women who had had sex education were less likely to have become pregnant than sexually active young women who had not had sex education (Zelnik and Kim, 1982). Finally, the institution of sex education programs in schools has been reported to reduce the incidence of gonorrhea by as much as 50 percent in a year's time (M. I. Levine, 1970).

PURPOSES OF SEX EDUCATION

SIECUS: The Sex Information and Education Council of the United States, an organization devoted to fostering sex education.

The Sex Information and Education Council of the United States (SIECUS), under the leadership of Dr. Mary Calderone, has been one of the most active groups promoting quality sex education. According to SIECUS, the goals of sex education should be:

1. To provide for the individual an adequate knowledge of his or her own physical, mental, and emotional maturation processes as related to sex.
2. To eliminate fears and anxieties relative to individual sexual development and adjustments.

3. To develop objective and understanding attitudes toward sex in all of its various manifestations—in the individual and in others.
4. To give the individual insight concerning her or his relationships to members of both genders and to help him or her understand their obligations and responsibilities to others.
5. To provide an appreciation of the positive satisfaction that wholesome human relations can bring in both individual and family living.
6. To build an understanding of the need for the moral values that are essential to provide rational bases for making decisions.
7. To provide enough knowledge about the misuses and aberrations of sex to enable individuals to protect themselves against exploitation and against injury to their physical or mental health.
8. To provide an incentive to work for a society in which such evils as prostitution and illegitimacy, archaic sex laws, irrational fears of sex, and sexual exploitation are nonexistent.
9. To provide the understanding and conditioning that will enable each individual to use his or her sexuality effectively and creatively in the several roles of spouse, parent, community member, and citizen. (Kirkendall, 1965)

I couldn't have said it better myself.

THE TEACHER

Suppose you have decided to start a program of sex education. Whether it is to be carried out in the school, in the home, or someplace else, the first thing you need is a teacher. What qualifications should this person have?[1]

First, the person should be fairly well educated in sexual matters. Reading a text such as this one or taking a university course in sexuality would be a good way to acquire the knowledge that is needed. But do not assume that a teacher has to have a Ph.D. in sex; the important qualifications are a good basic knowledge, a willingness to admit when he or she does not know the answer, and the patience to look things up (and a knowledge of where to look).

Equally important is the teacher's comfort with sexual topics. Even when parents or other adults willingly give accurate factual information to children about sex, they may still convey negative attitudes because they become anxious or blush while answering the child's questions or because they use euphemisms rather than direct sexual terms. Thus, it is important for the teacher to feel relaxed and comfortable in discussing sex. Some people are that way; others must work to learn this attitude. There are a number of ways to do this. For example, the teacher can role-play, with another adult, having sexual discussions with children. Comfort is gained with practice.

A good teacher is also a good listener who can assess what the child knows from the questions asked and who can understand what a child really wants to know when she or he asks a question. According to a joke, little Billy ran into the kitchen in his home one day after kindergarten and asked his mother where he had come from; she gritted her teeth, realized the time had come, and proceeded with a 15-minute discussion of intercourse, conception, and birth, blushing the whole time. Billy lis-

---

[1]The American Association of Sex Educators, Counselors, and Therapists is a good professional organization that can provide further information. See the Appendix at the back of this book for addresses and telephone numbers.

FIGURE 24.2

The use of the condom is explained in a sex education class in Kingston, Jamaica. The teenage pregnancy rate in Jamaica dropped by 80 percent two years after this sex education program was initiated.

tened, but at the end he appeared somewhat confused and walked away shaking his head and saying, "That's funny. Jimmy says he came from Illinois."

WHAT TO TEACH AT DIFFERENT AGES

Sex education is not something that can be carried out all at once in one week during fifth grade. Like teaching math, it is a process that must begin when children are small. They should learn simple concepts first, progressing to more difficult ones as they grow older. What one teaches at any particular age depends on the child's sexual behavior (see Chapter 11), sexual knowledge, and sexual interests at that age. This section will concentrate on theories and research that provide information on these last two points.

A Theoretical View: Piaget

Preartificialistic stage: According to Piaget, a stage in which preschool children believe that a baby has always existed and only wonder where it was before it came to their house.

Artificialistic stage: According to Piaget, a stage during which children (usually of elementary school age) know that a baby must be created but think it can be done in artificial ways as one might make a doll.

Naturalistic stage: According to Piaget, the stage at which children have a good biological understanding of how a baby is created; the shift to this stage usually occurs around age 12 or later.

The Swiss psychologist Jean Piaget believed that children are all little philosophers, constructing their own views of the universe that make sense; thus they pass through various stages of cognitive (intellectual) development during which they have different understandings of natural events.

Piaget believed that during the earliest phases of understanding about reproduction, at about ages 3 to 5, children are in a preartificialistic stage (Moore and Kendall, 1971). At this age, children believe that a baby, such as a little brother or sister, has always existed. They have no notion that something might have caused or created its existence. Instead, they only wonder where (geographically) the baby was before it was in their house.

In the second stage, children have artificialistic concepts of reproduction and believe that parents cause the creation of babies, although they may have bizarre ways of explaining how parents do this, as some of the following examples will show. This stage lasts from perhaps age 6 to age 11.

Finally, in the naturalistic stage, children come to have a more and more scientific understanding of processes involved in reproduction.

Children's Sex Knowledge

A few researchers have investigated what children know about sex and reproduction at various ages.

In one study, Israeli children aged 4 to 5½ were questioned about sex and reproduction (Kreitler and Kreitler, 1966). About 60 percent of the children could describe the sex organs of the opposite gender. More than 90 percent knew that a baby came from the mother's enlarged belly. But when asked what the mother does in order to get a baby, many of them responded that she must eat a lot or that she swallows a baby. These answers are reminiscent of Freud's notions. Only about 2 percent of the boys and one of the girls mentioned intercourse.

When the children were asked how the baby gets out, most said that the mother's belly had to be cut open. One wonders what the effects are when children hold such an alarming view of birth.

The children also were asked how the father helps in this process. Their answers typically involved things like feeding the mother, earning money, and helping the mother, once again demonstrating that they had no knowledge of intercourse.

One other interesting point emerged from this study. Some of the children were of European and American ancestry, while others were of non-Western ancestry (North African or Arab, for example). The sex knowledge of the children from these two groups differed greatly, with the Western children generally knowing considerably more. For example, 77 percent of the Western boys, but only 40 percent of the non-Western boys, could describe the sex organs of the opposite gender. This shows how much children's sex knowledge depends on their home environment.

This study was repeated in the United States with children aged 3 to 5½ (Moore and Kendall, 1971). The authors particularly noted the children's poor sexual vocabulary. When asked where the urine comes out, about half of the boys had a label ("penis" or some other word), compared with only 14 percent of the girls.[2] Thus many children did not know the correct names of the sexual organs. One wonders what the long-term effects of this lack of vocabulary might be—whether, for example, it might hinder people from communicating about sexual matters in adulthood. Most authorities in the field recommend that children be taught accurate labels from the first; it is, after all, just as easy to teach children to say "penis" as it is to teach them to say "peter."

As was true of the Israeli children, almost none of the children in this study knew about intercourse. When asked what a mother must do in order to have a baby, many gave responses like "go to the doctor" and "go to the hospital." Only 6 percent knew that the father had a role in reproduction, and only one child used the word "intercourse."

Stages of Understanding

Psychologist Anne Bernstein (1976; Bernstein and Cowan, 1975) has investigated children's understanding of reproduction, basing her research on Piaget's idea that children go through various stages in their understanding. She found that children do proceed through the following levels (stages) of understanding about reproduction.

---

[2]It occurs to me that it is probably not easy for girls to come up with such a label; probably "vulva" would be the most accurate.

F · O · C · U · S 24.1

ARE AMERICAN CHILDREN SEXUAL ILLITERATES?

Ronald and Juliette Goldman (1982) did a massive cross-cultural study of children's understanding of sexual matters. From their results, they concluded that American children are sexual illiterates.

The Goldmans did face-to-face interviews with children aged 5, 7, 9, 11, 13, and 15 in four different cultures: Australia, England, North America. and Sweden. A total of 838 children were interviewed. The Swedish sample is particularly interesting because there is compulsory sex education for all children in Swedish schools, beginning at age 8. It is also worth noting that the North American sample was originally planned to be a United States sample, but school officials in the United States were so uncooperative that the Goldmans had to go across the border from upstate New York to Canada (where they obtained more cooperation) in order to complete the sample.

The Goldmans were careful to avoid controversial topics such as homosexuality in the interview, and they questioned children only about their understanding of sexual concepts, not about their sexual behavior. They called the study "Children's Concepts of Development." These precautions were taken in order to produce a high rate of cooperation from parents. Parents in general were cooperative; only 20 percent of parents overall refused to allow their children to participate.

A comparison of the results from the North American children with those from children in the other three cultures led the Goldmans to conclude that the American children are strikingly lacking in sexual information. Some of the results are shown in Table 24.2. Notice, for example, that only 23 percent of North American 9-year-olds, but 60 percent of Austra-

LEVEL 1: GEOGRAPHY Most 3- to 4-year-olds believe that a baby has always existed and may believe that it was located somewhere else (geographically) before it got inside the mother. The following is an example of the responses of a Level 1 child:

> (How did the baby happen to be in your Mommy's tummy?) It just grows inside. (How did it get there?) It's there all the time. Mommy doesn't have to do anything. She waits until she feels it. (You said that the baby wasn't in there when you were there.) Yeah, then he was in the other place . . . in America. (In America?) Yeah, in somebody else's tummy. (Bernstein and Cowan, 1975, p. 86)

LEVEL 2: MANUFACTURING At around age 4, children begin to understand that something causes babies to come into existence. However, they think a manufacturing process is involved, as in the production of a refrigerator or a TV. A Level 2 child described how people get babies as follows:

TABLE 24.2

RESPONSES OF 9-YEAR-OLDS IN FOUR CULTURES IN THE GOLDMAN STUDY

Concept	Percent of Correct Answers Among			
	Australians	British	North Americans	Swedish
Knowing physical sex differences of newborn babies	60	35	23	40
Knowing correct terms for the genitals	50	33	20	*
Knowing length of gestation is 8 to 10 months	35	32	30	67
Knowing that one purpose of coitus is enjoyment	6	10	4	60
Knowing the meaning of the term "uterus"	0	0	0	23

*Owing to the difficulties of translating from the Swedish language, this percentage is not available.

Source: Ronald Goldman and Juliette Goldman. (1982). *Children's sexual thinking.* London: Routledge & Kegan Paul, pp. 197, 213, 240, 263, 354.

lian 9-year-olds, know the genital differences between newborn baby boys and girls. The Swedish children are consistently more knowledgeable than the American children, indicating the positive effects of sex education.

Some of the children's responses can only be classified as amusing. In response to the question "How can anyone know a newborn baby is a boy or a girl?" an 11-year-old English boy said, "If it's got a penis or not. If it has it's a boy. Girls have a virginia." And in all cultures there seems to be a lot of confusion about contraception. Hear are some responses:

The pill goes down the stomach and dissolves the baby and it goes out in the bowels. You should take three pills a day. (American boy, 7 years old)

If you don't want to start one, you don't get married. There's no other way. (English girl, 7 years old)

The tubes are tied, the vocal cords. (Australian girl, 15 years old)

If the Goldmans' conclusion is right, that American children are sexual illiterates, the remedy seems to be a massive program of sex education in the United States.

Source: Ronald Goldman and Juliette Goldman. (1982). *Children's sexual thinking.* London: Routledge & Kegan Paul.

Maybe they just paint the right bones. . . . Maybe they just paint the bones and paint the blood, and paint the blue blood. . . . (Bernstein and Cowan, 1975, p. 86)

LEVEL 3: TRANSITIONAL By age 7 or 8, children explain reproduction as a mixture of technology and physiology, but they stick to feasible occurrences. They no longer think that the mother opens up her tummy to let the baby out. Level 3 children may know that three things are involved in making a baby: a social relationship between two people, such as love or marriage; sexual intercourse; and the union of sperm and egg.

The combination of manufacturing ideas and biology ideas is illustrated by a Level 3 child's explanation of why the male's contribution is necessary:

Well, the father puts the shell. I forget what it's called, but he puts something in for the egg. If he didn't then a baby couldn't come. Because it needs the stuff that the father

F · O · C · U · S 24.2

QUESTIONS CHILDREN ASK ABOUT SEX

The following are typical questions that children ask at various ages:

THE PRIMARY GRADES

What is being born?
Where was I before I was born?
Why can't I have a baby?
Did I come from an egg?
Why can't I marry Daddy?

THE INTERMEDIATE GRADES

How do babies start?
How does the sperm get into the egg?
How can you tell if the baby will be a boy or a girl?
Do boys menstruate?
When are we old enough to mate?
Can you have a baby when you are 13 years old?
Does it hurt to have a baby?
Why do mothers nurse their babies?
Can a boy have a baby?
Do you menstruate the rest of your life once you start?

SEVENTH, EIGHTH, AND NINTH GRADES

About Dating

Is it bad or good to go steady?
Do you have to have a sense of humor to be popular?
What do you do if you're chicken to ask a girl to go on a date?
What do boys look for in a girl?

> gives. It helps it grow. I think that the stuff has the food part, maybe, and maybe it helps protect it. I think he gives the shell part, and the shell part, I think, is the skin. (Bernstein, 1976, p. 34)

In Piaget's terms, these children are in a transitional phase between the preoperational and the concrete operational stages of thought.

LEVEL 4: CONCRETE PHYSIOLOGY Level 4 and the successive levels are qualitatively different from the previous ones because children now have an understanding of the physical facts of life and of the importance of sperm and egg. At Levels 4, 5, and 6, they come increasingly closer to scientific understandings.

Though Level 4 children know about egg and sperm, they may not know why they have to unite. An 8-year-old said:

About Petting

Terms: What is petting; what is necking?
On a date, is it customary to kiss the girl after the date? If so, under what conditions should you do it?
How do you French-kiss a girl?
What should a girl do or say if her boyfriend wants to have sexual intercourse with her and she doesn't, but she still wants to keep him as a boyfriend?

About Terminology

What do these mean: nude, boner, queer, womb, testes, circumcise?

About Growth and Development

Is there any limit to a boy's sperm?
Is it milk in the girl's breast? Is the vagina between the girl's legs?
What does semen look like?
Does a girl ever have a wet dream?
Why does a boy's penis get hard and stiff when he gets sexually emotional?

About Menstruation

When do you start?
What is a period?
Why do some girls start menstruation later or earlier than others?
When girls start to menstruate, do they need Kotex?
Why are girls using Tampax?

About Masturbation

Is it bad for boys to masturbate?
What is masturbation?
Do all boys masturbate, and at what age?

About Homosexuality

Are there such things as homosexual women?
What is the difference between homosexuals, lesbians, and queers?

About Sexual Intercourse

Can boys possibly go to the bathroom during the time they make a woman pregnant? What position are the man and woman in when the man makes the woman pregnant?
Does sexual intercourse hurt?
What does "sexual intercourse" mean?

TENTH, ELEVENTH, AND TWELFTH GRADES

What is prostitution?
Is "making love" to a person the same as sexual intercourse?
What is an orgasm?
What is a virgin?

Source: Esther D. Schulz and Sally R. Williams. (1969). *Family life and sex education: Curriculum and instruction.* New York: Harcourt Brace & World. See also Ruth V. Byler. (1969). *Teach us what we want to know.* New York: Mental Health Materials Center, for the Connecticut State Board of Education.

> The man and the woman get together, and then they put a speck, then the man has his seed and the woman has an egg. They have to come together or else the baby won't really get hatched very well. The seed makes the egg grow. It's just like plants. If you plant a seed, a flower will grow. (Bernstein, 1976, p. 34)

LEVEL 5: PREFORMATION At level 5, children (usually 11- or 12-year-olds) believe that the baby already exists (is preformed) in either the sperm or the egg. They think that the other germ cell or intercourse simply makes conditions suitable for the baby to grow. For example:

> Well, if they're the man that made love to your mother, then your father because you really originally came out of him, and then went into your mother. Well, you were a

DENNIS the MENACE

"THAT'S FUNNY... MY DAD CAN TELL IF IT'S A BOY OR A GIRL JUST BY LOOKIN' AT THE BOTTOM OF ITS FEET."

FIGURE 24.3

Children often have inaccurate ideas about sex.

> sperm inside of him, there. So that you're the, you're really his daughter or son. 'Cause he was the one that really had you first. (Why must the egg be there for the sperm to develop into a baby?) 'Cause otherwise the sperm will have, uh, nothing to nourish it, or sort of keep it warm or, you know, able to move or something. Just has, it's not, just has to have the egg to be able to do something, develop. It just dies if it doesn't have the egg. (Bernstein and Cowan, 1975, p. 89)

LEVEL 6: PHYSICAL CAUSALITY Level 6 children, who are generally 12 or older, give a good physiological explanation of reproduction that includes the idea that the embryo begins its biological existence at the moment of conception and that it is the product of genetic material from both parents. A Level 6 child said:

> The sperm encounters one ovum, and one sperm breaks into the ovum which produces, the sperm makes like a cell, and the cell separates and divides. And so it's dividing, and the ovum goes through a tube and embeds itself in the wall of the, I think it's the fetus of the woman. (Bernstein and Cowan, 1975, p. 89)

Bernstein's findings have important implications for sex education (Bernstein, 1976). Educators should be aware of the level of the child's understanding and should not inundate him or her with information appropriate for a child three or four levels higher. Instead, there should be an attempt to clarify misunderstandings inherent in the child's beliefs. For example, a Level 1 child believes that a baby has always existed. To such a child, you might say, "To make a baby person, you need two grown-up persons, one a man and one a woman." To the Level 2 child, who believes that babies are manufactured, you might say, "That's an interesting way of looking at things. That's the way you'd make a doll. You would buy a head and some hair and put it all together. But making a real, live baby is different from making a doll or a cake or an airplane" (Bernstein, 1976, p. 35).

Children's Questions about Sex

Children's knowledge of and interest in sex are reflected in the questions they ask. In a study of children's questions about sex, it was found that many questions are asked at around age 5, a time when children are generally asking questions. Boys also tended to ask a lot of questions at around age 9, and girls at ages 9 and 13 (Byler, 1969; Hattendorf, 1932). The areas of sexual curiosity were (beginning with the most common) the origin of babies, the coming of another baby, intrauterine growth, the process of birth, the organs and functions of the body, physical gender differences, the relation of the father to reproduction, and marriage.

Sex educators have found that children tend to ask typical questions at various ages. A sampling of such questions is given in Focus 24.2.

Children's Dirty Jokes

We can also tell something about children's sexual knowledge and interest by the dirty jokes they tell.

Anthropologist Rosemary Zumwalt collected dirty jokes from girls between the ages of 7 and 10 as part of her study of children's folklore (1976). The following is typical of the jokes they told her:

> There's this little boy, and he wanted to take a bath with his dad. And his dad said, "If you promise not to look under the curtain." And then he took a shower, and he looked under the curtain. And he said, "Dad, what's that long hairy thing?" And the father says, "That's my banana."
>
> Then he asks his mom, "Can I take a shower with you, Mom?" She says, "If you promise not to look under the curtain." And they get into the shower, and he looks under the curtain. And he says, "Mom, what's that thing?" And she says, "That's my fruit bowl." And he says, "Mom, can I sleep with you and Dad?" And she says, "Yes, if you promise not to look under the covers." And he looks under the covers and says, "Mom, Dad's banana is in your fruit bowl!" (Zumwalt, 1976, p. 261)

Children's dirty jokes reflect several themes in their attitudes toward sexuality and in their interactions with their parents on the issue. First, children seem to view their parents as always trying to keep sex—such as nudity and sexual organs—a secret from them. The parents consistently tell children not to look under the cover, for example. Second, the jokes reflect children's fascination with sex, particularly with the penis, the vagina, the breasts, and intercourse. The jokes generally revolve around these topics and children's attempts to find out about them. Third, the jokes seem to satirize adults' use of euphemisms for sexual terms. The joke above hinges on a parent's using a term such as "banana" instead of "penis." Most frequently, the fanciful names used for the sexual organs involve food (banana, hot dog), power (light bulbs, light sockets), or animals (gorilla). Commenting on the bathtub-shower form of dirty joke, an authority said, "In all forms of the . . . joke, the wonderful humor to the child is the mocking of the parents' evasions, which are somehow so foolishly phrased. . ." (Legman, 1968, p. 53).

Teenagers have outgrown this sort of joke, but they tell a parallel one:

> This little boy walks into the bathroom, and he catches his mother naked. She was a little embarrassed. He said, "Mommy, what's that?" And she says, "Oh, that's where God hit me with an axe." And the little kid says, "Got you right in the cunt, eh?" (Zumwalt, 1976, p. 267)

Once again, this joke has the theme of a parent's embarrassment and use of evasions and euphemisms when dealing with sex. But now the child (teenager) reflects a sophistication about sex, perhaps even a greater sophistication than the parent has.

Sex educators should remember that children are aware of adults' attempts to "cover up" and of their embarrassment and their use of euphemisms, as these jokes indicate.

F · O · C · U · S 24.3

A SAMPLE SEX EDUCATION CURRICULUM

CONCEPTS TO BE LEARNED AT THE DIFFERENT GRADE LEVELS

Kindergarten and Grade 1

1. Use of correct terminology, such as "penis" and "breast"
2. Respecting the privacy and rights of others, such as privacy in the bathroom
3. The arrival of a new baby as a happy occasion
4. Safety going to and from school; what to do if offered a ride by a stranger

Grades 2 and 3

1. Understanding human growth and development
2. Understanding feelings (emotions), both one's own and those of others; understanding feelings of love and affection
3. Understanding how families and the community help each other

Grade 4

1. Body structures and functions, such as the circulatory system and the excretory system
2. Heredity
3. Being a good family member
4. Being a good friend
5. Growing up emotionally; acceptable ways to get rid of anger

Grade 5

1. Growth patterns and rates of development; the changes of puberty
2. Changes in the male and female reproductive organs

CURRICULUM

Space does not permit outlining a complex sex education curriculum here. Instead, a brief outline of major concepts to be covered in one major curriculum is given in Focus 24.3. Further references to curriculum materials are provided at the end of this chapter in "Suggestions for Further Reading."

Note that the sample curriculum in the Focus exemplifies several principles. First, sex education must be carried out at all grade levels. It cannot be accomplished all at once in a week (or a day) during the fifth or sixth grade. Curriculum materials are therefore geared to the age of the child and build on each other from year to year. For example, by the time conception and intercourse are discussed in

3. The baby, including embryonic development and birth
4. Good health habits
5. Living with parents and friends while growing up

Grade 6

1. Structure and function of cells
2. Emotions, including acceptability of "gender-inappropriate" emotions, such as crying by a boy
3. Sexual anatomy and hormones

Grade 7

1. Understanding one's personality and emotions; attraction to members of the opposite gender
2. Family structures in the United States, including families in which the mother holds a job outside the home and single-parent families
3. Male and female reproductive processes

Grade 8

1. Emotions, including the development of the sex drive and the need to control it
2. Dating, including necking and petting and problems related to dating
3. Continued discussion of the family
4. Review of the female and male reproductive processes

Grade 9

1. Mental and emotional health
2. Family relationships, including the development of independence and sound judgments
3. Boy-girl relationships, including dating, going steady, necking, and petting; understanding the meaning of the terms "sexual intercourse," "sexual relations," "premarital relations," and "premarital intercourse"

Grades 10 and 11

1. Psychosocial development; personality
2. Boy-girl relationships in light of both immediate and long-range goals
3. Family planning
4. Growth and reproduction

Grade 12

1. Preparation for marriage
2. Adjustments in marriage; potential problems
3. Planning for parenthood
4. Family living
5. Attitudes toward sex and sexual behavior; different value systems

Source: Growth patterns and sex education. *The Journal of School Health,* May 1967, pp. 1–136.

grade 6 or 7, the child is already familiar with parts of the anatomy and understands terms such as "penis," "vagina," and "uterus." Second, correct terminology should be taught from the beginning. Even children in kindergarten and first grade should learn terms such as "penis" and "vagina."[3] Third, the curriculum should reflect the

[3]The use of euphemisms and analogies by adults can cause children to have somewhat confused understandings of sex. One 4-year-old girl, when asked how a lady would get a baby to grow in her tummy, responded, "Get a duck." As it turns out, one widely distributed sex education book for children begins with a pencil dot (representing an ovum) and then proceeds through the sex lives of flowers, bees, rabbits, giraffes, chickens, and dogs before getting to humans. No wonder the little girl thought that in order to have a baby, you have to begin with a duck (Bernstein, 1976).

need to teach children about the emotional and social aspects of sex—such as dealing with sexual feelings and going on dates—as well as the biological aspects. These are important principles for any sex education curriculum.

SUMMARY

Most children receive their sex education from their peers, not from their parents; as a result, those who argue for sex education in the home rather than in the school are not being realistic. Most Americans actually do favor sex education in the school. Further, the presumed negative effects of sex education are not substantiated by the available data.

The purposes of sex education include providing children with an adequate knowledge of the physical and emotional aspects of sex and eliminating unwarranted fears and anxieties.

A good instructor in sex eduation must have some accurate knowledge about sex, must be comfortable discussing it, and must be good at listening to children's questions.

What one teaches in sex education at each age depends on what children are thinking about at that age. Acording to Piaget, children pass through various stages in their understanding of sex. First, they believe that a baby has always existed. Later they realize that the parents caused the baby's creation, though they have little idea of exactly how. Older children acquire a more and more scientific understanding of reproduction.

Children aged 4 to 5½ believe that eating something has to do with pregnancy and that birth may be accomplished by cutting open the mother's belly. Children generally do not know the correct names of the sexual organs. American children have a relatively poor understanding of sexual concepts.

Children's dirty jokes reflect their parents' attempts to hide sex from them, their parents' use of euphemisms rather than accurate terms, and their great fascination with sexual organs and intercourse.

REVIEW QUESTIONS

1. For most children, the major source of sex information is the mother. True or false?
2. Approximately 35 percent of American parents favor sex education in the schools. True or false?
3. Research on the effects of sex education indicates that those teenagers who had sex education in high school are more likely to engage in premarital intercourse and have a higher incidence of premarital pregnancies. True or false?
4. According to Piaget, children around the ages of 3 to 5 are in a preartificialistic stage in which they believe that a baby has always existed and only wonder where it was before it came to their house. True or false?
5. On the basis of their research, the Goldmans argue that North American children are sexual illiterates who possess less sexual knowledge than their counterparts in other cultures such as Australia and Sweden. True or false?
6. According to Bernstein's research on children's stages of understanding about sexual intercourse and conception, most children do not have a good physiological understanding until they reach Stage 6, when they are 12 years of age or older. True or false?
7. Analyses of children's dirty jokes indicate that children realize their parents try to keep sex a secret from them. True or false?

QUESTIONS FOR THOUGHT, DISCUSSION, AND DEBATE

1. Design a sample sex education curriculum for the schools, indicating what you think would be important to teach at various age levels and what your reasoning is behind your choices.
2. Debate the following topic. Resolved: A sex education unit, at least a week long, should be included in all grades in all schools.

SUGGESTIONS FOR FURTHER READING

Calderone, Mary S., and Ramey, James W. (1983). *Talking with your child about sex: Questions and answers for children from birth to puberty.* New York: Random House. An excellent guide for parents. Mary Calderone is one of America's leading sex educators.

Carpenter, George R. and Carpenter, Ann. (1975). *Babies come from people.* Salt Lake City, Utah: Coldstream. A good book for preschoolers. I used it with my three-year-old, preparing her for the arrival of her baby brother. She enjoyed it enormously and then "read" it to all her friends.

Fischer, H. L., Krajicek, M. J., and Borthick, W. A. (1973). *Sex education for the developmentally disabled.* Baltimore: University Park Press. Retarded children need sex education just as much as other children do, and this book provides a guide.

Gordon, Sol. (1975). *Let's make sex a household word: A guide for parents and children.* New York: John Day.

Growth patterns and sex education. *The Journal of School Health,* May 1967, 1–136. The whole issue is devoted to providing a detailed sex education curriculum for kindergarten through grade 12 (portions of which were summarized in Focus 24.3).

Mayle, P., Robins, A., and Walter, P. (1973) *Where did I come from?* Secaucus, N.J.: Lyle Stuart. A delightful sex education book for young children. Its companion volume—*What's happening to me?*—is for children approaching puberty.

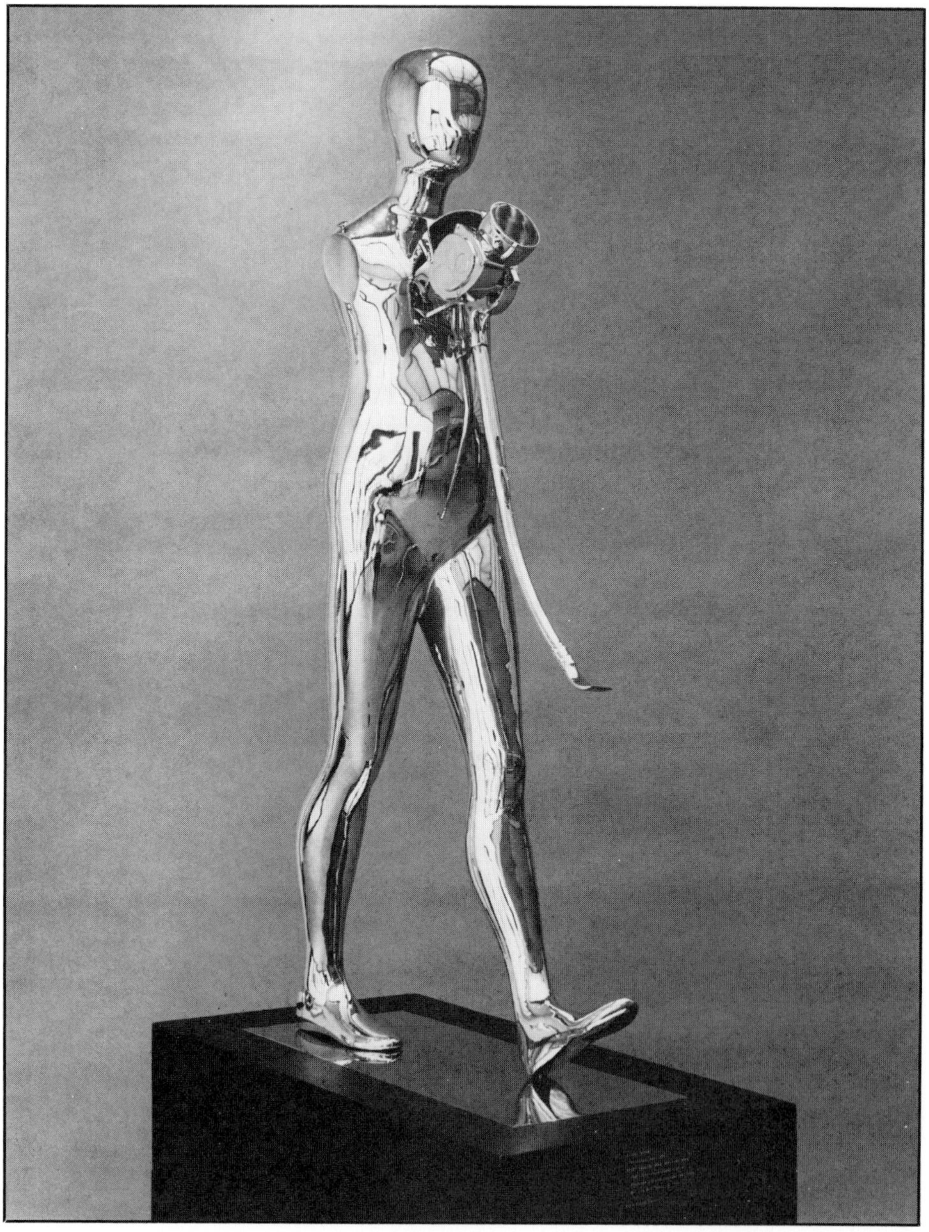

Ernest Trova: *Study from Falling Man Series: Walking Man*, 1964. Collection, The Museum of Modern Art, New York.

CHAPTER • 25

SEXUALITY IN THE FUTURE

We study the future the better to understand a present that will not stand still for inspection.*

*Source: Marshall McLuhan and George B. Leonard. (1974). The future of sex. In R. T. Francoeur and A. K. Francoeur (Eds.), *The future of sexual relations.* Englewood Cliffs, N.J.: Prentice-Hall, p. 15.

CHAPTER HIGHLIGHTS

I. TECHNOLOGIES
   - Artificial Insemination
   - Sperm Banks
   - Embryo Transplants
   - Test-Tube Babies
   - Cloning
   - Choosing Your Baby's Gender

II. LIFESTYLES
   - Relationships
   - Gender Roles

III. THE SEXUAL REVOLUTION: IS IT OVER?

IV. SOME HARD DECISIONS

There have been dramatic changes in sexuality in the last 30 years. Within our lifetimes, we will surely see more, equally dramatic changes. The changes that are occurrng are in two principle areas: technologies and lifestyles.

TECHNOLOGIES

Technological advances affect our sexuality. Perhaps the best example is the birth control pill. We are now able to separate sex from reproduction and (because of the way the pill is used) to separate contraception from sex. Surely the pill has contributed to the liberation of women and to changes in gender roles. It has probably also contributed to changes in sexual behavior and attitudes, in both premarital and marital sex.

Some recent scientific breakthroughs that may have an impact on sex in the future are discussed here.

Artificial Insemination

Artificial insemination: Artificially placing semen in the vagina or uterus in order to produce a pregnancy.

Artificial insemination involves artificially placing semen in the vagina to produce a pregnancy; thus it is a means of accomplishing reproduction without having sexual intercourse. Artificial insemination in animals was first done in 1776. In 1949, when British scientists successfully froze sperm without any apparent damage to it, a new era of reproductive technology for animals began (Francoeur, 1974). Today cattle are routinely bred by artificial insemination.

In humans, two kinds of artificial insemination have been used: artificial insemination by the husband (AIH) and artificial insemination by a donor (AID). AIH can be used when the husband has a low sperm count. Several samples of his semen are collected and pooled to make one sample with a higher count. This sample is then placed in the woman's vagina at the time of ovulation. AID is used when the husband is sterile. A donor provides semen to impregnate the wife. Estimates suggest that about 1 percent of all the children born in the United States today are conceived by means of artificial insemination (Francoeur, 1974).

Sperm Banks

Sperm bank: A place where sperm can be artificially frozen and stored.

Since it is now possible to freeze sperm, it is possible to store it, and that is just what some people are doing: using frozen human sperm banks. In 1972, there were 18 such facilities in the United States (Francoeur, 1974). The sperm banks open up many new possibilities for various life choices. For example, suppose that a couple decide, after having had two children, that they want a permanent method of contraception. The husband then has a vasectomy. Two years after he has the vasectomy, however, one of their children dies, and they very much want to have another baby. If the man has stored samples of his semen in a sperm bank, they can have another child.

FIGURE 25.1

The new technologies of sex.

Young men are also using sperm banks to store sperm before they undergo radiation therapy for cancer. They can later father children without fearing that they will transmit damaged chromosomes (as a result of the radiation) to their offspring.

One of the flashiest projects in this area is that of Robert K. Graham, a wealthy California businessman (*Time,* March 10, 1980). He started a sperm bank to collect "superior" sperm from scientists who have won a Nobel prize. He offers the sperm to young women who have a high IQ. At least five Nobel prizewinners have given donations, including physicist William Shockley. Graham provides a description of each scientist, and bright women applicants may choose whose sperm they want. Some Nobel winners are not amused, however. Burton Richter of Stanford, who received a Nobel prize in physics, reported that his students are beginning to ask him if he supplements his salary with stud fees.

Embryo Transplants

Embryo transplant: A technique in which a fertilized, developing egg (embryo) is artificially transferred from the uterus of one woman to the uterus of another.

In embryo transplantation, a fertilized, developing egg (embryo) is transferred from the uterus of one woman to the uterus of another woman. This technique may enable a woman who can conceive but who always miscarries early in the pregnancy to have a baby, with another woman serving as the "surrogate." The procedure also essentially can serve as the opposite of artificial insemination. That is, if a woman produces no viable eggs, her husband's sperm can be used to artificially inseminate another woman (who "donates" her egg), and the fertilized egg is then transferred from the donor to the mother.

Embryo transplants have been done routinely in cattle and rabbits since the 1950s. An important milestone was reached in 1975, when a female baboon gave birth to a healthy male infant baboon, after the embryo was transplanted from another female (Kraemer et al., 1976). This represented the first successful embryo transplant in a primate. Dr. John Buster of UCLA perfected the technique for use with humans, and the first two births resulting from the procedure were announced in 1984 (Brotman, 1984; Associated Press, 1984).

The technique will be a boon to some couples, but it raises some complex legal and ethical issues. For example, if a surrogate, or host, mother refused to give up the baby after it was born, what would be her rights? If she contracted German measles early in the pregnancy and the baby was deformed, who would be responsible for rearing it? New technologies often raise such ethical and legal issues, which in turn may require us to do some serious thinking about exactly what we mean by "parenthood."

Test-Tube Babies

It is possible for scientists to make sperm and egg unite outside the human body (in a "test tube"); the fertilized egg can then be implanted in the uterus of a woman and carried to term. This technique can be of great benefit to couples who are infertile because the woman's fallopian tubes are blocked (a fairly common cause of infertility). The woman's egg can be taken from her body and mixed with sperm from the husband, and the fertilized ovum can then be implanted in her uterus.

Test-tube baby: A baby who was created by fertilizing an egg outside the body and then implanting the fertilized egg into a woman's uterus.

A milestone was reached with the birth of Louise Brown in England on July 25, 1978. Obstetrician Patrick Steptoe and physiologist Robert Edwards had fertilized the mother's egg with her husband's sperm in a laboratory dish and implanted the embryo in the mother's uterus. The pregnancy went smoothly, and Louise was born healthy and normal, the first test-tube baby. Since then, the procedure has been repeated successfully many times.

FIGURE 25.2

"I ALREADY KNOW ABOUT THE BIRDS AND THE BEES, MOM; I WANT TO KNOW ABOUT ARTIFICIAL INSEMINATION, IN-VITRO FERTILIZATION AND SURROGATE MOTHERING!"

Cloning

Cloning (KLONE-ing): Reproduction of one or more genetically identical individuals from a single cell taken from a donor or parent.

Cloning is the reproduction of an individual from a single cell taken from a "donor" or "parent." The technique involves replacing the nucleus of an ovum with the nucleus from a body cell of the donor. This produces an embryo that is genetically identical to the donor. Normally, of course, a child has only half of its genes in common with the mother; the other half come from the father. Therefore, children are never genetically identical to either parent. But in cloning, no sperm is necessary, and the result is an individual who is genetically identical to the donor.

The concept of cloning raises ugly possibilities, such as an army of 100,000 genetically identical individuals. At present, cloning is on the brink of becoming scientifically feasible (see, for example, Galston, 1975). A breakthrough came with the first successful cloning of mice in 1981 (*Time,* January 19, 1981). The difficulties in doing this by now are mostly technical: the eggs of most mammals are so tiny that it is difficult to manipulate them in the ways necessary to achieve cloning. As an example, the human egg is approximately the size of the period at the end of this sentence.

Choosing Your Baby's Gender

Scientists are working on techniques that will allow couples to choose whether to have a boy or a girl. Such a technology would be good for parents who have six girls and really want a boy or for people who would like to have two children, one of each gender. Problems might arise, though. Some scientists fear that the result of being able to choose gender would be a great imbalance in our population, with many more males than females, since many couples prefer their first child to be a boy.

FIGURE 25.3

Louise Brown, the first test-tube baby.

LIFESTYLES

Sexual behavior and sexual lifestyles have changed in the last few decades. What will the trend be between now and the year 2000?

One of two trends might be predicted: a continuation of the liberation of sexuality or a reactionary movement toward sexual conservatism. Essentially the question is, is the sexual revolution over? Many new options for sexual lifestyles and gender roles opened up in the 1960s and 1970s. Let us discuss those first, and then look at what the trends for the 1980s and 1990s might be.

Relationships

In *The New Intimacy* (1973), Ron Mazur offers 12 possible alternative lifestyles or relationship patterns:

Monogamy (muh-NAH-guh-mee):
The pairing of one person with just one other person in a long-term relationship in which neither engages in sexual activity with others outside the relationship.

1. *Traditional* monogamy Traditional monogamy is a marriage between a man and a woman which is expected to last as long as both live. Sexual fidelity is to be observed, with neither partner having a sexual relationship with a person outside the marriage. Certainly historically and currently this has been the preferred lifestyle of millions. Perhaps the difference is that now it is more frequently *chosen,* by people who know that there are other alternatives.

2. *Child-free marriage* The traditional assumption has been that marriage includes children, but the possibility of a child-free marriage is increasingly being recognized. Advocates of this lifestyle point to the world population problem and the argument that not all people have the necessary qualities to be good parents.
3. *Single parenthood* The new "single parenthood" is much different from the "old illegitimacy." It now stems more from a growing independence of women, some of whom want children but not husbands. It also includes men who want to be adoptive parents but not husbands.
4. *Singlehood* With increasing mobility in society, and careers for women, singlehood is perceived by some to be a desirable option.
5. *Communes* The need and desire to share resources and experiences are common to those who choose communal living, groups of people living together (although not necessarily in the sexual sense). Doubtless with high interest rates and housing costs, communal living will increasingly become a reality and a necessity.
6. *Cohabitation* Cohabitation refers to two people living together, including having sexual relations, without being legally married (see Chapter 11). Some states recognize this legally as common law marriage. With more emphasis on graduate education and careers for both women and men, marriage is often postponed and more people may opt for cohabitation.
7. *Second-chance monogamy* It is common knowledge that the divorce rate is high, but it is also true that the remarriage rate of divorced persons is high; such persons are trying for second-chance monogamy, trying for a permanent, life-long relationship, hoping they are a bit wiser.
8. *Swinging and group sex* As discussed in Chapter 12, swinging involves a married couple exchanging partners sexually with another married couple. Although research shows that it is a minority phenomenon, it is interesting because it challenges the notion that marriage cannot survive without perfect fidelity.
9. *Family networks* Family networks are voluntary extended families who are not all blood relatives. One such network comprises a dozen people who went to graduate school together (Mazur, 1973). They and their families have been camping together for about 20 summers, and the children consider that they have numerous cousins, aunts, and uncles. They have contingency funds to help each other financially and they intervene in time of psychological crisis.
10. *Group marriage* Although it does not exist legally, group marriage consists of three or more people living together in a "marital" relationship. It is not a new concept; the Mormons in this country practiced polygamy, one form of group marriage, for many years. (For an extended discussion, see Constantine and Constantine, 1973).
11. *Synergamous marriage* Synergamous marriage is rather like double bigamy, and its possibilities have been explored in a novel by Robert Rimmer, *Thursday, My Love.* Adam is married and has a family. Angela is married and has a family. But Adam and Angela also marry (morally, not legally) each other. One sees at this point the limitless possibilities for alternative styles of relationships.
12. *Open-ended marriage* As discussed in Chapter 12, open-ended marriage refers to a marriage in which both partners are free to have sexual relationships with other people.

Whatever one's moral feelings about these various possibilities, they do illustrate the variety of sexual behaviors and relationships of which human beings ae capable.

Gender Roles

Spurred by the feminist movement and the more recent men's liberation movement, our society is undergoing substantial changes in gender roles. The majority of women now hold jobs outside the home, and women constitute about 40 percent of the work force. More women than ever before are seeking advanced degrees, and we see many more female faces in medical school and law school classes than before. My discussions with college students indicate that most young people, at least ideally, believe that their lives should not be restricted by gender roles.

Some scholars, though, believe that the public aspects of gender roles (such as women holding jobs outside the home) change much more quickly than the subtler, private aspects (such as who drives when both a man and a woman are in the car) (see, for example, Haavio-Mannila, 1967). Thus, while some indicators suggest that we are experiencing considerable change in gender roles, the subtle aspects may persist.

Many experts on gender roles believe that androgyny—in which both men and women are free to have both masculine and feminine characteristics—is the wave of the future (e.g., Bem, 1974).

FIGURE 25.4

Are androgynous people—and relationships—the trend for the future?

THE SEXUAL REVOLUTION: IS IT OVER?

In 1984 *Time* magazine ran a cover story entitled "Sex in the '80s: The revolution is over." The writers argued that the sexual revolution of the 1960s and 1970s—which tried to free people from repressive, Victorian standards, while maintaining that premarital sex, and even extramarital sex and vibrator sex were groovy—has come to a grinding halt. According to the authors, the trend for the 1980s is toward long-term, committed relationships. People are more interested in committing themselves to a single partner, than in finding 10 new partners with whom to have casual sex. Commitment, intimacy, and working at relationships are the new goals. People in increasing numbers are even taking the daring step of marriage.

What evidence is there for such trends? Are the authors at *Time* correct? *Psychology Today* surveyed its readers in 1969 and again in 1983 (Rubenstein, 1983). In 1969, at the height of the sexual revolt, only 17 percent of men and 29 percent of women said they believed that sex without love was unenjoyable or unacceptable. In 1983 those percentages had risen to 29 percent for men and 44 percent of women. Thus in 1983 there was increased rejection of casual sex. Although we must be wary of magazine surveys because of their sampling problems, these statistics give some indication that there is a trend toward more conservative sexual attitudes, and an increased emphasis on the importance of love in sexual relationships. Interestingly, in this survey sexual conservatism was greatest in the youngest age group; over 50 percent of those under 22 years of age felt that sex without love is unenjoyable or unacceptable. This youngest age group may give even more evidence of the trend for the future.

In a similar vein, sociologist John Scanzoni (1982) believes that the concept of "marital disintegration" that was widely publicized in the 1970s is, from a 1980s perspective, simply a myth. People in the 1980s are getting married—and remarried—in record numbers, and so one can scarcely say that marriage is obsolete. Surely the form of marriage is different today from what it was in the 1960s—there are far more two-paycheck marriages and more emphasis on egalitarian roles for husband and wife, for example—but it is still marriage, a long-term commitment to a relationship with another person.

Further evidence of the trend toward sexual conservatism comes from the data of sociologist Nancy Clatworthy (1980). She surveyed students at the Ohio State Uni-

FIGURE 25.5

Is the revolution over? Incidence of premarital intercourse among college students 1968–1980. (Clatworthy, 1980)

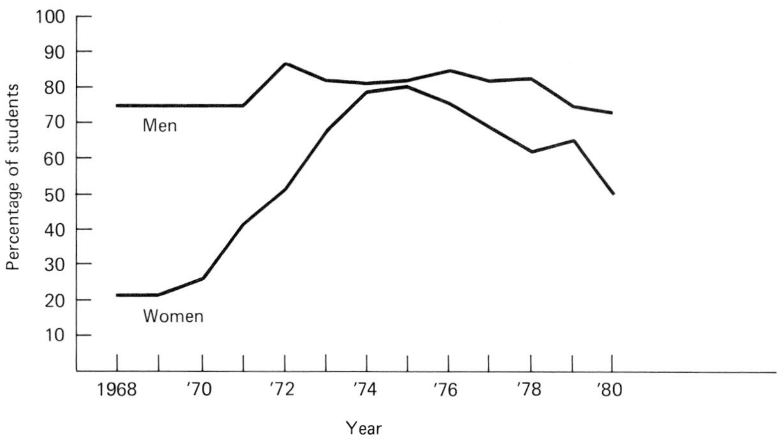

versity every year from 1968 to 1980. The results showed an increase in premarital intercourse for females from 21 percent in 1968 to 80 percent in 1975 (see Figure 25.5). But then the incidence fell to 50 percent in 1980. The rates for males show less of a dramatic trend, and generally fall around 75 percent for many years; but even for males, there was a peak incidence of 87 percent in 1972, and then a decline to 73 percent in 1980.

In sum, three sources of evidence indicate a more conservative trend in sexuality for the 1980s: attitudes about casual sex are more conservative, there is a resurgence of commitment to marriage, and the incidence of premarital intercourse (at least among females) seems to be declining. Of course, we are surely not seeing a return to the norms and behaviors of the 1950s, but neither are things as freewheeling as they were in 1975.

If the trend is away from radical, experimental sexuality, toward more traditional values of intimacy and relationship, what caused the reversal? Certainly the epidemic of sexually transmitted diseases is one factor (Lyons, 1983). The fear of herpes has caused many swinging singles to rethink their lifestyle. The threat of AIDS has had a similar impact among gays (Meredith, 1982; McWhirter and Mattison, 1983). Doubtless, too, there is disillusionment with the sexual revolution because it made more grandiose promises than it could keep. The Victorians promised that one could be good and successful and happy if one repressed all sexual desires. The sexual revolutionaries promised success and happiness if one expressed all sexual desires. Sex is nice, but it can't do all that.

SOME HARD DECISIONS

As a society, we typically await technological or lifestyle changes in sexuality passively. An alternative would be to do some social planning: to decide what we want our sexuality to be like in the future and then to shape technology to our values, rather than the reverse. Rather than wondering what the future will bring, we might take the future into our own hands and mold it.

Doing this would involve making some hard decisions about values. We would have to decide what a "good" sexual lifestyle is. What criterion would be used to decide that? That is a difficult question. As a beginning, however, I would suggest: "The question is which modification will be the most humane, most functional, most growth-promoting. . ." (Francoeur and Francoeur, 1974). We would do best to begin facing such issues.

FIGURE 25.6

Some argue that the sexual revolution is over and that people now want a return to long-term, deeply intimate relationships.

I hope that we can move away from viewing sex as something we must absolutely *not* do (to prove our virtue) or, alternatively, as something we *must* do (to prove our status or competence) and see it as an integrated, enriching part of our lives. A character in a novel expressed it well:

> He felt sorry for young people today, under such intense pressures to fill every available moment with sex. "Damned tiring, if nothing else. Well, in my day we were damned if we did, and now you're damned if you don't. Hope it levels off someday into something healthier than either one." (Byfield and Tedeschi, 1975, p. 162)

REVIEW QUESTIONS

1. The technique called _____ involves artificially placing semen in the vagina in order to produce a pregnancy.
2. An embryo transplant involves transferring a fertilized, developing egg from the uterus of one woman to the uterus of another. True or false?
3. Although embryo transplants have been done successfully in other species, the technique has not yet been done successfully in humans. True or false?
4. A test-tube baby is the result of artificially fertilizing an egg outside the body and then implanting it into a woman's uterus. True or false?
5. Marriage rates in the 1980s have declined substantially, indicating people's disillusionment with traditional marriage. True or false?
6. Surveys indicate that in the 1980s there is less approval of casual sex and a lower incidence of premarital sexual intercourse than there was in the 1960s or 1970s. True or false?

QUESTIONS FOR THOUGHT, DISCUSSION, AND DEBATE

1. From your observations on your own campus, do you agree with the notion that the sexual revolution is over?
2. How would you feel about being a surrogate mother in order to help an infertile couple?

SUGGESTION FOR FURTHER READING

Marin, Peter. (1983, July). A revolution's broken promises. *Psychology Today,* **17**(7), 50–57. Some second thoughts about the sexual revolution.

APPENDIX

DIRECTORY OF RESOURCES IN HUMAN SEXUALITY

I. HEALTH ISSUES: PREGNANCY, CONTRACEPTION, ABORTION, DISEASES

AIDS Hotline
1-800-342-AIDS

Operated by the U.S. Public Health Service, this hot line provides information and referrals on AIDS

American Cancer Society
777 Third Ave.
New York, NY 10017

Offers information and funds research on cancer

Association for Voluntary Sterilization, Inc.
122 East 42nd St.
New York, NY 10168

Offers information on sterilization

HELP
P.O. Box 100
Palo Alto, CA 94302

The American Social Health Association sponsors a program for herpes patients, including a newsletter and a telephone hotline.

La Leche International, Inc.
9616 Minneapolis Ave.
Franklin Park, IL 60123

Offers information on breast-feeding, organizes local support groups

National Abortion Rights Action League
1424 K St., N.W.
Washington, DC 20005
(202) 347–7774

A political action organization working at both state and national levels, dedicated to preserving a woman's right to legal abortion and also to teaching its members effective use of the political process to ensure abortion rights

National Genetics Foundation
555 W. 57th St.
New York, NY 10019

Offers information on genetic counseling

Planned Parenthood Federation of America
810 Seventh Ave.
New York, NY 10019
(212) 541–7800

PPFA is the nation's largest family planning agency. Through local clinics (check your telephone book) offers birth control instruction and prescriptions, pregnancy testing, voluntary sterilization, prenatal care, early abortion, pelvic and breast exams

Population Information Program
The Johns Hopkins University
624 North Broadway
Baltimore, MD 21205

Publishes *Population Reports,* frequent, up-to-date reports on contraception and family planning worldwide

Division of Sexually Transmitted Diseases
Centers for Disease Control
Atlanta, GA 30333

Offers the most up-to-date information on sexually transmitted diseases; administers federal program for control of STD

VD National Hotline of the American Social Health Assoc.
260 Sheridan Ave.
Palo Alto, CA 94306
1–800–227–8922 (national number)
1–800–982–5883 (California)
(8 A.M. to 8 P.M. PST)

Provides these toll-free numbers for telephone information on sexually transmitted diseases; also provides referrals to free or low-cost clinics or private physicians

II. SEX EDUCATION, SEX RESEARCH, AND SEX THERAPY

American Association of Sex Educators, Counselors, and Therapists
11 Dupont Circle, N.W., Suite 220
Washington, DC 20036
(202) 462–1171

This organization certifies sex educators, sex counselors, and sex therapists and provides other services associated with sex education and sex therapy

Current Research Updates in Human Sexuality
P.O. Box 2577
Bellingham, WA 98227
(206) 676–3611

A subscription service publishing a monthly listing of all journal articles dealing with human sexuality

Masters and Johnson Institute
24 South Kingshighway
St. Louis, MO 63108

A public foundation committed to sex research, sex therapy, and education

Sex Information and Education Council of the United States
80 Fifth Ave.
New York, NY 10011

Provides a library and information service on sex education, including curricula, bibliographies, and media

Society for the Scientific Study of Sex
P.O. Box 29795
Philadelphia, PA 19117

An organization devoted to promoting quality sex research; publishes *The Journal of Sex Research*

III. LIFESTYLE ISSUES

Thomas-Robert Ames, President
Coalition on Sexuality and Disability
853 Broadway, Suite 611
New York, NY 10003
(212) 242-3900

Sponsors workshops on sexuality and disabilities

The Janus Information Facility
c/o Paul A. Walker
1952 Union St.
San Francisco, CA 94123

Transsexual counseling

National Gay Task Force
80 Fifth Ave., Suite 1601
New York, NY 10011
(212) 741-5800

Offers information and support to gay men and lesbians and educational pamphlets, such as *About Coming Out.* Has a toll-free crisis line for reports of antigay violence and referral on AIDS, 1-800-221-7044 (national); (212) 807-6016 (in New York)

Society for the Study of Alternative Lifestyles
2742 Orangethorpe, Suite A
Fullerton, CA 92633

Devoted to the study and enjoyment of alternative sexual lifestyles

IV. MEDIA

Multi-Focus
1525 Franklin St.
San Francisco, CA 94109

Has the largest selection of sex education and sex therapy films available

V. SEXUAL VICTIMIZATION

National Center for the Prevention and Control of Rape (NCPCR)
National Institute of Mental Health
5600 Fishers Lane, Room 6C-12
Rockville, MD 20857

The NCPCR is the focal point in the National Institute of Mental Health for research, training, and public education activities in the area of rape and sexual assault of children and adults

Working Women's Institute
593 Park Ave.
New York, NY 10021

Builds public awareness of sexual harrassment on the job and builds systematic protection against it, through consultation and training with a variety of institutions and policy analysis

VI. FEMINISM AND WOMEN'S ISSUES

National Organization for Women
1401 New York Ave., N.W.
Washington, DC 20005–2102
(202) 347–2279

NOW seeks to take action to bring women into full participation in the mainstream of U.S. society now, exercising all the privileges and responsibilities thereof in truly equal partnership with men.

National PMS Society
3514 University Drive, Suite 5
Durham, NC 27707
(919) 489–6577

Offers information and support on PMS (premenstrual syndrome) and a national physician referral service

PEER: Project on Equal Education Rights
1413 K St., N.W., 9th Floor
Washington, DC 20005

Offers information on Title IX and its banning of sex discrimination in education

VII. JOURNALS

Alternative Lifestyles
Human Sciences Press
72 Fifth Ave.
New York, NY 10011

Archives of Sexual Behavior
Plenum Publishing Corp.
233 Spring St.
New York, NY 10013

Journal of Sex Education and Therapy
American Association of Sex Educators, Counselors, and Therapists
11 Dupont Circle, N.W.
Washington, DC 20036

Journal of Homosexuality
Haworth Press
28 East 22nd St.
New York, NY 10010

Journal of Sex Research
P.O. Box 29795
Philadelphia, PA 19117

Journal of Sex and Marital Therapy
Brunner/Mazel, Inc.
19 Union Square West
New York, NY 10003

Medical Aspects of Human Sexuality
Hospital Publications, Inc.
360 Lexington Ave.
New York, NY 10017

Sexuality and Disability
Human Sciences Press
72 Fifth Ave.
New York, NY 10011

Sexuality Today
ATCOM, Inc.
2315 Broadway
New York, NY 10024

ACKNOWLEDGMENTS

PHOTO CREDITS

Chapter 1 opening photo: Will Bradley, *Pausias and Glycera,* The Metropolitan Museum of Art, Gift of Fern Bradley Dufner, The Will Bradley Collection, 1952.

1.1 (*a*) AP/Wide World Photos (*b*) Culver Pictures, Inc.
1.2 The Kinsey Institute for Research
1.4 Malcolm S. Kirk
1.5 Ronald D. Nadler, Yerkes Regional Primate Research Center
1.6 From Philip Rawson, *Primitive Erotic Art.*

Chapter 2 opening photo: Auguste Rodin, *Love and Psyche,* The Metropolitan Museum of Art, Gift of Richard Anthony Stroag and Alexander Milliken Stewart, 1938.

2.1 Shirley Zeiberg, Photo Researchers, Inc.
2.2 Alice Kandell, Photo Researchers, Inc.
2.3 Leonard Freed, Magnum Photos, Inc.

Chapter 3 opening photo: Michelangelo, *Studies for the Libyan Sibyl,* The Metropolitan Museum of Art, Purchase, 1924, Joseph Pulitzer Bequest.

3.1 From D. Luciano, A. J. Vander, J. H. Sherman, *Human Anatomy and Physiology: Structure and Function* (2nd ed.) New York: McGraw-Hill, 1983.
3.3 From Betty Dodson, *Liberating Masturbation: A Meditation on Self-Love.* Copyright © 1974 by Betty Dodson
3.4 Anne Popkin
3.6 From D. Luciano, A. J. Vander, and J. H. Sherman, *Human Anatomy and Physiology: Structure and Function* (2nd ed.) New York: McGraw-Hill, 1983.
3.7 From D. Luciano, A. J. Vander, and J. H. Sherman, *Human Anatomy and Physiology: Structure and Function* (2nd ed.) New York: McGraw-Hill, 1983.
3.10 From D. Luciano, A. J. Vander, and J. H. Sherman, *Human Anatomy and Physiology: Structure and Function* (2nd ed.) New York: McGraw-Hill, 1983.
3.12 From D. Luciano, A. J. Vander, and J. H. Sherman, *Human Anatomy and Physiology: Structure and Function* (2nd ed.) New York: McGraw-Hill, 1983.
3.4 Anna Pomaska.

Chapter 4 opening photo: Edvard Munch, *Separation,* Scala/Art Resource.

4.2 Adapted from A. J. Vander, J. H. Sherman, and D. Luciano, *Human Physiology: The Mechanisms of Body Function.* (2nd ed.) New York: McGraw-Hill, 1975.
4.3 Adapted from A. J. Vander, J. H. Sherman, and D. Luciano, *Human Physiology: The Mechanisms of Body Function.* (2nd ed.) New York: McGraw-Hill, 1975.
4.5 AP/Wide World Photos
4.6 From J. Money and A. Ehrhardt, *Man and Woman, Boy and Girl.* Baltimore: Johns Hopkins, 1972, p. 167.
4.7 From W. A. Marshall, Sex Differences at Puberty. *Journal of Biosocial Science Supplement,* 1970, **2,** 31–41.
4.8 From J. M. Tanner, *Growth at Adolescence* (2nd ed.) Oxford: Blackwell Scientific Publications, 1962.

Chapter 5 opening photo: Imogen Cunningham, *The Wind,* The Metropolitan Museum of Art, Gift of Miss Imogen Cunningham, 1971.

5.1 Adapted from A. J. Vander, J. H. Sherman, and D. Luciano, *Human Physiology: The Mechanisms of Body Function.* (2nd ed.) New York: McGraw-Hill, 1975.
5.2 From R. J. Demarest and J. J. Sciarra, *Conception, Birth, and Contraception: A Visual Presentation.* (2nd ed.) New York: McGraw-Hill, 1976.
5.4 The Bettmann Archive, Inc.
5.5 Poem and graphic copyright © 1976 by *Women: A Journal of Liberation,* 3028 Greenmount Ave., Baltimore, MD 21218
5.6 Randy Matusow, 1984

Chapter 6 opening photo: Henry Moore, *Rocking Chair no. 2,* Hirshhorn Museum and Sculpture Garden, Smithsonian Institution.

6.3 (*a–b*) Courtesy of Landrum B. Shettles (*c–e*) Courtesy of Dr. Mark Evans, Division of Reproductive Genetics, Wayne State University, Hutzel Hospital (*f–g*) Courtesy of Landrum B. Shettles
6.5 (*a*) Heila Hammid, Photo Researchers, Inc. (*b*) Eugene Richards, Magnum Photos, Inc.

6.6 Fred Ward from Black Star
6.8 George Malave, Stock, Boston
6.9 Mary M. Thacher, Photo Researchers, Inc.
6.10 From J. A. Pritchard and P. C. McDonald, *Williams Obstetrics* (17th ed.). New York: Appleton-Century-Crofts, p. 332.

Chapter 7 opening photo: Claude Monet, *The Poplars,* The Metropolitan Museum of Art, Bequest of H. O. Havemeyer, 1929, H. O. Havemeyer Collection.

7.1 Ehrlich and Ehrlich
7.2 Culver Pictures, Inc.
7.3 (*a–c*) Planned Parenthood of New York City (*d*) Ortho Pharmaceutical Corp. (*e*) Russ Kinne, Photo Researchers, Inc.
7.4 Ortho Pharmaceutical Corp.
7.5 Ortho Pharmaceutical Corp.
7.6 Courtesy of Pharmacists Planning Service, Inc., P.O. Box 1336, Sausalito, CA. Copyright © Pharmacists Planning Service, Inc.
7.7 Jonathan Shrorey, 1984
7.10 Time Diagram by Karen Karlsson

Chapter 8 opening photo: Auguste Rodin, *Group: Eternal Springtime,* The Metropolitan Museum of Art, Bequest of Isaac D. Fletcher, 1917.

8.3 Reproductive Biology Research Foundation
8.4 Reproductive Biology Research Foundation
8.7 Time, Inc.
8.9 Paul Brown, Time Magazine

Chapter 9 opening photo: Pierre Bonnard, *L'Homme et La Femme,* SEF/Art Resource.

9.1 Rapho, Photo Researchers, Inc.
9.3 Reprinted by permission of the Putnam Publishing Group from Philip Rawson, *Erotic Art of the East.* Copyright © 1968 by Philip Rawson.
9.9 King Features Syndicate
9.10 King Features Syndicate
9.11 (*a–b*) Copyright © Randy Matusow, 1984.
9.12 Copyright © Randy Matusow, 1984

Chapter 10 opening photo: Jean Arp, *Leaves and Navels* (1929), oil and string on canvas, 13¾ x 10¾ inches. Collection, The Museum of Modern Art, New York. Purchase.

10.1 Copyright © Punch, ROTHCO
10.2 Culver Pictures, Inc.
10.3 United Artists Corp.
10.5 From Alfred C. Kinsey, Wardell B. Pomeroy, and Clyde F. Martin, *Sexual Behavior in the Human Male,* Philadelphia: Saunders, 1984, p. 502. Courtesy of The Institute for Sex Research.
10.6 Mitro, Rothco original, Rothco Cartoons, Inc.

Chapter 11 opening photo: Mary Cassat, *The Bath,* Scala/Art Resource.

11.1 Tana Hoban
11.2 Monkmeyer Press Photo Service
11.3 Copyright © Fredrik D. Bodin, Stock, Boston
11.4 Copyright © Donald Dietz, Stock, Boston
11.5 Adapted from Alfred C. Kinsey, Wardell B. Pomeroy, and Clyde F. Martin, *Sexual Behavior in the Human Male.* Philadelphia: Saunders, 1984 p. 502. Alfred C. Kinsey, Wardell B. Pomeroy, Clyde E. Martin, and Paul Gebhard, *Sexual Behavior in the Human Female.* Philadelphia: Saunders, 1953, p. 141. Courtesy of the Institute for Sex Research
11.6 Rapho, Photo Researchers, Inc.

Chapter 12 opening photos: Jean August Dominique Ingres, *Three Studies of a Male Nude,* The Metropolitan Museum of Art, Rogers Fund, 1919.
Davies, Arthur B., *Nude Studies,* The Metropolitan Museum of Art, Anonymous Gift, 1909.

12.1 Gunby, *STD Fact Sheet,* Gunby, 1983
12.2 Richard Kalver, Magnum Photos, Inc.
12.3 Bruce Davidson, Magnum Photos, Inc.

Chapter 13 opening photo: Henri Rousseau, *Rendezvous in the Forest.* Photograph courtesy of the National Gallery of Art, Washington, D.C.

13.1 Schultz, Courtesy United Feature Syndicate
13.2 (*a*) Susan Lapides, Design Conceptions, copyright © Joel Gordon (*b*) Charles Harbutt, Archive Pictures, Inc. (*c*) Joan Liftin, Archive Pictures, Inc.
13.3 Copyright © 1983, reprinted from *Psychology Today* magazine, American Psychological Association
13.4 Copyright © Randy Matusow, 1984

Chapter 14 opening photo: Henry Moore, *Family Group, 1946,* Hirshhorn Museum and Sculpture Garden, Smithsonian Institution.

14.1 From J. Elrod. The Ryatts. Copyright Field Enterprises, Inc. Courtesy of Field Newspaper Syndicate
14.2 Evelyn and George Malave, Stock, Boston, 1976
14.3 (*a*) M.I.T. Museum and Historical Collection (*b*) Supreme Court Historical Society
14.4 (*a–c*) Courtesy of David W. Foerster, M.D., and Charles L. Reynolds, M.D.
14.5 Courtesy of Dr. D. Laub, Gender Dysphoria Program, Department of Plastic and Reconstructive Surgery, Stanford University
14.6 New Times Magazine and Wide World Photos

Chapter 15 opening photos: Wilhelm Lehmbruck, *Kneeling Woman* (1911), cast stone, 69½ inches high, at base 56 x 27 inches, Collection, The Museum of Modern Art, New York, Abby Aldrich Rockefeller Fund.
Wilhelm Lehmbruck, *Standing Youth* (1913), cast stone, 7 feet 8 inches high, at base 36 x 26¾ inches, Collection, The Museum of Modern Art, New York, Gift of Abby Aldrich Rockefeller.

15.1 Copyright © Joel Gordon, 1981
15.2 Photo courtesy of J. R. Heinman
15.3 Copyright © 1983, reprinted from *Psychology Today* magazine, American Psychological Association
15.4 Bettye Lane, Nancy Palmer Photo Agency, Inc.

Chapter 16 opening photos: August Rodin, *The Embrace,* The Metropolitan Museum of Art, Kennedy Fund, 1910.

16.1 (*a*) Copyright © Joyce R. Wilson, 1978, Photo Researchers, Inc. (*b*) AP/Wide World Photos
16.2 Joel Gordon, 1980
16.3 Ira Kirschenbaum, Stock, Boston
16.5 (*a*) Bettye Lane, Photo Researchers, Inc. (*b*) UPI/Bettmann Archive
16.6 From *Victor, Victoria,* Time, Inc.

Chapter 17 opening photo: Richard Lidner, *The Meeting,* 1953, oil on canvas, 60 inches x 6 feet, Collection, The Museum of Modern Art, New York. Given anonymously.

17.2 (*a*) Eric Kroll (*b*) The New York Historical Society

17.3 The Bettmann Archive, Inc.
17.4 Copyright © Joel Gordon, 1981. All rights reserved
17.5 Jean C. Pigozzi, N.S.C., Archive Pictures, Inc.
17.6 The Bettmann Archive, Inc.
17.7 (*a*) Randy Matusow (*b*) Tribune Media Services, Inc.

Chapter 18 opening photo: Edvard Munch, *Jealousy,* Scala/Art Resource.

18.1 AP/Wide World Photos
18.4 Copyright © Randy Matusow, 1984

Chapter 19 opening photo: Toulouse-Lautrec, *Elles: Remme en corset-Conquete de Passage,* © 1985, Sotheby's Inc.

19.1 (*a*) Bob Adelman, Magnum Photos, Inc. (*b*) The New York Public Library
19.2 Richard Sobol, copyright © 1980, Stock, Boston
19.3 Guy Le Querrec, Magnum Photos, Inc.

Chapter 20 opening photo: Thomas Eakins, *Two Nude Men on Beach,* The Metropolitan Museum of Art, David A. McAlpin Fund, 1943.

20.5 Tony Guccione
20.6 V. Puglisi, Time, Inc., 1979

Chapter 21 opening photo: Peter Paul Rubens, *A Willow Tree.* Courtesy of the Trustees of the British Museum, London.

21.3 (*a–g*) Center for Disease Control, Atlanta
21.4 Center for Disease Control, Atlanta
21.6 Bettye Lane, Photo Researchers, Inc.
21.7 American Cancer Society
21.8 Randolph H. Buthrie, Jr., M.D., P.C.
21.9 Hazel Hankin, Stock, Boston

Chapter 22 opening photo: Peter Paul Rubens, *Virtue and Honor,* Museum Plantin-Moreteus.

22.1 Ploss & Bartles
22.2 Alinari, Art Resource, NY
22.3 Copyright © 1979 SIPA Press, from Black Star
22.4 Office of Sri Guradev, International Headquarters Integral Yoga Institute
22.5 (*a*) Daniel S. Brody, Stock, Boston (*b*) Jerry Berndt, Stock, Boston
22.6 Bettye Lane, Nancy Palmer
22.7 AP/Wide World Photos
22.8 AP/Wide World Photos

Chapter 23 opening photo: *Justice,* Art Resource.

23.1 (*a*) David Vance, quotation: Bill Hutchinson and James Kukar, Miami Magazine (*b*) Bettye Lane, Nancy Palmer
23.2 UPI/Bettmann News Photos
23.3 Copyright © 1976 The Chicago Sun Times. Reproduced by courtesy of Wil-Jo Associates, Inc., and Bill Mauldin.
23.4 UPI/Bettmann News Photos

Chapter 24 opening photo: Balthus, *The Living Room,* 1942, oil on canvas, 45¼ x 57⅞ inches, Collection, The Museum of Modern Art, New York, Estate of John Hay Whitney.

24.1 Jim Margulies, Rothco Cartoons, Inc.
24.2 From the "Oberlin Report," produced by Decade Media Inc.
24.3 "Dennis the Menace" used by permission of Hank Ketcham and copyright © by News Group Chicago, Inc.

Chapter 25 opening photo: *Study from Falling Man Series: Walking Man* (1964), chromium-plated bronze (cast 1965), 58⅝ x 11⅜ x 26½ inches, on chrome base recessed in marble base 4 to 6 inches high x 20⅛ x 35⅛ inches, Collection, The Museum of Modern Art, New York, Gift of Miss Viki Laura List.

25.1 Dana Summers, *The Orlando Sentinel,* Copley News Service
25.2 Dennis Renault, Rothco Cartoons, Inc.
25.3 United Press International Photo
25.4 AP/Wide World Photos
25.5 Nancy Clatworthy, Department of Sociology, Ohio State University, unpublished data
25.6 Copyright © Joel Gordon, 1978

TEXT QUOTATIONS

Boston Women's Health Book Collective. *Our bodies, ourselves.* New York: Simon & Schuster, 1973. Reprinted by permission of the publisher.

Brecher, E. M., and the Editors of Consumer Reports Books. *Love, sex, and aging.* Copyright © 1984 by Consumers Union of United States, Inc.

Burgess, Ann Wolbert, Editor, with Marieanne Lindequist Clark. *Child pornography and sex rings.* Lexington, Mass.: Lexington Books, D. C. Heath and Company. Copyright © 1984, D. C. Heath and Company. Reprinted by permission of the publisher.

Ferrara, A. J. My personal experience with AIDS. *American Psychologist,* 1984, **39,** 1285–1287. Reprinted by permission of the American Psychological Association.

The Gallup Poll.

Goldstein, B. *Human sexuality.* Copyright © 1976 by McGraw-Hill Book Co. Used with permission of the author and McGraw-Hill Book Co.

Hildebrand, M. An odd gastropod. In *Laugh & Love.* Hicksville, NY: Exposition Press, 1979. Reprinted by permission of the author.

Hunt, M. *Sexual behavior in the 1970s.* Copyright © 1974 by Playboy Press. Reprinted with permission of Playboy Press.

Kay. A poem by a London prostitute. In W. Young, *Eros Denied.* New York: Grove Press, 1964. Reprinted by permission of Wayland Young.

Money, J., and Ehrhardt. A. *Man and woman, boy and girl.* Baltimore: The Johns Hopkins University Press, 1972.

Piercy, M. Rape Poem. In *Living in the Open.* New York: Knopf, 1976. Reprinted by permission of Wallace & Sheil Agency, Inc. Copyright © 1974, 1976 by Marge Piercy.

Thompson, A. P. Extramarital sex: A review of the research literature. *Journal of Sex Research,* 1983, **19,** 1–22. Reprinted by permission of the author and *The Journal* *of Sex Research,* a publication of the Society for the Scientific Study of Sex.

Weideger, P. *Menstruation and menopause.* New York: Knopf, 1976. Copyright © 1975 by Paula Weideger. Reprinted by permission of Alfred A. Knopf, Inc.

Williams, E. R., and Caliendo, M. A. *Nutrition.* New York: McGraw-Hill, 1984. Reprinted by permission of the publisher.

BIBLIOGRAPHY

Abbey, A. (1982). Sex differences in attributions for friendly behavior: Do males misperceive females' friendliness. *Journal of Personality and Social Psychology,* **42**, 830–838.

Abel, Ernest L. (1980). Fetal alcohol syndrome. *Psychological Bulletin,* **87**, 29–50.

Abel, Ernest L. (1985). *Psychoactive drugs and sex.* New York: Plenum.

Abelson, Robert P. (1981). Psychological status of the script concept. *American Psychologist,* **36**, 715–729.

Abplanalp, Judith M. (1983). Premenstrual syndrome: A selective review. *Women and Health,* 107–123.

Abraham, Karl. (1953). *Selected papers on psychoanalysis.* New York: Basic Books.

Abramson, Paul R. (1977). Ethical requirements for research on human sexual behavior: From the perspectives of participating subjects. *Journal of Social Issues,* **33**, 184–192.

Abramson, Paul R., and Mechanic, Mindy B. (1983). Sex and the media: Three decades of best-selling books and major motion pictures. *Archives of Sexual Behavior,* **12**, 185–206.

Adams, Clifford R. (1966). An informal preliminary report on some factors relating to sexual responsiveness of certain college wives. In M. F. Martino (Ed.), *Sexual behavior and personality characteristics.* New York: Grove Press.

Adams, James F. (1973). *Understanding adolescence.* Boston: Allyn and Bacon.

Adams, J. W., et al. (1983). Sexual harassment of university students. *Journal of College Student Personnel,* **24**, 484–490.

Addiego, F., Belzer, E. G., Comolli, J., Moger, W., Perry, J. D., and Whipple, B. (1981). Female ejaculation: A case study. *Journal of Sex Research,* **17**, 13–21.

Adler, Nancy E. (1979). Abortion: A social-psychological perspective. *Journal of Social Issues,* **35**(1), 100–119.

Aiken, D. L. (1973, Sept. 26). Ex-sailor charges jail rape, stirs up storm. *The Advocate,* p. 5.

Albin, Rochelle S. (1977). Psychological studies of rape. *Signs,* **3**, 423–435.

Allen, Donald M. (1980). Young male prostitutes: A psychological study. *Archives of Sexual Behavior,* **9**, 399–426.

Allgeier, Elizabeth Rice, and Fogel, Arthur. (1978). Coital position and sex roles: Responses to cross-sex behavior in bed. *Journal of Consulting and Clinical Psychology,* **46**, 588–589.

Allgeier, Elizabeth R. (1976, May). Heterosexuality and sex-typing. Paper presented at meetings of the Mid-Western Psychological Association, Chicago.

Allgeier, Elizabeth R. (1981). The influence of androgynous identification on heterosexual relations. *Sex Roles,* **7**, 321–330.

Allgeier, Elizabeth R., and McCormick, Naomi B. (Eds.). (1982). *Changing boundaries: Gender roles and sexual behavior.* Palo Alto, CA: Mayfield.

American Cancer Society. (1980). *Cancer Facts & Figures.*

American Law Institute. (1962). *Model penal code: Proposed official draft.* Philadelphia: ALI.

American Psychological Association, Ad hoc Committee on Ethical Standards in Psychological Research. (1973). *Ethical principles in the conduct of research with human participants.* Washington, D.C.: APA.

Amir, Menachem. (1971). *Patterns in forcible rape.* Chicago: University of Chicago Press.

Andersen, Barbara L. (1981). A comparison of systematic desensitization and directed masturbation in the treatment of primary orgasmic dysfunction in females. *Journal of Consulting and Clinical Psychology,* **49**, 568–570.

Andersen, Barbara L. (1983). Primary orgasmic dysfunction: Diagnostic considerations and review of treatment. *Psychological Bulletin,* **93**, 105–136.

Andrews, Eva, and Cappon, Daniel. (1957). Autism and

schizophrenia in a child guidance clinic. *Canadian Psychiatric Association Journal,* **2**, 1–25.

Angrist, Shirley S. (1969). The study of sex roles. *Journal of Social Issues,* **25**, 215–232.

Anonymous. (1975). When a woman is attacked. In L. G. Schultz (Ed.), *Rape victimology.* Springfield, IL: Charles C. Thomas.

Anson, Robert S. (1977, Oct. 25). *The San Francisco Chronicle.*

Antle, Katharyn. (1978). Active involvement of expectant fathers in pregnancy: Some further considerations. *Journal of Obstetric, Gynecologic and Neonatal Nursing,* **7**(2), 7–12.

Aquinas, St. Thomas. (1968). *Summa theologica.* Vol. 43. (Thomas Gilly, O.P., Trans.). New York: McGraw-Hill.

Arafat, Ibtihaj S., and Cotton, Wayne L. (1974). Masturbation practices of males and females. *Journal of Sex Research,* **10**, 293–307.

Araoz, Daniel L. (1982). *Hypnosis and sex therapy.* New York: Brunner/Mazel.

A regular check for testicular tumors. (1980, Oct. 15). *Emergency Medicine,* **12**, 167–168.

Arehart-Treichal, J. (1974, May 11). Sperm don't like it hot. *Science News,* **105**, 309–310.

Aristotle. (1925). *Nicomachean ethics.* (W. D. Ross, Trans.) Oxford: Clarendon Press.

Associated Press. (1971), Aug. 28). German drug may reduce sex offenses. *Houston Chronicle.*

Associated Press. (1984, Mar. 25). Baby girl is born from transferred embryo. *New York Times.*

Athanasiou, Robert, et al. (1970). Sex. *Psychology Today,* **4**(2), 39–52.

Atkeson, Beverly M., et al. (1982). Victims of rape: Repeated assessment of depressive symptoms. *Journal of Consulting and Clinical Psychology,* **50**, 96–102.

Atwater, L. (1978, Aug.). Women in extramarital relationships: A case study in socio-sexuality. *Dissertation Abstracts International,* **39**(2–A), 1133.

Bach, G., and Wyden, P. (1969). *The imtimate enemy: How to fight fair in love and marriage.* New York: Morrow.

Bader, Louis. (1981). "Constitutional Law—Police Power—Equal Protection—Voluntary Sexual Deviate Intercourse Statute" *Duquesne Law Review,* **19**, 793–800.

Badgley, R. F., Caron, D. F., and Powell, M. G. (1977). *Report of the Committee on the Operation of the Abortion Law.* Ottawa: Minister of Supply and Services Canada.

Bancroft, John. (1974). *Deviant sexual behavior: Modification and assessment.* New York: Oxford University Press.

Bancroft, John. (1978). The prevention of sexual offenses. In C. B. Qualls et al. (Eds.), *The prevention of sexual disorders.* New York: Plenum.

Bandura, Albert. (1069). *Principles of behavior modification.* New York: Holt.

Bandura, Albert, and Walters, Richard H. (1963). *Social learning and personality development.* New York: Holt.

Barash, David P. (1977). *Sociobiology and behavior.* New York: Elsevier.

Barash, David P. (1982). *Sociobiology and behavior* (2nd ed.). New York: Elsevier.

Barbach, Lonnie G. (1975). *For yourself: The fulfillment of female sexuality.* Garden City, NY: Anchor Press/Doubleday.

Barclay, Andrew M. (1973). Sexual fantasies in men and women. *Medical Aspects of Human Sexuality,* **7**, 209–212.

Bardwick, Judith M. (1971). *Psychology of women: A study of biocultural conflicts.* New York: Harper & Row.

Barker, William J., and Perlman, Daniel. (1975). Volunteer bias and personality traits in sexual standards research. *Archives of Sexual Behavior,* **4**, 161–171.

Barlow, David H. (1973). Increasing heterosexual responsiveness in the treatment of sexual deviation: A review of the clinical and experimental evidence. *Behavior Therapy,* **4**, 655–671.

Barlow, D. H., Abel, G. G., and Blanchard, E. B. (1978). Gender identity change in transsexuals: Follow-up and replication. *Archives of General Psychiatry.*

Barlow, D. H., and Agras, W. S. (1973). Fading to increase heterosexual responsiveness in homosexuals. *Journal of Applied Behavior Analysis,* **6**, 355–366.

Barlow, D. H., Sakheim, D. K., and Beck, J. G. (1983). Anxiety increases sexual arousal. *Journal of Abnormal Psychology,* **92**, 49–54.

Barnett, W. (1973). *Sexual freedom and the Constitution.* Albuquerque: University of New Mexico Press.

Bart, Pauline B. (1971). Depression in middle-aged women. In V. G. Gornick and B. K. Moran (Eds.), *Women in sexist society.* New York: Basic Books.

Bartell, Gilbert D. (1970). Group sex among the mid-Americans. *Journal of Sex Research,* **6**, 113–130.

Beach, Frank A. (1947). Evolutionary changes in the physiological control of mating behavior in mammals. *Psychological Review,* **54**, 297–315.

Beach, Frank, and Merari, A. (1970). Coital behavior in dogs. V. Effects of estrogen and progesterone on mating and other forms of social behavior in the bitch. *Journal of Comparative and Physiological Psychology Monograph,* **70**(1), Part 2, 1–22.

Beatty, R. A. (1970). The genetics of the mammalian gamete. *Biological Review,* **45**, 73–119.

Beebe, J. L. (1983). Physician utilization of a gonococcal antibody screening test. *Sexually Transmitted Diseases,* **10**, 195–197.

Behrman, Richard E., and Rosen, Tove S. (1976). HEW Publication No. 05 76–128, 12–1–12–116.

Bell, Alan P. (1974a, summer). Childhood and adolescent sexuality. Address delivered at the Institute for Sex Research, Indiana University.

Bell, Alan P. (1974b). Homosexualities: Their range and

character. In *Nebraska symposium on motivation 1973.* Lincoln: University of Nebraska Press.

Bell, Alan P., and Weinberg, Martin S. (1978). *Homosexualities.* New York: Simon & Schuster.

Bell, A. P., Weinberg, M. S., and Hammersmith, S. K. (1981). *Sexual preference.* Bloomington: Indiana University Press.

Bell, N. J., and Carver, W. (1980). A reevaluation of gender label effects: Expectant mothers' responses to infants. *Child Development,* **51**, 925–927.

Bell, Robert R. (1966). *Premarital sex in a changing society.* Englewood Cliffs, N.J.: Prentice-Hall.

Bell, R. R.,Turner, S., and Rosen, L. (1975). A multivariate analysis of female extramarital coitus. *Journal of Marriage and the Family,* **37**, 375–384.

Belzer, E. G. (1981). Orgasmic expulsions of women: A review and heuristic inquiry. *Journal of Sex Research,* **17**, 1–12.

Bem, Sandra L. (1974). The measurement of psychological androgyny. *Journal of Consulting and Clinical Psychology,* **42**, 155–162.

Bem, Sandra L. (1975). Sex-role adaptability: One consequence of psychological androgyny. *Journal of Personality and Social Psychology,* **31**, 634–643.

Bem, Sandra L. (1981). Gender schema theory: A cognitive account of sex typing. *Psychological Review,* **88**, 354–364.

Bem, Sandra, L., and Bem, D. J. (1970). Case study of nonconscious ideology: Training the woman to know her place. In D. J. Bem (Ed.), *Beliefs, attitudes, and human affairs.* Belmont, Ca.: Brooks/Cole.

Bem, S. L., Martyna, W., and Watson, C. (1976). Sex-typing and androgyny: Further explorations of the expressive domain. *Journal of Personality and Social Psychology,* **34**, 1016–1023.

Benjamin, Harry, and Masters, R. E. L. (1964). *Prostitution and morality.* New York: Julian Press.

Benkert, O., Witt, W., Adam, W., and Leitz, A. (1979). Effects of testosterone undecanoate on sexual potency and the hypothalamic-pituitary-gonadal axis of impotent males. *Archives of Sexual Behavior,* **8**, 471–480.

Benney, M., Riesman, D., and Star, S. (1956). Age and sex in the interview. *American Journal of Sociology,* **62**, 143–152.

Benson, Donna J., and Thomson, Gregg E. (1982). Sexual harassment on a university campus: The confluence.of authority relations, sexual interest and gender stratification. *Social Problems,* **29**, 236–251.

Bentler, Peter M., and Abramson, Paul R. (1981). The science of sex research: Some methodological considerations. *Archives of Sexual Behavior,* **10**, 225–252.

Berardo, Felix. (1968). Widowhood status in the United States: Perspective on a neglected aspect of the family life-cycle. *Family Coordinator,* **17**, 191–203.

Berg, Phyllis A., and Hyde, Janet S. (1976, Aug.). Race and sex differences in causal attributions of success and failure. Paper presented at meetings of the American Psychological Association, Washington, D.C.

Berger, Charles J. (1980). Medical risks associated with "natural" family planning. *Advances in Planned Parenthood,* **15**(1), 1–2.

Berger, Raymond M. (1982). *Gay and gray: The older homosexual man.* Champaign, IL: University of Illinois Press.

Bergquist, Christer, et al. (1979). Inhibition of ovulation in women by intranasal treatment with a luteinizing hormone-releasing hormone agonist. *Contraception,* **19**, 497–506.

Berk, Bernard. (1977). Face-saving at the singles dance. *Social Problems,* 530–544.

Bermant, Gordon, and Davidson, Julian M. (1974). *Biological bases of sexual behavior.* New York: Harper & Row.

Bernard, Jesse. (1981). The good provider role: Its rise and fall. *American Psychologist,* **36**, 1–12.

Berne, Eric. (1970). *Sex in human loving.* New York: Simon & Schuster.

Bernstein, Anne C. (1976). How children learn about sex and birth. *Psychology Today,* **9**(8), 31.

Bernstein, Anne C., and Cowan, Philip A. (1975). Children's concepts of how people get babies. *Child Development,* **46**, 77–92.

Berscheid, Ellen, and Walster, Elaine. (1974). A little bit about love. In T. L. Huston (Ed.), *Foundations of interpersonal attraction.* New York: Academic Press.

Berscheid, Ellen, and Walster, Elaine. (1974). Physical attractiveness. *Advances in Experimental Social Psychology,* **7**, 157–215.

Berscheid, Ellen, et al. (1971). Physical attractiveness and dating choice: A test of the matching hypothesis. *Journal of Experimental Social Psychology,* **7**, 173–189.

Bess, Barbara E., and Janus, Samuel S. (1976). Prostitution. In B. J. Sadock et al. (Eds.), *The sexual experience.* Baltimore: Williams & Wilkins.

Bibring, Grete, et al. (1961). A study of the psychological processes in pregnancy and of the earliest mother-child relationship. *The psychoanalytic study of the child.* Vol. XVI. 9–72. New York: International Universities Press.

Beiber, Irving. (1976). A discussion of "Homosexuality: The ethical challenge." *Journal of Consulting and Clinical Psychology,* **44**, 163–166.

Biller, Henry and Meredith, D. (1975). *Father power.* New York: Anchor Books.

Billings, Andrew. (1979). Conflict resolution in distressed and nondistressed married couples. *Journal of Consulting and Clinical Psychology,* **47**, 368–376.

Billings, E. L., Billings, J. J., and Catarinch, M. (1974). *Atlas of the ovulation method.* Collegeville, MN: Liturgical Press.

Bingham, H. C. (1928). Sex development in apes. *Comparative Psychology Monographs,* **5**, 1–165.

Birchler, G. R., Weiss, R. L., and Vincent, J. P. (1975). Multimethod analysis of social reinforcement exchange between maritally distressed and nondistressed spouse and stranger dyads. *Journal of Personality and Social Psychology,* **31**, 349–360.

Birnbaum, Judith A. (1976). Life patterns and self-esteem in gifted family-oriented and career-committed women. In M. Mednick, L. W. Hoffman, and S. Tangri (Eds.), *Women: Social psychological perspectives on achievement.* New York: Psychological Dimensions.

Biskind, Morton S. (1947). The relation of nutritional deficiency to impaired libido and potency in the male. *Journal of Gerontology,* **2**, 303–314.

Blair, C. David, and Lanyon, Richard I. (1981). Exhibitionism: Etiology and treatment. *Psychological Bulletin,* **89**, 439–463.

Blanchard, R., Clemmensen, L. H., and Steiner, B. W. (1983). Gender reorientation and psychosocial adjustment in male-to-female transsexuals. *Archives of Sexual Behavior,* **12**, 503–510.

Blanchard, Ray, and Steiner, Betty W. (1983). Gender reorientation, psychological adjustment, and involvement with female partners in female-to-male transsexuals. *Archives of Sexual Behavior,* **12**, 149–158.

Blanchard, W. H. (1959). The group process in gang rape. *Journal of Social Psychology,* **49**, 259–266.

Block, Jeanne H. (1976). Issues, problems, and pitfalls in assessing sex differences. *Merrill-Palmer Quarterly,* **22**, 283–308.

Block, Jeanne H. (1983). Differential premises arising from differential socialization of the sexes: Some conjectures. *Child Development,* **54**, 1335–1354.

Blood, R., and Wolfe, D. N. (1960). *Husbands and wives.* Glencoe, IL: Free Press.

Blumstein, Philip W., and Schwartz, Pepper. (1974). Lesbianism and bisexuality. In E. Goode (Ed.), *Sexual deviance and sexual deviants.* New York: Morrow Press.

Blumstein, Philip W., and Schwartz, Pepper. (1976). Bisexual women. In J. P. Wiseman (Ed.), *The social psychology of sex.* New York: Harper & Row.

Blumstein, Philip, and Schwartz, Pepper. (1983). *American couples.* New York: William Morrow.

Boffey, Philip M. (1984, Oct. 9). Fast and accurate chlamydia test reported. *The New York Times,* C2.

Boggan, E. C., Haft, M. G., Lister, C., and Rupp, J. P. (1975). *The rights of gay people.* New York: Discus Books, Avon.

Bohmer, Carol. (1974). Judicial attitudes toward rape victims. *Judicature,* **57**, 303–307.

Bolles, Robert C. (1967). *Theory of motivation.* New York: Harper & Row.

Bonaparte, Marie. (1965). *Female sexuality.* New York: Grove Press. (First published by International Universities Press, 1953).

Boruchowitz, Robert C. (1973). Victimless crimes: A proposal to free the courts. *Judicature,* **57**, 69–78.

Boston Women's Health Book Collective. (1976). *Our bodies, ourselves.* New York: Simon & Schuster.

Boswell, John. (1980). *Christianity, social tolerance, and homosexuality.* Chicago: University of Chicago Press.

Brady, Katherine. (1978). *Father's days.* New York: Dell paperback.

Brandt, Anthony. (1982, Oct.). Avoiding couple karate: Lessons in the marital arts. *Psychology Today,* **16**(10), 38–43.

Breast cancer: Second thoughts about routine mammography. (1976). *Science,* **193**, 555.

Breasted, Mary. (1970). *Oh, sex education.* New York: Praeger.

Brecher, Edward M. (1975), Mar.–Apr.). Marijuana. *Consumer Reports,* **40**, 3–4.

Brecher, Edward M. (1984). *Love, sex, and aging.* Mount Vernon, N.Y.: Consumers Union.

Brecher, Ruth, and Brecher, Edward. (Eds.). (1966). *An analysis of human sexual response.* New York: Signet Books, New American Library.

Brent, Jonathan. (1976). A general introduction to privacy. *Massachusetts Law Quarterly,* **61**, 10–18.

Brenton, Myron. (1972). *Sex talk.* New York: Stein and Day.

Brim, O. G. (1976). Theories of the male mid-life crisis. *Counseling Psychologist,* **6**(1), 2–9.

Brinton, Crane. (1959). *A history of western morals.* New York: Harcourt Brace Jovanovich.

Broderick, Carlfred B. (1966a). Sexual behavior among preadolescents. *Journal of Social Issues,* **22**(2), 6–21.

Broderick, Carlfred B. (1966b). Socio-sexual development in a suburban community. *Journal of Sex Research,* **2**, 1–24.

Broderick, Carlfred B., and Bernard, Jessie. (1969). *The individual, sex, and society.* Baltimore: John Hopkins.

Brodsky, Carroll M. (1976). Rape at work. In M. J. Walker and S. L. Brodsky (Eds.), *Sexual assault: The victim and the rapist.* Lexington, MA: Lexington Books.

Bronson, F. (1968). Pheromonal influences on mammalian reproduction. In M. Diamond (Ed.), *Perspectives in reproduction and sexual behavior.* Bloomington: Indiana University Press.

Brotman, Harris. (1984, Jan. 8). Human embryo transplants. *The New York Times Magazine,* pp. 42 ff.

Broun, Heywood, and Leech, Margaret. (1927). *Anthony Comstock: Roundsman of the Lord.* New York: Boni.

Broverman, Inge K., et al. (1972). Sex-role stereotypes: A current appraisal. *Journal of Social Issues,* **28**(2), 59–78.

Brown, C., et al. (1978). Community standards, conservatism, and judgements of pornography. *Journal of Sex Research,* **14**, 81–95.

Brown, Daniel G. (1966). Female orgasm and sexual inadequacy. In Ruth Brecher and Edward Brecher (Eds.), *An analysis of human sexual response.* New York: Signet Books, New American Library.

Brown, M., Amoroso, D. M., and Ware, E. E. (1976). Behavioral effects of viewing pornography. *Journal of Social Psychology,* **98**, 235–245.

Brownmiller, Susan. (1975). *Against our will: Men, women, and rape.* New York: Simon & Schuster.

Bruce, H. M. (1969). Pheromones and behavior in mice. *Acta Neurologica Belgica,* **69**, 529–538.

Brueschke, Erich E., et al. (1979). Development of a reversible vas deferens occlusive device, VI. Long-term evaluation of flexible prosthetic devices. *Fertility and Sterility,* **31**, 575–586.

Bruser, M. (1969). Sporting activities during pregnancy. Cited in Sports and pregnancy. *Briefs: Footnotes on Maternity Care,* **33**(4), 51–53.

Brussel, J. A. (1971). Comment following Menachem Amir, Forcible rape. *Sexual Behavior,* **1**, 8.

Bryan, James H. (1965). Apprenticeships in prostitution. *Social Problems,* **12**, 278–297.

Bryant, C. D. (Ed.). (1977). *Sexual deviancy in social context.* New York: Franklin Watts.

Budoff, Penny W. (1980). *No more menstrual cramps and other good news.* New York: Putnam.

Buhrich, Neil, and Beaumont, Trina. (1981). Comparison of transvestism in Australia and America. *Archives of Sexual Behavior,* **10**, 269–280.

Bullough, Vern L. (1976). *Sexual variances in society and history.* New York: Wiley.

Bullough, Vern, and Bullough, B. (1978). *Prostitution: An illustrated social history.* New York: Crown Publishers.

Burgess, Ann W. (1984). *Child pornography and sex rings.* Lexington, MA: Lexington Books (D. C. Heath).

Burgess, Ann W., and Holmstrom, Linda L. (1974a). Rape trauma syndrome. *American Journal of Psychiatry,* **131**, 981–986.

Burgess, Ann W., and Holmstrom, Lynda L. (1974b). *Rape: Victims of crisis.* Bowie, MD: Robert J. Brady.

Burgess, Ann W. and Holmstrom, Lynda L. (1979). *Rape: Crisis and recovery.* Bowie, MD: Robert J. Brady.

Burton, Frances D. (1970). Sexual climax in *Macaca Mulatta. Proceedings of the Third International Congress on Primatology,* **3**, 180–191.

Bush, Trudy L., et al. (1983). Estrogen use and all-cause mortality. *Journal of the American Medical Association,* **249**, 903–906.

Buss, Arnold. (1966). *Psychopathology.* New York: Wiley.

Butler, Julius C., and Wagner, Nathaniel N. (1975). Sexuality during pregnancy and postpartum. In R. Green (Ed.), *Human sexuality: A health practitioner's text.* Baltimore: Williams & Wilkins.

Byfield, Barbara N., and Tedeschi, Frank L. (1975). *Solemn high murder.* Garder City, NY: Doubleday.

Byler, Ruth V. (1969). *Teach us what we want to know.* New York: Mental Health Materials Center, for the Connecticut State Board of Education.

Byrne, Donn. (1971). *The attraction paradigm.* New York: Academic Press.

Byrne, Donn. (1977, July). A pregnant pause in the sexual revolution. *Psychology Today,* **11**(2), 67–68.

Byrne, Donn. (1977). Social psychology and the study of sexual behavior. *Personality and Social Psychology Bulletin,* **3**, 3–30.

Byrne, Donn. (1983). Sex without contraception. In D. Byrne and W. A. Fisher (Eds.), *Adolescents, sex, and contraception.* Hillsdale, NJ: Lawrence Erlbaum.

Byrne, D., Ervin, C. E., and Lamberth, J. (1970). Continuity between the experimental study of attraction and real-life computer dating. *Journal of Personality and Social Psychology,* **16**, 157–165.

Callahan, Daniel. (1970). *Abortion, law, and morality.* New York: Macmillan.

Carpenter, C. R. (1942). Sexual behavior of free ranging rhesus monkeys (*Macaca mulatta*). *Journal of Comparative and Physiological Psychology,* **33**, 113–162.

Carpenter, Mary. (1979, Sept. 24). Physicians ponder popularity of pregnancy self-test kits. *Medical News,* **3**(14), 18.

Carroll, J., Volk, K., and Hyde, J. S. (1985). Differences between males and females in motives for engaging in sexual intercourse. *Archives of Sexual Behavior,* **14**, 131–139.

Catania, Joseph A., and White, Charles B. (1982). Sexuality in an aged sample: Cognitive determinants of masturbation. *Archives of Sexual Behavior,* **11**, 237–246.

Cates, R. M., et al. (1982). Premarital abuse: A social psychological perspective. *Journal of Family Issues,* **3**(1), 79–90.

Catterall, R. D. (1974). *A short textbook of venereology.* Philadelphia: Lippincott.

Caughey, Madeline S. (1974). The principle of harm and its application to laws criminalizing prostitution. *Denver Law Journal,* **51**, 235–262.

Centers for Disease Control. (1983). *Sexually transmitted disease statistical letter, 1982.* Atlanta: Centers for Disease Control.

Center for Disease Control. (1983, Jan. 6). Acquired immune deficiency syndrome (AIDS)—United States. *Morbidity and Mortality Weekly Report,* **32**, 688–691.

Chafetz, Janet S. (1974). *Masculine/feminine or human? An overview of the sociology of sex roles.* Itasca, IL: F. E. Peacock.

Chaikin, A. L., and Derlega, V. J. (1976). Norms affecting self-disclosure in men and women. *Journal of Consulting and Clinical Psychology,* **44**, 376–380.

Chambless, Dianne L., et al. (1982). The pubococcygeus and female orgasm: A correlational study with normal subjects. *Archives of Sexual Behavior,* **11**, 479–490.

Chappell, Duncan. (1976). Cross-cultural research on forcible rape. *International Journal of Criminology and Penology,* **4**, 295–304.

Chappell, D., Geis, G., and Fogarty, F. (1974). Forcible rape: Bibliography. *Journal of Criminal Law and Criminology,* **65**, 248–263.

Check, James V. P., and Malamuth, Neil M. (1984). Can

there be positive effects of participation in pornography experiments? *Journal of Sex Research,* **20**, 14–31.

Chein, I., Gerard, D., Lee, R., and Rosenfeld, E. (1964). *Narcotics, delinquency, and social policy.* London: Tavistock.

Chesler, Phyllis. (1972). *Women and madness.* Garden City, NY: Doubleday.

Chiazze, L., Jr., et al. (1968). The length and variability of the human menstrual cycle. *Journal of the American Medical Association,* **203**, 6.

Cimbalo, R. S., Faling, B., and Mousaw, P. (1976). The course of love: A cross-sectional design. *Psychological Reports,* **38**, 1292–1294.

Clanton, Gordon. (1973). The contemporary experience of adultery: Bob and Carol and Updike and Rimmer. In R. W. Libby and R. N. Whitehurst (Eds.), *Renovating marriage.* Danville, CA: Consensus Publishers.

Clark, Alexander L., and Wallin, Paul. (1964). The accuracy of husbands' and wives' reports of the frequency of marital coitus. *Population Studies,* **18**, 165–173.

Clarkson, Thomas B., and Alexander, Nancy J. (1980). Does vasectomy increase the risk of atherosclerosis? *Journal of Cardiovascular Medicine,* **5**(11).

Clarren, S. K., and Smith, D. W. (1978). The fetal alcohol syndrome. *New England Journal of Medicine,* **298**, 1063–1067.

Clatworthy, Nancy M. (1980). Morals and the ever-changing college student. Paper presented at North Central Sociological meetings, Dayton, Ohio.

Clement, U., Schmidt, G., and Kruse, M. (1984). Changes in sex differences in behavior: A replication of a study on West German students (1966–1981). *Archives of Sexual Behavior,* **13**, 99–120.

Cochran, W. G., Mosteller, F., and Tukey, J. W. (1953). Statistical problems of the Kinsey report. *Journal of the American Statistical Association,* **48**, 673–716.

Cofer, Charles N. (1972). *Motivation and emotion.* Glenview, IL: Scott Foresman.

Cohen, Michael W., and Friedman, Stanford B. (1975). Nonsexual motivation of adolescent sexual behavior. *Medical Aspects of Human Sexuality,* **9**(9), 9–31.

Cohen, M. L., Garofalo, R., Boucher, R., and Seghorn, T. (1971). The psychology of rapists. *Seminars in Psychiatry,* **3**, 307–327.

Cohn, Frederick. (1974). *Understanding human sexuality.* Englewood Cliffs, NJ: Prentice-Hall.

Cohn, Lawrence. (1983, Nov. 16). Pix less able but porn is stable. *Variety,* **313**(3), 1–2.

Cole, Theodore M. (1975). Sexuality: a health practitioner's text. Baltimore: Williams & Wilkins.

Coleman, Eli. (1982a). Changing approaches to the treatment of homosexuality: A review. In W. Paul et al. (Eds.), *Homosexuality: Social, psychological, and biological issues.* Beverly Hills: Sage.

Coleman, Eli. (1982b). Developmental stages of the coming-out process. In W. Paul et al. (Eds.), *Homosexuality: Social, psychological, and biological issues.* Beverly Hills: Sage.

Coleman, S., Piotrow, P. T., and Rinehart, W. (1979, Mar.). Tobacco: Hazards to health and human reproduction. *Population Reports,* Series L(1).

Comfort, Alex. (1971). Likelihood of human pheromones. *Nature,* **230**, 432–433.

Comfort, Alex. (1972). *The joy of sex.* New York: Crown.

Commission on Obscenity and Pornography. (1970). *The report of the commission on obscenity and pornography.* New York: Bantam Books.

Conn, Jacob H. (1948). Children's awareness of the origin of babies. *Journal of Child Psychiatry,* **1**, 3–57.

Constantine, Larry L., and Constantine, Joan M. (1973). *Group marriage: A study of contemporary multilateral marriage.* New York: Macmillan.

Coombs, N. R. (1974). Male prostitution: A psychosocial view of behavior. *American Journal of Orthopsychiatry,* **44**, 782.

Corrales, R. (1974). The influence of family life's cycle categories, marital power, spousal agreement, and communication styles upon marital satisfaction in the first six years of marriage. Unpublished doctoral dissertation, University of Minnesota.

Cox, D. J. (1983). Menstrual symptoms in college students: A controlled study. *Journal of Behavioral Medicine,* **6**, 335–338.

Cox, Harvey. (Ed.). (1968). *The situation ethics debate.* Philadelphia: Westminster Press.

Cozby, P. C. (1973). Self-disclosure: A literature review. *Psychological Bulletin,* **79**, 73–91.

Craven, J., and Polak, A. (1954). Cantharidin poisoning. *British Medical Journal,* **2**, 1386–1388.

Croft-Cooke, Rupert. (1972). *The unrecorded life of Oscar Wilde.* New York: McKay.

Croughan, Jack L., et al. (1981). A comparison of treated and untreated male cross-dressers. *Archives of Sexual Behavior,* **10**, 515–528.

Cushman, P. (1961). Sexual behavior in heroin addiction and methadone maintenance. *New York Sate Medical Journal,* 1972, **27**.

Dalton, Katharina. (1964). *The premenstrual syndrome.* Springfield, IL: Charles C. Thomas.

Dalton, Katharina. (1966). The influence of mother's menstruation on her child. *Proceedings of the Royal Society for Medicine,* **59**, 1014.

Dalton, Katharina. (1969). *The menstrual cycle.* New York: Pantheon.

Dalton, Katharina. (1979). *Once a month.* Ramona, CA: Hunter House.

Darrow, William. (1984). Meeting the AIDS dilemma. Address to the AASECT/SSSS convention, Boston.

Davidson, Julian M., et al. (1983). Maintenance of sexual function in a castrated man treated with ovarian steroids. *Archives of Sexual Behavior,* **12**, 263–274.

Davis, James A. (1980). *General social surveys, 1972–1980: Cumulative data.* Chicago: National Opinion Research Center. New Haven: Yale University, Roper Public Opinion Research Center.

Davis, John D. (1978). When boy meets girl: Sex roles and the negotiation of intimacy in an acquaintance exercise. *Journal of Personality and Social Psychology,* **36**, 684–692.

Davis, Keith E., and Braucht, G. Nicholas. (1973). Exposure to pornography, character and sexual deviance: A retrospective study. *Journal of Social Issues,* **29**, 183–196.

Davison, G. C. (1976). Homosexuality: The ethical challenge. *Journal of Consulting and Clinical Psychology,* **44**, 157–162.

Davison, G. C., and Neale, J. M. (1974). *Abnormal psychology: An experimental clinical approach.* New York: Wiley.

Davison, Gerald C. (1982). Politics, ethics, and therapy for homosexuality. In W. Paul, et al. (Eds.), *Homosexuality: Social, psychological, and biological issues.* Beverly Hills: Sage.

Deaux, Kay. (1976). *The behavior of women and men.* Belmont, CA: Brooks/Cole.

DeLamater, John, and MacCorquodale, Patricia. (1979). *Premarital sexuality: Attitudes, relationships, behavior.* Madison: University of Wisconsin Press.

DeLamater, John. (1981). The social control of sexuality. *Annual Review of Sociology,* **7**, 263–290.

DeLamater, John. (1982). Response effects of question content. In W. Dijkstra and J. Van der Zouwen (Eds.), *Response behavior in the survey–interview.* London: Academic Press.

Delaney, J., Lupton, M. J., and Toth, E. (1976). *The curse: A cultural history of menstruation.* New York: Dutton.

DeLora, Joann S., and Warren, Carol A. B. (1977). *Understanding sexual interaction.* Boston: Houghton Mifflin.

Derogatis, Leonard R., and King, Katherine M. (1981). The coital coronary: A reassessment of the concept. *Archives of Sexual Behavior,* **10**, 325–336.

Deschin, C. S. (1963). Teen-agers and venereal disease: A sociological study of 600 teen-agers in NYC social hygiene clinics. *American Journal of Nursing,* **63**, 63–67.

Dewsbury, Donald A. (1981). Effects of novelty on copulatory behavior: The Coolidge effect and related phenomena. *Psychological Bulletin,* **89**, 464–483.

Diamond, Milton. (1965). A critical evaluation of the ontogeny of human sexual behavior. *Quarterly Review of Biology,* **40**, 147–175.

Diamond, Milton. (1979). Sexual identity and sex roles. In V. Bullough (Ed.), *The frontiers of sex research.* Buffalo, NY: Prometheus Books.

Dickinson, Robert L. (1949). *Atlas of human sex anatomy.* Baltimore: Williams & Wilkins.

Dienstbier, R. A. (1977). Sex and violence: Can research have it both ways? *Journal of Communication,* **27**(3), 176–188.

Dietz, P. E., and Evans, B. (1982). Pornographic imagery and prevalence of paraphilia. *American Journal of Psychiatry,* **139**, 1493–1495.

Dishotsky, N., Loughman, W., Mogar, R., and Lipscomb, W. (1971). LSD and genetic damage. *Science,* **172**, 431–440.;

Ditkoff, Mitchell. (1978). Child pornography. *American Humane Society Magazine,* **16**(4), 30.

Ditman, Keith. (1964). Inhibition of ejaculation by chlorprothixens. *American Journal of Psychiatry,* **120**, 1004–1005.

Dixon, Joan K. (1984). The commencement of bisexual activity in swinging married women over age thirty. *Journal of Sex Research,* **20**, 71–90.

Doering, Charles, et al. (1975). A cycle of plasma testosterone in the human male. *Journal of Clinical Endocrinology and Metabolism,* **40**, 492.

Doering, Charles, et al. (1978). Plasma testosterone levels and psychologic measures in men over a 2-month period. In R. Friedman, et al. (Eds.), *Sex Differences in Behavior.* Huntington, NY: Krieger.

Donnerstein, Ed. (1980). Aggressive-erotica and violence against women. *Journal of Personality and Social Psychology,* **3**, 269–277.

Donnerstein, Ed, and Berkowitz, Leonard. (1981). Victim reactions in aggressive-erotic films as a factor in violence against women. *Journal of Personality and Social Psychology,* **41**, 710–724.

Donnerstein, Ed. (1983). Erotica and human aggression. In R. Geen and E. Donnerstein (Eds.), *Aggression: Theoretical and empirical reviews.* Vol. 2. New York: Academic Press.

Dorner, G. (1969, Feb. 2). Prophylaxie and therapie angeborener sexual deviationen. *Deutsche Medizinische Wochenschrift Sonderdruck.*

Dorner, G. (1976). *Hormones and brain differentiation.* Amsterdam: Elsevier.

Dotti, A., and Reda, M. (1975). Major tranquilizers and sexual function. In M. Sandler and G. L. Gessa (Eds.), *Sexual behavior: Pharmacology and biochemistry.* New York: Raven Press.

Doty, Richard L., et al. (1975). Changes in the intensity and pleasantness of human vaginal odors during the menstrual cycle. *Science,* **190**, 1316–1318.

Douglas, Mary. (1970). *Purity and danger: An analysis of concepts of pollution and taboo.* Baltimore: Penguin.

Dover, K. J. (1978). *Greek homosexuality.* Cambridge: Harvard University Press.

Doyle, J. A. (1983). *The male experience.* Dubuque, IA: Wm. C. Brown.

Dreger, Ralph M., et al. (1964). Behavioral classification project. *Journal of Consulting Psychology,* **28**, 1–13.

Driscoll, James P. (1971, Mar.–Apr.). Transsexuals. *Transaction,* 28–31.

Driscoll, R., Davis, K. E., and Lipetz, M. E. (1972). Parental interference and romantic love: The Romeo and Juliet effect. *Journal of Personality and Social Psychology,* **24**, 1–10.

Dunn, H. G., et al. (1977). Maternal cigarette smoking during pregnancy and the child's subsequent development: II. Neurologic and intellectual maturation to the age of 6½ years. *Canadian Journal of Public Health,* **68**, 470–517.

Dutton, Donald G., and Aron, Arthur P. (1974). Some evidence for heightened sexual attraction under conditions of high anxiety. *Journal of Personality and Social Psychology,* **30**, 470–517.

Dytrych, Z., Matejcek, Z., et al. (1975). Children born to women denied abortion. *Family Planning Perspectives,* **7**, 165–171.

Eakins, B. W., and Eakins, R. G. (1978). *Sex differences in human communication.* Boston: Houghton Mifflin.

Eastman, N. J. (1968, Nov.). The geographic distribution of pregnancy in the United States. National Research Council, Working Group on Relation of Nutrition to the Toxemias of Pregnancy. [Cited in L. M. Hellman and J. A. Pritchard, *Williams obstetrics* (14th ed.). New York: Appleton-Century-Crofts.]

Edelman, D. A., et al. (1983). Comparative trial of the contraceptive sponge and diaphragm: A preliminary report. *Journal of Reproductive Medicine,* **28**, 781–784.

Edwards, John N., and Booth, Alan. (1976). Sexual behavior in and out of marriage: An assessment of correlates. *Journal of Marriage and the Family,* 73–81.

Ehrhard, Anke, et al. (1985). Sexual orientation after prenatal exposure to exogenous estrogen. *Archives of Sexual Behavior,* **14**, 57–78.

Ehrlich, June, and Riesman, David. (1961). Age and authority in the interview. *Public Opinion Quarterly,* **23**, 39–56.

Ehrlich, Paul A., and Ehrlich, Anne H. (1972). *Population, resources, environment* (2nd ed.). San Francisco: Freeman.

Elder, Glen. (1969). Appearance and education in marriage mobility. *American Sociological Review,* **34**, 519–533.

Elias, James, and Gebhard, Paul. (1969). Sexuality and sexual learning in childhood. *Phi Delta Kappan,* **50**, 401–405.

Ellis, Albert. (1962). *The American sexual tragedy.* New York: Grove Press.

Ellis, Henry Havelock. (1939). *My life.* Boston: Houghton Mifflin.

Englander-Golden, P., et al. (1980, March). Female sexual arousal and the menstrual cycle. *Journal of Human Stress,* 42–48.

Erikson, Erik H. (1950). *Childhood and society.* New York: Norton.

Erikson, Erik H. (1968). *Identity: Youth and crisis.* New York: Norton.

Erwin, J., and Maple, Terru. (1976). Ambisexual behavior with male-male anal penetration in male rhesus monkeys. *Archives of Sexual Behavior,* **5**, 9–14.

Evans, R. B. (1970). Sixteen personality factor questionnaire scores of homosexual men. *Journal of Consulting and Clinical Psychology,* **34**, 212–215.

Everett, Guy M. (1975). Amyl nitrate ("poppers") as an aphrodisiac. In M. Sandler and G. L. Gessa (Eds.), *Sexual behavior: Pharmacology and biochemistry.* New York: Raven Press.

Eysenck, H. J., and Nias, D. K. B. (1978). *Sex, violence, and the media.* New York: Harper & Row.

Fahrenbach, H. B., Alexander, N. J., Senner, J. W., Fulgham, D. L., and Coon, L. J. (1980). Effect of vasectomy on the retinal vasculature of men. *Journal of Andrology,* **1**, 299–303.

Farkas, G. M., Sine, L. G., and Evans, I. M. (1978). Personality, sexuality, and demographic differences between volunteers and nonvolunteers for a laboratory study of male sexual behavior. *Archives of Sexual Behavior,* **7**, 513–520.

Fasteau, Marc F. (1974). *The male machine.* New York: McGraw-Hill.

Feder, H. H. (1984). Hormones and sexual behavior. *Annual Review of Psychology,* **35**, 165–200.

Federal Bureau of Investigation. (1973, 1975, 1979). *Uniform crime reports.*

Feild, Hubert S. (1978). Attitudes toward rape: A comparative analysis of police, rapists, crisis counselors, and citizens. *Journal of Personality and Social Psychology,* **36**, 156–179.

Feinbloom, Deborah H. (1976). Transvestites and transsexuals: *Mixed views.* New York: Delacorte Press.

Felman, Yehudi M., and Nikitas, James A. (1981). Nongonococcal urethritis. *Journal of the American Medical Association,* **245**, 381–386.

Felton, Gary, and Segelman, Florrie. (1978). Lamaze childbirth training and changes in belief about personal control. *Birth and the Family Journal,* **5**, 141–150.

Fensterheim, Herbert, and Kantor, Jerry S. (1980). The behavioral approach to sexual disorders. In B. J. Wolman and J. Money (Eds.), *Handbook of human sexuality.* Englewood Cliffs, NJ: Prentice-Hall.

Ferber, Andrew S., et al. (1967). Men with vasectomies: A study of medical, sexual, and psychosocial changes. *Psychosomatic Medicine,* **29**, 354–366.

Feshbach, Seymour, and Malamuth, Neal. (1978, Nov.). Sex and aggression: Proving the link. *Psychology Today,* **12**(6), 110.

Finkelhor, David. (1980). Sex among siblings: A survey on prevalence, variety and effects. *Archives of Sexual Behavior,* **9**, 171–194.

Fisher, C., et al. (1983). Patterns of female sexual arousal during sleep and waking: Vaginal thermo-conductance studies. *Archives of Sexual Behavior,* **12**, 97–122.

Fisher, J. D., et al. (1975, Sept.). Hands touching hands: Affective and evaluative effects of an interpersonal touch. Paper presented at meetings of the American Psychological Association, Chicago.

Fisher, Seymour. (1973) *Understanding the female orgasm.* New York: Basic Books.

Fisher, William A., Byrne, D. and White, L. A. (1983). Emotional barriers to contraception. In D. Byrne and W. A. Fisher (Eds.), *Adolescents, sex, and contraception.* Hillsdale, NJ: Lawrence Erlbaum.

Fishman, J. (1978). *Sex in prison.* New York: Hartwick Publications.

Fishman, Jack. (1980). Fatness, puberty, and ovulation. *New England Journal of Medicine,* **303**, 42–43.

Fleming, Michael Z., Jenkins, S. R., and Bugarin, C. (1980). Questioning current definitions of gender identity: Implications of the Bem Sex-Role Inventory for transsexuals. *Archives of Sexual Behavior,* **9**, 13–26.

Fleming, M., Steinman, C., and Boeknok, G. (1980). Methodological problems in assessing sex reassignment surgery: A reply to Meyer and Reter. *Archives of Sexual Behavior,* **9**, 451–456.

Fleming, Michael, et al. (1981). A study of pre- and post-surgical transsexuals: MMPI characteristics. *Archives of Sexual Behavior,* **10**, 161–170.

Fletcher, Joseph. (1966). *Situation ethics.* Philadelphia: Westminster Press.

Fletcher, Joseph. (1967). *Moral responsibility: Situation ethics at work.* Philadelphia: Westminster Press.

Ford, Clellan S., and Beach, Frank A. (1951). *Patterns of sexual behavior.* New York: Harper & Row.

Forer, Bertram R. (1972). Use of physical contact. In L. N. Soloman and B. Berzon (Eds.), *New perspectives on encounter groups.* San Francisco: Jossey-Bass.

Forgac, Gregory E., and Michaels, Edward J. (1982). Personality characteristics of two types of male exhibitionists. *Journal of Abnormal Psychology,* **91**, 287–293.

Forssman, H., and Thuwe, I. (1966). One hundred and twenty children born after application for therapeutic abortion refused. *Acta Psychiatrica Scandinavica,* **42**, 71–85.

Fox, C. A., et al. (1972). Studies on the relationship between plasma testosterone levels and human sexual activity. *Journal of Endocrinology,* **52**, 51–58.

Fox, Maurice, and Lipton, Helene L. (1983). AIDS—Two years later. *New England Journal of Medicine,* **309**, 609–610.

Francoeur, Anna K., and Francoeur, Robert T. (1974). Hot and cool sex: Closed and open marriage. In R. T. Francoeur and A. K. Francoeur, (Eds.), *The future of sexual relations.* Englewood Cliffs, NJ: Prentice-Hall.

Francoeur, Robert T. (1974). The technologies of man-made sex. In R. T. Francoeur and A. K. Francoeur (Eds.), *The future of sexual relations.* Englewood Cliffs, NJ: Prentice-Hall.

Francoeur, Robert. (1983, July). Drugs that screw up sex. *Forum.*

Frank, E., Anderson, C., and Rubinstein, D. (1978). Frequency of sexual dysfunction in "normal" couples. *New England Journal of Medicine,* **299**(3), 111–115.

Frank, Lawrence K. (1961). *The conduct of sex.* New York: Morrow.

Frank, R. T. (1931). The hormonal causes of premenstrual tension. *Archives of Neurological Psychiatry,* **26**, 1053.

Freedman, A. M. (1976). Drugs and sexual behavior. In B. J. Sadock et al. (Eds.), *The sexual experience.* Baltimore: Williams & Wilkins.

Freedman, Mark. (1975). Homosexuals may be healthier than straights. *Psychology Today,* **8**(10), 28–32.

Freud, Sigmund. (1924). *A general introduction to psychoanalysis.* New York: Permabooks, 1953. (Boni & Liveright edition, 1924).

Freud, S. (1948). The psychogenesis of a case of homosexuality in a woman (1920). In *The collected papers,* Vol. II. London: Hogarth. Pp. 202–231.

Friday, N. (1973). *My secret garden: Women's sexual fantasies.* New York: Simon & Schuster.

Friday, N. (1975). *Forbidden flowers: More Women's sexual fantasies.* New York: Simon & Schuster.

Frieze, Irene H. (1983). Causes and consequences of marital rape. *Signs,* **8**, 532–553.

Frisch, R. E., and McArthur, J. W. (1974). Menstrual cycles: Fatness as a determinant of minimum weight for height necessary for their maintenance or onset. *Science,* **185**, 949–951.

Fritz, Gregory S., Stoll, K., and Wagner, N. M. (1981). A comparison of males and females who were sexually molested as children. *Journal of Sex and Marital Therapy,* **7**, 54–59.

Frodi, A., Macaulay, J., and Thome, P. R. (1977). Are women always less aggressive than men? A review of the experimental literature. *Psychological Bulletin,* **84**, 634–660.

Fromm, Erich. (1956). *The art of loving.* New York: Harper & Row.

Fry, William F. (1976). Psychodynamics of sexual humor: Sex and the elderly. *Medical Aspects of Human Sexuality,* **10**(2), 140.

Fulton, Gere B. (1974). *Sexual awareness.* Boston: Holbrook Press.

Fulton, Gere B. (1977). Bioethics and health education: Some issues of the biological revolution. *Journal of School Health,* **47**, 205–211.

Fyfe, B. (1983). "Homophobia" or homosexual bias reconsidered. *Archives of Sexual Behavior,* **12**, 549–554.

Gagnon, F. (1950). Contribution to study of etiology and prevention of cancer of cervix or uterus. *American Journal of Obstetrics and Gynecology,* **60**, 516.

Gagnon, John H. (1965a). Female child victims of sex offenses. *Social Problems,* **13**, 176–192.

Gagnon, John H. (1965b). Sexuality and sexual learning in the child. *Psychiatry,* **28**, 212–228.

Gagnon, John H. (1977). *Human sexualities.* Glenview, IL: Scott, Foresman.

Gagnon, John H., and Simon, William. (Eds.). (1967). *Sexual deviance.* New York: Harper & Row.

Gagnon, John H., and Simon, William. (1973). *Sexual conduct: The social origins of human sexuality.* Chicago: Aldine.

Gallo, Maria Teresa de, and Alzate, Helo. (1976). Brothel prostitution in Columbia. *Archives of Sexual Behavior,* **5**, 1–7.

Galston, A. W. (1975). Here come the clones. *Natural History,* **84**, 72–75.

Garcia, Luis T. (1982). Sex-role orientation and stereotypes about male-female sexuality. *Sex Roles,* **8**, 863–876.

Garfinkel, Harold. (1967). *Studies in ethnomethodology.* Englewood Cliffs, NJ: Prentice-Hall.

Garner, Brian, and Smith, Richard W. (1977). Are there really any gay male athletes? An empirical survey. *Journal of Sex Research,* **13**, 22–34.

Garrett, Thomas, and Wright, Richard. (1975). Wives of rapists and incest offenders. *Journal of Sex Research,* **11**, 149–157.

Gartrell, Nanette K. (1982). Hormones and homosexuality. In W. Paul, et al. (Eds.), *Homosexuality: Social, psychological, and biological issues.* Beverly Hills: Sage.

Gartrell, Nanette K., Loriaux, D. L., and Chase, T. N. (1977). Plasma testosterone in homosexual and heterosexual women. *American Journal of Psychiatry,* **134**, 1117–1119.

Gay, Peter. (1984). *The bourgeois experience: Victoria to Freud.* New York: Oxford University Press.

Gebhard, Paul H. (1968). Postmarital coitus among widows and divorcees. In P. Bohannan (Ed.), *Divorce and after.* Garden City, NY: Doubleday.

Gebhard, Paul H. (1969, Mar.). Misconceptions about female prostitutes. *Medical Aspects of Human Sexuality,* **3**, 24–30.

Gebhard, Paul H. (1971). Human sexual behavior: A summary statement. In D. S. Marshall and R. C. Suggs (Eds.), *Human sexual behavior.* New York: Basic Books.

Gebhard, P. H., Gagnon, J. H., Pomeroy, W. B., and Christenson, C. V. (1965). *Sex offenders: An analysis of types.* New York: Harper & Row.

Geis, Gilbert. (1977). Forcible rape: An introdution. In D Chappell and R. Geis (Eds.) *Forcible rape.* New York: Columbia University Press.

Gibbens, R., Soothill, K., and Way, C. (1981). Sex offenses against young girls: A long-term record study. *Psychological Medicine,* **11**, 351–353.

Gillette, Paul J. (1972). *Vasectomy: The male sterilization operation.* New York: Paperback Library.

Gilmartin, Brian G. (1975). That swinging couple down the block. *Psychology Today,* **8**(9), 54.

Ginsberg, Barry G., and Vogelsong, Edward. (1977). Premarital relationship improvement by maximizing empathy and self-disclosure. The PRIMES program. In B. G. Guerney (Ed.), *Relationship enhancement.* San Francisco: Jossey-Bass.

Ginsberg, G. L., Frosch, W. A., and Shapiro, T. (1972). The new impotence. *Archives of General Psychiatry,* **26**(3), 218–220.

Gittelson, Natalie. (1980, Jan.). Marriage: What women expect and what they get. *McCall's,* 87–89.

Gladue, Brian A., Green, Richard, and Helman, R. E. (1984). Neuroendocrine response to estrogen and sexual orientation. *Science,* **225**, 1496–1498.

Glass, S. J., Deuel, H. J., and Wright, C. A. (1940). Sex hormone studies in male homosexuality. *Endocrinology,* **26**, 590–594.

Glass, S. J., and Johnson, R. W. (1944). Limitations and complications of organotherapy in male homosexuality. *Journal of Clinical Endocrinology,* **4**, 540–544.

Glassberg, B. Y. (1970). The quandary of a virginal male. *Family Coordinator,* **19**, 82–85.

Goergen, Donald. (1974). *The sexual celibate.* New York: Seabury Press.

Goffman, Erving. (1961). *Encounters: Two studies in the sociology of interaction.* Indianapolis: Bobbs-Merrill.

Gold, Alice R., and Adams, David B. (1981). Motivational factors affecting fluctuations of female sexual activity at menstruation. *Psychology of Women Quarterly,* **5**, 670–680.

Gold, Dolores, and Reis, Myrna. (1982). Male teacher effects on young children: A theoretical and empirical consideration. *Sex Roles,* **8**, 493–514.

Goldberg, Daniel C., et al. (1983). The Gräfenberg spot and female ejaculation: A review of initial hypotheses. *Journal of Sex and Marital Therapy,* **9**, 27–37.

Golde, Peggy, and Kogan, Nathan. (1959). A sentence completion procedure for assessing attitudes toward old people. *Journal of Gerontology,* **14**, 355–363.

Goldfoot, D. A., Westerberg-van Loon, W., Groeneveld, W., and Koos Slob, A. (1980). Behavioral and physiolgical evidence of sexual climax in the female stump-tailed macaque (*Macaca arctoides*). *Science,* **208**, 1477–1478.

Goldman, Ronald J., and Goldman, Juliette D. G. (1982). *Children's sexual thinking.* London: Routledge & Kegan Paul, pp. 197, 213, 240, 263, 354.

Goldman, Ronald, and Goldman, Juliette. (1982). *Children's sexual thinking.* London: Routledge and Kegan Paul.

Goldsmith, M. F. (1983). Modifications in prostate cancer operation preserve potency. *Journal of the American Medical Association,* **250**, 2897–2899.

Goldstein, Bernard. (1976). *Human sexuality.* New York: McGraw-Hill.

Goldstein, Michael J. (1973). Exposure to erotic stimuli and sexual deviance. *Journal of Social Issues,* **29**, 197–219.

Goldstein, Michael J., and Kant, Harold. (1973). *Pornography and sexual deviance.* Berkeley: University of California Press.

Goode, Erich. (1970). *The marijuana smokers.* New York: Basic Books.

Goode, Erich. (1981). Comments on the homosexual role. *Journal of Sex Research,* **17**, 54–65.

Gordon, E. M. (1967). Acceptance of pregnancy before and since oral contraception. *Obstetrics and Gynecology,* **29**, 144–146.

Gordon, R. E., and Gordon, K. K. (1967). Factors in postpartum emotional adjustment. *American Journal of Orthopsychiatry,* **37**, 359–360.

Gordon, R. E., Kapostons, E. F., and Gordon, K. K. (1965). Factors in postpartum emotional adjustment. *Obstetrics and Gynecology,* **25**, 158–166.

Gosselin, Chris, and Wilson, Glenn. (1980). *Sexual variations: Fetishism, sadomasochism, transvestism.* New York: Simon& Schuster.

Gottman, John, Markman, Howard, and Notarius, Cliff. (1977). The topography of marital conflict: A sequential analysis of verbal and noverbal behavior. *Journal of Marriage and the Family,* **39**, 461–478.

Gottman, John, Notarius, Cliff, Gonso, Jonni, and Markman, Howard. (1976). *A couple's guide to communication.* Champaign, IL: Research Press.

Gottman, John M. (1979). *Marital interaction: Experimental investigations.* New York: Academic Press.

Gottman, John M. (1980). Consistency of nonverbal affect and affect reciprocity in marital interaction. *Journal of Consulting and Clinical Psychology,* **48**, 711–717.

Gould, R. (1974, Apr). Vasectomy complications (an 1110 patient study). Paper presented at the twelfth annual meeting of the American Association of Planned Parenthood Physicians, Memphis.

Gove, W. R., and Tudor, Jeannette F. (1973). Adult sex roles and mental illness. *American Journal of Sociology,* **78**, 812–835.

Gray, A. H. (1922). *Men, women, and God.* New York: Association Press.

Great Britain Committee on Homosexual Offenses and Prostitution. (1963). *The Wolfenden report* (American ed.). New York: Stein and Day.

Green, B. L., Lee, R. R. and Lustig, N. (1974, Sept.). Conscious and unconscious factors in marital infidelity. *Medical Aspects of Human Sexuality,* 87–91, 97–98, 104–105.

Green, Richard M. (1966). Mythological, historical, and cross-cultural aspects of transsexualism. In H. Benjamin (Ed.), *The transsexual phenomenon.* New York: Julian Press.

Green, Richard. (1972). Homosexuality as mental illness. *International Journal of Psychiatry,* **10**, 77–98.

Green, Richard. (1975). Adults who want to change sex; adolescents who cross-dress; and children called "sissy" and "tomboy." In R. Green (Ed.), *Human sexuality: A health practitioner's text.* Baltimore: Williams & Wilkins.

Green, Richard. (1978). Sexual identity of 37 children raised by homosexual or transsexual parents. *American Journal of Psychiatry,* **135**, 692–687.

Green, Richard. (1978). Intervention and prevention: The child with cross-sex identity. In C. B. Qualls, et al. (Eds.), *The prevention of sexual disorders.* New York: Plenum.

Greene, F., Kirk, R. M., and Thompson, I. M. (1970). Retrograde ejaculation. *Medical Aspects of Human Sexuality,* **4**(12), 59–65.

Gregersen, Edgar. (1983). *Sexual practices: The story of human sexuality.* New York: Franklin Watts.

Griffin, Bernard Cardinal. (1956). Report of the Roman Catholic Advisory Commission on Prostitution and Homosexual Offenses and the Present Law. *Dublin Review,* **471**, 60–65.

Griffin, Susan. (1981). *Pornography and silence.* New York: Harper & Row.

Groat, H. Theodore, and Neal, A. G. (1975). A social psychological approach to family formation. In K. C. W. Kammeyer (Ed.), *Popuation studies: Selected essays and research* (2nd ed.). Chicago: Rand McNally.

Gross, Alan E. (1978). The male role and heterosexual behavior. *Journal of Social Issues,* **34**(1), 87–107.

Gross, Alan E., and Bellew-Smith, Martha (1983). A social psychological approach to reducing pregnancy risk in adolescence. In D. Byrne and W. A. Fisher (Eds.), *Adolescents, sex, and contraception.* Hillsdale, NJ: Lawrence Erlbaum.

Gruber, Kenneth J., Jones, R. J., and Freeman, M. H. (1982). Youth reactions to sexual assault. *Adolescence,* **17**, 541–551.

Gruntz, Louis G., Jr. (1974). Obscenity 1973: Remodeling the house that *Roth* built. *Loyola Law Review,* **20**, 159–174.

Guerney, Bernard G. (1977). *Relationship enhancement.* San Francisco: Jossey-Bass.

Gunby, Phil. (1983). Genital herpes research. *Journal of the American Medical Association,* **250**, 2417–2427.

Gutek, Barbara A., and Nakamura, C. Y. (1983). Gender roles and sexuality in the world of work. In E. R. Allgeier and N. B. McCormick (Eds.), *Changing boundaries: Gender roles and sexual behavior.* Palo Alto, CA: Mayfield.

Guttmacher, Allan F. (1947). The attitudes of 3381 physicians towards contraception and the contraceptives they prescribe. *Human Biology,* **12**, 1–12.

Haavio-Mannila, Elina. (1967). Sex differentiation in role expectations and performance. *Journal of Marriage and the Family,* **29**, 568–578.

Hackett, C. J. (1963). On the origin of the human treponematoses. *Bulletin of the World Health Organization,* **29**, 7–41.

Hafez, E. S. E. (Ed.). (1980). *Human reproduction: Conception and contraception.* Hagerstown, MD: Harper & Row.

Hahn, S. R., and Paige, K. E. (1980). American birth practices: A critical review. In J. E. Parsons (Ed.), *The psychobiology of sex differences and sex roles.* New York: McGraw-Hill, Hemisphere.

Haider, I. (1966). Thioridazine and sexual dysfunctions. *International Journal of Neuropsychiatry,* 255–257.

Hair, Paul. (1972). *Before the bawdy court.* London: Elek.

Halikas, J. A., Goodwin, P. H., and Guze, S. B. (1971). Marijuana effects: A survey of regular users. *Journal of the American Medical Association,* **217**, 692.

Hall, Judith A. (1978). Gender effects in decoding nonverbal cues. *Psychological Bulletin,* **85**, 845–857.

Halleck, S. (1967). Sex and mental health on the campus. *Journal of the American Medical Association,* **200**, 684.

Halverson, H. M. (1940). Genital and sphincter behavior of the male infant. *Journal of Genetic Psychology,* **43**, 95–136.

Hamilton, G. V. (1914). A study of sexual tendencies in monkeys and baboons. *Journal of Animal Behavior,* **4**, 295–318.

Hamilton, R. (1980). *The herpes book.* Los Angeles: J. P. Tarcher.

Hammond, Charles B., and Maxson, Wayne S. (1982). Current status of estrogen therapy for the menopause. *Fertility and Sterility,* **37**, 5–25.

Hand, J. R. (1970). Surgery of the penis and urethra. In M. F. Campbell and J. H. Harrison (Eds.), *Urology.* Vol. 3. Philadelphia: Saunders.

Hansfield, H. H. (1984, Jan. 20). Cause of acquired immune deficiency syndrome. *Journal of the American Medical Association,* **251**, 341.

Hansfield, H. A., Lipman, T. O., Harnisch, J. P., Tronca, E., and Holmes, K. K. (1975). Asymptomatc gonorrhea in men: Diagnosis, natural course, prevalence, and significance. *New England Journal of Medicine,* **290**(3), 117–123.

Harbison, R. D. and Mantilla-Plata, B. (1972). Prenatal toxicity, maternal distribution and placental transfer of tetrahydrocannabinol. *Journal of Pharmacology and Experimental Therapeutics,* **180**, 446–453.

Hariton, E. Barbara. (1973). The sexual fantasies of women. *Psychology Today,* **6**(10), 39–44.

Harlow, Harry F. (1959, June). Love in infant monkeys. *Scientific American,* **200**, 68–70.

Harlow, H. F., Harlow, M. K., and Hause, F. W. (1963). The maternal affectional system of rhesus monkeys. In H. L. Rheingold (Ed.), *Maternal behavior in mammals.* New York: Wiley.

Harris, Carol, et al. (1983, May 19). Immunodeficiency in female sexual partners of men with the acquired immuno-deficiency syndrome. *New England Journal of Medicine.* **308**.

Harris, G. W., and Levine, S. (1965). Sexual differentiation of the brain and its experimental control. *Journal of Physiology,* **181**, 379–400.

Hartley, Ruth E. (1959). Sex-role pressures in the socialization of the male child. *Psychological Reports,* **5**, 457–468.

Hartman, William E., and Fithian, Marilyn A. (1974). *Treatment of sexual dysfunction.* New York: Jason Aronson.

Hass, Aaron. (1979). *Teenage sexuality.* New York: Macmillan.

Hatcher, Robert A., et al. (1976). *Contraceptive technology, 1976–1977* (8th ed.). New York: Irvington.

Hatcher, Robert A., et al. (1980). *Contraceptive technology, 1980–1981* (10th ed.). New York: Irvington.

Hatcher, Robert A., et al. (1984). *Contraceptive technology 1984–1985* (12th ed.). New York: Irvington.

Hattendorf, K. W. (1932). A study of the questions of young children. *Jounal of Social Psychology,* **3**, 37–65.

Hayes, A. (1869). *Sexual physiology of woman.* Boston: Peabody Medical Institute.

Heath, Robert C. (1972). Pleasure and brain activity in man. *Journal of Nervous and Mental Disease,* **154**, 3–18.

Hegler, Sten, and Mortensen, Mei-Mei. (1977). Sexal behavior in elderly Danish males. In R. Gemme and C. C. Wheeler (Eds.) *Progress in sexology.* New York: Plenum.

Heilbrun, Carolyn G. (1973). *Toward a recognition of androgyny.* New York: Knopf.

Heim, Nikolaus. (1981). Sexual behavior of castrated sex offenders. *Archives of Sexual Behavior,* **10**, 11–20.

Heiman, Julia R. (1975). The physiology of erotica: Women's sexual arousal. *Psychology Today,* **8**(11), 90–94.

Heiman, J., LoPiccolo, L., and LoPiccolo, J.(1976). *Becoming orgasmic: A sexual growth program for women.* Englewood Cliffs, NJ: Prentice-Hall.

Hellerstein, Herman K., and Friedman, Ernest H. (1969, Mar.). Sexual activity and the post coronary patient. *Medical Aspects of Human Sexuality,* **3**, 70–74.

Hellman, L. M., and Pritchard, J. A. (1971). *Williams obstetrics* (14th ed.). New York: Appleton-Century-Crofts.

Helmreich, Robert L., Spence, Janet T., and Gibson, R. H. (1982). Sex-role attitudes: 1972–1980. *Personality and Social Psychology Bulletin,* **8**, 656–663.

Hembree, W. C., et al. (1976). Marihuana effects upon human gonadal function. In G. G. Nahas et al. (Eds.), *Marihuana: Chemistry, biochemistry, and cellular effects.* New York: Springer-Verlag.

Henahan, John. (1984). Honing the treatment of early breast cancer. *Journal of the American Medical Association,* **251**, 309–310.

Henderson, B. E., et al. (1978). Risk factors for cancer of the testis in young men. *International Journal of Cancer,* **23**, 98–602.

Henley, Nancy M. (1973a). The politics of touch. In P. Brown (Ed.), *Radical psychology.* New York: Harper & Row.

Henley, Nancy M. (1973). Status and sex: Some touching observations. *Bulletin of the Psychonomic Society,* **2**, 91–93.

Henslin, J. M. (Ed.). (1980). *Cohabitation: Its context and meaning in marriae and family in a changing society.* New York: The Free Press.

Herbert, J. (1966). The effect of estrogen applied directly to the genitalia upon the sexual attractiveness of the

female rhesus monkey. *Excerpta Medica International Congress Series,* **3**, 212.
Herbst, A. (1972). Clear cell adenocarcinoma of the genital tract in young females. *New England Journal of Medicine,* **287**(25), 1259–1264.
Herbst, Arthur L. (1979). Coitus and the fetus. *New England Journal of Medicine* **301**, 1235–1236.
Herman, Judith L. (1981). *Father-daughter incest.* Cambridge: Harvard University Press.
Herold, E. S., and Way, L. (1983). Oral-genital sexual behavior in a sample of university females. *Journal of Sex Research,* **19**, 327–338.
Heron, Alastair (Ed.). (1964). *Toward a Quaker view of sex* (Rev. ed.). London: Friends Service Committee.
Hersey, R. B. (1931). Emotional cycles in man. *Journal of Mental Science,* **77**, 151–169.
Heston, Leonard, and Shields, J. (1968). Homosexuality in twins: A family study and a registry study. *Archives of General Psychiatry,* **18**, 149–160.
Higgins, Glen E. (1978). Sexual response in spinal cord injured adults: A review of the literature. In J. LoPiccolo and L. LoPiccolo (Eds.), *Handbook of sex therapy.* New York: Plenum.
Higham, Eileen. (1980). Sexuality in the infant and neonate: Birth to two years. In B. B. Wolman and J. Money (Eds.), *Handbook of human sexuality.* Englewood Cliffs, NJ: Prentice-Hall.
Hill, C. T., Rubin, Z., and Peplau, L. A. (1976). Breakups before marriage: The end of 103 affairs. *Journal of Social Issues,* **32**(1).
Hite, Shere. (1976). *The Hite report.* New York: Macmillan.
Hite, Shere. (1981). *The Hite report on male sexuality.* New York: Alfred Knopf.
Hobart, C. Q. (1958). The incidence of romanticism during courtship. *Social Forces,* **36**, 364.
Hoffman, Louis W. (1974). Effects of maternal employment on the child: A review of the research. *Developmental Psychology,* **10**, 204–228.
Hollister, Leo E. (1975). The mystique of social drugs and sex. In M. Sandler and G. L. Gessa (Eds.), *Sexual behavior: Pharmacology and biochemistry.* New York: Raven Press.
Holmberg, A. R. (1946). The Siriono. Unpublished doctoral dissertation, Yale University. (Cited in Clellan S. Ford and Frank A. Beach, *Patterns of sexual behavior.* New York: Harper & Row.
Holmstrom, Lynda Lytle, and Burgess, Ann Wolbert. (1980). Sexual behavior of assailants during reported rapes. *Archives of Sexual Behavior,* **9**, 427–440.
Hong, Lawrence K. (1984). Survival of the fastest: On the origin of premature ejaculation. *Journal of Sex Research,* **20**, 109–122.
Hooker, Evelyn. (1957). The adjustment of the male overt homosexual. *Journal of Projective Techniques,* **21**, 18–31.
Hooker, Evelyn. (1965). An empirical study of some relations between sexual patterns and gender identity in male homosexuals. In J. Money (Ed.), *Sex research: New developments.* New York: Holt.
Hooper, R. R., et al. (1978). Cohort study of venereal disease. I: The risk of gonorrhea transmission from infected women to men. *American Journal of Epidemiology,* **108**, 136–144.
Hopkins, Joyce, Marcues, M., and Campbell, S. B. (1984). Postpartum depression: A critical review. *Psychological Bulletin,* **95**, 498–515.
Hopkins, J. Ray. (1977). Sexual behavior in adolescence. *Journal of Social Issues,* **33**(2), 67–85.
Hopkins, June H. (1969). The lesbian personality. *British Journal of Psychiatry,* **115**, 1433–1436.
Horgan, Dianne. (1983). The pregnant woman's place and where to find it. *Sex Roles,* **9**, 333–340.
Horner, Matina S. (1969). Fail: Bright women. *Psychology Today,* **3**(6), 36.
Horner, Matina S. (1970). Femininity and achievement: A basic inconsistency. In J. Bardwick et al. (Eds.), *Feminine personality and conflict.* Belmont, CA: Brooks/Cole.
Horner, Matina S. (1972). Toward an understanding of achievement-related conflicts in women. *Journal of Social Issues,* **28**(2), 157–175.
Horstman, W. (1972). Homosexuality and psychopathology. Unpublished doctoral dissertation, University of Oregon.
Housholder, Joanne, et al. (1982). Infants born to narcotic-addicted mothers. *Psychological Bulletin,* **92**, 453–468.
Houston, L. N. (1981). Romanticism and eroticism among black and white college students. *Adolescence,* **16**, 263–272.
Howard, Dale R., Lott, B., and Reilly, M. E. (1982). Sexual assault and harassment: A campus community study. *Signs,* 321.
Howard, J. L., Lipzin, M. B., and Reifler, C. B. (1973). Is pornography a problem? *Journal of Social Issues,* **29**, 133–145.
Hudson, Walter W., and Ricketts, Wendell A. (1980). A strategy for the measurement of homophobia. *Journal of Homosexuality,* **5**, 357–372.
Hughes, J. (1964). Failure to ejaculate with chlordiazepoxide. *American Journal of Psychiatry,* **121**, 610–611.
Humphreys, Laud. (1970). *Tearoom trade: Impersonal sex in public places.* Chicago: Aldine.
Hunt, Morton. (1966). *The world of the formerly married.* New York: McGraw-Hill.
Hunt, Morton. (1974). *Sexual behavior in the 1970s.* Chicago: Playboy Press.
Hunt, Morton, and Hunt, Bernice. (1977). *The divorce experience.* New York: McGraw-Hill.
Hurst, John. (1977, May 26). Children—A big profit item for the smut producers. *Los Angeles Times.*
Huttel, F., et al. (1972). A quantitative evaluation of psy-

chophrophylaxis in childbirth. *Journal of Psychosomatic Research,* **16**, 81–92.
Hyde, H. Montgomery. (1975). *Oscar Wilde.* New York: Farrar, Straus & Giroux.
Hyde, Janet S. (1981). How large are cognitive gender differences? A meta-analysis using omega squared and *d. American Psychologist,* **36**, 892–901.
Hyde, Janet S. (1984). How large are gender differences in aggression? A developmental meta-analysis. *Developmental Psychology,* **20**, 722–736.
Hyde, Janet S., and Rosenberg, B. G. (1976). *Half the human experience: The psychology of women.* Lexington, MA: Heath.

Idanpaan-Heikkila, J., et al. (1969). Placental transfer of tritiated-1-tetrahydrocannabinol. *New England Journal of Medicine,* **281**, 330.
Iffy, L., and Wingate, M. D. (1970). Risks of rhythm method of birth control. *Journal of Reproductive Medicine,* **3**(1), 11.
Imperato-McGinley, J., et al. (1974). Steroid 5 reductase deficiency in man: An inherited form of male pseudohermaphroditism. *Science,* **186**, 1213–1215.
Intelligence report. (1971, July 25). *Parade.*
Isbell, H. (1965). Prospectus in research on opiate addiction. In D. M. Wilner and G. G. Kasserbaum (Eds.), *Narcotics.* New York: McGraw-Hill.
Israel, Spencer L. (1967). *Diagnosis and treatment of menstrual disorders and sterility* (15th ed.). New York: Harper & Row.
Ivey, M. E., and Bardwick, Judih M. (1968). Patterns of affective fluctuation in the menstrual cycle. *Psychosomatic Medicine,* **30**, 336–345.

"J." (1969). *The sensuous woman.* New York: Lyle Stuart.
Jackman, N. R., O'Toole, R., and Geis, G. (1963). The self-image of the prostitute. *Sociological Quarterly,* **4**, 150–161.
Jacobson, N. S. (1978). Specific and non-specific factors in the effectiveness of a behavioral approach to marital discord. *Journal of Consulting and Clinical Psychology,* **46**, 442–452.
Jaffe, A. and Becker, R. E. (1984). Four new basic sex offenses: A fundamental shift in emphasis. *Illinois Bar Journal,* **72**, 400–403.
Jamison, K. R., Wellisch, D. K., and Pasnau, R. O. (1978). Psychological aspects of mastectomy. I. The woman's perspective. *American Journal of Psychiatry,* **135**, 432–436.
Jay, Karla, and Young, Allen (1979). *The gay report.* New York: Summit Books.
Jemail, Jay Ann, and Geer, James. (1977). Sexual scripts. In R. Gemme and C. C. Wheeler (Eds.), *Progress in sexology.* New York: Plenum.
Jensen, Gordon D. (1976a). Adolescent sexuality. In B. J. Sadock et al. (Eds.), *The sexual experience.* Baltimore: Williams & Wilkins.
Jensen, Gordon D. (1976b). Cross-cultural studies and animal studies of sex. In B. J. Sadock et al. (Eds.), *The sexual experience.* Baltimore: Williams & Wilkins.
Jensen, Soren B. (1981). Diabetic sexual dysfunction. *Archives of Sexual Behavior,* **10**, 493–504.
Jick, Hershel, et al. (1981). Vaginal spermicides and congenital disorders. *Journal of the American Medical Association,* **245**, 1329–1332.
Johnson, R. E. (1970). Some correlates of extramarital coitus. *Journal of Marriage and the Family,* **32**, 449–456.
Jones, Hardin, and Jones, Helen. (1977). *Sensual drugs.* New York: Cambridge University Press.
Jones, J. R. (1972). Plasma testosterone concentrations in female transsexuals. *Archives of Sexual Behavior,* **2**.
Jones, R. N., and Joe, V. C. (1980). Pornographic materials and commodity theory. *Journal of Applied Social Psychology,* **10**, 311–322.
Jones, W. C. (1976). *Doe v. commonwealth attorney:* Closing the door to a fundamental right to sexual privacy. *Denver Law Journal.* **53**, 553–576.
Jost, A. (1970). Hormonal factors in the sex differentiation of the mammalian foetus. *Philosophical Transactions of the Society of London,* Ser. B, **259**, 119–131.
Jourard, Sidney M. (1971). Some lethal aspects of the male role. In Sidney M. Jourard, *The transparent self.* Princeton, NJ: Van Nostrand.
Jourard, Sidney M., and Lasakow, P. (1958). Some factors in self-disclosure. *Journal of Abnormal and Social Psychology,* **56**, 91–98.
Justice, Blair, and Justice, Rita. (1979). *The broken taboo: Sex in the family.* New York: Human Sciences Press.

Kaats, Gilbert, and Davis, Keith. (1971). Effects of volunteer biases in studies of sexual behavior and attitudes. *Journal of Sex Research,* **7**, 26–34.
Kalisch, Philip A. and Kalisch, Beatrice J. (1984). Sex-role stereotyping of nurses and physicians on prime-time television. *Sex Roles,* **10**, 533–554.
Kallman, Franz J. (1952a). Comparative twin study on the genetic aspects of male homosexuality. *Journal of Nervous and Mental Disease,* **115**, 283–298.
Kallman, Franz J. (1952b). Twin and sibship study of overt male homosexuality. *American Journal of Human Genetics,* **4**, 136–146.
Kando, Thomas. (1973). *Sex change: The achievement of gender identity among feminized transsexuals.* Springfield, IL: Charles C. Thomas.
Kanin, Eugene J. (1969). Selected dyadic aspects of male sex aggression. *Journal of Sex Research,* **5**.
Kanin, E. J., Davidson, K. D., and Scheck, S. R. (1970). A research note on male-female differentials in the experience of heterosexual love. *Journal of Sex Research,* **6**, 64–72.

Kantner, John F., and Zelnik, Melvin. (1972). Sexual experience of young unmarried women in the United States. *Family Planning Perspectives,* **4**(4), 9–18.

Kantner, John F, and Zelnik, Melvin. (1973). Contraception and pregnancy: Experience of young unmarried women in the United States. *Family Planning Perspectives,* **5**(1), 21–35.

Kaplan, Helen S. (1974). *The new sex therapy.* New York: Brunner/Mazel.

Kaplan, Helen Singer. (1979). *Disorders of sexual desire.* New York: Simon & Schuster.

Kaplan, Helen S., and Sager, C. J. (1971, June). Sexual patterns at different ages. *Medical Aspects of Human Sexuality,* 10–23.

Karpman, Benjamin. (1954). *The sexual offender and his offenses.* New York: Julian Press.

Karr, Rodney K. (1978). Homosexual labeling and the male role. *Journal of Social Issues,* **34**(3), 73–83.

Kassel, Victor, (1976). Sex in nursing homes. *Medical Aspects of Human Sexuality,* **10**(3), 126.

Katchadourian, Herant L., and Lunde, D. T. (1975). *Fundamentals of human sexuality.* New York: Holt.

Katz, Kathryn D. (1982). Sexual Morality and the Constitution: *People v. Onofre. Albany Law Review,* **46**, 311–362.

Keane, Terence M., and Lisman, Stephan A. (1980). Alcohol and social anxiety in males: Behavioral, cognitive, and physiological effects. *Journal of Abnormal Psychology,* **89**, 213–223.

Kegel, A. H. (1952). Sexual functions of the pubococcygeus muscle. *Western Journal of Surgery,* **60**, 521–524.

Keller, J. F., Elliott, S. S., and Gunberg, E. (1982). Premarital sexual intercourse among single college students: A discriminant analysis. *Sex Roles,* **8**, 21–32.

Kemp, Karl H. (1974). Comment: Recent obscenity cases. *Arkansas Law Review,* **28**, 335–356.

Kempf, E. J. (1917). The social and sexual behavior of infrahuman primates with some comparable facts in human behavior. *Psychoanalytic Review,* **4**, 127–154.

Kenrick, D., et al. (1980). Sex differences, androgyny and approach responses to erotica: A new variation on an old volunteer problem. *Journal of Personality and Social Psychology,* **38**, 517–524.

Key, Mary R. (1975). *Male/female language.* Metuchen, NJ: Scarecrow Press.

Kilmann, Peter R., et al. (1981). Sex education: A review of its effects. *Archives of Sexual Behavior,* **10**, 177–206.

Kilmann, Peter R., and Mills, Katherine H. (1983). *All about sex therapy.* New York: Plenum.

Kilpatrick, D. G., Resick, P. A., and Veronen, L. J. (1981). Effects of a rape experience: A longitudinal study. *Journal of Social Issues,* **37**(4), 105–122.

Kimlicka, T., Cross, H., and Tarnai, J. (1983). A comparison of androgynous, feminine, masculine, and undifferentiated women on self-esteem body satisfaction, and sexual satisfaction. *Psychology of Women Quarterly,* **1**, 291–294.

Kinsey, A. C., Pomeroy, W. B., and Martin, C. E. (1948). *Sexual behavior in the human male.* Philadelphia: Saunders.

Kinsey, A. C., Pomeroy, W. B., Martin, C. E., and Gebhard, P. H. (1953). *Sexual behavior in the human female.* Philadelphia: Saunders.

Kirby, Douglas. (1977). The methods and methodological problems of sex research. In J. S. DeLora and C. A. B. Warren, *Understanding sexual interaction.* Boston: Houghton Mifflin.

Kirby, Douglas. (1984). *Sexuality education: An evaluation of programs and their effects.* Santa Cruz, CA: Network Publications.

Kirkendall, Lester A. (1965). *Sex education.* SIECUS Study Guide No. 1. New York: Sex Information and Education Council of the United States.

Klaus, Marshall A., et al. (1972). Maternal attachment: Importance of the first postpartum days. *New England Journal of Medicine,* **286**, 460–463.

Klaus, Marshall, and Kennell, John. (1970). Human maternal behavior at first contact with her young. *Pediatrics,* **46**, 187–192.

Klaus, Marshall, and Kennell, John. (1976). Human maternal and paternal behavior. In M. Klaus and J. Kennell (Eds.), *Maternal Infant Bonding.* St. Louis: Mosby.

Knowles, L. and Poorrkaj, H. (1974). Attitudes and behavior on viewing sexual activities in public places. *Sociology and Social Research,* **58**, 130–135.

Kohlberg, Lawrence. (1966). A cognitive-developmental analysis of children's sex-role concepts and attitudes. In E. E. Maccoby (Ed.), *The development of sex differences.* Stanford, CA: Stanford University Press.

Kohli, K. L., and Sobrero, A. J. (1973). Vasectomy: A study of psychosexual and general reactions. *Social Biology,* **20**, 298–302.

Kolodny, R. C., Masters, W. H., Kolodner, R. M., and Toro, G. (1974). Depression of plasma testosterone levels after chronic intensive marihuana use. *New England Journal of Medicine,* **290**, 872–874.

Koss, Mary P., and Oros, Cheryl J. (1982). Sexual experiences survey: A research instrument investigating sexual aggression and victimization. *Journal of Consulting and Clinical Psychology,* **50**, 455–457.

Kraemer, D., Moore, G., and Kramen, M. (1976). Baboon infant produced by embryo transfer. *Science,* **192**, 1246–1247.

Kreitler, Hans, and Kreitler, Shulamith. (1966). Children's concepts of sex and birth. *Child Development,* **37**, 363–378.

Kronhausen, Phyllis, and Kronhausen, Eberhard. (1964). *The sexually responsive woman.* New York: Grove Press.

Kutchinsky, Berl. (1973). The effect of easy availability of pornography on the incidence of sex crimes: The Danish experience. *Journal of Social Issues,* **29**, 163–181.

Kweskin, Sally, L., and Cook, Alicia S. (1982). Heterosexual and homosexual mothers' self-described sex-role behavior and ideal sex-role behavior in children. *Sex Roles,* **8**, 976–976.

Ladner, Joyce A. (1971). *Tomorrow's tomorrow: The black woman.* Garden City, NY: Doubleday.

Lakoff, Robin. (1973). Language and woman's place. *Language in Society,* **2**, 45–79.

Landesman, S. H., and Vierra, J. (1983). Acquired immune deficiency syndrome (AIDS): A review. *Archives of Internal Medicine,* **143**, 2307–2309.

Laner, M. R., and Thompson, J. (1982). Abuse and aggression in courting couples. *Deviant Behavior: An Interdisciplinary Journal,* **3**, 229–244.

Lange, James D., et al. (1981). Effects of demand for performance, self-monitoring of arousal and inceased sympathetic nervous system activity on male erectile response. *Archives of Sexual Behavior,* **10**, 443–464.

Langer, Ellen J., and Dweck, Carol S. (1973). *Personal politics: The psychology of making it.* Englewood Cliffs, NJ: Prentice-Hall.

Langevin, R., et al (1979). Experimental studies of the etiology of genital exhibitionism. *Archives of Sexual Behavior,* **8**, 307–332.

Lanson, Lucienne. (1975). *From woman to woman.* New York: Knopf.

Laumann, Edward O. (1969). Friends of urban men: An assessment of accuracy in reporting their socioeconomic attributes, mutual choice, and attitude agreement. *Sociometry,* **32**, 54–69.

Leavitt, Fred. (1974). *Drugs and behavior.* Philadelphia: Saunders.

Lecos, Chris. (1980, Oct.). Caution light on caffeine. *FDA Consumer,* 6–9.

Lederer, Laura. (Ed.) (1980). *Take back the night: Women on Pornography.* New York: William Morrow.

Lee, John Alan. (1974). Styles of loving. *Psychology Today,* **8**(5), 43–51.

Lee, John Alan. (1977). A typology of styles of loving. *Personality and Social Psychology Bulletin,* **3**, 173–182.

Legman, Gershon. (1968). *Rationale of the dirty joke.* New York: Grove Press.

Lieblum, Sandra R., and Pervin, L. A. (Eds.). (1980). *Principles and practice of sex therapy.* New York: Guilford Press.

Leiblum, S. R., Rosen, R. C., and Pierce, D. (1976). Group treatment format: Mixed sexual dysfunctions. *Archives of Sexual Behavior,* **5**, 313–322.

Leifer, Myra. (1980). *Psychological effects of motherhood: A study of first pregnancy.* New York: Praeger.

LeMagnen, J. (1952). Les pheromones olfactosexuals chez le rat blanc. *Archives des Sciences Physiologiques,* **6**, 295–332.

Lemere, Frederick, and Smith, James W. (1973). Alcohol-induced sexual impotence. *American Journal of Sex Research,* **8**, 268–285.

Levin, Robert J., and Levin, Amy. (1975, Sept.). Sexual pleasure: The surprising preferences of 100,000 women. *Redbook,* 51.

Levin, Robert J., and Levin, Amy. (1975, Oct.). The *Redbook* report on premarital and extramarital sex. *Redbook,* 38.

Levine, E. M., Gruenewald, D., and Shaiova, C. H. (1976). Behavioral differences and emotional conflict among male-to-female transsexuals. *Archives of Sexual Behavior,* **5**, 81–86.

Levine, M. I. (1970). Sex education in the public elementary and high school curriculum. In D. L. Taylor (Ed.), *Human sexual development.* Philadelphia: Davis.

Levinson, Daniel J. (1978). *The seasons of a man's life.* New York: Ballantine.

Leavitt, Eugene E. (1983). Estimating the duration of sexual behavior: A laboratory analog study. *Archives of Sexual Behavior,* **12**, 329–336.

Leavitt, E. E., and Klassen, A. D. (1974). Public attitudes toward homosexuality. *Journal of Homosexuality,* **1**, 29–43.

Lewis, C. S. (1960). *The four loves.* New York: Harcourt Brace Jovanovich.

LeWitter, Maximillian, and Abarbanel, Albert. (1973). Aging and sex. In A. Ellis and A. Abarbanel (Eds.), *The encyclopedia of sexual behavior.* New York: Jason Aronson.

Libby, Roger W. (1980). Make love not war? Sex, sexual meanings, and violence in a sample of university students. *Archives of Sexual Behavior,* **9**, 133–148.

Libby, Roger W., and Nass, Gilbert D. (1971). Parental views on teenage sexual behavior. *Journal of Sex Research,* **7**, 226–236.

Licklider, S. (1961). Jewish penile carcinoma. *Journal of Urology,* **86**, 98.

Linde, Randy, et al. (1981). Reversible inhibition of testicular steroidogenesis and spermatogenesis by a potent gonadotropin-releasing hormone agonist in normal men. *New England Journal of Medicine,* **305**, 663–667.

Lobitz, W. Charles, and LoPiccolo, Joseph. (1972). New methods in the behavioral treatment of sexual dysfunction. *Journal of Therapy and Experimental Psychiatry,* **3**, 265–271.

Lobsenz, Norman. (1974, Jan. 20). Sex and the senior citizen. *The New York Times Magazine,* 87–91.

Lockwood, Daniel. (1980). *Prison sexual violence.* New York: Elsevier.

LoPiccolo, Joseph, and Lobitz, Charles. (1972). The role of masturbation in the treatment of sexual dysfunction. *Archives of Sexual Behavior,* **2**, 163–171.

LoPiccolo, Leslie. (1980). Low sexual desire. In S. R. Leiblum and L. A. Pervin (Eds.), *Principles and practice of sex therapy.* New York: Guilford Press.

Loraine, J. A., Adampopoulos, D. A., Kirkhan, K. E., Ismail, A. A., and Dove, G. A. (1971). Patterns of hormone excretion in male and female homosexuals. *Nature,* **234**, 552–554.

Lorenz, Konrad. (1966). *On aggression.* New York: Harcourt Brace Jovanovich.

Louria, Donald B. (1970, Jan.). Sexual use of amyl nitrate. *Medical Aspects of Human Sexuality,* 89.

Lowenthal, M. F., et al. (1975). *Four stages of life: A comparative study of women and men facing transitions.* San Francisco: Jossey-Bass.

Lu, Y. (1952). Marital roles and marital adjustment. *Sociology and Social Research,* **36**, 364–368.

Luce, Gay. (1970). *Biological rhythms in psychiatry and medicine.* New York: Dover.

Luker, Kristin. (1975). *Taking chances: Abortion and the decision not to contracept.* Berkeley: University of California Press.

Lumby, M. E. (1978). Men who advertise for sex. *Journal of Homosexuality,* **4**, 63–72.

Lyons, Richard D. (1983, Oct. 4). Promiscuous sex believed declining in recent years. *The New York Times,* C1.

Maccoby, Eleanor E., and Jacklin, Carol N. (1974). *The psychology of sex differences.* Stanford, CA: Stanford University Press.

MacDonald, A. P. (1982). Research on sexual orientation: A bridge that touches both shores but doesn't meet in the middle. *Journal of Sex Education and Therapy,* **8**(1), 9–13.

MacDougald, D. (1961). Aphrodisiacs and anaphrodisiacs. In A. Ellis and A. Abarbanel (Eds.), *The encyclopedia of sexual behavior.* Vol I. New York: Hawthorn.

MacFarlane, J. A., et al. (1978). The relationship between mother and neonate. In S. Kitzinger and J. A. Davis (Eds.), *The place of birth.* Oxford: Oxford University Press.

Mack, Thomas M., et al. (1976). Estrogens and endometrial cancer in a retirement community. *New England Journal of Medicine,* **294**, 1262–1267.

MacKinnon, Catharine A. (1979). *Sexual harassment of working women.* New Haven: Yale University Press.

MacLean, Paul. (1962). New findings relevant to the evolution of psychosexual functions of the brain. *Journal of Nervous and Mental Disease,* **135**, 289–301.

MacLusky, Neil J., and Naftolin, Frederick. (1981). Sexual differentiation of the central nervous system. *Science,* **211**, 1294–1303.

MacNamara, Donal E. J., and Sagarin, Edward. (1977). *Sex, crime and the law.* New York: The Free Press.

Mahoney, E. R. (1983). *Human sexuality.* New York: McGraw-Hill.

Maisch, Herbert. (1972). *Incest.* New York: Stein and Day.

Makepeace, J. (1981). Courtship violence among college students. *Family Relations,* **30**, 97–102.

Malamuth, Neil M. (1981a). Rape proclivity in males. *Journal of Social Issues,* **37**(4), 138–157.

Malamuth, Neil M. (1981b). Rape fantasies as a function of exposure to violent sexual stimuli. *Archives of Sexual Behavior,* **10**, 33–48.

Malamuth, Neil M. (1984). Aggression against women: Cultural and individual causes. In N. Malamuth and E. Donnerstein (Eds.), *Pornography and sexual aggression.* New York: Academic Press.

Malamuth, Neil M., and Check, J. V. P. (1981). The effects of mass media exposure on acceptance of violence against women: A field experiment. *Journal of Research in Personality,* **15**, 436–446.

Malamuth, N., Feshbach, S., and Jaffee, Y. (1977). Sexual arousal and aggression: Recent experiments and theoretical issues. *Journal of Social Issues,* **33**, 110–133.

Malamuth, N. M., Heim, M., and Feshbach, S. (1980). Sexual responsiveness of college students to rape depictions: Inhibitory and disinhibitory effects. *Journal of Personality and Social Psychology,* **38**, 399–408.

Malamuth, Neil M., and Spinner, B. (1980). A longitudinal content analysis of sexual violence in the best-selling erotic magazines. *Journal of Sex Research,* **16**, 226–237.

Maletzky, B. M. (1974). "Assisted" covert sensitization in the treatment of exhibitionism. *Journal of Consulting and Clinical Psychology,* **42**, 34–40.

Maletsky, B. M. (1977). "Booster" sessions in aversion therapy: The permanency of treatment. *Behavior therapy,* **8**, 460–463.

Maletzky, B. M. (1980). Assisted covert sensitization. In D. J. Cox and R. J. Daitzman (Eds.), *Exhibitionism: Description, assessment, and treatment.* New York: Garland.

Malinowski, Bronislaw. (1929). *The sexual life of savages.* New York: Harcourt Brace Jovanovich.

Mamay, Patricia D., and Simpson, Richard L. (1981). Three female roles in television commercials. *Sex Roles,* **1**, 1223–1232.

Manabe, Y. (1969). Artificial abortion at mid-trimester by mechanical stimulation of the uterus. *American Journal of Obstetrics and Gynecology,* **105**, 132–146.

Mann, J., Sidman, J., and Starr, S. (1973). Evaluating social consequences of erotic films: An experimental approach. *Journal of Social Issues,* **29**, 113–131.

Marin, Peter. (1983, July). A revolution's broken promises. *Psychology Today,* **17**(7), 50–57.

Markman, Howard J. (1979). Application of a behavioral model of marriage in predicting relationship satisfaction of couples planning marriage. *Journal of Consulting and Clinical Psychology,* **47**, 743–749.

Markman, Howard J., and Floyd, Frank. (1980). Possibilities for the prevention of marital discord: A behavioral perspective. *American Journal of Family Therapy,* **8**, 29–48.

Markman, Howard J. (1981). Prediction of marital distress: A 5-year follow-up. *Journal of Consulting and Clinical Psychology,* **49**, 760–762.

Marks, Issac, and Gelder, Michael. (1967). Transvestism and fetishism: Clinical and psychological changes during faradic aversion. *British Journal of Psychiatry,* **113**, 711–729.

Marmor, Judd. (Ed.). (1965). *Sexual inversion: The multiple roots of homosexuality.* New York: Basic Books.

Marmor, Judd. (1969). Sex for nonsexual reasons. *Medical Aspects of Human Sexuality,* **3**(6), 8–21.

Marmor, Judd. (1971). "Normal" and "deviant" sexual

behavior. *Journal of the American Medical Association,* **217**, 165–170.

Marmor, Judd. (1976). Frigidity, dyspareunia, and vaginismus. In B. J. Sadock, et al. (Eds.), *The sexual experience.* Baltimore: Williams & Wilkins.

Marmor, Judd. (Ed.). (1980). *Homosexual behavior.* New York: Basic Books.

Marshall, P., Surridge, D., and Delva, N. (1981). The role of nocturnal penile tumescence in differentiating between organic and psychogenic impotence: The first stage of validation. *Archives of Sexual Behavior,* **10**, 1–10.

Martin, Clyde E. (1981). Factors affecting sexual functioning in 60–79-year-old married males. *Archives of Sexual Behavior,* **10**, 399–420.

Martin, Del, and Lyon, Phyllis. (1972). *Lesbian/woman.* San Francisco: Glide Publications.

Martinez, G. A., and Nalezienski, J. P. (1981). 1980 update: The recent trend in breastfeeding. *Pediatrics,* **67**(2), 260–263.

Martinson, Floyd M. (1973). *Infant and child sexuality: A sociological perspective.* St Peter, MN: Book Mark.

Marx, Jean L. (1976). Estrogen drugs: Do they increase the risk of cancer? *Science,* **191**, 838.

Maslow, Abraham H. (1968). *Toward a psychology of being* (2nd ed.). Princeton, NJ: Van Nostrand.

Maslow, Abraham H. (1970). *Motivation and personality* (2nd ed.). New York: Harper & Row.

Maslow, Abraham, and Sakoda, J. (1952). Volunteer-error in the Kinsey study. *Journal of Abnormal and Social Psychology,* **47**, 259–267.

Masters, William H., and Johnson, Virginia. (1966). *Human sexual response.* Boston: Little, Brown.

Masters, William H., and Johnson, Virginia. (1970). *Human sexual inadequacy.* Boston: Little, Brown.

Masters, William H., and Johnson, Virginia. (1974). What men stand to gain from women's liberation. In William H. Masters and Virginia Johnson, *The pleasure bond.* Boston: Little, Brown.

Masters, William H., and Johnson, Virginia. (1979). *Homosexuality in perspective.* Boston: Little, Brown.

Masters, William H., Johnson, Virginia E., and Kolodny, Robert C. (1982). *Human sexuality.* Boston: Little, Brown.

Maugh, Thomas H. (1981). Male "pill" blocks sperm enzyme. *Science,* 314.

May, Rollo. (1974). *Love and will.* New York: Dell Books.

Maykovich, M. K. (1976). Attitudes versus behavior in extramarital sexual relations. *Journal of Marriage and the Family,* **38**, 693–699.

Mayo, Clara, and Henley, Nancy M. (Eds.). (1981). *Gender and nonverbal behavior.* New York: Springer-Verlag.

Mazur, Ronald. (1973). *The new intimacy.* Boston: Beacon Press.

McArthur, Leslie Z., and Resko, Beth G. (1975). The portrayal of men and women in American television commercials. *Journal of Social Psychology,* **97**, 209–220.

McBride, Arthur F., and Hebb, D. O. (1948). Behavior of the captive bottlenose dolphin, *Tursiops truncatus. Journal of Comparative and Physciological Psychology,* **41**, 111–123.

McCaghy, Charles H. (1971). Child molesting. *Sexual Behavior,* **1**, 16–24.

McCary, James L. (1973). *Human sexuality.* Princeton, NJ: van Nostrand.

McCormick, Naomi B. (1979). Come-ons and put-offs: Unmarried students' strategies for having and avoiding sexual intercourse. *Psychology of Women Quarterly,* **4**, 194–211.

McCrary, J., and Gutierrez, L. (1979/80). The homosexual person in the military and in national security employment. *Journal of Homosexuality,* **5**(1/2), 115–146.

McDowell, Janet Dickey. (1983). Ethical implications of in vitro fertilization, *The Christian Century,* **100**, 936–938.

McGlothlin, W., Sparkes, R., and Arnold, D. (1970). Effect of LSD on human pregnancy. *Journal of the American Medical Association,* **212**, 1483–1487.

McGuire, R. J., Carlisle, J. M., and Young, B. G. (1965). Sexual deviations as conditioned behavior: A hypothesis. *Behavioral Research and Therapy,* **2**, 185–190.

McIntosh, Mary. (1968). The homosexual role. *Social Problems,* **16**(2), 185–190.

McKinlay, Sonja M., and Jeffreys, Margot. (1974). The menopausal syndrome. *British Journal of Preventive and Social Medicine,* **28**(2), 108.

McLuhan, Marshall, and Leonard, Geroge B. (1974). The future of sex. In R. T. Francoeur and A. K. Francoeur (Eds.), *The future of sexual relations.* Englewood Cliffs, NJ: Prentice-Hall.

McMillan, Julie R., et al. (1977). Women's language: Uncertainty or interpersonal sensitivity and emotionality? *Sex Roles,* **3**, 545–560.

McNeill, John J. (1976). *The church and the homosexual.* Kansas City: Sheed, Andrews, & McMeel.

McWhirter, David P., and Mattison, Andrew M. (1980). Treatment of sexual dysfunction in homosexual male couples. In S. R. Leiblum and L. A. Pervin (Eds.), *Principles and practice of sex therapy.* New York: Guilford Press.

McWhirter, David P., and Mattison, Andrew M. (1984). *The male couple: How relationships develop.* Englewood Cliffs, NJ: Prentice-Hall.

Mead, Margaret. (1935). *Sex and temperament in three primitive societies.* New York: Morrow.

Mead, Margaret, and Newton, Niles. (1967). Fatherhood. In S. A. Richardson and A. F. Guttmacher (Eds.), *Childbearing: Its social and psychological aspects.* Baltimore: Williams & Wilkins.

Meiselman, Karin. (1978). *Incest.* San Francisco: Jossey-Bass.

Meissner, William W. (1980). Psychoanalysis and sexual disorders. In B. J. Wolman and J. Money (Eds.), *Hand-*

book of human sexuality. Englewood Cliffs, NJ: Prentice-Hall.

Mendelsohn, Jack H., et al. (1974). Plasma testosterone levels before, during and after chronic marihuana smoking. *New England Journal of Medicine,* **291**, 1051–1055.

Meredith, Nikki. (1984, Jan.). The gay dilemma. *Psychology Today,* 56–62.

Mereson, Amy. (1983). Court throws out Akron ordinance, reaffirms abortion rights. *Civil Liberties,* No. 347, 8.

Messé, Madelyn R. and Geer, James H. (1985). Voluntary vaginal musculature contractions as an enhancer of sexual arousal. *Archives of Sexual Behavior,* **14**, 13–28.

Meyer, J. K. (1979). Sex reassignment. *Archives of General Psychiatry,* **36**, 1010–1015.

Meyer-Bahlburg, Heino F. L. (1980). Homosexual orientation in women and men: A hormonal basis? In J. E. Parsons (Ed.), *The psychobiology of sex differences and sex roles.* New York: McGraw-Hill.

Meyerowitz, Beth E. (1980). Psychosocial correlates of breast cancer and its treatments. *Psychological Bulletin,* **87**, 108–131.

Michael, R. P., Bonsall, R. W., and Warner, P. (1974). Human vaginal secretions: Volatile fatty acid content. *Science,* **186**, 1217–1219.

Michael, Richard P., and Keverne, E. B. (1968). Pheromones in the communication of sexual status in primates. *Nature,* **218**, 746–749.

Middleton, R. (1962). Brother-sister and father-daughter marriage in ancient Egypt. *American Sociological Review,* **27**, 603–611.

Migeon, C. J., Rivarola M. A., and Forest, M. G. (1968). Studies of androgens in transsexual subjects: Effects of estrogen therapy. *Johns Hopkins Medical Journal,* **123**, 128–133.

Milbauer, Barbara. (1983). *The law giveth: Legal aspects of the abortion controversy.* New York: Atheneum.

Millar, J. D. (1972). The national venereal disease problem. *Epidemic venereal disease: Proceedings of the Second International Symposium on Venereal Disease.* St Louis: American Social Health Association and Pfizer Laboratories.

Miller, S., Corrales, R., and Wachman, D. B. (1975). Recent progress in understanding and facilitating marital communication. *The Family Coordinator,* **24**, 143–152.

Miller, W., Nunnally, E., and Wachman, D. (1975). *Alive and aware.* Minneapolis: Interpersonal Communication Programs.

Mischel, Walter. (1969). Continuity and change in personality. *American Psychologist,* **24**, 1012–1018.

Mitchell, James, and Popkin, Michael. (1983). The pathophysiology of sexual dysfunction associated with antipsychotic drug therapy in males: A review. *Archives of Sexual Behavior,* **12**, 173–183.

Money, John, and Ehrhardt, Anke. (1972). *Man and woman, boy and girl.* Baltimore: Johns Hopkins.

Money, John, and Yankowitz, R. (1967). The sympathetic-inhibiting effects of the drug Ismelin on human male eroticism with a note on Mellaril. *Journal of Sex Research,* **3**, 69–82.

Montagu, Ashley. (1971). *Touching.* New York: Columbia University Press.

Montreal Health Press. (1972). *VD handbook.* Montreal: MHP.

Montreal Health Press. (1975). *Birth control handbook* (12th ed.). Montreal: MHP.

Moodbidri, S. B., et al. (1980). Measurement of inhibin. *Archives of Andrology,* **5**, 295–303.

Moore, James E., and Kendall, Dianne G. (1971). Children's concepts of reproduction. *Journal of Sex Research,* **7**, 42–61.

Morgan, Robin. (1978, Nov.). How to run the pornographers out of town (and preserve the first amendment). *Ms.* **55**, 78–80.

Morgan, Robin. (1980). Theory and practice: Pornography and rape. In L. Lederer (Ed.), *Take back the night: Women on pornography.* New York: William Morrow.

Morgentalev, Henry. (1982). *Abortion and contraception* Toronto: General Publishing.

Morin, Jack. (1981). *Anal pleasure and health.* Burlingame, CA: Down There Press.

Morin, Stephen F., and Garfinkle, Ellen M. (1978). Male homophobia. *Journal of Social Issues,* **34**(1), 29–47.

Morris, Norval J. (1973, Apr. 18). The law is a busy-body. *The New York Times Magazine,* 58–64.

Mosher, Donald L. (1973). Sex differences, sex experience, sex guilt and explicitly sexual films. *Journal of Social Issues,* **29**, 95–112.

Mueller, G. O. W. (1980). *Sexual conduct and the law* (2nd ed.). Dobbs Ferry, NY: Oceana Publications.

Mulvihill, D. J., et al. (1969). *Crimes of violence: A staff report to the National Commission on the Causes and Prevention of Violence.* Washington, D.C.: GPO.

Munjack, Dennis J., and Kanno, Pamela H. (1979). Retarded ejaculation: A review. *Archives of Sexual Behavior,* **8**, 139–150.

Murdock, George P. (1949). *Social structure.* New York: Macmillan.

Naeye, Richard L. (1979). Coitus and associated amniotic-fluid infections. *New England Journal of Medicine,* **301**, 1198–1200.

National Coordinating Group on Male Antifertility Agents. (1978). Gossypol—A new antifertility agent for males. *Chinese Medical Journal,* **4**, 417–428.

Nawy, Harold. (1973). In the pursuit of happiness? Consumers of erotica in San Francisco. *Journal of Social Issues,* **29**, 147–161.

Neiger, S. (1968). Sex potions. *Sexology,* 730–733.

Nemetz, G., Craig, K., and Reith, G. (1980). Treatment of female sexual dysfunction through symbolic modeling. In *Annual review of behavior therapy.* New York: Brunner/Mazel.

Neugarten, Bernice L., and Kraines, Ruth J. (1965). "Menopausal symptoms" in women of various ages. *Psychosomatic Medicine,* **27**, 266.

Newton, Esther. (1972). *Mothercamp: Female impersonators in America.* Englewood Cliffs, NJ: Prentice-Hall.

Newton, Niles A. (1972). Childbearing in broad perspective. In Boston Children's Medical Center. *Pregnancy, birth and the newborn baby.* New York: Delacorte Press.

Nickolls, L, and Teare, D. (1954). Poisoning by cantharidin. *British Medical Journal,* Part 2, 1384–1386.

Norton, G. R., and Jehu, D. (1984). The role of anxiety in sexual dysfunctions: A review. *Archives of Sexual Behavior,* **13**, 165–183.

Noss, John B. (1963). *Man's religions* (3rd ed.). New York: Macmillan.

Novak, Emil, and Novak, Edmund R. (1952). *Textbook of gynecology.* Baltimore: Williams & Wilkens.

Novak, E. R., Jones, G. S., and Jones, H. W. (1975). *Novak's textbook of gynecology* (9th ed.). Baltimore: Williams & Wilkins.

Novell, H. A. (1965). Psychological factors in premenstrual tension and dysmenorrhea. *Clinical Obstetrics and Gynecology,* **8**, 222–232.

Nyberg, K. L., and Alston, J. S. (1976/77). Analysis of public attitudes toward homosexual behavior. *Journal of Homosexuality,* **2**, 99–107.

Obzrut, L. (1976). Expectant fathers' perceptions of fathering. *American Journal of Nursing,* **76**, 1440–1442.

Offer, Daniel, and Simon, William. (1976). Stages of sexual development. In B. J. Sadock et al. (Eds.), *The sexual experience.* Baltimore: Williams & Wilkins.

Offer, D., Ostrov, E., and Howard, K. I. (1977). The self-image of adolescents: A study of four cultures. *Journal of Youth & Adolescence,* **6**, 265–279.

Olds, James. (1956). Pleasure centers in the brain. *Scientific American,* **193**, 105–116.

Olds, James, and Milner, Peter. (1954). Positive reinforcement produced by electrical stimulation of the septal area and other regions of the rat brain. *Journal of Comparative and Physiological Psychology,* **47**, 4–427.

Olds, Sally, and Eiger, M. S. (1973). *The complete book of breastfeeding.* New York: Bantam.

O'Neill, George, and O'Neill, Nena. (1972). *Open marriage: A new life style for couples.* New York: M. Evans.

O'Neill, Nena, and O'Neill, George. (1976). Marriage: A contemporary model. In B. J. Sadock, et al. (Eds.), *The sexual experience.* Baltimore: Williams & Wilkins.

Osofsky, Joy D., and Osofsky, Howard J. (1972). The psychological reactions of patients to legalized abortions. *American Journal of Orthopsychiatry,* **42**, 48–60.

Otto, H. A. (1963). Criteria for assessing family strengths. *Family Process,* **2**, 329–337.

Packer, H. L. (1968). *The limits of the criminal sanction.* Stanford, CA: Stanford University Press.

Paige, Karen E. (1971). Effects of oral contraceptives on affective fluctuations associated with the menstrual cycle. *Psychosomatic Medicine,* **33**, 515–537.

Paige, Karen E. (1973). Women learn to sing the menstrual blues. *Psychology Today,* **7**(4), 41.

Papalia, Diane E., and Olds, Sally W. (1975). *A child's world: Infancy through adolescence.* New York: McGraw-Hill.

Parke, Ross D. (1979). Perspectives on father-infant interaction. In J. D. Osofsky (Ed.), *Handbook of infant development.* New York: Wiley.

Parker, Graham. (1983). The legal regulation of sexual activity and the protection of females. *Osgoode Hall Law Journal,* **21**, 187–244.

Parlee, Mary Brown. (1973). The premenstrual syndrome. *Psychological Bulletin,* **80**, 454–465.

Parlee, Mary B. (1978, Apr.). The rhythms in men's lives. *Psychology Today,* 82–91.

Parnas, Raymond I. (1981). Legislative reform of prostitution laws: Keeping commercial sex out of sight and out of mind. *Santa Clara Law Review,* **21**, 669–696.

Parrinder, Geoffrey. (1980). *Sex in the world's religions.* New York: Oxford University Press.

Paul, William, et al. (Eds.). (1982). *Homosexuality: Social, psychological, and biological issues.* Beverly Hills: Sage.

Peplau, Letitia Anne. (1981, March). What homosexuals want in relationships. *Psychology Today,* **15**(3), 28–38.

Peplau, L. Anne, et al. (1978). Loving women: Attachment and autonomy in lesbian relationships. *Journal of Social Issues,* **34**(3), 7–27.

Peplau, Letitia Anne, and Amaro, Hortensia. (1982). Understanding lesbian relationships. In W. Paul et al (Eds.), *Homosexuality: Social, psychological, and biological issues.* Beverly Hills: Sage.

Peplau, L. A., Padesky, C. and Hamilton, M. (1982). Satisfaction in lesbian relationships. *Journal of Homosexuality,* **8**, 23–35.

Perloff, W. H. (1965). Hormones and homosexuality. In J. Marmor (Eds.), *Sexual inversion: The multiple roots of homosexuality.* New York: Basic Books.

Perry, Catherine D. (1980). Right of privacy challenges to prostitution statutes. *Washington University Law Quarterly,* **58**, 439–480.

Perry, John D., and Whipple, Beverly. (1981). Pelvic muscle strength of female ejaculators: Evidence in support of a new theory of orgasm. *Journal of Sex Research,* **17**, 22–39.

Persson, Goran (1980). Sexuality in a 70-year-old urban population. *Journal of Psychosomatic Research,* **24**, 335–342.

Peterson, Gail, et al. (1979). The role of some birth related variables on father attachment. *American Journal of Orthopsychiatry,* **40**, 330–338.

Peterson, W., Morese, K., and Kaltreider, D. (1965). Smoking and prematurity: A preliminary report based on a study of 7740 caucasians. *Obstetrics and Gynecology,* **26**, 775–779.

Peyster, A. (1979). Gossypol-proposed contraceptive for men passes the Ames test. *New England Journal of Medicine,* **301**, 275–276.

Pfeiffer, Eric. (1975). Sex and aging. In L. Gross (Ed.), *Sexual issues in marriage.* New York: Spectrum.

Pfeiffer, E., Verwoerdt, A., and Wang, H. S. (1968). Sexual behavior in aged men and women. *Archives of General Psychiatry,* **19**, 753–758.

Phillips, Leslie. (1977, Sept. 9). For women sexual harassment is an occupational hazard. *Boston Globe.*

Phoenix, C. H., Goy, R. W., Gerall, A. A., and Young, W. C. (1959). Organizing action of prenatally administered testosterone propionate on the tissues mediating mating behavior in the female guinea pig. *Endocrinology,* **65**, 369–382.

Pietropinto, A., and Simenauer, J. (1977). *Beyond the male myth.* New York: Times Books.

Pittenger, W. Norman. (1970). *Making sexuality human.* Philadelphia: Pilgrim Press.

Pittenger, W. Norman. (1974). *Love and control in sexuality.* Philadelphia: United Church Press.

Pittenger, W. Norman. (1976). A theological approach to understanding homosexuality. In Ruth T. Barnhouse and Urban T. Holmes III (Eds.), *Male and female.* New York: Seabury Press.

Pato. (1956). *Symposium.* In Irwin Edman (Ed.), *Tne works of Plato.* New York: Modern Library.

Platt, R., Rice, P. A., and McCormack, W. M. (1983). Risk of acquiring gonorrhea and prevalence of abnormal adnexal findings among women recently exposed to gonorrhea. *Journal of the American Medical Association,* **250**, 3205–3209.

Pleck, Joseph H. (1981). *The Myth of masculinity.* Cambridge, MA: MIT Press.

Pleck, Joseph H., and Sawyer, Jack. (1974). *Men and masculinity.* Englewood Cliffs, NJ: Prentice-Hall.

Pomeroy, Wa:rdell B. (1966). Normal vs. abnormal sex. *Sexology,* **32**, 436–439.

Pomeroy, Wardell B. (1972). *Dr. Kinsey and the Institute for Sex Research.* New York: Harper & Row.

Pomeroy, Wardell B. (1975). The diagnosis and treatment of transvestites and transsexuals. *Journal of Sex and Marital Therapy,* **1**, 215–224.

Pope Paul VI. (1968, July 30). *Humane vitae.* (English text in *The New York Times,* 20.)

Population Information Program. (1982). IUDs: An appropriate contraceptive for many women. *Population Reports,* Series B, No. 4, B101–B135.

Population Information Program. (1983). Vasectomy—Safe and simple. *Population Reports,* Series D, No. 4, D61–D100.

Powdermaker, Hortense. (1933). *Life in Lesu.* New York: Norton.

Presser, H. B., and Bumpass, L. L. (1972). The acceptability of contraceptive sterilization among U.S. couples: 1970. *Family Planning Perspectives,* **4**(4), 18.

Price, James H. (1981). Toxic shock syndrome—An update. *Journal of School Health.*

Prince, Virginia, and Butler, P. M. (1972). Survey of 504 cases of transvestism. *Psychological Reports,* **31**, 903–917.

Pritchard, J. A., and MacDonald, P. C. (1980). *Williams obstetrics* (16th ed.). NY: Appleton-Century-Crofts.

Qualls, C. Brandon. (1978). The prevention of sexual disorders. New York: Plenum.

Qualls, C. B., Wincze, J. P., and Barlow, D. H. (1978). *The prevention of sexual disorders.* New York: Plenum.

Rachman, S. (1966). Sexual fetishism: An experimental analogue. *Psychological Record,* **16**, 293–296.

Rada, R. T. (1975). Alcoholism and forcible rape. *American Journal of Psychiatry,* **132**, 444–446.

Radlove, Shirley. (1983). Sexual response and gender roles. In E. R. Allgeier and N. B. McCormick (Eds.), *Changing boundaries: Gender roles and sexual behavior.* Palo Alto, CA: Mayfield.

Rainwater, Lee. (1965). *Family design.* Chicago: Aldine.

Rainwater, Lee. (1971). Marital sexuality in four "cultures of poverty." In D. S. Marshall and R. C. Suggs (Eds.), *Human sexual behavior.* New York: Basic Books.

Ramcharan, S., Pellegrin, F. S., Ray, R., and Hsu, J-P. (1980). *The Walnut Creek contraceptive drug study: A prospective study of the side effects of oral contraceptives.* Vol. III. Washington. D.C.: Government Printing Office.

Ramey, Estelle. (1972, Spring). Men's cycles. *Ms.,* 8–14.

Ramsey, Glen V. (1943a). The sex information of younger boys. *American Journal of Orthopsychiatry,* **13**, 347–352.

Ramsey, Glen V. (1943b). The sexual development of boys. *American Journal of Psychology,* **56**, 217–233.

Raphael, Bette-Jane. (1973, Oct. 25). The myth of the male orgasm. *Village Voice.* [Reprinted in *Psychology Today,* **7**(8), 1974.]

Ravenholt, R., and Levinski, M. (1965). Smoking during pregnancy. *Lancet,* **1**, 961.

Raymond, Janice G. (1979). *The transsexual empire: The making of the she-male.* Boston: Beacon Press.

Reevy, William R. (1967). Child sexuality. In A. Ellis and A. Abarbanel (Eds.), *The encyclopedia of sexual behavior.* New York: Hawthorn.

Reilly, T., Carpenter, S., Dull, V., and Bartlett, K. (1982). The factorial survey technique: An approach to defining sexual harassment on campus. *Journal of Social Issues,* **38**(4), 99–110.

Reisenzein, Rainer. (1983). The Schachter theory of emotion: Two decades later. *Psychological Bulletin,* **94**, 239–264.

Reiss, Ira L. (1960). *Premarital sexual standards in America.* New York: Free Press.

Reiss, Ira L. (1961, Nov.). Sexual codes in teenage culture. *The Annals,* 53–62.

Reiss, Ira L. (1967). *The social context of premarital sexual permissiveness.* New York: Holt.

Renshaw, Domeena C. (1982). *Incest: Understanding and treatment.* Boston: Little, Brown.

Resick, Patricia, et al. (1981). Social adjustment of victims of sexual assault. *Journal of Consulting and Clinical Psychology,* **49**, 705–712.

Reuben, David. (1969). *Everything you always wanted to know about sex but were afraid to ask.* New York: Bantam Books.

Reynolds, Barry S. (1980). Biofeedback and facilitation of erection in men with erectile dysfunction. *Archives of Sexual Behavior,* **9**, 101–114.

Rhodes, Richard. (1972, Aug.). Sex and sin in Sheboygan. *Playboy,* 186–190.

Ribble, Margaret A. (1955). *The personality of the young child.* New York: Columbia University Press.

Rice, Berkeley. (1974). Rx: Sex for senior citizens. *Psychology Today,* **8**(1). 18–20.

Richards. David A. J. (1979). Sexual autonomy and the constitutional right to privacy: A case study in human rights and the unwritten constitution. *Hastings Law Journal,* **30**, 957–1018.

Richards, D. A. J. (1979–80). Homosexual acts and the constitutional right to privacy. *Journal of Homosexuality,* **5**(1/2), 43–66.

Richardson, Stephen A. (1972). People with cerebral palsy talk for themselves. *Developmental Medicine and Child Neurology.* **14**, 524–535.

Riddle, Dorothy I. (1978). Relating to children: Gays as role models. *Journal of Social Issues,* **34**(3), 38–58.

Ritzer, George. (1983). *Sociological theory.* New York: Knopf.

Rivera, Rhonda. (1979). Our straight-laced judges: The legal position of homosexual persons in the U. S. *Hastings Law Journal,* **30**, 799–955.

Rivera, Rhonda. (1980–81). Recent evelopments in sexual preference law. *Drake Law Review,* **30**, 311–346.

Rivera, Rhonda. (1982). Homosexuality and the law. In W. Paul, et al. (Eds.), *Homosexuality: Social, psychological. and biological issues.* Beverly Hills: Sage.

Roberto, Laura G. (1983). Issues in diagnosis and treatment of transsexualism. *Archives of Sexual Behavior,* **12**, 445–473.

Roberts, Elizabeth J. (Ed.) (1980). *Childhood sexual learning: The unwritten curriculum.* Cambridge, MA: Ballinger.

Roberts, E., Kline, D., and Gagnon, J. (1978). *Family life and sexual learning. A summary report.* Vol. I. Cambridge, MA: Population Education.

Robinson, B. E., Skeen, P., and Flake-Hobson, C. (1982). Sex role endorsement among homosexual men across the lifespan. *Archives of Sexual Behavior,* **11**, 355–360.

Robinson, D., and Rock, J. (1967). Intrascrotal hyperthermia induced by scrotal insulation: Effect on spermatogenesis. *Obstetrics and Gynecology,* **29**, 217.

Rogers, Carl R. (1951). *Client-centered therapy: Its current practice, implications, and theory.* Boston: Houghton Mifflin.

Rogers, Rex S. (1974). Woman, culture, and society: A theoretical overview. In M. S. Rosaldo and L. Lamphere (Eds.), *Woman, culture, and society.* Stanford, CA: Stanford University Press.

Rose, R. M. (1975). Testosterone, aggression, and homosexuality: A review of the literature and implications for future research. In E. J. Sachar (Ed.), *Topics in psychoendocrinology.* New York: Grune & Stratton.

Rosebury, Theodor. (1971). *Microbes and morals: The strange story of venereal disease.* New York: Viking.

Rosen, David H. (1974). *Lesbianism: A study of female homosexuality.* Springfield, IL: Charles C. Thomas.

Rosen, Ruth. (1982). *The lost sisterhood: Prostitution in America, 1900–1918.* Baltimore: Johns Hopkins Press.

Rosenbleet, C., and Pariente, B. J. (1973). The prostitution of the criminal law. *American Criminal Law Review,* **11**, 373–427.

Rosenkrantz, P. S., et al. (1968). Sex role stereotypes and self-concepts in college students. *Journal of Consulting and Clinical Psychology,* **32**, 287–295.

Rothchild, Ellen. (1975, Dec.). Answering young children's sex questions. *Medical Aspects of Human Sexuality,* 23.

Rotkin, I. D. (1962). Relation of adolescent coitus to cervical cancer risk. *Journal of the American Medical Association,* **179**, 110.

Rotkin, I. K. (1973). A comparison review of key epidemiological studies in cervical cancer related to current searches for transmissible agents. *Cancer Research,* **33**, 1353.

Rubin, Isadore. (1965). *Sexual life after sixty.* New York: Basic Books.

Rubin, Isadore. (1966). Sex after forty—and after seventy. In Ruth Brecher and Edward Brecher (Eds.), *An analysis of human sexual response.* New York: Signet Books, New American Library.

Rubin, Lillian B. (1979). *Women of a certain age: The midlife search for self.* New York: Harper & Row.

Rubin, Robert T., Reinisch, J. M., and Haskett, R. F. (1981). Postnatal gonadal steroid effects on human behavior. *Science,* **211**, 1318–1324.

Rubin, Zick. (1970). Measurement of romantic love. *Journal of Personality and Social Psychology,* **16**, 265–273.

Rubin, Zick. (1973). *Liking and loving: An invitation to social psychology.* New York: Holt.

Rubin, Zick, et al. (1980). Self-disclosure in dating couples: Sex roles and the ethic of openness. *Journal of Marriage and the Family,* **42**, 305–317.

Rubin, Z., Peplau L. A., and Hill, C. T. (1981). Loving and leaving: Sex differences in romantic attachments. *Sex Roles,* **1**, 821–836.

Rubenstein, Carin. (1983, July). The modern art of courtly love. *Psychology Today,* 40–49.

Ruble, Diane N. (1977). Premenstrual symptoms: A reinterpretation. *Science,* **197**, 291–292.

Ruble, D. N., Brooks-Gunn, J., and Clarke, A. (1980). Research on menstrual-related psychological changes: Alternative perspectives. In J. E. Parsons (Ed.), *The psychobiology of sex differences and sex roles.* New York: McGraw-Hill.

Ruble, Thomas L. (1983). Sex stereotypes: Issues of change in the 1970s. *Sex Roles,* **9**, 397–402.

Rush, Florence. (1980). Child pornography. In L. Lederer (Ed.), *Take back the night: Women on pornography.* New York: William Morrow.

Russell, Diana. (1975). *The politics of rape: The victim's perspective.* New York: Stein and Day.

Russell, Diana E. H. (1980). Pornography and violence: What does the new research say? In L. Lederer (Ed.), *Take back the night: Women on pornography.* New York: William Morrow.

Russell, Diana E. H. (1983). *Rape in marriage.* New York: Macmillan.

Russell, Diana E. H., and Howell, Nancy. (1983). The prevalence of rape in the United States revisited. *Signs,* **8**, 688–695.

Rylander, Gosta. (1969). Clinical and medico-criminological aspects of addiction to central stimulating drugs. In Folke Sjoqvist and Malcolm Tottie (Eds.), *Abuse of central stimulants.* New York: Raven Press.

Sacred Congregation for the Doctrine of the Faith. (1976, Jan. 16). Declaration on certain questions concerning sexual ethics. (English text in *The New York Times,* 2.)

Sadock, Benjamin J., and Sadock, Virginia A. (1976). Techniques of coitus. In B. J. Sadock et al. (Eds.), *The sexual experience.* Baltimore: Williams & Wilkins.

Saegert, S., Swap, W., and Zajonc, R. B. (1973). Exposure, context, an interpersonal attraction. *Journal of Personality and Social Psychology,* **25**, 234–242.

Safran, C. (1976, Nov.). What men do to women on the job: A shocking look at sexual harassment. *Redbook,* 148.

Sagarin, Edward. (1973). Power to the peephole. *Sexual Behavior,* **3**, 2–7.

Sagarin, Edward. (1977). Incest: Problems of definition and frequency. *Journal of Sex Research,* **13**, 126–135.

Saghir, M., and Robins, E. (1973). *Male and Female homosexuality.* Baltimore: Williams & Wilkins.

Salhanick, H. A., and Margulis, R. H. (1968). Hormonal physiology of the ovary. In J. J. Gold (Ed.), *Textbook of gynecologic endocrinology.* New York: Harper & Row.

Sanday, Peggy R. (1981). The socio-cultural context of rape: A cross-cultural study. *Journal of Social Issues,* **37**(4), 5–27.

Saral, Rein, et al (1981). Acyclovir prophylaxis of herpes-simplex-virus infection. *New England Journal of Medicine,* **305**, 63–67.

Sarrel, Philip, and Masters, William. (1982). Sexual molestation of men by women. *Archives of Sexual Behavior,* **11**, 117–132.

Sayers, Dorothy. (1946). *Unpopular opinions.* London: Gollancz.

Scanzoni, John. (1982). *Sexual bargaining* (2nd ed.). Chicago: University of Chicago Press.

Schachter, Stanley. (1964). The interaction of cognitive and physiological determinants of emotional state. In L. Berkowitz (Ed.), *Advances in experimental social psychology.* Vol. I. New York: Academic Press.

Schachter, Stanley, and Singer, J. F. (1962). Cognitive, social, and physiological determinants of emotional state. *Psychological Review,* **69**, 379–399.

Schafer, Sigrid. (1977). Sociosexual behavior in male and female homosexuals: A study in sex differences. *Archives of Sexual Behavior,* **6**, 355–364.

Schaffer, H. R., and Emerson, Peggy E. (1964). Patterns of response to physical contact in early human development. *Journal of Child Psychology and Psychiatry,* **5**, 1–13.

Schegloff, Emanuel A. (1979). Identification and recognition in telephone conversation openings. In G. Psathas (Ed.), *Everyday language: Studies in ethnomethodology.* New York: Irvington.

Schenker, J. G., and Evron, S. (1983). New concepts in the surgical management of tubal pregnancy and the consequent postoperative results. *Fertility and Sterility,* **40**, 709–723.

Schmidt, Gunter. (1977). Personal Communication.

Schmidt, Gunter and Schorsch, Eberhard. (1981). Psychosurgery of sexually deviant patients: Review and analysis of new empirical findings. *Archives of Sexual Behavior,* **10**, 301–323.

Schmidt, Gunter, and Sigusch, Volkmar. (1970). Sex differences in response to psychosexual stimulation by films and slides. *Journal of Sex Research,* **6**, 268–283.

Schmidt, G., Sigusch, V., and Schafer, S. (1973). Responses to reading erotic stories: Male-female differences. *Archives of Sexual Behavior,* **2**, 181–199.

Schmidt, Madeline H. (1970). Superiority of breast-feeding: Fact or fancy? *American Journal of Nursing,* **70**, 1488–1493.

Schneidman, Barbara, and McGuire, Linda. (1976). Group thrapy for nonorgasmic women: Two age levels. *Archives of Sexual Behavior,* **5**, 239–248.

Schofield, Alfred T., and Vaughan-Jackson, Percy. (1913). *What a boy should know.* New York: Cassell.

Schoof-Tams, K., Schlaegel, J., and Walczak, L. (1976). Differentiation of sexual morality between 11 and 16 years. *Archives of Sexual Behavior,* **5**, 353–370.

Schull, William J., and Neel, James V. (1965). *The effects of inbreeding on Japanese children.* New York: Harper & Row.

Schwartz, M. F., Kolodny, R. C., and Masters, W. H. (1980). Plasma testosterone levels of sexually functional and dysfunctional men. *Archives of Sexual Behavior,* **9**, 355–366.

Schwartz, Mark F., and Masters, W. H. (1983). Conceptual factors in the treatment of paraphilias: A preliminary report. *Journal of Sex and Marital Therapy,* **9**, 3–18.

Schwartz, P. (1981). The scientific study of rape. In R. Green and J. Wiener (Eds.), *Methodology in sex research.* Washington D.C.: U.S. Government Printing Office.

Sciarra, J. J., Markland, C., and Speidel, J. J. (1975). *Control of male fertility.* New York: Harper & Row.

Scott, John Paul. (1964). The effects of early experience on social behavior and organization. In W. Etkin (Ed.), *Social behavior and organization among vertebrates.* Chicago: University of Chicago Press.

Seavey, C. A., Katz, P. A., and Zalk, S. R. (1975). Baby X: The effect of gender labels on adult responses to infants. *Sex Roles,* 103–109.

Seeley, T. T., Abramson, P. R., Perry, L. B., Rothblatt, A. B., and Seeley, D. M. (1980). Thermographic measurement of sexual arousal: A methodological note. *Archives of Sexual Behavior,* **9**, 77–86.

Selkin, J. (1975). Rape. *Psychology Today,* **8**(8). 70.

Semans, J. (1956). Premature ejaculation: A new approach. *Southern Medical Journal,* **49**, 353–358.

Serrin, W. (1981, Feb. 9). Sex is a growing multimillion dollar business. *New York Times,* B1–B6.

Shaffer, Leigh S. (1977). The golden fleece: Anti-intellectualism and social science. *American Psychologist,* **32**, 814–823.

Shanor, Karen. (1978). *The sexual sensitivity of the American male.* New York: Ballantine Books.

Shaver, Phillip. (1976). Questions concerning fear of success and its conceptual relatives. *Sex Roles,* **2**, 305–320.

Sheehy, Gail. (1973). *Hustling: Prostitution in our wide open society.* New York: Delacorte Press.

Sherfey, Mary Jane. (1966). The evolution and nature of female sexuality in relation to psychoanalytic theory. *Journal of the American Psychoanalytic Association,* **14**, 28–128.

Sherman, Julia. (1971). *On the psychology of women: A survey of empirical studies.* Springfield, IL: Charles C. Thomas.

Shewaga, Duane. (1983). Note on *New York Ferber. Santa Clara Law Review,* **23**, 675–684.

Shoemaker, Donald J. (1977). The teeniest trollops: "Baby pros," "chickens," and child prostitutes. In C. D. Bryant (Ed.), *Sexual deviancy in social context.* New York: Franklin Watts. pp. 241–254.

Shope, David F. (1975). *Interpersonal sexuality.* Philadelphia: Saunders.

Shore, M. F. (1970, Dec.). Drugs can be dangerous during pregnancy and lactation. *Canadian Pharmaceutical Journal.*

Shouvlin, David P. (1981). Preventing the sexual exploitation of children: A model act. *Wake Forest Law Review,* **17**, 535–560.

Siegelman, Marvin. (1979). Adjustment of homosexual and heterosexual women: A cross-national replication. *Archives of Sexual Behavior,* **8**, 121–126.

Silber, Sherman. (1981). *The human male: From birth to old age.* New York: Scribner.

Simon Population Trust. (1969). Vasectomy: Follow-up of a thousand cases. Cambridge, England, **12**, 1–17. (Cited in W. M. Wiest and L. D. Janke. (1974). Methodological critique of research on psychological effects of vasectomy. *Psychosomatic Medicine,* **36**, 438–449.)

Slotkin, J. S. (1947). On a possible lack of incest regulations in Old Iran. *American Anthropologist,* **49**, 612–617.

Slovenko, Ralph. (1965). *Sexual behavior and the law.* Springfield, IL: Charles C. Thomas.

Smith, D. G. (1976). The social content of pornography. *Journal of Communication,* **26**, 16–33.

Smith, R. Spencer. (1976). Voyeurism: A review of literature. *Archives of Sexual Behavior,* **5**, 585–608.

Smith, Stuart L. (1975). Mood and the menstrual cycle. In E. J. Sachar (Ed.), *Topics in psychoendocrinology.* New York: Grune & Stratton.

Snelling, H. A. (1975). What is rape? In L. G. Schultz (Ed.), *Rape victimology.* Springfield, IL: Charles C. Thomas.

Snyder, Douglas K., and Berg, Phyllis. (1983). Determinants of sexual dissatisfaction in sexually distressed couples. *Archives of Sexual ehavior,* **12**, 237–246.

Somers, A. (1982). Sexual harassment in academe: Legal issues and definitions. *Journal of Social Issues,* **38**(4), 23–32.

Sommer, Barbara. (1973). The effect of menstruation on cognitive and perceptual-motor behavior: A review. *Psychosomatic Medicine,* **35**, 515–534.

Sorensen, Robet C. (1973). *Adolescent sexuality in contemporary America.* New York: World.

Sotile, Wayne M., and Kilmann, Peter R. (1977). Treatments of psychogenic female sexual dysfunctions. *Psychological Bulletin,* **84**, 619–633.

Southam, A. L., and Gonzaga, F. P. (1965). Systemic changes during the menstrual cycle. *American Journal of Obstetrics and Gynecology,* **91**, 142–165.

Spanier, Graham B. (1976). Formal and informal sex education as determinants of premarital sexual behavior. *Archives of Sexual Behavior,* **5**, 39–67.

Spanier, Graham B. (1977). Sources of sex information and premarital sexual behavior. *Journal of Sex Research,* **13**, 73–88.

Spanier, Graham B. (1979). Mate swapping: Marital enrichment or sexual experimentation? In G. B. Spanier (Ed.), *Human sexuality in a changing society.* Minneapolis: Burgess.

Spanier, Graham. (1983). Married and unmarried cohabitation in the United States: 1980. *Journal of Marriage and the Family,* **45**, 277–288.

Speidel, J. J. (1983). Steroidal contraception in the 80's: The role of current and new products. *Journal of Reproductive Medicine,* **28**, 759–769.

Speroff, L., Glass, R. H., and Kas, N. G. (1973). *Clinical gynecologic endocrinology and infertility.* Baltimore: Williams & Wilkins.

Spitz, Rene A. (1949). Autoeroticism: Some empirical findings and hypotheses on three of its manifestations in the first year of life. *The Psychoanalytic Study of the Child.* Vol. III–IV. New York: International Universities Press. Pp. 85–120.

Spivack, G., and Spotts, J. (1965). The Devereux Child Behavior Scale: Symptom behaviors in latency age children. *American Journal of Mental Retardation,* **69**, 839–853.

Staples, Robert. (1972). Research on black sexuality: Its implication for family life education and public policy. *The Family Coordinator,* **21**, 183–188.

St. Augustine. (1950). *The city of God.* (Marcus Dods, Trans.). New York: Modern Library.

Stein, Richard A. (1980). Sexual counseling and coronary heart disease. In S. R. Leiblum and L. A. Pervin (Eds.), *Principles and practice of sex therapy.* New York: Guilford Press.

Steinman, Debra L., et al. (1981). A comparison of male and female patterns of sexual arousal. *Archives of Sexual Behavior,* **10**, 529–548.

Stephan, W., Berscheid, E., and Walster, E. (1971). Sexual arousal and heterosexual perception. *Journal of Personality and Social Psychology,* **20**, 83–101.

Stephens, W. N. (1961). A cross-cultural study of menstrual taboos. *Genetic Psychology Monographs,* **64**, 385–416.

Stern, Mikhail. (1980). *Sex in the USSR.* New York: Times Books.

Stewart, W. F. R. (1979). *The sexual side of handicap: A guide for the caring professions.* Cambridge, England: Woodhead-Faulkner.

Stokes, K., Kilmann, P. R., and Wanlass, R. L. (1983). Sexual orientation and sex role conformity. *Archives of Sexual Behavior,* **12**, 427–434.

Stone, Abraham. (1931). *The practice of contraception.* Baltimore: Williams & Wilkins.

Storms, Michael D. (1980). Theories of sexual orientation. *Journal of Personality and Social Psychology,* **38**, 783–792.

Storms, Michael D. (1981). A theory of erotic orientation development. *Psychological Review,* **88**, 340–353.

Storms, Michael D. et al. (1981). Sexual scripts for women. *Sex Roles,* **1**, 699–708.

Stout, J. (1973, Aug. 25). Quaker tells of rape in D.C. Jail. *Washington Star-News.*

Sullivan, W. (1971, Jan. 24). Boys and girls are now maturing earlier. *The New York Times.*

Symons, Donald. (1979). *The evolution of human sexuality.* New York: Oxford University Press.

Szasz, Thomas S. (1965). Legal and moral aspects of homosexuality. In J. Marmor (Ed.) *Sexual inversion: The multiple roots of homosexuality.* New York: Basic Books.

Szasz, Thomas S. (1980). *Sex by prescription.* Garden City, NY, Anchor Press/Doubleday.

Talamini, John T. (1982). *Boys will be girls: The hidden world of the heterosexual male transvestite.* Washington, D.C.: University Press of America.

Tamir, Lois M. (1982). *Men in their forties: The transition to middle age.* New York: Springer.

Tangri, S., Burt, M. R., and Johnson, L. B. (1982). Sexual harassment at work: Three explanatory models. *Journal of Social Issues,* **38**(4), 33–54.

Tanner, James M. (1967). Puberty. In A. McLaren (Ed.), *Advances in reproductive physiology.* Vol. II. New York: Academic Press.

Tart, Charles. (1970). Marijuana intoxication: Common experience. *Nature,* **226**, 701–704.

Tart, Charles. (1971). *On being stoned.* Palo Alto, CA: Science and Behavior Books.

Tavris, Carol. (1977). Masculinity. *Psychology Today,* **10**(8), 34.

Tavris, C., and Sadd, S. (1975). *The Redbook report on female sexuality.* New York: Dell.

Taylor, Marylee C., and Hall, Judith A. (1982). Psychological androgyny: Theories, methods, and conclusions. *Psychological Bulletin,* **92**, 347–366.

Teen-age sex: Letting the pendulum swing. (1972, Aug. 21). *Time,* 34–38.

Terman, Lewis M. (1948). Kinsey's *Sexual behavior in the human male:* Some comments and criticisms. *Psychological Bulletin,* **45**, 443–459.

Terman, Lewis M. (1951). Correlates of orgasm adequacy in a group of 556 wives. *Journal of Psychology,* **32**, 115–172.

Terman, Lewis, et al. (1938). *Psychological factors in marital happiness.* New York: McGraw-Hill.

Thielicke, Helmut. (1964). *The ethics of sex.* New York: Harper & Row.

Thin, R. N. T., Williams, I. A., and Nicol, C. S. (1970). Direct and delayed methods of immunofluorescent diagnosis of gonorrhea in women. *British Journal of Venereal Disease,* **47**, 27–30.

Thomas, David J. (1982). San Francisco's 1979 White Night riot. In W. Paul, et al. (Eds.), *Homosexuality: Social, psychological, and biological issues.* Beverly Hills: Sage.

Thompson, Anthony P. (1983). Extramarital sex: A review of the research literature. *Journal of Sex Research,* **19**, 1–22.

Thorpe, L. P., Katz, B., and Lewis, R. T. (1961). *The psychology of abnormal behavior.* New York: Ronald Press.

Todd, J., et al. (1978). Toxic-shock syndrome associated with phase-group-I staphylococci. *Lancet,* **2**, 1116–1118.

Tordjman, Gilbert, et al. (1980). Advances in the vascular pathology of male erectile dysfunction. *Archives of Sexual Behavior,* **9**, 391–398.

Towne, J. E. (1955). Carcinoma of cervix in nulliparous and celibate women. *American Journal of Obstetrics and Gynecology,* **69**, 606.

Travis, Robert P., and Travis, Patricia Y. (1975). The pairing enrichment program: Actualizing the marriage. *Family Coordinator,* **24**, 161–165.

Tsai, M., Feldman-Summers, S., and Edgar, M. (1979). Childhood molestation: Variables related to differential impacts on psychosexual functioning in adult women. *Journal of Abnormal Psychology,* **88**, 407–417.

Tullman, Gerald M., et al. (1981). The pre- and post-therapy measurement of communication skills of couples undergoing sex therapy at the Masters & Johnson Institute. *Archives of Sexual Behavior,* **10**, 95–109.

Tutin, C. E. G., and McGinnis, P. R. (1981). Chimpanzee reproduction in the wild. In C. E. Graham (Ed.), *Reproductive biology of the great apes.* New York: Academic Press. Pp. 239–264.

Udry, J. Richard, and Eckland, Bruce K. (1984). Benefits of being attractive: Differential payoffs for men and women. *Psychological Reports,* **54**, 47–56.

Udry, J. Richard, and Morris, N. M. (1968). Distribution of coitus in the menstrual cycle. *Nature,* **220**, 593–596.

U.P.I. (1981, Nov. 5). Toxicologist warns against butyl nitrite. *Delaware Gazette,* 3.

Upton, (1983). The phasic approach to oral contraception: The triphasic concept and its clinical application. *International Journal of Fertility,* **28**(3), 121–140.

U.S. Bureau of the Census. (1976). *U.S. fact book: The American almanac.* New York: Grosset & Dunlap.

U.S. Department of Commerce. (1973). *Some demographic aspects of aging in the U.S.: Growth of the population 65 years and over.* Washington, D.C.: U.S. Government Printing Office.

U.S. Department of Labor. (1982). *20 facts on women workers.* Washington, D.C.: U.S. Department of Labor.

U.S. Public Health Service, Center for Disease Control. (1976a), Nov. 26). Comparative risks of three methods of midtrimester abortion. *Morbidity and Mortality Weekly Report,* 370.

U.S. Public Health Service, Center for Disease Control. (1976b). *VD fact sheet 1976.* HEW Publication No. (CDC) 77–8195.

U.S. Public Health Service, Center for Disease Control. (1977). *Abortion surveillance 1975.* Atlanta: CDC.

Vance, Ellen B., and Wagner, Nathaniel N. (1976). Written descriptions of orgasm: A study of sex differences. *Archives of Sexual Behavior,* **5**, 87–98.

Vandenberg, Steven G. (1972). Assortative mating, or who marries whom? *Behavior Genetics,* **2**, 127–158.

Vander, A. J., Sherman, J. H., and Luciano, D. S. (1975). *Human physiology.* New York: McGraw-Hill.

Velarde, Albert H., and Warlick, Mark. (1973). Massage parlors: The sensuality business. *Society,* **11**(1), 63–74.

Veronesi, Umberto, et al. (1981). Comparing radical mastectomy with quadrantectomy, axillary dissection, and radiotherapy in patients with small cancers of the breast. *New England Journal of Medicine,* **305**, 6–11.

Video turns big profit for porn products. (1982, Mar. 10). *Variety,* **306**, 35.

Vincent, J. P., Friedman, L. C., Nugent, J., and Messerly, L. (1979). Demand characteristics in observations of marital interaction. *Journal of Consulting and Clinical Psychology,* **47**, 557–566.

Vorherr, H., Messer, R. H. and Reid, D. (1983). Complications of tubal sterilization: Menstrual abnormalities and fibrocystic breast disease. *American Journal of Obstetrics and Gynecology,* **145**, 644–645.

Voss, Jacqueline R. (1980). Sex education: Evaluation and recommendations for future study. *Archives of Sexual Behavior,* **9**. 37–59.

Wabrek, Alan J., and Burchell, R. Clay. (1980). Male sexual dysfunction associated with coronary heart disease. *Archives of Sexual Behavior,* **9**, 69–75.

Wabrek, Alan J., and Wabrek, Carolyn J. (1975). Dyspareunia. *Journal of Sex and Marital Therapy,* **1**, 234–241.

Wagner, Nathanial, and Solberg, Don. (1974). Pregnancy and sexuality. *Medical Aspects of Human Sexuality,* **8**(3), 44–79.

Walfish, Steven, and Myerson, Marilyn. (1980). Sex role identity and attitudes toward sexuality. *Archives of Sexual Behavior,* **9**, 199–204.

Walker, Alexander M., et al. (1981). Hospitalization rates in vasectomized men. *Journal of the American Medical Association,* **245**, 2315–2317.

Wallace, Douglas H. (1973). Obscenity and contemporary standards: A survey. *Journal of Social Issues,* **29**, 53–68.

Wallerstein, Edward, (1980). *Circumcision: An American health fallacy.* New York: Springer.

Wallin, Paul. (1949). An appraisal of some methodological aspects of the Kinsey report. *American Sociological Review,* **14**, 197–210.

Walster, Elaine. (1978). Equity and extramarital sexuality. *Archives of Sexual Behavior,* **7**, 127–141.

Walster, Elaine, et al. (1973). "Playing hard-to-get": Understanding an elusive phenomenon. *Journal of Personality and Social Psychology,* **26**, 113–121.

Walster, Elaine, Walster, G. William. (1978). *A new look at love.* Reading, MA: Addison-Wesley.

Walster, E.. Walster, G. W., and Berscheid, E. (1978). *Equity theory and research.* Boston: Allyn and Bacon.

Walster, E., Walster, G. W., and Traupmann, J. (1978). Equity and premarital sex. *Journal of Personality and Social Psychology,* **36**, 82–92.

Walters, C., Shurley, J. T., and Parsons, O. A. (1962). Differences in male and female responses to underwater sensory deprivation: An exploratory study. *Journal of Nervous and Mental Disease,* **135**, 302–310.

Wampler, Karen S. (1982). The effectiveness of the Minnesota Couple Communication Program: A review of research. *Journal of Marital and Family Therapy,* 345–355.

Warren, Carol A. B. (1974). *Identity and community in the gay world.* New York: Wiley.

Weideger, Paula. (1976). *Menstruation and menopause.* New York: Knopf.

Weinberg, Martin S., and Williams, Colin. (1974). *Male homosexuals: Their problems and adaptations.* New York: Oxford University Press.

Weinberg, Samuel K. (1955). *Incest behavior.* New York: Citadel Press.

Weiner, L., et al. (1951). Carcinoma of the cervix in Jewish women. *American Journal of Obstetrics and Gynecology,* **61**, 418.

Weis, David L. (1983). Affective reactions of women to their initial experience of coitus. *Journal of Sex Research,* **19**, 209–237.

Weis, Kurt, and Borges, Sandra S. (1973). Victimology and rape: The case of the legitimate victim. *Issues in Criminology,* **8**(2), 71–115.

Weiss, Howard, D. (1973). Mechanism of erection. *Medical Aspects of Human Sexuality,* **7**(2), 21–40.

Weiss, Noel S., et al. (1976). Increasing incidence of endometrial cancer in the United States. *New England Journal of Medicine,* **294**, 1259–1261.

Weissman, M., and Klerman, G. (1977). Sex differences and the epidemiology of depression. *Archives of General Psychiatry,* **34**, 98–111.

Weitzman, L. J., Eifles, D., Hokada, E., and Ross, C. (1972). Sex role socialization in picture books for preschool children. *American Journal of Sociology,* **72**, 1125–1150.

Weller, Ronald A., and Halikas, James A.(1984). Marijuana use and sexual behavior. *Journal of Sex Research,* **20**, 186–193.

Werry, J. S., and Quay, H. S. (1971). The prevalence of behavior symptoms in younger elementary school children. *American Journal of Orthopsychiatry,* **41**, 136–143.;

Wertz, R. W., and Wertz, D. C. (1977). *Lying-in: A history of childbirth in America.* New York: Free Press.

Wessman, Alden E., and Ricks, David F. (1966). *Mood and personality.* New York: Holt.

Westoff, Charles. (194). Coital frequency and contraception. *Family Planning Perspectives,* **6**(3), 36–141.

Westoff, Charles, and Bumpass, Larry. (1973). The revolution in birth control practices of U.S. Roman Catholics. *Science,* **179**, 41–44.

Westoff, Charles F., and Jones, Elise F. (1977). Contraception and sterilization in the United States, 1965–1975. *Family Planning Perspectives,* **9**, 153–157.

Wheller, Garry D., et al. (1984). Reduced serum testosterone and prolactin levels in male distance runners. *Journal of the American Medical Association,* **252**, 514–516.

Wheeler, John, and Kilmann, Peter R. (1983). Comarital sexual behavior: Individual and relationship variables. *Archives of Sexual Behavior,* **12**, 295–306.

Whitam, F. L. (1977). The homosexual role: A reconsideration. *Journal of Sex Research,* **13**, 1–11.

Whitam, Frederick L. (1983). Culturally invariable properties of male homosexuality: Tentative conclusions from cross-cultural research. *Archives of Sexual Behavior,* **12**, 207–226.

White, Charles B. (1982). Sexual interest, attitudes, knowledge, and sexual history in relation to sexual behavior in the institutionalized aged. *Archives of Sexual Behavior,* **11**, 11–22.

White, David. (1981, Sept.). Pursuit of the ultimate aphrodisiac. *Psychology Today,* **15**(9), 9–12.

White, G. L., Fishbein, S., and Rutstein, J. (1981). Passionate love and the misattribution of arousal. *Journal of Personality and Social Psychology,* **41**, 56–62.

White, Gregory L., and Kight, T. D. (1984). Misattribution of arousal and attraction: Effects of salience of explanations for arousal. *Journal of Experimental Social Psychology,* **20**, 55–64.

White, Susan E., and Reamy, Kenneth. (1982). Sexuality and pregnancy: A review. *Archives of Sexual Behavior,* **11**, 429–444.

Whitehurst, R. N. (1972). Extramarital sex: Alienation or extension of normal behavior. In J. N. Edwards (Ed.), *Sex and society.* Chicago: Rand McNally.

Whiteside, D. C., et al. (1983). Factors associated with successful vaginal delivery after cesarean section. *Journal of Reproductive Medicine,* **28**, 785–788.

Wickler, Wolfgang. (1973). *The sexual code.* New York: Anchor Books. (Original in German, 1969).

Wiest, William M., and Janke, L. D. (1974). Methodological critique of research on psychological effects of vasectomy. *Psychosomatic Medicine,* **36**, 438–449.

Williams, Colin H., and Weinberg, Martin S. (1971). *Homosexuals and the military: A study of less than honorable discharge.* New York: Harper & Row.

Wills, G. (1977). Measuring the impact of erotica. *Psychology Today,* **11**(3), 30ff.

Wilson, E. O. (1975). *Sociobiology: The new synthesis.* Cambridge: Harvard University Press.

Wilson, G. T., and Lawson, D. M. (1978). Expectancies, alcohol, and sexual arousal in women. *Journal of Abnormal Psychology,* **87**, 358–367.

Wilson, W. Cody. (1973). Pornography: The emergence of a social issue and the beginning of psychological study. *Journal of Social Issues,* **29**, 7–17.

Wilson, W. Cody. (1975). The distribution of selected sexual attitudes and behaviors among the adult population of the United States. *Journal of Sex Research,* **11**, 46–64.

Wilson, W. Cody, and Abelson, Herbert I. (1973). Experience with and attitudes toward explicit sexual materials. *Journal of Social Issues,* **29**, 19–39.

Winick, Charles, and Kinsie, Paul M. (1972). Prostitutes. *Psychology Today,* **5**(9), 57.

Winn, Rhonda L., and Newton, Niles. (1982). Sexuality in aging: A study of 106 cultures. *Archives of Sexual Behavior,* **11**, 283–298.

Wolchik, S. A., Spencer, S. L., and Lisi, I. S. (1983). Volunteer bias in research employing vaginal measures of sexual arousal. *Archives of Sexual Behavior,* **12**, 399–408.

Wolfe, L. (1980, Sept.). The sexual profile of that Cosmopolitan girl. *Cosmopolitan,* 254–265.

Wolff, Charlotte. (1971). *Love between women.* New York: Harper & Row.

Women on Words and Images. (1972). *Dick and Jane as victims: Sex stereotyping in children's readers.* Princeton, NJ: Author.

Woods, James S. (1975). Drug effects on human sexual behavior. In N. F. Woods (Ed.), *Human sexuality in health and illness.* St Louis: Mosby.

Wright, L., Schaefer, A. B., and Solomons, G. (1979). *Encyclopedia of pediatric psychology,* Baltimore: University Park Press.

Wysor, Bettie. (1974). *The lesbian myth.* New York: Random House.

Yablonsky, L. (1979). *The extra-sex factor: Why over half of America's married men play around.* New York: Times Books.

Yalom, Irvin D. (1960). Aggression and forbiddenness in voyeurism. *Archives of General Psychiatry,* **3**, 317.

Yerushalmy, J. (1964). Mother's cigarette smoking and survival of infant. *American Journal of Obstetrics and Gynecology,* **88**, 505–518.

Yorburg, Betty. (1974). *Sexual identity: Sex roles and social change.* New York: Wiley.

Young, Wayland. (1970). Prostitution. In J. D. Douglas (Ed.), *Observations of deviance.* New York: Random House.

Zax, M., Sameroff, A., and Farnum, J. (1975). Childbirth education, maternal attitude and delivery. *American Journal of Obstetrics and Gynecology,* **123**, 185–190.

Zeiss, A. M., Rosen, G. M., and Zeiss, R. A. (1977). Orgasm during intercourse: A treatment strategy for women. *Journal of Consulting and Clinical Psychology,* **45**, 891–895.

Zellinger, P. A., et al. (1975). A commodity theory analysis of the effects of age restrictions upon pornographic materials. *Journal of Applied Psychology,* **60**, 94–99.

Zelnik, Melvin, and Kantner, John F. (1977). Sexual and contraceptive experience of young unmarried women in the United States, 1976 and 1971. *Family Planning Perspectives,* **9**(2), 55–71.

Zelnik, Melvin, and Kantner, John F. (1980). Sexual activity, contraceptive use and pregnancy among metropolitan-area teenagers: 1971–1979. *Family Planning Perspectives,* **12**(5), 230–237.

Zelnik, Melvin, and Kim, Young J. (1982). Sex education and its association with teenage sexual activity, pregnancy and contraceptive use. *Family Planning Perspectives,* **14**(3).

Zilbergeld, Bernie. (1975). Group treatment of sexual dysfunction in men without partners. *Journal of Sex and Marital Therapy,* **1**, 204–214.

Zilbergeld, Bernie. (1978). *Male sexuality.* Boston: Little, Brown.

Zilbergeld, Bernie, and Ellison, Carol Rinklieb. (1980). Desire discrepancies and arousal problems in sex therapy. In S. R. Leiblum and L. A. Pervin (Eds.), *Principles and practice of sex therapy.* New York: Guilford Press.

Zilbergeld, Bernie, and Evans, Michael. (1980, Aug.). The inadequacy of Masters and Johnson. *Psychology Today,* **14**(3), 28–43.

Zimmer, D. (1983). Interaction patterns and communication skills in sexually distressed, and normal couples: Two experimental studies. *Journal of Sex and Marital Therapy,* **9**, 251–265.

Zuckerman, M., Tushup, R., and Finner, S. (1976). Sexual attitudes and experience: Attitude and personality correlates and changes produced by a course in sexuality. *Journal of Consulting and Clinical Psychology.* **44**, 7–19.

Zuckerman, M., and Wheeler, L. (1975). To dispel fantasies about the fantasy-based measure of fear of success. *Psychological Bulletin,* **82**, 932–946.

Zumpe, Doris, and Michael, R. P. (1968). The clutching reaction and orgasm in the female rhesus monkey (*Macaca mulatta*). *Journal of Endocrinology,* **40**, 11–123.

Zumwalt, Rosemary. (1976). Plain and fancy: A content analysis of children's jokes dealing with adult sexuality. *Western Folklore,* **35**, 258–267.

Zussman, L., Zussman, S., Sunley, R., and Bjornson, E. (1981). Sexual response after hysterectomy—oophorectomy. *American Journal of Obstetrics and Gynecology,* **140**, 725–729.

GLOSSARY

Abortion The ending of a pregnancy and the expulsion of the contents of the uterus; may be spontaneous or induced by human intervention.

Abstinence (sexual) Not engaging in sexual activity.

Acquired immune deficiency syndrome (AIDS) A sexually transmitted disease that destroys the body's natural immunity to infection.

Adultery Sexual intercourse between a married person and someone other than her or his spouse.

Afterbirth The placenta and amniotic sac, which come out after the baby during childbirth.

Agape A Greek word meaning selfless love of others.

Ambisexual See *bisexual.*

Amenorrhea The absence of menstruation.

Amniocentesis A test done to determine whether a fetus has birth defects; done by removing amniotic fluid from the pregnant woman's uterus.

Amniotic fluid The watery fluid surrounding a developing fetus in the uterus.

Amyl nitrate A drug, usually inhaled, that some people use to prolong or intensify orgasm.

Anal intercourse Sexual behavior in which one person's penis is inserted into another's anus.

Analogous organs Organs in the male and female that have similar functions.

Anaphrodisiac A substance that decreases sexual desire.

Androgens "Male" sex hormones, produced in the testes; an example is testosterone. In females, the adrenal glands produce androgens.

Androgyny Having both feminine and masculine characteristics.

Anilingus Mouth-anus stimulation.

Anorgasmia The inability of a woman to orgasm; a sexual dysfunction.

Anus The opening of the rectum, located between the buttocks.

Aphrodisiac A substance that increases sexual desire.

Areola The dark circular area of skin surrounding the nipple of the breast.

Artificial insemination Artificially putting semen into a woman's vagina or uterus for the purpose of inducing pregnancy.

Asexual Without sexual desires.

Asymptomatic Having no symptoms.

Attachment A psychological bond that forms between an infant and the mother, father, or other care giver.

Autoeroticism Sexual self-stimulation; masturbation is one example.

Axillary hair Underarm hair.

Barr body A small, black dot appearing in the cells of genetic females; it represents an inactivated X chromosome.

Bartholin's glands Two tiny glands located on either side of the vaginal entrance.

Basal body temperature method One method of rhythm birth control.

Behavior therapy A system of therapy based on learning theory and focusing on the problem behavior, not the unconscious.

Bestiality Sexual contact with an animal; also called *zoophilia.*

Bisexual A person who has some sexual contacts with males and some with females.

Blastocyst A small mass of cells that results after several days of cell division by the fertilized egg.

Braxton-Hicks contractions Contractions of the uterus during pregnancy that are not part of actual labor.

Breech presentation Birth of a baby with buttocks or feet first.

Brothel A house of prostitution.

Bucchal smear A test of genetic gender.

Bulbourethral glands See *Cowper's glands.*

Butch A very masculine lesbian; may also refer to a very masculine male homosexual.

Candida albicans A yeast or fungus in the vagina; if its growth gets out of control, it causes vaginitis, or irritation of the vagina, with an accompanying discharge.

Carpopedal spasm A spastic contraction of the hands or feet which may occur during orgasm.

Castration The removal (usually by means of surgery) of the gonads (the testes in men or the ovaries in women).

Celibate Unmarried; also used to refer to someone who abstains from sexual activity.

Cervical cap A birth control device similar to the diaphragm.

Cervix The lower part of the uterus; the part next to the vagina.

Cesarean section Surgical delivery of a baby through an incision in the abdominal wall.

Chancre A painless open sore with a hard ridge around it; it is an early symptom of syphilis.

Chancroid A venereal disease.

Chastity Sexual abstinence.

Chlamydia An organism causing a sexually transmitted disease.

Cilia Tiny hairlike structures lining the vas deferens and the fallopian tubes.

Circumcision The surgical removal of the foreskin of the penis.

Climacteric See *menopause.*

Climax An orgasm.

Clitoridectomy Removal of the clitoris.

Clitoris A small, highly sensitive sexual organ in the female, located in front of the vaginal entrance.

Cloning Producing genetically identical individuals from a single parent.

Cognitive Relating to mental activity, such as thought, perception, understanding.

Cohabitation Living together.

Coitus Sexual intercourse; insertion of the penis into the vagina.

Coitus interruptus See *withdrawal.*

Coitus reservatus Sexual intercourse in which the man intentionally refrains fom ejaculating.

Colostrum A watery substance that is secreted from the breast at the end of pregnancy and during the first few days after delivery.

Conceptus The product of conception; sometimes used to refer to the embryo or fetus.

Condom A male contraceptive sheath that is placed over the penis.

Contraceptive sponge A polyurethane sponge containing a spermicide, which is placed in the vagina for contraceptive purposes.

Contraceptive technique A method of preventing conception.

Coprophilia A sexual variation in which arusal is associated with defecation or feces.

Copulation Sexual intercourse.

Corona The rim of tissue between the glans and the shaft of the penis.

Corpora cavernosa Two cylindrical masses of erectile tissue running the length of the penis; also present in the clitoris.

Corpus luteum The mass of cells remaining after a follicle has released an egg; it secretes progesterone.

Corpus spongiosum A cylinder of erectile tissue running the length of the penis.

Couvade The experiencing of the symptoms of pregnancy and labor by a male.

Cowper's glands A pair of glands that secrete substances into the male's urethra.

Crabs See *Pediculosis pubis.*

Cramps Painful menstruation, or dysmenorrhea.

Cremaster muscle A muscle in the scrotum.

Cryptorchidism Undescended testes.

Cul-de-sac The end of the vagina, past the cervix.

Culdoscopy A female sterilization procedure.

Culpotomy A female sterilization procedure.

Cunnilingus Mouth stimulation of the female genitals.

Cystitis Inflammation of the urinary bladder; the major symptom is a burning sensation while urinating.

Dartos muscle A muscle in the scrotum.

Decriminalization Removing criminal penalties for an activity that was previously defined as illegal.

Defloration The rupture of a virgin's hymen, through intercourse or other means.

Depo-Provera A drug containing synthetic hormones; used as an experimental form of birth control in women, as well as a treatment for male sex offenders.

Detumescence The return of an erect penis to the flaccid (unaroused) state.

Diaphragm A cap-shaped rubber contraceptive device that fits inside a woman's vagina over the cervix.

Diethylstilbestrol (DES) A potent estrogen drug used in the "morning-after" pill.

Dilate To enlarge; used to refer to the enlargement of the cervical opening during childbirth.

Dildo An artificial penis.

Douche To flush out the inside of the vagina with a liquid.

Drag queen A male homosexual who dresses in women's clothing.

Ductus deferens See *vas deferens.*

Dysmenorrhea Painful menstruation.

Dyspareunia Painful intercourse.

Ectopic pregnancy A pregnancy in which the fertilized egg implants somewhere other than the uterus.

Edema An excessive accumulation of fluid in a part of the body.

Effacement Thinning out of the cervix during childbirth.

Ejaculation The expulsion of semen from the penis, usually during orgasm.

Electra complex In Freudian theory, the little girl's sexual desires for her father; the female analogue of the Oedipus complex.

Embryo In humans, the term used to refer to the unborn young from the first to the eighth weeks after conception.

Embryo transplant A technique in which a fertilized, developing egg (embryo) is transferred from the uterus of one woman to the uterus of another woman.

Endocrine gland A gland that secretes substances (hormones) directly into the bloodstream.

Endometriosis A condition in which the endometrium grows in some place other than the uterus, such as the fallopian tubes.

Endometrium The inner lining of the uterus.

Epididymis Highly coiled tubules located on the edge of the testis; the site of sperm maturation.

E An incision that is sometimes made at the vaginal entrance during delivery.

Erectile dysfunction The inability to get or maintain an erection.

Erection An enlargement and hardening of the penis which occurs during sexual arousal.

Erogenous zones Areas of the body that are particularly sensitive to sexual stimulation.

Eros The Greek's term for passionate or erotic love.

Erotica Sexually arousing material that is not degrading to women, men, or children.

Erotophilia Feeling comfortable with sex, the opposite of erotophobia.

Erotophobia Feeling guilty and fearful about sex.

Estrogens A small group of "female" sex hormones; also produced in smaller quantities in males.

Estrus The period of ovulation and sexual activity in nonhuman female mammals.

Eunuch A castrated male.

Exhibitionist A person who derives sexual gratification from exposing his or her genitals to others.

Extramarital sex Sexual activity by a married person with someone other than her or his spouse.

Fallopian tube The tube extending from the uterus to the ovary.

Fellatio Mouth stimulation of the penis.

Femme A feminine lesbian.

Fertilization The union of sperm and egg, resulting in conception.

Fetal alcohol syndrome Disease of a newborn born to an alcoholic mother.

Fetishism A sexual variation in which an inanimate object causes sexual arousal.

Fetus In humans, the term used to refer to the unborn young from the third month after conception until birth.

Fimbriae Fingerlike projections at the end of the fallopian tube near the ovary.

Fitness In evolutionary theory, an individual's reproductive success.

Flaccid Not erect.

Follicle The capsule of cells surrounding an egg in the ovary.

Follicle-stimulating hormone (FSH) A hormone secreted by the pituitary; it stimulates follicle development in females and sperm production in males.

Follicular phase The first phase of the menstrual cycle, beginning just after menstruation.

Foreskin The sheath of skin covering the tip of the penis or clitoris.

Fornication Sexual intercourse between two unmarried people.

Fourchette The place where the inner lips come together behind the vaginal opening.

Frenulum A highly sensitive area of skin on the underside of the penis next to the glans.

Frigidity Lack of sexual response in a woman.

Gametes Sperm or eggs.

Gay Homosexual; particularly a male homosexual.

Gender The state of being male or female.

Gender dysphoria See *transsexual.*

Gender identity The psychological sense of one's own maleness or femaleness.

Gender role A cluster of socially defined expectations that people of one gender are expected to fulfill.

Genitals The sexual or reproductive organs.

Genital warts A sexually transmitted disease causing warts on the genitals.

Gerontophilia Sexual attraction to the elderly.

Gestation The period of pregnancy; the time from conception until birth.

Gigolo A male who sells his sexual services to women.

Glans The tip of the penis or clitoris.

Gonadotropin-releasing hormone (Gn-RH) A hormone secreted by the hypothalamus that regulates the pituitary's secretion of hormones.

Gonadotropins Pituitary hormones (FSH, LH) that stimulate the activity of the gonads.

Gonads The ovaries or testes.

Gonorrhea A common sexually transmitted disease.

Gossypol A substance used as a male contraceptive in China.

Gräfenberg spot A small gland on the front wall of the vagina, emptying into the urethra, which may be responsible for female ejaculation.

Granuloma inguinale A rare sexually transmitted disease.

Gynecomastia Temporary enlargement of a male's breasts during puberty.

Hegar's sign A sign of pregnancy based on a test done by a physician, in which a softening of the uterus is detected.

Hermaphrodite A person with both male and female sex glands, that is, both ovaries and testicular tissue (see also *pseudohermaphrodite*).

Herpes genitalis A disease characterized by painful bumps on the genitals.

Heterosexual A person who is sexually attracted to, or engages in sexual activity primarily with, members of the opposite gender.

Homologous organs Organs in the male and female that develop from the same embryonic tissue.

Homophobia Irrational fear of homosexuality.

Homosexual A person who is sexually attracted to, or engages in sexual activity primarily with, members of her or his own gender.

Homosocial A pattern of social grouping in which males associate with other males and females associate with other females.

Hormones Chemical substances secreted by the endocrine glands.

Human chorionic gonadotropin (HCG) A hormone produced by the placenta; HCG is what is detected in most pregnancy tests.

Hustlers Male prostitutes who sell their services to other males.

Hyaluronidase An enzyme secreted by the sperm that allows it to penetrate the egg.

Hymen A membrane that partially covers the vaginal opening.

Hypothalamus A part of the brain which is important in regulating certin body functions including sex hormone production.

Hysterectomy Surgical removal of the uterus.

Hysterotomy A method of abortion sometimes used during the second trimester.

Id In Freudian theory, the part of the personality containing the libido or sex drive.

Imperforate hymen A condition where the hymen is unusually thick and covers the vaginal entrance completely.

Implantation The burrowing of the fertilized egg into the lining of the uterus.

Impotence See *erectile dysfunction.*

Impregnate To make pregnant.

Incest Sexual activity between close relatives, such as a brother and sister.

Incest taboo A regulation prohibiting sexual activity between blood relatives.

Incidence The percentage of people giving a particular response.

Inguinal canal In the male, the passageway from the abdomen to the scrotum through which the testes usually descend shortly before birth.

Inhibin Substance produced by the testes, which regulates FH levels.

Inner lips Thin folds of skin on either side of the vaginal entrance.

Intercourse (sexual) Sexual activity in which the penis is inserted into the vagina; coitus (see also *anal intercourse.*

Interfemoral intercourse Sexual activity in which the penis moves between the thighs.

Interstitial cells Cells in the testes which manufacture male sex hormones; also called *Leydig cells.*

Interstitial-cell-stimulating hormone (ICSH) A hormone manufactured by the pituitary that stimulates the interstitial cells of the testes to produce testosterone; identical to the homone LH in the female.

Intrauterine device (IUD) A plastic or metal device that is inserted into the uterus for contraceptive purposes.

Introitus Entrance to the vagina.

Intromission Insertion of the penis into the vagina.

John Slang term for a prostitute's customer.

Kegel exercises Exercises to strengthen the muscle surrounding the genitals.

Kiddie porn Pictures or films of sexual acts with children.

Labia majora See *outer lips.*

Labia minora See *inner lips.*

Labor The series of processes involved in giving birth.

Lactation Secretion of milk from the female's breasts.

Lamaze method A method of "prepared" childbirth.

Laparoscopy A method of female sterilization.

Lesbian A female homosexual.

Leydig cells See *interstitial cells.*

Libido The sex drive.

Limbic system A set of structures in the interior of the brain, including the amygdala, hippocampus, and fornix; believed to be important for sexual behavior in both animals and humans.

Limerance Romantic love marked by preoccupation with the loved one.

Lochia A discharge from the uterus and vagina that occurs during the first few weeks after childbirth.

Luteinizing hormone (LH) A hormone secreted by the pituitary. In females, it causes ovulation; called *ICSH* in males.

Lymphogranuloma venereum (LGV) A virus-caused disease affecting the lymph glands in the genital region.

Mammary gland The milk-producing part of the breast.

Mammography X-rays for diagnosing breast cancer.

Masochism A sexual variation in which the person derives sexual pleasure from experiencing physical or mental pain.

Mastectomy Surgical removal of the breast.

Masturbation Self-stimulation of the genitals to produce sexual arousal.

Menage à trois A sexual relationship involving three people.

Menarche The first menstruation.

Menopause The gradual cessation of menstruation in a woman, generally at around age 50.

Menses The menstrual flow.

Menstruation A bloody discharge of the lining of the

uterus, generally occurring about once a month in women.

Midwife A person (often a nurse) trained as a birth attendant.

Mini-pill A birth control pill containing a low dose of progesterone and no estrogen.

Miscarriage A pregnancy that terminates on its own; spontaneous abortion.

Mittelschmerz Abdominal cramps at the time of ovulation.

Monilia A yeast infection of the vagina.

Monogamy The pairing of one person with just one other person in a long-term relationship in which neither engages in sexual activity with anyone else.

Mons pubis The fatty pad of tissue under the pubic hair; also called the *mons* or *mons veneris.*

Morning-after pill A pill containing a high dose of DES, which can be used in emergency situations for preventing pregnancy after intercourse has occurred.

Mucosa Mucous membrane.

Müllerian ducts In the embryo, a pair of ducts that eventually become part of the female reproductive system.

Multiparous A term used to refer to a woman who has had more than one baby.

Myotonia Muscle tension.

Necrophilia A sexual variation in which there is attraction to a corpse.

Nipples The pigmented tip of the breast, through which milk goes when a woman is breast-feeding.

Nocturnal emission Involuntary orgasm and ejaculation while asleep.

Nongonococcal urethritis An inflammation of the male's urethra not caused by gonorrhea.

Nulliparous A term used to refer to a woman who has never given birth to a baby.

Nymphomania An extraordinarily high, insatiable sex drive in a woman.

Obscenity Something that is offensive according to accepted standards of decency; the legal term for pornography.

Oedipus complex In Freudian theory, the sexual attraction of a little boy to his mother.

Onanism Withdrawal of the penis from the vagina before ejaculation; sometimes also used to refer to masturbation.

Operant conditioning The process of changing the frequency of a behavior (the operant) by following it with reinforcement or punishment.

Operational definition Defining a concept or term by how it is measured.

Oral-genital sex Sexual activity in which the mouth is used to stimulate the genitals.

Orchidectomy Surgical removal of the testes.

Orgasm An intense sensation that occurs at the peak of sexual arousal and is followed by release of sexual tensions.

Orgasmic platform The thickening of the walls of the outer third of the vagina that occurs during sexual arousal.

Outer lips The fatty pads of tissue lying on either side of the vaginal opening and inner lips.

Ovaries The paired sex glands in the female which produce ova (eggs) and sex hormones.

Oviduct Fallopian tube.

Ovulation Release of an egg by the ovaries.

Ovum Egg.

Oxytocin A hormone secreted by the pituitary which stimulates the contractions of the uterus during childbirth; also involved in breast-feeding.

Pander To produce a prostitute for a client; sometimes used to mean any catering to another's sexual desires.

Pap test The test for cervical cancer.

Paraphilia A sexual variation.

Parturition Childbirth.

Pederasty Sexual relations between a man and a boy; sometimes also used to mean anal intercourse.

Pediculosis pubis Lice attaching themselves to the roots of the pubic hair; crabs.

Pedophilia A sexual variation in which an adult is sexually attracted to children; child molesting.

Pelvic inflammatory disease Infection of the pelvic organs such as the oviducts.

Penis A male sexual organ.

Perineum The area between the vaginal opening and the anus.

Period The menstrual period.

Perversion A sexual deviation.

Phallus Penis.

Pheromones Chemical substances secreted outside the body that are important in communication between animals.

Phimosis A condition in which the foreskin is so tight that it cannot be pulled back.

Photoplethysmograph A device used to measure physiological sexual arousal in the female.

Pimp A prostitute's protector; one who procures a prostitute's services for another.;

Pituitary gland A gland located on the lower surface of the brain; it secretes several hormones important to sexual and reproductive functioning.

Placenta An organ formed on the wall of the uterus through which the fetus receives oxygen and nutrients and gets rid of waste products.

Plateau phase Masters and Johnson's term for the second phase of sexual response, occurring just before orgasm.

Population A group of people a researcher wants to study and make conclusions about.

Pornography Sexually arousing art, literature, or films.

Postpartum The period of time following childbirth.

Postpartum depression Mild to moderate depression in women following the birth of a baby.

Premarital intercourse Intercourse before marriage.

Premature ejaculation A sexual dysfunction in which the male ejaculates too soon.

Premenstrual syndrome (PMS) A combination of severe physical and psychological symptoms (such as depression and irritability) occurring in some women just before menstruation.

Prenatal Before birth.

Prepuce Foreskin.

Priapism A rare condition in which erections are long-lasting and painful.

Progesterone A female sex hormone produced by the corpus luteum in the ovary.

Prolactin A hormone secreted by the pituitary; it is involved in lactation.

Promiscuous A term used to refer to someone who engages in sexual activity with many different people.

Prophylactic A drug or device used to prevent disease, often specifically venereal disease; often used to mean "condom."

Prostaglandins Chemicals that stimulate the muscles of the uterus.

Prostate The gland in the male, located below the bladder, that secretes most of the fluid in semen.

Prostatitis An infection or inflammation of the prostate gland.

Prostitution Indiscriminate sexual activity for payment.

Pseudocyesis False pregnancy.

Pseudohermaphrodite An individual who has a mixture of male and female reproductive structures, so that it is not clear whether the individual is a male or a female.

Psychoanalytic theory A psychological theory originated by Freud; its basic assumption is that part of the human psyche is unconscious.

Puberty The period of time during which the body matures from that of a child to that of an adult capable of reproducing.

Pubic hair Hair on the lower abdomen and genital area, appearing at puberty.

Pubic lice See *Pediculosis pubis.*

Pubococcygeal muscle A muscle around the vaginal entrance.

Pudendum The external genitals of the female.

Rape Forcible sexual relations with an individual without that person's consent.

Refractory period The period following orgasm during which the male cannot be sexually aroused.

Resolution phase Masters and Johnson's term for the last phase of sexual response, in which the body returns to the unaroused state.

Retarded ejaculation A sexual dysfunction in which the male cannot have an orgasm, even though he is highly aroused.

Retrograde ejaculation A condition in which orgasm in the male is not accompanied by an external ejaculation; instead, the ejaculate goes into the urinary bladder.

Rhythm method A method of birth control that involves abstaining from sexual intercourse during the fertile days of the woman's menstrual cycle.

Sadism A sexual variation in which the person derives sexual pleasure from inflicting pain on someone else.

Salpingectomy See *tubal ligation.*

Salpingitis Infection of the fallopian tubes.

Satyriasis An extraordinarily high level of sex drive in a male.

Scripts What we have learned to be appropriate sequences of behavior.

Scrotum The pouch of skin that contains the testes.

Secondary sex characteristics The physical characteristics, other than the sex organs, that distinguish the male from the female; examples are the woman's breasts and the man's beard.

Semen The fluid that is ejaculated from the penis during orgasm; it contains sperm.

Seminal vesicles The two organs lying on either side of the prostate.

Seminiferous tubules Highly coiled tubules in the testes that manufacture sperm.

Sensate focus exercises Exercises prescribed by sex therapists to increase sexual response.

Sex-change operation The surgery done on transsexuals to change their anatomy to the other gender.

Sex flush A rashlike condition on the skin that occurs during sexual arousal.

Sexual dissatisfaction Masters and Johnson's term for homosexuals who are unhappy with their sexual orientation and seek therapy to become heterosexual.

Sexual dysfunction A problem with sexual responding that causes a person mental distress; examples are erectile dysfunction in men and anorgasmia in women.

Sexual harassment Unwanted imposition of sexual requirements in the context of a relationship of unequal power, such as an employer and an employee.

Sexual identity A person's sense of his or her own sexual nature, whether heterosexual, homosexual, or bisexual.

Situation ethics As defined by Joseph Fletcher, a way of making ethical decisions on the basis of the concrete situation and the persons involved, rather than on the basis of rules.

Skene's glands Glands opening into the urethra.

Smegma A cheesy substance formed under the foreskin of the penis.

Sociobiology A theory that applies evolutionary biology to understanding the social behavior of animals, including humans.

Sodomy An ambiguous legal term which may refer to anal intercourse, sexual relations with animals, or mouth-genital sex.

Spectatoring Acting as an observer or judge of one's own sexual performance.

Sperm The mature male reproductive cell, capable of fertilizing an egg.
Spermatogenesis The production of sperm.
Spermicide A substance that kills sperm.
Spirochete A spiral-shaped bacterium; one kind causes syphilis.
Sponge See *contraceptive sponge.*
Squeeze technique A form of therapy for premature ejaculation.
Statutory rape Sexual relations with a person who is below the legal "age of consent."
Sterile Incapable of reproducing.
Sterilization technique A procedure by which an individual is made incapable of reproducing.
Steroids A group of chemical substances including the sex hormones estrogen, progesterone, and testosterone.
Straight Heterosexual.
Structural-functionalism A sociological theory that views society as an interrelated set of structures that function together to maintain that society.
Surrogate An extra member of a sex therapy team who serves as a sexual partner for the client while in therapy.
Swinging An exchange of sex partners between married couples.
Syphilis A sexually transmitted disease.

Tearoom trade Impersonal sex in public places such as restrooms.
Teratogenic Producing defects in the fetus.
Testes The sex glands of the male, located in the scrotum; they manufacture sperm and sex hormones.
Testicle A testis.
Testosterone A hormone secreted by the testes in the male; it maintains secondary sex characteristics.
Toxemia A dangerous disease of pregnancy.
Toxic shock syndrome A sometimes fatal disease associated with tampon use.
Transsexual A person who feels that he or she is trapped in the body of the wrong gender; a person who undergoes a sex-change operation.
Transvestism Dressing in the clothing of the opposite gender.
Tribadism A sexual technique in which one woman lies on top of another, moving rhythmically to produce sexual pleasure.
Trichomoniasis A vaginal infection.
Trimester Three months.
Troilism A sexual variation in which three people engage in sexual activity together.
Tubal ligation A surgical method of female sterilization; also called salpingectomy.
Tumescence Swelling due to congestion with body fluids; erection.
Tyson's glands Glands under the foreskin of the penis that secrete a cheesy substance called smegma.

Umbilical cord The tube that connects the fetus to the placenta.
Urethra The tube through which urine leaves the bladder and passes out of the body; in males, also the tube through which semen is discharged.
Urophilia (or urolagnia) A sexual variation in which the person derives sexual pleasure from urine or urination.
Uterus The organ in the female in which the fetus develops.

Vacuum curettage A method of abortion that is performed during the first trimester.
Vagina The barrel-shaped organ in the female into which the penis is inserted during intercourse and through which a baby passes during birth.
Vaginal ring An experimental device for contraception.
Vaginismus A strong, spastic contraction of the muscles around the vagina, closing off the vaginal entrance and making intercourse impossible.
Vaginitis An inflammation or irritation of the vagina, usually due to infection.
Varicocele Essentially, varicose veins in the testes; may be related to infertility in men.
Vas deferens The ducts through which sperm pass on their way from the testes to the urethra.
Vasectomy A surgical procedure for male sterilization involving severing of the vas deferens.
Vasocongestion An accumulation of blood in the blood vessels of a region of the body, especially the genitals; a swelling or erection results.
Venereal disease A disease transmitted primarily by sexual intercourse.
Virgin A person who has never had sexual intercourse.
Volunteer bias A problem in sex research caused by some people refusing to participate, thus making it impossible to have a random sample.
Voyeurism A sexual variation in which the person derives sexual pleasure from watching nudes or watching others having sexual intercourse; also called *scoptophilia* and *Peeping Tomism.*
Vulva The collective term for the external genitals of the female; includes the mons, clitoris, inner and outer lips, and vaginal and urethral openings.

Wassermann test. A blood test for syphilis.
Wet dream See *Nocturnal emission.*
Withdrawal A method of birth control in which the male withdraws his penis from the vagina before he ejaculates.
Wolffian ducts Embryonic ducts which form part of the male's reproductive system.
Womb See *uterus.*

Zoophilia See *bestiality.*
Zygote The fertilized egg.

ANSWERS TO REVIEW QUESTIONS

CHAPTER 1. SEXUALITY IN PERSPECTIVE

1. T
2. T
3. F
4. F
5. T
6. F
7. T
8. gender
9. T
10. T

CHAPTER 2. THEORETICAL PERSPECTIVES ON SEXUALITY

1. sociobiology
2. libido
3. T
4. latency
5. T
6. F
7. T
8. F
9. T
10. F

CHAPTER 3. SEXUAL ANATOMY

1. clitoris
2. hymen
3. F
4. T
5. estrogen, progesterone
6. T
7. circumcision
8. F
9. T
10. prostate

CHAPTER 4. SEX HORMONES AND SEXUAL DIFFERENTIATION

1. hypothalamus
2. T
3. T
4. F
5. hypothalamus
6. ovaries
7. T
8. F
9. F
10. T

CHAPTER 5. MENSTRUATION AND MENOPAUSE

1. F
2. T
3. T
4. prostaglandins
5. T
6. F
7. T
8. Estrogen-replacement therapy
9. T
10. T

CHAPTER 6. CONCEPTION, PREGNANCY, AND CHILDBIRTH

1. F
2. F
3. F
4. Placenta
5. HCG or human chorionic gonadotropin
6. T
7. F
8. T
9. T
10. T

CHAPTER 7. BIRTH CONTROL AND ABORTION

1. estrogen and progestin (progesterone)
2. T
3. F
4. T
5. F
6. T
7. T
8. rhythm
9. the condom and vasectomy (male sterilization)
10. F

CHAPTER 8. THE PHYSIOLOGY OF SEXUAL RESPONSE

1. excitement, plateau, orgasm, resolution
2. vasocongestion
3. T
4. F
5. F
6. T
7. G-spot or Gräfenberg spot
8. F
9. Pheromones
10. F

CHAPTER 9. TECHNIQUES OF AROUSAL AND COMMUNICATION

1. F
2. T
3. F
4. cunnilingus
5. F
6. T
7. T
8. Leveling
9. F
10. T

CHAPTER 10. SEX RESEARCH

1. T
2. T
3. T
4. direct observation
5. F
6. T
7. F
8. Participant-observer study
9. F
10. F

CHAPTER 11. SEXUALITY AND THE LIFE CYCLE: CHILDHOOD AND ADOLESCENCE

1. F
2. F
3. T
4. T
5. T
6. T
7. F
8. serial monogamy
9. F
10. T

CHAPTER 12. SEXUALITY AND THE LIFE CYCLE: ADULTHOOD

1. T
2. T
3. F
4. T
5. F
6. Swinging
7. F
8. T
9. T
10. regular sexual expression

CHAPTER 13. LOVE AND ATTRACTION

1. Eros
2. T
3. T
4. F
5. F
6. T
7. physiological arousal
8. F
9. misattribution of arousal
10. F

CHAPTER 14. GENDER ROLES

1. T
2. T
3. T
4. F
5. F
6. T
7. T
8. Androgyny
9. Transsexual (or gender dysphoria)
10. T

CHAPTER 15. FEMALE SEXUALITY AND MALE SEXUALITY

1. T
2. T
3. 92; 58
4. F
5. T
6. F
7. T
8. F
9. T
10. T

CHAPTER 16. SEXUAL ORIENTATION: GAY, STRAIGHT, OR BI?

1. F
2. Homophobia
3. F
4. 80; 20
5. Tearoom trade
6. T
7. T
8. F
9. T
10. T

CHAPTER 17. VARIATIONS IN SEXUAL BEHAVIOR

1. T
2. Fetishism
3. T
4. masochist
5. F
6. satyriasis
7. F
8. F
9. T
10. T

CHAPTER 18. SEXUAL COERCION

1. T
2. victim-precipitated
3. F
4. F
5. T
6. F
7. T
8. F
9. T
10. T

CHAPTER 19. SEX FOR SALE

1. T
2. T
3. pimp
4. Gigolos
5. F
6. T
7. T
8. F
9. T
10. T

CHAPTER 20. SEXUAL DYSFUNCTION AND SEX THERAPY

1. Erectile dysfunction
2. T
3. T
4. F
5. T
6. Spectatoring
7. F
8. T
9. T
10. T

CHAPTER 21. SEXUALLY TRANSMITTED DISEASES

1. chlamydia or NGU
2. gonorrhea
3. F
4. T
5. genital herpes
6. T
7. F
8. F
9. F
10. F

CHAPTER 22. ETHICS, RELIGION, AND SEXUALITY

1. F
2. F
3. celibacy
4. Hindu
5. profamily
6. T
7. F
8. T
9. F
10. The New Morality

CHAPTER 23. SEX AND THE LAW

1. F
2. T
3. F
4. Sodomy
5. entrapment
6. T
7. obscene
8. T
9. F
10. F

CHAPTER 24. SEX EDUCATION

1. F
2. F
3. F
4. T
5. T
6. T
7. T

CHAPTER 25. SEXUALITY IN THE FUTURE

1. artificial insemination
2. T
3. F
4. T
5. F
6. T

INDEX